ALL GLORY TO ŚRĪ GURU AND GAURĀṄGA

ŚRĪMAD BHĀGAVATAM

of

KṚṢṆA-DVAIPĀYANA VYĀSA

तस्मात् सङ्कीर्तनं विष्णोर्जगन्मङ्गलमंहसाम् ।
महतामपि कौरव्य विद्ध्यैकान्तिकनिष्कृतम् ॥ ३१ ॥

tasmāt saṅkīrtanaṁ viṣṇor
jagan-maṅgalam aṁhasām
mahatām api kauravya
viddhy aikāntika-niṣkṛtam
(*Śrīmad-Bhāgavatam* 6.3.31)

Books by His Divine Grace
A. C. Bhaktivedanta Swami Prabhupāda:

Bhagavad-gītā As It Is
Śrīmad-Bhāgavatam (1st to 10th Cantos)
Śrī Caitanya-Caritāmṛta (9 vols.)
Kṛṣṇa, The Supreme Personality of Godhead
Teachings of Lord Caitanya
The Nectar of Devotion
The Nectar of Instruction
Śrī Īśopaniṣad
Light of the Bhāgavata
Easy Journey to Other Planets
The Science of Self-Realization
Kṛṣṇa Consciousness: The Topmost Yoga System
Perfect Questions, Perfect Answers
Teachings of Lord Kapila, the Son of Devahuti
Transcendental Teachings of Prahlāda Mahārāja
Teachings of Queen Kuntī
Kṛṣṇa, the Reservoir of Pleasure
The Path of Perfection
Life Comes from Life
Message of Godhead
The Perfection of Yoga
Beyond Birth and Death
On the Way to Kṛṣṇa
Rāja-vidyā: The King of Knowledge
Elevation to Kṛṣṇa Consciousness
Kṛṣṇa Consciousness: The Matchless Gift
Selected Verses from the Vedic Scriptures
Back to Godhead magazine (founder)

A complete catalogue is available upon request.
The Bhaktivedanta Book Trust, ISKCON Temple,
Hare Krishna Land, Juhu, Mumbai 400 049. India.
The above books are also available at ISKCON centers.
Please contact a center near to your place.

ŚRĪMAD BHĀGAVATAM

Sixth Canto

"Prescribed Duties for Mankind"

With the Original Sanskrit Text,
Its Roman Transliteration, Synonyms,
Translation and Elaborate Purports

by

His Divine Grace
A. C. Bhaktivedanta Swami Prabhupāda
Founder-*Ācārya* of the International Society for Krishna Consciousness

THE BHAKTIVEDANTA BOOK TRUST

Readers interested in the subject matter of this book are invited by The Bhaktivedanta Book Trust to correspond with its secretary at the following address:

The Bhaktivedanta Book Trust
Hare Krishna Land,
Juhu, Mumbai 400 049, India.

Website / E-mail :
www.indiabbt.com
admin@indiabbt.com

Śrīmad Bhāgavatam Sixth Canto (English)

First printing in India : 2,000 copies
Second to Seventeenth printings : 52,500 copies
Eighteenth printing, November 2018 : 7,000 copies

ISBN : 978-93-84564-08-7 (v. 8)
ISBN : 978-93-84564-00-1 (18-volume set)

Published and Printed by
The Bhaktivedanta Book Trust.

SJ1K

Table of Contents

CHAPTER FIVE

Nārada Muni Cursed by Prajāpati Dakṣa   231

Preface

We must know the present need of human society. And what is that need? Human society is no longer bounded by geographical limits to particular countries or communities. Human society is broader than in the Middle Ages, and the world tendency is toward one state or one human society. The ideals of spiritual communism, according to *Śrīmad-Bhāgavatam,* are based more or less on the oneness of the entire human society, nay, of the entire energy of living beings. The need is felt by great thinkers to make this a successful ideology. *Śrīmad-Bhāgavatam* will fill this need in human society. It begins, therefore, with an aphorism of Vedānta philosophy, *janmādy asya yataḥ,* to establish the ideal of a common cause.

Human society, at the present moment, is not in the darkness of oblivion. It has made rapid progress in the fields of material comforts, education and economic development throughout the entire world. But there is a pinprick somewhere in the social body at large, and therefore there are large-scale quarrels, even over less important issues. There is need of a clue as to how humanity can become one in peace, friendship and prosperity with a common cause. *Śrīmad-Bhāgavatam* will fill this need, for it is a cultural presentation for the respiritualization of the entire human society.

Śrīmad-Bhāgavatam should be introduced also in the schools and colleges, for it is recommended by the great student-devotee Prahlāda Mahārāja in order to change the demoniac face of society.

kaumāra ācaret prājño
dharmān bhāgavatān iha
durlabhaṁ mānuṣaṁ janma
tad apy adhruvam artha-dam

(*Bhāg.* 7.6.1)

Disparity in human society is due to lack of principles in a godless civilization. There is God, or the Almighty One, from whom everything emanates, by whom everything is maintained and in whom everything is merged to rest. Material science has tried to find the ultimate source of creation very insufficiently, but it is a fact that there is one ultimate source of everything that be. This ultimate source is explained rationally and authoritatively in the beautiful *Bhāgavatam,* or *Śrīmad-Bhāgavatam.*

Śrīmad-Bhāgavatam is the transcendental science not only for knowing the ultimate source of everything but also for knowing our relation with Him and our duty toward perfection of the human society on the basis of this perfect knowledge. It is powerful reading matter in the Sanskrit language, and it is now rendered into English elaborately so that simply by a careful reading one will know God perfectly well, so much so that the reader will be sufficiently educated to defend himself from the onslaught of atheists. Over and above this, the reader will be able to convert others to accepting God as a concrete principle.

Śrīmad-Bhāgavatam begins with the definition of the ultimate source. It is a bona fide commentary on the *Vedānta-sūtra* by the same author, Śrīla Vyāsadeva, and gradually it develops into nine cantos up to the highest state of God realization. The only qualification one needs to study this great book of transcendental knowledge is to proceed step by step cautiously and not jump forward haphazardly as with an ordinary book. It should be gone through chapter by chapter, one after another. The reading matter is so arranged with the original Sanskrit text, its English transliteration, synonyms, translation and purports so that one is sure to become a God-realized soul at the end of finishing the first nine cantos.

The Tenth Canto is distinct from the first nine cantos because it deals directly with the transcendental activities of the Personality of Godhead, Śrī Kṛṣṇa. One will be unable to capture the effects of the Tenth Canto without going through the first nine cantos. The book is complete in twelve cantos, each independent, but it is good for all to read them in small installments one after another.

I must admit my frailties in presenting *Śrīmad-Bhāgavatam,* but still I am hopeful of its good reception by the thinkers and leaders of society on the strength of the following statement of *Śrīmad-Bhāgavatam* (1.5.11):

tad-vāg-visargo janatāgha-viplavo
yasmin prati-ślokam abaddhavaty api
nāmāny anantasya yaśo 'ṅkitāni yac
chṛṇvanti gāyanti gṛṇanti sādhavaḥ

"On the other hand, that literature which is full of descriptions of the transcendental glories of the name, fame, form and pastimes of the unlimited Supreme Lord is a transcendental creation meant for bringing about a revolution in the impious life of a misdirected civilization. Such transcendental literature, even though irregularly composed, is heard, sung and accepted by purified men who are thoroughly honest."

Oṁ tat sat

A. C. Bhaktivedanta Swami

Introduction

"This *Bhāgavata Purāṇa* is as brilliant as the sun, and it has arisen just after the departure of Lord Kṛṣṇa to His own abode, accompanied by religion, knowledge, etc. Persons who have lost their vision due to the dense darkness of ignorance in the age of Kali shall get light from this *Purāṇa.*" (*Śrīmad-Bhāgavatam* 1.3.43)

The timeless wisdom of India is expressed in the *Vedas,* ancient Sanskrit texts that touch upon all fields of human knowledge. Originally preserved through oral tradition, the *Vedas* were first put into writing five thousand years ago by Śrīla Vyāsadeva, the "literary incarnation of God." After compiling the *Vedas,* Vyāsadeva set forth their essence in the aphorisms known as *Vedānta-sūtras. Śrīmad-Bhāgavatam* (*Bhāgavata Purāṇa*) is Vyāsadeva's commentary on his own *Vedānta-sūtras.* It was written in the maturity of his spiritual life under the direction of Nārada Muni, his spiritual master. Referred to as "the ripened fruit of the tree of Vedic literature," *Śrīmad-Bhāgavatam* is the most complete and authoritative exposition of Vedic knowledge.

After compiling the *Bhāgavatam,* Vyāsa imparted the synopsis of it to his son, the sage Śukadeva Gosvāmī. Śukadeva Gosvāmī subsequently recited the entire *Bhāgavatam* to Mahārāja Parīkṣit in an assembly of learned saints on the bank of the Ganges at Hastināpura (now Delhi). Mahārāja Parīkṣit was the emperor of the world and was a great *rājarṣi* (saintly king). Having received a warning that he would die within a week, he renounced his entire kingdom and retired to the bank of the Ganges to fast until death and receive spiritual enlightenment. The *Bhāgavatam* begins with Emperor Parīkṣit's sober inquiry to Śukadeva Gosvāmī: "You are the spiritual master of great saints and devotees. I am therefore begging you to show the way of perfection for all persons, and especially for one who is about to die. Please let me know what a man should hear, chant, remember and worship, and also what he should not do. Please explain all this to me."

Śukadeva Gosvāmī's answer to this question, and numerous other questions posed by Mahārāja Parīkṣit, concerning everything from the nature of the self to the origin of the universe, held the assembled sages in rapt attention continuously for the seven days leading up to the king's death. The sage Sūta Gosvāmī, who was present in that assembly when Śukadeva Gosvāmī first recited *Śrīmad-Bhāgavatam,* later repeated the *Bhāgavatam* before a gathering of sages in the forest of Naimiṣāraṇya. Those sages, concerned about the spiritual welfare of the people in general, had gathered to perform a long, continuous chain of sacrifices to counteract the degrading influence of the incipient age of Kali. In response to the sages' request that he speak the essence of Vedic wisdom, Sūta Gosvāmī repeated from memory the entire eighteen thousand verses of *Śrīmad-Bhāgavatam,* as spoken by Śukadeva Gosvāmī to Mahārāja Parīkṣit.

The reader of *Śrīmad-Bhāgavatam* hears Sūta Gosvāmī relate the questions of Mahārāja Parīkṣit and the answers of Śukadeva Gosvāmī. Also, Sūta Gosvāmī sometimes responds directly to questions put by Śaunaka Ṛṣi, the spokesman for the sages gathered at Naimiṣāraṇya. One therefore simultaneously hears two dialogues: one between Mahārāja Parīkṣit and Śukadeva Gosvāmī on the bank of the Ganges, and another at Naimiṣāraṇya between Sūta Gosvāmī and the sages at Naimiṣāraṇya forest, headed by Śaunaka Ṛṣi. Futhermore, while instructing King Parīkṣit, Śukadeva Gosvāmī often relates historical episodes and gives accounts of lengthy philosophical discussions between such great souls as Nārada Muni and Vasudeva. With this understanding of the history of the *Bhāgavatam,* the reader will easily be able to follow its intermingling of dialogues and events from various sources. Since philosophical wisdom, not chronological order, is most important in the text, one need only be attentive to the subject matter of *Śrīmad-Bhāgavatam* to appreciate fully its profound message.

The translators of this edition compare the *Bhāgavatam* to sugar candy—wherever you taste it, you will find it equally sweet and relishable. Therefore, to taste the sweetness of the *Bhāgavatam,* one may begin by reading any of its volumes. After such an introductory taste, however, the serious reader is best advised to go back to the First Canto and then proceed through the *Bhāgavatam,* canto after canto, in its natural order.

This edition of the *Bhāgavatam* is the first complete English translation of this important text with an elaborate commentary, and it is the first widely available to the English-speaking public. The first twelve volumes (Canto One through Canto Ten, Part One) are the product of the scholarly and devotional effort of His Divine Grace A. C. Bhaktivedanta Swami Prabhupāda, the founder-*ācārya* of the International Society for Krishna Consciousness and the world's most distinguished teacher of Indian religious and Philosophical thought. His consummate Sanskrit scholarship and intimate familiarity with Vedic culture and thought as well as the modern way of life combine to reveal to the West a magnificent exposition of this important classic. After the departure of Śrīla

Prabhupāda from this world in 1977, his monumental work of translating and annotating *Śrīmad-Bhāgavatam* has been continued by his disciples Hridayananda dāsa Goswami and Gopīparāṇadhana dāsa.

Readers will find this work of value for many reasons. For those interested in the classical roots of Indian civilization, it serves as a vast reservoir of detailed information on virtually every one of its aspects. For students of comparative philosophy and religion, the *Bhāgavatam* offers a penetrating view into the meaning of India's profound spiritual heritage. To sociologists and anthropologists, the *Bhāgavatam* reveals the practical workings of a peaceful and scientifically organized Vedic culture, whose institutions were integrated on the basis of a highly developed spiritual world view. Students of literature will discover the *Bhāgavatam* to be a masterpiece of majestic poetry. For students of psychology, the text provides important perspectives on the nature of consciousness, human behavior and the philosophical study of identity. Finally, to those seeking spiritual insight, the *Bhāgavatam* offers simple and practical guidance for attainment of the highest self-knowledge and realization of the Absolute Truth. The entire multivolume text, presented by the Bhaktivedanta Book Trust, promises to occupy a significant place in the intellectual, cultural and spiritual life of modern man for a long time to come.

—The Publishers

CHAPTER ONE

The History of the Life of Ajāmila

Throughout *Śrīmad-Bhāgavatam* there are descriptions of ten subject matters, including creation, subsequent creation and the planetary systems. Śukadeva Gosvāmī, the speaker of *Śrīmad-Bhāgavatam,* has already described creation, subsequent creation and the planetary systems in the Third, Fourth and Fifth Cantos. Now, in this Sixth Canto, which consists of nineteen chapters, he will describe *poṣaṇa,* or protection by the Lord.

The first chapter relates the history of Ajāmila, who was considered a greatly sinful man, but was liberated when four order carriers of Viṣṇu came to rescue him from the hands of the order carriers of Yamarāja. A full description of how he was liberated, having been relieved of the reactions of his sinful life, is given in this chapter. Sinful activities are painful both in this life and in the next. We should know for certain that the cause of all painful life is sinful action. On the path of fruitive work one certainly commits sinful activities, and therefore according to the considerations of *karma-kāṇḍa,* different types of atonement are recommended. Such methods of atonement, however, do not free one from ignorance, which is the root of sinful life. Consequently one is prone to commit sinful activities even after atonement, which is therefore very inadequate for purification. On the path of speculative knowledge one becomes free from sinful life by understanding things as they are. Therefore the acquirement of speculative knowledge is also considered a method of atonement. While performing fruitive activities one can become free from the actions of sinful life through austerity, penance, celibacy, control of the mind and senses, truthfulness and the practice of mystic *yoga.* By awakening knowledge one may also neutralize sinful reactions. Neither of these methods, however, can free one from the tendency to commit sinful activities.

By *bhakti-yoga* one can completely avoid the tendency for sinful life; other methods are not very feasible. Therefore the Vedic literature concludes that devotional service is more important than the methods of *karma-kāṇḍa* and *jñāna-kāṇḍa.* Only the path of devotional service is auspicious for everyone. Fruitive activities and speculative knowledge cannot independently liberate anyone, but devotional service, independent of *karma* and *jñāna,* is so potent that one who has fixed his mind at the lotus feet of Kṛṣṇa is guaranteed not to meet the Yamadūtas, the order carriers of Yamarāja, even in dreams.

To prove the strength of devotional service, Śukadeva Gosvāmī described the history of Ajāmila. Ajāmila was a resident of Kānyakubja (the modern Kanauj). He was trained by his parents to become a perfect *brāhmaṇa* by studying the *Vedas* and following the regulative principles, but because of his past, this youthful *brāhmaṇa* was somehow attracted by a prostitute, and because of her association he became most fallen and abandoned all regulative principles. Ajāmila begot in the womb of the prostitute ten sons, the last of whom was called Nārāyaṇa. At the time of Ajāmila's death, when the order carriers of Yamarāja came to take him, he loudly called the name Nārāyaṇa in fear because he was attached to his youngest son. Thus he remembered the original Nārāyaṇa, Lord Viṣṇu. Although he did not chant the holy name of Nārāyaṇa completely offenselessly, it acted nevertheless. As soon as he chanted the holy name of Nārāyaṇa, the order carriers of Lord Viṣṇu immediately appeared on the scene. A discussion ensued between the order carriers of Lord Viṣṇu and those of Yamarāja, and by hearing that discussion Ajāmila was liberated. He could then understand the bad effect of fruitive activities and could also understand how exalted is the process of devotional service.

TEXT 1

श्रीपरीक्षिदुवाच
निवृत्तिमार्गः कथित आदौ भगवता यथा ।
क्रमयोगोपलब्धेन ब्रह्मणा यदसंसृतिः ॥ १ ॥

śrī-parīkṣid uvāca
nivṛtti-mārgaḥ kathita
ādau bhagavatā yathā
krama-yogopalabdhena
brahmaṇā yad asaṁsṛtiḥ

śrī-parīkṣit uvāca—Mahārāja Parīkṣit said; *nivṛtti-mārgaḥ*—the path of liberation; *kathitaḥ*—described; *ādau*—in the beginning; *bhagavatā*—by Your Holiness; *yathā*—duly; *krama*—gradually; *yoga-upalabdhena*—obtained by the *yoga* process; *brahmaṇā*—along with Lord Brahmā (after reaching Brahmaloka); *yat*—by which way; *asaṁsṛtiḥ*—cessation of the repetition of birth and death.

TRANSLATION

Mahārāja Parīkṣit said: O my lord, O Śukadeva Gosvāmī, you have already described [in the Second Canto] the path of liberation [nivṛtti-mārga]. By following that path, one is certainly elevated gradually to the highest planetary system, Brahmaloka, from which one is promoted to the spiritual world along with Lord Brahmā. Thus one's repetition of birth and death in the material world ceases.

PURPORT

Since Mahārāja Parīkṣit was a Vaiṣṇava, when he heard the description, at the end of the Fifth Canto, of the different hellish conditions of life, he was very much concerned with how to liberate the conditioned souls from the clutches of *māyā* and take them back home, back to Godhead. Therefore he reminded his spiritual master, Śukadeva Gosvāmī, about the *nivṛtti-mārga,* or path of liberation, which he had described in the Second Canto. Mahārāja Parīkṣit, who at the time of death was fortunate to have met Śukadeva Gosvāmī, inquired from Śukadeva Gosvāmī about the path of liberation at that crucial time. Śukadeva Gosvāmī very much appreciated his question and congratulated him by saying:

varīyān eṣa te praśnaḥ
kṛto loka-hitaṁ nṛpa
ātmavit-sammataḥ puṁsāṁ
śrotavyādiṣu yaḥ paraḥ

"My dear King, your question is glorious because it is very beneficial for all kinds of people. The answer to this question is the prime subject matter for hearing, and it is approved by all transcendentalists." (*Bhāg.* 2.1.1)

Parīkṣit Mahārāja was astonished that the living entities in the conditional stage do not accept the path of liberation, devotional service, instead of suffering in so many hellish conditions. This is the symptom of a Vaiṣṇava. *Vāñchā-kalpa-tarubhyaś ca kṛpā-sindhubhya eva ca:* a Vaiṣṇava is an ocean of mercy. *Para-duḥkha-duḥkhī:* he is unhappy because of the unhappiness of others. Therefore Parīkṣit Mahārāja, being compassionate toward the conditioned souls suffering in hellish life, suggested that Śukadeva Gosvāmī continue describing the path of liberation, which he had explained in the beginning of *Śrīmad-Bhāgavatam.* The word *asaṁsṛti* is very important in this connection. *Saṁsṛti* refers to continuing on the path of birth and death.

Asaṁsṛti, on the contrary, refers to *nivṛtti-mārga,* or the path of liberation, by which one's birth and death cease and one gradually progresses to Brahmaloka, unless one is a pure devotee who does not care about going to the higher planetary systems, in which case one immediately returns home, back to Godhead, by executing devotional service (*tyaktvā dehaṁ punar janma naiti*). Parīkṣit Mahārāja, therefore, was very eager to hear from Śukadeva Gosvāmī about the path of liberation for the conditioned soul.

According to the opinion of the *ācāryas,* the word *krama-yogopalabdhena* indicates that by first performing *karma-yoga* and then *jñāna-yoga* and finally coming to the platform of *bhakti-yoga,* one can be liberated. *Bhakti-yoga,* however, is so powerful that it does not depend on *karma-yoga* or *jñāna-yoga. Bhakti-yoga* itself is so powerful that even an impious man with no assets in *karma-yoga* or an illiterate with no assets in *jñāna-yoga* can undoubtedly be elevated to the spiritual world if he simply adheres to *bhakti-yoga. Mām evaiṣyasy asaṁśayaḥ.* Kṛṣṇa says in *Bhagavad-gītā* (8.7) that by the process of *bhakti-yoga* one undoubtedly goes back to Godhead, back home to the spiritual world. *Yogīs,* however, instead of going directly to the spiritual world, sometimes want to see other planetary systems, and therefore they ascend to the planetary system where Lord Brahmā lives, as indicated here by the word *brahmaṇā.* At the time of dissolution, Lord Brahmā, along with all the inhabitants of Brahmaloka, goes directly to the spiritual world. This is confirmed in the *Vedas* as follows:

brahmaṇā saha te sarve
samprāpte pratisañcare
parasyānte kṛtātmānaḥ
praviśanti paraṁ padam

"Because of their exalted position, those who are on Brahmaloka at the time of dissolution go directly back home, back to Godhead, along with Lord Brahmā."

TEXT 2

प्रवृत्तिलक्षणश्चैव त्रैगुण्यविषयो मुने ।
योऽसावलीनप्रकृतेर्गुणसर्गः पुनः पुनः ॥ २ ॥

pravṛtti-lakṣaṇaś caiva
traiguṇya-viṣayo mune
yo'sāv alīna-prakṛter
guṇa-sargaḥ punaḥ punaḥ

pravṛtti—by inclination; *lakṣaṇaḥ*—symptomized; *ca*—also; *eva*—indeed; *trai-guṇya*—the three modes of nature; *viṣayaḥ*—possessing as objectives; *mune*—O great sage; *yaḥ*—which; *asau*—that; *alīna-prakṛteḥ*—of one who is not freed from the clutches of *māyā; guṇa-sargaḥ*—in which there is a creation of material bodies; *punaḥ punaḥ*—again and again.

TRANSLATION

O great sage Śukadeva Gosvāmī, unless the living entity is freed from the infection of the material modes of nature, he receives different types of bodies in which to enjoy or suffer, and according to the body, he is understood to have various inclinations. By following these inclinations he traverses the path called pravṛtti-mārga, by which one may be elevated to the heavenly planets, as you have already described [in the Third Canto].

PURPORT

As Lord Kṛṣṇa explains in *Bhagavad-gītā* (9.25):

yānti deva-vratā devān
pitṝn yānti pitṛ-vratāḥ
bhūtāni yānti bhūtejyā
yānti mad-yājino 'pi mām

"Those who worship the demigods will take birth among the demigods; those who worship ghosts and spirits will take birth among such beings; those who worship ancestors go to the ancestors; and those who worship Me will live with Me." Because of the influence of the various modes of nature, the living entities have various tendencies or propensities, and therefore they are qualified to achieve various destinations. As long as one is materially attached, he wants to be elevated to the heavenly planets because of his attraction to the material world. The Supreme Personality of Godhead declares, however, "Those who worship Me come to Me." If one has no information about the Supreme Lord and His abode, one tries to be elevated only to a higher material position, but when one concludes that in this material world there is nothing but repeated birth and death, he tries to return home, back to Godhead. If one attains that destination, he need never return to this material world (*yad gatvā na nivartante tad dhāma paramaṁ mama*). As Śrī Caitanya Mahāprabhu says in *Caitanya-caritāmṛta* (*Madhya* 19.151):

brahmāṇḍa bhramite kona bhāgyavān jīva
guru-kṛṣṇa-prasāde pāya bhakti-latā-bīja

"According to their *karma,* all living entities are wandering throughout the entire universe. Some of them are being elevated to the upper planetary systems, and some are going down into the lower planetary systems. Out of many millions of wandering living entities, one who is very fortunate gets an opportunity to associate with a bona fide spiritual master by the grace of Kṛṣṇa. By the mercy of both Kṛṣṇa and the spiritual master, such a person receives the seed of the creeper of devotional service." All living entities are rotating throughout the universe, going sometimes up to the higher planetary systems and sometimes down to the lower planets. This is the material disease, which is known as *pravṛtti-mārga.* When one becomes intelligent he takes to *nivṛtti-mārga,* the path of liberation, and thus instead of rotating within this material world, he returns home, back to Godhead. This is necessary.

TEXT 3

अधर्मलक्षणा नाना नरकाश्चानुवर्णिताः ।
मन्वन्तरश्च व्याख्यात आद्यः स्वायम्भुवो यतः ॥ ३ ॥

adharma-lakṣaṇā nānā
narakāś cānuvarṇitāḥ
manvantaraś ca vyākhyāta
ādyaḥ svāyambhuvo yataḥ

adharma-lakṣaṇāḥ—symptomized by impious activities; *nānā*—various; *narakāḥ*—hells; *ca*—also; *anuvarṇitāḥ*—have been described; *manu-antaraḥ*—the change of Manus [in one day of Brahmā there are fourteen Manus]; *ca*—also; *vyākhyātaḥ*—has been described; *ādyaḥ*—the original; *svāyambhuvaḥ*—directly the son of Lord Brahmā; *yataḥ*—wherein.

TRANSLATION

You have also described [at the end of the Fifth Canto] the varieties of hellish life that result from impious activities, and you have described [in the Fourth Canto] the first manvantara, which was presided over by Svāyambhuva Manu, the son of Lord Brahmā.

TEXTS 4–5

प्रियव्रतोत्तानपदोर्वंशस्तच्चरितानि च ।
द्वीपवर्षसमुद्राद्रिनद्युद्यानवनस्पतीन् ॥ ४ ॥

धरामण्डलसंस्थानं भागलक्षणमानतः ।
ज्योतिषां विवराणां च यथेदमसृजद्विभुः ॥ ५ ॥

priyavratottānapador
vaṁśas tac-caritāni ca
dvīpa-varṣa-samudrādri-
nady-udyāna-vanaspatīn

dharā-maṇḍala-saṁsthānaṁ
bhāga-lakṣaṇa-mānataḥ
jyotiṣāṁ vivarāṇāṁ ca
yathedam asṛjad vibhuḥ

priyavrata—of Priyavrata; *uttānapadoḥ*—and of Uttānapāda; *vaṁśaḥ*—the dynasty; *tat-caritāni*—their characteristics; *ca*—also; *dvīpa*—different planets; *varṣa*—lands; *samudra*—oceans and seas; *adri*—mountains; *nadī*—rivers; *udyāna*—gardens; *vanaspatīn*—and trees; *dharā-maṇḍala*—of the planet earth; *saṁsthānam*—situation; *bhāga*—according to divisions; *lakṣaṇa*—different symptoms; *mānataḥ*—and measurements; *jyotiṣām*—of the sun and other luminaries; *vivarāṇām*—of the lower planetary systems; *ca*—and; *yathā*—as; *idam*—this; *asṛjat*—created; *vibhuḥ*—the Supreme Personality of Godhead.

TRANSLATION

My dear lord, you have described the dynasties and characteristics of King Priyavrata and King Uttānapāda. The Supreme Personality of Godhead created this material world with various universes, planetary systems, planets and stars, with varied lands, seas, oceans, mountains, rivers, gardens and trees, all with different characteristics. These are divided among this planet earth, the luminaries in the sky and the lower planetary systems. You have very clearly described these planets and the living entities who live on them.

PURPORT

Here the words *yathedam asṛjad vibhuḥ* clearly indicate that the Supreme, the great, almighty Personality of Godhead, created this entire material world with its different varieties of planets, stars and so forth. Atheists try to conceal the hand of God, which is present in every creation, but they cannot explain how all these creations could come into existence without a competent intelligence and almighty power behind them. Simply to imagine or speculate is a waste of time. In *Bhagavad-gītā* (10.8), the Lord says, *ahaṁ sarvasya prabhavo:* "I am the origin of everything." *Mattaḥ sarvaṁ pravartate:* "Whatever exists in the creation emanates from Me." *Iti matvā bhajante māṁ budhā bhāva-samanvitāḥ:* "When one fully understands that I create everything by My omnipotence, one becomes firmly situated in devotional service and fully surrenders at My lotus feet." Unfortunately, the unintelligent cannot immediately understand Kṛṣṇa's supremacy. Nonetheless, if they associate with devotees and read authorized books, they may gradually come to the proper understanding, although this may take many, many births. As Kṛṣṇa says in *Bhagavad-gītā* (7.19):

bahūnāṁ janmanām ante
jñānavān māṁ prapadyate
vāsudevaḥ sarvam iti
sa mahātmā sudurlabhaḥ

"After many births and deaths, he who is actually in knowledge surrenders unto Me, knowing Me to be the cause of all causes and all that is. Such a great soul is very rare." Vāsudeva, Kṛṣṇa, is the creator of everything, and His energy is displayed in various ways. As explained in *Bhagavad-gītā* (7.4–5), a combination of the material energy (*bhūmir āpo'nalo vāyuḥ*) and the spiritual energy, the living entity, exists in every creation. Therefore the same principle, the combination of the supreme spirit and the material elements, is the cause of the cosmic manifestation.

TEXT 6

अधुनेह महाभाग यथैव नरकान्नरः ।
नानोग्रयातनान्नेयात्तन्मे व्याख्यातुमर्हसि ॥ ६ ॥

adhuneha mahā-bhāga
yathaiva narakān naraḥ
nānogra-yātanān neyāt
tan me vyākhyātum arhasi

adhunā—right now; *iha*—in this material world; *mahā-bhāga*—O greatly opulent and fortunate Śukadeva Gosvāmī; *yathā*—so that; *eva*—indeed; *narakān*—all the hellish conditions into which the impious are put; *naraḥ*—human beings; *nānā*—varieties of; *ugra*—terrible; *yātanān*—conditions of suffering; *na īyāt*—may not undergo; *tat*—that; *me*—to me; *vyākhyātum arhasi*—please describe.

TRANSLATION

O greatly fortunate and opulent Śukadeva Gosvāmī, now kindly tell me how human beings may be saved from having to enter hellish conditions in which they suffer terrible pains.

PURPORT

In the Twenty-sixth Chapter of the Fifth Canto, Śukadeva Gosvāmī has explained that people who commit sinful acts are forced to enter hellish planets and suffer. Now Mahārāja Parīkṣit, being a devotee, is concerned with how this can be stopped. A Vaiṣṇava is *para-duḥkha-duḥkhī;* in other words, he has no personal troubles, but he is very unhappy to see others in trouble. Prahlāda Mahārāja said, "My Lord, I have no personal problems, for I have learned how to glorify Your transcendental qualities and thus enter a trance of ecstasy. I do have a problem, however, for I am simply thinking of these rascals and fools who are busy with *māyā-sukha,* temporary happiness, without knowledge of devotional service unto You." This is the problem faced by a Vaiṣṇava. Because a Vaiṣṇava fully takes shelter of the Supreme Personality of Godhead, he personally has no problems, but because he is compassionate toward the fallen, conditioned souls, he is always thinking of plans to save them from their hellish life in this body and the next. Parīkṣit Mahārāja, therefore, anxiously wanted to know from Śukadeva Gosvāmī how humanity can be saved from gliding down to hell. Śukadeva Gosvāmī had already explained how people enter hellish life, and he could also explain how they could be saved from it. Intelligent men must take advantage of these instructions. Unfortunately, however, the entire world is lacking Kṛṣṇa consciousness, and therefore people are suffering from the grossest ignorance and do not even believe in a life after this one. To convince them of their next life is very difficult because they have become almost mad in their pursuit of material enjoyment. Nevertheless, our duty, the duty of all sane men, is to save them. Mahārāja Parīkṣit is the representative of one who can save them.

TEXT 7

श्रीशुक उवाच

न चेदिहैवापचितिं यथांहसः
कृतस्य कुर्यान्मनउक्तपाणिभिः ।

ध्रुवं स वै प्रेत्य नरकानुपैति
ये कीर्तिता मे भवतस्तिग्मयातनाः ॥ ७ ॥

śrī-śuka uvāca
na ced ihaivāpacitiṁ yathāṁhasaḥ
kṛtasya kuryān mana-ukta-pāṇibhiḥ
dhruvaṁ sa vai pretya narakān upaiti
ye kīrtitā me bhavatas tigma-yātanāḥ

śrī-śukaḥ uvāca—Śrīla Śukadeva Gosvāmī said; *na*—not; *cet*—if; *iha*—within this life; *eva*—certainly; *apacitim*—counteraction, atonement; *yathā*—duly; *aṁhasaḥ kṛtasya*—when one has performed sinful activities; *kuryāt*—performs; *manaḥ*—with the mind; *ukta*—words; *pāṇibhiḥ*—and with the senses; *dhruvam*—undoubtedly; *saḥ*—that person; *vai*—indeed; *pretya*—after death; *narakān*—different varieties of hellish conditions; *upaiti*—attains; *ye*—which; *kīrtitāḥ*—were already described; *me*—by me; *bhavataḥ*—unto you; *tigma-yātanāḥ*—in which there is very terrible suffering.

TRANSLATION

Śukadeva Gosvāmī replied: My dear King, if before one's next death whatever impious acts one has performed in this life with his mind, words and body are not counteracted through proper atonement according to the description of the Manu-saṁhitā and other dharma-śāstras, one will certainly enter the hellish planets after death and undergo terrible suffering, as I have previously described to you.

PURPORT

Śrīla Viśvanātha Cakravartī Ṭhākura mentions that although Mahārāja Parīkṣit was a pure devotee, Śukadeva Gosvāmī did not immediately speak to him about the strength of devotional service. As stated in *Bhagavad-gītā* (14.26):

māṁ ca yo'vyabhicāreṇa
bhakti-yogena sevate
sa guṇān samatītyaitān
brahma-bhūyāya kalpate

Devotional service is so strong that if one fully surrenders to Kṛṣṇa and takes fully to His devotional service, the reactions of his sinful life immediately stop.

Elsewhere in the *Gītā* (18.66), Lord Kṛṣṇa urges that one give up all other duties and surrender to Him, and He promises, *ahaṁ tvāṁ sarva-pāpebhyo mokṣayiṣyāmi:* "I shall free you from all sinful reactions and give you liberation." Therefore in response to the inquiries of Parīkṣit Mahārāja, Śukadeva Gosvāmī, his *guru,* could have immediately explained the principle of *bhakti,* but to test Parīkṣit Mahārāja's intelligence, he first prescribed atonement according to *karma-kāṇḍa,* the path of fruitive activities. For *karma-kāṇḍa* there are eighty authorized scriptures, such as *Manu-saṁhitā,* which are known as *dharma-śāstras.* In these scriptures one is advised to counteract his sinful acts by performing other types of fruitive action. This was the path first recommended by Śukadeva Gosvāmī to Mahārāja Parīkṣit, and actually it is a fact that one who does not take to devotional service must follow the decision of these scriptures by performing pious acts to counteract his impious acts. This is known as atonement.

TEXT 8

तस्मात्पुरैवाश्विह पापनिष्कृतौ
यतेत मृत्योरविपद्यतात्मना ।
दोषस्य दृष्ट्वा गुरुलाघवं यथा
भिषक् चिकित्सेत रुजां निदानवित् ॥ ८ ॥

tasmāt puraivāśv iha pāpa-niṣkṛtau
yateta mṛtyor avipadyatātmanā
doṣasya dṛṣṭvā guru-lāghavaṁ yathā
bhiṣak cikitseta rujāṁ nidānavit

tasmāt—therefore; *purā*—before; *eva*—indeed; *āśu*—very quickly; *iha*—in this life; *pāpa-niṣkṛtau*—to become free from the reaction of sinful activities; *yateta*—one should endeavor; *mṛtyoḥ*—death; *avipadyata*—not troubled by disease and old age; *ātmanā*—with a body; *doṣasya*—of the sinful activities; *dṛṣṭvā*—estimating; *guru-lāghavam*—the heaviness or lightness; *yathā*—just like; *bhiṣak*—a physician; *cikitseta*—would treat; *rujām*—of disease; *nidāna-vit*—one who is expert in diagnosis.

TRANSLATION

Therefore, before one's next death comes, as long as one's body is strong enough, one should quickly adopt the process of atonement according to śāstra; otherwise one's time will be lost, and the reactions of

his sins will increase. As an expert physician diagnoses and treats a disease according to its gravity, one should undergo atonement according to the severity of one's sins.

PURPORT

The *dharma-śāstras* like the *Manu-saṁhitā* prescribe that a man who has committed murder should be hanged and his own life sacrificed in atonement. Previously this system was followed all over the world, but since people are becoming atheists, they are stopping capital punishment. This is not wise. Herein it is said that a physician who knows how to diagnose a disease prescribes medicine accordingly. If the disease is very serious, the medicine must be strong. The weight of a murderer's sin is very great, and therefore according to *Manu-saṁhitā* a murderer must be killed. By killing a murderer the government shows mercy to him because if a murderer is not killed in this life, he will be killed and forced to suffer many times in future lives. Since people do not know about the next life and the intricate workings of nature, they manufacture their own laws, but they should properly consult the established injunctions of the *śāstras* and act accordingly. In India even today the Hindu community often takes advice from expert scholars regarding how to counteract sinful activities. In Christianity also there is a process of confession and atonement. Therefore atonement is required, and atonement must be undergone according to the gravity of one's sinful acts.

TEXT 9

श्रीराजोवाच
दृष्टश्रुताभ्यां यत्पापं जानन्नप्यात्मनोऽहितम् ।
करोति भूयो विवशः प्रायश्चित्तमथो कथम् ॥ ९ ॥

śrī-rājovāca
dṛṣṭa-śrutābhyāṁ yat pāpaṁ
jānann apy ātmano'hitam
karoti bhūyo vivaśaḥ
prāyaścittam atho katham

śrī-rājā uvāca—Parīkṣit Mahārāja replied; *dṛṣṭa*—by seeing; *śrutābhyām*—also by hearing (from the scriptures or lawbooks); *yat*—since; *pāpam*—sinful, criminal action; *jānan*—knowing; *api*—although; *ātmanaḥ*—of his self;

His Divine Grace
A. C. Bhaktivedanta Swami Prabhupāda
Founder-Ācārya of ISKCON and greatest exponent of Kṛṣṇa consciousness in the modern world

The order carriers of Yamarāja were snatching the soul from the core of Ajāmila's heart, but with resounding voices the messengers of Lord Viṣṇu forbade them to do so. (6.1.27–31)

On the bank of the Ganges at Hardwar, Ajāmila gave up his material body and regained his original, spiritual body, which was suitable for an associate of the Lord. Then, accompanied by the order carriers of Lord Viṣṇu, Ajāmila boarded a golden airplane for his journey back to the Lord's abode. (6.2.39–44)

When the ten Pracetās emerged from the sea, where they had been performing austerities, they saw that the entire surface of the earth was covered with trees. The Pracetās became very angry at the trees and, desiring to burn them to ashes, generated fire and wind from their mouths. Then Soma, the moon-god, appeared before the Pracetās to appease their anger. (6.4.4–6)

The Supreme Lord is known as Kṛṣṇa because His transcendental qualities make Him very attractive to all living entities. He especially displays His all-attractive feature in Vṛndāvana, where He sports with His cowherd boyfriends and other intimate associates. (6.4.34)

Lord Hari was very pleased by the prayers Dakṣa had offered, and thus He appeared before Dakṣa riding His carrier Garuḍa and accompanied by Nārada Muni, Nanda and all the principal demigods. (6.4.35–39)

Viśvarūpa, whom the demigods had engaged as their priest, instructed King Indra about the Nārāyaṇa armor, which enabled Indra to conquer the demons. (6.8.3–36)

From the southern side of the sacrificial fire came a fearful personality who looked like the destroyer of the entire creation at the end of the millennium. (6.9.11–17)

As the demigods looked on, Lord Indra cut off Vṛtrāsura's head with his thunderbolt. At that time the living spark came forth from Vṛtrāsura's body and returned home, back to Godhead. (6.12.32–33)

King Indra became enraged and threw one of his great clubs at Vṛtrāsura, but as the club flew toward him Vṛtrāsura easily caught it with his left hand. The powerful demon angrily struck the head of Indra's elephant with the club, making a tumultuous sound. Struck with

the club like a mountain struck by a thunderbolt, the elephant Airāvata, feeling great pain and spitting blood from its broken mouth, was pushed back fourteen yards. In extreme distress, the elephant fell, with Indra on its back. (6.11.6–11)

Because of killing the *brāhmaṇa* Vṛtrāsura, Indra suffered by having personified sinful reaction chase him in the form of a *caṇḍāla* woman. (6.13.12–14)

By mystic power, the great sage Nārada brought Citraketu's dead son back to life. Then the son spoke transcendental wisdom to enlighten the King. (6.16.1)

In the presence of his worshipable Lord, Citraketu felt great devotion and love, and he offered his respectful obeisances. (6.16.31)

As Mahā-Viṣṇu sleeps within the Causal Ocean, He exhales and inhales millions of universes. (6.16.37)

Once while King Citraketu was traveling in outer space on a brilliantly effulgent airplane given to him by Lord Viṣṇu, he saw Lord Śiva sitting in an assembly of saintly persons and embracing Parvati on his lap. (6.17.4–5)

ahitam—injurious; *karoti*—he acts; *bhūyaḥ*—again and again; *vivaśaḥ*—unable to control himself; *prāyaścittam*—atonement; *atho*—therefore; *katham*—what is the value of.

TRANSLATION

Mahārāja Parīkṣit said: One may know that sinful activity is injurious for him because he actually sees that a criminal is punished by the government and rebuked by people in general and because he hears from scriptures and learned scholars that one is thrown into hellish conditions in the next life for committing sinful acts. Nevertheless, in spite of such knowledge, one is forced to commit sins again and again, even after performing acts of atonement. Therefore, what is the value of such atonement?

PURPORT

In some religious sects a sinful man goes to a priest to confess his sinful acts and pay a fine, but then he again commits the same sins and returns to confess them again. This is the practice of a professional sinner. Parīkṣit Mahārāja's observations indicate that even five thousand years ago it was the practice of criminals to atone for their crimes but then commit the same crimes again, as if forced to do so. Therefore, owing to his practical experience, Parīkṣit Mahārāja saw that the process of repeatedly sinning and atoning is pointless. Regardless of how many times he is punished, one who is attached to sense enjoyment will commit sinful acts again and again until he is trained to refrain from enjoying his senses. The word *vivaśa* is used herein, indicating that even one who does not want to commit sinful acts will be forced to do so by habit. Parīkṣit Mahārāja therefore considered the process of atonement to have little value for saving one from sinful acts. In the following verse he further explains his rejection of this process.

TEXT 10

क्वचिन्निवर्ततेऽभद्रात्क्वचिच्चरति तत्पुनः ।
प्रायश्चित्तमथोऽपार्थं मन्ये कुञ्जरशौचवत् ॥ १० ॥

kvacin nivartate'bhadrāt
kvacic carati tat punaḥ
prāyaścittam atho'pārthaṁ
manye kuñjara-śaucavat

kvacit—sometimes; *nivartate*—ceases; *abhadrāt*—from sinful activity; *kvacit*—sometimes; *carati*—commits; *tat*—that (sinful activity); *punaḥ*—again; *prāyaścittam*—the process of atonement; *atho*—therefore; *apārtham*—useless; *manye*—I consider; *kuñjara-śaucavat*—exactly like the bathing of an elephant.

TRANSLATION

Sometimes one who is very alert so as not to commit sinful acts is victimized by sinful life again. I therefore consider this process of repeated sinning and atoning to be useless. It is like the bathing of an elephant, for an elephant cleanses itself by taking a full bath, but then throws dust over its head and body as soon as it returns to the land.

PURPORT

When Parīkṣit Mahārāja inquired how a human being could free himself from sinful activities so as not to be forced to go to hellish planetary systems after death, Śukadeva Gosvāmī answered that the process of counteracting sinful life is atonement. In this way Śukadeva Gosvāmī tested the intelligence of Mahārāja Parīkṣit, who passed the examination by refusing to accept this process as genuine. Now Parīkṣit Mahārāja is expecting another answer from his spiritual master, Śukadeva Gosvāmī.

TEXT 11

श्रीबादरायणिरुवाच
कर्मणा कर्मनिर्हारो न ह्यात्यन्तिक इष्यते ।
अविद्वदधिकारित्वात्प्रायश्चित्तं विमर्शनम् ॥ ११ ॥

śrī-bādarāyaṇir uvāca
karmaṇā karma-nirhāro
na hy ātyantika iṣyate
avidvad-adhikāritvāt
prāyaścittaṁ vimarśanam

śrī-bādarāyaṇiḥ uvāca—Śukadeva Gosvāmī, the son of Vyāsadeva, replied; *karmaṇā*—by fruitive activities; *karma-nirhāraḥ*—counteraction of fruitive activities; *na*—not; *hi*—indeed; *ātyantikaḥ*—final; *iṣyate*—becomes possible; *avidvat-adhikāritvāt*—from being without knowledge; *prāyaścittam*—real atonement; *vimarśanam*—full knowledge of Vedānta.

TRANSLATION

Śukadeva Gosvāmī, the son of Vedavyāsa, answered: My dear King, since acts meant to neutralize impious actions are also fruitive, they will not release one from the tendency to act fruitively. Persons who subject themselves to the rules and regulations of atonement are not at all intelligent. Indeed, they are in the mode of darkness. Unless one is freed from the mode of ignorance, trying to counteract one action through another is useless because this will not uproot one's desires. Thus even though one may superficially seem pious, he will undoubtedly be prone to act impiously. Therefore real atonement is enlightenment in perfect knowledge, Vedānta, by which one understands the Supreme Absolute Truth.

PURPORT

The *guru,* Śukadeva Gosvāmī, has examined Parīkṣit Mahārāja, and it appears that the King has passed one phase of the examination by rejecting the process of atonement because it involves fruitive activities. Now Śukadeva Gosvāmī is suggesting the platform of speculative knowledge. Progressing from *karma-kāṇḍa* to *jñāna-kāṇḍa,* he is proposing, *prāyaścittaṁ vimarśanam:* "Real atonement is full knowledge." *Vimarśana* refers to the cultivation of speculative knowledge. In *Bhagavad-gītā, karmīs,* who are lacking in knowledge, are compared to asses. Kṛṣṇa says in *Bhagavad-gītā* (7.15):

na māṁ duṣkṛtino mūḍhāḥ
prapadyante narādhamāḥ
māyayāpahṛta-jñānā
āsuraṁ bhāvam āśritāḥ

"Those miscreants who are grossly foolish, lowest among mankind, whose knowledge is stolen by illusion, and who partake of the atheistic nature of demons, do not surrender unto Me." Thus *karmīs* who engage in sinful acts and who do not know the true objective of life are called *mūḍhas,* asses. *Vimarśana,* however, is also explained in *Bhagavad-gītā* (15.15), where Kṛṣṇa says, *vedaiś ca sarvair aham eva vedyaḥ:* the purpose of Vedic study is to understand the Supreme Personality of Godhead. If one studies Vedānta but merely advances somewhat in speculative knowledge and does not understand the Supreme Lord, one remains the same *mūḍha.* As stated in *Bhagavad-gītā* (7.19), one attains real knowledge when he understands Kṛṣṇa and surrenders unto Him (*bahūnāṁ janmanām ante jñānavān māṁ prapadyate*). To become learned and free from material contamination, therefore, one should try to understand Kṛṣṇa, for thus one is immediately liberated from all pious and impious activities and their reactions.

TEXT 12

नाश्नतः पथ्यमेवान्नं व्याधयोऽभिभवन्ति हि ।
एवं नियमकृद्राजन् शनैः क्षेमाय कल्पते ॥ १२ ॥

nāśnataḥ pathyam evānnaṁ
vyādhayo'bhibhavanti hi
evaṁ niyamakṛd rājan
śanaiḥ kṣemāya kalpate

na—not; *aśnataḥ*—those who eat; *pathyam*—suitable; *eva*—indeed; *annam*—food; *vyādhayaḥ*—different types of disease; *abhibhavanti*—overcome; *hi*—indeed; *evam*—similarly; *niyama-kṛt*—one following regulative principles; *rājan*—O King; *śanaiḥ*—gradually; *kṣemāya*—for well-being; *kalpate*—becomes fit.

TRANSLATION

My dear King, if a diseased person eats the pure, uncontaminated food prescribed by a physician, he is gradually cured, and the infection of disease can no longer touch him. Similarly, if one follows the regulative principles of knowledge, he gradually progresses toward liberation from material contamination.

PURPORT

One is gradually purified if one cultivates knowledge, even through mental speculation, and strictly follows the regulative principles enjoined in the *śāstras* and explained in the next verse. Therefore the platform of *jñāna,* speculative knowledge, is better than the platform of *karma,* fruitive action. There is every chance of falling from the platform of *karma* to hellish conditions, but on the platform of *jñāna* one is saved from hellish life, although one is still not completely free from infection. The difficulty is that on the platform of *jñāna* one thinks that he has been liberated and has become Nārāyaṇa, or Bhagavān. This is another phase of ignorance.

ye'nye'ravindākṣa vimukta-māninas
tvayy asta-bhāvād aviśuddha-buddhayaḥ
āruhya kṛcchreṇa paraṁ padaṁ tataḥ
patanty adho'nādṛta-yuṣmad-aṅghrayaḥ
(*Bhāg.* 10.2.32)

Because of ignorance, one speculatively thinks himself liberated from material contamination although actually he is not. Therefore even if one rises to *brahma jñāna,* understanding of Brahman, one nevertheless falls down because of not taking shelter of the lotus feet of Kṛṣṇa. Nonetheless, *jñānīs* at least know what is sinful and what is pious, and they very cautiously act according to the injunctions of the *śāstras.*

TEXTS 13–14

तपसा ब्रह्मचर्येण शमेन च दमेन च ।
त्यागेन सत्यशौचाभ्यां यमेन नियमेन वा ॥ १३ ॥
देहवाग्बुद्धिजं धीरा धर्मज्ञाः श्रद्धयान्विताः ।
क्षिपन्त्यघं महदपि वेणुगुल्ममिवानलः ॥ १४ ॥

tapasā brahmacaryeṇa
śamena ca damena ca
tyāgena satya-śaucābhyāṁ
yamena niyamena vā

deha-vāg-buddhijaṁ dhīrā
dharmajñāḥ śraddhayānvitāḥ
kṣipanty aghaṁ mahad api
veṇu-gulmam ivānalaḥ

tapasā—by austerity or voluntary rejection of material enjoyment; *brahmacaryeṇa*—by celibacy (the first austerity); *śamena*—by controlling the mind; *ca*—and; *damena*—by fully controlling the senses; *ca*—also; *tyāgena*—by voluntarily giving charity to good causes; *satya*—by truthfulness; *śaucābhyām*—and by following regulative principles to keep oneself internally and externally clean; *yamena*—by avoiding cursing and violence; *niyamena*—by regularly chanting the holy name of the Lord; *vā*—and; *deha-vāk-buddhi-jam*—performed by the body, words and intelligence; *dhīrāḥ*—those who are sober; *dharma-jñāḥ*—fully imbued with knowledge of religious principles;

śraddhayā anvitāḥ—endowed with faith; *kṣipanti*—destroy; *agham*—all kinds of sinful activities; *mahat api*—although very great and abominable; *veṇu-gulmam*—the dried creepers beneath a bamboo tree; *iva*—like; *analaḥ*—fire.

TRANSLATION

To concentrate the mind, one must observe a life of celibacy and not fall down. One must undergo the austerity of voluntarily giving up sense enjoyment. One must then control the mind and senses, give charity, be truthful, clean and nonviolent, follow the regulative principles and regularly chant the holy name of the Lord. Thus a sober and faithful person who knows the religious principles is temporarily purified of all sins performed with his body, words and mind. These sins are like the dried leaves of creepers beneath a bamboo tree, which may be burned by fire although their roots remain to grow again at the first opportunity.

PURPORT

Tapaḥ is explained in the *smṛti-śāstra* as follows: *manasaś cendriyāṇāṁ ca aikāgryaṁ paramaṁ tapaḥ.* "Complete control of the mind and senses and their complete concentration on one kind of activity is called *tapaḥ.*" Our Kṛṣṇa consciousness movement is teaching people how to concentrate the mind on devotional service. This is first-class *tapaḥ. Brahmacarya,* the life of celibacy, has eight aspects: one should not think of women, speak about sex life, dally with women, look lustfully at women, talk intimately with women or decide to engage in sexual intercourse, nor should one endeavor for sex life or engage in sex life. One should not even think of women or look at them, to say nothing of talking with them. This is called first-class *brahmacarya.* If a *brahmacārī* or *sannyāsī* talks with a woman in a secluded place, naturally there will be a possibility of sex life without anyone's knowledge. Therefore a complete *brahmacārī* practices just the opposite. If one is a perfect *brahmacārī,* he can very easily control the mind and senses, give charity, speak truthfully and so forth. To begin, however, one must control the tongue and the process of eating.

In the *bhakti-mārga,* the path of devotional service, one must strictly follow the regulative principles by first controlling the tongue (*sevonmukhe hi jihvādau svayam eva sphuraty adaḥ*). The tongue (*jihvā*) can be controlled if one chants the Hare Kṛṣṇa *mahā-mantra,* does not speak of any subjects other than those concerning Kṛṣṇa and does not taste anything not offered to Kṛṣṇa. If one can control the tongue in this way, *brahmacarya* and other purifying processes will automatically follow. It will be explained in the next verse that the path of devotional service is completely perfect and is therefore superior to the path of fruitive activities and the path of knowledge. Quoting from the *Vedas,* Śrīla Vīrarāghava Ācārya explains that austerity involves observing fasts as fully as possible (*tapasānāśakena*). Śrīla Rūpa Gosvāmī has also advised that *atyāhāra,* too much eating, is an impediment to advancement in spiritual life. Also, in *Bhagavad-gītā* (6.17) Kṛṣṇa says:

yuktāhāra-vihārasya
yukta-ceṣṭasya karmasu
yukta-svapnāvabodhasya
yogo bhavati duḥkha-hā

"He who is temperate in his habits of eating, sleeping, working and recreation can mitigate all material pains by practicing the *yoga* system."

In text 14 the word *dhīrāḥ,* meaning "those who are undisturbed under all circumstances," is very significant. Kṛṣṇa tells Arjuna in *Bhagavad-gītā* (2.14):

mātrā-sparśās tu kaunteya
śītoṣṇa-sukha-duḥkha-dāḥ
āgamāpāyino'nityās
tāṁs titikṣasva bhārata

"O son of Kuntī, the nonpermanent appearance of happiness and distress, and their disappearance in due course, are like the appearance and disappearance of winter and summer seasons. They arise from sense perception, O scion of Bharata, and one must learn to tolerate them without being disturbed." In material life there are many disturbances (*adhyātmika, adhidaivika* and *adhibhautika*). One who has learned to tolerate these disturbances under all circumstances is called *dhīra.*

TEXT 15

केचित्केवलया भक्त्या वासुदेवपरायणाः ।
अघं धुन्वन्ति कार्त्स्न्येन नीहारमिव भास्करः ॥ १५ ॥

kecit kevalayā bhaktyā
vāsudeva-parāyaṇāḥ
aghaṁ dhunvanti kārtsnyena
nīhāram iva bhāskaraḥ

kecit—some people; *kevalayā bhaktyā*—by executing unalloyed devotional service; *vāsudeva*—to Lord Kṛṣṇa, the all-pervading Supreme

Personality of Godhead; *parāyaṇāḥ*—completely attached (only to such service, without dependence on austerity, penance, cultivation of knowledge or pious activities); *agham*—all kinds of sinful reactions; *dhunvanti*—destroy; *kārtsnyena*—completely (with no possibility that sinful desires will revive); *nīhāram*—fog; *iva*—like; *bhāskaraḥ*—the sun.

TRANSLATION

Only a rare person who has adopted complete, unalloyed devotional service to Kṛṣṇa can uproot the weeds of sinful actions with no possibility that they will revive. He can do this simply by discharging devotional service, just as the sun can immediately dissipate fog by its rays.

PURPORT

In the previous verse Śukadeva Gosvāmī gave the example that the dried leaves of creepers beneath a bamboo tree may be completely burnt to ashes by a fire, although the creepers may sprout again because the root is still in the ground. Similarly, because the root of sinful desire is not destroyed in the heart of a person who is cultivating knowledge but who has no taste for devotional service, there is a possibility that his sinful desires will reappear. As stated in *Śrīmad-Bhāgavatam* (10.14.4):

śreyaḥ-sṛtiṁ bhaktim udasya te vibho
kliśyanti ye kevala-bodha-labdhaye

Speculators who undergo great labor to gain a meticulous understanding of the material world by distinguishing between sinful and pious activities, but who are not situated in devotional service, are prone to material activities. They may fall down and become implicated in fruitive activities. If one becomes attached to devotional service, however, his desires for material enjoyment are automatically vanquished without separate endeavor. *Bhaktiḥ pareśānubhavo viraktir anyatra ca:* if one is advanced in Kṛṣṇa consciousness, material activities, both sinful and pious, automatically become distasteful to him. That is the test of Kṛṣṇa consciousness. Both pious and impious activities are actually due to ignorance because a living entity, as an eternal servant of Kṛṣṇa, has no need to act for his personal sense gratification. Therefore as soon as one is reclaimed to the platform of devotional service, he relinquishes his attachment for pious and impious activities and is interested only in what will satisfy Kṛṣṇa. This process of *bhakti,* devotional service to Kṛṣṇa (*vāsudeva-parāyaṇa*), relieves one from the reactions of all activities.

Since Mahārāja Parīkṣit was a great devotee. the answers of his *guru,* Śukadeva Gosvāmī, concerning *karma-kāṇḍa* and *jñāna-kāṇḍa* could not satisfy him. Therefore Śukadeva Gosvāmī, knowing very well the heart of his disciple, explained the transcendental bliss of devotional service. The word *kecit,* which is used in this verse, means. "a few people but not all." Not everyone can become Kṛṣṇa conscious. As Kṛṣṇa explains in *Bhagavad-gītā* (7.3):

manuṣyāṇāṁ sahasreṣu
kaścid yatati siddhaye
yatatām api siddhānāṁ
kaścin māṁ vetti tattvataḥ

"Out of many thousands among men, one may endeavor for perfection, and of those who have achieved perfection, hardly one knows Me in truth." Practically no one understands Kṛṣṇa as He is, for Kṛṣṇa cannot be understood through pious activities or attainment of the most elevated speculative knowledge. Actually the highest knowledge consists of understanding Kṛṣṇa. Unintelligent men who do not understand Kṛṣṇa are grossly puffed up, thinking that they are liberated or have themselves become Kṛṣṇa or Nārāyaṇa. This is ignorance.

To indicate the purity of *bhakti,* devotional service, Śrīla Rūpa Gosvāmī says in *Bhakti-rasāmṛta-sindhu* (1.1.11):

anyābhilāṣitā-śūnyaṁ
jñāna-karmādy-anāvṛtam
ānukūlyena kṛṣṇānu-
śīlanaṁ bhaktir uttamā

"One should render transcendental loving service to the Supreme Lord Kṛṣṇa favorably and without desire for material profit or gain through fruitive activities or philosophical speculation. That is called pure devotional service." Śrīla Rūpa Gosvāmī further explains that *bhakti* is *kleśaghnī śubhadā,* which means if one takes to devotional service, all kinds of unnecessary labor and material distress cease entirely and one achieves all good fortune. *Bhakti* is so powerful that it is also said to be *mokṣa-laghutākṛt;* in other words, it minimizes the importance of liberation.

Nondevotees must undergo material hardships because they are prone to commit sinful fruitive activities. The desire to commit sinful actions continues in their hearts due to ignorance. These sinful actions are divided into three categories—*pātaka, mahā-pātaka* and *atipātaka*—and also into two divisions; *prārabdha* and *aprārabdha. Prārabdha* refers to sinful reactions from which one is suffering at the present, and *aprārabdha* refers to sources of potential suffering. When the seeds (*bīja*) of sinful reactions have not yet fructified, the reactions are called *aprārabdha.* These seeds of sinful action are unseen, but they are unlimited, and no one can trace when they were first planted. Because of *prārabdha,* sinful reactions that have already fructified, one is seen to have taken birth in a low family or to be suffering from other miseries.

When one takes to devotional service, however, all phases of sinful life, including *prārabdha, aprārabdha* and *bīja,* are vanquished. In *Śrīmad-Bhāgavatam* (11.14.19) Lord Kṛṣṇa tells Uddhava:

yathāgniḥ susamṛddhārciḥ
karoty edhāṁsi bhasmasāt
tathā mad-viṣayā bhaktir
uddhavaināṁsi kṛtsnaśaḥ

"My dear Uddhava, devotional service in relationship with Me is like a blazing fire that can burn to ashes all the fuel of sinful activities supplied to it." How devotional service vanquishes the reactions of sinful life is explained in *Śrīmad-Bhāgavatam* (3.33.6) in a verse spoken during Lord Kapiladeva's instructions to His mother, Devahūti. Devahūti said:

yan-nāmadheya-śravaṇānukīrtanād
yat-prahvaṇād yat-smaraṇād api kvacit
śvādo'pi sadyaḥ savanāya kalpate
kutaḥ punas te bhagavan nu darśanāt

"My dear Lord, if even a person born in a family of dog-eaters hears and repeats the chanting of Your glories, offers respects to You and remembers You, he is immediately greater than a *brāhmaṇa* and is therefore eligible to perform sacrifices. Therefore, what is to be said of one who has seen You directly?"

In the *Padma Purāṇa* there is a statement that persons whose hearts are always attached to the devotional service of Lord Viṣṇu are immediately released from all the reactions of sinful life. These reactions generally exist in four phases. Some of them are ready to produce results immediately, some are in the form of seeds, some are unmanifested, and some are current. All such reactions are immediately nullified by devotional service. When devotional service is present in one's heart, desires to perform sinful activities have no place there. Sinful life is due to ignorance, which means forgetfulness of one's constitutional position as an eternal servant of God, but when one is fully Kṛṣṇa conscious he realizes that he is God's eternal servant.

In this regard, Śrīla Jīva Gosvāmī comments that *bhakti* may be divided into two divisions: (1) *santatā,* devotional service that continues incessantly with faith and love, and (2) *kādācitkī,* devotional service that does not continue incessantly but is sometimes awakened. Incessantly flowing devotional service (*santatā*) may also be divided into two categories: (1) service performed with slight attachment and (2) spontaneous devotional service. Intermittent devotional service (*kādācitkī*) may be divided into three categories: (1) *rāgābhāsamayī,* devotional service in which one is almost attached, (2) *rāgābhāsa-śūnya-svarūpa-bhūtā,* devotional service in which there is no spontaneous love but one likes the constitutional position of serving, and (3) *ābhāsa-rūpā,* a slight glimpse of devotional service. As for atonement, if one has caught even a slight glimpse of devotional service, all needs to undergo *prāyaścitta,* atonement, are superseded. Therefore atonement is certainly unnecessary when one has achieved spontaneous love and, above that, attachment with love, which are signs of increasing advancement in *kādācitkī.* Even in the stage of *ābhāsa-rūpā bhakti,* all the reactions of sinful life are uprooted and vanquished. Śrīla Jīva Gosvāmī expresses the opinion that the word *kārtsnyena* means that even if one has a desire to commit sinful actions, the roots of that desire are vanquished merely by *ābhāsa-rūpā bhakti.* The example of *bhāskara,* the sun, is most appropriate. The *ābhāsa* feature of *bhakti* is compared to twilight, and the accumulation of one's sinful activities is compared to fog. Since fog does not spread throughout the sky, the sun need do no more than merely manifest its first rays, and the fog immediately disappears. Similarly, if one has even a slight relationship with devotional service, all the fog of his sinful life is immediately vanquished.

TEXT 16

न तथा ह्यघवान् राजन् पूयेत तपआदिभिः ।
यथा कृष्णार्पितप्राणस्तत्पुरुषनिषेवया ॥ १६ ॥

na tathā hy aghavān rājan
pūyeta tapa-ādibhiḥ
yathā kṛṣṇārpita-prāṇas
tat-puruṣa-niṣevayā

na—not; *tathā*—so much; *hi*—certainly; *agha-vān*—a man full of sinful activities; *rājan*—O King; *pūyeta*—can become purified; *tapaḥ-ādibhiḥ*—by executing the principles of austerity, penance, *brahmacarya* and other purifying processes; *yathā*—as much as; *kṛṣṇa-arpita-prāṇaḥ*—the devotee whose life is fully Kṛṣṇa conscious; *tat-puruṣa-niṣevayā*—by engaging his life in the service of Kṛṣṇa's representative.

TRANSLATION

My dear King, if a sinful person engages in the service of a bona fide devotee of the Lord and thus learns how to dedicate his life unto the lotus feet of Kṛṣṇa, he can be completely purified. One cannot be purified merely by undergoing austerity, penance, brahmacarya and the other methods of atonement I have previously described.

PURPORT

Tat-puruṣa refers to a preacher of Kṛṣṇa consciousness, such as the spiritual master. Śrīla Narottama dāsa Ṭhākura has said, *chāḍiyā vaiṣṇava-sevā nistāra pāyeche kebā:* "Without serving a bona fide spiritual master, an ideal Vaiṣṇava, who can be delivered from the clutches of *māyā*?" This idea is also expressed in many other places. *Śrīmad-Bhāgavatam* (5.5.2) says, *mahat-sevāṁ dvāram āhur vimukteḥ:* if one desires liberation from the clutches of *māyā,* one must associate with a pure devotee *mahātmā.* A *mahātmā* is one who engages twenty-four hours daily in the loving service of the Lord. As Kṛṣṇa says in *Bhagavad-gītā* (9.13):

mahātmānas tu māṁ pārtha
daivīṁ prakṛtim āśritāḥ
bhajanty ananya-manaso
jñātvā bhūtādim avyayam

"O son of Pṛthā, those who are not deluded, the great souls, are under the protection of the divine nature. They are fully engaged in devotional service because they know Me as the Supreme Personality of Godhead, original and inexhaustible." Thus the symptom of a *mahātmā* is that he has no engagement other than service to Kṛṣṇa. One must render service to a Vaiṣṇava in order to get freed from sinful reactions, revive one's original Kṛṣṇa consciousness and be trained in how to love Kṛṣṇa. This is the result of *mahātma-sevā.* Of course, if one engages in the service of a pure devotee, the reactions of one's sinful life are vanquished automatically. Devotional service is necessary not to drive away an insignificant stock of sins, but to awaken our dormant love for Kṛṣṇa. As fog is vanquished at the first glimpse of sunlight, one's sinful reactions are automatically vanquished as soon as one begins serving a pure devotee; no separate endeavor is required.

The word *kṛṣṇārpita-prāṇaḥ* refers to a devotee who dedicates his life to serving Kṛṣṇa, not to being saved from the path to hellish life. A devotee is *nārāyaṇa-parāyaṇa,* or *vāsudeva-parāyaṇa,* which means that the path of Vāsudeva, or the devotional path, is his life and soul. *Nārāyaṇa-parāḥ sarve na kutaścana bibhyati* (*Bhāg.* 6.17.28): such a devotee is not afraid of going anywhere. There is a path toward liberation in the higher planetary systems and a path toward the hellish planets, but a *nārāyaṇa-para* devotee is unafraid wherever he is sent; he simply wants to remember Kṛṣṇa, wherever he may be. Such a devotee is unconcerned with hell and heaven; he is simply attached to rendering service to Kṛṣṇa. When a devotee is put into hellish conditions, he accepts them as Kṛṣṇa's mercy: *tat te'nukampāṁ susamīkṣamāṇaḥ* (*Bhāg.* 10.14.8). He does not protest, "Oh, I am such a great devotee of Kṛṣṇa. Why have I been put into this misery?" Instead he thinks, "This is Kṛṣṇa's mercy." Such an attitude is possible for a devotee who engages in the service of Kṛṣṇa's representative. This is the secret of success.

TEXT 17

सध्रीचीनो ह्ययं लोके पन्थाः क्षेमोऽकुतोभयः ।
सुशीलाः साधवो यत्र नारायणपरायणाः ॥ १७ ॥

sadhrīcīno hy ayaṁ loke
panthāḥ kṣemo'kuto-bhayaḥ
suśīlāḥ sādhavo yatra
nārāyaṇa-parāyaṇāḥ

sadhrīcīnaḥ—just appropriate; *hi*—certainly; *ayam*—this; *loke*—in the world; *panthāḥ*—path; *kṣemaḥ*—auspicious; *akutaḥ-bhayaḥ*—without fear; *su-śīlāḥ*—well-behaved; *sādhavaḥ*—saintly persons; *yatra*—wherein; *nārāyaṇa-parāyaṇāḥ*—those who have taken the path of Nārāyaṇa, devotional service, as their life and soul.

TRANSLATION

The path followed by pure devotees, who are well behaved and fully endowed with the best qualifications, is certainly the most auspicious path in this material world. It is free from fear, and it is authorized by the śāstras.

PURPORT

One should not think that the person who takes to *bhakti* is one who cannot perform the ritualistic ceremonies recommended in the *karma-kāṇḍa* section of the *Vedas* or is not sufficiently educated to speculate on spiritual subjects. Māyāvādīs generally allege that the *bhakti* path is for women and illiterates. This is a groundless accusation. The *bhakti* path is followed by the most learned scholars, such as the Gosvāmīs, Lord Caitanya Mahāprabhu and Rāmānujācārya. These are the actual followers of the *bhakti* path. Regardless of whether or not one is educated or aristocratic, one must follow in their footsteps. *Mahājano yena gataḥ sa panthāḥ:* one must follow the path of the *mahājanas.* The *mahājanas* are those who have taken to the path of devotional service (*suśīlāḥ sādhavo yatra nārāyaṇa-parāyaṇāḥ*), for these great personalities are the perfect persons. As stated in *Śrīmad-Bhāgavatam* (5.18.12):

yasyāsti bhaktir bhagavaty akiñcanā
sarvair guṇais tatra samāsate surāḥ

"One who has unflinching devotion to the Personality of Godhead has all the good qualities of the demigods." The less intelligent, however, misunderstand the *bhakti* path and therefore allege that it is for one who cannot execute ritualistic ceremonies or speculate. As confirmed here by the word *sadhrīcīnaḥ, bhakti* is the path that is appropriate, not the paths of *karma-kāṇḍa* and *jñāna-kāṇḍa.* Māyāvādīs may be *suśīlāḥ sādhavaḥ* (well-behaved saintly persons), but there is nevertheless some doubt about whether they are actually making progress, for they have not accepted the path of *bhakti.* On the other hand, those who follow the path of the *ācāryas* are *suśīlāḥ* and *sādhavaḥ,* but furthermore their path is *akuto-bhaya,* which means free from fear. One should fearlessly follow the twelve *mahājanas* and their line of disciplic succession and thus be liberated from the clutches of *māyā.*

TEXT 18

प्रायश्चित्तानि चीर्णानि नारायणपराङ्मुखम् ।
न निष्पुनन्ति राजेन्द्र सुराकुम्भमिवापगाः ॥ १८ ॥

prāyaścittāni cīrṇāni
nārāyaṇa-parāṅmukham
na niṣpunanti rājendra
surā-kumbham ivāpagāḥ

prāyaścittāni—processes of atonement; *cīrṇāni*—very nicely performed; *nārāyaṇa-parāṅmukham*—a nondevotee; *na niṣpunanti*—cannot purify; *rājendra*—O King; *surā-kumbham*—a pot containing liquor; *iva*—like; *āpa-gāḥ*—the waters of the rivers.

TRANSLATION

My dear King, as a pot containing liquor cannot be purified even if washed in the waters of many rivers, nondevotees cannot be purified by processes of atonement even if they perform them very well.

PURPORT

To take advantage of the methods of atonement, one must be at least somewhat devoted; otherwise there is no chance of one's being purified. It is clear from this verse that even those who take advantage of *karma-kāṇḍa* and *jñāna-kāṇḍa,* but are not at least slightly devoted cannot be purified simply by following these other paths. The word *prāyaścittāni* is plural in number to indicate both *karma-kāṇḍa* and *jñāna-kāṇḍa.* Narottama dāsa Ṭhākura therefore says, *karma-kāṇḍa, jñāna-kāṇḍa, kevala viṣera bhāṇḍa.* Thus Narottama dāsa Ṭhākura compares the paths of *karma-kāṇḍa* and *jñāna-kāṇḍa* to pots of poison. Liquor and poison are in the same category. According to this verse from *Śrīmad-Bhāgavatam,* a person who has heard a good deal about the path of devotional service, but who is not attached to it, who is not Kṛṣṇa conscious, is like a pot of liquor. Such a person cannot be purified without at least a slight touch of devotional service.

TEXT 19

सकृन्मनः कृष्णपदारविन्दयो-
निर्वेशितं तद्गुणरागि यैरिह ।
न ते यमं पाशभृतश्च तद्भटान्
स्वप्नेऽपि पश्यन्ति हि चीर्णनिष्कृताः ॥ १९ ॥

sakṛn manaḥ kṛṣṇa-padāravindayor
niveśitaṁ tad-guṇa-rāgi yair iha
na te yamaṁ pāśa-bhṛtaś ca tad-bhaṭān
svapne 'pi paśyanti hi cīrṇa-niṣkṛtāḥ

sakṛt—once only; *manaḥ*—the mind; *kṛṣṇa-pada-aravindayoḥ*—unto the two lotus feet of Lord Kṛṣṇa; *niveśitam*—completely surrendered; *tat*—of Kṛṣṇa; *guṇa-rāgi*—which is somewhat attached to the qualities, name, fame and paraphernalia; *yaiḥ*—by whom; *iha*—in this world; *na*—not; *te*—such persons; *yamam*—Yamarāja, the superintendent of death; *pāśa-bhṛtaḥ*—those who carry ropes (to catch sinful persons); *ca*—and; *tat*—his; *bhaṭān*

—order carriers; *svapne api*—even in dreams; *paśyanti*—see; *hi*—indeed; *cīrṇa-niṣkṛtāḥ*—who have performed the right type of atonement.

TRANSLATION

Although not having fully realized Kṛṣṇa, persons who have even once surrendered completely unto His lotus feet and who have become attracted to His name, form, qualities and pastimes are completely freed of all sinful reactions, for they have thus accepted the true method of atonement. Even in dreams, such surrendered souls do not see Yamarāja or his order carriers, who are equipped with ropes to bind the sinful.

PURPORT

Kṛṣṇa says in *Bhagavad-gītā* (18.66):

sarva-dharmān parityajya
mām ekaṁ śaraṇaṁ vraja
ahaṁ tvāṁ sarva-pāpebhyo
mokṣayiṣyāmi mā śucaḥ

"Abandon all varieties of religion and just surrender unto Me. I shall deliver you from all sinful reaction. Do not fear." This same principle is described here (*sakṛn manaḥ kṛṣṇa-padāravindayoḥ*). If by studying *Bhagavad-gītā* one decides to surrender to Kṛṣṇa, he is immediately freed from all sinful reactions. It is also significant that Śukadeva Gosvāmī, having several times repeated the words *vāsudeva-parāyaṇa* and *nārāyaṇa-parāyaṇa,* finally says *kṛṣṇa-padāravindayoḥ.* Thus he indicates that Kṛṣṇa is the origin of both Nārāyaṇa and Vāsudeva. Even though Nārāyaṇa and Vāsudeva are not different from Kṛṣṇa, simply by surrendering to Kṛṣṇa one fully surrenders to all His expansions, such as Nārāyaṇa, Vāsudeva and Govinda. As Kṛṣṇa says in *Bhagavad-gītā* (7.7), *mattaḥ parataraṁ nānyat:* "There is no truth superior to Me." There are many names and forms of the Supreme Personality of Godhead, but Kṛṣṇa is the supreme form (*kṛṣṇas tu bhagavān svayam*). Therefore Kṛṣṇa recommends to neophyte devotees that one should surrender unto Him only (*mām ekam*). Because neophyte devotees cannot understand what the forms of Nārāyaṇa, Vāsudeva and Govinda are, Kṛṣṇa directly says, *mām ekam.* Herein, this is also supported by the word *kṛṣṇa-padāravindayoḥ.* Nārāyaṇa does not speak personally, but Kṛṣṇa, or Vāsudeva, does, as in *Bhagavad-gītā* for example. Therefore, to follow the direction of *Bhagavad-gītā* means to surrender unto Kṛṣṇa, and to surrender in this way is the highest perfection of *bhakti-yoga.*

Parīkṣit Mahārāja had inquired from Śukadeva Gosvāmī how one can be saved from falling into the various conditions of hellish life. In this verse Śukadeva Gosvāmī answers that a soul who has surrendered to Kṛṣṇa certainly cannot go to *naraka,* hellish existence. To say nothing of going there, even in his dreams he does not see Yamarāja or his order carriers, who are able to take one there. In other words, if one wants to save himself from falling into *naraka,* hellish life, he should fully surrender to Kṛṣṇa. The word *sakṛt* is significant because it indicates that if one sincerely surrenders to Kṛṣṇa once, he is saved even if by chance he falls down by committing sinful activities. Therefore Kṛṣṇa says in *Bhagavad-gītā* (9.30):

api cet sudurācāro
bhajate mām ananya-bhāk
sādhur eva sa mantavyaḥ
samyag vyavasito hi saḥ

"Even if one commits the most abominable actions, if he is engaged in devotional service he is to be considered saintly because he is properly situated." If one never for a moment forgets Kṛṣṇa, he is safe even if by chance he falls down by committing sinful acts.

In the Second Chapter of *Bhagavad-gītā* (2.40) the Lord also says:

nehābhikrama-nāśo'sti
pratyavāyo na vidyate
svalpam apy asya dharmasya
trāyate mahato bhayāt

"In this endeavor there is no loss or diminution, and a little advancement on this path can protect one from the most dangerous type of fear."

Elsewhere in the *Gītā* (6.40) the Lord says, *na hi kalyāṇa-kṛt kaścid durgatiṁ tāta gacchati:* "One who performs auspicious activity is never overcome by evil." The highest *kalyāṇa* (auspicious) activity is to surrender to Kṛṣṇa. That is the only path by which to save oneself from falling down into hellish life. Śrīla Prabodhānanda Sarasvatī has confirmed this as follows:

kaivalyaṁ narakāyate tri-daśa-pūr ākāśa-puṣpāyate
durdāntendriya-kāla-sarpa-paṭalī protkhāta-daṁṣṭrāyate
viśvaṁ pūrṇa-sukhāyate vidhi-mahendrādiś ca kīṭāyate
yat-kāruṇya-kaṭākṣa-vaibhavavatāṁ taṁ gauram eva stumaḥ

The sinful actions of one who has surrendered unto Kṛṣṇa are compared to a snake with its poison fangs removed (*protkhāta-daṁṣṭrāyate*). Such a snake is no longer to be feared. Of course, one should not commit sinful activities on the strength of having surrendered to Kṛṣṇa. However, even if one who has surrendered to Kṛṣṇa happens to do something sinful because of his former habits, such sinful actions no longer have a destructive effect. Therefore one should adhere to the lotus feet of Kṛṣṇa very tightly and serve Him under the direction of the spiritual master. Thus in all conditions one will be *akuto-bhaya,* free from fear.

TEXT 20

अत्र चोदाहरन्तीममितिहासं पुरातनम् ।
दूतानां विष्णुयमयोः संवादस्तं निबोध मे ॥ २० ॥

atra codāharantīmam
itihāsaṁ purātanam
dūtānāṁ viṣṇu-yamayoḥ
saṁvādas taṁ nibodha me

atra—in this connection; *ca*—also; *udāharanti*—they give as an example; *imam*—this; *itihāsam*—the history (of Ajāmila); *purātanam*—which is very old; *dūtānām*—of the order carriers; *viṣṇu*—of Lord Viṣṇu; *yamayoḥ*—and of Yamarāja; *saṁvādaḥ*—the discussion; *tam*—that; *nibodha*—try to understand; *me*—from me.

TRANSLATION

In this regard, learned scholars and saintly persons describe a very old historical incident involving a discussion between the order carriers of Lord Viṣṇu and those of Yamarāja. Please hear of this from me.

PURPORT

The *Purāṇas,* or old histories, are sometimes neglected by unintelligent men who consider their descriptions mythological. Actually, the descriptions of the *Purāṇas,* or the old histories of the universe, are factual, although not chronological. The *Purāṇas* record the chief incidents that have occurred over many millions of years, not only on this planet but also on other planets within the universe. Therefore all learned and realized Vedic scholars speak with references to the incidents in the *Purāṇas.* Śrīla Rūpa Gosvāmī accepts the

Purāṇas to be as important as the *Vedas* themselves. Therefore in *Bhakti-rasāmṛta-sindhu* he quotes the following verse from the *Brahma-yāmala:*

śruti-smṛti-purāṇādi-
pañcarātra-vidhiṁ vinā
aikāntikī harer bhaktir
utpātāyaiva kalpate

"Devotional service of the Lord that ignores the authorized Vedic literatures like the *Upaniṣads, Purāṇas* and *Nārada-pañcarātra* is simply an unnecessary disturbance in society." A devotee of Kṛṣṇa must refer not only to the *Vedas,* but also to the *Purāṇas.* One should not foolishly consider the *Purāṇas* mythological. If they were mythological, Śukadeva Gosvāmī would not have taken the trouble to recite the old historical incidents concerning the life of Ajāmila. Now the history begins as follows.

TEXT 21

कान्यकुब्जे द्विजः कश्चिद्दासीपतिरजामिलः ।
नाम्ना नष्टसदाचारो दास्याः संसर्गदूषितः ॥ २१ ॥

kānyakubje dvijaḥ kaścid
dāsī-patir ajāmilaḥ
nāmnā naṣṭa-sadācāro
dāsyāḥ saṁsarga-dūṣitaḥ

kānya-kubje—in the city of Kānyakubja (Kanauj, a town near Kanpur); *dvijaḥ*—*brāhmaṇa; kaścit*—some; *dāsī-patiḥ*—the husband of a low-class woman or prostitute; *ajāmilaḥ*—Ajāmila; *nāmnā*—by name; *naṣṭa-sat-ācāraḥ*—who lost all brahminical qualities; *dāsyāḥ*—of the prostitute or maidservant; *saṁsarga-dūṣitaḥ*—contaminated by the association.

TRANSLATION

In the city known as Kānyakubja there was a brāhmaṇa named Ajāmila who married a prostitute maidservant and lost all his brahminical qualities because of the association of that low-class woman.

PURPORT

The fault of illicit connection with women is that it makes one lose all brahminical qualities. In India there is still a class of servants, called *śūdras,* whose maidservant wives are called *śūdrāṇīs.* Sometimes people who are very lusty establish relationships with such maidservants and sweeping women, since in the higher statuses of society they cannot indulge in the habit of woman hunting, which is strictly prohibited by social convention. Ajāmila, a qualified *brāhmaṇa* youth, lost all his brahminical qualities because of his association with a prostitute, but he was ultimately saved because he had begun the process of *bhakti-yoga.* Therefore in the previous verse, Śukadeva Gosvāmī spoke of the person who has only once surrendered himself at the lotus feet of the Lord (*manaḥ kṛṣṇa-padāravindayoḥ*) or has just begun the *bhakti-yoga* process. *Bhakti-yoga* begins with *śravaṇaṁ kīrtanaṁ viṣṇoḥ,* hearing and chanting of Lord Viṣṇu's names, as in the *mahā-mantra*—Hare Kṛṣṇa, Hare Kṛṣṇa, Kṛṣṇa Kṛṣṇa, Hare Hare/ Hare Rāma, Hare Rāma, Rāma Rāma, Hare Hare. Chanting is the beginning of *bhakti-yoga.* Therefore Śrī Caitanya Mahāprabhu declares:

harer nāma harer nāma
harer nāmaiva kevalam
kalau nāsty eva nāsty eva
nāsty eva gatir anyathā

"In this age of quarrel and hypocrisy the only means of deliverance is chanting the holy name of the Lord. There is no other way. There is no other way. There is no other way." The process of chanting the holy name of the Lord is always superbly effective, but it is especially effective in this age of Kali. Its practical effectiveness will now be explained by Śukadeva Gosvāmī through the history of Ajāmila, who was freed from the hands of the Yamadūtas simply because of chanting the holy name of Nārāyaṇa. Parīkṣit Mahārāja's original question was how to be freed from falling down into hell or into the hands of the Yamadūtas. In reply, Śukadeva Gosvāmī is citing this old historical example to convince Parīkṣit Mahārāja of the potency of *bhakti-yoga,* which begins simply with the chanting of the Lord's name. All the great authorities of *bhakti-yoga* recommend the devotional process beginning with the chanting of the holy name of Kṛṣṇa (*tan-nāma-grahaṇādibhiḥ*).

TEXT 22

बन्द्यक्षैः कैतवैश्चौर्यैर्गर्हितां वृत्तिमास्थितः ।
बिभ्रत्कुटुम्बमशुचिर्यातयामास देहिनः ॥ २२ ॥

bandy-akṣaiḥ kaitavaiś cauryair
garhitāṁ vṛttim āsthitaḥ

bibhrat kuṭumbam aśucir
yātayām āsa dehinaḥ

bandī-akṣaiḥ—by unnecessarily arresting someone; *kaitavaiḥ*—by cheating in gambling or throwing dice; *cauryaiḥ*—by committing theft; *garhitām*—condemned; *vṛttim*—professions; *āsthitaḥ*—who has undertaken (because of association with a prostitute); *bibhrat*—maintaining; *kuṭumbam*—his dependent wife and children; *aśuciḥ*—being most sinful; *yātayām āsa*—he gave trouble; *dehinaḥ*—to other living entities.

TRANSLATION

This fallen brāhmaṇa, Ajāmila, gave trouble to others by arresting them, by cheating them in gambling or by directly plundering them. This was the way he earned his livelihood and maintained his wife and children.

PURPORT

This verse indicates how degraded one becomes simply by indulging in illicit sex with a prostitute. Illicit sex is not possible with a chaste or aristocratic woman, but only with unchaste *śūdras.* The more society allows prostitution and illicit sex, the more impetus it gives to cheaters, thieves, plunderers, drunkards and gamblers. Therefore we first advise all the disciples in our Kṛṣṇa consciousness movement to avoid illicit sex, which is the beginning of all abominable life and which is followed by meat-eating, gambling and intoxication, one after another. Of course, restraint is very difficult, but it is quite possible if one fully surrenders to Kṛṣṇa, since all these abominable habits gradually become distasteful for a Kṛṣṇa conscious person. If illicit sex is allowed to increase in a society, however, the entire society will be condemned, for it will be full of rogues, thieves, cheaters and so forth.

TEXT 23

एवं निवसतस्तस्य लालयानस्य तत्सुतान् ।
कालोऽत्यगान्महान् राजन्नष्टाशीत्यायुषः समाः ॥ २३ ॥

evaṁ nivasatas tasya
lālayānasya tat-sutān
kālo 'tyagān mahān rājann
aṣṭāśītyāyuṣaḥ samāḥ

evam—in this way; *nivasataḥ*—living; *tasya*—of him (Ajāmila); *lālayānasya*—maintaining; *tat*—of her (the *śūdrāṇī*); *sutān*—sons; *kālaḥ*—time; *atyagāt*—passed away; *mahān*—a great amount; *rājan*—O King; *aṣṭāśītyā*—eighty-eight; *āyuṣaḥ*—of the duration of life; *samāḥ*—years.

TRANSLATION

My dear King, while he thus spent his time in abominable, sinful activities to maintain his family of many sons, eighty-eight years of his life passed by.

TEXT 24

तस्य प्रवयसः पुत्रा दश तेषां तु योऽवमः।
बालो नारायणो नाम्ना पित्रोश्च दयितो भृशम् ॥ २४॥

tasya pravayasaḥ putrā
daśa teṣāṁ tu yo'vamaḥ
bālo nārāyaṇo nāmnā
pitroś ca dayito bhṛśam

tasya—of him (Ajāmila); *pravayasaḥ*—who was very old; *putrāḥ*—sons; *daśa*—ten; *teṣām*—of all of them; *tu*—but; *yaḥ*—the one who; *avamaḥ*—the youngest; *bālaḥ*—child; *nārāyaṇaḥ*—Nārāyaṇa; *nāmnā*—by name; *pitroḥ*—of the father and mother; *ca*—and; *dayitaḥ*—dear; *bhṛśam*—very.

TRANSLATION

That old man Ajāmila had ten sons, of whom the youngest was a baby named Nārāyaṇa. Since Nārāyaṇa was the youngest of all the sons, he was naturally very dear to both his father and his mother.

PURPORT

The word *pravayasaḥ* indicates Ajāmila's sinfulness because although he was eighty-eight years old, he had a very young child. According to Vedic culture, one should leave home as soon as he has reached fifty years of age; one should not live at home and go on producing children. Sex life is allowed for twenty-five years, between the ages of twenty-five and forty-five or, at the most, fifty. After that one should give up the habit of sex life and leave home as a *vānaprastha* and then properly take *sannyāsa.* Ajāmila, however, because of his association with a prostitute, lost all brahminical culture and became most sinful, even in his so-called household life.

TEXT 25

स बद्धहृदयस्तस्मिन्नर्भके कलभाषिणि ।
निरीक्षमाणस्तल्लीलां मुमुदे जरठो भृशम् ॥ २५ ॥

sa baddha-hṛdayas tasminn
arbhake kala-bhāṣiṇi
nirīkṣamāṇas tal-līlāṁ
mumude jaraṭho bhṛśam

saḥ—he; *baddha-hṛdayaḥ*—being very attached; *tasmin*—to that; *arbhake*—small child; *kala-bhāṣiṇi*—who could not talk clearly but talked in broken language; *nirīkṣamāṇaḥ*—seeing; *tat*—his; *līlām*—pastimes (such as walking and talking to his father); *mumude*—enjoyed; *jaraṭhaḥ*—the old man; *bhṛśam*—very much.

TRANSLATION

Because of the child's broken language and awkward movements, old Ajāmila was very much attached to him. He always took care of the child and enjoyed the child's activities.

PURPORT

Here it is clearly mentioned that the child Nārāyaṇa was so young that he could not even speak or walk properly. Since the old man was very attached to the child, he enjoyed the child's activities, and because the child's name was Nārāyaṇa, the old man always chanted the holy name of Nārāyaṇa. Although he was referring to the small child and not to the original Nārāyaṇa, the name of Nārāyaṇa is so powerful that even by chanting his son's name he was becoming purified (*harer nāma harer nāma harer nāmaiva kevalam*). Śrīla Rūpa Gosvāmī has therefore declared that if one's mind is somehow or other attracted by the holy name of Kṛṣṇa (*tasmāt kenāpy upāyena manaḥ kṛṣṇe niveśayet*), one is on the path of liberation. It is customary in Hindu society for parents to give their children names like Kṛṣṇadāsa, Govinda dāsa, Nārāyaṇa dāsa and Vṛndāvana dāsa. Thus they chant the names Kṛṣṇa, Govinda, Nārāyaṇa and Vṛndāvana and get the chance to be purified.

TEXT 26

भुञ्जानः प्रपिबन् खादन् बालकंस्नेहयन्त्रितः ।
भोजयन् पाययन्मूढो न वेदागतमन्तकम् ॥ २६ ॥

bhuñjānaḥ prapiban khādan
bālakaṁ sneha-yantritaḥ
bhojayan pāyayan mūḍho
na vedāgatam antakam

bhuñjānaḥ—while eating; *prapiban*—while drinking; *khādan*—while chewing; *bālakam*—unto the child; *sneha-yantritaḥ*—being attached by affection; *bhojayan*—feeding; *pāyayan*—giving something to drink; *mūḍhaḥ*—the foolish man; *na*—not; *veda*—understood; *āgatam*—had arrived; *antakam*—death.

TRANSLATION

When Ajāmila chewed food and ate it, he called the child to chew and eat, and when he drank he called the child to drink also. Always engaged in taking care of the child and calling his name, Nārāyaṇa, Ajāmila could not understand that his own time was now exhausted and that death was upon him.

PURPORT

The Supreme Personality of Godhead is kind to the conditioned soul. Although this man completely forgot Nārāyaṇa, he was calling his child, saying, "Nārāyaṇa, please come eat this food. Nārāyaṇa, please come drink this milk." Somehow or other, therefore, he was attached to the name Nārāyaṇa. This is called *ajñāta-sukṛti.* Although calling for his son, he was unknowingly chanting the name of Nārāyaṇa, and the holy name of the Supreme Personality of Godhead is so transcendentally powerful that his chanting was being counted and recorded.

TEXT 27

स एवं वर्तमानोऽज्ञो मृत्युकाल उपस्थिते ।
मतिं चकार तनये बाले नारायणाह्वये ॥ २७ ॥

sa evaṁ vartamāno 'jño
mṛtyu-kāla upasthite

matiṁ cakāra tanaye
bāle nārāyaṇāhvaye

saḥ—that Ajāmila; *evam*—thus; *vartamānaḥ*—living; *ajñaḥ*—foolish; *mṛtyu-kāle*—when the time of death; *upasthite*—arrived; *matim cakāra*—concentrated his mind; *tanaye*—on his son; *bāle*—the child; *nārāyaṇa-āhvaye*—whose name was Nārāyaṇa.

TRANSLATION

When the time of death arrived for the foolish Ajāmila, he began thinking exclusively of his son Nārāyaṇa.

PURPORT

In the Second Canto of the *Śrīmad-Bhāgavatam* (2.1.6) Śukadeva Gosvāmī says:

etāvān sāṅkhya-yogābhyāṁ
svadharma-pariniṣṭhayā
janma-lābhaḥ paraḥ puṁsām
ante nārāyaṇa-smṛtiḥ

"The highest perfection of human life, achieved either by complete knowledge of matter and spirit, by acquirement of mystic powers, or by perfect discharge of one's occupational duty, is to remember the Personality of Godhead at the end of life." Somehow or other, Ajāmila consciously or unconsciously chanted the name of Nārāyaṇa at the time of death (*ante nārāyaṇa-smṛtiḥ*), and therefore he became all-perfect simply by concentrating his mind on the name of Nārāyaṇa.

It may also be concluded that Ajāmila, who was the son of a *brāhmaṇa,* was accustomed to worshiping Nārāyaṇa in his youth because in every *brāhmaṇa's* house there is worship of the *nārāyaṇa-śilā.* This system is still present in India; in a rigid *brāhmaṇa's* house, there is *nārāyaṇa-sevā,* worship of Nārāyaṇa. Therefore, although the contaminated Ajāmila was calling for his son, by concentrating his mind on the holy name of Nārāyaṇa he remembered the Nārāyaṇa he had very faithfully worshiped in his youth.

In this regard Śrīla Śrīdhara Svāmī expressed his verdict as follows: *etac ca tad-upalālanādi-śrī-nārāyaṇa-namoccāraṇa-māhātmyena tad-bhaktir evābhūd iti siddhāntopayogitvenāpi draṣṭavyam.* "According to the *bhakti-siddhānta,* it is to be analyzed that because Ajāmila constantly chanted his son's name,

Nārāyaṇa, he was elevated to the platform of *bhakti,* although he did not know it." Similarly, Śrīla Vīrarāghava Ācārya gives this opinion: *evaṁ vartamānaḥ sa dvijaḥ mṛtyu-kāle upasthite satyajño nārāyaṇākhye putra eva matiṁ cakāra matim āsaktām akarod ity arthaḥ.* "Although at the time of death he was chanting the name of his son, he nevertheless concentrated his mind upon the holy name of Nārāyaṇa." Śrīla Vijayadhvaja Tīrtha gives a similar opinion:

> *mṛtyu-kāle deha-viyoga-lakṣaṇa-kāle mṛtyoḥ sarva-doṣa-pāpa-harasya harer anugrahāt kāle datta-jñāna-lakṣaṇe upasthite hṛdi prakāśite tanaye pūrṇa-jñāne bāle pañca-varṣa-kalpe prādeśa-mātre nārāyaṇāhvaye mūrti-viśeṣe matiṁ smaraṇa-samarthaṁ cittaṁ cakāra bhaktyāsmarad ity arthaḥ.*

Directly or indirectly, Ajāmila factually remembered Nārāyaṇa at the time of death (*ante nārāyaṇa-smṛtiḥ).*

TEXTS 28–29

स पाशहस्तांस्त्रीन्दृष्ट्वा पुरुषानतिदारुणान् ।
वक्रतुण्डानूर्ध्वरोम्ण आत्मानं नेतुमागतान् ॥ २८ ॥
दूरे क्रीडनकासक्तं पुत्रं नारायणाह्वयम् ।
प्लावितेन स्वरेणोच्चैराजुहावाकुलेन्द्रियः ॥ २९ ॥

sa pāśa-hastāṁs trīn dṛṣṭvā
puruṣān ati-dāruṇān
vakra-tuṇḍān ūrdhva-romṇa
ātmānaṁ netum āgatān

dūre krīḍanakāsaktaṁ
putraṁ nārāyaṇāhvayam
plāvitena svareṇoccair
ājuhāvākulendriyaḥ

saḥ—that person (Ajāmila); *pāśa-hastān*—having ropes in their hands; *trīn*—three; *dṛṣṭvā*—seeing; *puruṣān*—persons; *ati-dāruṇān*—very fearful in their features; *vakra-tuṇḍān*—with twisted faces; *ūrdhva-romṇaḥ*—with hair standing on the body; *ātmānam*—the self; *netum*—to take away; *āgatān*—arrived; *dūre*—a short distance away; *krīḍanaka-āsaktam*—engaged in his play; *putram*—his child; *nārāyaṇa-āhvayam*—named Nārāyaṇa; *plāvitena*—with tearful eyes; *svareṇa*—with his voice; *uccaiḥ*—very loudly; *ājuhāva*—called; *ākula-indriyaḥ*—being full of anxiety.

TRANSLATION

Ajāmila then saw three awkward persons with deformed bodily features, fierce, twisted faces, and hair standing erect on their bodies. With ropes in their hands, they had come to take him away to the abode of Yamarāja. When he saw them he was extremely bewildered, and because of attachment to his child, who was playing a short distance away, Ajāmila began to call him loudly by his name. Thus with tears in his eyes he somehow or other chanted the holy name of Nārāyaṇa.

PURPORT

A person who performs sinful activities performs them with his body, mind and words. Therefore three order carriers from Yamarāja came to take Ajāmila to Yamarāja's abode. Fortunately, even though he was referring to his son, Ajāmila chanted the four syllables of the *hari-nāma* Nārāyaṇa, and therefore the order carriers of Nārāyaṇa, the Viṣṇudūtas, also immediately arrived there. Because Ajāmila was extremely afraid of the ropes of Yamarāja, he chanted the Lord's name with tearful eyes. Actually, however, he never meant to chant the holy name of Nārāyaṇa; he meant to call his son.

TEXT 30

निशम्य म्रियमाणस्य मुखतो हरिकीर्तनम्।
भर्तुर्नाम महाराज पार्षदाः सहसापतन् ॥ ३० ॥

niśamya mriyamāṇasya
mukhato hari-kīrtanam
bhartur nāma mahārāja
pārṣadāḥ sahasāpatan

niśamya—hearing; *mriyamāṇasya*—of the dying man; *mukhataḥ*—from the mouth; *hari-kīrtanam*—chanting of the holy name of the Supreme Personality of Godhead; *bhartuḥ nāma*—the holy name of their master; *mahā-rāja*—O King; *pārṣadāḥ*—the order carriers of Viṣṇu; *sahasā*—immediately; *āpatan*—arrived.

TRANSLATION

My dear King, the order carriers of Viṣṇu, the Viṣṇudūtas, immediately arrived when they heard the holy name of their master from the mouth of the dying Ajāmila, who had certainly chanted without offense because he had chanted in complete anxiety.

PURPORT

Śrīla Viśvanātha Cakravartī Ṭhākura remarks, *hari-kīrtanaṁ niśamyāpatan, katham-bhūtasya bhartur nāma bruvataḥ:* the order carriers of Lord Viṣṇu came because Ajāmila had chanted the holy name of Nārāyaṇa. They did not consider why he was chanting. While chanting the name of Nārāyaṇa, Ajāmila was actually thinking of his son, but simply because they heard Ajāmila chanting the Lord's name, the order carriers of Lord Viṣṇu, the Viṣṇudūtas, immediately came for Ajāmila's protection. *Hari-kīrtana* is actually meant to glorify the holy name, form, pastimes and qualities of the Lord. Ajāmila, however, did not glorify the form, qualities or paraphernalia of the Lord; he simply chanted the holy name. Nevertheless, that chanting was sufficient to cleanse him of all sinful activities. As soon as the Viṣṇudūtas heard their master's name being chanted, they immediately came. In this regard Śrīla Vijayadhvaja Tīrtha remarks: *anena putra-sneham antareṇa prācīnādṛṣṭa-balād udbhūtayā bhaktyā bhagavan-nāma-saṅkīrtanaṁ kṛtam iti jñāyate.* "Ajāmila chanted the name of Nārāyaṇa because of his excessive attachment to his son. Nevertheless, because of his past good fortune in having rendered devotional service to Nārāyaṇa, he apparently chanted the holy name in full devotional service and without offenses."

TEXT 31

विकर्षतोऽन्तर्हृदयाद्दासीपतिमजामिलम् ।
यमप्रेष्यान् विष्णुदूता वारयामासुरोजसा ॥ ३१ ॥

vikarṣato 'ntar hṛdayād
dāsī-patim ajāmilam
yama-preṣyān viṣṇudūtā
vārayām āsur ojasā

vikarṣataḥ—snatching; *antaḥ hṛdayāt*—from within the heart; *dāsī-patim*—the husband of the prostitute; *ajāmilam*—Ajāmila; *yama-preṣyān*—the messengers of Yamarāja; *viṣṇu-dūtāḥ*—the order carriers of Lord Viṣṇu; *vārayām āsuḥ*—forbade; *ojasā*—with resounding voices.

TRANSLATION

The order carriers of Yamarāja were snatching the soul from the core of the heart of Ajāmila, the husband of the prostitute, but with resounding

voices the messengers of Lord Viṣṇu, the Viṣṇudūtas, forbade them to do so.

PURPORT

A Vaiṣṇava, one who has surrendered to the lotus feet of Lord Viṣṇu, is always protected by Lord Viṣṇu's order carriers. Because Ajāmila had chanted the holy name of Nārāyaṇa, the Viṣṇudūtas not only immediately arrived on the spot but also at once ordered the Yamadūtas not to touch him. By speaking with resounding voices, the Viṣṇudūtas threatened to punish the Yamadūtas if they continued trying to snatch Ajāmila's soul from his heart. The order carriers of Yamarāja have jurisdiction over all sinful living entities, but the messengers of Lord Viṣṇu, the Viṣṇudūtas, are capable of punishing anyone, including Yamarāja, if he wrongs a Vaiṣṇava.

Materialistic scientists do not know where to find the soul within the body with their material instruments, but this verse clearly explains that the soul is within the core of the heart (*hṛdaya*); it is from the heart that the Yamadūtas were extracting the soul of Ajāmila. Similarly, we learn that the Supersoul, Lord Viṣṇu, is also situated within the heart (*īśvaraḥ sarva-bhūtānāṁ hṛd-deśe'rjuna tiṣṭhati*). In the *Upaniṣads* it is said that the Supersoul and the individual soul are living in the same tree of the body as two friendly birds. The Supersoul is said to be friendly because the Supreme Personality of Godhead is so kind to the original soul that when the original soul transmigrates from one body to another, the Lord goes with him. Furthermore, according to the desire and *karma* of the individual soul, the Lord, through the agency of *māyā,* creates another body for him.

The heart of the body is a mechanical arrangement. As the Lord says in *Bhagavad-gītā* (18.61):

īśvaraḥ sarva-bhūtānāṁ
hṛd-deśe'rjuna tiṣṭhati
bhrāmayan sarva-bhūtāni
yantrārūḍhāni māyayā

"The Supreme Lord is situated in everyone's heart, O Arjuna, and is directing the wanderings of all living entities, who are seated as on a machine, made of the material energy." *Yantra* means a machine, such as an automobile. The driver of the machine of the body is the individual soul, who is also its director or proprietor, but the supreme proprietor is the Supreme Personality of Godhead. One's body is created through the agency of *māyā* (*karmaṇā daiva-netreṇa*), and according to one's activities in this life, another vehicle is created, again under the supervision of *daivī māyā* (*daivī hy eṣā guṇamayī mama māyā duratyayā*). At the appropriate time, one's next body is immediately chosen, and both the individual soul and the Supersoul transfer to that particular bodily machine. This is the process of transmigration. During transmigration from one body to the next, the soul is taken away by the order carriers of Yamarāja and put into a particular type of hellish life (*naraka*) in order to become accustomed to the condition in which he will live in his next body.

TEXT 32

ऊचुर्निषेधितास्तांस्ते वैवस्वतपुरःसराः ।
के यूयं प्रतिषेद्धारो धर्मराजस्य शासनम् ॥ ३२ ॥

ūcur niṣedhitās tāṁs te
vaivasvata-puraḥsarāḥ
ke yūyaṁ pratiṣeddhāro
dharma-rājasya śāsanam

ūcuḥ—replied; *niṣedhitāḥ*—being forbidden; *tān*—to the order carriers of Lord Viṣṇu; *te*—they; *vaivasvata*—of Yamarāja; *puraḥ-sarāḥ*—the assistants or messengers; *ke*—who; *yūyam*—all of you; *pratiṣed-dhāraḥ*—who are opposing; *dharma-rājasya*—of the king of religious principles, Yamarāja; *śāsanam*—the ruling jurisdiction.

TRANSLATION

When the order carriers of Yamarāja, the son of the sungod, were thus forbidden, they replied: Who are you, sirs, that have the audacity to challenge the jurisdiction of Yamarāja?

PURPORT

According to the sinful activities of Ajāmila, he was within the jurisdiction of Yamarāja, the supreme judge appointed to consider the sins of the living entities. When forbidden to touch Ajāmila, the order carriers of Yamarāja were surprised because they had never been hindered in the execution of their duty by anyone within the three worlds.

TEXT 33

कस्य वा कुत आयाताः कस्मादस्य निषेधथ।
किं देवा उपदेवा या यूयं किं सिद्धसत्तमाः ॥ ३३ ॥

kasya vā kuta āyātāḥ
kasmād asya niṣedhatha
kiṁ devā upadevā yā
yūyaṁ kiṁ siddha-sattamāḥ

kasya—whose servants; *vā*—or; *kutaḥ*—from where; *āyātāḥ*—have you come; *kasmāt*—what is the reason; *asya*—(the taking away) of this Ajāmila; *niṣedhatha*—are you forbidding; *kim*—whether; *devāḥ*—demigods; *upadevāḥ*—sub-demigods; *yāḥ*—who; *yūyam*—all of you; *kim*—whether; *siddha-sat-tamāḥ*—the best of the perfect beings, the pure devotees.

TRANSLATION

Dear sirs, whose servants are you, where have you come from, and why are you forbidding us to touch the body of Ajāmila? Are you demigods from the heavenly planets, are you sub-demigods, or are you the best of devotees?

PURPORT

The most significant word used in this verse is *siddha-sattamāḥ,* which means "the best of the perfect." In *Bhagavad-gītā* (7.3) it is said, *manuṣyāṇāṁ sahasreṣu kaścid yatati siddhaye:* out of millions of persons, one may try to become *siddha,* perfect—or, in other words, self-realized. A self-realized person knows that he is not the body but a spiritual soul (*ahaṁ brahmāsmi*). At the present moment practically everyone is unaware of this fact, but one who understands this has attained perfection and is therefore called *siddha.* When one understands that the soul is part and parcel of the supreme soul and one thus engages in the devotional service of the supreme soul, one becomes *siddha-sattama.* One is then eligible to live in the Vaikuṇṭha planets or Kṛṣṇaloka. The word *siddha-sattama,* therefore, refers to a liberated, pure devotee.

Since the Yamadūtas are servants of Yamarāja, who is also one of the *siddha-sattamas,* they knew that a *siddha-sattama* is above the demigods and sub-demigods and, indeed, above all the living entities within this material world. The Yamadūtas therefore inquired why the Viṣṇudūtas were present where a sinful man was going to die.

It should also be noted that Ajāmila was not yet dead, for the Yamadūtas were trying to snatch the soul from his heart. They could not take the soul, however, and therefore Ajāmila was not yet dead. This will be revealed in later verses. Ajāmila was simply in an unconscious state when the argument was in progress between the Yamadūtas and the Viṣṇudūtas. The conclusion of the argument was to be a decision regarding who would claim the soul of Ajāmila.

TEXTS 34–36

सर्वे पद्मपलाशाक्षाः पीतकौशेयवाससः ।
किरीटिनः कुण्डलिनो लसत्पुष्करमालिनः ॥ ३४ ॥
सर्वे च नूत्नवयसः सर्वे चारुचतुर्भुजाः ।
धनुर्निषङ्गासिगदाशङ्खचक्राम्बुजश्रियः ॥ ३५ ॥
दिशो वितिमिरालोकाः कुर्वन्तः स्वेन तेजसा ।
किमर्थं धर्मपालस्य किङ्करान्नो निषेधथ ॥ ३६ ॥

sarve padma-palāśākṣāḥ
pīta-kauśeya-vāsasaḥ
kirīṭinaḥ kuṇḍalino
lasat-puṣkara-mālinaḥ

sarve ca nūtna-vayasaḥ
sarve cāru-caturbhujāḥ
dhanur-niṣaṅgāsi-gadā-
śaṅkha-cakrāmbuja-śriyaḥ

diśo vitimirālokāḥ
kurvantaḥ svena tejasā
kim arthaṁ dharma-pālasya
kiṅkarān no niṣedhatha

sarve—all of you; *padma-palāśa-akṣāḥ*—with eyes like the petals of a lotus flower; *pīta*—yellow; *kauśeya*—silk; *vāsasaḥ*—wearing garments; *kirīṭinaḥ*—with helmets; *kuṇḍalinaḥ*—with earrings; *lasat*—glittering; *puṣkara-mālinaḥ*—with a garland of lotus flowers; *sarve*—all of you; *ca*—also; *nūtna-vayasaḥ*—very youthful; *sarve*—all of you; *cāru*—very beautiful; *catuḥ-*

bhujāḥ—with four arms; *dhanuḥ*—bow; *niṣaṅga*—quiver of arrows; *asi*—sword; *gadā*—club; *śaṅkha*—conchshell; *cakra*—disc; *ambuja*—lotus flower; *śriyaḥ*—decorated with; *diśaḥ*—all directions; *vitimira*—without darkness; *ālokāḥ*—extraordinary illumination; *kurvantaḥ*—exhibiting; *svena*—by your own; *tejasā*—effulgence; *kim artham*—what is the purpose; *dharma-pālasya*—of Yamarāja, the maintainer of religious principles; *kiṅkarān*—servants; *naḥ*—us; *niṣedhatha*—you are forbidding.

TRANSLATION

The order carriers of Yamarāja said: Your eyes are just like the petals of lotus flowers. Dressed in yellow silken garments, decorated with garlands of lotuses, and wearing very attractive helmets on your heads and earrings on your ears, you all appear fresh and youthful. Your four long arms are decorated with bows and quivers of arrows and with swords, clubs, conchshells, discs and lotus flowers. Your effulgence has dissipated the darkness of this place with extraordinary illumination. Now, sirs, why are you obstructing us?

PURPORT

Before even being introduced to a foreigner, one becomes acquainted with him through his dress, bodily features and behavior and can thus understand his position. Therefore when the Yamadūtas saw the Viṣṇudūtas for the first time, they were surprised. They said, "By your bodily features you appear to be very exalted gentlemen, and you have such celestial power that you have dissipated the darkness of this material world with your own effulgences. Why then should you endeavor to stop us from executing our duty?" It will be explained that the Yamadūtas, the order carriers of Yamarāja, mistakenly considered Ajāmila sinful. They did not know that although he was sinful throughout his entire life, he was purified by constantly chanting the holy name of Nārāyaṇa. In other words, unless one is a Vaiṣṇava, one cannot understand the activities of a Vaiṣṇava.

The dress and bodily features of the residents of Vaikuṇṭhaloka are properly described in these verses. The residents of Vaikuṇṭha, who are decorated with garlands and yellow silken garments, have four arms holding various weapons. Thus they conspicuously resemble Lord Viṣṇu. They have the same bodily features as Nārāyaṇa because they have attained the liberation of *sārūpya,* but they nevertheless act as servants. All the residents of Vaikuṇṭhaloka know perfectly well that their master is Nārāyaṇa, or Kṛṣṇa, and that they are all His servants. They are all self-realized souls who are *nitya-mukta,* everlastingly liberated. Although they could conceivably declare themselves Nārāyaṇa or Viṣṇu, they never do so; they always remain Kṛṣṇa conscious and serve the Lord faithfully. Such is the atmosphere of Vaikuṇṭhaloka. Similarly, one who learns the faithful service of Lord Kṛṣṇa through the Kṛṣṇa consciousness movement will always remain in Vaikuṇṭhaloka and have nothing to do with the material world.

TEXT 37

श्रीशुक उवाच
इत्युक्ते यमदूतैस्तेवासुदेवोक्तकारिणः ।
तान् प्रत्यूचुः प्रहस्येदं मेघनिर्ह्रादया गिरा ॥ ३७॥

śrī-śuka uvāca
ity ukte yamadūtais te
vāsudevokta-kāriṇaḥ
tān pratyūcuḥ prahasyedaṁ
megha-nirhrādayā girā

śrī-śukaḥ uvāca—Śrī Śukadeva Gosvāmī said; *iti*—thus; *ukte*—being addressed; *yamadūtaiḥ*—by the messengers of Yamarāja; *te*—they; *vāsudeva-ukta-kāriṇaḥ*—who are always ready to execute the orders of Lord Vāsudeva (being personal associates of Lord Viṣṇu who have obtained the liberation of *sālokya*); *tān*—unto them; *pratyūcuḥ*—replied; *prahasya*—smiling; *idam*—this; *megha-nirhrādayā*—resounding like a rumbling cloud; *girā*—with voices.

TRANSLATION

Śukadeva Gosvāmī continued: Being thus addressed by the messengers of Yamarāja, the servants of Vāsudeva smiled and spoke the following words in voices as deep as the sound of rumbling clouds.

PURPORT

The Yamadūtas were surprised to see that the Viṣṇudūtas, although polite, were hindering the rule of Yamarāja. Similarly, the Viṣṇudūtas were also surprised that the Yamadūtas, although claiming to be servants of Yamarāja, the supreme judge of religious principles, were unaware of the principles of religious action. Thus the Viṣṇudūtas smiled, thinking, "What is this nonsense they are speaking? If they are actually servants of Yamarāja they should know that Ajāmila is not a suitable candidate for them to carry off."

TEXT 38

श्रीविष्णुदूता ऊचुः
यूयं वै धर्मराजस्य यदि निर्देशकारिणः ।
ब्रूत धर्मस्य नस्तत्त्वं यच्चाधर्मस्य लक्षणम् ॥ ३८ ॥

śrī-viṣṇudūtā ūcuḥ
yūyaṁ vai dharma-rājasya
yadi nirdeśa-kāriṇaḥ
brūta dharmasya nas tattvaṁ
yac cādharmasya lakṣaṇam

śrī-viṣṇudūtāḥ ūcuḥ—the blessed messengers of Lord Viṣṇu spoke; *yūyam*—all of you; *vai*—indeed; *dharma-rājasya*—of King Yamarāja, who knows the religious principles; *yadi*—if; *nirdeśa-kāriṇaḥ*—order carriers; *brūta*—just speak; *dharmasya*—of religious principles; *naḥ*—unto us; *tattvam*—the truth; *yat*—that which; *ca*—also; *adharmasya*—of impious activities; *lakṣaṇam*—symptoms.

TRANSLATION

The blessed messengers of Lord Viṣṇu, the Viṣṇudūtas, said: If you are actually servants of Yamarāja, you must explain to us the meaning of religious principles and the symptoms of irreligion.

PURPORT

This inquiry by the Viṣṇudūtas to the Yamadūtas is most important. A servant must know the instructions of his master. The servants of Yamarāja claimed to be carrying out his orders, and therefore the Viṣṇudūtas very intelligently asked them to explain the symptoms of religious and irreligious principles. A Vaiṣṇava knows these principles perfectly well because he is well acquainted with the instructions of the Supreme Personality of Godhead. The Supreme Lord says, *sarva-dharmān parityajya mām ekaṁ śaraṇaṁ vraja:* "Give up all other varieties of religion and just surrender unto Me." Therefore surrender unto the Supreme Personality of Godhead is the actual principle of religion. Those who have surrendered to the principles of material nature instead of to Kṛṣṇa are all impious, regardless of their material position.

Unaware of the principles of religion, they do not surrender to Kṛṣṇa, and therefore they are considered sinful rascals, the lowest of men, and fools bereft of all knowledge. As Kṛṣṇa says in *Bhagavad-gītā* (7.15):

na māṁ duṣkṛtino mūḍhāḥ
prapadyante narādhamāḥ
māyayāpahṛta-jñānā
āsuraṁ bhāvam āśritāḥ

"Those miscreants who are grossly foolish, lowest among mankind, whose knowledge is stolen by illusion, and who partake of the atheistic nature of demons, do not surrender unto Me." One who has not surrendered to Kṛṣṇa does not know the true principle of religion; otherwise he would have surrendered.

The question posed by the Viṣṇudūtas was very suitable. One who represents someone else must fully know that person's mission. The devotees in the Kṛṣṇa consciousness movement must therefore be fully aware of the mission of Kṛṣṇa and Lord Caitanya; otherwise they will be considered foolish. All devotees, especially preachers, must know the philosophy of Kṛṣṇa consciousness so as not to be embarrassed and insulted when they preach.

TEXT 39

कथंस्विद् ध्रियते दण्डः किं वास्य स्थानमीप्सितम् ।
दण्ड्याः किं कारिणः सर्वे आहोस्वित्कतिचिन्नृणाम् ॥ ३९ ॥

kathaṁ svid dhriyate daṇḍaḥ
kiṁ vāsya sthānam īpsitam
daṇḍyāḥ kiṁ kāriṇaḥ sarve
āho svit katicin nṛṇām

katham svit—by which means; *dhriyate*—is imposed; *daṇḍaḥ*—punishment; *kim*—what; *vā*—or; *asya*—of this; *sthānam*—the place; *īpsitam*—desirable; *daṇḍyāḥ*—punishable; *kim*—whether; *kāriṇaḥ*—fruitive actors; *sarve*—all; *āho svit*—or whether; *katicit*—some; *nṛṇām*—of the human beings.

TRANSLATION

What is the process of punishing others? Who are the actual candidates

for punishment? Are all karmīs engaged in fruitive activities punishable, or only some of them?

PURPORT

One who has the power to punish others should not punish everyone. There are innumerable living entities, the majority of whom are in the spiritual world and are *nitya-mukta,* everlastingly liberated. There is no question of judging these liberated living beings. Only a small fraction of the living entities, perhaps one fourth, are in the material world. And the major portion of the living entities in the material world—8,000,000 of the 8,400,000 forms of life—are lower than human beings. They are not punishable, for under the laws of material nature they are automatically evolving. Human beings, who are advanced in consciousness, are responsible, but not all of them are punishable. Those engaged in advanced pious activities are beyond punishment. Only those who engage in sinful activities are punishable. Therefore the Viṣṇudūtas particularly inquired about who is punishable and why Yamarāja has been designated to discriminate between who is punishable and who is not. How is one to be judged? What is the basic principle of authority? These are the questions raised by the Viṣṇudūtas.

TEXT 40

यमदूता ऊचुः

वेदप्रणिहितो धर्मो ह्यधर्मस्तद्विपर्ययः ।
वेदो नारायणः साक्षात्स्वयम्भूरिति शुश्रुम ॥ ४० ॥

yamadūtā ūcuḥ
veda-praṇihito dharmo
hy adharmas tad-viparyayaḥ
vedo nārāyaṇaḥ sākṣāt
svayambhūr iti śuśruma

yamadūtāḥ ūcuḥ—the order carriers of Yamarāja said; *veda*—by the four *Vedas* (*Sāma, Yajur, Ṛg* and *Atharva*); *praṇihitaḥ*—prescribed; *dharmaḥ*—religious principles; *hi*—indeed; *adharmaḥ*—irreligious principles; *tat-viparyayaḥ*—the opposite of that (that which is not supported by Vedic injunctions); *vedaḥ*—the *Vedas,* books of knowledge; *nārāyaṇaḥ sākṣāt*—directly the Supreme Personality of Godhead (being the words of Nārāyaṇa);

svayam-bhūḥ—self-born, self-sufficient (appearing only from the breath of Nārāyaṇa and not being learned from anyone else); *iti*—thus; *śuśruma*—we have heard.

TRANSLATION

The Yamadūtas replied: That which is prescribed in the Vedas constitutes dharma, the religious principles, and the opposite of that is irreligion. The Vedas are directly the Supreme Personality of Godhead, Nārāyaṇa, and are self-born. This we have heard from Yamarāja.

PURPORT

The servants of Yamarāja replied quite properly. They did not manufacture principles of religion or irreligion. Instead, they explained what they had heard from the authority Yamarāja. *Mahājano yena gataḥ sa panthāḥ:* one should follow the *mahājana,* the authorized person. Yamarāja is one of twelve authorities. Therefore the servants of Yamarāja, the Yamadūtas, replied with perfect clarity when they said *śuśruma* ("we have heard"). The members of modern civilization manufacture defective religious principles through speculative concoction. This is not *dharma.* They do not know what is *dharma* and what is *adharma.* Therefore, as stated in the beginning of *Śrīmad-Bhāgavatam, dharmaḥ projjhita-kaitavo'tra: dharma* not supported by the *Vedas* is rejected from *śrīmad-bhāgavata-dharma. Bhāgavata-dharma* comprises only that which is given by the Supreme Personality of Godhead. *Bhāgavata-dharma* is *sarva-dharmān parityajya mām ekaṁ śaraṇaṁ vraja:* one must accept the authority of the Supreme Personality of Godhead and surrender to Him and whatever He says. That is *dharma.* Arjuna, for example, thinking that violence was *adharma,* was declining to fight, but Kṛṣṇa urged him to fight. Arjuna abided by the orders of Kṛṣṇa, and therefore he is actually a *dharmī* because the order of Kṛṣṇa is *dharma.* Kṛṣṇa says in *Bhagavad-gītā* (15.15), *vedaiś ca sarvair aham eva vedyaḥ:* "The real purpose of *veda,* knowledge, is to know Me." One who knows Kṛṣṇa perfectly is liberated. As Kṛṣṇa says in *Bhagavad-gītā* (4.9):

janma karma ca me divyam
evaṁ yo vetti tattvataḥ
tyaktvā dehaṁ punar janma
naiti mām eti so'rjuna

"One who knows the transcendental nature of My appearance and activities does not, upon leaving the body, take his birth again in this material world, but attains My eternal abode, O Arjuna." One who understands Kṛṣṇa and abides by His order is a candidate for returning home, back to Godhead. It may be concluded that *dharma,* religion, refers to that which is ordered in the *Vedas,* and *adharma,* irreligion, refers to that which is not supported in the *Vedas.*

Dharma is not actually manufactured by Nārāyaṇa. As stated in the *Vedas, asya mahato bhūtasya niśvasitam etad yad ṛg-vedaḥ iti:* the injunctions of *dharma* emanate from the breathing of Nārāyaṇa, the supreme living entity. Nārāyaṇa exists eternally and breathes eternally, and therefore *dharma,* the injunctions of Nārāyaṇa, also exist eternally. Śrīla Madhvācārya, the original *ācārya* for those who belong to the Mādhva-Gauḍīya *sampradāya,* says:

vedānāṁ prathamo vaktā
harir eva yato vibhuḥ
ato viṣṇv-ātmakā vedā
ity āhur veda-vādinaḥ

The transcendental words of the *Vedas* emanated from the mouth of the Supreme Personality of Godhead. Therefore the Vedic principles should be understood to be Vaiṣṇava principles because Viṣṇu is the origin of the *Vedas.* The *Vedas* contain nothing besides the instructions of Viṣṇu, and one who follows the Vedic principles is a Vaiṣṇava. The Vaiṣṇava is not a member of a manufactured community of this material world. A Vaiṣṇava is a real knower of the *Vedas,* as confirmed in *Bhagavad-gītā* (*vedaiś ca sarvair aham eva vedyaḥ*).

TEXT 41

येन स्वधाम्न्यमी भावा रजःसत्त्वतमोमयाः ।
गुणनामक्रियारूपैर्विभाव्यन्ते यथातथम् ॥ ४१ ॥

yena sva-dhāmny amī bhāvā
rajaḥ-sattva-tamomayāḥ
guṇa-nāma-kriyā-rūpair
vibhāvyante yathā-tatham

yena—by whom (Nārāyaṇa); *sva-dhāmni*—although in His own place, the spiritual world; *amī*—all these; *bhāvāḥ*—manifestations; *rajaḥ-sattva-tamaḥ-mayāḥ*—created by the three modes of material nature (passion, goodness and ignorance); *guṇa*—qualities; *nāma*—names; *kriyā*—activities; *rūpaiḥ*—and with forms; *vibhāvyante*—are variously manifested; *yathā-tatham*—exactly to the right point.

TRANSLATION

The supreme cause of all causes, Nārāyaṇa, is situated in His own abode in the spiritual world, but nevertheless He controls the entire cosmic manifestation according to the three modes of material nature—sattva-guṇa, rajo-guṇa and tamo-guṇa. In this way all living entities are awarded different qualities, different names [such as brāhmaṇa, kṣatriya and vaiśya], different duties according to the varṇāśrama institution, and different forms. Thus Nārāyaṇa is the cause of the entire cosmic manifestation.

PURPORT

The *Vedas* inform us:

na tasya kāryaṁ karaṇaṁ ca vidyate
na tat-samaś cābhyadhikaś ca dṛśyate
parāsya śaktir vividhaiva śrūyate
svābhāvikī jñāna-bala-kriyā ca
(*Śvetāśvatara Upaniṣad* 6.8)

Nārāyaṇa, the Supreme Personality of Godhead, is almighty, omnipotent. He has multifarious energies, and therefore He is able to remain in His own abode and without endeavor supervise and manipulate the entire cosmic manifestation through the interaction of the three modes of material nature—*sattva-guṇa, rajo-guṇa* and *tamo-guṇa.* These interactions create different forms, bodies, activities and changes, which all occur perfectly. Because the Lord is perfect, everything works as if He were directly supervising and taking part in it. Atheistic men, however, being covered by the three modes of material nature, cannot see Nārāyaṇa to be the supreme cause behind all activities. As Kṛṣṇa says in *Bhagavad-gītā* (7.13):

tribhir guṇamayair bhāvair
ebhiḥ sarvam idaṁ jagat
mohitaṁ nābhijānāti
mām ebhyaḥ param avyayam

"Deluded by the three modes, the whole world does not know Me, who am above the modes and inexhaustible." Because unintelligent agnostics are *mohita,* illusioned by the three modes of material nature, they cannot understand that Nārāyaṇa, Kṛṣṇa, is the supreme cause of all activities. As stated in *Brahma-saṁhitā* (5.1):

īśvaraḥ paramaḥ kṛṣṇaḥ
sac-cid-ānanda-vigrahaḥ
anādir ādir govindaḥ
sarva-kāraṇa-kāraṇam

"Kṛṣṇa, who is known as Govinda, is the supreme controller. He has an eternal, blissful, spiritual body. He is the origin of all. He has no other origin, for He is the prime cause of all causes."

TEXT 42

सूर्योऽग्निः खं मरुद्देवः सोमः सन्ध्याहनी दिशः ।
कं कुः स्वयं धर्म इति ह्येते दैह्यस्य साक्षिणः ॥ ४२ ॥

sūryo'gniḥ khaṁ marud devaḥ
somaḥ sandhyāhanī diśaḥ
kaṁ kuḥ svayaṁ dharma iti
hy ete daihyasya sākṣiṇaḥ

sūryaḥ—the sun- god; *agniḥ*—the fire; *kham*—the sky; *marut*—the air; *devaḥ*—the demigods; *somaḥ*—the moon; *sandhyā*—evening; *ahanī*—the day and night; *diśaḥ*—the directions; *kam*—the water; *kuḥ*—the land; *svayam*—personally; *dharmaḥ*—Yamarāja or the Supersoul; *iti*—thus; *hi*—indeed; *ete*—all of these; *daihyasya*—of a living entity embodied in the material elements; *sākṣiṇaḥ*—witnesses.

TRANSLATION

The sun, fire, sky, air, demigods, moon, evening, day, night, directions, water, land and Supersoul Himself all witness the activities of the living entity.

PURPORT

The members of some religious sects, especially Christians, do not believe in the reactions of *karma.* We once had a discussion with a learned Christian professor who argued that although people are generally punished after the witnesses of their misdeeds are examined, where are the witnesses responsible for one's suffering the reactions of past *karma*? To such a person the answer by the Yamadūtas is given here. A conditioned soul thinks that he is working stealthily and that no one can see his sinful activities, but we can understand from the *śāstras* that there are many witnesses, including the sun, fire, sky, air, moon, demigods, evening, day, night, directions, water, land and the Supersoul Himself, who sits with the individual soul within his heart. Where is the dearth of witnesses? The witnesses and the Supreme Lord both exist, and therefore so many living entities are elevated to higher planetary systems or degraded to lower planetary systems, including the hellish planets. There are no discrepancies, for everything is arranged perfectly by the management of the Supreme God (*svābhāvikī jñāna-bala-kriyā ca*). The witnesses mentioned in this verse are also mentioned in other Vedic literatures:

āditya-candrāv anilo'nalaś ca
dyaur bhūmir āpo hṛdayaṁ yamaś ca
ahaś ca rātriś ca ubhe ca sandhye
dharmo'pi jānāti narasya vṛttam

TEXT 43

एतैरधर्मो विज्ञातः स्थानं दण्डस्य युज्यते ।
सर्वे कर्मानुरोधेन दण्डमर्हन्ति कारिणः ॥ ४३ ॥

etair adharmo vijñātaḥ
sthānaṁ daṇḍasya yujyate
sarve karmānurodhena
daṇḍam arhanti kāriṇaḥ

etaiḥ—by all these (witnesses, beginning from the sun- god); *adharmaḥ*—deviation from the regulative principles; *vijñātaḥ*—is known; *sthānam*—the proper place; *daṇḍasya*—of punishment; *yujyate*—is accepted as; *sarve*—all; *karma-anurodhena*—with consideration of the activities performed; *daṇḍam*—punishment; *arhanti*—deserve; *kāriṇaḥ*—the performers of sinful activities.

TRANSLATION

The candidates for punishment are those who are confirmed by these many witnesses to have deviated from their prescribed regulative duties. Everyone engaged in fruitive activities is suitable to be subjected to punishment according to his sinful acts.

TEXT 44

सम्भवन्ति हि भद्राणि विपरीतानि चानघाः ।
कारिणां गुणसङ्गोऽस्ति देहवान् न ह्यकर्मकृत् ॥ ४४ ॥

sambhavanti hi bhadrāṇi
viparītāni cānaghāḥ
kāriṇāṁ guṇa-saṅgo'sti
dehavān na hy akarma-kṛt

sambhavanti—there are; *hi*—indeed; *bhadrāṇi*—auspicious, pious activities; *viparītāni*—just the opposite (inauspicious, sinful activities); *ca*—also; *anaghāḥ*—O sinless inhabitants of Vaikuṇṭha; *kāriṇām*—of the fruitive workers; *guṇa-saṅgaḥ*—contamination of the three modes of nature; *asti*—there is; *deha-vān*—anyone who has accepted this material body; *na*—not; *hi*—indeed; *akarma-kṛt*—without performing action.

TRANSLATION

O inhabitants of Vaikuṇṭha, you are sinless, but those within this material world are all karmīs, whether acting piously or impiously. Both kinds of action are possible for them because they are contaminated by the three modes of nature and must act accordingly. One who has accepted a material body cannot be inactive, and sinful action is inevitable for one acting under the modes of material nature. Therefore all the living entities within this material world are punishable.

PURPORT

The difference between human beings and nonhuman beings is that a human is supposed to act according to the direction of the *Vedas.* Unfortunately, men manufacture their own ways of acting, without reference to the *Vedas.* Therefore all of them commit sinful actions and are punishable.

TEXT 45

येन यावान् यथाधर्मो धर्मो वेह समीहितः ।
स एव तत्फलं भुङ्क्ते तथा तावदमुत्र वै ॥ ४५ ॥

yena yāvān yathādharmo
dharmo veha samīhitaḥ
sa eva tat-phalaṁ bhuṅkte
tathā tāvad amutra vai

yena—by which person; *yāvān*—to which extent; *yathā*—in which manner; *adharmaḥ*—irreligious activities; *dharmaḥ*—religious activities; *vā*—or; *iha*—in this life; *samīhitaḥ*—performed; *saḥ*—that person; *eva*—indeed; *tat-phalam*—the particular result of that; *bhuṅkte*—enjoys or suffers; *tathā*—in that way; *tāvat*—to that extent; *amutra*—in the next life; *vai*—indeed.

TRANSLATION

In proportion to the extent of one's religious or irreligious actions in this life, one must enjoy or suffer the corresponding reactions of his karma in the next.

PURPORT

As stated in *Bhagavad-gītā* (14.18):

ūrdhvaṁ gacchanti sattva-sthā
madhye tiṣṭhanti rājasāḥ
jaghanya-guṇa-vṛtti-sthā
adho gacchanti tāmasāḥ

Those who act in the mode of goodness are promoted to higher planetary systems to become demigods, those who act in an ordinary way and do not commit excessively sinful acts remain within this middle planetary system, and those who perform abominable sinful actions must go down to hellish life.

TEXT 46

यथेह देवप्रवरास्त्रैविध्यमुपलभ्यते ।
भूतेषु गुणवैचित्र्यात्तथान्यत्रानुमीयते ॥ ४६ ॥

yatheha deva-pravarās
trai-vidhyam upalabhyate
bhūteṣu guṇa-vaicitryāt
tathānyatrānumīyate

yathā—just as; *iha*—in this life; *deva-pravarāḥ*—O best of the demigods; *trai-vidhyam*—three kinds of attributes; *upalabhyate*—are achieved; *bhūteṣu*—among all living entities; *guṇa-vaicitryāt*—because of the diversity of the contamination by the three modes of nature; *tathā*—similarly; *anyatra*—in other places; *anumīyate*—it is inferred.

TRANSLATION

O best of the demigods, we can see three different varieties of life, which are due to the contamination of the three modes of nature. The living entities are thus known as peaceful, restless and foolish; as happy, unhappy or in-between; or as religious, irreligious and semireligious. We can deduce that in the next life these three kinds of material nature will similarly act.

PURPORT

The actions and reactions of the three modes of material nature are visible in this life. For example, some people are very happy, some are very distressed, and some are in mixed happiness and distress. This is the result of past association with the modes of material nature—goodness, passion and ignorance. Since these varieties are visible in this life, we may assume that the living entities, according to their association with the different modes of material nature, will be happy, distressed or between the two in their next lives also. Therefore the best policy is to disassociate oneself from the three modes of material nature and be always transcendental to their contamination. This is possible only when one fully engages in the devotional service of the Lord. As Kṛṣṇa confirms in *Bhagavad-gītā* (14.26):

māṁ ca yo'vyabhicāreṇa
bhakti-yogena sevate
sa guṇān samatītyaitān
brahma-bhūyāya kalpate

"One who engages in full devotional service, who does not fall down under any circumstance, at once transcends the modes of material nature and thus comes to the spiritual platform." Unless one is fully absorbed in the service of the Lord, one is subject to the contamination of the three modes of material nature and must therefore suffer from distress or mixed happiness and distress.

TEXT 47

वर्तमानोऽन्ययोः कालो गुणाभिज्ञापको यथा ।
एवं जन्मान्ययोरेतद्धर्माधर्मनिदर्शनम् ॥ ४७ ॥

vartamāno'nyayoḥ kālo
guṇābhijñāpako yathā

evaṁ janmānyayor etad
dharmādharma-nidarśanam

vartamānaḥ—the present; *anyayoḥ*—of the past and future; *kālaḥ*—time; *guṇa-abhijñāpakaḥ*—making known the qualities; *yathā*—just as; *evam*—thus; *janma*—birth; *anyayoḥ*—of the past and future births; *etat*—this; *dharma*—religious principles; *adharma*—irreligious principles; *nidarśanam*—indicating.

TRANSLATION

Just as springtime in the present indicates the nature of springtimes in the past and future, so this life of happiness, distress or a mixture of both gives evidence concerning the religious and irreligious activities of one's past and future lives.

PURPORT

Our past and future are not very difficult to understand, for time is under the contamination of the three modes of material nature. As soon as spring arrives, the usual exhibition of various types of fruits and flowers automatically becomes manifest, and therefore we may conclude that spring in the past was adorned with similar fruits and flowers and will be so adorned in the future also. Our repetition of birth and death is taking place within time, and according to the influence of the modes of nature, we are receiving various types of bodies and being subjected to various conditions.

TEXT 48

मनसैव पुरे देवः पूर्वरूपं विपश्यति ।
अनुमीमांसतेऽपूर्वं मनसा भगवानजः ॥ ४८ ॥

manasaiva pure devaḥ
pūrva-rūpaṁ vipaśyati
anumīmāṁsate'pūrvaṁ
manasā bhagavān ajaḥ

manasā—by the mind; *eva*—indeed; *pure*—in his abode, or within everyone's heart like the Supersoul; *devaḥ*—the demigod Yamarāja (*dīvyatīti devaḥ*, one who is always brilliant and illuminated is called *deva*); *pūrva-rūpam*—the past religious or irreligious condition; *vipaśyati*—

completely observes; *anumīmāṁsate*—he considers; *apūrvam*—the future condition; *manasā*—with his mind; *bhagavān*—who is omnipotent; *ajaḥ*—as good as Lord Brahmā.

TRANSLATION

The omnipotent Yamarāja is as good as Lord Brahmā, for while situated in his own abode or in everyone's heart like the Paramātmā, he mentally observes the past activities of a living entity and thus understands how the living entity will act in future lives.

PURPORT

One should not consider Yamarāja an ordinary living being. He is as good as Lord Brahmā. He has the complete cooperation of the Supreme Lord, who is situated in everyone's heart, and therefore, by the grace of the Supersoul, he can see the past, present and future of a living being from within. The word *anumīmāṁsate* means that he can decide in consultation with the Supersoul. *Anu* means "following." The actual decisions concerning the next lives of the living entities are made by the Supersoul, and they are carried out by Yamarāja.

TEXT 49

यथाज्ञस्तमसा युक्त उपास्ते व्यक्तमेव हि ।
न वेद पूर्वमपरं नष्टजन्मस्मृतिस्तथा ॥ ४९ ॥

yathājñas tamasā yukta
upāste vyaktam eva hi
na veda pūrvam aparaṁ
naṣṭa-janma-smṛtis tathā

yathā—just as; *ajñaḥ*—an ignorant living being; *tamasā*—in sleep; *yuktaḥ*—engaged; *upāste*—acts according to; *vyaktam*—a body manifested in a dream; *eva*—certainly; *hi*—indeed; *na veda*—does not know; *pūrvam*—the past body; *aparam*—the next body; *naṣṭa*—lost; *janma-smṛtiḥ*—the remembrance of birth; *tathā*—similarly.

TRANSLATION

As a sleeping person acts according to the body manifested in his dreams and accepts it to be himself, so one identifies with his present body, which he acquired because of his past religious or irreligious actions, and is unable to know his past or future lives.

PURPORT

A man engages in sinful activities because he does not know what he did in his past life to get his present materially conditioned body, which is subjected to the threefold miseries. As stated by Ṛṣabhadeva in *Śrīmad-Bhāgavatam* (5.5.4), *nūnaṁ pramattaḥ kurute vikarma:* a human being who is mad after sense gratification does not hesitate to act sinfully. *Yad indriya-prītaya āpṛṇoti:* he performs sinful actions simply for sense gratification. *Na sādhu manye:* this is not good. *Yata ātmano'yam asann api kleśada āsa dehaḥ:* because of such sinful actions, one receives another body in which to suffer as he is suffering in his present body because of his past sinful activities.

It should be understood that a person who does not have Vedic knowledge always acts in ignorance of what he has done in the past, what he is doing at the present and how he will suffer in the future. He is completely in darkness. Therefore the Vedic injunction is, *tamasi mā:* "Don't remain in darkness." *Jyotir gama:* "Try to go to the light." The light or illumination is Vedic knowledge, which one can understand when he is elevated to the mode of goodness or when he transcends the mode of goodness by engaging in devotional service to the spiritual master and the Supreme Lord. This is described in the *Śvetāśvatara Upaniṣad* (6.23):

yasya deve parā bhaktir
yathā deve tathā gurau
tasyaite kathitā hy arthāḥ
prakāśante mahātmanaḥ

"Unto those great souls who have implicit faith in both the Lord and the spiritual master, all the imports of Vedic knowledge are automatically revealed." The *Vedas* enjoin, *tad-vijñānārthaṁ sa gurum evābhigacchet:* one must approach a spiritual master who has full knowledge of the *Vedas* and be faithfully directed by him in order to become a devotee of the Lord. Then the knowledge of the *Vedas* will be revealed. When the Vedic knowledge is revealed, one need no longer remain in the darkness of material nature.

According to his association with the material modes of nature—goodness, passion and ignorance—a living entity gets a particular type of body. The example of one who associates with the mode of goodness is a qualified *brāhmaṇa.* Such a *brāhmaṇa* knows past, present and future because he consults the Vedic literature and sees through the eyes of *śāstra* (*śāstra-cakṣuḥ*). He can understand what his past life was, why be is in the present body, and how he can obtain liberation from the clutches of *māyā* and not accept another material body. This is all possible when one is situated in the mode of goodness. Generally, however, the living entities are engrossed in the modes of passion and ignorance.

In any case, one receives an inferior or superior body at the discretion of the Supreme Personality of Godhead, Paramātmā. As stated in the previous verse:

manasaiva pure devaḥ
pūrva-rūpaṁ vipaśyati
anumīmāṁsate'pūrvaṁ
manasā bhagavān ajaḥ

Everything depends on *bhagavān,* or *ajaḥ,* the unborn. Why doesn't one please Bhagavān to receive a better body? The answer is *ajñas tamasā:* because of gross ignorance. One who is in complete darkness cannot know what his past life was or what his next life will be; he is simply interested in his present body. Even though he has a human body, a person in the mode of ignorance and interested only in his present body is like an animal, for an animal, being covered by ignorance, thinks that the ultimate goal of life and happiness is to eat as much as possible. A human being must be educated to understand his past life and how he can endeavor for a better life in the future. There is even a book, called *Bhṛgu-saṁhitā,* which reveals information about one's past, present and future lives according to astrological calculations. Somehow or other one must be enlightened about his past, present and future. One who is interested only in his present body and who tries to enjoy his senses to the fullest extent is understood to be engrossed in the mode of ignorance. His future is very, very dark. Indeed, the future is always dark for one who is grossly covered by ignorance. Especially in this age, human society is covered by the mode of ignorance, and therefore everyone thinks his present body to be everything, without consideration of the past or future.

TEXT 50

पञ्चभिः कुरुते स्वार्थान् पञ्च वेदाथ पञ्चभिः ।
एकस्तु षोडशेन त्रीन् स्वयं सप्तदशोऽश्नुते ॥ ५० ॥

pañcabhiḥ kurute svārthān
pañca vedātha pañcabhiḥ
ekas tu ṣoḍaśena trīn
svayaṁ saptadaśo'śnute

pañcabhiḥ—with the five working senses (voice, arms, legs, anus and genitals); *kurute*—performs; *sva-arthān*—his desired interests; *pañca*—the five objects of the senses (sound, form, touch, aroma and taste); *veda*—knows; *atha*—thus; *pañcabhiḥ*—by the five senses of perception (hearing, seeing, smelling, tasting and feeling); *ekaḥ*—the one; *tu*—but; *ṣoḍaśena*—by these fifteen items and the mind; *trīn*—the three categories of experience (happiness, distress and a mixture of both); *svayam*—he, the living entity himself; *saptadaśaḥ*—the seventeenth item; *aśnute*—enjoys.

TRANSLATION

Above the five senses of perception, the five working senses and the five objects of the senses is the mind, which is the sixteenth element. Above the mind is the seventeenth element, the soul, the living being himself, who, in cooperation with the other sixteen, enjoys the material world alone. The living being enjoys three kinds of situations, namely happy, distressful and mixed.

PURPORT

Everyone engages in work with his hands, legs and other senses just to achieve a certain goal according to his concocted ideas. One tries to enjoy the five sense objects, namely form, sound, taste, aroma and touch, not knowing the actual goal of life, which is to satisfy the Supreme Lord. Because of disobeying the Supreme Lord, one is put into material conditions, and he then tries to improve his situation in a concocted way, not desiring to follow the instructions of the Supreme Personality of Godhead. Nevertheless, the Supreme Lord is so kind that He comes Himself to instruct the bewildered living entity how to act obediently and then gradually return home, back to Godhead, where he can attain an eternal, peaceful life of bliss and knowledge. The living entity has a body, which is a very complicated combination of the material elements, and with this body he struggles alone, as indicated in this verse by the words *ekas tu.* For example, if one is struggling in the ocean, he must swim through it alone. Although many other men and aquatics are swimming in the ocean, he must take care of himself because no one else will help him. Therefore this verse indicates that the seventeenth item, the soul, must work alone. Although he tries to create society, friendship and love, no one will be able to help him but Kṛṣṇa, the Supreme Lord. Therefore his only concern should be how to satisfy Kṛṣṇa. That is also what Kṛṣṇa wants (*sarva-dharmān parityajya mām ekaṁ śaraṇaṁ vraja*). People bewildered by material conditions try to be united, but although they strive for unity among men and nations, all their attempts are futile. Everyone must struggle alone for existence with the many elements of nature. Therefore one's only hope, as Kṛṣṇa advises, is to surrender to Him, for He can help one become free from the ocean of nescience. Śrī Caitanya Mahāprabhu therefore prayed:

ayi nanda-tanuja kiṅkaraṁ
patitaṁ māṁ viṣame bhavāmbudhau
kṛpayā tava pāda-paṅkaja-
sthita-dhūlī-sadṛśaṁ vicintaya

" O Kṛṣṇa, beloved son of Nanda Mahārāja, I am Your eternal servant, but somehow or other I have fallen into this ocean of nescience, and although I am struggling very hard, there is no way I can save myself. If You kindly pick me up and fix me as one of the particles of dust at Your lotus feet, that will save me."

In a similar way, Bhaktivinoda Ṭhākura sang:

anādi karama-phale, paḍi' bhavārṇava-jale,
taribāre nā dekhi upāya

"My dear Lord, I cannot remember when I somehow or other fell into this ocean of nescience, and now I can find no way to rescue myself." We should remember that everyone is responsible for his own life. If an individual becomes a pure devotee of Kṛṣṇa, he is then delivered from the ocean of nescience.

TEXT 51

तदेतत् षोडशकलं लिङ्गं शक्तित्रयं महत् ।
धत्तेऽनुसंसृतिं पुंसि हर्षशोकभयार्तिदाम् ॥ ५१ ॥

tad etat ṣoḍaśa-kalaṁ
liṅgaṁ śakti-trayaṁ mahat
dhatte'nusaṁsṛtiṁ puṁsi
harṣa-śoka-bhayārtidām

tat—therefore; *etat*—this; *ṣoḍaśa-kalam*—made of sixteen parts (namely the ten senses, the mind and the five sense objects); *liṅgam*—the subtle body; *śakti-trayam*—the effect of the three modes of material nature; *mahat*—insurmountable; *dhatte*—gives; *anusaṁsṛtim*—almost perpetual rotation and transmigration in different types of bodies; *puṁsi*—unto the living entity; *harṣa*—jubilation; *śoka*—lamentation; *bhaya*—fear; *ārti*—misery; *dām*—which gives.

TRANSLATION

The subtle body is endowed with sixteen parts—the five knowledge-acquiring senses, the five working senses, the five objects of sense gratification, and the mind. This subtle body is an effect of the three modes of material nature. It is composed of insurmountably strong desires, and therefore it causes the living entity to transmigrate from one body to another in human life, animal life and life as a demigod. When the living entity gets the body of a demigod, he is certainly very jubilant, when he gets a human body he is always in lamentation, and when he gets the body of an animal, he is always afraid. In all conditions, however, he is actually miserable. His miserable condition is called saṁsṛti, or transmigration in material life.

PURPORT

The sum and substance of material conditional life is explained in this verse. The living entity, the seventeenth element, is struggling alone, life after life. This struggle is called *saṁsṛti,* or material conditional life. In *Bhagavad-gītā* it is said that the force of material nature is insurmountably strong (*daivī hy eṣā guṇamayī mama māyā duratyayā*). Material nature harasses the living entity in different bodies, but if the living entity surrenders to the Supreme Personality of Godhead, he becomes free from this entanglement, as confirmed in *Bhagavad-gītā* (*mām eva ye prapadyante māyām etāṁ taranti te*). Thus his life becomes successful.

TEXT 52

देह्यज्ञोऽजितषड्वर्गो नेच्छन् कर्माणि कार्यते ।
कोशकार इवात्मानं कर्मणाच्छाद्य मुह्यति ॥ ५२ ॥

dehy ajño 'jita-ṣaḍ-vargo
necchan karmāṇi kāryate
kośakāra ivātmānaṁ
karmaṇācchādya muhyati

dehī—the embodied soul; *ajñaḥ*—without perfect knowledge; *ajita-ṣaṭ-vargaḥ*—who has not controlled the senses of perception and the mind; *na icchan*—without desiring; *karmāṇi*—activities for material benefit; *kāryate* —is caused to perform; *kośakāraḥ*—the silkworm; *iva*—like; *ātmānam*—himself; *karmaṇā*—by fruitive activities; *ācchādya*—covering; *muhyati* —becomes bewildered.

TRANSLATION

The foolish embodied living entity, inept at controlling his senses and mind, is forced to act according to the influence of the modes of material nature, against his desires. He is like a silkworm that uses its own saliva to create a cocoon and then becomes trapped in it, with no possibility of getting out. The living entity traps himself in a network of his own fruitive activities and then can find no way to release himself. Thus he is always bewildered, and repeatedly he dies.

PURPORT

As already explained, the influence of the modes of nature is very strong. The living entity entangled in different types of fruitive activity is like a silkworm trapped in a cocoon. Getting free is very difficult unless he is helped by the Supreme Personality of Godhead.

TEXT 53

न हि कश्चित्क्षणमपि जातु तिष्ठत्यकर्मकृत् ।
कार्यते ह्यवशः कर्म गुणैः स्वाभाविकैर्बलात् ॥ ५३ ॥

na hi kaścit kṣaṇam api
jātu tiṣṭhaty akarma-kṛt
kāryate hy avaśaḥ karma
guṇaiḥ svābhāvikair balāt

na—not; *hi*—indeed; *kaścit*—anyone; *kṣaṇam api*—even for a moment; *jātu*—at any time; *tiṣṭhati*—remains; *akarma-kṛt*—without doing anything; *kāryate*—he is caused to perform; *hi*—indeed; *avaśaḥ*—automatically; *karma* —fruitive activities; *guṇaiḥ*—by the three modes of nature; *svābhāvikaiḥ*—which are produced by his own tendencies in previous lives; *balāt*—by force.

TRANSLATION

Not a single living entity can remain unengaged even for a moment. One must act by his natural tendency according to the three modes of

material nature because this natural tendency forcibly makes him work in a particular way.

PURPORT

The *svābhāvika,* or one's natural tendency, is the most important factor in action. One's natural tendency is to serve because a living entity is an eternal servant of God. The living entity wants to serve, but because of his forgetfulness of his relationship with the Supreme Lord, he serves under the modes of material nature and manufactures various modes of service, such as socialism, humanitarianism and altruism. However, one should be enlightened in the tenets of *Bhagavad-gītā* and accept the instruction of the Supreme Personality of Godhead that one give up all natural tendencies for material service under different names and take to the service of the Lord. One's original natural tendency is to act in Kṛṣṇa consciousness because one's real nature is spiritual. The duty of a human being is to understand that since he is essentially spirit, he must abide by the spiritual tendency and not be carried away by material tendencies. Śrīla Bhaktivinoda Ṭhākura has therefore sung:

(miche) māyāra vaśe, yāccha bhese',
khāccha hābuḍubu, bhāi

"My dear brothers, you are being carried away by the waves of material energy and are suffering in many miserable conditions. Sometimes you are drowning in the waves of material nature, and sometimes you are tossed like a swimmer struggling in the ocean." As confirmed by Bhaktivinoda Ṭhākura, this tendency to be battered by the waves of *māyā* can be changed to one's original, natural tendency, which is spiritual, when the living entity comes to understand that he is eternally *kṛṣṇa-dāsa,* a servant of God, Kṛṣṇa.

(jīva) kṛṣṇa-dāsa, ei viśvāsa,
karle ta' āra duḥkha nāi

If instead of serving *māyā* under different names, one turns his service attitude toward the Supreme Lord, he is then safe, and there is no more difficulty. If one returns to his original, natural tendency in the human form of life by understanding the perfect knowledge given by Kṛṣṇa Himself in the Vedic literature, one's life is successful.

TEXT 54

लब्ध्वा निमित्तमव्यक्तं व्यक्ताव्यक्तं भवत्युत।
यथायोनि यथाबीजं स्वभावेन बलीयसा ॥ ५४॥

labdhvā nimittam avyaktaṁ
vyaktāvyaktaṁ bhavaty uta
yathā-yoni yathā-bījaṁ
svabhāvena balīyasā

labdhvā—having gotten; *nimittam*—the cause; *avyaktam*—unseen or unknown to the person; *vyakta-avyaktam*—manifested and unmanifested, or the gross body and the subtle body; *bhavati*—come into being; *uta*—certainly; *yathā-yoni*—exactly like the mother; *yathā-bījam*—exactly like the father; *sva-bhāvena*—by the natural tendency; *balīyasā*—which is very powerful.

TRANSLATION

The fruitive activities a living being performs, whether pious or impious, are the unseen cause for the fulfillment of his desires. This unseen cause is the root for the living entity's different bodies. Because of his intense desire, the living entity takes birth in a particular family and receives a body which is either like that of his mother or like that of his father. The gross and subtle bodies are created according to his desire.

PURPORT

The gross body is a product of the subtle body. As stated in *Bhagavad-gītā* (8.6):

yaṁ yaṁ vāpi smaran bhāvaṁ
tyajaty ante kalevaram
taṁ tam evaiti kaunteya
sadā tad-bhāva-bhāvitaḥ

"Whatever state of being one remembers when he quits his body, that state he will attain without fail." The atmosphere of the subtle body at the time of death is created by the activities of the gross body. Thus the gross body acts during one's lifetime, and the subtle body acts at the time of death. The subtle body, which is called *liṅga,* the body of desire, is the background for the development of a particular type of gross body, which is either like that of one's mother or like that of one's father. According to the *Ṛg Veda,* if at the time of sex the secretions of the mother are more profuse than those of the father, the child will receive a female body, and if the secretions of the father are more profuse than those of the mother, the child will receive a male body. These are the subtle laws of nature, which act according to the desire of the living entity. If a human being is taught to change his subtle body by developing a consciousness of Kṛṣṇa, at the time of death the subtle body will create a gross body in which he will be a devotee of Kṛṣṇa, or if he is still more perfect, he will not take another material body but will immediately get a spiritual body and thus return home, back to Godhead. This is the process of the transmigration of the soul. Therefore instead of trying to unite human society through pacts for sense gratification that can never be achieved, it is clearly desirable to teach people how to become Kṛṣṇa conscious and return home, back to Godhead. This is true now and, indeed, at any time.

TEXT 55

एष प्रकृतिसङ्गेन पुरुषस्य विपर्ययः ।
आसीत् स एव नचिरादीशसङ्गाद्विलीयते ॥ ५५ ॥

eṣa prakṛti-saṅgena
puruṣasya viparyayaḥ
āsīt sa eva na cirād
īśa-saṅgād vilīyate

eṣaḥ—this; *prakṛti-saṅgena*—because of association with the material nature; *puruṣasya*—of the living entity; *viparyayaḥ*—a situation of forgetfulness or an awkward position; *āsīt*—came to be; *saḥ*—that position; *eva*—indeed; *na*—not; *cirāt*—taking a long time; *īśa-saṅgāt*—from the association of the Supreme Lord; *vilīyate*—is vanquished.

TRANSLATION

Since the living entity is associated with material nature, he is in an awkward position, but if in the human form of life he is taught how to associate with the Supreme Personality of Godhead or His devotee, this position can be overcome.

PURPORT

The word *prakṛti* means material nature, and *puruṣa* may also refer to the Supreme Personality of Godhead. If one wants to continue his association with *prakṛti,* the female energy of Kṛṣṇa, and be separated from Kṛṣṇa by the illusion that he is able to enjoy *prakṛti,* he must continue in his conditional life. If he changes his consciousness, however, and associates with the supreme, original person (*puruṣaṁ śāśvatam*), or with His associates, he can get out of the entanglement of material nature. As confirmed in *Bhagavad-gītā* (4.9), *janma karma ca me divyam evaṁ yo vetti tattvataḥ:* one must simply understand the Supreme Person, Kṛṣṇa, in terms of His form, name, activities and pastimes. This will keep one always in the association of Kṛṣṇa. *Tyaktvā dehaṁ punar janma naiti mām eti so 'rjuna:* thus after giving up his gross material body, one accepts not another gross body but a spiritual body in which to return home, back to Godhead. Thus one ends the tribulation caused by his association with the material energy. In summary, the living entity is an eternal servant of God, but he comes to the material world and is bound by material conditions because of his desire to lord it over matter. Liberation means giving up this false consciousness and reviving one's original service to the Lord. This return to one's original life is called *mukti,* as confirmed in *Śrīmad-Bhāgavatam* (*muktir hitvānyathā rūpaṁ svarūpeṇa vyavasthitiḥ*).

TEXTS 56–57

अयं हि श्रुतसम्पन्नः शीलवृत्तगुणालयः ।
धृतव्रतो मृदुर्दान्तः सत्यवाङ्मन्त्रविच्छुचिः ॥ ५६ ॥
गुर्वग्न्यतिथिवृद्धानां शुश्रूषुरनहङ्कृतः ।
सर्वभूतसुहृत्साधुर्मितवागनसूयकः ॥ ५७ ॥

ayaṁ hi śruta-sampannaḥ
śīla-vṛtta-guṇālayaḥ
dhṛta-vrato mṛdur dāntaḥ
satya-vāṅ mantra-vic chuciḥ

gurv-agny-atithi-vṛddhānāṁ
śuśrūṣur anahaṅkṛtaḥ
sarva-bhūta-suhṛt sādhur
mita-vāg anasūyakaḥ

ayam—this person (known as Ajāmila); *hi*—indeed; *śruta-sampannaḥ*—well educated in Vedic knowledge; *śīla*—of good character; *vṛtta*—good conduct; *guṇa*—and good qualities; *ālayaḥ*—the reservoir; *dhṛta-vrataḥ*—fixed in the execution of the Vedic injunctions; *mṛduḥ*—very mild; *dāntaḥ*—completely controlling the mind and senses; *satya-vāk*—always truthful; *mantra-vit*—knowing how to chant the Vedic hymns; *śuciḥ*—always very neat and clean; *guru*—the spiritual master; *agni*—the fire god; *atithi*—guests; *vṛddhānām*—and of the old household members; *śuśrūṣuḥ*—very respectfully engaged in the service; *anahaṅkṛtaḥ*—without pride or false prestige; *sarva-bhūta-suhṛt*—friendly to all living entities; *sādhuḥ*—well-behaved (no one could find any fault in his character); *mita-vāk*—talking with great care not to speak nonsense; *anasūyakaḥ*—not envious.

TRANSLATION

In the beginning this brāhmaṇa named Ajāmila studied all the Vedic literatures. He was a reservoir of good character, good conduct and good qualities. Firmly established in executing all the Vedic injunctions, he was very mild and gentle, and he kept his mind and senses under control. Furthermore, he was always truthful, he knew how to chant the Vedic mantras, and he was also very pure. Ajāmila was very respectful to his spiritual master, the fire-god, guests, and the elderly members of his household. Indeed, he was free from false prestige. He was upright, benevolent to all living entities, and well behaved. He would never speak nonsense or envy anyone.

PURPORT

The order carriers of Yamarāja, the Yamadūtas, are explaining the factual position of piety and impiety and how a living entity is entangled in this material world. Describing the history of Ajāmila's life, the Yamadūtas relate that in the beginning he was a learned scholar of the Vedic literature. He was well-behaved, neat and clean, and very kind to everyone. In fact, he had all good qualities. In other words, he was like a perfect *brāhmaṇa.* A *brāhmaṇa* is expected to be perfectly pious, to follow all the regulative principles and to have all good qualities. The symptoms of piety are explained in these verses. Śrīla Vīrarāghava Ācārya comments that *dhṛta-vrata* means *dhṛtaṁ vrataṁ strī-saṅga-rāhityātmaka-brahmacarya-rūpam.* In other words, Ajāmila followed the rules and regulations of celibacy as a perfect *brahmacārī* and was very softhearted, truthful, clean and pure. How he fell down in spite of all these qualities and thus came to be threatened with punishment by Yamarāja will be described in the following verses.

TEXTS 58–60

एकदासौ वनं यातः पितृसन्देशकृद् द्विजः ।
आदाय तत आवृत्तः फलपुष्पसमित्कुशान् ॥ ५८ ॥
ददर्श कामिनं कञ्चिच्छूद्रं सह भुजिष्यया ।
पीत्वा च मधु मैरेयं मदाघूर्णितनेत्रया ॥ ५९ ॥
मत्तया विश्लथन्नीव्या व्यपेतं निरपत्रपम् ।
क्रीडन्तमनुगायन्तं हसन्तमनयान्तिके ॥ ६० ॥

ekadāsau vanaṁ yātaḥ
pitṛ-sandeśa-kṛd dvijaḥ
ādāya tata āvṛttaḥ
phala-puṣpa-samit-kuśān

dadarśa kāminaṁ kañcic
chūdraṁ saha bhujiṣyayā
pītvā ca madhu maireyaṁ
madāghūrṇita-netrayā

mattayā viślathan-nīvyā
vyapetaṁ nirapatrapam
krīḍantam anugāyantaṁ
hasantam anayāntike

ekadā—once upon a time; *asau*—this Ajāmila; *vanam yātaḥ*—went to the forest; *pitṛ*—of his father; *sandeśa*—the order; *kṛt*—carrying out; *dvijaḥ*—the *brāhmaṇa; ādāya*—collecting; *tataḥ*—from the forest; *āvṛttaḥ*—returning; *phala-puṣpa*—fruits and flowers; *samit-kuśān*—two kinds of grass, known as *samit* and *kuśa; dadarśa*—saw; *kāminam*—very lusty; *kañcit*—someone; *śūdram*—a fourth-class man, a *śūdra; saha*—along with; *bhujiṣyayā*—an ordinary maidservant or prostitute; *pītvā*—after drinking; *ca*—also; *madhu*—nectar; *maireyam*—made of the *soma* flower; *mada*—by intoxication; *āghūrṇita*—moving; *netrayā*—her eyes; *mattayā*—intoxicated; *viślathat-nīvyā*—whose dress was slackened; *vyapetam*—fallen from proper behavior; *nirapatrapam*—without fear of public opinion; *krīḍantam*—engaged in enjoyment; *anugāyantam*—singing; *hasantam*—smiling; *anayā*—with her; *antike*—close by.

TRANSLATION

Once this brāhmaṇa Ajāmila, following the order of his father, went to the forest to collect fruit, flowers and two kinds of grass, called samit and kuśa. On the way home, he came upon a śūdra, a very lusty, fourth-class man, who was shamelessly embracing and kissing a prostitute. The śūdra was smiling, singing and enjoying as if this were proper behavior. Both the śūdra and the prostitute were drunk. The prostitute's eyes were rolling in intoxication, and her dress had become loose. Such was the condition in which Ajāmila saw them.

PURPORT

While traveling along the public way, Ajāmila came upon a fourth-class man and a prostitute, who are vividly described here. Drunkenness was sometimes manifest even in bygone ages, although not very frequently. In this age of Kali, however, such sin is to be seen everywhere, for people all over the world have become shameless. Long ago, when he saw the scene of the drunken *śūdra* and the prostitute, Ajāmila, who was a perfect *brahmacārī,* was affected. Nowadays such sin is visible in so many places, and we must consider the position of a *brahmacārī* student who sees such behavior. For such a *brahmacārī* to remain steady is very difficult unless he is extremely strong in following the regulative principles. Nevertheless, if one takes to Kṛṣṇa consciousness very seriously, he can withstand the provocation created by sin. In our Kṛṣṇa consciousness movement we prohibit illicit sex, intoxication, meat-eating and gambling. In Kali-yuga, a drunk, half-naked woman embracing a drunk man is a very common sight, especially in the Western countries, and restraining oneself after seeing such things is very difficult. Nevertheless, if by the grace of Kṛṣṇa one adheres to the regulative principles and chants the Hare Kṛṣṇa *mantra,* Kṛṣṇa will certainly protect him. Indeed, Kṛṣṇa says that His devotee is never vanquished (*kaunteya pratijānīhi na me bhaktaḥ praṇaśyati*). Therefore all the disciples practicing Kṛṣṇa consciousness should obediently follow the regulative principles and remain fixed in chanting the holy name of the Lord. Then there need be no fear. Otherwise one's position is very dangerous, especially in this Kali-yuga.

TEXT 61

दृष्ट्वा तां कामलिप्तेन बाहुना परिरम्भिताम् ।
जगाम हृच्छयवशं सहसैव विमोहितः ॥ ६१ ॥

dṛṣṭvā tāṁ kāma-liptena
bāhunā parirambhitām
jagāma hṛc-chaya-vaśaṁ
sahasaiva vimohitaḥ

dṛṣṭvā—by seeing; *tām*—her (the prostitute); *kāma-liptena*—decorated with turmeric to incite lusty desires; *bāhunā*—with the arm; *parirambhitām*—embraced; *jagāma*—went; *hṛt-śaya*—of lusty desires within the heart; *vaśam*—under the control; *sahasā*—suddenly; *eva*—indeed; *vimohitaḥ*—being illusioned.

TRANSLATION

The śūdra, his arm decorated with turmeric powder, was embracing the prostitute. When Ajāmila saw her, the dormant lusty desires in his heart awakened, and in illusion he fell under their control.

PURPORT

It is said that if one's body is smeared with turmeric, it attracts the lusty desires of the opposite sex. The word *kāma-liptena* indicates that the *śūdra* was decorated with turmeric smeared on his body.

TEXT 62

स्तम्भयन्नात्मनात्मानं यावत्सत्त्वं यथाश्रुतम् ।
न शशाक समाधातुं मनो मदनवेपितम् ॥ ६२ ॥

stambhayann ātmanātmānaṁ
yāvat sattvaṁ yathā-śrutam
na śaśāka samādhātuṁ
mano madana-vepitam

stambhayan—trying to control; *ātmanā*—by the intelligence; *ātmānam*—the mind; *yāvat sattvam*—as far as possible for him; *yathā-śrutam*—by remembering the instruction (of celibacy, *brahmacarya,* not even to see a woman); *na*—not; *śaśāka*—was able; *samādhātum*—to restrain; *manaḥ*—the mind; *madana-vepitam*—agitated by Cupid or lusty desire.

TRANSLATION

As far as possible he patiently tried to remember the instructions of the śāstras not even to see a woman. With the help of this knowledge and his

intellect, he tried to control his lusty desires, but because of the force of Cupid within his heart, he failed to control his mind.

PURPORT

Unless one is very strong in knowledge, patience and proper bodily, mental and intellectual behavior, controlling one's lusty desires is extremely difficult. Thus after seeing a man embracing a young woman and practically doing everything required for sex life, even a fully qualified *brāhmaṇa,* as described above, could not control his lusty desires and restrain himself from pursuing them. Because of the force of materialistic life, to maintain self-control is extremely difficult unless one is specifically under the protection of the Supreme Personality of Godhead through devotional service.

TEXT 63

तन्निमित्तस्मरव्याजग्रहग्रस्तो विचेतनः ।
तामेव मनसा ध्यायन् स्वधर्माद्विरराम ह ॥ ६३ ॥

tan-nimitta-smara-vyāja-
graha-grasto vicetanaḥ
tām eva manasā dhyāyan
sva-dharmād virarāma ha

tat-nimitta—caused by the sight of her; *smara-vyāja*—taking advantage of his thinking of her always; *graha-grastaḥ*—being caught by an eclipse; *vicetanaḥ*—having completely forgotten his real position; *tām*—her; *eva*—certainly; *manasā*—by the mind; *dhyāyan*—meditating upon; *sva-dharmāt*—from the regulative principles executed by a *brāhmaṇa; virarāma ha*—he completely ceased.

TRANSLATION

In the same way that the sun and moon are eclipsed by a low planet, the brāhmaṇa lost all his good sense. Taking advantage of this situation, he always thought of the prostitute, and within a short time he took her as a servant in his house and abandoned all the regulative principles of a brāhmaṇa.

PURPORT

By speaking this verse, Śukadeva Gosvāmī wants to impress upon the mind of the reader that Ajāmila's exalted position as a *brāhmaṇa* was vanquished by his association with the prostitute, so much so that he forgot all his brahminical activities. Nevertheless, at the end of his life, by chanting the four syllables of the name Nārāyaṇa, he was saved from the gravest danger of falling down. *Svalpam apy asya dharmasya trāyate mahato bhayāt:* even a little devotional service can save one from the greatest danger. Devotional service, which begins with chanting of the holy name of the Lord, is so powerful that even if one falls down from the exalted position of a *brāhmaṇa* through sexual indulgence, he can be saved from all calamities if he somehow or other chants the holy name of the Lord. This is the extraordinary power of the Lord's holy name. Therefore in *Bhagavad-gītā* it is advised that one not forget the chanting of the holy name even for a moment (*satataṁ kīrtayanto māṁ yatantaś ca dṛḍha-vratāḥ*). There are so many dangers in this material world that one may fall down from an exalted position at any time. Yet if one keeps himself always pure and steady by chanting the Hare Kṛṣṇa *mahā-mantra,* he will be safe without a doubt.

TEXT 64

तामेव तोषयामास पित्र्येणार्थेन यावता ।
ग्राम्यैर्मनोरमैः कामैः प्रसीदेत यथा तथा ॥ ६४ ॥

tām eva toṣayām āsa
pitryeṇārthena yāvatā
grāmyair manoramaiḥ kāmaiḥ
prasīdeta yathā tathā

tām—her (the prostitute); *eva*—indeed; *toṣayām āsa*—he tried to please; *pitryeṇa*—he got from his father's hard labor; *arthena*—by the money; *yāvatā*—as long as possible; *grāmyaiḥ*—material; *manaḥ-ramaiḥ*—pleasing to her mind; *kāmaiḥ*—by presentations for sense enjoyment; *prasīdeta*—she would be satisfied; *yathā*—so that; *tathā*—in that way.

TRANSLATION

Thus Ajāmila began spending whatever money he had inherited from his father to satisfy the prostitute with various material presentations so that she would remain pleased with him. He gave up all his brahminical activities to satisfy the prostitute.

PURPORT

There are many instances throughout the world in which even a purified person, being attracted by a prostitute, spends all the money he has inherited. Prostitute hunting is so abominable that the desire for sex with a prostitute can ruin one's character, destroy one's exalted position and plunder all one's money. Therefore illicit sex is strictly prohibited. One should be satisfied with his married wife, for even a slight deviation will create havoc. A Kṛṣṇa conscious *gṛhastha* should always remember this. He should always be satisfied with one wife and be peaceful simply by chanting the Hare Kṛṣṇa *mantra.* Otherwise at any moment he may fall down from his good position, as exemplified in the case of Ajāmila.

TEXT 65

विप्रां स्वभार्यामप्रौढां कुले महति लम्भिताम् ।
विससर्जाचिरात्पापः स्वैरिण्यापाङ्गविद्धधीः ॥ ६५ ॥

viprāṁ sva-bhāryām aprauḍhāṁ
kule mahati lambhitām
visasarjācirāt pāpaḥ
svairiṇyāpāṅga-viddha-dhīḥ

viprām—the daughter of a *brāhmaṇa; sva-bhāryām*—his wife; *aprauḍhām*—not very old (youthful); *kule*—from a family; *mahati*—very respectable; *lambhitām*—married; *visasarja*—he gave up; *acirāt*—very soon; *pāpaḥ*—being sinful; *svairiṇyā*—of the prostitute; *apāṅga-viddha-dhīḥ*—his intelligence pierced by the lustful glance.

TRANSLATION

Because his intelligence was pierced by the lustful glance of the prostitute, the victimized brāhmaṇa Ajāmila engaged in sinful acts in her association. He even gave up the company of his very beautiful young wife, who came from a very respectable brāhmaṇa family.

PURPORT

Customarily everyone is eligible to inherit his father's property, and Ajāmila also inherited the money of his father. But what did he do with the money? Instead of engaging the money in the service of Kṛṣṇa, he engaged it in the service of a prostitute. Therefore he was condemned and was punishable by Yamarāja. How did this happen? He was victimized by the dangerous lustful glance of a prostitute.

TEXT 66

यतस्ततश्चोपनिन्ये न्यायतोऽन्यायतो धनम् ।
बभारास्याः कुटुम्बिन्याः कुटुम्बं मन्दधीरयम् ॥ ६६ ॥

yatas tataś copaninye
nyāyato'nyāyato dhanam
babhārāsyāḥ kuṭumbinyāḥ
kuṭumbaṁ manda-dhīr ayam

yataḥ tataḥ—wherever possible, however possible; *ca*—and; *upaninye*—he got; *nyāyataḥ*—properly; *anyāyataḥ*—improperly; *dhanam*—money; *babhāra*—he maintained; *asyāḥ*—of her; *kuṭum-binyāḥ*—possessing many sons and daughters; *kuṭumbam*—the family; *manda-dhīḥ*—bereft of all intelligence; *ayam*—this person (Ajāmila).

TRANSLATION

Although born of a brāhmaṇa family, this rascal, bereft of intelligence because of the prostitute's association, earned money somehow or other, regardless of whether properly or improperly, and used it to maintain the prostitute's sons and daughters.

TEXT 67

यदसौ शास्त्रमुल्लङ्घ्य स्वैरचार्यतिगर्हितः ।
अवर्तत चिरं कालमघायुरशुचिर्मलात् ॥ ६७ ॥

yad asau śāstram ullaṅghya
svaira-cāry ati-garhitaḥ
avartata ciraṁ kālam
aghāyur aśucir malāt

yat—because; *asau*—this *brāhmaṇa; śāstram ullaṅghya*—transgressing the laws of *śāstra; svaira-cārī*—acting irresponsibly; *ati-garhitaḥ*—very much condemned; *avartata*—passed; *ciram kālam*—a long time; *agha-āyuḥ*—whose life was full of sinful activities; *aśuciḥ*—unclean; *malāt*—because of impurity.

TRANSLATION

This brāhmaṇa irresponsibly spent his long lifetime transgressing all the rules and regulations of the holy scripture, living extravagantly and eating food prepared by a prostitute. Therefore he is full of sins. He is unclean and is addicted to forbidden activities.

PURPORT

Food prepared by an unclean, sinful man or woman, especially a prostitute, is extremely infectious. Ajāmila ate such food, and therefore he was subject to be punished by Yamarāja.

TEXT 68

तत एनं दण्डपाणेः सकाशं कृतकिल्बिषम् ।
नेष्यामोऽकृतनिर्वेशं यत्र दण्डेन शुद्ध्यति ॥ ६८ ॥

tata enaṁ daṇḍa-pāṇeḥ
sakāśaṁ kṛta-kilbiṣam
neṣyāmo'kṛta-nirveśaṁ
yatra daṇḍena śuddhyati

tataḥ—therefore; *enam*—him; *daṇḍa-pāṇeḥ*—of Yamarāja, who is authorized to punish; *sakāśam*—in the presence; *kṛta-kilbiṣam*—who has regularly committed all sinful activities; *neṣyāmaḥ*—we shall take; *akṛta-nirveśam*—who has not undergone atonement; *yatra*—where; *daṇḍena*—by punishment; *śuddhyati*—he will be purified.

TRANSLATION

This man Ajāmila did not undergo atonement. Therefore because of his sinful life, we must take him into the presence of Yamarāja for punishment. There, according to the extent of his sinful acts, he will be punished and thus purified.

PURPORT

The Viṣṇudūtas had forbidden the Yamadūtas to take Ajāmila to Yamarāja, and therefore the Yamadūtas explained that taking such a man to Yamarāja was appropriate. Since Ajāmila had not undergone atonement for his sinful acts, he was to be taken to Yamarāja to be purified. When a man commits murder he becomes sinful, and therefore he also must be killed; otherwise after death he must suffer many sinful reactions. Similarly, punishment by Yamarāja is a process of purification for the most abominable sinful persons. Therefore the Yamadūtas requested the Viṣṇudūtas not to obstruct their taking Ajāmila to Yamarāja.

Thus end the Bhaktivedanta purports of the Sixth Canto, First Chapter, of the Śrīmad-Bhāgavatam, entitled *"The History of the Life of Ajāmila."*

CHAPTER TWO

Ajāmila Delivered by the Viṣṇudūtas

In this chapter the messengers from Vaikuṇṭha explain to the Yamadūtas the glories of chanting the holy name of the Lord. The Viṣṇudūtas said, "Now impious acts are being performed even in an assembly of devotees, for a person who is not punishable is going to be punished in the assembly of Yamarāja. The mass of people are helpless and must depend upon the government for their safety and security, but if the government takes advantage of this to harm the citizens, where will they go? We see perfectly that Ajāmila should not be punished, although you are attempting to take him to Yamarāja for punishment."

It was due to Ajāmila's glorifying the holy name of the Supreme Lord that he was not punishable. The Viṣṇudūtas explained this as follows: "Simply by once chanting the holy name of Nārāyaṇa, this *brāhmaṇa* has become free from the reactions of sinful life. Indeed, he has been freed not only from the sins of this life, but from the sins of many, many thousands of other lives. He has already undergone true atonement for all his sinful actions. If one atones according to the directions of the *śāstras,* one does not actually become free from sinful reactions, but if one chants the holy name of the Lord, even a glimpse of such chanting can immediately free one from all sins. Chanting the glories of the Lord's holy name awakens all good fortune. Therefore there is no doubt that Ajāmila, being completely free from all sinful reactions, should not be punished by Yamarāja."

As they were saying this, the Viṣṇudūtas released Ajāmila from the ropes of the Yamadūtas and left for their own abode. The *brāhmaṇa* Ajāmila, however, offered his respectful obeisances to the Viṣṇudūtas. He could understand how fortunate he was to have chanted the holy name of Nārāyaṇa at the end of his life. Indeed, he could realize the full significance of this good fortune. Having thoroughly understood the discussion between the Yamadūtas and the Viṣṇudūtas, he became a pure devotee of the Supreme Personality of Godhead. He lamented very much for how very sinful he had been, and he condemned himself again and again.

Finally, because of his association with the Viṣṇudūtas, Ajāmila, his original consciousness aroused, gave up everything and went to Hardwar, where he engaged in devotional service without deviation, always thinking of the

Supreme Personality of Godhead. Thus the Viṣṇudūtas went there, seated him on a golden throne and took him away to Vaikuṇṭhaloka.

In summary, although the sinful Ajāmila meant to call his son, the holy name of Lord Nārāyaṇa, even though chanted in the preliminary stage, *nāmābhāsa,* was able to give him liberation. Therefore one who chants the holy name of the Lord with faith and devotion is certainly exalted. He is protected even in his material, conditional life.

TEXT 1

श्रीबादरायणिरुवाच

एवं ते भगवद्दूता यमदूताभिभाषितम् ।
उपधार्याथ तान् राजन् प्रत्याहुर्नयकोविदाः ॥ १ ॥

śrī-bādarāyaṇir uvāca
evaṁ te bhagavad-dūtā
yamadūtābhibhāṣitam
upadhāryātha tān rājan
pratyāhur naya-kovidāḥ

śrī-bādarāyaṇiḥ uvāca—Śukadeva Gosvāmī, the son of Vyāsadeva, said; *evam*—thus; *te*—they; *bhagavat-dūtāḥ*—the servants of Lord Viṣṇu; *yamadūta*—by the servants of Yamarāja; *abhibhāṣitam*—what was spoken; *upadhārya*—hearing; *atha*—then; *tān*—unto them; *rājan*—O King; *pratyāhuḥ*—replied properly; *naya-kovidāḥ*—being conversant in good arguments or good logic.

TRANSLATION

Śukadeva Gosvāmī said: My dear King, the servants of Lord Viṣṇu are always very expert in logic and arguments. After hearing the statements of the Yamadūtas, they replied as follows.

TEXT 2

श्रीविष्णुदूता ऊचुः

अहो कष्टं धर्मदृशामधर्मः स्पृशते सभाम् ।
यत्रादण्ड्येष्वपापेषु दण्डो यैर्ध्रियते वृथा ॥ २ ॥

śrī-viṣṇudūtā ūcuḥ
aho kaṣṭaṁ dharma-dṛśām
adharmaḥ spṛśate sabhām

yatrādaṇḍyeṣv apāpeṣu
daṇḍo yair dhriyate vṛthā

śrī-viṣṇudūtāḥ ūcuḥ—the Viṣṇudūtas said; *aho*—alas; *kaṣṭam*—how painful it is; *dharma-dṛśām*—of persons interested in maintaining religion; *adharmaḥ*—irreligion; *spṛśate*—is affecting; *sabhām*—the assembly; *yatra*—wherein; *adaṇḍyeṣu*—upon persons not to be punished; *apāpeṣu*—who are sinless; *daṇḍaḥ*—punishment; *yaiḥ*—by whom; *dhriyate*—is being allotted; *vṛthā*—unnecessarily.

TRANSLATION

The Viṣṇudūtas said: Alas, how painful it is that irreligion is being introduced into an assembly where religion should be maintained. Indeed, those in charge of maintaining the religious principles are needlessly punishing a sinless, unpunishable person.

PURPORT

The Viṣṇudūtas accused the Yamadūtas of violating the religious principles by attempting to drag Ajāmila to Yamarāja for punishment. Yamarāja is the officer appointed by the Supreme Personality of Godhead to judge religious and irreligious principles and to punish people who are irreligious. However, if completely sinless people are punished, the entire assembly of Yamarāja is contaminated. This principle applies not only in the assembly of Yamarāja, but throughout human society also.

In human society, properly maintaining religious principles is the duty of the king's court or the government. Unfortunately, in this *yuga,* Kali-yuga, the religious principles are tampered with, and the government cannot properly judge who is to be punished and who is not. It is said that in the Kali-yuga if one cannot spend money in court, one cannot get justice. Indeed, in courts of justice it is often found that magistrates are bribed for favorable judgments. Sometimes religious men who preach the Kṛṣṇa consciousness movement for the benefit of the entire populace are arrested and harassed by the police and courts. The Viṣṇudūtas, who are Vaiṣṇavas, lamented for these very regrettable facts. Because of their spiritual compassion for all the fallen souls, Vaiṣṇavas go out to preach according to the standard method of all religious principles, but unfortunately, because of the influence of Kali-yuga, Vaiṣṇavas who have dedicated their lives to preaching the glories of the Lord are sometimes harassed and punished by courts on false charges of disturbing the peace.

TEXT 3

प्रजानां पितरो ये च शास्तारः साधवः समाः ।
यदि स्यात्तेषु वैषम्यं कं यान्ति शरणं प्रजाः ॥ ३ ॥

prajānāṁ pitaro ye ca
śāstāraḥ sādhavaḥ samāḥ
yadi syāt teṣu vaiṣamyaṁ
kaṁ yānti śaraṇaṁ prajāḥ

prajānām—of the citizens; *pitaraḥ*—protectors, guardians (kings or government servants); *ye*—they who; *ca*—and; *śāstāraḥ*—give instructions concerning law and order; *sādhavaḥ*—endowed with all good qualities; *samāḥ*—equal to everyone; *yadi*—if; *syāt*—there is; *teṣu*—among them; *vaiṣamyam*—partiality; *kam*—what; *yānti*—will go to; *śaraṇam*—shelter; *prajāḥ*—the citizens.

TRANSLATION

A king or governmental official should be so well qualified that he acts as a father, maintainer and protector of the citizens because of affection and love. He should give the citizens good advice and instructions according to the standard scriptures and should be equal to everyone. Yamarāja does this, for he is the supreme master of justice, and so do those who follow in his footsteps. However, if such persons become polluted and exhibit partiality by punishing an innocent, blameless person, where will the citizens go to take shelter for their maintenance and security?

PURPORT

The king, or in modern times the government, should act as the guardian of the citizens by teaching them the proper goal of life. The human form of life is especially meant for realization of one's self and one's relationship with the Supreme Personality of Godhead because this cannot be realized in animal life. The duty of the government, therefore, is to take charge of training all the citizens in such a way that by a gradual process they will be elevated to the spiritual platform and will realize the self and his relationship with God. This principle was followed by kings like Mahārāja Yudhiṣṭhira, Mahārāja Parīkṣit, Lord Rāmacandra, Mahārāja Ambarīṣa and Prahlāda Mahārāja. The leaders of the government must be very honest and religious because otherwise all the affairs of the state will suffer. Unfortunately, in the name of democracy, rogues and thieves are electing other rogues and thieves to the most important posts in the government. Recently this has been proven in America, where the president had to be condemned and dragged down from his post by the citizens. This is only one case, but there are many others. Because of the importance of the Kṛṣṇa consciousness movement, people should be Kṛṣṇa conscious and should not vote for anyone who is not Kṛṣṇa conscious. Then there will be actual peace and prosperity in the state. When a Vaiṣṇava sees mismanagement in the government, he feels great compassion in his heart and tries his best to purify the situation by spreading the Hare Kṛṣṇa movement.

TEXT 4

यद्यदाचरति श्रेयानितरस्तत्तदीहते ।
स यत्प्रमाणं कुरुते लोकस्तदनुवर्तते ॥ ४ ॥

yad yad ācarati śreyān
itaras tat tad īhate
sa yat pramāṇaṁ kurute
lokas tad anuvartate

yat yat—whatever; *ācarati*—executes; *śreyān*—a first-class man with full knowledge of religious principles; *itaraḥ*—the subordinate man; *tat tat*—that; *īhate*—performs; *saḥ*—he (the great man); *yat*—whatever; *pramāṇam*—as evidence or as the right thing; *kurute*—accepts; *lokaḥ*—the general public; *tat*—that; *anuvartate*—follows.

TRANSLATION

The mass of people follow the example of a leader in society and imitate his behavior. They accept as evidence whatever the leader accepts.

PURPORT

Although Ajāmila was not punishable, the Yamadūtas were insisting on taking him away to Yamarāja for punishment. This was *adharma,* contrary to religious principles. The Viṣṇudūtas feared that if such irreligious acts were allowed, the management of human society would be spoiled. In modern times, the Kṛṣṇa consciousness movement is trying to introduce the right principles of management for human society, but unfortunately the governments of Kali-yuga do not properly support the Hare Kṛṣṇa movement because they do not appreciate its valuable service. The Hare Kṛṣṇa movement is the right movement for ameliorating the fallen condition of human society, and therefore governments and public leaders in every part of the world should support this movement to completely rectify humanity's sinful condition.

TEXTS 5–6

यस्याङ्के शिर आधाय लोकः स्वपिति निर्वृतः ।
स्वयं धर्ममधर्मं वा न हि वेद यथा पशुः ॥ ५ ॥
स कथं न्यर्पितात्मानं कृतमैत्रमचेतनम् ।
विस्रम्भणीयो भूतानां सघृणो दोग्धुमर्हति ॥ ६ ॥

yasyāṅke śira ādhāya
lokaḥ svapiti nirvṛtaḥ
svayaṁ dharmam adharmaṁ vā
na hi veda yathā paśuḥ

sa kathaṁ nyarpitātmānaṁ
kṛta-maitram acetanam
visrambhaṇīyo bhūtānāṁ
saghṛṇo dogdhum arhati

yasya—of whom; *aṅke*—on the lap; *śiraḥ*—the head; *ādhāya*—placing; *lokaḥ*—the general mass of people; *svapiti*—sleep; *nirvṛtaḥ*—in peace; *svayam*—personally; *dharmam*—religious principles or the goal of life; *adharmam*—irreligious principles; *vā*—or; *na*—not; *hi*—indeed; *veda*—know; *yathā*—exactly like; *paśuḥ*—an animal; *saḥ*—such a person; *katham*—how; *nyarpita-ātmānam*—unto the living entity who has fully surrendered; *kṛta-maitram*—endowed with good faith and friendship; *acetanam*—with undeveloped consciousness, foolish; *visrambhaṇīyaḥ*—deserving to be the object of faith; *bhūtānām*—of the living entities; *sa-ghṛṇaḥ*—who has a soft heart for the good of all people; *dogdhum*—to give pain; *arhati*—is able.

TRANSLATION

People in general are not very advanced in knowledge by which to discriminate between religion and irreligion. The innocent, unenlightened citizen is like an ignorant animal sleeping in peace with its head on the lap of its master, faithfully believing in the master's protection. If a leader is actually kindhearted and deserves to be the object of a living entity's faith,

how can he punish or kill a foolish person who has fully surrendered in good faith and friendship?

PURPORT

The Sanskrit word *viśvasta-ghāta* refers to one who breaks faith or causes a breach of trust. The mass of people should always feel security because of the government's protection. Therefore, how regrettable it is for the government itself to cause a breach of trust and put the citizens in difficulty for political reasons. We actually saw during the partition days in India that although Hindus and Muslims were living together peacefully, manipulation by politicians suddenly aroused feelings of hatred between them, and thus the Hindus and Muslims killed one another over politics. This is a sign of Kali-yuga. In this age, animals are kept nicely sheltered, completely confident that their masters will protect them, but unfortunately as soon as the animals are fat, they are immediately sent for slaughter. Such cruelty is condemned by Vaiṣṇavas like the Viṣṇudūtas. Indeed, the hellish conditions already described await the sinful men responsible for such suffering. One who betrays the confidence of a living entity who takes shelter of him in good faith, whether that living entity be a human being or an animal, is extremely sinful. Because such betrayals now go unpunished by the government, all of human society is terribly contaminated. The people of this age are therefore described as *mandāḥ sumanda-matayo manda-bhāgyā hy upadrutāḥ.* As a consequence of such sinfulness, men are condemned (*mandāḥ*), their intelligence is unclear (*sumanda-matayaḥ*), they are unfortunate (*manda-bhāgyāḥ*), and therefore they are always disturbed by many problems (*upadrutāḥ*). This is their situation in this life, and after death they are punished in hellish conditions.

TEXT 7

अयं हि कृतनिर्वेशो जन्मकोट्यंहसामपि ।
यद् व्याजहार विवशो नाम स्वस्त्ययनं हरेः ॥ ७ ॥

ayaṁ hi kṛta-nirveśo
janma-koṭy-aṁhasām api
yad vyājahāra vivaśo
nāma svasty-ayanaṁ hareḥ

ayam—this person (Ajāmila); *hi*—indeed; *kṛta-nirveśaḥ*—has undergone all kinds of atonement; *janma*—of births; *koṭi*—of millions; *aṁhasām*—for the sinful activities; *api*—even; *yat*—because; *vyājahāra*—he has chanted; *vivaśaḥ*—in a helpless condition; *nāma*—the holy name; *svasti-ayanam*—the means of liberation; *hareḥ*—of the Supreme Personality of Godhead.

TRANSLATION

Ajāmila has already atoned for all his sinful actions. Indeed, he has atoned not only for sins performed in one life but for those performed in millions of lives, for in a helpless condition he chanted the holy name of Nārāyaṇa. Even though he did not chant purely, he chanted without offense, and therefore he is now pure and eligible for liberation.

PURPORT

The Yamadūtas had considered only the external situation of Ajāmila. Since he was extremely sinful throughout his life, they thought he should be taken to Yamarāja and did not know that he had become free from the reactions of all his sins. The Viṣṇudūtas therefore instructed that because he had chanted the four syllables of the name Nārāyaṇa at the time of his death, he was freed from all sinful reactions. In this regard Śrīla Viśvanātha Cakravartī Ṭhākura quotes the following verses from the *smṛti-śāstra:*

nāmno hi yāvatī śaktiḥ
pāpa-nirharaṇe hareḥ
tāvat kartuṁ na śaknoti
pātakaṁ pātakī naraḥ

"Simply by chanting one holy name of Hari, a sinful man can counteract the reactions to more sins than he is able to commit." (*Bṛhad-viṣṇu Purāṇa*)

avaśenāpi yan-nāmni
kīrtite sarva-pātakaiḥ
pumān vimucyate sadyaḥ
siṁha-trastair mṛgair iva

"If one chants the holy name of the Lord, even in a helpless condition or without desiring to do so, all the reactions of his sinful life depart, just as when a lion roars, all the small animals flee in fear." (*Garuḍa Purāṇa*)

sakṛd uccāritaṁ yena
harir ity akṣara-dvayam
baddha-parikaras tena
mokṣāya gamanaṁ prati

"By once chanting the holy name of the Lord, which consists of the two syllables *ha-ri,* one guarantees his path to liberation." (*Skanda Purāṇa*)

These are some of the reasons why the Viṣṇudūtas objected to the Yamadūtas' taking Ajāmila to the court of Yamarāja.

TEXT 8

एतेनैव ह्यघोनोऽस्य कृतं स्यादघनिष्कृतम् ।
यदा नारायणायेति जगाद चतुरक्षरम् ॥ ८ ॥

etenaiva hy aghono'sya
kṛtaṁ syād agha-niṣkṛtam
yadā nārāyaṇāyeti
jagāda catur-akṣaram

etena—by this (chanting); *eva*—indeed; *hi*—certainly; *aghonaḥ*—who possesses sinful reactions; *asya*—of this (Ajāmila); *kṛtam*—performed; *syāt*—is; *agha*—of sins; *niṣkṛtam*—complete atonement; *yadā*—when; *nārāyaṇa*—O Nārāyaṇa (the name of his son); *āya*—please come; *iti*—thus; *jagāda*—he chanted; *catuḥ-akṣaram*—the four syllables (*nā-rā-ya-ṇa*).

TRANSLATION

The Viṣṇudūtas continued: Even previously, while eating and at other times, this Ajāmila would call his son, saying, "My dear Nārāyaṇa, please come here." Although calling the name of his son, he nevertheless uttered the four syllables nā-rā-ya-ṇa. Simply by chanting the name of Nārāyaṇa in this way, he sufficiently atoned for the sinful reactions of millions of lives.

PURPORT

Previously, when engaged in sinful activities to maintain his family, Ajāmila chanted the name of Nārāyaṇa without offenses. To chant the holy name of the Lord just to counteract one's sinful activities, or to commit sinful activities on the strength of chanting the holy name, is offensive (*nāmno balād yasya hi pāpa-buddhiḥ*). But although Ajāmila engaged in sinful activities, he never chanted the holy name of Nārāyaṇa to counteract them; he simply chanted the name Nārāyaṇa to call his son. Therefore his chanting was effective. Because of chanting the holy name of Nārāyaṇa in this way, he had already vanquished the accumulated sinful reactions of many, many lives. In the beginning he was pure, but although he later committed many sinful acts, he was offenseless because he did not chant the holy name of Nārāyaṇa to counteract them. One who always chants the holy name of the Lord without offenses is always pure. As confirmed in this verse Ajāmila was already sinless, and because he chanted the name of Nārāyaṇa he remained sinless. It did not matter that he was calling his son; the name itself was effective.

TEXTS 9–10

स्तेनः सुरापो मित्रध्रुग् ब्रह्महा गुरुतल्पगः ।
स्त्रीराजपितृगोहन्ता ये च पातकिनोऽपरे ॥ ९ ॥
सर्वेषामप्यघवतामिदमेव सुनिष्कृतम् ।
नामव्याहरणं विष्णोर्यतस्तद्विषया मतिः ॥ १० ॥

stenaḥ surā-po mitra-dhrug
brahma-hā guru-talpa-gaḥ
strī-rāja-pitṛ-go-hantā
ye ca pātakino'pare

sarveṣām apy aghavatām
idam eva suniṣkṛtam
nāma-vyāharaṇaṁ viṣṇor
yatas tad-viṣayā matiḥ

stenaḥ—one who steals; *surā-paḥ*—a drunkard; *mitra-dhruk*—one who turns against a friend or relative; *brahma-hā*—one who kills a *brāhmaṇa; guru-talpa-gaḥ*—one who indulges in sex with the wife of his teacher or *guru; strī*—women; *rāja*—king; *pitṛ*—father; *go*—of cows; *hantā*—the killer; *ye*—those who; *ca*—also; *pātakinaḥ*—committed sinful activities; *apare*—many others; *sarveṣām*—of all of them; *api*—although; *agha-vatām*—persons who have committed many sins; *idam*—this; *eva*—certainly; *su-niṣkṛtam*—perfect atonement; *nāma-vyāharaṇam*—chanting of the holy name; *viṣṇoḥ*—of Lord Viṣṇu; *yataḥ*—because of which; *tat-viṣayā*—on the person who chants the holy name; *matiḥ*—His attention.

TRANSLATION

The chanting of the holy name of Lord Viṣṇu is the best process of atonement for a thief of gold or other valuables, for a drunkard, for one who betrays a friend or relative, for one who kills a brāhmaṇa, or for one who indulges in sex with the wife of his guru or another superior. It is also

the best method of atonement for one who murders women, the king or his father, for one who slaughters cows, and for all other sinful men. Simply by chanting the holy name of Lord Viṣṇu, such sinful persons may attract the attention of the Supreme Lord, who therefore considers, "Because this man has chanted My holy name, My duty is to give him protection."

TEXT 11

न निष्कृतैरुदितैर्ब्रह्मवादिभि-
स्तथा विशुद्ध्यत्यघवान् व्रतादिभिः ।
यथा हरेर्नामपदैरुदाहृतै-
स्तदुत्तमश्लोकगुणोपलम्भकम् ॥ ११ ॥

na niṣkṛtair uditair brahma-vādibhis
tathā viśuddhyaty aghavān vratādibhiḥ
yathā harer nāma-padair udāhṛtais
tad uttamaśloka-guṇopalambhakam

na—not; *niṣkṛtaiḥ*—by the processes of atonement; *uditaiḥ*—prescribed; *brahma-vādibhiḥ*—by learned scholars such as Manu; *tathā*—to that extent; *viśuddhyati*—becomes purified; *agha-vān*—a sinful man; *vrata-ādibhiḥ*—by observing the vows and regulative principles; *yathā*—as; *hareḥ*—of Lord Hari; *nāma-padaiḥ*—by the syllables of the holy name; *udāhṛtaiḥ*—chanted; *tat*—that; *uttamaśloka*—of the Supreme Personality of Godhead; *guṇa*—of the transcendental qualities; *upalambhakam*—reminding one.

TRANSLATION

By following the Vedic ritualistic ceremonies or undergoing atonement, sinful men do not become as purified as by chanting once the holy name of Lord Hari. Although ritualistic atonement may free one from sinful reactions, it does not awaken devotional service, unlike the chanting of the Lord's names, which reminds one of the Lord's fame, qualities, attributes, pastimes and paraphernalia.

PURPORT

Śrīla Viśvanātha Cakravartī Ṭhākura comments that the chanting of the holy name of the Lord has special significance that distinguishes it from the Vedic ritualistic ceremonies of atonement for severe, more severe or most severe sinful actions. There are twenty types of religious scriptures called *dharma-śāstras,* beginning with the *Manu-saṁhitā* and *Parāśara-saṁhitā,* but herein it is stressed that although one may become free from the reactions of the most sinful activities by following the religious principles of these scriptures, this cannot promote a sinful man to the stage of loving service to the Lord. On the other hand, chanting the holy name of the Lord even once not only frees one immediately from the reactions of the greatest sins, but also raises one to the platform of rendering loving service to the Supreme Personality of Godhead, who is described as *uttamaśloka* because He is famous for His glorious activities. Thus one serves the Lord by remembering His form, His attributes and pastimes. Śrīla Viśvanātha Cakravartī Ṭhākura explains that this is all possible simply by chanting the Lord's holy name because of the Lord's omnipotence. What cannot be achieved through the performance of Vedic rituals can be easily achieved through the chanting of the Lord's holy name. To chant the holy name and dance in ecstasy is so easy and sublime that one can achieve all the benefits of spiritual life simply by following this process. Therefore Śrī Caitanya Mahāprabhu declares, *paraṁ vijayate śrī-kṛṣṇa-saṅkīrtanam:* "All glories to Śrī Kṛṣṇa *saṅkīrtana*!" The *saṅkīrtana* movement we have started offers the best process for becoming purified of all sinful reactions and coming immediately to the platform of spiritual life.

TEXT 12

नैकान्तिकं तद्धि कृतेऽपि निष्कृते
मनः पुनर्धावति चेदसत्पथे ।
तत्कर्मनिर्हारमभीप्सतां हरे-
र्गुणानुवादः खलु सत्त्वभावनः ॥ १२ ॥

naikāntikaṁ tad dhi kṛte'pi niṣkṛte
manaḥ punar dhāvati ced asat-pathe
tat karma-nirhāram abhīpsatāṁ harer
guṇānuvādaḥ khalu sattva-bhāvanaḥ

na—not; *aikāntikam*—absolutely cleansed; *tat*—the heart; *hi*—because; *kṛte*—very nicely performed; *api*—although; *niṣkṛte*—atonement; *manaḥ*—the mind; *punaḥ*—again; *dhāvati*—runs; *cet*—if; *asat-pathe*—on the path of material activities; *tat*—therefore; *karma-nirhāram*—cessation of the fruitive reactions of material activities; *abhīpsatām*—for those who seriously want;

hareḥ—of the Supreme Personality of Godhead; *guṇa-anuvādaḥ*—constant chanting of the glories; *khalu*—indeed; *sattva-bhāvanaḥ*—actually purifying one's existence.

TRANSLATION

The ritualistic ceremonies of atonement recommended in the religious scriptures are insufficient to cleanse the heart absolutely because after atonement one's mind again runs toward material activities. Consequently, for one who wants liberation from the fruitive reactions of material activities, the chanting of the Hare Kṛṣṇa mantra, or glorification of the name, fame and pastimes of the Lord, is recommended as the most perfect process of atonement because such chanting eradicates the dirt from one's heart completely.

PURPORT

The statements in this verse have been confirmed previously in *Śrīmad-Bhāgavatam* (1.2.17):

śṛṇvatāṁ sva-kathāḥ kṛṣṇaḥ
puṇya-śravaṇa-kīrtanaḥ
hṛdy antaḥ-stho hy abhadrāṇi
vidhunoti suhṛt satām

"Śrī Kṛṣṇa, the Personality of Godhead, who is the Paramātmā [Supersoul] in everyone's heart and the benefactor of the truthful devotee, cleanses desire for material enjoyment from the heart of the devotee who relishes His messages, which are in themselves virtuous when properly heard and chanted." It is the special mercy of the Supreme Lord that as soon as He knows that one is glorifying His name, fame and attributes, He personally helps cleanse the dirt from one's heart. Therefore simply by such glorification one not only becomes purified, but also achieves the results of pious activities (*puṇya-śravaṇa-kīrtana*). *Puṇya-śravaṇa-kīrtana* refers to the process of devotional service. Even if one does not understand the meaning of the Lord's name, pastimes or attributes, one is purified simply by hearing or chanting of them. Such purification is called *sattva-bhāvana.*

One's main purpose in human life should be to purify his existence and achieve liberation. As long as one has a material body, one is understood to be impure. In such an impure, material condition, one cannot enjoy a truly blissful life, although everyone seeks it. Therefore *Śrīmad-Bhāgavatam* (5.5.1) says, *tapo divyaṁ putrakā yena sattvaṁ śuddhyet:* one must perform *tapasya,* austerity, to purify his existence in order to come to the spiritual platform. The *tapasya* of chanting and glorifying the name, fame and attributes of the Lord is a very easy purifying process by which everyone can be happy. Therefore everyone who desires the ultimate cleansing of his heart must adopt this process. Other processes, such as *karma, jñāna* and *yoga,* cannot cleanse the heart absolutely.

TEXT 13

अथैनं मापनयत कृताशेषाघनिष्कृतम् ।
यदसौ भगवन्नाम म्रियमाणः समग्रहीत् ॥ १३ ॥

athainaṁ māpanayata
kṛtāśeṣāgha-niṣkṛtam
yad asau bhagavan-nāma
mriyamāṇaḥ samagrahīt

atha—therefore; *enam*—him (Ajāmila); *mā*—do not; *apanayata*—try to take; *kṛta*—already done; *aśeṣa*—unlimited; *agha-niṣkṛtam*—atonement for his sinful actions; *yat*—because; *asau*—he; *bhagavat-nāma*—the holy name of the Supreme Personality of Godhead; *mriyamāṇaḥ*—while dying; *samagrahīt*—perfectly chanted.

TRANSLATION

At the time of death, this Ajāmila helplessly and very loudly chanted the holy name of the Lord, Nārāyaṇa. That chanting alone has already freed him from the reactions of all sinful life. Therefore, O servants of Yamarāja, do not try to take him to your master for punishment in hellish conditions.

PURPORT

The Viṣṇudūtas, who are superior authorities, gave orders to the Yamadūtas, who did not know that Ajāmila was no longer subject to tribulation in hellish life for his past sins. Although he had chanted the holy name Nārāyaṇa to indicate his son, the holy name is so transcendentally powerful that he was automatically freed because he had chanted the holy name while dying (*ante nārāyaṇa-smṛtiḥ*). As Kṛṣṇa confirms in *Bhagavad-gītā* (7.28):

yeṣāṁ tv anta-gataṁ pāpaṁ
janānāṁ puṇya-karmaṇām

te dvandva-moha-nirmuktā
bhajante māṁ dṛḍha-vratāḥ

"Persons who have acted piously in previous lives and in this life, whose sinful actions are completely eradicated and who are freed from the duality of delusion, engage themselves in My service with determination." Unless one is freed from all sinful reactions, one cannot be promoted to the platform of devotional service. Elsewhere in *Bhagavad-gītā* (8.5) it is stated:

anta-kāle ca mām eva
smaran muktvā kalevaram
yaḥ prayāti sa mad-bhāvaṁ
yāti nāsty atra saṁśayaḥ

If one remembers Kṛṣṇa, Nārāyaṇa, at the time of death, one is certainly eligible to return immediately home, back to Godhead.

TEXT 14

साङ्केत्यं पारिहास्यं वा स्तोभं हेलनमेव वा।
वैकुण्ठनामग्रहणमशेषाघहरं विदुः ॥ १४ ॥

sāṅketyaṁ pārihāsyaṁ vā
stobhaṁ helanam eva vā
vaikuṇṭha-nāma-grahaṇam
aśeṣāgha-haraṁ viduḥ

sāṅketyam—as an assignation; *pārihāsyam*—jokingly; *vā*—or; *stobham*—as musical entertainment; *helanam*—neglectfully; *eva*—certainly; *vā*—or; *vaikuṇṭha*—of the Lord; *nāma-grahaṇam*—chanting the holy name; *aśeṣa*—unlimited; *agha-haram*—neutralizing the effect of sinful life; *viduḥ*—advanced transcendentalists know.

TRANSLATION

One who chants the holy name of the Lord is immediately freed from the reactions of unlimited sins, even if he chants indirectly [to indicate something else], jokingly, for musical entertainment, or even neglectfully. This is accepted by all the learned scholars of the scriptures.

TEXT 15

पतितः स्खलितो भग्नः सन्दष्टस्तप्त आहतः।
हरिरित्यवशेनाह पुमान्नार्हति यातनाः ॥ १५ ॥

patitaḥ skhalito bhagnaḥ
sandaṣṭas tapta āhataḥ
harir ity avaśenāha
pumān nārhati yātanāḥ

patitaḥ—fallen down; *skhalitaḥ*—slipped; *bhagnaḥ*—having broken his bones; *sandaṣṭaḥ*—bitten; *taptaḥ*—severely attacked by fever or similar painful conditions; *āhataḥ*—injured; *hariḥ*—Lord Kṛṣṇa; *iti*—thus; *avaśena*—accidentally; *āha*—chants; *pumān*—a person; *na*—not; *arhati*—deserves; *yātanāḥ*—hellish conditions.

TRANSLATION

If one chants the holy name of Hari and then dies because of an accidental misfortune, such as falling from the top of a house, slipping and suffering broken bones while traveling on the road, being bitten by a serpent, being afflicted with pain and high fever, or being injured by a weapon, one is immediately absolved from having to enter hellish life, even though he is sinful.

PURPORT

As stated in *Bhagavad-gītā* (8.6):

yaṁ yaṁ vāpi smaran bhāvaṁ
tyajaty ante kalevaram
taṁ tam evaiti kaunteya
sadā tad-bhāva-bhāvitaḥ

"Whatever state of being one remembers when he quits his body, that state he will attain without fail." If one practices chanting the Hare Kṛṣṇa *mantra,* he is naturally expected to chant Hare Kṛṣṇa when he meets with some accident. Even without such practice, however, if one somehow or other chants the holy name of the Lord (Hare Kṛṣṇa) when he meets with an accident and dies, he will be saved from hellish life after death.

TEXT 16

गुरूणां च लघूनां च गुरूणि च लघूनि च ।
प्रायश्चित्तानि पापानां ज्ञात्वोक्तानि महर्षिभिः ॥ १६ ॥

gurūṇāṁ ca laghūnāṁ ca
gurūṇi ca laghūni ca

prāyaścittāni pāpānāṁ
jñātvoktāni maharṣibhiḥ

gurūṇām—heavy; *ca*—and; *laghūnām*—light; *ca*—also; *gurūṇi*—heavy; *ca*—and; *laghūni*—light; *ca*—also; *prāyaścittāni*—the processes of atonement; *pāpānām*—of sinful activities; *jñātvā*—knowing perfectly well; *uktāni*—have been prescribed; *mahā-ṛṣibhiḥ*—by great sages.

TRANSLATION

Authorities who are learned scholars and sages have carefully ascertained that one should atone for the heaviest sins by undergoing a heavy process of atonement and one should atone for lighter sins by undergoing lighter atonement. Chanting the Hare Kṛṣṇa mantra, however, vanquishes all the effects of sinful activities, regardless of whether heavy or light.

PURPORT

In this regard, Śrīla Viśvanātha Cakravartī Ṭhākura describes an incident that took place when Sāmba was rescued from the punishment of the Kauravas. Sāmba fell in love with the daughter of Duryodhana, and since according to *kṣatriya* custom one is not offered a *kṣatriya's* daughter unless he displays his chivalrous valor, Sāmba abducted her. Consequently Sāmba was arrested by the Kauravas. Later, when Lord Balarāma came to rescue him, there was an argument about Sāmba's release. Since the argument was not settled, Balarāma showed His power in such a way that all of Hastināpura trembled and would have been vanquished as if by a great earthquake. Then the matter was settled, and Sāmba married Duryodhana's daughter. The purport is that one should take shelter of Kṛṣṇa-Balarāma, the Supreme Personality of Godhead, whose protective power is so great that it cannot be equaled in the material world. However powerful the reactions of one's sins, they will immediately be vanquished if one chants the name of Hari, Kṛṣṇa, Balarāma or Nārāyaṇa.

TEXT 17

तैस्तान्यघानि पूयन्ते तपोदानव्रतादिभिः ।
नाधर्मजं तद्धृदयं तदपीशाङ्घ्रिसेवया ॥ १७ ॥

tais tāny aghāni pūyante
tapo-dāna-vratādibhiḥ

nādharmajaṁ tad-dhṛdayaṁ
tad apīśāṅghri-sevayā

taiḥ—by those; *tāni*—all those; *aghāni*—sinful activities and their results; *pūyante*—become vanquished; *tapaḥ*—austerity; *dāna*—charity; *vrata-ādibhiḥ*—by vows and other such activities; *na*—not; *adharma-jam*—produced from irreligious actions; *tat*—of that; *hṛdayam*—the heart; *tat*—that; *api*—also; *īśa-aṅghri*—of the lotus feet of the Lord; *sevayā*—by service.

TRANSLATION

Although one may neutralize the reactions of sinful life through austerity, charity, vows and other such methods, these pious activities cannot uproot the material desires in one's heart. However, if one serves the lotus feet of the Personality of Godhead, he is immediately freed from all such contaminations.

PURPORT

As stated in *Śrīmad-Bhāgavatam* (11.2.42), *bhaktiḥ pareśānubhavo viraktir anyatra ca:* devotional service is so powerful that one who performs devotional service is immediately freed from all sinful desires. All desires within this material world are sinful because material desire means sense gratification, which always involves action that is more or less sinful. Pure *bhakti,* however, is *anyābhilāṣitā-śūnya;* in other words, it is free from material desires, which result from *karma* and *jñāna.* One who is situated in devotional service no longer has material desires, and therefore he is beyond sinful life. Material desires should be completely stopped. Otherwise, although one's austerities, penances and charity may free one from sin for the time being, one's desires will reappear because his heart is impure. Thus he will act sinfully and suffer.

TEXT 18

अज्ञानादथवा ज्ञानादुत्तमश्लोकनाम यत् ।
सङ्कीर्तितमघं पुंसो दहेदेधो यथानलः ॥ १८ ॥

ajñānād athavā jñānād
uttamaśloka-nāma yat
saṅkīrtitam aghaṁ puṁso
dahed edho yathānalaḥ

ajñānāt—out of ignorance; *athavā*—or; *jñānāt*—with knowledge; *uttamaśloka*—of the Supreme Personality of Godhead; *nāma*—the holy name; *yat*—that which; *saṅkīrtitam*—chanted; *agham*—sin; *puṁsaḥ*—of a person; *dahet*—burns to ashes; *edhaḥ*—dry grass; *yathā*—just as; *analaḥ*—fire.

TRANSLATION

As a fire burns dry grass to ashes, so the holy name of the Lord, whether chanted knowingly or unknowingly, burns to ashes, without fail, all the reactions of one's sinful activities.

PURPORT

Fire will act, regardless of whether handled by an innocent child or by someone well aware of its power. For example, if a field of straw or dry grass is set afire, either by an elderly man who knows the power of fire or by a child who does not, the grass will be burned to ashes. Similarly, one may or may not know the power of chanting the Hare Kṛṣṇa *mantra,* but if one chants the holy name he will become free from all sinful reactions.

TEXT 19

यथागदं वीर्यतममुपयुक्तं यदृच्छया ।
अजानतोऽप्यात्मगुणं कुर्यान्मन्त्रोऽप्युदाहृतः ॥ १९ ॥

yathāgadaṁ vīryatamam
upayuktaṁ yadṛcchayā
ajānato'py ātma-guṇaṁ
kuryān mantro'py udāhṛtaḥ

yathā—just like; *agadam*—medicine; *vīrya-tamam*—very powerful; *upayuktam*—properly taken; *yadṛcchayā*—somehow or other; *ajānataḥ*—by a person without knowledge; *api*—even; *ātma-guṇam*—its own potency; *kuryāt*—manifests; *mantraḥ*—the Hare Kṛṣṇa *mantra; api*—also; *udāhṛtaḥ*—chanted.

TRANSLATION

If a person unaware of the effective potency of a certain medicine takes that medicine or is forced to take it, it will act even without his knowledge because its potency does not depend on the patient's understanding. Similarly, even though one does not know the value of chanting the holy

name of the Lord, if one chants knowingly or unknowingly, the chanting will be very effective.

PURPORT

In the Western countries, where the Hare Kṛṣṇa movement is spreading, learned scholars and other thoughtful men are realizing its effectiveness. For example, Dr. J. Stillson Judah, a learned scholar, has been very much attracted to this movement because he has actually seen that it is turning hippies addicted to drugs into pure Vaiṣṇavas who voluntarily become servants of Kṛṣṇa and humanity. Even a few years ago, such hippies did not know the Hare Kṛṣṇa *mantra,* but now they are chanting it and becoming pure Vaiṣṇavas. Thus they are becoming free from all sinful activities, such as illicit sex, intoxication, meat-eating and gambling. This is practical proof of the effectiveness of the Hare Kṛṣṇa movement, which is supported in this verse. One may or may not know the value of chanting the Hare Kṛṣṇa *mantra,* but if one somehow or other chants it, he will immediately be purified, just as one who takes a potent medicine will feel its effects, regardless of whether he takes it knowingly or unknowingly.

TEXT 20

श्रीशुक उवाच
त एवं सुविनिर्णीय धर्मं भागवतं नृप ।
तं याम्यपाशान्निर्मुच्य विप्रं मृत्योरमूमुचन् ॥ २० ॥

śrī-śuka uvāca
ta evaṁ suvinirṇīya
dharmaṁ bhāgavataṁ nṛpa
taṁ yāmya-pāśān nirmucya
vipraṁ mṛtyor amūmucan

śrī-śukaḥ uvāca—Śrī Śukadeva Gosvāmī said; *te*—they (the order carriers of Lord Viṣṇu); *evam*—thus; *su-vinirṇīya*—perfectly ascertaining; *dharmam*—real religion; *bhāgavatam*—in terms of devotional service; *nṛpa*—O King; *tam*—him (Ajāmila); *yāmya-pāśāt*—from the bondage of the order carriers of Yamarāja; *nirmucya*—releasing; *vipram*—the *brāhmaṇa; mṛtyoḥ*—from death; *amūmucan*—rescued.

TRANSLATION

Śrī Śukadeva Gosvāmī continued: My dear King, having thus perfectly judged the principles of devotional service with reasoning and arguments,

the order carriers of Lord Viṣṇu released the brāhmaṇa Ajāmila from the bondage of the Yamadūtas and saved him from imminent death.

TEXT 21

इति प्रत्युदिता याम्या दूता यात्वा यमान्तिकम् ।
यमराज्ञे यथा सर्वमाचचक्षुररिन्दम ॥ २१ ॥

iti pratyuditā yāmyā
dūtā yātvā yamāntikam
yama-rājñe yathā sarvam
ācacakṣur arindama

iti—thus; *pratyuditāḥ*—having been replied to (by the order carriers of Viṣṇu); *yāmyāḥ*—the servants of Yamarāja; *dūtāḥ*—the messengers; *yātvā*—going; *yama-antikam*—to the abode of Lord Yamarāja; *yama-rājñe*—unto King Yamarāja; *yathā*—duly; *sarvam*—everything; *ācacakṣuḥ*—informed in full detail; *arindama*—O subduer of the enemies.

TRANSLATION

My dear Mahārāja Parīkṣit, O subduer of all enemies, after the servants of Yamarāja had been answered by the order carriers of Lord Viṣṇu, they went to Yamarāja and explained to him everything that had happened.

PURPORT

In this verse the word *pratyuditāḥ* is very significant. The servants of Yamarāja are so powerful that they can never be hindered anywhere, but this time they were baffled and disappointed in their attempt to take away a man they considered sinful. Therefore they immediately returned to Yamarāja and described to him everything that had happened.

TEXT 22

द्विजः पाशाद्विनिर्मुक्तो गतभीः प्रकृतिं गतः ।
ववन्दे शिरसा विष्णोः किङ्करान् दर्शनोत्सवः ॥ २२ ॥

dvijaḥ pāśād vinirmukto
gata-bhīḥ prakṛtiṁ gataḥ
vavande śirasā viṣṇoḥ
kiṅkarān darśanotsavaḥ

dvijaḥ—the *brāhmaṇa* (Ajāmila); *pāśāt*—from the noose; *vinirmuktaḥ*—being released; *gata-bhīḥ*—freed from fear; *prakṛtim gataḥ*—came to his senses; *vavande*—offered his respectful obeisances; *śirasā*—by bowing his head; *viṣṇoḥ*—of Lord Viṣṇu; *kiṅkarān*—unto the servants; *darśana-utsavaḥ*—very pleased by seeing them.

TRANSLATION

Having been released from the nooses of Yamarāja's servants, the brāhmaṇa Ajāmila, now free from fear, came to his senses and immediately offered obeisances to the Viṣṇudūtas by bowing his head at their lotus feet. He was extremely pleased by their presence, for he had seen them save his life from the hands of the servants of Yamarāja.

PURPORT

Vaiṣṇavas are also Viṣṇudūtas because they carry out the orders of Kṛṣṇa. Lord Kṛṣṇa is very eager for all the conditioned souls rotting in this material world to surrender to Him and be saved from material pangs in this life and punishment in hellish conditions after death. A Vaiṣṇava therefore tries to bring conditioned souls to their senses. Those who are fortunate like Ajāmila are saved by the Viṣṇudūtas, or Vaiṣṇavas, and thus they return back home, back to Godhead.

TEXT 23

तं विवक्षुमभिप्रेत्य महापुरुषकिङ्कराः ।
सहसा पश्यतस्तस्य तत्रान्तर्दधिरेऽनघ ॥ २३ ॥

taṁ vivakṣum abhipretya
mahāpuruṣa-kiṅkarāḥ
sahasā paśyatas tasya
tatrāntardadhire'nagha

tam—him (Ajāmila); *vivakṣum*—desiring to speak; *abhipretya*—understanding; *mahāpuruṣa-kiṅkarāḥ*—the order carriers of Lord Viṣṇu; *sahasā*—suddenly; *paśyataḥ tasya*—while he looked on; *tatra*—there; *antardadhire*—disappeared; *anagha*—O sinless Mahārāja Parīkṣit.

TRANSLATION

O sinless Mahārāja Parīkṣit, the order carriers of the Supreme Personality of Godhead, the Viṣṇudūtas, saw that Ajāmila was attempting to say something, and thus they suddenly disappeared from his presence.

PURPORT

The *śāstras* say:

pāpiṣṭhā ye durācārā
deva-brāhmaṇa-nindakāḥ
apathya-bhojanās teṣām
akāle maraṇaṁ dhruvam

"For persons who are *pāpiṣṭha,* very sinful, and *durācāra,* misbehaved or very unclean in their habits, who are against the existence of God, who disrespect Vaiṣṇavas and *brāhmaṇas,* and who eat anything and everything, untimely death is sure." It is said that in Kali-yuga one has a maximum lifetime of one hundred years, but as people become degraded, the duration of their lives decreases (*prāyeṇālpāyuṣaḥ*). Because Ajāmila was now free from all sinful reactions, his lifetime was extended, even though he was to have died immediately. When the Viṣṇudūtas saw Ajāmila trying to say something to them, they disappeared to give him a chance to glorify the Supreme Lord. Since all his sinful reactions had been vanquished, he was now prepared to glorify the Lord. Indeed, one cannot glorify the Lord unless one is completely free from all sinful activities. This is confirmed by Kṛṣṇa Himself in *Bhagavad-gītā* (7.28):

yeṣāṁ tv anta-gataṁ pāpaṁ
janānāṁ puṇya-karmaṇām
te dvandva-moha-nirmuktā
bhajante māṁ dṛḍha-vratāḥ

"Persons who have acted piously in previous lives and in this life, whose sinful actions are completely eradicated and who are freed from the duality of delusion, engage themselves in My service with determination." The Viṣṇudūtas made Ajāmila aware of devotional service so that He might immediately become fit to return home, back to Godhead. To increase his eagerness to glorify the Lord, they disappeared so that he would feel separation in their absence. In the mode of separation, glorification of the Lord is very intense.

TEXTS 24–25

अजामिलोऽप्यथाकर्ण्य दूतानां यमकृष्णयोः ।
धर्मं भागवतं शुद्धं त्रैवेद्यं च गुणाश्रयम् ॥ २४ ॥

भक्तिमान् भगवत्याशु माहात्म्यश्रवणाद्धरेः ।
अनुतापो महानासीत्स्मरतोऽशुभमात्मनः ॥ २५ ॥

ajāmilo'py athākarṇya
dūtānāṁ yama-kṛṣṇayoḥ
dharmaṁ bhāgavataṁ śuddhaṁ
trai-vedyaṁ ca guṇāśrayam

bhaktimān bhagavaty āśu
māhātmya-śravaṇād dhareḥ
anutāpo mahān āsīt
smarato'śubham ātmanaḥ

ajāmilaḥ—Ajāmila; *api*—also; *atha*—thereafter; *ākarṇya*—hearing; *dūtānām*—of the order carriers; *yama-kṛṣṇayoḥ*—of Yamarāja and Lord Kṛṣṇa; *dharmam*—actual religious principles; *bhāgavatam*—as described in *Śrīmad-Bhāgavatam,* or concerning the relationship between the living being and the Supreme Personality of Godhead; *śuddham*—pure; *trai-vedyam*—mentioned in three *Vedas; ca*—also; *guṇa-aśrayam*—material religion, under the modes of material nature; *bhakti-mān*—a pure devotee (cleansed of the modes of material nature); *bhagavati*—unto the Supreme Personality of Godhead; *āśu*—immediately; *māhātmya*—glorification of the name, fame, etc.; *śravaṇāt*—because of hearing; *hareḥ*—of Lord Hari; *anutāpaḥ*—regret; *mahān*—very great; *āsīt*—there was; *smarataḥ*—remembering; *aśubham*—all the inglorious activities; *ātmanaḥ*—done by himself.

TRANSLATION

After hearing the discourses between the Yamadūtas and the Viṣṇudūtas, Ajāmila could understand the religious principles that act under the three modes of material nature. These principles are mentioned in the three Vedas. He could also understand the transcendental religious principles, which are above the modes of material nature and which concern the relationship between the living being and the Supreme Personality of Godhead. Furthermore, Ajāmila heard glorification of the name, fame, qualities and pastimes of the Supreme Personality of Godhead. He thus became a perfectly pure devotee. He could then remember his past sinful activities, which he greatly regretted having performed.

PURPORT

In *Bhagavad-gītā* (2.45) Lord Kṛṣṇa told Arjuna:

traiguṇya-viṣayā vedā
nistraiguṇyo bhavārjuna
nirdvandvo nitya-sattva-stho
niryoga-kṣema ātmavān

"The *Vedas* mainly deal with the subject of the three modes of material nature. Rise above these modes, O Arjuna. Be transcendental to all of them. Be free from all dualities and from all anxieties for gain and safety, and be established in the Self." The Vedic principles certainly prescribe a gradual process for rising to the spiritual platform, but if one remains attached to the Vedic principles, there is no chance of his being elevated to spiritual life. Kṛṣṇa therefore advised Arjuna to perform devotional service, which is the process of transcendental religion. The transcendental position of devotional service is also confirmed in *Śrīmad-Bhāgavatam* (1.2.6). *Sa vai puṁsāṁ paro dharmo yato bhaktir adhokṣaje. Bhakti,* devotional service, is *paro dharmaḥ,* transcendental *dharma;* it is not material *dharma.* People generally think that religion should be pursued for material profit. This may be suitable for persons interested in material life, but one who is interested in spiritual life should be attached to *paro dharmaḥ,* the religious principles by which one becomes a devotee of the Supreme Lord (*yato bhaktir adhokṣaje*). The *bhāgavata* religion teaches that the Lord and the living entity are eternally related and that the duty of the living entity is to surrender to the Lord. When one is situated on the platform of devotional service, one is freed from impediments and completely satisfied (*ahaituky apratihatā yayātmā suprasīdati*). Having been elevated to that platform, Ajāmila began to lament for his past materialistic activities and glorify the name, fame, form and pastimes of the Supreme Personality of Godhead.

TEXT 26

अहो मे परमं कष्टमभूदविजितात्मनः ।
येन विप्लावितं ब्रह्म वृषल्यां जायतात्मना ॥ २६ ॥

aho me paramaṁ kaṣṭam
abhūd avijitātmanaḥ
yena viplāvitaṁ brahma
vṛṣalyāṁ jāyatātmanā

aho—alas; *me*—my; *paramam*—extreme; *kaṣṭam*—miserable condition; *abhūt*—became; *avijita-ātmanaḥ*—because my senses were uncontrolled; *yena*—by which; *viplāvitam*—destroyed; *brahma*—all my brahminical qualifications; *vṛṣalyām*—through a *śūdrāṇī,* a maidservant; *jāyatā*—being born; *ātmanā*—by me.

TRANSLATION

Ajāmila said: Alas, being a servant of my senses, how degraded I became! I fell down from my position as a duly qualified brāhmaṇa and begot children in the womb of a prostitute.

PURPORT

The men of the higher classes—the *brāhmaṇas, kṣatriyas* and *vaiśyas*—do not beget children in the wombs of lower-class women. Therefore the custom in Vedic society is to examine the horoscopes of a girl and boy being considered for marriage to see whether their combination is suitable. Vedic astrology reveals whether one has been born in the *vipra-varṇa, kṣatriya-varṇa, vaiśya-varṇa* or *śūdra-varṇa,* according to the three qualities of material nature. This must be examined because a marriage between a boy of the *vipra-varṇa* and a girl of the *śūdra-varṇa* is incompatible; married life would be miserable for both husband and wife. Consequently a boy should marry a girl of the same category. Of course, this is *trai-guṇya,* a material calculation according to the *Vedas,* but if the boy and girl are devotees there need be no such considerations. A devotee is transcendental, and therefore in a marriage between devotees, the boy and girl form a very happy combination.

TEXT 27

धिङ्मां विगर्हितं सद्भिर्दुष्कृतं कुलकज्जलम्।
हित्वा बालां सतीं योऽहंसुरापीमसतीमगाम् ॥ २७॥

dhiṅ māṁ vigarhitaṁ sadbhir
duṣkṛtaṁ kula-kajjalam
hitvā bālāṁ satīṁ yo'haṁ
surā-pīm asatīm agām

dhik mām—all condemnation upon me; *vigarhitam*—condemned; *sadbhiḥ*—by honest men; *duṣkṛtam*—who has committed sinful acts; *kula-kajjalam*—who has defamed the family tradition; *hitvā*—giving up; *bālām*

—a young wife; *satīm*—chaste; *yaḥ*—who; *aham*—I; *surā-pīm*—with a woman accustomed to drinking wine; *asatīm*—unchaste; *agām*—I had sexual intercourse.

TRANSLATION

Alas, all condemnation upon me! I acted so sinfully that I degraded my family tradition. Indeed, I gave up my chaste and beautiful young wife to have sexual intercourse with a fallen prostitute accustomed to drinking wine. All condemnation upon me!

PURPORT

This is the mentality of one who is becoming a pure devotee. When one is elevated to the platform of devotional service by the grace of the Lord and the spiritual master, one first regrets his past sinful activities. This helps one advance in spiritual life. The Viṣṇudūtas had given Ajāmila the chance to become a pure devotee, and the duty of a pure devotee is to regret his past sinful activities in illicit sex, intoxication, meat-eating and gambling. Not only should one give up his past bad habits, but he must always regret his past sinful acts. This is the standard of pure devotion.

TEXT 28

वृद्धावनाथौ पितरौ नान्यबन्धू तपस्विनौ ।
अहो मयाधुना त्यक्तावकृतज्ञेन नीचवत् ॥ २८ ॥

vṛddhāv anāthau pitarau
nānya-bandhū tapasvinau
aho mayādhunā tyaktāv
akṛtajñena nīcavat

vṛddhau—old; *anāthau*—who had no other person to look after their comforts; *pitarau*—my father and mother; *na anya-bandhū*—who had no other friend; *tapasvinau*—who underwent great difficulties; *aho*—alas; *mayā*—by me; *adhunā*—at that moment; *tyaktau*—were given up; *akṛta-jñena*—ungrateful; *nīca-vat*—like the most abominable low-class person.

TRANSLATION

My father and mother were old and had no other son or friend to look after them. Because I did not take care of them, they lived with great

difficulty. Alas, like an abominable lower-class man, I ungratefully left them in that condition.

PURPORT

According to Vedic civilization, everyone has the responsibility for taking care of *brāhmaṇas,* old men, women, children and cows. This is the duty of everyone, especially an upper-class person. Because of his association with a prostitute, Ajāmila abandoned all his duties. Regretting this, Ajāmila now considered himself quite fallen.

TEXT 29

सोऽहं व्यक्तं पतिष्यामि नरके भृशदारुणे ।
धर्मघ्नाः कामिनो यत्र विन्दन्ति यमयातनाः ॥ २९ ॥

so'haṁ vyaktaṁ patiṣyāmi
narake bhṛśa-dāruṇe
dharma-ghnāḥ kāmino yatra
vindanti yama-yātanāḥ

saḥ—such a person; *aham*—I; *vyaktam*—it is now clear; *patiṣyāmi*—will fall down; *narake*—in hell; *bhṛśa-dāruṇe*—most miserable; *dharma-ghnāḥ*—they who break the principles of religion; *kāminaḥ*—who are too lusty; *yatra*—where; *vindanti*—undergo; *yama-yātanāḥ*—the miserable conditions imposed by Yamarāja.

TRANSLATION

It is now clear that as a consequence of such activities, a sinful person like me must be thrown into hellish conditions meant for those who have broken religious principles and must there suffer extreme miseries.

TEXT 30

किमिदं स्वप्न आहोस्वित् साक्षाद् दृष्टमिहाद्भुतम् ।
क्व याता अद्य ते ये मां व्यकर्षन् पाशपाणयः ॥ ३० ॥

kim idaṁ svapna āho svit
sākṣād dṛṣṭam ihādbhutam
kva yātā adya te ye māṁ
vyakarṣan pāśa-pāṇayaḥ

kim—whether; *idam*—this; *svapne*—in a dream; *āho svit*—or; *sākṣāt*—directly; *dṛṣṭam*—seen; *iha*—here; *adbhutam*—wonderful; *kva*—where; *yātāḥ*—have gone; *adya*—now; *te*—all of them; *ye*—who; *mām*—me; *vyakarṣan*—were dragging; *pāśa-pāṇayaḥ*—with ropes in their hands.

TRANSLATION

Was this a dream I saw, or was it reality? I saw fearsome men with ropes in their hands coming to arrest me and drag me away. Where have they gone?

TEXT 31

अथ ते क्व गताः सिद्धाश्चत्वारश्चारुदर्शनाः ।
व्यामोचयन्नीयमानं बद्ध्वा पाशैरधो भुवः ॥ ३१ ॥

atha te kva gatāḥ siddhāś
catvāraś cāru-darśanāḥ
vyāmocayan nīyamānaṁ
baddhvā pāśair adho bhuvaḥ

atha—thereafter; *te*—those persons; *kva*—where; *gatāḥ*—went; *siddhāḥ*—liberated; *catvāraḥ*—four personalities; *cāru-darśanāḥ*—extremely beautiful to see; *vyāmocayan*—they released; *nīyamānam*—me, who was being carried away; *baddhvā*—being arrested; *pāśaiḥ*—by ropes; *adhaḥ bhuvaḥ*—downward to the hellish region.

TRANSLATION

And where have those four liberated and very beautiful persons gone who released me from arrest and saved me from being dragged down to the hellish regions?

PURPORT

As we have learned from the descriptions in the Fifth Canto, the hellish planets are situated in the lower portions of this universe. Therefore they are called *adho bhuvaḥ.* Ajāmila could understand that the Yamadūtas had come from that region.

TEXT 32

अथापि मे दुर्भगस्य विबुधोत्तमदर्शने ।
भवितव्यं मङ्गलेन येनात्मा मे प्रसीदति ॥ ३२ ॥

athāpi me durbhagasya
vibudhottama-darśane
bhavitavyaṁ maṅgalena
yenātmā me prasīdati

atha—therefore; *api*—although; *me*—of me; *durbhagasya*—so unfortunate; *vibudha-uttama*—exalted devotees; *darśane*—because of seeing; *bhavitavyam*—there must be; *maṅgalena*—auspicious activities; *yena*—by which; *ātmā*—self; *me*—my; *prasīdati*—actually becomes happy.

TRANSLATION

I am certainly most abominable and unfortunate to have merged in an ocean of sinful activities, but nevertheless, because of my previous spiritual activities, I could see those four exalted personalities who came to rescue me. Now I feel exceedingly happy because of their visit.

PURPORT

As stated in *Caitanya-caritāmṛta* (*Madhya* 22.54):

'sādhu-saṅga', 'sādhu-saṅga'—sarva-śāstre kaya
lava-mātra sādhu-saṅge sarva-siddhi haya

"Association with devotees is recommended by all the *śāstras* because by even a moment of such association one can receive the seed for all perfection." In the beginning of his life Ajāmila was certainly very pure, and he associated with devotees and *brāhmaṇas;* because of that pious activity, even though he was fallen, he was inspired to name his son Nārāyaṇa. Certainly this was due to good counsel given from within by the Supreme Personality of Godhead. As the Lord says in *Bhagavad-gītā* (15.15), *sarvasya cāhaṁ hṛdi sanniviṣṭo mattaḥ smṛtir jñānam apohanaṁ ca:* "I am seated in everyone's heart, and from Me come remembrance, knowledge and forgetfulness." The Lord, who is situated in everyone's heart, is so kind that if one has ever rendered service to Him, the Lord never forgets him. Thus the Lord, from within, gave Ajāmila the opportunity to name his youngest son Nārāyaṇa so that in affection he would constantly call "Nārāyaṇa! Nārāyaṇa!" and thus be saved from the most fearful and dangerous condition at the time of his death. Such is the mercy of Kṛṣṇa. *Guru-kṛṣṇa-prasāde pāya bhakti-latā-bīja:* by the mercy of the *guru* and Kṛṣṇa, one receives the seed of *bhakti.* This association saves a devotee from the greatest fear. In our Kṛṣṇa consciousness movement we therefore change a devotee's name to a form that reminds him of Viṣṇu. If at the time of death the devotee can remember his own name, such as Kṛṣṇadāsa or Govinda dāsa, he can be saved from the greatest danger. Therefore the change of names at the time of initiation is essential. The Kṛṣṇa consciousness movement is so meticulous that it gives one a good opportunity to remember Kṛṣṇa somehow or other.

TEXT 33

अन्यथा म्रियमाणस्य नाशुचेर्वृषलीपतेः ।
वैकुण्ठनामग्रहणं जिह्वा वक्तुमिहार्हति ॥ ३३ ॥

anyathā mriyamāṇasya
nāśucer vṛṣalī-pateḥ
vaikuṇṭha-nāma-grahaṇaṁ
jihvā vaktum ihārhati

anyathā—otherwise; *mriyamāṇasya*—of a person who is just ready for death; *na*—not; *aśuceḥ*—most unclean; *vṛṣalī-pateḥ*—the keeper of a prostitute; *vaikuṇṭha*—of the Lord of Vaikuṇṭha; *nāma-grahaṇam*—the chanting of the holy name; *jihvā*—the tongue; *vaktum*—to speak; *iha*—in this situation; *arhati*—is able.

TRANSLATION

Were it not for my past devotional service, how could I, a most unclean keeper of a prostitute, have gotten an opportunity to chant the holy name of Vaikuṇṭhapati when I was just ready to die? Certainly it could not have been possible.

PURPORT

The name Vaikuṇṭhapati, which means "the master of the spiritual world," is not different from the name Vaikuṇṭha. Ajāmila, who was now a realized soul, could understand that because of his past spiritual activities in devotional service, he had gotten this opportunity to chant the holy name of Vaikuṇṭhapati in his horrible condition at the time of death.

TEXT 34

क्व चाहं कितवः पापो ब्रह्मघ्नो निरपत्रपः ।
क्व च नारायणेत्येतद्भगवन्नाम मङ्गलम् ॥ ३४ ॥

kva cāhaṁ kitavaḥ pāpo
brahma-ghno nirapatrapaḥ
kva ca nārāyaṇety etad
bhagavan-nāma maṅgalam

kva—where; *ca*—also; *aham*—I; *kitavaḥ*—a cheater; *pāpaḥ*—all sins personified; *brahma-ghnaḥ*—the killer of my brahminical culture; *nirapatrapaḥ*—shameless; *kva*—where; *ca*—also; *nārāyaṇa*—Nārāyaṇa; *iti*—thus; *etat*—this; *bhagavat-nāma*—the holy name of the Supreme Personality of Godhead; *maṅgalam*—all-auspicious.

TRANSLATION

Ajāmila continued: I am a shameless cheater who has killed his brahminical culture. Indeed, I am sin personified. Where am I in comparison to the all-auspicious chanting of the holy name of Lord Nārāyaṇa?

PURPORT

Those engaged in broadcasting the holy name of Nārāyaṇa, Kṛṣṇa, through the Kṛṣṇa consciousness movement should always consider what our position was before we came and what it is now. We had fallen into abominable lives as meat-eaters, drunkards and woman hunters who performed all kinds of sinful activities, but now we have been given the opportunity to chant the Hare Kṛṣṇa *mantra.* Therefore we should always appreciate this opportunity. By the grace of the Lord we are opening many branches, and we should use this good fortune to chant the holy name of the Lord and serve the Supreme Personality of Godhead directly. We must be conscious of the difference between our present and past conditions and should always be very careful not to fall from the most exalted life.

TEXT 35

सोऽहं तथा यतिष्यामि यतचित्तेन्द्रियानिलः ।
यथा न भूय आत्मानमन्धे तमसि मज्जये ॥ ३५ ॥

so'haṁ tathā yatiṣyāmi
yata-cittendriyānilaḥ
yathā na bhūya ātmānam
andhe tamasi majjaye

saḥ—such a person; *aham*—I; *tathā*—in that way; *yatiṣyāmi*—I shall endeavor; *yata-citta-indriya*—controlling the mind and senses; *anilaḥ*—and the internal airs; *yathā*—so that; *na*—not; *bhūyaḥ*—again; *ātmānam*—my soul; *andhe*—in darkness; *tamasi*—in ignorance; *majjaye*—I drown.

TRANSLATION

I am such a sinful person, but since I have now gotten this opportunity, I must completely control my mind, life and senses and always engage in devotional service so that I may not fall again into the deep darkness and ignorance of material life.

PURPORT

Every one of us should have this determination. We have been elevated to an exalted position by the mercy of Kṛṣṇa and the spiritual master, and if we remember that this is a great opportunity and pray to Kṛṣṇa that we will not fall again, our lives will be successful.

TEXTS 36–37

विमुच्य तमिमं बन्धमविद्याकामकर्मजम् ।
सर्वभूतसुहृच्छान्तो मैत्रः करुण आत्मवान् ॥ ३६ ॥
मोचये ग्रस्तमात्मानं योषिन्मय्यात्ममायया ।
विक्रीडितो ययैवाहं क्रीडामृग इवाधमः ॥ ३७ ॥

vimucya tam imaṁ bandham
avidyā-kāma-karmajam
sarva-bhūta-suhṛc chānto
maitraḥ karuṇa ātmavān

mocaye grastam ātmānaṁ
yoṣin-mayyātma-māyayā
vikrīḍito yayaivāhaṁ
krīḍā-mṛga ivādhamaḥ

vimucya—having become free from; *tam*—that; *imam*—this; *bandham*—bondage; *avidyā*—due to ignorance; *kāma*—due to lusty desire; *karma-jam*—caused by activities; *sarva-bhūta*—of all living entities; *suhṛt*—friend; *śāntaḥ*—very peaceful; *maitraḥ*—friendly; *karuṇaḥ*—merciful; *ātma-vān*—self-realized; *mocaye*—I shall disentangle; *grastam*—encaged; *ātmānam*—my soul; *yoṣit-mayyā*—in the form of woman; *ātma-māyayā*—by the illusory energy of the Lord; *vikrīḍitaḥ*—played with; *yayā*—by which; *eva*—

certainly; *aham*—I; *krīḍā-mṛgaḥ*—a controlled animal; *iva*—like; *adhamaḥ* —so fallen.

TRANSLATION

Because of identifying oneself with the body, one is subjected to desires for sense gratification, and thus one engages in many different types of pious and impious action. This is what constitutes material bondage. Now I shall disentangle myself from my material bondage, which has been caused by the Supreme Personality of Godhead's illusory energy in the form of a woman. Being a most fallen soul, I was victimized by the illusory energy and have become like a dancing dog led around by a woman's hand. Now I shall give up all lusty desires and free myself from this illusion. I shall become a merciful, well-wishing friend to all living entities and always absorb myself in Kṛṣṇa consciousness.

PURPORT

This should be the standard of determination for all Kṛṣṇa conscious persons. A Kṛṣṇa conscious person should free himself from the clutches of *māyā,* and he should also be compassionate to all others suffering in those clutches. The activities of the Kṛṣṇa consciousness movement are meant not only for oneself but for others also. This is the perfection of Kṛṣṇa consciousness. One who is interested in his own salvation is not as advanced in Kṛṣṇa consciousness as one who feels compassion for others and who therefore propagates the Kṛṣṇa consciousness movement. Such an advanced devotee will never fall down, for Kṛṣṇa will give him special protection. That is the sum and substance of the Kṛṣṇa consciousness movement. Everyone is like a play toy in the hands of the illusory energy and is acting as she moves him. One should come to Kṛṣṇa consciousness to release oneself and also to release others.

TEXT 38

ममाहमिति देहादौ हित्वामिथ्यार्थधीर्मतिम् ।
धास्ये मनो भगवति शुद्धं तत्कीर्तनादिभिः ॥ ३८ ॥

mamāham iti dehādau
hitvāmithyārtha-dhīr matim
dhāsye mano bhagavati
śuddhaṁ tat-kīrtanādibhiḥ

mama—my; *aham*—I; *iti*—thus; *deha-ādau*—in the body and things related to the body; *hitvā*—giving up; *amithyā*—not false; *artha*—on values; *dhīḥ*—with my consciousness; *matim*—the attitude; *dhāsye*—I shall engage; *manaḥ*—my mind; *bhagavati*—on the Supreme Personality of Godhead; *śuddham*—pure; *tat*—His name; *kīrtana-ādibhiḥ*—by chanting, hearing and so on.

TRANSLATION

Simply because I chanted the holy name of the Lord in the association of devotees, my heart is now becoming purified. Therefore I shall not fall victim again to the false lures of material sense gratification. Now that I have become fixed in the Absolute Truth, henceforward I shall not identify myself with the body. I shall give up false conceptions of "I" and "mine" and fix my mind on the lotus feet of Kṛṣṇa.

PURPORT

How a living entity becomes a victim of the material condition is lucidly explained in this verse. The beginning is to misidentify the body as one's self. Therefore *Bhagavad-gītā* begins with the spiritual instruction that one is not the body, but is within the body. This consciousness can be possible only if one chants the holy name of Kṛṣṇa, the Hare Kṛṣṇa *mahā-mantra,* and always keeps oneself in the association of devotees. This is the secret of success. Therefore we stress that one should chant the holy name of the Lord and keep oneself free from the contaminations of this material world, especially the contaminations of lusty desires for illicit sex, meat-eating, intoxication and gambling. With determination, one should vow to follow these principles and thus be saved from the miserable condition of material existence. The first necessity is to become freed from the bodily concept of life.

TEXT 39

इति जातसुनिर्वेदः क्षणसङ्गेन साधुषु ।
गङ्गाद्वारमुपेयाय मुक्तसर्वानुबन्धनः ॥ ३९ ॥

iti jāta-sunirvedaḥ
kṣaṇa-saṅgena sādhuṣu
gaṅgā-dvāram upeyāya
mukta-sarvānubandhanaḥ

iti—thus; *jāta-sunirvedaḥ*—(Ajāmila) who had become detached from the material conception of life; *kṣaṇa-saṅgena*—by a moment's association;

sādhuṣu—with devotees; *gaṅgā-dvāram*—to Hardwar (*hari-dvāra*), the doorway to Hari (because the Ganges begins there, Hardwar is also called *gaṅgā-dvāra*); *upeyāya*—went; *mukta*—being freed from; *sarva-anubandhanaḥ*—all kinds of material bondage.

TRANSLATION

Because of a moment's association with devotees [the Viṣṇudūtas], Ajāmila detached himself from the material conception of life with determination. Thus freed from all material attraction, he immediately started for Hardwar.

PURPORT

The word *mukta-sarvānubandhanaḥ* indicates that after this incident, Ajāmila, not caring for his wife and children, went straight to Hardwar for further advancement in his spiritual life. Our Kṛṣṇa consciousness movement now has centers in Vṛndāvana and Navadvīpa so that those who want to live a retired life, whether they be devotees or not, can go there and with determination give up the bodily concept of life. One is welcome to live in those holy places for the rest of his life in order to achieve the highest success by the very simple method of chanting the holy name of the Lord and taking *prasāda.* Thus one may return home, back to Godhead. We do not have a center in Hardwar, but Vṛndāvana and Śrīdhāma Māyāpur are better for devotees than any other places. The Caitanya Candrodaya temple offers one a good opportunity to associate with devotees. Let us all take advantage of this opportunity.

TEXT 40

स तस्मिन् देवसदन आसीनो योगमास्थितः ।
प्रत्याहृतेन्द्रियग्रामो युयोज मन आत्मनि ॥ ४० ॥

sa tasmin deva-sadana
āsīno yogam āsthitaḥ
pratyāhṛtendriya-grāmo
yuyoja mana ātmani

saḥ—he (Ajāmila); *tasmin*—at that place (Hardwar); *deva-sadane*—in one Viṣṇu temple; *āsīnaḥ*—being situated; *yogam āsthitaḥ*—performed *bhakti-yoga; pratyāhṛta*—withdrawn from all activities of sense gratification; *indriya-grāmaḥ*—his senses; *yuyoja*—he fixed; *manaḥ*—the mind; *ātmani* —on the self or the Supersoul, the Supreme Personality of Godhead.

TRANSLATION

In Hardwar, Ajāmila took shelter at a Viṣṇu temple, where he executed the process of bhakti-yoga. He controlled his senses and fully applied his mind in the service of the Lord.

PURPORT

The devotees who have joined the Kṛṣṇa consciousness movement may live comfortably in our many temples and engage in the devotional service of the Lord. Thus they can control the mind and senses and achieve the highest success in life. This is the process descending from time immemorial. Learning from the life of Ajāmila, we should vow with determination to do what is necessary to follow this path.

TEXT 41

ततो गुणेभ्य आत्मानं वियुज्यात्मसमाधिना ।
युयुजे भगवद्धाम्नि ब्रह्मण्यनुभवात्मनि ॥ ४१ ॥

tato guṇebhya ātmānaṁ
viyujyātma-samādhinā
yuyuje bhagavad-dhāmni
brahmaṇy anubhavātmani

tataḥ—thereafter; *guṇebhyaḥ*—from the modes of material nature; *ātmānam*—the mind; *viyujya*—detaching; *ātma-samādhinā*—by being fully engaged in devotional service; *yuyuje*—engaged; *bhagavat-dhāmni*—in the form of the Lord; *brahmaṇi*—which is Parabrahman (not idol worship); *anubhava-ātmani*—which is always thought of (beginning from the lotus feet and gradually progressing upward).

TRANSLATION

Ajāmila fully engaged in devotional service. Thus he detached his mind from the process of sense gratification and became fully absorbed in thinking of the form of the Lord.

PURPORT

If one worships the Deity in the temple, one's mind will naturally be absorbed in thought of the Lord and His form. There is no distinction between the form of the Lord and the Lord Himself. Therefore *bhakti-yoga* is the most easy system of *yoga. Yogīs* try to concentrate their minds upon the form of the Supersoul, Viṣṇu, within the heart, but this same objective is easily achieved when one's mind is absorbed in the Deity worshiped in the temple. In every temple there is a transcendental form of the Lord, and one may easily think of this form. By seeing the Lord during *ārati,* by offering *bhoga* and by constantly thinking of the form of the Deity, one becomes a first-class *yogī.* This is the best process of *yoga,* as confirmed by the Supreme Personality of Godhead in *Bhagavad-gītā* (6.47):

yoginām api sarveṣāṁ
mad-gatenāntarātmanā
śraddhāvān bhajate yo māṁ
sa me yuktatamo mataḥ

"Of all *yogīs,* he who always abides in Me with great faith, worshiping Me in transcendental loving service, is most intimately united with Me in *yoga* and is the highest of all." The first-class *yogī* is he who controls his senses and detaches himself from material activities by always thinking of the form of the Lord.

TEXT 42

यर्ह्युपारतधीस्तस्मिन्नद्राक्षीत्पुरुषान् पुरः ।
उपलभ्योपलब्धान् प्राग् ववन्दे शिरसा द्विजः ॥ ४२ ॥

yarhy upārata-dhīs tasminn
adrākṣīt puruṣān puraḥ
upalabhyopalabdhān prāg
vavande śirasā dvijaḥ

yarhi—when; *upārata-dhīḥ*—his mind and intelligence were fixed; *tasmin*—at that time; *adrākṣīt*—had seen; *puruṣān*—the persons (the order carriers of Lord Viṣṇu); *puraḥ*—before him; *upalabhya*—getting; *upalabdhān*—who were gotten; *prāk*—previously; *vavande*—offered obeisances; *śirasā*—by the head; *dvijaḥ*—the *brāhmaṇa.*

TRANSLATION

When his intelligence and mind were fixed upon the form of the Lord, the brāhmaṇa Ajāmila once again saw before him four celestial persons. He could understand that they were those he had seen previously, and thus he offered them his obeisances by bowing down before them.

PURPORT

The Viṣṇudūtas who had rescued Ajāmila came before him again when his mind was firmly fixed upon the form of the Lord. The Viṣṇudūtas had gone away for some time to give Ajāmila a chance to become firmly fixed in meditation upon the Lord. Now that his devotion had matured, they returned to take him. Understanding that the same Viṣṇudūtas had returned, Ajāmila offered them his obeisances by bowing down before them.

TEXT 43

हित्वा कलेवरं तीर्थे गङ्गायां दर्शनादनु ।
सद्यः स्वरूपं जगृहे भगवत्पार्श्ववर्तिनाम् ॥ ४३ ॥

hitvā kalevaraṁ tīrthe
gaṅgāyāṁ darśanād anu
sadyaḥ svarūpaṁ jagṛhe
bhagavat-pārśva-vartinām

hitvā—giving up; *kalevaram*—the material body; *tīrthe*—in the holy place; *gaṅgāyām*—on the bank of the Ganges; *darśanāt anu*—after seeing; *sadyaḥ*—immediately; *sva-rūpam*—his original spiritual form; *jagṛhe*—he assumed; *bhagavat-pārśva-vartinām*—which is fit for an associate of the Lord.

TRANSLATION

Upon seeing the Viṣṇudūtas, Ajāmila gave up his material body at Hardwar on the bank of the Ganges. He regained his original spiritual body, which was a body appropriate for an associate of the Lord.

PURPORT

The Lord says in *Bhagavad-gītā* (4.9):

janma karma ca me divyam
evaṁ yo vetti tattvataḥ
tyaktvā dehaṁ punar janma
naiti mām eti so'rjuna

"One who knows the transcendental nature of My appearance and activities does not, upon leaving the body, take his birth again in this material world, but attains My eternal abode, O Arjuna."

The result of perfection in Kṛṣṇa consciousness is that after giving up one's material body, one is immediately transferred to the spiritual world in one's original spiritual body to become an associate of the Supreme Personality of Godhead. Some devotees go to Vaikuṇṭhaloka, and others go to Goloka Vṛndāvana to become associates of Kṛṣṇa.

TEXT 44

साकं विहायसा विप्रो महापुरुषकिङ्करैः ।
हैमं विमानमारुह्य ययौ यत्र श्रियः पतिः ॥ ४४ ॥

sākaṁ vihāyasā vipro
mahāpuruṣa-kiṅkaraiḥ
haimaṁ vimānam āruhya
yayau yatra śriyaḥ patiḥ

sākam—along; *vihāyasā*—by the path in the sky, or the airways; *vipraḥ*—the *brāhmaṇa* (Ajāmila); *mahāpuruṣa-kiṅkaraiḥ*—with the order carriers of Lord Viṣṇu; *haimam*—made of gold; *vimānam*—an airplane; *āruhya*—boarding; *yayau*—went; *yatra*—where; *śriyaḥ patiḥ*—Lord Viṣṇu, the husband of the goddess of fortune.

TRANSLATION

Accompanied by the order carriers of Lord Viṣṇu, Ajāmila boarded an airplane made of gold. Passing through the airways, he went directly to the abode of Lord Viṣṇu, the husband of the goddess of fortune.

PURPORT

For many years, material scientists have tried to go to the moon, but they are still unable to go there. However, the spiritual airplanes from the spiritual planets can take one back home, back to Godhead, in a second. The speed of such a spiritual plane can only be imagined. Spirit is finer than the mind, and everyone has experience of how swiftly the mind travels from one place to another. Therefore one can imagine the swiftness of the spiritual form by comparing it to the speed of the mind. In less than even a moment, a perfect devotee can return home, back to Godhead, immediately after giving up his material body.

TEXT 45

एवं स विप्लावितसर्वधर्मा
दास्याः पतिः पतितो गर्ह्यकर्मणा ।
निपात्यमानो निरये हतव्रतः
सद्यो विमुक्तो भगवन्नाम गृह्णन् ॥ ४५ ॥

evaṁ sa viplāvita-sarva-dharmā
dāsyāḥ patiḥ patito garhya-karmaṇā
nipātyamāno niraye hata-vrataḥ
sadyo vimukto bhagavan-nāma gṛhṇan

evam—in this way; *saḥ*—he (Ajāmila); *viplāvita-sarva-dharmāḥ*—who gave up all religious principles; *dāsyāḥ patiḥ*—the husband of a prostitute; *patitaḥ*—fallen; *garhya-karmaṇā*—by being engaged in abominable activities; *nipātyamānaḥ*—falling; *niraye*—in hellish life; *hata-vrataḥ*—who broke all his vows; *sadyaḥ*—immediately; *vimuktaḥ*—liberated; *bhagavat-nāma*—the holy name of the Lord; *gṛhṇan*—chanting.

TRANSLATION

Ajāmila was a brāhmaṇa who because of bad association had given up all brahminical culture and religious principles. Becoming most fallen, he stole, drank and performed other abominable acts. He even kept a prostitute. Thus he was destined to be carried away to hell by the order carriers of Yamarāja, but he was immediately rescued simply by a glimpse of the chanting of the holy name Nārāyaṇa.

TEXT 46

नातः परं कर्मनिबन्धकृन्तनं
मुमुक्षतां तीर्थपदानुकीर्तनात् ।
न यत्पुनः कर्मसु सज्जते मनो
रजस्तमोभ्यां कलिलं ततोऽन्यथा ॥ ४६ ॥

nātaḥ paraṁ karma-nibandha-kṛntanaṁ
mumukṣatāṁ tīrtha-padānukīrtanāt
na yat punaḥ karmasu sajjate mano
rajas-tamobhyāṁ kalilaṁ tato'nyathā

na—not; *ataḥ*—therefore; *param*—better means; *karma-nibandha*—the obligation to suffer or undergo tribulations as a result of fruitive activities; *kṛntanam*—that which can completely cut off; *mumukṣatām*—of persons desiring to get out of the clutches of material bondage; *tīrtha-pada*—about the Supreme Personality of Godhead, at whose feet all the holy places stand; *anukīrtanāt*—than constantly chanting under the direction of the bona fide spiritual master; *na*—not; *yat*—because; *punaḥ*—again; *karmasu*—in fruitive activities; *sajjate*—becomes attached; *manaḥ*—the mind; *rajaḥ-tamobhyām*—by the modes of passion and ignorance; *kalilam*—contaminated; *tataḥ*—thereafter; *anyathā*—by any other means.

TRANSLATION

Therefore one who desires freedom from material bondage should adopt the process of chanting and glorifying the name, fame, form and pastimes of the Supreme Personality of Godhead, at whose feet all the holy places stand. One cannot derive the proper benefit from other methods, such as pious atonement, speculative knowledge and meditation in mystic yoga, because even after following such methods one takes to fruitive activities again, unable to control his mind, which is contaminated by the base qualities of nature, namely passion and ignorance.

PURPORT

It has actually been seen that even after achieving so-called perfection, many *karmīs, jñānīs* and *yogīs* become attached to material activities again. Many so-called *svāmīs* and *yogīs* give up material activities as false (*jagan mithyā*), but after some time they nevertheless resume material activities by opening hospitals and schools or performing other activities for the benefit of the public. Sometimes they participate in politics, although still falsely declaring themselves *sannyāsīs,* members of the renounced order. The perfect conclusion, however, is that if one actually desires to get out of the material world, he must take to devotional service, which begins with *śravaṇaṁ kīrtanaṁ viṣṇoḥ:* chanting and hearing the glories of the Lord. The Kṛṣṇa consciousness movement has actually proved this. In the Western countries, many young boys who were addicted to drugs and who had many other bad habits, which they could not give up, abandoned all those propensities and very seriously engaged in chanting the glories of the Lord as soon as they joined the Kṛṣṇa consciousness movement. In other words, this process is the perfect method of atonement for actions performed in *rajaḥ* and *tamaḥ* (passion and ignorance). As stated in *Śrīmad-Bhāgavatam* (1.2.19):

tadā rajas-tamo-bhāvāḥ
kāma-lobhādayaś ca ye
ceta etair anāviddhaṁ
sthitaṁ sattve prasīdati

As a result of *rajaḥ* and *tamaḥ,* one becomes increasingly lusty and greedy, but when one takes to the process of chanting and hearing, one comes to the platform of goodness and becomes happy. As he advances in devotional service, all his doubts are completely eradicated (*bhidyate hṛdaya-granthiś chidyante sarva-saṁśayāḥ*). Thus the knot of his desire for fruitive activities is cut to pieces.

TEXTS 47–48

य एतं परमं गुह्यमितिहासमघापहम् ।
शृणुयाच्छ्रद्धया युक्तो यश्च भक्त्यानुकीर्तयेत् ॥ ४७ ॥
न वै स नरकं याति नेक्षितो यमकिङ्करैः ।
यद्यप्यमङ्गलो मर्त्यो विष्णुलोके महीयते ॥ ४८ ॥

ya etaṁ paramaṁ guhyam
itihāsam aghāpaham
śṛṇuyāc chraddhayā yukto
yaś ca bhaktyānukīrtayet

na vai sa narakaṁ yāti
nekṣito yama-kiṅkaraiḥ
yady apy amaṅgalo martyo
viṣṇu-loke mahīyate

yaḥ—anyone who; *etam*—this; *paramam*—very; *guhyam*—confidential; *itihāsam*—historical narration; *agha-apaham*—which frees one from all reactions to sins; *śṛṇuyāt*—hears; *śraddhayā*—with faith; *yuktaḥ*—endowed; *yaḥ*—one who; *ca*—also; *bhaktyā*—with great devotion; *anukīrtayet*—repeats; *na*—not; *vai*—indeed; *saḥ*—such a person; *narakam*—to hell; *yāti*—goes; *na*—not; *īkṣitaḥ*—is observed; *yama-kiṅkaraiḥ*—by the order carriers of Yamarāja; *yadi api*—although; *amaṅgalaḥ*—inauspicious; *martyaḥ*—a living entity with a material body; *viṣṇu-loke*—in the spiritual world; *mahīyate*—is welcomed and respectfully received.

TRANSLATION

Because this very confidential historical narration has the potency to vanquish all sinful reactions, one who hears or describes it with faith and

devotion is no longer doomed to hellish life, regardless of his having a material body and regardless of how sinful he may have been. Indeed, the Yamadūtas, who carry out the orders of Yamarāja, do not approach him even to see him. After giving up his body, he returns home, back to Godhead, where he is very respectfully received and worshiped.

TEXT 49

म्रियमाणो हरेर्नाम गृणन् पुत्रोपचारितम् ।
अजामिलोऽप्यगाद्धाम किमुत श्रद्धया गृणन् ॥ ४९ ॥

mriyamāṇo harer nāma
gṛṇan putropacāritam
ajāmilo'py agād dhāma
kim uta śraddhayā gṛṇan

mriyamāṇaḥ—at the time of death; *hareḥ nāma*—the holy name of Hari; *gṛṇan*—chanting; *putra-upacāritam*—indicating his son; *ajāmilaḥ*—Ajāmila; *api*—even; *agāt*—went; *dhāma*—to the spiritual world; *kim uta*—what to speak of; *śraddhayā*—with faith and love; *gṛṇan*—chanting.

TRANSLATION

While suffering at the time of death, Ajāmila chanted the holy name of the Lord, and although the chanting was directed toward his son, he nevertheless returned home, back to Godhead. Therefore if one faithfully and inoffensively chants the holy name of the Lord, where is the doubt that he will return to Godhead?

PURPORT

At the time of death one is certainly bewildered because his bodily functions are in disorder. At that time, even one who throughout his life has practiced chanting the holy name of the Lord may not be able to chant the Hare Kṛṣṇa *mantra* very distinctly. Nevertheless, such a person receives all the benefits of chanting the holy name. While the body is fit, therefore, why should we not chant the holy name of the Lord loudly and distinctly? If one does so, it is quite possible that even at the time of death he will be properly able to chant the holy name of the Lord with love and faith. In conclusion, one who chants the holy name of the Lord constantly is guaranteed to return home, back to Godhead, without a doubt.

Supplementary note to this chapter.

Śrīla Viśvanātha Cakravartī Ṭhākura's commentary to texts 9 and 10 of this chapter form a dialogue concerning how one can become free from all sinful reactions simply by chanting the holy name of the Lord.

Someone may say, "It may be accepted that by chanting the holy name of the Lord one becomes freed from all the reactions of sinful life. However, if one commits sinful acts in full consciousness, not only once but many, many times, he is unable to free himself from the reactions of such sins even after atoning for them for twelve years or more. How is it possible, then, that simply by once chanting the holy name of the Lord one immediately becomes freed from the reactions of such sins?"

Śrīla Viśvanātha Cakravartī Ṭhākura replies by quoting verses 9 and 10 of this chapter: "The chanting of the holy name of Lord Viṣṇu is the best process of atonement for a thief of gold or other valuables, for a drunkard, for one who betrays a friend or relative, for one who kills a *brāhmaṇa,* or for one who indulges in sex with the wife of his *guru* or another superior. It is also the best method of atonement for one who murders women, the king or his father, for one who slaughters cows, and for all other sinful men. Simply by chanting the holy name of Lord Viṣṇu, such sinful persons may attract the attention of the Supreme Lord, who therefore considers "Because this man has chanted My holy name, My duty is to give him protection.'"

One may atone for sinful life and vanquish all sinful reactions by chanting the holy name, although this is not called atonement. Ordinary atonement may temporarily protect a sinful person, but it does not completely cleanse his heart of the deep-rooted desire to commit sinful acts. Therefore atonement is not as powerful as the chanting of the holy name of the Lord. In the *śāstras* it is said that if a person only once chants the holy name and completely surrenders unto the lotus feet of the Lord, the Lord immediately considers him His ward and is always inclined to give him protection. This is confirmed by Śrīdhara Svāmī. Thus when Ajāmila was in great danger of being carried off by the order carriers of Yamarāja, the Lord immediately sent His personal order carriers to protect him, and because Ajāmila was freed from all sinful reactions, the Viṣṇudūtas spoke on his behalf.

Ajāmila had named his son Nārāyaṇa, and because he loved the boy very much, he would call him again and again. Although he was calling for his son, the name itself was powerful because the name Nārāyaṇa is not different from the Supreme Lord Nārāyaṇa. When Ajāmila named his son Nārāyaṇa, all the reactions of his sinful life were neutralized, and as he continued calling his son and thus chanting the holy name of Nārāyaṇa thousands of times, he was actually unconsciously advancing in Kṛṣṇa consciousness.

One may argue, "Since he was constantly chanting the name of Nārāyaṇa, how was it possible for him to be associating with a prostitute and thinking of wine?" By his sinful actions he was bringing suffering upon himself again and again, and therefore one may say that his ultimate chanting of Nārāyaṇa was the cause of his being freed. However, his chanting would then have been a *nāma-aparādha. Nāmno balād yasya hi pāpa-buddhiḥ:* one who continues to act sinfully and tries to neutralize his sins by chanting the holy name of the Lord is a *nāma-aparādhī,* an offender to the holy name. In response it may be said that Ajāmila's chanting was inoffensive because he did not chant the name of Nārāyaṇa with the purpose of counteracting his sins. He did not know that he was addicted to sinful actions, nor did he know that his chanting of the name of Nārāyaṇa was neutralizing them. Thus he did not commit a *nāma-aparādha,* and his repeated chanting of the holy name of Nārāyaṇa while calling his son may be called pure chanting. Because of this pure chanting, Ajāmila unconsciously accumulated the results of *bhakti.* Indeed, even his first utterance of the holy name was sufficient to nullify all the sinful reactions of his life. To cite a logical example, a fig tree does not immediately yield fruits, but in time the fruits are available. Similarly, Ajāmila's devotional service grew little by little, and therefore although he committed very sinful acts, the reactions did not affect him. In the *śāstras* it is said that if one chants the holy name of the Lord even once, the reactions of past, present or future sinful life do not affect him. To give another example, if one extracts the poison fangs of a serpent, this saves the serpent's future victims from poisonous effects, even if the serpent bites repeatedly. Similarly, if a devotee chants the holy name even once inoffensively, this protects him eternally. He need only wait for the results of the chanting to mature in due course of time.

Thus end the Bhaktivedanta purports of the Sixth Canto, Second Chapter, of the Śrīmad-Bhāgavatam, *entitled "Ajāmila Delivered by the Viṣṇudūtas."*

CHAPTER THREE

Yamarāja Instructs His Messengers

As related in this chapter, the Yamadūtas approached Yamarāja, who very exhaustively explained *bhāgavata-dharma,* the religious principle of devotional service. Yamarāja thus satisfied the Yamadūtas, who had been very disappointed. Yamarāja said, "Although Ajāmila was calling for his son, he chanted the holy name of the Lord, Nārāyaṇa, and simply by a glimpse of the chanting of the holy name, he immediately achieved the association of Lord Viṣṇu's order carriers, who saved him from your attempt to arrest him. This is quite all right. It is a fact that even a chronically sinful person who chants the holy name of the Lord, although not completely without offenses, does not take another material birth."

By chanting the holy name of the Lord, Ajāmila had met four order carriers of Lord Viṣṇu. They were very beautiful and had quickly come to rescue him. Yamarāja now described them. "The Viṣṇudūtas are all pure devotees of the Lord, the Supreme Person in regard to the creation, maintenance and annihilation of this cosmic manifestation. Neither King Indra, Varuṇa, Śiva, Brahmā, the seven *ṛṣis* nor I myself can understand the transcendental activities of the Supreme Lord, who is self-sufficient and beyond the reach of the material senses. With material senses, no one can attain enlightenment about Him. The Lord, the master of the illusory energy, possesses transcendental qualities for the good fortune of everyone, and His devotees are also qualified in that way. The devotees, concerned only with rescuing the fallen souls from this material world, apparently take birth in different places in the material world just to save the conditioned souls. If one is somewhat interested in spiritual life, the devotees of the Lord protect him in many ways."

Yamarāja continued, "The essence of *sanātana-dharma,* or eternal religion, is extremely confidential. No one but the Lord Himself can deliver that confidential religious system to human society. It is by the mercy of the Lord that the transcendental system of religion can be understood by His pure devotees, and specifically by the twelve *mahājanas*-Lord Brahmā, Nārada Muni, Lord Śiva, the Kumāras, Kapila, Manu, Prahlāda, Janaka, Bhīṣma, Bali, Śukadeva Gosvāmī and me. Other learned scholars, headed by Jaimini, are almost always covered by the illusory energy, and therefore they are more or less attracted by the flowery language of the three *Vedas,* namely *Ṛg, Yajur* and *Sāma,* which are called *trayī.* Instead of becoming pure devotees, people captivated by the flowery words of these three *Vedas* are interested in the Vedic ritualistic ceremonies. They cannot understand the glories of chanting the holy name of the Lord. Intelligent persons, however, take to the devotional service of the Lord. When they chant the holy name of the Lord without offenses, they are no longer subject to my rulings. If by chance they commit some sinful act, they are protected by the holy name of the Lord because that is where their interest lies. The four weapons of the Lord, especially the club and the Sudarśana *cakra,* always protect the devotees. One who chants, hears or remembers the holy name of the Lord without duplicity, or who prays or offers obeisances to the Lord, becomes perfect, whereas even a learned person may be called to hell if he is bereft of devotional service."

After Yamarāja thus described the glories of the Lord and His devotees, Śukadeva Gosvāmī further explained the potency of chanting the holy name and the futility of performing Vedic ritualistic ceremonies and pious activities for atonement.

TEXT 1

श्रीराजोवाच
निशम्य देवः स्वभटोपवर्णितं
प्रत्याह किं तानपि धर्मराजः ।
एवं हताज्ञो विहतान्मुरारे-
नैंदेशिकैर्यस्य वशे जनोऽयम् ॥ १ ॥

śrī-rājovāca
niśamya devaḥ sva-bhaṭopavarṇitaṁ
pratyāha kiṁ tān api dharmarājaḥ
evaṁ hatājño vihatān murārer
naideśikair yasya vaśe jano'yam

śrī-rājā uvāca—the King said; *niśamya*—after hearing; *devaḥ*—Lord Yamarāja; *sva-bhaṭa*—of his own servants; *upavarṇitam*—the statements; *pratyāha*—replied; *kim*—what; *tān*—unto them; *api*—also; *dharma-rājaḥ*—Yamarāja, the superintendent of death and the judge of religious and irreligious activities; *evam*—thus; *hata-ājñaḥ*—whose order was foiled; *vihatān*—who were defeated; *murāreḥ naideśikaiḥ*—by the order carriers of Murāri, Kṛṣṇa; *yasya*—of whom; *vaśe*—under the subjugation; *janaḥ ayam*—all the people of the world.

TRANSLATION

King Parīkṣit said: O my lord, O Śukadeva Gosvāmī, Yamarāja is the controller of all living entities in terms of their religious and irreligious activities, but his order had been foiled. When his servants, the Yamadūtas, informed him of their defeat by the Viṣṇudūtas, who had stopped them from arresting Ajāmila, what did he reply?

PURPORT

Śrīla Viśvanātha Cakravartī Ṭhākura says that although the statements of the Yamadūtas were fully upheld by Vedic principles, the statements of the Viṣṇudūtas were triumphant. This was confirmed by Yamarāja himself.

TEXT 2

यमस्य देवस्य न दण्डभङ्गः
कुतश्चनर्षे श्रुतपूर्व आसीत् ।
एतन्मुने वृश्चति लोकसंशयं
न हि त्वदन्य इति मे विनिश्चितम् ॥ २ ॥

yamasya devasya na daṇḍa-bhaṅgaḥ
kutaścanarṣe śruta-pūrva āsīt
etan mune vṛścati loka-saṁśayaṁ
na hi tvad-anya iti me viniścitam

yamasya—of Yamarāja; *devasya*—the demigod in charge of judgment; *na*—not; *daṇḍa-bhaṅgaḥ*—the breaking of the order; *kutaścana*—from anywhere; *ṛṣe*—O great sage; *śruta-pūrvaḥ*—heard before; *āsīt*—was; *etat*—this; *mune*—O great sage; *vṛścati*—can eradicate; *loka-saṁśayam*—the doubt of people; *na*—not; *hi*—indeed; *tvat-anyaḥ*—anyone other than you; *iti*—thus; *me*—by me; *viniścitam*—concluded.

TRANSLATION

O great sage, never before has it been heard anywhere that an order from Yamarāja has been baffled. Therefore I think that people will have doubts about this that no one but you can eradicate. Since that is my firm conviction, kindly explain the reasons for these events.

TEXT 3

श्रीशुक उवाच
भगवत्पुरुषै राजन् याम्याः प्रतिहतोद्यमाः ।
पतिं विज्ञापयामासुर्यमं संयमनीपतिम् ॥ ३ ॥

śrī-śuka uvāca
bhagavat-puruṣai rājan
yāmyāḥ pratihatodyamāḥ
patiṁ vijñāpayām āsur
yamaṁ saṁyamanī-patim

śrī-śukaḥ uvāca—Śukadeva Gosvāmī said; *bhagavat-puruṣaiḥ*—by the order carriers of the Lord, the Viṣṇudūtas; *rājan*—O King; *yāmyāḥ*—the order carriers of Yamarāja; *pratihata-udyamāḥ*—whose efforts were defeated; *patim*—their master; *vijñāpayām āsuḥ*—informed; *yamam*—Yamarāja; *saṁyamanī-patim*—the master of the city Saṁyamanī.

TRANSLATION

Śrī Śukadeva Gosvāmī replied: My dear King, when the order carriers of Yamarāja were baffled and defeated by the order carriers of Viṣṇu, they approached their master, the controller of Saṁyamanī-purī and master of sinful persons, to tell him of this incident.

TEXT 4

यमदूता ऊचुः
कति सन्तीह शास्तारो जीवलोकस्य वै प्रभो ।
त्रैविध्यं कुर्वतः कर्म फलाभिव्यक्तिहेतवः ॥ ४ ॥

yamadūtā ūcuḥ
kati santīha śāstāro
jīva-lokasya vai prabho
trai-vidhyaṁ kurvataḥ karma
phalābhivyakti-hetavaḥ

yamadūtāḥ ūcuḥ—the order carriers of Yamarāja said; *kati*—how many; *santi*—are there; *iha*—in this world; *śāstāraḥ*—controllers or rulers; *jīva-lokasya*—of this material world; *vai*—indeed; *prabho*—O master; *trai-vidhyam*—under the three modes of material nature; *kurvataḥ*—

performing; *karma*—activity; *phala*—of the results; *abhivyakti*—of the manifestation; *hetavaḥ*—causes.

TRANSLATION

The Yamadūtas said: Our dear lord, how many controllers or rulers are there in this material world? How many causes are responsible for manifesting the various results of activities performed under the three modes of material nature [sattva-guṇa, rajo-guṇa and tamo-guṇa]?

PURPORT

Śrīla Viśvanātha Cakravartī Ṭhākura says that the Yamadūtas, the order carriers of Yamarāja, were so disappointed that they asked their master, almost in great anger, whether there were many masters other than him. Furthermore, because the Yamadūtas had been defeated and their master could not protect them, they were inclined to say that there was no need to serve such a master. If a servant cannot carry out the orders of his master without being defeated, what is the use of serving such a powerless master?

TEXT 5

यदि स्युर्बहवो लोके शास्तारो दण्डधारिणः ।
कस्य स्यातां न वा कस्य मृत्युश्चामृतमेव वा ॥ ५ ॥

yadi syur bahavo loke
śāstāro daṇḍa-dhāriṇaḥ
kasya syātāṁ na vā kasya
mṛtyuś cāmṛtam eva vā

yadi—if; *syuḥ*—there are; *bahavaḥ*—many; *loke*—in this world; *śāstāraḥ*—rulers or controllers; *daṇḍa-dhāriṇaḥ*—who punish the sinful men; *kasya*—of whom; *syātām*—there may be; *na*—not; *vā*—or; *kasya*—of whom; *mṛtyuḥ*—distress or unhappiness; *ca*—and; *amṛtam*—happiness; *eva*—certainly; *vā*—or.

TRANSLATION

If in this universe there are many rulers and justices who disagree about punishment and reward, their contradictory actions will neutralize each other, and no one will be punished or rewarded. Otherwise, if their contradictory acts fail to neutralize each other, everyone will have to be both punished and rewarded.

PURPORT

Because the Yamadūtas had been unsuccessful in carrying out the order of Yamarāja, they doubted whether Yamarāja actually had the power to punish the sinful. Although they had gone to arrest Ajāmila, following Yamarāja's order, they found themselves unsuccessful because of the order of some higher authority. Therefore they were unsure of whether there were many authorities or only one. If there were many authorities who gave different judgments, which could be contradictory, a person might be wrongly punished or wrongly rewarded, or he might be neither punished nor rewarded. According to our experience in the material world, a person punished in one court may appeal to another. Thus the same man may be either punished or rewarded according to different judgments. However, in the law of nature or the court of the Supreme Personality of Godhead there cannot be such contradictory judgments. The judges and their judgments must be perfect and free from contradictions. Actually the position of Yamarāja was very awkward in the case of Ajāmila because the Yamadūtas were right in attempting to arrest Ajāmila, but the Viṣṇudūtas had baffled them. Although Yamarāja, under these circumstances, was accused by both the Viṣṇudūtas and the Yamadūtas, he is perfect in administering justice because he is empowered by the Supreme Personality of Godhead. Therefore he will explain what his real position is and how everyone is controlled by the supreme controller, the Personality of Godhead.

TEXT 6

किन्तु शास्तृबहुत्वे स्याद्बहूनामिह कर्मिणाम्।
शास्तृत्वमुपचारो हि यथा मण्डलवर्तिनाम् ॥ ६ ॥

kintu śāstṛ-bahutve syād
bahūnām iha karmiṇām
śāstṛtvam upacāro hi
yathā maṇḍala-vartinām

kintu—but; *śāstṛ*—of governors or judges; *bahutve*—in the plurality; *syāt*—there may be; *bahūnām*—of many; *iha*—in this world; *karmiṇām*—persons performing actions; *śāstṛtvam*—departmental management; *upacāraḥ*—administration; *hi*—indeed; *yathā*—just like; *maṇḍala-vartinām*—of the departmental heads.

TRANSLATION

The Yamadūtas continued: Since there are many different karmīs, or workers, there may be different judges or rulers to give them justice, but just as one central emperor controls different departmental rulers, there must be one supreme controller to guide all the judges.

PURPORT

In governmental management there may be departmental officials to give justice to different persons, but the law must be one, and that central law must control everyone. The Yamadūtas could not imagine that two judges would give two different verdicts in the same case, and therefore they wanted to know who the central judge is. The Yamadūtas were certain that Ajāmila was a most sinful man, but although Yamarāja wanted to punish him, the Viṣṇudūtas excused him. This was a puzzling situation that the Yamadūtas wanted Yamarāja to clarify.

TEXT 7

अतस्त्वमेको भूतानां सेश्वराणामधीश्वरः ।
शास्ता दण्डधरो नृणां शुभाशुभविवेचनः ॥ ७ ॥

atas tvam eko bhūtānāṁ
seśvarāṇām adhīśvaraḥ
śāstā daṇḍa-dharo nṛṇāṁ
śubhāśubha-vivecanaḥ

ataḥ—as such; *tvam*—you; *ekaḥ*—one; *bhūtānām*—of all living beings; *sa-īśvarāṇām*—including all the demigods; *adhīśvaraḥ*—the supreme master; *śāstā*—the supreme ruler; *daṇḍa-dharaḥ*—the supreme administrator of punishment; *nṛṇām*—of human society; *śubha-aśubha-vivecanaḥ*—who discriminates between what is auspicious and inauspicious.

TRANSLATION

The supreme judge must be one, not many. It was our understanding that you are that supreme judge and that you have jurisdiction even over the demigods. Our impression was that you are the master of all living entities, the supreme authority who discriminates between the pious and impious activities of all human beings.

TEXT 8

तस्य ते विहितो दण्डो न लोके वर्ततेऽधुना।
चतुर्भिरद्भुतैः सिद्धैराज्ञा ते विप्रलम्भिता ॥ ८ ॥

tasya te vihito daṇḍo
na loke vartate'dhunā
caturbhir adbhutaiḥ siddhair
ājñā te vipralambhitā

tasya—of the influence; *te*—of you; *vihitaḥ*—ordained; *daṇḍaḥ*—punishment; *na*—not; *loke*—within this world; *vartate*—exists; *adhunā*—now; *caturbhiḥ*—by four; *adbhutaiḥ*—very wonderful; *siddhaiḥ*—perfected persons; *ājñā*—the order; *te*—your; *vipralambhitā*—surpassed.

TRANSLATION

But now we see that the punishment ordained under your authority is no longer effective, since your order has been transgressed by four wonderful and perfect persons.

PURPORT

The Yamadūtas had been under the impression that Yamarāja was the only person in charge of administering justice. They were fully confident that no one could counteract his judgments, but now, to their surprise, his order had been violated by the four wonderful persons from Siddhaloka.

TEXT 9

नीयमानं तवादेशादस्माभिर्यातनागृहान् ।
व्यामोचयन् पातकिनं छित्त्वा पाशान् प्रसह्य ते ॥ ९ ॥

nīyamānaṁ tavādeśād
asmābhir yātanā-gṛhān
vyāmocayan pātakinaṁ
chittvā pāśān prasahya te

nīyamānam—being brought; *tava ādeśāt*—by your order; *asmābhiḥ*—by us; *yātanā-gṛhān*—to the torture chambers, the hellish planets; *vyāmocayan*—released; *pātakinam*—the sinful Ajāmila; *chittvā*—cutting; *pāśān*—the ropes; *prasahya*—by force; *te*—they.

TRANSLATION

We were bringing the most sinful Ajāmila toward the hellish planets, following your order, when those beautiful persons from Siddhaloka forcibly cut the knots of the ropes with which we were arresting him.

PURPORT

Śrīla Viśvanātha Cakravartī Ṭhākura remarks that the Yamadūtas wanted to bring the Viṣṇudūtas before Yamarāja. If Yamarāja could then have punished the Viṣṇudūtas, the Yamadūtas would have been satisfied.

TEXT 10

तांस्ते वेदितुमिच्छामो यदि नो मन्यसे क्षमम् ।
नारायणेत्यभिहिते मा भैरित्याययुर्द्रुतम् ॥ १० ॥

tāṁs te veditum icchāmo
yadi no manyase kṣamam
nārāyaṇety abhihite
mā bhair ity āyayur drutam

tān—about them; *te*—from you; *veditum*—to know; *icchāmaḥ*—we wish; *yadi*—if; *naḥ*—for us; *manyase*—you think; *kṣamam*—suitable; *nārāyaṇa*—Nārāyaṇa; *iti*—thus; *abhihite*—being uttered; *mā*—do not; *bhaiḥ*—fear; *iti*—thus; *āyayuḥ*—they arrived; *drutam*—very soon.

TRANSLATION

As soon as the sinful Ajāmila uttered the name Nārāyaṇa, these four beautiful men immediately arrived and reassured him, saying, "Do not fear. Do not fear." We wish to know about them from Your Lordship. If you think we are able to understand them, kindly describe who they are.

PURPORT

The order carriers of Yamarāja, being very much aggrieved because of their defeat by the four Viṣṇudūtas, wanted to bring them before Yamarāja and, if possible, punish them. Otherwise they desired to commit suicide. Before pursuing either course, however, they wanted to know about the Viṣṇudūtas from Yamarāja, who is also omniscient.

TEXT 11

श्रीबादरायणिरुवाच
इति देवः स आपृष्टः प्रजासंयमनो यमः ।
प्रीतः स्वदूतान् प्रत्याह स्मरन् पादाम्बुजं हरेः ॥ ११ ॥

śrī-bādarāyaṇir uvāca
iti devaḥ sa āpṛṣṭaḥ
prajā-saṁyamano yamaḥ
prītaḥ sva-dūtān pratyāha
smaran pādāmbujaṁ hareḥ

śrī-bādarāyaṇiḥ uvāca—Śukadeva Gosvāmī said; *iti*—thus; *devaḥ*—the demigod; *saḥ*—he; *āpṛṣṭaḥ*—being questioned; *prajā-saṁyamanaḥ yamaḥ*—Lord Yamarāja, who controls the living entities; *prītaḥ*—being pleased; *sva-dūtān*—to his own servants; *pratyāha*—replied; *smaran*—remembering; *pāda-ambujam*—the lotus feet; *hareḥ*—of Hari, the Personality of Godhead.

TRANSLATION

Śrī Śukadeva Gosvāmī said: Thus having been questioned, Lord Yamarāja, the supreme controller of the living entities, was very pleased with his order carriers because of hearing from them the holy name of Nārāyaṇa. He remembered the lotus feet of the Lord and began to reply.

PURPORT

Śrīla Yamarāja, the supreme controller of the living entities in terms of their pious and impious activities, was very pleased with his servants because they had chanted the holy name of Nārāyaṇa in his dominion. Yamarāja has to deal with men who are all sinful and who can hardly understand Nārāyaṇa. Consequently when his order carriers uttered the name of Nārāyaṇa, he was extremely pleased, for he also is a Vaiṣṇava.

TEXT 12

यम उवाच
परो मदन्यो जगतस्तस्थुषश्च
ओतं प्रोतं पटवद्यत्र विश्वम् ।
यदंशतोऽस्य स्थितिजन्मनाशा
नस्योतवद् यस्य वशे च लोकः ॥ १२ ॥

yama uvāca
paro mad-anyo jagatas tasthuṣaś ca
otaṁ protaṁ paṭavad yatra viśvam
yad-aṁśato'sya sthiti-janma-nāśā
nasy otavad yasya vaśe ca lokaḥ

yamaḥ uvāca—Yamarāja replied; *paraḥ*—superior; *mat*—than me; *anyaḥ*—another; *jagataḥ*—of all moving things; *tasthuṣaḥ*—of nonmoving things; *ca*—and; *otam*—crosswise; *protam*—lengthwise; *paṭavat*—like a woven cloth; *yatra*—in whom; *viśvam*—the cosmic manifestation; *yat*—of whom; *aṁśataḥ*—from the partial expansions; *asya*—of this universe; *sthiti*—the maintenance; *janma*—the creation; *nāśāḥ*—the annihilation; *nasi*—in the nose; *ota-vat*—like the rope; *yasya*—of whom; *vaśe*—under the control; *ca*—and; *lokaḥ*—the whole creation.

TRANSLATION

Yamarāja said: My dear servants, you have accepted me as the Supreme, but factually I am not. Above me, and above all the other demigods, including Indra and Candra, is the one supreme master and controller. The partial manifestations of His personality are Brahmā, Viṣṇu and Śiva, who are in charge of the creation, maintenance and annihilation of this universe. He is like the two threads that form the length and breadth of a woven cloth. The entire world is controlled by Him just as a bull is controlled by a rope in its nose.

PURPORT

The order carriers of Yamarāja suspected that there was a ruler even above Yamarāja. To eradicate their doubts, Yamarāja immediately replied, "Yes, there is one supreme controller above everything." Yamarāja is in charge of some of the moving living entities, namely the human beings, but the animals, who also move, are not under his control. Only human beings have consciousness of right and wrong, and among them only those who perform sinful activities come under the control of Yamarāja. Therefore although Yamarāja is a controller, he is only a departmental controller of a few living entities. There are other demigods who control many other departments, but above them all is one supreme controller, Kṛṣṇa. *Īśvaraḥ paramaḥ kṛṣṇaḥ sac-cid-ānanda-vigrahaḥ:* the supreme controller is Kṛṣṇa. Others, who control their own departments in the affairs of the universe, are insignificant in comparison to Kṛṣṇa, the supreme controller. Kṛṣṇa says in *Bhagavad-gītā*

(7.7), *mattaḥ parataraṁ nānyat kiñcid asti dhanañjaya:* "My dear Dhanañjaya [Arjuna], no one is superior to Me." Therefore Yamarāja immediately cleared away the doubts of his assistants, the Yamadūtas, by confirming that there is a supreme controller above all others.

Śrīla Madhvācārya explains that the words *otaṁ protam* refer to the cause of all causes. The Supreme Lord is both vertical and horizontal to the cosmic manifestation. This is confirmed by the following verse from the *Skanda Purāṇa:*

yathā kanthā-paṭāḥ sūtra
otāḥ protāś ca sa sthitāḥ
evaṁ viṣṇāv idaṁ viśvam
otaṁ protaṁ ca saṁsthitam

Like the two threads, horizontal and vertical, of which a quilt is manufactured, Lord Viṣṇu is situated as the vertical and horizontal cause of the cosmic manifestation.

TEXT 13

यो नामभिर्वाचि जनं निजायां
बध्नाति तन्त्यामिव दामभिर्गाः ।
यस्मै बलिं त इमे नामकर्म-
निबन्धबद्धाश्चकिता वहन्ति ॥ १३ ॥

yo nāmabhir vāci janaṁ nijāyāṁ
badhnāti tantryām iva dāmabhir gāḥ
yasmai baliṁ ta ime nāma-karma-
nibandha-baddhāś cakitā vahanti

yaḥ—He who; *nāmabhiḥ*—by different names; *vāci*—to the Vedic language; *janam*—all people; *nijāyām*—which has emanated from Himself; *badhnāti*—binds; *tantryām*—to a rope; *iva*—like; *dāmabhiḥ*—by cords; *gāḥ*—bulls; *yasmai*—unto whom; *balim*—a small presentation of taxes; *te*—all of them; *ime*—these; *nāma-karma*—of names and different activities; *nibandha*—by the obligations; *baddhāḥ*—bound; *cakitāḥ*—being fearful; *vahanti*—carry.

TRANSLATION

Just as the driver of a bullock cart ties ropes through the nostrils of his bulls to control them, the Supreme Personality of Godhead binds all

men through the ropes of His words in the Vedas, which set forth the names and activities of the distinct orders of human society [brāhmaṇa, kṣatriya, vaiśya and śūdra]. In fear, the members of these orders all worship the Supreme Lord by offering Him presentations according to their respective activities.

PURPORT

In this material world, everyone is conditioned, regardless of who he is. One may be a human being, a demigod or an animal, tree or plant, but everything is controlled by the laws of nature, and behind this natural control is the Supreme Personality of Godhead. This is confirmed by *Bhagavad-gītā* (9.10), wherein Kṛṣṇa says, *mayādhyakṣeṇa prakṛtiḥ sūyate sa-carācaram:* "The material nature is working under My direction and producing all moving and nonmoving beings." Thus Kṛṣṇa is behind the natural machine, which works under His control.

Apart from other living entities, the living being in the human form of body is systematically controlled by the Vedic injunctions in terms of the divisions of *varṇa* and *āśrama.* A human being is expected to follow the rules and regulations of *varṇa* and *āśrama;* otherwise he cannot escape punishment by Yamarāja. The point is that every human being is expected to elevate himself to the position of a *brāhmaṇa,* the most intelligent man, and then one must transcend that position to become a Vaiṣṇava. This is the perfection of life. The *brāhmaṇa, kṣatriya, vaiśya* and *śūdra* can elevate themselves by worshiping the Lord according to their activities (*sve sve karmaṇy abhirataḥ saṁsiddhiṁ labhate naraḥ*). The divisions of *varṇa* and *āśrama* are necessary to insure the proper execution of duties and peaceful existence for everyone, but everyone is directed to worship the Supreme Lord, who is all-pervading (*yena sarvam idaṁ tatam*). The Supreme Lord exists vertically and horizontally (*otaṁ protam*), and therefore if one follows the Vedic injunctions by worshiping the Supreme Lord according to one's ability, his life will be perfect. As stated in *Śrīmad-Bhāgavatam* (1.2.13):

ataḥ pumbhir dvija-śreṣṭhā
varṇāśrama-vibhāgaśaḥ
svanuṣṭhitasya dharmasya
saṁsiddhir hari-toṣaṇam

"O best among the twice-born, it is therefore concluded that the highest perfection one can achieve, by discharging his prescribed duties [*dharma*] according to caste divisions and orders of life, is to please the Lord Hari." The *varṇāśrama* institution offers the perfect process for making one eligible to return home, back to Godhead, because the aim of every *varṇa* and *āśrama* is to please the Supreme Lord. One can please the Lord under the direction of a bona fide spiritual master, and if one does so his life is perfect. The Supreme Lord is worshipable, and everyone worships Him directly or indirectly. Those who worship Him directly get the results of liberation quickly, whereas the liberation of those who serve Him indirectly is delayed.

The words *nāmabhir vāci* are very important. In the *varṇāśrama* institution, there are different names—*brāhmaṇa, kṣatriya, vaiśya, śūdra, brahmacārī, gṛhastha, vānaprastha* and *sannyāsī.* The *vāk,* or Vedic injunctions, give directions for all these divisions. Everyone is expected to offer obeisances to the Supreme Lord and perform duties as indicated in the *Vedas.*

TEXTS 14–15

अहं महेन्द्रो निर्ऋतिः प्रचेताः
सोमोऽग्निरीशः पवनो विरिञ्चिः ।
आदित्यविश्वे वसवोऽथ साध्या
मरुद्गणा रुद्रगणाः ससिद्धाः ॥ १४ ॥
अन्ये च ये विश्वसृजोऽमरेशा
भृग्वादयोऽस्पृष्टरजस्तमस्काः ।
यस्येहितं न विदुः स्पृष्टमायाः
सत्त्वप्रधाना अपि किं ततोऽन्ये ॥ १५ ॥

ahaṁ mahendro nirṛtiḥ pracetāḥ
somo'gnir īśaḥ pavano viriñciḥ
āditya-viśve vasavo'tha sādhyā
marud-gaṇā rudra-gaṇāḥ sasiddhāḥ

anye ca ye viśva-sṛjo'mareśā
bhṛgv-ādayo'spṛṣṭa-rajas-tamaskāḥ
yasyehitaṁ na viduḥ spṛṣṭa-māyāḥ
sattva-pradhānā api kiṁ tato'nye

aham—I, Yamarāja; *mahendraḥ*—Indra, the King of heaven; *nirṛtiḥ*—Nirṛti; *pracetāḥ*—Varuṇa, the controller of water; *somaḥ*—the moon; *agniḥ*—fire; *īśaḥ*—Lord Śiva; *pavanaḥ*—the demigod of the air; *viriñciḥ*—Lord

Brahmā; *āditya*—the sun; *viśve*—Viśvāsu; *vasavaḥ*—the eight Vasus; *atha*—also; *sādhyāḥ*—the demigods; *marut-gaṇāḥ*—masters of the wind; *rudra-gaṇāḥ*—the expansions of Lord Śiva; *sa-siddhāḥ*—with the inhabitants of Siddhaloka; *anye*—others; *ca*—and; *ye*—who; *viśva-sṛjaḥ*—Marīci and the other creators of the universal affairs; *amara-īśāḥ*—the demigods like Bṛhaspati; *bhṛgu-ādayaḥ*—the great sages headed by Bhṛgu; *aspṛṣṭa*—who have not been contaminated; *rajaḥ-tamaskāḥ*—by the lower modes of material nature (*rajo-guṇa* and *tamo-guṇa*); *yasya*—of whom; *īhitam*—the activity; *na viduḥ*—do not know; *spṛṣṭa-māyāḥ*—who are illusioned by the illusory energy; *sattva-pradhānāḥ*—chiefly in the mode of goodness; *api*—although; *kim*—what to speak of; *tataḥ*—than them; *anye*—others.

TRANSLATION

I, Yamarāja; Indra, the King of heaven; Nirṛti; Varuṇa; Candra, the moon god; Agni; Lord Śiva; Pavana; Lord Brahmā; Sūrya, the sun-god; Viśvāsu; the eight Vasus; the Sādhyas; the Maruts; the Rudras; the Siddhas; and Marīci and the other great ṛṣis engaged in maintaining the departmental affairs of the universe, as well as the best of the demigods headed by Bṛhaspati, and the great sages headed by Bhṛgu are all certainly freed from the influence of the two base material modes of nature, namely passion and ignorance. Nevertheless, although we are in the mode of goodness, we cannot understand the activities of the Supreme Personality of Godhead. What, then, is to be said of others, who, under illusion, merely speculate to know God?

PURPORT

The men and other living entities within this cosmic manifestation are controlled by the three modes of nature. For the living entities controlled by the base qualities of nature, passion and ignorance, there is no possibility of understanding God. Even those in the mode of goodness, like the many demigods and great *ṛṣis* described in these verses, cannot understand the activities of the Supreme Personality of Godhead. As stated in *Bhagavad-gītā,* one who is situated in the devotional service of the Lord is transcendental to all the material qualities. Therefore the Lord personally says that no one can understand Him but the *bhaktas,* who are transcendental to all material qualities (*bhaktyā mām abhijānāti*). As stated by Bhīṣmadeva to Mahārāja Yudhiṣṭhira in *Śrīmad-Bhāgavatam* (1.9.16):

na hy asya karhicid rājan
pumān veda vidhitsitam
yad-vijijñāsayā yuktā
muhyanti kavayo'pi hi

"O King, no one can know the plan of the Lord [Śrī Kṛṣṇa]. Even though great philosophers inquire exhaustively, they are bewildered." No one, therefore, can understand God by speculative knowledge. Indeed, by speculation one will be bewildered (*muhyanti*). This is also confirmed by the Lord Himself in *Bhagavad-gītā* (7.3):

manuṣyāṇāṁ sahasreṣu
kaścid yatati siddhaye
yatatām api siddhānāṁ
kaścin māṁ vetti tattvataḥ

Among many thousands of men, one may endeavor for perfection, and even among the *siddhas,* those who have already become perfect, only one who adopts the process of *bhakti,* devotional service, can understand Kṛṣṇa.

TEXT 16

यं वै न गोभिर्मनसासुभिर्वा
हृदा गिरा वासुभृतो विचक्षते ।
आत्मानमन्तर्हृदि सन्तमात्मनां
चक्षुर्यथैवाकृतयस्ततः परम् ॥ १६ ॥

yaṁ vai na gobhir manasāsubhir vā
hṛdā girā vāsu-bhṛto vicakṣate
ātmānam antar-hṛdi santam ātmanāṁ
cakṣur yathaivākṛtayas tataḥ param

yam—whom; *vai*—indeed; *na*—not; *gobhiḥ*—by the senses; *manasā*—by the mind; *asubhiḥ*—by the life breath; *vā*—or; *hṛdā*—by thoughts; *girā*—by words; *vā*—or; *asu-bhṛtaḥ*—the living entities; *vicakṣate*—see or know; *ātmānam*—the Supersoul; *antaḥ-hṛdi*—within the core of the heart; *santam*—existing; *ātmanām*—of the living entities; *cakṣuḥ*—the eyes; *yathā*—just like; *eva*—indeed; *ākṛtayaḥ*—the different parts or limbs of the body; *tataḥ*—than them; *param*—higher.

TRANSLATION

As the different limbs of the body cannot see the eyes, the living entities cannot see the Supreme Lord, who is situated as the Supersoul in everyone's heart. Not by the senses, by the mind, by the life air, by thoughts within the heart, or by the vibration of words can the living entities ascertain the real situation of the Supreme Lord.

PURPORT

Although the different parts of the body do not have the power to see the eyes, the eyes direct the movements of the body's different parts. The legs move forward because the eyes see what is in front of them, and the hand touches because the eyes see touchable entities. Similarly, every living being acts according to the direction of the Supersoul, who is situated within the heart. As the Lord Himself confirms in *Bhagavad-gītā* (15.15), *sarvasya cāhaṁ hṛdi sanniviṣṭo mattaḥ smṛtir jñānam apohanaṁ ca:* "I am sitting in everyone's heart and giving directions for remembrance, knowledge and forgetfulness." Elsewhere in *Bhagavad-gītā* it is stated, *īśvaraḥ sarva-bhūtānāṁ hṛd-deśe 'rjuna tiṣṭhati:* "The Supreme Lord, as the Supersoul, is situated within the heart." The living entity cannot do anything without the sanction of the Supersoul. The Supersoul is acting at every moment, but the living entity cannot understand the form and activities of the Supersoul by manipulating his senses. The example of the eyes and the bodily limbs is very appropriate. If the limbs could see, they could walk forward without the help of the eyes, but that is impossible. Although one cannot see the Supersoul in one's heart through sensual activities, His direction is necessary.

TEXT 17

तस्यात्मतन्त्रस्य हरेरधीशितुः
परस्य मायाधिपतेर्महात्मनः ।
प्रायेण दूता इह वै मनोहरा-
श्चरन्ति तद्रूपगुणस्वभावाः ॥ १७ ॥

tasyātma-tantrasya harer adhīśituḥ
parasya māyādhipater mahātmanaḥ
prāyeṇa dūtā iha vai manoharāś
caranti tad-rūpa-guṇa-svabhāvāḥ

tasya—of Him; *ātma-tantrasya*—being self-sufficient, not dependent on any other person; *hareḥ*—the Supreme Personality of Godhead; *adhīśituḥ*—who is the master of everything; *parasya*—the Transcendence; *māyā-adhipateḥ*—the master of the illusory energy; *mahā-ātmanaḥ*—of the Supreme Soul; *prāyeṇa*—almost; *dūtāḥ*—the order carriers; *iha*—in this world; *vai*—indeed; *manoharāḥ*—pleasing in their dealings and bodily features; *caranti*—they move; *tat*—of Him; *rūpa*—possessing the bodily features; *guṇa*—the transcendental qualities; *svabhāvāḥ*—and nature.

TRANSLATION

The Supreme Personality of Godhead is self-sufficient and fully independent. He is the master of everyone and everything, including the illusory energy. He has His form, qualities and features; and similarly His order carriers, the Vaiṣṇavas, who are very beautiful, possess bodily features, transcendental qualities and a transcendental nature almost like His. They always wander within this world with full independence.

PURPORT

Yamarāja was describing the Supreme Personality of Godhead, the supreme controller, but the order carriers of Yamarāja were very eager to know about the Viṣṇudūtas, who had defeated them in their encounter with Ajāmila. Yamarāja therefore stated that the Viṣṇudūtas resemble the Supreme Personality of Godhead in their bodily features, transcendental qualities and nature. In other words, the Viṣṇudūtas, or Vaiṣṇavas, are almost as qualified as the Supreme Lord. Yamarāja informed the Yamadūtas that the Viṣṇudūtas are no less powerful than Lord Viṣṇu. Since Viṣṇu is above Yamarāja, the Viṣṇudūtas are above the Yamadūtas. Persons protected by the Viṣṇudūtas, therefore, cannot be touched by the Yamadūtas.

TEXT 18

भूतानि विष्णोः सुरपूजितानि
दुर्दर्शलिङ्गानि महाद्भुतानि ।
रक्षन्ति तद्भक्तिमतः परेभ्यो
मत्तश्च मर्त्यानथ सर्वतश्च ॥ १८ ॥

bhūtāni viṣṇoḥ sura-pūjitāni
durdarśa-liṅgāni mahādbhutāni

rakṣanti tad-bhaktimataḥ parebhyo
mattaś ca martyān atha sarvataś ca

bhūtāni—living entities or servants; *viṣṇoḥ*—of Lord Viṣṇu; *sura-pūjitāni*—who are worshiped by the demigods; *durdarśa-liṅgāni*—possessing forms not easily seen; *mahā-adbhutāni*—greatly wonderful; *rakṣanti*—they protect; *tat-bhakti-mataḥ*—the devotees of the Lord; *parebhyaḥ*—from others who are inimical; *mattaḥ*—from me (Yamarāja) and my order carriers; *ca*—and; *martyān*—the human beings; *atha*—thus; *sarvataḥ*—from everything; *ca*—and.

TRANSLATION

The order carriers of Lord Viṣṇu, who are worshiped even by the demigods, possess wonderful bodily features exactly like those of Viṣṇu and are very rarely seen. The Viṣṇudūtas protect the devotees of the Lord from the hands of enemies, from envious persons and even from my jurisdiction, as well as from natural disturbances.

PURPORT

Yamarāja has specifically described the qualities of the Viṣṇudūtas to convince his own servants not to be envious of them. Yamarāja warned the Yamadūtas that the Viṣṇudūtas are worshiped with respectful obeisances by the demigods and are always very alert to protect the devotees of the Lord from the hands of enemies, from natural disturbances and from all dangerous conditions in this material world. Sometimes the members of the Kṛṣṇa Consciousness Society are afraid of the impending danger of world war and ask what would happen to them if a war should occur. In all kinds of danger, they should be confident of their protection by the Viṣṇudūtas or the Supreme Personality of Godhead, as confirmed in *Bhagavad-gītā* (*kaunteya pratijānīhi na me bhaktaḥ praṇaśyati*). Material danger is not meant for devotees. This is also confirmed in *Śrīmad-Bhāgavatam. Padaṁ padaṁ yad vipadāṁ na teṣām:* in this material world there are dangers at every step, but they are not meant for devotees who have fully surrendered unto the lotus feet of the Lord. The pure devotees of Lord Viṣṇu may rest assured of the Lord's protection, and as long as they are in this material world they should fully engage in devotional service by preaching the cult of Śrī Caitanya Mahāprabhu and Lord Kṛṣṇa, namely the Hare Kṛṣṇa movement of Kṛṣṇa consciousness.

TEXT 19

धर्मं तु साक्षाद्भगवत्प्रणीतं
न वै विदुर्ऋषयो नापि देवाः ।
न सिद्धमुख्या असुरा मनुष्याः
कुतो नु विद्याधरचारणादयः ॥ १९ ॥

dharmaṁ tu sākṣād bhagavat-praṇītaṁ
na vai vidur ṛṣayo nāpi devāḥ
na siddha-mukhyā asurā manuṣyāḥ
kuto nu vidyādhara-cāraṇādayaḥ

dharmam—real religious principles, or bona fide laws of religion; *tu*—but; *sākṣāt*—directly; *bhagavat*—by the Supreme Personality of Godhead; *praṇītam*—enacted; *na*—not; *vai*—indeed; *viduḥ*—they know; *ṛṣayaḥ*—the great *ṛṣis* such as Bhṛgu; *na*—not; *api*—also; *devāḥ*—the demigods; *na*—nor; *siddha-mukhyāḥ*—the chief leaders of Siddhaloka; *asurāḥ*—the demons; *manuṣyāḥ*—the inhabitants of Bhūrloka, the human beings; *kutaḥ*—where; *nu*—indeed; *vidyādhara*—the lesser demigods known as Vidyādharas; *cāraṇa*—the residents of the planets where people are by nature great musicians and singers; *ādayaḥ*—and so on.

TRANSLATION

Real religious principles are enacted by the Supreme Personality of Godhead. Although fully situated in the mode of goodness, even the great ṛṣis who occupy the topmost planets cannot ascertain the real religious principles, nor can the demigods or the leaders of Siddhaloka, to say nothing of the asuras, ordinary human beings, Vidyādharas and Cāraṇas.

PURPORT

When challenged by the Viṣṇudūtas to describe the principles of religion, the Yamadūtas said, *veda-praṇihito dharmaḥ:* the religious principles are the principles enacted in the Vedic literature. They did not know, however, that the Vedic literature contains ritualistic ceremonies that are not transcendental, but are meant to keep peace and order among materialistic persons in the material world. Real religious principles are *nistraiguṇya,* above the three modes of material nature, or transcendental. The Yamadūtas did not know these transcendental religious principles, and therefore when prevented from arresting Ajāmila they were surprised. Materialistic persons who attach all their faith to the Vedic rituals are described in *Bhagavad-gītā* (2.42), wherein Kṛṣṇa says, *veda-vāda-ratāḥ pārtha nānyad astīti vādinaḥ:* the supposed followers of the *Vedas* say that there is nothing beyond the Vedic ceremonies. Indeed, there is a group of men in India who are very fond of the Vedic rituals, not understanding the meaning of these rituals, which are intended to elevate one gradually to the transcendental platform of knowing Kṛṣṇa (*vedaiś ca sarvair aham eva vedyaḥ*). Those who do not know this principle but who simply attach their faith to the Vedic rituals are called *veda-vāda-ratāḥ.*

Herein it is stated that the real religious principle is that which is given by the Supreme Personality of Godhead. That principle is stated in *Bhagavad-gītā. Sarva-dharmān parityajya mām ekaṁ śaraṇaṁ vraja:* one should give up all other duties and surrender unto the lotus feet of Kṛṣṇa. That is the real religious principle everyone should follow. Even though one follows Vedic scriptures, one may not know this transcendental principle, for it is not known to everyone. To say nothing of human beings, even the demigods in the upper planetary systems are unaware of it. This transcendental religious principle must be understood from the Supreme Personality of Godhead directly or from His special representative, as stated in the next verses.

TEXTS 20–21

स्वयम्भूर्नारदः शम्भुः कुमारः कपिलो मनुः ।
प्रह्लादो जनको भीष्मो बलिर्वैयासकिर्वयम् ॥ २० ॥
द्वादशैते विजानीमो धर्मं भागवतं भटाः ।
गुह्यं विशुद्धं दुर्बोधं यं ज्ञात्वामृतमश्नुते ॥ २१ ॥

svayambhūr nāradaḥ śambhuḥ
kumāraḥ kapilo manuḥ
prahlādo janako bhīṣmo
balir vaiyāsakir vayam

dvādaśaite vijānīmo
dharmaṁ bhāgavataṁ bhaṭāḥ
guhyaṁ viśuddhaṁ durbodhaṁ
yaṁ jñātvāmṛtam aśnute

svayambhūḥ—Lord Brahmā; *nāradaḥ*—the great saint Nārada; *śambhuḥ*—Lord Śiva; *kumāraḥ*—the four Kumāras; *kapilaḥ*—Lord Kapila; *manuḥ*—

Svāyambhuva Manu; *prahlādaḥ*—Prahlāda Mahārāja; *janakaḥ*—Janaka Mahārāja; *bhīṣmaḥ*—Grandfather Bhīṣma; *baliḥ*—Bali Mahārāja; *vaiyāsakiḥ* —Śukadeva, the son of Vyāsadeva; *vayam*—we; *dvādaśa*—twelve; *ete*—these; *vijānīmaḥ*—know; *dharmam*—real religious principles; *bhāgavatam* —which teach a person how to love the Supreme Personality of Godhead; *bhaṭāḥ*—O my dear servants; *guhyam*—very confidential; *viśuddham*—transcendental, not contaminated by the material modes of nature; *durbodham*—not easily understood; *yam*—which; *jñātvā*—understanding; *amṛtam*—eternal life; *aśnute*—he enjoys.

TRANSLATION

Lord Brahmā, Bhagavān Nārada, Lord Śiva, the four Kumāras, Lord Kapila [the son of Devahūti], Svāyambhuva Manu, Prahlāda Mahārāja, Janaka Mahārāja, Grandfather Bhīṣma, Bali Mahārāja, Śukadeva Gosvāmī and I myself know the real religious principle. My dear servants, this transcendental religious principle, which is known as bhāgavata-dharma, or surrender unto the Supreme Lord and love for Him, is uncontaminated by the material modes of nature. It is very confidential and difficult for ordinary human beings to understand, but if by chance one fortunately understands it, he is immediately liberated, and thus he returns home, back to Godhead.

PURPORT

In *Bhagavad-gītā* Lord Kṛṣṇa refers to *bhāgavata-dharma* as the most confidential religious principle (*sarva-guhyatamam, guhyād guhyataram*). Kṛṣṇa says to Arjuna, "Because you are My very dear friend, I am explaining to you the most confidential religion." *Sarva-dharmān parityajya mām ekaṁ śaraṇaṁ vraja:* "Give up all other duties and surrender unto Me." One may ask, "If this principle is very rarely understood, what is the use of it?" In answer, Yamarāja states herein that this religious principle is understandable if one follows the *paramparā* system of Lord Brahmā, Lord Śiva, the four Kumāras and the other standard authorities. There are four lines of disciplic succession: one from Lord Brahmā, one from Lord Śiva, one from Lakṣmī, the goddess of fortune, and one from the Kumāras. The disciplic succession from Lord Brahmā is called the Brahma -sampradāya, the succession from Lord Śiva (Śambhu) is called the Rudra- sampradāya, the one from the goddess of fortune, Lakṣmījī, is called the Śrī- sampradāya, and the one from the Kumāras is called the Kumāra sampradāya. One must take shelter of one of these four *sampradāyas* in order to understand the most confidential religious system. In the *Padma Purāṇa* it is said, *sampradāya-vihīnā ye mantrās te niṣphalā matāḥ:* if one does not follow the four recognized disciplic successions, his *mantra* or initiation is useless. In the present day there are many *apasampradāyas,* or *sampradāyas* which are not bona fide, which have no link to authorities like Lord Brahmā, Lord Śiva, the Kumāras or Lakṣmī. People are misguided by such *sampradāyas.* The *śāstras* say that being initiated in such a *sampradāya* is a useless waste of time, for it will never enable one to understand the real religious principles.

TEXT 22

एतावानेव लोकेऽस्मिन् पुंसां धर्मः परः स्मृतः ।
भक्तियोगो भगवति तन्नामग्रहणादिभिः ॥ २२ ॥

etāvān eva loke'smin
puṁsāṁ dharmaḥ paraḥ smṛtaḥ
bhakti-yogo bhagavati
tan-nāma-grahaṇādibhiḥ

etāvān—this much; *eva*—indeed; *loke asmin*—in this material world; *puṁsām*—of the living entities; *dharmaḥ*—the religious principles; *paraḥ*—transcendental; *smṛtaḥ*—recognized; *bhakti-yogaḥ*—*bhakti-yoga,* or devotional service; *bhagavati*—to the Supreme Personality of Godhead (not to the demigods); *tat*—His; *nāma*—of the holy name; *grahaṇa-ādibhiḥ*—beginning with chanting.

TRANSLATION

Devotional service, beginning with the chanting of the holy name of the Lord, is the ultimate religious principle for the living entity in human society.

PURPORT

As stated in the previous verse, *dharmaṁ bhāgavatam,* real religious principles, are *bhāgavata-dharma,* the principles described in *Śrīmad-Bhāgavatam* itself or in *Bhagavad-gītā,* the preliminary study of the *Bhāgavatam.* What are these principles? The *Bhāgavatam* says, *dharmaḥ projjhita-kaitavo'tra :* in *Śrīmad-Bhāgavatam* there are no cheating religious systems. Everything in the *Bhāgavatam* is directly connected with the Supreme Personality of Godhead. The *Bhāgavatam* further says, *sa vai puṁsāṁ paro dharmo yato bhaktir adhokṣaje:* the supreme religion is that which teaches its followers how to love the Supreme Personality of Godhead, who is beyond the reach of experimental knowledge. Such a religious system begins with *tan-nāma-grahaṇa,* chanting of the holy name of the Lord (*śravaṇaṁ kīrtanaṁ viṣṇoḥ smaraṇaṁ pāda-sevanam*). After chanting the holy name of the Lord and dancing in ecstasy, one gradually sees the form of the Lord, the pastimes of the Lord and the transcendental qualities of the Lord. This way one fully understands the situation of the Personality of Godhead. One can come to this understanding of the Lord, how He descends into the material world, how He takes His births and what activities He performs, but one can know this only by executing devotional service. As stated in *Bhagavad-gītā, bhaktyā mām abhijānāti:* simply by devotional service one can understand everything about the Supreme Lord. If one fortunately understands the Supreme Lord in this way, the result is *tyaktvā dehaṁ punar janma naiti:* after giving up his material body, he no longer has to take birth in this material world. Instead, he returns home, back to Godhead. That is the ultimate perfection. Therefore Kṛṣṇa says in *Bhagavad-gītā* (8.15):

mām upetya punar janma
duḥkhālayam aśāśvatam
nāpnuvanti mahātmānaḥ
saṁsiddhiṁ paramāṁ gatāḥ

"After attaining Me, the great souls, who are *yogīs* in devotion, never return to this temporary world, which is full of miseries, because they have attained the highest perfection."

TEXT 23

नामोच्चारणमाहात्म्यं हरेः पश्यत पुत्रकाः ।
अजामिलोऽपि येनैव मृत्युपाशादमुच्यत ॥ २३ ॥

nāmoccāraṇa-māhātmyaṁ
hareḥ paśyata putrakāḥ
ajāmilo'pi yenaiva
mṛtyu-pāśād amucyata

nāma—of the holy name; *uccāraṇa*—of the pronouncing; *māhātmyam*—the exalted position; *hareḥ*—of the Supreme Lord; *paśyata*—just see; *putrakāḥ*—O my dear servants, who are like my sons; *ajāmilaḥ api*—even Ajāmila (who was considered greatly sinful); *yena*—by the chanting of which; *eva*—certainly; *mṛtyu-pāśāt*—from the ropes of death; *amucyata*—was delivered.

TRANSLATION

My dear servants, who are as good as my sons, just see how glorious is the chanting of the holy name of the Lord. The greatly sinful Ajāmila chanted only to call his son, not knowing that he was chanting the Lord's holy name. Nevertheless, by chanting the holy name of the Lord, he remembered Nārāyaṇa, and thus he was immediately saved from the ropes of death.

PURPORT

There is no need to conduct research into the significance of the chanting of the Hare Kṛṣṇa *mantra.* The history of Ajāmila is sufficient proof of the power of the Lord's holy name and the exalted position of a person who chants the holy name incessantly. Therefore Śrī Caitanya Mahāprabhu advised:

harer nāma harer nāma
harer nāmaiva kevalam
kalau nāsty eva nāsty eva
nāsty eva gatir anyathā

In this age of Kali, no one can perform all the ritualistic ceremonies for becoming liberated; that is extremely difficult. Therefore all the *śāstras* and all the *ācāryas* have recommended that in this age one chant the holy name.

TEXT 24

एतावतालमघनिर्हरणाय पुंसां
सङ्कीर्तनं भगवतो गुणकर्मनाम्नाम् ।
विक्रुश्य पुत्रमघवान् यदजामिलोऽपि
नारायणेति म्रियमाण इयाय मुक्तिम् ॥ २४ ॥

etāvatālam agha-nirharaṇāya puṁsāṁ
saṅkīrtanaṁ bhagavato guṇa-karma-nāmnām
vikruśya putram aghavān yad ajāmilo'pi
nārāyaṇeti mriyamāṇa iyāya muktim

etāvatā—with this much; *alam*—sufficient; *agha-nirharaṇāya*—for taking away the reactions of sinful activities; *puṁsām*—of human beings;

saṅkīrtanam—the congregational chanting; *bhagavataḥ*—of the Supreme Personality of Godhead; *guṇa*—of the transcendental qualities; *karma-nāmnām*—and of His names according to His activities and pastimes; *vikruśya*—crying to without offense; *putram*—his son; *aghavān*—the sinful; *yat*—since; *ajāmilaḥ api*—even Ajāmila; *nārāyaṇa*—the Lord's name, Nārāyaṇa; *iti*—thus; *mriyamāṇaḥ*—dying; *iyāya*—achieved; *muktim*—liberation.

TRANSLATION

Therefore it should be understood that one is easily relieved from all sinful reactions by chanting the holy name of the Lord and chanting of His qualities and activities. This is the only process recommended for relief from sinful reactions. Even if one chants the holy name of the Lord with improper pronunciation, he will achieve relief from material bondage if he chants without offenses. Ajāmila, for example, was extremely sinful, but while dying he merely chanted the holy name, and although calling his son, he achieved complete liberation because he remembered the name of Nārāyaṇa.

PURPORT

In the assembly of Raghunātha dāsa Gosvāmī's father, Haridāsa Ṭhākura confirmed that simply by chanting the holy name of the Lord one is liberated, even if he does not chant completely inoffensively. *Smārta-brāhmaṇas* and Māyāvādīs do not believe that one can achieve liberation in this way, but the truth of Haridāsa Ṭhākura's statement is supported by many quotations from *Śrīmad-Bhāgavatam.*

In his commentary on this verse, for example, Śrīdhara Svāmī gives the following quotation:

sāyaṁ prātar gṛṇan bhaktyā
duḥkha-grāmād vimucyate

"If one always chants the holy name of the Lord with great devotion in the evening and in the morning, one can become free from all material miseries." Another quotation confirms that one can achieve liberation if one hears the holy name of the Lord constantly, every day with great respect (*anudinam idam ādareṇa śṛṇvan*). Another quotation says:

śravaṇaṁ kīrtanaṁ dhyānaṁ
harer adbhuta-karmaṇaḥ

janma-karma-guṇānāṁ ca
tad-arthe'khila-ceṣṭitam

"One should always chant and hear about the extraordinarily wonderful activities of the Lord, one should meditate upon these activities, and one should endeavor to please the Lord." (*Bhāg.* 11.3.27)

Śrīdhara Svāmī also quotes from the *Purāṇas, pāpa-kṣayaś ca bhavati smaratāṁ tam ahar-niśam:* "One can become free from all sinful reactions simply by remembering the lotus feet of the Lord day and night [*ahar-niśam*]." Furthermore, he quotes from *Bhāgavatam* (6.3.31):

tasmāt saṅkīrtanaṁ viṣṇor
jagan-maṅgalam aṁhasām
mahatām api kauravya
viddhy aikāntika-niṣkṛtam

All these quotations prove that one who constantly engages in chanting and hearing of the holy activities, name, fame and form of the Lord is liberated. As stated wonderfully in this verse, *etāvatālam agha-nirharaṇāya puṁsām:* simply by uttering the name of the Lord, one is freed from all sinful reactions.

The word *alam,* which is used in this verse, indicates that simply uttering the holy name of the Lord is sufficient. This word is used with different imports. As stated in the *Amara-kośa,* the most authorized dictionary in the Sanskrit language, *alaṁ bhūṣaṇa-paryāpti-śakti-vāraṇa-vācakam:* the word *alam* is used to mean "ornament," "sufficiency," "power" and "restraint." Here the word *alam* is used to indicate that there is no need of any other process, for the chanting of the holy name of the Lord is sufficient. Even if one chants imperfectly, one becomes free from all sinful reactions by chanting.

This power of chanting the holy name was proved by the liberation of Ajāmila. When Ajāmila chanted the holy name of Nārāyaṇa, he did not precisely remember the Supreme Lord; instead, he remembered his own son. At the time of death, Ajāmila certainly was not very clean; indeed, he was famous as a great sinner. Furthermore, one's physiological condition is completely disturbed at the time of death, and in such an awkward condition it would certainly have been very difficult for Ajāmila to have chanted clearly. Nevertheless, Ajāmila achieved liberation simply by chanting the holy name of the Lord. Therefore, what is to be said of those who are not sinful like Ajāmila? It is to be concluded that with a strong vow one should chant the holy name of the Lord—Hare Kṛṣṇa, Hare Kṛṣṇa, Kṛṣṇa Kṛṣṇa, Hare Hare/ Hare

Rāma, Hare Rāma, Rāma Rāma, Hare Hare—for thus one will certainly be delivered from the clutches of *māyā* by the grace of Kṛṣṇa.

The chanting of the Hare Kṛṣṇa *mantra* is recommended even for persons who commit offenses, because if they continue chanting they will gradually chant offenselessly. By chanting the Hare Kṛṣṇa *mantra* without offenses, one increases his love for Kṛṣṇa. As stated by Śrī Caitanya Mahāprabhu, *premā pum-artho mahān:* one's main concern should be to increase one's attachment to the Supreme Personality of Godhead and to increase one's love for Him.

In this regard Śrīla Viśvanātha Cakravartī Ṭhākura quotes the following verse from *Śrīmad-Bhāgavatam* (11.19.24):

evaṁ dharmair manuṣyāṇām
uddhavātmani vedinām
mayi sañjāyate bhaktiḥ
ko'nyo'rtho'syāvaśiṣyate

"My dear Uddhava, the supreme religious system for human society is that by which one can awaken his dormant love for Me." Commenting on this verse, Śrīla Viśvanātha Cakravartī Ṭhākura describes the word *bhakti* by saying *premaivoktaḥ. Kaḥ anyaḥ arthaḥ asya:* in the presence of *bhakti,* what is the necessity of liberation?

Śrīla Viśvanātha Cakravartī Ṭhākura also quotes this verse from the *Padma Purāṇa:*

nāmāparādha-yuktānāṁ
nāmāny eva haranty agham
aviśrānti-prayuktāni
tāny evārtha-karāṇi ca

Even if in the beginning one chants the Hare Kṛṣṇa *mantra* with offenses, one will become free from such offenses by chanting again and again. *Pāpa-kṣayaś ca bhavati smaratāṁ tam ahar-niśam:* one becomes free from all sinful reactions if one chants day and night, following the recommendation of Śrī Caitanya Mahāprabhu. It was Śrī Caitanya Mahāprabhu who quoted the following verse:

harer nāma harer nāma
harer nāmaiva kevalam
kalau nāsty eva nāsty eva
nāsty eva gatir anyathā

"In this age of quarrel and hypocrisy the only means of deliverance is chanting the holy name of the Lord. There is no other way. There is no other way. There is no other way." If the members of the Kṛṣṇa consciousness movement strictly follow this recommendation of Śrī Caitanya Mahāprabhu, their position will always be secure.

TEXT 25

प्रायेण वेद तदिदं न महाजनोऽयं
देव्या विमोहितमतिर्बत माययालम् ।
त्रय्यां जडीकृतमतिर्मधुपुष्पितायां
वैतानिके महति कर्मणि युज्यमानः ॥ २५ ॥

prāyeṇa veda tad idaṁ na mahājano'yaṁ
devyā vimohita-matir bata māyayālam
trayyāṁ jaḍī-kṛta-matir madhu-puṣpitāyāṁ
vaitānike mahati karmaṇi yujyamānaḥ

prāyeṇa—almost always; *veda*—know; *tat*—that; *idam*—this; *na*—not; *mahājanaḥ*—great personalities besides Svayambhū, Śambhu and the other ten; *ayam*—this; *devyā*—by the energy of the Supreme Personality of Godhead; *vimohita-matiḥ*—whose intelligence is bewildered; *bata*—indeed; *māyayā*—by the illusory energy; *alam*—greatly; *trayyām*—in the three *Vedas; jaḍī-kṛta-matiḥ*—whose intelligence has been dulled; *madhu-puṣpitāyām*—in the flowery Vedic language describing the results of ritualistic performances; *vaitānike*—in the performances mentioned in the *Vedas; mahati*—very great; *karmaṇi*—fruitive activities; *yujyamānaḥ*—being engaged.

TRANSLATION

Because they are bewildered by the illusory energy of the Supreme Personality of Godhead, Yājñavalkya and Jaimini and other compilers of the religious scriptures cannot know the secret, confidential religious system of the twelve mahājanas. They cannot understand the transcendental value of performing devotional service or chanting the Hare Kṛṣṇa mantra. Because their minds are attracted to the ritualistic ceremonies mentioned in the Vedas—especially the Yajur Veda, Sāma Veda and Ṛg Veda—their intelligence has become dull. Thus they are busy collecting the ingredients for ritualistic ceremonies that yield only

temporary benefits, such as elevation to Svargaloka for material happiness. They are not attracted to the saṅkīrtana movement; instead, they are interested in dharma, artha, kāma and mokṣa.

PURPORT

Since one may easily achieve the highest success by chanting the holy name of the Lord, one may ask why there are so many Vedic ritualistic ceremonies and why people are attracted to them. This verse answers that question. As stated in *Bhagavad-gītā* (15.15), *vedaiś ca sarvair aham eva vedyaḥ:* the real purpose of studying the *Vedas* is to approach the lotus feet of Lord Kṛṣṇa. Unfortunately, unintelligent people bewildered by the grandeur of Vedic *yajñas* want to see gorgeous sacrifices performed. They want Vedic *mantras* chanted and huge amounts of money spent for such ceremonies. Sometimes we have to observe the Vedic ritualistic ceremonies to please such unintelligent men. Recently, when we established a large Kṛṣṇa-Balarāma temple in Vṛndāvana, we were obliged to have Vedic ceremonies enacted by *brāhmaṇas* because the inhabitants of Vṛndāvana, especially the *smārta-brāhmaṇas,* would not accept Europeans and Americans as bona fide *brāhmaṇas.* Thus we had to engage *brāhmaṇas* to perform costly *yajñas.* In spite of these *yajñas,* the members of our Society performed *saṅkīrtana* loudly with *mṛdaṅgas,* and I considered the *saṅkīrtana* more important than the Vedic ritualistic ceremonies. Both the ceremonies and the *saṅkīrtana* were going on simultaneously. The ceremonies were meant for persons interested in Vedic rituals for elevation to heavenly planets (*jaḍī-kṛta-matir madhu-puṣpitāyām*), whereas the *saṅkīrtana* was meant for pure devotees interested in pleasing the Supreme Personality of Godhead. We would simply have performed *saṅkīrtana,* but then the inhabitants of Vṛndāvana would not have taken the installation ceremony seriously. As explained here, the Vedic performances are meant for those whose intelligence has been dulled by the flowery language of the *Vedas,* which describe fruitive activities intended to elevate one to the higher planets.

Especially in this age of Kali, *saṅkīrtana* alone is sufficient. If the members of our temples in the different parts of the world simply continue *saṅkīrtana* before the Deity, especially before Śrī Caitanya Mahāprabhu, they will remain perfect. There is no need of any other performances. Nevertheless, to keep oneself clean in habits and mind, Deity worship and other regulative principles are required. Śrīla Jīva Gosvāmī says that although *saṅkīrtana* is sufficient for the perfection of life, the *arcanā,* or worship of the Deity in the temple, must continue in order that the devotees may stay clean and pure. Śrīla Bhaktisiddhānta Sarasvatī Ṭhākura therefore recommended that one follow both processes simultaneously. We strictly follow his principle of performing Deity worship and *saṅkīrtana* along parallel lines. This we should continue.

TEXT 26

एवं विमृश्य सुधियो भगवत्यनन्ते
सर्वात्मना विदधते खलु भावयोगम् ।
ते मे न दण्डमर्हन्त्यथ यद्यमीषां
स्यात् पातकं तदपि हन्त्युरुगायवादः ॥ २६ ॥

evaṁ vimṛśya sudhiyo bhagavaty anante
sarvātmanā vidadhate khalu bhāva-yogam
te me na daṇḍam arhanty atha yady amīṣāṁ
syāt pātakaṁ tad api hanty urugāya-vādaḥ

evam—thus; *vimṛśya*—considering; *su-dhiyaḥ*—those whose intelligence is sharp; *bhagavati*—unto the Supreme Personality of Godhead; *anante*—the unlimited; *sarva-ātmanā*—with all their heart and soul; *vidadhate*—take to; *khalu*—indeed; *bhāva-yogam*—the process of devotional service; *te*—such persons; *me*—my; *na*—not; *daṇḍam*—punishment; *arhanti*—deserve; *atha*—therefore; *yadi*—if; *amīṣām*—of them; *syāt*—there is; *pātakam*—some sinful activity; *tat*—that; *api*—also; *hanti*—destroys; *urugāya-vādaḥ*—the chanting of the holy name of the Supreme Lord.

TRANSLATION

Considering all these points, therefore, intelligent men decide to solve all problems by adopting the devotional service of chanting the holy name of the Lord, who is situated in everyone's heart and who is a mine of all auspicious qualities. Such persons are not within my jurisdiction for punishment. Generally they never commit sinful activities, but even if by mistake or because of bewilderment or illusion they sometimes commit sinful acts, they are protected from sinful reactions because they always chant the Hare Kṛṣṇa mantra.

PURPORT

In this regard Śrīla Viśvanātha Cakravartī Ṭhākura quotes the following verse from the prayers of Lord Brahmā (*Bhāg.* 10.14.29):

athāpi te deva padāmbuja-dvaya-
prasāda-leśānugṛhīta eva hi
jānāti tattvaṁ bhagavan-mahimno
na cānya eko'pi ciraṁ vicinvan

The purport is that even though one is a very learned scholar of the Vedic *śāstras,* he may be completely unaware of the existence of the Supreme Personality of Godhead and His name, fame, qualities and so forth, whereas one who is not a great scholar can understand the position of the Supreme Personality of Godhead if he somehow or other becomes a pure devotee of the Lord by engaging in devotional service. Therefore this verse spoken by Yamarāja says, *evaṁ vimṛśya sudhiyo bhagavati:* those who engage in the loving service of the Lord become *sudhiyaḥ,* intelligent, but this is not so of a Vedic scholar who does not understand Kṛṣṇa's name, fame and qualities. A pure devotee is one whose intelligence is clear; he is truly thoughtful because he engages in the service of the Lord—not as a matter of show, but with love, with his mind, words and body. Nondevotees may make a show of religion, but it is not very effective because although they ostentatiously attend a temple or church, they are thinking of something else. Such persons are neglecting their religious duty and are punishable by Yamarāja. But a devotee who commits sinful acts, which he may do unwillingly or accidentally because of his former habits, is excused. That is the value of the *saṅkīrtana* movement.

TEXT 27

ते देवसिद्धपरिगीतपवित्रगाथा
ये साधवः समदृशो भगवत्प्रपन्नाः ।
तान् नोपसीदत हरेर्गदयाभिगुप्तान्
नैषां वयं न च वयः प्रभवाम दण्डे ॥ २७ ॥

te deva-siddha-parigīta-pavitra-gāthā
ye sādhavaḥ samadṛśo bhagavat-prapannāḥ
tān nopasīdata harer gadayābhiguptān
naiṣāṁ vayaṁ na ca vayaḥ prabhavāma daṇḍe

te—they; *deva*—by the demigods; *siddha*—and the inhabitants of Siddhaloka; *parigīta*—sung; *pavitra-gāthāḥ*—whose pure narrations; *ye*—who; *sādhavaḥ*—devotees; *samadṛśaḥ*—who see everyone equally; *bhagavat-prapannāḥ*—being surrendered to the Supreme Personality of

Godhead; *tān*—them; *na*—not; *upasīdata*—should go near; *hareḥ*—of the Supreme Personality of Godhead; *gadayā*—by the club; *abhiguptān*—being fully protected; *na*—not; *eṣām*—of these; *vayam*—we; *na ca*—and also not; *vayaḥ*—unlimited time; *prabhavāma*—are competent; *daṇḍe*—in punishing.

TRANSLATION

My dear servants, please do not approach such devotees, for they have fully surrendered to the lotus feet of the Supreme Personality of Godhead. They are equal to everyone, and their narrations are sung by the demigods and the inhabitants of Siddhaloka. Please do not even go near them. They are always protected by the club of the Supreme Personality of Godhead, and therefore Lord Brahmā and I and even the time factor are not competent to chastise them.

PURPORT

In effect, Yamarāja warned his servants, "My dear servants, despite what you may have done previously to disturb the devotees, henceforward you should stop. The actions of devotees who have surrendered unto the lotus feet of the Lord and who constantly chant the holy name of the Lord are praised by the demigods and the residents of Siddhaloka. Those devotees are so respectable and exalted that Lord Viṣṇu personally protects them with the club in His hand. Therefore, regardless of what you have done this time, henceforward you should not approach such devotees; otherwise you will be killed by the club of Lord Viṣṇu. This is my warning. Lord Viṣṇu has a club and *cakra* to punish nondevotees. Do not risk punishment by attempting to disturb the devotees. Not to speak of you, if even Lord Brahmā or I were to punish them, Lord Viṣṇu would punish us. Therefore do not disturb the devotees any further."

TEXT 28

तानानयध्वमसतो विमुखान् मुकुन्द-
पादारविन्दमकरन्दरसादजस्रम् ।
निष्किञ्चनैः परमहंसकुलैरसङ्गै-
र्जुष्टाद् गृहे निरयवर्त्मनि बद्धतृष्णान्॥ २८॥

tān ānayadhvam asato vimukhān mukunda-
pādāravinda-makaranda-rasād ajasram
niṣkiñcanaiḥ paramahaṁsa-kulair asaṅgair
juṣṭād gṛhe niraya-vartmani baddha-tṛṣṇān

tān—them; *ānayadhvam*—bring before me; *asataḥ*—nondevotees (those who have not taken to Kṛṣṇa consciousness); *vimukhān*—who have turned against; *mukunda*—of Mukunda, the Supreme Personality of Godhead; *pāda-aravinda*—of the lotus feet; *makaranda*—of the honey; *rasāt*—the taste; *ajasram*—continuously; *niṣkiñcanaiḥ*—by persons completely free from material attachment; *paramahaṁsa-kulaiḥ*—by the *paramahaṁsas,* the most exalted personalities; *asaṅgaiḥ*—who have no material attachment; *juṣṭāt*—which is enjoyed; *gṛhe*—to household life; *niraya-vartmani*—the path leading to hell; *baddha-tṛṣṇān*—whose desires are bound.

TRANSLATION

Paramahaṁsas are exalted persons who have no taste for material enjoyment and who drink the honey of the Lord's lotus feet. My dear servants, bring to me for punishment only persons who are averse to the taste of that honey, who do not associate with paramahaṁsas and who are attached to family life and worldly enjoyment, which form the path to hell.

PURPORT

After warning the Yamadūtas not to approach the devotees, Yamarāja now indicates who is to be brought before him. He specifically advises the Yamadūtas to bring him the materialistic persons who are attached to household life merely for sex. As stated in *Śrīmad-Bhāgavatam, yan maithunādi-gṛhamedhi-sukhaṁ hi tuccham:* people are attached to household life for sex only. They are always harassed in many ways by their material engagements, and their only happiness is that after working very hard all day, at night they sleep and indulge in sex. *Nidrayā hriyate naktaṁ vyavāyena ca vā vayaḥ:* at night, materialistic householders sleep or indulge in sex life. *Divā cārthehayā rajan kuṭumba-bharaṇena vā:* during the day they are busy trying to find out where money is, and if they get money they spend it to maintain their families. Yamarāja specifically advises his servants to bring these persons to him for punishment and not to bring the devotees, who always lick the honey at the lotus feet of the Lord, who are equal to everyone, and who try to preach Kṛṣṇa consciousness because of sympathy for all living entities. Devotees are not liable to punishment by Yamarāja, but persons who have no information of Kṛṣṇa consciousness cannot be protected by their material life of so-called family enjoyment. *Śrīmad-Bhāgavatam* says (2.1.4):

dehāpatya-kalatrādiṣv
ātma-sainyeṣv asatsv api
teṣāṁ pramatto nidhanaṁ
paśyann api na paśyati

Such persons complacently believe that their nations, communities or families can protect them, unaware that all such fallible soldiers will be destroyed in due course of time. In conclusion, one should try to associate with persons who engage in devotional service twenty-four hours a day.

TEXT 29

जिह्वा न वक्ति भगवद्गुणनामधेयं
चेतश्च न स्मरति तच्चरणारविन्दम् ।
कृष्णाय नो नमति यच्छिर एकदापि
तानानयध्वमसतोऽकृतविष्णुकृत्यान् ॥ २९ ॥

jihvā na vakti bhagavad-guṇa-nāmadheyaṁ
cetaś ca na smarati tac-caraṇāravindam
kṛṣṇāya no namati yac-chira ekadāpi
tān ānayadhvam asato 'kṛta-viṣṇu-kṛtyān

jihvā—the tongue; *na*—not; *vakti*—chants; *bhagavat*—of the Supreme Personality of Godhead; *guṇa*—transcendental qualities; *nāma*—and the holy name; *dheyam*—imparting; *cetaḥ*—the heart; *ca*—also; *na*—not; *smarati*—remembers; *tat*—His; *caraṇa-aravindam*—lotus feet; *kṛṣṇāya*—unto Lord Kṛṣṇa through His Deity in the temple; *no*—not; *namati*—bows; *yat*—whose; *śiraḥ*—head; *ekadā api*—even once; *tān*—them; *ānayadhvam*—bring before me; *asataḥ*—the nondevotees; *akṛta*—not performing; *viṣṇu-kṛtyān*—duties toward Lord Viṣṇu.

TRANSLATION

My dear servants, please bring to me only those sinful persons who do not use their tongues to chant the holy name and qualities of Kṛṣṇa, whose hearts do not remember the lotus feet of Kṛṣṇa even once, and whose heads do not bow down even once before Lord Kṛṣṇa. Send me those who do not perform their duties toward Viṣṇu, which are the only duties in human life. Please bring me all such fools and rascals.

PURPORT

The word *viṣṇu-kṛtyān* is very important in this verse because the purpose of human life is to please Lord Viṣṇu. *Varṇāśrama-dharma* is also meant for that purpose. As stated in the *Viṣṇu Purāṇa* (3.8.9):

varṇāśramācāravatā
puruṣeṇa paraḥ pumān
viṣṇur ārādhyate panthā
nānyat tat-toṣa-kāraṇam

Human society is meant to follow strictly the *varṇāśrama-dharma,* which divides society into four social divisions (*brāhmaṇa, kṣatriya, vaiśya* and *śūdra*) and four spiritual divisions (*brahmacarya, gṛhastha, vānaprastha* and *sannyāsa*). *Varṇāśrama-dharma* easily brings one nearer to Lord Viṣṇu, who is the only true objective in human society. *Na te viduḥ svārtha-gatiṁ hi viṣṇum:* unfortunately, however, people do not know that their self-interest is to return home, back to Godhead, or to approach Lord Viṣṇu. *Durāśayā ye bahir-artha-māninaḥ:* instead, they are simply bewildered. Every human being is expected to perform duties meant for approaching Lord Viṣṇu. Therefore Yamarāja advises the Yamadūtas to bring him those persons who have forgotten their duties toward Viṣṇu (*akṛta-viṣṇu-kṛtyān*). One who does not chant the holy name of Viṣṇu (Kṛṣṇa), who does not bow down to the Deity of Viṣṇu, and who does not remember the lotus feet of Viṣṇu is punishable by Yamarāja. In summary, all *avaiṣṇavas,* persons unconcerned with Lord Viṣṇu, are punishable by Yamarāja.

TEXT 30

तत् क्षम्यतां स भगवान् पुरुषः पुराणो
नारायणः स्वपुरुषैर्यदसत्कृतं नः ।
स्वानामहो न विदुषां रचिताञ्जलीनां
क्षान्तिर्गरीयसि नमः पुरुषाय भूम्ने ॥ ३० ॥

tat kṣamyatāṁ sa bhagavān puruṣaḥ purāṇo
nārāyaṇaḥ sva-puruṣair yad asat kṛtaṁ naḥ
svānām aho na viduṣāṁ racitāñjalīnāṁ
kṣāntir garīyasi namaḥ puruṣāya bhūmne

tat—that; *kṣamyatām*—let it be excused; *saḥ*—He; *bhagavān*—the Supreme Personality of Godhead; *puruṣaḥ*—the Supreme Person; *purāṇaḥ*

—the oldest; *nārāyaṇaḥ*—Lord Nārāyaṇa; *sva-puruṣaiḥ*—by my own servants; *yat*—which; *asat*—impudence; *kṛtam*—performed; *naḥ*—of us; *svānām*—of my own men; *aho*—alas; *na viduṣām*—not knowing; *racita-añjalīnām*—folding our hands together to beg Your pardon; *kṣāntiḥ*—forgiveness; *garīyasi*—in the glorious; *namaḥ*—respectful obeisances; *puruṣāya*—unto the person; *bhūmne*—supreme and all-pervading.

TRANSLATION

[Then Yamarāja, considering himself and his servants to be offenders, spoke as follows, begging pardon from the Lord.] O my Lord, my servants have surely committed a great offense by arresting a Vaiṣṇava such as Ajāmila. O Nārāyaṇa, O supreme and oldest person, please forgive us. Because of our ignorance, we failed to recognize Ajāmila as a servant of Your Lordship, and thus we have certainly committed a great offense. Therefore with folded hands we beg Your pardon. My Lord, since You are supremely merciful and are always full of good qualities, please pardon us. We offer our respectful obeisances unto You.

PURPORT

Lord Yamarāja took upon himself the responsibility for the offense committed by his servants. If the servant of an establishment makes a mistake, the establishment takes responsibility for it. Although Yamarāja is above offenses, his servants, practically with his permission, went to arrest Ajāmila, which was a great offense. The *nyāya-śāstra* confirms, *bhṛtyāparādhe svāmino daṇḍaḥ:* if a servant makes a mistake, the master is punishable because he is responsible for the offense. Taking this seriously, Yamarāja, along with his servants, prayed with folded hands to be excused by the Supreme Personality of Godhead, Nārāyaṇa.

TEXT 31

तस्मात् सङ्कीर्तनं विष्णोर्जगन्मङ्गलमंहसाम् ।
महतामपि कौरव्य विद्ध्यैकान्तिकनिष्कृतम् ॥ ३१ ॥

tasmāt saṅkīrtanaṁ viṣṇor
jagan-maṅgalam aṁhasām
mahatām api kauravya
viddhy aikāntika-niṣkṛtam

tasmāt—therefore; *saṅkīrtanam*—the congregational chanting of the holy name; *viṣṇoḥ*—of Lord Viṣṇu; *jagat-maṅgalam*—the most auspicious performance within this material world; *aṁhasām*—for sinful activities; *mahatām api*—even though very great; *kauravya*—O descendant of the Kuru family; *viddhi*—understand; *aikāntika*—the ultimate; *niṣkṛtam*—atonement.

TRANSLATION

Śukadeva Gosvāmī continued: My dear King, the chanting of the holy name of the Lord is able to uproot even the reactions of the greatest sins. Therefore the chanting of the saṅkīrtana movement is the most auspicious activity in the entire universe. Please try to understand this so that others will take it seriously.

PURPORT

We should note that although Ajāmila chanted the name of Nārāyaṇa imperfectly, he was delivered from all sinful reactions. The chanting of the holy name is so auspicious that it can free everyone from the reactions of sinful activities. One should not conclude that one may continue to sin with the intention of chanting Hare Kṛṣṇa to neutralize the reactions. Rather, one should be very careful to be free from all sins and never think of counteracting sinful activities by chanting the Hare Kṛṣṇa *mantra,* for this is another offense. If by chance a devotee accidentally performs some sinful activity, the Lord will excuse him, but one should not intentionally perform sinful acts.

TEXT 32

शृण्वतां गृणतां वीर्याण्युद्दामानि हरेर्मुहुः ।
यथा सुजातया भक्त्या शुद्ध्येन्नात्मा व्रतादिभिः ॥ ३२ ॥

śṛṇvatāṁ gṛṇatāṁ vīryāṇy
uddāmāni harer muhuḥ
yathā sujātayā bhaktyā
śuddhyen nātmā vratādibhiḥ

śṛṇvatām—of those hearing; *gṛṇatām*—and chanting; *vīryāṇi*—the wonderful activities; *uddāmāni*—able to counteract sin; *hareḥ*—of the Supreme Personality of Godhead; *muhuḥ*—always; *yathā*—as; *su-jātayā*—easily brought forth; *bhaktyā*—by devotional service; *śuddhyet*—may be purified; *na*—not; *ātmā*—the heart and soul; *vrata-ādibhiḥ*—by performing ritualistic ceremonies.

TRANSLATION

One who constantly hears and chants the holy name of the Lord and hears and chants about His activities can very easily attain the platform of pure devotional service, which can cleanse the dirt from one's heart. One cannot achieve such purification merely by observing vows and performing Vedic ritualistic ceremonies.

PURPORT

One may very easily practice chanting and hearing the holy name of the Lord and thus become ecstatic in spiritual life. *Padma Purāṇa* states:

nāmāparādha-yuktānāṁ
nāmāny eva haranty agham
aviśrānti-prayuktāni
tāny evārtha-karāṇi ca

Even if one chants the Hare Kṛṣṇa *mahā-mantra* offensively, one can avoid offenses by continuously chanting without deviation. One who becomes accustomed to this practice will always remain in a pure transcendental position, untouchable by sinful reactions. Śukadeva Gosvāmī especially requested King Parīkṣit to note this fact very carefully. There is no profit, however, in executing the Vedic ritualistic ceremonies. By performing such activities one may go to the higher planetary systems, but as stated in *Bhagavad-gītā* (9.21), *kṣīṇe puṇye martya-lokaṁ viśanti:* when the period of one's enjoyment in the heavenly planets is terminated because of the limited extent of the results of one's pious activities, one must return to earth. Thus there is no use in endeavoring to travel up and down in the universe. It is better to chant the holy name of the Lord so that one may become fully purified and eligible to return home, back to Godhead. That is the aim of life, and that is the perfection of life.

TEXT 33

कृष्णाङ्घ्रिपद्ममधुलिण् न पुनर्विसृष्ट-
मायागुणेषु रमते वृजिनावहेषु ।
अन्यस्तु कामहत आत्मरजः प्रमार्ष्टु-
मीहेत कर्म यत एव रजः पुनः स्यात् ॥ ३३ ॥

kṛṣṇāṅghri-padma-madhu-liṇ na punar visṛṣṭa-
māyā-guṇeṣu ramate vṛjināvaheṣu

anyas tu kāma-hata ātma-rajaḥ pramārṣṭum
īheta karma yata eva rajaḥ punaḥ syāt

kṛṣṇa-aṅghri-padma—of the lotus feet of Lord Kṛṣṇa; *madhu*—the honey; *liṭ*—one who licks; *na*—not; *punaḥ*—again; *visṛṣṭa*—already renounced; *māyā-guṇeṣu*—in the material modes of nature; *ramate*—desires to enjoy; *vṛjina-avaheṣu*—which brings distress; *anyaḥ*—another; *tu*—however; *kāma-hataḥ*—being enchanted by lust; *ātma-rajaḥ*—the sinful infection of the heart; *pramārṣṭum*—to cleanse; *īheta*—may perform; *karma*—activities; *yataḥ*—after which; *eva*—indeed; *rajaḥ*—the sinful activity; *punaḥ*—again; *syāt*—appears.

TRANSLATION

Devotees who always lick the honey from the lotus feet of Lord Kṛṣṇa do not care at all for material activities, which are performed under the three modes of material nature and which bring only misery. Indeed, devotees never give up the lotus feet of Kṛṣṇa to return to material activities. Others, however, who are addicted to Vedic rituals because they have neglected the service of the Lord's lotus feet and are enchanted by lusty desires, sometimes perform acts of atonement. Nevertheless, being incompletely purified, they return to sinful activities again and again.

PURPORT

A devotee's duty is to chant the Hare Kṛṣṇa *mantra.* One may sometimes chant with offenses and sometimes without offenses, but if one seriously adopts this process, he will achieve perfection, which cannot be achieved through Vedic ritualistic ceremonies of atonement. Persons who are attached to the Vedic ritualistic ceremonies, but do not believe in devotional service, who advise atonement, but do not appreciate the chanting of the Lord's holy name, fail to achieve the highest perfection. Devotees, therefore, being completely detached from material enjoyment, never give up Kṛṣṇa consciousness for Vedic ritualistic ceremonies. Those who are attached to Vedic ritualistic ceremonies because of lusty desires are subjected to the tribulations of material existence again and again. Mahārāja Parīkṣit has compared their activities to *kuñjara-śauca,* the bathing of an elephant.

TEXT 34

इत्थं स्वभर्तृगदितं भगवन्महित्वं
संस्मृत्य विस्मितधियो यमकिङ्करास्ते ।

नैवाच्युताश्रयजनं प्रतिशङ्कमाना
द्रष्टुं च बिभ्यति ततः प्रभृति स्म राजन् ॥ ३४॥

ittharn svabhartṛ-gaditaṁ bhagavan-mahitvaṁ
saṁsmṛtya vismita-dhiyo yama-kiṅkarās te
naivācyutāśraya-janaṁ pratiśaṅkamānā
draṣṭuṁ ca bibhyati tataḥ prabhṛti sma rājan

ittham—of such power; *sva-bhartṛ-gaditam*—explained by their master (Yamarāja); *bhagavat-mahitvam*—the extraordinary glory of the Supreme Personality of Godhead and His name, fame, form and attributes; *saṁsmṛtya*—remembering; *vismita-dhiyaḥ*—whose minds were struck with wonder; *yama-kiṅkarāḥ*—all the servants of Yamarāja; *te*—they; *na*—not; *eva*—indeed; *acyuta-āśraya-janam*—a person sheltered by the lotus feet of Acyuta, Lord Kṛṣṇa; *pratiśaṅkamānāḥ*—always fearing; *draṣṭum*—to see; *ca*—and; *bibhyati*—they are afraid; *tataḥ prabhṛti*—beginning from then; *sma*—indeed; *rājan*—O King.

TRANSLATION

After hearing from the mouth of their master about the extraordinary glories of the Lord and His name, fame and attributes, the Yamadūtas were struck with wonder. Since then, as soon as they see a devotee, they fear him and dare not look at him again.

PURPORT

Since this incident, the Yamadūtas have given up the dangerous behavior of approaching devotees. For the Yamadūtas, a devotee is dangerous.

TEXT 35

इतिहासमिमं गुह्यं भगवान् कुम्भसम्भवः ।
कथयामास मलय आसीनो हरिमर्चयन् ॥ ३५॥

itihāsam imaṁ guhyaṁ
bhagavān kumbha-sambhavaḥ
kathayām āsa malaya
āsīno harim arcayan

itihāsam—history; *imam*—this; *guhyam*—very confidential; *bhagavān*—the most powerful; *kumbha-sambhavaḥ*—Agastya Muni, the son of Kumbha;

kathayām āsa—explained; *malaye*—in the Malaya Hills; *āsīnaḥ*—residing; *harim arcayan*—worshiping the Supreme Personality of Godhead.

TRANSLATION

When the great sage Agastya, the son of Kumbha, was residing in the Malaya Hills and worshiping the Supreme Personality of Godhead, I approached him, and he explained to me this confidential history.

Thus end the Bhaktivedanta purports of the Sixth Canto, Third Chapter, of the Śrīmad-Bhāgavatam, *entitled "Yamarāja Instructs His Messengers."*

CHAPTER FOUR

The Haṁsa-guhya Prayers Offered to the Lord by Prajāpati Dakṣa

After Mahārāja Parīkṣit appealed to Śukadeva Gosvāmī to describe in further detail the creation of the living entities within this universe, Śukadeva Gosvāmī informed him that when the Pracetās, the ten sons of Prācīnabarhi, entered the sea to execute austerities, the planet earth was neglected because of the absence of a king. Naturally many weeds and unnecessary trees grew, and no food grains were produced. Indeed, all the land became like a forest. When the ten Pracetās came out of the sea and saw the entire world full of trees, they were very angry with the trees and decided to destroy them all to rectify the situation. Thus the Pracetās created wind and fire to burn the trees to ashes. Soma, however, the king of the moon and the king of all vegetation, forbade the Pracetās to destroy the trees, since the trees are the source of fruit and flowers for all living beings. Just to satisfy the Pracetās, Soma gave them a beautiful girl born of Pramlocā Apsarā. By the semen of all the Pracetās, Dakṣa was born of that girl.

In the beginning, Dakṣa created all the demigods, demons and human beings, but when he found the population not increasing properly, he took *sannyāsa* and went to Vindhya Mountain, where be underwent severe austerities and offered Lord Viṣṇu a particular prayer known as *Haṁsa-guhya,* by which Lord Viṣṇu became very pleased with him. The contents of the prayer were as follows.

"The Supreme Personality of Godhead, the Supersoul, Lord Hari, is the controller of both the living entities and the material nature. He is self-sufficient and self-effulgent. As the subject matter of perception is not the cause of our perceiving senses, so the living entity, although within his body, does not cause his eternal friend the Supersoul, who is the cause of creation of all the senses. Because of the living entity's ignorance, his senses are engaged with material objects. Since the living entity is alive, he can understand the creation of this material world to some extent, but he cannot understand the Supreme Personality of Godhead, who is beyond the conception of the body, mind and intelligence. Nevertheless, great sages who are always in meditation can see the personal form of the Lord within their hearts."

"Since an ordinary living being is materially contaminated, his words and intelligence are also material. Therefore he cannot ascertain the Supreme Personality of Godhead by manipulating his material senses. The conception of God derived through the material senses is inaccurate because the Supreme Lord is beyond the material senses, but when one engages his senses in devotional service, the eternal Supreme Personality of Godhead is revealed on the platform of the soul. When that Supreme Godhead becomes the aim of one's life, one is said to have attained spiritual knowledge."

"The Supreme Brahman is the cause of all causes because He originally existed before the creation. He is the original cause of everything, both material and spiritual, and His existence is independent. However, the Lord has a potency called *avidyā,* the illusory energy, which induces the false arguer to think himself perfect and which induces the illusory energy to bewilder the conditioned soul. That Supreme Brahman, the Supersoul, is very affectionate to His devotees. To bestow mercy upon them, He discloses His form, name, attributes and qualities to be worshiped within this material world."

"Unfortunately, however, those who are materially absorbed worship various demigods. As the air passes over a lotus flower and carries the scent of the flower with it, or as the air sometimes carries dust and therefore assumes colors, the Supreme Personality of Godhead appears as the various demigods according to the desires of His various foolish worshipers, but actually He is the supreme truth, Lord Viṣṇu. To fulfill the desires of His devotees, He appears in various incarnations, and therefore there is no need to worship the demigods."

Being very satisfied by the prayers of Dakṣa, Lord Viṣṇu appeared before Dakṣa with eight arms. The Lord was dressed in yellow garments and had a blackish complexion. Understanding that Dakṣa was very eager to follow the path of enjoyment, the Lord awarded him the potency to enjoy the illusory energy. The Lord offered him the daughter of Pañcajana named Asiknī, who was suitable for Mahārāja Dakṣa to enjoy in sex. Indeed, Dakṣa received his name because he was very expert in sex life. After awarding this benediction, Lord Viṣṇu disappeared.

TEXTS 1–2

श्रीराजोवाच

देवासुरनृणां सर्गो नागानां मृगपक्षिणाम् ।
सामासिकस्त्वया प्रोक्तो यस्तु स्वायम्भुवेऽन्तरे ॥ १ ॥

तस्यैव व्यासमिच्छामि ज्ञातुं ते भगवन् यथा ।
अनुसर्गं यया शक्त्या ससर्ज भगवान् परः ॥ २ ॥

śrī-rājovāca
devāsura-nṛṇāṁ sargo
nāgānāṁ mṛga-pakṣiṇām
sāmāsikas tvayā prokto
yas tu svāyambhuve'ntare

tasyaiva vyāsam icchāmi
jñātuṁ te bhagavan yathā
anusargaṁ yayā śaktyā
sasarja bhagavān paraḥ

śrī-rājā uvāca—the King said; *deva-asura-nṛṇām*—of the demigods, the demons and the human beings; *sargaḥ*—the creation; *nāgānām*—of the Nāgas (serpentine living entities); *mṛga-pakṣiṇām*—of the beasts and birds; *sāmāsikaḥ*—briefly; *tvayā*—by you; *proktaḥ*—described; *yaḥ*—which; *tu*—however; *svāyambhuve*—of Svāyambhuva Manu; *antare*—within the period; *tasya*—of this; *eva*—indeed; *vyāsam*—the detailed account; *icchāmi*—I wish; *jñātum*—to know; *te*—from you; *bhagavan*—O my lord; *yathā*—as well as; *anusargam*—the subsequent creation; *yayā*—by which; *śaktyā*—potency; *sasarja*—created; *bhagavān*—the Supreme Personality of Godhead; *paraḥ*—transcendental.

TRANSLATION

The blessed King said to Śukadeva Gosvāmī: My dear lord, the demigods, demons, human beings, Nāgas, beasts and birds were created during the reign of Svāyambhuva Manu. You have spoken about this creation briefly [in the Third Canto]. Now I wish to know about it elaborately. I also wish to know about the potency of the Supreme Personality of Godhead by which He brought about the secondary creation.

TEXT 3

श्रीसूत उवाच
इति सम्प्रश्नमाकर्ण्य राजर्षेर्बादरायणिः ।
प्रतिनन्द्य महायोगी जगाद मुनिसत्तमाः ॥ ३ ॥

śrī-sūta uvāca
iti sampraśnam ākarṇya
rājarṣer bādarāyaṇiḥ
pratinandya mahā-yogī
jagāda muni-sattamāḥ

śrī-sūtaḥ uvāca—Sūta Gosvāmī said; *iti*—thus; *sampraśnam*—the inquiry; *ākarṇya*—hearing; *rājarṣeḥ*—of King Parīkṣit; *bādarāyaṇiḥ*—Śukadeva Gosvāmī; *pratinandya*—praising; *mahā-yogī*—the great *yogī; jagāda*—replied; *muni-sattamāḥ*—O best of the sages.

TRANSLATION

Sūta Gosvāmī said: O great sages [assembled at Naimiṣāraṇya], after the great yogi Śukadeva Gosvāmī heard King Parīkṣit's inquiry, he praised it and thus replied.

TEXT 4

श्रीशुक उवाच
यदा प्रचेतसः पुत्रा दश प्राचीनबर्हिषः ।
अन्तःसमुद्रादुन्मग्ना ददृशुर्गां द्रुमैर्वृताम् ॥ ४ ॥

śrī-śuka uvāca
yadā pracetasaḥ putrā
daśa prācīnabarhiṣaḥ
antaḥ-samudrād unmagnā
dadṛśur gāṁ drumair vṛtām

śrī-śukaḥ uvāca—Śukadeva Gosvāmī said; *yadā*—when; *pracetasaḥ*—the Pracetās; *putrāḥ*—the sons; *daśa*—ten; *prācīnabarhiṣaḥ*—of King Prācīnabarhi; *antaḥ-samudrāt*—from within the ocean; *unmagnāḥ*—emerged; *dadṛśuḥ*—they saw; *gām*—the entire planet; *drumaiḥ vṛtām*—covered with trees.

TRANSLATION

Śukadeva Gosvāmī said: When the ten sons of Prācīnabarhi emerged from the waters, in which they were performing austerities, they saw that the entire surface of the world was covered by trees.

PURPORT

When King Prācīnabarhi was performing Vedic rituals in which the killing of animals was recommended, Nārada Muni, out of compassion, advised him to stop. Prācīnabarhi understood Nārada properly and then left the kingdom to perform austerities in the forest. His ten sons, however, were performing austerities within the water, and therefore there was no king to see to the management of the world. When the ten sons, the Pracetās, came out of the water, they saw that the earth was overrun with trees.

When the government neglects agriculture, which is necessary for the production of food, the land becomes covered with unnecessary trees. Of course, many trees are useful because they produce fruits and flowers, but many other trees are unnecessary. They could be used as fuel and the land cleared and used for agriculture. When the government is negligent, less grain is produced. As stated in *Bhagavad-gītā* (18.44), *kṛṣi-go-rakṣya-vāṇijyaṁ vaiśya-karma svabhāva jam:* the proper engagements for *vaiśyas,* according to their nature, are to farm and to protect cows. The duty of the government and the *kṣatriyas* is to see that the members of the third class, the *vaiśyas,* who are neither *brāhmaṇas* nor *kṣatriyas,* are thus properly engaged. *Kṣatriyas* are meant to protect human beings, whereas *vaiśyas* are meant to protect useful animals, especially cows.

TEXT 5

द्रुमेभ्यः क्रुध्यमानास्ते तपोदीपितमन्यवः ।
मुखतो वायुमग्निं च ससृजुस्तद्दिधक्षया ॥ ५ ॥

drumebhyaḥ krudhyamānās te
tapo-dīpita-manyavaḥ
mukhato vāyum agniṁ ca
sasṛjus tad-didhakṣayā

drumebhyaḥ—unto the trees; *krudhyamānāḥ*—being very angry; *te*—they (the ten sons of Prācīnabarhi); *tapaḥ-dīpita-manyavaḥ*—whose anger was inflamed because of long austerities; *mukhataḥ*—from the mouth; *vāyum*—wind; *agnim*—fire; *ca*—and; *sasṛjuḥ*—they created; *tat*—those forests; *didhakṣayā*—with the desire to burn.

TRANSLATION

Because of having undergone long austerities in the water, the Pracetās were very angry at the trees. Desiring to burn them to ashes, they generated wind and fire from their mouths.

PURPORT

Here the word *tapo-dīpita-manyavaḥ* indicates that persons who have undergone severe austerity (*tapasya*) are endowed with great mystic power, as evinced by the Pracetās, who created fire and wind from their mouths. Although devotees undergo severe *tapasya,* however, they are *vimanyavaḥ, sādhavaḥ,* which means that they are never angry. They are always decorated with good qualities. *Bhāgavatam* (3.25.21) states:

titikṣavaḥ kāruṇikāḥ
suhṛdaḥ sarva-dehinām
ajāta-śatravaḥ śāntāḥ
sādhavaḥ sādhu-bhūṣaṇāḥ

A *sādhu,* a devotee, is never angry. Actually the real feature of devotees who undergo *tapasya,* austerity, is forgiveness. Although a Vaiṣṇava has sufficient power in *tapasya,* he does not become angry when put into difficulty. If one undergoes *tapasya* but does not become a Vaiṣṇava, however, one does not develop good qualities. For example, Hiraṇyakaśipu and Rāvaṇa also performed great austerities, but they did so to demonstrate their demoniac tendencies. Vaiṣṇavas must meet many opponents while preaching the glories of the Lord, but Śrī Caitanya Mahāprabhu recommends that they not become angry while preaching. Lord Caitanya Mahāprabhu has given this formula: *tṛṇād api sunīcena taror api sahiṣṇunā/ amāninā mānadena kīrtanīyaḥ sadā hariḥ.* "One should chant the holy name of the Lord in a humble state of mind, thinking oneself lower than the straw in the street; one should be more tolerant than a tree, devoid of all sense of false prestige and should be ready to offer all respect to others. In such a state of mind one can chant the holy name of the Lord constantly." Those engaged in preaching the glories of the Lord should be humbler than grass and more tolerant than a tree; then they can preach the glories of the Lord without difficulty.

TEXT 6

ताभ्यां निर्दह्यमानांस्तानुपलभ्य कुरूद्वह ।
राजोवाच महान् सोमो मन्युं प्रशमयन्निव ॥ ६ ॥

tābhyāṁ nirdahyamānāṁs tān
upalabhya kurūdvaha
rājovāca mahān somo
manyuṁ praśamayann iva

tābhyām—by the wind and fire; *nirdahyamānān*—being burned; *tān*—them (the trees); *upalabhya*—seeing; *kurūdvaha*—O Mahārāja Parīkṣit; *rājā*—the king of the forest; *uvāca*—said; *mahān*—the great; *somaḥ*—predominating deity of the moon, Somadeva; *manyum*—the anger; *praśamayan*—pacifying; *iva*—like.

TRANSLATION

My dear King Parīkṣit, when Soma, the king of the trees and predominating deity of the moon, saw the fire and wind burning all the trees to ashes, he felt great sympathy because he is the maintainer of all herbs and trees. To appease the anger of the Pracetās, Soma spoke as follows.

PURPORT

It is understood from this verse that the predominating deity of the moon is the maintainer of all the trees and plants throughout the universe. It is due to the moonshine that trees and plants grow very luxuriantly. Therefore how can we accept the so-called scientists whose moon expeditions have informed us that there are no trees or vegetation on the moon? Śrīla Viśvanātha Cakravartī Ṭhākura says, *somo vṛkṣādhiṣṭhātā sa eva vṛkṣāṇāṁ rājā:* Soma, the predominating deity of the moon, is the king of all vegetation. How can we believe that the maintainer of vegetation has no vegetation on his own planet?

TEXT 7

न द्रुमेभ्यो महाभागा दीनेभ्यो द्रोग्धुमर्हथ ।
विवर्धयिषवो यूयं प्रजानां पतयः स्मृताः ॥ ७ ॥

na drumebhyo mahā-bhāgā
dīnebhyo drogdhum arhatha
vivardhayiṣavo yūyaṁ
prajānāṁ patayaḥ smṛtāḥ

na—not; *drumebhyaḥ*—the trees; *mahā-bhāgāḥ*—O greatly fortunate ones; *dīnebhyaḥ*—who are very poor; *drogdhum*—to burn to ashes; *arhatha*—you deserve; *vivardhayiṣavaḥ*—desiring to bring about an increase; *yūyam*—you; *prajānām*—of all living entities who have taken shelter of you; *patayaḥ*—the masters or protectors; *smṛtāḥ*—known as.

TRANSLATION

O greatly fortunate ones, you should not kill these poor trees by burning them to ashes. Your duty is to wish the citizens [prajās] all prosperity and to act as their protectors.

PURPORT

It is indicated herein that the government or king has the duty of protecting not only the human beings, but all other living entities, including animals, trees and plants. No living entity should be killed unnecessarily.

TEXT 8

अहो प्रजापतिपतिर्भगवान् हरिरव्ययः ।
वनस्पतीनोषधीश्च ससर्जोर्जमिषं विभुः ॥ ८ ॥

aho prajāpati-patir
bhagavān harir avyayaḥ
vanaspatīn oṣadhīś ca
sasarjorjam iṣaṁ vibhuḥ

aho—alas; *prajāpati-patiḥ*—the Lord of all the lords of created beings; *bhagavān hariḥ*—the Supreme Personality of Godhead, Hari; *avyayaḥ*—indestructible; *vanaspatīn*—the trees and plants; *oṣadhīḥ*—the herbs; *ca*—and; *sasarja*—created; *ūrjam*—invigorating; *iṣam*—food; *vibhuḥ*—the Supreme Being.

TRANSLATION

The Supreme Personality of Godhead, Śrī Hari, is the master of all living entities, including all the prajāpatis, such as Lord Brahmā. Because He is the all-pervading and indestructible master, He has created all these trees and vegetables as eatables for other living entities.

PURPORT

Soma, the predominating deity of the moon, reminded the Pracetās that this vegetation had been created by the Lord of lords to provide food for everyone. If the Pracetās tried to kill them off, their own subjects would also suffer, for trees are also required for food.

TEXT 9

अन्नं चराणामचरा ह्यपदः पादचारिणाम् ।
अहस्ता हस्तयुक्तानां द्विपदां च चतुष्पदः ॥ ९ ॥

annaṁ carāṇām acarā
hy apadaḥ pāda-cāriṇām
ahastā hasta-yuktānāṁ
dvi-padāṁ ca catuṣ-padaḥ

annam—food; *carāṇām*—of those that move on wings; *acarāḥ*—the nonmoving (fruits and flowers); *hi*—indeed; *apadaḥ*—the living entities without legs, like the grass; *pāda-cāriṇām*—of the animals who move on legs, like the cows and buffalo; *ahastāḥ*—animals without hands; *hasta-yuktānām*—of the animals with hands, like the tigers; *dvi-padām*—of human beings, who have two legs; *ca*—and; *catuḥ-padaḥ*—the four-legged animals like the deer.

TRANSLATION

By nature's arrangement, fruits and flowers are considered the food of insects and birds; grass and other legless living entities are meant to be the food of four-legged animals like cows and buffalo; animals that cannot use their front legs as hands are meant to be the food of animals like tigers, which have claws; and four-legged animals like deer and goats, as well as food grains, are meant to be the food of human beings.

PURPORT

By nature's law, or the arrangement of the Supreme Personality of Godhead, one kind of living entity is eatable by other living entities. As mentioned herein, *dvi-padāṁ ca catuṣ-padaḥ:* the four-legged animals (*catuṣ-padaḥ*), as well as food grains, are eatables for human beings (*dvi-padām*). These four-legged animals are those such as deer and goats, not cows, which are meant to be protected. Generally the men of the higher classes of society—the *brāhmaṇas, kṣatriyas* and *vaiśyas*—do not eat meat. Sometimes *kṣatriyas* go to the forest to kill animals like deer because they have to learn the art of killing, and sometimes they eat the animals also. *Śūdras,* too, eat animals such as goats. Cows, however, are never meant to be killed or eaten by human beings. In every *śāstra,* cow killing is vehemently condemned. Indeed, one who kills a cow must suffer for as many years as there are hairs on the body of a cow. *Manu-saṁhitā* says, *pravṛttir eṣā bhūtānāṁ nivṛttis tu mahā-phalā:* we have many tendencies in this material world, but in human life one is meant to learn how to curb those tendencies. Those who desire to eat meat may satisfy the demands of their tongues by eating lower animals, but they should never kill cows, who are actually accepted as the mothers of human society because they supply milk. The *śāstra* especially recommends, *kṛṣi-gorakṣya:* the *vaiśya* section of humanity should arrange for the food of the entire society through agricultural activities and should give full protection to the cows, which are the most useful animals because they supply milk to human society.

TEXT 10

यूयं च पित्रान्वादिष्टा देवदेवेन चानघाः ।
प्रजासर्गाय हि कथं वृक्षान् निर्दग्धुमर्हथ ॥ १० ॥

yūyaṁ ca pitrānvādiṣṭā
deva-devena cānaghāḥ
prajā-sargāya hi kathaṁ
vṛkṣān nirdagdhum arhatha

yūyam—you; *ca*—also; *pitrā*—by your father; *anvādiṣṭāḥ*—ordered; *deva-devena*—by the Personality of Godhead, the master of the masters; *ca*—also; *anaghāḥ*—O sinless ones; *prajā-sargāya*—for generating the population; *hi*—indeed; *katham*—how; *vṛkṣān*—the trees; *nirdagdhum*—to burn to ashes; *arhatha*—are able.

TRANSLATION

O pure-hearted ones, your father, Prācīnabarhi, and the Supreme Personality of Godhead have ordered you to generate population. Therefore how can you burn to ashes these trees and herbs, which are needed for the maintenance of your subjects and descendants?

TEXT 11

आतिष्ठत सतां मार्गं कोपं यच्छत दीपितम् ।
पित्रा पितामहेनापि जुष्टं वः प्रपितामहैः ॥ ११ ॥

ātiṣṭhata satāṁ mārgaṁ
kopaṁ yacchata dīpitam

pitrā pitāmahenāpi
juṣṭaṁ vaḥ prapitāmahaiḥ

ātiṣṭhata—just follow; *satām mārgam*—the path of the great saintly personalities; *kopam*—the anger; *yacchata*—subdue; *dīpitam*—which is now awakened; *pitrā*—by the father; *pitāmahena api*—and by the grandfather; *juṣṭam*—executed; *vaḥ*—your; *prapitāmahaiḥ*—by the great-grandfathers.

TRANSLATION

The path of goodness traversed by your father, grandfather and great-grandfathers is that of maintaining the subjects [prajās], including the men, animals and trees. That is the path you should follow. Unnecessary anger is contrary to your duty. Therefore I request you to control your anger.

PURPORT

Here the words *pitrā pitāmahenāpi juṣṭaṁ vaḥ prapitāmahaiḥ* depict an honest royal family, consisting of the kings, their father, their grandfather and their great-grandfathers. Such a royal family has a prestigious position because it maintains the citizens, or *prajās.* The word *prajā* refers to one who has taken birth within the jurisdiction of the government. The exalted royal families were conscious that all living beings, whether human, animal or lower than animal, should be given protection. The modern democratic system cannot be exalted in this way because the leaders elected strive only for power and have no sense of responsibility. In a monarchy, a king with a prestigious position follows the great deeds of his forefathers. Thus Soma, the king of the moon, here reminds the Pracetās about the glories of their father, grandfather and great-grandfathers.

TEXT 12

तोकानां पितरौ बन्धू दृशः पक्ष्म स्त्रियाः पतिः ।
पतिः प्रजानां भिक्षूणां गृह्यज्ञानां बुधः सुहृत् ॥ १२ ॥

tokānāṁ pitarau bandhū
dṛśaḥ pakṣma striyāḥ patiḥ
patiḥ prajānāṁ bhikṣūṇāṁ
gṛhy ajñānāṁ budhaḥ suhṛt

tokānām—of children; *pitarau*—the two parents; *bandhū*—the friends; *dṛśaḥ*—of the eye; *pakṣma*—the eyelid; *striyāḥ*—of the woman; *patiḥ*—the husband; *patiḥ*—the protector; *prajānām*—of the subjects; *bhikṣūṇām*—of the beggars; *gṛhī*—the householder; *ajñānām*—of the ignorant; *budhaḥ*—the learned; *su-hṛt*—the friend.

TRANSLATION

As the father and mother are the friends and maintainers of their children, as the eyelid is the protector of the eye, as the husband is the maintainer and protector of a woman, as the householder is the maintainer and protector of beggars, and as the learned is the friend of the ignorant, so the king is the protector and giver of life to all his subjects. The trees are also subjects of the king. Therefore they should be given protection.

PURPORT

By the supreme will of the Personality of Godhead, there are various protectors and maintainers for helpless living entities. The trees are also considered *prajās,* subjects of the king, and therefore the duty of the monarch is to protect even the trees, not to speak of others. The king is duty-bound to protect the living entities in his kingdom. Thus although the parents are directly responsible for the protection and maintenance of their children, the duty of the king is to see that all parents do their duty properly. Similarly, the king is also responsible for overseeing the other protectors mentioned in this verse. It may also be noted that the beggars who should be maintained by the householders are not professional beggars, but *sannyāsīs* and *brāhmaṇas,* to whom the householders should supply food and clothing.

TEXT 13

अन्तर्देहेषु भूतानामात्मास्ते हरिरीश्वरः ।
सर्वं तद्धिष्ण्यमीक्षध्वमेवं वस्तोषितो ह्यसौ ॥ १३ ॥

antar deheṣu bhūtānām
ātmāste harir īśvaraḥ
sarvaṁ tad-dhiṣṇyam īkṣadhvam
evaṁ vas toṣito hy asau

antaḥ deheṣu—within the bodies (in the cores of the hearts); *bhūtānām*—of all living entities; *ātmā*—the Supersoul; *āste*—resides; *hariḥ*—the Supreme Personality of Godhead; *īśvaraḥ*—the Lord or director; *sarvam*—all;

tat-dhiṣṇyam—His place of residence; *īkṣadhvam*—try to see; *evam*—in this way; *vaḥ*—with you; *toṣitaḥ*—satisfied; *hi*—indeed; *asau*—that Supreme Personality of Godhead.

TRANSLATION

The Supreme Personality of Godhead is situated as the Supersoul within the cores of the hearts of all living entities, whether moving or nonmoving, including men, birds, animals, trees and, indeed, all living entities. Therefore you should consider every body a residence or temple of the Lord. By such vision you will satisfy the Lord. You should not angrily kill these living entities in the forms of trees.

PURPORT

As stated in *Bhagavad-gītā* and confirmed by all the Vedic scriptures, *īśvaraḥ sarva-bhūtānāṁ hṛd-deśe'rjuna tiṣṭhati:* the Supersoul is situated within everyone's heart. Therefore, since everyone's body is the residence of the Supreme Lord, one should not destroy the body because of unnecessary envy. That will dissatisfy the Supersoul. Soma told the Pracetās that because they had tried to satisfy the Supersoul, now they should not displease Him.

TEXT 14

यः समुत्पतितं देह आकाशान्मन्युमुल्बणम् ।
आत्मजिज्ञासया यच्छेत् स गुणानतिवर्तते ॥ १४ ॥

yaḥ samutpatitaṁ deha
ākāśān manyum ulbaṇam
ātma-jijñāsayā yacchet
sa guṇān ativartate

yaḥ—anyone who; *samutpatitam*—suddenly awakened; *dehe*—in the body; *ākāśāt*—from the sky; *manyum*—anger; *ulbaṇam*—powerful; *ātma-jijñāsayā*—by inquiry into spiritual realization or self-realization; *yacchet*—subdues; *saḥ*—that person; *guṇān*—the modes of material nature; *ativartate*—transcends.

TRANSLATION

One who inquires into self-realization and thus subdues his powerful anger—which awakens suddenly in the body as if falling from the sky—transcends the influence of the modes of material nature.

PURPORT

When one becomes angry, he forgets himself and his situation, but if one is able to consider his situation by knowledge, one transcends the influence of the modes of material nature. One is always a servant of lusty desires, anger, greed, illusion, envy and so forth, but if one obtains sufficient strength in spiritual advancement, one can control them. One who obtains such control will always be transcendentally situated, untouched by the modes of material nature. This is only possible when one fully engages in the service of the Lord. As the Lord says in *Bhagavad-gītā* (14.26):

māṁ ca yo'vyabhicāreṇa
bhakti-yogena sevate
sa guṇān samatītyaitān
brahma-bhūyāya kalpate

"One who engages in full devotional service, who does not fall down in any circumstance, at once transcends the modes of material nature and thus comes to the spiritual platform." By engaging one in devotional service, the Kṛṣṇa consciousness movement keeps one always transcendental to anger, greed, lust, envy and so forth. One must perform devotional service because otherwise one will become victimized by the modes of material nature.

TEXT 15

अलं दग्धैर्द्रुमैर्दीनैः खिलानां शिवमस्तु वः ।
वार्क्षी ह्येषा वरा कन्या पत्नीत्वे प्रतिगृह्यताम् ॥ १५ ॥

alaṁ dagdhair drumair dīnaiḥ
khilānāṁ śivam astu vaḥ
vārkṣī hy eṣā varā kanyā
patnītve pratigṛhyatām

alam—enough; *dagdhaiḥ*—with burning; *drumaiḥ*—the trees; *dīnaiḥ*—poor; *khilānām*—of the remainder of the trees; *śivam*—all good fortune; *astu*—let there be; *vaḥ*—of you; *vārkṣī*—raised by the trees; *hi*—indeed; *eṣā*—this; *varā*—choice; *kanyā*—daughter; *patnītve*—into wifehood; *pratigṛhyatām*—let her be accepted.

TRANSLATION

There is no need to burn these poor trees any longer. Let whatever trees still remain be happy. Indeed, you should also be happy. Now, here

is a beautiful, well-qualified girl named Māriṣā, who was raised by the trees as their daughter. You may accept this beautiful girl as your wife.

TEXT 16

इत्यामन्त्र्य वरारोहां कन्यामाप्सरसीं नृप ।
सोमो राजा ययौ दत्त्वा ते धर्मेणोपयेमिरे ॥ १६ ॥

ity āmantrya varārohāṁ
kanyām āpsarasīṁ nṛpa
somo rājā yayau dattvā
te dharmeṇopayemire

iti—thus; *āmantrya*—addressing; *vara-ārohām*—possessing high, beautiful hips; *kanyām*—the girl; *āpsarasīm*—born of an Apsarā; *nṛpa*—O King; *somaḥ*—Soma, the predominating deity of the moon; *rājā*—the king; *yayau*—returned; *dattvā*—delivering; *te*—they; *dharmeṇa*—according to religious principles; *upayemire*—married.

TRANSLATION

Śukadeva Gosvāmī continued: My dear King, after thus pacifying the Pracetās, Soma, the king of the moon, gave them the beautiful girl born of Pramlocā Apsarā. The Pracetās all received Pramlocā's daughter, who had high, very beautiful hips, and married her according to the religious system.

TEXT 17

तेभ्यस्तस्यां समभवद् दक्षः प्राचेतसः किल ।
यस्य प्रजाविसर्गेण लोका आपूरितास्त्रयः ॥ १७ ॥

tebhyas tasyāṁ samabhavad
dakṣaḥ prācetasaḥ kila
yasya prajā-visargeṇa
lokā āpūritās trayaḥ

tebhyaḥ—from all the Pracetās; *tasyām*—in her; *samabhavat*—was generated; *dakṣaḥ*—Dakṣa, the expert in begetting children; *prācetasaḥ*—the son of the Pracetās; *kila*—indeed; *yasya*—of whom; *prajā-visargeṇa*—by the generation of living entities; *lokāḥ*—the worlds; *āpūritāḥ*—filled; *trayaḥ*—three.

TRANSLATION

In the womb of that girl the Pracetās all begot a son named Dakṣa, who filled the three worlds with living entities.

PURPORT

Dakṣa was first born during the reign of Svāyambhuva Manu, but because of offending Lord Śiva he was punished by having the head of a goat substituted for his own head. Thus insulted, he had to give up that body, and in the sixth *manvantara,* called the Cākṣuṣa *manvantara,* he was born of the womb of Māriṣā as Dakṣa. In this connection Śrīla Viśvanātha Cakravartī Ṭhākura quotes this verse:

cākṣuṣe tv antare prāpte
prāk-sarge kāla-vidrute
yaḥ sasarja prajā iṣṭāḥ
sa dakṣo daiva-coditaḥ

"His previous body had been destroyed, but he, the same Dakṣa, inspired by the supreme will, created all the desired living entities in the Cākṣuṣa *manvantara.*" (*Bhāg.* 4.30.49) Thus Dakṣa regained his previous opulence and again begot thousands and millions of children to fill the three worlds.

TEXT 18

यथा ससर्ज भूतानि दक्षो दुहितृवत्सलः ।
रेतसा मनसा चैव तन्ममावहितः शृणु ॥ १८ ॥

yathā sasarja bhūtāni
dakṣo duhitṛ-vatsalaḥ
retasā manasā caiva
tan mamāvahitaḥ śṛṇu

yathā—as; *sasarja*—created; *bhūtāni*—the living entities; *dakṣaḥ*—Dakṣa; *duhitṛ-vatsalaḥ*—who is very affectionate to his daughters; *retasā*—by semen; *manasā*—by the mind; *ca*—also; *eva*—indeed; *tat*—that; *mama*—from me; *avahitaḥ*—being attentive; *śṛṇu*—please hear.

TRANSLATION

Śukadeva Gosvāmī continued: Please hear from me with great attention how Prajāpati Dakṣa, who was very affectionate to his daughters,

created different types of living entities through his semen and through his mind.

PURPORT

The word *duhitṛ-vatsalaḥ* indicates that all the *prajās* were born from Dakṣa's daughters. Śrīla Viśvanātha Cakravartī Ṭhākura says that apparently Dakṣa had no son.

TEXT 19

मनसैवासृजत्पूर्वं प्रजापतिरिमाः प्रजाः ।
देवासुरमनुष्यादीन्नभःस्थलजलौकसः ॥ १९ ॥

manasaivāsṛjat pūrvaṁ
prajāpatir imāḥ prajāḥ
devāsura-manuṣyādīn
nabhaḥ-sthala-jalaukasaḥ

manasā—by the mind; *eva*—indeed; *asṛjat*—created; *pūrvam*—in the beginning; *prajāpatiḥ*—the *prajāpati* (Dakṣa); *imāḥ*—these; *prajāḥ*—living entities; *deva*—the demigods; *asura*—the demons; *manuṣya-ādīn*—and other living entities, headed by the human beings; *nabhaḥ*—in the skies; *sthala*—on the land; *jala*—or within the water; *okasaḥ*—who have their abodes.

TRANSLATION

With his mind, Prajāpati Dakṣa first created all kinds of demigods, demons, human beings, birds, beasts, aquatics and so on.

TEXT 20

तमबृंहितमालोक्य प्रजासर्गं प्रजापतिः ।
विन्ध्यपादानुपव्रज्य सोऽचरद् दुष्करं तपः ॥ २० ॥

tam abṛṁhitam ālokya
prajā-sargaṁ prajāpatiḥ
vindhya-pādān upavrajya
so'carad duṣkaraṁ tapaḥ

tam—that; *abṛṁhitam*—not increasing; *ālokya*—seeing; *prajā-sargam*—the creation of the living entities; *prajāpatiḥ*—Dakṣa, the generator of living entities; *vindhya-pādān*—the mountains near the Vindhya mountain range; *upavrajya*—going to; *saḥ*—he; *acarat*—executed; *duṣkaram*—very difficult; *tapaḥ*—austerities.

TRANSLATION

But when Prajāpati Dakṣa saw that he was not properly generating all kinds of living entities, he approached a mountain near the Vindhya mountain range, and there he executed very difficult austerities.

TEXT 21

तत्राघमर्षणं नाम तीर्थं पापहरं परम् ।
उपस्पृश्यानुसवनं तपसातोषयद्धरिम् ॥ २१ ॥

tatrāghamarṣaṇaṁ nāma
tīrthaṁ pāpa-haraṁ param
upaspṛśyānusavanaṁ
tapasātoṣayad dhariṁ

tatra—there; *aghamarṣaṇam*—Aghamarṣaṇa; *nāma*—named; *tīrtham*—the holy place; *pāpa-haram*—suitable for destroying all sinful reactions; *param*—best; *upaspṛśya*—performing *ācamana* and bathing; *anusavanam*—regularly; *tapasā*—by austerity; *atoṣayat*—caused pleasure; *harim*—to the Supreme Personality of Godhead.

TRANSLATION

Near that mountain was a very holy place named Aghamarṣaṇa. There Prajāpati Dakṣa executed ritualistic ceremonies and satisfied the Supreme Personality of Godhead, Hari, by engaging in great austerities to please Him.

TEXT 22

अस्तौषीद्धंसगुह्येन भगवन्तमधोक्षजम् ।
तुभ्यं तदभिधास्यामि कस्यातुष्यद् यथा हरिः ॥ २२ ॥

astauṣīd dhaṁsa-guhyena
bhagavantam adhokṣajam
tubhyaṁ tad abhidhāsyāmi
kasyātuṣyad yathā hariḥ

astauṣīt—satisfied; *haṁsa-guhyena*—by the celebrated prayers known as *Haṁsa-guhya; bhagavantam*—the Supreme Personality of Godhead; *adhokṣajam*—who is beyond the reach of the senses; *tubhyam*—unto you; *tat*—that; *abhidhāsyāmi*—I shall explain; *kasya*—with Dakṣa, the *prajāpati; atuṣyat*—was satisfied; *yathā*—how; *hariḥ*—the Supreme Personality of Godhead.

TRANSLATION

My dear King, I shall fully explain to you the Haṁsa-guhya prayers, which were offered to the Supreme Personality of Godhead by Dakṣa, and I shall explain how the Lord was pleased with him for those prayers.

PURPORT

It is to be understood that the *Haṁsa-guhya* prayers were not composed by Dakṣa, but were existing in the Vedic literature.

TEXT 23

श्रीप्रजापतिरुवाच
नमः परायावितथानुभूतये
गुणत्रयाभासनिमित्तबन्धवे ।
अदृष्टधाम्ने गुणतत्त्वबुद्धिभि-
र्निवृत्तमानाय दधे स्वयम्भुवे ॥ २३ ॥

śrī-prajāpatir uvāca
namaḥ parāyāvitathānubhūtaye
guṇa-trayābhāsa-nimitta-bandhave
adṛṣṭa-dhāmne guṇa-tattva-buddhibhir
nivṛtta-mānāya dadhe svayambhuve

śrī-prajāpatiḥ uvāca—the *prajāpati* Dakṣa said; *namaḥ*—all respectful obeisances; *parāya*—unto the Transcendence; *avitatha*—correct; *anubhūtaye*—unto Him whose spiritual potency brings about realization of Him; *guṇa-traya*—of the three material modes of nature; *ābhāsa*—of the living entities who have the appearance; *nimitta*—and of the material energy; *bandhave*—unto the controller; *adṛṣṭa-dhāmne*—who is not perceived in His abode; *guṇa-tattva-buddhibhiḥ*—by the conditioned souls whose poor intelligence dictates that real truth is found in the manifestations of the three modes of material nature; *nivṛtta-mānāya*—who has surpassed all material measurements and calculations; *dadhe*—I offer; *svayambhuve*—unto the Supreme Lord, who is manifest with no cause.

TRANSLATION

Prajāpati Dakṣa said: The Supreme Personality of Godhead is transcendental to the illusory energy and the physical categories it produces. He possesses the potency for unfailing knowledge and supreme willpower, and He is the controller of the living entities and the illusory energy. The conditioned souls who have accepted this material manifestation as everything cannot see Him, for He is above the evidence of experimental knowledge. Self-evident and self-sufficient, He is not caused by any superior cause. Let me offer my respectful obeisances unto Him.

PURPORT

The transcendental position of the Supreme Personality of Godhead is explained herewith. He is not perceivable by the conditioned souls, who are accustomed to material vision and cannot understand that the Supreme Personality of Godhead exists in His abode, which is beyond that vision. Even if a materialistic person could count all the atoms in the universe, he would still be unable to understand the Supreme Personality of Godhead. As confirmed in *Brahma-saṁhitā* (5.34):

panthās tu koṭi-śata-vatsara-saṁpragamyo
vāyor athāpi manaso muni-puṅgavānām
so'py asti yat-prapada-sīmny avicintya-tattve
govindam ādi-puruṣaṁ tam ahaṁ bhajāmi

The conditioned souls may try to understand the Supreme Personality of Godhead for many billions of years through their mental speculative processes, traveling at the speed of the mind or the wind, but still the Absolute Truth will remain inconceivable to them because a materialistic person cannot measure the length and breadth of the Supreme Personality of Godhead's unlimited existence. If the Absolute Truth is beyond measurement, one may ask, how can one realize Him? The answer is given here by the word *svayambhuve:* one may understand Him or not, but nevertheless He is existing in His own spiritual potency.

TEXT 24

न यस्य सख्यं पुरुषोऽवैति सख्युः
सखा वसन् संवसतः पुरेऽस्मिन् ।
गुणो यथा गुणिनो व्यक्तदृष्टे-
स्तस्मै महेशाय नमस्करोमि ॥ २४ ॥

na yasya sakhyaṁ puruṣo'vaiti sakhyuḥ
sakhā vasan saṁvasataḥ pure'smin
guṇo yathā guṇino vyakta-dṛṣṭes
tasmai maheśāya namaskaromi

na—not; *yasya*—whose; *sakhyam*—fraternity; *puruṣaḥ*—the living entity; *avaiti*—knows; *sakhyuḥ*—of the supreme friend; *sakhā*—the friend; *vasan*—living; *saṁvasataḥ*—of the one living with; *pure*—in the body; *asmin*—this; *guṇaḥ*—the object of sense perception; *yathā*—just like; *guṇinaḥ*—of its respective sense organ; *vyakta-dṛṣṭeḥ*—who oversees the material manifestation; *tasmai*—unto Him; *mahā-īśāya*—unto the supreme controller; *namaskaromi*—I offer my obeisances.

TRANSLATION

As the sense objects [form, taste, touch, smell and sound] cannot understand how the senses perceive them, so the conditioned soul, although residing in his body along with the Supersoul, cannot understand how the supreme spiritual person, the master of the material creation, directs his senses. Let me offer my respectful obeisances unto that Supreme Person, who is the supreme controller.

PURPORT

The individual soul and the Supreme Soul live together within the body. This is confirmed in the *Upaniṣads* by the analogy that two friendly birds live in one tree—one bird eating the fruit of the tree and the other simply witnessing and directing. Although the individual living being, who is compared to the bird that is eating, is sitting with his friend the Supreme Soul, the individual living being cannot see Him. Actually the Supersoul is directing the workings of his senses in the enjoyment of sense objects, but as these sense objects cannot see the senses, the conditioned soul cannot see the directing soul. The conditioned soul has desires, and the Supreme Soul fulfills them, but the conditioned soul is unable to see the Supreme Soul. Thus

Prajāpati Dakṣa offers his obeisances to the Supreme Soul, the Supersoul, even though unable to see Him. Another example given is that although ordinary citizens work under the direction of the government, they cannot understand how they are being governed or what the government is. In this regard, Madhvācārya quotes the following verse from the *Skanda Purāṇa:*

yathā rājñaḥ priyatvaṁ tu
bhṛtyā vedena cātmanaḥ
tathā jīvo na yat-sakhyaṁ
vetti tasmai namo'stu te

"As the various servants in the different departments of big establishments cannot see the supreme managing director under whom they are working, the conditioned souls cannot see the supreme friend sitting within their bodies. Let us therefore offer our respectful obeisances unto the Supreme, who is invisible to our material eyes."

TEXT 25

देहोऽसवोऽक्षा मनवो भूतमात्रा-
मात्मानमन्यं च विदुः परं यत्।
सर्वं पुमान् वेद गुणांश्च तज्ज्ञो
न वेद सर्वज्ञमनन्तमीडे ॥ २५ ॥

deho'savo'kṣā manavo bhūta-mātrām
ātmānam anyaṁ ca viduḥ paraṁ yat
sarvaṁ pumān veda guṇāṁś ca taj-jño
na veda sarva-jñam anantam īḍe

dehaḥ—this body; *asavaḥ*—the life airs; *akṣāḥ*—the different senses; *manavaḥ*—the mind, understanding, intellect and ego; *bhūta-mātrām*—the five gross material elements and the sense objects (form, taste, sound and so on); *ātmānam*—themselves; *anyam*—any other; *ca*—and; *viduḥ*—know; *param*—beyond; *yat*—that which; *sarvam*—everything; *pumān*—the living being; *veda*—knows; *guṇān*—the qualities of the material nature; *ca*—and; *tat-jñaḥ*—knowing those things; *na*—not; *veda*—knows; *sarva-jñam*—unto the omniscient; *anantam*—the unlimited; *īḍe*—I offer my respectful obeisances.

TRANSLATION

Because they are only matter, the body, the life airs, the external and internal senses, the five gross elements and the subtle sense objects [form, taste, smell, sound and touch] cannot know their own nature, the nature of the other senses or the nature of their controllers. But the living being, because of his spiritual nature, can know his body, the life airs, the senses, the elements and the sense objects, and he can also know the three qualities that form their roots. Nevertheless, although the living being is completely aware of them, he is unable to see the Supreme Being, who is omniscient and unlimited. I therefore offer my respectful obeisances unto Him.

PURPORT

Material scientists can make an analytical study of the physical elements, the body, the senses, the sense objects and even the air that controls the vital force, but still they cannot understand that above all these is the real spirit soul. In other words, the living entity, because of his being a spirit soul, can understand all the material objects, or, when self-realized, he can understand the Paramātmā, upon whom *yogīs* meditate. Nevertheless, the living being, even if advanced, cannot understand the Supreme Being, the Personality of Godhead, for He is *ananta,* unlimited, in all six opulences.

TEXT 26

यदोपरामो मनसो नामरूप-
रूपस्य दृष्टस्मृतिसम्प्रमोषात् ।
य ईयते केवलया स्वसंस्थया
हंसाय तस्मै शुचिसद्मने नमः ॥ २६ ॥

yadoparāmo manaso nāma-rūpa-
rūpasya dṛṣṭa-smṛti-sampramoṣāt
ya īyate kevalayā sva-saṁsthayā
haṁsāya tasmai śuci-sadmane namaḥ

yadā—when in trance; *uparāmaḥ*—complete cessation; *manasaḥ*—of the mind; *nāma-rūpa*—material names and forms; *rūpasya*—of that by which they appear; *dṛṣṭa*—of material vision; *smṛti*—and of remembrance; *sampramoṣāt*—due to the destruction; *yaḥ*—who (the Supreme Personality of Godhead); *īyate*—is perceived; *kevalayā*—with spiritual; *sva-saṁsthayā*—His own original form; *haṁsāya*—unto the supreme pure; *tasmai*—unto Him; *śuci-sadmane*—who is realized only in the pure state of spiritual existence; *namaḥ*—I offer my respectful obeisances.

TRANSLATION

When one's consciousness is completely purified of the contamination of material existence, gross and subtle, without being agitated as in the working and dreaming states, and when the mind is not dissolved as in suṣupti, deep sleep, one comes to the platform of trance. Then one's material vision and the memories of the mind, which manifests names and forms, are vanquished. Only in such a trance is the Supreme Personality of Godhead revealed. Thus let us offer our respectful obeisances unto the Supreme Personality of Godhead, who is seen in that uncontaminated, transcendental state.

PURPORT

There are two stages of God realization. One is called *sujñeyam,* or very easily understood (generally by mental speculation), and the other is called *durjñeyam,* understood only with difficulty. Paramātmā realization and Brahman realization are considered *sujñeyam,* but realization of the Supreme Personality of Godhead is *durjñeyam.* As described here, one attains the ultimate realization of the Personality of Godhead when one gives up the activities of the mind—thinking, feeling and willing—or, in other words, when mental speculation stops. This transcendental realization is above *suṣupti,* deep sleep. In our gross conditional stage we perceive things through material experience and remembrance, and in the subtle stage we perceive the world in dreams. The process of vision also involves remembrance and also exists in a subtle form. Above gross experience and dreams is *suṣupti,* deep sleep, and when one comes to the completely spiritual platform, transcending deep sleep, he attains trance, *viśuddha-sattva,* or *vasudeva-sattva,* in which the Personality of Godhead is revealed.

Ataḥ śrī-kṛṣṇa-nāmādi na bhaved grāhyam indriyaiḥ : as long as one is situated in duality, on the sensual platform, gross or subtle, realization of the original Personality of Godhead is impossible. *Sevonmukhe hi jihvādau svayam eva sphuraty adaḥ:* but when one engages his senses in the service of the Lord—specifically, when one engages the tongue in chanting the Hare Kṛṣṇa *mantra* and tasting only Kṛṣṇa *prasāda* with a spirit of service—the Supreme

Personality of Godhead is revealed. This is indicated in this verse by the word *śuci-sadmane. Śuci* means purified. By the spirit of rendering service with one's senses, one's entire existence becomes *śuci-sadma,* the platform of uncontaminated purity. Dakṣa therefore offers his respectful obeisances unto the Supreme Personality of Godhead, who is revealed on the platform of *śuci-sadma.* In this regard Śrīla Viśvanātha Cakravartī Ṭhākura quotes the following prayer by Lord Brahmā from the *Śrīmad-Bhāgavatam* (10.14.6): *tathāpi bhūman mahimāguṇasya te viboddhum arhaty amalāntar-ātmabhiḥ.* "One whose heart has become completely purified, my Lord, can understand the transcendental qualities of Your Lordship and can understand the greatness of Your activities."

TEXTS 27–28

मनीषिणोऽन्तर्हृदि संनिवेशितं
स्वशक्तिभिर्नवभिश्च त्रिवृद्भिः ।
वह्निं यथा दारुणि पाञ्चदश्यं
मनीषया निष्कर्षन्ति गूढम् ॥ २७ ॥
स वै ममाशेषविशेषमाया-
निषेधनिर्वाणसुखानुभूतिः ।
स सर्वनामा स च विश्वरूपः
प्रसीदतामनिरुक्तात्मशक्तिः ॥ २८ ॥

manīṣiṇo'ntar-hṛdi sanniveśitaṁ
sva-śaktibhir navabhiś ca trivṛdbhiḥ
vahniṁ yathā dāruṇi pāñcadaśyaṁ
manīṣayā niṣkarṣanti gūḍham

sa vai mamāśeṣa-viśeṣa-māyā-
niṣedha-nirvāṇa-sukhānubhūtiḥ
sa sarva-nāmā sa ca viśva-rūpaḥ
prasīdatām aniruktātma-śaktiḥ

manīṣiṇaḥ—great learned *brāhmaṇas* performing ritualistic ceremonies and sacrifices; *antaḥ-hṛdi*—within the core of the heart; *sanniveśitam*—being situated; *sva-śaktibhiḥ*—with His own spiritual potencies; *navabhiḥ*—also with the nine different material potencies (the material nature, the total material energy, the ego, the mind and the five objects of the senses); *ca*—

and (the five gross material elements and the ten acting and knowledge-gathering senses); *trivṛdbhiḥ*—by the three material modes of nature; *vahnim*—fire; *yathā*—just like; *dāruṇi*—within wood; *pāñcadaśyam*—produced by chanting the fifteen hymns known as Sāmidhenī *mantras; manīṣayā*—by purified intelligence; *niṣkarṣanti*—extract; *gūḍham*—although not manifesting; *saḥ*—that Supreme Personality of Godhead; *vai*—indeed; *mama*—toward me; *aśeṣa*—all; *viśeṣa*—varieties; *māyā*—of the illusory energy; *niṣedha*—by the process of negation; *nirvāṇa*—of liberation; *sukha-anubhūtiḥ*—who is realized by transcendental bliss; *saḥ*—that Supreme Personality of Godhead; *sarva-nāmā*—who is the source of all names; *saḥ*—that Supreme Personality of Godhead; *ca*—also; *viśva-rūpaḥ*—the gigantic form of the universe; *prasīdatām*—may He be merciful; *anirukta*—inconceivable; *ātma-śaktiḥ*—the reservoir of all spiritual potencies.

TRANSLATION

Just as great learned brāhmaṇas who are expert in performing ritualistic ceremonies and sacrifices can extract the fire dormant within wooden fuel by chanting the fifteen Sāmidhenī mantras, thus proving the efficacy of the Vedic mantras, so those who are actually advanced in consciousness—in other words, those who are Kṛṣṇa conscious—can find the Supersoul, who by His own spiritual potency is situated within the heart. The heart is covered by the three modes of material nature and the nine material elements [material nature, the total material energy, the ego, the mind and the five objects of sense gratification], and also by the five material elements and the ten senses. These twenty-seven elements constitute the external energy of the Lord. Great yogīs meditate upon the Lord, who is situated as the Supersoul, Paramātmā, within the core of the heart. May that Supersoul be pleased with me. The Supersoul is realized when one is eager for liberation from the unlimited varieties of material life. One actually attains such liberation when he engages in the transcendental loving service of the Lord and realizes the Lord because of his attitude of service. The Lord may be addressed by various spiritual names, which are inconceivable to the material senses. When will that Supreme Personality of Godhead be pleased with me?

PURPORT

In his commentary to this verse, Śrīla Viśvanātha Cakravartī Ṭhākura uses the word *durvijñeyam,* which means "very difficult to realize." The pure stage of existence is described in *Bhagavad-gītā* (7.28), wherein Kṛṣṇa says:

yeṣāṁ tv anta-gataṁ pāpaṁ
janānāṁ puṇya-karmaṇām
te dvandva-moha-nirmuktā
bhajante māṁ dṛḍha-vratāḥ

"Persons who have acted piously in previous lives and in this life, whose sinful actions are completely eradicated and who are freed from the duality of delusion, engage themselves in My service with determination."

Elsewhere in *Bhagavad-gītā* (9.14) the Lord says:

satataṁ kīrtayanto māṁ
yatantaś ca dṛḍha-vratāḥ
namasyantaś ca māṁ bhaktyā
nitya-yuktā upāsate

"Always chanting My glories, endeavoring with great determination, bowing down before Me, these great souls perpetually worship Me with devotion."

One can understand the Supreme Personality of Godhead after transcending all material impediments. Therefore Lord Kṛṣṇa also says in the *Gītā* (7.3):

manuṣyāṇāṁ sahasreṣu
kaścid yatati siddhaye
yatatām api siddhānāṁ
kaścin māṁ vetti tattvataḥ

"Out of many thousands among men, one may endeavor for perfection, and of those who have achieved perfection, hardly one knows Me in truth."

To understand Kṛṣṇa, the Supreme Personality of Godhead, one must undergo severe penances and austerities, but since the path of devotional service is perfect, by following this process one can very easily come to the spiritual platform and understand the Lord. This, too, is confirmed in *Bhagavad-gītā* (18.55), wherein Kṛṣṇa says:

bhaktyā mām abhijānāti
yāvān yaś cāsmi tattvataḥ
tato māṁ tattvato jñātvā
viśate tad-anantaram

"One can understand the Supreme Personality of Godhead as He is only by devotional service. And when one is in full consciousness of the Supreme Lord by such devotion, he can enter into the kingdom of God."

Thus although the subject matter is *durvijñeyam,* extremely difficult to understand, it becomes easy if one follows the prescribed method. Coming in touch with the Supreme Personality of Godhead is possible through pure devotional service, which begins with *śravaṇaṁ kīrtanaṁ viṣṇoḥ.* In this regard, Śrīla Viśvanātha Cakravartī Ṭhākura quotes a verse from *Śrīmad-Bhāgavatam* (2.8.5): *praviṣṭaḥ karṇa-randhreṇa svānāṁ bhāva-saroruham.* The process of hearing and chanting enters the core of the heart, and in this way one becomes a pure devotee. By continuing this process, one comes to the stage of transcendental love, and then he appreciates the transcendental name, form, qualities and pastimes of the Supreme Personality of Godhead. In other words, a pure devotee, by devotional service, is able to see the Supreme Personality of Godhead despite many material impediments, which are all various energies of the Supreme Personality of Godhead. Easily making his way through these impediments, a devotee comes directly in contact with the Supreme Personality of Godhead. After all, the material impediments described in these verses are but various energies of the Lord. When a devotee is eager to see the Supreme Personality of Godhead, he prays to the Lord:

ayi nanda-tanuja kiṅkaraṁ
patitaṁ māṁ viṣame bhavāmbudhau
kṛpayā tava pāda-paṅkaja-
sthita-dhūlī-sadṛśaṁ vicintaya

"O son of Mahārāja Nanda [Kṛṣṇa], I am Your eternal servitor, yet somehow or other I have fallen into the ocean of birth and death. Please pick me up from this ocean of death and place me as one of the atoms at Your lotus feet." Being pleased with the devotee, the Lord turns all his material impediments into spiritual service. In this connection Śrīla Viśvanātha Cakravartī Ṭhākura quotes a verse from the *Viṣṇu Purāṇa:*

hlādinī sandhinī samvit
tvayy ekā sarva-saṁsthitau
hlāda-tāpa-karī miśrā
tvayi no guṇa-varjite

In the material world, the spiritual energy of the Supreme Personality of Godhead is manifested as *tāpa-karī,* which means "causing miseries." Everyone hankers for happiness, but although happiness originally comes from the pleasure potency of the Supreme Personality of Godhead, in the material world, because of material activities, the pleasure potency of the Lord becomes a source of miseries (*hlāda-tāpa-karī*). False happiness in the material world is the source of distress, but when one's endeavors for happiness are redirected toward the satisfaction of the Supreme Personality of Godhead, this *tāpa-karī* element of misery is vanquished. An example given in this connection is that extracting fire from wood is certainly difficult, but when the fire comes out it burns the wood to ashes. In other words, experiencing the Supreme Personality of Godhead is extremely difficult for those devoid of devotional service, but everything becomes easier for a devotee, and thus he can very easily meet the Supreme Lord.

Here the prayers say that the form of the Lord is beyond the jurisdiction of material form and is therefore inconceivable. A devotee prays, however, "My dear Lord, be pleased with me so that I may very easily see Your transcendental form and potency." Nondevotees try to understand the Supreme Brahman by discussions of *neti neti. Niṣedha-nirvāṇa-sukhānubhūtiḥ:* a devotee, however, simply by chanting the holy name of the Lord, avoids such laborious speculations and realizes the existence of the Lord very easily.

TEXT 29

यद्यन्निरुक्तं वचसा निरूपितं
धियाक्षभिर्वा मनसोत यस्य ।
मा भूत् स्वरूपं गुणरूपं हि तत्तत्
स वै गुणापायविसर्गलक्षणः ॥ २९ ॥

yad yan niruktaṁ vacasā nirūpitaṁ
dhiyākṣabhir vā manasota yasya
mā bhūt svarūpaṁ guṇa-rūpaṁ hi tat tat
sa vai guṇāpāya-visarga-lakṣaṇaḥ

yat yat—whatever; *niruktam*—expressed; *vacasā*—by words; *nirūpitam*—ascertained; *dhiyā*—by so-called meditation or intelligence; *akṣabhiḥ*—by the senses; *vā*—or; *manasā*—by the mind; *uta*—certainly; *yasya*—of whom; *mā bhūt*—may not be; *sva-rūpam*—the actual form of the Lord; *guṇa-rūpam*—consisting of the three qualities; *hi*—indeed; *tat tat*—that; *saḥ*—that Supreme Personality of Godhead; *vai*—indeed; *guṇa-apāya*—the cause of the annihilation of everything made of the material modes of nature; *visarga*—and the creation; *lakṣaṇaḥ*—appearing as.

TRANSLATION

Anything expressed by material vibrations, anything ascertained by material intelligence and anything experienced by the material senses or concocted within the material mind is but an effect of the modes of material nature and therefore has nothing to do with the real nature of the Supreme Personality of Godhead. The Supreme Lord is beyond the creation of this material world, for He is the source of the material qualities and creation. As the cause of all causes, He exists before the creation and after the creation. I wish to offer my respectful obeisances unto Him.

PURPORT

One who manufactures names, forms, qualities or paraphernalia pertaining to the Supreme Personality of Godhead cannot understand Him, since He is beyond creation. The Supreme Lord is the creator of everything, and this means that He existed when there was no creation. In other words, His name, form and qualities are not materially created entities; they are transcendental always. Therefore by our material concoctions, vibrations and thoughts we cannot ascertain the Supreme Lord. This is explained in the verse *ataḥ śrī-kṛṣṇa-nāmādi na bhaved grāhyam indriyaiḥ.*

Prācetasa, Dakṣa, herein offers prayers unto the Transcendence, not to anyone within the material creation. Only fools and rascals think God a material creation. This is confirmed by the Lord Himself in *Bhagavad-gītā* (9.11):

avajānanti māṁ mūḍhā
mānuṣīṁ tanum āśritam
paraṁ bhāvam ajānanto
mama bhūta-maheśvaram

"Fools deride Me when I descend in the human form. They do not know My transcendental nature and My supreme dominion over all that be." Therefore, one must receive knowledge from a person to whom the Lord has revealed Himself; there is no value in creating an imaginary name or form for the Lord. Śrīpāda Śaṅkarācārya was an impersonalist, but nevertheless he said, *nārāyaṇaḥ paro'vyaktāt:* Nārāyaṇa, the Supreme Personality of Godhead, is not a person of the material world. We cannot assign Nārāyaṇa a material designation, as the foolish attempt to do when they speak of *daridra-nārāyaṇa* (poor Nārāyaṇa). Nārāyaṇa is always transcendental, beyond this material creation. How can He become *daridra-nārāyaṇa*? Poverty is found within this material world, but in the spiritual world, there is no such thing as poverty. Therefore the idea of *daridra-nārāyaṇa* is merely a concoction.

Dakṣa very carefully points out that material designations cannot be names of the worshipable Lord: *yad yan niruktaṁ vacasā nirūpitam. Nirukta* refers to the Vedic dictionary. One cannot properly understand the Supreme Personality of Godhead merely by picking up expressions from a dictionary. In praying to the Lord, Dakṣa does not wish material names and forms to be the objects of his worship; rather, he wants to worship the Lord, who existed before the creation of material dictionaries and names. As confirmed in the *Vedas, yato vāco nivartante/ aprāpya manasā saha:* the name, form, attributes and paraphernalia of the Lord cannot be ascertained through a material dictionary. However, if one reaches the transcendental platform of understanding the Supreme Personality of Godhead, he becomes well acquainted with everything, material and spiritual. This is confirmed in another Vedic *mantra: tam eva viditvāti mṛtyum eti.* If one can somehow or other, by the grace of the Lord, understand the transcendental position of the Lord, one becomes eternal. This is further confirmed by the Lord Himself in *Bhagavad-gītā* (4.9):

janma karma ca me divyam
evaṁ yo vetti tattvataḥ
tyaktvā dehaṁ punar janma
naiti mām eti so'rjuna

"One who knows the transcendental nature of My appearance and activities does not, upon leaving the body, take his birth again in this material world, but attains My eternal abode, O Arjuna." Simply by understanding the Supreme Lord, one goes beyond birth, death, old age and disease. Śrīla Śukadeva Gosvāmī therefore advised Mahārāja Parīkṣit in *Śrīmad-Bhāgavatam* (2.1.5):

tasmād bhārata sarvātmā
bhagavān īśvaro hariḥ
śrotavyaḥ kīrtitavyaś ca
smartavyaś cecchatābhayam

"O descendant of King Bharata, one who desires to be free from all miseries must hear, glorify and also remember the Personality of Godhead, who is the Supersoul, the controller and the savior from all miseries."

TEXT 30

यस्मिन् यतो येन च यस्य यस्मै
यद् यो यथा कुरुते कार्यते च।
परावरेषां परमं प्राक् प्रसिद्धं
तद् ब्रह्म तद्धेतुरनन्यदेकम् ॥ ३० ॥

yasmin yato yena ca yasya yasmai
yad yo yathā kurute kāryate ca
parāvareṣāṁ paramaṁ prāk prasiddhaṁ
tad brahma tad dhetur ananyad ekam

yasmin—in whom (the Supreme Personality of Godhead or the supreme place of repose); *yataḥ*—from whom (everything emanates); *yena*—by whom (everything is enacted); *ca*—also; *yasya*—to whom everything belongs; *yasmai*—to whom (everything is offered); *yat*—which; *yaḥ*—who; *yathā*—as; *kurute*—executes; *kāryate*—is performed; *ca*—also; *para-avareṣām*—of both, in the material and spiritual existence; *paramam*—the supreme; *prāk*—the origin; *prasiddham*—well known to everyone; *tat*—that; *brahma*—the Supreme Brahman; *tat hetuḥ*—the cause of all causes; *ananyat*—having no other cause; *ekam*—one without a second.

TRANSLATION

The Supreme Brahman, Kṛṣṇa, is the ultimate resting place and source of everything. Everything is done by Him, everything belongs to Him, and everything is offered to Him. He is the ultimate objective, and whether acting or causing others to act, He is the ultimate doer. There are many causes, high and low, but since He is the cause of all causes, He is well known as the Supreme Brahman who existed before all activities. He is one without a second and has no other cause. I therefore offer my respects unto Him.

PURPORT

The Supreme Personality of Godhead, Kṛṣṇa, is the original cause, as confirmed in *Bhagavad-gītā* (*ahaṁ sarvasya prabhavaḥ*). Even this material world, which is conducted under the modes of material nature, is caused by the Supreme Personality of Godhead, who therefore also has an intimate relationship with the material world. If the material world were not a part of His body, the Supreme Lord, the supreme cause, would be incomplete. Therefore we hear, *vāsudevaḥ sarvam iti sa mahātmā su-durlabhaḥ:* if one knows that Vāsudeva is the original cause of all causes, he becomes a perfect *mahātmā.*

The *Brahma-saṁhitā* (5.1) declares:

īśvaraḥ paramaḥ kṛṣṇaḥ
sac-cid-ānanda-vigrahaḥ
anādir ādir govindaḥ
sarva-kāraṇa-kāraṇam

"Kṛṣṇa, who is known as Govinda, is the supreme controller. He has an eternal, blissful, spiritual body. He is the origin of all. He has no other origin, for He is the prime cause of all causes." The Supreme Brahman (*tad brahma*) is the cause of all causes, but He has no cause. *Anādir ādir govindaḥ sarva-kāraṇa-kāraṇam:* Govinda, Kṛṣṇa, is the original cause of all causes, but He has no cause for His appearance as Govinda. Govinda expands in multifarious forms, but nevertheless they are one. As confirmed by Madhvācārya, *ananyaḥ sadṛśābhāvād eko rūpādy-abhedataḥ:* Kṛṣṇa has no cause nor any equal, and He is one because His various forms, as *svāṁśa* and *vibhinnāṁśa,* are nondifferent from Himself.

TEXT 31

यच्छक्तयो वदतां वादिनां वै
विवादसंवादभुवो भवन्ति ।
कुर्वन्ति चैषां मुहुरात्ममोहं
तस्मै नमोऽनन्तगुणाय भूम्ने ॥ ३१ ॥

yac-chaktayo vadatāṁ vādināṁ vai
vivāda-saṁvāda-bhuvo bhavanti
kurvanti caiṣāṁ muhur ātma-mohaṁ
tasmai namo'nanta-guṇāya bhūmne

yat-śaktayaḥ—whose multifarious potencies; *vadatām*—speaking different philosophies; *vādinām*—of the speakers; *vai*—indeed; *vivāda*—of argument; *saṁvāda*—and agreement; *bhuvaḥ*—the causes; *bhavanti*—are; *kurvanti*—create; *ca*—and; *eṣām*—of them (the theorists); *muhuḥ*—continuously; *ātma-moham*—bewilderment regarding the existence of the soul; *tasmai*—unto Him; *namaḥ*—my respectful obeisances; *ananta*—

unlimited; *guṇāya*—possessing transcendental attributes; *bhūmne*—the all-pervading Godhead.

TRANSLATION

Let me offer my respectful obeisances unto the all-pervading Supreme Personality of Godhead, who possesses unlimited transcendental qualities. Acting from within the cores of the hearts of all philosophers, who propagate various views, He causes them to forget their own souls while sometimes agreeing and sometimes disagreeing among themselves. Thus He creates within this material world a situation in which they are unable to come to a conclusion. I offer my obeisances unto Him.

PURPORT

Since time immemorial or since the creation of the cosmic manifestation, the conditioned souls have formed various parties of philosophical speculation, but this is not true of the devotees. Nondevotees have different ideas of creation, maintenance and annihilation, and therefore they are called *vādīs* and *prativādīs*—proponents and counterproponents. It is understood from the statement of *Mahābhārata* that there are many *munis,* or speculators:

tarko'pratiṣṭhaḥ śrutayo vibhinnā
nāsāv ṛṣir yasya mataṁ na bhinnam

All speculators must disagree with other speculators; otherwise, why should there be so many opposing parties concerned with ascertaining the supreme cause?

Philosophy means finding the ultimate cause. As *Vedānta-sūtra* very reasonably says, *athāto brahma jijñāsā:* human life is meant for understanding the ultimate cause. Devotees accept that the ultimate cause is Kṛṣṇa because this conclusion is supported by all Vedic literature and also by Kṛṣṇa Himself, who says, *ahaṁ sarvasya prabhavaḥ:* "I am the source of everything." Devotees have no problem understanding the ultimate cause of everything, but nondevotees must face many opposing elements because everyone who wants to be a prominent philosopher invents his own way. In India there are many parties of philosophers, such as the *dvaita-vādīs, advaita-vādīs, vaiśeṣikas, mīmāṁsakas,* Māyāvādīs and *svabhāva-vādīs,* and each of them opposes the others. Similarly, in the Western countries there are also many philosophers with different views of creation, life, maintenance and annihilation. Thus it is undoubtedly a fact that there are countless philosophers throughout the world, each of them contradicting the others.

Now, one might ask why there are so many philosophers if the ultimate goal of philosophy is one. Undoubtedly the ultimate cause is one—the Supreme Brahman. As Arjuna told Kṛṣṇa in *Bhagavad-gītā* (10.12):

paraṁ brahma paraṁ dhāma
pavitraṁ paramaṁ bhavān
puruṣaṁ śāśvataṁ divyam
ādi-devam ajaṁ vibhum

"You are the Supreme Brahman, the ultimate, the supreme abode and purifier, the Absolute Truth and the eternal divine person. You are the primal God, transcendental and original, and You are the unborn and all-pervading beauty." Nondevotee speculators, however, do not accept an ultimate cause (*sarva-kāraṇa-kāraṇam*). Because they are ignorant and bewildered concerning the soul and its activities, even though some of them have a vague idea of the soul, many controversies arise, and the philosophical speculators can never reach a conclusion. All of these speculators are envious of the Supreme Personality of Godhead, and as Kṛṣṇa says in *Bhagavad-gītā* (16.19–20):

tān ahaṁ dviṣataḥ krūrān
saṁsāreṣu narādhamān
kṣipāmy ajasram aśubhān
āsurīṣv eva yoniṣu

āsurīṁ yonim āpannā
mūḍhā janmani janmani
mām aprāpyaiva kaunteya
tato yānty adhamāṁ gatim

"Those who are envious and mischievous, who are the lowest among men, are cast by Me into the ocean of material existence, into various demoniac species of life. Attaining repeated birth among the species of demoniac life, such persons can never approach Me. Gradually they sink down to the most abominable type of existence." Because of their envy of the Supreme Personality of Godhead, nondevotees are born in demoniac families life after life. They are great offenders, and because of their offenses the Supreme Lord keeps them always bewildered. *Kurvanti caiṣāṁ muhur ātma-moham:* the

Lord, the Supreme Personality of Godhead, purposely keeps them in darkness (*ātma-mohaṁ*).

The great authority Parāśara, the father of Vyāsadeva, explains the Supreme Personality of Godhead thus:

jñāna-śakti-balaiśvarya-
vīrya-tejāṁsy aśeṣataḥ
bhagavac-chabda-vācyāni
vinā heyair guṇādibhiḥ

The demoniac speculators cannot understand the transcendental qualities, form, pastimes, strength, knowledge and opulence of the Supreme Personality of Godhead, which are all free from material contamination (*vinā heyair guṇādibhiḥ*). These speculators are envious of the existence of the Lord. *Jagad āhur anīśvaram:* their conclusion is that the entire cosmic manifestation has no controller, but is just working naturally. Thus they are kept in constant darkness, birth after birth, and cannot understand the real cause of all causes. This is the reason why there are so many schools of philosophical speculation.

TEXT 32

अस्तीति नास्तीति च वस्तुनिष्ठयो-
रेकस्थयोर्भिन्नविरुद्धधर्मणोः ।
अवेक्षितं किञ्चन योगसांख्ययोः
समं परं ह्यनुकूलं बृहत्तत् ॥ ३२ ॥

astīti nāstīti ca vastu-niṣṭhayor
eka-sthayor bhinna-viruddha-dharmaṇoḥ
avekṣitaṁ kiñcana yoga-sāṅkhyayoḥ
samaṁ paraṁ hy anukūlaṁ bṛhat tat

asti—there is; *iti*—thus; *na*—not; *asti*—there is; *iti*—thus; *ca*—and; *vastu-niṣṭhayoḥ*—professing knowledge of the ultimate cause; *eka-sthayoḥ*—with one and the same subject matter, establishing Brahman; *bhinna*—demonstrating different; *viruddha-dharmaṇoḥ*—and opposing characteristics; *avekṣitam*—perceived; *kiñcana*—that something which; *yoga-sāṅkhyayoḥ*—of mystic *yoga* and the Sāṅkhya philosophy (analysis of the ways of nature); *samam*—the same; *param*—transcendental; *hi*—indeed; *anukūlam*—dwelling place; *bṛhat tat*—that ultimate cause.

TRANSLATION

There are two parties—namely, the theists and the atheists. The theist, who accepts the Supersoul, finds the spiritual cause through mystic yoga. The Sāṅkhyite, however, who merely analyzes the material elements, comes to a conclusion of impersonalism and does not accept a supreme cause—whether Bhagavān, Paramātmā or even Brahman. Instead, he is preoccupied with the superfluous, external activities of material nature. Ultimately, however, both parties demonstrate the Absolute Truth because although they offer opposing statements, their object is the same ultimate cause. They are both approaching the same Supreme Brahman, to whom I offer my respectful obeisances.

PURPORT

Actually there are two sides to this argument. Some say that the Absolute has no form (*nirākāra*), and others say that the Absolute has a form (*sākāra*). Therefore the word form is the common factor, although some accept it (*asti* or *astika*) whereas others try to negate it (*nāsti* or *nāstika*). Since the devotee considers the word "form" (*ākāra*) the common factor for both, he offers his respectful obeisances to the form, although others may go on arguing about whether the Absolute has a form or not.

In this verse the word *yoga-sāṅkhyayoḥ* is very important. *Yoga* means *bhakti-yoga* because *yogīs* also accept the existence of the all-pervading Supreme Soul and try to see that Supreme Soul within their hearts. As stated in *Śrīmad-Bhāgavatam* (12.13.1), *dhyānāvasthita-tad-gatena manasā paśyanti yaṁ yoginaḥ.* The devotee tries to come directly in touch with the Supreme Personality of Godhead, whereas the *yogī* tries to find the Supersoul within the heart by meditation. Thus, both directly and indirectly, *yoga* means *bhakti-yoga.* Sāṅkhya, however, means physical study of the cosmic situation through speculative knowledge. This is generally known as *jñāna-śāstra.* The Sāṅkhyites are attached to the impersonal Brahman, but the Absolute Truth is known in three ways. *Brahmeti paramātmeti bhagavān iti śabdyate:* the Absolute Truth is one, but some accept Him as impersonal Brahman, some as the Supersoul existing everywhere, and some as Bhagavān, the Supreme Personality of Godhead. The central point is the Absolute Truth.

Although the impersonalists and personalists fight with one another, they focus upon the same Parabrahman, the same Absolute Truth. In the *yoga-śāstras,* Kṛṣṇa is described as follows: *kṛṣṇaṁ piśaṅgāmbaram ambujekṣaṇaṁ catur-bhujaṁ śaṅkha-gadādy-udāyudham.* Thus the pleasing appearance of the Supreme Personality of Godhead's bodily features, His limbs and His dress are described. The *sāṅkhya-śāstra,* however, denies the existence of the Lord's transcendental form. The *sāṅkhya-śāstra* says that the Supreme Absolute Truth has no hands, no legs and no name: *hy anāma-rūpa-guṇa-pāṇi-pādam acakṣur aśrotram ekam advitīyam api nāma-rūpādikaṁ nāsti.* The Vedic *mantras* say, *apāṇi-pādo javano grahītā:* the Supreme Lord has no legs and hands, but He can accept whatever is offered to Him. Actually such statements accept that the Supreme has hands and legs, but deny that He has material hands and legs. This is why the Absolute is called *aprākṛta.* Kṛṣṇa, the Supreme Personality of Godhead, has a *sac-cid-ānanda-vigraha,* a form of eternity, knowledge and bliss, not a material form. The Sāṅkhyites, or *jñānīs,* deny the material form, and the devotees also know very well that the Absolute Truth, Bhagavān, has no material form.

īśvaraḥ paramaḥ kṛṣṇaḥ
sac-cid-ānanda-vigrahaḥ
anādir ādir govindaḥ
sarva-kāraṇa-kāraṇam

"Kṛṣṇa, who is known as Govinda, is the supreme controller. He has an eternal, blissful, spiritual body. He is the origin of all. He has no other origin, for He is the prime cause of all causes." The conception of the Absolute without hands and legs and the conception of the Absolute with hands and legs are apparently contradictory, but they both coincide with the same truth about the Supreme Absolute Person. Therefore the word *vastu-niṣṭhayoḥ,* which is used herein, indicates that both the *yogīs* and Sāṅkhyites have faith in the reality, but are arguing about it from the different viewpoints of material and spiritual identities. Parabrahman, or *bṛhat,* is the common point. The Sāṅkhyites and *yogīs* are both situated in that same Brahman, but they differ because of different angles of vision.

The directions given by the *bhakti-śāstra* point one in the perfect direction because the Supreme Personality of Godhead says in *Bhagavad-gītā, bhaktyā mām abhijānāti:* "Only by devotional service am I to be known." The *bhaktas* know that the Supreme Person has no material form, whereas the *jñānīs* simply deny the material form. One should therefore take shelter of the *bhakti-mārga,* the path of devotion; then everything will be clear. *Jñānīs* concentrate on the *virāṭ-rūpa,* the gigantic universal form of the Lord. This is a good system in the beginning for those who are extremely materialistic, but there is no need to think continuously of the *virāṭ-rūpa.* When Arjuna was shown the *virāṭ-rūpa* of Kṛṣṇa, he saw it, but he did not want to see it perpetually. He therefore requested the Lord to return to His original form as two-armed Kṛṣṇa. In conclusion, learned scholars find no contradictions in the devotees' concentration upon the spiritual form of the Lord (*īśvaraḥ paramaḥ kṛṣṇaḥ sac-cid-ānanda-vigrahaḥ*). In this regard, Śrīla Madhvācārya says that less intelligent nondevotees think that their conclusion is the ultimate, but because devotees are completely learned, they can understand that the Supreme Personality of Godhead is the ultimate goal.

TEXT 33

योऽनुग्रहार्थं भजतां पादमूल-
मनामरूपो भगवाननन्तः ।
नामानि रूपाणि च जन्मकर्मभि-
र्भेजे स मह्यं परमः प्रसीदतु ॥ ३३ ॥

yo'nugrahārthaṁ bhajatāṁ pāda-mūlam
anāma-rūpo bhagavān anantaḥ
nāmāni rūpāṇi ca janma-karmabhir
bheje sa mahyaṁ paramaḥ prasīdatu

yaḥ—who (the Supreme Personality of Godhead); *anugraha-artham*—to show His causeless mercy; *bhajatām*—to the devotees who always render devotional service; *pāda-mūlam*—to His transcendental lotus feet; *anāma*—with no material name; *rūpaḥ*—or material form; *bhagavān*—the Supreme Personality of Godhead; *anantaḥ*—unlimited, all-pervading and eternally existing; *nāmāni*—transcendental holy names; *rūpāṇi*—His transcendental forms; *ca*—also; *janma-karmabhiḥ*—with His transcendental birth and activities; *bheje*—manifests; *saḥ*—He; *mahyam*—unto me; *paramaḥ*—the Supreme; *prasīdatu*—may He be merciful.

TRANSLATION

The Supreme Personality of Godhead, who is inconceivably opulent, who is devoid of all material names, forms and pastimes, and who is all-pervading, is especially merciful to the devotees who worship His lotus feet. Thus He exhibits transcendental forms and names with His different pastimes. May that Supreme Personality of Godhead, whose form is eternal and full of knowledge and bliss, be merciful to me.

PURPORT

In regard to the significant word *anāma-rūpaḥ,* Śrī Śrīdhara Svāmī says, *prākṛta-nāma-rūpa-rahito'pi.* The word *anāma,* which means "having no name," indicates that the Supreme Personality of Godhead has no material name. Simply by chanting the name of Nārāyaṇa to call his son, Ajāmila attained salvation. This means that Nārāyaṇa is not an ordinary mundane name; it is nonmaterial. The word *anāma,* therefore, indicates that the names of the Supreme Lord do not belong to this material world. The vibration of the Hare Kṛṣṇa *mahā-mantra* is not a material sound, and similarly the form of the Lord and His appearance and activities are all nonmaterial. To show His causeless mercy to the devotees, as well as to the nondevotees, Kṛṣṇa, the Supreme Personality of Godhead, appears in this material world with names, forms and pastimes, all of which are transcendental. Unintelligent men who cannot understand this think that these names, forms and pastimes are material, and therefore they deny that He has a name or a form.

Considered with scrutiny, the conclusion of nondevotees, who say that God has no name, and that of devotees, who know that His name is not material, are practically the same. The Supreme Personality of Godhead has no material name, form, birth, appearance or disappearance, but nevertheless, He takes His birth (*janma*). As stated in *Bhagavad-gītā* (4.6):

ajo'pi sann avyayātmā
bhūtānām īśvaro'pi san
prakṛtiṁ svām adhiṣṭhāya
sambhavāmy ātma-māyayā

Although the Lord is unborn (*aja*) and His body never undergoes material changes, He nevertheless appears as an incarnation, maintaining Himself always in the transcendental stage (*śuddha-sattva*). Thus He exhibits His transcendental forms, names and activities. That is His special mercy toward His devotees. Others may continue merely arguing about whether the Absolute Truth has form or not, but when a devotee, by the grace of the Lord, sees the Lord personally, he becomes spiritually ecstatic.

Unintelligent persons say that the Lord does nothing. Actually He has nothing to do, but nevertheless He has to do everything, because without His sanction no one can do anything. The unintelligent, however, cannot see how He is working and how the entire material nature is working under His direction. His different potencies work perfectly.

na tasya kāryaṁ karaṇaṁ ca vidyate
na tat-samaś cābhyadhikaś ca dṛśyate
parāsya śaktir vividhaiva śrūyate
svābhāvikī jñāna-bala-kriyā ca
(Śvetāśvatara Upaniṣad 6.8)

He has nothing to do personally, for since His potencies are perfect, everything is immediately done by His will. Persons to whom the Supreme Personality of Godhead is not revealed cannot see how He is working, and therefore they think that even if there is God, He has nothing to do or has no particular name.

Actually the Lord's name already exists because of His transcendental activities. The Lord is sometimes called *guṇa-karma-nāma* because He is named according to His transcendental activities. For example, *Kṛṣṇa* means "all-attractive." This is the Lord's name because His transcendental qualities make Him very attractive. As a small boy He lifted Govardhana Hill, and in His childhood He killed many demons. Such activities are very attractive, and therefore He is sometimes called Giridhārī, Madhusūdana, Agha-niṣūdana and so on. Because He acted as the son of Nanda Mahārāja, He is called Nanda-tanuja. These names already exist, but since nondevotees cannot understand the names of the Lord, He is sometimes called *anāma,* or nameless. This means that He has no material names. All His activities are spiritual, and therefore He has spiritual names.

Generally, less intelligent men are under the impression that the Lord has no form. Therefore He appears in His original form as Kṛṣṇa, *sac-cid-ānanda-vigraha,* to carry out His mission of participating in the Battle of Kurukṣetra and pastimes to protect the devotees and vanquish the demons (*paritrāṇāya sādhūnāṁ vināśāya ca duṣkṛtām*). This is His mercy. For those who think that He has no form and no work to do, Kṛṣṇa comes to show that indeed He works. He works so gloriously that no one else can perform such uncommon acts. Although He appeared as a human being, He married 16,108 wives, which is impossible for a human being to do. The Lord performs such activities to show people how great He is, how affectionate He is and how merciful He is. Although His original name is Kṛṣṇa (*kṛṣṇas tu bhagavān svayam*), He acts in unlimited ways, and therefore according to His work He has many, many thousands of names.

TEXT 34

यः प्राकृतैर्ज्ञानपथैर्जनानां
यथाशयं देहगतो विभाति ।

यथानिलः पार्थिवमाश्रितो गुणं
स ईश्वरो मे कुरुतां मनोरथम् ॥ ३४ ॥

yaḥ prākṛtair jñāna-pathair janānāṁ
yathāśayaṁ deha-gato vibhāti
yathānilaḥ pārthivam āśrito guṇaṁ
sa īśvaro me kurutāṁ manoratham

yaḥ—who; *prākṛtaiḥ*—lower grade; *jñāna-pathaiḥ*—by the paths of worship; *janānām*—of all living entities; *yathā-āśayam*—according to the desire; *deha-gataḥ*—situated within the core of the heart; *vibhāti*—manifests; *yathā*—just as; *anilaḥ*—the air; *pārthivam*—earthly; *āśritaḥ*—receiving; *guṇam*—the quality (like flavor and color); *saḥ*—He; *īśvaraḥ*—the Supreme Personality of Godhead; *me*—my; *kurutām*—may He fulfill; *manoratham*—desire (for devotional service).

TRANSLATION

As the air carries various characteristics of the physical elements, like the aroma of a flower or colors resulting from a mixture of dust in the air, the Lord appears through lower systems of worship according to one's desires, although He appears as the demigods and not in His original form. What is the use of these other forms? May the original Supreme Personality of Godhead please fulfill my desires.

PURPORT

The impersonalists imagine the various demigods to be forms of the Lord. For example, the Māyāvādīs worship five demigods (*pañcopāsanā*). They do not actually believe in the form of the Lord, but for the sake of worship they imagine some form to be God. Generally they imagine a form of Viṣṇu, a form of Śiva, and forms of Gaṇeśa, the sun-god and Durgā. This is called *pañcopāsanā.* Dakṣa, however, wanted to worship not an imaginary form, but the supreme form of Lord Kṛṣṇa.

In this regard, Śrīla Viśvanātha Cakravartī Ṭhākura describes the difference between the Supreme Personality of Godhead and an ordinary living being. As pointed out in a previous verse, *sarvaṁ pumān veda guṇāṁś ca taj-jño na veda sarva-jñam anantam īḍe:* the omnipotent Supreme Lord knows everything, but the living being does not actually know the Supreme Personality of Godhead. As Kṛṣṇa says in *Bhagavad-gītā,* "I know everything, but no one knows Me." This is the difference between the Supreme Lord and an ordinary living being. In a prayer in *Śrīmad-Bhāgavatam,* Queen Kuntī says, "My dear Lord, You exist inside and outside, yet no one can see You."

The conditioned soul cannot understand the Supreme Personality of Godhead by speculative knowledge or by imagination. One must therefore know the Supreme Personality of Godhead by the grace of the Supreme Personality of Godhead. He reveals Himself, but He cannot be understood by speculation. As stated in *Śrīmad-Bhāgavatam* (10.14.29):

athāpi te deva padāmbuja-dvaya-
prasāda-leśānugṛhīta eva hi
jānāti tattvaṁ bhagavan-mahimno
na cānya eko'pi ciraṁ vicinvan

"My Lord, if one is favored by even a slight trace of the mercy of Your lotus feet, he can understand the greatness of Your personality. But those who speculate to understand the Supreme Personality of Godhead are unable to know You, even though they continue to study the *Vedas* for many years."

This is the verdict of the *śāstra.* An ordinary man may be a great philosopher and may speculate upon what the Absolute Truth is, what His form is and where He is existing, but be cannot understand these truths. *Sevonmukhe hi jihvādau svayam eva sphuraty adaḥ:* one can understand the Supreme Personality of Godhead only through devotional service. This is also explained by the Supreme Personality of Godhead Himself in *Bhagavad-gītā* (18.55). *Bhaktyā mām abhijānāti yāvān yaś cāsmi tattvataḥ:* "One can understand the Supreme Personality of Godhead as He is only by devotional service." Unintelligent persons want to imagine or concoct a form of the Supreme Personality of Godhead, but devotees want to worship the actual Personality of Godhead. Therefore Dakṣa prays, "One may think of You as personal, impersonal or imaginary, but I wish to pray to Your Lordship that You fulfill my desires to see You as You actually are."

Śrīla Viśvanātha Cakravartī Ṭhākura comments that this verse is especially meant for the impersonalist, who thinks that he himself is the Supreme because there is no difference between the living being and God. The Māyāvādī philosopher thinks that there is only one Supreme Truth and that he is also that Supreme Truth. Actually this is not knowledge but foolishness, and this verse is especially meant for such fools, whose knowledge has been stolen by illusion (*māyayāpahṛta-jñānāḥ*). Viśvanātha Cakravartī Ṭhākura says that such persons, *jñāni-māninaḥ,* think themselves very advanced, but actually they are unintelligent.

In regard to this verse, Śrīla Madhvācārya says:

svadeha-sthaṁ hariṁ prāhur
adhamā jīvam eva tu
madhyamāś cāpy anirṇītaṁ
jīvād bhinnaṁ janārdanam

There are three classes of men—the lowest (*adhama*), those in the middle (*madhyama*), and the best (*uttama*). The lowest (*adhama*) think that there is no difference between God and the living entity except that the living entity is under designations whereas the Absolute Truth has no designations. In their opinion, as soon as the designations of the material body are dissolved, the *jīva,* the living entity, will mix with the Supreme. They give the argument of *ghaṭākāśa-paṭākāśa,* in which the body is compared to a pot with the sky within and the sky without. When the pot breaks, the sky inside becomes one with the sky outside, and so the impersonalists say that the living being becomes one with the Supreme. This is their argument, but Śrīla Madhvācārya says that such an argument is put forward by the lowest class of men. Another class of men cannot ascertain what the actual form of the Supreme is, but they agree that there is a Supreme who controls the activities of the ordinary living being. Such philosophers are accepted as mediocre. The best, however, are those who understand the Supreme Lord (*sac-cid-ānanda-vigraha*). *Pūrṇānandādi-guṇakaṁ sarva jīva-vilakṣaṇam:* His form is completely spiritual, full of bliss, and completely distinct from that of the conditioned soul or any other living entity. *Uttamās tu hariṁ prāhus tāratamyena teṣu ca:* such philosophers are the best because they know that the Supreme Personality of Godhead reveals Himself differently to worshipers in various modes of material nature. They know that there are thirty-three million demigods just to convince the conditioned soul that there is a supreme power and to induce him to agree to worship one of these demigods so that by the association of devotees he may be able to understand that Kṛṣṇa is the Supreme Personality of Godhead. As Lord Kṛṣṇa says in *Bhagavad-gītā, mattaḥ parataraṁ nānyat kiñcid asti dhanañjaya:* "There is no truth superior to Me." *Aham ādir hi devānām:* "I am the origin of all the demigods." *Ahaṁ sarvasya prabhavaḥ:* "I am superior to everyone, even Lord Brahmā, Lord Śiva and the other demigods." These are the conclusions of the *śāstra,* and one who accepts these conclusions should be considered a first-class philosopher. Such a philosopher knows that the

Supreme Personality of Godhead is the Lord of the demigods (*deva-deveśvaraṁ sūtram ānandaṁ prāṇa-vedinaḥ*).

TEXTS 35–39

श्रीशुक उवाच

इति स्तुतः संस्तुवतः स तस्मिन्नघमर्षणे ।
प्रादुरासीत् कुरुश्रेष्ठ भगवान् भक्तवत्सलः ॥ ३५ ॥
कृतपादः सुपर्णांसे प्रलम्बाष्टमहाभुजः ।
चक्रशङ्खासिचर्मेषुधनुःपाशगदाधरः ॥ ३६ ॥
पीतवासा घनश्यामः प्रसन्नवदनेक्षणः ।
वनमालानिवीताङ्गो लसच्छ्रीवत्सकौस्तुभः ॥ ३७ ॥
महाकिरीटकटकः स्फुरन्मकरकुण्डलः ।
काञ्च्यङ्गुलीयवलयनूपुराङ्गदभूषितः ॥ ३८ ॥
त्रैलोक्यमोहनं रूपं बिभ्रत् त्रिभुवनेश्वरः ।
वृतो नारदनन्दाद्यैः पार्षदैः सुरयूथपैः ।
स्तूयमानोऽनुगायद्भिः सिद्धगन्धर्वचारणैः ॥ ३९ ॥

śrī-śuka uvāca
iti stutaḥ saṁstuvataḥ
sa tasminn aghamarṣaṇe
prādurāsīt kuru-śreṣṭha
bhagavān bhakta-vatsalaḥ

kṛta-pādaḥ suparṇāṁse
pralambāṣṭa-mahā-bhujaḥ
cakra-śaṅkhāsi-carmeṣu-
dhanuḥ-pāśa-gadā-dharaḥ

pīta-vāsā ghana-śyāmaḥ
prasanna-vadanekṣaṇaḥ
vana-mālā-nivītāṅgo
lasac-chrīvatsa-kaustubhaḥ

mahā-kirīṭa-kaṭakaḥ
sphuran-makara-kuṇḍalaḥ
kāñcy-aṅgulīya-valaya-
nūpurāṅgada-bhūṣitaḥ

trailokya-mohanaṁ rūpaṁ
bibhrat tribhuvaneśvaraḥ
vṛto nārada-nandādyaiḥ
pārṣadaiḥ sura-yūthapaiḥ
stūyamāno'nugāyadbhiḥ
siddha-gandharva-cāraṇaiḥ

śrī-śukaḥ uvāca—Śrī Śukadeva Gosvāmī said; *iti*—thus; *stutaḥ*—being praised; *saṁstuvataḥ*—of Dakṣa, who was offering prayers; *saḥ*—that Supreme Personality of Godhead; *tasmin*—in that; *aghamarṣaṇe*—holy place celebrated as Aghamarṣaṇa; *prādurāsīt*—appeared; *kuru-śreṣṭha*—O best of the Kuru dynasty; *bhagavān*—the Supreme Personality of Godhead; *bhakta-vatsalaḥ*—who is very kind to His devotees; *kṛta-pādaḥ*—whose lotus feet were placed; *suparṇa-aṁse*—on the shoulders of His carrier, Garuḍa; *pralamba*—very long; *aṣṭa-mahā-bhujaḥ*—possessing eight mighty arms; *cakra*—disc; *śaṅkha*—conchshell; *asi*—sword; *carma*—shield; *iṣu*—arrow; *dhanuḥ*—bow; *pāśa*—rope; *gadā*—club; *dharaḥ*—holding; *pīta-vāsāḥ*—with yellow garments; *ghana-śyāmaḥ*—whose bodily hue was intense blue-black; *prasanna*—very cheerful; *vadana*—whose face; *īkṣaṇaḥ*—and glance; *vana-mālā*—by a garland of forest flowers; *nivīta-aṅgaḥ*—whose body was adorned from the neck down to the feet; *lasat*—shining; *śrīvatsa-kaustubhaḥ*—the jewel known as Kaustubha and the mark of Śrīvatsa; *mahā-kirīṭa*—of a very large and gorgeous helmet; *kaṭakaḥ*—a circle; *sphurat*—glittering; *makara-kuṇḍalaḥ*—earrings resembling sharks; *kāñcī*—with a belt; *aṅgulīya*—finger rings; *valaya*—bracelets; *nūpura*—ankle bells; *aṅgada*—upper-arm bracelets; *bhūṣitaḥ*—decorated; *trai-lokya-mohanam*—captivating the three worlds; *rūpam*—His bodily features; *bibhrat*—shining; *tri-bhuvana*—of the three worlds; *īśvaraḥ*—the Supreme Lord; *vṛtaḥ*—surrounded; *nārada*—by exalted devotees, headed by Nārada; *nanda-ādyaiḥ*—and others, like Nanda; *pārṣadaiḥ*—who are all eternal associates; *sura-yūthapaiḥ*—as well as by the heads of the demigods; *stūyamānaḥ*—being glorified; *anugāyadbhiḥ*—singing after Him; *siddha-gandharva-cāraṇaiḥ*—by the Siddhas, Gandharvas and Cāraṇas.

TRANSLATION

Śrī Śukadeva Gosvāmī said: The Supreme Personality of Godhead, Hari, who is extremely affectionate to His devotees, was very pleased by the prayers offered by Dakṣa, and thus He appeared at that holy place known

as Aghamarṣaṇa. O Mahārāja Parīkṣit, best of the Kuru dynasty, the Lord's lotus feet rested on the shoulders of His carrier, Garuḍa, and He appeared with eight long, mighty, very beautiful arms. In His hands He held a disc, conchshell, sword, shield, arrow, bow, rope and club—in each hand a different weapon, all brilliantly shining. His garments were yellow and His bodily hue deep bluish. His eyes and face were very cheerful, and from His neck to His feet hung a long garland of flowers. His chest was decorated with the Kaustubha jewel and the mark of Śrīvatsa. On His head was a gorgeous round helmet, and His ears were decorated with earrings resembling sharks. All these ornaments were uncommonly beautiful. The Lord wore a golden belt on His waist, bracelets on His arms, rings on His fingers, and ankle bells on His feet. Thus decorated by various ornaments, Lord Hari, who is attractive to all the living entities of the three worlds, is known as Puruṣottama, the best personality. He was accompanied by great devotees like Nārada, Nanda and all the principal demigods, led by the heavenly king, Indra, and the residents of various upper planetary systems such as Siddhaloka, Gandharvaloka and Cāraṇaloka. Situated on both sides of the Lord and behind Him as well, these devotees offered Him prayers continuously.

TEXT 40

रूपं तन्महदाश्चर्यं विचक्ष्यागतसाध्वसः ।
ननाम दण्डवद् भूमौ प्रहृष्टात्मा प्रजापतिः ॥ ४० ॥

rūpaṁ tan mahad-āścaryaṁ
vicakṣyāgata-sādhvasaḥ
nanāma daṇḍavad bhūmau
prahṛṣṭātmā prajāpatiḥ

rūpam—transcendental form; *tat*—that; *mahat-āścaryam*—greatly wonderful; *vicakṣya*—seeing; *āgata-sādhvasaḥ*—in the beginning becoming afraid; *nanāma*—offered obeisances; *daṇḍa-vat*—like a stick; *bhūmau*—on the ground; *prahṛṣṭa-ātmā*—being pleased in his body, mind and soul; *prajāpatiḥ*—the *prajāpati* known as Dakṣa.

TRANSLATION

Seeing that wonderful and effulgent form of the Supreme Personality of Godhead, Prajāpati Dakṣa was first somewhat afraid, but then he was

very pleased to see the Lord, and he fell to the ground like a stick [daṇḍavat] to offer his respects to the Lord.

TEXT 41

न किञ्चनोदीरयितुमशकत् तीव्रया मुदा।
आपूरितमनोद्वारैर्ह्रदिन्य इव निर्झरैः ॥ ४१ ॥

na kiñcanodīrayitum
aśakat tīvrayā mudā
āpūrita-manodvārair
hradinya iva nirjharaiḥ

na—not; *kiñcana*—anything; *udīrayitum*—to speak; *aśakat*—he was able; *tīvrayā*—by very great; *mudā*—happiness; *āpūrita*—filled; *manaḥ-dvāraiḥ*—by the senses; *hradinyaḥ*—the rivers; *iva*—like; *nirjharaiḥ*—by torrents from the mountain.

TRANSLATION

As rivers are filled by water flowing from a mountain, all of Dakṣa's senses were filled with pleasure. Because of his highly elevated happiness, Dakṣa could not say anything, but simply remained flat on the ground.

PURPORT

When one actually realizes or sees the Supreme Personality of Godhead, he is filled with complete happiness. For example, when Dhruva Mahārāja saw the Lord in his presence, he said, *svāmin kṛtārtho 'smi varaṁ na yāce:* "My dear Lord, I have nothing to ask from You. Now I am completely satisfied." Similarly, when Prajāpati Dakṣa saw the Supreme Lord in his presence, he simply fell flat, unable to speak or ask Him for anything.

TEXT 42

तं तथावनतं भक्तं प्रजाकामं प्रजापतिम् ।
चित्तज्ञः सर्वभूतानामिदमाह जनार्दनः ॥ ४२ ॥

taṁ tathāvanataṁ bhaktaṁ
prajā-kāmaṁ prajāpatim
citta-jñaḥ sarva-bhūtānām
idam āha janārdanaḥ

tam—him (Prajāpati Dakṣa); *tathā*—in that way; *avanatam*—prostrated before Him; *bhaktam*—a great devotee; *prajā-kāmam*—desiring to increase the population; *prajāpatim*—unto the *prajāpati* (Dakṣa); *citta-jñaḥ*—who can understand the hearts; *sarva-bhūtānām*—of all living entities; *idam*—this; *āha*—said; *janārdanaḥ*—the Supreme Personality of Godhead, who can appease everyone's desires.

TRANSLATION

Although Prajāpati Dakṣa could not say anything, when the Lord, who knows everyone's heart, saw His devotee prostrate in that manner and desiring to increase the population, He addressed him as follows.

TEXT 43

श्रीभगवानुवाच
प्राचेतस महाभाग संसिद्धस्तपसा भवान् ।
यच्छ्रद्धया मत्परया मयि भावं परं गतः ॥ ४३ ॥

śrī-bhagavān uvāca
prācetasa mahā-bhāga
saṁsiddhas tapasā bhavān
yac chraddhayā mat-parayā
mayi bhāvaṁ paraṁ gataḥ

śrī-bhagavān uvāca—the Supreme Personality of Godhead said; *prācetasa*—O My dear Prācetasa; *mahā-bhāga*—O you who are so fortunate; *saṁsiddhaḥ*—perfected; *tapasā*—by your austerities; *bhavān*—your good self; *yat*—because; *śraddhayā*—by great faith; *mat-parayā*—whose object is Me; *mayi*—in Me; *bhāvam*—ecstasy; *param*—supreme; *gataḥ*—attained.

TRANSLATION

The Supreme Personality of Godhead said: O most fortunate Prācetasa, because of your great faith in Me, you have attained the supreme devotional ecstasy. Indeed, because of your austerities, combined with exalted devotion, your life is now successful. You have achieved complete perfection.

PURPORT

As the Lord Himself confirms in *Bhagavad-gītā* (8.15), one reaches the highest perfection when he attains the fortune of realizing the Supreme Personality of Godhead:

mām upetya punar janma
duḥkhālayam aśāśvatam
nāpnuvanti mahātmānaḥ
saṁsiddhiṁ paramāṁ gatāḥ

"After attaining Me, the great souls, who are *yogīs* in devotion, never return to this temporary world, which is full of miseries, because they have attained the highest perfection." Therefore the Kṛṣṇa consciousness movement teaches one to follow the path toward the topmost perfection simply by performing devotional service.

TEXT 44

प्रीतोऽहं ते प्रजानाथ यत्तेऽस्योद्बृंहणं तपः ।
ममैष कामो भूतानां यद् भूयासुर्विभूतयः ॥ ४४ ॥

prīto 'haṁ te prajā-nātha
yat te 'syodbṛṁhaṇaṁ tapaḥ
mamaiṣa kāmo bhūtānāṁ
yad bhūyāsur vibhūtayaḥ

prītaḥ—very much pleased; *aham*—I; *te*—with you; *prajā-nātha*—O king of population; *yat*—because; *te*—your; *asya*—of this material world; *udbṛṁhaṇam*—causing increase; *tapaḥ*—austerity; *mama*—My; *eṣaḥ*—this; *kāmaḥ*—desire; *bhūtānām*—of the living entities; *yat*—which; *bhūyāsuḥ*—may there be; *vibhūtayaḥ*—advancement in all respects.

TRANSLATION

My dear Prajāpati Dakṣa, you have performed extreme austerities for the welfare and growth of the world. My desire also is that everyone within this world be happy. I am therefore very pleased with you because you are endeavoring to fulfill My desire for the welfare of the entire world.

PURPORT

After every dissolution of the material cosmos, all the living entities take shelter in the body of Kāraṇodakaśāyī Viṣṇu, and when creation takes place again, they come forth from His body in their various species to resume their activities. Why does the creation take place in such a way that the living entities are put into conditioned life to suffer the threefold miseries imposed upon them by the material nature? Here the Lord says to Dakṣa, "You desire to benefit all living entities, and that is also My desire." The living entities who come in contact with the material world are meant to be corrected. All the living entities within this material world have revolted against the service of the Lord, and therefore they remain within this material world as ever conditioned, *nitya-baddha,* taking birth again and again. There is a chance, of course, of their being liberated, but nevertheless the conditioned souls, not taking advantage of this opportunity, continue in a life of sense enjoyment, and thus they are punished by birth and death again and again. This is the law of nature. As the Lord says in *Bhagavad-gītā* (7.14):

daivī hy eṣā guṇa-mayī
mama māyā duratyayā
mām eva ye prapadyante
māyām etāṁ taranti te

"This divine energy of Mine, consisting of the three modes of material nature, is difficult to overcome. But those who have surrendered unto Me can easily cross beyond it." Elsewhere in *Bhagavad-gītā* (15.7) the Lord says:

mamaivāṁśo jīva-loke
jīva-bhūtaḥ sanātanaḥ
manaḥ ṣaṣṭhānīndriyāṇi
prakṛti-sthāni karṣati

"The living entities in this conditioned world are My eternal, fragmental parts. Due to conditioned life, they are struggling very hard with the six senses, which include the mind." The living entity's struggle for existence within the material world is due to his rebellious nature. Unless a living entity surrenders to Kṛṣṇa, he must continue this life of struggle.

The Kṛṣṇa consciousness movement is not a fad. It is a bona fide movement intended to promote the welfare of all conditioned souls by trying to elevate everyone to the platform of Kṛṣṇa consciousness. If one does not come to this platform, he must continue in material existence perpetually, sometimes in the upper planets and sometimes in the lower planets. As confirmed in *Caitanya-caritāmṛta* (*Madhya* 20.118), *kabhu svarge uṭhāya, kabhu narake ḍubāya:* the conditioned soul sometimes descends into nescience and sometimes gets some relief by being relatively freed from it. This is the life of the conditioned soul.

Prajāpati Dakṣa is trying to benefit the conditioned souls by begetting them to give them a life with a chance for liberation. Liberation means surrender to Kṛṣṇa. If one begets children with the purpose of training them to surrender to Kṛṣṇa, fatherhood is very good. Similarly, when the spiritual master trains the conditioned souls to become Kṛṣṇa conscious, his position is successful. If one gives the conditioned souls a chance to become Kṛṣṇa conscious, all his activities are approved by the Supreme Personality of Godhead, who is extremely pleased, as stated here (*prīto'ham*). Following the examples of the previous *ācāryas,* all the members of the Kṛṣṇa consciousness movement should try to benefit the conditioned souls by inducing them to become Kṛṣṇa conscious and giving them all facilities to do so. Such activities constitute real welfare work. By such activities, a preacher or anyone who endeavors to spread Kṛṣṇa consciousness is recognized by the Supreme Personality of Godhead. As the Lord Himself confirms in *Bhagavad-gītā* (18.68–69):

ya idaṁ paramaṁ guhyaṁ
mad-bhakteṣv abhidhāsyati
bhaktiṁ mayi parāṁ kṛtvā
mām evaiṣyaty asaṁśayaḥ

na ca tasmān manuṣyeṣu
kaścin me priya-kṛttamaḥ
bhavitā na ca me tasmād
anyaḥ priyataro bhuvi

"For one who explains the supreme secret to the devotees, devotional service is guaranteed, and at the end he will come back to Me. There is no servant in this world more dear to Me than he, nor will there ever be one more dear."

TEXT 45

ब्रह्मा भवो भवन्तश्च मनवो विबुधेश्वराः ।
विभूतयो मम ह्येता भूतानां भूतिहेतवः ॥ ४५ ॥

brahmā bhavo bhavantaś ca
manavo vibudheśvarāḥ
vibhūtayo mama hy etā
bhūtānāṁ bhūti-hetavaḥ

brahmā—Lord Brahmā; *bhavaḥ*—Lord Śiva; *bhavantaḥ*—all of you *prajāpatis; ca*—and; *manavaḥ*—the Manus; *vibudha-īśvarāḥ*—all the different demigods (such as the sun, the moon, Venus, Mars and Jupiter, who are all in charge of various activities for the welfare of the world); *vibhūtayaḥ*—expansions of energy; *mama*—My; *hi*—indeed; *etāḥ*—all these; *bhūtānām*—of all the living entities; *bhūti*—of welfare; *hetavaḥ*—causes.

TRANSLATION

Lord Brahmā, Lord Śiva, the Manus, all the other demigods in the higher planetary systems, and you prajāpatis, who are increasing the population, are working for the benefit of all living entities. Thus you expansions of My marginal energy are incarnations of My various qualities.

PURPORT

There are various types of incarnations or expansions of the Supreme Personality of Godhead. The expansions of His personal self, or *viṣṇu-tattva,* are called *svāṁśa* expansions, whereas the living entities, who are not *viṣṇu-tattva* but *jīva-tattva,* are called *vibhinnāṁśa,* separated expansions. Although Prajāpati Dakṣa is not on the same level as Lord Brahmā and Lord Śiva, he is compared to them because he engages in the service of the Lord. In the service of the Personality of Godhead, it is not that Lord Brahmā is considered very great while an ordinary human being trying to preach the glories of the Lord is considered very low. There are no such distinctions. Regardless of whether materially high or materially low, anyone engaged in the service of the Lord is spiritually very dear to Him. In this regard, Śrīla Madhvācārya gives this quotation from the *Tantra-nirṇaya:*

viśeṣa-vyakti-pātratvād
brahmādyās tu vibhūtayaḥ
tad-antaryāmiṇaś caiva
matsyādyā vibhavāḥ smṛtāḥ

From Lord Brahmā down, all the living entities engaged in the service of the Lord are extraordinary and are called *vibhūti.* As the Lord says in *Bhagavad-gītā* (10.41):

yad yad vibhūtimat sattvaṁ
śrīmad ūrjitam eva vā
tat tad evāvagaccha tvaṁ
mama tejo-'ṁśa-sambhavam

"Know that all beautiful, glorious and mighty creations spring from but a spark of My splendor." A living entity especially empowered to act on behalf of the

Lord is called *vibhūti,* whereas the *viṣṇu-tattva* incarnations of the Lord, such as the Matsya *avatāra* (*keśava dhṛta-mīna-śarīra jaya jagad-īśa hare*), are called *vibhava.*

TEXT 46

तपो मे हृदयं ब्रह्मंस्तनुर्विद्या क्रियाकृतिः ।
अङ्गानि क्रतवो जाता धर्म आत्मासवः सुराः ॥ ४६ ॥

tapo me hṛdayaṁ brahmaṁs
tanur vidyā kriyākṛtiḥ
aṅgāni kratavo jātā
dharma ātmāsavaḥ surāḥ

tapaḥ—austerities like mental control, mystic *yoga* and meditation; *me*—My; *hṛdayam*—heart; *brahman*—O *brāhmaṇa; tanuḥ*—the body; *vidyā*—the knowledge derived from Vedic scripture; *kriyā*—spiritual activities; *ākṛtiḥ*—form; *aṅgāni*—the limbs of the body; *kratavaḥ*—the ritualistic ceremonies and sacrifices mentioned in the Vedic literature; *jātāḥ*—completed; *dharmaḥ*—the religious principles for executing the ritualistic ceremonies; *ātmā*—My soul; *asavaḥ*—life airs; *surāḥ*—the demigods who execute My orders in different departments of the material world.

TRANSLATION

My dear brāhmaṇa, austerity in the form of meditation is My heart, Vedic knowledge in the form of hymns and mantras constitutes My body, and spiritual activities and ecstatic emotions are My actual form. The ritualistic ceremonies and sacrifices, when properly conducted, are the various limbs of My body, the unseen good fortune proceeding from pious or spiritual activities constitutes My mind, and the demigods who execute My orders in various departments are My life and soul.

PURPORT

Sometimes atheists argue that since God is invisible to their eyes, they do not believe in God. For them the Supreme Lord is describing a method by which one can see God in His impersonal form. Intelligent persons can see God in His personal form, as stated in the *śāstras,* but if one is very eager to see the Supreme Personality of Godhead immediately, face to face, he can see the Supreme Lord through this description, which portrays the various internal and external parts of His body.

To engage in *tapasya,* or denial of material activities, is the first principle of spiritual life. Then there are spiritual activities, such as the performance of Vedic ritualistic sacrifices, study of the Vedic knowledge, meditation upon the Supreme Personality of Godhead, and chanting of the Hare Kṛṣṇa *mahā-mantra.* One should also respect the demigods and understand how they are situated, how they act and how they manage the activities of the various departments of this material world. In this way one can see how God is existing and how everything is managed perfectly because of the presence of the Supreme Lord. As the Lord says in *Bhagavad-gītā* (9.10):

mayādhyakṣeṇa prakṛtiḥ
sūyate sa-carācaram
hetunānena kaunteya
jagad viparivartate

"This material nature is working under My direction, O son of Kuntī, and it is producing all moving and nonmoving beings. By its rule this manifestation is created and annihilated again and again." If one is unable to see the Supreme Lord although He is present as Kṛṣṇa in His various incarnations, one may see the Supreme Lord's impersonal feature, according to the direction of the *Vedas,* by seeing the activities of material nature.

Anything done under the direction of the Vedic injunctions is called *dharma,* as described by the order carriers of Yamarāja (*Bhāg.* 6.1.40):

veda-praṇihito dharmo
hy adharmas tad-viparyayaḥ
vedo nārāyaṇaḥ sākṣāt
svayambhūr iti śuśruma

"That which is prescribed in the *Vedas* constitutes *dharma,* the religious principles, and the opposite of that is irreligion. The *Vedas* are directly the Supreme Personality of Godhead, Nārāyaṇa, and are self-born. This we have heard from Yamarāja."

In this connection, Śrīla Madhvācārya comments:

tapo'bhimānī rudras tu
viṣṇor hṛdayam āśritaḥ
vidyā rūpā tathaivomā
viṣṇos tanum upāśritā

śṛṅgārādy-ākṛti-gataḥ
kriyātmā pāka-śāsanaḥ
aṅgeṣu kratavaḥ sarve
madhya-dehe ca dharma-rāṭ
prāṇo vāyuś citta-gato
brahmādyāḥ sveṣu devatāḥ

The various demigods are all acting under the protection of the Supreme Personality of Godhead, and according to their various actions the demigods are differently named.

TEXT 47

अहमेवासमेवाग्रे नान्यत् किञ्चान्तरं बहिः ।
संज्ञानमात्रमव्यक्तं प्रसुप्तमिव विश्वतः ॥ ४७ ॥

aham evāsam evāgre
nānyat kiñcāntaraṁ bahiḥ
saṁjñāna-mātram avyaktaṁ
prasuptam iva viśvataḥ

aham—I, the Supreme Personality of Godhead; *eva*—only; *āsam*—was; *eva*—certainly; *agre*—in the beginning, before the creation; *na*—not; *anyat*—other; *kiñca*—anything; *antaram*—besides Me; *bahiḥ*—external (since the cosmic manifestation is external to the spiritual world, the spiritual world existed when there was no material world); *saṁjñāna-mātram*—only the consciousness of the living entities; *avyaktam*—unmanifested; *prasuptam*—sleeping; *iva*—like; *viśvataḥ*—all over.

TRANSLATION

Before the creation of this cosmic manifestation, I alone existed with My specific spiritual potencies. Consciousness was then unmanifested, just as one's consciousness is unmanifested during the time of sleep.

PURPORT

The word *aham* indicates a person. As explained in the *Vedas, nityo nityānāṁ cetanaś cetanānām:* the Lord is the supreme eternal among innumerable eternals and the supreme living being among the innumerable living beings. The Lord is a person who also has impersonal features. As stated in *Śrīmad-Bhāgavatam* (1.2.11):

vadanti tat tattva-vidas
tattvaṁ yaj jñānam advayam
brahmeti paramātmeti
bhagavān iti śabdyate

"Learned transcendentalists who know the Absolute Truth call this nondual substance Brahman, Paramātmā or Bhagavān." Consideration of the Paramātmā and impersonal Brahman arose after the creation; before the creation, only the Supreme Personality of Godhead existed. As firmly declared in *Bhagavad-gītā* (18.55), the Lord can be understood only by *bhakti-yoga.* The ultimate cause, the supreme cause of creation, is the Supreme Personality of Godhead, who can be understood only by *bhakti-yoga.* He cannot be understood by speculative philosophical research or by meditation, since all such processes came into existence after the material creation. The impersonal and localized conceptions of the Supreme Lord are more or less materially contaminated. The real spiritual process, therefore, is *bhakti-yoga.* As the Lord says, *bhaktyā mām abhijānāti:* "Only by devotional service can I be understood." Before the creation, the Lord existed as a person, as indicated here by the word *aham.* When Prajāpati Dakṣa saw Him as a person, who was beautifully dressed and ornamented, he actually experienced the meaning of this word *aham* through devotional service.

Each person is eternal. Because the Lord says that He existed as a person before the creation (*agre*) and will also exist after the annihilation, the Lord is a person eternally. Śrīla Viśvanātha Cakravartī Ṭhākura therefore quotes these verses from *Śrīmad-Bhāgavatam* (10.9.13–14):

na cāntar na bahir yasya
na pūrvaṁ nāpi cāparam
pūrvāparaṁ bahiś cāntar
jagato yo jagac ca yaḥ

taṁ matvātmajam avyaktaṁ
martya-liṅgam adhokṣajam
gopikolūkhale dāmnā
babandha prākṛtaṁ yathā

The Personality of Godhead appeared in Vṛndāvana as the son of mother Yaśodā, who bound the Lord with rope just as an ordinary mother binds a material child. There are actually no divisions of external and internal for the form of the Supreme Personality of Godhead (*sac-cid-ānanda-vigraha*), but when He appears in His own form the unintelligent think Him an ordinary person. *Avajānanti māṁ mūḍhā mānuṣīṁ tanum āśritam:* although He comes in His own body, which never changes, *mūḍhas,* the unintelligent, think that the impersonal Brahman has assumed a material body to come in the form of a person. Ordinary living beings assume material bodies, but the Supreme Personality of Godhead does not. Since the Supreme Personality of Godhead is the supreme consciousness, it is stated herein that *saṁjñāna-mātram,* the original consciousness, Kṛṣṇa consciousness, was unmanifested before the creation, although the consciousness of the Supreme Personality of Godhead is the origin of everything. The Lord says in *Bhagavad-gītā* (2.12), "Never was there a time when I did not exist, nor you, nor all these kings; nor in the future shall any of us cease to be." Thus the Lord's person is the Absolute Truth in the past, present and future.

In this regard, Madhvācārya quotes two verses from the *Matsya Purāṇa:*

nānā-varṇo haris tv eko
bahu-śīrṣa-bhujo rūpāt
āsīl laye tad-anyat tu
sūkṣma-rūpaṁ śriyaṁ vinā

asuptaḥ supta iva ca
mīlitākṣo'bhavad dhariḥ
anyatrānādarād viṣṇau
śrīś ca līneva kathyate
sūkṣmatvena harau sthānāl
līnam anyad apīṣyate

After the annihilation of everything, the Supreme Lord, because of His *sac-cid-ānanda-vigraha,* remains in His original form, but since the other living entities have material bodies, the matter merges into matter, and the subtle form of the spirit soul remains within the body of the Lord. The Lord does not sleep, but the ordinary living entities remain asleep until the next creation. An unintelligent person thinks that the opulence of the Supreme Lord is nonexistent after the annihilation, but that is not a fact. The opulence of the Supreme Personality of Godhead remains as it is in the spiritual world; only in the material world is everything dissolved. *Brahma-līna,* merging into the Supreme Brahman, is not actual *līna,* or annihilation, for the subtle form remaining in the Brahman effulgence will return to the material world after the material creation and again assume a material form. This is described as *bhūtvā bhūtvā pralīyate.* When the material body is annihilated, the spirit soul remains in a subtle form, which later assumes another material body. This is true for the conditioned souls, but the Supreme Personality of Godhead remains eternally in His original consciousness and spiritual body.

TEXT 48

मय्यनन्तगुणेऽनन्ते गुणतो गुणविग्रहः ।
यदासीत् तत एवाद्यः स्वयम्भूः समभूदजः ॥ ४८ ॥

mayy ananta-guṇe'nante
guṇato guṇa-vigrahaḥ
yadāsīt tata evādyaḥ
svayambhūḥ samabhūd ajaḥ

mayi—in Me; *ananta-guṇe*—possessing unlimited potency; *anante*—unlimited; *guṇataḥ*—from My potency known as *māyā; guṇa-vigrahaḥ*—the universe, which is a result of the modes of nature; *yadā*—when; *āsīt*—it came into existence; *tataḥ*—therein; *eva*—indeed; *ādyaḥ*—the first living being; *svayambhūḥ*—Lord Brahmā; *samabhūt*—was born; *ajaḥ*—although not from a material mother.

TRANSLATION

I am the reservoir of unlimited potency, and therefore I am known as unlimited or all-pervading. From My material energy the cosmic manifestation appeared within Me, and in this universal manifestation appeared the chief being, Lord Brahmā, who is your source and is not born of a material mother.

PURPORT

This is a description of the history of the universal creation. The first cause is the Lord Himself, the Supreme Person. From Him, Brahmā is created, and Brahmā takes charge of the affairs of the universe. The universal affairs of the material creation depend upon the material energy of the Supreme Personality of Godhead, who is therefore the cause of the material creation. The entire cosmic manifestation is described herein as *guṇa-vigrahaḥ,* the form of the Lord's qualities. From the cosmic universal form, the first creation is Lord Brahmā, who is the cause of all living entities. In this regard, Śrīla Madhvācārya describes the unlimited attributes of the Lord:

praty-ekaśo guṇānāṁ tu
niḥsīmatvam udīryate
tadānantyaṁ tu guṇatas
te cānantā hi saṅkhyayā
ato'nanta-guṇo viṣṇur
guṇato'nanta eva ca

Parāsya śaktir vividhaiva śrūyate: the Lord has innumerable potencies, all of which are unlimited. Therefore the Lord Himself and all His qualities, forms, pastimes and paraphernalia are also unlimited. Because Lord Viṣṇu has unlimited attributes, He is known as Ananta.

TEXTS 49–50

स वै यदा महादेवो मम वीर्योपबृंहितः ।
मेने खिलमिवात्मानमुद्यतः स्वर्गकर्मणि ॥ ४९ ॥
अथ मेऽभिहितो देवस्तपोऽतप्यत दारुणम् ।
नव विश्वसृजो युष्मान् येनादावसृजद् विभुः ॥ ५० ॥

sa vai yadā mahādevo
mama vīryopabṛṁhitaḥ
mene khilam ivātmānam
udyataḥ svarga-karmaṇi

atha me'bhihito devas
tapo'tapyata dāruṇam
nava viśva-sṛjo yuṣmān
yenādāv asṛjad vibhuḥ

saḥ—that Lord Brahmā; *vai*—indeed; *yadā*—when; *mahā-devaḥ*—the chief of all the demigods; *mama*—My; *vīrya-upabṛṁhitaḥ*—being increased by the potency; *mene*—thought; *khilam*—incapable; *iva*—as if; *ātmānam*—himself; *udyataḥ*—attempting; *svarga-karmaṇi*—in the creation of the universal affairs; *atha*—at that time; *me*—by Me; *abhihitaḥ*—advised; *devaḥ*—that Lord Brahmā; *tapaḥ*—austerity; *atapyata*—performed; *dāruṇam*—extremely difficult; *nava*—nine; *viśva-sṛjaḥ*—important personalities to create the universe; *yuṣmān*—all of you; *yena*—by whom; *ādau*—in the beginning; *asṛjat*—created; *vibhuḥ*—the great.

TRANSLATION

When the chief lord of the universe, Lord Brahmā [Svayambhū], having been inspired by My energy, was attempting to create, he thought himself incapable. Therefore I gave him advice, and in accordance with My instructions he underwent extremely difficult austerities. Because of these austerities, the great Lord Brahmā was able to create nine personalities, including you, to help him in the functions of creation.

PURPORT

Nothing is possible without *tapasya.* Lord Brahmā, however, was empowered to create this entire universe because of his austerities. The more we engage in austerities, the more we become powerful by the grace of the Lord. Therefore Ṛṣabhadeva advised His sons, *tapo divyaṁ putrakā yena sattvaṁ śuddhyed:* "One should engage in penance and austerity to attain the divine position of devotional service. By such activity, one's heart is purified." (*Bhāg.* 5.5.1) In our material existence we are impure, and therefore we cannot do anything wonderful, but if we purify our existence by *tapasya,* we can do wonderful things by the grace of the Lord. Therefore *tapasya* is very important, as stressed in this verse.

TEXT 51

एषा पञ्चजनस्याङ्ग दुहिता वै प्रजापतेः ।
असिक्नी नाम पत्नीत्वे प्रजेश प्रतिगृह्यताम् ॥ ५१ ॥

eṣā pañcajanasyāṅga
duhitā vai prajāpateḥ
asiknī nāma patnītve
prajeśa pratigṛhyatām

eṣā—this; *pañcajanasya*—of Pañcajana; *aṅga*—O My dear son; *duhitā*—the daughter; *vai*—indeed; *prajāpateḥ*—another *prajāpati; asiknī nāma*—of the name Asiknī; *patnītve*—as your wife; *prajeśa*—O *prajāpati; pratigṛhyatām*—let her be accepted.

TRANSLATION

O My dear son Dakṣa, Prajāpati Pañcajana has a daughter named Asiknī, whom I offer to you so that you may accept her as your wife.

TEXT 52

मिथुनव्यवायधर्मस्त्वं प्रजासर्गमिमं पुनः ।
मिथुनव्यवायधर्मिण्यां भूरिशो भावयिष्यसि ॥ ५२ ॥

mithuna-vyavāya-dharmas tvaṁ
prajā-sargam imaṁ punaḥ
mithuna-vyavāya-dharmiṇyāṁ
bhūriśo bhāvayiṣyasi

mithuna—of man and woman; *vyavāya*—sexual activities; *dharmaḥ*—who accepts by religious performance; *tvam*—you; *prajā-sargam*—creation of living entities; *imam*—this; *punaḥ*—again; *mithuna*—of man and woman united; *vyavāya-dharmiṇyām*—in her according to the religious performance of sexual intercourse; *bhūriśaḥ*—manifold; *bhāvayiṣyasi*—you will cause to be.

TRANSLATION

Now unite in sexual life as man and woman, and in this way, by sexual intercourse, you will be able to beget hundreds of children in the womb of this girl to increase the population.

PURPORT

The Lord says in *Bhagavad-gītā* (7.11), *dharmāviruddho bhūteṣu kāmo'smi:* "I am sex that is not contrary to religious principles." Sexual intercourse ordained by the Supreme Personality of Godhead is *dharma,* a religious principle, but it is not intended for sense enjoyment. Indulgence in sense enjoyment through sexual intercourse is not allowed by the Vedic principles. One may follow the natural tendency for sex life only to beget children. Therefore the Lord told Dakṣa in this verse, "This girl is offered to you only for sex life to beget children, not for any other purpose. She is very fertile, and therefore you will be able to have as many children as you can beget."

Śrīla Viśvanātha Cakravartī Ṭhākura remarks in this connection that Dakṣa was given the facility for unlimited sexual intercourse. In Dakṣa's previous life he was also known as Dakṣa, but in the course of performing sacrifices he offended Lord Śiva, and thus his head was replaced with that of a goat. Then Dakṣa gave up his life because of his degraded condition, but because he maintained the same unlimited sexual desires, he underwent austerities by which he satisfied the Supreme Lord, who then gave him unlimited potency for sexual intercourse.

It should be noted that although such a facility for sexual intercourse is achieved by the grace of the Supreme Personality of Godhead, this facility is not offered to advanced devotees, who are free from material desires (*anyābhilāṣitā-śūnyam*). In this connection it may be noted that if the American boys and girls engaged in the Kṛṣṇa consciousness movement want to advance in Kṛṣṇa consciousness to achieve the supreme benefit of loving service to the Lord, they should refrain from indulging in this facility for sex life. Therefore we advise that one should at least refrain from illicit sex. Even if there are opportunities for sex life, one should voluntarily accept the limitation of having sex only for progeny, not for any other purpose. Kardama Muni was also given the facility for sex life, but he had only a slight desire for it. Therefore after begetting children in the womb of Devahūti, Kardama Muni became completely renounced. The purport is that if one wants to return home, back to Godhead, one should voluntarily refrain from sex life. Sex should be accepted only as much as needed, not unlimitedly.

One should not think that Dakṣa received the favor of the Lord by receiving the facilities for unlimited sex. Later verses will reveal that Dakṣa again committed an offense, this time at the lotus feet of Nārada. Therefore although sex life is the topmost enjoyment in the material world and although one may have an opportunity for sexual enjoyment by the grace of God, this entails a risk of committing offenses. Dakṣa was open to such offenses, and therefore, strictly speaking, he was not actually favored by the Supreme Lord. One should not seek the favor of the Lord for unlimited potency in sex life.

TEXT 53

त्वत्तोऽधस्तात् प्रजाः सर्वा मिथुनीभूय मायया।
मदीयया भविष्यन्ति हरिष्यन्ति च मे बलिम् ॥५३॥

tvatto'dhastāt prajāḥ sarvā
mithunī-bhūya māyayā
madīyayā bhaviṣyanti
hariṣyanti ca me balim

tvattaḥ—you; *adhastāt*—after; *prajāḥ*—the living entities; *sarvāḥ*—all; *mithunī-bhūya*—having sex life; *māyayā*—because of the influence or facilities given by the illusory energy; *madīyayā*—My; *bhaviṣyanti*—they will become; *hariṣyanti*—they will offer; *ca*—also; *me*—unto Me; *balim*—presentations.

TRANSLATION

After you give birth to many hundreds and thousands of children, they will also be captivated by My illusory energy and will engage, like You, in sexual intercourse. But because of My mercy to you and them, they will also be able to give Me presentations in devotion.

TEXT 54

श्रीशुक उवाच
इत्युक्त्वा मिषतस्तस्य भगवान् विश्वभावनः ।
स्वप्नोपलब्धार्थ इव तत्रैवान्तर्दधे हरिः ॥ ५४ ॥

śrī-śuka uvāca
ity uktvā miṣatas tasya
bhagavān viśva-bhāvanaḥ
svapnopalabdhārtha iva
tatraivāntardadhe hariḥ

śrī-śukaḥ uvāca—Śukadeva Gosvāmī continued to speak; *iti*—thus; *uktvā*—saying; *miṣataḥ tasya*—while he (Dakṣa) was personally looking on; *bhagavān*—the Supreme Personality of Godhead; *viśva-bhāvanaḥ*—who creates the universal affairs; *svapna-upalabdha-arthaḥ*—an object obtained in dreaming; *iva*—like; *tatra*—there; *eva*—certainly; *antardadhe*—disappeared; *hariḥ*—the Lord, the Supreme Personality of Godhead.

TRANSLATION

Śukadeva Gosvāmī continued: After the creator of the entire universe, the Supreme Personality of Godhead, Hari, had spoken in this way in the presence of Prajāpati Dakṣa, He immediately disappeared as if He were an object experienced in a dream.

Thus end the Bhaktivedanta purports of the Sixth Canto, Fourth Chapter, of the Śrīmad-Bhāgavatam, *entitled "The Haṁsa-guhya Prayers Offered to the Lord by Prajāpati Dakṣa."*

CHAPTER FIVE

Nārada Muni Cursed by Prajāpati Dakṣa

This chapter relates how all the sons of Dakṣa were delivered from the clutches of the material energy by following the advice of Nārada, who was therefore cursed by Dakṣa.

Influenced by the external energy of Lord Viṣṇu, Prajāpati Dakṣa begot ten thousand sons in the womb of his wife, Pāñcajanī. These sons, who were all of the same character and mentality, were known as the Haryaśvas. Ordered by their father to create more and more population, the Haryaśvas went west to the place where the River Sindhu (now the Indus) meets the Arabian Sea. In those days this was the site of a holy lake named Nārāyaṇa-saras, where there were many saintly persons. The Haryaśvas began practicing austerities, penances and meditation, which are the engagements of the highly exalted renounced order of life. However, when Śrīla Nārada Muni saw these boys engaged in such commendable austerities simply for material creation, he thought it better to release them from this tendency. Nārada Muni described to the boys their ultimate goal of life and advised them not to become ordinary *karmīs* to beget children. Thus all the sons of Dakṣa became enlightened and left, never to return.

Prajāpati Dakṣa, who was very sad at the loss of his sons, begot one thousand more sons in the womb of his wife, Pāñcajanī, and ordered them to increase progeny. These sons, who were named the Savalāśvas, also engaged in worshiping Lord Viṣṇu to beget children, but Nārada Muni convinced them to become mendicants and not beget children. Foiled twice in his attempts to increase population, Prajāpati Dakṣa became most angry at Nārada Muni and cursed him, saying that in the future he would not be able to stay anywhere. Since Nārada Muni, being fully qualified, was fixed in tolerance, he accepted Dakṣa's curse.

TEXT 1

श्रीशुक उवाच

तस्यां स पाञ्चजन्यां वै विष्णुमायोपबृंहितः ।
हर्यश्वसंज्ञानयुतं पुत्रानजनयद् विभुः ॥ १ ॥

śrī-śuka uvāca
tasyāṁ sa pāñcajanyāṁ vai
viṣṇu-māyopabṛṁhitaḥ
haryaśva-saṁjñān ayutaṁ
putrān ajanayad vibhuḥ

śrī-śukaḥ uvāca—Śrī Śukadeva Gosvāmī said; *tasyām*—in her; *saḥ*—Prajāpati Dakṣa; *pāñcajanyām*—his wife named Pāñcajanī; *vai*—indeed; *viṣṇu-māyā-upabṛṁhitaḥ*—being made capable by the illusory energy of Lord Viṣṇu; *haryaśva-saṁjñān*—named the Haryaśvas; *ayutam*—ten thousand; *putrān*—sons; *ajanayat*—begot; *vibhuḥ*—being powerful.

TRANSLATION

Śrīla Śukadeva Gosvāmī continued: Impelled by the illusory energy of Lord Viṣṇu, Prajāpati Dakṣa begot ten thousand sons in the womb of Pāñcajanī [Asiknī]. My dear King, these sons were called the Haryaśvas.

TEXT 2

अपृथग्धर्मशीलास्ते सर्वे दाक्षायणा नृप ।
पित्रा प्रोक्ताः प्रजासर्गे प्रतीचीं प्रययुर्दिशम् ॥ २ ॥

apṛthag-dharma-śīlās te
sarve dākṣāyaṇā nṛpa
pitrā proktāḥ prajā-sarge
pratīcīṁ prayayur diśam

apṛthak—alike in; *dharma-śīlāḥ*—good character and behavior; *te*—they; *sarve*—all; *dākṣāyaṇāḥ*—the sons of Dakṣa; *nṛpa*—O King; *pitrā*—by their father; *proktāḥ*—ordered; *prajā-sarge*—to increase the population; *pratīcīm*—western; *prayayuḥ*—they went to; *diśam*—the direction.

TRANSLATION

My dear King, all the sons of Prajāpati Dakṣa were alike in being very gentle and obedient to the orders of their father. When their father ordered them to beget children, they all went in the western direction.

TEXT 3

तत्र नारायणसरस्तीर्थं सिन्धुसमुद्रयोः ।
सङ्गमो यत्र सुमहन्मुनिसिद्धनिषेवितम् ॥ ३ ॥

tatra nārāyaṇa-saras
tīrthaṁ sindhu-samudrayoḥ
saṅgamo yatra sumahan
muni-siddha-niṣevitam

tatra—in that direction; *nārāyaṇa-saraḥ*—the lake named Nārāyaṇa-saras; *tīrtham*—very holy place; *sindhu-samudrayoḥ*—of the River Sindhu and the sea; *saṅgamaḥ*—confluence; *yatra*—where; *su-mahat*—very great; *muni*—by sages; *siddha*—and perfected human beings; *niṣevitam*—frequented.

TRANSLATION

In the west, where the River Sindhu meets the sea, there is a great place of pilgrimage known as Nārāyaṇa-saras. Many sages and others advanced in spiritual consciousness live there.

TEXTS 4–5

तदुपस्पर्शनादेव विनिर्धूतमलाशयाः ।
धर्मे पारमहंस्ये च प्रोत्पन्नमतयोऽप्युत ॥ ४ ॥
तेपिरे तप एवोग्रं पित्रादेशेन यन्त्रिताः ।
प्रजाविवृद्धये यत्तान् देवर्षिस्तान् ददर्श ह ॥ ५ ॥

tad-upasparśanād eva
vinirdhūta-malāśayāḥ
dharme pāramahaṁsye ca
protpanna-matayo'py uta

tepire tapa evograṁ
pitrādeśena yantritāḥ
prajā-vivṛddhaye yattān
devarṣis tān dadarśa ha

tat—of that holy place; *upasparśanāt*—from bathing in that water or touching it; *eva*—only; *vinirdhūta*—completely washed away; *mala-āśayāḥ*—whose impure desires; *dharme*—to the practices; *pāramahaṁsye*—executed by the topmost class of *sannyāsīs; ca*—also; *protpanna*—highly inclined; *matayaḥ*—whose minds; *api uta*—although; *tepire*—they executed; *tapaḥ*—penances; *eva*—certainly; *ugram*—severe; *pitṛ-ādeśena*—by the order of their father; *yantritāḥ*—engaged; *prajā-vivṛddhaye*—for the purpose of increasing the population; *yattān*—ready; *devarṣiḥ*—the great sage Nārada; *tān*—them; *dadarśa*—visited; *ha*—indeed.

TRANSLATION

In that holy place, the Haryaśvas began regularly touching the lake's waters and bathing in them. Gradually becoming very much purified, they became inclined toward the activities of paramahaṁsas. Nevertheless, because their father had ordered them to increase the population, they performed severe austerities to fulfill his desires. One day, when the great sage Nārada saw those boys performing such fine austerities to increase the population, Nārada approached them.

TEXTS 6–8

उवाच चाथ हर्यश्वाः कथं स्रक्ष्यथ वै प्रजाः ।
अदृष्ट्वान्तं भुवो यूयं बालिशा बत पालकाः ॥ ६ ॥
तथैकपुरुषं राष्ट्रं बिलं चादृष्टनिर्गमम् ।
बहुरूपां स्त्रियं चापि पुमांसं पुंश्चलीपतिम् ॥ ७ ॥
नदीमुभयतोवाहां पञ्चपञ्चाद्भुतं गृहम् ।
क्वचिद्धंसं चित्रकथं क्षौरपव्यं स्वयं भ्रमि ॥ ८ ॥

uvāca cātha haryaśvāḥ
kathaṁ srakṣyatha vai prajāḥ
adṛṣṭvāntaṁ bhuvo yūyaṁ
bāliśā bata pālakāḥ

tathaika-puruṣaṁ rāṣṭraṁ
bilaṁ cādṛṣṭa-nirgamam
bahu-rūpāṁ striyaṁ cāpi
pumāṁsaṁ puṁścalī-patim

nadīm ubhayato vāhāṁ
pañca-pañcādbhutaṁ gṛham
kvacid dhaṁsaṁ citra-kathaṁ
kṣaura-pavyaṁ svayaṁ bhrami

uvāca—he said; *ca*—also; *atha*—thus; *haryaśvāḥ*—O Haryaśvas, sons of Prajāpati Dakṣa; *katham*—why; *srakṣyatha*—you will beget; *vai*—indeed; *prajāḥ*—progeny; *adṛṣṭvā*—having not seen; *antam*—the end; *bhuvaḥ*—of this earth; *yūyam*—all of you; *bāliśāḥ*—inexperienced; *bata*—alas; *pālakāḥ* —although ruling princes; *tathā*—so also; *eka*—one; *puruṣam*—man; *rāṣṭram*—kingdom; *bilam*—the hole; *ca*—also; *adṛṣṭa-nirgamam*—from which there is no coming out; *bahu-rūpām*—taking many forms; *striyam*—the woman; *ca*—and; *api*—even; *pumāṁsam*—the man; *puṁścalī-patim* —the husband of a prostitute; *nadīm*—a river; *ubhayataḥ*—in both ways; *vāhām*—which flows; *pañca-pañca*—of five multiplied by five (twenty-five); *adbhutam*—a wonder; *gṛham*—the house; *kvacit*—somewhere; *haṁsam*—a swan; *citra-katham*—whose story is wonderful; *kṣaura-pavyam*—made of sharp razors and thunderbolts; *svayam*—itself; *bhrami*—revolving.

TRANSLATION

The great sage Nārada said: My dear Haryaśvas, you have not seen the extremities of the earth. There is a kingdom where only one man lives and where there is a hole from which, having entered, no one emerges. A woman there who is extremely unchaste adorns herself with various attractive dresses, and the man who lives there is her husband. In that kingdom, there is a river flowing in both directions, a wonderful home made of twenty-five materials, a swan that vibrates various sounds, and an automatically revolving object made of sharp razors and thunderbolts. You have not seen all this, and therefore you are inexperienced boys without advanced knowledge. How, then, will you create progeny?

PURPORT

Nārada Muni saw that the boys known as the Haryaśvas were already purified because of living in that holy place and were practically ready for liberation. Why then should they be encouraged to become entangled in family life, which is so dark that once having entered it one cannot leave it? Through this analogy, Nārada Muni asked them to consider why they should follow their father's order to be entangled in family life. Indirectly, he asked them to find within the cores of their hearts the situation of the Supersoul, Lord Viṣṇu, for then they would truly be experienced. In other words, one who is too involved in his material environment and does not look within the core of his heart is increasingly entangled in the illusory energy. Nārada Muni's purpose was to get the sons of Prajāpati Dakṣa to divert their attention toward spiritual realization instead of involving themselves in the ordinary but complicated affairs of propagation. The same advice was given by Prahlāda Mahārāja to his father (*Bhāg.* 7.5.5):

tat sādhu manye'sura-varya dehināṁ
sadā samudvigna-dhiyām asad-grahāt
hitvātma-pātaṁ gṛham andha-kūpaṁ
vanaṁ gato yad dharim āśrayeta

In the dark well of family life, one is always full of anxiety because of having accepted a temporary body. If one wants to free himself from this anxiety, one should immediately leave family life and take shelter of the Supreme Personality of Godhead in Vṛndāvana. Nārada Muni advised the Haryaśvas not to enter household life. Since they were already advanced in spiritual knowledge, why should they be entangled in that way?

TEXT 9

कथं स्वपितुरादेशमविद्वांसो विपश्चितः ।
अनुरूपमविज्ञाय अहो सर्गं करिष्यथ ॥ ९ ॥

kathaṁ sva-pitur ādeśam
avidvāṁso vipaścitaḥ
anurūpam avijñāya
aho sargaṁ kariṣyatha

katham—how; *sva-pituḥ*—of your own father; *ādeśam*—the order; *avidvāṁsaḥ*—ignorant; *vipaścitaḥ*—who knows everything; *anurūpam*—suitable for you; *avijñāya*—without knowing; *aho*—alas; *sargam*—the creation; *kariṣyatha*—you will perform.

TRANSLATION

Alas, your father is omniscient, but you do not know his actual order. Without knowing the actual purpose of your father, how will you create progeny?

TEXT 10

श्रीशुक उवाच
तन्निशम्याथ हर्यश्वा औत्पत्तिकमनीषया ।
वाचःकूटं तु देवर्षेः स्वयं विममृशुर्धिया ॥ १० ॥

śrī-śuka uvāca
tan niśamyātha haryaśvā
autpattika-manīṣayā

vācaḥ kūṭaṁ tu devarṣeḥ
svayaṁ vimamṛśur dhiyā

śrī-śukaḥ uvāca—Śrī Śukadeva Gosvāmī said; *tat*—that; *niśamya*—hearing; *atha*—thereafter; *haryaśvāḥ*—all the sons of Prajāpati Dakṣa; *autpattika*—naturally awakened; *manīṣayā*—by possessing the power to consider; *vācaḥ*—of the speech; *kūṭam*—the enigma; *tu*—but; *devarṣeḥ*—of Nārada Muni; *svayam*—themselves; *vimamṛśuḥ*—reflected upon; *dhiyā*—with full intelligence.

TRANSLATION

Śrī Śukadeva Gosvāmī said: Hearing these enigmatic words of Nārada Muni, the Haryaśvas considered them with their natural intelligence, without help from others.

TEXT 11

भूः क्षेत्रं जीवसंज्ञं यदनादि निजबन्धनम् ।
अदृष्ट्वा तस्य निर्वाणं किमसत्कर्मभिर्भवेत् ॥ ११ ॥

bhūḥ kṣetraṁ jīva-saṁjñaṁ yad
anādi nija-bandhanam
adṛṣṭvā tasya nirvāṇaṁ
kim asat-karmabhir bhavet

bhūḥ—the earth; *kṣetram*—the field of activities; *jīva-saṁjñam*—the designation of the spiritual living being who is bound by different results of activity; *yat*—which; *anādi*—existing since time immemorial; *nija-bandhanam*—causing his own bondage; *adṛṣṭvā*—without seeing; *tasya*—of this; *nirvāṇam*—the cessation; *kim*—what benefit; *asat-karmabhiḥ*—with temporary fruitive activities; *bhavet*—there can be.

TRANSLATION

[The Haryaśvas understood the meaning of Nārada's words as follows.] The word "bhūḥ" ["the earth"] refers to the field of activities. The material body, which is a result of the living being's actions, is his field of activities, and it gives him false designations. Since time immemorial, he has received various types of material bodies, which are the roots of bondage to the material world. If one foolishly engages in temporary fruitive

activities and does not look toward the cessation of this bondage, what will be the benefit of his actions?

PURPORT

Nārada Muni spoke to the Haryaśvas, the sons of Prajāpati Dakṣa, about ten allegorical subjects—the king, the kingdom, the river, the house, the physical elements and so forth. After considering these by themselves, the Haryaśvas could understand that the living entity encaged in his body seeks happiness, but takes no interest in how to become free from his encagement. This is a very important verse, since all the living entities in the material world are very active, having obtained their particular types of bodies. A man works all day and night for sense gratification, and animals like hogs and dogs also work for sense gratification all day and night. Birds, beasts and all other conditioned living entities engage in various activities without knowledge of the soul encaged within the body. Especially in the human form of body, one's duty is to act in such a way that he can release himself from his encagement, but without the instructions of Nārada or his representative in the disciplic succession, people blindly engage in bodily activities to enjoy *māyā-sukha*—flickering, temporary happiness. They do not know how to become free from their material encagement. Ṛṣabhadeva therefore said that such activity is not at all good, since it encages the soul again and again in a body subjected to the threefold miseries of the material condition.

The Haryaśvas, the sons of Prajāpati Dakṣa, could immediately understand the purport of Nārada's instructions. Our Kṛṣṇa consciousness movement is especially meant for such enlightenment. We are trying to enlighten humanity so that people may come to the understanding that they should work hard in *tapasya* for self-realization and freedom from the continuous bondage of birth, death, old age and disease in one body after another. *Māyā,* however, is very strong; she is expert in putting impediments in the way of this understanding. Therefore sometimes one comes to the Kṛṣṇa consciousness movement but again falls into the clutches of *māyā,* not understanding the importance of this movement.

TEXT 12

एक एवेश्वरस्तुर्यो भगवान् स्वाश्रयः परः ।
तमदृष्ट्वाभवं पुंसः किमसत्कर्मभिर्भवेत् ॥ १२ ॥

eka eveśvaras turyo
bhagavān svāśrayaḥ paraḥ

tam adṛṣṭvābhavaṁ puṁsaḥ
kim asat-karmabhir bhavet

ekaḥ—one; *eva*—indeed; *īśvaraḥ*—supreme controller; *turyaḥ*—the fourth transcendental category; *bhagavān*—the Supreme Personality of Godhead; *sva-āśrayaḥ*—independent, being His own shelter; *paraḥ*—beyond this material creation; *tam*—Him; *adṛṣṭvā*—not seeing; *abhavam*—who is not born or created; *puṁsaḥ*—of a man; *kim*—what benefit; *asat-karmabhiḥ*—with temporary fruitive activities; *bhavet*—there can be.

TRANSLATION

[Nārada Muni had said that there is a kingdom where there is only one male. The Haryaśvas realized the purport of this statement.] The only enjoyer is the Supreme Personality of Godhead, who observes everything, everywhere. He is full of six opulences and fully independent of everyone else. He is never subject to the three modes of material nature, for He is always transcendental to this material creation. If the members of human society do not understand Him, the Supreme, through their advancement in knowledge and activities, but simply work very hard like cats and dogs all day and night for temporary happiness, what will be the benefit of their activities?

PURPORT

Nārada Muni had mentioned a kingdom where there is only one king with no competitor. The complete spiritual world, and specifically the cosmic manifestation, has only one proprietor or enjoyer—the Supreme Personality of Godhead, who is beyond this material manifestation. The Lord has therefore been described as *turya,* existing on the fourth platform. He has also been described as *abhava.* The word *bhava,* which means "takes birth," comes from the word *bhū,* "to be." As stated in *Bhagavad-gītā* (8.19), *bhūtvā bhūtvā pralīyate:* the living entities in the material world must be repeatedly born and destroyed. The Supreme Personality of Godhead, however, is neither *bhūtvā* nor *pralīyate;* He is eternal. In other words, He is not obliged to take birth like human beings or animals, which repeatedly take birth and die because of ignorance of the soul. The Supreme Personality of Godhead, Kṛṣṇa, is not subjected to such changes of body, and one who thinks otherwise is considered a fool (*avajānanti māṁ mūḍhā mānuṣīṁ tanum āśritam*). Nārada Muni advises that human beings not waste their time simply jumping like cats and monkeys, without real benefit. The duty of the human being is to understand the Supreme Personality of Godhead.

TEXT 13

पुमान् नैवैति यद् गत्वा बिलस्वर्गं गतो यथा ।
प्रत्यग्धामाविद इह किमसत्कर्मभिर्भवेत् ॥ १३ ॥

pumān naivaiti yad gatvā
bila-svargaṁ gato yathā
pratyag-dhāmāvida iha
kim asat-karmabhir bhavet

pumān—a human being; *na*—not; *eva*—indeed; *eti*—comes back; *yat*—to which; *gatvā*—having gone; *bila-svargam*—to the region of the lower planetary system known as Pātāla; *gataḥ*—gone; *yathā*—like; *pratyak-dhāma*—the effulgent spiritual world; *avidaḥ*—of the unintelligent man; *iha*—in this material world; *kim*—what benefit; *asat-karmabhiḥ*—with temporary fruitive activities; *bhavet*—there can be.

TRANSLATION

[Nārada Muni had described that there is a bila, or hole, from which, having entered, one does not return. The Haryaśvas understood the meaning of this allegory.] Hardly once has a person who has entered the lower planetary system called Pātāla been seen to return. Similarly, if one enters the Vaikuṇṭha-dhāma [pratyag-dhāma], he does not return to this material world. If there is such a place, from which, having gone, one does not return to the miserable material condition of life, what is the use of jumping like monkeys in the temporary material world and not seeing or understanding that place? What will be the profit?

PURPORT

As stated in *Bhagavad-gītā* (15.6), *yad gatvā na nivartante tad dhāma paramaṁ mama:* there is a region from which, having gone, one does not return to the material world. This region has been repeatedly described. Elsewhere in *Bhagavad-gītā* (4.9), Kṛṣṇa says:

janma karma ca me divyam
evaṁ yo vetti tattvataḥ
tyaktvā dehaṁ punar janma
naiti mām eti so'rjuna

"One who knows the transcendental nature of My appearance and activities does not, upon leaving the body, take his birth again in this material world, but attains My eternal abode, O Arjuna."

If one can properly understand Kṛṣṇa, who has already been described as the Supreme King, he does not return here after giving up his material body. This fact has been described in this verse of *Śrīmad-Bhāgavatam. Pumān naivaiti yad gatvā:* he does not return to this material world, but returns home, back to Godhead, to live an eternally blissful life of knowledge. Why do people not care about this? What will be the benefit of taking birth again in this material world, sometimes as a human being, sometimes a demigod and sometimes a cat or dog? What is the benefit of wasting time in this way? Kṛṣṇa has very definitely asserted in *Bhagavad-gītā* (8.15):

mām upetya punar janma
duḥkhālayam aśāśvatam
nāpnuvanti mahātmānaḥ
saṁsiddhiṁ paramāṁ gatāḥ

"After attaining Me, the great souls, who are *yogīs* in devotion, never return to this temporary world, which is full of miseries, because they have attained the highest perfection." One's real concern should be to free himself from the repetition of birth and death and attain the topmost perfection of life by living with the Supreme King in the spiritual world. In these verses the sons of Dakṣa repeatedly say, *kim asat-karmabhir bhavet:* "What is the use of impermanent fruitive activities?"

TEXT 14

नानारूपात्मनो बुद्धिः स्वैरिणीव गुणान्विता ।
तन्निष्ठामगतस्येह किमसत्कर्मभिर्भवेत् ॥ १४ ॥

nānā-rūpātmano buddhiḥ
svairiṇīva guṇānvitā
tan-niṣṭhām agatasyeha
kim asat-karmabhir bhavet

nānā—various; *rūpā*—who has forms or dresses; *ātmanaḥ*—of the living entity; *buddhiḥ*—the intelligence; *svairiṇī*—a prostitute who freely decorates herself with different types of cloths and ornaments; *iva*—like; *guṇa-anvitā*—endowed with the mode of passion, and so on; *tat-niṣṭhām*

—the cessation of that; *agatasya*—of one who has not obtained; *iha*—in this material world; *kim asat-karmabhiḥ bhavet*—what is the use of performing temporary fruitive activities.

TRANSLATION

[Nārada Muni had described a woman who is a professional prostitute. The Haryaśvas understood the identity of this woman.] Mixed with the mode of passion, the unsteady intelligence of every living entity is like a prostitute who changes dresses just to attract one's attention. If one fully engages in temporary fruitive activities, not understanding how this is taking place, what does he actually gain?

PURPORT

A woman who has no husband declares herself independent, which means that she becomes a prostitute. A prostitute generally dresses herself in various fashions intended to attract a man's attention to the lower part of her body. Today it has become a much advertised fashion for a woman to go almost naked, covering the lower part of her body only slightly, in order to draw the attention of a man to her private parts for sexual enjoyment. The intelligence engaged to attract a man to the lower part of the body is the intelligence of a professional prostitute. Similarly, the intelligence of a living entity who does not turn his attention toward Kṛṣṇa or the Kṛṣṇa consciousness movement simply changes dresses like a prostitute. What is the benefit of such foolish intelligence? One should be intelligently conscious in such a way that he need no longer change from one body to another.

Karmīs change their professions at any moment, but a Kṛṣṇa conscious person does not change his profession, for his only profession is to attract the attention of Kṛṣṇa by chanting the Hare Kṛṣṇa *mantra* and living a very simple life, without following daily changes of fashion. In our Kṛṣṇa consciousness movement, fashionable persons are taught to adopt one fashion—the dress of a Vaiṣṇava with a shaved head and *tilaka.* They are taught to be always clean in mind, dress and eating in order to be fixed in Kṛṣṇa consciousness. What is the use of changing one's dress, sometimes wearing long hair and a long beard and sometimes dressing otherwise? This is not good. One should not waste his time in such frivolous activities. One should always be fixed in Kṛṣṇa consciousness and take the cure of devotional service with firm determination.

TEXT 15

तत्सङ्गभ्रंशितैश्वर्यं संसरन्तं कुभार्यवत् ।
तद्गतीरबुधस्येह किमसत्कर्मभिर्भवेत् ॥ १५ ॥

tat-saṅga-bhraṁśitaiśvaryaṁ
saṁsarantaṁ kubhāryavat
tad-gatīr abudhasyeha
kim asat-karmabhir bhavet

tat-saṅga—by association with the prostitute of intelligence; *bhraṁśita*—taken away; *aiśvaryam*—the opulence of independence; *saṁsarantam*—undergoing the material way of life; *ku-bhārya-vat*—exactly like a person who has a polluted wife; *tat-gatīḥ*—the movements of the polluted intelligence; *abudhasya*—of one who does not know; *iha*—in this world; *kim asat-karmabhiḥ bhavet*—what can be the benefit of performing temporary fruitive activities.

TRANSLATION

[Nārada Muni had also spoken of a man who is the husband of the prostitute. The Haryaśvas understood this as follows.] If one becomes the husband of a prostitute, he loses all independence. Similarly, if a living entity has polluted intelligence, he prolongs his materialistic life. Frustrated by material nature, he must follow the movements of the intelligence, which brings various conditions of happiness and distress. If one performs fruitive activities under such conditions, what will be the benefit?

PURPORT

Polluted intelligence has been compared to a prostitute. One who has not purified his intelligence is said to be controlled by that prostitute. As stated in *Bhagavad-gītā* (2.41), *vyavasāyātmikā buddhir ekeha kuru-nandana:* those who are actually serious are conducted by one kind of intelligence, namely, intelligence in Kṛṣṇa consciousness. *Bahu-śākhā hy anantāś ca buddhayo'vyavasāyinām:* one who is not fixed in proper intelligence discovers many modes of life. Thus involved in material activities, he is exposed to the different modes of material nature and subjected to varieties of so-called happiness and distress. If a man becomes the husband of a prostitute, he cannot be happy, and similarly one who follows the dictations of material intelligence and material consciousness will never be happy.

One must judiciously understand the activities of material nature. As stated in *Bhagavad-gītā* (3.27):

prakṛteḥ kriyamāṇāni
guṇaiḥ karmāṇi sarvaśaḥ
ahaṅkāra-vimūḍhātmā
kartāham iti manyate

"The bewildered spirit soul, under the influence of the three modes of material nature, thinks himself to be the doer of activities, which are in actuality carried out by nature." Although one follows the dictations of material nature, he happily thinks himself the master or husband of material nature. Scientists, for example, try to be the masters of material nature, life after life, not caring to understand the Supreme Person, under whose direction everything within this material world is moving. Trying to be the masters of material nature, they are imitation gods who declare to the public that scientific advancement will one day be able to avoid the so-called control of God. In fact, however, the living being, unable to control the rulings of God, is forced to associate with the prostitute of polluted intelligence and accept various material bodies. As stated in *Bhagavad-gītā* (13.22):

puruṣaḥ prakṛti-stho hi
bhuṅkte prakṛti-jān guṇān
kāraṇaṁ guṇa-saṅgo'sya
sad-asad-yoni-janmasu

"The living entity in material nature thus follows the ways of life, enjoying the three modes of nature. This is due to his association with that material nature. Thus he meets with good and evil amongst various species." If one fully engages in temporary fruitive activities and does not solve this real problem, what profit will he gain?

TEXT 16

सृष्ट्यप्ययकरीं मायां वेलाकूलान्तवेगिताम् ।
मत्तस्य तामविज्ञस्य किमसत्कर्मभिर्भवेत् ॥ १६ ॥

sṛṣṭy-apyaya-karīṁ māyāṁ
velā-kūlānta-vegitām
mattasya tām avijñasya
kim asat-karmabhir bhavet

sṛṣṭi—creation; *apyaya*—dissolution; *karīm*—one who causes; *māyām*—the illusory energy; *velā-kūla-anta*—near the banks; *vegitām*—being very rapid; *mattasya*—of one who is mad; *tām*—that material nature; *avijñasya*—who does not know; *kim asat-karmabhiḥ bhavet*—what benefit can there be by performing temporary fruitive activities.

TRANSLATION

[Nārada Muni had said that there is a river flowing in both directions. The Haryaśvas understood the purport of this statement.] Material nature functions in two ways—by creation and dissolution. Thus the river of material nature flows both ways. A living entity who unknowingly falls in this river is submerged in its waves, and since the current is swifter near the banks of the river, he is unable to get out. What will be the benefit of performing fruitive activities in that river of māyā?

PURPORT

One may be submerged in the waves of the river of *māyā,* but one may also get free from the waves by coming to the banks of knowledge and austerity. Near these banks, however, the waves are very strong. If one does not understand how he is being tossed by the waves, but simply engages in temporary fruitive activities, what benefit will he derive?

In the *Brahma-saṁhitā* (5.44) there is this statement:

sṛṣṭi-sthiti-pralaya-sādhana-śaktir ekā
chāyeva yasya bhuvanāni bibharti durgā

The *māyā-śakti,* Durgā, is in charge of *sṛṣṭi-sthiti-pralaya,* creation and dissolution, and she acts under the direction of the Supreme Lord (*mayādhyakṣeṇa prakṛtiḥ sūyate sa-carācaram*). When one falls in the river of nescience, he is always tossed here and there by the waves, but the same *māyā* can also save him when be surrenders to Kṛṣṇa, or becomes Kṛṣṇa conscious. Kṛṣṇa consciousness is knowledge and austerity. A Kṛṣṇa conscious person takes knowledge from the Vedic literature, and at the same time he must practice austerities.

To attain freedom from material life, one must take to Kṛṣṇa consciousness. Otherwise, if one very busily engages in the so-called advancement of science, what benefit will he derive? If one is carried away by the waves of nature, what is the meaning of being a great scientist or philosopher? Mundane science and philosophy are also material creations. One must understand how *māyā* works and how one can be released from the tossing waves of the river of nescience. That is one's first duty.

TEXT 17

पञ्चविंशतितत्त्वानां पुरुषोऽद्भुतदर्पणः ।
अध्यात्ममबुधस्येह किमसत्कर्मभिर्भवेत् ॥ १७ ॥

pañca-viṁśati-tattvānāṁ
puruṣo'dbhuta-darpaṇaḥ
adhyātmam abudhasyeha
kim asat-karmabhir bhavet

pañca-viṁśati—twenty-five; *tattvānām*—of the elements; *puruṣaḥ*—the Supreme Personality of Godhead; *adbhuta-darpaṇaḥ*—the wonderful manifester; *adhyātmam*—the overseer of all causes and effects; *abudhasya*—of one who does not know; *iha*—in this world; *kim asat-karmabhiḥ bhavet*—what can be the benefit of engaging in temporary fruitive activities.

TRANSLATION

[Nārada Muni had said that there is a house made of twenty-five elements. The Haryaśvas understood this analogy.] The Supreme Lord is the reservoir of the twenty-five elements, and as the Supreme Being, the conductor of cause and effect, He causes their manifestation. If one engages in temporary fruitive activities, not knowing that Supreme Person, what benefit will he derive?

PURPORT

Philosophers and scientists conduct scholarly research to find the original cause, but they should do so scientifically, not whimsically or through fantastic theories. The science of the original cause is explained in various Vedic literatures. *Athāto brahma jijñāsā/janmādy asya yataḥ.* The *Vedānta-sūtra* explains that one should inquire about the Supreme Soul. Such inquiry about the Supreme is called *brahma jijñāsā.* The Absolute Truth, *tattva,* is explained in *Śrīmad-Bhāgavatam* (1.2.11):

vadanti tat tattva-vidas
tattvaṁ yaj jñānam advayam
brahmeti paramātmeti
bhagavān iti śabdyate

"Learned transcendentalists who know the Absolute Truth call this nondual substance Brahman, Paramātmā or Bhagavān." The Absolute Truth appears to neophytes as impersonal Brahman and to advanced mystic *yogīs* as Paramātmā, the Supersoul, but devotees, who are further advanced, understand the Absolute Truth as the Supreme Lord, Viṣṇu.

This material cosmic manifestation is an expansion of the energy of Lord Kṛṣṇa, or Lord Viṣṇu.

eka-deśa-sthitasyāgner
jyotsnā vistāriṇī yathā
parasya brahmaṇaḥ śaktis
tathedam akhilaṁ jagat

"Whatever we see in this world is but an expansion of various energies of the Supreme Personality of Godhead, who is like a fire that spreads illumination for a long distance although it is situated in one place." (*Viṣṇu Purāṇa*) The entire cosmic manifestation is an expansion of the Supreme Lord. Therefore if one does not conduct research to find the supreme cause, but instead falsely engages in frivolous, temporary activities, what is the use of demanding recognition as an important scientist or philosopher? If one does not know the ultimate cause, what is the use of his scientific and philosophical research?

The *puruṣa,* the original person—Bhagavān, Viṣṇu—can be understood only by devotional service. *Bhaktyā mām abhijānāti yāvān yaś cāsmi tattvataḥ:* only by devotional service can one understand the Supreme Person, who is behind everything. One must try to understand that the material elements are the separated, inferior energy of the Lord and that the living entity is the Lord's spiritual energy. Whatever we experience, including matter and the spirit soul, the living force, is but a combination of two energies of Lord Viṣṇu—the inferior energy and the superior energy. One should seriously study the facts concerning creation, maintenance and devastation, as well as the permanent place from which one never need return (*yad gatvā na nivartante*). Human society should study this, but instead of culturing such knowledge, people are attracted to temporary happiness and sense gratification, culminating in bottomless, topless passion. There is no profit in such activities; one must engage himself in the Kṛṣṇa consciousness movement.

TEXT 18

ऐश्वरं शास्त्रमुत्सृज्य बन्धमोक्षानुदर्शनम् ।
विविक्तपदमज्ञाय किमसत्कर्मभिर्भवेत् ॥ १८ ॥

aiśvaraṁ śāstram utsṛjya
bandha-mokṣānudarśanam
vivikta-padam ajñāya
kim asat-karmabhir bhavet

aiśvaram—bringing understanding of God, or Kṛṣṇa consciousness; *śāstram*—the Vedic literature; *utsṛjya*—giving up; *bandha*—of bondage; *mokṣa*—and of liberation; *anudarśanam*—informing about the ways; *vivikta-padam*—distinguishing spirit from matter; *ajñāya*—not knowing; *kim asat-karmabhiḥ bhavet*—what can be the use of temporary fruitive activities.

TRANSLATION

[Nārada Muni had spoken of a swan. That swan is explained in this verse.] The Vedic literatures [śāstras] vividly describe how to understand the Supreme Lord, the source of all material and spiritual energy. Indeed, they elaborately explain these two energies. The swan [haṁsa] is one who discriminates between matter and spirit, who accepts the essence of everything, and who explains the means of bondage and the means of liberation. The words of scriptures consist of variegated vibrations. If a foolish rascal leaves aside the study of these śāstras to engage in temporary activities, what will be the result?

PURPORT

The Kṛṣṇa consciousness movement is very eager to present Vedic literature in modern languages, especially Western languages such as English, French and German. The leaders of the Western world, the Americans and Europeans, have become the idols of modern civilization because the Western people are very sophisticated in temporary activities for the advancement of material civilization. A sane man, however, can see that all such grand activities, although perhaps very important for temporary life, have nothing to do with eternal life. The entire world is imitating the materialistic civilization of the West, and therefore the Kṛṣṇa consciousness movement is very much interested in giving the Western people knowledge by translating the original Sanskrit Vedic literatures into Western languages.

The word *vivikta-padam* refers to the path of logical discourses concerning the aim of life. If one does not discuss that which is important in life, one is put into darkness and must struggle for existence. What, then, is the benefit of his advancement in knowledge? The people of the West are seeing their students becoming hippies, despite gorgeous arrangements for university education. The Kṛṣṇa consciousness movement, however, is trying to convert misguided, drug-addicted students to the service of Kṛṣṇa and engage them in the best welfare activities for human society.

TEXT 19

कालचक्रं भ्रमि तीक्ष्णं सर्वं निष्कर्षयज्जगत् ।
स्वतन्त्रमबुधस्येह किमसत्कर्मभिर्भवेत् ॥ १९ ॥

kāla-cakraṁ bhrami tīkṣṇaṁ
sarvaṁ niṣkarṣayaj jagat
svatantram abudhasyeha
kim asat-karmabhir bhavet

kāla-cakram—the wheel of eternal time; *bhrami*—revolving automatically; *tīkṣṇam*—very sharp; *sarvam*—all; *niṣkarṣayat*—driving; *jagat*—the world; *sva-tantram*—independent, not caring for the so-called scientists and philosophers; *abudhasya*—of one who does not know (this principle of time); *iha*—in this material world; *kim asat-karmabhiḥ bhavet*—what is the use of engaging in temporary fruitive activities.

TRANSLATION

[Nārada Muni had spoken of a physical object made of sharp blades and thunderbolts. The Haryaśvas understood this allegory as follows.] Eternal time moves very sharply, as if made of razors and thunderbolts. Uninterrupted and fully independent, it drives the activities of the entire world. If one does not try to study the eternal element of time, what benefit can he derive from performing temporary material activities?

PURPORT

This verse explains the words *kṣaura-pavyaṁ svayaṁ bhrami,* which especially refer to the orbit of eternal time. It is said that time and tide wait for no man. According to the moral instructions of the great politician Cāṇakya Paṇḍita:

āyuṣaḥ kṣaṇa eko'pi
na labhyaḥ svarṇa-koṭibhiḥ
na cen nirarthakaṁ nītiḥ
kā ca hānis tato'dhikā

Even a moment of one's lifetime could not be returned in exchange for millions of dollars. Therefore one should consider how much loss one suffers if he wastes even a moment of his life for nothing. Living like an animal, not understanding the goal of life, one foolishly thinks that there is no eternity and that his life span of fifty, sixty, or, at the most, one hundred years, is everything. This is the greatest foolishness. Time is eternal, and in the material world one passes through different phases of his eternal life. Time is compared herein to a sharp razor. A razor is meant to shave the hair from one's face, but if not carefully handled, the razor will cause disaster. One is advised not to create a disaster by misusing his lifetime. One should be extremely careful to utilize the span of his life for spiritual realization, or Kṛṣṇa consciousness.

TEXT 20

शास्त्रस्य पितुरादेशं यो न वेद निवर्तकम्।
कथं तदनुरूपाय गुणविस्रम्भ्युपक्रमेत् ॥ २० ॥

śāstrasya pitur ādeśaṁ
yo na veda nivartakam
kathaṁ tad-anurūpāya
guṇa-visrambhy upakramet

śāstrasya—of the scriptures; *pituḥ*—of the father; *ādeśam*—the instruction; *yaḥ*—one who; *na*—not; *veda*—understands; *nivartakam*—which brings about the cessation of the material way of life; *katham*—how; *tat-anurūpāya*—to follow the instruction of the *śāstras; guṇa-visrambhī*—a person entangled in the three modes of material nature; *upakramet*—can engage in the creation of progeny.

TRANSLATION

[Nārada Muni had asked how one could ignorantly defy one's own father. The Haryaśvas understood the meaning of this question.] One must accept the original instructions of the śāstra. According to Vedic civilization, one is offered a sacred thread as a sign of second birth. One takes his second birth by dint of having received instructions in the śāstra from a bona fide spiritual master. Therefore, śāstra, scripture, is the real father. All the śāstras instruct that one should end his material way of life. If one does not know the purpose of the father's orders, the śāstras, he is ignorant. The words of a material father who endeavors to engage his son in material activities are not the real instructions of the father.

PURPORT

Bhagavad-gītā (16.7) says, *pravṛttiṁ ca nivṛttiṁ ca janā na vidur āsurāḥ:* demons, who are less than human beings but are not called animals, do not know the meaning of *pravṛtti* and *nivṛtti,* work to be done and work not to be done. In the material world, every living entity has a desire to lord it over the material world as much as possible. This is called *pravṛtti-mārga.* All the *śāstras,* however, advise *nivṛtti-mārga,* or release from the materialistic way of life. Apart from the *śāstras* of the Vedic civilization, which is the oldest of the world, other *śāstras* agree on this point. For example, in the Buddhist *śāstras* Lord Buddha advises that one achieve *nirvāṇa* by giving up the materialistic way of life. In the Bible, which is also *śāstra,* one will find the same advice: one should cease materialistic life and return to the kingdom of God. In any *śāstra* one may examine, especially the Vedic *śāstra,* the same advice is given: one should give up his materialistic life and return to his original, spiritual life. Śaṅkarācārya also propounds the same conclusion. *Brahma satyaṁ jagan mithyā:* this material world or materialistic life is simply illusion, and therefore one should stop his illusory activities and come to the platform of Brahman.

The word *śāstra* refers to the scriptures, particularly the Vedic books of knowledge. The *Vedas—Sāma, Yajur, Ṛg* and *Atharva*—and any other books deriving knowledge from these *Vedas* are considered Vedic literatures. *Bhagavad-gītā* is the essence of all Vedic knowledge, and therefore it is the scripture whose instructions should be especially accepted. In this essence of all *śāstras,* Kṛṣṇa personally advises that one give up all other duties and surrender unto Him (*sarva-dharmān parityajya mām ekaṁ śaraṇaṁ vraja*).

One should be initiated into following the principles of *śāstra.* In offering initiation, our Kṛṣṇa consciousness movement asks one to come to the conclusion of *śāstra* by taking the advice of the supreme speaker of the *śāstra,* Kṛṣṇa, forgetting the principles of the materialistic way of life. Therefore the principles we advise are no illicit sex, no intoxication, no gambling and no meat-eating. These four types of engagement will enable an intelligent person to get free from the materialistic life and return home, back to Godhead.

In regard to the instructions of the father and mother, it may be said that every living entity, including even the insignificant cats, dogs and serpents, takes birth of a father and mother. Therefore, getting a material father and mother is not a problem. In every form of life, birth after birth, the living entity gets a father and mother. In human society, however, if one is satisfied with his material father and mother and their instructions and does not make further progress by accepting a spiritual master and being educated in the *śāstras,* he certainly remains in darkness. The material father and mother are important only if they are interested in educating their son to become free from the clutches of death. As instructed by Ṛṣabhadeva (*Bhāg.* 5.5.18): *pitā na sa syāj jananī na sā syāt/ na mocayed yaḥ samupeta-mṛtyum.* One should not strive to become a mother or father if one cannot save one's dependent son from the impending danger of death. A parent who does not know how to save his son has no value because such fathers and mothers may be had in any form of life, even among the cats, dogs and so on. Only a father and mother who can elevate their son to the spiritual platform are bona fide parents. Therefore according to the Vedic system it is said, *janmanā jāyate śūdraḥ:* one is born of a material father and mother as a *śūdra.* The purpose of life, however, is to become a *brāhmaṇa,* a first-class man.

A first-class intelligent man is called a *brāhmaṇa* because he knows the Supreme Brahman, the Absolute Truth. According to the Vedic instructions, *tad-vijñānārthaṁ sa gurum evābhigacchet:* to know this science, one must approach a bona fide *guru,* a spiritual master who will initiate the disciple with the sacred thread so that he may understand the Vedic knowledge. *Janmanā jāyate śūdraḥ saṁskārād dhi bhaved dvijaḥ.* Becoming a *brāhmaṇa* through the endeavor of a bona fide spiritual master is called *saṁskāra.* After initiation, one is engaged in study of the *śāstra,* which teaches the student how to gain release from materialistic life and return home, back to Godhead.

The Kṛṣṇa consciousness movement is teaching this higher knowledge of retiring from materialistic life to return to Godhead, but unfortunately many parents are not very satisfied with this movement. Aside from the parents of our students, many businessmen are also dissatisfied because we teach our students to abandon intoxication, meat-eating, illicit sex and gambling. If the Kṛṣṇa consciousness movement spreads, the so-called businessmen will have to close their slaughterhouses, breweries and cigarette factories. Therefore they are also very much afraid. However, we have no alternative than to teach our disciples to free themselves from materialistic life. We must instruct them in the opposite of material life to save them from the repetition of birth and death.

Nārada Muni, therefore, advised the Haryaśvas, the sons of Prajāpati Dakṣa, that instead of begetting progeny, it would be better to leave and achieve the perfection of spiritual understanding according to the instructions of the *śāstras.* The importance of the *śāstras* is mentioned in *Bhagavad-gītā* (16.23):

yaḥ śāstra-vidhim utsṛjya
vartate kāma-kārataḥ
na sa siddhim avāpnoti
na sukhaṁ na parāṁ gatim

"One who disregards the injunctions of the *śāstras* and acts whimsically, as he likes, never achieves the perfection of life, not to speak of happiness. Nor does he return home to the spiritual world."

TEXT 21

इति व्यवसिता राजन् हर्यश्वा एकचेतसः ।
प्रययुस्तं परिक्रम्य पन्थानमनिवर्तनम् ॥ २१ ॥

iti vyavasitā rājan
haryaśvā eka-cetasaḥ
prayayus taṁ parikramya
panthānam anivartanam

iti—thus; *vyavasitāḥ*—being fully convinced by the instructions of Nārada Muni; *rājan*—O King; *haryaśvāḥ*—the sons of Prajāpati Dakṣa; *eka-cetasaḥ*—all being of the same opinion; *prayayuḥ*—left; *tam*—Nārada Muni; *parikramya*—circumambulating; *panthānam*—on the path; *anivartanam*—which does not bring one back again to this material world.

TRANSLATION

Śukadeva Gosvāmī continued: My dear King, after hearing the instructions of Nārada, the Haryaśvas, the sons of Prajāpati Dakṣa, were firmly convinced. They all believed in his instructions and reached the same conclusion. Having accepted him as their spiritual master, they circumambulated that great sage and followed the path by which one never returns to this world.

PURPORT

From this verse we can understand the meaning of initiation and the duties of a disciple and spiritual master. The spiritual master never instructs his disciple, "Take a *mantra* from me, pay me some money, and by practicing this *yoga* system you will become very expert in materialistic life." This is not the duty of a spiritual master. Rather, the spiritual master teaches the disciple how to give up materialistic life, and the disciple's duty is to assimilate his instructions and ultimately follow the path back home, back to Godhead, from whence no one returns to this material world.

After hearing the instructions of Nārada Muni, the Haryaśvas, the sons of Prajāpati Dakṣa, decided not to be entangled in materialistic life by begetting hundreds of children and having to take care of them. This would have been unnecessarily entangling. The Haryaśvas did not consider pious and impious activities. Their materialistic father had instructed them to increase the population, but because of the words of Nārada Muni, they could not heed that instruction. Nārada Muni, as their spiritual master, gave them the śāstric instructions that they should give up this material world, and as bona fide disciples they followed his instructions. One should not endeavor to wander to different planetary systems within this universe, for even if one goes to the topmost planetary system, Brahmaloka, one must return again (*kṣīṇe puṇye martya-lokaṁ viśanti*). The endeavors of *karmīs* are a useless waste of time. One should endeavor to return home, back to Godhead. This is the perfection of life. As the Lord says in *Bhagavad-gītā* (8.16):

ābrahma-bhuvanāl lokāḥ
punar āvartino'rjuna
mām upetya tu kaunteya
punar janma na vidyate

"From the highest planet in the material world down to the lowest, all are places of misery wherein repeated birth and death take place. But one who attains to My abode, O son of Kuntī, never takes birth again."

TEXT 22

स्वरब्रह्मणि निर्भातहृषीकेशपदाम्बुजे ।
अखण्डं चित्तमावेश्य लोकाननुचरन्मुनिः ॥ २२ ॥

svara-brahmaṇi nirbhāta-
hṛṣīkeśa-padāmbuje
akhaṇḍaṁ cittam āveśya
lokān anucaran muniḥ

svara-brahmaṇi—in spiritual sound; *nirbhāta*—placing clearly before the mind; *hṛṣīkeśa*—of the Supreme Personality of Godhead, Kṛṣṇa, the master of the senses; *padāmbuje*—the lotus feet; *akhaṇḍam*—unbroken; *cittam*—

consciousness; *āveśya*—engaging; *lokān*—all the planetary systems; *anucarat* —traveled around; *muniḥ*—the great sage Nārada Muni.

TRANSLATION

The seven musical notes—ṣa, ṛ, gā, ma, pa, dha and ni—are used in musical instruments, but originally they come from the Sāma Veda. The great sage Nārada vibrates sounds describing the pastimes of the Supreme Lord. By such transcendental vibrations, such as Hare Kṛṣṇa, Hare Kṛṣṇa, Kṛṣṇa Kṛṣṇa, Hare Hare/ Hare Rāma, Hare Rāma, Rāma Rāma, Hare Hare, he fixes his mind at the lotus feet of the Lord. Thus he directly perceives Hṛṣīkeśa, the master of the senses. After delivering the Haryaśvas, Nārada Muni continued traveling throughout the planetary systems, his mind always fixed at the lotus feet of the Lord.

PURPORT

The goodness of the great sage Nārada Muni is described herewith. He always chants about the pastimes of the Lord and delivers the fallen souls back to Godhead. In this regard, Śrīla Bhaktivinoda Ṭhākura has sung:

nārada-muni, bājāya vīṇā,
'rādhikā-ramaṇa'-nāme
nāma amani, udita haya,
bhakata-gīta-sāme

amiya-dhārā, variṣe ghana,
śravaṇa-yugale giyā
bhakata-jana, saghane nāce,
bhariyā āpana hiyā

mādhurī-pūra, āsaba paśi',
mātāya jagata-jane
keha vā kāṅde, keha vā nāce,
keha māte mane mane

pañca-vadana, nārade dhari',
premera saghana rola
kamalāsana, nāciyā bale,
'bola bola hari bola'

sahasrānana, parama-sukhe,
'hari hari' bali' gāya

nāma-prabhāve, mātila viśva,
nāma-rasa sabe pāya

śrī-kṛṣṇa-nāma, rasane sphuri',
purā 'la āmāra āśa
śrī-rūpa-pade, yācaye ihā,
bhakativinoda dāsa

The purport of this song is that Nārada Muni, the great soul, plays a stringed instrument called a *vīṇā,* vibrating the sound *rādhikā-ramaṇa,* which is another name for Kṛṣṇa. As soon as he strokes the strings, all the devotees begin responding, making a very beautiful vibration. Accompanied by the stringed instrument, the singing seems like a shower of nectar, and all the devotees dance in ecstasy to the fullest extent of their satisfaction. While dancing, they appear madly intoxicated with ecstasy, as if drinking the beverage called *mādhurī-pūra.* Some of them cry, some of them dance, and some of them, although unable to dance publicly, dance within their hearts. Lord Śiva embraces Nārada Muni and begins talking in an ecstatic voice, and seeing Lord Śiva dancing with Nārada, Lord Brahmā also joins, saying, "All of you kindly chant 'Hari bol! Hari bol!' " The King of heaven, Indra, also gradually joins with great satisfaction and begins dancing and chanting "Hari bol! Hari bol!" In this way, by the influence of the transcendental vibration of the holy name of God, the whole universe becomes ecstatic. Bhaktivinoda Ṭhākura says, "When the universe becomes ecstatic, my desire is satisfied. I therefore pray unto the lotus feet of Rūpa Gosvāmī that this chanting of *harer nāma* may go on nicely like this."

Lord Brahmā is the *guru* of Nārada Muni, who is the *guru* of Vyāsadeva, and Vyāsadeva is the *guru* of Madhvācārya. Thus the Gauḍīya Mādhva *sampradāya* is in the disciplic succession from Nārada Muni. The members of this disciplic succession—in other words, the members of the Kṛṣṇa consciousness movement—should follow in the footsteps of Nārada Muni by chanting the transcendental vibration Hare Kṛṣṇa, Hare Kṛṣṇa, Kṛṣṇa Kṛṣṇa, Hare Hare/ Hare Rāma, Hare Rāma, Rāma Rāma, Hare Hare. They should go everywhere to deliver the fallen souls by vibrating the Hare Kṛṣṇa *mantra* and the instructions of *Bhagavad-gītā, Śrīmad-Bhāgavatam* and *Caitanya-caritāmṛta.* That will please the Supreme Personality of Godhead. One can spiritually advance if one actually follows the instructions of Nārada Muni. If one pleases Nārada Muni, then the Supreme Personality of Godhead, Hṛṣīkeśa, is also pleased (*yasya prasādād bhagavat-prasādaḥ*). The immediate spiritual master is the representative of Nārada Muni; there is no difference between the instructions of Nārada Muni and those of the present spiritual master. Both Nārada Muni and the present spiritual master speak the same teachings of Kṛṣṇa, who says in *Bhagavad-gītā* (18.65–66):

man-manā bhava mad-bhakto
mad-yājī māṁ namaskuru
mām evaiṣyasi satyaṁ te
pratijāne priyo'si me

sarva-dharmān parityajya
mām ekaṁ śaraṇaṁ vraja
ahaṁ tvāṁ sarva-pāpebhyo
mokṣayiṣyāmi mā śucaḥ

"Always think of Me and become My devotee. Worship Me and offer your homage unto Me. Thus you will come to Me without fail. I promise you this because you are My very dear friend. Abandon all varieties of religion and just surrender unto Me. I shall deliver you from all sinful reaction. Do not fear."

TEXT 23

नाशं निशम्य पुत्राणां नारदाच्छीलशालिनाम् ।
अन्वतप्यत कः शोचन् सुप्रजस्त्वं शुचां पदम् ॥ २३ ॥

nāśaṁ niśamya putrāṇāṁ
nāradāc chīla-śālinām
anvatapyata kaḥ śocan
suprajastvaṁ śucāṁ padam

nāśam—the loss; *niśamya*—hearing of; *putrāṇām*—of his sons; *nāradāt*—from Nārada; *śīla-śālinām*—who were the best of well-behaved persons; *anvatapyata*—suffered; *kaḥ*—Prajāpati Dakṣa; *śocan*—lamenting; *suprajastvam*—having ten thousand well-behaved sons; *śucām*—of lamentation; *padam*—position.

TRANSLATION

The Haryaśvas, the sons of Prajāpati Dakṣa, were very well behaved, cultured sons, but unfortunately, because of the instructions of Nārada Muni, they deviated from the order of their father. When Dakṣa heard this news, which was brought to him by Nārada Muni, he began to lament.

Although he was the father of such good sons, he had lost them all. Certainly this was lamentable.

PURPORT

The Haryaśvas, the sons of Prajāpati Dakṣa, were certainly well behaved, learned and advanced, and in accordance with the order of their father they went to perform austerities to beget good sons for their family. But Nārada Muni took advantage of their good behavior and culture to properly direct them not to be involved with this material world, but to use their culture and knowledge to end their material affairs. The Haryaśvas abided by the order of Nārada Muni, but when news of this was brought to Prajāpati Dakṣa, the *prajāpati,* instead of being happy with the actions of Nārada Muni, was extremely sorrowful. Similarly, we are trying to bring as many young men as possible to the Kṛṣṇa consciousness movement for their ultimate benefit, but the parents of the young men joining this movement, being very sorry, are lamenting and making counterpropaganda. Of course, Prajāpati Dakṣa did not make propaganda against Nārada Muni, but later, as we shall see, Dakṣa cursed Nārada Muni for his benevolent activities. This is the way of materialistic life. A materialistic father and mother want to engage their sons in begetting children, striving for improved economic conditions and rotting in materialistic life. They are not unhappy when their children become spoiled, useless citizens, but they lament when they join the Kṛṣṇa consciousness movement to achieve the ultimate goal of life. This animosity between parents and the Kṛṣṇa consciousness movement has existed since time immemorial. Even Nārada Muni was condemned, not to speak of others. Nevertheless, Nārada Muni never gives up his mission. To deliver as many fallen souls as possible, he continues playing his musical instrument and vibrating the transcendental sound Hare Kṛṣṇa, Hare Kṛṣṇa, Kṛṣṇa Kṛṣṇa, Hare Hare/ Hare Rāma, Hare Rāma, Rāma Rāma, Hare Hare.

TEXT 24

स भूयः पाञ्चजन्यायामजेन परिसान्त्वितः ।
पुत्रानजनयद् दक्षः सवलाश्वान् सहस्रिणः ॥ २४ ॥

sa bhūyaḥ pāñcajanyāyām
ajena parisāntvitaḥ
putrān ajanayad dakṣaḥ
savalāśvān sahasriṇaḥ

saḥ—Prajāpati Dakṣa; *bhūyaḥ*—again; *pāñcajanyāyām*—in the womb of his wife Asiknī, or Pāñcajanī; *ajena*—by Lord Brahmā; *parisāntvitaḥ*—being pacified; *putrān*—sons; *ajanayat*—begot; *dakṣaḥ*—Prajāpati Dakṣa; *savalāśvān*—named the Savalāśvas; *sahasriṇaḥ*—numbering one thousand.

TRANSLATION

When Prajāpati Dakṣa was lamenting for his lost children, Lord Brahmā pacified him with instructions, and thereafter Dakṣa begot one thousand more children in the womb of his wife, Pāñcajanī. This time his sons were known as the Savalāśvas.

PURPORT

Prajāpati Dakṣa was so named because he was very expert in begetting children. (The word *dakṣa* means "expert.") First he begot ten thousand children in the womb of his wife, and when the children were lost—when they returned home, back to Godhead—he begot another set of children, known as the Savalāśvas. Prajāpati Dakṣa is very expert in begetting children, and Nārada Muni is very expert in delivering all the conditioned souls back home, back to Godhead. Therefore the materialistic experts do not agree with the spiritual expert Nārada Muni, but this does not mean that Nārada Muni will give up his engagement of chanting the Hare Kṛṣṇa *mantra.*

TEXT 25

ते च पित्रा समादिष्टाः प्रजासर्गे धृतव्रताः ।
नारायणसरो जग्मुर्यत्र सिद्धाः स्वपूर्वजाः ॥ २५ ॥

te ca pitrā samādiṣṭāḥ
prajā-sarge dhṛta-vratāḥ
nārāyaṇa-saro jagmur
yatra siddhāḥ sva-pūrvajāḥ

te—these sons (the Savalāśvas); *ca*—and; *pitrā*—by their father; *samādiṣṭāḥ*—being ordered; *prajā-sarge*—in increasing progeny or population; *dhṛta-vratāḥ*—accepted vows; *nārāyaṇa-saraḥ*—the holy lake named Nārāyaṇa-saras; *jagmuḥ*—went to; *yatra*—where; *siddhāḥ*—perfected; *sva-pūrva-jāḥ*—their older brothers, who had previously gone there.

TRANSLATION

In accordance with their father's order to beget children, the second group of sons also went to Nārāyaṇa-saras, the same place where their brothers had previously attained perfection by following the instructions of Nārada. Undertaking great vows of austerity, the Savalāśvas remained at that holy place.

PURPORT

Prajāpati Dakṣa sent his second group of sons to the same place where his previous sons had attained perfection. He did not hesitate to send his second group of sons to the same place, although they too might become victims of Nārada's instructions. According to the Vedic culture, one should be trained in spiritual understanding as a *brahmacārī* before entering household life to beget children. This is the Vedic system. Thus Prajāpati Dakṣa sent his second group of sons for cultural improvement, despite the risk that because of the instructions of Nārada they might become as intelligent as their older brothers. As a dutiful father, he did not hesitate to allow his sons to receive cultural instructions concerning the perfection of life; he depended upon them to choose whether to return home, back to Godhead, or to rot in this material world in various species of life. In all circumstances, the duty of the father is to give cultural education to his sons, who must later decide which way to go. Responsible fathers should not hinder their sons who are making cultural advancement in association with the Kṛṣṇa consciousness movement. This is not a father's duty. The duty of a father is to give his son complete freedom to make his choice after becoming spiritually advanced by following the instructions of the spiritual master.

TEXT 26

तदुपस्पर्शनादेव विनिर्धूतमलाशयाः ।
जपन्तो ब्रह्म परमं तेपुस्तत्र महत् तपः ॥ २६ ॥

tad-upasparśanād eva
vinirdhūta-malāśayāḥ
japanto brahma paramaṁ
tepus tatra mahat tapaḥ

tat—of that holy place; *upasparśanāt*—by bathing regularly in the water; *eva*—indeed; *vinirdhūta*—completely purified; *mala-āśayāḥ*—of all the dirt within the heart; *japantaḥ*—chanting or murmuring; *brahma*—*mantras* beginning with *oṁ* (such as *oṁ tad viṣṇoḥ paramaṁ padaṁ sadā paśyanti sūrayaḥ*); *paramam*—the ultimate goal; *tepuḥ*—performed; *tatra*—there; *mahat*—great; *tapaḥ*—penances.

TRANSLATION

At Nārāyaṇa-saras, the second group of sons performed penances in the same way as the first. They bathed in the holy water, and by its touch all the dirty material desires in their hearts were cleansed away. They murmured mantras beginning with oṁkāra and underwent a severe course of austerities.

PURPORT

Every Vedic *mantra* is called *brahma* because each *mantra* is preceded by the *brahmākṣara* (*aum* or *oṁkāra*). For example, *oṁ namo bhagavate vāsudevāya.* Lord Kṛṣṇa says in *Bhagavad-gītā* (7.8), *praṇavaḥ sarva-vedeṣu:* "In all the Vedic *mantras,* I am represented by *praṇava,* or *oṁkāra.*" Thus chanting of the Vedic *mantras* beginning with *oṁkāra* is directly chanting of Kṛṣṇa's name. There is no difference. Whether one chants *oṁkāra* or addresses the Lord as "Kṛṣṇa," the meaning is the same, but Śrī Caitanya Mahāprabhu has recommended that in this age one chant the Hare Kṛṣṇa *mantra* (*harer nāma eva kevalam*). Although there is no difference between Hare Kṛṣṇa and the Vedic *mantras* beginning with *oṁkāra,* Śrī Caitanya Mahāprabhu, the leader of the spiritual movement for this age, has recommended that one chant Hare Kṛṣṇa, Hare Kṛṣṇa, Kṛṣṇa Kṛṣṇa, Hare Hare/ Hare Rāma, Hare Rāma, Rāma Rāma, Hare Hare.

TEXTS 27–28

अब्भक्षाः कतिचिन्मासान् कतिचिद् वायुभोजनाः ।
आराधयन् मन्त्रमिममभ्यस्यन्त इडस्पतिम् ॥ २७ ॥
ॐ नमो नारायणाय पुरुषाय महात्मने ।
विशुद्धसत्त्वधिष्ण्याय महाहंसाय धीमहि ॥ २८ ॥

ab-bhakṣāḥ katicin māsān
katicid vāyu-bhojanāḥ
ārādhayan mantram imam
abhyasyanta iḍaspatim

oṁ namo nārāyaṇāya
puruṣāya mahātmane
viśuddha-sattva-dhiṣṇyāya
mahā-haṁsāya dhīmahi

ap-bhakṣāḥ—drinking only water; *katicit māsān*—for some months; *katicit*—for some; *vāyu-bhojanāḥ*—merely breathing, or eating air; *ārādhayan*—worshiped; *mantram imam*—this *mantra,* which is nondifferent from Nārāyaṇa; *abhyasyantaḥ*—practicing; *iḍaḥ-patim*—the master of all *mantras,* Lord Viṣṇu; *oṁ* —O Lord; *namaḥ*—respectful obeisances; *nārāyaṇāya*—unto Lord Nārāyaṇa; *puruṣāya*—the Supreme Person; *mahā-ātmane*—the exalted Supersoul; *viśuddha-sattva-dhiṣṇyāya*—who is always situated in the transcendental abode; *mahā-haṁsāya*—the great swanlike Personality of Godhead; *dhīmahi*—we always offer.

TRANSLATION

For a few months the sons of Prajāpati Dakṣa drank only water and ate only air. Thus undergoing great austerities, they recited this mantra: "Let us offer our respectful obeisances unto Nārāyaṇa, the Supreme Personality of Godhead, who is always situated in His transcendental abode. Since He is the Supreme Person [paramahaṁsa], let us offer our respectful obeisances unto Him."

PURPORT

From these verses it is apparent that the chanting of the *mahā-mantra* or the Vedic *mantras* must be accompanied by severe austerities. In Kali-yuga, people cannot undergo severe austerities like those mentioned herein—drinking only water and eating only air for many months. One cannot imitate such a process. But at least one must undergo some austerity by giving up four unwanted principles, namely illicit sex, meat-eating, intoxication and gambling. Anyone can easily practice this *tapasya,* and then the chanting of the Hare Kṛṣṇa *mantra* will be effective without delay. One should not give up the process of austerity. If possible, one should bathe in the waters of the Ganges or Yamunā, or in the absence of the Ganges and Yamunā one may bathe in the water of the sea. This is an item of austerity. Our Kṛṣṇa consciousness movement has therefore established two very large centers, one in Vṛndāvana and another in Māyāpur, Navadvīpa. There one may bathe in the Ganges or Yamunā, chant the Hare Kṛṣṇa *mantra* and thus become perfect and return home, back to Godhead.

TEXT 29

इति तानपि राजेन्द्र प्रजासर्गधियो मुनिः ।
उपेत्य नारदः प्राह वाचःकूटानि पूर्ववत् ॥ २९ ॥

iti tān api rājendra
prajā-sarga-dhiyo muniḥ
upetya nāradaḥ prāha
vācaḥ kūṭāni pūrvavat

iti—thus; *tān*—them (the sons of Prajāpati Dakṣa known as the Savalāśvas); *api*—also; *rājendra*—O King Parīkṣit; *prajā-sarga-dhiyaḥ*—who were under the impression that begetting children was the most important duty; *muniḥ*—the great sage; *upetya*—approaching; *nāradaḥ*—Nārada; *prāha*—said; *vācaḥ*—words; *kūṭāni*—enigmatic; *pūrva-vat*—as he had done previously.

TRANSLATION

O King Parīkṣit, Nārada Muni approached these sons of Prajāpati Dakṣa, who were engaged in tapasya to beget children, and spoke enigmatic words to them just as he had spoken to their elder brothers.

TEXT 30

दाक्षायणाः संश्रृणुत गदतो निगमं मम ।
अन्विच्छतानुपदवीं भ्रातॄणां भ्रातृवत्सलाः ॥ ३० ॥

dākṣāyaṇāḥ saṁśṛṇuta
gadato nigamaṁ mama
anvicchatānupadavīṁ
bhrātṝṇāṁ bhrātṛ-vatsalāḥ

dākṣāyaṇāḥ—O sons of Prajāpati Dakṣa; *saṁśṛṇuta*—please hear with attention; *gadataḥ*—who am speaking; *nigamam*—instruction; *mama*—my; *anvicchata*—follow; *anupadavīm*—the path; *bhrātṝṇām*—of your brothers; *bhrātṛ-vatsalāḥ*—O you who are very much affectionate to your brothers.

TRANSLATION

O sons of Dakṣa, please hear my words of instruction attentively. You are all very affectionate to your elder brothers, the Haryaśvas. Therefore you should follow their path.

PURPORT

Nārada Muni encouraged Prajāpati Dakṣa's second group of sons by awakening their natural affinity for their brothers. He urged them to follow their older brothers if they were at all affectionate toward them. Family affection is very strong, and therefore Nārada Muni followed this tactic of reminding them of their family relationship with the Haryaśvas. Generally the word *nigama* refers to the *Vedas,* but here *nigama* refers to the instructions contained in the *Vedas. Śrīmad-Bhāgavatam* says, *nigama-kalpa-taror galitaṁ phalam:* the Vedic instructions are like a tree, of which *Śrīmad-Bhāgavatam* is the ripened fruit. Nārada Muni is engaged in distributing this fruit, and therefore he instructed Vyāsadeva to write this *Mahā-purāṇa, Śrīmad-Bhāgavatam,* for the benefit of ignorant human society.

anarthopaśamaṁ sākṣād
bhakti-yogam adhokṣaje
lokasyājānato vidvāṁś
cakre sātvata-saṁhitām

"The material miseries of the living entity, which are superfluous to him, can be directly mitigated by the linking process of devotional service. But the mass of people do not know this, and therefore the learned Vyāsadeva compiled this Vedic literature, which is in relation to the Supreme Truth." (*Bhāg.* 1.7.6) People are suffering because of ignorance and are following a wrong path for happiness. This is called *anartha.* These material activities will never make them happy, and therefore Nārada instructed Vyāsadeva to record the instructions of *Śrīmad-Bhāgavatam.* Vyāsadeva actually followed Nārada and did this. *Śrīmad-Bhāgavatam* is the supreme instruction of the *Vedas. Galitaṁ phalam:* the ripened fruit of the *Vedas* is *Śrīmad-Bhāgavatam.*

TEXT 31

भ्रातॄणां प्रायणं भ्राता योऽनुतिष्ठति धर्मवित् ।
स पुण्यबन्धुः पुरुषो मरुद्भिः सह मोदते ॥ ३१ ॥

bhrātṝṇāṁ prāyaṇaṁ bhrātā
yo 'nutiṣṭhati dharmavit
sa puṇya-bandhuḥ puruṣo
marudbhiḥ saha modate

bhrātṝṇām—of elder brothers; *prāyaṇam*—the path; *bhrātā*—a faithful brother; *yaḥ*—one who; *anutiṣṭhati*—follows; *dharma-vit*—knowing the religious principles; *saḥ*—that; *puṇya-bandhuḥ*—highly pious; *puruṣaḥ*—person; *marudbhiḥ*—the demigods of the winds; *saha*—with; *modate*—enjoys life.

TRANSLATION

A brother aware of the principles of religion follows in the footsteps of his elder brothers. Because of being highly elevated, such a pious brother gets the opportunity to associate and enjoy with demigods like the Maruts, who are all affectionate to their brothers.

PURPORT

According to their belief in various material relationships, people are promoted to various planets. Here it is said that one who is very faithful to his brothers should follow a path similar to theirs and get the opportunity for promotion to Marudloka. Nārada Muni advised Prajāpati Dakṣa's second group of sons to follow their elder brothers and be promoted to the spiritual world.

TEXT 32

एतावदुक्त्वा प्रययौ नारदोऽमोघदर्शनः ।
तेऽपि चान्वगमन् मार्गं भ्रातॄणामेव मारिष ॥ ३२ ॥

etāvad uktvā prayayau
nārado 'mogha-darśanaḥ
te 'pi cānvagaman mārgaṁ
bhrātṝṇām eva māriṣa

etāvat—this much; *uktvā*—speaking; *prayayau*—departed from that place; *nāradaḥ*—the great sage Nārada; *amogha-darśanaḥ*—whose glance is all-auspicious; *te*—they; *api*—also; *ca*—and; *anvagaman*—followed; *mārgam*—the path; *bhrātṝṇām*—of their previous brothers; *eva*—indeed; *māriṣa*—O great Āryan king.

TRANSLATION

Śukadeva Gosvāmī continued: O best of the advanced Āryans, after saying this much to the sons of Prajāpati Dakṣa, Nārada Muni, whose merciful glance never goes in vain, left as he had planned. The sons of Dakṣa followed their elder brothers. Not attempting to produce children, they engaged themselves in Kṛṣṇa consciousness.

TEXT 33

सध्रीचीनं प्रतीचीनं परस्यानुपथं गताः ।
नाद्यापि ते निवर्तन्ते पश्चिमा यामिनीरिव ॥ ३३ ॥

sadhrīcīnaṁ pratīcīnaṁ
parasyānupathaṁ gatāḥ
nādyāpi te nivartante
paścimā yāminīr iva

sadhrīcīnam—completely correct; *pratīcīnam*—obtainable by adopting a mode of life aimed at the highest goal, devotional service; *parasya*—of the Supreme Lord; *anupatham*—the pathway; *gatāḥ*—taking to; *na*—not; *adya api*—even until today; *te*—they (the sons of Prajāpati Dakṣa); *nivartante*—have come back; *paścimāḥ*—western (those that have past); *yāminīḥ*—nights; *iva*—like.

TRANSLATION

The Savalāśvas took to the correct path, which is obtainable by a mode of life meant to achieve devotional service, or the mercy of the Supreme Personality of Godhead. Like nights that have gone to the west, they have not returned even until now.

TEXT 34

एतस्मिन् काल उत्पातान् बहून् पश्यन् प्रजापतिः ।
पूर्ववन्नारदकृतं पुत्रनाशमुपाशृणोत् ॥ ३४ ॥

etasmin kāla utpātān
bahūn paśyan prajāpatiḥ
pūrvavan nārada-kṛtaṁ
putra-nāśam upāśṛṇot

etasmin—at this; *kāle*—time; *utpātān*—disturbances; *bahūn*—many; *paśyan*—seeing; *prajāpatiḥ*—Prajāpati Dakṣa; *pūrva-vat*—like before; *nārada*—by the great sage Nārada Muni; *kṛtam*—done; *putra-nāśam*—the loss of his children; *upāśṛṇot*—he heard of.

TRANSLATION

At this time, Prajāpati Dakṣa observed many inauspicious signs, and he heard from various sources that his second group of sons, the Savalāśvas,

had followed the path of their elder brothers in accordance with the instructions of Nārada.

TEXT 35

चुक्रोध नारदायासौ पुत्रशोकविमूर्च्छितः ।
देवर्षिमुपलभ्याह रोषाद्विस्फुरिताधरः ॥ ३५ ॥

cukrodha nāradāyāsau
putra-śoka-vimūrcchitaḥ
devarṣim upalabhyāha
roṣād visphuritādharaḥ

cukrodha—became very angry; *nāradāya*—at the great sage Nārada Muni; *asau*—that one (Dakṣa); *putra-śoka*—due to lamentation for the loss of his children; *vimūrcchitaḥ*—almost fainting; *devarṣim*—the great sage Devarṣi Nārada; *upalabhya*—seeing; *āha*—he said; *roṣāt*—out of great anger; *visphurita*—trembling; *adharaḥ*—whose lips.

TRANSLATION

When he heard that the Savalāśvas had also left this world to engage in devotional service, Dakṣa was angry at Nārada, and he almost fainted due to lamentation. When Dakṣa met Nārada, Dakṣa's lips began trembling in anger, and he spoke as follows.

PURPORT

Śrīla Viśvanātha Cakravartī Ṭhākura comments that Nārada Muni had delivered the entire family of Svāyambhuva Manu, beginning with Priyavrata and Uttānapāda. He had delivered Uttānapāda's son Dhruva and had even delivered Prācīnabarhi, who was engaged in fruitive activities. Nevertheless, he could not deliver Prajāpati Dakṣa. Prajāpati Dakṣa saw Nārada before him because Nārada had personally come to deliver him. Nārada Muni took the opportunity to approach Prajāpati Dakṣa in his bereavement because the time of bereavement is a suitable time for appreciating *bhakti-yoga.* As stated in *Bhagavad-gītā* (7.16), four kinds of men—*ārta* (one who is distressed), *arthārthī* (one in need of money), *jijñāsu* (one who is inquisitive) and *jñānī* (a person in knowledge)—try to understand devotional service. Prajāpati Dakṣa was in great distress because of the loss of his sons, and therefore Nārada took the opportunity to instruct him regarding liberation from material bondage.

TEXT 36

श्रीदक्ष उवाच
अहो असाधो साधूनां साधुलिङ्गेन नस्त्वया ।
असाध्वकार्यर्भकाणां भिक्षोर्मार्गः प्रदर्शितः ॥ ३६ ॥

śrī-dakṣa uvāca
aho asādho sādhūnāṁ
sādhu-liṅgena nas tvayā
asādhv akāry arbhakāṇāṁ
bhikṣor mārgaḥ pradarśitaḥ

śrī-dakṣaḥ uvāca—Prajāpati Dakṣa said; *aho asādho*—O greatly dishonest nondevotee; *sādhūnām*—of the society of devotees and great sages; *sādhu-liṅgena*—wearing the dress of a saintly person; *naḥ*—unto us; *tvayā*—by you; *asādhu*—a dishonesty; *akāri*—has been done; *arbhakāṇām*—of poor boys who were very inexperienced; *bhikṣoḥ mārgaḥ*—the path of a beggar or mendicant *sannyāsī; pradarśitaḥ*—shown.

TRANSLATION

Prajāpati Dakṣa said: Alas, Nārada Muni, you wear the dress of a saintly person, but you are not actually a saint. Indeed, although I am now in gṛhastha life, I am a saintly person. By showing my sons the path of renunciation, you have done me an abominable injustice.

PURPORT

Śrī Caitanya Mahāprabhu said, *sannyāsīra alpa chidra sarva-loke gāya* (*Cc. Madhya* 12.51). In society one will find many *sannyāsīs, vānaprasthas, gṛhasthas* and *brahmacārīs,* but if all of them properly live in accordance with their duties, they are understood to be *sādhus.* Prajāpati Dakṣa was certainly a *sādhu* because he had executed such great austerities that the Supreme Personality of Godhead, Lord Viṣṇu, had appeared before him. Nevertheless, he had a fault-finding mentality. He improperly thought Nārada Muni to be *asādhu,* or nonsaintly, because Nārada had foiled his intentions. Desiring to train his sons to become *gṛhasthas* fully equipped with knowledge, Dakṣa had sent them to execute austerities by Nārāyaṇa-saras. Nārada Muni, however, taking advantage of their highly elevated position in austerity, instructed them to become Vaiṣṇavas in the renounced order. This is the duty of Nārada Muni and his followers. They must show everyone the path of renouncing this material world and returning home, back to Godhead. Prajāpati Dakṣa, however, could not see the exaltedness of the duties Nārada Muni performed in relation to his sons. Unable to appreciate Nārada Muni's behavior, Dakṣa accused Nārada of being *asādhu.*

The words *bhikṣor mārga,* "the path of the renounced order," are very significant in this regard. A *sannyāsī* is called *tridaṇḍi-bhikṣu* because his duty is to beg alms from the homes of *gṛhasthas* and to give the *gṛhasthas* spiritual instructions. A *sannyāsī* is allowed to beg from door to door, but a *gṛhastha* cannot do so. *Gṛhasthas* may earn their living according to the four divisions of spiritual life. A *brāhmaṇa gṛhastha* may earn his livelihood by becoming a learned scholar and teaching people in general how to worship the Supreme Personality of Godhead. He may also assume the duty of worship himself. Therefore it is said that only *brāhmaṇas* may engage in Deity worship, and they may accept as *prasāda* whatever people offer the Deity. Although a *brāhmaṇa* may sometimes accept charity, it is not for his personal maintenance but for the worship of the Deity. Thus a *brāhmaṇa* does not stock anything for his future use. Similarly, *kṣatriyas* may collect taxes from the citizens, and they must also protect the citizens, enforce rules and regulations, and maintain law and order. *Vaiśyas* should earn their livelihood through agriculture and cow protection, and *śūdras* should maintain their livelihood by serving the three higher classes. Unless one becomes a *brāhmaṇa,* one cannot take *sannyāsa. Sannyāsīs* and *brahmacārīs* may beg alms door to door, but a *gṛhastha* cannot.

Prajāpati Dakṣa condemned Nārada Muni because Nārada, a *brahmacārī* who could beg from door to door, had made *sannyāsīs* of Dakṣa's sons, who were being trained to be *gṛhasthas.* Dakṣa was extremely angry at Nārada because he thought that Nārada had done him a great injustice. According to Dakṣa's opinion, Nārada Muni had misled Dakṣa's inexperienced sons (*asādhv akāry arbhakāṇām*). Dakṣa regarded his sons as innocent boys who had been misled when Nārada showed them the renounced order of life. Because of all these considerations, Prajāpati Dakṣa charged that Nārada Muni was *asādhu* and should not have adopted the dress of a *sādhu.*

Sometimes a saintly person is misunderstood by *gṛhasthas,* especially when he instructs their young sons to accept Kṛṣṇa consciousness. Generally a *gṛhastha* thinks that unless one enters *gṛhastha* life he cannot properly enter the renounced order. If a young man immediately adopts the path of the renounced order in accordance with the instructions of Nārada or a member of his disciplic succession, his parents become very angry. This same phenomenon is occurring in our Kṛṣṇa consciousness movement because we are instructing all the young boys in the Western countries to follow the path of renunciation. We allow *gṛhastha* life, but a *gṛhastha* also follows the path of renunciation. Even a *gṛhastha* has to give up so many bad habits that his parents think his life has been practically destroyed. We allow no meat-eating, no illicit sex, no gambling and no intoxication, and consequently the parents wonder how, if there are so many no's, one's life can be positive. In the Western countries especially, these four prohibited activities practically constitute the life and soul of the modern population. Therefore parents sometimes dislike our movement, just as Prajāpati Dakṣa disliked the activities of Nārada and accused Nārada of dishonesty. Nevertheless, although parents may be angry at us, we must perform our duty without hesitation because we are in the disciplic succession from Nārada Muni.

People addicted to householder life wonder how one can give up the enjoyment of *gṛhastha* life, which is a concession for sex enjoyment, simply to become a mendicant in Kṛṣṇa consciousness. They do not know that the householder's concession for sex life cannot be regulated unless one accepts the life of a mendicant. The Vedic civilization therefore enjoins that at the end of one's fiftieth year one must give up household life. This is compulsory. However, because modern civilization is misled, householders want to remain in family life until death, and therefore they are suffering. In such cases, the disciples of Nārada Muni advise all the members of the younger generation to join the Kṛṣṇa consciousness movement immediately. There is nothing wrong in this.

TEXT 37

ऋणैस्त्रिभिरमुक्तानाममीमांसितकर्मणाम् ।
विघातः श्रेयसः पाप लोकयोरुभयोः कृतः ॥ ३७ ॥

ṛṇais tribhir amuktānām
amīmāṁsita-karmaṇām
vighātaḥ śreyasaḥ pāpa
lokayor ubhayoḥ kṛtaḥ

ṛṇaiḥ—from the debts; *tribhiḥ*—three; *amuktānām*—of persons not freed; *amīmāṁsita*—not considering; *karmaṇām*—the path of duty; *vighātaḥ*—ruin; *śreyasaḥ*—of the path of good fortune; *pāpa*—O most sinful (Nārada Muni); *lokayoḥ*—of the worlds; *ubhayoḥ*—both; *kṛtaḥ*—done.

TRANSLATION

Prajāpati Dakṣa said: My sons were not at all freed from their three debts. Indeed, they did not properly consider their obligations. O Nārada Muni, O personality of sinful action, you have obstructed their progress toward good fortune in this world and the next because they are still indebted to the saintly persons, the demigods and their father.

PURPORT

As soon as a *brāhmaṇa* takes birth, he assumes three kinds of debts—debts to great saints, debts to the demigods and debts to his father. The son of a *brāhmaṇa* must undergo celibacy (*brahmacarya*) to clear his debts to the saintly persons, he must perform ritualistic ceremonies to clear his debts to the demigods, and he must beget children to become free from his debts to his father. Prajāpati Dakṣa argued that although the renounced order is recommended for liberation, one cannot attain liberation unless one fulfills his obligations to the demigods, the saints and his father. Since Dakṣa's sons had not liberated themselves from these three debts, how could Nārada Muni have led them to the renounced order of life? Apparently, Prajāpati Dakṣa did not know the final decision of the *śāstras.* As stated in *Śrīmad-Bhāgavatam* (11.5.41):

devarṣi-bhūtāpta-nṛṇāṁ pitṝṇāṁ
na kiṅkaro nāyam ṛṇī ca rājan
sarvātmanā yaḥ śaraṇaṁ śaraṇyaṁ
gato mukundaṁ parihṛtya kartam

Everyone is indebted to the demigods, to living entities in general, to his family, to the *pitās* and so on, but if one fully surrenders to Kṛṣṇa, Mukunda, who can give one liberation, even if one performs no *yajñas,* one is freed from all debts. Even if one does not repay his debts, he is freed from all debts if he renounces the material world for the sake of the Supreme Personality of Godhead, whose lotus feet are the shelter of everyone. This is the verdict of the *śāstra.* Therefore Nārada Muni was completely right in instructing the sons of Prajāpati Dakṣa to renounce this material world immediately and take shelter of the Supreme Personality of Godhead. Unfortunately, Prajāpati Dakṣa, the father of the Haryaśvas and Savalāśvas, did not understand the great service rendered by Nārada Muni. Dakṣa therefore addressed him as *pāpa* (the personality of sinful activities) and *asādhu* (a nonsaintly person). Since Nārada Muni was a great saint and Vaiṣṇava, he tolerated all such accusations from Prajāpati Dakṣa. He merely performed his duty as a Vaiṣṇava by delivering all the sons of Prajāpati Dakṣa, enabling them to return home, back to Godhead.

TEXT 38

एवं त्वं निरनुक्रोशो बालानां मतिभिद्धरेः ।
पार्षदमध्ये चरसि यशोहा निरपत्रपः ॥ ३८ ॥

evaṁ tvaṁ niranukrośo
bālānāṁ mati-bhid dhareḥ
pārṣada-madhye carasi
yaśo-hā nirapatrapaḥ

evam—thus; *tvam*—you (Nārada); *niranukrośaḥ*—without compassion; *bālānām*—of innocent, inexperienced boys; *mati-bhit*—contaminating the consciousness; *hareḥ*—of the Supreme Personality of Godhead; *pārṣada-madhye*—among the personal associates; *carasi*—travel; *yaśaḥ-hā*—defaming the Supreme Personality of Godhead; *nirapatrapaḥ*—(although you do not know what you are doing, you are executing sinful activities) without shame.

TRANSLATION

Prajāpati Dakṣa continued: Thus committing violence against other living entities and yet claiming to be an associate of Lord Viṣṇu, you are defaming the Supreme Personality of Godhead. You needlessly created a mentality of renunciation in innocent boys, and therefore you are shameless and devoid of compassion. How could you travel with the personal associates of the Supreme Lord?

PURPORT

This mentality of Prajāpati Dakṣa still continues even today. When young boys join the Kṛṣṇa consciousness movement, their fathers and so-called guardians are very angry at the propounder of the Kṛṣṇa consciousness movement because they think that their sons have been unnecessarily induced to deprive themselves of the material enjoyments of eating, drinking and merrymaking. *Karmīs,* fruitive workers, think that one should fully enjoy his present life in this material world and also perform some pious activities to be promoted to higher planetary systems for further enjoyment in the next life. A *yogī,* however, especially a *bhakti-yogī,* is callous to the opinions of this material world. He is not interested in traveling to the higher planetary systems of the demigods to enjoy a long life in an advanced materialistic civilization. As stated by Prabodhānanda Sarasvatī, *kaivalyaṁ narakāyate tridaśa-pūr ākāśa-puṣpāyate:* for a devotee, merging into the Brahman existence is hellish, and life in the higher planetary systems of the demigods is a will-o'-the-wisp, a phantasmagoria with no real existence at all. A pure devotee is not interested in yogic perfection, travel to higher planetary systems, or oneness with Brahman. He is interested only in rendering service to the Personality of Godhead. Since Prajāpati Dakṣa was a *karmī,* he could not appreciate the great service Nārada Muni had rendered his eleven thousand sons. Instead, he accused Nārada Muni of being sinful and charged that because Nārada Muni was associated with the Supreme Personality of Godhead, the Lord would also be defamed. Thus Dakṣa criticized that Nārada Muni was an offender to the Lord although he was known as an associate of the Lord.

TEXT 39

ननु भागवता नित्यं भूतानुग्रहकातराः ।
ऋते त्वां सौहृदघ्नं वै वैरङ्करमवैरिणाम् ॥ ३९ ॥

nanu bhāgavatā nityaṁ
bhūtānugraha-kātarāḥ
ṛte tvāṁ sauhṛda-ghnaṁ vai
vairaṅ-karam avairiṇām

nanu—now; *bhāgavatāḥ*—devotees of the Supreme Personality of Godhead; *nityam*—eternally; *bhūta-anugraha-kātarāḥ*—very much anxious to bestow benedictions upon the fallen conditioned souls; *ṛte*—except; *tvām*—yourself; *sauhṛda-ghnam*—a breaker of friendship (therefore not countable among the *bhāgavatas,* or devotees of the Lord); *vai*—indeed; *vairam-karam*—you create enmity; *avairiṇām*—toward persons who are not enemies.

TRANSLATION

All the devotees of the Lord but you are very kind to the conditioned souls and are eager to benefit others. Although you wear the dress of a devotee, you create enmity with people who are not your enemies, or you break friendship and create enmity between friends. Are you not ashamed of posing as a devotee while performing these abominable actions?

PURPORT

Such are the criticisms that must be borne by the servants of Nārada Muni in the disciplic succession. Through the Kṛṣṇa consciousness movement, we are trying to train young people to become devotees and return home, back to Godhead, by following rigid regulative principles, but our service is appreciated neither in India nor abroad in the Western countries where we are endeavoring to spread this Kṛṣṇa consciousness movement. In India the caste *brāhmaṇas* have become enemies of the Kṛṣṇa consciousness movement because we elevate foreigners, who are supposed to be *mlecchas* and *yavanas,* to the position of *brāhmaṇas.* We train them in austerities and penances and recognize them as *brāhmaṇas* by awarding them sacred threads. Thus the caste *brāhmaṇas* of India are very displeased by our activities in the Western world. In the West also, the parents of the young people who join this movement have also become enemies. We have no business creating enemies, but the process is such that nondevotees will always be inimical toward us. Nevertheless, as stated in the *śāstras,* a devotee should be both tolerant and merciful. Devotees engaged in preaching should be prepared to be accused by ignorant persons, and yet they must be very merciful to the fallen conditioned souls. If one can execute his duty in the disciplic succession of Nārada Muni, his service will surely be recognized. As the Lord says in *Bhagavad-gītā* (18.68–69):

ya idaṁ paramaṁ guhyaṁ
mad-bhakteṣv abhidhāsyati
bhaktiṁ mayi parāṁ kṛtvā
mām evaiṣyaty asaṁśayaḥ

na ca tasmān manuṣyeṣu
kaścin me priya-kṛttamaḥ
bhavitā na ca me tasmād
anyaḥ priyataro bhuvi

"For one who explains the supreme secret to the devotees, devotional service is guaranteed, and at the end he will come back to Me. There is no servant in this world more dear to Me than he, nor will there ever be one more dear." Let us continue preaching the message of Lord Kṛṣṇa and not be afraid of enemies. Our only duty is to satisfy the Lord by this preaching, which will be accepted as service by Lord Caitanya and Lord Kṛṣṇa. We must sincerely serve the Lord and not be deterred by so-called enemies.

In this verse the word *sauhṛda-ghnam* ("a breaker of friendship") is used. Because Nārada Muni and the members of his disciplic succession disrupt friendships and family life, they are sometimes accused of being *sauhṛda-ghnam,* creators of enmity between relatives. Actually such devotees are friends of every living entity (*suhṛdaṁ sarva-bhūtānām*), but they are misunderstood to be enemies. Preaching can be a difficult, thankless task, but a preacher must follow the orders of the Supreme Lord and be unafraid of materialistic persons.

TEXT 40

नेत्थं पुंसां विरागः स्यात् त्वया केवलिना मृषा ।
मन्यसे यद्युपशमं स्नेहपाशनिकृन्तनम् ॥ ४० ॥

netthaṁ puṁsāṁ virāgaḥ syāt
tvayā kevalinā mṛṣā
manyase yady upaśamaṁ
sneha-pāśa-nikṛntanam

na—not; *ittham*—in this way; *puṁsām*—of persons; *virāgaḥ*—renunciation; *syāt*—is possible; *tvayā*—by you; *kevalinā mṛṣā*—possessing knowledge falsely; *manyase*—you think; *yadi*—if; *upaśamam*—renunciation of material enjoyment; *sneha-pāśa*—the bonds of affection; *nikṛntanam*—cutting.

TRANSLATION

Prajāpati Dakṣa continued: If you think that simply awakening the sense of renunciation will detach one from the material world, I must say that unless full knowledge is awakened, simply changing dresses as you have done cannot possibly bring detachment.

PURPORT

Prajāpati Dakṣa was correct in stating that changing one's dress cannot detach one from this material world. The *sannyāsīs* of Kali-yuga who change their robes from white to saffron and then think they can do whatever they like are more abominable than materialistic *gṛhasthas.* This is not recommended anywhere. Prajāpati Dakṣa was right in pointing out this defect, but he did not know that Nārada Muni had aroused the spirit of renunciation in the Haryaśvas and Savalāśvas through full knowledge. Such enlightened renunciation is desirable. One should enter the renounced order with full knowledge (*jñāna-vairāgya*), for the perfection of life is possible for one who renounces this material world in that way. This elevated stage can be reached very easily, as supported by the statements of *Śrīmad-Bhāgavatam* (1.2.7):

vāsudeve bhagavati
bhakti-yogaḥ prayojitaḥ
janayaty āśu vairāgyaṁ
jñānaṁ ca yad ahaitukam

"By rendering devotional service unto the Personality of Godhead, Śrī Kṛṣṇa, one immediately acquires causeless knowledge and detachment from the world." If one seriously engages in devotional service to Lord Vāsudeva, *jñāna* and *vairāgya* are automatically manifest in one's person. There is no doubt of this. Prajāpati Dakṣa's accusation that Nārada had not actually elevated his sons to the platform of knowledge was not factual. All the sons of Prajāpati Dakṣa had first been raised to the platform of *jñāna* and had then automatically renounced this world. In summary, unless one's knowledge is awakened, renunciation cannot take place, for without elevated knowledge one cannot give up attachment for material enjoyment.

TEXT 41

नानुभूय न जानाति पुमान् विषयतीक्ष्णताम् ।
निर्विद्यते स्वयं तस्मान्न तथा भिन्नधीः परैः ॥ ४१ ॥

nānubhūya na jānāti
pumān viṣaya-tīkṣṇatām
nirvidyate svayaṁ tasmān
na tathā bhinna-dhīḥ paraiḥ

na—not; *anubhūya*—experiencing; *na*—not; *jānāti*—knows; *pumān*—a person; *viṣaya-tīkṣṇatām*—the sharpness of material enjoyment; *nirvidyate*—becomes aloof; *svayam*—himself; *tasmāt*—from that; *na tathā*—not like that; *bhinna-dhīḥ*—whose intelligence is changed; *paraiḥ*—by others.

TRANSLATION

Material enjoyment is indeed the cause of all unhappiness, but one cannot give it up unless one has personally experienced how much suffering it is. Therefore one should be allowed to remain in so-called

material enjoyment while simultaneously advancing in knowledge to experience the misery of this false material happiness. Then, without help from others, one will find material enjoyment detestful. Those whose minds are changed by others do not become as renounced as those who have personal experience.

PURPORT

It is said that unless a woman becomes pregnant, she cannot understand the trouble of giving birth to a child. *Bandhyā ki bujhibe prasava-vedanā.* The word *bandhyā* means a sterile woman. Such a woman cannot give birth to a child. How, then, can she perceive the pain of delivery? According to the philosophy of Prajāpati Dakṣa, a woman should first become pregnant and then experience the pain of childbirth. Then, if she is intelligent, she will not want to be pregnant again. Actually. However. this is not a fact. Sex enjoyment is so strong that a woman becomes pregnant and suffers at the time of childbirth, but she becomes pregnant again, despite her experience. According to Dakṣa's philosophy, one should become implicated in material enjoyment so that after experiencing the distress of such enjoyment. one will automatically renounce. Material nature, however, is so strong that although a man suffers at every step, he will not cease his attempts to enjoy (*tṛpyanti neha kṛpaṇā bahu-duḥkha-bhājaḥ*). Under the circumstances, unless one gets the association of a devotee like Nārada Muni or his servant in the disciplic succession, one's dormant spirit of renunciation cannot be awakened. It is not a fact that because material enjoyment involves so many painful conditions one will automatically become detached. One needs the blessings of a devotee like Nārada Muni. Then one can renounce his attachment for the material world. The young boys and girls of the Kṛṣṇa consciousness movement have given up the spirit of material enjoyment not because of practice but by the mercy of Lord Śrī Caitanya Mahāprabhu and His servants.

TEXT 42

यन्नस्त्वं कर्मसन्धानां साधूनां गृहमेधिनाम् ।
कृतवानसि दुर्मर्षं विप्रियं तव मर्षितम् ॥ ४२ ॥

yan nas tvaṁ karma-sandhānāṁ
sādhūnāṁ gṛhamedhinām
kṛtavān asi durmarṣaṁ
vipriyaṁ tava marṣitam

yat—which; *naḥ*—unto us; *tvam*—you; *karma-sandhānām*—who strictly follow the fruitive ritualistic ceremonies according to Vedic injunctions; *sādhūnām*—who are honest (because we honestly seek elevated social standards and bodily comfort); *gṛha-medhinām*—although situated with a wife and children; *kṛtavān asi*—have created; *durmarṣam*—unbearable; *vipriyam*—wrong; *tava*—your; *marṣitam*—forgiven.

TRANSLATION

Although I live in household life with my wife and children, I honestly follow the Vedic injunctions by engaging in fruitive activities to enjoy life without sinful reactions. I have performed all kinds of yajñas, including the deva-yajña, ṛṣi-yajña, pitṛ-yajña and nṛ-yajña. Because these yajñas are called vratas [vows], I am known as a gṛhavrata. Unfortunately, you have given me great displeasure by misguiding my sons, for no reason, to the path of renunciation. This can be tolerated once.

PURPORT

Prajāpati Dakṣa wanted to prove that he had been most tolerant in not having said anything when Nārada Muni, for no reason, induced his ten thousand innocent sons to adopt the path of renunciation. Sometimes householders are accused of being *gṛhamedhīs,* for *gṛhamedhīs* are satisfied with family life without spiritual advancement. *Gṛhasthas,* however, are different because although *gṛhasthas* live in householder life with their wives and children, they are eager for spiritual advancement. Wanting to prove that he had been magnanimous to Nārada Muni, Prajāpati Dakṣa stressed that when Nārada had misled his first sons, Dakṣa had taken no action; he had been kind and tolerant. He was aggrieved, however, because Nārada Muni had misled his sons for a second time. Therefore he wanted to prove that Nārada Muni, although dressed like a *sādhu,* was not actually a *sādhu;* he himself, although a householder, was a greater *sādhu* than Nārada Muni.

TEXT 43

तन्तुकृन्तन यन्नस्त्वमभद्रमचरः पुनः ।
तस्माल्लोकेषु ते मूढ न भवेद्भ्रमतः पदम् ॥ ४३ ॥

tantu-kṛntana yan nas tvam
abhadram acaraḥ punaḥ

tasmāl lokeṣu te mūḍha
na bhaved bhramataḥ padam

tantu-kṛntana—O mischief-monger who have mercilessly separated my sons from me; *yat*—which; *naḥ*—unto us; *tvam*—you; *abhadram*—an inauspicious thing; *acaraḥ*—have done; *punaḥ*—again; *tasmāt*—therefore; *lokeṣu*—in all the planetary systems within the universe; *te*—of you; *mūḍha* —O rascal not knowing how to act; *na*—not; *bhavet*—there may be; *bhramataḥ*—who are wandering; *padam*—an abode.

TRANSLATION

You have made me lose my sons once, and now you have again done the same inauspicious thing. Therefore you are a rascal who does not know how to behave toward others. You may travel all over the universe, but I curse you to have no residence anywhere.

PURPORT

Because Prajāpati Dakṣa was a *gṛhamedhī* who wanted to remain in household life, he thought that if Nārada Muni could not remain in one place, but had to travel all over the world, that would be a great punishment for him. Actually, however, such a punishment is a boon for a preacher. A preacher is known as *parivrājakācārya*—an *ācārya,* or teacher, who always travels for the benefit of human society. Prajāpati Dakṣa cursed Nārada Muni by saying that although he had the facility to travel all over the universe, he would never be able to stay in one place. In the *parampara* system from Nārada Muni, I have also been cursed. Although I have many centers that would be suitable places of residence, I cannot stay anywhere, for I have been cursed by the parents of my young disciples. Since the Kṛṣṇa consciousness movement was started, I have traveled all over the world two or three times a year, and although I am provided comfortable places to stay wherever I go, I cannot stay anywhere for more than three days or a week. I do not mind this curse by the parents of my disciples, but now it is necessary that I stay in one place to finish another task—this translation of *Śrīmad-Bhāgavatam.* If my young disciples, especially those who have taken *sannyāsa,* take charge of traveling all over the world, it may be possible for me to transfer the curse of the parents to these young preachers. Then I may sit down conveniently in one place for the work of translation.

TEXT 44

श्रीशुक उवाच
प्रतिजग्राह तद् बाढं नारदः साधुसम्मतः ।
एतावान् साधुवादो हि तितिक्षेतेश्वरः स्वयम् ॥ ४४ ॥

śrī-śuka uvāca
pratijagrāha tad bāḍhaṁ
nāradaḥ sādhu-sammataḥ
etāvān sādhu-vādo hi
titikṣeteśvaraḥ svayam

śrī-śukaḥ uvāca—Śrī Śukadeva Gosvāmī said; *pratijagrāha*—accepted; *tat*—that; *bāḍham*—so be it; *nāradaḥ*—Nārada Muni; *sādhu-sammataḥ*—who is an approved *sādhu; etāvān*—this much; *sādhu-vādaḥ*—appropriate for a saintly person; *hi*—indeed; *titikṣeta*—he may tolerate; *īśvaraḥ*—although able to curse Prajāpati Dakṣa; *svayam*—himself.

TRANSLATION

Śrī Śukadeva Gosvāmī continued: My dear King, since Nārada Muni is an approved saintly person, when cursed by Prajāpati Dakṣa he replied, tad bāḍham: "Yes, what you have said is good. I accept this curse." He could have cursed Prajāpati Dakṣa in return, but because he is a tolerant and merciful sādhu, he took no action.

PURPORT

As stated in *Śrīmad-Bhāgavatam* (3.25.21):

titikṣavaḥ kāruṇikāḥ
suhṛdaḥ sarva-dehinām
ajāta-śatravaḥ śāntāḥ
sādhavaḥ sādhu-bhūṣaṇāḥ

"The symptoms of a *sādhu* are that he is tolerant, merciful and friendly to all living entities. He has no enemies, he is peaceful, he abides by the scriptures, and all his characteristics are sublime." Because Nārada Muni is the most elevated of *sādhus,* devotees, to deliver Prajāpati Dakṣa he silently tolerated the curse. Śrī Caitanya Mahāprabhu has taught this principle to all His devotees:

tṛṇād api sunīcena
taror api sahiṣṇunā
amāninā mānadena
kīrtanīyaḥ sadā hariḥ

"One should chant the holy name of the Lord in a humble state of mind, thinking oneself lower than the straw in the street; one should be more tolerant than a tree, devoid of all sense of false prestige and should be ready to offer all respects to others. In such a state of mind one can chant the holy name of the Lord constantly." Following the orders of Śrī Caitanya Mahāprabhu, one who preaches the glories of the Lord all over the world or all over the universe should be humbler than grass and more tolerant than a tree because a preacher cannot live an easygoing life. Indeed, a preacher must face many impediments. Not only is he sometimes cursed, but sometimes he must also suffer personal injury. For example, when Nityānanda Prabhu went to preach Kṛṣṇa consciousness to the two roguish brothers Jagāi and Mādhāi, they injured Him and made His head bleed, but nevertheless, He tolerantly delivered the two rogues, who became perfect Vaiṣṇavas. This is the duty of a preacher. Lord Jesus Christ even tolerated crucifixion. Therefore the curse against Nārada was not very astonishing, and he tolerated it.

Now, it may be asked why Nārada Muni stayed in the presence of Prajāpati Dakṣa and tolerated all his accusations and curses. Was that for Dakṣa's deliverance? The answer is yes. Śrīla Viśvanātha Cakravartī Ṭhākura says that after being insulted by Prajāpati Dakṣa, Nārada Muni should have left immediately, but he purposely stayed to hear all Dakṣa's strong words so that Dakṣa might be relieved of his anger. Prajāpati Dakṣa was not an ordinary man; he had accumulated the results of many pious activities. Therefore Nārada Muni expected that after delivering his curse, Dakṣa, satisfied and freed from anger, would repent his misbehavior and thus get a chance to become a Vaiṣṇava and be delivered. When Jagāi and Mādhāi offended Lord Nityānanda, Lord Nityānanda stood tolerantly, and therefore both brothers fell at His lotus feet and repented. Consequently they later became perfect Vaiṣṇavas.

Thus end the Bhaktivedanta purports of the Sixth Canto, Fifth Chapter, of the Śrīmad-Bhāgavatam, *entitled "Nārada Muni Cursed by Prajāpati Dakṣa."*

CHAPTER SIX

The Progeny of the Daughters of Dakṣa

As described in this chapter, Prajāpati Dakṣa begot sixty daughters in the womb of his wife Asiknī. These daughters were given in charity to various persons to increase the population. Since these offspring of Dakṣa were women, Nārada Muni did not try to lead them toward the renounced order of life. Thus the daughters were saved from Nārada Muni. Ten of the daughters were given in marriage to Dharmarāja, thirteen to Kaśyapa Muni, and twenty-seven to the moon god, Candra. In this way fifty daughters were distributed, and of the other ten daughters, four were given to Kaśyapa and two each to Bhūta, Aṅgirā and Kṛśāśva. One should know that it is because of the union of these sixty daughters with various exalted personalities that the entire universe was filled with various kinds of living entities, such as human beings, demigods, demons, beasts, birds and serpents.

TEXT 1

श्रीशुक उवाच
ततः प्राचेतसोऽसिक्न्यामनुनीतः स्वयम्भुवा ।
षष्टिं सञ्जनयामास दुहितृः पितृवत्सलाः ॥ १ ॥

śrī-śuka uvāca
tataḥ prācetaso'siknyām
anunītaḥ svayambhuvā
ṣaṣṭiṁ sañjanayām āsa
duhitṝḥ pitṛ-vatsalāḥ

śrī-śukaḥ uvāca—Śrī Śukadeva Gosvāmī said; *tataḥ*—after that incident; *prācetasaḥ*—Dakṣa; *asiknyām*—in his wife named Asiknī; *anunītaḥ*—pacified; *svayambhuvā*—by Lord Brahmā; *ṣaṣṭim*—sixty; *sañjanayām āsa*—begot; *duhitṝḥ*—daughters; *pitṛ-vatsalāḥ*—all very affectionate to their father.

TRANSLATION

Śrī Śukadeva Gosvāmī said: My dear King, thereafter, at the request of Lord Brahmā, Prajāpati Dakṣa, who is known as Prācetasa, begot sixty daughters in the womb of his wife Asiknī. All the daughters were very affectionate toward their father.

PURPORT

After the incidents concerning the loss of his many sons, Dakṣa repented his misunderstanding with Nārada Muni. Lord Brahmā then saw Dakṣa and instructed him to beget children again. This time Dakṣa was very cautious to beget female children instead of male children so that Nārada Muni would not disturb them by urging them to accept the renounced order. Females are not meant for the renounced order of life; they should be faithful to their good husbands, for if a husband is competent for liberation, his wife will also achieve liberation with him. As stated in the *śāstra,* the results of a husband's pious activities are shared by his wife. Therefore a woman's duty is to be very chaste and faithful to her husband. Then without separate endeavor she will share in all the profit the husband earns.

TEXT 2

दश धर्माय कायादाद्द्विषट् त्रिणव चेन्दवे ।
भूताङ्गिरःकृशाश्वेभ्यो द्वे द्वे तार्क्ष्याय चापराः ॥ २ ॥

daśa dharmāya kāyādād
dvi-ṣaṭ tri-ṇava cendave
bhūtāṅgiraḥ-kṛśāśvebhyo
dve dve tārkṣyāya cāparāḥ

daśa—ten; *dharmāya*—unto King Dharma, Yamarāja; *kāya*—unto Kaśyapa; *adāt*—gave; *dvi-ṣaṭ*—twice six and one (thirteen); *tri-nava*—thrice nine (twenty-seven); *ca*—also; *indave*—unto the moon god; *bhūta-aṅgiraḥ-kṛśāśvebhyaḥ*—unto Bhūta, Aṅgirā and Kṛśāśva; *dve dve*—two each; *tārkṣyāya*—again unto Kaśyapa; *ca*—and; *aparāḥ*—the balance.

TRANSLATION

He gave ten daughters in charity to Dharmarāja [Yamarāja], thirteen to Kaśyapa [first twelve and then one more], twenty-seven to the moon god, and two each to Aṅgirā, Kṛśāśva and Bhūta. The other four daughters were given to Kaśyapa. [Thus Kaśyapa received seventeen daughters in all.]

TEXT 3

नामधेयान्यमूषां त्वं सापत्यानां च मे शृणु ।
यासां प्रसूतिप्रसवैर्लोका आपूरितास्त्रयः ॥ ३ ॥

nāmadheyāny amūṣāṁ tvaṁ
sāpatyānāṁ ca me śṛṇu
yāsāṁ prasūti-prasavair
lokā āpūritās trayaḥ

nāmadheyāni—the different names; *amūṣām*—of them; *tvam*—you; *sa-apatyānām*—with their offspring; *ca*—and; *me*—from me; *śṛṇu*—please hear; *yāsām*—of all of whom; *prasūti-prasavaiḥ*—by so many children and descendants; *lokāḥ*—the worlds; *āpūritāḥ*—populated; *trayaḥ*—three (the upper, middle and lower worlds).

TRANSLATION

Now please hear from me the names of all these daughters and their descendants, who filled all the three worlds.

TEXT 4

भानुर्लम्बा ककुद्यामिर्विश्वा साध्या मरुत्वती ।
वसुर्मुहूर्ता सङ्कल्पा धर्मपत्न्यः सुताञ् शृणु ॥ ४ ॥

bhānur lambā kakud yāmir
viśvā sādhyā marutvatī
vasur muhūrtā saṅkalpā
dharma-patnyaḥ sutāñ śṛṇu

bhānuḥ—Bhānu; *lambā*—Lambā; *kakut*—Kakud; *yāmiḥ*—Yāmi; *viśvā*—Viśvā; *sādhyā*—Sādhyā; *marutvatī*—Marutvatī; *vasuḥ*—Vasu; *muhūrtā*—Muhūrtā; *saṅkalpā*—Saṅkalpā; *dharma-patnyaḥ*—the wives of Yamarāja; *sutān*—their sons; *śṛṇu*—now hear of.

TRANSLATION

The ten daughters given to Yamarāja were named Bhānu, Lambā, Kakud, Yāmi, Viśvā, Sādhyā, Marutvatī, Vasu, Muhūrtā and Saṅkalpā. Now hear the names of their sons.

TEXT 5

भानोस्तु देवऋषभ इन्द्रसेनस्ततो नृप ।
विद्योत आसील्लम्बायास्ततश्च स्तनयित्नवः ॥ ५ ॥

bhānos tu deva-ṛṣabha
indrasenas tato nṛpa
vidyota āsīl lambāyās
tataś ca stanayitnavaḥ

bhānoḥ—from the womb of Bhānu; *tu*—of course; *deva-ṛṣabhaḥ*—Deva-ṛṣabha; *indrasenaḥ*—Indrasena; *tataḥ*—from him (Deva-ṛṣabha); *nṛpa*—O King; *vidyotaḥ*—Vidyota; *āsīt*—appeared; *lambāyāḥ*—from the womb of Lambā; *tataḥ*—from him; *ca*—and; *stanayitnavaḥ*—all the clouds.

TRANSLATION

O King, a son named Deva-ṛṣabha was born from the womb of Bhānu, and from him came a son named Indrasena. From the womb of Lambā came a son named Vidyota, who generated all the clouds.

TEXT 6

ककुदः सङ्कटस्तस्य कीकटस्तनयो यतः ।
भुवो दुर्गाणि यामेयः स्वर्गो नन्दिस्ततोऽभवत् ॥ ६ ॥

kakudaḥ saṅkaṭas tasya
kīkaṭas tanayo yataḥ
bhuvo durgāṇi yāmeyaḥ
svargo nandis tato'bhavat

kakudaḥ—from the womb of Kakud; *saṅkaṭaḥ*—Saṅkaṭa; *tasya*—from him; *kīkaṭaḥ*—Kīkaṭa; *tanayaḥ*—son; *yataḥ*—from whom; *bhuvaḥ*—of the earth; *durgāṇi*—many demigods, protectors of this universe (which is called Durgā); *yāmeyaḥ*—of Yāmi; *svargaḥ*—Svarga; *nandiḥ*—Nandi; *tataḥ*—from him (Svarga); *abhavat*—was born.

TRANSLATION

From the womb of Kakud came the son named Saṅkaṭa, whose son was named Kīkaṭa. From Kīkaṭa came the demigods named Durgā. From Yāmi came the son named Svarga, whose son was named Nandi.

TEXT 7

विश्वेदेवास्तु विश्वाया अप्रजांस्तान् प्रचक्षते ।
साध्योगणश्च साध्याया अर्थसिद्धिस्तु तत्सुतः ॥ ७ ॥

viśve-devās tu viśvāyā
aprajāṁs tān pracakṣate
sādhyo-gaṇaś ca sādhyāyā
arthasiddhis tu tat-sutaḥ

viśve-devāḥ—the demigods named the Viśvadevas; *tu*—but; *viśvāyāḥ*—from Viśvā; *aprajān*—without sons; *tān*—them; *pracakṣate*—it is said; *sādhyaḥ-gaṇaḥ*—the demigods named the Sādhyas; *ca*—and; *sādhyāyāḥ*—from the womb of Sādhyā; *arthasiddhiḥ*—Arthasiddhi; *tu*—but; *tat-sutaḥ*—the son of the Sādhyas.

TRANSLATION

The sons of Viśvā were the Viśvadevas, who had no progeny. From the womb of Sādhyā came the Sādhyas, who had a son named Arthasiddhi.

TEXT 8

मरुत्वांश्च जयन्तश्च मरुत्वत्या बभूवतुः ।
जयन्तो वासुदेवांश उपेन्द्र इति यं विदुः ॥ ८ ॥

marutvāṁś ca jayantaś ca
marutvatyā babhūvatuḥ
jayanto vāsudevāṁśa
upendra iti yaṁ viduḥ

marutvān—Marutvān; *ca*—also; *jayantaḥ*—Jayanta; *ca*—and; *marutvatyāḥ*—from Marutvatī; *babhūvatuḥ*—took birth; *jayantaḥ*—Jayanta; *vāsudeva-aṁśaḥ*—an expansion of Vāsudeva; *upendraḥ*—Upendra; *iti*—thus; *yam*—whom; *viduḥ*—they know.

TRANSLATION

The two sons who took birth from the womb of Marutvatī were Marutvān and Jayanta. Jayanta, who is an expansion of Lord Vāsudeva, is known as Upendra.

TEXT 9

मौहूर्तिका देवगणा मुहूर्तायाश्च जज्ञिरे ।
ये वै फलं प्रयच्छन्ति भूतानां स्वस्वकालजम् ॥ ९ ॥

mauhūrtikā deva-gaṇā
muhūrtāyāś ca jajñire

ye vai phalaṁ prayacchanti
bhūtānāṁ sva-sva-kālajam

mauhūrtikāḥ—Mauhūrtikas; *deva-gaṇāḥ*—the demigods; *muhūrtāyāḥ*—from the womb of Muhūrtā; *ca*—and; *jajñire*—took birth; *ye*—all of whom; *vai*—indeed; *phalam*—result; *prayacchanti*—deliver; *bhūtānām*—of the living entities; *sva-sva*—their own; *kāla-jam*—born of time.

TRANSLATION

The demigods named the Mauhūrtikas took birth from the womb of Muhūrtā. These demigods deliver the results of actions to the living entities of their respective times.

TEXTS 10–11

सङ्कल्पायास्तु सङ्कल्पः कामः सङ्कल्पजः स्मृतः ।
वसवोऽष्टौ वसोः पुत्रास्तेषां नामानि मे शृणु ॥ १० ॥
द्रोणः प्राणो ध्रुवोऽर्कोऽग्निर्दोषो वास्तुर्विभावसुः ।
द्रोणस्याभिमतेः पत्न्या हर्षशोकभयादयः ॥ ११ ॥

saṅkalpāyās tu saṅkalpaḥ
kāmaḥ saṅkalpajaḥ smṛtaḥ
vasavo 'ṣṭau vasoḥ putrās
teṣāṁ nāmāni me śṛṇu

droṇaḥ prāṇo dhruvo 'rko 'gnir
doṣo vāstur vibhāvasuḥ
droṇasyābhimateḥ patnyā
harṣa-śoka-bhayādayaḥ

saṅkalpāyāḥ—from the womb of Saṅkalpā; *tu*—but; *saṅkalpaḥ*—Saṅkalpa; *kāmaḥ*—Kāma; *saṅkalpa-jaḥ*—the son of Saṅkalpā; *smṛtaḥ*—known; *vasavaḥ aṣṭau*—the eight Vasus; *vasoḥ*—of Vasu; *putrāḥ*—the sons; *teṣām*—of them; *nāmāni*—the names; *me*—from me; *śṛṇu*—just hear; *droṇaḥ*—Droṇa; *prāṇaḥ*—Prāṇa; *dhruvaḥ*—Dhruva; *arkaḥ*—Arka; *agniḥ*—Agni; *doṣaḥ*—Doṣa; *vāstuḥ*—Vāstu; *vibhāvasuḥ*—Vibhāvasu; *droṇasya*—of Droṇa; *abhimateḥ*—from Abhimati; *patnyāḥ*—the wife; *harṣa-śoka-bhaya-ādayaḥ*—the sons named Harṣa, Śoka, Bhaya and so on.

TRANSLATION

The son of Saṅkalpā was known as Saṅkalpa, and from him lust was born. The sons of Vasu were known as the eight Vasus. Just hear their names from me: Droṇa, Prāṇa, Dhruva, Arka, Agni, Doṣa, Vāstu and Vibhāvasu. From Abhimati, the wife of the Vasu named Droṇa, were generated the sons named Harṣa, Śoka, Bhaya and so on.

TEXT 12

प्राणस्योर्जस्वती भार्या सह आयुः पुरोजवः ।
ध्रुवस्य भार्या धरणिरसूत विविधाः पुरः ॥ १२ ॥

prāṇasyorjasvatī bhāryā
saha āyuḥ purojavaḥ
dhruvasya bhāryā dharaṇir
asūta vividhāḥ puraḥ

prāṇasya—of Prāna; *ūrjasvatī*—Ūrjasvatī; *bhāryā*—the wife; *sahaḥ*—Saha; *āyuḥ*—Āyus; *purojavaḥ*—Purojava; *dhruvasya*—of Dhruva; *bhāryā*—the wife; *dharaṇiḥ*—Dharaṇi; *asūta*—gave birth to; *vividhāḥ*—the various; *puraḥ*—cities and towns.

TRANSLATION

Ūrjasvatī, the wife of Prāṇa, gave birth to three sons, named Saha, Āyus and Purojava. The wife of Dhruva was known as Dharaṇi, and from her womb various cities took birth.

TEXT 13

अर्कस्य वासना भार्या पुत्रास्तर्षादयः स्मृताः ।
अग्नेर्भार्या वसोर्धारा पुत्रा द्रविणकादयः ॥ १३ ॥

arkasya vāsanā bhāryā
putrās tarṣādayaḥ smṛtāḥ
agner bhāryā vasor dhārā
putrā draviṇakādayaḥ

arkasya—of Arka; *vāsanā*—Vāsanā; *bhāryā*—the wife; *putrāḥ*—the sons; *tarṣa-ādayaḥ*—named Tarṣa and so on; *smṛtāḥ*—celebrated; *agneḥ*—of Agni; *bhāryā*—wife; *vasoḥ*—the Vasu; *dhārā*—Dhārā; *putrāḥ*—the sons; *draviṇaka-ādayaḥ*—known as Draviṇaka and so on.

TRANSLATION

From the womb of Vāsanā, the wife of Arka, came many sons, headed by Tarṣa. Dhārā, the wife of the Vasu named Agni, gave birth to many sons, headed by Draviṇaka.

TEXT 14

स्कन्दश्च कृत्तिकापुत्रो ये विशाखादयस्ततः ।
दोषस्य शर्वरीपुत्रः शिशुमारो हरेः कला ॥ १४ ॥

skandaś ca kṛttikā-putro
ye viśākhādayas tataḥ
doṣasya śarvarī-putraḥ
śiśumāro hareḥ kalā

skandaḥ—Skanda; *ca*—also; *kṛttikā-putraḥ*—the son of Kṛttikā; *ye*—all of whom; *viśākha-ādayaḥ*—headed by Viśākha; *tataḥ*—from him (Skanda); *doṣasya*—of Doṣa; *śarvarī-putraḥ*—the son of his wife Śarvarī; *śiśumāraḥ*—Śiśumāra; *hareḥ kalā*—an expansion of the Supreme Personality of Godhead.

TRANSLATION

From Kṛttikā, another wife of Agni, came the son named Skanda, Kārttikeya, whose sons were headed by Viśākha. From the womb of Śarvarī, the wife of the Vasu named Doṣa, came the son named Śiśumāra, who was an expansion of the Supreme Personality of Godhead.

TEXT 15

वास्तोराङ्गिरसीपुत्रो विश्वकर्माकृतीपतिः ।
ततो मनुश्चाक्षुषोऽभूद् विश्वे साध्या मनोः सुताः ॥ १५ ॥

vāstor āṅgirasī-putro
viśvakarmākṛtī-patiḥ
tato manuś cākṣuṣo'bhūd
viśve sādhyā manoḥ sutāḥ

vāstoḥ—of Vāstu; *āṅgirasī*—of his wife named Āṅgirasī; *putraḥ*—the son; *viśvakarmā*—Viśvakarmā; *ākṛtī-patiḥ*—the husband of Ākṛtī; *tataḥ*—from them; *manuḥ cākṣuṣaḥ*—the Manu named Cākṣuṣa; *abhūt*—was born; *viśve*—the Viśvadevas; *sādhyāḥ*—the Sādhyas; *manoḥ*—of Manu; *sutāḥ*—the sons.

TRANSLATION

From Āṅgirasī, the wife of the Vasu named Vāstu, was born the great architect Viśvakarmā. Viśvakarmā became the husband of Ākṛtī, from whom the Manu named Cākṣuṣa was born. The sons of Manu were known as the Viśvadevas and Sādhyas.

TEXT 16

विभावसोरसूतोषा व्युष्टं रोचिषमातपम् ।
पञ्चयामोऽथ भूतानि येन जाग्रति कर्मसु ॥ १६ ॥

vibhāvasor asūtoṣā
vyuṣṭaṁ rociṣam ātapam
pañcayāmo'tha bhūtāni
yena jāgrati karmasu

vibhāvasoḥ—of Vibhāvasu; *asūta*—gave birth to; *ūṣā*—named Ūṣā; *vyuṣṭam*—Vyuṣṭa; *rociṣam*—Rociṣa; *ātapam*—Ātapa; *pañcayāmaḥ*—Pañcayāma; *atha*—thereafter; *bhūtāni*—the living entities; *yena*—by whom; *jāgrati*—are awakened; *karmasu*—in material activities.

TRANSLATION

Ūṣā, the wife of Vibhāvasu, gave birth to three sons—Vyuṣṭa, Rociṣa and Ātapa. From Ātapa came Pañcayāma, the span of day, who awakens all living entities to material activities.

TEXTS 17–18

सरूपासूत भूतस्य भार्या रुद्रांश्च कोटिशः ।
रैवतोऽजो भवो भीमो वाम उग्रो वृषाकपिः ॥ १७ ॥
अजैकपादहिर्ब्रध्नो बहुरूपो महानिति ।
रुद्रस्य पार्षदाश्चान्ये घोराः प्रेतविनायकाः ॥ १८ ॥

sarūpāsūta bhūtasya
bhāryā rudrāṁś ca koṭiśaḥ
raivato 'jo bhavo bhīmo
vāma ugro vṛṣākapiḥ

ajaikapād ahirbradhno
bahurūpo mahān iti

rudrasya pārṣadāś cānye
ghorāḥ preta-vināyakāḥ

sarūpā—Sarūpā; *asūta*—gave birth; *bhūtasya*—of Bhūta; *bhāryā*—the wife; *rudrān*—Rudras; *ca*—and; *koṭiśaḥ*—ten million; *raivataḥ*—Raivata; *ajaḥ*—Aja; *bhavaḥ*—Bhava; *bhīmaḥ*—Bhīma; *vāmaḥ*—Vāma; *ugraḥ*—Ugra; *vṛṣākapiḥ*—Vṛṣākapi; *ajaikapāt*—Ajaikapāt; *ahirbradhnaḥ*—Ahirbradhna; *bahurūpaḥ*—Bahurūpa; *mahān*—Mahān; *iti*—thus; *rudrasya*—of these Rudras; *pārṣadāḥ*—their associates; *ca*—and; *anye*—other; *ghorāḥ*—very fearful; *preta*—ghosts; *vināyakāḥ*—and hobgoblins.

TRANSLATION

Sarūpā, the wife of Bhūta, gave birth to the ten million Rudras, of whom the eleven principle Rudras were Raivata, Aja, Bhava, Bhīma, Vāma, Ugra, Vṛṣākapi, Ajaikapāt, Ahirbradhna, Bahurūpa and Mahān. Their associates, the ghosts and goblins, who are very fearful, were born of the other wife of Bhūta.

PURPORT

Śrīla Viśvanātha Cakravartī Ṭhākura comments that Bhūta had two wives. One of them, Sarūpā, gave birth to the eleven Rudras, and the other wife gave birth to the associates of the Rudras known as the ghosts and hobgoblins.

TEXT 19

प्रजापतेरङ्गिरसः स्वधा पत्नी पितॄनथ ।
अथर्वाङ्गिरसं वेदं पुत्रत्वे चाकरोत् सती ॥ १९ ॥

prajāpater aṅgirasaḥ
svadhā patnī pitṝn atha
atharvāṅgirasaṁ vedaṁ
putratve cākarot satī

prajāpateḥ aṅgirasaḥ—of another *prajāpati,* known as Aṅgirā; *svadhā*—Svadhā; *patnī*—his wife; *pitṝn*—the Pitās; *atha*—thereafter; *atharva-āṅgirasam*—Atharvāṅgirasa; *vedam*—the personified *Veda; putratve*—as the son; *ca*—and; *akarot*—accepted; *satī*—Satī.

TRANSLATION

The prajāpati Aṅgirā had two wives, named Svadhā and Satī. The wife named Svadhā accepted all the Pitās as her sons, and Satī accepted the Atharvāṅgirasa Veda as her son.

TEXT 20

कृशाश्वोऽर्चिषि भार्यायां धूमकेतुमजीजनत् ।
धिषणायां वेदशिरो देवलं वयुनं मनुम् ॥ २० ॥

kṛśāśvo'rciṣi bhāryāyāṁ
dhūmaketum ajījanat
dhiṣaṇāyāṁ vedaśiro
devalaṁ vayunaṁ manum

kṛśāśvaḥ—Kṛśāśva; *arciṣi*—Arcis; *bhāryāyām*—in his wife; *dhūmaketum*—to Dhūmaketu; *ajījanat*—gave birth; *dhiṣaṇāyām*—in the wife known as Dhiṣaṇā; *vedaśiraḥ*—Vedaśirā; *devalam*—Devala; *vayunam*—Vayuna; *manum*—Manu.

TRANSLATION

Kṛśāśva had two wives, named Arcis and Dhiṣaṇā. In the wife named Arcis he begot Dhūmaketu and in Dhiṣaṇā he begot four sons, named Vedaśirā, Devala, Vayuna and Manu.

TEXTS 21–22

तार्क्ष्यस्य विनता कद्रूः पतङ्गी यामिनीति च ।
पतङ्ग्यसूत पतगान् यामिनी शलभानथ ॥ २१ ॥
सुपर्णासूत गरुडं साक्षाद् यज्ञेशवाहनम् ।
सूर्यसूतमनूरुं च कद्रूर्नागाननेकशः ॥ २२ ॥

tārkṣyasya vinatā kadrūḥ
pataṅgī yāminīti ca
pataṅgy asūta patagān
yāminī śalabhān atha

suparṇāsūta garuḍaṁ
sākṣād yajñeśa-vāhanam
sūrya-sūtam anūruṁ ca
kadrūr nāgān anekaśaḥ

tārkṣyasya—of Kaśyapa, whose other name is Tārkṣya; *vinatā*—Vinatā; *kadrūḥ*—Kadrū; *pataṅgī*—Pataṅgī; *yāminī*—Yāminī; *iti*—thus; *ca*—and; *pataṅgī*—Pataṅgī; *asūta*—gave birth; *patagān*—to birds of different varieties; *yāminī*—Yāminī; *śalabhān*—(gave birth to) locusts; *atha*—thereafter; *suparṇā*—the wife named Vinatā; *asūta*—gave birth; *garuḍam*—to the celebrated bird known as Garuḍa; *sākṣāt*—directly; *yajñeśa-vāhanam*—the carrier of the Supreme Personality of Godhead, Viṣṇu; *sūrya-sūtam*—the chariot driver of the sun-god; *anūrum*—Anūru; *ca*—and; *kadrūḥ*—Kadrū; *nāgān*—serpents; *anekaśaḥ*—in varieties.

TRANSLATION

Kaśyapa, who is also named Tārkṣya, had four wives—Vinatā [Suparṇā], Kadrū, Pataṅgī and Yāminī. Pataṅgī gave birth to many kinds of birds, and Yāminī gave birth to locusts. Vinatā [Suparṇā] gave birth to Garuḍa, the carrier of Lord Viṣṇu, and to Anūru, or Aruṇa, the chariot driver of the sun-god. Kadrū gave birth to different varieties of serpents.

TEXT 23

कृत्तिकादीनि नक्षत्राणीन्दोः पत्न्यस्तु भारत ।
दक्षशापात् सोऽनपत्यस्तासु यक्ष्मग्रहार्दितः ॥ २३ ॥

kṛttikādīni nakṣatrāṇ-
īndoḥ patnyas tu bhārata
dakṣa-śāpāt so'napatyas
tāsu yakṣma-grahārditaḥ

kṛttikā-ādīni—headed by Kṛttikā; *nakṣatrāṇi*—the constellations; *indoḥ*—of the moon-god; *patnyaḥ*—the wives; *tu*—but; *bhārata*—O Mahārāja Parīkṣit, descendant of the dynasty of Bharata; *dakṣa-śāpāt*—because of being cursed by Dakṣa; *saḥ*—the moon-god; *anapatyaḥ*—without children; *tāsu*—in so many wives; *yakṣma-graha-arditaḥ*—being oppressed by a disease that brings about gradual destruction.

TRANSLATION

O Mahārāja Parīkṣit, best of the Bhāratas, the constellations named Kṛttikā were all wives of the moon-god. However, because Prajāpati Dakṣa had cursed him to suffer from a disease causing gradual destruction, the moon-god could not beget children in any of his wives.

PURPORT

Because the moon-god was very much attached to Rohiṇī, he neglected all his other wives. Therefore, seeing the bereavement of these daughters, Prajāpati Dakṣa became angry and cursed him.

TEXTS 24–26

पुनः प्रसाद्य तं सोमः कला लेभे क्षये दिताः ।
शृणु नामानि लोकानां मातॄणां शङ्कराणि च ॥ २४ ॥
अथ कश्यपपत्नीनां यत्प्रसूतमिदं जगत् ।
अदितिर्दितिर्दनुः काष्ठा अरिष्टा सुरसा इला ॥ २५ ॥
मुनिः क्रोधवशा ताम्रा सुरभिः सरमा तिमिः ।
तिमेर्यादोगणा आसन् श्वापदाः सरमासुताः ॥ २६ ॥

punaḥ prasādya taṁ somaḥ
kalā lebhe kṣaye ditāḥ
śṛṇu nāmāni lokānāṁ
mātṝṇāṁ śaṅkarāṇi ca

atha kaśyapa-patnīnāṁ
yat-prasūtam idaṁ jagat
aditir ditir danuḥ kāṣṭhā
ariṣṭā surasā ilā

muniḥ krodhavaśā tāmrā
surabhiḥ saramā timiḥ
timer yādo-gaṇā āsan
śvāpadāḥ saramā-sutāḥ

punaḥ—again; *prasādya*—pacifying; *tam*—him (Prajāpati Dakṣa); *somaḥ*—the moon-god; *kalāḥ*—portions of light; *lebhe*—achieved; *kṣaye*—in gradual destruction (the dark fortnight); *ditāḥ*—removed; *śṛṇu*—please hear; *nāmāni*—all the names; *lokānām*—of the planets; *mātṝṇām*—of the mothers; *śaṅkarāṇi*—pleasing; *ca*—also; *atha*—now; *kaśyapa-patnīnām*—of the wives of Kaśyapa; *yat-prasūtam*—from whom was born; *idam*—this; *jagat*—whole universe; *aditiḥ*—Aditi; *ditiḥ*—Diti; *danuḥ*—Danu; *kāṣṭhā*—Kāṣṭhā; *ariṣṭā*—Ariṣṭā; *surasā*—Surasā; *ilā*—Ilā; *muniḥ*—Muni; *krodhavaśā*—Krodhavaśā; *tāmrā*—Tāmrā; *surabhiḥ*—Surabhi; *saramā*—Saramā; *timiḥ*—Timi; *timeḥ*—from Timi; *yādaḥ-gaṇāḥ*—the aquatics; *āsan*—appeared;

śvāpadāḥ—the ferocious animals like the lions and tigers; *saramā-sutāḥ*—the children of Saramā.

TRANSLATION

Thereafter the King of the moon pacified Prajāpati Dakṣa with courteous words and thus regained the portions of light he had lost during his disease. Nevertheless he could not beget children. The moon loses his shining power during the dark fortnight, and in the bright fortnight it is manifest again. O King Parīkṣit, now please hear from me the names of Kaśyapa's wives, from whose wombs the population of the entire universe has come. They are the mothers of almost all the population of the entire universe, and their names are very auspicious to hear. They are Aditi, Diti, Danu, Kāṣṭhā, Ariṣṭā, Surasā, Ilā, Muni, Krodhavaśā, Tāmrā, Surabhi, Saramā and Timi. From the womb of Timi all the aquatics took birth, and from the womb of Saramā the ferocious animals like the tigers and lions took birth.

TEXT 27

सुरभेर्महिषागावो ये चान्ये द्विशफा नृप ।
ताम्रायाः श्येनगृध्राद्या मुनेरप्सरसां गणाः ॥ २७ ॥

surabher mahiṣā gāvo
ye cānye dviśaphā nṛpa
tāmrāyāḥ śyena-gṛdhrādyā
muner apsarasāṁ gaṇāḥ

surabheḥ—from the womb of Surabhi; *mahiṣāḥ*—buffalo; *gāvaḥ*—cows; *ye*—who; *ca*—also; *anye*—others; *dvi-śaphāḥ*—having cloven hooves; *nṛpa*—O King; *tāmrāyāḥ*—from Tāmrā; *śyena*—eagles; *gṛdhra-ādyāḥ*—vultures and so on; *muneḥ*—from Muni; *apsarasām*—of angels; *gaṇāḥ*—the groups.

TRANSLATION

My dear King Parīkṣit, from the womb of Surabhi the buffalo, cow and other animals with cloven hooves took birth, from the womb of Tāmrā the eagles, vultures and other large birds of prey took birth, and from the womb of Muni the angels took birth.

TEXT 28

दन्दशूकादयः सर्पा राजन् क्रोधवशात्मजाः ।
इलाया भूरुहाः सर्वे यातुधानाश्च सौरसाः ॥ २८ ॥

dandaśūkādayaḥ sarpā
rājan krodhavaśātmajāḥ
ilāyā bhūruhāḥ sarve
yātudhānāś ca saurasāḥ

dandaśūka-ādayaḥ—headed by the *dandaśūka* snakes; *sarpāḥ*—reptiles; *rājan*—O King; *krodhavaśā-ātma-jāḥ*—born from Krodhavaśā; *ilāyāḥ*—from the womb of Ilā; *bhūruhāḥ*—the creepers and trees; *sarve*—all; *yātudhānāḥ*—the cannibals (Rākṣasas); *ca*—also; *saurasāḥ*—from the womb of Surasā.

TRANSLATION

The sons born of Krodhavaśā were the serpents known as dandaśūka, as well as other serpents and the mosquitoes. All the various creepers and trees were born from the womb of Ilā. The Rākṣasas, bad spirits, were born from the womb of Surasā.

TEXTS 29–31

अरिष्टायास्तु गन्धर्वाः काष्ठाया द्विशफेतराः ।
सुता दनोरेकषष्टिस्तेषां प्राधानिकाञ् शृणु ॥ २९ ॥
द्विमूर्धा शम्बरोऽरिष्टो हयग्रीवो विभावसुः ।
अयोमुखः शङ्कुशिराः स्वर्भानुः कपिलोऽरुणः ॥ ३० ॥
पुलोमा वृषपर्वा च एकचक्रोऽनुतापनः ।
धूम्रकेशो विरूपाक्षो विप्रचित्तिश्च दुर्जयः ॥ ३१ ॥

ariṣṭāyās tu gandharvāḥ
kāṣṭhāyā dviśaphetarāḥ
sutā danor eka-ṣaṣṭis
teṣāṁ prādhānikāñ śṛṇu

dvimūrdhā śambaro'riṣṭo
hayagrīvo vibhāvasuḥ
ayomukhaḥ śaṅkuśirāḥ
svarbhānuḥ kapilo'ruṇaḥ

pulomā vṛṣaparvā ca
ekacakro'nutāpanaḥ
dhūmrakeśo virūpākṣo
vipracittiś ca durjayaḥ

ariṣṭāyāḥ—from the womb of Ariṣṭā; *tu*—but; *gandharvāḥ*—the Gandharvas; *kāṣṭhāyāḥ*—from the womb of Kāṣṭhā; *dvi-śapha-itarāḥ*—animals such as horses, which do not have cloven hooves; *sutāḥ*—sons; *danoḥ*—from the womb of Danu; *eka-ṣaṣṭiḥ*—sixty-one; *teṣām*—of them; *prādhānikān*—the important ones; *śṛṇu*—hear; *dvimūrdhā*—Dvimūrdhā; *śambaraḥ*—Śambara; *ariṣṭaḥ*—Ariṣṭa; *hayagrīvaḥ*—Hayagrīva; *vibhāvasuḥ*—Vibhāvasu; *ayomukhaḥ*—Ayomukha; *śaṅkuśirāḥ*—Śaṅkuśirā; *svarbhānuḥ*—Svarbhānu; *kapilaḥ*—Kapila; *aruṇaḥ*—Aruṇa; *pulomā*—Pulomā; *vṛṣaparvā*—Vṛṣaparvā; *ca*—also; *ekacakraḥ*—Ekacakra; *anutāpanaḥ*—Anutāpana; *dhūmrakeśaḥ*—Dhūmrakeśa; *virūpākṣaḥ*—Virūpākṣa; *vipracittiḥ*—Vipracitti; *ca*—and; *durjayaḥ*—Durjaya.

TRANSLATION

The Gandharvas were born from the womb of Ariṣṭā, and animals whose hooves are not split, such as the horse, were born from the womb of Kāṣṭhā. O King, from the womb of Danu came sixty-one sons, of whom these eighteen were very important: Dvimūrdhā, Śambara, Ariṣṭa, Hayagrīva, Vibhāvasu, Ayomukha, Śaṅkuśirā, Svarbhānu, Kapila, Aruṇa, Pulomā, Vṛṣaparvā, Ekacakra, Anutāpana, Dhūmrakeśa, Virūpākṣa, Vipracitti and Durjaya.

TEXT 32

स्वर्भानोः सुप्रभां कन्यामुवाह नमुचिः किल ।
वृषपर्वणस्तु शर्मिष्ठां ययातिर्नाहुषो बली ॥ ३२ ॥

svarbhānoḥ suprabhāṁ kanyām
uvāha namuciḥ kila
vṛṣaparvaṇas tu śarmiṣṭhāṁ
yayātir nāhuṣo balī

svarbhānoḥ—of Svarbhānu; *suprabhām*—Suprabhā; *kanyām*—the daughter; *uvāha*—married; *namuciḥ*—Namuci; *kila*—indeed; *vṛṣaparvaṇaḥ*—of Vṛṣaparvā; *tu*—but; *śarmiṣṭhām*—Śarmiṣṭhā; *yayātiḥ*—King Yayāti; *nāhuṣaḥ*—the son of Nahuṣa; *balī*—very powerful.

TRANSLATION

The daughter of Svarbhānu named Suprabhā was married by Namuci. The daughter of Vṛṣaparvā named Śarmiṣṭhā was given to the powerful King Yayāti, the son of Nahuṣa.

TEXTS 33–36

वैश्वानरसुता याश्च चतस्रश्चारुदर्शनाः ।
उपदानवी हयशिरा पुलोमा कालका तथा ॥ ३३ ॥
उपदानवीं हिरण्याक्षः क्रतुर्हयशिरां नृप ।
पुलोमां कालकां च द्वे वैश्वानरसुते तु कः ॥ ३४ ॥
उपयेमेऽथ भगवान् कश्यपो ब्रह्मचोदितः ।
पौलोमाः कालकेयाश्च दानवा युद्धशालिनः ॥ ३५ ॥
तयोः षष्टिसहस्राणि यज्ञघ्नांस्ते पितुः पिता ।
जघान स्वर्गतो राजन्नेक इन्द्रप्रियङ्करः ॥ ३६ ॥

vaiśvānara-sutā yāś ca
catasraś cāru-darśanāḥ
upadānavī hayaśirā
pulomā kālakā tathā

upadānavīṁ hiraṇyākṣaḥ
kratur hayaśirāṁ nṛpa
pulomāṁ kālakāṁ ca dve
vaiśvānara-sute tu kaḥ

upayeme'tha bhagavān
kaśyapo brahma-coditaḥ
paulomāḥ kālakeyāś ca
dānavā yuddha-śālinaḥ

tayoḥ ṣaṣṭi-sahasrāṇi
yajña-ghnāṁs te pituḥ pitā
jaghāna svar-gato rājann
eka indra-priyaṅkaraḥ

vaiśvānara-sutāḥ—the daughters of Vaiśvānara; *yāḥ*—who; *ca*—and; *catasraḥ*—four; *cāru-darśanāḥ*—very, very beautiful; *upadānavī*—Upadānavī; *hayaśirā*—Hayaśirā; *pulomā*—Pulomā; *kālakā*—Kālakā; *tathā*—as well; *upadānavīm*—Upadānavī; *hiraṇyākṣaḥ*—the demon Hiraṇyākṣa; *kratuḥ*—Kratu; *hayaśirām*—Hayaśirā; *nṛpa*—O King; *pulomām kālakām ca*—Pulomā and Kālakā; *dve*—the two; *vaiśvānara-sute*—daughters of Vaiśvānara; *tu*—but; *kaḥ*—the *prajāpati; upayeme*—married; *atha*—then;

bhagavān—the most powerful; *kaśyapaḥ*—Kaśyapa Muni; *brahma-coditaḥ*—requested by Lord Brahmā; *paulomāḥ kālakeyāḥ ca*—the Paulomas and Kālakeyas; *dānavāḥ*—demons; *yuddha-śālinaḥ*—very fond of fighting; *tayoḥ*—of them; *ṣaṣṭi-sahasrāṇi*—sixty thousand; *yajña-ghnān*—who were disturbing sacrifices; *te*—your; *pituḥ*—of the father; *pitā*—the father; *jaghāna*—killed; *svaḥ-gataḥ*—in the heavenly planets; *rājan*—O King; *ekaḥ*—alone; *indra-priyam-karaḥ*—to please King Indra.

TRANSLATION

Vaiśvānara, the son of Danu, had four beautiful daughters, named Upadānavī, Hayaśirā, Pulomā and Kālakā. Hiraṇyākṣa married Upadānavī, and Kratu married Hayaśirā. Thereafter, at the request of Lord Brahmā, Prajāpati Kaśyapa married Pulomā and Kālakā, the other two daughters of Vaiśvānara. From the wombs of these two wives of Kaśyapa came sixty thousand sons, headed by Nivātakavaca, who are known as the Paulomas and the Kālakeyas. They were physically very strong and expert in fighting, and their aim was to disturb the sacrifices performed by the great sages. My dear King, when your grandfather Arjuna went to the heavenly planets, he alone killed all these demons, and thus King Indra became extremely affectionate toward him.

TEXT 37

विप्रचित्तिः सिंहिकायां शतं चैकमजीजनत् ।
राहुज्येष्ठं केतुशतं ग्रहत्वं य उपागताः ॥ ३७ ॥

vipracittiḥ siṁhikāyāṁ
śataṁ caikam ajījanat
rāhu-jyeṣṭhaṁ ketu-śataṁ
grahatvaṁ ya upāgatāḥ

vipracittiḥ—Vipracitti; *siṁhikāyām*—in the womb of his wife Siṁhikā; *śatam*—to one hundred; *ca*—and; *ekam*—one; *ajījanat*—gave birth; *rāhu-jyeṣṭham*—among whom Rāhu is the oldest; *ketu-śatam*—one hundred Ketus; *grahatvam*—planethood; *ye*—all of whom; *upāgatāḥ*—obtained.

TRANSLATION

In his wife Siṁhikā, Vipracitti begot one hundred and one sons, of whom the eldest is Rāhu and the others are the one hundred Ketus. All of them attained positions in the influential planets.

TEXTS 38–39

अथातः श्रूयतां वंशो योऽदितेरनुपूर्वशः ।
यत्र नारायणो देवः स्वांशेनावातरद्विभुः ॥ ३८ ॥
विवस्वानर्यमा पूषा त्वष्टाथ सविता भगः ।
धाता विधाता वरुणो मित्रः शत्रु उरुक्रमः ॥ ३९ ॥

athātaḥ śrūyatāṁ vaṁśo
yo'diter anupūrvaśaḥ
yatra nārāyaṇo devaḥ
svāṁśenāvātarad vibhuḥ

vivasvān aryamā pūṣā
tvaṣṭātha savitā bhagaḥ
dhātā vidhātā varuṇo
mitraḥ śatru urukramaḥ

atha—thereafter; *ataḥ*—now; *śrūyatām*—let it be heard; *vaṁśaḥ*—the dynasty; *yaḥ*—which; *aditeḥ*—from Aditi; *anupūrvaśaḥ*—in chronological order; *yatra*—wherein; *nārāyaṇaḥ*—the Supreme Personality of Godhead; *devaḥ*—the Lord; *sva-aṁśena*—by His own plenary expansion; *avātarat*—descended; *vibhuḥ*—the Supreme; *vivasvān*—Vivasvān; *aryamā*—Aryamā; *pūṣā*—Pūṣā; *tvaṣṭā*—Tvaṣṭā; *atha*—thereafter; *savitā*—Savitā; *bhagaḥ*—Bhaga; *dhātā*—Dhātā; *vidhātā*—Vidhātā; *varuṇaḥ*—Varuṇa; *mitraḥ*—Mitra; *śatruḥ*—Śatru; *urukramaḥ*—Urukrama.

TRANSLATION

Now please hear me as I describe the descendants of Aditi in chronological order. In this dynasty the Supreme Personality of Godhead Nārāyaṇa descended by His plenary expansion. The names of the sons of Aditi are as follows: Vivasvān, Aryamā, Pūṣā, Tvaṣṭā, Savitā, Bhaga, Dhātā, Vidhātā, Varuṇa, Mitra, Śatru and Urukrama.

TEXT 40

विवस्वतः श्राद्धदेवं संज्ञासूयत वै मनुम् ।
मिथुनं च महाभागा यमं देवं यमीं तथा ।
सैव भूत्वाथ वडवा नासत्यौ सुषुवे भुवि ॥ ४० ॥

vivasvataḥ śrāddhadevaṁ
saṁjñāsūyata vai manum
mithunaṁ ca mahā-bhāgā
yamaṁ devaṁ yamīṁ tathā
saiva bhūtvātha vaḍavā
nāsatyau suṣuve bhuvi

vivasvataḥ—of the sun-god; *śrāddhadevam*—named Śrāddhadeva; *saṁjñā*—Saṁjñā; *asūyata*—gave birth; *vai*—indeed; *manum*—to Manu; *mithunam*—twins; *ca*—and; *mahā-bhāgā*—the fortunate Saṁjñā; *yamam*—to Yamarāja; *devam*—the demigod; *yamīm*—to his sister named Yamī; *tathā*—as well as; *sā*—she; *eva*—also; *bhūtvā*—becoming; *atha*—then; *vaḍavā*—a mare; *nāsatyau*—to the Aśvinī-kumāras; *suṣuve*—gave birth; *bhuvi*—on this earth.

TRANSLATION

Saṁjñā, the wife of Vivasvān, the sun-god, gave birth to the Manu named Śrāddhadeva, and the same fortunate wife also gave birth to the twins Yamarāja and the River Yamunā. Then Yamī, while wandering on the earth in the form of a mare, gave birth to the Aśvinī-kumāras.

TEXT 41

छाया शनैश्चरं लेभे सावर्णिं च मनुं ततः ।
कन्यां च तपतीं या वै वव्रे संवरणं पतिम् ॥ ४१ ॥

chāyā śanaiścaraṁ lebhe
sāvarṇiṁ ca manuṁ tataḥ
kanyāṁ ca tapatīṁ yā vai
vavre saṁvaraṇaṁ patim

chāyā—Chāyā, another wife of the sun god; *śanaiścaram*—Saturn; *lebhe*—begot; *sāvarṇim*—Sāvarṇi; *ca*—and; *manum*—the Manu; *tataḥ*—from him (Vivasvān); *kanyām*—one daughter; *ca*—as well as; *tapatīm*—named Tapatī; *yā*—who; *vai*—indeed; *vavre*—married; *saṁvaraṇam*—Saṁvaraṇa; *patim*—husband.

TRANSLATION

Chāyā, another wife of the sun-god, begot two sons named Śanaiścara and Sāvarṇi Manu, and one daughter, Tapatī, who married Saṁvaraṇa.

TEXT 42

अर्यम्णो मातृका पत्नी तयोश्चर्षणयः सुताः ।
यत्र वै मानुषी जातिर्ब्रह्मणा चोपकल्पिता ॥ ४२ ॥

aryamṇo mātṛkā patnī
tayoś carṣaṇayaḥ sutāḥ
yatra vai mānuṣī jātir
brahmaṇā copakalpitā

aryamṇaḥ—of Aryamā; *mātṛkā*—Mātṛkā; *patnī*—the wife; *tayoḥ*—by their union; *carṣaṇayaḥ sutāḥ*—many sons who were learned scholars; *yatra*—wherein; *vai*—indeed; *mānuṣī*—human; *jātiḥ*—species; *brahmaṇā*—by Lord Brahmā; *ca*—and; *upakalpitā*—was created.

TRANSLATION

From the womb of Mātṛkā, the wife of Aryamā, were born many learned scholars. Among them Lord Brahmā created the human species, which are endowed with an aptitude for self-examination.

TEXT 43

पूषानपत्यः पिष्टादो भग्नदन्तोऽभवत् पुरा ।
योऽसौ दक्षाय कुपितं जहास विवृतद्विजः ॥ ४३ ॥

pūṣānapatyaḥ piṣṭādo
bhagna-danto'bhavat purā
yo'sau dakṣāya kupitaṁ
jahāsa vivṛta-dvijaḥ

pūṣā—Pūṣā; *anapatyaḥ*—without children; *piṣṭa-adaḥ*—who lives by eating flour; *bhagna-dantaḥ*—with broken teeth; *abhavat*—became; *purā*—formerly; *yaḥ*—who; *asau*—that; *dakṣāya*—at Dakṣa; *kupitam*—very angry; *jahāsa*—laughed; *vivṛta-dvijaḥ*—uncovering his teeth.

TRANSLATION

Pūṣā had no sons. When Lord Śiva was angry at Dakṣa, Pūṣā had laughed at Lord Śiva and shown his teeth. Therefore he lost his teeth and had to live by eating only ground flour.

TEXT 44

त्वष्टुर्दैत्यात्मजा भार्या रचना नाम कन्यका।
संनिवेशस्तयोर्जज्ञे विश्वरूपश्च वीर्यवान् ॥ ४४ ॥

tvaṣṭur daityātmajā bhāryā
racanā nāma kanyakā
sanniveśas tayor jajñe
viśvarūpaś ca vīryavān

tvaṣṭuḥ—of Tvaṣṭā; *daitya-ātma-jā*—the daughter of a demon; *bhāryā*—wife; *racanā*—Racanā; *nāma*—named; *kanyakā*—a maiden; *sanniveśaḥ*—Sanniveśa; *tayoḥ*—of those two; *jajñe*—was born; *viśvarūpaḥ*—Viśvarūpa; *ca*—and; *vīryavān*—very powerful in bodily strength.

TRANSLATION

Racanā, the daughter of the Daityas, became the wife of Prajāpati Tvaṣṭā. By his semina he begot in her womb two very powerful sons named Sanniveśa and Viśvarūpa.

TEXT 45

तं वव्रिरे सुरगणा स्वस्त्रीयं द्विषतामपि।
विमतेन परित्यक्ता गुरुणाङ्गिरसेन यत्॥ ४५ ॥

taṁ vavrire sura-gaṇā
svasrīyaṁ dviṣatām api
vimatena parityaktā
guruṇāṅgirasena yat

tam—him (Viśvarūpa); *vavrire*—accepted as a priest; *sura-gaṇāḥ*—the demigods; *svasrīyam*—the son of a daughter; *dviṣatām*—of the inimical demons; *api*—although; *vimatena*—being disrespected; *parityaktāḥ*—who were given up; *guruṇā*—by their spiritual master; *āṅgirasena*—Bṛhaspati; *yat*—since.

TRANSLATION

Although Viśvarūpa was the son of the daughter of their eternal enemies the demons, the demigods accepted him as their priest in

accordance with the order of Brahmā when they were abandoned by their spiritual master, Bṛhaspati, whom they had disrespected.

Thus end the Bhaktivedanta purports to the Sixth Canto, Sixth Chapter, of the Śrīmad-Bhāgavatam, *entitled "The Progeny of the Daughters of Dakṣa."*

CHAPTER SEVEN

Indra Offends His Spiritual Master, Bṛhaspati.

As related in this chapter, Indra, the King of heaven, committed an offense at the feet of his spiritual master, Bṛhaspati. Bṛhaspati therefore left the demigods, who then had no priest. However, at the request of the demigods, Viśvarūpa, the son of the *brāhmaṇa* Tvaṣṭā, became their priest.

Once upon a time, Indra, the King of the demigods, was sitting with his wife Śacīdevī and being praised by various demigods like the Siddhas, Cāraṇas and Gandharvas when Bṛhaspati, the spiritual master of the demigods, entered the assembly. Indra, being too absorbed in material opulence, forgot himself and did not respect Bṛhaspati, who thus became aware of Indra's pride in his material opulence and immediately disappeared from the assembly to teach him a lesson. Indra became most repentant, understanding that because of his opulence he had forgotten to respect his spiritual master. He left the palace to beg pardon from his spiritual master, but could not find Bṛhaspati anywhere.

Because of his disrespectful behavior toward his spiritual master, Indra lost all his opulence and was conquered by the demons, who defeated the demigods in a great fight and occupied Indra's throne. King Indra, along with the other demigods, later took shelter of Lord Brahmā. Understanding the situation, Lord Brahmā chastised the demigods for their offense to their spiritual master. Following Lord Brahmā's orders, the demigods accepted Viśvarūpa, who was a *brāhmaṇa* and the son of Tvaṣṭā, as their priest. Then they performed *yajñas* under the priesthood of Viśvarūpa and were able to conquer the demons.

TEXT 1

श्रीराजोवाच

कस्य हेतोः परित्यक्ता आचार्येणात्मनः सुराः ।
एतदाचक्ष्व भगवञ्छिष्याणामक्रमं गुरौ ॥ १ ॥

śrī-rājovāca
kasya hetoḥ parityaktā
ācāryeṇātmanaḥ surāḥ

etad ācakṣva bhagavañ
chiṣyāṇām akramaṁ gurau

śrī-rājā uvāca—the King inquired; *kasya hetoḥ*—for what reason; *parityaktāḥ*—rejected; *ācāryeṇa*—by the spiritual master, Bṛhaspati; *ātmanaḥ*—of himself; *surāḥ*—all the demigods; *etat*—this; *ācakṣva*—kindly describe; *bhagavan*—O great sage (Śukadeva Gosvāmī); *śiṣyāṇām*—of the disciples; *akramam*—the offense; *gurau*—unto the spiritual master.

TRANSLATION

Mahārāja Parīkṣit inquired from Śukadeva Gosvāmī: O great sage, why did the spiritual master of the demigods, Bṛhaspati, reject the demigods, who were his own disciples? What offense did the demigods commit against their spiritual master? Please describe to me this incident.

PURPORT

Śrīla Viśvanātha Cakravartī Ṭhākura comments:

saptame guruṇā tyaktair
devair daitya-parājitaiḥ
viśvarūpo gurutvena
vṛto brahmopadeśataḥ

"This Seventh Chapter describes how Bṛhaspati was offended by the demigods, how he left them and the demigods were defeated, and how the demigods, following the instructions of Lord Brahmā, accepted Viśvarūpa as the priest to perform their sacrifice."

TEXTS 2–8

श्रीबादरायणिरुवाच

इन्द्रस्त्रिभुवनैश्वर्यमदोल्लङ्घितसत्पथः ।
मरुद्भिर्वसुभी रुद्रैरादित्यैर्ऋभुभिर्नृप ॥ २ ॥
विश्वेदेवैश्च साध्यैश्च नासत्याभ्यां परिश्रितः ।
सिद्धचारणगन्धर्वैर्मुनिभिर्ब्रह्मवादिभिः ॥ ३ ॥
विद्याधराप्सरोभिश्च किन्नरैः पतगोरगैः ।
निषेव्यमाणो मघवान् स्तूयमानश्च भारत ॥ ४ ॥
उपगीयमानो ललितमास्थानाध्यासनाश्रितः ।
पाण्डुरेणातपत्रेण चन्द्रमण्डलचारुणा ॥ ५ ॥

युक्तश्चान्यैः पारमेष्ठ्यैश्चामरव्यजनादिभिः ।
विराजमानः पौलम्या सहार्धासनया भृशम् ॥ ६ ॥
स यदा परमाचार्यं देवानामात्मनश्च ह ।
नाभ्यनन्दत संप्राप्तं प्रत्युत्थानासनादिभिः ॥ ७ ॥
वाचस्पतिं मुनिवरं सुरासुरनमस्कृतम् ।
नोच्चचालासनादिन्द्रः पश्यन्नपि सभागतम् ॥ ८ ॥

śrī-bādarāyaṇir uvāca
indras tribhuvanaiśvarya-
madollaṅghita-satpathaḥ
marudbhir vasubhī rudrair
ādityair ṛbhubhir nṛpa

viśvedevaiś ca sādhyaiś ca
nāsatyābhyāṁ pariśritaḥ
siddha-cāraṇa-gandharvair
munibhir brahmavādibhiḥ

vidyādharāpsarobhiś ca
kinnaraiḥ patagoragaiḥ
niṣevyamāṇo maghavān
stūyamānaś ca bhārata

upagīyamāno lalitam
āsthānādhyāsanāśritaḥ
pāṇḍureṇātapatreṇa
candra-maṇḍala-cāruṇā

yuktaś cānyaiḥ pārameṣṭhyaiś
cāmara-vyajanādibhiḥ
virājamānaḥ paulamyā
sahārdhāsanayā bhṛśam

sa yadā paramācāryaṁ
devānām ātmanaś ca ha
nābhyanandata samprāptaṁ
pratyutthānāsanādibhiḥ

vācaspatiṁ muni-varaṁ
surāsura-namaskṛtam

noccacālāsanād indraḥ
paśyann api sabhāgatam

śrī-bādarāyaṇiḥ uvāca—Śrī Śukadeva Gosvāmī replied; *indraḥ*—King Indra; *tri-bhuvana-aiśvarya*—because of possessing all the material opulences of the three worlds; *mada*—due to pride; *ullaṅghita*—who has transgressed; *sat-pathaḥ*—the path of Vedic civilization; *marudbhiḥ*—by the wind demigods, known as the Maruts; *vasubhiḥ*—by the eight Vasus; *rudraiḥ*—by the eleven Rudras; *ādityaiḥ*—by the Ādityas; *ṛbhubhiḥ*—by the Ṛbhus; *nṛpa*—O King; *viśvedevaiḥ ca*—and by the Viśvadevas; *sādhyaiḥ*—by the Sādhyas; *ca*—also; *nāsatyābhyām*—by the two Aśvinī-kumāras; *pariśritaḥ*—surrounded; *siddha*—by the inhabitants of Siddhaloka; *cāraṇa*—the Cāraṇas; *gandharvaiḥ*—and the Gandharvas; *munibhiḥ*—by the great sages; *brahmavādibhiḥ*—by greatly learned impersonalist scholars; *vidyādhara-apsarobhiḥ ca*—and by the Vidyādharas and Apsarās; *kinnaraiḥ*—by the Kinnaras; *pataga-uragaiḥ*—by the Patagas (birds) and Uragas (snakes); *niṣevyamāṇaḥ*—being served; *maghavān*—King Indra; *stūyamānaḥ ca*—and being offered prayers; *bhārata*—O Mahārāja Parīkṣit; *upagīyamānaḥ*—being sung before; *lalitam*—very sweetly; *āsthāna*—in his assembly; *adhyāsana-āśritaḥ*—situated on the throne; *pāṇḍureṇa*—white; *ātapatreṇa*—with an umbrella over the head; *candra-maṇḍala-cāruṇā*—as beautiful as the circle of the moon; *yuktaḥ*—endowed; *ca anyaiḥ*—and by other; *pārameṣṭhyaiḥ*—symptoms of an exalted king; *cāmara*—by yak-tail; *vyajana-ādibhiḥ*—fans and other paraphernalia; *virājamānaḥ*—shining; *paulamyā*—his wife, Śacī; *saha*—with; *ardha-āsanayā*—who occupied half the throne; *bhṛśam*—greatly; *saḥ*—he (Indra); *yadā*—when; *parama-ācāryam*—the most exalted *ācārya,* spiritual master; *devānām*—of all the demigods; *ātmanaḥ*—of himself; *ca*—and; *ha*—indeed; *na*—not; *abhyanandata*—welcomed; *samprāptam*—having appeared in the assembly; *pratyutthāna*—by getting up from the throne; *āsana-ādibhiḥ*—and by a seat and other greetings; *vācaspatim*—the priest of the demigods, Bṛhaspati; *muni-varam*—the best of all the sages; *sura-asura-namaskṛtam*—who is respected by both the demigods and the *asuras; na*—not; *uccacāla*—did get up; *āsanāt*—from the throne; *indraḥ*—Indra; *paśyan api*—although seeing; *sabhā-āgatam*—entering the assembly.

TRANSLATION

Śukadeva Gosvāmī said: O King, once upon a time, the King of heaven, Indra, being extremely proud because of his great opulence of the three

worlds, transgressed the law of Vedic etiquette. Seated on his throne, he was surrounded by the Maruts, Vasus, Rudras, Ādityas, Ṛbhus, Viśvadevas, Sādhyas, Aśvinī-kumāras, Siddhas, Cāraṇas and Gandharvas and by great saintly persons. Also surrounding him were the Vidyādharas, Apsarās, Kinnaras, Patagas [birds] and Uragas [snakes]. All of them were offering Indra their respects and services, and the Apsarās and Gandharvas were dancing and singing with very sweet musical instruments. Over Indra's head was a white umbrella as effulgent as the full moon. Fanned by yak-tail whisks and served with all the paraphernalia of a great king, Indra was sitting with his wife, Śacīdevī, who occupied half the throne, when the great sage Bṛhaspati appeared in that assembly. Bṛhaspati, the best of the sages, was the spiritual master of Indra and the demigods and was respected by the demigods and demons alike. Nevertheless, although Indra saw his spiritual master before him, he did not rise from his own seat or offer a seat to his spiritual master, nor did Indra offer him a respectful welcome. Indra did nothing to show him respect.

TEXT 9

ततो निर्गत्य सहसा कविराङ्गिरसः प्रभुः ।
आययौ स्वगृहं तूष्णीं विद्वान् श्रीमदविक्रियाम् ॥ ९ ॥

tato nirgatya sahasā
kavir āṅgirasaḥ prabhuḥ
āyayau sva-gṛhaṁ tūṣṇīṁ
vidvān śrī-mada-vikriyām

tataḥ—thereafter; *nirgatya*—going out; *sahasā*—suddenly; *kaviḥ*—the great learned sage; *āṅgirasaḥ*—Bṛhaspati; *prabhuḥ*—the master of the demigods; *āyayau*—returned; *sva-gṛham*—to his home; *tūṣṇīm*—being silent; *vidvān*—having known; *śrī-mada-vikriyām*—deterioration because of madness due to opulence.

TRANSLATION

Bṛhaspati knew everything that would happen in the future. Seeing Indra's transgression of etiquette, he completely understood that Indra was puffed up by his material opulence. Although able to curse Indra, he did not do so. Instead, he left the assembly and in silence returned to his home.

TEXT 10

तर्ह्येव प्रतिबुध्येन्द्रो गुरुहेलनमात्मनः ।
गर्हयामास सदसि स्वयमात्मानमात्मना ॥ १० ॥

tarhy eva pratibudhyendro
guru-helanam ātmanaḥ
garhayām āsa sadasi
svayam ātmānam ātmanā

tarhi—then, immediately; *eva*—indeed; *pratibudhya*—realizing; *indraḥ*—King Indra; *guru-helanam*—disrespect to the spiritual master; *ātmanaḥ*—his own; *garhayām āsa*—reproached; *sadasi*—in that assembly; *svayam*—personally; *ātmānam*—himself; *ātmanā*—by himself.

TRANSLATION

Indra, the King of heaven, could immediately understand his mistake. Realizing he had disrespected his spiritual master, he condemned himself in the presence of all the members of the assembly.

TEXT 11

अहो बत मयासाधु कृतं वै दभ्रबुद्धिना ।
यन्मयैश्वर्यमत्तेन गुरुः सदसि कात्कृतः ॥ ११ ॥

aho bata mayāsādhu
kṛtaṁ vai dabhra-buddhinā
yan mayaiśvarya-mattena
guruḥ sadasi kātkṛtaḥ

aho—alas; *bata*—indeed; *mayā*—by me; *asādhu*—disrespectful; *kṛtam*—the action done; *vai*—certainly; *dabhra-buddhinā*—being of less intelligence; *yat*—because; *mayā*—by me; *aiśvarya-mattena*—being very proud of material opulence; *guruḥ*—the spiritual master; *sadasi*—in this assembly; *kāt-kṛtaḥ*—mistreated.

TRANSLATION

Alas, what a regrettable deed I have committed because of my lack of intelligence and my pride in my material opulences. I failed to show

respect to my spiritual master when he entered this assembly, and thus I have insulted him.

TEXT 12

को गृध्येत् पण्डितो लक्ष्मीं त्रिपिष्टपपतेरपि।
ययाहमासुरं भावं नीतोऽद्य विबुधेश्वरः ॥ १२ ॥

ko gṛdhyet paṇḍito lakṣmīṁ
tripiṣṭapa-pater api
yayāham āsuraṁ bhāvaṁ
nīto'dya vibudheśvaraḥ

kaḥ—who; *gṛdhyet*—would accept; *paṇḍitaḥ*—a learned man; *lakṣmīm*—opulences; *tri-piṣṭa-pa-pateḥ api*—although I am the King of the demigods; *yayā*—by which; *aham*—I; *āsuram*—demoniac; *bhāvam*—mentality; *nītaḥ*—carried to; *adya*—now; *vibudha*—of the demigods, who are in the mode of goodness; *īśvaraḥ*—the King.

TRANSLATION

Although I am King of the demigods, who are situated in the mode of goodness, I was proud of a little opulence and polluted by false ego. Under the circumstances, who in this world would accept such riches at the risk of falling down? Alas! I condemn my wealth and opulence.

PURPORT

Śrī Caitanya Mahāprabhu prayed to the Supreme Personality of Godhead, *na dhanaṁ na janaṁ na sundarīṁ kavitāṁ vā jagad-īśa kāmaye:* "O my Lord, I do not aspire for material opulence or wealth, nor do I want a great number of followers to accept me as their leader, nor do I want a very beautiful wife to please me." *Mama janmani janmanīśvare bhavatād bhaktir ahaitukī tvayi:* "I do not even want liberation. All I want, life after life, is to be a faithful servant of Your Lordship." According to the laws of nature, when one is extremely opulent one becomes degraded, and this is true both individually and collectively. The demigods are situated in the mode of goodness, but sometimes even one who is situated in such an exalted position as King Indra, the king of all the demigods, falls down because of material opulence. We are now actually seeing this in America. The entire American nation has tried to advance in material opulence without striving to produce ideal human beings. The result is that Americans are now regretting the wholesale criminality of American society and are wondering how America has become so lawless and unmanageable. As stated in *Śrīmad-Bhāgavatam* (7.5.31), *na te viduḥ svārtha-gatiṁ hi viṣṇum:* persons who are unenlightened do not know the aim of life, which is to return home, back to Godhead. Therefore, both individually and collectively, they try to enjoy so-called material comforts, and they become addicted to wine and women. The men produced in such a society are less than fourth class. They are the unwanted population known as *varṇa-saṅkara,* and as stated in *Bhagavad-gītā,* an increase of *varṇa-saṅkara* population creates a hellish society. This is the society in which Americans now find themselves.

Fortunately, however, the Hare Kṛṣṇa movement has come to America, and many fortunate young men are giving serious attention to this movement, which is creating ideal men of first-class character, men who completely refrain from meat-eating, illicit sex, intoxication and gambling. If the American people are serious about curbing the degraded criminal life of their nation, they must take to the Kṛṣṇa consciousness movement and try to create the kind of human society advised in *Bhagavad-gītā* (*cātur-varṇyaṁ mayā sṛṣṭaṁ guṇa-karma-vibhāgaśaḥ*). They must divide their society into first-class men, second-class men, third-class men and fourth-class men. Since they are now creating only men who are less than fourth class, how can they avoid the dangers of a criminal society? Long, long ago, Lord Indra regretted his disrespect to his spiritual master, Bṛhaspati. Similarly, it is advised that the American people regret their mistaken advancement in civilization. They should take advice from the spiritual master, the representative of Kṛṣṇa. If they do so, they will be happy, and theirs will be an ideal nation to lead the entire world.

TEXT 13

यः पारमेष्ठ्यं धिषणमधितिष्ठन् न कञ्चन।
प्रत्युत्तिष्ठेदिति ब्रूयुर्धर्मं ते न परं विदुः ॥ १३ ॥

yaḥ pārameṣṭhyaṁ dhiṣaṇam
adhitiṣṭhan na kañcana
pratyuttiṣṭhed iti brūyur
dharmaṁ te na paraṁ viduḥ

yaḥ—anyone who; *pārameṣṭhyam*—royal; *dhiṣaṇam*—throne; *adhitiṣṭhan*—sitting on; *na*—not; *kañcana*—anyone; *pratyuttiṣṭhet*—should rise before; *iti*—thus; *brūyuḥ*—those who say; *dharmam*—the codes of religion; *te*—they; *na*—not; *param*—higher; *viduḥ*—know.

TRANSLATION

If a person says, "One who is situated on the exalted throne of a king should not stand up to show respect to another king or a brāhmaṇa," it is to be understood that he does not know the superior religious principles.

PURPORT

Śrīla Viśvanātha Cakravartī Ṭhākura says in this regard that when a president or king is sitting on his throne, he does not need to show respect to everyone who comes within his assembly, but he must show respect to superiors like his spiritual master, *brāhmaṇas* and Vaiṣṇavas. There are many examples of how he should act. When Lord Kṛṣṇa was sitting on His throne and Nārada fortunately entered His assembly, even Lord Kṛṣṇa immediately stood up with His officers and ministers to offer respectful obeisances to Nārada. Nārada knew that Kṛṣṇa is the Supreme Personality of Godhead, and Kṛṣṇa knew that Nārada was His devotee, but although Kṛṣṇa is the Supreme Lord and Nārada is the Lord's devotee, the Lord observed the religious etiquette. Since Nārada was a *brahmacārī,* a *brāhmaṇa* and an exalted devotee, even Kṛṣṇa, while acting as a king, offered His respectful obeisances unto Nārada. Such is the conduct visible in the Vedic civilization. A civilization in which the people do not know how the representative of Nārada and Kṛṣṇa should be respected, how society should be formed and how one should advance in Kṛṣṇa consciousness—a society concerned only with manufacturing new cars and new skyscrapers every year and then breaking them to pieces and making new ones—may be technologically advanced, but it is not a human civilization. A human civilization is advanced when its people follow the *cātur-varṇya* system, the system of four orders of life. There must be ideal, first-class men to act as advisors, second-class men to act as administrators, third-class men to produce food and protect cows, and fourth-class men who obey the three higher classes of society. One who does not follow the standard system of society should be considered a fifth-class man. A society without Vedic laws and regulations will not be very helpful to humanity. As stated in this verse, *dharmaṁ te na paraṁ viduḥ:* such a society does not know the aim of life and the highest principle of religion.

TEXT 14

तेषां कुपथदेष्टॄणां पततां तमसि ह्यधः ।
ये श्रद्दध्युर्वचस्ते वै मज्जन्त्यश्मप्लवा इव ॥ १४ ॥

teṣāṁ kupatha-deṣṭṝṇāṁ
patatāṁ tamasi hy adhaḥ
ye śraddadhyur vacas te vai
majjanty aśma-plavā iva

teṣām—of them (the misleaders); *ku-patha-deṣṭṝṇām*—who show the path of danger; *patatām*—themselves falling; *tamasi*—in darkness; *hi*—indeed; *adhaḥ*—down; *ye*—anyone who; *śraddadhyuḥ*—place faith in; *vacaḥ*—the words; *te*—they; *vai*—indeed; *majjanti*—sink; *aśma-plavāḥ*—boats made of stone; *iva*—like.

TRANSLATION

Leaders who have fallen into ignorance and who mislead people by directing them to the path of destruction [as described in the previous verse] are, in effect, boarding a stone boat, and so too are those who blindly follow them. A stone boat would be unable to float and would sink in the water with its passengers. Similarly, those who mislead people go to hell, and their followers go with them.

PURPORT

As stated in the Vedic literature (*Bhāg.* 11.20.17):

nṛ-deham ādyaṁ sulabhaṁ sudurlabhaṁ
plavaṁ sukalpaṁ guru-karṇa-dhāram

We, the conditioned souls, have fallen in the ocean of nescience, but the human body fortunately provides us a good opportunity to cross the ocean because the human body is like a very good boat. When directed by a spiritual master acting as the captain, the boat can very easily cross the ocean. Furthermore, the boat is helped across by favorable winds, which are the instructions of Vedic knowledge. If one does not take advantage of all these facilities to cross the ocean of nescience, he is certainly committing suicide.

One who boards a boat made of stone is doomed. To be elevated to the stage of perfection, humanity must first give up false leaders who present boats of stone. All of human society is in such a dangerous position that to be rescued it must abide by the standard instructions of the *Vedas.* The cream of these instructions appears in the form of *Bhagavad-gītā.* One should not take shelter of any other instructions, for *Bhagavad-gītā* gives direct instructions on how to fulfill the aim of human life. Lord Śrī Kṛṣṇa therefore says, *sarva-dharmān parityajya mām ekaṁ śaraṇaṁ vraja:* "Give up all other processes of religion and simply surrender to Me." Even if one does not accept Lord Kṛṣṇa as the Supreme Personality of Godhead, His instructions are so exalted and beneficial for humanity that if one follows His instructions one will be saved. Otherwise one will be cheated by unauthorized meditation and gymnastic methods of *yoga.* Thus one will board a boat of stone, which will sink and drown all its passengers. Unfortunately, although the American people are extremely eager to get out of materialistic chaos, they are sometimes found to patronize the makers of stone boats. That will not help them. They must take the proper boat offered by Kṛṣṇa in the form of the Kṛṣṇa consciousness movement. Then they will be easily saved. In this regard Śrīla Viśvanātha Cakravartī Ṭhākura comments: *aśmamayaḥ plavo yeṣāṁ te yathā majjantaṁ plavam anumajjanti tatheti rāja-nīty-upadeṣṭṛṣu sva-sabhyeṣu kopo vyañjitaḥ.* If society is guided by political diplomacy, with one nation maneuvering against another, it will certainly sink like a stone boat. Political maneuvering and diplomacy will not save human society. People must take to Kṛṣṇa consciousness to understand the aim of life, to understand God, and to fulfill the human mission.

TEXT 15

अथाहममराचार्यमगाधधिषणं द्विजम् ।
प्रसादयिष्ये निशठः शीर्ष्णा तच्चरणं स्पृशन् ॥ १५ ॥

athāham amarācāryam
agādha-dhiṣaṇaṁ dvijam
prasādayiṣye niśaṭhaḥ
śīrṣṇā tac-caraṇaṁ spṛśan

atha—therefore; *aham*—I; *amara-ācāryam*—the spiritual master of the demigods; *agādha-dhiṣaṇam*—whose spiritual knowledge is deep; *dvijam*—the perfect *brāhmaṇa; prasādayiṣye*—I shall please; *niśaṭhaḥ*—without duplicity; *śīrṣṇā*—with my head; *tat-caraṇam*—his lotus feet; *s pṛśan*—touching.

TRANSLATION

King Indra said: Therefore with great frankness and without duplicity I shall now bow my head at the lotus feet of Bṛhaspati, the spiritual master of the demigods. Because he is in the mode of goodness, he is fully aware of all knowledge and is the best of the brāhmaṇas. Now I shall touch his lotus feet and offer my obeisances unto him to try to satisfy him.

PURPORT

Coming to his senses, King Indra realized that he was not a very sincere disciple of his spiritual master, Bṛhaspati. Therefore he decided that henceforward he would be *niśaṭha,* nonduplicitous. *Niśaṭhaḥ śīrṣṇā-tac-caraṇaṁ spṛśan:* he decided to touch his head to the feet of his spiritual master. From this example, we should learn this principle enunciated by Viśvanātha Cakravartī Ṭhākura:

yasya prasādād bhagavat-prasādo
yasyāprasādān na gatiḥ kuto'pi

"By the mercy of the spiritual master one is benedicted by the mercy of Kṛṣṇa. Without the grace of the spiritual master, one cannot make any advancement." A disciple should never be a hypocrite or be unfaithful to his spiritual master. In *Śrīmad-Bhāgavatam* (11.17.27), the spiritual master is also called *ācārya. Ācāryaṁ māṁ vijānīyān:* the Supreme Personality of Godhead says that one should respect the spiritual master, accepting him as the Lord Himself. *Nāvamanyeta karhicit:* one should not disrespect the *ācārya* at any time. *Na martya-buddhyāsūyeta:* one should never think the *ācārya* an ordinary person. Familiarity sometimes breeds contempt, but one should be very careful in one's dealings with the *ācārya. Agādha-dhiṣaṇaṁ dvijam:* the *ācārya* is a perfect *brāhmaṇa* and has unlimited intelligence in guiding the activities of his disciple. Therefore Kṛṣṇa advises in *Bhagavad-gītā* (4.34):

tad viddhi praṇipātena
paripraśnena sevayā
upadekṣyanti te jñānaṁ
jñāninas tattva-darśinaḥ

"Just try to learn the truth by approaching a spiritual master. Inquire from him submissively and render service unto him. The self-realized soul can impart knowledge unto you because he has seen the truth." One should fully surrender unto the spiritual master, and with service (*sevayā*) one should approach him for further spiritual enlightenment.

TEXT 16

एवं चिन्तयतस्तस्य मघोनो भगवान् गृहात् ।
बृहस्पतिर्गतोऽदृष्टां गतिमध्यात्ममायया ॥ १६ ॥

evaṁ cintayatas tasya
maghono bhagavān gṛhāt
bṛhaspatir gato 'dṛṣṭāṁ
gatim adhyātma-māyayā

evam—thus; *cintayataḥ*—while thinking very seriously; *tasya*—he; *maghonaḥ*—Indra; *bhagavān*—the most powerful; *gṛhāt*—from his home; *bṛhaspatiḥ*—Bṛhaspati; *gataḥ*—went; *adṛṣṭām*—invisible; *gatim*—to a state; *adhyātma*—due to being highly elevated in spiritual consciousness; *māyayā*—by his potency.

TRANSLATION

While Indra, the King of the demigods, thought in this way and repented in his own assembly, Bṛhaspati, the most powerful spiritual master, understood his mind. Thus he became invisible to Indra and left home, for Bṛhaspati was spiritually more powerful than King Indra.

TEXT 17

गुरोर्नाधिगतः संज्ञां परीक्षन् भगवान् स्वराट् ।
ध्यायन् धिया सुरैर्युक्तः शर्म नालभतात्मनः ॥ १७ ॥

guror nādhigataḥ saṁjñāṁ
parīkṣan bhagavān svarāṭ
dhyāyan dhiyā surair yuktaḥ
śarma nālabhatātmanaḥ

guroḥ—of his spiritual master; *na*—not; *adhigataḥ*—finding; *saṁjñām*—trace; *parīkṣan*—searching vigorously all around; *bhagavān*—the most powerful Indra; *svarāṭ*—independent; *dhyāyan*—meditating; *dhiyā*—by wisdom; *suraiḥ*—by the demigods; *yuktaḥ*—surrounded; *śarma*—peace; *na*—not; *alabhata*—obtained; *ātmanaḥ*—of the mind.

TRANSLATION

Although Indra searched vigorously with the assistance of the other demigods, he could not find Bṛhaspati. Then Indra thought, "Alas, my spiritual master has become dissatisfied with me, and now I have no means of achieving good fortune." Although Indra was surrounded by demigods, he could not find peace of mind.

TEXT 18

तच्छ्रुत्वैवासुराः सर्व आश्रित्यौशनसं मतम् ।
देवान् प्रत्युद्यमं चक्रुर्दुर्मदा आततायिनः ॥ १८ ॥

tac chrutvaivāsurāḥ sarva
āśrityauśanasaṁ matam
devān pratyudyamaṁ cakrur
durmadā ātatāyinaḥ

tat śrutvā—hearing that news; *eva*—indeed; *asurāḥ*—the demons; *sarve*—all; *āśritya*—taking shelter of; *auśanasam*—of Śukrācārya; *matam*—the instruction; *devān*—the demigods; *pratyudyamam*—action against; *cakruḥ*—performed; *durmadāḥ*—not very intelligent; *ātatāyinaḥ*—equipped with arms for fighting.

TRANSLATION

Hearing of the pitiable condition of King Indra, the demons, following the instructions of their guru, Śukrācārya, equipped themselves with weapons and declared war against the demigods.

TEXT 19

तैर्विसृष्टेषुभिस्तीक्ष्णैर्निर्भिन्नाङ्गोरुबाहवः ।
ब्रह्माणं शरणं जग्मुः सहेन्द्रा नतकन्धराः ॥ १९ ॥

tair visṛṣṭeṣubhis tīkṣṇair
nirbhinnāṅgoru-bāhavaḥ
brahmāṇaṁ śaraṇaṁ jagmuḥ
sahendrā nata-kandharāḥ

taiḥ—by them (the demons); *visṛṣṭa*—thrown; *iṣubhiḥ*—by the arrows; *tīkṣṇaiḥ*—very sharp; *nirbhinna*—pierced all over; *aṅga*—bodies; *uru*—

thighs; *bāhavaḥ*—and arms; *brahmāṇam*—of Lord Brahmā; *śaraṇam*—the shelter; *jagmuḥ*—approached; *saha-indrāḥ*—with King Indra; *nata-kandharāḥ*—their heads bent downward.

TRANSLATION

The demigods' heads, thighs and arms and the other parts of their bodies were injured by the sharp arrows of the demons. The demigods, headed by Indra, saw no other course than to immediately approach Lord Brahmā with bowed heads for shelter and proper instruction.

TEXT 20

तांस्तथाभ्यर्दितान् वीक्ष्य भगवानात्मभूरजः ।
कृपया परया देव उवाच परिसान्त्वयन् ॥ २० ॥

tāṁs tathābhyarditān vīkṣya
bhagavān ātmabhūr ajaḥ
kṛpayā parayā deva
uvāca parisāntvayan

tān—them (the demigods); *tathā*—in that way; *abhyarditān*—afflicted by the weapons of the demons; *vīkṣya*—seeing; *bhagavān*—the most powerful; *ātma-bhūḥ*—Lord Brahmā; *ajaḥ*—who was not born like an ordinary human being; *kṛpayā*—out of causeless mercy; *parayā*—great; *devaḥ*—Lord Brahmā; *uvāca*—said; *parisāntvayan*—pacifying them.

TRANSLATION

When the most powerful Lord Brahmā saw the demigods coming toward him, their bodies gravely injured by the arrows of the demons, he pacified them by his great causeless mercy and spoke as follows.

TEXT 21

श्रीब्रह्मोवाच
अहो बत सुरश्रेष्ठा ह्यभद्रं वः कृतं महत् ।
ब्रह्मिष्ठं ब्राह्मणं दान्तमैश्वर्यान्नाभ्यनन्दत ॥ २१ ॥

śrī-brahmovāca
aho bata sura-śreṣṭhā
hy abhadraṁ vaḥ kṛtaṁ mahat

brahmiṣṭhaṁ brāhmaṇaṁ dāntam
aiśvaryān nābhyanandata

śrī-brahmā uvāca—Lord Brahmā said; *aho*—alas; *bata*—it is very astonishing; *sura-śreṣṭhāḥ*—O best of the demigods; *hi*—indeed; *abhadram*—injustice; *vaḥ*—by you; *kṛtam*—done; *mahat*—great; *brahmiṣṭham*—a person fully obedient to the Supreme Brahman; *brāhmaṇam*—a *brāhmaṇa; dāntam*—who has fully controlled the mind and senses; *aiśvaryāt*—because of your material opulence; *na*—not; *abhyanandata*—welcomed properly.

TRANSLATION

Lord Brahmā said: O best of the demigods, unfortunately, because of madness resulting from your material opulence, you failed to receive Bṛhaspati properly when he came to your assembly. Because he is aware of the Supreme Brahman and fully in control of his senses, he is the best of the brāhmaṇas. Therefore it is very astonishing that you have acted impudently toward him.

PURPORT

Lord Brahmā recognized the brahminical qualifications of Bṛhaspati, who was the spiritual master of the demigods because of his awareness of the Supreme Brahman. Bṛhaspati was very much in control of his senses and mind, and therefore he was a most qualified *brāhmaṇa.* Lord Brahmā chastised the demigods for not properly respecting this *brāhmaṇa,* who was their *guru.* Lord Brahmā wanted to impress upon the demigods that one's *guru* should not be disrespected under any circumstances. When Bṛhaspati entered the assembly of the demigods, they and their king, Indra, took him for granted. Since he came every day, they thought, they did not need to show him special respect. As it is said, familiarity breeds contempt. Being very much displeased, Bṛhaspati immediately left Indra's palace. Thus all the demigods, headed by Indra, became offenders at the lotus feet of Bṛhaspati, and Lord Brahmā, being aware of this, condemned their neglect. In a song we sing every day, Narottama dāsa Ṭhākura says, *cakṣu-dāna dila yei, janme janme prabhu sei:* the *guru* gives spiritual insight to the disciple, and therefore the *guru* should be considered his master, life after life. Under no circumstances should the *guru* be disrespected, but the demigods, being puffed up by their material possessions, were disrespectful to their *guru.* Therefore *Śrīmad-Bhāgavatam* (11.17.27) advises, *ācāryaṁ māṁ vijānīyān nāvamanyeta karhicit/ na martya-*

buddhyāsūyeta: the *ācārya* should always be offered respectful obeisances; one should never envy the *ācārya,* considering him an ordinary human being.

TEXT 22

तस्यायमनयस्यासीत् परेभ्यो वः पराभवः ।
प्रक्षीणेभ्यः स्ववैरिभ्यः समृद्धानां च यत् सुराः ॥ २२ ॥

tasyāyam anayasyāsīt
parebhyo vaḥ parābhavaḥ
prakṣīṇebhyaḥ sva-vairibhyaḥ
samṛddhānāṁ ca yat surāḥ

tasya—that; *ayam*—this; *anayasya*—of your ungrateful activity; *āsīt*—was; *parebhyaḥ*—by others; *vaḥ*—of all of you; *parābhavaḥ*—the defeat; *prakṣīṇebhyaḥ*—although they were weak; *sva-vairibhyaḥ*—by your own enemies, who were previously defeated by you; *samṛddhānām*—being yourselves very opulent; *ca*—and; *yat*—which; *surāḥ*—O demigods.

TRANSLATION

Because of your misbehavior toward Bṛhaspati, you have been defeated by the demons. My dear demigods, since the demons were weak, having been defeated by you several times, how else could you, who were so advanced in opulence, be defeated by them?

PURPORT

The *devas* are celebrated for fighting with the *asuras* perpetually. In such fights the *asuras* were always defeated, but this time the demigods were defeated. Why? The reason, as stated here, was that they had offended their spiritual master. Their impudent disrespect of their spiritual master was the cause of their defeat by the demons. As stated in the *śāstras,* when one disrespects a respectable superior, one loses his longevity and the results of his pious activities, and in this way one is degraded.

TEXT 23

मघवन् द्विषतः पश्य प्रक्षीणान् गुर्वतिक्रमात् ।
सम्प्रत्युपचितान् भूयः काव्यमाराध्य भक्तितः ।
आददीरन् निलयनं ममापि भृगुदेवताः ॥ २३ ॥

maghavan dviṣataḥ paśya
prakṣīṇān gurv-atikramāt
sampraty upacitān bhūyaḥ
kāvyam ārādhya bhaktitaḥ
ādadīran nilayanaṁ
mamāpi bhṛgu-devatāḥ

maghavan—O Indra; *dviṣataḥ*—your enemies; *paśya*—just see; *prakṣīṇān*—being very weak (formerly); *guru-atikramāt*—because of disrespecting their *guru,* Śukrācārya; *samprati*—at the present moment; *upacitān*—powerful; *bhūyaḥ*—again; *kāvyam*—their spiritual master, Śukrācārya; *ārādhya*—worshiping; *bhaktitaḥ*—with great devotion; *ādadīran*—may take away; *nilayanam*—the abode, Satyaloka; *mama*—my; *api*—even; *bhṛgu-devatāḥ*—who are now strong devotees of Śukrācārya, the disciple of Bhṛgu.

TRANSLATION

O Indra, your enemies, the demons, were extremely weak because of their disrespect toward Śukrācārya, but since they have now worshiped Śukrācārya with great devotion, they have again become powerful. By their devotion to Śukrācārya, they have increased their strength so much that now they are even able to easily seize my abode from me.

PURPORT

Lord Brahmā wanted to point out to the demigods that by the strength of the *guru* one can become most powerful within this world, and by the displeasure of the *guru* one can lose everything. This is confirmed by the song of Viśvanātha Cakravartī Ṭhākura:

yasya prasādād bhagavat-prasādo
yasyāprasādān na gatiḥ kuto'pi

"By the mercy of the spiritual master one is benedicted by the mercy of Kṛṣṇa. Without the grace of the spiritual master, one cannot make any advancement." Although the demons are insignificant in comparison to Lord Brahmā, because of the strength of their *guru* they were so powerful that they could even seize Brahmaloka from Lord Brahmā. We therefore pray to the spiritual master:

mūkaṁ karoti vācālaṁ
paṅguṁ laṅghayate girim

yat-kṛpā tam ahaṁ vande
śrī-guruṁ dīna-tāraṇam

By the mercy of the *guru,* even a dumb man can become the greatest orator, and even a lame man can cross mountains. As advised by Lord Brahmā, one should remember this śāstric injunction if one desires success in his life.

TEXT 24

त्रिपिष्टपं किं गणयन्त्यभेद्य-
मन्त्रा भृगूणामनुशिक्षितार्थाः ।
न विप्रगोविन्दगवीश्वराणां
भवन्त्यभद्राणि नरेश्वराणाम् ॥ २४ ॥

tripiṣṭapaṁ kiṁ gaṇayanty abhedya-
mantrā bhṛgūṇām anuśikṣitārthāḥ
na vipra-govinda-gav-īśvarāṇāṁ
bhavanty abhadrāṇi nareśvarāṇām

tri-piṣṭa-pam—all the demigods, including Lord Brahmā; *kim*—what; *gaṇayanti*—they care for; *abhedya-mantrāḥ*—whose determination to carry out the orders of the spiritual master is unbreakable; *bhṛgūṇām*—of the disciples of Bhṛgu Muni like Śukrācārya; *anuśikṣita-arthāḥ*—deciding to follow the instructions; *na*—not; *vipra*—the *brāhmaṇas; govinda*—the Supreme Personality of Godhead, Kṛṣṇa; *go*—the cows; *īśvarāṇām*—of persons favoring or considering worshipable; *bhavanti*—are; *abhadrāṇi*—any misfortunes; *nara-īśvarāṇām*—or of kings who follow this principle.

TRANSLATION

Because of their firm determination to follow the instructions of Śukrācārya, his disciples, the demons, are now unconcerned about the demigods. In fact, kings or others who have determined faith in the mercy of brāhmaṇas, cows and the Supreme Personality of Godhead, Kṛṣṇa, and who always worship these three are always strong in their position.

PURPORT

From the instructions of Lord Brahmā it is understood that everyone should very faithfully worship the *brāhmaṇas,* the Supreme Personality of Godhead and the cows. The Supreme Personality of Godhead is *go-brāhmaṇa-hitāya ca:* He is always very kind to cows and *brāhmaṇas.* Therefore one who worships Govinda must satisfy Him by worshiping the *brāhmaṇas* and cows. If a government worships the *brāhmaṇas,* the cows and Kṛṣṇa, Govinda, it is never defeated anywhere; otherwise it must always be defeated and condemned everywhere. At the present moment, all over the world, governments have no respect for *brāhmaṇas,* cows and Govinda, and consequently there are chaotic conditions all over the world. In summary, although the demigods were very powerful in material opulence, the demons defeated them in battle because the demigods had behaved disrespectfully toward a *brāhmaṇa,* Bṛhaspati, who was their spiritual master.

TEXT 25

तद् विश्वरूपं भजताशु विप्रं
तपस्विनं त्वाष्ट्रमथात्मवन्तम् ।
सभाजितोऽर्थान् स विधास्यते वो
यदि क्षमिष्यध्वमुतास्य कर्म ॥ २५ ॥

tad viśvarūpaṁ bhajatāśu vipraṁ
tapasvinaṁ tvāṣṭram athātmavantam
sabhājito'rthān sa vidhāsyate vo
yadi kṣamiṣyadhvam utāsya karma

tat—therefore; *viśvarūpam*—Viśvarūpa; *bhajata*—just worship as *guru; āśu*—immediately; *vipram*—who is a perfect *brāhmaṇa; tapasvinam*—undergoing great austerities and penances; *tvāṣṭram*—the son of Tvaṣṭā; *atha*—as well as; *ātma-vantam*—very independent; *sabhājitaḥ*—being worshiped; *arthān*—the interests; *saḥ*—he; *vidhāsyate*—will execute; *vaḥ*—of all of you; *yadi*—if; *kṣamiṣyadhvam*—you tolerate; *uta*—indeed; *asya*—his; *karma*—activities (to support the Daityas).

TRANSLATION

O demigods, I instruct you to approach Viśvarūpa, the son of Tvaṣṭā, and accept him as your guru. He is a pure and very powerful brāhmaṇa undergoing austerity and penances. Pleased by your worship, he will fulfill your desires, provided that you tolerate his being inclined to side with the demons.

PURPORT

Lord Brahmā advised the demigods to accept the son of Tvaṣṭā as their spiritual master although he was always inclined toward the benefit of the *asuras.*

TEXT 26

श्रीशुक उवाच
त एवमुदिता राजन् ब्रह्मणा विगतज्वराः ।
ऋषिं त्वाष्ट्रमुपव्रज्य परिष्वज्येदमब्रुवन् ॥ २६ ॥

śrī-śuka uvāca
ta evam uditā rājan
brahmaṇā vigata-jvarāḥ
ṛṣiṁ tvāṣṭram upavrajya
pariṣvajyedam abruvan

śrī-śukaḥ uvāca—Śukadeva Gosvāmī said; *te*—all the demigods; *evam*—thus; *uditāḥ*—being advised; *rājan*—O King Parīkṣit; *brahmaṇā*—by Lord Brahmā; *vigata-jvarāḥ*—being relieved from the aggrievement caused by the demons; *ṛṣim*—the great sage; *tvāṣṭram*—to the son of Tvaṣṭā; *upavrajya*—going; *pariṣvajya*—embracing; *idam*—this; *abruvan*—spoke.

TRANSLATION

Śrīla Śukadeva Gosvāmī continued: Thus advised by Lord Brahmā and relieved of their anxiety, all the demigods went to the sage Viśvarūpa, the son of Tvaṣṭā. My dear King, they embraced him and spoke as follows.

TEXT 27

श्रीदेवा ऊचुः
वयं तेऽतिथयः प्राप्ता आश्रमं भद्रमस्तु ते ।
कामः सम्पाद्यतां तात पितॄणां समयोचितः ॥ २७ ॥

śrī-devā ūcuḥ
vayaṁ te'tithayaḥ prāptā
āśramaṁ bhadram astu te
kāmaḥ sampādyatāṁ tāta
pitṝṇāṁ samayocitaḥ

śrī-devāḥ ūcuḥ—the demigods said; *vayam*—we; *te*—your; *atithayaḥ*—guests; *prāptāḥ*—arrived at; *āśramam*—your abode; *bhadram*—good fortune; *astu*—let there be; *te*—unto you; *kāmaḥ*—the desire; *sampādyatām*—let it be executed; *tāta*—O darling; *pitṝṇām*—of us, who are just like your fathers; *samayocitaḥ*—suitable to the present time.

TRANSLATION

The demigods said: Beloved Viśvarūpa, may there be all good fortune for you. We, the demigods, have come to your āśrama as your guests. Please try to fulfill our desires according to the time, since we are on the level of your parents.

TEXT 28

पुत्राणां हि परो धर्मः पितृशुश्रूषणं सताम् ।
अपि पुत्रवतां ब्रह्मन् किमुत ब्रह्मचारिणाम् ॥ २८ ॥

putrāṇāṁ hi paro dharmaḥ
pitṛ-śuśrūṣaṇaṁ satām
api putravatāṁ brahman
kim uta brahmacāriṇām

putrāṇām—of sons; *hi*—indeed; *paraḥ*—superior; *dharmaḥ*—religious principle; *pitṛ-śuśrūṣaṇam*—the service of the parents; *satām*—good; *api*—even; *putra-vatām*—of those who have sons; *brahman*—O dear *brāhmaṇa; kim uta*—what to speak; *brahmacāriṇām*—of *brahmacārīs.*

TRANSLATION

O brāhmaṇa, the highest duty of a son, even though he has sons of his own, is to serve his parents, and what to speak of a son who is abrahmacārī?

TEXTS 29–30

आचार्यो ब्रह्मणो मूर्तिः पिता मूर्तिः प्रजापतेः ।
भ्राता मरुत्पतेर्मूर्तिर्माता साक्षात् क्षितेस्तनुः ॥ २९ ॥
दयाया भगिनी मूर्तिर्धर्मस्यात्मातिथिः स्वयम् ।
अग्नेरभ्यागतो मूर्तिः सर्वभूतानि चात्मनः ॥ ३० ॥

ācāryo brahmaṇo mūrtiḥ
pitā mūrtiḥ prajāpateḥ

bhrātā marutpater mūrtir
mātā sākṣāt kṣites tanuḥ

dayāyā bhaginī mūrtir
dharmasyātmātithiḥ svayam
agner abhyāgato mūrtiḥ
sarva-bhūtāni cātmanaḥ

ācāryaḥ—the teacher or spiritual master who instructs Vedic knowledge by his personal behavior; *brahmaṇaḥ*—of all the *Vedas; mūrtiḥ*—the personification; *pitā*—the father; *mūrtiḥ*—the personification; *prajāpateḥ*—of Lord Brahmā; *bhrātā*—the brother; *marut-pateḥ mūrtiḥ*—the personification of Indra; *mātā*—the mother; *sākṣāt*—directly; *kṣiteḥ*—of the earth; *tanuḥ*—the body; *dayāyāḥ*—of mercy; *bhaginī*—the sister; *mūrtiḥ*—the personification; *dharmasya*—of religious principles; *ātma*—the self; *atithiḥ*—the guest; *svayam*—personally; *agneḥ*—of the fire-god; *abhyāgataḥ*—the invited guest; *mūrtiḥ*—the personification; *sarva-bhūtāni*—all living entities; *ca*—and; *ātmanaḥ*—of the Supreme Lord Viṣṇu.

TRANSLATION

The ācārya, the spiritual master who teaches all the Vedic knowledge and gives initiation by offering the sacred thread, is the personification of all the Vedas. Similarly, a father personifies Lord Brahmā; a brother, King Indra; a mother, the planet earth; and a sister, mercy. A guest personifies religious principles, an invited guest personifies the demigod Agni, and all living entities personify Lord Viṣṇu, the Supreme Personality of Godhead.

PURPORT

According to the moral instructions of Cāṇakya Paṇḍita, *ātmavat sarva-bhūteṣu:* one should observe all living entities to be on the same level as oneself. This means that no one should be neglected as inferior; because Paramātmā is seated in everyone's body, everyone should be respected as a temple of the Supreme Personality of Godhead. This verse describes the different ways in which one should respect a *guru,* a father, a brother, a sister, a guest and so on.

TEXT 31

तस्मात् पितॄणामार्तानामार्तिं परपराभवम् ।
तपसापनयंस्तात सन्देशं कर्तुमर्हसि ॥ ३१ ॥

tasmāt pitṝṇām ārtānām
ārtiṁ para-parābhavam
tapasāpanayaṁs tāta
sandeśaṁ kartum arhasi

tasmāt—therefore; *pitṝṇām*—of the parents; *ārtānām*—who are in distress; *ārtim*—the grief; *para-parābhavam*—being defeated by the enemies; *tapasā*—by the strength of your austerities; *apanayan*—taking away; *tāta*—O dear son; *sandeśam*—our desire; *kartum arhasi*—you deserve to execute.

TRANSLATION

Dear son, we have been defeated by our enemies, and therefore we are very much aggrieved. Please mercifully fulfill our desires by relieving our distress through the strength of your austerities. Please fulfill our prayers.

TEXT 32

वृणीमहे त्वोपाध्यायं ब्रह्मिष्ठं ब्राह्मणं गुरुम् ।
यथाञ्जसा विजेष्यामः सपत्नांस्तव तेजसा ॥ ३२ ॥

vṛṇīmahe tvopādhyāyaṁ
brahmiṣṭhaṁ brāhmaṇaṁ gurum
yathāñjasā vijeṣyāmaḥ
sapatnāṁs tava tejasā

vṛṇīmahe—we choose; *tvā*—you; *upādhyāyam*—as teacher and spiritual master; *brahmiṣṭham*—being perfectly aware of the Supreme Brahman; *brāhmaṇam*—a qualified *brāhmaṇa; gurum*—the perfect spiritual master; *yathā*—so that; *añjasā*—very easily; *vijeṣyāmaḥ*—we shall defeat; *sapatnān*—our rivals; *tava*—your; *tejasā*—by the power of austerity.

TRANSLATION

Since you are completely aware of the Supreme Brahman, you are a perfect brāhmaṇa, and therefore you are the spiritual master of all orders of life. We accept you as our spiritual master and director so that by the power of your austerity we may easily defeat the enemies who have conquered us.

PURPORT

One must approach a particular type of *guru* to execute a particular type of duty. Therefore although Viśvarūpa was inferior to the demigods, the demigods accepted him as their *guru* to conquer the demons.

TEXT 33

न गर्हयन्ति ह्यर्थेषु यविष्ठाङ्घ्र्यभिवादनम् ।
छन्दोभ्योऽन्यत्र न ब्रह्मन् वयो ज्यैष्ठ्यस्य कारणम् ॥ ३३ ॥

na garhayanti hy artheṣu
yaviṣṭhāṅghry-abhivādanam
chandobhyo'nyatra na brahman
vayo jyaiṣṭhyasya kāraṇam

na—not; *garhayanti*—forbid; *hi*—indeed; *artheṣu*—in acquiring interests; *yaviṣṭha-aṅghri*—at the lotus feet of a junior; *abhivādanam*—offering obeisances; *chandobhyaḥ*—the Vedic *mantras; anyatra*—apart from; *na*—not; *brahman*—O *brāhmaṇa; vayaḥ*—age; *jyaiṣṭhyasya*—of seniority; *kāraṇam*—the cause.

TRANSLATION

The demigods continued: Do not fear criticism for being younger than us. Such etiquette does not apply in regard to Vedic mantras. Except in relationship to Vedic mantras, seniority is determined by age, but one may offer respectful obeisances even to a younger person who is advanced in chanting Vedic mantras. Therefore although you are junior in relationship to us, you may become our priest without hesitation.

PURPORT

It is said, *vṛddhatvaṁ vayasā vinā:* one may be senior without being advanced in age. Even if one is not old, one gains seniority if he is senior in knowledge. Viśvarūpa was junior in relationship to the demigods because he was their nephew, but the demigods wanted to accept him as their priest, and therefore he would have to accept obeisances from them. The demigods explained that this should not be a cause for hesitation; he could become their priest because he was advanced in Vedic knowledge. Similarly, Cāṇakya Paṇḍita advises, *nīcād apy uttamaṁ jñānam:* one may accept education from a member of a lower social order. The *brāhmaṇas,* the members of the most elevated *varṇa,* are teachers, but a person in a lower family, such as a family of *kṣatriyas, vaiśyas* or even *śūdras,* may be accepted as a teacher if he has knowledge. Śrī Caitanya Mahāprabhu approved of this when He expressed this opinion before Rāmānanda Rāya (*Cc. Madhya* 8.128):

kibā vipra, kibā nyāsī, śūdra kene naya
yei kṛṣṇa-tattva-vettā, sei'guru' haya

It does not matter whether one is a *brāhmaṇa, śūdra, gṛhastha* or *sannyāsī.* These are all material designations. A spiritually advanced person has nothing to do with such designations. Therefore, if one is advanced in the science of Kṛṣṇa consciousness, regardless of his position in human society, he may become a spiritual master.

TEXT 34

श्रीऋषिरुवाच
अभ्यर्थितः सुरगणैः पौरहित्ये महातपाः ।
स विश्वरूपस्तानाह प्रसन्नः श्लक्ष्णया गिरा ॥ ३४॥

śrī-ṛṣir uvāca
abhyarthitaḥ sura-gaṇaiḥ
paurahitye mahā-tapāḥ
sa viśvarūpas tān āha
prasannaḥ ślakṣṇayā girā

śrī-ṛṣiḥ uvāca—Śukadeva Gosvāmī continued to speak; *abhyarthitaḥ*—being requested; *sura-gaṇaiḥ*—by the demigods; *paurahitye*—in accepting the priesthood; *mahā-tapāḥ*—highly advanced in austerity and penances; *saḥ*—he; *viśvarūpaḥ*—Viśvarūpa; *tān*—to the demigods; *āha*—spoke; *prasannaḥ*—being satisfied; *ślakṣṇayā*—sweet; *girā*—with words.

TRANSLATION

Śukadeva Gosvāmī continued: When all the demigods requested the great Viśvarūpa to be their priest, Viśvarūpa, who was advanced in austerities, was very pleased. He replied to them as follows.

TEXT 35

श्रीविश्वरूप उवाच
विगर्हितं धर्मशीलैर्ब्रह्मवर्चउपव्ययम् ।
कथं नु मद्विधो नाथा लोकेशैरभियाचितम् ।
प्रत्याख्यास्यति तच्छिष्यः स एव स्वार्थ उच्यते ॥ ३५॥

śrī-viśvarūpa uvāca
vigarhitaṁ dharma-śīlair
brahmavarca-upavyayam
kathaṁ nu mad-vidho nāthā
lokeśair abhiyācitam
pratyākhyāsyati tac-chiṣyaḥ
sa eva svārtha ucyate

śrī-viśvarūpaḥ uvāca—Śrī Viśvarūpa said; *vigarhitam*—condemned; *dharma-śīlaiḥ*—by persons respectful to the religious principles; *brahma-varcaḥ*—of brahminical strength or power; *upavyayam*—causes loss; *katham*—how; *nu*—indeed; *mat-vidhaḥ*—a person like me; *nāthāḥ*—O lords; *loka-īśaiḥ*—by the ruling powers of different planets; *abhiyācitam*—request; *pratyākhyāsyati*—will refuse; *tat-śiṣyaḥ*—who is on the level of their disciple; *saḥ*—that; *eva*—indeed; *sva-arthaḥ*—real interest; *ucyate*—is described as.

TRANSLATION

Śrī Viśvarūpa said: O demigods, although the acceptance of priesthood is decried as causing the loss of previously acquired brahminical power, how can someone like me refuse to accept your personal request? You are all exalted commanders of the entire universe. I am your disciple and must take many lessons from you. Therefore I cannot refuse you. I must agree for my own benefit.

PURPORT

The professions of a qualified *brāhmaṇa* are *paṭhana, pāṭhana, yajana, yājana, dāna* and *pratigraha.* The words *yajana* and *yājana* mean that a *brāhmaṇa* becomes the priest of the populace for the sake of their elevation. One who accepts the post of spiritual master neutralizes the sinful reactions of the *yajamāna,* the one on whose behalf he performs *yajña.* Thus the results of the pious acts previously performed by the priest or spiritual master are diminished. Therefore priesthood is not accepted by learned *brāhmaṇas.* Nevertheless, the greatly learned *brāhmaṇa* Viśvarūpa became the priest of the demigods because of his profound respect for them.

TEXT 36

अकिञ्चनानां हि धनं शिलोञ्छनं
तेनेह निर्वर्तितसाधुसत्क्रियः ।

कथं विगर्ह्यं नु करोम्यधीश्वराः
पौरोधसं हृष्यति येन दुर्मतिः ॥ ३६ ॥

akiñcanānāṁ hi dhanaṁ śiloñchanaṁ
teneha nirvartita-sādhu-satkriyaḥ
kathaṁ vigarhyaṁ nu karomy adhīśvarāḥ
paurodhasaṁ hṛṣyati yena durmatiḥ

akiñcanānām—of persons who have taken to austerities and penances to become detached from worldly possessions; *hi*—certainly; *dhanam*—the wealth; *śila*—the collecting of grains left in the field; *uñchanam*—and the collecting of grains left in the wholesale marketplace; *tena*—by that means; *iha*—here; *nirvartita*—accomplishing; *sādhu*—of the exalted devotees; *sat-kriyaḥ*—all the pious activities; *katham*—how; *vigarhyam*—reproachable; *nu*—indeed; *karomi*—I shall execute; *adhīśvarāḥ*—O great governors of the planetary systems; *paurodhasam*—the duty of priesthood; *hṛṣyati*—is pleased; *yena*—by which; *durmatiḥ*—one who is less intelligent.

TRANSLATION

O exalted governors of various planets, the true brāhmaṇa, who has no material possessions, maintains himself by the profession of accepting śiloñchana. In other words, he picks up grains left in the field and on the ground in the wholesale marketplace. By this means, householder brāhmaṇas who actually abide by the principles of austerity and penance maintain themselves and their families and perform all necessary pious activities. A brāhmaṇa who desires to achieve happiness by gaining wealth through professional priesthood must certainly have a very low mind. How shall I accept such priesthood?

PURPORT

A first-class *brāhmaṇa* does not accept any rewards from his disciples or *yajamānas.* Practicing austerities and penances, he instead goes to the agricultural field and collects food grains left by the agriculturalists to be collected by *brāhmaṇas.* Similarly, such *brāhmaṇas* go to marketplaces where grains are purchased and sold wholesale, and there they collect grains left by the merchants. In this way, such exalted *brāhmaṇas* maintain their bodies and families. Such priests never demand anything from their disciples to live in opulence, imitating *kṣatriyas* or *vaiśyas.* In other words, a pure *brāhmaṇa* voluntarily accepts a life of poverty and lives in complete dependence on the mercy of the Lord. Not very many years ago, a *brāhmaṇa* in Kṛṣṇanagara, near Navadvīpa, was offered some help from the local Zamindar, Vraja Kṛṣṇacandra. The *brāhmaṇa* refused to accept the help. He said that since he was very happy in his householder life, taking rice given by his disciples and cooking vegetables of tamarind leaves, there was no question of taking help from the Zamindar. The conclusion is that although a *brāhmaṇa* may receive much opulence from his disciples, he should not utilize the rewards of his priesthood for his personal benefit; he must use them for the service of the Supreme Personality of Godhead.

TEXT 37

तथापि न प्रतिब्रूयां गुरुभिः प्रार्थितं कियत् ।
भवतां प्रार्थितं सर्वं प्राणैरर्थैश्च साधये ॥ ३७ ॥

tathāpi na pratibrūyāṁ
gurubhiḥ prārthitaṁ kiyat
bhavatāṁ prārthitaṁ sarvaṁ
prāṇair arthaiś ca sādhaye

tathā api—still; *na*—not; *pratibrūyām*—I may refuse; *gurubhiḥ*—by persons on the level of my spiritual master; *prārthitam*—request; *kiyat*—of small value; *bhavatām*—of all of you; *prārthitam*—the desire; *sarvam*—whole; *prāṇaiḥ*—by my life; *arthaiḥ*—by my possessions; *ca*—also; *sādhaye*—I shall execute.

TRANSLATION

All of you are my superiors. Therefore although accepting priesthood is sometimes reproachable, I cannot refuse even a small request from you. I agree to be your priest. I shall fulfill your request by dedicating my life and possessions.

TEXT 38

श्रीबादरायणिरुवाच
तेभ्य एवं प्रतिश्रुत्य विश्वरूपो महातपाः ।
पौरहित्यं वृतश्चक्रे परमेण समाधिना ॥ ३८ ॥

śrī-bādarāyaṇir uvāca
tebhya evaṁ pratiśrutya
viśvarūpo mahā-tapāḥ

paurahityaṁ vṛtaś cakre
parameṇa samādhinā

śrī-bādarāyaṇiḥ uvāca—Śrī Śukadeva Gosvāmī said; *tebhyaḥ*—unto them (the demigods); *evam*—thus; *pratiśrutya*—promising; *viśvarūpaḥ*—Viśvarūpa; *mahā-tapāḥ*—the most exalted personality; *paurahityam*—the priesthood; *vṛtaḥ*—surrounded by them; *cakre*—executed; *parameṇa*—supreme; *samādhinā*—with attention.

TRANSLATION

Śrī Śukadeva Gosvāmī continued: O King, after making this promise to the demigods, the exalted Viśvarūpa, surrounded by the demigods, performed the necessary priestly activities with great enthusiasm and attention.

PURPORT

The word *samādhinā* is very important. *Samādhi* means complete absorption with an undiverted mind. Viśvarūpa, who was a most learned *brāhmaṇa,* not only accepted the request of the demigods, but took their request seriously and performed the activities of priesthood with an undiverted mind. In other words, he accepted the priesthood not for material gain, but to profit the demigods. Such is the duty of a priest. The word *puraḥ* means "family," and *hita* means "benefit." Thus the word *purohita* indicates that the priest is the well-wisher of the family. Another meaning of the word *puraḥ* is "first." A priest's first duty is to see that his disciples benefit spiritually and materially by all means. Then he is satisfied. A priest should never be interested in performing Vedic rituals for his personal benefit.

TEXT 39

सुरद्विषां श्रियं गुप्तामौशनस्यापि विद्यया ।
आच्छिद्यादान्महेन्द्राय वैष्णव्या विद्यया विभुः ॥ ३९ ॥

sura-dviṣāṁ śriyaṁ guptām
auśanasyāpi vidyayā
ācchidyādān mahendrāya
vaiṣṇavyā vidyayā vibhuḥ

sura-dviṣām—of the enemies of the demigods; *śriyam*—the opulence; *guptām*—protected; *auśanasya*—of Śukrācārya; *api*—although; *vidyayā*—

by the talents; *ācchidya*—collecting; *adāt*—delivered; *mahā-indrāya*—unto King Indra; *vaiṣṇavyā*—of Lord Viṣṇu; *vidyayā*—by a prayer; *vibhuḥ*—the most powerful Viśvarūpa.

TRANSLATION

The opulence of the demons, who are generally known as the enemies of the demigods, was protected by the talents and tactics of Śukrācārya, but Viśvarūpa, who was most powerful, composed a protective prayer known as the Nārāyaṇa-kavaca. By this intelligent mantra, he took away the opulence of the demons and gave it to Mahendra, the King of heaven.

PURPORT

The distinction between the demigods (*devas*) and demons (*asuras*) is that the demigods are all devotees of Lord Viṣṇu whereas the demons are devotees of demigods like Lord Śiva, Goddess Kālī and Goddess Durgā. Sometimes the demons are also devotees of Lord Brahmā. For example, Hiraṇyakaśipu was a devotee of Lord Brahmā, Rāvaṇa was a devotee of Lord Śiva, and Mahiṣāsura was a devotee of Goddess Durgā. The demigods are devotees of Lord Viṣṇu (*viṣṇu-bhaktaḥ smṛto daiva*), whereas the demons (*āsuras tad-viparyayaḥ*) are always against the *viṣṇu-bhaktas,* or Vaiṣṇavas. To oppose the Vaiṣṇavas, the demons become devotees of Lord Śiva, Lord Brahmā, Kālī, Durgā, and so on. In the days of yore, many long years ago, there was animosity between the *devas* and the *asuras,* and the same spirit still continues, for the devotees of Lord Śiva and Goddess Durgā are always envious of Vaiṣṇavas, who are devotees of Lord Viṣṇu. This strain between the devotees of Lord Śiva and Lord Viṣṇu has always existed. In the higher planetary systems, fights between the demons and the demigods continue for a long, long time.

Herein we see that Viśvarūpa made for the demigods a protective covering, saturated with a Viṣṇu *mantra.* Sometimes the Viṣṇu *mantra* is called Viṣṇu-jvara, and the Śiva *mantra* is called Śiva-jvara. We find in the *śāstras* that sometimes the Śiva-jvara and Viṣṇu-jvara are employed in the fights between the demons and the demigods.

The word *sura-dviṣām,* which in this verse means "of the enemies of the demigods," also refers to the atheists. *Śrīmad-Bhāgavatam* elsewhere says that Lord Buddha appeared for the purpose of bewildering the demons or atheists. The Supreme Personality of Godhead always awards His benediction to devotees. The Lord Himself confirms this in *Bhagavad-gītā* (9.31):

kaunteya pratijānīhi
na me bhaktaḥ praṇaśyati

"O son of Kuntī, declare it boldly that My devotee never perishes."

TEXT 40

यया गुप्तः सहस्राक्षो जिग्येऽसुरचमूर्विभुः ।
तां प्राह स महेन्द्राय विश्वरूप उदारधीः ॥ ४० ॥

yayā guptaḥ sahasrākṣo
jigye'sura-camūr vibhuḥ
tāṁ prāha sa mahendrāya
viśvarūpa udāra-dhīḥ

yayā—by which; *guptaḥ*—protected; *sahasra-akṣaḥ*—the thousand-eyed demigod, Indra; *jigye*—conquered; *asura*—of the demons; *camūḥ*—military power; *vibhuḥ*—becoming very powerful; *tām*—that; *prāha*—spoke; *saḥ*—he; *mahendrāya*—unto the King of heaven, Mahendra; *viśvarūpaḥ*—Viśvarūpa; *udāra-dhīḥ*—very broad-minded.

TRANSLATION

Viśvarūpa, who was most liberal, spoke to King Indra [Sahasrākṣa] the secret hymn that protected Indra and conquered the military power of the demons.

Thus end the Bhaktivedanta purports to the Sixth Canto, Seventh Chapter, of the Śrīmad-Bhāgavatam, *entitled "Indra Offends His Spiritual Master, Bṛhaspati."*

CHAPTER EIGHT

The Nārāyaṇa-kavaca Shield

This chapter describes how Indra, the King of heaven, was victorious over the soldiers of the demons, and it also describes the shield of the Viṣṇu *mantra.*

To take protection from this shield, one must first touch *kuśa* grass and wash one's mouth with *ācamana-mantras.* One should observe silence and then place the eight-syllable Viṣṇu *mantra* on the parts of his body and place the twelve-syllable *mantra* on his hands. The eight-syllable *mantra* is *oṁ namo nārāyaṇāya.* This *mantra* should be distributed all over the front and back of the body. The twelve-syllable *mantra,* which begins with the *praṇava, oṁkāra,* is *oṁ namo bhagavate vāsudevāya.* One syllable should be placed on each of the fingers and should be preceded by the *praṇava, oṁkāra.* Thereafter, one must chant *oṁ viṣṇave namaḥ,* which is a six-syllable *mantra.* One must progressively place the syllables of the *mantra* on the heart, the head, between the two eyebrows, on the *śikhā* and between the eyes, and then one should chant *maḥ astrāya phaṭ* and with this *mantra* protect himself from all directions. *Nādevo devam arcayet:* one who has not risen to the level of a *deva* cannot chant this *mantra.* According to this direction of the *śāstra,* one must think himself qualitatively nondifferent from the Supreme.

After finishing this dedication, one must offer a prayer to the eight-armed Lord Viṣṇu, who sits on the shoulders of Garuḍadeva. One also has to think of the fish incarnation, Vāmana, Kūrma, Nṛsiṁha, Varāha, Paraśurāma, Rāmacandra (the elder brother of Lakṣmaṇa), Nara-Nārāyaṇa, Dattātreya (an empowered incarnation), Kapila, Sanat-kumāra, Hayagrīva, Nārada-deva (the incarnation of a devotee), Dhanvantari, Ṛṣabha-deva, Yajña, Balarāma, Vyāsadeva, Buddhadeva and Keśava. One should also think of Govinda, the master of Vṛndāvana, and one should think of Nārāyaṇa, the master of the spiritual sky. One should think of Madhusūdana, Tridhāmā, Mādhava, Hṛṣīkeśa, Padmanābha, Janārdana, Dāmodara and Viśveśvara, as well as the Supreme Personality of Godhead Kṛṣṇa Himself. After offering prayers to the Lord's personal expansions known as the *svāṁśa* and *śaktyāveśa-avatāras,* one should pray to the weapons of Lord Nārāyaṇa, such as the Sudarśana, *gadā, śaṅkha, khaḍga* and bow.

After explaining this process, Śukadeva Gosvāmī told Mahārāja Parīkṣit how Viśvarūpa, the brother of Vṛtrāsura, described the glories of the Nārāyaṇa-kavaca to Indra.

TEXTS 1–2

श्रीराजोवाच
यया गुप्तः सहस्त्राक्षः सवाहान् रिपुसैनिकान् ।
क्रीडन्निव विनिर्जित्य त्रिलोक्या बुभुजे श्रियम् ॥ १ ॥
भगवंस्तन्ममाख्याहि वर्म नारायणात्मकम् ।
यथाततायिनः शत्रून् येन गुप्तोऽजयन्मृधे ॥ २ ॥

śrī-rājovāca
yayā guptaḥ sahasrākṣaḥ
savāhān ripu-sainikān
krīḍann iva vinirjitya
tri-lokyā bubhuje śriyam

bhagavaṁs tan mamākhyāhi
varma nārāyaṇātmakam
yathātatāyinaḥ śatrūn
yena gupto'jayan mṛdhe

śrī-rājā uvāca—King Parīkṣit said; *yayā*—by which (the spiritual armor); *guptaḥ*—protected; *sahasra-akṣaḥ*—the thousand-eyed King Indra; *sa-vāhān*—with their carriers; *ripu-sainikān*—the soldiers and commanders of the enemies; *krīḍan iva*—just like playing; *vinirjitya*—conquering; *tri-lokyāḥ*—of the three worlds (the higher, middle and lower planetary systems); *bubhuje*—enjoyed; *śriyam*—the opulence; *bhagavan*—O great sage; *tat*—that; *mama*—unto me; *ākhyāhi*—please explain; *varma*—defensive armor made of a *mantra; nārāyaṇa-ātmakam*—consisting of the mercy of Nārāyaṇa; *yathā*—in which way; *ātatāyinaḥ*—who were endeavoring to kill him; *śatrūn*—enemies; *yena*—by which; *guptaḥ*—being protected; *ajayat*—conquered; *mṛdhe*—in the fight.

TRANSLATION

King Parīkṣit inquired from Śukadeva Gosvāmī: My lord, kindly explain the Viṣṇu mantra armor that protected King Indra and enabled him to conquer his enemies, along with their carriers, and enjoy the opulence of the three worlds. Please explain to me that Nārāyaṇa armor, by which King Indra achieved success in battle, conquering the enemies who were endeavoring to kill him.

TEXT 3

श्रीबादरायणिरुवाच
वृतः पुरोहितस्त्वाष्ट्रो महेन्द्रायानुपृच्छते ।
नारायणाख्यं वर्माह तदिहैकमनाः शृणु ॥ ३ ॥

śrī-bādarāyaṇir uvāca
vṛtaḥ purohitas tvāṣṭro
mahendrāyānupṛcchate
nārāyaṇākhyaṁ varmāha
tad ihaika-manāḥ śṛṇu

śrī-bādarāyaṇiḥ uvāca—Śrī Śukadeva Gosvāmī said; *vṛtaḥ*—the chosen; *purohitaḥ*—priest; *tvāṣṭraḥ*—the son of Tvaṣṭā; *mahendrāya*—unto King Indra; *anupṛcchate*—after he (Indra) inquired; *nārāyaṇa-ākhyam*—named Nārāyaṇa-kavaca; *varma*—defensive armor made of a *mantra; āha*—he said; *tat*—that; *iha*—this; *eka-manāḥ*—with great attention; *śṛṇu*—hear from me.

TRANSLATION

Śrī Śukadeva Gosvāmī said: King Indra, the leader of the demigods, inquired about the armor known as Nārāyaṇa-kavaca from Viśvarūpa, who was engaged by the demigods as their priest. Please hear Viśvarūpa's reply with great attention.

TEXTS 4–6

श्रीविश्वरूप उवाच
धौताङ्घ्रिपाणिराचम्य सपवित्र उदङ्मुखः ।
कृतस्वाङ्गकरन्यासो मन्त्राभ्यां वाग्यतः शुचिः ॥ ४ ॥
नारायणपरं वर्म सन्नह्येद् भय आगते ।
पादयोर्जानुनोरूर्वोरुदरे हृद्यथोरसि ॥ ५ ॥
मुखे शिरस्यानुपूर्व्यादोङ्कारादीनि विन्यसेत् ।
ॐ नमो नारायणायेति विपर्ययमथापि वा ॥ ६ ॥

śrī-viśvarūpa uvāca
dhautāṅghri-pāṇir ācamya
sapavitra udaṅ-mukhaḥ
kṛta-svāṅga-kara-nyāso
mantrābhyāṁ vāg-yataḥ śuciḥ

nārāyaṇa-paraṁ varma
sannahyed bhaya āgate
pādayor jānunor ūrvor
udare hṛdy athorasi

mukhe śirasy ānupūrvyād
oṁkārādīni vinyaset
oṁ namo nārāyaṇāyeti
viparyayam athāpi vā

śrī-viśvarūpaḥ uvāca—Śrī Viśvarūpa said; *dhauta*—having completely washed; *aṅghri*—feet; *pāṇiḥ*—hands; *ācamya*—performing *ācamana* (sipping a little water three times after chanting the prescribed *mantra*); *sa-pavitraḥ*—wearing rings made of *kuśa* grass (on the ring finger of each hand); *udak-mukhaḥ*—sitting facing the north; *kṛta*—making; *sva-aṅga-kara-nyāsaḥ*—mental assignment of the eight parts of the body and twelve parts of the hands; *mantrābhyām*—with the two *mantras* (*oṁ namo bhagavate vāsudevāya* and *oṁ namo nārāyaṇāya*); *vāk-yataḥ*—keeping oneself silent; *śuciḥ*—being purified; *nārāyaṇa-param*—fully intent on Lord Nārāyaṇa; *varma*—armor; *sannahyet*—put on oneself; *bhaye*—when fear; *āgate*—has come; *pādayoḥ*—on the two legs; *jānunoḥ*—on the two knees; *ūrvoḥ*—on the two thighs; *udare*—on the abdomen; *hṛdi*—on the heart; *atha*—thus; *urasi*—on the chest; *mukhe*—on the mouth; *śirasi*—on the head; *ānupūrvyāt*—one after another; *oṁkāra-ādīni*—beginning with *oṁkāra; vinyaset*—one should place; *oṁ*—the *praṇava; namaḥ*—obeisances; *nārāyaṇāya*—unto Nārāyaṇa, the Supreme Personality of Godhead; *iti*—thus; *viparyayam*—the reverse; *atha api*—moreover; *vā*—or.

TRANSLATION

Viśvarūpa said: If some form of fear arrives, one should first wash his hands and legs clean and then perform ācamana by chanting this mantra: oṁ apavitraḥ pavitro vā sarvāvasthāṁ gato'pi vā/ yaḥ smaret puṇḍarīkākṣaṁ sa bahyābhyantaraḥ śuciḥ/ śrī-viṣṇu śrī-viṣṇu śrī-viṣṇu. Then one should touch kuśa grass and sit gravely and silently, facing north. When completely purified, one should touch the mantra composed of eight syllables to the eight parts of his body and touch the mantra composed of twelve syllables to his hands. Thus, in the following manner, he should bind himself with the Nārāyaṇa coat of armor. First, while

chanting the mantra composed of eight syllables [oṁ namo nārāyaṇāya], beginning with the praṇava, the syllable oṁ, one should touch his hands to eight parts of his body, starting with the two feet and progressing systematically to the knees, thighs, abdomen, heart, chest, mouth and head. Then one should chant the mantra in reverse, beginning from the last syllable [ya], while touching the parts of his body in the reverse order. These two processes are known as utpatti-nyāsa and saṁhāra-nyāsa respectively.

TEXT 7

करन्यासं ततः कुर्याद् द्वादशाक्षरविद्यया ।
प्रणवादियकारान्तमङ्गुल्यङ्गुष्ठपर्वसु ॥ ७ ॥

kara-nyāsaṁ tataḥ kuryād
dvādaśākṣara-vidyayā
praṇavādi-ya-kārāntam
aṅguly-aṅguṣṭha-parvasu

kara-nyāsam—the ritual known as *kara-nyāsa,* which assigns the syllables of the *mantra* to the fingers; *tataḥ*—thereafter; *kuryāt*—should execute; *dvādaśa-akṣara*—composed of twelve syllables; *vidyayā*—with the *mantra; praṇava-ādi*—beginning with the *oṁkāra; ya-kāra-antam*—ending with the syllable *ya; aṅguli*—on the fingers, beginning with the index finger; *aṅguṣṭha-parvasu*—to the joints of the thumbs.

TRANSLATION

Then one should chant the mantra composed of twelve syllables [oṁ namo bhagavate vāsudevāya]. Preceding each syllable by the oṁkāra, one should place the syllables of the mantra on the tips of his fingers, beginning with the index finger of the right hand and concluding with the index finger of the left. The four remaining syllables should be placed on the joints of the thumbs.

TEXTS 8–10

न्यसेद्धृदय ओङ्कारं विकारमनु मूर्धनि ।
षकारं तु भ्रुवोर्मध्ये णकारं शिखया न्यसेत् ॥ ८ ॥
वेकारं नेत्रयोर्युञ्ज्यान्नकारं सर्वसन्धिषु ।
मकारमस्त्रमुद्दिश्य मन्त्रमूर्तिर्भवेद् बुधः ॥ ९ ॥

सविसर्गं फडन्तं तत् सर्वदिक्षु विनिर्दिशेत् ।
ॐ विष्णवे नम इति ॥ १० ॥

nyased dhṛdaya oṁkāraṁ
vi-kāram anu mūrdhani
ṣa-kāraṁ tu bhruvor madhye
ṇa-kāraṁ śikhayā nyaset

ve-kāraṁ netrayor yuñjyān
na-kāraṁ sarva-sandhiṣu
ma-kāram astram uddiśya
mantra-mūrtir bhaved budhaḥ

savisargaṁ phaḍ-antaṁ tat
sarva-dikṣu vinirdiśet
oṁ viṣṇave nama iti

nyaset—should place; *hṛdaye*—on the heart; *oṁkāram*—the *praṇava, oṁkāra; vi-kāram*—the syllable *vi* of *viṣṇave; anu*—thereafter; *mūrdhani*—on the top of the head; *ṣa-kāram*—the syllable *ṣa; tu*—and; *bhruvoḥ madhye*—between the two eyebrows; *ṇa-kāram*—the syllable *ṇa; śikhayā*—on the *śikhā* on the head; *nyaset*—should place; *vekāram*—the syllable *ve; netrayoḥ*—between the two eyes; *yuñjyāt*—should be placed; *na-kāram*—the syllable *na* of the word *namaḥ; sarva-sandhiṣu*—on all the joints; *ma-kāram*—the syllable *ma* of the word *namaḥ; astram*—a weapon; *uddiśya*—thinking; *mantra-mūrtiḥ*—the form of the *mantra; bhavet*—should become; *budhaḥ*—an intelligent person; *sa-visargam*—with the *visarga* (*ḥ*); *phaṭ-antam*—ending with the sound *phaṭ; tat*—that; *sarva-dikṣu*—in all directions; *vinirdiśet*—should fix; *oṁ*—*praṇava; viṣṇave*—unto Lord Viṣṇu; *namaḥ*—obeisances; *iti*—thus.

TRANSLATION

One must then chant the mantra of six syllables [oṁ viṣṇave namaḥ]. One should place the syllable "oṁ" on his heart, the syllable "vi" on the top of his head, the syllable "ṣa" between his eyebrows, the syllable "ṇa" on his tuft of hair [śikhā], and the syllable "ve" between his eyes. The chanter of the mantra should then place the syllable "na" on all the joints of his body and meditate on the syllable "ma" as being a weapon. He should thus become the perfect personification of the mantra. Thereafter, adding

visarga to the final syllable "ma," he should chant the mantra "maḥ astrāya phaṭ" in all directions, beginning from the east. In this way, all directions will be bound by the protective armor of the mantra.

TEXT 11

आत्मानं परमं ध्यायेद् ध्येयं षट्शक्तिभिर्युतम् ।
विद्यातेजस्तपोमूर्तिमिमं मन्त्रमुदाहरेत् ॥ ११ ॥

ātmānaṁ paramaṁ dhyāyed
dhyeyaṁ ṣaṭ-śaktibhir yutam
vidyā-tejas-tapo-mūrtim
imaṁ mantram udāharet

ātmānam—the self; *paramam*—the supreme; *dhyāyet*—one should meditate on; *dhyeyam*—worthy to be meditated on; *ṣaṭ-śaktibhiḥ*—the six opulences; *yutam*—possessed of; *vidyā*—learning; *tejaḥ*—influence; *tapaḥ*—austerity; *mūrtim*—personified; *imam*—this; *mantram*—*mantra; udāharet*—should chant.

TRANSLATION

After finishing this chanting, one should think himself qualitatively one with the Supreme Personality of Godhead, who is full in six opulences and is worthy to be meditated upon. Then one should chant the following protective prayer to Lord Nārāyaṇa, the Nārāyaṇa-kavaca.

TEXT 12

ॐ हरिर्विदध्यान्मम सर्वरक्षां
न्यस्ताङ्घ्रिपद्मः पतगेन्द्रपृष्ठे ।
दरारिचर्मासिगदेषुचाप-
पाशान् दधानोऽष्टगुणोऽष्टबाहुः ॥ १२ ॥

oṁ harir vidadhyān mama sarva-rakṣāṁ
nyastāṅghri-padmaḥ patagendra-pṛṣṭhe
darāri-carmāsi-gadeṣu-cāpa-
pāśān dadhāno 'ṣṭa-guṇo 'ṣṭa-bāhuḥ

oṁ—O Lord; *hariḥ*—the Supreme Personality of Godhead; *vidadhyāt*—may He bestow; *mama*—my; *sarva-rakṣām*—protection from all sides; *nyasta*

—placed; *aṅghri-padmaḥ*—whose lotus feet; *patagendra-pṛṣṭhe*—on the back of Garuḍa, the king of all birds; *dara*—conchshell; *ari*—disc; *carma*—shield; *asi*—sword; *gadā*—club; *iṣu*—arrows; *cāpa*—bow; *pāśān*—ropes; *dadhānaḥ*—holding; *aṣṭa*—possessing eight; *guṇaḥ*—perfections; *aṣṭa*—eight; *bāhuḥ*—arms.

TRANSLATION

The Supreme Lord, who sits on the back of the bird Garuḍa, touching him with His lotus feet, holds eight weapons—the conchshell, disc, shield, sword, club, arrows, bow and ropes. May that Supreme Personality of Godhead protect me at all times with His eight arms. He is all-powerful because He fully possesses the eight mystic powers [aṇimā, laghimā, etc.].

PURPORT

Thinking oneself one with the Supreme is called *ahaṅgrahopāsanā.* Through *ahaṅgrahopāsanā* one does not become God, but he thinks of himself as qualitatively one with the Supreme. Understanding that as a spirit soul he is equal in quality to the supreme soul the way the water of a river is of the same nature as the water of the sea, one should meditate upon the Supreme Lord, as described in this verse, and seek His protection. The living entities are always subordinate to the Supreme. Consequently their duty is to always seek the mercy of the Lord in order to be protected by Him in all circumstances.

TEXT 13

जलेषु मां रक्षतु मत्स्यमूर्ति-
यादोगणेभ्यो वरुणस्य पाशात् ।
स्थलेषु मायावटुवामनोऽव्यात्
त्रिविक्रमः खेऽवतु विश्वरूपः ॥ १३ ॥

jaleṣu māṁ rakṣatu matsya-mūrtir
yādo-gaṇebhyo varuṇasya pāśāt
sthaleṣu māyāvaṭu-vāmano 'vyāt
trivikramaḥ khe 'vatu viśvarūpaḥ

jaleṣu—in the water; *mām*—me; *rakṣatu*—protect; *matsya-mūrtiḥ*—the Supreme Lord in the form of a great fish; *yādaḥ-gaṇebhyaḥ*—from fierce aquatic animals; *varuṇasya*—of the demigod known as Varuṇa; *pāśāt*—from the arresting rope; *sthaleṣu*—on the land; *māyā-vaṭu*—the merciful form of the Lord as a dwarf; *vāmanaḥ*—named Vāmanadeva; *avyāt*—may He protect; *trivikramaḥ*—Trivikrama, whose three gigantic steps took the three worlds from Bali; *khe*—in the sky; *avatu*—may the Lord protect; *viśvarūpaḥ*—the gigantic universal form.

TRANSLATION

May the Lord, who assumes the body of a great fish, protect me in the water from the fierce animals that are associates of the demigod Varuṇa. By expanding His illusory energy, the Lord assumed the form of the dwarf Vāmana. May Vāmana protect me on the land. Since the gigantic form of the Lord, Viśvarūpa, conquers the three worlds, may He protect me in the sky.

PURPORT

This *mantra* seeks the protection of the Supreme Personality of Godhead in the water, land and sky in His incarnations as the fish, Vāmanadeva and the Viśvarūpa.

TEXT 14

दुर्गेष्वटव्याजिमुखादिषु प्रभुः
पायान्नृसिंहोऽसुरयूथपारिः ।
विमुञ्चतो यस्य महाट्टहासं
दिशो विनेदुर्न्यपतंश्च गर्भाः ॥ १४ ॥

durgeṣv aṭavy-āji-mukhādiṣu prabhuḥ
pāyān nṛsiṁho'sura-yūthapāriḥ
vimuñcato yasya mahāṭṭa-hāsaṁ
diśo vinedur nyapataṁś ca garbhāḥ

durgeṣu—in places where travel is very difficult; *aṭavi*—in the dense forest; *āji-mukha-ādiṣu*—on the war front and so on; *prabhuḥ*—the Supreme Lord; *pāyāt*—may He protect; *nṛsiṁhaḥ*—Lord Nṛsiṁhadeva; *asura-yūthapa*—of Hiraṇyakaśipu, the leader of the demons; *ariḥ*—the enemy; *vimuñcataḥ*—releasing; *yasya*—of whom; *mahā-aṭṭa-hāsam*—great and fearful laughing; *diśaḥ*—all the directions; *vineduḥ*—resounded through; *nyapatan*—fell down; *ca*—and; *garbhāḥ*—the embryos of the wives of the demons.

TRANSLATION

May Lord Nṛsiṁhadeva, who appeared as the enemy of Hiraṇyakaśipu, protect me in all directions. His loud laughing vibrated in all directions and caused the pregnant wives of the asuras to have miscarriages. May that Lord be kind enough to protect me in difficult places like the forest and battlefront.

TEXT 15

रक्षत्वसौ माध्वनि यज्ञकल्पः
स्वदंष्ट्रयोन्नीतधरो वराहः ।
रामोऽद्रिकूटेष्वथ विप्रवासे
सलक्ष्मणोऽव्याद् भरताग्रजोऽस्मान् ॥ १५ ॥

rakṣatv asau mādhvani yajña-kalpaḥ
sva-daṁṣṭrayonnīta-dharo varāhaḥ
rāmo'dri-kūṭeṣv atha vipravāse
salakṣmaṇo'vyād bharatāgrajo'smān

rakṣatu—may the Lord protect; *asau*—that; *mā*—me; *adhvani*—on the street; *yajña-kalpaḥ*—who is ascertained by performance of ritualistic ceremonies; *sva-daṁṣṭrayā*—by His own tusk; *unnīta*—raising; *dharaḥ*—the planet earth; *varāhaḥ*—Lord Boar; *rāmaḥ*—Lord Rāma; *adri-kūṭeṣu*—on the summits of the mountains; *atha*—then; *vipravāse*—in foreign countries; *sa-lakṣmaṇaḥ*—with His brother Lakṣmaṇa; *avyāt*—may He protect; *bharata-agrajaḥ*—the elder brother of Mahārāja Bharata; *asmān*—us.

TRANSLATION

The Supreme indestructible Lord is ascertained through the performance of ritualistic sacrifices and is therefore known as Yajñeśvara. In His incarnation as Lord Boar, He raised the planet earth from the water at the bottom of the universe and kept it on His pointed tusks. May that Lord protect me from rogues on the street. May Paraśurāma protect me on the tops of mountains, and may the elder brother of Bharata, Lord Rāmacandra, along with His brother Lakṣmaṇa, protect me in foreign countries.

PURPORT

There are three Rāmas. One Rāma is Paraśurāma (Jāmadāgnya), another

Rāma is Lord Rāmacandra, and a third Rāma is Lord Balarāma. In this verse the words *rāmo 'dri-kūṭeṣv atha* indicate Lord Paraśurāma. The brother of Bharata Mahārāja and Lakṣmaṇa is Lord Rāmacandra.

TEXT 16

मामुग्रधर्मादखिलात् प्रमादा-
न्नारायणः पातु नरश्च हासात् ।
दत्तस्त्वयोगादथ योगनाथः
पायाद्गुणेशः कपिलः कर्मबन्धात् ॥ १६ ॥

mām ugra-dharmād akhilāt pramādān
nārāyaṇaḥ pātu naraś ca hāsāt
dattas tv ayogād atha yoga-nāthaḥ
pāyād guṇeśaḥ kapilaḥ karma-bandhāt

mām—me; *ugra-dharmāt*—from unnecessary religious principles; *akhilāt*—from all kinds of activities; *pramādāt*—which are enacted in madness; *nārāyaṇaḥ*—Lord Nārāyaṇa; *pātu*—may He protect; *naraḥ ca*—and Nara; *hāsāt*—from unnecessary pride; *dattaḥ*—Dattātreya; *tu*—of course; *ayogāt*—from the path of false *yoga; atha*—indeed; *yoga-nāthaḥ*—the master of all mystic powers; *pāyāt*—may He protect; *guṇa-īśaḥ*—the master of all spiritual qualities; *kapilaḥ*—Lord Kapila; *karma-bandhāt*—from the bondage of fruitive activities.

TRANSLATION

May Lord Nārāyaṇa protect me from unnecessarily following false religious systems and falling from my duties due to madness. May the Lord in His appearance as Nara protect me from unnecessary pride. May Lord Dattātreya, the master of all mystic power, protect me from falling while performing bhakti-yoga, and may Lord Kapila, the master of all good qualities, protect me from the material bondage of fruitive activities.

TEXT 17

सनत्कुमारोऽवतु कामदेवा-
द्धयशीर्षा मां पथि देवहेलनात् ।
देवर्षिवर्यः पुरुषार्चनान्तरात्
कूर्मो हरिर्मां निरयादशेषात् ॥ १७ ॥

sanat-kumāro'vatu kāmadevād
dhayaśīrṣā māṁ pathi deva-helanāt
devarṣi-varyaḥ puruṣārcanāntarāt
kūrmo harir māṁ nirayād aśeṣāt

sanat-kumāraḥ—the great *brahmacārī* named Sanat-kumāra; *avatu*—may he protect; *kāma-devāt*—from the hands of Cupid or lusty desire; *haya-śīrṣā*—Lord Hayagrīva, the incarnation of the Lord whose head is like that of a horse; *mām*—me; *pathi*—on the path; *deva-helanāt*—from neglecting to offer respectful obeisances to *brāhmaṇas,* Vaiṣṇavas and the Supreme Lord; *devarṣi-varyaḥ*—the best of the saintly sages, Nārada; *puruṣa-arcana-antarāt*—from the offenses in worshiping the Deity; *kūrmaḥ*—Lord Kūrma, the tortoise; *hariḥ*—the Supreme Personality of Godhead; *mām*—me; *nirayāt*—from hell; *aśeṣāt*—unlimited.

TRANSLATION

May Sanat-kumāra protect me from lusty desires. As I begin some auspicious activity, may Lord Hayagrīva protect me from being an offender by neglecting to offer respectful obeisances to the Supreme Lord. May Devarṣi Nārada protect me from committing offenses in worshiping the Deity, and may Lord Kūrma, the tortoise, protect me from falling to the unlimited hellish planets.

PURPORT

Lusty desires are very strong in everyone, and they are the greatest impediment to the discharge of devotional service. Therefore those who are very much influenced by lusty desires are advised to take shelter of Sanat-kumāra, the great *brahmacārī* devotee. Nārada Muni, who is the guide for *arcana,* is the author of the *Nārada-pañcarātra,* which prescribes the regulative principles for worshiping the Deity. Everyone engaged in Deity worship, whether at home or in the temple, should always seek the mercy of Devarṣi Nārada in order to avoid the thirty-two offenses while worshiping the Deity. These offenses in Deity worship are mentioned in *The Nectar of Devotion.*

TEXT 18

धन्वन्तरिर्भगवान् पात्वपथ्याद्
द्वन्द्वाद् भयादृषभो निर्जितात्मा ।

यज्ञश्च लोकादवताज्जनान्ताद्
बलो गणात् क्रोधवशादहीन्द्रः ॥ १८ ॥

dhanvantarir bhagavān pātv apathyād
dvandvād bhayād ṛṣabho nirjitātmā
yajñaś ca lokād avatāj janāntād
balo gaṇāt krodha-vaśād ahīndraḥ

dhanvantariḥ—the incarnation Dhanvantari, the physician; *bhagavān*—the Supreme Personality of Godhead; *pātu*—may He protect me; *apathyāt*—from things injurious to the health, such as meat and intoxicants; *dvandvāt*—from duality; *bhayāt*—from fear; *ṛṣabhaḥ*—Lord Ṛṣabhadeva; *nirjita-ātmā*—who fully controlled his mind and self; *yajñaḥ*—Yajña; *ca*—and; *lokāt*—from the defamation of the populace; *avatāt*—may He protect; *jana-antāt*—from dangerous positions created by other people; *balaḥ*—Lord Balarāma; *gaṇāt*—from the hordes of; *krodha-vaśāt*—the angry serpents; *ahīndraḥ*—Lord Balarāma in the form of the serpent Śeṣa Nāga.

TRANSLATION

May the Supreme Personality of Godhead in His incarnation as Dhanvantari relieve me from undesirable eatables and protect me from physical illness. May Lord Ṛṣabhadeva, who conquered His inner and outer senses, protect me from fear produced by the duality of heat and cold. May Yajña protect me from defamation and harm from the populace, and may Lord Balarāma as Śeṣa protect me from envious serpents.

PURPORT

To live within this material world, one must face many dangers, as described herein. For example, undesirable food poses a danger to health, and therefore one must give up such food. The Dhanvantari incarnation can protect us in this regard. Since Lord Viṣṇu is the Supersoul of all living entities, if He likes He can save us from *adhibhautika* disturbances, disturbances from other living entities. Lord Balarāma is the Śeṣa incarnation, and therefore He can save us from angry serpents or envious persons, who are always ready to attack.

TEXT 19

द्वैपायनो भगवानप्रबोधाद्
बुद्धस्तु पाषण्डगणप्रमादात् ।

कल्किः कलेः कालमलात् प्रपातु
धर्मावनायोरुकृतावतारः ॥ १९ ॥

dvaipāyano bhagavān aprabodhād
buddhas tu pāṣaṇḍa-gaṇa-pramādāt
kalkiḥ kaleḥ kāla-malāt prapātu
dharmāvanāyoru-kṛtāvatāraḥ

dvaipāyanaḥ—Śrīla Vyāsadeva, the giver of all Vedic knowledge; *bhagavān*—the most powerful incarnation of the Supreme Personality of Godhead; *aprabodhāt*—from ignorance of the *śāstra; buddhaḥ tu*—also Lord Buddha; *pāṣaṇḍa-gaṇa*—of atheists creating disillusionment for innocent persons; *pramādāt*—from the madness; *kalkiḥ*—Lord Kalki, the incarnation of Keśava; *kaleḥ*—of this Kali-yuga; *kāla-malāt*—from the darkness of the age; *prapātu*—may He protect; *dharma-avanāya*—for the protection of religious principles; *uru*—very great; *kṛta-avatāraḥ*—who took an incarnation.

TRANSLATION

May the Personality of Godhead in His incarnation as Vyāsadeva protect me from all kinds of ignorance resulting from the absence of Vedic knowledge. May Lord Buddhadeva protect me from activities opposed to Vedic principles and from laziness that causes one to madly forget the Vedic principles of knowledge and ritualistic action. May Kalkideva, the Supreme Personality of Godhead, who appeared as an incarnation to protect religious principles, protect me from the dirt of the age of Kali.

PURPORT

This verse mentions various incarnations of the Supreme Personality of Godhead who appear for various purposes. Śrīla Vyāsadeva, Mahāmuni, compiled the Vedic literature for the benefit of all human society. If one wants to be protected from the reactions of ignorance even in this age of Kali, one may consult the books left by Śrīla Vyāsadeva, namely the four *Vedas* (*Sāma, Yajur, Ṛg* and *Atharva*), the 108 *Upaniṣads, Vedānta-sūtra* (*Brahma-sūtra*), *Mahābhārata, Śrīmad-Bhāgavatam Mahā-Purāṇa* (Vyāsadeva's commentary on the *Brahma-sūtra*) and the other seventeen *Purāṇas.* Only by the mercy of Śrīla Vyāsadeva do we have so many volumes of transcendental knowledge to save us from the clutches of ignorance.

As described by Śrīla Jayadeva Gosvāmī in his *Daśāvatāra-stotra,* Lord Buddha apparently decried the Vedic knowledge:

nindasi yajña-vidher ahaha śruti-jātaṁ
sadaya-hṛdaya-darśita-paśu-ghātam
keśava dhṛta-buddha-śarīra jaya jagad-īśa hare

The mission of Lord Buddha was to save people from the abominable activity of animal killing and to save the poor animals from being unnecessarily killed. When *pāṣaṇḍīs* were cheating by killing animals on the plea of sacrificing them in Vedic *yajñas,* the Lord said, "If the Vedic injunctions allow animal killing, I do not accept the Vedic principles." Thus he actually saved people who acted according to Vedic principles. One should therefore surrender to Lord Buddha so that he can help one avoid misusing the injunctions of the *Vedas.*

The Kalki *avatāra* is the fierce incarnation who vanquishes the class of the atheists born in this age of Kali. Now, in the beginning of Kali-yuga, many irreligious principles are in effect, and as Kali-yuga advances, many pseudo religious principles will certainly be introduced, and people will forget the real religious principles enunciated by Lord Kṛṣṇa before the beginning of Kali-yuga, namely principles of surrender unto the lotus feet of the Lord. Unfortunately, because of Kali-yuga, foolish people do not surrender to the lotus feet of Kṛṣṇa. Even most people who claim to belong to the Vedic system of religion are actually opposed to the Vedic principles. Every day they manufacture a new type of *dharma* on the plea that whatever one manufactures is also a path of liberation. Atheistic men generally say, *yata mata tata patha.* According to this view, there are hundreds and thousands of different opinions in human society, and each opinion is a valid religious principle. This philosophy of rascals has killed the religious principles mentioned in the *Vedas,* and such philosophies will become increasingly influential as Kali-yuga progresses. In the last stage of Kali-yuga, Kalkideva, the fierce incarnation of Keśava, will descend to kill all the atheists and will save only the devotees of the Lord.

TEXT 20

मां केशवो गदया प्रातरव्याद्
गोविन्द आसङ्गवमात्तवेणुः ।
नारायणः प्राह्ण उदात्तशक्ति-
र्मध्यन्दिने विष्णुररीन्द्रपाणिः ॥ २० ॥

māṁ keśavo gadayā prātar avyād
govinda āsaṅgavam ātta-veṇuḥ
nārāyaṇaḥ prāhṇa udātta-śaktir
madhyan-dine viṣṇur arīndra-pāṇiḥ

mām—me; *keśavaḥ*—Lord Keśava; *gadayā*—by His club; *prātaḥ*—in the morning hours; *avyāt*—may He protect; *govindaḥ*—Lord Govinda; *āsaṅgavam*—during the second part of the day; *ātta-veṇuḥ*—holding His flute; *nārāyaṇaḥ*—Lord Nārāyaṇa with four hands; *prāhṇaḥ*—during the third part of the day; *udātta-śaktiḥ*—controlling different types of potencies; *madhyam-dine*—during the fourth part of the day; *viṣṇuḥ*—Lord Viṣṇu; *arīndra-pāṇiḥ*—bearing the disc in His hand to kill the enemies.

TRANSLATION

May Lord Keśava protect me with His club in the first portion of the day, and may Govinda, who is always engaged in playing His flute, protect me in the second portion of the day. May Lord Nārāyaṇa, who is equipped with all potencies, protect me in the third part of the day, and may Lord Viṣṇu, who carries a disc to kill His enemies, protect me in the fourth part of the day.

PURPORT

According to Vedic astronomical calculations, day and night are each divided into thirty *ghaṭikās* (twenty-four minutes), instead of twelve hours. Generally, each day and each night is divided into six parts consisting of five *ghaṭikās.* In each of these six portions of the day and night, the Lord may be addressed for protection according to different names. Lord Keśava, the proprietor of the holy place of Mathurā, is the Lord of the first portion of the day, and Govinda, the Lord of Vṛndāvana, is the master of the second portion.

TEXT 21

देवोऽपराह्णे मधुहोग्रधन्वा
सायं त्रिधामावतु माधवो माम् ।
दोषे हृषीकेश उतार्धरात्रे
निशीथ एकोऽवतु पद्मनाभः ॥ २१ ॥

devo'parāhṇe madhu-hogradhanvā
sāyaṁ tri-dhāmāvatu mādhavo mām

doṣe hṛṣīkeśa utārdha-rātre
niśītha eko'vatu padmanābhaḥ

devaḥ—the Lord; *aparāhṇe*—in the fifth part of the day; *madhu-hā*—named Madhusūdana; *ugra-dhanvā*—bearing the very fearful bow known as Śārṅga; *sāyam*—the sixth part of the day; *tri-dhāmā*—manifesting as the three deities Brahmā, Viṣṇu and Maheśvara; *avatu*—may He protect; *mādhavaḥ*—named Mādhava; *mām*—me; *doṣe*—during the first portion of the night; *hṛṣīkeśaḥ*—Lord Hṛṣīkeśa; *uta*—also; *ardha-rātre*—during the second part of the night; *niśīthe*—during the third part of the night; *ekaḥ*—alone; *avatu*—may He protect; *padmanābhaḥ*—Lord Padmanābha.

TRANSLATION

May Lord Madhusūdana, who carries a bow very fearful for the demons, protect me during the fifth part of the day. In the evening, may Lord Mādhava, appearing as Brahmā, Viṣṇu and Maheśvara, protect me, and in the beginning of night may Lord Hṛṣīkeśa protect me. At the dead of night [in the second and third parts of night] may Lord Padmanābha alone protect me.

TEXT 22

श्रीवत्सधामापररात्र ईशः
प्रत्यूष ईशोऽसिधरो जनार्दनः ।
दामोदरोऽव्यादनुसन्ध्यं प्रभाते
विश्वेश्वरो भगवान् कालमूर्तिः ॥ २२ ॥

śrīvatsa-dhāmāpara-rātra īśaḥ
pratyūṣa īśo'si-dharo janārdanaḥ
dāmodaro'vyād anusandhyaṁ prabhāte
viśveśvaro bhagavān kāla-mūrtiḥ

śrīvatsa-dhāmā—the Lord, on whose chest the mark of Śrīvatsa is resting; *apara-rātre*—in the fourth part of the night; *īśaḥ*—the Supreme Lord; *pratyūṣe*—in the end of the night; *īśaḥ*—the Supreme Lord; *asi-dharaḥ*—carrying a sword in the hand; *janārdanaḥ*—Lord Janārdana; *dāmodaraḥ*—Lord Dāmodara; *avyāt*—may He protect; *anusandhyam*—during each junction or twilight; *prabhāte*—in the early morning (the sixth part of the night); *viśva-īśvaraḥ*—the Lord of the whole universe; *bhagavān*—the Supreme Personality of Godhead; *kāla-mūrtiḥ*—the personification of time.

TRANSLATION

May the Supreme Personality of Godhead, who bears the Śrīvatsa on His chest, protect me after midnight until the sky becomes pinkish. May Lord Janārdana, who carries a sword in His hand, protect me at the end of night [during the last four ghaṭikās of night]. May Lord Dāmodara protect me in the early morning, and may Lord Viśveśvara protect me during the junctions of day and night.

TEXT 23

चक्रं युगान्तानलतिग्मनेमि
भ्रमत् समन्ताद् भगवत्प्रयुक्तम् ।
दन्दग्धि दन्दग्ध्यरिसैन्यमाशु
कक्षं यथा वातसखो हुताशः ॥ २३ ॥

cakraṁ yugāntānala-tigma-nemi
bhramat samantād bhagavat-prayuktam
dandagdhi dandagdhy ari-sainyam āśu
kakṣaṁ yathā vāta-sakho hutāśaḥ

cakram—the disc of the Lord; *yuga-anta*—at the end of the millennium; *anala*—like the fire of devastation; *tigma-nemi*—with a sharp rim; *bhramat*—wandering; *samantāt*—on all sides; *bhagavat-prayuktam*—being engaged by the Lord; *dandagdhi dandagdhi*—please burn completely, please burn completely; *ari-sainyam*—the army of our enemies; *āśu*—immediately; *kakṣam*—dry grass; *yathā*—like; *vāta-sakhaḥ*—the friend of the wind; *hutāśaḥ*—blazing fire.

TRANSLATION

Set into motion by the Supreme Personality of Godhead and wandering in all the four directions, the disc of the Supreme Lord has sharp edges as destructive as the fire of devastation at the end of the millennium. As a blazing fire burns dry grass to ashes with the assistance of the breeze, may that Sudarśana cakra burn our enemies to ashes.

TEXT 24

गदेऽशनिस्पर्शनविस्फुलिङ्गे
निष्पिण्ढि निष्पिण्ढ्यजितप्रियासि ।
कुष्माण्डवैनायकयक्षरक्षो-
भूतग्रहांश्चूर्णय चूर्णयारीन् ॥ २४ ॥

gade'śani-sparśana-visphuliṅge
niṣpiṇḍhi niṣpiṇḍhy ajita-priyāsi
kuṣmāṇḍa-vaināyaka-yakṣa-rakṣo-
bhūta-grahāṁś cūrṇaya cūrṇayārīn

gade—O club in the hands of the Supreme Personality of Godhead; *aśani*—like thunderbolts; *sparśana*—whose touch; *visphuliṅge*—giving off sparks of fire; *niṣpiṇḍhi niṣpiṇḍhi*—pound to pieces, pound to pieces; *ajita-priyā*—very dear to the Supreme Personality of Godhead; *asi*—you are; *kuṣmāṇḍa*—imps named Kuṣmāṇḍas; *vaināyaka*—ghosts named Vaināyakas; *yakṣa*—ghosts named Yakṣas; *rakṣaḥ*—ghosts named Rākṣasas; *bhūta*—ghosts named Bhūtas; *grahān*—and evil demons named Grahas; *cūrṇaya*—pulverize; *cūrṇaya*—pulverize; *arīn*—my enemies.

TRANSLATION

O club in the hand of the Supreme Personality of Godhead, you produce sparks of fire as powerful as thunderbolts, and you are extremely dear to the Lord. I am also His servant. Therefore kindly help me pound to pieces the evil living beings known as Kuṣmāṇḍas, Vaināyakas, Yakṣas, Rākṣasas, Bhūtas and Grahas. Please pulverize them.

TEXT 25

त्वं यातुधानप्रमथप्रेतमातृ-
पिशाचविप्रग्रहघोरदृष्टीन् ।
दरेन्द्र विद्रावय कृष्णपूरितो
भीमस्वनोऽरेर्हृदयानि कम्पयन् ॥ २५ ॥

tvaṁ yātudhāna-pramatha-preta-mātṛ-
piśāca-vipragraha-ghora-dṛṣṭīn
darendra vidrāvaya kṛṣṇa-pūrito
bhīma-svano'rer hṛdayāni kampayan

tvam—you; *yātudhāna*—Rākṣasas; *pramatha*—Pramathas; *preta*—Pretas; *mātṛ*—Mātās; *piśāca*—Piśācas; *vipra-graha*—*brāhmaṇa* ghosts; *ghora-dṛṣṭīn*—who have very fearful eyes; *darendra*—O Pāñcajanya, the conchshell in the hands of the Lord; *vidrāvaya*—drive away; *kṛṣṇa-pūritaḥ*—being filled with air from the mouth of Kṛṣṇa; *bhīma-svanaḥ*—sounding extremely fearful; *areḥ*—of the enemy; *hṛdayāni*—the cores of the hearts; *kampayan*—causing to tremble.

TRANSLATION

O best of conchshells, O Pāñcajanya in the hands of the Lord, you are always filled with the breath of Lord Kṛṣṇa. Therefore you create a fearful sound vibration that causes trembling in the hearts of enemies like the Rākṣasas, Pramatha ghosts, Pretas, Mātās, Piśācas and brāhmaṇa ghosts with fearful eyes.

TEXT 26

त्वं तिग्मधारासिवरारिसैन्य-
मीशप्रयुक्तो मम छिन्धि छिन्धि ।
चक्षूंषि चर्मञ्छतचन्द्र छादय
द्विषामघोनां हर पापचक्षुषाम् ॥ २६ ॥

tvaṁ tigma-dhārāsi-varāri-sainyam
īśa-prayukto mama chindhi chindhi
cakṣūṁṣi carmañ chata-candra chādaya
dviṣām aghonāṁ hara pāpa-cakṣuṣām

tvam—you; *tigma-dhāra-asi-vara*—O best of swords possessing very sharp blades; *ari-sainyam*—the soldiers of the enemy; *īśa-prayuktaḥ*—being engaged by the Supreme Personality of Godhead; *mama*—my; *chindhi chindhi*—chop to pieces, chop to pieces; *cakṣūṁṣi*—the eyes; *carman*—O shield; *śata-candra*—possessing brilliant circles like a hundred moons; *chādaya*—please cover; *dviṣām*—of those who are envious of me; *aghonām*—who are completely sinful; *hara*—please take away; *pāpa-cakṣuṣām*—of those whose eyes are very sinful.

TRANSLATION

O king of sharp-edged swords, you are engaged by the Supreme Personality of Godhead. Please cut the soldiers of my enemies to pieces.

Please cut them to pieces! O shield marked with a hundred brilliant moonlike circles, please cover the eyes of the sinful enemies. Pluck out their sinful eyes.

TEXTS 27–28

यन्नो भयं ग्रहेभ्योऽभूत् केतुभ्यो नृभ्य एव च ।
सरीसृपेभ्यो दंष्ट्रिभ्यो भूतेभ्योंऽहोभ्य एव च ॥ २७ ॥
सर्वाण्येतानि भगवन्नामरूपानुकीर्तनात् ।
प्रयान्तु संक्षयं सद्यो ये नः श्रेयःप्रतीपकाः ॥ २८ ॥

yan no bhayaṁ grahebhyo'bhūt
ketubhyo nṛbhya eva ca
sarīsṛpebhyo daṁṣṭribhyo
bhūtebhyo'ṁhobhya eva ca

sarvāṇy etāni bhagavan-
nāma-rūpānukīrtanāt
prayāntu saṅkṣayaṁ sadyo
ye naḥ śreyaḥ-pratīpakāḥ

yat—which; *naḥ*—our; *bhayam*—fear; *grahebhyaḥ*—from the Graha demons; *abhūt*—was; *ketubhyaḥ*—from meteors, or falling stars; *nṛbhyaḥ*—from envious human beings; *eva ca*—also; *sarīsṛpebhyaḥ*—from snakes or scorpions; *daṁṣṭribhyaḥ*—from animals with fierce teeth like tigers, wolves and boars; *bhūtebhyaḥ*—from ghosts or the material elements (earth, water, fire, etc.); *aṁhobhyaḥ*—from sinful activities; *eva ca*—as well as; *sarvāṇi etāni*—all these; *bhagavat-nāma-rūpa-anukīrtanāt*—by glorifying the transcendental form, name, attributes and paraphernalia of the Supreme Personality of Godhead; *prayāntu*—let them go; *saṅkṣayam*—to complete destruction; *sadyaḥ*—immediately; *ye*—which; *naḥ*—our; *śreyaḥ-pratīpakāḥ*—hindrances to well-being.

TRANSLATION

May the glorification of the transcendental name, form, qualities and paraphernalia of the Supreme Personality of Godhead protect us from the influence of bad planets, meteors, envious human beings, serpents, scorpions, and animals like tigers and wolves. May it protect us from ghosts and the material elements like earth, water, fire and air, and may

it also protect us from lightning and our past sins. We are always afraid of these hindrances to our auspicious life. Therefore, may they all be completely destroyed by the chanting of the Hare Kṛṣṇa mahā-mantra.

TEXT 29

गरुडो भगवान् स्तोत्रस्तोभश्छन्दोमयः प्रभुः ।
रक्षत्वशेषकृच्छ्रेभ्यो विष्वक्सेनः स्वनामभिः ॥ २९ ॥

garuḍo bhagavān stotra-
stobhaś chandomayaḥ prabhuḥ
rakṣatv aśeṣa-kṛcchrebhyo
viṣvaksenaḥ sva-nāmabhiḥ

garuḍaḥ—His Holiness Garuḍa, the carrier of Lord Viṣṇu; *bhagavān*—as powerful as the Supreme Personality of Godhead; *stotra-stobhaḥ*—who is glorified by selected verses and songs; *chandaḥ-mayaḥ*—the personified *Vedas; prabhuḥ*—the lord; *rakṣatu*—may He protect; *aśeṣa-kṛcchrebhyaḥ*—from unlimited miseries; *viṣvaksenaḥ*—Lord Viṣvaksena; *sva-nāmabhiḥ*—by His holy names.

TRANSLATION

Lord Garuḍa, the carrier of Lord Viṣṇu, is the most worshipable lord, for he is as powerful as the Supreme Lord Himself. He is the personified Vedas and is worshiped by selected verses. May he protect us from all dangerous conditions, and may Lord Viṣvaksena, the Personality of Godhead, also protect us from all dangers by His holy names.

TEXT 30

सर्वापद्भ्यो हरेर्नामरूपयानायुधानि नः ।
बुद्धीन्द्रियमनःप्राणान् पान्तु पार्षदभूषणाः ॥ ३० ॥

sarvāpadbhyo harer nāma-
rūpa-yānāyudhāni naḥ
buddhīndriya-manaḥ-prāṇān
pāntu pārṣada-bhūṣaṇāḥ

sarva-āpadbhyaḥ—from all kinds of danger; *hareḥ*—of the Supreme Personality of Godhead; *nāma*—the holy name; *rūpa*—the transcendental form; *yāna*—the carriers; *āyudhāni*—and all the weapons; *naḥ*—our; *buddhi*—intelligence; *indriya*—senses; *manaḥ*—mind; *prāṇān*—life air; *pāntu*—

may they protect and maintain; *pārṣada-bhūṣaṇāḥ*—the decorations who are personal associates.

TRANSLATION

May the Supreme Personality of Godhead's holy names, His transcendental forms, His carriers and all the weapons decorating Him as personal associates protect our intelligence, senses, mind and life air from all dangers.

PURPORT

There are various associates of the transcendental Personality of Godhead, and His weapons and carrier are among them. In the spiritual world, nothing is material. The sword, bow, club, disc and everything decorating the personal body of the Lord are spiritual living force. Therefore the Lord is called *advaya-jñāna,* indicating that there is no difference between Him and His names, forms, qualities, weapons and so on. Anything pertaining to Him is in the same category of spiritual existence. They are all engaged in the service of the Lord in varieties of spiritual forms.

TEXT 31

यथा हि भगवानेव वस्तुतः सदसच्च यत्।
सत्येनानेन नः सर्वे यान्तु नाशमुपद्रवाः ॥ ३१ ॥

yathā hi bhagavān eva
vastutaḥ sad asac ca yat
satyenānena naḥ sarve
yāntu nāśam upadravāḥ

yathā—just as; *hi*—indeed; *bhagavān*—the Supreme Personality of Godhead; *eva*—undoubtedly; *vastutaḥ*—at the ultimate issue; *sat*—manifested; *asat*—unmanifested; *ca*—and; *yat*—whatever; *satyena*—by the truth; *anena*—this; *naḥ*—our; *sarve*—all; *yāntu*—let them go; *nāśam*—to annihilation; *upadravāḥ*—disturbances.

TRANSLATION

The subtle and gross cosmic manifestation is material, but nevertheless it is nondifferent from the Supreme Personality of Godhead because He is ultimately the cause of all causes. Cause and effect are factually one because the cause is present in the effect. Therefore the Absolute Truth,

the Supreme Personality of Godhead, can destroy all our dangers by any of His potent parts.

TEXTS 32–33

यथैकात्म्यानुभावानां विकल्परहितः स्वयम् ।
भूषणायुधलिङ्गाख्या धत्ते शक्तीः स्वमायया ॥ ३२ ॥
तेनैव सत्यमानेन सर्वज्ञो भगवान् हरिः ।
पातु सर्वैः स्वरूपैर्नः सदा सर्वत्र सर्वगः ॥ ३३ ॥

yathaikātmyānubhāvānāṁ
vikalpa-rahitaḥ svayam
bhūṣaṇāyudha-liṅgākhyā
dhatte śaktīḥ sva-māyayā

tenaiva satya-mānena
sarva-jño bhagavān hariḥ
pātu sarvaiḥ svarūpair naḥ
sadā sarvatra sarva-gaḥ

yathā—just as; *aikātmya*—in terms of oneness manifested in varieties; *anubhāvānām*—of those thinking; *vikalpa-rahitaḥ*—the absence of difference; *svayam*—Himself; *bhūṣaṇa*—decorations; *āyudha*—weapons; *liṅga-ākhyāḥ*—characteristics and different names; *dhatte*—possesses; *śaktīḥ*—potencies like wealth, influence, power, knowledge, beauty and renunciation; *sva-māyayā*—by expanding His spiritual energy; *tena eva*—by that; *satya-mānena*—true understanding; *sarva-jñaḥ*—omniscient; *bhagavān*—the Supreme Personality of Godhead; *hariḥ*—who can take away all the illusion of the living entities; *pātu*—may He protect; *sarvaiḥ*—with all; *sva-rūpaiḥ*—His forms; *naḥ*—us; *sadā*—always; *sarvatra*—everywhere; *sarva-gaḥ*—who is all-pervasive.

TRANSLATION

The Supreme Personality of Godhead, the living entities, the material energy, the spiritual energy and the entire creation are all individual substances. In the ultimate analysis, however, together they constitute the supreme one, the Personality of Godhead. Therefore those who are advanced in spiritual knowledge see unity in diversity. For such advanced persons, the Lord's bodily decorations, His name, His fame, His attributes and forms and the weapons in His hand are manifestations of the strength

of His potency. According to their elevated spiritual understanding, the omniscient Lord, who manifests various forms, is present everywhere. May He always protect us everywhere from all calamities.

PURPORT

A person highly elevated in spiritual knowledge knows that nothing exists but the Supreme Personality of Godhead. This is also confirmed in *Bhagavad-gītā* (9.4) where Lord Kṛṣṇa says, *mayā tatam idaṁ sarvam,* indicating that everything we see is an expansion of His energy. This is confirmed in the *Viṣṇu Purāṇa* (1.22.52):

eka-deśa-sthitasyāgner
jyotsnā vistāriṇī yathā
parasya brahmaṇaḥ śaktis
tathedam akhilaṁ jagat

As a fire, although existing in one place, can expand its light and heat everywhere, so the omnipotent Lord, the Supreme Personality of Godhead, although situated in His spiritual abode, expands Himself everywhere, in both the material and spiritual worlds, by His various energies. Since both cause and effect are the Supreme Lord, there is no difference between cause and effect. Consequently the ornaments and weapons of the Lord, being expansions of His spiritual energy, are not different from Him. There is no difference between the Lord and His variously presented energies. This is also confirmed in the *Padma Purāṇa:*

nāma cintāmaṇiḥ kṛṣṇaś
caitanya-rasa-vigrahaḥ
pūrṇaḥ śuddho nitya-mukto
'bhinnatvān nāma-nāminoḥ

The holy name of the Lord is fully identical with the Lord, not partially. The word *pūrṇa* means "complete." The Lord is omnipotent and omniscient, and similarly, His name, form, qualities, paraphernalia and everything pertaining to Him are complete, pure, eternal and free from material contamination. The prayer to the ornaments and carriers of the Lord is not false, for they are as good as the Lord. Since the Lord is all-pervasive, He exists in everything, and everything exists in Him. Therefore even worship of the Lord's weapons or ornaments has the same potency as worship of the Lord. Māyāvādīs refuse to accept the form of the Lord, or they say that the form of the Lord is *māyā,* or false, but one should note very carefully that this is not acceptable. Although the Lord's original form and His impersonal expansion are one, the Lord maintains His form, qualities and abode eternally. Therefore this prayer says, *pātu sarvaiḥ svarūpair naḥ sadā sarvatra sarva-gaḥ:* "May the Lord, who is all-pervasive in His various forms, protect us everywhere." The Lord is always present everywhere by His name, form, qualities, attributes and paraphernalia, and they all have equal power to protect the devotees. Śrīla Madhvācārya explains this as follows:

eka eva paro viṣṇur
bhūṣāheti dhvajeṣv ajaḥ
tat-tac-chakti-pradatvena
svayam eva vyavasthitaḥ
satyenānena māṁ devaḥ
pātu sarveśvaro hariḥ

TEXT 34

विदिक्षु दिक्षूर्ध्वमधः समन्ता-
दन्तर्बहिर्भगवान् नारसिंहः ।
प्रहापयँल्लोकभयं स्वनेन
स्वतेजसा ग्रस्तसमस्ततेजाः ॥ ३४ ॥

vidikṣu dikṣūrdhvam adhaḥ samantād
antar bahir bhagavān nārasiṁhaḥ
prahāpayal̐ loka-bhayaṁ svanena
sva-tejasā grasta-samasta-tejāḥ

vidikṣu—in all corners; *dikṣu*—in all directions (east, west, north and south); *ūrdhvam*—above; *adhaḥ*—below; *samantāt*—on all sides; *antaḥ*—internally; *bahiḥ*—externally; *bhagavān*—the Supreme Personality of Godhead; *nārasiṁhaḥ*—in the form of Nṛsiṁhadeva (half-lion and half-man); *prahāpayan*—completely destroying; *loka-bhayam*—fear created by animals, poison, weapons, water, air, fire and so on; *svanena*—by His roar or the vibration of His name by His devotee Prahlāda Mahārāja; *sva-tejasā*—by His personal effulgence; *grasta*—covered; *samasta*—all other; *tejāḥ*—influences.

TRANSLATION

Prahlāda Mahārāja loudly chanted the holy name of Lord Nṛsiṁhadeva. May Lord Nṛsiṁhadeva, roaring for His devotee Prahlāda Mahārāja,

protect us from all fear of dangers created by stalwart leaders in all directions through poison, weapons, water, fire, air and so on. May the Lord cover their influence by His own transcendental influence. May Nṛsiṁha-deva protect us in all directions and in all corners, above, below, within and without.

TEXT 35

मघवन्निदमाख्यातं वर्म नारायणात्मकम् ।
विजेष्यसेऽञ्जसा येन दंशितोऽसुरयूथपान् ॥ ३५ ॥

maghavann idam ākhyātaṁ
varma nārāyaṇātmakam
vijeṣyase 'ñjasā yena
daṁśito 'sura-yūthapān

maghavan—O King Indra; *idam*—this; *ākhyātam*—described; *varma*—mystic armor; *nārāyaṇa-ātmakam*—related to Nārāyaṇa; *vijeṣyase*—you will conquer; *añjasā*—very easily; *yena*—by which; *daṁśitaḥ*—being protected; *asura-yūthapān*—the chief leaders of the demons.

TRANSLATION

Viśvarūpa continued: O Indra, this mystic armor related to Lord Nārāyaṇa has been described by me to you. By putting on this protective covering, you will certainly be able to conquer the leaders of the demons.

TEXT 36

एतद् धारयमाणस्तु यं यं पश्यति चक्षुषा ।
पदा वा संस्पृशेत् सद्यः साध्वसात् स विमुच्यते ॥ ३६ ॥

etad dhārayamāṇas tu
yaṁ yaṁ paśyati cakṣuṣā
padā vā saṁspṛśet sadyaḥ
sādhvasāt sa vimucyate

etat—this; *dhārayamāṇaḥ*—a person employing; *tu*—but; *yam yam*—whomever; *paśyati*—he sees; *cakṣuṣā*—by his eyes; *padā*—by his feet; *vā*—or; *saṁspṛśet*—may touch; *sadyaḥ*—immediately; *sādhvasāt*—from all fear; *saḥ*—he; *vimucyate*—is freed.

TRANSLATION

If one employs this armor, whomever he sees with his eyes or touches with his feet is immediately freed from all the above-mentioned dangers.

TEXT 37

न कुतश्चिद् भयं तस्य विद्यां धारयतो भवेत् ।
राजदस्युग्रहादिभ्यो व्याध्यादिभ्यश्च कर्हिचित् ॥ ३७ ॥

na kutaścid bhayaṁ tasya
vidyāṁ dhārayato bhavet
rāja-dasyu-grahādibhyo
vyādhy-ādibhyaś ca karhicit

na—not; *kutaścit*—from anywhere; *bhayam*—fear; *tasya*—of him; *vidyām*—this mystical prayer; *dhārayataḥ*—employing; *bhavet*—may appear; *rāja*—from the government; *dasyu*—from rogues and thieves; *graha-ādibhyaḥ*—from demons and so on; *vyādhi-ādibhyaḥ*—from diseases and so on; *ca*—also; *karhicit*—at any time.

TRANSLATION

This prayer, Nārāyaṇa-kavaca, constitutes subtle knowledge transcendentally connected with Nārāyaṇa. One who employs this prayer is never disturbed or put in danger by the government, by plunderers, by evil demons or by any type of disease.

TEXT 38

इमां विद्यां पुरा कश्चित् कौशिको धारयन् द्विजः ।
योगधारणया स्वाङ्गं जहौ स मरुधन्वनि ॥ ३८ ॥

imāṁ vidyāṁ purā kaścit
kauśiko dhārayan dvijaḥ
yoga-dhāraṇayā svāṅgaṁ
jahau sa maru-dhanvani

imām—this; *vidyām*—prayer; *purā*—formerly; *kaścit*—someone; *kauśikaḥ*—Kauśika; *dhārayan*—using; *dvijaḥ*—a *brāhmaṇa; yoga-dhāraṇayā*—by mystic power; *sva-aṅgam*—his own body; *jahau*—gave up; *saḥ*—he; *maru-dhanvani*—in the desert.

TRANSLATION

O King of heaven, a brāhmaṇa named Kauśika formerly used this armor when he purposely gave up his body in the desert by mystic power.

TEXT 39

तस्योपरि विमानेन गन्धर्वपतिरेकदा ।
ययौ चित्ररथः स्त्रीभिर्वृतो यत्र द्विजक्षयः ॥ ३९ ॥

tasyopari vimānena
gandharva-patir ekadā
yayau citrarathaḥ strībhir
vṛto yatra dvija-kṣayaḥ

tasya—his dead body; *upari*—above; *vimānena*—by airplane; *gandharva-patiḥ*—the King of Gandharvaloka, Citraratha; *ekadā*—once upon a time; *yayau*—went; *citrarathaḥ*—Citraratha; *strībhiḥ*—by many beautiful women; *vṛtaḥ*—surrounded; *yatra*—where; *dvija-kṣayaḥ*—the *brāhmaṇa* Kauśika had died.

TRANSLATION

Surrounded by many beautiful women, Citraratha, the King of Gandharvaloka, was once passing in his airplane over the brāhmaṇa's body at the spot where the brāhmaṇa had died.

TEXT 40

गगनान्न्यपतत् सद्यः सविमानो ह्यवाक्शिराः ।
स वालिखिल्यवचनादस्थीन्यादाय विस्मितः ।
प्रास्य प्राचीसरस्वत्यां स्नात्वा धाम स्वमन्वगात् ॥ ४० ॥

gaganān nyapatat sadyaḥ
savimāno hy avāk-śirāḥ
sa vālikhilya-vacanād
asthīny ādāya vismitaḥ
prāsya prācī-sarasvatyāṁ
snātvā dhāma svam anvagāt

gaganāt—from the sky; *nyapatat*—fell; *sadyaḥ*—suddenly; *sa-vimānaḥ*—with his airplane; *hi*—certainly; *avāk-śirāḥ*—with his head downward; *saḥ*

—he; *vālikhilya*—of the great sages named the Vālikhilyas; *vacanāt*—by the instructions; *asthīni*—all the bones; *ādāya*—taking; *vismitaḥ*—struck with wonder; *prāsya*—throwing; *prācī-sarasvatyām*—in the River Sarasvatī, which flows to the east; *snātvā*—bathing in that river; *dhāma*—to the abode; *svam*—his own; *anvagāt*—returned.

TRANSLATION

Suddenly Citraratha was forced to fall from the sky headfirst with his airplane. Struck with wonder, he was ordered by the great sages named the Vālikhilyas to throw the brāhmaṇa's bones in the nearby River Sarasvatī. He had to do this and bathe in the river before returning to his own abode.

TEXT 41

श्रीशुक उवाच
य इदं शृणुयात् काले यो धारयति चादृतः ।
तं नमस्यन्ति भूतानि मुच्यते सर्वतो भयात् ॥ ४१ ॥

śrī-śuka uvāca
ya idaṁ śṛṇuyāt kāle
yo dhārayati cādṛtaḥ
taṁ namasyanti bhūtāni
mucyate sarvato bhayāt

śrī-śukaḥ uvāca—Śrī Śukadeva Gosvāmī said; *yaḥ*—anyone who; *idam*—this; *śṛṇuyāt*—may hear; *kāle*—at a time of fear; *yaḥ*—anyone who; *dhārayati*—employs this prayer; *ca*—also; *ādṛtaḥ*—with faith and adoration; *tam*—unto him; *namasyanti*—offer respectful obeisances; *bhūtāni*—all living beings; *mucyate*—is released; *sarvataḥ*—from all; *bhayāt*—fearful conditions.

TRANSLATION

Śrī Śukadeva Gosvāmī said: My dear Mahārāja Parīkṣit, one who employs this armor or hears about it with faith and veneration when afraid because of any conditions in the material world is immediately freed from all dangers and is worshiped by all living entities.

TEXT 42

एतां विद्यामधिगतो विश्वरूपाच्छतक्रतुः ।
त्रैलोक्यलक्ष्मीं बुभुजे विनिर्जित्य मृधेऽसुरान् ॥ ४२ ॥

etāṁ vidyām adhigato
viśvarūpāc chatakratuḥ
trailokya-lakṣmīṁ bubhuje
vinirjitya mṛdhe'surān

etām—this; *vidyām*—prayer; *adhigataḥ*—received; *viśvarūpāt*—from the *brāhmaṇa* Viśvarūpa; *śata-kratuḥ*—Indra, the King of heaven; *trailokya-lakṣmīm*—all the opulence of the three worlds; *bubhuje*—enjoyed; *vinirjitya*—conquering; *mṛdhe*—in battle; *asurān*—all the demons.

TRANSLATION

King Indra, who performed one hundred sacrifices, received this prayer of protection from Viśvarūpa. After conquering the demons, he enjoyed all the opulences of the three worlds.

PURPORT

This mystical mantric armor given by Viśvarūpa to Indra, the King of heaven, acted powerfully, with the effect that Indra was able to conquer the *asuras* and enjoy the opulence of the three worlds without impediments. In this regard, Madhvācārya points out:

vidyāḥ karmāṇi ca sadā
guroḥ prāptāḥ phala-pradāḥ
anyathā naiva phaladāḥ
prasannoktāḥ phala-pradāḥ

One must receive all kinds of *mantras* from a bona fide spiritual master; otherwise the *mantras* will not be fruitful. This is also indicated in *Bhagavad-gītā* (4.34):

tad viddhi praṇipātena
paripraśnena sevayā
upadekṣyanti te jñānaṁ
jñāninas tattva-darśinaḥ

"Just try to learn the truth by approaching a spiritual master. Inquire from him submissively and render service unto him. The self-realized soul can impart knowledge unto you because he has seen the truth." All *mantras* should be received through the authorized *guru*, and the disciple must satisfy the *guru* in all respects, after surrendering at his lotus feet. In the *Padma Purāṇa* it is also said, *sampradāya-vihīnā ye mantrās te niṣphalā matāḥ.* There are four *sampradāyas,* or disciplic successions, namely the Brahma-sampradāya, the Rudra-sampradāya, the Śrī-sampradāya and the Kumāra-sampradāya. If one wants to advance in spiritual power, one must receive his *mantras* from one of these bona fide *sampradāyas;* otherwise he will never successfully advance in spiritual life.

Thus end the Bhaktivedanta purports of the Sixth Canto, Eighth Chapter, of the Śrīmad-Bhāgavatam, *entitled "The Nārāyaṇa-kavaca Shield."*

CHAPTER NINE

Appearance of the Demon Vṛtrāsura

As described in this chapter, Indra, the King of heaven, killed Viśvarūpa, and therefore Viśvarūpa's father performed a *yajña* to kill Indra. When Vṛtrāsura appeared from that *yajña,* the demigods, in fear, sought shelter of the Supreme Personality of Godhead and glorified Him.

Because of affection for the demons, Viśvarūpa secretly supplied them the remnants of *yajña.* When Indra learned about this, he beheaded Viśvarūpa, but he later regretted killing Viśvarūpa because Viśvarūpa was a *brāhmaṇa.* Although competent to neutralize the sinful reactions for killing a *brāhmaṇa,* Indra did not do so. Instead he accepted the reactions. Later, he distributed these reactions among the land, water, trees and women in general. Since the land accepted one fourth of the sinful reactions, a portion of the land turned into desert. The trees were also given one fourth of the sinful reactions, and therefore they drip sap, which is prohibited for drinking. Because women accepted one fourth of the sinful reactions, they are untouchable during their menstrual period. Since water was also infested with sinful reactions, when bubbles appear in water it cannot be used for any purpose.

After Viśvarūpa was killed, his father, Tvaṣṭā, performed a sacrifice to kill King Indra. Unfortunately, if *mantras* are chanted irregularly, they yield an opposite result. This happened when Tvaṣṭā performed this *yajña.* While performing the sacrifice to kill Indra, Tvaṣṭā chanted a *mantra* to increase Indra's enemies, but because he chanted the *mantra* wrong, the sacrifice produced an *asura* named Vṛtrāsura, of whom Indra was the enemy. When Vṛtrāsura was generated from the sacrifice, his fierce features made the whole world afraid, and his personal effulgence diminished even the power of the demigods. Finding no other means of protection, the demigods began to worship the Supreme Personality of Godhead, the enjoyer of all the results of sacrifice, who is supreme throughout the entire universe. The demigods all worshiped Him because ultimately no one but Him can protect a living entity from fear and danger. Seeking shelter of a demigod instead of worshiping the Supreme Personality of Godhead is compared to trying to cross the ocean by grasping the tail of a dog. A dog can swim, but that does not mean that one can cross the ocean by grasping a dog's tail.

Being pleased with the demigods, the Supreme Personality of Godhead advised them to approach Dadhīci to beg him for the bones of his own body. Dadhīci would comply with the request of the demigods, and with the help of his bones Vṛtrāsura could be killed.

TEXT 1

श्रीशुक उवाच
तस्यासन् विश्वरूपस्य शिरांसि त्रीणि भारत।
सोमपीथं सुरापीथमन्नादमिति शुश्रुम ॥ १ ॥

śrī-śuka uvāca
tasyāsan viśvarūpasya
śirāṁsi trīṇi bhārata
soma-pīthaṁ surā-pītham
annādam iti śuśruma

śrī-śukaḥ uvāca—Śrī Śukadeva Gosvāmī said; *tasya*—of him; *āsan*—there were; *viśvarūpasya*—of Viśvarūpa, the priest of the demigods; *śirāṁsi*—heads; *trīṇi*—three; *bhārata*—O Mahārāja Parīkṣit; *soma-pītham*—used for drinking the beverage *soma; surā-pītham*—used for drinking wine; *anna-adam*—used for eating; *iti*—thus; *śuśruma*—I have heard by the *paramparā* system.

TRANSLATION

Śrī Śukadeva Gosvāmī continued: Viśvarūpa, who was engaged as the priest of the demigods, had three heads. He used one to drink the beverage soma-rasa, another to drink wine and the third to eat food. O King Parīkṣit, thus I have heard from authorities.

PURPORT

One cannot directly perceive the kingdom of heaven, its king and other inhabitants, or how they perform their various engagements, for no one can go to the heavenly planets. Although modern scientists have invented many powerful space vehicles, they cannot even go to the moon, not to speak of other planets. By direct experience one cannot learn anything beyond the range of human perception. One must hear from authorities. Therefore Śukadeva Gosvāmī, a great personality, says, "What I am describing to you, O King, is what I have heard from authoritative sources." This is the Vedic system. The Vedic knowledge is called *śruti* because it must be received by being heard from authorities. It is beyond the realm of our false experimental knowledge.

TEXT 2

स वै बर्हिषि देवेभ्यो भागं प्रत्यक्षमुच्चकैः ।
अददद् यस्य पितरो देवाः सप्रश्रयं नृप ॥ २ ॥

sa vai barhiṣi devebhyo
bhāgaṁ pratyakṣam uccakaiḥ
adadad yasya pitaro
devāḥ sapraśrayaṁ nṛpa

saḥ—he (Viśvarūpa); *vai*—indeed; *barhiṣi*—in the sacrificial fire; *devebhyaḥ*—unto the particular demigods; *bhāgam*—the proper share; *pratyakṣam*—visibly; *uccakaiḥ*—by loud chanting of the *mantras; adadat*—offered; *yasya*—of whom; *pitaraḥ*—the fathers; *devāḥ*—demigods; *sa-praśrayam*—very humbly in a gentle voice; *nṛpa*—O King Parīkṣit.

TRANSLATION

O Mahārāja Parīkṣit, the demigods were related to Viśvarūpa from his father's side, and therefore he visibly offered clarified butter in the fire while chanting mantras such as "indrāya idaṁ svāhā" ["this is meant for King Indra"] and "idam agnaye" ["this is for the demigod of fire"]. He loudly chanted these mantras and offered each of the demigods his proper share.

TEXT 3

स एव हि ददौ भागं परोक्षमसुरान् प्रति ।
यजमानोऽवहद् भागं मातृस्नेहवशानुगः ॥ ३ ॥

sa eva hi dadau bhāgaṁ
parokṣam asurān prati
yajamāno'vahad bhāgaṁ
mātṛ-sneha-vaśānugaḥ

saḥ—he (Viśvarūpa); *eva*—indeed; *hi*—certainly; *dadau*—offered; *bhāgam*—share; *parokṣam*—without the knowledge of the demigods; *asurān*—the demons; *prati*—unto; *yajamānaḥ*—performing sacrifice; *avahat*—offered; *bhāgam*—share; *mātṛ-sneha*—by affection for his mother; *vaśa-anugaḥ*—being compelled.

TRANSLATION

Although offering clarified butter in the sacrificial fire in the name of the demigods, without the knowledge of the demigods he also offered

oblations to the demons because they were his relatives through his mother.

PURPORT

Because of Viśvarūpa's affection for the families of both the demigods and the demons, he appeased the Supreme Lord on behalf of both dynasties. When he offered oblations in the fire on behalf of the *asuras,* he did so secretly, without the knowledge of the demigods.

TEXT 4

तद् देवहेलनं तस्य धर्मालीकं सुरेश्वरः ।
आलक्ष्य तरसा भीतस्तच्छीर्षाण्यच्छिनद् रुषा ॥ ४ ॥

tad deva-helanaṁ tasya
dharmālīkaṁ sureśvaraḥ
ālakṣya tarasā bhītas
tac-chīrṣāṇy acchinad ruṣā

tat—that; *deva-helanam*—offense to the demigods; *tasya*—of him (Viśvarūpa); *dharma-alīkam*—cheating in religious principles (pretending to be the priest of the demigods, but secretly acting as the priest of the demons also); *sura-īśvaraḥ*—the king of the demigods; *ālakṣya*—observing; *tarasā*—quickly; *bhītaḥ*—being afraid (that the demons would gain strength by being blessed by Viśvarūpa); *tat*—his (Viśvarūpa's); *śīrṣāṇi*—heads; *acchinat*—cut off; *ruṣā*—with great anger.

TRANSLATION

Once upon a time, however, the King of heaven, Indra, understood that Viśvarūpa was secretly cheating the demigods by offering oblations on behalf of the demons. He became extremely afraid of being defeated by the demons, and in great anger at Viśvarūpa he cut Viśvarūpa's three heads from his shoulders.

TEXT 5

सोमपीथं तु यत् तस्य शिर आसीत् कपिञ्जलः ।
कलविङ्कः सुरापीथमन्नादं यत् स तित्तिरिः ॥ ५ ॥

soma-pīthaṁ tu yat tasya
śira āsīt kapiñjalaḥ

kalaviṅkaḥ surā-pītham
annādaṁ yat sa tittiriḥ

soma-pītham—used for drinking *soma-rasa; tu*—however; *yat*—which; *tasya*—of him (Viśvarūpa); *śiraḥ*—the head; *āsīt*—became; *kapiñjalaḥ*—a francolin partridge; *kalaviṅkaḥ*—a sparrow; *surā-pītham*—meant for drinking wine; *anna-adam*—used for eating food; *yat*—which; *saḥ*—that; *tittiriḥ*—a common partridge.

TRANSLATION

Thereafter, the head meant for drinking soma-rasa was transformed into a kapiñjala [francolin partridge]. Similarly, the head meant for drinking wine was transformed into a kalaviṅka [sparrow], and the head meant for eating food became a tittiri [common partridge].

TEXT 6

ब्रह्महत्यामञ्जलिना जग्राह यदपीश्वरः ।
संवत्सरान्ते तदघं भूतानां स विशुद्धये ।
भूम्यम्बुद्रुमयोषिद्भ्यश्चतुर्धा व्यभजद्धरिः ॥ ६ ॥

brahma-hatyām añjalinā
jagrāha yad apīśvaraḥ
saṁvatsarānte tad aghaṁ
bhūtānāṁ sa viśuddhaye
bhūmy-ambu-druma-yoṣidbhyaś
caturdhā vyabhajad dhariḥ

brahma-hatyām—the sinful reaction for killing a *brāhmaṇa; añjalinā*—with folded hands; *jagrāha*—assumed the responsibility for; *yat api*—although; *īśvaraḥ*—very powerful; *saṁvatsara-ante*—after one year; *tat agham*—that sinful reaction; *bhūtānām*—of the material elements; *saḥ*—he; *viśuddhaye*—for purification; *bhūmi*—unto the earth; *ambu*—water; *druma*—trees; *yoṣidbhyaḥ*—and unto women; *caturdhā*—in four divisions; *vyabhajat*—divided; *hariḥ*—King Indra.

TRANSLATION

Although Indra was so powerful that he could neutralize the sinful reactions for killing a brāhmaṇa, he repentantly accepted the burden of these reactions with folded hands. He suffered for one year, and then to

purify himself he distributed the reactions for this sinful killing among the earth, water, trees and women.

TEXT 7

भूमिस्तुरीयं जग्राह खातपूरवरेण वै ।
ईरिणं ब्रह्महत्याया रूपं भूमौ प्रदृश्यते ॥ ७ ॥

bhūmis turīyaṁ jagrāha
khāta-pūra-vareṇa vai
īriṇaṁ brahma-hatyāyā
rūpaṁ bhūmau pradṛśyate

bhūmiḥ—the earth; *turīyam*—one fourth; *jagrāha*—accepted; *khāta-pūra*—of the filling of holes; *vareṇa*—because of the benediction; *vai*—indeed; *īriṇam*—the deserts; *brahma-hatyāyāḥ*—of the reaction for killing a *brāhmaṇa; rūpam*—form; *bhūmau*—on the earth; *pradṛśyate*—is visible.

TRANSLATION

In return for King Indra's benediction that ditches in the earth would be filled automatically, the land accepted one fourth of the sinful reactions for killing a brāhmaṇa. Because of those sinful reactions, we find many deserts on the surface of the earth.

PURPORT

Because deserts are manifestations of the earth's diseased condition, no auspicious ritualistic ceremony can be performed in a desert. Persons destined to live in deserts are understood to be sharing the reactions for the sin of *brahma-hatyā,* the killing of a *brāhmaṇa.*

TEXT 8

तुर्यं छेदविरोहेण वरेण जगृहुर्द्रुमाः ।
तेषां निर्यासरूपेण ब्रह्महत्या प्रदृश्यते ॥ ८ ॥

turyaṁ cheda-viroheṇa
vareṇa jagṛhur drumāḥ
teṣāṁ niryāsa-rūpeṇa
brahma-hatyā pradṛśyate

turyam—one fourth; *cheda*—although being cut; *viroheṇa*—of growing again; *vareṇa*—because of the benediction; *jagṛhuḥ*—accepted; *drumāḥ*—

the trees; *teṣām*—of them; *niryāsa-rūpeṇa*—by the liquid oozing from the trees; *brahma-hatyā*—the reaction for killing a *brāhmaṇa; pradṛśyate*—is visible.

TRANSLATION

In return for Indra's benediction that their branches and twigs would grow back when trimmed, the trees accepted one fourth of the reactions for killing a brāhmaṇa. These reactions are visible in the flowing of sap from trees. [Therefore one is forbidden to drink this sap.]

TEXT 9

शश्वत्कामवरेणांहस्तुरीयं जगृहुः स्त्रियः ।
रजोरूपेण तास्वंहो मासि मासि प्रदृश्यते ॥ ९ ॥

śaśvat-kāma-vareṇāṁhas
turīyaṁ jagṛhuḥ striyaḥ
rajo-rūpeṇa tāsv aṁho
māsi māsi pradṛśyate

śaśvat—perpetual; *kāma*—of sexual desire; *vareṇa*—because of the benediction; *aṁhaḥ*—the sinful reaction for killing a *brāhmaṇa; turīyam*—one fourth; *jagṛhuḥ*—accepted; *striyaḥ*—women; *rajaḥ-rūpeṇa*—in the form of the menstrual period; *tāsu*—in them; *aṁhaḥ*—the sinful reaction; *māsi māsi*—every month; *pradṛśyate*—is visible.

TRANSLATION

In return for Lord Indra's benediction that they would be able to enjoy lusty desires continuously, even during pregnancy for as long as sex is not injurious to the embryo, women accepted one fourth of the sinful reactions. As a result of those reactions, women manifest the signs of menstruation every month.

PURPORT

Women as a class are very lusty, and apparently their continuous lusty desires are never satisfied. In return for Lord Indra's benediction that there would be no cessation to their lusty desires, women accepted one fourth of the sinful reactions for killing a *brāhmaṇa*.

TEXT 10

द्रव्यभूयोवरेणापस्तुरीयं जगृहुर्मलम् ।
तासु बुद्बुदफेनाभ्यां दृष्टं तद्धरति क्षिपन् ॥ १० ॥

dravya-bhūyo-vareṇāpas
turīyaṁ jagṛhur malam
tāsu budbuda-phenābhyāṁ
dṛṣṭaṁ tad dharati kṣipan

dravya—other things; *bhūyaḥ*—of increasing; *vareṇa*—by the benediction; *āpaḥ*—water; *turīyam*—one fourth; *jagṛhuḥ*—accepted; *malam*—the sinful reaction; *tāsu*—in the water; *budbuda-phenābhyām*—by bubbles and foam; *dṛṣṭam*—visible; *tat*—that; *harati*—one collects; *kṣipan*—throwing away.

TRANSLATION

And in return for King Indra's benediction that water would increase the volume of other substances with which it was mixed, water accepted one fourth of the sinful reactions. Therefore there are bubbles and foam in water. When one collects water, these should be avoided.

PURPORT

If water is mixed with milk, fruit juice or other similar substances, it increases their volume, and no one can understand which has increased. In return for this benediction, water accepted one fourth of Indra's sinful reactions. These sinful reactions are visible in foam and bubbles. Therefore one should avoid foam and bubbles while collecting drinking water.

TEXT 11

हतपुत्रस्ततस्त्वष्टा जुहावेन्द्राय शत्रवे ।
इन्द्रशत्रो विवर्धस्व माचिरं जहि विद्विषम् ॥ ११ ॥

hata-putras tatas tvaṣṭā
juhāvendrāya śatrave
indra-śatro vivardhasva
mā ciraṁ jahi vidviṣam

hata-putraḥ—who lost his son; *tataḥ*—thereafter; *tvaṣṭā*—Tvaṣṭā; *juhāva*—performed a sacrifice; *indrāya*—of Indra; *śatrave*—for creating an enemy; *indra-śatro*—O enemy of Indra; *vivardhasva*—increase; *mā*—not; *ciram*—after a long time; *jahi*—kill; *vidviṣam*—your enemy.

TRANSLATION

After Viśvarūpa was killed, his father, Tvaṣṭā, performed ritualistic ceremonies to kill Indra. He offered oblations in the sacrificial fire, saying, "O enemy of Indra, flourish to kill your enemy without delay."

PURPORT

There was some defect in Tvaṣṭā's chanting of the *mantra* because he chanted it long instead of short, and therefore the meaning changed. Tvaṣṭā intended to chant the word *indra-śatro,* meaning, "O enemy of Indra." In this *mantra,* the word *indra* is in the possessive case (*ṣaṣṭhī*), and the word *indra-śatro* is called a *tat-puruṣa* compound (*tatpuruṣa-samāsa*). Unfortunately, instead of chanting the *mantra* short, Tvaṣṭā chanted it long, and its meaning changed from "the enemy of Indra" to "Indra, who is an enemy." Consequently instead of an enemy of Indra's, there emerged the body of Vṛtrāsura, of whom Indra was the enemy.

TEXT 12

अथान्वाहार्यपचनादुत्थितो घोरदर्शनः ।
कृतान्त इव लोकानां युगान्तसमये यथा ॥ १२ ॥

athānvāhārya-pacanād
utthito ghora-darśanaḥ
kṛtānta iva lokānāṁ
yugānta-samaye yathā

atha—thereafter; *anvāhārya-pacanāt*—from the fire known as Anvāhārya; *utthitaḥ*—arisen; *ghora-darśanaḥ*—appearing very fearful; *kṛtāntaḥ*—personified annihilation; *iva*—like; *lokānām*—of all the planets; *yuga-anta*—of the end of the millennium; *samaye*—at the time; *yathā*—just as.

TRANSLATION

Thereafter, from the southern side of the sacrificial fire known as Anvāhārya came a fearful personality who looked like the destroyer of the entire creation at the end of the millennium.

TEXTS 13–17

विष्वग्विवर्धमानं तमिषुमात्रं दिने दिने ।
दग्धशैलप्रतीकाशं सन्ध्याभ्रानीकवर्चसम् ॥ १३ ॥
तप्तताम्रशिखाश्मश्रुं मध्याह्नार्कोग्रलोचनम् ॥ १४ ॥
देदीप्यमाने त्रिशिखे शूल आरोप्य रोदसी ।
नृत्यन्तमुन्नदन्तं च चालयन्तं पदा महीम् ॥ १५ ॥
दरीगम्भीरवक्त्रेण पिबता च नभस्तलम् ।
लिहता जिह्वयर्क्षाणि ग्रसता भुवनत्रयम् ॥ १६ ॥
महता रौद्रदंष्ट्रेण जृम्भमाणं मुहुर्मुहुः ।
वित्रस्ता दुद्रुवुर्लोका वीक्ष्य सर्वे दिशो दश ॥ १७ ॥

viṣvag vivardhamānaṁ tam
iṣu-mātraṁ dine dine
dagdha-śaila-pratīkāśaṁ
sandhyābhrānīka-varcasam

tapta-tāmra-śikhā-śmaśruṁ
madhyāhnārkogra-locanam

dedīpyamāne tri-śikhe
śūla āropya rodasī
nṛtyantam unnadantaṁ ca
cālayantaṁ padā mahīm

darī-gambhīra-vaktreṇa
pibatā ca nabhastalam
lihatā jihvayarkṣāṇi
grasatā bhuvana-trayam

mahatā raudra-daṁṣṭreṇa
jṛmbhamāṇaṁ muhur muhuḥ
vitrastā dudruvur lokā
vīkṣya sarve diśo daśa

viṣvak—all around; *vivardhamānam*—increasing; *tam*—him; *iṣu-mātram*—an arrow's flight; *dine dine*—day after day; *dagdha*—burnt; *śaila*—mountain; *pratīkāśam*—resembling; *sandhyā*—in the evening; *abhra-anīka*

—like an array of clouds; *varcasam*—having an effulgence; *tapta*—melted; *tāmra*—like copper; *śikhā*—hair; *śmaśrum*—moustache and beard; *madhyāhna*—at midday; *arka*—like the sun; *ugra-locanam*—having powerful eyes; *dedīpyamāne*—blazing; *tri-śikhe*—three-pointed; *śūle*—on his spear; *āropya*—keeping; *rodasī*—heaven and earth; *nṛtyantam*—dancing; *unnadantam*—shouting loudly; *ca*—and; *cālayantam*—moving; *padā*—by his foot; *mahīm*—the earth; *darī-gambhīra*—as deep as a cave; *vaktreṇa*—by the mouth; *pibatā*—drinking; *ca*—also; *nabhastalam*—the sky; *lihatā*—licking up; *jihvayā*—by the tongue; *ṛkṣāṇi*—the stars; *grasatā*—swallowing; *bhuvana-trayam*—the three worlds; *mahatā*—very great; *raudra-daṁṣṭreṇa*—with fearful teeth; *jṛmbhamāṇam*—yawning; *muhuḥ muhuḥ*—again and again; *vitrastāḥ*—fearful; *dudruvuḥ*—ran; *lokāḥ*—people; *vīkṣya*—seeing; *sarve*—all; *diśaḥ daśa*—ten directions.

TRANSLATION

Like arrows released in the four directions, the demon's body grew, day after day. Tall and blackish, he appeared like a burnt hill and was as lustrous as a bright array of clouds in the evening. The hair on the demon's body and his beard and moustache were the color of melted copper, and his eyes were piercing like the midday sun. He appeared unconquerable, as if holding the three worlds on the points of his blazing trident. Dancing and shouting with a loud voice, he made the entire surface of the earth tremble as if from an earthquake. As he yawned again and again, he seemed to be trying to swallow the whole sky with his mouth, which was as deep as a cave. He seemed to be licking up all the stars in the sky with his tongue and eating the entire universe with his long, sharp teeth. Seeing this gigantic demon, everyone, in great fear, ran here and there in all directions.

TEXT 18

येनावृता इमे लोकास्तपसा त्वाष्ट्रमूर्तिना ।
स वै वृत्र इति प्रोक्तः पापः परमदारुणः ॥ १८ ॥

yenāvṛtā ime lokās
tapasā tvāṣṭra-mūrtinā
sa vai vṛtra iti proktaḥ
pāpaḥ parama-dāruṇaḥ

yena—by whom; *āvṛtāḥ*—covered; *ime*—all these; *lokāḥ*—planets; *tapasā*—by the austerity; *tvāṣṭra-mūrtinā*—in the form of the son of Tvaṣṭā; *saḥ*—he; *vai*—indeed; *vṛtraḥ*—Vṛtra; *iti*—thus; *proktaḥ*—called; *pāpaḥ*—personified sin; *parama-dāruṇaḥ*—very fearful.

TRANSLATION

That very fearful demon, who was actually the son of Tvaṣṭā, covered all the planetary systems by dint of austerity. Therefore he was named Vṛtra, or one who covers everything.

PURPORT

In the *Vedas* it is said, *sa imāl̐ lokān āvṛṇot tad vṛtrasya vṛtratvam:* because the demon covered all the planetary systems, his name was Vṛtrāsura.

TEXT 19

तं निजघ्नुरभिद्रुत्य सगणा विबुधर्षभाः ।
स्वैः स्वैर्दिव्यास्त्रशस्त्रौघैः सोऽग्रसत् तानि कृत्स्नशः ॥ १९ ॥

taṁ nijaghnur abhidrutya
sagaṇā vibudharṣabhāḥ
svaiḥ svair divyāstra-śastraughaiḥ
so'grasat tāni kṛtsnaśaḥ

tam—him; *nijaghnuḥ*—struck; *abhidrutya*—running to; *sa-gaṇāḥ*—with soldiers; *vibudha-ṛṣabhāḥ*—all the great demigods; *svaiḥ svaiḥ*—with their own respective; *divya*—transcendental; *astra*—bows and arrows; *śastra-oghaiḥ*—different weapons; *saḥ*—he (Vṛtra); *agrasat*—swallowed; *tāni*—them (the weapons); *kṛtsnaśaḥ*—all together.

TRANSLATION

The demigods, headed by Indra, charged the demon with their soldiers, striking him with their own transcendental bows and arrows and other weapons but Vṛtrāsura swallowed all their weapons.

TEXT 20

ततस्ते विस्मिताः सर्वे विषण्णा ग्रस्ततेजसः ।
प्रत्यञ्चमादिपुरुषमुपतस्थुः समाहिताः ॥ २० ॥

tatas te vismitāḥ sarve
viṣaṇṇā grasta-tejasaḥ

pratyañcam ādi-puruṣam
upatasthuḥ samāhitāḥ

tataḥ—thereafter; *te*—they (the demigods); *vismitāḥ*—being struck with wonder; *sarve*—all; *viṣaṇṇāḥ*—being very morose; *grasta-tejasaḥ*—having lost all their personal strength; *pratyañcam*—to the Supersoul; *ādi-puruṣam*—the original person; *upatasthuḥ*—prayed; *samāhitāḥ*—all gathered together.

TRANSLATION

Struck with wonder and disappointment upon seeing the strength of the demon, the demigods lost their own strength. Therefore they all met together to try to please the Supersoul, the Supreme Personality of Godhead, Nārāyaṇa, by worshiping Him.

TEXT 21

श्रीदेवा ऊचुः
वाय्वम्बराग्न्यप्क्षितयस्त्रिलोका
ब्रह्मादयो ये वयमुद्विजन्तः ।
हराम यस्मै बलिमन्तकोऽसौ
बिभेति यस्मादरणं ततो नः ॥ २१ ॥

śrī-devā ūcuḥ
vāyv-ambarāgny-ap-kṣitayas tri-lokā
brahmādayo ye vayam udvijantaḥ
harāma yasmai balim antako'sau
bibheti yasmād araṇaṁ tato naḥ

śrī-devāḥ ūcuḥ—the demigods said; *vāyu*—composed of air; *ambara*—sky; *agni*—fire; *ap*—water; *kṣitayaḥ*—and land; *tri-lokāḥ*—the three worlds; *brahma-ādayaḥ*—beginning from Lord Brahmā; *ye*—who; *vayam*—we; *udvijantaḥ*—being very much afraid; *harāma*—offer; *yasmai*—unto whom; *balim*—presentation; *antakaḥ*—the destroyer, death; *asau*—that; *bibheti*—fears; *yasmāt*—from whom; *araṇam*—shelter; *tataḥ*—therefore; *naḥ*—our.

TRANSLATION

The demigods said: The three worlds are created by the five elements—namely ether, air, fire, water and earth—which are controlled by various demigods, beginning from Lord Brahmā. Being very much afraid that the

time factor will end our existence, we offer presentations unto time by performing our work as time dictates. The time factor himself, however, is afraid of the Supreme Personality of Godhead. Therefore let us now worship that Supreme Lord, who alone can give us full protection.

PURPORT

When one is afraid of being killed, one must take shelter of the Supreme Personality of Godhead. He is worshiped by all the demigods, beginning from Brahmā, although they are in charge of the various elements of this material world. The words *bibheti yasmāt* indicate that all the demons, regardless of how great and powerful, fear the Supreme Personality of Godhead. The demigods, being afraid of death, took shelter of the Lord and offered Him these prayers. Although the time factor is fearful to everyone, fear personified is afraid of the Supreme Lord, who is therefore known as *abhaya,* fearless. Taking shelter of the Supreme Lord brings actual fearlessness, and therefore the demigods decided to take shelter of the Lord.

TEXT 22

अविस्मितं तं परिपूर्णकामं
स्वेनैव लाभेन समं प्रशान्तम् ।
विनोपसर्पत्यपरं हि बालिशः
श्वलाङ्गुलेनातितितर्ति सिन्धुम् ॥ २२ ॥

avismitaṁ taṁ paripūrṇa-kāmaṁ
svenaiva lābhena samaṁ praśāntam
vinopasarpaty aparaṁ hi bāliśaḥ
śva-lāṅgulenātititarti sindhum

avismitam—who is never struck with wonder; *tam*—Him; *paripūrṇa-kāmam*—who is fully satisfied; *svena*—by His own; *eva*—indeed; *lābhena*—achievements; *samam*—equipoised; *praśāntam*—very steady; *vinā*—without; *upasarpati*—approaches; *aparam*—another; *hi*—indeed; *bāliśaḥ*—a fool; *śva*—of a dog; *lāṅgulena*—by the tail; *atititarti*—wants to cross; *sindhum*—the sea.

TRANSLATION

Free from all material conceptions of existence and never wonder-struck by anything, the Lord is always jubilant and fully satisfied by His own spiritual perfection. He has no material designations, and therefore He is

steady and unattached. That Supreme Personality of Godhead is the only shelter of everyone. Anyone desiring to be protected by others is certainly a great fool who desires to cross the sea by holding the tail of a dog.

PURPORT

A dog can swim in the water, but if a dog dives in the ocean and someone wants to cross the ocean by holding the dog's tail, he is certainly fool number one. A dog cannot cross the ocean, nor can a person cross the ocean by catching a dog's tail. Similarly, one who desires to cross the ocean of nescience should not seek the shelter of any demigod or anyone else but the fearless shelter of the Supreme Personality of Godhead. *Śrīmad-Bhāgavatam* (10.14.58) therefore says:

samāśritā ye pada-pallava-plavaṁ
mahat-padaṁ puṇya-yaśo-murāreḥ
bhavāmbudhir vatsa-padaṁ paraṁ padaṁ
padaṁ padaṁ yad vipadāṁ na teṣām

The Lord's lotus feet are an indestructible boat, and if one takes shelter of that boat he can easily cross the ocean of nescience. Consequently there are no dangers for a devotee although he lives within this material world, which is full of dangers at every step. One should seek the shelter of the all-powerful instead of trying to be protected by one's own concocted ideas.

TEXT 23

यस्योरुशृङ्गे जगतीं स्वनावं
मनुर्यथाबध्य ततार दुर्गम् ।
स एव नस्त्वाष्ट्रभयाद् दुरन्तात्
त्राताश्रितान् वारिचरोऽपि नूनम् ॥ २३ ॥

yasyoru-śṛṅge jagatīṁ sva-nāvaṁ
manur yathābadhya tatāra durgam
sa eva nas tvāṣṭra-bhayād durantāt
trātāśritān vāricaro'pi nūnam

yasya—of whom; *uru*—very strong and high; *śṛṅge*—on the horn; *jagatīm*—in the form of the world; *sva-nāvam*—his own boat; *manuḥ*—Manu, King Satyavrata; *yathā*—just as; *ābadhya*—binding; *tatāra*—crossed; *durgam*—the very difficult to cross (inundation); *saḥ*—He (the Supreme

Personality of Godhead); *eva*—certainly; *naḥ*—us; *tvāṣṭra-bhayāt*—from fear of the son of Tvaṣṭā; *durantāt*—endless; *trātā*—deliverer; *āśritān*—dependents (like us); *vāri-caraḥ api*—although taking the form of a fish; *nūnam*—indeed.

TRANSLATION

The Manu named King Satyavrata formerly saved himself by tying the small boat of the entire world to the horn of the Matsya avatāra, the fish incarnation. By the grace of the Matsya avatāra, Manu saved himself from the great danger of the flood. May that same fish incarnation save us from the great and fearful danger caused by the son of Tvaṣṭā.

TEXT 24

पुरा स्वयम्भूरपि संयमाम्भ-
स्युदीर्णवातोर्मिरवैः कराले ।
एकोऽरविन्दात् पतितस्ततार
तस्माद् भयाद् येन स नोऽस्तु पारः ॥ २४ ॥

purā svayambhūr api saṁyamāmbhasy
udīrṇa-vātormi-ravaiḥ karāle
eko'ravindāt patitas tatāra
tasmād bhayād yena sa no'stu pāraḥ

purā—formerly (during the time of creation); *svayambhūḥ*—Lord Brahmā; *api*—also; *saṁyama-ambhasi*—in the water of inundation; *udīrṇa*—very high; *vāta*—of wind; *ūrmi*—and of waves; *ravaiḥ*—by the sounds; *karāle*—very fearful; *ekaḥ*—alone; *aravindāt*—from the lotus seat; *patitaḥ*—almost fallen; *tatāra*—escaped; *tasmāt*—from that; *bhayāt*—fearful situation; *yena*—by whom (the Lord); *saḥ*—He; *naḥ*—of us; *astu*—let there be; *pāraḥ*—deliverance.

TRANSLATION

In the beginning of creation, a tremendous wind caused fierce waves of inundating water. The great waves made such a horrible sound that Lord Brahmā almost fell from his seat on the lotus into the water of devastation, but he was saved with the help of the Lord. Thus we also expect the Lord to protect us from this dangerous condition.

TEXT 25

य एक ईशो निजमायया नः
ससर्ज येनानुसृजाम विश्वम् ।
वयं न यस्यापि पुरः समीहतः
पश्याम लिङ्गं पृथगीशमानिनः ॥ २५ ॥

ya eka īśo nija-māyayā naḥ
sasarja yenānusṛjāma viśvam
vayaṁ na yasyāpi puraḥ samīhataḥ
paśyāma liṅgaṁ pṛthag īśa-māninaḥ

yaḥ—He who; *ekaḥ*—one; *īśaḥ*—controller; *nija-māyayā*—by His transcendental potency; *naḥ*—us; *sasarja*—created; *yena*—by whom (through whose mercy); *anusṛjāma*—we also create; *viśvam*—the universe; *vayam*—we; *na*—not; *yasya*—of whom; *api*—although; *puraḥ*—in front of us; *samīhataḥ*—of Him who is acting; *paśyāma*—see; *liṅgam*—the form; *pṛthak*—separate; *īśa*—as controllers; *māninaḥ*—thinking of ourselves.

TRANSLATION

The Supreme Personality of Godhead, who created us by His external potency and by whose mercy we expand the creation of the universe, is always situated before us as the Supersoul, but we cannot see His form. We are unable to see Him because all of us think that we are separate and independent gods.

PURPORT

Here is an explanation of why the conditioned soul cannot see the Supreme Personality of Godhead face to face. Even though the Lord appears before us as Lord Kṛṣṇa or Lord Rāmacandra and lives in human society as a leader or king, the conditioned soul cannot understand Him. *Avajānanti māṁ mūḍhā mānuṣīṁ tanum āśritam:* rascals (*mūḍhas*) deride the Supreme Personality of Godhead, thinking Him an ordinary human being. However insignificant we are, we think that we are also God, that we can create a universe or that we can create another God. This is why we cannot see or understand the Supreme Personality of Godhead. In this regard, Śrīla Madhvācārya says:

liṅgam eva paśyāmaḥ
kadācid abhimānas tu

devānām api sann iva
prāyaḥ kāleṣu nāsty eva
tāratamyena so'pi tu

We are all conditioned to various degrees, but we think that we are God. This is why we cannot understand who God is or see Him face to face.

TEXTS 26–27

यो नः सपत्नैर्भृशमर्द्यमानान्
देवर्षितिर्यङ्नृषु नित्य एव ।
कृतावतारस्तनुभिः स्वमायया
कृत्वात्मसात् पाति युगे युगे च ॥ २६ ॥
तमेव देवं वयमात्मदैवतं
परं प्रधानं पुरुषं विश्वमन्यम् ।
व्रजाम सर्वे शरणं शरण्यं
स्वानां स नो धास्यति शं महात्मा ॥ २७ ॥

yo naḥ sapatnair bhṛśam ardyamānān
devarṣi-tiryaṅ-nṛṣu nitya eva
kṛtāvatāras tanubhiḥ sva-māyayā
kṛtvātmasāt pāti yuge yuge ca

tam eva devaṁ vayam ātma-daivataṁ
paraṁ pradhānaṁ puruṣaṁ viśvam anyam
vrajāma sarve śaraṇaṁ śaraṇyaṁ
svānāṁ sa no dhāsyati śaṁ mahātmā

yaḥ—He who; *naḥ*—us; *sapatnaiḥ*—by our enemies, the demons; *bhṛśam*—almost always; *ardyamānān*—being persecuted; *deva*—among the demigods; *ṛṣi*—the saintly persons; *tiryak*—the animals; *nṛṣu*—and men; *nityaḥ*—always; *eva*—certainly; *kṛta-avatāraḥ*—appearing as an incarnation; *tanubhiḥ*—with different forms; *sva-māyayā*—by His internal potency; *kṛtvā ātmasāt*—considering very near and dear to Him; *pāti*—protects; *yuge yuge*—in every millennium; *ca*—and; *tam*—Him; *eva*—indeed; *devam*—the Supreme Lord; *vayam*—all of us; *ātma-daivatam*—the Lord of all living entities; *param*—transcendental; *pradhānam*—the original cause of the total material energy; *puruṣam*—the supreme enjoyer; *viśvam*—whose energy constitutes this universe; *anyam*—separately situated; *vrajāma*—we approach; *sarve*—all; *śaraṇam*—shelter; *śaraṇyam*—suitable as shelter; *svānām*—unto His own devotees; *saḥ*—He; *naḥ*—unto us; *dhāsyati*—shall give; *śam*—good fortune; *mahātmā*—the Supersoul.

TRANSLATION

By His inconceivable internal potency, the Supreme Personality of Godhead expands into various transcendental bodies as Vāmanadeva, the incarnation of strength among the demigods; Paraśurāma, the incarnation among saints; Nṛsiṁhadeva and Varāha, incarnations among animals; and Matsya and Kūrma, incarnations among aquatics. He accepts various transcendental bodies among all types of living entities, and among human beings He especially appears as Lord Kṛṣṇa and Lord Rāma. By His causeless mercy, He protects the demigods, who are always harassed by the demons. He is the supreme worshipable Deity of all living entities. He is the supreme cause, represented as the male and female creative energies. Although different from this universe, He exists in His universal form [virāṭ-rūpa]. In our fearful condition, let us take shelter of Him, for we are sure that the Supreme Lord, the Supreme Soul, will give us His protection.

PURPORT

In this verse, the Supreme Personality of Godhead, Viṣṇu, is ascertained to be the original cause of creation. Śrīdhara Svāmī, in his commentary *Bhāvārtha-dīpikā,* replies to the idea that *prakṛti* and *puruṣa* are the causes of the cosmic manifestation. As stated herein, *paraṁ pradhānaṁ puruṣaṁ viśvam anyam:* "He is the supreme cause, represented as the male and female creative energies. Although different from this universe, He exists in His universal form [*virāṭa-rūpa*]." The word *prakṛti,* which is used to indicate the source of generation, refers to the material energy of the Supreme Lord, and the word *puruṣa* refers to the living entities, who are the superior energy of the Lord. Both the *prakṛti* and *puruṣa* ultimately enter the Supreme Lord, as stated in *Bhagavad-gītā* (*prakṛtiṁ yānti māmikām*).

Although *prakṛti* and *puruṣa* superficially appear to be the causes of the material manifestation, both are emanations of different energies of the Supreme Lord. Therefore the Supreme Lord is the cause of *prakṛti* and *puruṣa.* He is the original cause (*sarva-kāraṇa-kāraṇam*). The *Nāradīya Purāṇa* says:

avikāro'pi paramaḥ
prakṛtis tu vikāriṇī

anupraviśya govindaḥ
prakṛtiś cābhidhīyate

Both the *prakṛti* and *puruṣa,* which are inferior and superior energies, are emanations from the Supreme Personality of Godhead. As explained in *Bhagavad-gītā* (*gām āviśya*), the Lord enters the *prakṛti,* and then the *prakṛti* creates different manifestations. The *prakṛti* is not independent or beyond His energies. Vāsudeva, Lord Śrī Kṛṣṇa, is the original cause of everything. Therefore the Lord says in *Bhagavad-gītā* (10.8):

ahaṁ sarvasya prabhavo
mattaḥ sarvaṁ pravartate
iti matvā bhajante māṁ
budhā bhāva-samanvitāḥ

"I am the source of all spiritual and material worlds. Everything emanates from Me. The wise who perfectly know this engage in My devotional service and worship Me with all their hearts." In *Śrīmad-Bhāgavatam* (2.9.33) the Lord also says, *aham evāsam evāgre:* "Only I existed before the creation." This is confirmed in the *Brahmāṇḍa Purāṇa* as follows:

smṛtir avyavadhānena
prakṛtitvam iti sthitiḥ
ubhayātmaka-sūtitvād
vāsudevaḥ paraḥ pumān
prakṛtiḥ puruṣaś ceti
śabdair eko'bhidhīyate

To generate the universe, the Lord acts indirectly as the *puruṣa* and directly as the *prakṛti.* Because both energies emanate from Lord Vāsudeva, the all-pervasive Supreme Personality of Godhead, He is known as both *prakṛti* and *puruṣa.* Therefore Vāsudeva is the cause of everything (*sarva-kāraṇa-kāraṇam*).

TEXT 28

श्रीशुक उवाच
इति तेषां महाराज सुराणामुपतिष्ठताम् ।
प्रतीच्यां दिश्यभूदाविः शङ्खचक्रगदाधरः ॥ २८ ॥

śrī-śuka uvāca
iti teṣāṁ mahārāja
surāṇām upatiṣṭhatām

pratīcyāṁ diśy abhūd āviḥ
śaṅkha-cakra-gadā-dharaḥ

śrī-śukaḥ uvāca—Śrī Śukadeva Gosvāmī said; *iti*—thus; *teṣām*—of them; *mahārāja*—O King; *surāṇām*—of the demigods; *upatiṣṭhatām*—praying; *pratīcyām*—inside; *diśi*—in the direction; *abhūt*—became; *āviḥ*—visible; *śaṅkha-cakra-gadā-dharaḥ*—bearing the transcendental weapons: the conchshell, disc and club.

TRANSLATION

Śrī Śukadeva Gosvāmī said: My dear King, when all the demigods offered Him their prayers, the Supreme Personality of Godhead, Lord Hari, carrying His weapons, the conchshell, disc and club, appeared first within their hearts and then before them.

TEXTS 29–30

आत्मतुल्यैः षोडशभिर्विना श्रीवत्सकौस्तुभौ ।
पर्युपासितमुन्निद्रशरदम्बुरुहेक्षणम् ॥ २९ ॥
दृष्ट्वा तमवनौ सर्व ईक्षणाह्लादविक्लवाः ।
दण्डवत् पतिता राजञ्छनैरुत्थाय तुष्टुवुः ॥ ३० ॥

ātma-tulyaiḥ ṣoḍaśabhir
vinā śrīvatsa-kaustubhau
paryupāsitam unnidra-
śarad-amburuhekṣaṇam

dṛṣṭvā tam avanau sarva
īkṣaṇāhlāda-viklavāḥ
daṇḍavat patitā rājañ
chanair utthāya tuṣṭuvuḥ

ātma-tulyaiḥ—almost equal to Himself; *ṣoḍaśabhiḥ*—by sixteen (servants); *vinā*—without; *śrīvatsa-kaustubhau*—the Śrīvatsa mark and Kaustubha jewel; *paryupāsitam*—being attended on all sides; *unnidra*—blooming; *śarat*—of the autumn; *amburuha*—like lotus flowers; *īkṣaṇam*—having eyes; *dṛṣṭvā*—seeing; *tam*—Him (the Supreme Personality of Godhead, Nārāyaṇa); *avanau*—on the ground; *sarve*—all of them; *īkṣaṇa*—from directly seeing; *āhlāda*—with happiness; *viklavāḥ*—being overwhelmed;

daṇḍa-vat—like a stick; *patitāḥ*—fell; *rājan*—O King; *śanaiḥ*—slowly; *utthāya*—standing up; *tuṣṭuvuḥ*—offered prayers.

TRANSLATION

Surrounding and serving the Supreme Personality of Godhead, Nārāyaṇa, were sixteen personal attendants, decorated with ornaments and appearing exactly like Him but without the mark of Śrīvatsa and the Kaustubha jewel. O King, when all the demigods saw the Supreme Lord in that posture, smiling with eyes like the petals of lotuses grown in autumn, they were overwhelmed with happiness and immediately fell down like rods, offering daṇḍavats. Then they slowly rose and pleased the Lord by offering Him prayers.

PURPORT

In Vaikuṇṭhaloka the Supreme Personality of Godhead has four hands and decorations like the Śrīvatsa mark on His chest and the gem known as Kaustubha. These are special indications of the Supreme Personality of Godhead. The Lord's personal attendants and other devotees in Vaikuṇṭha have the same features, except for the Śrīvatsa mark and the Kaustubha gem.

TEXT 31

श्रीदेवा ऊचुः
नमस्ते यज्ञवीर्याय वयसे उत ते नमः ।
नमस्ते ह्यस्तचक्राय नमः सुपुरुहूतये ॥ ३१ ॥

śrī-devā ūcuḥ
namas te yajña-vīryāya
vayase uta te namaḥ
namas te hy asta-cakrāya
namaḥ supuru-hūtaye

śrī-devāḥ ūcuḥ—the demigods said; *namaḥ*—obeisances; *te*—unto You; *yajña-vīryāya*—unto the Supreme Personality of Godhead, who is able to give the results of sacrifice; *vayase*—who is the time factor, which ends the results of *yajña; uta*—although; *te*—unto You; *namaḥ*—obeisances; *namaḥ*—obeisances; *te*—unto You; *hi*—indeed; *asta-cakrāya*—who throws the disc; *namaḥ*—respectful obeisances; *supuru-hūtaye*—having varieties of transcendental names.

TRANSLATION

The demigods said: O Supreme Personality of Godhead, You are competent to give the results of sacrifice, and You are also the time factor that destroys all such results in due course. You are the one who releases the cakra to kill the demons. O Lord, who possesses many varieties of names, we offer our respectful obeisances unto You.

TEXT 32

यत् ते गतीनां तिसृणामीशितुः परमं पदम् ।
नार्वाचीनो विसर्गस्य धातर्वेदितुमर्हति ॥ ३२ ॥

yat te gatīnāṁ tisṛṇām
īśituḥ paramaṁ padam
nārvācīno visargasya
dhātar veditum arhati

yat—which; *te*—of You; *gatīnām tisṛṇām*—of the three destinations (the heavenly planets, the earthly planets and hell); *īśituḥ*—who are the controller; *paramam padam*—the supreme abode, Vaikuṇṭhaloka; *na*—not; *arvācīnaḥ*—a person appearing after; *visargasya*—the creation; *dhātaḥ*—O supreme controller; *veditum*—to understand; *arhati*—is able.

TRANSLATION

O supreme controller, You control the three destinations [promotion to the heavenly planets, birth as a human being, and condemnation in hell], yet Your supreme abode is Vaikuṇṭha-dhāma. Since we appeared after You created this cosmic manifestation, Your activities are impossible for us to understand. We therefore have nothing to offer You but our humble obeisances.

PURPORT

An inexperienced man generally does not know what to beg from the Supreme Personality of Godhead. Everyone is under the jurisdiction of the created material world, and no one knows what benediction to ask when praying to the Supreme Lord. People generally pray to be promoted to the heavenly planets because they have no information of Vaikuṇṭhaloka. Śrīla Madhvācārya quotes the following verse:

deva-lokāt pitṛ-lokāt
nirayāc cāpi yat param
tisṛbhyaḥ paramaṁ sthānaṁ
vaiṣṇavaṁ viduṣāṁ gatiḥ

There are different planetary systems, known as Devaloka (the planets of the demigods), Pitṛloka (the planet of the Pitās) and Niraya (the hellish planets). When one transcends these various planetary systems and enters Vaikuṇṭhaloka, he achieves the ultimate resort of the Vaiṣṇavas. Vaiṣṇavas have nothing to do with the other planetary systems.

TEXT 33

ॐ नमस्तेऽस्तु भगवन् नारायण वासुदेवादिपुरुष महापुरुष महानुभाव परममङ्गल परमकल्याण परमकारुणिक केवल जगदाधार लोकैकनाथ सर्वेश्वर लक्ष्मीनाथ परमहंसपरिव्राजकैः परमेणात्मयोगसमाधिना परिभावितपरिस्फुटपारमहंस्यधर्मेणोद्घाटिततमःकपाटद्वारे चित्तेऽपावृत आत्मलोके स्वयमुपलब्धनिजसुखानुभवो भवान् ॥ ३३ ॥

oṁ namas te'stu bhagavan nārāyaṇa vāsudevādi-puruṣa mahā-puruṣa mahānubhāva parama-maṅgala parama-kalyāṇa parama-kāruṇika kevala jagad-ādhāra lokaika-nātha sarveśvara lakṣmī-nātha paramahaṁsa-parivrājakaiḥ parameṇātma-yoga-samādhinā paribhāvita-parisphuṭa-pāramahaṁsya-dharmeṇodghāṭita-tamaḥ-kapāṭa-dvāre citte'pāvṛta ātma-loke svayam upalabdha-nija-sukhānubhavo bhavān.

oṁ—O Lord; *namaḥ*—respectful obeisances; *te*—unto You; *astu*—let there be; *bhagavan*—O Supreme Personality of Godhead; *nārāyaṇa*—the resort of all living entities, Nārāyaṇa; *vāsudeva*—Lord Vāsudeva, Śrī Kṛṣṇa; *ādi-puruṣa*—the original person; *mahā-puruṣa*—the most exalted personality; *mahā-anubhāva*—the supremely opulent; *parama-maṅgala*—the most auspicious; *parama-kalyāṇa*—the supreme benediction; *parama-kāruṇika*—the supremely merciful; *kevala*—changeless; *jagat-ādhāra*—the support of the cosmic manifestation; *loka-eka-nātha*—the only proprietor of all the planetary systems; *sarva-īśvara*—the supreme controller; *lakṣmī-nātha*—the husband of the goddess of fortune; *paramahaṁsa-parivrājakaiḥ*—by the topmost *sannyāsīs* wandering all over the world; *parameṇa*—by supreme;

ātma-yoga-samādhinā—absorption in *bhakti-yoga; paribhāvita*—fully purified; *parisphuṭa*—and fully manifested; *pāramahaṁsya-dharmeṇa*—by executing the transcendental process of devotional service; *udghāṭita*—pushed open; *tamaḥ*—of illusory existence; *kapāṭa*—in which the door; *dvāre*—existing as the entrance; *citte*—in the mind; *apāvṛte*—without contamination; *ātma-loke*—in the spiritual world; *svayam*—personally; *upalabdha*—experiencing; *nija*—personal; *sukha-anubhavaḥ*—perception of happiness; *bhavān*—Your Lordship.

TRANSLATION

O Supreme Personality of Godhead, O Nārāyaṇa, O Vāsudeva, original person! O most exalted person, supreme experience, welfare personified! O supreme benediction, supremely merciful and changeless! O support of the cosmic manifestation, sole proprietor of all planetary systems, master of everything and husband of the goddess of fortune! Your Lordship is realized by the topmost sannyāsīs, who wander about the world to preach Kṛṣṇa consciousness, fully absorbed in samādhi through bhakti-yoga. Because their minds are concentrated upon You, they can receive the conception of Your personality in their fully purified hearts. When the darkness in their hearts is completely eradicated and You are revealed to them, the transcendental bliss they enjoy is the transcendental form of Your Lordship. No one but such persons can realize You. Therefore we simply offer You our respectful obeisances.

PURPORT

The Supreme Personality of Godhead has numerous transcendental names pertaining to different grades of revelation to various grades of devotees and transcendentalists. When He is realized in His impersonal form He is called the Supreme Brahman, when realized as the Paramātmā He is called *antaryāmī,* and when He expands Himself in different forms for material creation He is called Kṣīrodakaśāyī Viṣṇu, Garbhodakaśāyī Viṣṇu and Kāraṇodakaśāyī Viṣṇu. When He is realized as Vāsudeva, Saṅkarṣaṇa, Pradyumna and Aniruddha—the Caturvyūha, who are beyond the three forms of Viṣṇu—He is the Vaikuṇṭha Nārāyaṇa. Above realization of Nārāyaṇa is realization of Baladeva, and above that is realization of Kṛṣṇa. All these realizations are possible when one engages fully in devotional service. The covered core of one's heart is then completely open to receiving an understanding of the Supreme Personality of Godhead in His various forms.

TEXT 34

दुरवबोध इव तवायं विहारयोगो यदशरणोऽशरीर इदमनवेक्षितास्मत्समवाय आत्मनैवाविक्रियमाणेन सगुणमगुणः सृजसि पासि हरसि ॥ ३४॥

duravabodha iva tavāyaṁ vihāra-yogo yad aśaraṇo'śarīra idam anavekṣitāsmat-samavāya ātmanaivāvikriyamāṇena saguṇam aguṇaḥ sṛjasi pāsi harasi.

duravabodhaḥ—difficult to understand; *iva*—quite; *tava*—Your; *ayam*—this; *vihāra-yogaḥ*—engagement in the pastimes of material creation, maintenance and annihilation; *yat*—which; *aśaraṇaḥ*—not dependent on any other support; *aśarīraḥ*—without having a material body; *idam*—this; *anavekṣita*—without waiting for; *asmat*—of us; *samavāyaḥ*—the cooperation; *ātmanā*—by Your own self; *eva*—indeed; *avikriyamāṇena*—without being transformed; *sa-guṇam*—the material modes of nature; *aguṇaḥ*—although transcendental to such material qualities; *sṛjasi*—You create; *pāsi*—maintain; *harasi*—annihilate.

TRANSLATION

O Lord, You need no support, and although You have no material body, You do not need cooperation from us. Since You are the cause of the cosmic manifestation and You supply its material ingredients without being transformed, You create, maintain and annihilate this cosmic manifestation by Yourself. Nevertheless, although You appear engaged in material activity, You are transcendental to all material qualities. Consequently these transcendental activities of Yours are extremely difficult to understand.

PURPORT

The *Brahma-saṁhitā* (5.37) says, *goloka eva nivasaty akhilātma-bhūtaḥ:* the Supreme Personality of Godhead, Kṛṣṇa, is always situated in Goloka Vṛndāvana. It is also said, *vṛndāvanaṁ parityajya padam ekaṁ na gacchati:* Kṛṣṇa never goes even a step from Vṛndāvana. Nevertheless, although Kṛṣṇa is situated in His own abode, Goloka Vṛndāvana, He is simultaneously all-pervading and is therefore present everywhere. This is very difficult for a conditioned soul to understand, but devotees can understand how Kṛṣṇa, without undergoing any changes, can simultaneously be in His abode and be all-pervasive. The demigods are understood to be various limbs of the Supreme Lord's body, although the Supreme Lord has no material body and does not need anyone's help. He is spread everywhere (*mayā tatam idaṁ sarvaṁ jagad avyakta-mūrtinā*). Nevertheless, He is not present everywhere in His spiritual form. According to the Māyāvāda philosophy, the Supreme Truth, being all-pervasive, does not need a transcendental form. The Māyāvādīs suppose that since His form is distributed everywhere, He has no form. This is untrue. The Lord keeps His transcendental form, and at the same time He extends everywhere, in every nook and corner of the material creation.

TEXT 35

अथ तत्र भवान् किं देवदत्तवदिह गुणविसर्गपतितः पारतन्त्र्येण स्वकृतकुशलाकुशलं फलमुपाददात्याहोस्विदात्माराम उपशमशीलः समञ्जसदर्शन उदास्त इति ह वाव न विदामः ॥ ३५ ॥

atha tatra bhavān kiṁ devadattavad iha guṇa-visarga-patitaḥ
pāratantryeṇa sva-kṛta-kuśalākuśalaṁ phalam upādadāty āhosvid
ātmārāma upaśama-śīlaḥ samañjasa-darśana udāsta iti ha vāva na
vidāmaḥ.

atha—therefore; *tatra*—in that; *bhavān*—Your Lordship; *kim*—whether; *deva-datta-vat*—like an ordinary human being, forced by the fruits of his activities; *iha*—in this material world; *guṇa-visarga-patitaḥ*—fallen in a material body impelled by the modes of material nature; *pāratantryeṇa*—by dependence on the conditions of time, space, activity and nature; *sva-kṛta*—executed by oneself; *kuśala*—auspicious; *akuśalam*—inauspicious; *phalam*—results of action; *upādadāti*—accepts; *āhosvit*—or; *ātmārāmaḥ*—completely self-satisfied; *upaśama-śīlaḥ*—self-controlled in nature; *samañjasa-darśanaḥ*—not deprived of full spiritual potencies; *udāste*—remains neutral as the witness; *iti*—thus; *ha vāva*—certainly; *na vidāmaḥ*—we do not understand.

TRANSLATION

These are our inquiries. The ordinary conditioned soul is subject to the material laws, and he thus receives the fruits of his actions. Does Your Lordship, like an ordinary human being, exist within this material world in a body produced by the material modes? Do You enjoy or suffer the good or bad results of actions under the influence of time, past work and so forth? Or, on the contrary, are You present here only as a neutral witness who is self-sufficient, free from all material desires, and always full of spiritual potency? We certainly cannot understand Your actual position.

PURPORT

In *Bhagavad-gītā* Kṛṣṇa says that He descends to this material world for two purposes, namely *paritrāṇāya sādhūnāṁ vināśāya ca duṣkṛtām*—to relieve the devotees and kill demons or nondevotees. These two kinds of action are the same for the Absolute Truth. When the Lord comes to punish the demons, He bestows His favor upon them, and similarly when He delivers His devotees and gives them relief, He also bestows His favor. Thus the Lord bestows His favor equally upon the conditioned souls. When a conditioned soul gives relief to others he acts piously, and when he gives trouble to others he acts impiously, but the Lord is neither pious nor impious; He is always full in His spiritual potency, by which He shows equal mercy to the punishable and the protectable. The Lord is *apāpa-viddham;* He is never contaminated by the reactions of so-called sinful activities. When Kṛṣṇa was present on this earth, He killed many inimical nondevotees, but they all received *sārūpya;* in other words, they returned to their original spiritual bodies. One who does not know the Lord's position says that God is unkind to him but merciful to others. Actually the Lord says in *Bhagavad-gītā* (9.29), *samo'haṁ sarva-bhūteṣu na me dveṣyo'sti na priyaḥ:* "I am equal to everyone. No one is My enemy, and no one is My friend." But He also says, *ye bhajanti tu māṁ bhaktyā mayi te teṣu cāpy aham:* "If one becomes My devotee and fully surrenders unto Me, I give him special attention."

TEXT 36

न हि विरोध उभयं भगवत्यपरिमितगुणगण ईश्वरेऽनवगाह्यमाहात्म्येऽर्वाचीन-
विकल्पवितर्कविचारप्रमाणाभासकुतर्कशास्त्रकलिलान्तःकरणाश्रयदुरवग्रह
-वादिनां विवादानवसर उपरतसमस्तमायामये केवल एवात्ममायामन्तर्धाय को
न्वर्थो दुर्घट इव भवति स्वरूपद्वयाभावात् ॥ ३६ ॥

na hi virodha ubhayaṁ bhagavaty aparimita-guṇa-gaṇa īśvare'nav-
agāhya-māhātmye'rvācīna-vikalpa-vitarka-vicāra-pramāṇābhāsa-ku-
tarka-śāstra-kalilāntaḥkaraṇāśraya-duravagraha-vādināṁ
vivādānavasara uparata-samasta-māyāmaye kevala evātma-māyām an-
tardhāya ko nv artho durghaṭa iva bhavati svarūpa-dvayābhāvāt.

na—not; *hi*—certainly; *virodhaḥ*—contradiction; *ubhayam*—both; *bhagavati*—in the Supreme Personality of Godhead; *aparimita*—unlimited; *guṇa-gaṇe*—whose transcendental attributes; *īśvare*—in the supreme controller; *anavagāhya*—possessing; *māhātmye*—unfathomable ability and glories; *arvācīna*—recent; *vikalpa*—full of equivocal calculations; *vitarka*—opposing arguments; *vicāra*—judgments; *pramāṇa-ābhāsa*—imperfect evidence; *kutarka*—useless arguments; *śāstra*—by unauthorized scriptures; *kalila*—agitated; *antaḥkaraṇa*—minds; *āśraya*—whose shelter; *duravagraha*—with wicked obstinacies; *vādinām*—of theorists; *vivāda*—of the controversies; *anavasare*—not within the range; *uparata*—withdrawn; *samasta*—from whom all; *māyā-maye*—illusory energy; *kevale*—without a second; *eva*—indeed; *ātma-māyām*—the illusory energy, which can do and undo the inconceivable; *antardhāya*—placing between; *kaḥ*—what; *nu*—indeed; *arthaḥ*—meaning; *durghaṭaḥ*—impossible; *iva*—as it were; *bhavati*—is; *sva-rūpa*—natures; *dvaya*—of two; *abhāvāt*—due to the absence.

TRANSLATION

O Supreme Personality of Godhead, all contradictions can be reconciled in You. O Lord, since You are the Supreme Person, the reservoir of unlimited spiritual qualities, the supreme controller, Your unlimited glories are inconceivable to the conditioned souls. Many modern theologians argue about right and wrong without knowing what is actually right. Their arguments are always false and their judgments inconclusive because they have no authorized evidence with which to gain knowledge of You. Because their minds are agitated by scriptures containing false conclusions, they are unable to understand the truth concerning You. Furthermore, because of polluted eagerness to arrive at the right conclusion, their theories are incapable of revealing You, who are transcendental to their material conceptions. You are one without a second, and therefore in You contradictions like doing and not doing, happiness and distress, are not contradictory. Your potency is so great that it can do and undo anything as You like. With the help of that potency, what is impossible for You? Since there is no duality in Your constitutional position, You can do everything by the influence of Your energy.

PURPORT

The Supreme Personality of Godhead, being self-sufficient, is full of transcendental bliss (*ātmārāma*). He enjoys bliss in two ways—when He appears happy and when He appears distressed. Distinctions and contradictions are impossible in Him because only from Him have they emanated. The Supreme Personality of Godhead is the reservoir of all knowledge, all potency, all strength, opulence and influence. There is no limit to His powers. Since He is full in all transcendental attributes, nothing abominable from the material world can exist in Him. He is transcendental and spiritual, and therefore conceptions of material happiness and distress do not apply to Him.

We should not be astonished to find contradictions in the Supreme Personality of Godhead. Actually there are no contradictions. That is the meaning of His being supreme. Because He is all-powerful, He is not subject to the conditioned soul's arguments regarding His existence or nonexistence. He is pleased to protect His devotees by killing their enemies. He enjoys both the killing and the protecting.

Such freedom from duality applies not only to the Lord but also to His devotees. In Vṛndāvana, the damsels of Vrajabhūmi enjoy transcendental bliss in the company of the Supreme Personality of Godhead, Kṛṣṇa, and they feel the same transcendental bliss in separation when Kṛṣṇa and Balarāma leave Vṛndāvana for Mathurā. There is no question of material pains or pleasures for either the Supreme Personality of Godhead or His pure devotees, although they are sometimes superficially said to be distressed or happy. One who is *ātmārāma* is blissful in both ways.

Nondevotees cannot understand the contradictions present in the Supreme Lord or His devotees. Therefore in *Bhagavad-gītā* the Lord says, *bhaktyā mām abhijānāti:* the transcendental pastimes can be understood through devotional service; to nondevotees they are inconceivable. *Acintyāḥ khalu ye bhāvā na tāṁs tarkeṇa yojayet:* the Supreme Lord and His form, name, pastimes and paraphernalia are inconceivable to nondevotees, and one should not try to understand such realities simply by logical arguments. They will not bring one to the right conclusion about the Absolute Truth.

TEXT 37

समविषममतीनां मतमनुसरसि यथा रज्जुखण्डः सर्पादिधियाम् ॥ ३७ ॥

sama-viṣama-matīnāṁ matam anusarasi yathā rajju-khaṇḍaḥ sarpādi-dhiyām.

sama—equal or proper; *viṣama*—and unequal or mistaken; *matīnām*—of those having intelligence; *matam*—conclusion; *anusarasi*—You follow; *yathā*—just as; *rajju-khaṇḍaḥ*—a piece of rope; *sarpa-ādi*—a snake, etc.; *dhiyām*—of those who perceive.

TRANSLATION

A rope causes fear for a bewildered person who considers it a snake, but not for a person with proper intelligence who knows it to be only a rope. Similarly, You, as the Supersoul in everyone's heart, inspire fear or fearlessness according to one's intelligence, but in You there is no duality.

PURPORT

In *Bhagavad-gītā* (4.11) the Lord says, *ye yathā māṁ prapadyante tāṁs tathaiva bhajāmy aham:* "As one surrenders unto Me, I reward him accordingly." The Supreme Personality of Godhead is the reservoir of everything, including all knowledge, all truth and all contradictions. The example cited herein is very appropriate. A rope is one truth, but some mistake it for a snake, whereas others know it to be a rope. Similarly, devotees who know the Supreme Personality of Godhead do not see contradictions in Him, but nondevotees regard Him as the snakelike source of all fear. For example, when Nṛsiṁhadeva appeared, Prahlāda Mahārāja saw the Lord as the supreme solace, whereas his father, a demon, saw Him as the ultimate death. As stated in *Śrīmad-Bhāgavatam* (11.2.37), *bhayaṁ dvitīyābhiniveśataḥ syāt:* fear results from being absorbed in duality. When one is in knowledge of duality, one knows both fear and bliss. The same Supreme Lord is a source of bliss to devotees and fear to nondevotees who have a poor fund of knowledge. God is one, but people understand the Absolute Truth from different angles of vision. The unintelligent see contradictions in Him, but sober devotees find no contradictions.

TEXT 38

स एव हि पुनः सर्ववस्तुनि वस्तुस्वरूपः सर्वेश्वरः सकलजगत्कारणकारणभूतः
सर्वप्रत्यगात्मत्वात् सर्वगुणाभासोपलक्षित एक एव पर्यवशेषितः ॥ ३८ ॥

sa eva hi punaḥ sarva-vastuni vastu-svarūpaḥ sarveśvaraḥ sakala-jagat-
kāraṇa-kāraṇa-bhūtaḥ sarva-pratyag-ātmatvāt sarva-
guṇābhāsopalakṣita eka eva paryavaśeṣitaḥ.

saḥ—He (the Supreme Personality of Godhead); *eva*—indeed; *hi*—certainly; *punaḥ*—again; *sarva-vastuni*—in everything, material and spiritual; *vastu-svarūpaḥ*—the substance; *sarva-īśvaraḥ*—the controller of everything; *sakala-jagat*—of the whole universe; *kāraṇa*—of the causes; *kāraṇa-bhūtaḥ*

—existing as the cause; *sarva-pratyak-ātmatvāt*—because of being the Supersoul of every living being, or being present in everything, even the atom; *sarva-guṇa*—of all the effects of the material modes of nature (such as intelligence and the senses); *ābhāsa*—by the manifestations; *upalakṣitaḥ*—perceived; *ekaḥ*—alone; *eva*—indeed; *paryavaśeṣitaḥ*—left remaining.

TRANSLATION

With deliberation, one will see that the Supreme Soul, although manifested in different ways, is actually the basic principle of everything. The total material energy is the cause of the material manifestation, but the material energy is caused by Him. Therefore He is the cause of all causes, the manifester of intelligence and the senses. He is perceived as the Supersoul of everything. Without Him, everything would be dead. You, as that Supersoul, the supreme controller, are the only one remaining.

PURPORT

The words *sarva-vastuni vastu-svarūpaḥ* indicate that the Supreme Lord is the active principle of everything. As described in the *Brahma-saṁhitā* (5.35):

eko'py asau racayituṁ jagad-aṇḍa-koṭiṁ
yac-chaktir asti jagad-aṇḍa-cayā yad-antaḥ
aṇḍāntara-stha-paramāṇu-cayāntara-sthaṁ
govindam ādi-puruṣaṁ tam ahaṁ bhajāmi

"I worship the Personality of Godhead, Govinda, who enters the existence of every universe and every atom by one of His plenary portions and thus manifests His infinite energy throughout the material creation." By His one plenary portion as Paramātmā, *antaryāmī,* the Lord is all-pervading throughout the unlimited universes. He is the *pratyak,* or *antaryāmī,* of all living entities. The Lord says in *Bhagavad-gītā* (13.3), *kṣetrajñaṁ cāpi māṁ viddhi sarva-kṣetreṣu bhārata:* "O scion of Bharata, you should understand that I am also the knower in all bodies." Because the Lord is the Supersoul, He is the active principle of every living entity and even the atom (*aṇḍāntara-stha-paramāṇu-cayāntara-stham*). He is the actual reality. According to various stages of intelligence, one realizes the presence of the Supreme in everything through the manifestations of His energy. The entire world is permeated by the three *guṇas,* and one can understand His presence according to one's modes of material nature.

TEXT 39

अथ ह वाव तव महिमामृतरससमुद्रविप्रुषा सकृदवलीढया स्वमनसि निष्यन्द-मानानवरतसुखेन विस्मारितदृष्टश्रुतविषयसुखलेशाभासाः परमभागवता एकान्तिनो भगवति सर्वभूतप्रियसुहृदि सर्वात्मनि नितरां निरन्तरं निर्वृतमनसः कथमु ह वा एते मधुमथन पुनः स्वार्थकुशला ह्यात्मप्रियसुहृदः साधवस्त्व-च्चरणाम्बुजानुसेवां विसृजन्ति न यत्र पुनरयं संसारपर्यावर्तः ॥ ३९ ॥

atha ha vāva tava mahimāmṛta-rasa-samudra-vipruṣā sakṛd avalīḍhayā sva-manasi niṣyandamānānavarata-sukhena vismārita-dṛṣṭa-śruta-viṣaya-sukha-leśābhāsāḥ parama-bhāgavatā ekāntino bhagavati sarva-bhūta-priya-suhṛdi sarvātmani nitarāṁ nirantaraṁ nirvṛta-manasaḥ katham u ha vā ete madhumathana punaḥ svārtha-kuśalā hy ātma-priya-suhṛdaḥ sādhavas tvac-caraṇāmbujānusevāṁ visṛjanti na yatra punar ayaṁ saṁsāra-paryāvartaḥ.

atha ha—therefore; *vāva*—indeed; *tava*—Your; *mahima*—of glories; *amṛta*—of the nectar; *rasa*—of the mellow; *samudra*—of the ocean; *vipruṣā*—by a drop; *sakṛt*—only once; *avalīḍhayā*—tasted; *sva-manasi*—in his mind; *niṣyandamāna*—flowing; *anavarata*—continuously; *sukhena*—by the transcendental bliss; *vismārita*—forgotten; *dṛṣṭa*—from material sight; *śruta*—and sound; *viṣaya-sukha*—of the material happiness; *leśa-ābhāsāḥ*—the dim reflection of a tiny portion; *parama-bhāgavatāḥ*—great, exalted devotees; *ekāntinaḥ*—who have faith only in the Supreme Lord and nothing else; *bhagavati*—in the Supreme Personality of Godhead; *sarva-bhūta*—to all living entities; *priya*—who is dearmost; *suhṛdi*—the friend; *sarva-ātmani*—the Supersoul of all; *nitarām*—completely; *nirantaram*—continuously; *nirvṛta*—with happiness; *manasaḥ*—those whose minds; *katham*—how; *u ha*—then; *vā*—or; *ete*—these; *madhu-mathana*—O killer of the Madhu demon; *punaḥ*—again; *sva-artha-kuśalāḥ*—who are expert in the interest of life; *hi*—indeed; *ātma-priya-suhṛdaḥ*—who have accepted You as the Supersoul, dearmost lover and friend; *sādhavaḥ*—the devotees; *tvat-caraṇa-ambuja-anusevām*—service to the lotus feet of Your Lordship; *visṛjanti*—can give up; *na*—not; *yatra*—wherein; *punaḥ*—again; *ayam*—this; *saṁsāra-paryāvartaḥ*—repetition of birth and death within the material world.

TRANSLATION

Therefore, O killer of the Madhu demon, incessant transcendental bliss flows in the minds of those who have even once tasted but a drop of the

nectar from the ocean of Your glories. Such exalted devotees forget the tiny reflection of so-called material happiness produced from the material senses of sight and sound. Free from all desires, such devotees are the real friends of all living entities. Offering their minds unto You and enjoying transcendental bliss, they are expert in achieving the real goal of life. O Lord, You are the soul and dear friend of such devotees, who never need return to this material world. How could they give up engagement in Your devotional service?

PURPORT

Although nondevotees, because of their meager knowledge and speculative habits, cannot understand the real nature of the Lord, a devotee who has once tasted the nectar from the Lord's lotus feet can realize what transcendental pleasure there is in the Lord's devotional service. A devotee knows that simply by rendering service to the Lord, he serves everyone. Therefore devotees are real friends to all living entities. Only a pure devotee can preach the glories of the Lord for the benefit of all conditioned souls.

TEXT 40

त्रिभुवनात्मभवन त्रिविक्रम त्रिनयन त्रिलोकमनोहरानुभाव तवैव विभूतयो दितिजदनुजादयश्चापि तेषामुपक्रमसमयोऽयमिति स्वात्ममायया सुरनरमृगमि-श्रितजलचराकृतिभिर्यथापराधं दण्डं दण्डधर दधर्थ एवमेनमपि भगवञ्जहि त्वा-ष्ट्रमुत यदि मन्यसे ॥ ४० ॥

tri-bhuvanātma-bhavana trivikrama tri-nayana tri-loka-
manoharānubhāva tavaiva vibhūtayo ditija-danujādayaś cāpi teṣām
upakrama-samayo'yam iti svātma-māyayā sura-nara-mṛga-miśrita-
jalacarākṛtibhir yathāparādhaṁ daṇḍaṁ daṇḍa-dhara dadhartha evam
enam api bhagavañ jahi tvāṣṭram uta yadi manyase.

tri-bhuvana-ātma-bhavana—O Lord, You are the shelter of the three worlds because You are the Supersoul of the three worlds; *tri-vikrama*—O Lord, who assumes the form of Vāmana, Your power and opulence are distributed throughout the three worlds; *tri-nayana*—O maintainer and seer of the three worlds; *tri-loka-manohara-anubhāva*—O You who are perceived as the most beautiful within the three worlds; *tava*—of You; *eva*—certainly; *vibhūtayaḥ*—the expansions of energy; *diti-ja-danu-ja-ādayaḥ*—the demoniac sons of Diti, and the Dānavas, another type of demon; *ca*—and; *api*

—also (the human beings); *teṣām*—of all of them; *upakrama-samayaḥ*—the time of enterprise; *ayam*—this; *iti*—thus; *sva-ātma-māyayā*—by Your own energy; *sura-nara-mṛga-miśrita-jalacara-ākṛtibhiḥ*—with different forms like those of the demigods, human beings, animals, mixtures and aquatics (the incarnations Vāmana, Lord Rāmacandra, Kṛṣṇa, Varāha, Hayagrīva, Nṛsiṁha, Matsya and Kūrma); *yathā-aparādham*—according to their offenses; *daṇḍam*—punishment; *daṇḍa-dhara*—O supreme chastiser; *dadhartha*—You awarded; *evam*—thus; *enam*—this one (Vṛtrāsura); *api*—also; *bhagavan*—O Supreme Personality of Godhead; *jahi*—kill; *tvāṣṭram*—the son of Tvaṣṭā; *uta*—indeed; *yadi manyase*—if You think it proper.

TRANSLATION

O Lord, O personified three worlds, father of the three worlds! O strength of the three worlds, in the form of the Vāmana incarnation! O three-eyed form of Nṛsiṁhadeva! O most beautiful person within the three worlds! Everything and everyone, including human beings and even the Daitya demons and the Dānavas, is but an expansion of Your energy. O supremely powerful one, You have always appeared in Your forms as the various incarnations to punish the demons as soon as they become very powerful. You appear as Lord Vāmanadeva, Lord Rāma and Lord Kṛṣṇa. You appear sometimes as an animal like Lord Boar, sometimes a mixed incarnation like Lord Nṛsiṁhadeva and Lord Hayagrīva, and sometimes an aquatic like Lord Fish and Lord Tortoise. Assuming such various forms, You have always punished the demons and Dānavas. We therefore pray that Your Lordship appear today as another incarnation, if You so desire, to kill the great demon Vṛtrāsura.

PURPORT

There are two kinds of devotees, known as *sakāma* and *akāma.* Pure devotees are *akāma,* whereas devotees in the upper planetary systems, such as the demigods, are called *sakāma* because they still want to enjoy material opulence. Because of their pious activities, the *sakāma* devotees are promoted to the higher planetary systems, but at heart they still desire to lord it over the material resources. The *sakāma* devotees are sometimes disturbed by the demons and Rākṣasas, but the Lord is so kind that He always saves them by appearing as an incarnation. The Lord's incarnations are so powerful that Lord Vāmanadeva covered the entire universe with two steps and therefore had no place for His third step. The Lord is called Trivikrama because He showed His strength by delivering the entire universe with merely three steps.

The difference between *sakāma* and *akāma* devotees is that when *sakāma* devotees, like the demigods, fall into difficulty, they approach the Supreme Personality of Godhead for relief, whereas *akāma* devotees, even in the greatest danger, never disturb the Lord for material benefits. Even if an *akāma* devotee is suffering, he thinks this is due to his past impious activities and agrees to suffer the consequences. He never disturbs the Lord. *Sakāma* devotees immediately pray to the Lord as soon as they are in difficulty, but they are regarded as pious because they consider themselves fully dependent on the mercy of the Lord. As stated in *Śrīmad-Bhāgavatam* (10.14.8):

tat te'nukampāṁ susamīkṣamāṇo
bhuñjāna evātma-kṛtaṁ vipākam
hṛd-vāg-vapurbhir vidadhan namas te
jīveta yo mukti-pade sa dāya-bhāk

Even while suffering in the midst of difficulties, devotees simply offer their prayers and service more enthusiastically. In this way they become firmly fixed in devotional service and eligible to return home, back to Godhead, without a doubt. *Sakāma* devotees, of course, achieve from the Lord the results they desire from their prayers, but they do not immediately become fit to return to Godhead. It is to be noted herein that Lord Viṣṇu, in His various incarnations, is always the protector of His devotees. Śrīla Madhvācārya says: *vividhaṁ bhāva-pātratvāt sarve viṣṇor vibhūtayaḥ.* Kṛṣṇa is the original Personality of Godhead (*kṛṣṇas tu bhagavān svayam*). All the other incarnations proceed from Lord Viṣṇu.

TEXT 41

अस्माकं तावकानां ततत नतानां हरे तव चरणनलिनयुगलध्यानानु-बद्धहृदयनिगडानां स्वलिङ्गविवरणेनात्मसात्कृतानामनुकम्पानुरञ्जितविशदरुचिर-शिशिरस्मितावलोकेन विगलितमधुरमुखरसामृतकलया चान्तस्तापमनघार्हसि शमयितुम् ॥ ४१ ॥

asmākaṁ tāvakānāṁ tatatata natānāṁ hare tava caraṇa-nalina-yugala-dhyānānubaddha-hṛdaya-nigaḍānāṁ sva-liṅga-vivaraṇenātmasāt-kṛtānām anukampānurañjita-viśada-rucira-śiśira-smitāvalokena vigalita-madhura-mukha-rasāmṛta-kalayā cāntas tāpam anaghārhasi śamayitum.

asmākam—of us; *tāvakānām*—who are wholly and solely dependent upon You; *tata-tata*—O grandfather, father of the father; *natānām*—who are fully surrendered unto You; *hare*—O Lord Hari; *tava*—Your; *caraṇa*—on the feet; *nalina-yugala*—like two blue lotus flowers; *dhyāna*—by meditation; *anubaddha*—bound; *hṛdaya*—in the heart; *nigaḍānām*—whose chains; *sva-liṅga-vivaraṇena*—by manifesting Your own form; *ātmasāt-kṛtānām*—of those You have accepted as Your own; *anukampā*—by compassion; *anurañjita*—being colored; *viśada*—bright; *rucira*—very pleasing; *śiśira*—cool; *smita*—with a smile; *avalokena*—by Your glance; *vigalita*—melted with compassion; *madhura-mukha-rasa*—of the very sweet words from Your mouth; *amṛta-kalayā*—by the drops of nectar; *ca*—and; *antaḥ*—within the cores of our hearts; *tāpam*—the great pain; *anagha*—O supreme pure; *arhasi*—You deserve; *śamayitum*—to curb.

TRANSLATION

O supreme protector, O grandfather, O supreme pure, O Lord! We are all surrendered souls at Your lotus feet. Indeed, our minds are bound to Your lotus feet in meditation by chains of love. Now please manifest Your incarnation. Accepting us as Your own eternal servants and devotees, be pleased with us and sympathetic toward us. By Your love-filled glance, with its cool and pleasing smile of sympathy, and by the sweet, nectarean words emanating from Your beautiful face, free us from the anxiety caused by this Vṛtrāsura, who always pains the cores of our hearts.

PURPORT

Lord Brahmā is considered the father of the demigods, but Kṛṣṇa, or Lord Viṣṇu, is the father of Brahmā because Brahmā took birth from the lotus flower growing from the Lord's abdomen.

TEXT 42

अथ भगवंस्तवास्माभिरखिलजगदुत्पत्तिस्थितिलयनिमित्तायमानदिव्यमाया
विनोदस्यसकलजीवनिकायानामन्तर्हृदयेषु बहिरपि च ब्रह्मप्रत्यगात्मस्वरूपेण
प्रधानरूपेण च यथादेशकालदेहावस्थानविशेषं तदुपादानोपलम्भकतयानुभवतः
सर्वप्रत्ययसाक्षिण आकाशशरीरस्य साक्षात्परब्रह्मणः परमात्मनः कियानिह
वार्थविशेषो विज्ञापनीयः स्याद् विस्फुलिङ्गादिभिरिव हिरण्यरेतसः ॥ ४२ ॥

atha bhagavaṁs tavāsmābhir akhila-jagad-utpatti-sthiti-laya-nimit-
tāyamāna-divya-māyā-vinodasya sakala-jīva-nikāyānām antar-
hṛdayeṣu bahir api ca brahma-pratyag-ātma-svarūpeṇa pradhāna-
rūpeṇa ca yathā-deśa-kāla-dehāvasthāna-viśeṣaṁ tad-

upādānopalambhakatayānubhavataḥ sarva-pratyaya-sākṣiṇa ākāśa-śarīrasya sākṣāt para-brahmaṇaḥ paramātmanaḥ kiyān iha vārtha-viśeṣo vijñāpanīyaḥ syād visphuliṅgādibhir iva hiraṇya-retasaḥ.

atha—therefore; *bhagavan*—O Lord; *tava*—of You; *asmābhiḥ*—by us; *akhila*—all; *jagat*—of the material world; *utpatti*—of the creation; *sthiti*—maintenance; *laya*—and annihilation; *nimittāyamāna*—being the cause; *divya-māyā*—with the spiritual energy; *vinodasya*—of You, who amuse Yourself; *sakala*—all; *jīva-nikāyānām*—of the hordes of living entities; *antaḥ-hṛdayeṣu*—in the cores of the hearts; *bahiḥ api*—externally also; *ca*—and; *brahma*—of impersonal Brahman, or the Absolute Truth; *pratyak-ātma*—of the Supersoul; *sva-rūpeṇa*—by Your forms; *pradhāna-rūpeṇa*—by Your form as the external ingredients; *ca*—also; *yathā*—according to; *deśa-kāla-deha-avasthāna*—of country, time, body and position; *viśeṣam*—the particulars; *tat*—of them; *upādāna*—of the material causes; *upalambhakatayā*—by being the exhibitor; *anubhavataḥ*—witnessing; *sarva-pratyaya-sākṣiṇaḥ*—the witness of all different activities; *ākāśa-śarīrasya*—the Supersoul of the whole universe; *sākṣāt*—directly; *para-brahmaṇaḥ*—the Supreme Absolute Truth; *paramātmanaḥ*—the Supersoul; *kiyān*—of what extent; *iha*—herein; *vā*—or; *artha-viśeṣaḥ*—special necessity; *vijñāpanīyaḥ*—to be informed; *syāt*—may be; *visphuliṅga-ādibhiḥ*—by the sparks of the fire; *iva*—like; *hiraṇya-retasaḥ*—to the original fire.

TRANSLATION

O Lord, as the small sparks of a fire cannot possibly perform the actions of the whole fire, we sparks of Your Lordship cannot inform You of the necessities of our lives. You are the complete whole. Therefore, of what do we need to inform You? You know everything because You are the original cause of the cosmic manifestation, the maintainer and the annihilator of the entire universal creation. You always engage in Your pastimes with Your spiritual and material energies, for You are the controller of all these varied energies. You exist within all living entities, within the cosmic manifestation, and also beyond them. You exist internally as Parabrahman and externally as the ingredients of the material creation. Therefore, although manifested in various stages, at different times and places, and in various bodies, You, the Personality of Godhead, are the original cause of all causes. Indeed, You are the original element. You are the witness of all activities, but because You are as great as the sky, You are never touched by any of them. You are the witness of

everything as Parabrahman and Paramātmā. O Supreme Personality of Godhead, nothing is unknown to You.

PURPORT

The Absolute Truth exists in three phases of spiritual understanding—Brahman, Paramātmā and Bhagavān (*brahmeti paramātmeti bhagavān iti śabdyate*). Bhagavān, the Supreme Personality of Godhead, is the cause of Brahman and Paramātmā. Brahman, the impersonal Absolute Truth, is all-pervading, and Paramātmā is locally situated in everyone's heart, but Bhagavān, who is worshipable by the devotees, is the original cause of all causes. A pure devotee is aware that since nothing is unknown to the Supreme Personality of Godhead, He need not be informed of a devotee's conveniences and inconveniences. A pure devotee knows that there is no need to ask the Absolute Truth for any material necessities. Therefore, while informing the Supreme Lord about their distress in being attacked by Vṛtrāsura, the demigods apologized for offering prayers for their safety. A neophyte devotee, of course, approaches the Supreme Lord for relief from distress or poverty, or for speculative knowledge of the Lord. *Bhagavad-gītā* (7.16) mentions four kinds of pious men who begin devotional service to the Lord—one who is distressed (*ārta*), one in need of money (*arthārthī*), one who is inquisitive (*jijñāsu*) and one who is searching for the Absolute Truth (*jñānī*). A pure devotee, however, knows that since the Lord is omnipresent and omniscient, there is no need to offer prayers or worship Him for one's personal benefit. A pure devotee always engages in the service of the Lord without demanding anything. The Lord is present everywhere and knows the necessities of His devotees; consequently there is no need to disturb Him by asking Him for material benefits.

TEXT 43

अत एव स्वयं तदुपकल्पयास्माकं भगवतः परमगुरोस्तव चरणशतपलाशच्छायां
विविधवृजिनसंसारपरिश्रमोपशमनीमुपसृतानां वयं यत्कामेनोपसादिताः ॥ ४३ ॥

ata eva svayaṁ tad upakalpayāsmākaṁ bhagavataḥ parama-guros tava
caraṇa-śata-palāśac-chāyāṁ vividha-vṛjina-saṁsāra-
pariśramopaśamanīm upasṛtānāṁ vayaṁ yat-kāmenopasāditāḥ.

ata eva—therefore; *svayam*—Yourself; *tat*—that; *upakalpaya*—please arrange; *asmākam*—of us; *bhagavataḥ*—of the Supreme Personality of

Godhead; *parama-guroḥ*—the supreme spiritual master; *tava*—of You; *caraṇa*—of the feet; *śata-palāśat*—like lotus flowers with hundreds of petals; *chāyām*—the shade; *vividha*—various; *vṛjina*—with dangerous positions; *saṁsāra*—of this conditioned life; *pariśrama*—the pain; *upaśamanīm*—relieving; *upasṛtānām*—the devotees who have taken shelter at Your lotus feet; *vayam*—we; *yat*—for which; *kāmena*—by the desires; *upasāditāḥ*—caused to come near (the shelter of Your lotus feet).

TRANSLATION

Dear Lord, You are omniscient, and therefore You know very well why we have taken shelter at Your lotus feet, which provide shade that gives relief from all material disturbances. Since You are the supreme spiritual master and You know everything, we have sought shelter of Your lotus feet for instruction. Please give us relief by counteracting our present distress. Your lotus feet are the only shelter for a fully surrendered devotee and are the only means for subduing all the tribulations of this material world.

PURPORT

One need only seek shelter of the shade of the Lord's lotus feet. Then all the material tribulations that disturb him will be subdued, just as when one comes under the shadow of a big tree, the disturbances caused by the heat of the scorching sun are immediately mitigated, without one's asking for relief. Therefore the whole concern of the conditioned soul should be the lotus feet of the Lord. The conditioned soul suffering from various tribulations because of existing in this material world can be relieved only when he seeks shelter at the Lord's lotus feet.

TEXT 44

अथो ईश जहि त्वाष्ट्रं ग्रसन्तं भुवनत्रयम् ।
ग्रस्तानि येन नः कृष्ण तेजांस्यस्त्रायुधानि च ॥ ४४ ॥

atho īśa jahi tvāṣṭraṁ
grasantaṁ bhuvana-trayam
grastāni yena naḥ kṛṣṇa
tejāṁsy astrāyudhāni ca

atho—therefore; *īśa*—O supreme controller; *jahi*—kill; *tvāṣṭram*—the demon Vṛtrāsura, son of Tvaṣṭā; *grasantam*—who is devouring; *bhuvana-*

trayam—the three worlds; *grastāni*—devoured; *yena*—by whom; *naḥ*—our; *kṛṣṇa*—O Lord Kṛṣṇa; *tejāṁsi*—all strength and prowess; *astra*—arrows; *āyudhāni*—and other weapons; *ca*—also.

TRANSLATION

Therefore, O Lord, O supreme controller, O Lord Kṛṣṇa, please annihilate this dangerous demon Vṛtrāsura, Tvaṣṭā's son, who has already swallowed all our weapons, our paraphernalia for fighting, and our strength and influence.

PURPORT

The Lord says in *Bhagavad-gītā* (7.15–16):

na māṁ duṣkṛtino mūḍhāḥ
prapadyante narādhamāḥ
māyayāpahṛta-jñānā
āsuraṁ bhāvam āśritāḥ

catur-vidhā bhajante māṁ
janāḥ sukṛtino 'rjuna
ārto jijñāsur arthārthī
jñānī ca bharatarṣabha

"Those miscreants who are grossly foolish, lowest among mankind, whose knowledge is stolen by illusion, and who partake of the atheistic nature of demons, do not surrender unto Me. O best among the Bhāratas [Arjuna], four kinds of pious men render devotional service unto Me—the distressed, the desirer of wealth, the inquisitive, and he who is searching for knowledge of the Absolute."

The four classes of neophyte devotees who approach the Supreme Personality of Godhead to offer devotional service because of material motives are not pure devotees, but the advantage for such materialistic devotees is that they sometimes give up their material desires and become pure. When the demigods are utterly helpless, they approach the Supreme Personality of Godhead in grief and with tears in their eyes, praying to the Lord, and thus they become almost pure devotees, free from material desires. Admitting that they have forgotten pure devotional service because of extensive material opportunities, they fully surrender to the Lord, leaving to His consideration whether to maintain them or annihilate them. Such surrender is necessary. Bhaktivinoda Ṭhākura sings, *mārabi rākhabi—yo icchā tohārā:* "O Lord, I fully surrender unto Your lotus feet. Now, as You desire, You may protect me or annihilate me. You have the full right to do either."

TEXT 45

हंसाय दह्रनिलयाय निरीक्षकाय
कृष्णाय मृष्टयशसे निरुपक्रमाय।
सत्संग्रहाय भवपान्थनिजाश्रमाप्ता-
वन्ते परीष्टगतये हरये नमस्ते ॥ ४५ ॥

haṁsāya dahra-nilayāya nirīkṣakāya
kṛṣṇāya mṛṣṭa-yaśase nirupakramāya
sat-saṁgrahāya bhava-pāntha-nijāśramāptāv
ante parīṣṭa-gataye haraye namas te

haṁsāya—unto the most exalted and pure (*pavitraṁ paramam,* the supreme pure); *dahra*—in the core of the heart; *nilayāya*—whose abode; *nirīkṣakāya*—supervising the activities of the individual soul; *kṛṣṇāya*—unto the Supersoul, who is a partial manifestation of Kṛṣṇa; *mṛṣṭa-yaśase*—whose reputation is very bright; *nirupakramāya*—who has no beginning; *sat-saṁgrahāya*—understood only by pure devotees; *bhava- pāntha-nija-āśrama-āptau*—being obtainment of the shelter of Kṛṣṇa for persons within this material world; *ante*—at the ultimate end; *parīṣṭa-gataye*—unto Him who is the ultimate goal, the highest success of life; *haraye*—unto the Supreme Personality of Godhead; *namaḥ*—respectful obeisances; *te*—unto You.

TRANSLATION

O Lord, O supreme pure, You live within the core of everyone's heart and observe all the desires and activities of the conditioned souls. O Supreme Personality of Godhead known as Lord Kṛṣṇa, Your reputation is bright and illuminating. You have no beginning, for You are the beginning of everything. This is understood by pure devotees because You are easily accessible to the pure and truthful. When the conditioned souls are liberated and sheltered at Your lotus feet after roving throughout the material world for many millions of years, they attain the highest success of life. Therefore, O Lord, O Supreme Personality of Godhead, we offer our respectful obeisances at Your lotus feet.

PURPORT

The demigods certainly wanted Lord Viṣṇu to relieve their anxiety, but now they directly approach Lord Kṛṣṇa, for although there is no difference between Lord Kṛṣṇa and Lord Viṣṇu, Kṛṣṇa descends to this planet in His Vāsudeva feature for the purpose of *paritrāṇāya sādhūnāṁ vināśāya ca duṣkṛtām*—protecting His devotees and annihilating the miscreants. Demons, or atheists, always disturb the demigods, or devotees, and therefore Kṛṣṇa descends to punish the atheists and demons and fulfill the desire of His devotees. Kṛṣṇa, being the original cause of everything, is the Supreme Person, above even Viṣṇu and Nārāyaṇa, although there is no difference between these different forms of the Lord. As explained in *Brahma-saṁhitā* (5.46):

dīpārcir eva hi daśāntaram abhyupetya
dīpāyate vivṛta-hetu-samāna-dharmā
yas tādṛg eva hi ca viṣṇutayā vibhāti
govindam ādi-puruṣaṁ tam ahaṁ bhajāmi

Kṛṣṇa expands Himself as Viṣṇu the way a bright candle kindles another. Although there is no difference between the power of one candle and another, Kṛṣṇa is compared to the original candle.

The word *mṛṣṭa-yaśase* is significant herein because Kṛṣṇa is always famous for relieving His devotee from danger. A devotee who has sacrificed everything for the service of Kṛṣṇa and whose only source of relief is the Lord is known as *akiñcana.*

As expressed in the prayers offered by Queen Kuntī, the Lord is *akiñcana-vitta,* the property of such a devotee. Those who are liberated from the bondage of conditioned life are elevated to the spiritual world, where they achieve five kinds of liberation—*sāyujya, sālokya, sārūpya, sārṣṭi* and *sāmīpya.* They personally associate with the Lord in five mellows—*śānta, dāsya, sakhya, vātsalya* and *mādhurya.* These *rasas* are all emanations from Kṛṣṇa. As described by Viśvanātha Cakravartī Ṭhākura, the original mellow, *ādi-rasa,* is conjugal love. Kṛṣṇa is the origin of pure and spiritual conjugal love.

TEXT 46

श्रीशुक उवाच
अथैवमीडितो राजन् सादरं त्रिदशैर्हरिः ।
स्वमुपस्थानमाकर्ण्य प्राह तानभिनन्दितः ॥ ४६ ॥

śrī-śuka uvāca
athaivam īḍito rājan
sādaraṁ tri-daśair hariḥ
svam upasthānam ākarṇya
prāha tān abhinanditaḥ

śrī-śukaḥ uvāca—Śrī Śukadeva Gosvāmī said; *atha*—thereafter; *evam*—in this way; *īḍitaḥ*—being worshiped and offered obeisances; *rājan*—O King; *sa-ādaram*—with proper respect; *tri-daśaiḥ*—by all the demigods from the higher planetary systems; *hariḥ*—the Supreme Personality of Godhead; *svam upasthānam*—their prayer glorifying Him; *ākarṇya*—hearing; *prāha*—replied; *tān*—unto them (the demigods); *abhinanditaḥ*—being pleased.

TRANSLATION

Śrī Śukadeva Gosvāmī continued: O King Parīkṣit, when the demigods offered the Lord their sincere prayers in this way, the Lord listened by His causeless mercy. Being pleased, He then replied to the demigods.

TEXT 47

श्रीभगवानुवाच
प्रीतोऽहं वः सुरश्रेष्ठा मदुपस्थानविद्यया ।
आत्मैश्वर्यस्मृतिः पुंसां भक्तिश्चैव यया मयि ॥ ४७ ॥

śrī-bhagavān uvāca
prīto 'haṁ vaḥ sura-śreṣṭhā
mad-upasthāna-vidyayā
ātmaiśvarya-smṛtiḥ puṁsāṁ
bhaktiś caiva yayā mayi

śrī-bhagavān uvāca—the Supreme Personality of Godhead said; *prītaḥ*—pleased; *aham*—I; *vaḥ*—of you; *sura-śreṣṭhāḥ*—O best of the demigods; *mat-upasthāna-vidyayā*—by the highly advanced knowledge and prayers offered unto Me; *ātma-aiśvarya-smṛtiḥ*—remembrance of the exalted transcendental position of Me, the Supreme Personality of Godhead; *puṁsām*—of men; *bhaktiḥ*—devotional service; *ca*—and; *eva*—certainly; *yayā*—by which; *mayi*—unto Me.

TRANSLATION

The Supreme Personality of Godhead said: O beloved demigods, you have offered your prayers to Me with great knowledge, and I am certainly most pleased with you. A person is liberated by such knowledge, and thus he remembers My exalted position, which is above the conditions of material life. Such a devotee is fully purified by offering prayers in full knowledge. This is the source of devotional service to Me.

PURPORT

Another name of the Supreme Personality of Godhead is Uttamaśloka, which means that He is offered prayers with selected verses. *Bhakti* means *śravaṇaṁ kīrtanaṁ viṣṇoḥ,* chanting and hearing about Lord Viṣṇu. Impersonalists cannot be purified, for they do not offer personal prayers to the Supreme Personality of Godhead. Even though they sometimes offer prayers, the prayers are not directed toward the Supreme Person. Impersonalists sometimes show their incomplete knowledge by addressing the Lord as being nameless. They always offer prayers indirectly, saying, "You are this, You are that," but they do not know to whom they are praying. A devotee, however, always offers personal prayers. A devotee says, *govindam ādi-puruṣaṁ tam ahaṁ bhajāmi:* "I offer my respectful obeisances unto Govinda, unto Kṛṣṇa." That is the way to offer prayers. If one continues to offer such personal prayers to the Supreme Personality of Godhead, he is eligible to become a pure devotee and return home, back to Godhead.

TEXT 48

किं दुरापं मयि प्रीते तथापि विबुधर्षभाः ।
मय्येकान्तमतिर्नान्यन्मत्तो वाञ्छति तत्त्ववित् ॥ ४८ ॥

kiṁ durāpaṁ mayi prīte
tathāpi vibudharṣabhāḥ
mayy ekānta-matir nānyan
matto vāñchati tattva-vit

kim—what; *durāpam*—difficult to obtain; *mayi*—when I; *prīte*—satisfied; *tathāpi*—still; *vibudha-ṛṣabhāḥ*—O best of the intelligent demigods; *mayi*—in Me; *ekānta*—exclusively fixed; *matiḥ*—whose attention; *na anyat*—not anything other; *mattaḥ*—than Me; *vāñchati*—desires; *tattva-vit*—one who knows the truth.

TRANSLATION

O best of the intelligent demigods, although it is true that nothing is difficult for one to obtain when I am pleased with him, a pure devotee, whose mind is exclusively fixed upon Me, does not ask Me for anything but the opportunity to engage in devotional service.

PURPORT

When the demigods finished offering their prayers, they anxiously waited for their enemy Vṛtrāsura to be killed. This means that the demigods are not pure devotees. Although without difficulty one can get anything he desires if the Lord is pleased, the demigods aspire for material profit by pleasing the Lord. The Lord wanted the demigods to pray for unalloyed devotional service, but instead they prayed for an opportunity to kill their enemy. This is the difference between a pure devotee and a devotee on the material platform. Indirectly, the Lord regretted that the demigods did not ask for pure devotional service.

TEXT 49

न वेद कृपणः श्रेय आत्मनो गुणवस्तुदृक् ।
तस्य तानिच्छतो यच्छेद् यदि सोऽपि तथाविधः ॥ ४९ ॥

na veda kṛpaṇaḥ śreya
ātmano guṇa-vastu-dṛk
tasya tān icchato yacched
yadi so'pi tathā-vidhaḥ

na—not; *veda*—knows; *kṛpaṇaḥ*—a miserly living entity; *śreyaḥ*—the ultimate necessity; *ātmanaḥ*—of the soul; *guṇa-vastu-dṛk*—who is attracted by the creation of the modes of material nature; *tasya*—of him; *tān*—things created by the material energy; *icchataḥ*—desiring; *yacchet*—one bestows; *yadi*—if; *saḥ api*—he also; *tathā-vidhaḥ*—of the kind (a foolish *kṛpaṇa* who does not know his real self-interest).

TRANSLATION

Those who think material assets to be everything or to be the ultimate goal of life are called misers [kṛpaṇas]. They do not know the ultimate necessity of the soul. Moreover, if one awards that which is desired by such fools, he must also be considered foolish.

PURPORT

There are two classes of men—namely the *kṛpaṇa* and the *brāhmaṇa.* A *brāhmaṇa* is one who knows Brahman, the Absolute Truth, and who thus knows his real interest. A *kṛpaṇa,* however, is one who has a material, bodily concept of life. Not knowing how to utilize his human or demigod life, a *kṛpaṇa* is attracted by things created by the material modes of nature. The *kṛpaṇas,* who always desire material benefits, are foolish, whereas *brāhmaṇas,* who always desire spiritual benefits, are intelligent. If a *kṛpaṇa,* not knowing his self-interest, foolishly asks for something material, one who awards it to him is also foolish. Kṛṣṇa, however, is not a foolish person; He is supremely intelligent. If someone comes to Kṛṣṇa asking for material benefits, Kṛṣṇa does not award him the material things he desires. Instead, the Lord gives him intelligence so that he will forget his material desires and become attached to the Lord's lotus feet. In such cases, although the *kṛpaṇa* offers prayers to Lord Kṛṣṇa for material things, the Lord takes away whatever material possessions the *kṛpaṇa* has and gives him the sense to become a devotee. As stated by the Lord in the *Caitanya-caritāmṛta* (*Madhya* 22.39):

āmi-vijña, ei mūrkhe 'viṣaya' kene diba?
sva-caraṇāmṛta diyā 'viṣaya' bhulāiba

"Since I am very intelligent, why should I give this fool material prosperity? Instead I shall induce him to take the nectar of the shelter of My lotus feet and make him forget illusory material enjoyment." If one sincerely prays to God for material possessions in exchange for devotional service, the Lord, who is not foolish like such an unintelligent devotee, shows him special favor by taking away whatever material possessions he has and gradually giving him the intelligence to be satisfied only by rendering service to His lotus feet. Śrīla Viśvanātha Cakravartī Ṭhākura comments in this regard that if a foolish child requests his mother to give him poison, the mother, being intelligent, will certainly not give him poison, even though he requests it. A materialist does not know that to accept material possessions means to accept poison, or the repetition of birth and death. An intelligent person, a *brāhmaṇa,* aspires for liberation from material bondage. That is the real self-interest of a human being.

TEXT 50

स्वयं निःश्रेयसं विद्वान् न वक्त्यज्ञाय कर्म हि ।
न राति रोगिणोऽपथ्यं वाञ्छतोऽपि भिषक्तमः ॥ ५० ॥

svayaṁ niḥśreyasaṁ vidvān
na vakty ajñāya karma hi
na rāti rogiṇo'pathyaṁ
vāñchato'pi bhiṣaktamaḥ

svayam—personally; *niḥśreyasam*—the supreme goal of life, namely the means of obtaining ecstatic love for the Supreme Personality of Godhead; *vit-vān*—one who is accomplished in devotional service; *na*—not; *vakti*—teaches; *ajñāya*—unto a foolish person not conversant with the ultimate goal of life; *karma*—fruitive activities; *hi*—indeed; *na*—not; *rāti*—administers; *rogiṇaḥ*—unto the patient; *apathyam*—something unconsumable; *vāñchataḥ*—desiring; *api*—although; *bhiṣak-tamaḥ*—an experienced physician.

TRANSLATION

A pure devotee who is fully accomplished in the science of devotional service will never instruct a foolish person to engage in fruitive activities for material enjoyment, not to speak of helping him in such activities. Such a devotee is like an experienced physician, who never encourages a patient to eat food injurious to his health, even if the patient desires it.

PURPORT

Here is the difference between the benedictions awarded by the demigods and those awarded by the Supreme Personality of Godhead, Viṣṇu. Devotees of the demigods ask for benedictions simply for sense gratification, and therefore they have been described in *Bhagavad-gītā* (7.20) as bereft of intelligence.

kāmais tais tair hṛta-jñānāḥ
prapadyante'nya-devatāḥ
taṁ taṁ niyamam āsthāya
prakṛtyā niyatāḥ svayā

"Those whose minds are distorted by material desires surrender unto demigods and follow the particular rules and regulations of worship according to their own natures."

Conditioned souls are generally bereft of intelligence because of profound desires for sense gratification. They do not know what benedictions to ask. Therefore nondevotees are advised in the *śāstras* to worship various demigods to achieve material benefits. For example, if one wants a beautiful wife, he is advised to worship Umā, or goddess Durgā. If one wants to be cured of a disease, he is advised to worship the sun-god. All requests for benedictions from the demigods, however, are due to material lust. The benedictions will be finished at the end of the cosmic manifestation, along with those who bestow them. If one approaches Lord Viṣṇu for benedictions, the Lord will give him a benediction that will help him return home, back to Godhead. This is also confirmed by the Lord Himself in *Bhagavad-gītā* (10.10):

teṣāṁ satata-yuktānāṁ
bhajatāṁ prīti-pūrvakam
dadāmi buddhi-yogaṁ taṁ
yena mām upayānti te

Lord Viṣṇu, or Lord Kṛṣṇa, instructs a devotee who constantly engages in His service how to approach Him at the end of his material body. The Lord says in *Bhagavad-gītā* (4.9):

janma karma ca me divyam
evaṁ yo vetti tattvataḥ
tyaktvā dehaṁ punar janma
naiti mām eti so 'rjuna

"One who knows the transcendental nature of My appearance and activities, does not, upon leaving the body, take his birth again in this material world, but attains My eternal abode, O Arjuna." This is the benediction of Lord Viṣṇu, Kṛṣṇa. After giving up his body, a devotee returns home, back to Godhead.

A devotee may foolishly ask for material benedictions, but Lord Kṛṣṇa does not give him such benedictions, despite the devotee's prayers. Therefore people who are very attached to material life do not generally become devotees of Kṛṣṇa or Viṣṇu. Instead they become devotees of the demigods (*kāmais tais tair hṛta jñānāḥ prapadyante 'nya-devatāḥ*). The benedictions of the demigods, however, are condemned in *Bhagavad-gītā. Antavat tu phalaṁ teṣāṁ tad bhavaty alpa-medhasām:* "Men of small intelligence worship the demigods, and their fruits are limited and temporary." A non-Vaiṣṇava, one who is not engaged in the service of the Supreme Personality of Godhead, is considered a fool with a small quantity of brain substance.

TEXT 51

मघवन् यात भद्रं वो दध्यञ्चमृषिसत्तमम् ।
विद्याव्रततपःसारं गात्रं याचत मा चिरम् ॥ ५१ ॥

maghavan yāta bhadraṁ vo
dadhyañcam ṛṣi-sattamam
vidyā-vrata-tapaḥ-sāraṁ
gātraṁ yācata mā ciram

maghavan—O Indra; *yāta*—go; *bhadram*—good fortune; *vaḥ*—to all of you; *dadhyañcam*—to Dadhyañca; *ṛṣi-sat-tamam*—the most exalted saintly person; *vidyā*—of education; *vrata*—vow; *tapaḥ*—and austerities; *sāram*—the essence; *gātram*—his body; *yācata*—ask for; *mā ciram*—without delay.

TRANSLATION

O Maghavan [Indra], all good fortune unto you. I advise you to approach the exalted saint Dadhyañca [Dadhīci]. He has become very accomplished in knowledge, vows and austerities, and his body is very strong. Go ask him for his body without delay.

PURPORT

Everyone in this material world, from Lord Brahmā down to the ant, is eager to keep his body comfortable. A pure devotee may also be comfortable, but he is not eager for such a benediction. Since Maghavan, the King of heaven, still aspired for a comfortable bodily situation, Lord Viṣṇu advised him to ask Dadhyañca for his body, which was very strong due to his knowledge, vows and austerity.

TEXT 52

स वा अधिगतो दध्यङ्ङश्विभ्यां ब्रह्म निष्कलम् ।
यद् वा अश्वशिरो नाम तयोरमरतां व्यधात् ॥ ५२ ॥

sa vā adhigato dadhyaṅṅ
aśvibhyāṁ brahma niṣkalam
yad vā aśvaśiro nāma
tayor amaratāṁ vyadhāt

saḥ—he; *vā*—certainly; *adhigataḥ*—having obtained; *dadhyaṅ*—Dadhyañca; *aśvibhyām*—to the two Aśvinī-kumāras; *brahma*—spiritual knowledge; *niṣkalam*—pure; *yat vā*—by which; *aśvaśiraḥ*—Aśvaśira; *nāma*—named; *tayoḥ*—of the two; *amaratām*—liberation in one's life; *vyadhāt*—awarded.

TRANSLATION

That saintly Dadhyañca, who is also known as Dadhīci, personally assimilated the spiritual science and then delivered it to the Aśvinī-kumāras. It is said that Dadhyañca gave them mantras through the head of a horse. Therefore the mantras are called Aśvaśira. After obtaining the mantras of spiritual science from Dadhīci, the Aśvinī-kumāras became jīvan-mukta, liberated even in this life.

PURPORT

The following story is narrated by many *ācāryas* in their commentaries:

niśamyātharvaṇaṁ dakṣaṁ pravargya-brahmavidyayoḥ. dadhyañcaṁ samupāgamya tam ūcatur athāśvinau. bhagavan dehi nau vidyām iti śrutvā sa cābravīt. karmaṇy avasthito'dyāhaṁ paścād vakṣyāmi gacchatam. tayor nirgatayor eva śakra āgatya taṁ munim. uvāca bhiṣajor vidyāṁ mā vādīr aśvinor mune. yadi mad-vākyam ullaṅghya bravīṣi sahasaiva te. śiraś-chindyāṁ na sandeha ity uktvā sa yayau hariḥ. indre gate tathābhyetya nāsatyāv ūcatur dvijam. tan-mukhād indra-gaditaṁ śrutvā tāv ūcatuḥ punaḥ. āvāṁ tava śiraś chittvā pūrvam aśvasya mastakam. sandhāsyāvas tato brūhi tena vidyāṁ ca nau dvija. tasminn indreṇa sañchinne punaḥ sandhāya mastakam. nijaṁ te dakṣiṇāṁ dattvā gamiṣyāvo yathāgatam. etac chrutvā tadovāca dadhyaṅṅ ātharvaṇas tayoḥ pravargyaṁ brahma-vidyāṁ ca sat-kṛto'satya-śaṅkitaḥ.

The great saint Dadhīci had perfect knowledge of how to perform fruitive activities, and he had advanced spiritual knowledge as well. Knowing this, the Aśvinī-kumāras once approached him and begged him to instruct them in spiritual science (*brahma-vidyā*). Dadhīci Muni replied, "I am now engaged in arranging sacrifices for fruitive activities. Come back some time later." When the Aśvinī-kumāras left, Indra, the King of heaven, approached Dadhīci and said, "My dear Muni, the Aśvinī-kumāras are only physicians. Please do not instruct them in spiritual science. If you impart the spiritual science to them despite my warning, I shall punish you by cutting off your head." After warning Dadhīci in this way, Indra returned to heaven. The Aśvinī-kumāras, who understood Indra's desires, returned and begged Dadhīci for *brahma-vidyā.* When the great saint Dadhīci informed them of Indra's threat, the Aśvinī-kumāras replied, "Let us first cut off your head and replace it with the head of a horse. You can instruct *brahma-vidyā* through the horse's head, and when Indra returns and cuts off that head, we shall reward you and restore your original head." Since Dadhīci had promised to impart *brahma-vidyā* to the Aśvinī-kumāras, he agreed to their proposal. Therefore, because Dadhīci imparted *brahma-vidyā* through the mouth of a horse, this *brahma-vidyā* is also known as Aśvaśira.

TEXT 53

दध्यङ्ङाथर्वणस्त्वष्ट्रे वर्माभेद्यं मदात्मकम् ।
विश्वरूपाय यत् प्रादात् त्वष्टा यत् त्वमधास्ततः ॥ ५३ ॥

dadhyaṅṅ ātharvaṇas tvaṣṭre
varmābhedyaṁ mad-ātmakam
viśvarūpāya yat prādāt
tvaṣṭā yat tvam adhās tataḥ

dadhyaṅ—Dadhyañca; *ātharvaṇaḥ*—the son of Atharvā; *tvaṣṭre*—unto Tvaṣṭā; *varma*—the protective covering known as Nārāyaṇa-kavaca; *abhedyam*—invincible; *mat-ātmakam*—consisting of Myself; *viśvarūpāya*—unto Viśvarūpa; *yat*—which; *prādāt*—delivered; *tvaṣṭā*—Tvaṣṭā; *yat*—which; *tvam*—you; *adhāḥ*—received; *tataḥ*—from him.

TRANSLATION

Dadhyañca's invincible protective covering known as the Nārāyaṇa-kavaca was given to Tvaṣṭā, who delivered it to his son Viśvarūpa, from whom you have received it. Because of this Nārāyaṇa-kavaca, Dadhīci's body is now very strong. You should therefore beg him for his body.

TEXT 54

युष्मभ्यं याचितोऽश्विभ्यां धर्मज्ञोऽङ्गानि दास्यति ।
ततस्तैरायुधश्रेष्ठो विश्वकर्मविनिर्मितः ।
येन वृत्रशिरो हर्ता मत्तेजउपबृंहितः ॥ ५४ ॥

yuṣmabhyaṁ yācito'śvibhyāṁ
dharma-jño'ṅgāni dāsyati
tatas tair āyudha-śreṣṭho
viśvakarma-vinirmitaḥ
yena vṛtra-śiro hartā
mat-teja-upabṛṁhitaḥ

yuṣmabhyam—for all of you; *yācitaḥ*—being asked; *aśvibhyām*—by the Aśvinī-kumāras; *dharma-jñaḥ*—Dadhīci, who knows the principles of religion; *aṅgāni*—his limbs; *dāsyati*—will give; *tataḥ*—after that; *taiḥ*—by those bones; *āyudha*—of weapons; *śreṣṭhaḥ*—the most powerful (the thunderbolt); *viśvakarma-vinirmitaḥ*—manufactured by Viśvakarmā; *yena*—

by which; *vṛtra-śiraḥ*—the head of Vṛtrāsura; *hartā*—will be taken away; *mat-tejaḥ*—by My strength; *upabṛṁhitaḥ*—increased.

TRANSLATION

When the Aśvinī-kumāras beg for Dadhyañca's body on your behalf, he will surely give it because of affection. Do not doubt this, for Dadhyañca is very experienced in religious understanding. When Dadhyañca awards you his body, Viśvakarmā will prepare a thunderbolt from his bones. This thunderbolt will certainly kill Vṛtrāsura because it will be invested with My power.

TEXT 55

तस्मिन् विनिहते यूयं तेजोऽस्त्रायुधसम्पदः ।
भूयः प्राप्स्यथ भद्रं वो न हिंसन्ति च मत्परान् ॥ ५५ ॥

tasmin vinihate yūyaṁ
tejo-'strāyudha-sampadaḥ
bhūyaḥ prāpsyatha bhadraṁ vo
na hiṁsanti ca mat-parān

tasmin—when he (Vṛtrāsura); *vinihate*—is killed; *yūyam*—all of you; *tejaḥ*—power; *astra*—arrows; *āyudha*—other weapons; *sampadaḥ*—and opulence; *bhūyaḥ*—again; *prāpsyatha*—will obtain; *bhadram*—all good fortune; *vaḥ*—unto you; *na*—not; *hiṁsanti*—hurt; *ca*—also; *mat-parān*—My devotees.

TRANSLATION

When Vṛtrāsura is killed because of My spiritual strength, you will regain your strength, weapons and wealth. Thus there will be all good fortune for all of you. Although Vṛtrāsura can destroy all the three worlds, do not fear that he will harm you. He is also a devotee and will never be envious of you.

PURPORT

A devotee of the Lord is never envious of anyone, what to speak of other devotees. As revealed later, Vṛtrāsura was also a devotee. Therefore he was not expected to be envious of the demigods. Indeed, of his own accord, he would try to benefit the demigods. A devotee does not hesitate to give up his own body for a better cause. Cāṇakya Paṇḍita said, *san-nimitte varaṁ tyāgo vināśe niyate sati.* After all, all one's material possessions, including his body, will be destroyed in due course of time. Therefore if the body and other possessions can be utilized for a better cause, a devotee never hesitates to give up even his own body. Because Lord Viṣṇu wanted to save the demigods, Vṛtrāsura, even though able to swallow the three worlds, would agree to be killed by the demigods. For a devotee there is no difference between living and dying because in this life a devotee engages in devotional service, and after giving up his body, he engages in the same service in the spiritual world. His devotional service is never hindered.

Thus end the Bhaktivedanta purports to the Ninth Chapter, Sixth Canto, of the Śrīmad-Bhāgavatam, *entitled "Appearance of the Demon Vṛtrāsura."*

CHAPTER TEN

The Battle Between the Demigods and Vṛtrāsura

As described in this chapter, after Indra obtained the body of Dadhīci, a thunderbolt was prepared from Dadhīci's bones, and a fight took place between Vṛtrāsura and the demigods.

Following the order of the Supreme Personality of Godhead, the demigods approached Dadhīci Muni and begged for his body. Dadhīci Muni, just to hear from the demigods about the principles of religion, jokingly refused to relinquish his body, but for higher purposes he thereafter agreed to give it up, for after death the body is usually eaten by low animals like dogs and jackals. Dadhīci Muni first merged his gross body made of five elements into the original stock of five elements and then engaged his soul at the lotus feet of the Supreme Personality of Godhead. Thus he gave up his gross body. With the help of Viśvakarmā, the demigods then prepared a thunderbolt from Dadhīci's bones. Armed with the thunderbolt weapon, they prepared themselves to fight and got up on the backs of elephants.

At the end of Satya-yuga and the beginning of Tretā-yuga, a great fight took place between the demigods and the *asuras.* Unable to tolerate the effulgence of the demigods, the *asuras* fled the battle, leaving Vṛtrāsura, their commander in chief, to fight for himself. Vṛtrāsura, however, seeing the demons fleeing, instructed them in the importance of fighting and dying in the battlefield. One who is victorious in battle gains material possessions, and one who dies in the battlefield attains a residence at once in the celestial heavens. In either way, the fighter benefits.

TEXT 1

श्रीबादरायणिरुवाच
इन्द्रमेवं समादिश्य भगवान् विश्वभावनः ।
पश्यतामनिमेषाणां तत्रैवान्तर्दधे हरिः ॥ १ ॥

śrī-bādarāyaṇir uvāca
indram evaṁ samādiśya
bhagavān viśva-bhāvanaḥ

paśyatām animeṣāṇāṁ
tatraivāntardadhe hariḥ

śrī-bādarāyaṇiḥ uvāca—Śrī Śukadeva Gosvāmī said; *indram*—Indra, the heavenly King; *evam*—thus; *samādiśya*—after instructing; *bhagavān*—the Supreme Personality of Godhead; *viśva-bhāvanaḥ*—the original cause of all cosmic manifestations; *paśyatām animeṣāṇām*—while the demigods were looking on; *tatra*—then and there; *eva*—indeed; *antardadhe*—disappeared; *hariḥ*—the Lord.

TRANSLATION

Śrī Śukadeva Gosvāmī said: After instructing Indra in this way, the Supreme Personality of Godhead, Hari, the cause of the cosmic manifestation, then and there disappeared from the presence of the onlooking demigods.

TEXT 2

तथाभियाचितो देवैर्ऋषिराथर्वणो महान्।
मोदमान उवाचेदं प्रहसन्निव भारत ॥ २ ॥

tathābhiyācito devair
ṛṣir ātharvaṇo mahān
modamāna uvācedaṁ
prahasann iva bhārata

tathā—in that manner; *abhiyācitaḥ*—being begged; *devaiḥ*—by the demigods; *ṛṣiḥ*—the great saintly person; *ātharvaṇaḥ*—Dadhīci, the son of Atharvā; *mahān*—the great personality; *modamānaḥ*—being merry; *uvāca*—said; *idam*—this; *prahasan*—smiling; *iva*—somewhat; *bhārata*—O Mahārāja Parīkṣit.

TRANSLATION

O King Parīkṣit, following the Lord's instructions, the demigods approached Dadhīci, the son of Atharvā. He was very liberal, and when they begged him to give them his body, he at once partially agreed. However, just to hear religious instructions from them, he smiled and jokingly spoke as follows.

TEXT 3

अपि वृन्दारका यूयं न जानीथ शरीरिणाम् ।
संस्थायां यस्त्वभिद्रोहो दुःसहश्चेतनापहः ॥ ३ ॥

api vṛndārakā yūyaṁ
na jānītha śarīriṇām
saṁsthāyāṁ yas tv abhidroho
duḥsahaś cetanāpahaḥ

api—although; *vṛndārakāḥ*—O demigods; *yūyam*—all of you; *na jānītha*—do not know; *śarīriṇām*—of those who have material bodies; *saṁsthāyām*—at the time of death, or while quitting this body; *yaḥ*—which; *tu*—then; *abhidrohaḥ*—severe pain; *duḥsahaḥ*—unbearable; *cetana*—the consciousness; *apahaḥ*—which takes away.

TRANSLATION

O elevated demigods, at the time of death, severe, unbearable pain takes away the consciousness of all living entities who have accepted material bodies. Don't you know about this pain?

TEXT 4

जिजीविषूणां जीवानामात्मा प्रेष्ठ इहेप्सितः ।
क उत्सहेत तं दातुं भिक्षमाणाय विष्णवे ॥ ४ ॥

jijīviṣūṇāṁ jīvānām
ātmā preṣṭha ihepsitaḥ
ka utsaheta taṁ dātuṁ
bhikṣamāṇāya viṣṇave

jijīviṣūṇām—aspiring to remain alive; *jīvānām*—of all living entities; *ātmā*—the body; *preṣṭhaḥ*—very dear; *iha*—here; *īpsitaḥ*—desired; *kaḥ*—who; *utsaheta*—can bear; *tam*—that body; *dātum*—to deliver; *bhikṣamāṇāya*—begging; *viṣṇave*—even to Lord Viṣṇu.

TRANSLATION

In this material world, every living entity is very much addicted to his material body. Struggling to keep his body forever, everyone tries to protect it by all means, even at the sacrifice of all his possessions.

Therefore, who would be prepared to deliver his body to anyone, even if it were demanded by Lord Viṣṇu?

PURPORT

It is said, *ātmānaṁ sarvato rakṣet tato dharmaṁ tato dhanam:* one must protect his body by all means; then he may protect his religious principles and thereafter his possessions. This is the natural desire of all living entities. No one wants to give up his body unless it is forcibly given away. Even though the demigods said that they were demanding Dadhīci's body for their benefit in accordance with the order of Lord Viṣṇu, Dadhīci superficially refused to give them his body.

TEXT 5

श्रीदेवा ऊचुः

किं नु तद् दुस्त्यजं ब्रह्मन् पुंसां भूतानुकम्पिनाम्।
भवद्विधानां महतां पुण्यश्लोकेड्यकर्मणाम् ॥ ५ ॥

śrī-devā ūcuḥ
kiṁ nu tad dustyajaṁ brahman
puṁsāṁ bhūtānukampinām
bhavad-vidhānāṁ mahatāṁ
puṇya-ślokeḍya-karmaṇām

śrī-devāḥ ūcuḥ—the demigods said; *kim*—what; *nu*—indeed; *tat*—that; *dustyajam*—difficult to give up; *brahman*—O exalted *brāhmaṇa; puṁsām*—of persons; *bhūta-anukampinām*—who are very sympathetic toward the suffering living entities; *bhavat-vidhānām*—like Your Lordship; *mahatām*—who are very great; *puṇya-śloka-īḍya-karmaṇām*—whose pious activities are praised by all great souls.

TRANSLATION

The demigods replied: O exalted brāhmaṇa, pious persons like you, whose activities are praiseworthy, are very kind and affectionate to people in general. What can't such pious souls give for the benefit of others? They can give everything, including their bodies.

TEXT 6

नूनं स्वार्थपरो लोको न वेद परसंकटम्।
यदि वेद न याचेत नेति नाह यदीश्वरः ॥ ६ ॥

nūnaṁ svārtha-paro loko
na veda para-saṅkaṭam
yadi veda na yāceta
neti nāha yad īśvaraḥ

nūnam—certainly; *sva-artha-paraḥ*—interested only in sense gratification in this life or the next; *lokaḥ*—materialistic people in general; *na*—not; *veda*—know; *para-saṅkaṭam*—the pain of others; *yadi*—if; *veda*—know; *na*—not; *yāceta*—would ask; *na*—no; *iti*—thus; *na āha*—does not say; *yat*—since; *īśvaraḥ*—able to give charity.

TRANSLATION

Those who are too self-interested beg something from others, not knowing of others' pain. But if the beggar knew the difficulty of the giver, he would not ask for anything. Similarly, he who is able to give charity does not know the beggar's difficulty, for otherwise he would not refuse to give the beggar anything he might want as charity.

PURPORT

This verse describes two people—one who gives charity and one who begs for it. A beggar should not ask charity from a person who is in difficulty. Similarly, one who is able to give charity should not deny a beggar. These are the moral instructions of the *śāstra.* Cāṇakya Paṇḍita says, *san-nimitte varaṁ tyāgo vināśe niyate sati:* everything within this material world will be destroyed, and therefore one should use everything for good purposes. If one is advanced in knowledge, he must always be prepared to sacrifice anything for a better cause. At the present moment the entire world is in a dangerous position under the spell of a godless civilization. The Kṛṣṇa consciousness movement needs many exalted, learned persons who will sacrifice their lives to revive God consciousness throughout the world. We therefore invite all men and women advanced in knowledge to join the Kṛṣṇa consciousness movement and sacrifice their lives for the great cause of reviving the God consciousness of human society.

TEXT 7

श्रीऋषिरुवाच
धर्मं वः श्रोतुकामेन यूयं मे प्रत्युदाहृताः ।
एष वः प्रियमात्मानं त्यजन्तं संत्यजाम्यहम् ॥ ७ ॥

śrī-ṛṣir uvāca
dharmaṁ vaḥ śrotu-kāmena
yūyaṁ me pratyudāhṛtāḥ
eṣa vaḥ priyam ātmānaṁ
tyajantaṁ santyajāmy aham

śrī-ṛṣiḥ uvāca—the great saint Dadhīci said; *dharmam*—the principles of religion; *vaḥ*—from you; *śrotu-kāmena*—by the desire to hear; *yūyam*—you; *me*—by me; *pratyudāhṛtāḥ*—replied to the contrary; *eṣaḥ*—this; *vaḥ*—for you; *priyam*—dear; *ātmānam*—body; *tyajantam*—leaving me anyway, today or tomorrow; *santyajāmi*—give up; *aham*—I.

TRANSLATION

The great sage Dadhīci said: Just to hear from you about religious principles, I refused to offer my body at your request. Now, although my body is extremely dear to me, I must give it up for your better purposes since I know that it will leave me today or tomorrow.

TEXT 8

योऽध्रुवेणात्मना नाथा न धर्मं न यशः पुमान् ।
ईहेत भूतदयया स शोच्यः स्थावरैरपि ॥ ८ ॥

yo'dhruveṇātmanā nāthā
na dharmaṁ na yaśaḥ pumān
īheta bhūta-dayayā
sa śocyaḥ sthāvarair api

yaḥ—anyone who; *adhruveṇa*—impermanent; *ātmanā*—by the body; *nāthāḥ*—O lords; *na*—not; *dharmam*—religious principles; *na*—not; *yaśaḥ*—fame; *pumān*—a person; *īheta*—endeavors for; *bhūta-dayayā*—by mercy for the living beings; *saḥ*—that person; *śocyaḥ*—pitiable; *sthāvaraiḥ*—by the immobile creatures; *api*—even.

TRANSLATION

O demigods, one who has no compassion for humanity in its suffering and does not sacrifice his impermanent body for the higher causes of religious principles or eternal glory is certainly pitied even by the immovable beings.

PURPORT

In this regard, a very exalted example was set by Lord Śrī Caitanya Mahāprabhu and the six Gosvāmīs of Vṛndāvana. Concerning Śrī Caitanya Mahāprabhu it is said in *Śrīmad-Bhāgavatam* (11.5.34):

tyaktvā sudustyaja-surepsita-rājya-lakṣmīṁ
dharmiṣṭha ārya-vacasā yad agād araṇyam
māyā-mṛgaṁ dayitayepsitam anvadhāvad
vande mahā-puruṣa te caraṇāravindam

"We offer our respectful obeisances unto the lotus feet of the Lord, upon whom one should always meditate. He left His householder life, leaving aside His eternal consort, whom even the denizens of heaven adore. He went into the forest to deliver the fallen souls, who are put into illusion by material energy." To accept *sannyāsa* means to commit civil suicide, but *sannyāsa* is compulsory, at least for every *brāhmaṇa,* every first-class human being. Śrī Caitanya Mahāprabhu had a very young and beautiful wife and a very affectionate mother. Indeed, the affectionate dealings of His family members were so pleasing that even the demigods could not expect such happiness at home. Nevertheless, for the deliverance of all the fallen souls of the world, Śrī Caitanya Mahāprabhu took *sannyāsa* and left home when He was only twenty-four years old. He lived a very strict life as a *sannyāsī,* refusing all bodily comforts. Similarly, His disciples the six Gosvāmīs were ministers who held exalted positions in society, but they also left everything to join the movement of Śrī Caitanya Mahāprabhu. Śrīnivāsa Ācārya says:

tyaktvā tūrṇam aśeṣa-maṇḍala-pati-śreṇīṁ sadā tucchavat
bhūtvā dīna-gaṇeśakau karuṇayā kaupīna-kanthāśritau

These Gosvāmīs left their very comfortable lives as ministers, Zamindars and learned scholars and joined Śrī Caitanya Mahāprabhu's movement, just to show mercy to the fallen souls of the world (*dīna-gaṇeśakau karuṇayā*). Accepting very humble lives as mendicants, wearing no more than loincloths and torn quilts (*kaupīna-kantha*), they lived in Vṛndāvana and followed Śrī Caitanya Mahāprabhu's order to excavate Vṛndāvana's lost glories.

Similarly, everyone else with a materially comfortable condition in this world should join the Kṛṣṇa consciousness movement to elevate the fallen souls. The words *bhūta-dayayā, māyā-mṛgaṁ dayitayepsitam* and *dīna-gaṇeśakau karuṇayā* all convey the same sense. These are very significant words for those interested in elevating human society to a proper understanding of life. One should join the Kṛṣṇa consciousness movement, following the examples of such great personalities as Śrī Caitanya Mahāprabhu, the six Gosvāmīs and, before them, the great sage Dadhīci. Instead of wasting one's life for temporary bodily comforts, one should always be prepared to give up one's life for better causes. After all, the body will be destroyed. Therefore one should sacrifice it for the glory of distributing religious principles throughout the world.

TEXT 9

एतावानव्ययो धर्मः पुण्यश्लोकैरुपासितः ।
यो भूतशोकहर्षाभ्यामात्मा शोचति हृष्यति ॥ ९ ॥

etāvān avyayo dharmaḥ
puṇya-ślokair upāsitaḥ
yo bhūta-śoka-harṣābhyām
ātmā śocati hṛṣyati

etāvān—this much; *avyayaḥ*—imperishable; *dharmaḥ*—religious principle; *puṇya-ślokaiḥ*—by famous persons who are celebrated as pious; *upāsitaḥ*—recognized; *yaḥ*—which; *bhūta*—of the living beings; *śoka*—by the distress; *harṣābhyām*—and by the happiness; *ātmā*—the mind; *śocati*—laments; *hṛṣyati*—feels happiness.

TRANSLATION

If one is unhappy to see the distress of other living beings and happy to see their happiness, his religious principles are appreciated as imperishable by exalted persons who are considered pious and benevolent.

PURPORT

One generally follows different types of religious principles or performs various occupational duties according to the body given to him by the modes of material nature. In this verse, however, real religious principles are explained. Everyone should be unhappy to see others in distress and happy to see others happy. *Ātmavat sarva-bhūteṣu:* one should feel the happiness and distress of others as his own. It is on this basis that the Buddhist religious principle of nonviolence—*ahiṁsaḥ parama-dharmaḥ*—is established. We feel pain when someone disturbs us, and therefore we should not inflict pain upon other living beings. Lord Buddha's mission was to stop unnecessary animal killing, and therefore he preached that the greatest religious principle is nonviolence.

One cannot continue killing animals and at the same time be a religious man. That is the greatest hypocrisy. Jesus Christ said, "Do not kill," but hypocrites nevertheless maintain thousands of slaughterhouses while posing as Christians. Such hypocrisy is condemned in this verse. One should be happy to see others happy, and one should be unhappy to see others unhappy. This is the principle to be followed. Unfortunately, at the present moment so-called philanthropists and humanitarians advocate the happiness of humanity at the cost of the lives of poor animals. That is not recommended herein. This verse clearly says that one should be compassionate to all living entities. Regardless of whether human, animal, tree or plant, all living entities are sons of the Supreme Personality of Godhead. Lord Kṛṣṇa says in *Bhagavad-gītā* (14.4):

sarva-yoniṣu kaunteya
mūrtayaḥ sambhavanti yāḥ
tāsāṁ brahma mahad yonir
ahaṁ bīja-pradaḥ pitā

"It should be understood that all species of life, O son of Kuntī, are made possible by birth in this material nature, and that I am the seed-giving father." The different forms of these living entities are only their external dresses. Every living being is actually a spirit soul, a part and parcel of God. Therefore one should not favor only one kind of living being. A Vaiṣṇava sees all living entities as part and parcel of God. As the Lord says in *Bhagavad-gītā* (5.18 and 18.54):

vidyā-vinaya-sampanne
brāhmaṇe gavi hastini
śuni caiva śvapāke ca
paṇḍitāḥ sama-darśinaḥ

"The humble sage, by virtue of true knowledge, sees with equal vision a learned and gentle *brāhmaṇa,* a cow, an elephant, a dog and a dog-eater [outcaste]."

brahma-bhūtaḥ prasannātmā
na śocati na kāṅkṣati
samaḥ sarveṣu bhūteṣu
mad-bhaktiṁ labhate parām

"One who is transcendentally situated at once realizes the Supreme Brahman and becomes fully joyful. He never laments nor desires to have anything. he is equally disposed to every living entity. In that state he attains pure devotional service unto Me." A Vaiṣṇava, therefore, is truly a perfect person because he laments to see others unhappy and feels joy at seeing others happy. A Vaiṣṇava is *para-duḥkha-duḥkhī;* he is always unhappy to see the conditioned souls in an unhappy state of materialism. Therefore a Vaiṣṇava is always busy preaching Kṛṣṇa consciousness throughout the world.

TEXT 10

अहो दैन्यमहो कष्टं पारक्यैः क्षणभङ्गुरैः ।
यन्नोपकुर्यादस्वार्थैर्मर्त्यः स्वज्ञातिविग्रहैः ॥ १० ॥

aho dainyam aho kaṣṭaṁ
pārakyaiḥ kṣaṇa-bhaṅguraiḥ
yan nopakuryād asvārthair
martyaḥ sva-jñāti-vigrahaiḥ

aho—alas; *dainyam*—a miserable condition; *aho*—alas; *kaṣṭam*—simply tribulation; *pārakyaiḥ*—which after death are eatable by dogs and jackals; *kṣaṇa-bhaṅguraiḥ*—perishable at any moment; *yat*—because; *na*—not; *upakuryāt*—would help; *a-sva-arthaiḥ*—not meant for self-interest; *martyaḥ*—a living entity destined to die; *sva*—with his wealth; *jñāti*—relatives and friends; *vigrahaiḥ*—and his body.

TRANSLATION

This body, which is eatable by jackals and dogs after death, does not actually do any good for me, the spirit soul. It is usable only for a short time and may perish at any moment. The body and its possessions, its riches and relatives, must all be engaged for the benefit of others, or else they will be sources of tribulation and misery.

PURPORT

Similar advice is also given in *Śrīmad-Bhāgavatam* (10.22.35):

etāvaj janma-sāphalyaṁ
dehinām iha dehiṣu
prāṇair arthair dhiyā vācā
śreya-ācaraṇaṁ sadā

"It is the duty of every living being to perform welfare activities for the benefit of others with his life, wealth, intelligence and words." This is the mission of life. One's own body and the bodies of his friends and relatives, as well as one's own riches and everything else one has, should be engaged for the benefit of others. This is the mission of Śrī Caitanya Mahāprabhu. As stated in *Caitanya-caritāmṛta* (*Ādi* 9.41):

bhārata-bhūmite haila manuṣya-janma yāra
janma sārthaka kari' kara para-upakāra

"One who has taken birth as a human being in the land of India [Bhārata-varṣa] should make his life successful and work for the benefit of all other people."

The word *upakuryāt* means *para-upakāra,* helping others. Of course, in human society there are many institutions to help others, but because philanthropists do not know how to help others, their propensity for philanthropy is ineffectual. They do not know the ultimate goal of life (*śreya ācaraṇam*), which is to please the Supreme Lord. If all philanthropic and humanitarian activities were directed toward achieving the ultimate goal of life—to please the Supreme Personality of Godhead—they would all be perfect. Humanitarian work without Kṛṣṇa is nothing. Kṛṣṇa must be brought to the center of all our activities; otherwise no activity will have value.

TEXT 11

श्रीबादरायणिरुवाच
एवं कृतव्यवसितो दध्यङ्ङाथर्वणस्तनुम् ।
परे भगवति ब्रह्मण्यात्मानं सन्नयञ्जहौ ॥ ११ ॥

śrī-bādarāyaṇir uvāca
evaṁ kṛta-vyavasito
dadhyaṅṅ ātharvaṇas tanum
pare bhagavati brahmaṇy
ātmānaṁ sannayañ jahau

śrī-bādarāyaṇiḥ uvāca—Śrī Śukadeva Gosvāmī said; *evam*—thus; *kṛta-vyavasitaḥ*—making certain of what to do (in giving his body to the demigods); *dadhyaṅ*—Dadhīci Muni; *ātharvaṇaḥ*—the son of Atharvā; *tanum*—his body; *pare*—to the Supreme; *bhagavati*—Personality of Godhead; *brahmaṇi*—the Supreme Brahman; *ātmānam*—himself, the spirit soul; *sannayan*—offering; *jahau*—gave up.

TRANSLATION

Śrī Śukadeva Gosvāmī said: Dadhīci Muni, the son of Atharvā, thus resolved to give his body to the service of the demigods. He placed himself, the spirit soul, at the lotus feet of the Supreme Personality of Godhead and in this way gave up his gross material body made of five elements.

PURPORT

As indicated by the words *pare bhagavati brahmaṇy ātmānaṁ sannayan,* Dadhīci placed himself, as spirit soul, at the lotus feet of the Supreme Personality of Godhead. In this regard, one may refer to the incident of Dhṛtarāṣṭra's leaving his body, as described in the First Canto of *Śrīmad-Bhāgavatam* (1.13.55). Dhṛtarāṣṭra analytically divided his gross material body into the five different elements of which it was made—earth, water, fire, air and ether—and distributed them to the different reservoirs of these elements; in other words, he merged these five elements into the original *mahat-tattva.* By identifying his material conception of life, he gradually separated his spirit soul from material connections and placed himself at the lotus feet of the Supreme Personality of Godhead. The example given in this connection is that when an earthen pot is broken, the small portion of the sky within the pot is united with the large sky outside the pot. Māyāvādī philosophers misunderstand this description of *Śrīmad-Bhāgavatam.* Therefore Śrī Rāmānuja Svāmī, in his book *Vedānta-tattva-sāra,* has described that this merging of the soul means that after separating himself from the material body made of eight elements—earth, water, fire, air, ether, false ego, mind and intelligence—the individual soul engages himself in devotional service to the Supreme Personality of Godhead in His eternal form (*īśvaraḥ paramaḥ kṛṣṇaḥ sac-cid-ānanda-vigrahaḥ/ anādir ādir govindaḥ sarva-kāraṇa-kāraṇam*). The material cause of the material elements absorbs the material body, and the spiritual soul assumes its original position. As described by Śrī Caitanya Mahāprabhu, *jīvera'svarūpa' haya-kṛṣṇera'nitya-dāsa':* the constitutional position of the living entity is that he is the eternal servant of Kṛṣṇa. When one overcomes the material body through cultivation of spiritual knowledge and devotional service, one can revive his own position and thus engage in the service of the Lord.

TEXT 12

यताक्षासुमनोबुद्धिस्तत्त्वदृग् ध्वस्तबन्धनः ।
आस्थितः परमं योगं न देहं बुबुधे गतम् ॥ १२ ॥

yatākṣāsu-mano-buddhis
tattva-dṛg dhvasta-bandhanaḥ
āsthitaḥ paramaṁ yogaṁ
na dehaṁ bubudhe gatam

yata—controlled; *akṣa*—senses; *asu*—the life air; *manaḥ*—the mind; *buddhiḥ*—intelligence; *tattva-dṛk*—one who knows the *tattvas,* the material and spiritual energies; *dhvasta-bandhanaḥ*—liberated from bondage; *āsthitaḥ*—being situated in; *paramam*—the supreme; *yogam*—absorption, trance; *na*—not; *deham*—the material body; *bubudhe*—perceived; *gatam*—left.

TRANSLATION

Dadhīci Muni controlled his senses, life force, mind and intelligence and became absorbed in trance. Thus he cut all his material bonds. He could not perceive how his material body became separated from his self.

PURPORT

The Lord says in *Bhagavad-gītā* (8.5):

anta-kāle ca mām eva
smaran muktvā kalevaram
yaḥ prayāti sa mad-bhāvaṁ
yāti nāsty atra saṁśayaḥ

"Whoever, at the time of death, quits his body remembering Me alone, at once attains My nature. Of this there is no doubt." Of course, one must practice before one is overcome by death, but the perfect *yogī,* namely the devotee, dies in trance, thinking of Kṛṣṇa. He does not feel his material body being separated from his soul; the soul is immediately transferred to the spiritual world. *Tyaktvā dehaṁ punar janma naiti mām eti:* the soul does not enter the womb of a material mother again, but is transferred back home, back to Godhead. This *yoga, bhakti-yoga,* is the highest *yoga* system, as explained by the Lord Himself in *Bhagavad-gītā* (6.47):

yoginām api sarveṣāṁ
mad-gatenāntarātmanā
śraddhāvān bhajate yo māṁ
sa me yuktatamo mataḥ

"Of all *yogīs,* he who always abides in Me with great faith, worshiping Me in transcendental loving service, is most intimately united with Me in *yoga* and is the highest of all." The *bhakti-yogī* always thinks of Kṛṣṇa, and therefore at the time of death he can very easily transfer himself to Kṛṣṇaloka, without even perceiving the pains of death.

TEXTS 13–14

अथेन्द्रो वज्रमुद्यम्य निर्मितं विश्वकर्मणा ।
मुनेः शक्तिभिरुत्सिक्तो भगवत्तेजसान्वितः ॥ १३ ॥
वृतो देवगणैः सर्वैर्गजेन्द्रोपर्यशोभत ।
स्तूयमानो मुनिगणैस्त्रैलोक्यं हर्षयन्निव ॥ १४ ॥

athendro vajram udyamya
nirmitaṁ viśvakarmaṇā
muneḥ śaktibhir utsikto
bhagavat-tejasānvitaḥ

vṛto deva-gaṇaiḥ sarvair
gajendropary aśobhata
stūyamāno muni-gaṇais
trailokyaṁ harṣayann iva

atha—thereafter; *indraḥ*—the King of heaven; *vajram*—the thunderbolt; *udyamya*—firmly taking up; *nirmitam*—manufactured; *viśvakarmaṇā*—by Viśvakarmā; *muneḥ*—of the great sage, Dadhīci; *śaktibhiḥ*—by the power; *utsiktaḥ*—saturated; *bhagavat*—of the Supreme Personality of Godhead; *tejasā*—with spiritual power; *anvitaḥ*—endowed; *vṛtaḥ*—encircled; *deva-gaṇaiḥ*—by the other demigods; *sarvaiḥ*—all; *gajendra*—of his elephant carrier; *upari*—upon the back; *aśobhata*—shone; *stūyamānaḥ*—being offered prayers; *muni-gaṇaiḥ*—by the saintly persons; *trai-lokyam*—to the three worlds; *harṣayan*—causing pleasure; *iva*—as it were.

TRANSLATION

Thereafter, King Indra very firmly took up the thunderbolt manufactured by Viśvakarmā from the bones of Dadhīci. Charged with the exalted power of Dadhīci Muni and enlightened by the power of the Supreme Personality of Godhead, Indra rode on the back of his carrier, Airāvata, surrounded by all the demigods, while all the great sages offered him praise. Thus he shone very beautifully, pleasing the three worlds as he rode off to kill Vṛtrāsura.

TEXT 15

वृत्रमभ्यद्रवच्छत्रुमसुरानीकयूथपैः ।
पर्यस्तमोजसा राजन् क्रुद्धो रुद्र इवान्तकम् ॥ १५ ॥

vṛtram abhyadravac chatrum
asurānīka-yūthapaiḥ
paryastam ojasā rājan
kruddho rudra ivāntakam

vṛtram—Vṛtrāsura; *abhyadravat*—attacked; *śatrum*—the enemy; *asura-anīka-yūthapaiḥ*—by the commanders or captains of the soldiers of the *asuras; paryastam*—surrounded; *ojasā*—with great force; *rājan*—O King; *kruddhaḥ*—being angry; *rudraḥ*—an incarnation of Lord Śiva; *iva*—like; *antakam*—Antaka, or Yamarāja.

TRANSLATION

My dear King Parīkṣit, as Rudra, being very angry at Antaka [Yamarāja] had formerly run toward Antaka to kill him, Indra angrily and with great force attacked Vṛtrāsura, who was surrounded by the leaders of the demoniac armies.

TEXT 16

ततः सुराणामसुरै रणः परमदारुणः ।
त्रेतामुखे नर्मदायामभवत् प्रथमे युगे ॥ १६ ॥

tataḥ surāṇām asurai
raṇaḥ parama-dāruṇaḥ
tretā-mukhe narmadāyām
abhavat prathame yuge

tataḥ—thereafter; *surāṇām*—of the demigods; *asuraiḥ*—with the demons; *raṇaḥ*—a great battle; *parama-dāruṇaḥ*—very fearful; *tretā-mukhe*—in the beginning of Tretā-yuga; *narmadāyām*—on the bank of the River Narmadā; *abhavat*—took place; *prathame*—in the first; *yuge*—millennium.

TRANSLATION

Thereafter, at the end of Satya-yuga and the beginning of Tretā-yuga, a fierce battle took place between the demigods and the demons on the bank of the Narmadā.

PURPORT

Herein the Narmadā does not mean the Narmadā River in India. The five sacred rivers in India—Gaṅgā, Yamunā, Narmadā, Kāverī and Kṛṣṇā—are all celestial. Like the Ganges River, the Narmadā River also flows in the higher planetary systems. The battle between the demigods and the demons took place in the higher planets.

The words *prathame yuge* mean "in the beginning of the first millennium," that is to say, in the beginning of the Vaivasvata *manvantara.* In one day of Brahmā there are fourteen Manus, who each live for seventy-one millenniums. The four *yugas*—Satya, Tretā, Dvāpara and Kali—constitute one millennium. We are presently in the *manvantara* of Vaivasvata Manu, who is mentioned in *Bhagavad-gītā* (*imaṁ vivasvate yogaṁ proktavān aham avyayam/ vivasvān manave prāha*). We are now in the twenty-eighth millennium of Vaivasvata Manu, but this fight took place in the beginning of Vaivasvata Manu's first millennium. One can historically calculate how long ago the battle took place. Since each millennium consists of 4,300,000 years and we are now in the twenty-eighth millennium, some 120,400,000 years have passed since the battle took place on the bank of the River Narmadā.

TEXTS 17–18

रुद्रैर्वसुभिरादित्यैरश्विभ्यां पितृवह्निभिः ।
मरुद्भिर्ऋभुभिः साध्यैर्विश्वेदेवैर्मरुत्पतिम् ॥ १७ ॥
दृष्ट्वा वज्रधरं शक्रं रोचमानं स्वया श्रिया ।
नामृष्यन्नसुरा राजन् मृधे वृत्रपुरःसराः ॥ १८ ॥

rudrair vasubhir ādityair
aśvibhyāṁ pitṛ-vahnibhiḥ
marudbhir ṛbhubhiḥ sādhyair
viśvedevair marut-patim

dṛṣṭvā vajra-dharaṁ śakraṁ
rocamānaṁ svayā śriyā
nāmṛṣyann asurā rājan
mṛdhe vṛtra-puraḥsarāḥ

rudraiḥ—by the Rudras; *vasubhiḥ*—by the Vasus; *ādityaiḥ*—by the Ādityas; *aśvibhyām*—by the Aśvinī-kumāras; *pitṛ*—by the Pitās; *vahnibhiḥ*—

and the Vahnis; *marudbhiḥ*—by the Maruts; *ṛbhubhiḥ*—by the Ṛbhus; *sādhyaiḥ*—by the Sādhyas; *viśve-devaiḥ*—by the Viśvadevas; *marut-patim*—Indra, the heavenly King; *dṛṣṭvā*—seeing; *vajra-dharam*—bearing the thunderbolt; *śakram*—another name of Indra; *rocamānam*—shining; *svayā*—by his own; *śriyā*—opulence; *na*—not; *amṛṣyan*—tolerated; *asurāḥ*—all the demons; *rājan*—O King; *mṛdhe*—in the fight; *vṛtra-puraḥsarāḥ*—headed by Vṛtrāsura.

TRANSLATION

O King, when all the asuras came onto the battlefield, headed by Vṛtrāsura, they saw King Indra carrying the thunderbolt and surrounded by the Rudras, Vasus, Ādityas, Aśvinī-kumāras, Pitās, Vahnis, Maruts, Ṛbhus, Sādhyas and Viśvadevas. Surrounded by his company, Indra shone so brightly that his effulgence was intolerable to the demons.

TEXTS 19–22

नमुचिः शम्बरोऽनर्वा द्विमूर्धा ऋषभोऽसुरः ।
हयग्रीवः शङ्कुशिरा विप्रचित्तिरयोमुखः ॥ १९ ॥
पुलोमा वृषपर्वा च प्रहेतिर्हेतिरुत्कलः ।
दैतेया दानवा यक्षा रक्षांसि च सहस्रशः ॥ २० ॥
सुमालिमालिप्रमुखाः कार्तस्वरपरिच्छदाः ।
प्रतिषिध्येन्द्रसेनाग्रं मृत्योरपि दुरासदम् ॥ २१ ॥
अभ्यर्दयन्नसंभ्रान्ताः सिंहनादेन दुर्मदाः ।
गदाभिः परिघैर्बाणैः प्रासमुद्गरतोमरैः ॥ २२ ॥

namuciḥ śambaro'narvā
dvimūrdhā ṛṣabho'suraḥ
hayagrīvaḥ śaṅkuśirā
vipracittir ayomukhaḥ

pulomā vṛṣaparvā ca
prahetir hetir utkalaḥ
daiteyā dānavā yakṣā
rakṣāṁsi ca sahasraśaḥ

sumāli-māli-pramukhāḥ
kārtasvara-paricchadāḥ

pratiṣidhyendra-senāgraṁ
mṛtyor api durāsadam

abhyardayann asambhrāntāḥ
siṁha-nādena durmadāḥ
gadābhiḥ parighair bāṇaiḥ
prāsa-mudgara-tomaraiḥ

namuciḥ—Namuci; *śambaraḥ*—Śambara; *anarvā*—Anarvā; *dvimūrdhā*—Dvimūrdhā; *ṛṣabhaḥ*—Ṛṣabha; *asuraḥ*—Asura; *hayagrīvaḥ*—Hayagrīva; *śaṅkuśirāḥ*—Śaṅkuśirā; *vipracittiḥ*—Vipracitti; *ayomukhaḥ*—Ayomukha; *pulomā*—Pulomā; *vṛṣaparvā*—Vṛṣaparvā; *ca*—also; *prahetiḥ*—Praheti; *hetiḥ*—Heti; *utkalaḥ*—Utkala; *daiteyāḥ*—the Daityas; *dānavāḥ*—the Dānavas; *yakṣāḥ*—the Yakṣas; *rakṣāṁsi*—the Rākṣasas; *ca*—and; *sahasraśaḥ*—by the thousands; *sumāli-māli-pramukhāḥ*—others, headed by Sumāli and Māli; *kārtasvara*—of gold; *paricchadāḥ*—dressed in ornaments; *pratiṣidhya*—keeping back; *indra-senā-agram*—the front of Indra's army; *mṛtyoḥ*—for death; *api*—even; *durāsadam*—difficult to approach; *abhyardayan*—harassed; *asambhrāntāḥ*—without fear; *siṁha-nādena*—with a sound like a lion; *durmadāḥ*—furious; *gadābhiḥ*—with clubs; *parighaiḥ*—with iron-studded bludgeons; *bāṇaiḥ*—with arrows; *prāsa-mudgara-tomaraiḥ*—with barbed missiles, mallets and lances.

TRANSLATION

Many hundreds and thousands of demons, demi-demons, Yakṣas, Rākṣasas [man-eaters] and others, headed by Sumāli and Māli, resisted the armies of King Indra, which even death personified cannot easily overcome. Among the demons were Namuci, Śambara, Anarvā, Dvimūrdhā, Ṛṣabha, Asura, Hayagrīva, Śaṅkuśirā, Vipracitti, Ayomukha, Pulomā, Vṛṣaparvā, Praheti, Heti and Utkala. Roaring tumultuously and fearlessly like lions, these invincible demons, all dressed in golden ornaments, gave pain to the demigods with weapons like clubs, bludgeons, arrows, barbed darts, mallets and lances.

TEXT 23

शूलैः परश्वधैः खड्गैः शतघ्नीभिर्भुशुण्डिभिः ।
सर्वतोऽवाकिरन् शस्त्रैरस्त्रैश्च विबुधर्षभान् ॥ २३ ॥

śūlaiḥ paraśvadhaiḥ khaḍgaiḥ
śataghnībhir bhuśuṇḍibhiḥ
sarvato'vākiran śastrair
astraiś ca vibudharṣabhān

śūlaiḥ—by spears; *paraśvadhaiḥ*—by axes; *khaḍgaiḥ*—by swords; *śataghnībhiḥ*—by *śataghnīs; bhuśuṇḍibhiḥ*—by *bhuśuṇḍis; sarvataḥ*—all around; *avākiran*—scattered; *śastraiḥ*—with weapons; *astraiḥ*—with arrows; *ca*—and; *vibudha-ṛṣabhān*—the chiefs of the demigods.

TRANSLATION

Armed with lances, tridents, axes, swords and other weapons like śataghnīs and bhuśuṇḍis, the demons attacked from different directions and scattered all the chiefs of the demigod armies.

TEXT 24

न तेऽदृश्यन्त संछन्नाः शरजालैः समन्ततः ।
पुङ्खानुपुङ्खपतितैर्ज्योतींषीव नभोघनैः ॥ २४ ॥

na te 'dṛśyanta sañchannāḥ
śara-jālaiḥ samantataḥ
puṅkhānupuṅkha-patitair
jyotīṁṣīva nabho-ghanaiḥ

na—not; *te*—they (the demigods); *adṛśyanta*—were seen; *sañchannāḥ*—being completely covered; *śara-jālaiḥ*—by networks of arrows; *samantataḥ*—all around; *puṅkha-anupuṅkha*—one arrow after another; *patitaiḥ*—falling; *jyotīṁṣi iva*—like the stars in the sky; *nabhaḥ-ghanaiḥ*—by the dense clouds.

TRANSLATION

As the stars in the sky cannot be seen when covered by dense clouds, the demigods, being completely covered by networks of arrows falling upon them one after another, could not be seen.

TEXT 25

न ते शस्त्रास्त्रवर्षौघा ह्यासेदुः सुरसैनिकान् ।
छिन्नाः सिद्धपथे देवैर्लघुहस्तैः सहस्रधा ॥ २५ ॥

na te śastrāstra-varṣaughā
hy āseduḥ sura-sainikān
chinnāḥ siddha-pathe devair
laghu-hastaiḥ sahasradhā

na—not; *te*—those; *śastra-astra-varṣa-oghāḥ*—showers of arrows and other weapons; *hi*—indeed; *āseduḥ*—reached; *sura-sainikān*—the armies of the demigods; *chinnāḥ*—cut; *siddha-pathe*—in the sky; *devaiḥ*—by the demigods; *laghu-hastaiḥ*—quick-handed; *sahasradhā*—into thousands of pieces.

TRANSLATION

The showers of various weapons and arrows released to kill the soldiers of the demigods did not reach them because the demigods, acting quickly, cut the weapons into thousands of pieces in the sky.

TEXT 26

अथ क्षीणास्त्रशस्त्रौघा गिरिशृङ्गद्रुमोपलैः ।
अभ्यवर्षन् सुरबलं चिच्छिदुस्तांश्च पूर्ववत् ॥ २६ ॥

atha kṣīṇāstra-śastraughā
giri-śṛṅga-drumopalaiḥ
abhyavarṣan sura-balaṁ
cicchidus tāṁś ca pūrvavat

atha—thereupon; *kṣīṇa*—being reduced; *astra*—of the arrows released by *mantras; śastra*—and weapons; *oghāḥ*—the multitudes; *giri*—of mountains; *śṛṅga*—with the peaks; *druma*—with trees; *upalaiḥ*—and with stones; *abhyavarṣan*—showered; *sura-balam*—the soldiers of the demigods; *cicchiduḥ*—broke to pieces; *tān*—them; *ca*—and; *pūrva-vat*—as before.

TRANSLATION

As their weapons and mantras decreased, the demons began showering mountain peaks, trees and stones upon the demigod soldiers, but the demigods were so powerful and expert that they nullified all these weapons by breaking them to pieces in the sky as before.

TEXT 27

तानक्षतान् स्वस्तिमतो निशाम्य
शस्त्रास्त्रपूगैरथ वृत्रनाथाः ।

द्रुमैर्दृषद्भिर्विविधाद्रिशृङ्गै-
रविक्षतांस्तत्रसुरिन्द्रसैनिकान् ॥ २७ ॥

tān akṣatān svastimato niśāmya
śastrāstra-pūgair atha vṛtra-nāthāḥ
drumair dṛṣadbhir vividhādri-śṛṅgair
avikṣatāṁs tatrasur indra-sainikān

tān—them (the soldiers of the demigods); *akṣatān*—not injured; *svasti-matah*—being very healthy; *niśāmya*—seeing; *śastra-astra-pūgaiḥ*—by the bunches of weapons and *mantras; atha*—thereupon; *vṛtra-nāthāḥ*—the soldiers led by Vṛtrāsura; *drumaiḥ*—by the trees; *dṛṣadbhiḥ*—by the stones; *vividha*—various; *adri*—of mountains; *śṛṅgaiḥ*—by the peaks; *avikṣatān*—not injured; *tatrasuḥ*—became afraid; *indra-sainikān*—the soldiers of King Indra.

TRANSLATION

When the soldiers of the demons, commanded by Vṛtrāsura, saw that the soldiers of King Indra were quite well, having not been injured at all by their volleys of weapons, not even by the trees, stones and mountain peaks, the demons were very much afraid.

TEXT 28

सर्वे प्रयासा अभवन् विमोघाः
कृताः कृता देवगणेषु दैत्यैः ।
कृष्णानुकूलेषु यथा महत्सु
क्षुद्रैः प्रयुक्ता ऊषती रूक्षवाचः ॥ २८ ॥

sarve prayāsā abhavan vimoghāḥ
kṛtāḥ kṛtā deva-gaṇeṣu daityaiḥ
kṛṣṇānukūleṣu yathā mahatsu
kṣudraiḥ prayuktā ūṣatī rūkṣa-vācaḥ

sarve—all; *prayāsāḥ*—endeavors; *abhavan*—were; *vimoghāḥ*—futile; *kṛtāḥ*—performed; *kṛtāḥ*—again performed; *deva-gaṇeṣu*—unto the demigods; *daityaiḥ*—by the demons; *kṛṣṇa-anukūleṣu*—who were always protected by Kṛṣṇa; *yathā*—just as; *mahatsu*—unto the Vaiṣṇavas; *kṣudraiḥ*—by insignificant persons; *prayuktāḥ*—used; *ūṣatīḥ*—unfavorable; *rūkṣa*—rough; *vācaḥ*—words.

TRANSLATION

When insignificant persons use rough words to cast false, angry accusations against saintly persons, their fruitless words do not disturb the great personalities. Similarly, all the efforts of the demons against the demigods, who were favorably situated under the protection of Kṛṣṇa, were futile.

PURPORT

There is a Bengali saying that if a vulture curses a cow to die, the curse will not be effective. Similarly, accusations made by demoniac persons against devotees of Kṛṣṇa cannot have any effect. The demigods are devotees of Lord Kṛṣṇa, and therefore the curses of the demons were futile.

TEXT 29

ते स्वप्रयासं वितथं निरीक्ष्य
हरावभक्ता हतयुद्धदर्पाः ।
पलायनायाजिमुखे विसृज्य
पतिं मनस्ते दधुरात्तसाराः ॥ २९ ॥

te sva-prayāsaṁ vitathaṁ nirīkṣya
harāv abhaktā hata-yuddha-darpāḥ
palāyanāyāji-mukhe visṛjya
patiṁ manas te dadhur ātta-sārāḥ

te—they (the demons); *sva-prayāsam*—their own endeavors; *vitatham*—fruitless; *nirīkṣya*—seeing; *harau abhaktāḥ*—the *asuras,* those who are not devotees of the Supreme Personality of Godhead; *hata*—defeated; *yuddha-darpāḥ*—their pride in fighting; *palāyanāya*—for leaving the battlefield; *āji-mukhe*—in the very beginning of the battle; *visṛjya*—leaving aside; *patim*—their commander, Vṛtrāsura; *manaḥ*—their minds; *te*—all of them; *dadhuḥ*—gave; *ātta-sārāḥ*—whose prowess was taken away.

TRANSLATION

The asuras, who are never devotees of Lord Kṛṣṇa, the Supreme Personality of Godhead, lost their pride in fighting when they found all their endeavors futile. Leaving aside their leader even in the very beginning of the fight, they decided to flee because all their prowess had been taken away by the enemy.

TEXT 30

वृत्रोऽसुरांस्ताननुगान् मनस्वी
प्रधावतः प्रेक्ष्य बभाष एतत् ।
पलायितं प्रेक्ष्य बलं च भग्नं
भयेन तीव्रेण विहस्य वीरः ॥ ३० ॥

vṛtro 'surāṁs tān anugān manasvī
pradhāvataḥ prekṣya babhāṣa etat
palāyitaṁ prekṣya balaṁ ca bhagnaṁ
bhayena tīvreṇa vihasya vīraḥ

vṛtraḥ—Vṛtrāsura, the commander of the demons; *asurān*—all the demons; *tān*—them; *anugān*—his followers; *manasvī*—the great-minded; *pradhāvataḥ*—fleeing; *prekṣya*—observing; *babhāṣa*—spoke; *etat*—this; *palāyitam*—fleeing; *prekṣya*—seeing; *balam*—army; *ca*—and; *bhagnam*—broken; *bhayena*—out of fear; *tīvreṇa*—intense; *vihasya*—smiling; *vīraḥ*—the great hero.

TRANSLATION

Seeing his army broken and all the asuras, even those known as great heroes, fleeing the battlefield out of intense fear, Vṛtrāsura, who was truly a great-minded hero, smiled and spoke the following words.

TEXT 31

कालोपपन्नां रुचिरां मनस्विनां
जगाद वाचं पुरुषप्रवीरः ।
हे विप्रचित्ते नमुचे पुलोमन्
मयानर्वञ्छम्बर मे शृणुध्वम् ॥ ३१ ॥

kālopapannāṁ rucirāṁ manasvināṁ
jagāda vācaṁ puruṣa-pravīraḥ
he vipracitte namuce puloman
mayānarvañ chambara me śṛṇudhvam

kāla-upapannām—suitable to the time and circumstances; *rucirām*—very beautiful; *manasvinām*—to the great, deep-minded personalities; *jagāda*—spoke; *vācam*—words; *puruṣa-pravīraḥ*—the hero among heroes, Vṛtrāsura;

he—O; *vipracitte*—Vipracitti; *namuce*—O Namuci; *puloman*—O Pulomā; *maya*—O Maya; *anarvan*—O Anarvā; *śambara*—O Śambara; *me*—from me; *śṛṇudhvam*—please hear.

TRANSLATION

According to his position and the time and circumstances, Vṛtrāsura, the hero among heroes, spoke words that were much to be appreciated by thoughtful men. He called to the heroes of the demons, "O Vipracitti! O Namuci! O Pulomā! O Maya, Anarvā and Śambara! Please hear me and do not flee."

TEXT 32

जातस्य मृत्युर्ध्रुव एव सर्वतः
प्रतिक्रिया यस्य न चेह क्लृप्ता ।
लोको यशश्चाथ ततो यदि ह्यमुं
को नाम मृत्युं न वृणीत युक्तम् ॥ ३२ ॥

jātasya mṛtyur dhruva eva sarvataḥ
pratikriyā yasya na ceha kḷptā
loko yaśaś cātha tato yadi hy amuṁ
ko nāma mṛtyuṁ na vṛṇīta yuktam

jātasya—of one who has taken birth (all living beings); *mṛtyuḥ*—death; *dhruvaḥ*—inevitable; *eva*—indeed; *sarvataḥ*—everywhere in the universe; *pratikriyā*—counteraction; *yasya*—of which; *na*—not; *ca*—also; *iha*—in this material world; *kḷptā*—devised; *lokaḥ*—promotion to higher planets; *yaśaḥ*—reputation and glory; *ca*—and; *atha*—then; *tataḥ*—from that; *yadi*—if; *hi*—indeed; *amum*—that; *kaḥ*—who; *nāma*—indeed; *mṛtyum*—death; *na*—not; *vṛṇīta*—would accept; *yuktam*—suitable.

TRANSLATION

Vṛtrāsura said: All living entities who have taken birth in this material world must die. Surely, no one in this world has found any means to be saved from death. Even providence has not provided a means to escape it. Under the circumstances, death being inevitable, if one can gain promotion to the higher planetary systems and be always celebrated here by dying a suitable death, what man will not accept such a glorious death?

PURPORT

If by dying one can be elevated to the higher planetary systems and be ever-famous after his death, who is so foolish that he will refuse such a glorious death? Similar advice was also given by Kṛṣṇa to Arjuna. "My dear Arjuna," the Lord said, "do not desist from fighting. If you gain victory in the fight, you will enjoy a kingdom, and even if you die you will be elevated to the heavenly planets." Everyone should be ready to die while performing glorious deeds. A glorious person is not meant to meet death like cats and dogs.

TEXT 33

द्वौ संमताविह मृत्यू दुरापौ
यद् ब्रह्मसंधारणया जितासुः ।
कलेवरं योगरतो विजह्याद्
यदग्रणीर्वीरशयेऽनिवृत्तः ॥ ३३ ॥

dvau sammatāv iha mṛtyū durāpau
yad brahma-sandhāraṇayā jitāsuḥ
kalevaraṁ yoga-rato vijahyād
yad agraṇīr vīra-śaye 'nivṛttaḥ

dvau—two; *sammatau*—approved (by *śāstra* and great personalities); *iha*—in this world; *mṛtyū*—deaths; *durāpau*—extremely rare; *yat*—which; *brahma-sandhāraṇayā*—with concentration on Brahman, Paramātmā or Parabrahma, Kṛṣṇa; *jita-asuḥ*—controlling the mind and senses; *kalevaram*—the body; *yoga-rataḥ*—being engaged in the performance of *yoga; vijahyāt*—one may leave; *yat*—which; *agraṇīḥ*—taking the lead; *vīra-śaye*—on the battlefield; *anivṛttaḥ*—not turning back.

TRANSLATION

There are two ways to meet a glorious death, and both are very rare. One is to die after performing mystic yoga, especially bhakti-yoga, by which one can control the mind and living force and die absorbed in thought of the Supreme Personality of Godhead. The second is to die on the battlefield, leading the army and never showing one's back. These two kinds of death are recommended in the śāstra as glorious.

Thus end the Bhaktivedanta purports of the Sixth Canto, Tenth Chapter, of the Śrīmad-Bhāgavatam, *entitled "The Battle Between the Demigods and Vṛtrāsura."*

CHAPTER ELEVEN

The Transcendental Qualities of Vṛtrāsura

This chapter describes Vṛtrāsura's great qualities. When the prominent commanders of the demons fled, not hearing Vṛtrāsura's advice, Vṛtrāsura condemned them all as cowards. Speaking very bravely, he stood alone to face the demigods. When the demigods saw Vṛtrāsura's attitude, they were so afraid that they practically fainted, and Vṛtrāsura began trampling them down. Unable to tolerate this, Indra, the King of the demigods, threw his club at Vṛtrāsura, but Vṛtrāsura was such a great hero that he easily caught the club with his left hand and used it to beat Indra's elephant. Struck by the blow of Vṛtrāsura, the elephant was pushed back fourteen yards and fell, with Indra on its back.

King Indra had first accepted Viśvarūpa as his priest and thereafter killed him. Reminding Indra of his heinous activities, Vṛtrāsura said, "If one is a devotee of the Supreme Personality of Godhead, Lord Viṣṇu, and depends on Lord Viṣṇu in every respect, then victory, opulence and peace of mind are all inevitably available. Such a person has nothing for which to aspire in the three worlds. The Supreme Lord is so kind that He especially favors such a devotee by not giving him opulence that will hamper his devotional service. Therefore I wish to give up everything for the service of the Lord. I wish always to chant the glories of the Lord and engage in His service. Let me become unattached to my worldly family and make friendships with the devotees of the Lord. I do not desire to be promoted to the higher planetary systems, even to Dhruvaloka or Brahmaloka, nor do I desire an unconquerable position within this material world. I have no need for such things."

TEXT 1

श्रीशुक उवाच

त एवं शंसतो धर्मं वचः पत्युरचेतसः ।
नैवागृह्णन्त सम्भ्रान्ताः पलायनपरा नृप ॥ १ ॥

śrī-śuka uvāca
ta evaṁ śaṁsato dharmaṁ
vacaḥ patyur acetasaḥ

naivāgṛhṇanta sambhrāntāḥ
palāyana-parā nṛpa

śrī-śukaḥ uvāca—Śrī Śukadeva Gosvāmī said; *te*—they; *evam*—thus; *śaṁsataḥ*—praising; *dharmam*—the principles of religion; *vacaḥ*—the words; *patyuḥ*—of their master; *acetasaḥ*—their minds being very disturbed; *na*—not; *eva*—indeed; *agṛhṇanta*—accepted; *sambhrāntāḥ*—fearful; *palāyana-parāḥ*—intent upon fleeing; *nṛpa*—O King.

TRANSLATION

Śrī Śukadeva Gosvāmī said: O King, Vṛtrāsura, the commander in chief of the demons, advised his lieutenants in the principles of religion, but the cowardly demoniac commanders, intent upon fleeing the battlefield, were so disturbed by fear that they could not accept his words.

TEXTS 2–3

विशीर्यमाणां पृतनामासुरीमसुरर्षभः ।
कालानुकूलैस्त्रिदशैः काल्यमानामनाथवत् ॥ २ ॥
दृष्ट्वातप्यत संक्रुद्ध इन्द्रशत्रुरमर्षितः ।
तान् निवार्यौजसा राजन् निर्भर्त्स्येदमुवाच ह ॥ ३ ॥

viśīryamāṇāṁ pṛtanām
āsurīm asurarṣabhaḥ
kālānukūlais tridaśaiḥ
kālyamānām anāthavat

dṛṣṭvātapyata saṅkruddha
indra-śatrur amarṣitaḥ
tān nivāryaujasā rājan
nirbhartsyedam uvāca ha

viśīryamāṇām—being shattered; *pṛtanām*—the army; *āsurīm*—of the demons; *asura-ṛṣabhaḥ*—the best of the *asuras,* Vṛtrāsura; *kāla-anukūlaiḥ*—following the circumstances presented by time; *tridaśaiḥ*—by the demigods; *kālyamānām*—being chased; *anātha-vat*—as if no one were there to protect them; *dṛṣṭvā*—seeing; *atapyata*—felt pain; *saṅkruddhaḥ*—being very angry; *indra-śatruḥ*—Vṛtrāsura, the enemy of Indra; *amarṣitaḥ*—unable to tolerate; *tān*—them (the demigods); *nivārya*—blocking; *ojasā*—with great force;

rājan—O King Parīkṣit; *nirbhartsya*—rebuking; *idam*—this; *uvāca*—said; *ha*—indeed.

TRANSLATION

O King Parīkṣit, the demigods, taking advantage of a favorable opportunity presented by time, attacked the army of the demons from the rear and began driving away the demoniac soldiers, scattering them here and there as if their army had no leader. Seeing the pitiable condition of his soldiers, Vṛtrāsura, the best of the asuras, who was called Indraśatru, the enemy of Indra, was very much aggrieved. Unable to tolerate such reverses, he stopped and forcefully rebuked the demigods, speaking the following words in an angry mood.

TEXT 4

किं व उच्चरितैर्मातुर्धावद्भिः पृष्ठतो हतैः ।
न हि भीतवधः श्लाघ्यो न स्वर्ग्यः शूरमानिनाम् ॥ ४ ॥

kiṁ va uccaritair mātur
dhāvadbhiḥ pṛṣṭhato hataiḥ
na hi bhīta-vadhaḥ ślāghyo
na svargyaḥ śūra-māninām

kim—what is the benefit; *vaḥ*—for you; *uccaritaiḥ*—with those like the stool; *mātuḥ*—of the mother; *dhāvadbhiḥ*—running away; *pṛṣṭhataḥ*—from the back; *hataiḥ*—killed; *na*—not; *hi*—certainly; *bhīta-vadhaḥ*—the killing of a person who is afraid; *ślāghyaḥ*—glorious; *na*—nor; *svargyaḥ*—leading to the heavenly planets; *śūra-māninām*—of persons who consider themselves heroes.

TRANSLATION

O demigods, these demoniac soldiers have taken birth uselessly. Indeed, they have come from the bodies of their mothers exactly like stool. What is the benefit of killing such enemies from behind while they are running in fear? One who considers himself a hero should not kill an enemy who is afraid of losing his life. Such killing is never glorious, nor can it promote one to the heavenly planets.

PURPORT

Vṛtrāsura rebuked both the demigods and the demoniac soldiers because the demons were running in fear of their lives and the demigods were killing them from behind. The actions of both were abominable. When a fight takes place, the opposing parties must be prepared to fight like heroes. A hero never runs from the field of battle. He always fights face to face, determined to gain victory or lay down his life in the fight. That is heroic. Killing an enemy from behind is also inglorious. When an enemy turns his back and runs in fear of his life, he should not be killed. This is the etiquette of military science.

Vṛtrāsura insulted the demoniac soldiers by comparing them to the stool of their mothers. Both stool and a cowardly son come from the abdomen of the mother, and Vṛtrāsura said that there is no difference between them. A similar comparison was given by Tulasī dāsa, who commented that a son and urine both come from the same channel. In other words, semen and urine both come from the genitals, but semen produces a child whereas urine produces nothing. Therefore if a child is neither a hero nor a devotee, he is not a son but urine. Similarly, Cāṇakya Paṇḍita also says:

ko'rthaḥ putreṇa jātena
yo na vidvān na dhārmikaḥ
kāṇena cakṣuṣā kiṁ vā
cakṣuḥ pīḍaiva kevalam

"What is the use of a son who is neither glorious nor devoted to the Lord? Such a son is like a blind eye, which simply gives pain but cannot help one see."

TEXT 5

यदि वः प्रधने श्रद्धा सारं वा क्षुल्लका हृदि ।
अग्रे तिष्ठत मात्रं मे न चेद् ग्राम्यसुखे स्पृहा ॥ ५ ॥

yadi vaḥ pradhane śraddhā
sāraṁ vā kṣullakā hṛdi
agre tiṣṭhata mātraṁ me
na ced grāmya-sukhe spṛhā

yadi—if; *vaḥ*—of you; *pradhane*—in battle; *śraddhā*—faith; *sāram*—patience; *vā*—or; *kṣullakāḥ*—O insignificant ones; *hṛdi*—in the core of the heart; *agre*—in front; *tiṣṭhata*—just stand; *mātram*—for a moment; *me*—of me; *na*—not; *cet*—if; *grāmya-sukhe*—in sense gratification; *spṛhā*—desire.

TRANSLATION

O insignificant demigods, if you truly have faith in your heroism, if you have patience in the cores of your hearts and if you are not ambitious for sense gratification, please stand before me for a moment.

PURPORT

Rebuking the demigods, Vṛtrāsura challenged, "O demigods, if you are actually heroes, stand before me now and try to show your prowess. If you do not wish to fight, if you are afraid of losing your lives, I shall not kill you, for unlike you, I am not so evil minded as to kill persons who are neither heroic nor willing to fight. If you have faith in your heroism, please stand before me."

TEXT 6

एवं सुरगणान् क्रुद्धो भीषयन् वपुषा रिपून् ।
व्यनदत् सुमहाप्राणो येन लोका विचेतसः ॥ ६ ॥

evaṁ sura-gaṇān kruddho
bhīṣayan vapuṣā ripūn
vyanadat sumahā-prāṇo
yena lokā vicetasaḥ

evam—thus; *sura-gaṇān*—the demigods; *kruddhaḥ*—being very angry; *bhīṣayan*—terrifying; *vapuṣā*—by his body; *ripūn*—his enemies; *vyanadat*—roared; *su-mahā-prāṇaḥ*—the most powerful Vṛtrāsura; *yena*—by which; *lokāḥ*—all people; *vicetasaḥ*—unconscious.

TRANSLATION

Śukadeva Gosvāmī said: Vṛtrāsura, the angry and most powerful hero, terrified the demigods with his stout and strongly built body. When he roared with a resounding voice, nearly all living entities fainted.

TEXT 7

तेन देवगणाः सर्वे वृत्रविस्फोटनेन वै ।
निपेतुर्मूर्च्छिता भूमौ यथैवाशनिना हताः ॥ ७ ॥

tena deva-gaṇāḥ sarve
vṛtra-visphoṭanena vai
nipetur mūrcchitā bhūmau
yathaivāśaninā hatāḥ

tena—by that; *deva-gaṇāḥ*—the demigods; *sarve*—all; *vṛtra-visphoṭanena*—the tumultuous sound of Vṛtrāsura; *vai*—indeed; *nipetuḥ*—fell; *mūrcchitāḥ*—fainted; *bhūmau*—on the ground; *yathā*—just as if; *eva*—indeed; *aśaninā*—by a thunderbolt; *hatāḥ*—struck.

TRANSLATION

When all the demigods heard Vṛtrāsura's tumultuous roar, which resembled that of a lion, they fainted and fell to the ground as if struck by thunderbolts.

TEXT 8

ममर्द पद्भ्यां सुरसैन्यमातुरं
निमीलिताक्षं रणरङ्गदुर्मदः ।
गां कम्पयन्नुद्यतशूल ओजसा
नालं वनं यूथपतिर्यथोन्मदः ॥ ८ ॥

mamarda padbhyāṁ sura-sainyam āturaṁ
nimīlitākṣaṁ raṇa-raṅga-durmadaḥ
gāṁ kampayann udyata-śūla ojasā
nālaṁ vanaṁ yūtha-patir yathonmadaḥ

mamarda—trampled; *padbhyām*—by his feet; *sura-sainyam*—the army of the demigods; *āturam*—who were very afraid; *nimīlita-akṣam*—closing their eyes; *raṇa-raṅga-durmadaḥ*—arrogant on the battlefield; *gām*—the surface of the globe; *kampayan*—causing to tremble; *udyata-śūlaḥ*—taking up his trident; *ojasā*—with his strength; *nālam*—of hollow bamboo sticks; *vanam*—a forest; *yūtha-patiḥ*—an elephant; *yathā*—just as; *unmadaḥ*—maddened.

TRANSLATION

As the demigods closed their eyes in fear, Vṛtrāsura, taking up his trident and making the earth tremble with his great strength, trampled the demigods beneath his feet on the battlefield the way a mad elephant tramples hollow bamboos in the forest.

TEXT 9

विलोक्य तं वज्रधरोऽत्यमर्षितः
स्वशत्रवेऽभिद्रवते महागदाम् ।

चिक्षेप तामापततीं सुदुःसहां
जग्राह वामेन करेण लीलया ॥ ९ ॥

vilokya taṁ vajra-dharo 'tyamarṣitaḥ
sva-śatrave 'bhidravate mahā-gadām
cikṣepa tām āpatatīṁ suduḥsahāṁ
jagrāha vāmena kareṇa līlayā

vilokya—seeing; *tam*—him (Vṛtrāsura); *vajra-dharaḥ*—the carrier of the thunderbolt (King Indra); *ati*—very much; *amarṣitaḥ*—intolerant; *sva*—his own; *śatrave*—toward the enemy; *abhidravate*—running; *mahā-gadām*—a very powerful club; *cikṣepa*—threw; *tām*—that (club); *āpatatīm*—flying toward him; *su-duḥsahām*—very difficult to counteract; *jagrāha*—caught; *vāmena*—with his left; *kareṇa*—hand; *līlayā*—very easily.

TRANSLATION

Seeing Vṛtrāsura's disposition, Indra, the King of heaven, became intolerant and threw at him one of his great clubs, which are extremely difficult to counteract. However, as the club flew toward him, Vṛtrāsura easily caught it with his left hand.

TEXT 10

स इन्द्रशत्रुः कुपितो भृशं तया
महेन्द्रवाहं गदयोरुविक्रमः ।
जघान कुम्भस्थल उन्नदन् मृधे
तत्कर्म सर्वे समपूजयन्नृप ॥ १० ॥

sa indra-śatruḥ kupito bhṛśaṁ tayā
mahendra-vāhaṁ gadayoru-vikramaḥ
jaghāna kumbha-sthala unnadan mṛdhe
tat karma sarve samapūjayan nṛpa

saḥ—that; *indra-śatruḥ*—Vṛtrāsura; *kupitaḥ*—being angry; *bhṛśam*—very much; *tayā*—with that; *mahendra-vāham*—the elephant who is the carrier of Indra; *gadayā*—by the club; *uru-vikramaḥ*—who is famous for his great strength; *jaghāna*—struck; *kumbha-sthale*—on the head; *unnadan*—roaring loudly; *mṛdhe*—in that fight; *tat karma*—that action (striking the head of Indra's elephant with the club in his left hand); *sarve*—all the soldiers (on both sides); *samapūjayan*—glorified; *nṛpa*—O King Parīkṣit.

TRANSLATION

O King Parīkṣit, the powerful Vṛtrāsura, the enemy of King Indra, angrily struck the head of Indra's elephant with that club, making a tumultuous sound on the battlefield. For this heroic deed, the soldiers on both sides glorified him.

TEXT 11

ऐरावतो वृत्रगदाभिमृष्टो
विघूर्णितोऽद्रिः कुलिशाहतो यथा।
अपासरद् भिन्नमुखः सहेन्द्रो
मुञ्चन्नसृक् सप्तधनुर्भृशार्तः ॥ ११ ॥

airāvato vṛtra-gadābhimṛṣṭo
vighūrṇito'driḥ kuliśāhato yathā
apāsarad bhinna-mukhaḥ sahendro
muñcann asṛk sapta-dhanur bhṛśārtaḥ

airāvataḥ—Airāvata, the elephant of King Indra; *vṛtra-gadā-abhimṛṣṭaḥ*—struck by the club in Vṛtrāsura's hand; *vighūrṇitaḥ*—shaken; *adriḥ*—a mountain; *kuliśa*—by a thunderbolt; *āhataḥ*—struck; *yathā*—just like; *apāsarat*—was pushed back; *bhinna-mukhaḥ*—having a broken mouth; *saha-indraḥ*—with King Indra; *muñcan*—spitting; *asṛk*—blood; *sapta-dhanuḥ*—a distance measured by seven bows (approximately fourteen yards); *bhṛśa*—very severely; *ārtaḥ*—aggrieved.

TRANSLATION

Struck with the club by Vṛtrāsura like a mountain struck by a thunderbolt, the elephant Airāvata, feeling great pain and spitting blood from its broken mouth, was pushed back fourteen yards. In great distress, the elephant fell, with Indra on its back.

TEXT 12

न सन्नवाहाय विषण्णचेतसे
प्रायुङ्क्त भूयः स गदां महात्मा।

इन्द्रोऽमृतस्यन्दिकराभिमर्श-
वीतव्यथक्षतवाहोऽवतस्थे ॥ १२ ॥

na sanna-vāhāya viṣaṇṇa-cetase
prāyuṅkta bhūyaḥ sa gadāṁ mahātmā
indro 'mṛta-syandi-karābhimarśa-
vīta-vyatha-kṣata-vāho 'vatasthe

na—not; *sanna*—fatigued; *vāhāya*—upon him whose carrier; *viṣaṇṇa-cetase*—morose in the core of his heart; *prāyuṅkta*—used; *bhūyaḥ*—again; *saḥ*—he (Vṛtrāsura); *gadām*—the club; *mahā-ātmā*—the great soul (who refrained from striking Indra with the club when he saw Indra morose and aggrieved); *indraḥ*—Indra; *amṛta-syandi-kara*—of his hand, which produces nectar; *abhimarśa*—by the touch; *vīta*—was relieved; *vyatha*—from pains; *kṣata*—and cuts; *vāhaḥ*—whose carrier elephant; *avatasthe*—stood there.

TRANSLATION

When he saw Indra's carrier elephant thus fatigued and injured and when he saw Indra morose because his carrier had been harmed in that way, the great soul Vṛtrāsura, following religious principles, refrained from again striking Indra with the club. Taking this opportunity, Indra touched the elephant with his nectar-producing hand, thus relieving the animal's pain and curing its injuries. Then the elephant and Indra both stood silently.

TEXT 13

स तं नृपेन्द्राहवकाम्यया रिपुं
वज्रायुधं भ्रातृहणं विलोक्य।
स्मरंश्च तत्कर्म नृशंसमंहः
शोकेन मोहेन हसञ्जगाद ॥ १३ ॥

sa taṁ nṛpendrāhava-kāmyayā ripuṁ
vajrāyudhaṁ bhrātṛ-haṇaṁ vilokya
smaraṁś ca tat-karma nṛ-śaṁsam aṁhaḥ
śokena mohena hasañ jagāda

saḥ—he (Vṛtrāsura); *tam*—him (the King of heaven, Indra); *nṛpa-indra*—O King Parīkṣit; *āhava-kāmyayā*—with a desire to fight; *ripum*—his enemy; *vajra-āyudham*—whose weapon was the thunderbolt (made from the bones of Dadhīci); *bhrātṛ-haṇam*—who was the killer of his brother; *vilokya*—seeing; *smaran*—remembering; *ca*—and; *tat-karma*—his activities; *nṛ-śaṁsam*—cruel; *aṁhaḥ*—a great sin; *śokena*—with lamentation; *mohena*—by bewilderment; *hasan*—laughing; *jagāda*—said.

TRANSLATION

O King, when the great hero Vṛtrāsura saw Indra, his enemy, the killer of his brother, standing before him with a thunderbolt in his hand, desiring to fight, Vṛtrāsura remembered how Indra had cruelly killed his brother. Thinking of Indra's sinful activities, he became mad with lamentation and forgetfulness. Laughing sarcastically, he spoke as follows.

TEXT 14

श्रीवृत्र उवाच
दिष्ट्या भवान् मे समवस्थितो रिपु-
यो ब्रह्महा गुरुहा भ्रातृहा च ।
दिष्ट्यानृणोऽद्याहमसत्तम त्वया
मच्छूलनिर्भिन्नदृषद्धृदाचिरात् ॥ १४ ॥

śrī-vṛtra uvāca
diṣṭyā bhavān me samavasthito ripur
yo brahma-hā guru-hā bhrātṛ-hā ca
diṣṭyānṛṇo 'dyāham asattama tvayā
mac-chūla-nirbhinna-dṛṣad-dhṛdācirāt

śrī-vṛtraḥ uvāca—the great hero Vṛtrāsura said; *diṣṭyā*—by good fortune; *bhavān*—Your Lordship; *me*—of me; *samavasthitaḥ*—situated (in front); *ripuḥ*—my enemy; *yaḥ*—who; *brahma-hā*—the killer of a *brāhmaṇa; guru-hā*—the killer of your *guru; bhrātṛ-hā*—the killer of my brother; *ca*—also; *diṣṭyā*—by good fortune; *anṛṇaḥ*—free from debt (to my brother); *adya*—today; *aham*—I; *asat-tama*—O most abominable one; *tvayā*—through you; *mat-śūla*—by my trident; *nirbhinna*—being pierced; *dṛṣat*—like stone; *hṛdā*—whose heart; *acirāt*—very soon.

TRANSLATION

Śrī Vṛtrāsura said: He who has killed a brāhmaṇa, he who has killed his spiritual master—indeed, he who has killed my brother—is now, by good

fortune, standing before me face to face as my enemy. O most abominable one, when I pierce your stonelike heart with my trident, I shall be freed from my debt to my brother.

TEXT 15

यो नोऽग्रजस्यात्मविदो द्विजाते-
गुरोरपापस्य च दीक्षितस्य ।
विश्रभ्य खड्गेन शिरांस्यवृश्चत्
पशोरिवाकरुणः स्वर्गकामः ॥ १५ ॥

yo no 'grajasyātma-vido dvijāter
guror apāpasya ca dīkṣitasya
viśrabhya khaḍgena śirāṁsy avṛścat
paśor ivākaruṇaḥ svarga-kāmaḥ

yaḥ—he who; *naḥ*—our; *agra-jasya*—of the elder brother; *ātma-vidaḥ*—who was fully self-realized; *dvi-jāteḥ*—a qualified *brāhmaṇa; guroḥ*—your spiritual master; *apāpasya*—free from all sinful activities; *ca*—also; *dīkṣitasya*—appointed as the initiator of your *yajña; viśrabhya*—trustfully; *khaḍgena*—by your sword; *śirāṁsi*—the heads; *avṛścat*—cut off; *paśoḥ*—of an animal; *iva*—like; *akaruṇaḥ*—merciless; *svarga-kāmaḥ*—desiring the heavenly planets.

TRANSLATION

Only for the sake of living in the heavenly planets, you killed my elder brother—a self-realized, sinless, qualified brāhmaṇa who had been appointed your chief priest. He was your spiritual master, but although you entrusted him with the performance of your sacrifice, you later mercilessly severed his heads from his body the way one butchers an animal.

TEXT 16

श्रीह्रीदयाकीर्तिभिरुज्झितं त्वां
स्वकर्मणा पुरुषादैश्च गर्ह्यम् ।
कृच्छ्रेण मच्छूलविभिन्नदेह-
मस्पृष्टवह्निं समदन्ति गृध्राः ॥ १६ ॥

śrī-hrī-dayā-kīrtibhir ujjhitaṁ tvāṁ
sva-karmaṇā puruṣādaiś ca garhyam
kṛcchreṇa mac-chūla-vibhinna-deham
aspṛṣṭa-vahniṁ samadanti gṛdhrāḥ

śrī—opulence or beauty; *hrī*—shame; *dayā*—mercy; *kīrtibhiḥ*—and glory; *ujjhitam*—bereft of; *tvām*—you; *sva-karmaṇā*—by your own activities; *puruṣa-adaiḥ*—by the Rākṣasas (man-eaters); *ca*—and; *garhyam*—condemnable; *kṛcchreṇa*—with great difficulty; *mat-śūla*—by my trident; *vibhinna*—pierced; *deham*—your body; *aspṛṣṭa-vahnim*—not even touched by fire; *samadanti*—will eat; *gṛdhrāḥ*—the vultures.

TRANSLATION

Indra, you are bereft of all shame, mercy, glory and good fortune. Deprived of these good qualities by the reactions of your fruitive activities, you are to be condemned even by the man-eaters [Rākṣasas]. Now I shall pierce your body with my trident, and after you die with great pain, even fire will not touch you; only the vultures will eat your body.

TEXT 17

अन्येऽनु ये त्वेह नृशंसमज्ञा
यदुद्यतास्त्राः प्रहरन्ति मह्यम् ।
तैर्भूतनाथान् सगणान् निशात-
त्रिशूलनिर्भिन्नगलैर्यजामि ॥ १७ ॥

anye 'nu ye tveha nṛ-śaṁsam ajñā
yad udyatāstrāḥ praharanti mahyam
tair bhūta-nāthān sagaṇān niśāta-
triśūla-nirbhinna-galair yajāmi

anye—others; *anu*—follow; *ye*—who; *tvā*—you; *iha*—in this connection; *nṛ-śaṁsam*—very cruel; *ajñāḥ*—persons unaware of my prowess; *yat*—if; *udyata-astrāḥ*—with their swords raised; *praharanti*—attack; *mahyam*—me; *taiḥ*—with those; *bhūta-nāthān*—to such leaders of the ghosts as Bhairava; *sa-gaṇān*—with their hordes; *niśāta*—sharpened; *tri-śūla*—by the trident; *nirbhinna*—separated or pierced; *galaiḥ*—having their necks; *yajāmi*—I shall offer sacrifices.

TRANSLATION

You are naturally cruel. If the other demigods, unaware of my prowess, follow you by attacking me with raised weapons, I shall sever their heads with this sharp trident. With those heads I shall perform a sacrifice to Bhairava and the other leaders of the ghosts, along with their hordes.

TEXT 18

अथो हरे मे कुलिशेन वीर
हर्ता प्रमथ्यैव शिरो यदीह ।
तत्रानृणो भूतबलिं विधाय
मनस्विनां पादरजः प्रपत्स्ये ॥ १८ ॥

atho hare me kuliśena vīra
hartā pramathyaiva śiro yadīha
tatrānṛṇo bhūta-baliṁ vidhāya
manasvināṁ pāda-rajaḥ prapatsye

atho—otherwise; *hare*—O King Indra; *me*—of me; *kuliśena*—by your thunderbolt; *vīra*—O great hero; *hartā*—you cut off; *pramathya*—destroying my army; *eva*—certainly; *śiraḥ*—head; *yadi*—if; *iha*—in this battle; *tatra*—in that case; *anṛṇaḥ*—relieved of all debts in this material world; *bhūta-balim*—a presentation for all living entities; *vidhāya*—arranging; *manasvinām*—of great sages like Nārada Muni; *pāda-rajaḥ*—the dust of the lotus feet; *prapatsye*—I shall achieve.

TRANSLATION

But if in this battle you cut off my head with your thunderbolt and kill my soldiers, O Indra, O great hero, I shall take great pleasure in offering my body to other living entities [such as jackals and vultures]. I shall thus be relieved of my obligations to the reactions of my karma, and my fortune will be to receive the dust from the lotus feet of great devotees like Nārada Muni.

PURPORT

Śrī Narottama dāsa Ṭhākura sings:

ei chaya gosāñi yāra, mui tāra dāsa
tāṅ' sabāra pada-reṇu mora pañca-grāsa

"I am the servant of the six Gosvāmīs, and the dust of their lotus feet provides my five kinds of food." A Vaiṣṇava always desires the dust of the lotus feet of previous *ācāryas* and Vaiṣṇavas. Vṛtrāsura was certain that he would be killed in the battle with Indra, because this was the desire of Lord Viṣṇu. He was prepared for death because he knew that after his death he was destined to return home, back to Godhead. This is a great destination, and it is achieved by the grace of a Vaiṣṇava. *Chāḍiyā vaiṣṇava-sevā nistāra pāyeche kebā:* no one has ever gone back to Godhead without being favored by a Vaiṣṇava. In this verse, therefore, we find the words *manasvināṁ pāda-rajaḥ prapatsye:* "I shall receive the dust of the lotus feet of great devotees." The word *manasvinām* refers to great devotees who always think of Kṛṣṇa. They are always peaceful, thinking of Kṛṣṇa, and therefore they are called *dhīra.* The best example of such a devotee is Nārada Muni. If one receives the dust of the lotus feet of a *manasvī,* a great devotee, he certainly returns home, back to Godhead.

TEXT 19

सुरेश कस्मान्न हिनोषि वज्रं
पुरः स्थिते वैरिणि मय्यमोघम् ।
मा संशयिष्ठा न गदेव वज्रः
स्यान्निष्फलः कृपणार्थेव याच्ञा ॥ १९ ॥

sureśa kasmān na hinoṣi vajraṁ
puraḥ sthite vairiṇi mayy amogham
mā saṁśayiṣṭhā na gadeva vajraḥ
syān niṣphalaḥ kṛpaṇārtheva yācñā

sura-īśa—O King of the demigods; *kasmāt*—why; *na*—not; *hinoṣi*—you hurl; *vajram*—the thunderbolt; *puraḥ sthite*—standing in front; *vairiṇi*—your enemy; *mayi*—at me; *amogham*—which is infallible (your thunderbolt); *mā* —do not; *saṁśayiṣṭhāḥ*—doubt; *na*—not; *gadā iva*—like the club; *vajraḥ*—the thunderbolt; *syāt*—may be; *niṣphalaḥ*—with no result; *kṛpaṇa*—from a miserly person; *arthā*—for money; *iva*—like; *yācñā*—a request.

TRANSLATION

O King of the demigods, since I, your enemy, am standing before you, why don't you hurl your thunderbolt at me? Although your attack upon me with your club was certainly useless, like a request of money from a

miser, the thunderbolt you carry will not be useless. You need have no doubts about this.

PURPORT

When King Indra threw his club at Vṛtrāsura, Vṛtrāsura caught it in his left hand and retaliated by using it to strike the head of Indra's elephant. Thus Indra's attack was a disastrous failure. Indeed, Indra's elephant was injured and thrown back fourteen yards. Therefore even though Indra stood with the thunderbolt to hurl against Vṛtrāsura, he was doubtful, thinking that the thunderbolt might also fail. Vṛtrāsura, however, being a Vaiṣṇava, assured Indra that the thunderbolt would not fail, for Vṛtrāsura knew that it had been prepared in accordance with the instructions of Lord Viṣṇu. Although Indra had doubts because he could not understand that Lord Viṣṇu's order never fails, Vṛtrāsura understood Lord Viṣṇu's purpose. Vṛtrāsura was eager to be killed by the thunderbolt manufactured according to Lord Viṣṇu's instructions because he was sure that he would thus return home, back to Godhead. He was simply waiting for the opportunity of the thunderbolt's being released. In effect, therefore, Vṛtrāsura told Indra, "If you want to kill me, since I am your enemy, take this opportunity. Kill me. You will gain victory, and I shall go back to Godhead. Your deed will be equally beneficial for both of us. Do it immediately."

TEXT 20

नन्वेष वज्रस्तव शक्र तेजसा
हरेर्दधीचेस्तपसा च तेजितः ।
तेनैव शत्रुं जहि विष्णुयन्त्रितो
यतो हरिर्विजयः श्रीर्गुणास्ततः ॥ २० ॥

nanv eṣa vajras tava śakra tejasā
harer dadhīces tapasā ca tejitaḥ
tenaiva śatruṁ jahi viṣṇu-yantrito
yato harir vijayaḥ śrīr guṇās tataḥ

nanu—certainly; *eṣaḥ*—this; *vajraḥ*—thunderbolt; *tava*—of yours; *śakra*—O Indra; *tejasā*—by the prowess; *hareḥ*—of Lord Viṣṇu, the Supreme Personality of Godhead; *dadhīceḥ*—of Dadhīci; *tapasā*—by the austerities; *ca*—as well as; *tejitaḥ*—empowered; *tena*—with that; *eva*—certainly; *śatrum*

—your enemy; *jahi*—kill; *viṣṇu-yantritaḥ*—ordered by Lord Viṣṇu; *yataḥ*—wherever; *hariḥ*—Lord Viṣṇu; *vijayaḥ*—victory; *śrīḥ*—opulences; *guṇāḥ*—and other good qualities; *tataḥ*—there.

TRANSLATION

O Indra, King of heaven, the thunderbolt you carry to kill me has been empowered by the prowess of Lord Viṣṇu and the strength of Dadhīci's austerities. Since you have come here to kill me in accordance with Lord Viṣṇu's order, there is no doubt that I shall be killed by the release of your thunderbolt. Lord Viṣṇu has sided with you. Therefore your victory, opulence and all good qualities are assured.

PURPORT

Vṛtrāsura not only assured King Indra that the thunderbolt was invincible, but also encouraged Indra to use it against him as soon as possible. Vṛtrāsura was eager to die with the stroke of the thunderbolt sent by Lord Viṣṇu so that he could immediately return home, back to Godhead. By hurling the thunderbolt, Indra would gain victory and enjoy the heavenly planets, remaining in the material world for repeated birth and death. Indra wanted to gain victory over Vṛtrāsura and thereby become happy, but that would not at all be happiness. The heavenly planets are just below Brahmaloka, but as stated by the Supreme Lord, Kṛṣṇa, *ābrahma-bhuvanāl lokāḥ punar āvartino 'rjuna :* even if one achieves Brahmaloka, he must still fall to the lower planetary systems again and again. However, if one goes back to Godhead, he never returns to this material world. By killing Vṛtrāsura, Indra would not actually gain; he would remain in the material world. Vṛtrāsura, however, would go to the spiritual world. Therefore victory was destined for Vṛtrāsura, not for Indra.

TEXT 21

अहं समाधाय मनो यथाह नः
सङ्कर्षणस्तच्चरणारविन्दे ।
त्वद्वज्ररंहोलुलितग्राम्यपाशो
गतिं मुनेर्याम्यपविद्धलोकः ॥ २१ ॥

ahaṁ samādhāya mano yathāha naḥ
saṅkarṣaṇas tac-caraṇāravinde

tvad-vajra-raṁho-lulita-grāmya-pāśo
gatiṁ muner yāmy apaviddha-lokaḥ

aham—I; *samādhāya*—fixing firmly; *manaḥ*—the mind; *yathā*—just as; *āha*—said; *naḥ*—our; *saṅkarṣaṇaḥ*—Lord Saṅkarṣaṇa; *tat-caraṇa-aravinde*—at His lotus feet; *tvat-vajra*—of your thunderbolt; *raṁhaḥ*—by the force; *lulita*—torn; *grāmya*—of material attachment; *pāśaḥ*—the rope; *gatim*—the destination; *muneḥ*—of Nārada Muni and other devotees; *yāmi*—I shall achieve; *apaviddha*—giving up; *lokaḥ*—this material world (where one desires all kinds of impermanent things).

TRANSLATION

By the force of your thunderbolt, I shall be freed of material bondage and shall give up this body and this world of material desires. Fixing my mind upon the lotus feet of Lord Saṅkarṣaṇa, I shall attain the destination of such great sages as Nārada Muni, just as Lord Saṅkarṣaṇa has said.

PURPORT

The words *ahaṁ samādhāya manaḥ* indicate that the most important duty at the time of death is to concentrate one's mind. If one can fix his mind on the lotus feet of Kṛṣṇa, Viṣṇu, Saṅkarṣaṇa or any Viṣṇu *mūrti,* his life will be successful. To be killed while fixing his mind at the lotus feet of Saṅkarṣaṇa, Vṛtrāsura asked Indra to release his *vajra,* or thunderbolt. He was destined to be killed by the thunderbolt given by Lord Viṣṇu; there was no question of its being baffled. Therefore Vṛtrāsura requested Indra to release the thunderbolt immediately, and he prepared himself by fixing his mind at the lotus feet of Kṛṣṇa. A devotee is always ready to give up his material body, which is described herein as *grāmya-pāśa,* the rope of material attachment. The body is not at all good; it is simply a cause of bondage to the material world. Unfortunately, even though the body is destined for destruction, fools and rascals invest all their faith in the body and are never eager to return home, back to Godhead.

TEXT 22

पुंसां किलैकान्तधियां स्वकानां
याः सम्पदो दिवि भूमौ रसायाम्।
न राति यद् द्वेष उद्वेग आधि-
र्मदः कलिर्व्यसनं संप्रयासः ॥ २२ ॥

puṁsāṁ kilaikānta-dhiyāṁ svakānāṁ
yāḥ sampado divi bhūmau rasāyām
na rāti yad dveṣa udvega ādhir
madaḥ kalir vyasanaṁ samprayāsaḥ

puṁsām—unto persons; *kila*—certainly; *ekānta-dhiyām*—who are advanced in spiritual consciousness; *svakānām*—who are recognized by the Supreme Personality of Godhead as His own; *yāḥ*—which; *sampadaḥ*—opulences; *divi*—in the upper planetary systems; *bhūmau*—in the middle planetary systems; *rasāyām*—and in the lower planetary systems; *na*—not; *rāti*—bestows; *yat*—from which; *dveṣaḥ*—envy; *udvegaḥ*—anxiety; *ādhiḥ*—mental agitation; *madaḥ*—pride; *kaliḥ*—quarrel; *vyasanam*—distress due to loss; *samprayāsaḥ*—great endeavor.

TRANSLATION

Persons who fully surrender at the lotus feet of the Supreme Personality of Godhead and always think of His lotus feet are accepted and recognized by the Lord as His own personal assistants or servants. The Lord never bestows upon such servants the brilliant opulences of the upper, lower and middle planetary systems of this material world. When one possesses material opulence in any of these three divisions of the universe, his possessions naturally increase his enmity, anxiety, mental agitation, pride and belligerence. Thus one goes through much endeavor to increase and maintain his possessions, and he suffers great unhappiness when he loses them.

PURPORT

In *Bhagavad-gītā* (4.11) the Lord says:

ye yathā māṁ prapadyante
tāṁs tathaiva bhajāmy aham
mama vartmānuvartante
manuṣyāḥ pārtha sarvaśaḥ

"As devotees surrender unto Me, I reward them accordingly. Everyone follows My path in all respects, O son of Pṛthā." Both Indra and Vṛtrāsura were certainly devotees of the Lord, although Indra took instructions from Viṣṇu to kill Vṛtrāsura. The Lord was actually more favorable to Vṛtrāsura because after being killed by Indra's thunderbolt, Vṛtrāsura would go back to Godhead, whereas the victorious Indra would rot in this material world. Because both of them were devotees, the Lord awarded them the respective benedictions they wanted. Vṛtrāsura never wanted material possessions, for he knew very well the nature of such possessions. To accumulate material possessions, one must labor very hard, and when he gets them he creates many enemies because this material world is always full of rivalry. If one becomes rich, his friends or relatives are envious. For *ekānta-bhaktas,* unalloyed devotees, Kṛṣṇa therefore never provides material possessions. A devotee sometimes needs some material possessions for preaching, but the possessions of a preacher are not like those of a *karmī.* A *karmī's* possessions are achieved as a result of *karma,* but those of a devotee are arranged by the Supreme Personality of Godhead just to facilitate his devotional activities. Because a devotee never uses material possessions for any purpose other than the service of the Lord, the possessions of a devotee are not to be compared to those of a *karmī.*

TEXT 23

त्रैवर्गिकायासविघातमस्मत्-
पतिर्विधत्ते पुरुषस्य शक्र ।
ततोऽनुमेयो भगवत्प्रसादो
यो दुर्लभोऽकिञ्चनगोचरोऽन्यैः ॥ २३ ॥

trai-vargikāyāsa-vighātam asmat-
patir vidhatte puruṣasya śakra
tato 'numeyo bhagavat-prasādo
yo durlabho 'kiñcana-gocaro 'nyaiḥ

trai-vargika—for the three objectives, namely religiosity, economic development, and satisfaction of the senses; *āyāsa*—of endeavor; *vighātam*—the ruin; *asmat*—our; *patiḥ*—Lord; *vidhatte*—performs; *puruṣasya*—of a devotee; *śakra*—O Indra; *tataḥ*—whereby; *anumeyaḥ*—to be inferred; *bhagavat-prasādaḥ*—the special mercy of the Supreme Personality of Godhead; *yaḥ*—which; *durlabhaḥ*—very difficult to obtain; *akiñcana-gocaraḥ*—within the reach of the unalloyed devotees; *anyaiḥ*—by others, who aspire for material happiness.

TRANSLATION

Our Lord, the Supreme Personality of Godhead, forbids His devotees to endeavor uselessly for religion, economic development and sense

gratification. O Indra, one can thus infer how kind the Lord is. Such mercy is obtainable only by unalloyed devotees, not by persons who aspire for material gains.

PURPORT

There are four objectives in human life—namely, religiosity (*dharma*), economic development (*artha*), sense gratification (*kāma*), and liberation (*mokṣa*) from the bondage of material existence. People generally aspire for religiosity, economic development and sense gratification, but a devotee has no other desire than to serve the Supreme Personality of Godhead both in this life and in the next. The special mercy for the unalloyed devotee is that the Lord saves him from hard labor to achieve the results of religion, economic development and sense gratification. Of course, if one wants such benefits, the Lord certainly awards them. Indra, for example, although a devotee, was not much interested in release from material bondage; instead, he desired sense gratification and a high standard of material happiness in the heavenly planets. Vṛtrāsura, however, being an unalloyed devotee, aspired only to serve the Supreme Personality of Godhead. Therefore the Lord arranged for him to go back to Godhead after his bodily bondage was destroyed by Indra. Vṛtrāsura requested Indra to release his thunderbolt against him as soon as possible so that both he and Indra would benefit according to their proportionate advancement in devotional service.

TEXT 24

अहं हरे तव पादैकमूल-
दासानुदासो भवितास्मि भूयः ।
मनः स्मरेतासुपतेर्गुणांस्ते
गृणीत वाक् कर्म करोतु कायः ॥ २४ ॥

ahaṁ hare tava pādaika-mūla-
dāsānudāso bhavitāsmi bhūyaḥ
manaḥ smaretāsu-pater guṇāṁs te
gṛṇīta vāk karma karotu kāyaḥ

aham—I; *hare*—O my Lord; *tava*—of Your Lordship; *pāda-eka-mūla*—whose only shelter is the lotus feet; *dāsa-anudāsaḥ*—the servant of Your servant; *bhavitāsmi*—shall I become; *bhūyaḥ*—again; *manaḥ*—my mind; *smareta*—may remember; *asu-pateḥ*—of the Lord of my life; *guṇān*—the attributes; *te*—of Your Lordship; *gṛṇīta*—may chant; *vāk*—my words; *karma*—activities of service to You; *karotu*—may perform; *kāyaḥ*—my body.

TRANSLATION

O my Lord, O Supreme Personality of Godhead, will I again be able to be a servant of Your eternal servants who find shelter only at Your lotus feet? O Lord of my life, may I again become their servant so that my mind may always think of Your transcendental attributes, my words always glorify those attributes, and my body always engage in the loving service of Your Lordship?

PURPORT

This verse gives the sum and substance of devotional life. One must first become a servant of the servant of the servant of the Lord (*dāsānudāsa*). Śrī Caitanya Mahāprabhu advised, and He also showed by His own example, that a living entity should always desire to be a servant of the servant of the servant of Kṛṣṇa, the maintainer of the *gopīs* (*gopī-bhartuḥ pada-kamalayor dāsa-dāsānudāsaḥ*). This means that one must accept a spiritual master who comes in the disciplic succession and is a servant of the servant of the Lord. Under his direction, one must then engage one's three properties, namely his body, mind and words. The body should be engaged in physical activity under the order of the master, the mind should think of Kṛṣṇa incessantly, and one's words should be engaged in preaching the glories of the Lord. If one is thus engaged in the loving service of the Lord, one's life is successful.

TEXT 25

न नाकपृष्ठं न च पारमेष्ठ्यं
न सार्वभौमं न रसाधिपत्यम् ।
न योगसिद्धीरपुनर्भवं वा
समञ्जस त्वा विरहय्य काङ्क्षे ॥ २५ ॥

na nāka-pṛṣṭhaṁ na ca pārameṣṭhyaṁ
na sārva-bhaumaṁ na rasādhipatyam
na yoga-siddhīr apunar-bhavaṁ vā
samañjasa tvā virahayya kāṅkṣe

na—not; *nāka-pṛṣṭham*—the heavenly planets or Dhruvaloka; *na*—nor; *ca*—also; *pārameṣṭhyam*—the planet on which Lord Brahmā resides; *na*—

nor; *sārva-bhaumam*—sovereignty of the whole earthly planetary system; *na*—nor; *rasā-ādhipatyam*—sovereignty of the lower planetary systems; *na*—nor; *yoga-siddhīḥ*—eight kinds of mystic yogic power (*aṇimā, laghimā, mahimā,* etc.); *apunaḥ-bhavam*—liberation from rebirth in a material body; *vā*—or; *samañjasa*—O source of all opportunities; *tvā*—You; *virahayya*—being separated from; *kāṅkṣe*—I desire.

TRANSLATION

O my Lord, source of all opportunities, I do not desire to enjoy in Dhruvaloka, the heavenly planets or the planet where Lord Brahmā resides, nor do I want to be the supreme ruler of all the earthly planets or the lower planetary systems. I do not desire to be master of the powers of mystic yoga, nor do I want liberation if I have to give up Your lotus feet.

PURPORT

A pure devotee never desires to gain material opportunities by rendering transcendental loving service to the Lord. A pure devotee desires only to engage in loving service to the Lord in the constant association of the Lord and His eternal associates, as stated in the previous verse (*dāsānudāso bhavitāsmi*). As confirmed by Narottama dāsa Ṭhākura:

tāṅdera caraṇa sevi bhakta-sane vāsa
janame janame haya, ei abhilāṣa

To serve the Lord and the servants of His servants, in the association of devotees, is the only objective of a pure, unalloyed devotee.

TEXT 26

अजातपक्षा इव मातरं खगाः
स्तन्यं यथा वत्सतराः क्षुधार्ताः ।
प्रियं प्रियेव व्युषितं विषण्णा
मनोऽरविन्दाक्ष दिदृक्षते त्वाम् ॥ २६ ॥

ajāta-pakṣā iva mātaraṁ khagāḥ
stanyaṁ yathā vatsatarāḥ kṣudh-ārtāḥ
priyaṁ priyeva vyuṣitaṁ viṣaṇṇā
mano'ravindākṣa didṛkṣate tvām

ajāta-pakṣāḥ—who have not yet grown wings; *iva*—like; *mātaram*—the mother; *khagāḥ*—small birds; *stanyam*—the milk from the udder; *yathā*—just as; *vatsatarāḥ*—the young calves; *kṣudh-ārtāḥ*—distressed by hunger; *priyam*—the beloved or husband; *priyā*—the wife or lover; *iva*—like; *vyuṣitam*—who is away from home; *viṣaṇṇā*—morose; *manaḥ*—my mind; *aravinda-akṣa*—O lotus-eyed one; *didṛkṣate*—wants to see; *tvām*—You.

TRANSLATION

O lotus-eyed Lord, as baby birds that have not yet developed their wings always look for their mother to return and feed them, as small calves tied with ropes await anxiously the time of milking, when they will be allowed to drink the milk of their mothers, or as a morose wife whose husband is away from home always longs for him to return and satisfy her in all respects, I always yearn for the opportunity to render direct service unto You.

PURPORT

A pure devotee always yearns to associate personally with the Lord and render service unto Him. The examples given in this regard are most appropriate. A small baby bird is practically never satisfied except when the mother bird comes to feed it, a small calf is not satisfied unless allowed to suck the milk from the mother's udder, and a chaste, devoted wife whose husband is away from home is never satisfied until she has the association of her beloved husband.

TEXT 27

ममोत्तमश्लोकजनेषु सख्यं
संसारचक्रे भ्रमतः स्वकर्मभिः ।
त्वन्माययात्मात्मजदारगेहे-
ष्वासक्तचित्तस्य न नाथ भूयात् ॥ २७ ॥

mamottamaśloka-janeṣu sakhyaṁ
saṁsāra-cakre bhramataḥ sva-karmabhiḥ
tvan-māyayātmātmaja-dāra-geheṣv
āsakta-cittasya na nātha bhūyāt

mama—my; *uttama-śloka-janeṣu*—among devotees who are simply attached to the Supreme Personality of Godhead; *sakhyam*—friendship;

saṁsāra-cakre—in the cycle of birth and death; *bhramataḥ*—who am wandering; *sva-karmabhiḥ*—by the results of my own fruitive activities; *tvat-māyayā*—by Your external energy; *ātma*—to the body; *ātma-ja*—children; *dāra*—wife; *geheṣu*—and home; *āsakta*—attached; *cittasya*--whose mind; *na*—not; *nātha*—O my Lord; *bhūyāt*—may there be.

TRANSLATION

O my Lord, my master, I am wandering throughout this material world as a result of my fruitive activities. Therefore I simply seek friendship in the association of Your pious and enlightened devotees. My attachment to my body, wife, children and home is continuing by the spell of Your external energy, but I wish to be attached to them no longer. Let my mind, my consciousness and everything I have be attached only to You.

Thus end the Bhaktivedanta purports to the Sixth Canto, Eleventh Chapter, of the Śrīmad-Bhāgavatam, *entitled "The Transcendental Qualities of Vṛtrāsura."*

CHAPTER TWELVE

Vṛtrāsura's Glorious Death

This chapter describes how Indra, the King of heaven, killed Vṛtrāsura despite great reluctance.

After Vṛtrāsura finished speaking, he released his trident against King Indra with great anger, but Indra, using his thunderbolt, which was many times more powerful than the trident, broke the trident to pieces and cut off one of Vṛtrāsura's arms. Nevertheless, Vṛtrāsura used his remaining arm to strike Indra with an iron mace, making the thunderbolt fall from Indra's hand. Indra, being very ashamed of this, did not pick up the thunderbolt from the ground, but Vṛtrāsura encouraged King Indra to pick it up and fight. Vṛtrāsura then spoke to King Indra as follows, instructing him very well.

"The Supreme Personality of Godhead," he said, "is the cause of victory and defeat. Not knowing that the Supreme Lord is the cause of all causes, fools and rascals try to take credit for victory or defeat themselves, but everything is actually under the control of the Lord. No one but Him has any independence. The *puruṣa* (the enjoyer) and *prakṛti* (the enjoyed) are under the control of the Lord, for it is by His supervision that everything works systematically. Not seeing the hand of the Supreme in every action, a fool considers himself the ruler and controller of everything. When one understands, however, that the real controller is the Supreme Personality of Godhead, he is freed from the relativities of the world, such as distress, happiness, fear and impurity." Thus Indra and Vṛtrāsura not only fought, but also engaged in philosophical discourses. Then they began to fight again.

This time Indra was more powerful, and he severed Vṛtrāsura's remaining arm. Vṛtrāsura then assumed a gigantic form and swallowed King Indra, but Indra, being protected by the talisman known as Nārāyaṇa-kavaca, was able to protect himself even within Vṛtrāsura's body. Thus he emerged from Vṛtrāsura's abdomen and severed the demon's head from his body with his powerful thunderbolt. Severing the demon's head took one complete year to accomplish.

TEXT 1

श्रीऋषिरुवाच

एवं जिहासुर्नृप देहमाजौ
मृत्युं वरं विजयान्मन्यमानः ।

शूलं प्रगृह्याभ्यपतत् सुरेन्द्रं
यथा महापुरुषं कैटभोऽप्सु ॥ १ ॥

śrī-ṛṣir uvāca
evaṁ jihāsur nṛpa deham ājau
mṛtyuṁ varaṁ vijayān manyamānaḥ
śūlaṁ pragṛhyābhyapatat surendraṁ
yathā mahā-puruṣaṁ kaiṭabho'psu

śrī-ṛṣiḥ uvāca—Śrī Śukadeva Gosvāmī said; *evam*—thus; *jihāsuḥ*—very eager to give up; *nṛpa*—O King Parīkṣit; *deham*—the body; *ājau*—in battle; *mṛtyum*—death; *varam*—better; *vijayāt*—than victory; *manyamānaḥ*—thinking; *śūlam*—trident; *pragṛhya*—taking up; *abhyapatat*—attacked; *sura-indram*—the King of heaven, Indra; *yathā*—just as; *mahā-puruṣam*—the Supreme Personality of Godhead; *kaiṭabhaḥ*—the demon Kaiṭabha; *apsu*—when the whole universe was inundated.

TRANSLATION

Śukadeva Gosvāmī said: Desiring to give up his body, Vṛtrāsura considered death in the battle preferable to victory. O King Parīkṣit, he vigorously took up his trident and with great force attacked Lord Indra, the King of heaven, just as Kaiṭabha had forcefully attacked the Supreme Personality of Godhead when the universe was inundated.

PURPORT

Although Vṛtrāsura repeatedly encouraged Indra to kill him with the thunderbolt, King Indra was morose at having to kill such a great devotee and was hesitant to throw it. Vṛtrāsura, disappointed that King Indra was reluctant despite his encouragement, took the initiative very forcefully by throwing his trident at Indra. Vṛtrāsura was not at all interested in victory; he was interested in being killed so that he could immediately return home, back to Godhead. As confirmed in *Bhagavad-gītā* (4.9), *tyaktvā dehaṁ punar janma naiti:* after giving up his body, a devotee immediately returns to Lord Kṛṣṇa and never returns to accept another body. This was Vṛtrāsura's interest.

TEXT 2

ततो युगान्ताग्निकठोरजिह्व-
माविध्य शूलं तरसासुरेन्द्रः ।

क्षिप्त्वा महेन्द्राय विनद्य वीरो
हतोऽसि पापेति रुषा जगाद ॥ २ ॥

tato yugāntāgni-kaṭhora-jihvam
āvidhya śūlaṁ tarasāsurendraḥ
kṣiptvā mahendrāya vinadya vīro
hato 'si pāpeti ruṣā jagāda

tataḥ—thereafter; *yuga-anta-agni*—like the fire at the end of every millennium; *kaṭhora*—sharp; *jihvam*—possessing points; *āvidhya*—twirling; *śūlam*—the trident; *tarasā*—with great force; *asura-indraḥ*—the great hero of the demons, Vṛtrāsura; *kṣiptvā*—throwing; *mahā-indrāya*—unto King Indra; *vinadya*—roaring; *vīraḥ*—the great hero (Vṛtrāsura); *hataḥ*—killed; *asi*—you are; *pāpa*—O sinful one; *iti*—thus; *ruṣā*—with great anger; *jagāda*—be cried out.

TRANSLATION

Then Vṛtrāsura, the great hero of the demons, whirled his trident, which had points like the flames of the blazing fire at the end of the millennium. With great force and anger he threw it at Indra, roaring and exclaiming loudly, "O sinful one, thus shall I kill you!"

TEXT 3

ख आपतत् तद् विचलद् ग्रहोल्कव-
न्निरीक्ष्य दुष्प्रेक्ष्यमजातविक्लवः ।
वज्रेण वज्री शतपर्वणाच्छिनद्
भुजं च तस्योरगराजभोगम् ॥ ३ ॥

kha āpatat tad vicalad graholkavan
nirīkṣya duṣprekṣyam ajāta-viklavaḥ
vajreṇa vajrī śata-parvaṇācchinad
bhujaṁ ca tasyoraga-rāja-bhogam

khe—in the sky; *āpatat*—flying toward him; *tat*—that trident; *vicalat*—rotating; *graha-ulka-vat*—like a falling star; *nirīkṣya*—observing; *duṣprekṣyam*—unbearable to see; *ajāta-viklavaḥ*—not afraid; *vajreṇa*—with the thunderbolt; *vajrī*—Indra, the holder of the thunderbolt; *śata-parvaṇā*—possessing one hundred joints; *ācchinat*—cut; *bhujam*—the arm; *ca*—and;

tasya—of him (Vṛtrāsura); *uraga-rāja*—of the great serpent Vāsuki; *bhogam*—like the body.

TRANSLATION

Flying in the sky, Vṛtrāsura's trident resembled a brilliant meteor. Although the blazing weapon was difficult to look upon, King Indra, unafraid, cut it to pieces with his thunderbolt. Simultaneously, he cut off one of Vṛtrāsura's arms, which was as thick as the body of Vāsuki, the King of the serpents.

TEXT 4

छिन्नैकबाहुः परिघेण वृत्रः
संरब्ध आसाद्य गृहीतवज्रम् ।
हनौ तताडेन्द्रमथामरेभं
वज्रं च हस्तान्न्यपतन्मघोनः ॥ ४ ॥

chinnaika-bāhuḥ parigheṇa vṛtraḥ
saṁrabdha āsādya gṛhīta-vajram
hanau tatāḍendram athāmarebhaṁ
vajraṁ ca hastān nyapatan maghonaḥ

chinna—cut off; *eka*—one; *bāhuḥ*—whose arm; *parigheṇa*—with a mace of iron; *vṛtraḥ*—Vṛtrāsura; *saṁrabdhaḥ*—being very angry; *āsādya*—reaching; *gṛhīta*—taking up; *vajram*—the thunderbolt; *hanau*—on the jaw; *tatāḍa*—struck; *indram*—Lord Indra; *atha*—also; *amara-ibham*—his elephant; *vajram*—the thunderbolt; *ca*—and; *hastāt*—from the hand; *nyapatat*—fell; *maghonaḥ*—of King Indra.

TRANSLATION

Although one of his arms was severed from his body, Vṛtrāsura angrily approached King Indra and struck him on the jaw with an iron mace. He also struck the elephant that carried Indra. Thus Indra dropped the thunderbolt from his hand.

TEXT 5

वृत्रस्य कर्मातिमहाद्भुतं तत्
सुरासुराश्चारणसिद्धसङ्घाः ।

अपूजयंस्तत् पुरुहूतसंकटं
निरीक्ष्य हा हेति विचुक्रुशुर्भृशम् ॥ ५ ॥

vṛtrasya karmāti-mahādbhutaṁ tat
surāsurāś cāraṇa-siddha-saṅghāḥ
apūjayaṁs tat puruhūta-saṅkaṭaṁ
nirīkṣya hā heti vicukruśur bhṛśam

vṛtrasya—of Vṛtrāsura; *karma*—the accomplishment; *ati*—very; *mahā*—greatly; *adbhutam*—wonderful; *tat*—that; *sura*—the demigods; *asurāḥ*—and the demons; *cāraṇa*—the Cāraṇas; *siddha-saṅghāḥ*—and the society of Siddhas; *apūjayan*—glorified; *tat*—that; *puruhūta-saṅkaṭam*—the dangerous position of Indra; *nirīkṣya*—seeing; *hā hā*—alas, alas; *iti*—thus; *vicukruśuḥ*—lamented; *bhṛśam*—very much.

TRANSLATION

The denizens of various planets, like the demigods, demons, Cāraṇas and Siddhas, praised Vṛtrāsura's deed, but when they observed that Indra was in great danger, they lamented, "Alas! Alas!"

TEXT 6

इन्द्रो न वज्रं जगृहे विलज्जित-
श्च्युतं स्वहस्तादरिसन्निधौ पुनः ।
तमाह वृत्रो हर आत्तवज्रो
जहि स्वशत्रुं न विषादकालः ॥ ६ ॥

indro na vajraṁ jagṛhe vilajjitaś
cyutaṁ sva-hastād ari-sannidhau punaḥ
tam āha vṛtro hara ātta-vajro
jahi sva-śatruṁ na viṣāda-kālaḥ

indraḥ—King Indra; *na*—not; *vajram*—the thunderbolt; *jagṛhe*—took up; *vilajjitaḥ*—being ashamed; *cyutam*—fallen; *sva-hastāt*—from his own hand; *ari-sannidhau*—in front of his enemy; *punaḥ*—again; *tam*—unto him; *āha*—said; *vṛtraḥ*—Vṛtrāsura; *hare*—O Indra; *ātta-vajraḥ*—taking up your thunderbolt; *jahi*—kill; *sva-śatrum*—your enemy; *na*—not; *viṣāda-kālaḥ*—the time for lamentation.

TRANSLATION

Having dropped the thunderbolt from his hand in the presence of his enemy, Indra was practically defeated and was very much ashamed. He dared not pick up his weapon again. Vṛtrāsura, however, encouraged him, saying, "Take up your thunderbolt and kill your enemy. This is not the time to lament your fate."

TEXT 7

युयुत्सतां कुत्रचिदाततायिनां
जयः सदैकत्र न वै परात्मनाम्।
विनैकमुत्पत्तिलयस्थितीश्वरं
सर्वज्ञमाद्यं पुरुषं सनातनम् ॥ ७ ॥

yuyutsatāṁ kutracid ātatāyināṁ
jayaḥ sadaikatra na vai parātmanām
vinaikam utpatti-laya-sthitīśvaraṁ
sarvajñam ādyaṁ puruṣaṁ sanātanam

yuyutsatām—of those who are belligerent; *kutracit*—sometimes; *ātatāyinām*—armed with weapons; *jayaḥ*—victory; *sadā*—always; *ekatra*—in one place; *na*—not; *vai*—indeed; *para-ātmanām*—of the subordinate living entities, who work only under the direction of the Supersoul; *vinā*—except; *ekam*—one; *utpatti*—of the creation; *laya*—annihilation; *sthiti*—and maintenance; *īśvaram*—the controller; *sarva-jñam*—who knows everything (past, present and future); *ādyam*—the original; *puruṣam*—enjoyer; *sanātanam*—eternal.

TRANSLATION

Vṛtrāsura continued: O Indra, no one is guaranteed of being always victorious but the original enjoyer, the Supreme Personality of Godhead, Bhagavān. He is the cause of creation, maintenance and annihilation, and He knows everything. Being dependent and being obliged to accept material bodies, belligerent subordinates are sometimes victorious and sometimes defeated.

PURPORT

The Lord says in *Bhagavad-gītā* (15.15):

sarvasya cāhaṁ hṛdi sanniviṣṭo
mattaḥ smṛtir jñānam apohanaṁ ca

"I am seated in everyone's heart, and from Me come remembrance, knowledge and forgetfulness." When two parties fight, the fighting actually goes on under the direction of the Supreme Personality of Godhead, who is Paramātmā, the Supersoul. Elsewhere in the *Gītā* (3.27) the Lord says:

prakṛteḥ kriyamāṇāni
guṇaiḥ karmāṇi sarvaśaḥ
ahaṅkāra-vimūḍhātmā
kartāham iti manyate

"The bewildered spirit soul, under the influence of the three modes of material nature, thinks himself the doer of activities that are in actuality carried out by nature." The living entities work only under the direction of the Supreme Lord. The Lord gives orders to material nature, and she arranges facilities for the living entities. The living entities are not independent, although they foolishly think themselves the doers (*kartā*).

Victory is always with the Supreme Personality of Godhead. As for the subordinate living entities, they fight under the arrangement of the Supreme Personality of Godhead. Victory or defeat is not actually theirs; it is an arrangement by the Lord through the agency of material nature. Pride in victory, or moroseness in defeat, is useless. One should fully depend on the Supreme Personality of Godhead, who is responsible for the victory and defeat of all living entities. The Lord advises, *niyataṁ kuru karma tvaṁ karma jyāyo hy akarmaṇaḥ:* "Perform your prescribed duty, for action is better than inaction." The living entity is ordered to act according to his position. Victory or defeat depends on the Supreme Lord. *Karmaṇy evādhikāras te mā phaleṣu kadācana:* "You have a right to perform your prescribed duty, but you are not entitled to the fruits of actions." One must act sincerely, according to his position. Victory or defeat depends on the Lord.

Vṛtrāsura encouraged Indra, saying, "Don't be morose because of my victory. There is no need to stop fighting. Instead, you should go on with your duty. When Kṛṣṇa desires, you will certainly be victorious." This verse is very instructive for sincere workers in the Kṛṣṇa consciousness movement. We should not be jubilant in victory or morose in defeat. We should make a sincere effort to implement the will of Kṛṣṇa, or Śrī Caitanya Mahāprabhu, and we should not be concerned with victory and defeat. Our only duty is to work sincerely, so that our activities may be recognized by Kṛṣṇa.

TEXT 8

लोकाः सपाला यस्येमे श्वसन्ति विवशा वशे ।
द्विजा इव शिचा बद्धाः स काल इह कारणम् ॥ ८ ॥

lokāḥ sapālā yasyeme
śvasanti vivaśā vaśe
dvijā iva śicā baddhāḥ
sa kāla iha kāraṇam

lokāḥ—the worlds; *sa-pālāḥ*—with their chief deities or controllers; *yasya*—of whom; *ime*—all these; *śvasanti*—live; *vivaśāḥ*—fully dependent; *vaśe*—under the control; *dvijāḥ*—birds; *iva*—like; *śicā*—by a net; *baddhāḥ*—bound; *saḥ*—that; *kālaḥ*—time factor; *iha*—in this; *kāraṇam*—the cause.

TRANSLATION

All living beings in all the planets of this universe, including the presiding deities of all the planets, are fully under the control of the Lord. They work like birds caught in a net, who cannot move independently.

PURPORT

The difference between the *suras* and the *asuras* is that the *suras* know that nothing can happen without the desire of the Supreme Personality of Godhead, whereas the *asuras* cannot understand the supreme will of the Lord. In this fight, Vṛtrāsura is actually the *sura,* whereas Indra is the *asura.* No one can act independently; rather, everyone acts under the direction of the Supreme Personality of Godhead. Therefore victory and defeat come according to the results of one's *karma,* and the judgment is given by the Supreme Lord (*karmaṇā-daiva-netreṇa*). Since we act under the control of the Supreme according to our *karma,* no one is independent, from Brahmā down to the insignificant ant. Whether we are defeated or victorious, the Supreme Lord is always victorious because everyone acts under His directions.

TEXT 9

ओजः सहो बलं प्राणममृतं मृत्युमेव च ।
तमज्ञाय जनो हेतुमात्मानं मन्यते जडम् ॥ ९ ॥

ojaḥ saho balaṁ prāṇam
amṛtaṁ mṛtyum eva ca

tam ajñāya jano hetum
ātmānaṁ manyate jaḍam

ojaḥ—the strength of the senses; *sahaḥ*—the strength of the mind; *balam*—the strength of the body; *prāṇam*—the living condition; *amṛtam*—immortality; *mṛtyum*—death; *eva*—indeed; *ca*—also; *tam*—Him (the Supreme Lord); *ajñāya*—without knowing; *janaḥ*—a foolish person; *hetum*—the cause; *ātmānam*—the body; *manyate*—considers; *jaḍam*—although as good as stone.

TRANSLATION

Our sensory prowess, mental power, bodily strength, living force, immortality and mortality are all subject to the superintendence of the Supreme Personality of Godhead. Not knowing this, foolish people think the dull material body to be the cause of their activities.

TEXT 10

यथा दारुमयी नारी यथा पत्रमयो मृगः ।
एवं भूतानि मघवन्नीशतन्त्राणि विद्धि भोः ॥ १० ॥

yathā dārumayī nārī
yathā patramayo mṛgaḥ
evaṁ bhūtāni maghavann
īśa-tantrāṇi viddhi bhoḥ

yathā—just as; *dāru-mayī*—made of wood; *nārī*—a woman; *yathā*—just as; *patra-mayaḥ*—made of leaves; *mṛgaḥ*—an animal; *evam*—thus; *bhūtāni*—all things; *maghavan*—O King Indra; *īśa*—the Supreme Personality of Godhead; *tantrāṇi*—depending upon; *viddhi*—please know; *bhoḥ*—O sir.

TRANSLATION

O King Indra, as a wooden doll that looks like a woman or as an animal made of grass and leaves cannot move or dance independently, but depends fully on the person who handles it, all of us dance according to the desire of the supreme controller, the Personality of Godhead. No one is independent.

PURPORT

This is confirmed in *Caitanya-caritāmṛta* (*Ādi* 5.142):

ekale īśvara kṛṣṇa, āra saba bhṛtya
yāre yaiche nācāya, se taiche kare nṛtya

"Lord Kṛṣṇa alone is the supreme controller, and all others are His servants. They dance as He makes them do so." We are all servants of Kṛṣṇa; we have no independence. We are dancing according to the desire of the Supreme Personality of Godhead, but out of ignorance and illusion we think we are independent of the supreme will. Therefore it is said:

īśvaraḥ paramaḥ kṛṣṇaḥ
sac-cid-ānanda-vigrahaḥ
anādir ādir govindaḥ
sarva-kāraṇa-kāraṇam

"Kṛṣṇa, who is known as Govinda, is the supreme controller. He has an eternal, blissful, spiritual body. He is the origin of all. He has no other origin, for He is the prime cause of all causes." (*Brahma-saṁhitā* 5.1)

TEXT 11

पुरुषः प्रकृतिर्व्यक्तमात्मा भूतेन्द्रियाशयाः ।
शक्नुवन्त्यस्य सर्गादौ न विना यदनुग्रहात् ॥ ११ ॥

puruṣaḥ prakṛtir vyaktam
ātmā bhūtendriyāśayāḥ
śaknuvanty asya sargādau
na vinā yad-anugrahāt

puruṣaḥ—the generator of the total material energy; *prakṛtiḥ*—the material energy or material nature; *vyaktam*—the principles of manifestation (*mahat-tattva*); *ātmā*—the false ego; *bhūta*—the five material elements; *indriya*—the ten senses; *āśayāḥ*—the mind, intelligence and consciousness; *śaknuvanti*—are able; *asya*—of this universe; *sarga-ādau*—in the creation, etc.; *na*—not; *vinā*—without; *yat*—of whom; *anugrahāt*—the mercy.

TRANSLATION

The three puruṣas—Kāraṇodakaśāyī Viṣṇu, Garbhodakaśāyī Viṣṇu and Kṣīrodakaśāyī Viṣṇu—the material nature, the total material energy, the

false ego, the five material elements, the material senses, the mind, the intelligence and consciousness cannot create the material manifestation without the direction of the Supreme Personality of Godhead.

PURPORT

As confirmed in the *Viṣṇu Purāṇa, parasya brahmaṇaḥ śaktis tathedam akhilaṁ jagat:* whatever manifestations we experience are nothing but various energies of the Supreme Personality of Godhead. These energies cannot create anything independently. This is also confirmed by the Lord Himself in *Bhagavad-gītā* (9.10): *mayādhyakṣeṇa prakṛtiḥ sūyate sa-carācaram.* "This material nature is working under My direction, O son of Kuntī, and it is producing all moving and unmoving living beings." Only under the direction of the Lord, the Supreme Person, can *prakṛti,* which is manifested in twenty-four elements, create different situations for the living entity. In the *Vedas* the Lord says:

madīyaṁ mahimānaṁ ca
parabrahmeti śabditam
vetsyasy anugṛhītaṁ me
sampraśnair vivṛtaṁ hṛdi

"Since everything is a manifestation of My energy, I am known as Parabrahman. Therefore everyone should hear from Me about My glorious activities." The Lord also says in *Bhagavad-gītā* (10.2), *aham ādir hi devānām:* "I am the origin of all the demigods." Therefore the Supreme Personality of Godhead is the origin of everything, and no one is independent of Him. Śrīla Madhvācārya also says, *anīśa-jīva-rūpeṇa:* the living entity is *anīśa,* never the controller, but is always controlled. Therefore when a living entity becomes proud of being an independent *īśvara,* or god, that is his foolishness. Such foolishness is described in the following verse.

TEXT 12

अविद्वानेवमात्मानं मन्यतेऽनीशमीश्वरम् ।
भूतैः सृजति भूतानि ग्रसते तानि तैः स्वयम् ॥ १२ ॥

avidvān evam ātmānaṁ
manyate 'nīśam īśvaram
bhūtaiḥ sṛjati bhūtāni
grasate tāni taiḥ svayam

avidvān—one who is foolish, without knowledge; *evam*—thus; *ātmānam*—himself; *manyate*—considers; *anīśam*—although totally dependent on others; *īśvaram*—as the supreme controller, independent; *bhūtaiḥ*—by the living entities; *sṛjati*—He (the Lord) creates; *bhūtāni*—other living entities; *grasate*—He devours; *tāni*—them; *taiḥ*—by other living beings; *svayam*—Himself.

TRANSLATION

A foolish, senseless person cannot understand the Supreme Personality of Godhead. Although always dependent, he falsely thinks himself the Supreme. If one thinks, "According to one's previous fruitive actions, one's material body is created by the father and mother, and the same body is annihilated by another agent, as another animal is devoured by a tiger," this is not proper understanding. The Supreme Personality of Godhead Himself creates and devours the living beings through other living beings.

PURPORT

According to the conclusion of the philosophy known as *karma-mīmāṁsā,* one's *karma,* or previous fruitive activity, is the cause of everything, and therefore there is no need to work. Those who arrive at this conclusion are foolish. When a father creates a child, he does not do so independently; he is induced to do so by the Supreme Lord. As the Lord Himself says in *Bhagavad-gītā* (15.15), *sarvasya cāhaṁ hṛdi sanniviṣṭo mattaḥ smṛtir jñānam apohanaṁ ca:* "I am in everyone's heart, and from Me come remembrance, knowledge and forgetfulness." Unless one receives dictation from the Supreme Personality of Godhead, who sits within everyone's heart, one cannot be induced to create anything. Therefore the father and mother are not the creators of the living entity. According to the living entity's *karma,* fruitive activities, he is put into the semen of the father, who injects the living entity into the womb of the mother. Then according to the body of the mother and father (*yathā-yoni yathā-bījam*), the living entity accepts a body and takes birth to suffer or enjoy. Therefore the Supreme Lord is the original cause of one's birth. Similarly, the Supreme Lord is the cause of one's being killed. No one is independent; everyone is dependent. The true conclusion is that the only independent person is the Supreme Personality of Godhead.

TEXT 13

आयुः श्रीः कीर्तिरैश्वर्यमाशिषः पुरुषस्य याः ।
भवन्त्येव हि तत्काले यथानिच्छोर्विपर्ययाः ॥ १३ ॥

āyuḥ śrīḥ kīrtir aiśvaryam
āśiṣaḥ puruṣasya yāḥ
bhavanty eva hi tat-kāle
yathānicchor viparyayāḥ

āyuḥ—longevity; *śrīḥ*—opulence; *kīrtiḥ*—fame; *aiśvaryam*—power; *āśiṣaḥ*—benedictions; *puruṣasya*—of the living entity; *yāḥ*—which; *bhavanti*—arise; *eva*—indeed; *hi*—certainly; *tat-kāle*—at that proper time; *yathā*—just as; *anicchoḥ*—of one not desiring; *viparyayāḥ*—reverse conditions.

TRANSLATION

Just as a person not inclined to die must nonetheless give up his longevity, opulence, fame and everything else at the time of death, so, at the appointed time of victory, one can gain all these when the Supreme Lord awards them by His mercy.

PURPORT

It is not good to be falsely puffed up, saying that by one's own effort one has become opulent, learned, beautiful and so on. All such good fortune is achieved through the mercy of the Lord. From another point of view, no one wants to die, and no one wants to be poor or ugly. Therefore, why does the living entity, against his will, receive such unwanted troubles? It is due to the mercy or chastisement of the Supreme Personality of Godhead that one gains or loses everything material. No one is independent; everyone is dependent on the mercy or chastisement of the Supreme Lord. There is a common saying in Bengal that the Lord has ten hands. This means that He has control everywhere—in the eight directions and up and down. If He wants to take everything away from us with His ten hands, we cannot protect anything with our two hands. Similarly, if He wants to bestow benedictions upon us with His ten hands, we cannot factually receive them all with our two hands; in other words, the benedictions exceed our ambitions. The conclusion is that even though we do not wish to be separated from our possessions, sometimes the Lord forcibly takes them from us; and sometimes He showers such benedictions upon us that we are unable to receive them all. Therefore either in opulence or in distress we are not independent; everything is dependent on the sweet will of the Supreme Personality of Godhead.

TEXT 14

तस्मादकीर्तियशसोर्जयापजययोरपि ।
समः स्यात् सुखदुःखाभ्यां मृत्युजीवितयोस्तथा ॥ १४ ॥

tasmād akīrti-yaśasor
jayāpajayayor api
samaḥ syāt sukha-duḥkhābhyāṁ
mṛtyu-jīvitayos tathā

tasmāt—therefore (because of being fully dependent on the pleasure of the Supreme Personality of Godhead); *akīrti*—of defamation; *yaśasoḥ*—and fame; *jaya*—of victory; *apajayayoḥ*—and defeat; *api*—even; *samaḥ*—equal; *syāt*—one should be; *sukha-duḥkhābhyām*—with the distress and happiness; *mṛtyu*—of death; *jīvitayoḥ*—or of living; *tathā*—as well as.

TRANSLATION

Since everything is dependent on the supreme will of the Personality of Godhead, one should be equipoised in fame and defamation, victory and defeat, life and death. In their effects, represented as happiness and distress, one should maintain oneself in equilibrium, without anxiety.

TEXT 15

सत्त्वं रजस्तम इति प्रकृतेर्नात्मनो गुणाः ।
तत्र साक्षिणमात्मानं यो वेद स न बध्यते ॥ १५ ॥

sattvaṁ rajas tama iti
prakṛter nātmano guṇāḥ
tatra sākṣiṇam ātmānaṁ
yo veda sa na badhyate

sattvam—the mode of goodness; *rajaḥ*—the mode of passion; *tamaḥ*—the mode of ignorance; *iti*—thus; *prakṛteḥ*—of the material nature; *na*—not; *ātmanaḥ*—of the spirit soul; *guṇāḥ*—the qualities; *tatra*—in such a position;

sākṣiṇam—an observer; *ātmānam*—the self; *yaḥ*—anyone who; *veda*—knows; *saḥ*—he; *na*—not; *badhyate*—is bound.

TRANSLATION

One who knows that the three qualities—goodness, passion and ignorance—are not qualities of the soul but qualities of material nature, and who knows that the pure soul is simply an observer of the actions and reactions of these qualities, should be understood to be a liberated person. He is not bound by these qualities.

PURPORT

As the Lord explains in *Bhagavad-gītā* (18.54):

brahma-bhūtaḥ prasannātmā
na śocati na kāṅkṣati
samaḥ sarveṣu bhūteṣu
mad-bhaktiṁ labhate parām

"One who is transcendentally situated at once realizes the Supreme Brahman and becomes fully joyful. He never laments or desires to have anything; he is equally disposed to every living entity. In that state he attains pure devotional service unto Me." When one attains self-realization, the *brahma-bhūta* stage, one knows that whatever happens during his life is due to the contamination of the modes of material nature. The living being, the pure soul, has nothing to do with these modes. In the midst of the hurricane of the material world, everything changes very quickly, but if one remains silent and simply observes the actions and reactions of the hurricane, he is understood to be liberated. The real qualification of the liberated soul is that he remains Kṛṣṇa conscious, undisturbed by the actions and reactions of the material energy. Such a liberated person is always jubilant. He never laments or aspires for anything. Since everything is supplied by the Supreme Lord, the living entity, being fully dependent on Him, should not protest or accept anything in terms of his personal sense gratification; rather, he should receive everything as the mercy of the Lord and remain steady in all circumstances.

TEXT 16

पश्य मां निर्जितं शत्रु वृक्णायुधभुजं मृधे।
घटमानं यथाशक्ति तव प्राणजिहीर्षया ॥ १६ ॥

paśya māṁ nirjitaṁ śatru
vṛkṇāyudha-bhujaṁ mṛdhe
ghaṭamānaṁ yathā-śakti
tava prāṇa-jihīrṣayā

paśya—look; *mām*—at me; *nirjitam*—already defeated; *śatru*—O enemy; *vṛkṇa*—cut off; *āyudha*—my weapon; *bhujam*—and my arm; *mṛdhe*—in this fight; *ghaṭamānam*—still trying; *yathā-śakti*—according to my ability; *tava*—of you; *prāṇa*—the life; *jihīrṣayā*—with the desire to take away.

TRANSLATION

O my enemy, just look at me. I have already been defeated, for my weapon and arm have been cut to pieces. You have already overwhelmed me, but nonetheless, with a desire to kill you, I am trying my best to fight. I am not at all morose, even under such adverse conditions. Therefore you should give up your moroseness and continue fighting.

PURPORT

Vṛtrāsura was so great and powerful that in effect he was acting as the spiritual master of Indra. Although Vṛtrāsura was on the verge of defeat, he was not at all affected. He knew that he was going to be defeated by Indra, and he voluntarily accepted that, but since he was supposed to be Indra's enemy, he tried his best to kill Indra. Thus he performed his duty. One should perform his duty under all circumstances, even though one may know what the result will be.

TEXT 17

प्राणग्लहोऽयं समर इष्वक्षो वाहनासनः ।
अत्र न ज्ञायतेऽमुष्य जयोऽमुष्य पराजयः ॥ १७ ॥

prāṇa-glaho'yaṁ samara
iṣv-akṣo vāhanāsanaḥ
atra na jñāyate'muṣya
jayo'muṣya parājayaḥ

prāṇa-glahaḥ—life is the stake; *ayam*—this; *samaraḥ*—battle; *iṣu-akṣaḥ*—the arrows are the dice; *vāhana-āsanaḥ*—the carriers such as the horses and elephants are the game board; *atra*—here (in this gambling match); *na*—not; *jñāyate*—is known; *amuṣya*—of that one; *jayaḥ*—victory; *amuṣya*—of that one; *parājayaḥ*—defeat.

TRANSLATION

O my enemy, consider this battle a gambling match in which our lives are the stakes, the arrows are the dice, and the animals acting as carriers are the game board. No one can understand who will be defeated and who will be victorious. It all depends on providence.

TEXT 18

श्रीशुक उवाच
इन्द्रो वृत्रवचः श्रुत्वा गतालीकमपूजयत् ।
गृहीतवज्रः प्रहसंस्तमाह गतविस्मयः ॥ १८ ॥

śrī-śuka uvāca
indro vṛtra-vacaḥ śrutvā
gatālīkam apūjayat
gṛhīta-vajraḥ prahasaṁs
tam āha gata-vismayaḥ

śrī-śukaḥ uvāca—Śrī Śukadeva Gosvāmī said; *indraḥ*—King Indra; *vṛtra-vacaḥ*—the words of Vṛtrāsura; *śrutvā*—hearing; *gata-alīkam*—without duplicity; *apūjayat*—worshiped; *gṛhīta-vajraḥ*—taking up the thunderbolt; *prahasan*—smiling; *tam*—unto Vṛtrāsura; *āha*—said; *gata-vismayaḥ*—giving up his wonder.

TRANSLATION

Śukadeva Gosvāmī said: Hearing the straightforward, instructive words of Vṛtrāsura, King Indra praised him and again took the thunderbolt in his hand. Without bewilderment or duplicity, he then smiled and spoke to Vṛtrāsura as follows.

PURPORT

King Indra, the greatest of the demigods, was astonished to hear the instructions of Vṛtrāsura, who was supposed to be a demon. He was struck with wonder that a demon could speak so intelligently. Then he remembered great devotees like Prahlāda Mahārāja and Bali Mahārāja, who had been born in the families of demons, and thus he came to his senses. Even so-called demons sometimes have exalted devotion for the Supreme Personality of Godhead. Therefore Indra smiled reassuringly at Vṛtrāsura.

TEXT 19

इन्द्र उवाच
अहो दानव सिद्धोऽसि यस्य ते मतिरीदृशी ।
भक्तः सर्वात्मनात्मानं सुहृदं जगदीश्वरम् ॥ १९ ॥

indra uvāca
aho dānava siddho'si
yasya te matir īdṛśī
bhaktaḥ sarvātmanātmānaṁ
suhṛdaṁ jagad-īśvaram

indraḥ uvāca—Indra said; *aho*—hello; *dānava*—O demon; *siddhaḥ asi*—you are now perfect; *yasya*—whose; *te*—your; *matiḥ*—consciousness; *īdṛśī*—such as this; *bhaktaḥ*—a great devotee; *sarva-ātmanā*—without diversion; *ātmānam*—to the Supersoul; *suhṛdam*—the greatest friend; *jagat-īśvaram*—to the Supreme Personality of Godhead.

TRANSLATION

Indra said: O great demon, I see by your discrimination and endurance in devotional service, despite your dangerous position, that you are a perfect devotee of the Supreme Personality of Godhead, the Supersoul and friend of everyone.

PURPORT

As stated in *Bhagavad-gītā* (6.22):

yaṁ labdhvā cāparaṁ lābhaṁ
manyate nādhikaṁ tataḥ
yasmin sthito na duḥkhena
guruṇāpi vicālyate

"Established in Kṛṣṇa consciousness, one never departs from the truth, and upon gaining this he thinks there is no greater gain. Being situated in such a position, one is never shaken, even in the midst of the greatest difficulty." An unalloyed devotee is never disturbed by any kind of trying circumstance. Indra was surprised to see that Vṛtrāsura, undisturbed, was fixed in devotional service to the Lord, for such a mentality is impossible for a demon. However, by the grace of the Supreme Personality of Godhead, anyone can become an exalted devotee (*striyo vaiśyās tathā śūdrās te'pi yānti paraṁ gatim*). An unalloyed devotee is sure to return home, back to Godhead.

TEXT 20

भवानतार्षीन्मायां वै वैष्णवीं जनमोहिनीम् ।
यद् विहायासुरं भावं महापुरुषतां गतः ॥ २० ॥

bhavān atārṣīn māyāṁ vai
vaiṣṇavīṁ jana-mohinīm
yad vihāyāsuraṁ bhāvaṁ
mahā-puruṣatāṁ gataḥ

bhavān—your good self; *atārṣīt*—has surmounted; *māyām*—the illusory energy; *vai*—indeed; *vaiṣṇavīm*—of Lord Viṣṇu; *jana-mohinīm*—which deludes the mass of people; *yat*—since; *vihāya*—giving up; *āsuram*—of the demons; *bhāvam*—the mentality; *mahā-puruṣatām*—the position of an exalted devotee; *gataḥ*—obtained.

TRANSLATION

You have surmounted the illusory energy of Lord Viṣṇu, and because of this liberation, you have given up the demoniac mentality and have attained the position of an exalted devotee.

PURPORT

Lord Viṣṇu is the *mahā-puruṣa.* Therefore one who becomes a Vaiṣṇava attains the position of a *mahā-pauruṣya.* This position was attained by Mahārāja Parīkṣit. It is said in the *Padma Purāṇa* that the distinction between a demigod and a demon is that a demigod is a devotee of Lord Viṣṇu whereas a demon is just the opposite: *viṣṇu-bhaktaḥ smṛto daiva āsuras tad-viparyayaḥ.* Vṛtrāsura was considered a demon, but actually he was more than qualified as a devotee, or *mahā-pauruṣya.* If one somehow becomes a devotee of the Supreme Lord, whatever his position, he can be brought to the position of a perfect person. This is possible if an unalloyed devotee tries to serve the Lord by delivering him in this way. Therefore Śukadeva Gosvāmī says in *Śrīmad-Bhāgavatam* (2.4.18):

kirāta-hūṇāndhra-pulinda-pulkaśā
ābhīra-śumbhā yavanāḥ khasādayaḥ
ye 'nye ca pāpā yad-apāśrayāśrayāḥ
śudhyanti tasmai prabhaviṣṇave namaḥ

"Kirātas, Hūṇas, Āndhras, Pulindas, Pulkaśas, Ābhīras, Śumbhas, Yavanas and members of the Khasa races, and even others addicted to sinful acts can be purified by taking shelter of the devotees of the Lord, for He is the supreme power. I beg to offer my respectful obeisances unto Him." Anyone can be purified if he takes shelter of a pure devotee and molds his character according to the pure devotee's direction. Then, even if one is a Kirāta, Āndhra, Pulinda or whatever, he can be purified and elevated to the position of a *mahā-pauruṣya.*

TEXT 21

खल्विदं महदाश्चर्यं यद् रजःप्रकृतेस्तव ।
वासुदेवे भगवति सत्त्वात्मनि दृढा मतिः ॥ २१ ॥

khalv idaṁ mahad āścaryaṁ
yad rajaḥ-prakṛtes tava
vāsudeve bhagavati
sattvātmani dṛḍhā matiḥ

khalu—indeed; *idam*—this; *mahat āścaryam*—great wonder; *yat*—which; *rajaḥ*—influenced by the mode of passion; *prakṛteḥ*—whose nature; *tava*—of you; *vāsudeve*—in Lord Kṛṣṇa; *bhagavati*—the Supreme Personality of Godhead; *sattva-ātmani*—who is situated in pure goodness; *dṛḍhā*—firm; *matiḥ*—consciousness.

TRANSLATION

O Vṛtrāsura, demons are generally conducted by the mode of passion. Therefore, what a great wonder it is that although you are a demon, you have adopted the mentality of a devotee and have fixed your mind on the Supreme Personality of Godhead, Vāsudeva, who is always situated in pure goodness.

PURPORT

King Indra wondered how Vṛtrāsura could have been elevated to the position of an exalted devotee. As for Prahlāda Mahārāja, he was initiated by

Nārada Muni, and therefore it was possible for him to become a great devotee, although he was born in a family of demons. For Vṛtrāsura, however, Indra could not detect such causes. Therefore he was struck with wonder that Vṛtrāsura was such an exalted devotee that he could fix his mind without deviation upon the lotus feet of Lord Kṛṣṇa, Vāsudeva.

TEXT 22

यस्य भक्तिर्भगवति हरौ निःश्रेयसेश्वरे ।
विक्रीडतोऽमृताम्भोधौ किं क्षुद्रैः खातकोदकैः ॥ २२ ॥

yasya bhaktir bhagavati
harau niḥśreyaseśvare
vikrīḍato'mṛtāmbhodhau
kiṁ kṣudraiḥ khātakodakaiḥ

yasya—of whom; *bhaktiḥ*—devotional service; *bhagavati*—to the Supreme Personality of Godhead; *harau*—Lord Hari; *niḥśreyasa-īśvare*—the controller of the supreme perfection of life, or supreme liberation; *vikrīḍataḥ*—swimming or playing; *amṛta-ambhodhau*—in the ocean of nectar; *kim*—what is the use; *kṣudraiḥ*—with small; *khātaka-udakaiḥ*—ditches of water.

TRANSLATION

A person fixed in the devotional service of the Supreme Lord, Hari, the Lord of the highest auspiciousness, swims in the ocean of nectar. For him what is the use of the water in small ditches?

PURPORT

Vṛtrāsura has formerly prayed (*Bhāg.* 6.11.25), *na nāka-pṛṣṭhaṁ na ca pārameṣṭhyaṁ na sārva-bhaumaṁ na rasādhipatyam.* "I do not want the facilities for happiness on Brahmaloka, Svargaloka or even Dhruvaloka, not to speak of this earth or the lower planets. I simply want to return home, back to Godhead." This is the determination of a pure devotee. A pure devotee is never attracted to any exalted position within this material world. He simply wants to associate with the Supreme Personality of Godhead like the inhabitants of Vṛndāvana—Śrīmatī Rādhārāṇī, the *gopīs,* Kṛṣṇa's father and mother (Nanda Mahārāja and Yaśodā), Kṛṣṇa's friends and Kṛṣṇa's servants. He wants to associate with Kṛṣṇa's atmosphere of Vṛndāvana's beauty. These are the highest ambitions of a devotee of Kṛṣṇa. Devotees of Lord Viṣṇu may aspire for a position in Vaikuṇṭhaloka, but a devotee of Kṛṣṇa never aspires even for the facilities of Vaikuṇṭha; he wants to return to Goloka Vṛndāvana and associate with Lord Kṛṣṇa in His eternal pastimes. Any material happiness is like water in a ditch, whereas the spiritual happiness eternally enjoyed in the spiritual world is like an ocean of nectar in which a devotee wants to swim.

TEXT 23

श्रीशुक उवाच
इति ब्रुवाणावन्योन्यं धर्मजिज्ञासया नृप ।
युयुधाते महावीर्याविन्द्रवृत्रौ युधाम्पती ॥ २३ ॥

śrī-śuka uvāca
iti bruvāṇāv anyonyaṁ
dharma-jijñāsayā nṛpa
yuyudhāte mahā-vīryāv
indra-vṛtrau yudhām patī

śrī-śukaḥ uvāca—Śrī Śukadeva Gosvāmī said; *iti*—thus; *bruvāṇau*—speaking; *anyonyam*—to one another; *dharma-jijñāsayā*—with a desire to know the supreme, ultimate religious principle (devotional service); *nṛpa*—O King; *yuyudhāte*—fought; *mahā-vīryau*—both very powerful; *indra*—King Indra; *vṛtrau*—and Vṛtrāsura; *yudhām patī*—both great military commanders.

TRANSLATION

Śrī Śukadeva Gosvāmī said: Vṛtrāsura and King Indra spoke about devotional service even on the battlefield, and then as a matter of duty they again began fighting. My dear King, both of them were great fighters and were equally powerful.

TEXT 24

आविध्य परिघं वृत्रः कार्ष्णायसमरिन्दमः ।
इन्द्राय प्राहिणोद् घोरं वामहस्तेन मारिष ॥ २४ ॥

āvidhya parighaṁ vṛtraḥ
kārṣṇāyasam arindamaḥ
indrāya prāhiṇod ghoraṁ
vāma-hastena māriṣa

āvidhya—whirling; *parigham*—the club; *vṛtraḥ*—Vṛtrāsura; *kārṣṇa-ayasam*—made of iron; *arim-damaḥ*—who was competent to subdue his enemy; *indrāya*—at Indra; *prāhiṇot*—threw; *ghoram*—very fearful; *vāma-hastena*—with his left hand; *māriṣa*—O best of kings, Mahārāja Parīkṣit.

TRANSLATION

O Mahārāja Parīkṣit, Vṛtrāsura, who was completely able to subdue his enemy, took his iron club, whirled it around, aimed it at Indra and then threw it at him with his left hand.

TEXT 25

स तु वृत्रस्य परिघं करं च करभोपमम् ।
चिच्छेद युगपद् देवो वज्रेण शतपर्वणा ॥ २५ ॥

sa tu vṛtrasya parighaṁ
karaṁ ca karabhopamam
ciccheda yugapad devo
vajreṇa śata-parvaṇā

saḥ—he (King Indra); *tu*—however; *vṛtrasya*—of Vṛtrāsura; *parigham*—the iron club; *karam*—his hand; *ca*—and; *karabha-upamam*—as strong as the trunk of an elephant; *ciccheda*—cut to pieces; *yugapat*—simultaneously; *devaḥ*—Lord Indra; *vajreṇa*—with the thunderbolt; *śata-parvaṇā*—having one hundred joints.

TRANSLATION

With his thunderbolt named Śataparvan, Indra simultaneously cut to pieces Vṛtrāsura's club and his remaining hand.

TEXT 26

दोर्भ्यामुत्कृत्तमूलाभ्यां बभौ रक्तस्रवोऽसुरः ।
छिन्नपक्षो यथा गोत्रः खाद् भ्रष्टो वज्रिणा हतः ॥ २६ ॥

dorbhyām utkṛtta-mūlābhyāṁ
babhau rakta-sravo'suraḥ
chinna-pakṣo yathā gotraḥ
khād bhraṣṭo vajriṇā hataḥ

dorbhyām—from the two arms; *utkṛtta-mūlābhyām*—cut from the very root; *babhau*—was; *rakta-sravaḥ*—profusely discharging blood; *asuraḥ*—Vṛtrāsura; *chinna-pakṣaḥ*—whose wings are cut; *yathā*—just as; *gotraḥ*—a mountain; *khāt*—from the sky; *bhraṣṭaḥ*—falling; *vajriṇā*—by Indra, the carrier of the thunderbolt; *hataḥ*—struck.

TRANSLATION

Vṛtrāsura, bleeding profusely, his two arms cut off at their roots, looked very beautiful, like a flying mountain whose wings have been cut to pieces by Indra.

PURPORT

It appears from the statement of this verse that sometimes there are flying mountains and that their wings are cut by the thunderbolt of Indra. Vṛtrāsura's huge body resembled such a mountain.

TEXTS 27–29

महाप्राणो महावीर्यो महासर्प इव द्विपम् ।
कृत्वाधरां हनुं भूमौ दैत्यो दिव्युत्तरां हनुम् ।
नभोगम्भीरवक्त्रेण लेलिहोल्बणजिह्वया ॥ २७ ॥
दंष्ट्राभिः कालकल्पाभिर्ग्रसन्निव जगत्त्रयम् ।
अतिमात्रमहाकाय आक्षिपंस्तरसा गिरीन् ॥ २८ ॥
गिरिराट् पादचारीव पद्भ्यां निर्जरयन् महीम् ।
जग्रास स समासाद्य वज्रिणं सहवाहनम् ॥ २९ ॥

mahā-prāṇo mahā-vīryo
mahā-sarpa iva dvipam
kṛtvādharāṁ hanuṁ bhūmau
daityo divy uttarāṁ hanum
nabho-gambhīra-vaktreṇa
leliholbaṇa-jihvayā

daṁṣṭrābhiḥ kāla-kalpābhir
grasann iva jagat-trayam
atimātra-mahā-kāya
ākṣipaṁs tarasā girīn

giri-rāṭ pāda-cārīva
padbhyāṁ nirjarayan mahīm
jagrāsa sa samāsādya
vajriṇaṁ saha-vāhanam

mahā-prāṇaḥ—very great in bodily strength; *mahā-vīryaḥ*—showing uncommon prowess; *mahā-sarpaḥ*—the biggest snake; *iva*—like; *dvipam*—an elephant; *kṛtvā*—placing; *adharām*—the lower; *hanum*—jaw; *bhūmau*—on the ground; *daityaḥ*—the demon; *divi*—in the sky; *uttarām hanum*—the upper jaw; *nabhaḥ*—like the sky; *gambhīra*—deep; *vaktreṇa*—with his mouth; *leliha*—like a snake; *ulbaṇa*—fearful; *jihvayā*—with a tongue; *daṁṣṭrābhiḥ*—with teeth; *kāla-kalpābhiḥ*—exactly like the time factor, or death; *grasan*—devouring; *iva*—as if; *jagat-trayam*—the three worlds; *ati-mātra*—very high; *mahā-kāyaḥ*—whose great body; *ākṣipan*—shaking; *tarasā*—with great force; *girīn*—the mountains; *giri-rāṭ*—the Himalaya Mountains; *pāda-cārī*—moving on foot; *iva*—as if; *padbhyām*—by his feet; *nirjarayan*—crushing; *mahīm*—the surface of the world; *jagrāsa*—swallowed; *saḥ*—he; *samāsādya*—reaching; *vajriṇam*—Indra, who carries the thunderbolt; *saha-vāhanam*—with his carrier, the elephant.

TRANSLATION

Vṛtrāsura was very powerful in physical strength and influence. He placed his lower jaw on the ground and his upper jaw in the sky. His mouth became very deep, like the sky itself, and his tongue resembled a large serpent. With his fearful, deathlike teeth, he seemed to be trying to devour the entire universe. Thus assuming a gigantic body, the great demon Vṛtrāsura shook even the mountains and began crushing the surface of the earth with his legs, as if he were the Himalayas walking about. He came before Indra and swallowed him and Airāvata, his carrier, just as a big python might swallow an elephant.

TEXT 30

वृत्रग्रस्तं तमालोक्य सप्रजापतयः सुराः ।
हा कष्टमिति निर्विण्णाश्चुक्रुशुः समहर्षयः ॥ ३० ॥

vṛtra-grastaṁ tam ālokya
saprajāpatayaḥ surāḥ

hā kaṣṭam iti nirviṇṇāś
cukruśuḥ samaharṣayaḥ

vṛtra-grastam—swallowed by Vṛtrāsura; *tam*—him (Indra); *ālokya*—seeing; *sa-prajāpatayaḥ*—with Lord Brahmā and other *prajāpatis; surāḥ*—all the demigods; *hā*—alas; *kaṣṭam*—what a tribulation; *iti*—thus; *nirviṇṇāḥ*—being very morose; *cukruśuḥ*—lamented; *sa-mahā-ṛṣayaḥ*—with the great sages.

TRANSLATION

When the demigods, along with Brahmā, other prajāpatis and other great saintly persons, saw that Indra had been swallowed by the demon, they became very morose. "Alas," they lamented. "What a calamity! What a calamity!"

TEXT 31

निगीर्णोऽप्यसुरेन्द्रेण न ममारोदरं गतः ।
महापुरुषसन्नद्धो योगमायाबलेन च ॥ ३१ ॥

nigīrṇo'py asurendreṇa
na mamārodaraṁ gataḥ
mahāpuruṣa-sannaddho
yoga-māyā-balena ca

nigīrṇaḥ—swallowed; *api*—although; *asura-indreṇa*—by the best of the demons, Vṛtrāsura; *na*—not; *mamāra*—died; *udaram*—the abdomen; *gataḥ*—reaching; *mahā-puruṣa*—by the armor of the Supreme Lord, Nārāyaṇa; *sannaddhaḥ*—being protected; *yoga-māyā-balena*—by the mystic power that Indra himself possessed; *ca*—also.

TRANSLATION

The protective armor of Nārāyaṇa, which Indra possessed, was identical with Nārāyaṇa Himself, the Supreme Personality of Godhead. Protected by that armor and by his own mystic power, King Indra, although swallowed by Vṛtrāsura, did not die within the demon's belly.

TEXT 32

भित्त्वा वज्रेण तत्कुक्षिं निष्क्रम्य बलभिद् विभुः ।
उच्चकर्त शिरः शत्रोर्गिरिश्रृङ्गमिवौजसा ॥ ३२ ॥

bhittvā vajreṇa tat-kukṣiṁ
niṣkramya bala-bhid vibhuḥ
uccakarta śiraḥ śatror
giri-śṛṅgam ivaujasā

bhittvā—piercing; *vajreṇa*—by the thunderbolt; *tat-kukṣim*—the abdomen of Vṛtrāsura; *niṣkramya*—getting out; *bala-bhit*—the slayer of the demon Bala; *vibhuḥ*—the powerful Lord Indra; *uccakarta*—cut off; *śiraḥ*—the head; *śatroḥ*—of the enemy; *giri-śṛṅgam*—the peak of a mountain; *iva*—like; *ojasā*—with great force.

TRANSLATION

With his thunderbolt, King Indra, who was also extremely powerful, pierced through Vṛtrāsura's abdomen and came out. Indra, the killer of the demon Bala, then immediately cut off Vṛtrāsura's head, which was as high as the peak of a mountain.

TEXT 33

वज्रस्तु तत्कन्धरमाशुवेगः
कृन्तन् समन्तात् परिवर्तमानः ।
न्यपातयत् तावदहर्गणेन
यो ज्योतिषामयने वार्त्रहत्ये ॥ ३३ ॥

vajras tu tat-kandharam āśu-vegaḥ
kṛntan samantāt parivartamānaḥ
nyapātayat tāvad ahar-gaṇena
yo jyotiṣām ayane vārtra-hatye

vajraḥ—the thunderbolt; *tu*—but; *tat-kandharam*—his neck; *āśu-vegaḥ*—although very fast; *kṛntan*—cutting; *samantāt*—all around; *parivartamānaḥ*—revolving; *nyapātayat*—caused to fall; *tāvat*—so many; *ahaḥ-gaṇena*—by days; *yaḥ*—which; *jyotiṣām*—of the luminaries like the sun and moon; *ayane*—in moving to both sides of the equator; *vārtra-hatye*—at the time suitable for killing Vṛtrāsura.

TRANSLATION

Although the thunderbolt revolved around Vṛtrāsura's neck with great speed, separating his head from his body took one complete year—360

days, the time in which the sun, moon and other luminaries complete a northern and southern journey. Then, at the suitable time for Vṛtrāsura to be killed, his head fell to the ground.

TEXT 34

तदा च खे दुन्दुभयो विनेदु-
गन्धर्वसिद्धाः समहर्षिसङ्घाः ।
वार्त्रघ्नलिङ्गैस्तमभिष्टुवाना
मन्त्रैर्मुदा कुसुमैरभ्यवर्षन् ॥ ३४ ॥

tadā ca khe dundubhayo vinedur
gandharva-siddhāḥ samaharṣi-saṅghāḥ
vārtra-ghna-liṅgais tam abhiṣṭuvānā
mantrair mudā kusumair abhyavarṣan

tadā—at that time; *ca*—also; *khe*—in the higher planetary systems in the sky; *dundubhayaḥ*—the kettledrums; *vineduḥ*—sounded; *gandharva*—the Gandharvas; *siddhāḥ*—and the Siddhas; *sa-maharṣi-saṅghāḥ*—with the assembly of saintly persons; *vārtra-ghna-liṅgaiḥ*—celebrating the prowess of the killer of Vṛtrāsura; *tam*—him (Indra); *abhiṣṭuvānāḥ*—praising; *mantraiḥ*—by various *mantras; mudā*—with great pleasure; *kusumaiḥ*—with flowers; *abhyavarṣan*—showered.

TRANSLATION

When Vṛtrāsura was killed, the Gandharvas and Siddhas in the heavenly planets beat kettledrums in jubilation. With Vedic hymns they celebrated the prowess of Indra, the killer of Vṛtrāsura, praising Indra and showering flowers upon him with great pleasure.

TEXT 35

वृत्रस्य देहान्निष्क्रान्तमात्मज्योतिररिन्दम ।
पश्यतां सर्वदेवानामलोकं समपद्यत ॥ ३५ ॥

vṛtrasya dehān niṣkrāntam
ātma-jyotir arindama
paśyatāṁ sarva-devānām
alokaṁ samapadyata

vṛtrasya—of Vṛtrāsura; *dehāt*—from the body; *niṣkrāntam*—coming out; *ātma-jyotiḥ*—the spirit soul, which was as brilliant as the effulgence of Brahman; *arim-dama*—O King Parīkṣit, subduer of enemies; *paśyatām*—were watching; *sarva-devānām*—while all the demigods; *alokam*—the supreme abode, filled with the Brahman effulgence; *samapadyata*—achieved.

TRANSLATION

O King Parīkṣit, subduer of enemies, the living spark then came forth from Vṛtrāsura's body and returned home, back to Godhead. While all the demigods looked on, he entered the transcendental world to become an associate of Lord Saṅkarṣaṇa.

PURPORT

Śrīla Viśvanātha Cakravartī Ṭhākura explains that Indra, not Vṛtrāsura, was actually killed. He says that when Vṛtrāsura swallowed King Indra and his carrier, the elephant, he thought, "Now I have killed Indra, and therefore there is no more need of fighting. Now let me return home, back to Godhead." Thus he stopped all his bodily activities and became situated in trance. Taking advantage of the silence of Vṛtrāsura's body, Indra pierced the demon's abdomen, and because of Vṛtrāsura's trance, Indra was able to come out. Now, Vṛtrāsura was in *yoga-samādhi,* and therefore although King Indra wanted to cut his throat, the demon's neck was so stiff that Indra's thunderbolt took 360 days to cut it to pieces. Actually it was the body left by Vṛtrāsura that was cut to pieces by Indra; Vṛtrāsura himself was not killed. In his original consciousness, Vṛtrāsura returned home, back to Godhead, to become an associate of Lord Saṅkarṣaṇa. Here the word *alokam* means the transcendental world, Vaikuṇṭhaloka, where Saṅkarṣaṇa eternally resides.

Thus end the Bhaktivedanta purports of the Sixth Canto, Twelfth Chapter, of the Śrīmad-Bhāgavatam, *entitled "Vṛtrāsura's Glorious Death."*

CHAPTER THIRTEEN

King Indra Afflicted by Sinful Reaction

This chapter describes Indra's fear at having killed a *brāhmaṇa* (Vṛtrāsura), and it also describes how he fled and was saved by the grace of Lord Viṣṇu.

When all the demigods requested Indra to kill Vṛtrāsura, he refused because Vṛtrāsura was a *brāhmaṇa.* The demigods, however, encouraged Indra not to fear killing him because Indra was protected by the Nārāyaṇa-kavaca, or the Supreme Personality of Godhead Himself, Lord Nārāyaṇa. Even by a glimpse of the chanting of Nārāyaṇa's name, one becomes free from all the sinful reactions of killing a woman, a cow or a *brāhmaṇa.* The demigods advised Indra to perform an *aśvamedha* sacrifice, by which Nārāyaṇa would be pleased, for the performer of such a sacrifice is not implicated in sinful reactions even if he kills the entire universe.

Following this instruction from the demigods, King Indra fought Vṛtrāsura, but when Vṛtrāsura was killed, everyone was satisfied but King Indra, who knew Vṛtrāsura's position. This is the nature of a great personality. Even if a great personality acquires some opulence, he is always ashamed and regretful if he acquires it illegally. Indra could understand that he was certainly entangled by sinful reactions for killing a *brāhmaṇa.* Indeed, he could see sinful reaction personified following him, and thus he fled here and there in fear, thinking of how to rid himself of his sins. He went to Mānasa-sarovara, and there, under the protection of the goddess of fortune, he meditated for one thousand years. During this time, Nahuṣa reigned over the heavenly planets as the representative of Indra. Unfortunately, however, he was attracted by the beauty of Indra's wife, Śacīdevī, and because of his sinful desire he had to accept the body of a serpent in his next life. Indra later performed a great sacrifice with the help of exalted *brāhmaṇas* and saints. In this way he was released from the reactions of his sinful killing of a *brāhmaṇa.*

TEXT 1

श्रीशुक उवाच

वृत्रे हते त्रयो लोका विना शक्रेण भूरिद ।

सपाला ह्यभवन् सद्यो विज्वरा निर्वृतेन्द्रियाः ॥ १ ॥

śrī-śuka uvāca
vṛtre hate trayo lokā
vinā śakreṇa bhūrida
sapālā hy abhavan sadyo
vijvarā nirvṛtendriyāḥ

śrī-śukaḥ uvāca—Śrī Śukadeva Gosvāmī said; *vṛtre hate*—when Vṛtrāsura was killed; *trayaḥ lokāḥ*—the three planetary systems (upper, middle and lower); *vinā*—except; *śakreṇa*—Indra, who is also called Śakra; *bhūri-da*—O Mahārāja Parīkṣit, giver of great charity; *sa-pālāḥ*—with the rulers of the various planets; *hi*—indeed; *abhavan*—became; *sadyaḥ*—immediately; *vijvarāḥ*—without fear of death; *nirvṛta*—very much pleased; *indriyāḥ*—whose senses.

TRANSLATION

Śrī Śukadeva Gosvāmī said: O King Parīkṣit, who are so charitably disposed, when Vṛtrāsura was killed, all the presiding deities and everyone else in the three planetary systems was immediately pleased and free from trouble—everyone, that is, except Indra.

TEXT 2

देवर्षिपितृभूतानि दैत्या देवानुगाः स्वयम् ।
प्रतिजग्मुः स्वधिष्ण्यानि ब्रह्मेशेन्द्रादयस्ततः ॥ २ ॥

devarṣi-pitṛ-bhūtāni
daityā devānugāḥ svayam
pratijagmuḥ sva-dhiṣṇyāni
brahmeśendrādayas tataḥ

deva—demigods; *ṛṣi*—great saintly persons; *pitṛ*—the inhabitants of Pitṛloka; *bhūtāni*—and the other living entities; *daityāḥ*—demons; *deva-anugāḥ*—the inhabitants of other planets following the principles of the demigods; *svayam*—independently (without asking permission from Indra); *pratijagmuḥ*—returned; *sva-dhiṣṇyāni*—to their respective planets and homes; *brahma*—Lord Brahmā; *īśa*—Lord Śiva; *indra-ādayaḥ*—and the demigods headed by Indra; *tataḥ*—thereafter.

TRANSLATION

Thereafter, the demigods, the great saintly persons, the inhabitants of Pitṛloka and Bhūtaloka, the demons, the followers of the demigods, and

also Lord Brahmā, Lord Śiva and the demigods subordinate to Indra all returned to their respective homes. While departing, however, no one spoke to Indra.

PURPORT

In this connection Śrīla Viśvanātha Cakravartī Ṭhākura comments:

brahmeśendrādaya iti; indrasya sva-dhiṣṇya-gamanaṁ nopapadyate vṛtra-vadha-kṣaṇa eva brahma-hatyopadrava-prāpteḥ; tasmāt tata ity anena mānasa-sarovarād āgatya pravartitād aśvamedhāt parata iti vyākhyeyam.

Lord Brahmā, Lord Śiva and the other demigods returned to their respective abodes, but Indra did not, for he was disturbed at having killed Vṛtrāsura, who was actually a *brāhmaṇa.* After killing Vṛtrāsura, Indra went to the Mānasa-sarovara Lake to become free from sinful reactions. When he left the lake, he performed an *aśvamedha-yajña* and then returned to his own abode.

TEXT 3

श्रीराजोवाच
इन्द्रस्यानिर्वृतेर्हेतुं श्रोतुमिच्छामि भो मुने ।
येनासन् सुखिनो देवा हरेर्दुःखं कुतोऽभवत् ॥ ३ ॥

śrī-rājovāca
indrasyānirvṛter hetuṁ
śrotum icchāmi bho mune
yenāsan sukhino devā
harer duḥkhaṁ kuto'bhavat

śrī-rājā uvāca—King Parīkṣit inquired; *indrasya*—of King Indra; *anirvṛteḥ*—of the moroseness; *hetum*—the reason; *śrotum*—to hear; *icchāmi*—I wish; *bhoḥ*—O my lord; *mune*—O great sage, Śukadeva Gosvāmī; *yena*—by which; *āsan*—were; *sukhinaḥ*—very happy; *devāḥ*—all the demigods; *hareḥ*—of Indra; *duḥkham*—moroseness; *kutaḥ*—from where; *abhavat*—was.

TRANSLATION

Mahārāja Parīkṣit inquired from Śukadeva Gosvāmī: O great sage, what was the reason for Indra's unhappiness? I wish to hear about this. When he killed Vṛtrāsura, all the demigods were extremely happy. Why, then, was Indra himself unhappy?

PURPORT

This, of course, is a very intelligent question. When a demon is killed, certainly all the demigods are happy. In this case, however, when all the demigods were happy because of Vṛtrāsura's having been killed, Indra was unhappy. Why? It may be suggested that Indra was unhappy because he knew that he had killed a great devotee and *brāhmaṇa.* Vṛtrāsura outwardly appeared to be a demon, but inwardly he was a great devotee and therefore a great *brāhmaṇa.*

Herein it is clearly indicated that a person who is not at all demoniac, such as Prahlāda Mahārāja and Bali Mahārāja, may outwardly be a demon or be born in a family of demons. Therefore in terms of real culture one should not be considered a demigod or demon simply according to birth. In his dealings while fighting with Indra, Vṛtrāsura proved himself a great devotee of the Supreme Personality of Godhead. Furthermore, as soon as he finished fighting with Indra and was apparently killed, Vṛtrāsura was transferred to Vaikuṇṭhaloka to become an associate of Saṅkarṣaṇa. Indra knew this, and therefore he was morose at having killed such a demon, who was actually a Vaiṣṇava or *brāhmaṇa.*

A Vaiṣṇava is already a *brāhmaṇa,* although a *brāhmaṇa* may not be a Vaiṣṇava. The *Padma Purāṇa* says:

ṣaṭ-karma-nipuṇo vipro
mantra-tantra-viśāradaḥ
avaiṣṇavo gurur na syād
vaiṣṇavaḥ śva-paco guruḥ

One may be a *brāhmaṇa* in terms of his culture and family and may be expert in Vedic knowledge (*mantra-tantra-viśāradaḥ*), but if he is not a Vaiṣṇava, he cannot be a *guru.* This means that an expert *brāhmaṇa* may not be a Vaiṣṇava, but a Vaiṣṇava is already a *brāhmaṇa.* A millionaire may very easily possess hundreds and thousands of dollars, but a person with hundreds and thousands of dollars is not necessarily a millionaire. Vṛtrāsura was a perfect Vaiṣṇava, and therefore he was also a *brāhmaṇa.*

TEXT 4

श्रीशुक उवाच
वृत्रविक्रमसंविग्नाः सर्वे देवाः सहर्षिभिः ।
तद्वधायार्थयन्निन्द्रं नैच्छद् भीतो बृहद्वधात् ॥४॥

śrī-śuka uvāca
vṛtra-vikrama-saṁvignāḥ
sarve devāḥ saharṣibhiḥ
tad-vadhāyārthayann indraṁ
naicchad bhīto bṛhad-vadhāt

śrī-śukaḥ uvāca—Śrī Śukadeva Gosvāmī said; *vṛtra*—of Vṛtrāsura; *vikrama*—by the powerful activities; *saṁvignāḥ*—being full of anxieties; *sarve*—all; *devāḥ*—the demigods; *saha ṛṣibhiḥ*—with the great sages; *tat-vadhāya*—for the killing of him; *ārthayan*—requested; *indram*—Indra; *na aicchat*—declined; *bhītaḥ*—being afraid; *bṛhat-vadhāt*—due to killing a *brāhmaṇa.*

TRANSLATION

Śrī Śukadeva Gosvāmī answered: When all the great sages and demigods were disturbed by the extraordinary power of Vṛtrāsura, they had assembled to ask Indra to kill him. Indra, however, being afraid of killing a brāhmaṇa, declined their request.

TEXT 5

इन्द्र उवाच
स्त्रीभूद्रुमजलैरेनो विश्वरूपवधोद्भवम् ।
विभक्तमनुगृह्णद्भिर्वृत्रहत्यां क्व मार्ज्म्यहम् ॥ ५ ॥

indra uvāca
strī-bhū-druma-jalair eno
viśvarūpa-vadhodbhavam
vibhaktam anugṛhṇadbhir
vṛtra-hatyāṁ kva mārjmy aham

indraḥ uvāca—King Indra replied; *strī*—by women; *bhū*—the earth; *druma*—the trees; *jalaiḥ*—and water; *enaḥ*—this (sin); *viśvarūpa*—of Viśvarūpa; *vadha*—from the killing; *udbhavam*—produced; *vibhaktam*—divided; *anugṛhṇadbhiḥ*—showing their favor (to me); *vṛtra-hatyām*—the killing of Vṛtra; *kva*—how; *mārjmi*—shall become free from; *aham*—I.

TRANSLATION

King Indra replied: When I killed Viśvarūpa, I received extensive sinful reactions, but I was favored by the women, land, trees and water, and

therefore I was able to divide the sin among them. But now if I kill Vṛtrāsura, another brāhmaṇa, how shall I free myself from the sinful reactions?

TEXT 6

श्रीशुक उवाच
ऋषयस्तदुपाकर्ण्य महेन्द्रमिदमब्रुवन् ।
याजयिष्याम भद्रं ते हयमेधेन मा स्म भैः ॥ ६ ॥

śrī-śuka uvāca
ṛṣayas tad upākarṇya
mahendram idam abruvan
yājayiṣyāma bhadraṁ te
hayamedhena mā sma bhaiḥ

śrī-śukaḥ uvāca—Śrī Śukadeva Gosvāmī said; *ṛṣayaḥ*—the great sages; *tat*—that; *upākarṇya*—hearing; *mahā-indram*—unto King Indra; *idam*—this; *abruvan*—spoke; *yājayiṣyāmaḥ*—we shall perform a great sacrifice; *bhadram*—good fortune; *te*—unto you; *hayamedhena*—by the horse sacrifice; *mā sma bhaiḥ*—do not be afraid.

TRANSLATION

Śrī Śukadeva Gosvāmī said: Hearing this, the great sages replied to King Indra, "O King of heaven, all good fortune unto you. Do not fear. We shall perform an aśvamedha sacrifice to release you from any sin you may accrue by killing the brāhmaṇa."

TEXT 7

हयमेधेन पुरुषं परमात्मानमीश्वरम् ।
इष्ट्वा नारायणं देवं मोक्ष्यसेऽपि जगद्वधात् ॥ ७ ॥

hayamedhena puruṣaṁ
paramātmānam īśvaram
iṣṭvā nārāyaṇaṁ devaṁ
mokṣyase'pi jagad-vadhāt

hayamedhena—by the sacrifice known as *aśvamedha; puruṣam*—the Supreme Person; *paramātmānam*—the Supersoul; *īśvaram*—the supreme controller; *iṣṭvā*—worshiping; *nārāyaṇam*—Lord Nārāyaṇa; *devam*—the Supreme Lord; *mokṣyase*—you will be liberated; *api*—even; *jagat-vadhāt*—from the sin for killing the whole world.

TRANSLATION

The ṛṣis continued: O King Indra, by performing an aśvamedha sacrifice and thereby pleasing the Supreme Personality of Godhead, who is the Supersoul, Lord Nārāyaṇa, the supreme controller, one can be relieved even of the sinful reactions for killing the entire world, not to speak of killing a demon like Vṛtrāsura.

TEXTS 8–9

ब्रह्महा पितृहा गोघ्नो मातृहाचार्यहाघवान् ।
श्वादः पुल्कसको वापि शुद्ध्येरन् यस्य कीर्तनात् ॥ ८ ॥

तमश्वमेधेन महामखेन
श्रद्धान्वितोऽस्माभिरनुष्ठितेन ।
हत्वापि सब्रह्मचराचरं त्वं
न लिप्यसे किं खलनिग्रहेण ॥ ९ ॥

brahma-hā pitṛ-hā go-ghno
mātṛ-hācārya-hāghavān
śvādaḥ pulkasako vāpi
śuddhyeran yasya kīrtanāt

tam aśvamedhena mahā-makhena
śraddhānvito'smābhir anuṣṭhitena
hatvāpi sabrahma-carācaraṁ tvaṁ
na lipyase kiṁ khala-nigraheṇa

brahma-hā—a person who has killed a *brāhmaṇa; pitṛ-hā*—a person who has killed his father; *go-ghnaḥ*—a person who has killed a cow; *mātṛ-hā*—a person who has killed his mother; *ācārya-hā*—a person who has killed his spiritual master; *agha-vān*—such a sinful person; *śva-adaḥ*—a dog-eater; *pulkasakaḥ*—a *caṇḍāla,* one who is less than a *śūdra; vā*—or; *api*—even; *śuddhyeran*—may be purified; *yasya*—of whom (Lord Nārāyaṇa); *kīrtanāt*—from chanting the holy name; *tam*—Him; *aśvamedhena*—by the *aśvamedha* sacrifice; *mahā-makhena*—the topmost of all sacrifices; *śraddhā-anvitaḥ*—

endowed with faith; *asmābhiḥ*—by us; *anuṣṭhitena*—conducted or managed; *hatvā*—killing; *api*—even; *sa-brahma-cara-acaram*—all the living entities, including the *brāhmaṇas; tvam*—you; *na*—not; *lipyase*—are contaminated; *kim*—what then; *khala-nigraheṇa*—by killing one disturbing demon.

TRANSLATION

One who has killed a brāhmaṇa, one who has killed a cow or one who has killed his father, mother or spiritual master can be immediately freed from all sinful reactions simply by chanting the holy name of Lord Nārāyaṇa. Other sinful persons, such as dog-eaters and caṇḍālas, who are less than śūdras, can also be freed in this way. But you are a devotee, and we shall help you by performing the great horse sacrifice. If you please Lord Nārāyaṇa in that way, why should you be afraid? You will be freed even if you kill the entire universe, including the brāhmaṇas, not to speak of killing a disturbing demon like Vṛtrāsura.

PURPORT

It is said in the Bṛhad-viṣṇu Purāṇa:

nāmno hi yāvatī śaktiḥ
pāpa-nirharaṇe hareḥ
tāvat kartuṁ na śaknoti
pātakaṁ pātakī naraḥ

Also, in the *Prema-vivarta* by Jagadānanda Paṇḍita it is said:

eka kṛṣṇa-nāme pāpīra yata pāpa-kṣaya
bahu janme sei pāpī karite nāraya

This means that by once chanting the holy name of the Lord, one can be freed from the reactions of more sins that he can even imagine performing. The holy name is so spiritually potent that simply by chanting the holy name one can be freed from the reactions to all sinful activities. What, then, is to be said of those who chant the holy name regularly or worship the Deity regularly? For such purified devotees, freedom from sinful reaction is certainly assured. This does not mean, however, that one should intentionally commit sinful acts and think himself free from the reactions because he is chanting the holy name. Such a mentality is a most abominable offense at the lotus feet of the holy name. *Nāmno balād yasya hi pāpa-buddhiḥ:* the Lord's holy name certainly has the potency to neutralize all sinful activities, but if one repeatedly and intentionally commits sins while chanting the holy name, he is most condemned.

These verses name the performers of various sinful deeds. In the *Manu-saṁhitā* the following names are given. A son begotten by a *brāhmaṇa* and born from the womb of a *śūdra* mother is called a *pāraśava* or *niṣāda,* a hunter accustomed to stealing. A son begotten by a *niṣāda* in the womb of a *śūdra* woman is called a *pukkasa.* A child begotten by a *kṣatriya* in the womb of the daughter of a *śūdra* is called an *ugra.* A child begotten by a *śūdra* in the womb of the daughter of a *kṣatriya* is called a *kṣattā.* A child begotten by a *kṣatriya* in the womb of a lower-class woman is called a *śvāda,* or dog-eater. All such offspring are considered extremely sinful, but the holy name of the Supreme Personality of Godhead is so strong that all of them can be purified simply by chanting the Hare Kṛṣṇa *mantra.*

The Hare Kṛṣṇa movement offers everyone a chance to be purified, regardless of birth or family. As confirmed in *Śrīmad-Bhāgavatam* (2.4.18):

kirāta-hūṇāndhra-pulinda-pulkaśā
ābhīra-śumbhā yavanāḥ khasādayaḥ
ye'nye ca pāpā yad-apāśrayāśrayāḥ
śudhyanti tasmai prabhaviṣṇave namaḥ

"Kirātas, Hūṇas, Āndhras, Pulindas, Pulkaśas, Ābhīras, Śumbhas, Yavanas, members of the Khasa races, and even others addicted to sinful acts can be purified by taking shelter of devotees of the Lord, for He is the supreme power. I beg to offer my respectful obeisances unto Him." Even such sinful persons can certainly all be purified if they chant the holy name of the Lord under the direction of a pure devotee.

Herein the sages encourage King Indra to kill Vṛtrāsura even at the risk of *brahma-hatyā,* the killing of a *brāhmaṇa,* and they guarantee to release him from sinful reactions by performing an *aśvamedha-yajña.* Such purposefully devised atonement, however, cannot relieve the performer of sinful acts. This will be seen from the following verse.

TEXT 10

श्रीशुक उवाच
एवं सञ्चोदितो विप्रैर्मरुत्वानहनद्रिपुम् ।
ब्रह्महत्या हते तस्मिन्नाससाद वृषाकपिम् ॥ १० ॥

śrī-śuka uvāca
evaṁ sañcodito viprair
marutvān ahanad ripum
brahma-hatyā hate tasminn
āsasāda vṛṣākapim

śrī-śukaḥ uvāca—Śrī Śukadeva Gosvāmī said; *evam*—thus; *sañcoditaḥ*—being encouraged; *vipraiḥ*—by the *brāhmaṇas; marutvān*—Indra; *ahanat*—killed; *ripum*—his enemy, Vṛtrāsura; *brahma-hatyā*—the sinful reaction for killing a *brāhmaṇa; hate*—was killed; *tasmin*—when he (Vṛtrāsura); *āsasāda*—approached; *vṛṣākapim*—Indra, who is also named Vṛṣākapi.

TRANSLATION

Śrī Śukadeva Gosvāmī said: Encouraged by the words of the sages, Indra killed Vṛtrāsura, and when he was killed the sinful reaction for killing a brāhmaṇa [brahma-hatyā] certainly took shelter of Indra.

PURPORT

After killing Vṛtrāsura, Indra could not surpass the *brahma-hatyā,* the sinful reactions for killing a *brāhmaṇa.* Formerly he had killed one *brāhmaṇa,* Viśvarūpa, out of circumstantial anger, but this time, following the advice of the sages, he killed another *brāhmaṇa* purposely. Therefore the sinful reaction was greater than before. Indra could not be relieved from the reaction simply by performing sacrifices for atonement. He had to undergo a severe series of sinful reactions, and when he was freed by such suffering, the *brāhmaṇas* allowed him to perform the horse sacrifice. The planned execution of sinful deeds on the strength of chanting the holy name of the Lord or undergoing *prāyaścitta,* atonement, cannot give relief to anyone, even to Indra or Nahuṣa. Nahuṣa was officiating for Indra while Indra, absent from heaven, was going here and there to gain release from his sinful reactions.

TEXT 11

तयेन्द्रः स्मासहत् तापं निर्वृतिर्नामुमाविशत् ।
ह्रीमन्तं वाच्यतां प्राप्तं सुखयन्त्यपि नो गुणाः ॥ ११ ॥

tayendraḥ smāsahat tāpaṁ
nirvṛtir nāmum āviśat

hrīmantaṁ vācyatāṁ prāptaṁ
sukhayanty api no guṇāḥ

tayā—by that action; *indraḥ*—King Indra; *sma*—indeed; *asahat*—suffered; *tāpam*—misery; *nirvṛtiḥ*—happiness; *na*—not; *amum*—him; *āviśat*—entered; *hrīmantam*—one who is shameful; *vācyatām*—ill fame; *prāptam*—obtaining; *sukhayanti*—give pleasure; *api*—although; *no*—not; *guṇāḥ*—good qualifications like possessing opulence.

TRANSLATION

Following the advice of the demigods, Indra killed Vṛtrāsura, and he suffered because of this sinful killing. Although the other demigods were happy, he could not derive happiness from the killing of Vṛtrāsura. Indra's other good qualities, such as tolerance and opulence, could not help him in his grief.

PURPORT

One cannot be happy by committing sinful acts, even if one is endowed with material opulence. Indra found this to be true. People began to blaspheme him, saying, "This person has killed a *brāhmaṇa* for the sake of enjoying heavenly material happiness." Therefore in spite of being King of heaven and enjoying material opulence, Indra was always unhappy because of the accusations of the populace.

TEXTS 12–13

तां ददर्शानुधावन्तीं चाण्डालीमिव रूपिणीम् ।
जरया वेपमानाङ्गीं यक्ष्मग्रस्तामसृक्पटाम् ॥ १२ ॥
विकीर्य पलितान् केशांस्तिष्ठ तिष्ठेति भाषिणीम् ।
मीनगन्ध्यसुगन्धेन कुर्वतीं मार्गदूषणम् ॥ १३ ॥

tāṁ dadarśānudhāvantīṁ
cāṇḍālīm iva rūpiṇīm
jarayā vepamānāṅgīṁ
yakṣma-grastām asṛk-paṭām

vikīrya palitān keśāṁs
tiṣṭha tiṣṭheti bhāṣiṇīm
mīna-gandhy-asu-gandhena
kurvatīṁ mārga-dūṣaṇam

tām—the sinful reaction; *dadarśa*—he saw; *anudhāvantīm*—chasing; *cāṇḍālīm*—a woman of the lowest class; *iva*—like; *rūpiṇīm*—taking a form; *jarayā*—because of old age; *vepamāna-aṅgīm*—whose bodily limbs were trembling; *yakṣma-grastām*—infected with tuberculosis; *asṛk-paṭām*—whose clothes were covered with blood; *vikīrya*—scattering; *palitān*—grayed; *keśān*—hair; *tiṣṭha tiṣṭha*—wait, wait; *iti*—thus; *bhāṣiṇīm*—calling; *mīna-gandhi*—the smell of fish; *asu*—whose breath; *gandhena*—by the odor; *kurvatīm*—bringing about; *mārga-dūṣaṇam*—the pollution of the whole street.

TRANSLATION

Indra saw personified sinful reaction chasing him, appearing like a caṇḍāla woman, a woman of the lowest class. She seemed very old, and all the limbs of her body trembled. Because she was afflicted with tuberculosis, her body and garments were covered with blood. Breathing an unbearable fishy odor that polluted the entire street, she called to Indra, "Wait! Wait!"

PURPORT

When a person is afflicted with tuberculosis, he often vomits blood, which makes his garments bloody.

TEXT 14

नभो गतो दिशः सर्वाः सहस्राक्षो विशाम्पते ।
प्रागुदीचीं दिशं तूर्णं प्रविष्टो नृप मानसम् ॥ १४ ॥

nabho gato diśaḥ sarvāḥ
sahasrākṣo viśāmpate
prāg-udīcīṁ diśaṁ tūrṇaṁ
praviṣṭo nṛpa mānasam

nabhaḥ—to the sky; *gataḥ*—going; *diśaḥ*—to the directions; *sarvāḥ*—all; *sahasra-akṣaḥ*—Indra, who is endowed with one thousand eyes; *viśāmpate*—O King; *prāk-udīcīm*—to the northeast; *diśam*—direction; *tūrṇam*—very speedily; *praviṣṭaḥ*—entered; *nṛpa*—O King; *mānasam*—the lake known as Mānasa-sarovara.

TRANSLATION

O King, Indra first fled to the sky, but there also he saw the woman of personified sin chasing him. This witch followed him wherever he went. At last he very quickly went to the northeast and entered the Mānasa-sarovara Lake.

TEXT 15

स आवसत्पुष्करनालतन्तू-
नलब्धभोगो यदिहाग्निदूतः ।
वर्षाणि साहस्रमलक्षितोऽन्तः
सञ्चिन्तयन् ब्रह्मवधाद् विमोक्षम् ॥ १५ ॥

sa āvasat puṣkara-nāla-tantūn
alabdha-bhogo yad ihāgni-dūtaḥ
varṣāṇi sāhasram alakṣito'ntaḥ
sañcintayan brahma-vadhād vimokṣam

saḥ—he (Indra); *āvasat*—lived; *puṣkara-nāla-tantūn*—in the network of the fibers of a lotus stem; *alabdha-bhogaḥ*—not getting any material comfort (practically starving for all material needs); *yat*—which; *iha*—here; *agni-dūtaḥ*—the fire-god messenger; *varṣāṇi*—celestial years; *sāhasram*—one thousand; *alakṣitaḥ*—invisible; *antaḥ*—within his heart; *sañcintayan*—always thinking of; *brahma-vadhāt*—from the killing of a *brāhmaṇa; vimokṣam*—liberation.

TRANSLATION

Always thinking of how he could be relieved from the sinful reaction for killing a brāhmaṇa, King Indra, invisible to everyone, lived in the lake for one thousand years in the subtle fibers of the stem of a lotus. The fire-god used to bring him his share of all yajñas, but because the fire-god was afraid to enter the water, Indra was practically starving.

TEXT 16

तावत्त्रिणाकं नहुषः शशास
विद्यातपोयोगबलानुभावः ।
स सम्पदैश्वर्यमदान्धबुद्धि-
र्नीतस्तिरश्चां गतिमिन्द्रपत्न्या ॥ १६ ॥

tāvat triṇākaṁ nahuṣaḥ śaśāsa
vidyā-tapo-yoga-balānubhāvaḥ
sa sampad-aiśvarya-madāndha-buddhir
nītas tiraścāṁ gatim indra-patnyā

tāvat—for so long; *triṇākam*—the heavenly planet; *nahuṣaḥ*—Nahuṣa; *śaśāsa*—ruled; *vidyā*—by education; *tapaḥ*—austerities; *yoga*—mystic power; *bala*—and strength; *anubhāvaḥ*—being equipped; *saḥ*—he (Nahuṣa); *sampat*—of so much wealth; *aiśvarya*—and opulence; *mada*—by the madness; *andha*—blinded; *buddhiḥ*—his intelligence; *nītaḥ*—was brought; *tiraścām*—of a snake; *gatim*—to the destination; *indra-patnyā*—by Indra's wife Śacīdevī.

TRANSLATION

As long as King Indra lived in the water, wrapped in the stem of the lotus, Nahuṣa was equipped with the ability to rule the heavenly kingdom, due to his knowledge, austerity and mystic power. Nahuṣa, however, blinded and maddened by power and opulence, made undesirable proposals to Indra's wife with a desire to enjoy her. Thus Nahuṣa was cursed by a brāhmaṇa and later became a snake.

TEXT 17

ततो गतो ब्रह्मगिरोपहूत
ऋतम्भरध्याननिवारिताघः ।
पापस्तु दिग्देवतया हतौजा-
स्तं नाभ्यभूदवितं विष्णुपत्न्या ॥ १७ ॥

tato gato brahma-giropahūta
ṛtambhara-dhyāna-nivāritāghaḥ
pāpas tu digdevatayā hataujās
taṁ nābhyabhūd avitaṁ viṣṇu-patnyā

tataḥ—thereafter; *gataḥ*—gone; *brahma*—of the *brāhmaṇas; girā*—by the words; *upahūtaḥ*—being invited; *ṛtambhara*—on the Supreme Lord, who maintains truth; *dhyāna*—by meditation; *nivārita*—impeded; *aghaḥ*—whose sin; *pāpaḥ*—the sinful activity; *tu*—then; *dik-devatayā*—by the demigod Rudra; *hata-ojāḥ*—with all prowess diminished; *tam*—him (Indra); *na abhyabhūt*—could not overcome; *avitam*—being protected; *viṣṇu-patnyā*—by Lord Viṣṇu's wife, the goddess of fortune.

TRANSLATION

Indra's sins were diminished by the influence of Rudra, the demigod of all directions. Because Indra was protected by the goddess of fortune, Lord Viṣṇu's wife, who resides in the lotus clusters of Mānasa-sarovara Lake, Indra's sins could not affect him. Indra was ultimately relieved of all the reactions of his sinful deeds by strictly worshiping Lord Viṣṇu. Then he was called back to the heavenly planets by the brāhmaṇas and reinstated in his position.

TEXT 18

तं च ब्रह्मर्षयोऽभ्येत्य हयमेधेन भारत ।
यथावद्दीक्षयाञ्चक्रुः पुरुषाराधनेन ह ॥ १८ ॥

taṁ ca brahmarṣayo'bhyetya
hayamedhena bhārata
yathāvad dīkṣayāñ cakruḥ
puruṣārādhanena ha

tam—him (Lord Indra); *ca*—and; *brahma-ṛṣayaḥ*—the great saints and *brāhmaṇas; abhyetya*—approaching; *hayamedhena*—with an *aśvamedha* sacrifice; *bhārata*—O King Parīkṣit; *yathāvat*—according to the rules and regulations; *dīkṣayām cakruḥ*—initiated; *puruṣa-ārādhanena*—which consists of worship of the Supreme Person, Hari; *ha*—indeed.

TRANSLATION

O King, when Lord Indra reached the heavenly planets, the saintly brāhmaṇas approached him and properly initiated him into a horse sacrifice [aśvamedha-yajña] meant to please the Supreme Lord.

TEXTS 19–20

अथेज्यमाने पुरुषे सर्वदेवमयात्मनि ।
अश्वमेधे महेन्द्रेण वितते ब्रह्मवादिभिः ॥ १९ ॥
स वै त्वाष्ट्रवधो भूयानपि पापचयो नृप ।
नीतस्तेनैव शून्याय नीहार इव भानुना ॥ २० ॥

athejyamāne puruṣe
sarva-devamayātmani
aśvamedhe mahendreṇa
vitate brahma-vādibhiḥ

sa vai tvāṣṭra-vadho bhūyān
api pāpa-cayo nṛpa
nītas tenaiva śūnyāya
nīhāra iva bhānunā

atha—therefore; *ijyamāne*—when worshiped; *puruṣe*—the Supreme Personality of Godhead; *sarva*—all; *deva-maya-ātmani*—the Supersoul and maintainer of the demigods; *aśvamedhe*—through the *aśvamedha-yajña; mahā-indreṇa*—by King Indra; *vitate*—being administered; *brahma-vādibhiḥ*—by the saints and *brāhmaṇas* expert in Vedic knowledge; *saḥ*—that; *vai*—indeed; *tvāṣṭra-vadhaḥ*—the killing of Vṛtrāsura, the son of Tvaṣṭā; *bhūyāt*—may be; *api*—although; *pāpa-cayaḥ*—mass of sin; *nṛpa*—O King; *nītaḥ*—was brought; *tena*—by that (the horse sacrifice); *eva*—certainly; *śūnyāya*—to nothing; *nīhāraḥ*—fog; *iva*—like; *bhānunā*—by the brilliant sun.

TRANSLATION

The horse sacrifice performed by the saintly brāhmaṇas relieved Indra of the reactions to all his sins because he worshiped the Supreme Personality of Godhead in that sacrifice. O King, although he had committed a gravely sinful act, it was nullified at once by that sacrifice, just as fog is vanquished by the brilliant sunrise.

TEXT 21

स वाजिमेधेन यथोदितेन
वितायमानेन मरीचिमिश्रैः ।
इष्ट्वाधियज्ञं पुरुषं पुराण-
मिन्द्रो महानास विधूतपापः ॥ २१ ॥

sa vājimedhena yathoditena
vitāyamānena marīci-miśraiḥ
iṣṭvādhiyajñaṁ puruṣaṁ purāṇam
indro mahān āsa vidhūta-pāpaḥ

saḥ—he (Indra); *vājimedhena*—by the *aśvamedha* sacrifice; *yathā*—just as; *uditena*—described; *vitāyamānena*—being performed; *marīci-miśraiḥ*—by the priests, headed by Marīci; *iṣṭvā*—worshiping; *adhiyajñam*—the Supreme Supersoul; *puruṣam purāṇam*—the original Personality of Godhead; *indraḥ*—King Indra; *mahān*—worshipable; *āsa*—became; *vidhūta-pāpaḥ*—being cleansed of all sinful reactions.

TRANSLATION

King Indra was favored by Marīci and the other great sages. They performed the sacrifice just according to the rules and regulations, worshiping the Supreme Personality of Godhead, the Supersoul, the original person. Thus Indra regained his exalted position and was again honored by everyone.

TEXTS 22–23

इदं महाख्यानमशेषपाप्मनां
प्रक्षालनं तीर्थपदानुकीर्तनम् ।
भक्त्युच्छ्रयं भक्तजनानुवर्णनं
महेन्द्रमोक्षं विजयं मरुत्वतः ॥ २२ ॥
पठेयुराख्यानमिदं सदा बुधाः
शृण्वन्त्यथो पर्वणि पर्वणीन्द्रियम् ।
धन्यं यशस्यं निखिलाघमोचनं
रिपुञ्जयं स्वस्त्ययनं तथायुषम् ॥ २३ ॥

idaṁ mahākhyānam aśeṣa-pāpmanāṁ
prakṣālanaṁ tīrthapadānukīrtanam
bhakty-ucchrayaṁ bhakta-janānuvarṇanaṁ
mahendra-mokṣaṁ vijayaṁ marutvataḥ

paṭheyur ākhyānam idaṁ sadā budhāḥ
śṛṇvanty atho parvaṇi parvaṇīndriyam
dhanyaṁ yaśasyaṁ nikhilāgha-mocanaṁ
ripuñjayaṁ svasty-ayanaṁ tathāyuṣam

idam—this; *mahā-ākhyānam*—great historical incident; *aśeṣa-pāpmanām*—of unlimited numbers of sinful acts; *prakṣālanam*—cleansing; *tīrthapada-anukīrtanam*—glorifying the Supreme Personality of Godhead, who is known as Tīrthapada; *bhakti*—of devotional service; *ucchrayam*—in which there is an increase; *bhakta-jana*—the devotees; *anuvarṇanam*—describing; *mahā-indra-mokṣam*—the liberation of the King of heaven; *vijayam*—the victory; *marutvataḥ*—of King Indra; *paṭheyuḥ*—should read; *ākhyānam*—narration; *idam*—this; *sadā*—always; *budhāḥ*—learned scholars; *śṛṇvanti*—continue to hear; *atho*—as well; *parvaṇi parvaṇi*—on the occasion of great festivals; *indriyam*—which makes the senses sharp; *dhanyam*—brings wealth; *yaśasyam*—brings fame; *nikhila*—all; *agha-mocanam*—releasing from sins; *ripum-jayam*—makes one victorious over his enemies; *svasti-ayanam*—brings good fortune for all; *tathā*—so also; *āyuṣam*—longevity.

TRANSLATION

In this very great narrative there is glorification of the Supreme Personality of Godhead, Nārāyaṇa, there are statements about the exaltedness of devotional service, there are descriptions of devotees like Indra and Vṛtrāsura, and there are statements about King Indra's release from sinful life and about his victory in fighting the demons. By understanding this incident, one is relieved of all sinful reactions. Therefore the learned are always advised to read this narration. If one does so, one will become expert in the activities of the senses, his opulence will increase, and his reputation will become widespread. One will also be relieved of all sinful reactions, he will conquer all his enemies, and the duration of his life will increase. Because this narration is auspicious in all respects, learned scholars regularly hear and repeat it on every festival day.

Thus ends the Bhaktivedanta purports of the Sixth Canto, Thirteenth Chapter, of the Śrīmad-Bhāgavatam, *entitled "King Indra Afflicted by Sinful Reaction."*

CHAPTER FOURTEEN

King Citraketu's Lamentation

In this Fourteenth Chapter, Parīkṣit Mahārāja asks his spiritual master, Śukadeva Gosvāmī, how such a demon as Vṛtrāsura could become an exalted devotee. In this connection the previous life of Vṛtrāsura is discussed. This involves the story of Citraketu and how he was victimized by lamentation because of the death of his son.

Among many millions of living entities, the number of human beings is extremely small, and among human beings who are actually religious, only some are eager to be liberated from material existence. Among many thousands of people who desire relief from material existence, one is freed from the association of unwanted persons or is relieved of material contamination. And among many millions of such liberated persons, one may become a devotee of Lord Nārāyaṇa. Therefore such devotees are extremely rare. Since *bhakti,* devotional service, is not ordinary, Parīkṣit Mahārāja was astonished that an *asura* could rise to the exalted position of a devotee. Being doubtful, Parīkṣit Mahārāja inquired from Śukadeva Gosvāmī, who then described Vṛtrāsura with reference to his previous birth as Citraketu, the King of Śūrasena.

Citraketu, who had no sons, got an opportunity to meet the great sage Aṅgirā. When Aṅgirā inquired from the King about his welfare, the King expressed his moroseness, and therefore by the grace of the great sage, the King's first wife, Kṛtadyuti, gave birth to a son, who was the cause of both happiness and lamentation. Upon the birth of this son, the King and all the residents of the palace were very happy. The co-wives of Kṛtadyuti, however, were envious, and later they administered poison to the child. Citraketu was overwhelmed by shock at his son's death. Then Nārada Muni and Aṅgirā went to see him.

TEXT 1

श्रीपरीक्षिदुवाच

रजस्तमःस्वभावस्य ब्रह्मन् वृत्रस्य पाप्मनः ।
नारायणे भगवति कथमासीद् दृढा मतिः ॥ १ ॥

śrī-parīkṣid uvāca
rajas-tamaḥ-svabhāvasya
brahman vṛtrasya pāpmanaḥ
nārāyaṇe bhagavati
katham āsīd dṛḍhā matiḥ

śrī-parīkṣit uvāca—King Parīkṣit inquired; *rajaḥ*—of the mode of passion; *tamaḥ*—and of the mode of ignorance; *sva-bhāvasya*—having a nature; *brahman*—O learned *brāhmaṇa; vṛtrasya*—of Vṛtrāsura; *pāpmanaḥ*—who was supposedly sinful; *nārāyaṇe*—in Lord Nārāyaṇa; *bhagavati*—the Supreme Personality of Godhead; *katham*—how; *āsīt*—was there; *dṛḍhā*—very strong; *matiḥ*—consciousness.

TRANSLATION

King Parīkṣit inquired from Śukadeva Gosvāmī: O learned brāhmaṇa, demons are generally sinful, being obsessed with the modes of passion and ignorance. How, then, could Vṛtrāsura have attained such exalted love for the Supreme Personality of Godhead, Nārāyaṇa?

PURPORT

In this material world, everyone is obsessed with the modes of passion and ignorance. However, unless one conquers these modes and comes to the platform of goodness, there is no chance of one's becoming a pure devotee. This is confirmed by Lord Kṛṣṇa Himself in *Bhagavad-gītā* (7.28):

yeṣāṁ tv anta-gataṁ pāpaṁ
janānāṁ puṇya-karmaṇām
te dvandva-moha-nirmuktā
bhajante māṁ dṛḍha-vratāḥ

"Persons who have acted piously in previous lives and in this life, whose sinful actions are completely eradicated and who are freed from the duality of delusion, engage themselves in My service with determination." Since Vṛtrāsura was among the demons, Mahārāja Parīkṣit wondered how it was possible for him to have become such an exalted devotee.

TEXT 2

देवानां शुद्धसत्त्वानामृषीणां चामलात्मनाम् ।
भक्तिर्मुकुन्दचरणे न प्रायेणोपजायते ॥ २ ॥

devānāṁ śuddha-sattvānām
ṛṣīṇāṁ cāmalātmanām
bhaktir mukunda-caraṇe
na prāyeṇopajāyate

devānām—of the demigods; *śuddha-sattvānām*—whose minds are purified; *ṛṣīṇām*—of great saintly persons; *ca*—and; *amala-ātmanām*—who have purified their existence; *bhaktiḥ*—devotional service; *mukunda-caraṇe*—to the lotus feet of Mukunda, the Lord, who can give liberation; *na*—not; *prāyeṇa*—almost always; *upajāyate*—develops.

TRANSLATION

Demigods situated in the mode of goodness and great saints cleansed of the dirt of material enjoyment hardly ever render pure devotional service at the lotus feet of Mukunda. [Therefore how could Vṛtrāsura have become such a great devotee?]

TEXT 3

रजोभिः समसंख्याताः पार्थिवैरिह जन्तवः ।
तेषां ये केचनेहन्ते श्रेयो वै मनुजादयः ॥ ३ ॥

rajobhiḥ sama-saṅkhyātāḥ
pārthivair iha jantavaḥ
teṣāṁ ye kecanehante
śreyo vai manujādayaḥ

rajobhiḥ—with the atoms; *sama-saṅkhyātāḥ*—having the same numerical strength; *pārthivaiḥ*—of the earth; *iha*—in this world; *jantavaḥ*—the living entities; *teṣām*—of them; *ye*—those who; *kecana*—some; *īhante*—act; *śreyaḥ*—for religious principles; *vai*—indeed; *manuja-ādayaḥ*—the human beings and so on.

TRANSLATION

In this material world there are as many living entities as atoms. Among these living entities, a very few are human beings, and among them, few are interested in following religious principles.

TEXT 4

प्रायो मुमुक्षवस्तेषां केचनैव द्विजोत्तम ।
मुमुक्षूणां सहस्रेषु कश्चिन्मुच्येत सिध्यति ॥ ४ ॥

prāyo mumukṣavas teṣāṁ
kecanaiva dvijottama
mumukṣūṇāṁ sahasreṣu
kaścin mucyeta sidhyati

prāyaḥ—almost always; *mumukṣavaḥ*—persons interested in liberation; *teṣām*—of them; *kecana*—some; *eva*—indeed; *dvija-uttama*—O best of the *brāhmaṇas; mumukṣūṇām*—of those who desire to be liberated; *sahasreṣu*—in many thousands; *kaścit*—someone; *mucyeta*—may be actually liberated; *sidhyati*—someone is perfect.

TRANSLATION

O best of the brāhmaṇas, Śukadeva Gosvāmī, out of many persons who follow religious principles, only a few desire liberation from the material world. Among many thousands who desire liberation, one may actually achieve liberation, giving up material attachment to society, friendship, love, country, home, wife and children. And among many thousands of such liberated persons, one who can understand the true meaning of liberation is very rare.

PURPORT

There are four classes of men, namely *karmīs, jñānīs, yogīs* and *bhaktas.* This statement pertains especially to *karmīs* and *jñānīs.* A *karmī* tries to be happy within this material world by changing from one body to another. His objective is bodily comfort, either in this planet or in another. When such a person becomes a *jñānī,* however, he aspires for liberation from material bondage. Among many such persons who aspire for liberation, one may actually be liberated during his life. Such a person gives up his attachment for society, friendship, love, country, family, wife and children. Among many such persons, who are in the *vānaprastha* stage, one may understand the value of becoming a *sannyāsī,* completely accepting the renounced order of life.

TEXT 5

मुक्तानामपि सिद्धानां नारायणपरायणः ।
सुदुर्लभः प्रशान्तात्मा कोटिष्वपि महामुने ॥ ५ ॥

muktānām api siddhānāṁ
nārāyaṇa-parāyaṇaḥ
su-durlabhaḥ praśāntātmā
koṭiṣv api mahā-mune

muktānām—of those who are liberated during this life (who are unattached to the bodily comforts of society, friendship and love); *api*—even; *siddhānām*—who are perfect (because they understand the insignificance of bodily comforts); *nārāyaṇa-parāyaṇaḥ*—a person who has concluded that Nārāyaṇa is the Supreme; *su-durlabhaḥ*—very rarely found; *praśānta*—fully pacified; *ātmā*—whose mind; *koṭiṣu*—out of millions and trillions;* api—even; *mahā-mune*—O great sage.

TRANSLATION

O great sage, among many millions who are liberated and perfect in knowledge of liberation, one may be a devotee of Lord Nārāyaṇa, or Kṛṣṇa. Such devotees, who are fully peaceful, are extremely rare.

PURPORT

Śrīla Viśvanātha Cakravartī Ṭhākura gives the following purport to this verse. Simply desiring *mukti,* or liberation, is insufficient; one must become factually liberated. When one understands the futility of the materialistic way of life, one becomes advanced in knowledge, and therefore he situates himself in the *vānaprastha* order, unattached to family, wife and children. One should then further progress to the platform of *sannyāsa,* the actual renounced order, never to fall again and be afflicted by materialistic life. Even though one desires to be liberated, this does not mean he is liberated. Only rarely is someone liberated. Indeed, although many men take *sannyāsa* to become liberated, because of their imperfections they again become attached to women, material activities, social welfare work and so on.

Jñānīs, yogīs and *karmīs* devoid of devotional service are called offenders. Śrī Caitanya Mahāprabhu says, *māyāvādī kṛṣṇe aparādhī:* one who thinks that everything is *māyā* instead of thinking that everything is Kṛṣṇa is called an *aparādhī,* or offender. Although the Māyāvādīs, impersonalists, are offenders at the lotus feet of Kṛṣṇa, they may nonetheless be counted among the *siddhas,* those who have realized the self. They may be considered nearer to spiritual perfection because at least they have realized what spiritual life

* The word *koṭi* means ten million. Its plural means millions and trillions.

is. If such a person becomes *nārāyaṇa-parāyaṇa,* a devotee of Lord Nārāyaṇa, he is better than a *jīvan-mukta,* one who is liberated or perfect. This requires higher intelligence.

There are two kinds of *jñānīs.* One is inclined to devotional service and the other to impersonal realization. Impersonalists generally undergo great endeavor for no tangible benefit, and therefore it is said that they are husking paddy that has no grain (*sthūla-tuṣāvaghātinaḥ*). The other class of *jñānīs,* whose *jñāna* is mixed with *bhakti,* are also of two kinds—those who are devoted to the so-called false form of the Supreme Personality of Godhead and those who understand the Supreme Personality of Godhead as *sac-cid-ānanda-vigraha,* the actual spiritual form. The Māyāvādī devotees worship Nārāyaṇa or Viṣṇu with the idea that Viṣṇu has accepted a form of *māyā* and that the ultimate truth is actually impersonal. The pure devotee, however, never thinks that Viṣṇu has accepted a body of *māyā;* instead, he knows perfectly well that the original Absolute Truth is the Supreme Person. Such a devotee is actually situated in knowledge. He never merges in the Brahman effulgence. As stated in *Śrīmad-Bhāgavatam* (10.2.32):

ye 'nye 'ravindākṣa vimukta-māninas
tvayy asta-bhāvād aviśuddha-buddhayaḥ
āruhya kṛcchreṇa paraṁ padaṁ tataḥ
patanty adho 'nādṛta-yuṣmad-aṅghrayaḥ

"O Lord, the intelligence of those who think themselves liberated but who have no devotion is impure. Even though they rise to the highest point of liberation by dint of severe penances and austerities, they are sure to fall down again into material existence, for they do not take shelter at Your lotus feet." Evidence of this same point is also given in *Bhagavad-gītā* (9.11), wherein the Lord says:

avajānanti māṁ mūḍhā
mānuṣīṁ tanum āśritam
paraṁ bhāvam ajānanto
mama bhūta-maheśvaram

"Fools deride Me when I descend in the human form. They do not know My transcendental nature and My supreme dominion over all that be." When rascals (*mūḍhas*) see that Kṛṣṇa acts exactly like a human being, they deride the transcendental form of the Lord because they do not know the *paraṁ bhāvam,* His transcendental form and activities. Such persons are further described in *Bhagavad-gītā* (9.12) as follows:

moghāśā mogha-karmāṇo
mogha-jñānā vicetasaḥ
rākṣasīm āsurīṁ caiva
prakṛtiṁ mohinīṁ śritāḥ

"Those who are thus bewildered are attracted by demoniac and atheistic views. In that deluded condition, their hopes for liberation, their fruitive activities and their culture of knowledge are all defeated." Such persons do not know that Kṛṣṇa's body is not material. There is no distinction between Kṛṣṇa's body and His soul, but because less intelligent men see Kṛṣṇa as a human being, they deride Him. They cannot imagine how a person like Kṛṣṇa could be the origin of everything (*govindam ādi-puruṣaṁ tam ahaṁ bhajāmi*). Such persons are described as *moghāśāḥ,* baffled in their hopes. Whatever they desire for the future will be baffled. Even if they apparently engage in devotional service, they are described as *moghāśāḥ* because they ultimately desire to merge into the Brahman effulgence.

Those who aspire to be elevated to the heavenly planets by devotional service will also be frustrated, because this is not the result of devotional service. However, they are also given a chance to engage in devotional service and be purified. As stated in *Śrīmad-Bhāgavatam* (1.2.17):

śṛṇvatāṁ sva-kathāḥ kṛṣṇaḥ
puṇya-śravaṇa-kīrtanaḥ
hṛdy antaḥ-stho hy abhadrāṇi
vidhunoti suhṛt satām

"Śrī Kṛṣṇa, the Personality of Godhead, who is the Paramātmā [Supersoul] in everyone's heart and the benefactor of the truthful devotee, cleanses desire for material enjoyment from the heart of the devotee who relishes His messages, which are in themselves virtuous when properly heard and chanted."

Unless the dirt within the core of one's heart is cleansed away, one cannot become a pure devotee. Therefore the word *su-durlabhaḥ* ("very rarely found") is used in this verse. Not only among hundreds and thousands, but among millions of perfectly liberated souls, a pure devotee is hardly ever found. Therefore the words *koṭiṣv api* are used herein. Śrīla Madhvācārya gives the following quotations from the *Tantra Bhāgavata:*

nava-koṭyas tu devānām
ṛṣayaḥ sapta-koṭayaḥ
nārāyaṇāyanāḥ sarve
ye kecit tat-parāyaṇāḥ

"There are ninety million demigods and seventy million sages, who are all called *nārāyaṇāyana,* devotees of Lord Nārāyaṇa. Among them, only a few are called *nārāyaṇa-parāyaṇa.*"

nārāyaṇāyanā devā
ṛṣy-ādyās tat-parāyaṇāḥ
brahmādyāḥ kecanaiva syuḥ
siddho yogya-sukhaṁ labhan

The difference between the *siddhas* and *nārāyaṇa-parāyaṇas* is that direct devotees are called *nārāyaṇa-parāyaṇas* whereas those who perform various types of mystic *yoga* are called *siddhas.*

TEXT 6

वृत्रस्तु स कथं पापः सर्वलोकोपतापनः ।
इत्थं दृढमतिः कृष्ण आसीत् संग्राम उल्बणे ॥ ६ ॥

vṛtras tu sa kathaṁ pāpaḥ
sarva-lokopatāpanaḥ
itthaṁ dṛḍha-matiḥ kṛṣṇa
āsīt saṅgrāma ulbaṇe

vṛtraḥ—Vṛtrāsura; *tu*—but; *saḥ*—he; *katham*—how; *pāpaḥ*—although sinful (getting the body of a demon); *sarva-loka*—of all the three worlds; *upatāpanaḥ*—the cause of suffering; *ittham*—such; *dṛḍha-matiḥ*—firmly fixed intelligence; *kṛṣṇe*—in Kṛṣṇa; *āsīt*—there was; *saṅgrāme ulbaṇe*—in the great blazing fire of battle.

TRANSLATION

Vṛtrāsura was situated in the blazing fire of battle and was an infamous, sinful demon, always engaged in giving troubles and anxieties to others. How could such a demon become so greatly Kṛṣṇa conscious?

PURPORT

It has been described that a *nārāyaṇa-parāyaṇa,* a pure devotee, is rarely found even among millions and millions of persons. Therefore Parīkṣit Mahārāja was surprised that Vṛtrāsura, whose purpose was to give trouble and anxiety to others, was one of these devotees, even on a battlefield. What was the reason for Vṛtrāsura's advancement?

TEXT 7

अत्र नः संशयो भूयाञ्छ्रोतुं कौतूहलं प्रभो।
यः पौरुषेण समरे सहस्राक्षमतोषयत् ॥ ७ ॥

atra naḥ saṁśayo bhūyāñ
chrotuṁ kautūhalaṁ prabho
yaḥ pauruṣeṇa samare
sahasrākṣam atoṣayat

atra—in this connection; *naḥ*—our; *saṁśayaḥ*—doubt; *bhūyān*—great; *śrotum*—to hear; *kautūhalam*—eagerness; *prabho*—O my lord; *yaḥ*—he who; *pauruṣeṇa*—by bravery and strength; *samare*—in battle; *sahasra-akṣam*—Lord Indra, who has one thousand eyes; *atoṣayat*—pleased.

TRANSLATION

My dear lord, Śukadeva Gosvāmī, although Vṛtrāsura was a sinful demon, he showed the prowess of a most exalted kṣatriya and satisfied Lord Indra in battle. How could such a demon be a great devotee of Lord Kṛṣṇa? These contradictions have caused me great doubt, and they have made me eager to hear of this from you.

TEXT 8

श्रीसूत उवाच
परीक्षितोऽथ संप्रश्नं भगवान् बादरायणिः।
निशम्य श्रद्दधानस्य प्रतिनन्द्य वचोऽब्रवीत् ॥ ८ ॥

śrī-sūta uvāca
parīkṣito'tha sampraśnaṁ
bhagavān bādarāyaṇiḥ
niśamya śraddadhānasya
pratinandya vaco'bravīt

śrī-sūtaḥ uvāca—Śrī Sūta Gosvāmī said; *parīkṣitaḥ*—of Mahārāja Parīkṣit; *atha*—thus; *sampraśnam*—the perfect question; *bhagavān*—the most powerful; *bādarāyaṇiḥ*—Śukadeva Gosvāmī, the son of Vyāsadeva; *niśamya*—hearing; *śraddadhānasya*—of his disciple, who was so faithful in understanding the truth; *pratinandya*—congratulating; *vacaḥ*—words; *abravīt*—spoke.

TRANSLATION

Śrī Sūta Gosvāmī said: After hearing Mahārāja Parīkṣit's very intelligent question, Śukadeva Gosvāmī, the most powerful sage, began answering his disciple with great affection.

TEXT 9

श्रीशुक उवाच
श्रृणुष्वावहितो राजन्नितिहासमिमं यथा ।
श्रुतं द्वैपायनमुखान्नारदाद्देवलादपि ॥ ९ ॥

śrī-śuka uvāca
śṛṇuṣvāvahito rājann
itihāsam imaṁ yathā
śrutaṁ dvaipāyana-mukhān
nāradād devalād api

śrī-śukaḥ uvāca—Śrī Śukadeva Gosvāmī said; *śṛṇuṣva*—please hear; *avahitaḥ*—with great attention; *rājan*—O King; *itihāsam*—history; *imam*—this; *yathā*—just as; *śrutam*—heard; *dvaipāyana*—of Vyāsadeva; *mukhāt*—from the mouth; *nāradāt*—from Nārada; *devalāt*—from Devala Ṛṣi; *api*—also.

TRANSLATION

Śrī Śukadeva Gosvāmī said: O King, I shall speak to you the same history I have heard from the mouths of Vyāsadeva, Nārada and Devala. Please listen with attention.

TEXT 10

आसीद्राजा सार्वभौमः शूरसेनेषु वै नृप ।
चित्रकेतुरिति ख्यातो यस्यासीत् कामधुङ्मही ॥ १० ॥

āsīd rājā sārvabhaumaḥ
śūraseneṣu vai nṛpa
citraketur iti khyāto
yasyāsīt kāmadhuṅ mahī

āsīt—there was; *rājā*—one king; *sārva-bhaumaḥ*—an emperor of the entire surface of the globe; *śūraseneṣu*—in the country known as Śūrasena; *vai*—indeed; *nṛpa*—O King; *citraketuḥ*—Citraketu; *iti*—thus; *khyātaḥ*—celebrated; *yasya*—of whom; *āsīt*—was; *kāma-dhuk*—supplying all the necessities; *mahī*—the earth.

TRANSLATION

O King Parīkṣit, in the province of Śūrasena there was a king named Citraketu, who ruled the entire earth. During his reign, the earth produced all the necessities for life.

PURPORT

Here the most significant statement is that the earth completely produced all the necessities of life during the time of King Citraketu. As stated in the *Īśopaniṣad* (Mantra 1):

īśāvāsyam idaṁ sarvaṁ
yat kiñca jagatyāṁ jagat
tena tyaktena bhuñjīthā
mā gṛdhaḥ kasya svid dhanam

"Everything animate or inanimate that is within the universe is controlled and owned by the Lord. One should therefore accept only those things necessary for himself, which are set aside as his quota, and one should not accept other things, knowing well to whom they belong." Kṛṣṇa, the supreme controller, has created the material world, which is completely perfect and free from scarcity. The Lord supplies the necessities of all living entities. These necessities come from the earth, and thus the earth is the source of supply. When there is a good ruler, that source produces the necessities of life abundantly. However, when there is not such a good ruler, there will be scarcity. This is the significance of the word *kāmadhuk*. Elsewhere in *Śrīmad-Bhāgavatam* (1.10.4) it is said, *kāmaṁ vavarṣa parjanyaḥ sarva-kāma-dughā mahī:* "During the reign of Mahārāja Yudhiṣṭhira, the clouds showered all the water that people needed, and the earth produced all the necessities of men in profusion." We have experience that in some seasons the rains produce abundance and in other seasons there is scarcity. We have no control over the earth's productiveness, for it is naturally under the full control of the Supreme Personality of Godhead. By His order, the Lord can make the earth produce sufficiently or insufficiently. If a pious king rules the earth according to the śāstric injunctions, there will naturally be regular rainfall and sufficient produce to provide for all men. There will be no question of exploitation, for everyone will have enough. Black-marketeering and other corrupt dealings will then automatically stop. Simply ruling the land cannot solve man's problems unless the leader has spiritual capabilities. He must be like Mahārāja Yudhiṣṭhira, Parīkṣit Mahārāja or Rāmacandra. Then all the inhabitants of the land will be extremely happy.

TEXT 11

तस्य भार्यासहस्राणां सहस्राणि दशाभवन् ।
सान्तानिकश्चापि नृपो न लेभे तासु सन्ततिम् ॥ ११ ॥

tasya bhāryā-sahasrāṇāṁ
sahasrāṇi daśābhavan
sāntānikaś cāpi nṛpo
na lebhe tāsu santatim

tasya—of him (King Citraketu); *bhāryā*—of wives; *sahasrāṇām*—of thousands; *sahasrāṇi*—thousands; *daśa*—ten; *abhavan*—there were; *sāntānikaḥ*—quite capable of begetting sons; *ca*—and; *api*—although; *nṛpaḥ*—the King; *na*—not; *lebhe*—obtained; *tāsu*—in them; *santatim*—a son.

TRANSLATION

This Citraketu had ten million wives, but although he was capable of producing children, he did not receive a child from any of them. By chance, all the wives were barren.

TEXT 12

रूपौदार्यवयोजन्मविद्यैश्वर्यश्रियादिभिः ।
सम्पन्नस्य गुणैः सर्वैश्चिन्ता बन्ध्यापतेरभूत् ॥ १२ ॥

rūpaudārya-vayo-janma-
vidyaiśvarya-śriyādibhiḥ

sampannasya guṇaiḥ sarvaiś
cintā bandhyā-pater abhūt

rūpa—with beauty; *audārya*—magnanimity; *vayaḥ*—youth; *janma*—aristocratic birth; *vidyā*—education; *aiśvarya*—opulence; *śriya-ādibhiḥ*—wealth and so on; *sampannasya*—endowed; *guṇaiḥ*—with good qualities; *sarvaiḥ*—all; *cintā*—anxiety; *bandhyā-pateḥ*—of Citraketu, the husband of so many sterile wives; *abhūt*—there was.

TRANSLATION

Citraketu, the husband of these millions of wives, was endowed with a beautiful form, magnanimity and youth. He was born in a high family, he had a complete education, and he was wealthy and opulent. Nevertheless, in spite of being endowed with all these assets, he was full of anxiety because he did not have a son.

PURPORT

It appears that the King first married one wife, but she could not bear a child. Then he married a second, a third, a fourth and so on, but none of the wives could bear children. In spite of the material assets of *janmaiśvarya-śruta-śrī*—birth in an aristocratic family with full opulence, wealth, education and beauty—he was very much aggrieved because in spite of having so many wives, he had no son. Certainly his grief was natural. *Gṛhastha* life does not mean having a wife and no children. Cāṇakya Paṇḍita says, *putra-hīnaṁ gṛhaṁ śūnyam:* if a family man has no son, his home is no better than a desert. The King was certainly most unhappy that he could not get a son, and this is why he had married so many times. *Kṣatriyas* especially are allowed to marry more than one wife, and this King did so. Nonetheless, he had no issue.

TEXT 13

न तस्य संपदः सर्वा महिष्यो वामलोचनाः ।
सार्वभौमस्य भूश्चेयमभवन् प्रीतिहेतवः ॥ १३ ॥

na tasya sampadaḥ sarvā
mahiṣyo vāma-locanāḥ
sārvabhaumasya bhūś ceyam
abhavan prīti-hetavaḥ

na—not; *tasya*—of him (Citraketu); *sampadaḥ*—the great opulences; *sarvāḥ*—all; *mahiṣyaḥ*—the queens; *vāma-locanāḥ*—having very attractive eyes; *sārva-bhaumasya*—of the emperor; *bhūḥ*—land; *ca*—also; *iyam*—this; *abhavan*—were; *prīti-hetavaḥ*—sources of pleasure.

TRANSLATION

His queens all had beautiful faces and attractive eyes, yet neither his opulences, his hundreds and thousands of queens, nor the lands of which he was the supreme proprietor were sources of happiness for him.

TEXT 14

तस्यैकदा तु भवनमङ्गिरा भगवानृषिः ।
लोकाननुचरन्नेतानुपागच्छद्यदृच्छया ॥ १४ ॥

tasyaikadā tu bhavanam
aṅgirā bhagavān ṛṣiḥ
lokān anucarann etān
upāgacchad yadṛcchayā

tasya—of him; *ekadā*—once upon a time; *tu*—but; *bhavanam*—to the palace; *aṅgirāḥ*—Aṅgirā; *bhagavān*—very powerful; *ṛṣiḥ*—sage; *lokān*—planets; *anucaran*—traveling around; *etān*—these; *upāgacchat*—came; *yadṛcchayā*—suddenly.

TRANSLATION

Once upon a time, when the powerful sage named Aṅgirā was traveling all over the universe without engagement, by his sweet will he came to the palace of King Citraketu.

TEXT 15

तं पूजयित्वा विधिवत्प्रत्युत्थानार्हणादिभिः ।
कृतातिथ्यमुपासीदत्सुखासीनं समाहितः ॥ १५ ॥

taṁ pūjayitvā vidhivat
pratyutthānārhaṇādibhiḥ
kṛtātithyam upāsīdat
sukhāsīnaṁ samāhitaḥ

tam—him; *pūjayitvā*—after worshiping; *vidhi-vat*—according to the rules and regulations for receiving exalted guests; *pratyutthāna*—by standing from the throne; *arhaṇa-ādibhiḥ*—offering worship and so on; *kṛta-atithyam*—who was given hospitality; *upāsīdat*—sat down near; *sukha-āsīnam*—who was seated very comfortably; *samāhitaḥ*—controlling his mind and senses.

TRANSLATION

Citraketu immediately stood up from his throne and offered him worship. He offered drinking water and eatables and in this way performed his duty as a host to a great guest. When the ṛṣi was seated very comfortably, the King, restraining his mind and senses, sat on the ground at the side of the ṛṣi's feet.

TEXT 16

महर्षिस्तमुपासीनं प्रश्रयावनतं क्षितौ ।
प्रतिपूज्य महाराज समाभाष्येदमब्रवीत् ॥ १६ ॥

maharṣis tam upāsīnaṁ
praśrayāvanataṁ kṣitau
pratipūjya mahārāja
samābhāṣyedam abravīt

mahā-ṛṣiḥ—the great sage; *tam*—unto him (the King); *upāsīnam*—sitting near; *praśraya-avanatam*—bowing in humility; *kṣitau*—on the ground; *pratipūjya*—congratulating; *mahārāja*—O King Parīkṣit; *samābhāṣya*—addressing; *idam*—this; *abravīt*—said.

TRANSLATION

O King Parīkṣit, when Citraketu, bent low in humility, was seated at the lotus feet of the great sage, the sage congratulated him for his humility and hospitality. The sage addressed him in the following words.

TEXT 17

अङ्गिरा उवाच

अपि तेऽनामयं स्वस्ति प्रकृतीनां तथात्मनः ।
यथा प्रकृतिभिर्गुप्तः पुमान् राजा च सप्तभिः ॥ १७ ॥

aṅgirā uvāca
api te'nāmayaṁ svasti
prakṛtīnāṁ tathātmanaḥ
yathā prakṛtibhir guptaḥ
pumān rājā ca saptabhiḥ

aṅgirāḥ uvāca—the great sage Aṅgirā said; *api*—whether; *te*—of you; *anāmayam*—health; *svasti*—auspiciousness; *prakṛtīnām*—of your royal elements (associates and paraphernalia); *tathā*—as well as; *ātmanaḥ*—of your own body, mind and soul; *yathā*—like; *prakṛtibhiḥ*—by the elements of material nature; *guptaḥ*—protected; *pumān*—the living being; *rājā*—the king; *ca*—also; *saptabhiḥ*—by seven.

TRANSLATION

The great sage Aṅgirā said: My dear King, I hope that your body and mind and your royal associates and paraphernalia are well. When the seven properties of material nature [the total material energy, the ego and the five objects of sense gratification] are in proper order, the living entity within the material elements is happy. Without these seven elements one cannot exist. Similarly, a king is always protected by seven elements—his instructor (svāmī or guru), his ministers, his kingdom, his fort, his treasury, his royal order and his friends.

PURPORT

As it is quoted by Śrīdhara Svāmī in his *Bhāgavatam* commentary:

svāmy-amātyau janapadā
durga-draviṇa-sañcayāḥ
daṇḍo mitraṁ ca tasyaitāḥ
sapta-prakṛtayo matāḥ

A king is not alone. He first has his spiritual master, the supreme guide. Then come his ministers, his kingdom, his fortifications, his treasury, his system of law and order, and his friends or allies. If these seven are properly maintained, the king is happy. Similarly, as explained in *Bhagavad-gītā* (*dehino'smin yathā dehe*), the living entity, the soul, is within the material covering of the *mahat-tattva,* ego and *pañca-tanmātrā,* the five objects of sense gratification. When these seven are in proper order, the living entity is in a mood of pleasure. Generally when the associates of the king are quiet and obedient, the king can be happy. Therefore the great sage Aṅgirā Ṛṣi inquired about the King's personal health and the good fortune of his seven associates. When we inquire from a friend whether everything is well, we are concerned not only with his personal self but also with his family, his source of income, and his assistants or servants. All of them must be well, and then a person can be happy.

TEXT 18

आत्मानं प्रकृतिष्वद्धा निधाय श्रेय आप्नुयात् ।
राज्ञा तथा प्रकृतयो नरदेवाहिताधयः ॥ १८ ॥

ātmānaṁ prakṛtiṣv addhā
nidhāya śreya āpnuyāt
rājñā tathā prakṛtayo
naradevāhitādhayaḥ

ātmānam—himself; *prakṛtiṣu*—under these seven royal elements; *addhā*—directly; *nidhāya*—placing; *śreyaḥ*—ultimate happiness; *āpnuyāt*—may obtain; *rājñā*—by the king; *tathā*—so also; *prakṛtayaḥ*—the dependent royal elements; *nara-deva*—O King; *āhita-adhayaḥ*—offering wealth and other items.

TRANSLATION

O King, O lord of humanity, when a king directly depends upon his associates and follows their instructions, he is happy. Similarly, when his associates offer their gifts and activities to the king and follow his orders, they are also happy.

PURPORT

The actual happiness of a king and his dependents is described in this verse. A king should not simply give orders to his dependents because he is supreme; sometimes he must follow their instructions. Similarly, the dependents should depend on the king. This mutual dependence will make everyone happy.

TEXT 19

अपि दाराः प्रजामात्या भृत्याः श्रेण्योऽथ मन्त्रिणः ।
पौरा जानपदा भूपा आत्मजा वशवर्तिनः ॥ १९ ॥

api dārāḥ prajāmātyā
bhṛtyāḥ śreṇyo'tha mantriṇaḥ
paurā jānapadā bhūpā
ātmajā vaśa-vartinaḥ

api—whether; *dārāḥ*—wives; *prajā*—citizens; *amātyāḥ*—and secretaries; *bhṛtyāḥ*—servants; *śreṇyaḥ*—merchants; *atha*—as well as; *mantriṇaḥ*—ministers; *paurāḥ*—inmates of the palace; *jānapadāḥ*—the provincial governors; *bhūpāḥ*—landholders; *ātma-jāḥ*—sons; *vaśa-vartinaḥ*—under your full control.

TRANSLATION

O King, are your wives, citizens, secretaries and servants and the merchants who sell spices and oil under your control? Are you also in full control of ministers, the inhabitants of your palace, your provincial governors, your sons and your other dependents?

PURPORT

The master or king and his subordinates should be interdependent. Through cooperation, both of them can be happy.

TEXT 20

यस्यात्मानुवशश्चेत्स्यात्सर्वे तद्वशगा इमे ।
लोकाः सपाला यच्छन्ति सर्वे बलिमतन्द्रिताः ॥ २० ॥

yasyātmānuvaśaś cet syāt
sarve tad-vaśagā ime
lokāḥ sapālā yacchanti
sarve balim atandritāḥ

yasya—of whom; *ātmā*—mind; *anuvaśaḥ*—under control; *cet*—if; *syāt*—may be; *sarve*—all; *tat-vaśa-gāḥ*—under the control of him; *ime*—these; *lokāḥ*—the worlds; *sa-pālāḥ*—with their governors; *yacchanti*—offer; *sarve*—all; *balim*—contribution; *atandritāḥ*—becoming free from laziness.

TRANSLATION

If the king's mind is fully controlled, all his family members and governmental officers are subordinate to him. His provincial governors

present taxes on time, without resistance, and what to speak of lesser servants?

PURPORT

Aṅgirā Ṛṣi asked the King whether his mind was also under control. This is most essential for happiness.

TEXT 21

आत्मनः प्रीयते नात्मा परतः स्वत एव वा ।
लक्षयेऽलब्धकामं त्वां चिन्तया शबलं मुखम् ॥ २१ ॥

ātmanaḥ prīyate nātmā
parataḥ svata eva vā
lakṣaye'labdha-kāmaṁ tvāṁ
cintayā śabalaṁ mukham

ātmanaḥ—of you; *prīyate*—is pleased; *na*—not; *ātmā*—the mind; *parataḥ*—due to other causes; *svataḥ*—due to yourself; *eva*—indeed; *vā*—or; *lakṣaye*—I can see; *alabdha-kāmam*—not achieving your desired goals; *tvām*—you; *cintayā*—by anxiety; *śabalam*—pale; *mukham*—face.

TRANSLATION

O King Citraketu, I can observe that your mind is not pleased. You seem not to have achieved your desired goal. Is this because of you yourself, or has it been caused by others? Your pale face reflects your deep anxiety.

TEXT 22

एवं विकल्पितो राजन् विदुषा मुनिनापि सः ।
प्रश्रयावनतोऽभ्याह प्रजाकामस्ततो मुनिम् ॥ २२ ॥

evaṁ vikalpito rājan
viduṣā munināpi saḥ
praśrayāvanato'bhyāha
prajā-kāmas tato munim

evam—thus; *vikalpitaḥ*—questioned; *rājan*—O King Parīkṣit; *viduṣā*—greatly learned; *muninā*—by the philosopher; *api*—although; *saḥ*—he (King Citraketu); *praśraya-avanataḥ*—being bent low due to humility; *abhyāha*—

replied; *prajā-kāmaḥ*—desiring offspring; *tataḥ*—thereafter; *munim*—to the great sage.

TRANSLATION

Śukadeva Gosvāmī said: O King Parīkṣit, although the great sage Aṅgirā knew everything, he inquired from the King in this way. Thus King Citraketu, desiring a son, bent low in great humility and spoke to the great sage as follows.

PURPORT

Since the face is the index to the mind, a saintly person can study the condition of one's mind by seeing his face. When Aṅgirā Ṛṣi remarked about the King's discolored face, King Citraketu explained the cause of his anxiety as follows.

TEXT 23

चित्रकेतुरुवाच

भगवन् किं न विदितं तपोज्ञानसमाधिभिः ।
योगिनां ध्वस्तपापानां बहिरन्तः शरीरिषु ॥ २३ ॥

citraketur uvāca
bhagavan kiṁ na viditaṁ
tapo-jñāna-samādhibhiḥ
yogināṁ dhvasta-pāpānāṁ
bahir antaḥ śarīriṣu

citraketuḥ uvāca—King Citraketu replied; *bhagavan*—O most powerful sage; *kim*—what; *na*—not; *viditam*—is understood; *tapaḥ*—by austerity; *jñāna*—knowledge; *samādhibhiḥ*—and by *samādhi* (trance, transcendental meditation); *yoginām*—by the great *yogīs* or devotees; *dhvasta-pāpānām*—who are fully freed from all sinful reactions; *bahiḥ*—externally; *antaḥ*—internally; *śarīriṣu*—in conditioned souls, who have material bodies.

TRANSLATION

King Citraketu said: O great lord Aṅgirā, because of austerity, knowledge and transcendental samādhi, you are freed from all the reactions of sinful life. Therefore, as a perfect yogī, you can understand everything external and internal regarding embodied, conditioned souls like us.

TEXT 24

तथापि पृच्छतो ब्रूयां ब्रह्मन्नात्मनि चिन्तितम् ।
भवतो विदुषश्चापि चोदितस्त्वदनुज्ञया ॥ २४ ॥

tathāpi pṛcchato brūyāṁ
brahmann ātmani cintitam
bhavato viduṣaś cāpi
coditas tvad-anujñayā

tathāpi—still; *pṛcchataḥ*—asking; *brūyām*—let me speak; *brahman*—O great *brāhmaṇa; ātmani*—in the mind; *cintitam*—anxiety; *bhavataḥ*—to you; *viduṣaḥ*—who know everything; *ca*—and; *api*—although; *coditaḥ*—being inspired; *tvat*—your; *anujñayā*—by the order.

TRANSLATION

O great soul, you are aware of everything, yet you are asking me why I am full of anxiety. Therefore, in response to your order, let me disclose the cause.

TEXT 25

लोकपालैरपि प्रार्थ्याः साम्राज्यैश्वर्यसम्पदः ।
न नन्दयन्त्यप्रजं मां क्षुत्तृट्कामामिवापरे ॥ २५ ॥

loka-pālair api prārthyāḥ
sāmrājyaiśvarya-sampadaḥ
na nandayanty aprajaṁ māṁ
kṣut-tṛṭ-kāmam ivāpare

loka-pālaiḥ—by great demigods; *api*—even; *prārthyāḥ*—desirable; *sāmrājya*—a great empire; *aiśvarya*—material opulence; *sampadaḥ*—possessions; *na nandayanti*—do not give pleasure; *aprajam*—because of having no son; *mām*—unto me; *kṣut*—hunger; *tṛṭ*—thirst; *kāmam*—desiring to satisfy; *iva*—like; *apare*—other enjoyable sense objects.

TRANSLATION

As a person aggrieved by hunger and thirst is not pleased by the external gratification of flower garlands or sandalwood pulp, I am not

pleased with my empire, opulence or possessions, which are desirable even for great demigods, because I have no son.

TEXT 26

ततः पाहि महाभाग पूर्वैः सह गतं तमः ।
यथा तरेम दुष्पारं प्रजया तद् विधेहि नः ॥ २६ ॥

tataḥ pāhi mahā-bhāga
pūrvaiḥ saha gataṁ tamaḥ
yathā tarema duṣpāraṁ
prajayā tad vidhehi naḥ

tataḥ—therefore, because of this; *pāhi*—kindly save; *mahā-bhāga*—O great sage; *pūrvaiḥ saha*—along with my forefathers; *gatam*—gone; *tamaḥ*—to darkness; *yathā*—so that; *tarema*—we can cross; *duṣpāram*—very difficult to cross; *prajayā*—by getting a son; *tat*—that; *vidhehi*—kindly do; *naḥ*—for us.

TRANSLATION

Therefore, O great sage, please save me and my forefathers, who are descending to the darkness of hell because I have no progeny. Kindly do something so that I may have a son to deliver us from hellish conditions.

PURPORT

According to Vedic civilization, one gets married simply to have a son, who is needed to offer oblations to his forefathers. King Citraketu responsibly desired to beget a child so that he and his forefathers might be delivered from the darkest regions. He was concerned with how to get *piṇḍa,* oblations, in the next life, not only for himself but also for his forefathers. Therefore he requested Aṅgirā Ṛṣi to favor him by doing something that could help him get a son.

TEXT 27

श्रीशुक उवाच
इत्यर्थितः स भगवान् कृपालुर्ब्रह्मणः सुतः ।
श्रपयित्वा चरुं त्वाष्ट्रं त्वष्टारमयजद् विभुः ॥ २७ ॥

śrī-śuka uvāca
ity arthitaḥ sa bhagavān
kṛpālur brahmaṇaḥ sutaḥ
śrapayitvā caruṁ tvāṣṭraṁ
tvaṣṭāram ayajad vibhuḥ

śrī-śukaḥ uvāca—Śrī Śukadeva Gosvāmī said; *iti*—thus; *arthitaḥ*—being requested; *saḥ*—he (Aṅgirā Ṛṣi); *bhagavān*—the most powerful; *kṛpāluḥ*—being very merciful; *brahmaṇaḥ*—of Lord Brahmā; *sutaḥ*—a son (born of Lord Brahmā's mind); *śrapayitvā*—after causing to cook; *carum*—a specific oblation of sweetrice; *tvāṣṭram*—meant for the demigod known as Tvaṣṭā; *tvaṣṭāram*—Tvaṣṭā; *ayajat*—he worshiped; *vibhuḥ*—the great sage.

TRANSLATION

In response to the request of Mahārāja Citraketu, Aṅgirā Ṛṣi, who was born of Lord Brahmā's mind, was very merciful toward him. Because the sage was a greatly powerful personality, he performed a sacrifice by offering oblations of sweetrice to Tvaṣṭā.

TEXT 28

ज्येष्ठा श्रेष्ठा च या राज्ञो महिषीणां च भारत ।
नाम्ना कृतद्युतिस्तस्यै यज्ञोच्छिष्टमदाद् द्विजः ॥ २८ ॥

jyeṣṭhā śreṣṭhā ca yā rājño
mahiṣīṇāṁ ca bhārata
nāmnā kṛtadyutis tasyai
yajñocchiṣṭam adād dvijaḥ

jyeṣṭhā—the senior; *śreṣṭhā*—the most perfect; *ca*—and; *yā*—she who; *rājñaḥ*—of the King; *mahiṣīṇām*—among all the queens; *ca*—also; *bhārata*—O Mahārāja Parīkṣit, the best of the Bhāratas; *nāmnā*—by name; *kṛtadyutiḥ*—Kṛtadyuti; *tasyai*—unto her; *yajña*—of the sacrifice; *ucchiṣṭam*—the remnants of food; *adāt*—delivered; *dvijaḥ*—the great sage (Aṅgirā).

TRANSLATION

O Parīkṣit Mahārāja, best of the Bhāratas, the remnants of the food offered in the yajña were given by the great sage Aṅgirā to the first and most perfect among Citraketu's millions of queens, whose name was Kṛtadyuti.

TEXT 29

अथाह नृपतिं राजन् भवितैकस्तवात्मजः ।
हर्षशोकप्रदस्तुभ्यमिति ब्रह्मसुतो ययौ ॥ २९ ॥

athāha nṛpatiṁ rājan
bhavitaikas tavātmajaḥ
harṣa-śoka-pradas tubhyam
iti brahma-suto yayau

atha—thereafter; *āha*—said; *nṛpatim*—unto the King; *rājan*—O King Citraketu; *bhavitā*—there will be; *ekaḥ*—one; *tava*—your; *ātmajaḥ*—son; *harṣa-śoka*—jubilation and lamentation; *pradaḥ*—who will give; *tubhyam*—unto you; *iti*—thus; *brahma-sutaḥ*—Aṅgirā Ṛṣi, the son of Lord Brahmā; *yayau*—left.

TRANSLATION

Thereafter, the great sage told the King, "O great King, now you will have a son who will be the cause of both jubilation and lamentation." The sage then left, without waiting for Citraketu's response.

PURPORT

The word *harṣa* means "jubilation," and *śoka* means "lamentation." The King was overwhelmed with joy when he understood that he would have a son. Because of his great jubilation, he could not actually understand the statement of the sage Aṅgirā. He accepted it to mean that there would certainly be jubilation because of the birth of his future son, but that he would be the King's only son and, being very proud of his great wealth and empire, would not be very obedient to his father. Thus the King was satisfied, thinking, "Let there be a son. It does not matter if he is not very obedient." In Bengal there is a proverb that instead of having no maternal uncle, it is better to have a maternal uncle who is blind. The King accepted this philosophy, thinking that a disobedient son would be better than no son at all. The great sage Cāṇakya Paṇḍita says:

ko'rthaḥ putreṇa jātena
yo na vidvān na dhārmikaḥ
kāṇena cakṣuṣā kiṁ vā
cakṣuḥ pīḍaiva kevalam

"What is the use of a son who is neither a learned scholar nor a devotee? Such a son is like a blind, diseased eye, which always causes suffering." Nevertheless, the material world is so polluted that one wants to have a son even though he is useless. This attitude was represented in the history of King Citraketu.

TEXT 30

सापि तत्प्राशनादेव चित्रकेतोरधारयत् ।
गर्भं कृतद्युतिर्देवी कृत्तिकाग्नेरिवात्मजम् ॥ ३० ॥

sāpi tat-prāśanād eva
citraketor adhārayat
garbhaṁ kṛtadyutir devī
kṛttikāgner ivātmajam

sā—she; *api*—even; *tat-prāśanāt*—by eating the remnants of food from the great sacrifice; *eva*—indeed; *citraketoḥ*—from King Citraketu; *adhārayat*—bore; *garbham*—pregnancy; *kṛtadyutiḥ*—Queen Kṛtadyuti; *devī*—the goddess; *kṛttikā*—Kṛttikā; *agneḥ*—from Agni; *iva*—as; *ātma-jam*—a son.

TRANSLATION

As Kṛttikādevī, after receiving the semen of Lord Śiva from Agni, conceived a child named Skanda [Kārttikeya], Kṛtadyuti, having received semen from Citraketu, became pregnant after eating remnants of food from the yajña performed by Aṅgirā.

TEXT 31

तस्या अनुदिनं गर्भः शुक्लपक्ष इवोडुपः ।
ववृधे शूरसेनेशतेजसा शनकैर्नृप ॥ ३१ ॥

tasyā anudinaṁ garbhaḥ
śukla-pakṣa ivoḍupaḥ
vavṛdhe śūraseneśa-
tejasā śanakair nṛpa

tasyāḥ—her; *anudinam*—day after day; *garbhaḥ*—embryo; *śukla-pakṣe*—during the fortnight of the waxing moon; *iva*—like; *uḍupaḥ*—the moon; *vavṛdhe*—gradually developed; *śūrasena-īśa*—of the King of Śūrasena; *tejasā*—by the semen; *śanakaiḥ*—little by little; *nṛpa*—O King Parīkṣit.

TRANSLATION

After receiving semen from Mahārāja Citraketu, the King of Śūrasena, Queen Kṛtadyuti gradually developed in her pregnancy, O King Parīkṣit, just as the moon develops during the bright fortnight.

TEXT 32

अथ काल उपावृत्ते कुमारः समजायत ।
जनयन् शूरसेनानां शृण्वतां परमां मुदम् ॥ ३२ ॥

atha kāla upāvṛtte
kumāraḥ samajāyata
janayan śūrasenānāṁ
śṛṇvatāṁ paramāṁ mudam

atha—thereafter; *kāle upāvṛtte*—in due course of time; *kumāraḥ*—the son; *samajāyata*—took birth; *janayan*—creating; *śūrasenānām*—of the inhabitants of Śūrasena; *śṛṇvatām*—hearing; *paramām*—the highest; *mudam*—delight.

TRANSLATION

Thereafter, in due course of time, a son was born to the King. Hearing news of this, all the inhabitants of the state of Śūrasena were extremely pleased.

TEXT 33

हृष्टो राजा कुमारस्य स्नातः शुचिरलंकृतः ।
वाचयित्वाशिषो विप्रैः कारयामास जातकम् ॥ ३३ ॥

hṛṣṭo rājā kumārasya
snātaḥ śucir alaṅkṛtaḥ
vācayitvāśiṣo vipraiḥ
kārayām āsa jātakam

hṛṣṭaḥ—very happy; *rājā*—the King; *kumārasya*—of his newly born son; *snātaḥ*—having bathed; *śuciḥ*—being purified; *alaṅkṛtaḥ*—being decorated with ornaments; *vācayitvā*—having caused to be spoken; *āśiṣaḥ*—words of benediction; *vipraiḥ*—by learned *brāhmaṇas; kārayām āsa*—caused to be performed; *jātakam*—the birth ceremony.

TRANSLATION

King Citraketu was especially pleased. After purifying himself by bathing and by decorating himself with ornaments, he engaged learned brāhmaṇas in offering benedictions to the child and performing the birth ceremony.

TEXT 34

तेभ्यो हिरण्यं रजतं वासांस्याभरणानि च ।
ग्रामान् हयान् गजान् प्रादाद् धेनूनामर्बुदानि षट् ॥ ३४ ॥

tebhyo hiraṇyaṁ rajataṁ
vāsāṁsy ābharaṇāni ca
grāmān hayān gajān prādād
dhenūnām arbudāni ṣaṭ

tebhyaḥ—unto them (the learned *brāhmaṇas*); *hiraṇyam*—gold; *rajatam*—silver; *vāsāṁsi*—garments; *ābharaṇāni*—ornaments; *ca*—also; *grāmān*—villages; *hayān*—horses; *gajān*—elephants; *prādāt*—gave in charity; *dhenūnām*—of cows; *arbudāni*—groups of one hundred million; *ṣaṭ*—six.

TRANSLATION

Unto the brāhmaṇas who took part in the ritualistic ceremony the King gave charity of gold, silver, garments, ornaments, villages, horses and elephants, as well as sixty crores of cows [six hundred million cows].

TEXT 35

ववर्ष कामानन्येषां पर्जन्य इव देहिनाम् ।
धन्यं यशस्यमायुष्यं कुमारस्य महामनाः ॥ ३५ ॥

vavarṣa kāmān anyeṣāṁ
parjanya iva dehinām
dhanyaṁ yaśasyam āyuṣyaṁ
kumārasya mahā-manāḥ

vavarṣa—showered, gave in charity; *kāmān*—all desirable things; *anyeṣām*—of others; *parjanyaḥ*—a cloud; *iva*—like; *dehinām*—of all living entities; *dhanyam*—with the desire for an increase of opulence; *yaśasyam*—an increase of reputation; *āyuṣyam*—and an increase of the duration of life; *kumārasya*—of the newly born child; *mahā-manāḥ*—the beneficent King Citraketu.

TRANSLATION

As a cloud indiscriminately pours water on the earth, the beneficent King Citraketu, to increase the reputation, opulence and longevity of his son, distributed like rainfall all desirable things to everyone.

TEXT 36

कृच्छ्रलब्धेऽथ राजर्षेस्तनयेऽनुदिनं पितुः ।
यथा निःस्वस्य कृच्छ्राप्ते धने स्नेहोऽन्ववर्धत ॥ ३६ ॥

kṛcchra-labdhe'tha rājarṣes
tanaye'nudinaṁ pituḥ
yathā niḥsvasya kṛcchrāpte
dhane sneho'nvavardhata

kṛcchra—with great difficulty; *labdhe*—gained; *atha*—thereafter; *rāja-ṛṣeḥ*—of the pious King Citraketu; *tanaye*—for the son; *anudinam*—day after day; *pituḥ*—of the father; *yathā*—exactly as; *niḥsvasya*—of a poor man; *kṛcchra-āpte*—gained after great difficulty; *dhane*—for riches; *snehaḥ*—affection; *anvavardhata*—increased.

TRANSLATION

When a poor man gets some money after great difficulty, his affection for the money increases daily. Similarly, when King Citraketu, after great difficulty, received a son, his affection for the son increased day after day.

TEXT 37

मातुस्त्वतितरां पुत्रे स्नेहो मोहसमुद्भवः ।
कृतद्युतेः सपत्नीनां प्रजाकामज्वरोऽभवत् ॥ ३७ ॥

mātus tv atitarāṁ putre
sneho moha-samudbhavaḥ
kṛtadyuteḥ sapatnīnāṁ
prajā-kāma-jvaro'bhavat

mātuḥ—of the mother; *tu*—also; *atitarām*—excessively; *putre*—for the son; *snehaḥ*—affection; *moha*—out of ignorance; *samudbhavaḥ*—produced; *kṛtadyuteḥ*—of Kṛtadyuti; *sapatnīnām*—of the co-wives; *prajā-kāma*—of a desire to have sons; *jvaraḥ*—a fever; *abhavat*—there was.

TRANSLATION

The mother's attraction and attention to the son, like that of the child's father, excessively increased. The other wives, seeing Kṛtadyuti's son, were very much agitated, as if by high fevers, with a desire to have sons.

TEXT 38

चित्रकेतोरतिप्रीतिर्यथा दारे प्रजावति ।
न तथान्येषु सञ्जज्ञे बालं लालयतोऽन्वहम् ॥ ३८ ॥

citraketor atiprītir
yathā dāre prajāvati
na tathānyeṣu sañjajñe
bālaṁ lālayato'nvaham

citraketoḥ—of King Citraketu; *atiprītiḥ*—excessive attraction; *yathā*—just as; *dāre*—unto the wife; *prajā-vati*—who begot a son; *na*—not; *tathā*—like that; *anyeṣu*—unto the others; *sañjajñe*—arose; *bālam*—the son; *lālayataḥ*—taking care of; *anvaham*—constantly.

TRANSLATION

As King Citraketu fostered his son very carefully, his affection for Queen Kṛtadyuti increased, but gradually he lost affection for the other wives, who had no sons.

TEXT 39

ताः पर्यतप्यन्नात्मानं गर्हयन्त्योऽभ्यसूयया ।
आनपत्येन दुःखेन राज्ञश्चानादरेण च ॥ ३९ ॥

tāḥ paryatapyann ātmānaṁ
garhayantyo'bhyasūyayā
ānapatyena duḥkhena
rājñaś cānādareṇa ca

tāḥ—they (the queens who did not have sons); *paryatapyan*—lamented; *ātmānam*—themselves; *garhayantyaḥ*—condemning; *abhyasūyayā*—out of envy; *ānapatyena*—due to being without sons; *duḥkhena*—by unhappiness; *rājñaḥ*—of the King; *ca*—also; *anādareṇa*—due to negligence; *ca*—also.

TRANSLATION

The other queens were extremely unhappy due to their being sonless. Because of the King's negligence toward them, they condemned themselves in envy and lamented.

TEXT 40

धिगप्रजां स्त्रियं पापां पत्युश्चागृहसम्मताम् ।
सुप्रजाभिः सपत्नीभिर्दासीमिव तिरस्कृताम् ॥ ४० ॥

dhig aprajāṁ striyaṁ pāpāṁ
patyuś cāgṛha-sammatām
suprajābhiḥ sapatnībhir
dāsīm iva tiraskṛtām

dhik—all condemnation; *aprajām*—without a son; *striyam*—upon a woman; *pāpām*—full of sinful activities; *patyuḥ*—by the husband; *ca*—also; *a-gṛha-sammatām*—who is not honored at home; *su-prajābhiḥ*—who have sons; *sapatnībhiḥ*—by co-wives; *dāsīm*—a maidservant; *iva*—exactly like; *tiraskṛtām*—dishonored.

TRANSLATION

A wife who has no sons is neglected at home by her husband and dishonored by her co-wives exactly like a maidservant. Certainly such a woman is condemned in every respect because of her sinful life.

PURPORT

As stated by Cāṇakya Paṇḍita:

mātā yasya gṛhe nāsti
bhāryā cāpriya-vādinī
araṇyaṁ tena gantavyaṁ
yathāraṇyaṁ tathā gṛham

"A person who has no mother at home and whose wife does not speak sweetly should go to the forest. For such a person, living at home and living in the forest are equal." Similarly, for a woman who has no son, who is not cared for by her husband and whose co-wives neglect her, treating her like a maidservant, to go to the forest is better than to remain at home.

TEXT 41

दासीनां को नु सन्तापः स्वामिनः परिचर्यया ।
अभीक्ष्णं लब्धमानानां दास्या दासीव दुर्भगाः ॥ ४१ ॥

dāsīnāṁ ko nu santāpaḥ
svāminaḥ paricaryayā
abhīkṣṇaṁ labdha-mānānāṁ
dāsyā dāsīva durbhagāḥ

dāsīnām—of the maidservants; *kaḥ*—what; *nu*—indeed; *santāpaḥ*—lamentation; *svāminaḥ*—unto the husband; *paricaryayā*—by rendering service; *abhīkṣṇam*—constantly; *labdha-mānānām*—honored; *dāsyāḥ*—of the maidservant; *dāsī iva*—like a maidservant; *durbhagāḥ*—most unfortunate.

TRANSLATION

Even maidservants who are constantly engaged in rendering service to the husband are honored by the husband, and thus they have nothing for which to lament. Our position, however, is that we are maidservants of the maidservant. Therefore we are most unfortunate.

TEXT 42

एवं सन्दह्यमानानां सपत्न्याः पुत्रसम्पदा ।
राज्ञोऽसम्मतवृत्तीनां विद्वेषो बलवानभूत् ॥ ४२ ॥

evaṁ sandahyamānānāṁ
sapatnyāḥ putra-sampadā
rājño'sammata-vṛttīnāṁ
vidveṣo balavān abhūt

evam—thus; *sandahyamānānām*—of the queens, who were constantly burning in lamentation; *sapatnyāḥ*—of the co-wife Kṛtadyuti; *putra-sampadā*—due to the opulence of a son; *rājñaḥ*—by the King; *asammata-vṛttīnām*—not being very much favored; *vidveṣaḥ*—envy; *balavān*—very strong; *abhūt*—became.

TRANSLATION

Śrī Śukadeva Gosvāmī continued: Being neglected by their husband and seeing Kṛtadyuti's opulence in possessing a son, Kṛtadyuti's co-wives always burned in envy, which became extremely strong.

TEXT 43

विद्वेषनष्टमतयः स्त्रियो दारुणचेतसः ।
गरं ददुः कुमाराय दुर्मर्षा नृपतिं प्रति ॥ ४३ ॥

vidveṣa-naṣṭa-matayaḥ
striyo dāruṇa-cetasaḥ
garaṁ daduḥ kumārāya
durmarṣā nṛpatiṁ prati

vidveṣa-naṣṭa-matayaḥ—whose intelligence was lost in envy; *striyaḥ*—the women; *dāruṇa-cetasaḥ*—being very hardhearted; *garam*—poison; *daduḥ*—administered; *kumārāya*—unto the boy; *durmarṣāḥ*—being intolerant; *nṛpatim*—the King; *prati*—upon.

TRANSLATION

As their envy increased, they lost their intelligence. Being extremely hardhearted and unable to tolerate the King's neglect, they finally administered poison to the son.

TEXT 44

कृतद्युतिरजानन्ती सपत्नीनामघं महत् ।
सुप्त एवेति सञ्चिन्त्य निरीक्ष्य व्यचरद् गृहे ॥ ४४ ॥

kṛtadyutir ajānantī
sapatnīnām aghaṁ mahat
supta eveti sañcintya
nirīkṣya vyacarad gṛhe

kṛtadyutiḥ—Queen Kṛtadyuti; *ajānantī*—being unaware of; *sapatnīnām*—of her co-wives; *agham*—sinful act; *mahat*—very great; *suptaḥ*—sleeping; *eva*—indeed; *iti*—thus; *sañcintya*—thinking; *nirīkṣya*—looking at; *vyacarat*—was walking; *gṛhe*—at home.

TRANSLATION

Unaware of the poison administered by her co-wives, Queen Kṛtadyuti walked within the house, thinking that her son was sleeping deeply. She did not understand that he was dead.

TEXT 45

शयानं सुचिरं बालमुपधार्य मनीषिणी ।
पुत्रमानय मे भद्रे इति धात्रीमचोदयत् ॥ ४५ ॥

śayānaṁ suciraṁ bālam
upadhārya manīṣiṇī
putram ānaya me bhadre
iti dhātrīm acodayat

śayānam—lying down; *su-ciram*—for a long time; *bālam*—the son; *upadhārya*—thinking; *manīṣiṇī*—very intelligent; *putram*—the son; *ānaya*—bring; *me*—unto me; *bhadre*—O gentle friend; *iti*—thus; *dhātrīm*—unto the nurse; *acodayat*—gave the order.

TRANSLATION

Thinking that her child had been sleeping for a long time, Queen Kṛtadyuti, who was certainly very intelligent, ordered the nurse, "My dear friend, please bring my son here."

TEXT 46

सा शयानमुपव्रज्य दृष्ट्वा चोत्तारलोचनम् ।
प्राणेन्द्रियात्मभिस्त्यक्तं हतास्मीत्यपतद्भुवि ॥ ४६ ॥

sā śayānam upavrajya
dṛṣṭvā cottāra-locanam
prāṇendriyātmabhis tyaktaṁ
hatāsmīty apatad bhuvi

sā—she (the maidservant); *śayānam*—lying down; *upavrajya*—going to; *dṛṣṭvā*—seeing; *ca*—also; *uttāra-locanam*—his eyes turned upward (as are those of a dead body); *prāṇa-indriya-ātmabhiḥ*—by the life force, senses and mind; *tyaktam*—abandoned; *hatā asmi*—now I am doomed; *iti*—thus; *apatat*—fell down; *bhuvi*—on the ground.

TRANSLATION

When the maidservant approached the child, who was lying down, she saw that his eyes were turned upward. There were no signs of life, all his

senses having stopped, and she could understand that the child was dead. Seeing this, she immediately cried, "Now I am doomed," and fell to the ground.

TEXT 47

तस्यास्तदाकर्ण्य भृशातुरं स्वरं
घ्नन्त्याः कराभ्यामुर उच्चकैरपि ।
प्रविश्य राज्ञी त्वरयात्मजान्तिकं
ददर्श बालं सहसा मृतं सुतम् ॥ ४७ ॥

tasyās tadākarṇya bhṛśāturaṁ svaraṁ
ghnantyāḥ karābhyām ura uccakair api
praviśya rājñī tvarayātmajāntikaṁ
dadarśa bālaṁ sahasā mṛtaṁ sutam

tasyāḥ—of her (the maidservant); *tadā*—at that time; *ākarṇya*—hearing; *bhṛśa-āturam*—highly regretful and agitated; *svaram*—voice; *ghnantyāḥ*—striking; *karābhyām*—with the hands; *uraḥ*—the chest; *uccakaiḥ*—loudly; *api*—also; *praviśya*—entering; *rājñī*—the Queen; *tvarayā*—hastily; *ātmaja-antikam*—near her son; *dadarśa*—she saw; *bālam*—the child; *sahasā*—suddenly; *mṛtam*—dead; *sutam*—son.

TRANSLATION

In great agitation, the maidservant struck her breast with both hands and cried loudly in regretful words. Hearing her loud voice, the Queen immediately came, and when she approached her son, she saw that he was suddenly dead.

TEXT 48

पपात भूमौ परिवृद्धया शुचा ।
मुमोह विभ्रष्टशिरोरुहाम्बरा ॥ ४८ ॥

papāta bhūmau parivṛddhayā śucā
mumoha vibhraṣṭa-śiroruhāmbarā

papāta—fell down; *bhūmau*—on the ground; *parivṛddhayā*—highly increased; *śucā*—out of lamentation; *mumoha*—she became unconscious; *vibhraṣṭa*—scattered; *śiroruha*—hair; *ambarā*—and dress.

TRANSLATION

In great lamentation, her hair and dress in disarray, the Queen fell to the ground unconscious.

TEXT 49

ततो नृपान्तःपुरवर्तिनो जना
नराश्च नार्यश्च निशम्य रोदनम् ।
आगत्य तुल्यव्यसनाः सुदुःखिता-
स्ताश्च व्यलीकं रुरुदुः कृतागसः ॥ ४९ ॥

tato nṛpāntaḥpura-vartino janā
narāś ca nāryaś ca niśamya rodanam
āgatya tulya-vyasanāḥ suduḥkhitās
tāś ca vyalīkaṁ ruruduḥ kṛtāgasaḥ

tataḥ—thereafter; *nṛpa*—O King; *antaḥpura-vartinaḥ*—the inhabitants of the palace; *janāḥ*—all the people; *narāḥ*—the men; *ca*—and; *nāryaḥ*—the women; *ca*—also; *niśamya*—hearing; *rodanam*—loud crying; *āgatya*—coming; *tulya-vyasanāḥ*—being equally aggrieved; *su-duḥkhitāḥ*—very greatly lamenting; *tāḥ*—they; *ca*—and; *vyalīkam*—pretentiously; *ruruduḥ*—cried; *kṛta-āgasaḥ*—who had committed the offense (by giving the poison).

TRANSLATION

O King Parīkṣit, hearing the loud crying, all the inhabitants of the palace came, both men and women. Being equally aggrieved, they also began to cry. The queens who had administered the poison also cried pretentiously, knowing full well their offense.

TEXTS 50–51

श्रुत्वा मृतं पुत्रमलक्षितान्तकं
विनष्टदृष्टिः प्रपतन् स्खलन् पथि ।
स्नेहानुबन्धैधितया शुचा भृशं
विमूर्च्छितोऽनुप्रकृतिर्द्विजैर्वृतः ॥ ५० ॥
पपात बालस्य स पादमूले
मृतस्य विस्रस्तशिरोरुहाम्बरः ।

दीर्घं श्वसन् बाष्पकलोपरोधतो
निरुद्ध कण्ठो न शशाक भाषितुम्॥ ५१ ॥

śrutvā mṛtaṁ putram alakṣitāntakaṁ
vinaṣṭa-dṛṣṭiḥ prapatan skhalan pathi
snehānubandhaidhitayā śucā bhṛśaṁ
vimūrcchito'nuprakṛtir dvijair vṛtaḥ

papāta bālasya sa pāda-mūle
mṛtasya visrasta-śiroruhāmbaraḥ
dīrghaṁ śvasan bāṣpa-kaloparodhato
niruddha-kaṇṭho na śaśāka bhāṣitum

śrutvā—hearing; *mṛtam*—dead; *putram*—the son; *alakṣita-antakam*—the cause of death being unknown; *vinaṣṭa-dṛṣṭiḥ*—unable to see properly; *prapatan*—constantly falling down; *skhalan*—slipping; *pathi*—on the road; *sneha-anubandha*—because of affection; *edhitayā*—increasing; *śucā*—by lamentation; *bhṛśam*—greatly; *vimūrcchitaḥ*—becoming unconscious; *anuprakṛtiḥ*—followed by ministers and other officers; *dvijaiḥ*—by learned *brāhmaṇas; vṛtaḥ*—surrounded; *papāta*—fell down; *bālasya*—of the boy; *saḥ*—he (the King); *pāda-mūle*—at the feet; *mṛtasya*—of the dead body; *visrasta*—scattered; *śiroruha*—hair; *ambaraḥ*—and dress; *dīrgham*—long; *śvasan*—breathing; *bāṣpa-kalā-uparodhataḥ*—due to crying with tearful eyes; *niruddha-kaṇṭhaḥ*—having a choked voice; *na*—not; *śaśāka*—was able; *bhāṣitum*—to speak.

TRANSLATION

When King Citraketu heard of his son's death from unknown causes, he became almost blind. Because of his great affection for his son, his lamentation grew like a blazing fire, and as he went to see the dead child, he kept slipping and falling on the ground. Surrounded by his ministers and other officers and the learned brāhmaṇas present, the King approached and fell unconscious at the child's feet, his hair and dress scattered. When the King, breathing heavily, regained consciousness, his eyes were tearful, and he could not speak.

TEXT 52

पतिं निरीक्ष्योरुशुचार्पितं तदा
मृतं च बालं सुतमेकसन्ततिम्।

जनस्य राज्ञी प्रकृतेश्च हृद्रुजं
सती दधाना विललाप चित्रधा ॥ ५२ ॥

patiṁ nirīkṣyoru-śucārpitaṁ tadā
mṛtaṁ ca bālaṁ sutam eka-santatim
janasya rājñī prakṛteś ca hṛd-rujaṁ
satī dadhānā vilalāpa citradhā

patim—the husband; *nirīkṣya*—by seeing; *uru*—greatly; *śuca*—with lamentation; *arpitam*—pained; *tadā*—at that time; *mṛtam*—dead; *ca*—and; *bālam*—the child; *sutam*—the son; *eka-santatim*—the only son in the family; *janasya*—of all the other people gathered there; *rājñī*—the Queen; *prakṛteḥ ca*—as well as of the officers and ministers; *hṛt-rujam*—the pains within the core of the heart; *satī dadhānā*—increasing; *vilalāpa*—lamented; *citradhā*—in varieties of ways.

TRANSLATION

When the Queen saw her husband, King Citraketu, merged in great lamentation and saw the dead child, who was the only son in the family, she lamented in various ways. This increased the pain in the cores of the hearts of all the inhabitants of the palace, the ministers and all the brāhmaṇas.

TEXT 53

स्तनद्वयं कुङ्कुमपङ्कमण्डितं
निषिञ्चती साञ्जनबाष्पबिन्दुभिः ।
विकीर्य केशान् विगलत्स्रजः सुतं
शुशोच चित्रं कुररीव सुस्वरम् ॥ ५३ ॥

stana-dvayaṁ kuṅkuma-paṅka-maṇḍitaṁ
niṣiñcatī sāñjana-bāṣpa-bindubhiḥ
vikīrya keśān vigalat-srajaḥ sutaṁ
śuśoca citraṁ kurarīva susvaram

stana-dvayam—her two breasts; *kuṅkuma*—with *kuṅkuma* powder (which is generally sprayed on the breasts of women); *paṅka*—ointment; *maṇḍitam*—decorated; *niṣiñcatī*—moistening; *sa-añjana*—mixed with the eye ointment; *bāṣpa*—of tears; *bindubhiḥ*—by drops; *vikīrya*—scattering;

keśān—hair; *vigalat*—was falling down; *srajaḥ*—on which the flower garland; *sutam*—for her son; *śuśoca*—lamented; *citram*—variegated; *kurarī iva*—like a *kurarī* bird; *su-svaram*—in a very sweet voice.

TRANSLATION

The garland of flowers decorating the Queen's head fell, and her hair scattered. Falling tears melted the collyrium on her eyes and moistened her breasts, which were covered with kuṅkuma powder. As she lamented the loss of her son, her loud crying resembled the sweet sound of a kurarī bird.

TEXT 54

अहो विधातस्त्वमतीव बालिशो
यस्त्वात्मसृष्ट्यप्रतिरूपमीहसे ।
परे नु जीवत्यपरस्य या मृति-
र्विपर्ययश्चेत्त्वमसि ध्रुवः परः ॥ ५४ ॥

aho vidhātas tvam atīva bāliśo
yas tv ātma-sṛṣṭy-apratirūpam īhase
pare nu jīvaty aparasya yā mṛtir
viparyayaś cet tvam asi dhruvaḥ paraḥ

aho—alas (in great lamentation); *vidhātaḥ*—O Providence; *tvam*—You; *atīva*—very much; *bāliśaḥ*—inexperienced; *yaḥ*—who; *tu*—indeed; *ātma-sṛṣṭi*—of Your own creation; *apratirūpam*—just the opposite; *īhase*—You are performing and desiring; *pare*—while the father or the elder; *nu*—indeed; *jīvati*—is living; *aparasya*—of one who was born later; *yā*—which; *mṛtiḥ*—death; *viparyayaḥ*—contradictory; *cet*—if; *tvam*—You; *asi*—are; *dhruvaḥ*—indeed; *paraḥ*—an enemy.

TRANSLATION

Alas, O Providence, O Creator, You are certainly inexperienced in creation, for during the lifetime of a father You have caused the death of his son, thus acting in opposition to Your creative laws. If You are determined to contradict these laws, You are certainly the enemy of living entities and are never merciful.

PURPORT

This is the way a conditioned soul condemns the supreme creator when he meets reverses. Sometimes he accuses the Supreme Personality of

Godhead of being crooked because some people are happy and some are not. Here the Queen blames supreme providence for her son's death. Following the creative laws, a father should die first and then his son. If the creative laws are changed according to the whims of providence, then providence certainly should not be considered merciful, but must be considered inimical to the created being. Actually it is not the creator, but the conditioned soul who is inexperienced. He does not know how the subtle laws of fruitive activity work, and without knowledge of these laws of nature, he ignorantly criticizes the Supreme Personality of Godhead.

TEXT 55

न हि क्रमश्चेदिह मृत्युजन्मनोः
शरीरिणामस्तु तदात्मकर्मभिः ।
यः स्नेहपाशो निजसर्गवृद्धये
स्वयं कृतस्ते तमिमं विवृश्चसि ॥ ५५ ॥

na hi kramaś ced iha mṛtyu-janmanoḥ
śarīriṇām astu tad ātma-karmabhiḥ
yaḥ sneha-pāśo nija-sarga-vṛddhaye
svayaṁ kṛtas te tam imaṁ vivṛścasi

na—not; *hi*—indeed; *kramaḥ*—chronological order; *cet*—if; *iha*—in this material world; *mṛtyu*—of death; *janmanoḥ*—and of birth; *śarīriṇām*—of the conditioned souls, who have accepted material bodies; *astu*—let it be; *tat*—that; *ātma-karmabhiḥ*—by the results of one's *karma* (fruitive activities); *yaḥ*—that which; *sneha-pāśaḥ*—bondage of affection; *nija-sarga*—Your own creation; *vṛddhaye*—to increase; *svayam*—personally; *kṛtaḥ*—made; *te*—by You; *tam*—that; *imam*—this; *vivṛścasi*—you are cutting.

TRANSLATION

My Lord, You may say that there is no law that a father must die in the lifetime of his son and that a son must be born in the lifetime of his father, since everyone lives and dies according to his own fruitive activity. However, if fruitive activity is so strong that birth and death depend upon it, there is no need of a controller, or God. Again, if You say that a controller is needed because the material energy does not have the power to act, one may answer that if the bonds of affection You have created are disturbed

by fruitive action, no one will raise children with affection; instead, everyone will cruelly neglect his children. Since You have cut the bonds of affection that compel a parent to raise his child, You appear inexperienced and unintelligent.

PURPORT

As stated in the *Brahma-saṁhitā, karmāṇi nirdahati kintu ca bhakti-bhājām:* one who has taken to Kṛṣṇa consciousness, devotional service, is not affected by the results of *karma.* In this verse, *karma* has been stressed on the basis of *karma-mīmāṁsā* philosophy, which says that one must act according to his *karma* and that a supreme controller must give the results of *karma.* The subtle laws of *karma,* which are controlled by the Supreme, cannot be understood by ordinary conditioned souls. Therefore Kṛṣṇa says that one who can understand Him and how He is acting, controlling everything by subtle laws, immediately becomes freed by His grace. That is the statement of *Brahma-saṁhitā* (*karmāṇi nirdahati kintu ca bhakti-bhājām*). One should take to devotional service without reservations and surrender everything to the supreme will of the Lord. That will make one happy in this life and the next.

TEXT 56

त्वं तात नार्हसि च मां कृपणामनाथां
त्यक्तुं विचक्ष्व पितरं तव शोकतप्तम्।
अञ्जस्तरेम भवताप्रजदुस्तरं यद्
ध्वान्तं न याह्यकरुणेन यमेन दूरम् ॥५६॥

tvaṁ tāta nārhasi ca māṁ kṛpaṇām anāthāṁ
tyaktuṁ vicakṣva pitaraṁ tava śoka-taptam
añjas tarema bhavatāpraja-dustaraṁ yad
dhvāntaṁ na yāhy akaruṇena yamena dūram

tvam—you; *tāta*—my dear son; *na*—not; *arhasi*—ought; *ca*—and; *mām*—me; *kṛpaṇām*—very poor; *anāthām*—without a protector; *tyaktum*—to give up; *vicakṣva*—look; *pitaram*—at the father; *tava*—your; *śoka-taptam*—affected by so much lamentation; *añjaḥ*—easily; *tarema*—we can cross; *bhavatā*—by you; *apraja-dustaram*—very difficult to cross for one without a son; *yat*—which; *dhvāntam*—the kingdom of darkness; *na yāhi*—do not go away; *akaruṇena*—merciless; *yamena*—with Yamarāja; *dūram*—any further.

TRANSLATION

My dear son, I am helpless and very much aggrieved. You should not give up my company. Just look at your lamenting father. We are helpless because without a son we shall have to suffer the distress of going to the darkest hellish regions. You are the only hope by which we can get out of these dark regions. Therefore I request you not to go any further with the merciless Yama.

PURPORT

According to the Vedic injunctions, one must accept a wife just to beget a son who can deliver one from the clutches of Yamarāja. Unless one has a son to offer oblations to the *pitās,* or forefathers, one must suffer in Yamarāja's kingdom. King Citraketu was very much aggrieved, thinking that because his son was going away with Yamarāja, he himself would again suffer. The subtle laws exist for the *karmīs;* if one becomes a devotee, he has no more obligations to the laws of *karma.*

TEXT 57

उत्तिष्ठ तात त इमे शिशवो वयस्या-
स्त्वामाह्वयन्ति नृपनन्दन संविहर्तुम् ।
सुप्तश्चिरं ह्यशनया च भवान् परीतो
भुङ्क्ष्व स्तनं पिब शुचो हर नः स्वकानाम् ॥ ५७ ॥

uttiṣṭha tāta ta ime śiśavo vayasyās
tvām āhvayanti nṛpa-nandana saṁvihartum
suptaś ciraṁ hy aśanayā ca bhavān parīto
bhuṅkṣva stanaṁ piba śuco hara naḥ svakānām

uttiṣṭha—kindly get up; *tāta*—my dear son; *te*—they; *ime*—all these; *śiśavaḥ*—children; *vayasyāḥ*—playmates; *tvām*—you; *āhvayanti*—are calling; *nṛpa-nandana*—O son of the King; *saṁvihartum*—to play with; *suptaḥ*—you have slept; *ciram*—for a long time; *hi*—indeed; *aśanayā*—by hunger; *ca*—also; *bhavān*—you; *parītaḥ*—overcome; *bhuṅkṣva*—please eat; *stanam*—at the breast (of your mother); *piba*—drink; *śucaḥ*—lamentation; *hara*—just dissipate; *naḥ*—of us; *svakānām*—your relatives.

TRANSLATION

My dear son, you have slept a long time. Now please get up. Your playmates are calling you to play. Since you must be very hungry, please get up and suck my breast and dissipate our lamentation.

TEXT 58

नाहं तनूज ददृशे हतमङ्गला ते
मुग्धस्मितं मुदितवीक्षणमाननाब्जम् ।
किं वा गतोऽस्यपुनरन्वयमन्यलोकं
नीतोऽघृणेन न शृणोमि कला गिरस्ते ॥ ५८ ॥

nāhaṁ tanūja dadṛśe hata-maṅgalā te
mugdha-smitaṁ mudita-vīkṣaṇam ānanābjam
kiṁ vā gato'sy apunar-anvayam anya-lokaṁ
nīto'ghṛṇena na śṛṇomi kalā giras te

na—not; *aham*—I; *tanū-ja*—my dear son (born of my body); *dadṛśe*—saw; *hata-maṅgalā*—because of my being the most unfortunate; *te*—your; *mugdha-smitam*—with charming smiling; *mudita-vīkṣaṇam*—with closed eyes; *ānana-abjam*—lotus face; *kiṁ vā*—whether; *gataḥ*—gone away; *asi*—you are; *a-punaḥ-anvayam*—from which one does not return; *anya-lokam*—to another planet, or the planet of Yamarāja; *nītaḥ*—having been taken away; *aghṛṇena*—by the cruel Yamarāja; *na*—not; *śṛṇomi*—I can hear; *kalāḥ*—very pleasing; *giraḥ*—utterances; *te*—your.

TRANSLATION

My dear son, I am certainly most unfortunate, for I can no longer see your mild smiling. You have closed your eyes forever. I therefore conclude that you have been taken from this planet to another, from which you will not return. My dear son, I can no longer hear your pleasing voice.

TEXT 59

श्रीशुक उवाच

विलपन्त्या मृतं पुत्रमिति चित्रविलापनैः ।
चित्रकेतुर्भृशं तप्तो मुक्तकण्ठो रुरोद ह ॥ ५९ ॥

śrī-śuka uvāca
vilapantyā mṛtaṁ putram
iti citra-vilāpanaiḥ
citraketur bhṛśaṁ tapto
mukta-kaṇṭho ruroda ha

śrī-śukaḥ uvāca—Śrī Śukadeva Gosvāmī said; *vilapantyā*—with the woman who was lamenting; *mṛtam*—dead; *putram*—for the son; *iti*—thus; *citra-vilāpanaiḥ*—with various lamentations; *citraketuḥ*—King Citraketu; *bhṛśam*—very much; *taptaḥ*—aggrieved; *mukta-kaṇṭhaḥ*—loudly; *ruroda*—cried; *ha*—indeed.

TRANSLATION

Śrī Śukadeva Gosvāmī continued: Accompanied by his wife, who was thus lamenting for her dead son, King Citraketu began crying loudly with an open mouth, being greatly aggrieved.

TEXT 60

तयोर्विलपतोः सर्वे दम्पत्योस्तदनुव्रताः ।
रुरुदुः स्म नरा नार्यः सर्वमासीदचेतनम् ॥ ६० ॥

tayor vilapatoḥ sarve
dampatyos tad-anuvratāḥ
ruruduḥ sma narā nāryaḥ
sarvam āsīd acetanam

tayoḥ—while the two of them; *vilapatoḥ*—were lamenting; *sarve*—all; *dam-patyoḥ*—the King, along with his wife; *tat-anuvratāḥ*—their followers; *ruruduḥ*—cried loudly; *sma*—indeed; *narāḥ*—the male members; *nāryaḥ*—the female members; *sarvam*—the whole kingdom; *āsīt*—became; *acetanam*—almost unconscious.

TRANSLATION

As the King and Queen lamented, all their male and female followers joined them in crying. Because of the sudden accident, all the citizens of the kingdom were almost unconscious.

TEXT 61

एवं कश्मलमापन्नं नष्टसंज्ञमनायकम् ।
ज्ञात्वाङ्गिरा नाम ऋषिराजगाम सनारदः ॥ ६१ ॥

evaṁ kaśmalam āpannaṁ
naṣṭa-saṁjñam anāyakam
jñātvāṅgirā nāma ṛṣir
ājagāma sanāradaḥ

evam—thus; *kaśmalam*—misery; *āpannam*—having gotten; *naṣṭa*—lost; *saṁjñam*—consciousness; *anāyakam*—without help; *jñātvā*—knowing; *aṅgirāḥ*—Aṅgirā; *nāma*—named; *ṛṣiḥ*—the saintly person; *ājagāma*—came; *sa-nāradaḥ*—with Nārada Muni.

TRANSLATION

When the great sage Aṅgirā understood that the King was almost dead in an ocean of lamentation, he went there with Nārada Ṛṣi.

Thus end the Bhaktivedanta purports of the Sixth Canto, Fourteenth Chapter, of the Śrīmad-Bhāgavatam, *entitled "King Citraketu's Lamentation."*

CHAPTER FIFTEEN

The Saints Nārada and Aṅgirā Instruct King Citraketu

In this chapter, Aṅgirā Ṛṣi, along with Nārada, consoles Citraketu as far as possible. Aṅgirā and Nārada Ṛṣi came to relieve the King from excessive lamentation by instructing him about the spiritual significance of life.

The great saints Aṅgirā and Nārada explained that the relationship between father and son is not factual; it is simply a representation of the illusory energy. The relationship did not exist before, nor will it stay in the future. By the arrangement of time, the relationship exists only in the present. One should not lament for temporary relationships. The entire cosmic manifestation is temporary; although not unreal, it is not factual. By the direction of the Supreme Personality of Godhead, everything created in the material world is transient. By a temporary arrangement, a father begets a child, or a living entity becomes the child of a so-called father. This temporary arrangement is made by the Supreme Lord. Neither the father nor the son exists independently.

As the King listened to the great sages, he was relieved from his false lamentation, and then he inquired about their identity. The great sages presented who they were and instructed that all sufferings are due to the bodily conception of life. When one understands his spiritual identity and surrenders to the Supreme Personality of Godhead, the supreme spiritual person, one becomes actually happy. When one searches for happiness in matter, one must certainly lament for bodily relationships. Self-realization means spiritual realization of one's relationship with Kṛṣṇa. Such realization ends one's miserable material life.

TEXT 1

श्रीशुक उवाच

ऊचतुर्मृतकोपान्ते पतितं मृतकोपमम् ।
शोकाभिभूतं राजानं बोधयन्तौ सदुक्तिभिः ॥ १ ॥

śrī-śuka uvāca
ūcatur mṛtakopānte
patitaṁ mṛtakopamam
śokābhibhūtaṁ rājānaṁ
bodhayantau sad-uktibhiḥ

śrī-śukaḥ uvāca—Śrī Śukadeva Gosvāmī said; *ūcatuḥ*—they spoke; *mṛtaka*—the dead body; *upānte*—near; *patitam*—fallen; *mṛtaka-upamam*—exactly like another dead body; *śoka-abhibhūtam*—very much aggrieved by lamentation; *rājānam*—to the King; *bodhayantau*—giving instruction; *sat-uktibhiḥ*—by instructions that are factual, not temporary.

TRANSLATION

Śrī Śukadeva Gosvāmī said: While King Citraketu, overcome by lamentation, lay like a dead body at the side of the dead body of his son, the two great sages Nārada and Aṅgirā instructed him about spiritual consciousness as follows.

TEXT 2

कोऽयं स्यात् तव राजेन्द्र भवान् यमनुशोचति ।
त्वं चास्य कतमः सृष्टौ पुरेदानीमतः परम् ॥ २ ॥

ko'yaṁ syāt tava rājendra
bhavān yam anuśocati
tvaṁ cāsya katamaḥ sṛṣṭau
puredānīm ataḥ param

kaḥ—who; *ayam*—this; *syāt*—is; *tava*—to you; *rāja-indra*—O best of kings; *bhavān*—Your Lordship; *yam*—whom; *anuśocati*—laments over; *tvam*—you; *ca*—and; *asya*—to him (the dead boy); *katamaḥ*—who; *sṛṣṭau*—in the birth; *purā*—previously; *idānīm*—at this time, at the present; *ataḥ param*—and hereafter, in the future.

TRANSLATION

O King, what relationship does the dead body for which you lament have with you, and what relationship do you have with him? You may say that you are now related as father and son, but do you think this relationship existed before? Does it truly exist now? Will it continue in the future?

PURPORT

The instructions given by Nārada and Aṅgirā Muni are the true spiritual instructions for the illusioned conditioned soul. This world is temporary, but because of our previous *karma* we come here and accept bodies, creating temporary relationships in terms of society, friendship, love, nationality and community, which are all finished at death. These temporary relationships did not exist in the past, nor will they exist in the future. Therefore at the present moment the so-called relationships are illusions.

TEXT 3

यथा प्रयान्ति संयान्ति स्रोतोवेगेन बालुकाः ।
संयुज्यन्ते वियुज्यन्ते तथा कालेन देहिनः ॥ ३ ॥

yathā prayānti saṁyānti
sroto-vegena bālukāḥ
saṁyujyante viyujyante
tathā kālena dehinaḥ

yathā—just as; *prayānti*—move apart; *saṁyānti*—come together; *srotaḥ-vegena*—by the force of waves; *bālukāḥ*—the small particles of sand; *saṁyujyante*—they are united; *viyujyante*—they are separated; *tathā*—similarly; *kālena*—by time; *dehinaḥ*—the living entities who have accepted material bodies.

TRANSLATION

O King, as small particles of sand sometimes come together and are sometimes separated due to the force of the waves, the living entities who have accepted material bodies sometimes come together and are sometimes separated by the force of time.

PURPORT

The misunderstanding of the conditioned soul is the bodily conception of life. The body is material, but within the body is the soul. This is spiritual understanding. Unfortunately, one who is in ignorance, under the spell of material illusion, accepts the body to be the self. He cannot understand that the body is matter. Like small particles of sand, bodies come together and are separated by the force of time, and people falsely lament for unification and separation. Unless one knows this, there is no question of happiness. Therefore in *Bhagavad-gītā* (2.13) this is the first instruction given by the Lord:

dehino'smin yathā dehe
kaumāraṁ yauvanaṁ jarā
tathā dehāntara-prāptir
dhīras tatra na muhyati

"As the embodied soul continually passes, in this body, from boyhood to youth to old age, the soul similarly passes into another body at death. The self-realized soul is not bewildered by such a change." We are not the body; we are spiritual beings trapped in the body. Our real interest lies in understanding this simple fact. Then we can make further spiritual progress. Otherwise, if we remain in the bodily conception of life, our miserable material existence will continue forever. Political adjustments, social welfare work, medical assistance and the other programs we have manufactured for peace and happiness will never endure. We shall have to undergo the sufferings of material life one after another. Therefore material life is said to be *duḥkhālayam aśāśvatam;* it is a reservoir of miserable conditions.

TEXT 4

यथा धानासु वै धाना भवन्ति न भवन्ति च ।
एवं भूतानि भूतेषु चोदितानीशमायया ॥ ४ ॥

yathā dhānāsu vai dhānā
bhavanti na bhavanti ca
evaṁ bhūtāni bhūteṣu
coditānīśa-māyayā

yathā—just as; *dhānāsu*—through seeds of paddy; *vai*—indeed; *dhānāḥ*—grains; *bhavanti*—are generated; *na*—not; *bhavanti*—are generated; *ca*—also; *evam*—in this way; *bhūtāni*—the living entities; *bhūteṣu*—in other living entities; *coditāni*—impelled; *īśa-māyayā*—by the potency or power of the Supreme Personality of Godhead.

TRANSLATION

When seeds are sown in the ground, they sometimes grow into plants and sometimes do not. Sometimes the ground is not fertile, and the sowing of seeds is unproductive. Similarly, sometimes a prospective father, being impelled by the potency of the Supreme Lord, can beget a child, but sometimes conception does not take place. Therefore one should not

lament over the artificial relationship of parenthood, which is ultimately controlled by the Supreme Lord.

PURPORT

Mahārāja Citraketu was actually not destined to get a son. Therefore although he married hundreds and thousands of wives, all of them proved barren, and he could not beget even one child. When Aṅgirā Ṛṣi came to see the King, the King requested the great sage to enable him to have at least one son. Because of the blessing of Aṅgirā Ṛṣi, a child was sent by the grace of *māyā,* but the child was not to live for long. Therefore in the beginning Aṅgirā Ṛṣi told the King that he would beget a child who would cause jubilation and lamentation.

King Citraketu was not destined to get a child by providence, or the will of the Supreme. Just as sterile grain cannot produce more grain, a sterile person, by the will of the Supreme Lord, cannot beget a child. Sometimes a child is born even to an impotent father and sterile mother, and sometimes a potent father and fertile mother are childless. Indeed, sometimes a child is born despite contraceptive methods, and therefore the parents kill the child in the womb. In the present age, killing children in the womb has become a common practice. Why? When contraceptive methods are taken, why don't they act? Why is a child sometimes produced so that the father and mother have to kill it in the womb? We must conclude that our arrangement of so-called scientific knowledge cannot determine what will take place; what is enacted actually depends on the supreme will. It is by the supreme will that we are situated in certain conditions in terms of family, community and personality. These are all arrangements of the Supreme Lord according to our desires under the spell of *māyā,* illusion. In devotional life, therefore, one should not desire anything, since everything depends on the Supreme Personality of Godhead. As stated in *Bhakti-rasāmṛta-sindhu* (1.1.11):

anyābhilāṣitā-śūnyaṁ
jñāna-karmādy-anāvṛtam
ānukūlyena kṛṣṇānu-
śīlanaṁ bhaktir uttamā

"One should render transcendental loving service to the Supreme Lord Kṛṣṇa favorably and without desire for material profit or gain through fruitive activities or philosophical speculation. That is called pure devotional service." One should act only to develop Kṛṣṇa consciousness. For everything else, one should fully depend upon the Supreme Person. We should not create plans that will ultimately make us frustrated.

TEXT 5

वयं च त्वं च ये चेमे तुल्यकालाश्चराचराः ।
जन्ममृत्योर्यथा पश्चात् प्राङ्नैवमधुनापि भोः ॥ ५ ॥

vayaṁ ca tvaṁ ca ye ceme
tulya-kālāś carācarāḥ
janma-mṛtyor yathā paścāt
prāṅ naivam adhunāpi bhoḥ

vayam—we (the great sages and the ministers and adherents of the King); *ca*—and; *tvam*—you; *ca*—also; *ye*—who; *ca*—also; *ime*—these; *tulya-kālāḥ*—assembled at the same time; *cara-acarāḥ*—moving and not moving; *janma*—birth; *mṛtyoḥ*—and death; *yathā*—just as; *paścāt*—after; *prāk*—before; *na*—not; *evam*—thus; *adhunā*—at present; *api*—although; *bhoḥ*—O King.

TRANSLATION

O King, both you and we—your advisers, wives and ministers—as well as everything moving and not moving throughout the entire cosmos at this time, are in a temporary situation. Before our birth this situation did not exist, and after our death it will exist no longer. Therefore our situation now is temporary, although it is not false.

PURPORT

The Māyāvādī philosophers say, *brahma satyaṁ jagan mithyā:* Brahman, the living being, is factual, but his present bodily situation is false. According to the Vaiṣṇava philosophy, however, the present situation is not false but temporary. It is like a dream. A dream does not exist before one falls asleep, nor does it continue after one awakens. The period for dreaming exists only between these two, and therefore it is false in the sense that it is impermanent. Similarly, the entire material creation, including our own creation and those of others, is impermanent. We do not lament for the situation in a dream before the dream takes place or after it is over, and so during the dream, or during a dreamlike situation, one should not accept it as factual and lament about it. This is real knowledge.

TEXT 6

भूतैर्भूतानि भूतेशः सृजत्यवति हन्ति च ।
आत्मसृष्टैरस्वतन्त्रैरनपेक्षोऽपि बालवत् ॥ ६ ॥

bhūtair bhūtāni bhūteśaḥ
sṛjaty avati hanti ca
ātma-sṛṣṭair asvatantrair
anapekṣo'pi bālavat

bhūtaiḥ—by some living beings; *bhūtāni*—other living entities; *bhūta-īśaḥ*—the Supreme Personality of Godhead, the master of everything; *sṛjati*—creates; *avati*—maintains; *hanti*—kills; *ca*—also; *ātma-sṛṣṭaiḥ*—who are created by Him; *asvatantraiḥ*—not independent; *anapekṣaḥ*—not interested (in creation); *api*—although; *bāla-vat*—like a boy.

TRANSLATION

The Supreme Personality of Godhead, the master and proprietor of everything, is certainly not interested in the temporary cosmic manifestation. Nonetheless, just as a boy at the beach creates something in which he is not interested, the Lord, keeping everything under His control, causes creation, maintenance and annihilation. He creates by engaging a father to beget a son, He maintains by engaging a government or king to see to the public's welfare, and He annihilates through agents for killing, such as snakes. The agents for creation, maintenance and annihilation have no independent potency, but because of the spell of the illusory energy, one thinks himself the creator, maintainer and annihilator.

PURPORT

No one can independently create, maintain or annihilate. *Bhagavad-gītā* (3.27) therefore says:

prakṛteḥ kriyamāṇāni
guṇaiḥ karmāṇi sarvaśaḥ
ahaṅkāra-vimūḍhātmā
kartāham iti manyate

"The bewildered spirit soul, under the influence of the three modes of material nature, thinks himself the doer of activities that are in actuality carried out by nature." *Prakṛti,* material nature, as directed by the Supreme Personality of

Godhead, induces all living entities to create, maintain or annihilate according to the modes of nature. But the living entity, without knowledge of the Supreme Person and His agent the material energy, thinks that he is the doer. In fact, he is not at all the doer. As an agent of the supreme doer, the Supreme Lord, one should abide by the Lord's orders. The present chaotic conditions of the world are due to the ignorance of leaders who forget that they have been appointed to act by the Supreme Personality of Godhead. Because they have been appointed by the Lord, their duty is to consult the Lord and act accordingly. The book for consultation is *Bhagavad-gītā,* in which the Supreme Lord gives directions. Therefore those who are engaged in creation, maintenance and annihilation should consult the Supreme Person, who has appointed them, and should act accordingly. Then everyone will be satisfied, and there will be no disturbances.

TEXT 7

देहेन देहिनो राजन् देहाद्देहोऽभिजायते ।
बीजादेव यथा बीजं देह्यर्थ इव शाश्वतः ॥ ७ ॥

dehena dehino rājan
dehād deho'bhijāyate
bījād eva yathā bījaṁ
dehy artha iva śāśvataḥ

dehena—by the body; *dehinaḥ*—of the father possessing a material body; *rājan*—O King; *dehāt*—from the body (of the mother); *dehaḥ*—another body; *abhijāyate*—takes birth; *bījāt*—from one seed; *eva*—indeed; *yathā*—just as; *bījam*—another seed; *dehī*—a person who has accepted a material body; *arthaḥ*—the material elements; *iva*—like; *śāśvataḥ*—eternal.

TRANSLATION

As from one seed another seed is generated, O King, so from one body [the body of the father], through another body [the body of the mother], a third body is generated [the body of a son]. As the elements of the material body are eternal, the living entity who appears through these material elements is also eternal.

PURPORT

From *Bhagavad-gītā* we understand that there are two energies, namely the superior energy and inferior energy. Inferior energy consists of the five gross and three subtle material elements. The living entity, who represents the superior energy, appears in different types of bodies through these elements by the manipulation or supervision of the material energy. Actually both the material and spiritual energies—matter and spirit—exist eternally as potencies of the Supreme Personality of Godhead. The potent entity is the Supreme Person. Since the spiritual energy, the living being, who is part and parcel of the Supreme Lord, desires to enjoy this material world, the Lord gives him a chance to accept different types of material bodies and enjoy or suffer in different material conditions. Factually, the spiritual energy, the living entity who desires to enjoy material things, is manipulated by the Supreme Lord. The so-called father and mother have nothing to do with the living entity. As a result of his own choice and *karma,* the living being takes different bodies through the agency of so-called fathers and mothers.

TEXT 8

देहदेहिविभागोऽयमविवेककृतः पुरा ।
जातिव्यक्तिविभागोऽयं यथा वस्तुनि कल्पितः ॥ ८ ॥

deha-dehi-vibhāgo'yam
aviveka-kṛtaḥ purā
jāti-vyakti-vibhāgo'yaṁ
yathā vastuni kalpitaḥ

deha—of this body; *dehi*—and the proprietor of the body; *vibhāgaḥ*—the division; *ayam*—this; *aviveka*—from ignorance; *kṛtaḥ*—made; *purā*—from time immemorial; *jāti*—of the class or caste; *vyakti*—and the individual; *vibhāgaḥ*—division; *ayam*—this; *yathā*—just as; *vastuni*—in the original object; *kalpitaḥ*—imagined.

TRANSLATION

Divisions of generalization and specification, such as nationality and individuality, are the imaginations of persons who are not advanced in knowledge.

PURPORT

Actually there are two energies—material and spiritual. Both of them are ever-existing because they are emanations from the eternal truth, the Supreme Lord. Because the individual soul, the individual living entity, has desired to act in forgetfulness of his original identity since time immemorial, he is accepting different positions in material bodies and being designated according to many divisions of nationality, community, society, species and so on.

TEXT 9

श्रीशुक उवाच

एवमाश्वासितो राजा चित्रकेतुर्द्विजोक्तिभिः ।
विमृज्य पाणिना वक्त्रमाधिम्लानमभाषत ॥ ९ ॥

śrī-śuka uvāca
evam āśvāsito rājā
citraketur dvijoktibhiḥ
vimṛjya pāṇinā vaktram
ādhi-mlānam abhāṣata

śrī-śukaḥ uvāca—Śrī Śukadeva Gosvāmī said; *evam*—thus; *āśvāsitaḥ*—being enlightened or given hope; *rājā*—the King; *citraketuḥ*—Citraketu; *dvija-uktibhiḥ*—by the instructions of the great *brāhmaṇas* (Nārada and Aṅgirā Ṛṣi); *vimṛjya*—wiping off; *pāṇinā*—by the hand; *vaktram*—his face; *ādhi-mlānam*—shriveled due to lamentation; *abhāṣata*—spoke intelligently.

TRANSLATION

Śrī Śukadeva Gosvāmī continued: Thus enlightened by the instructions of Nārada and Aṅgirā, King Citraketu became hopeful with knowledge. Wiping his shriveled face with his hand, the King began to speak.

TEXT 10

श्रीराजोवाच

कौ युवां ज्ञानसम्पन्नौ महिष्ठौ च महीयसाम् ।
अवधूतेन वेषेण गूढाविह समागतौ ॥ १० ॥

śrī-rājovāca
kau yuvāṁ jñāna-sampannau
mahiṣṭhau ca mahīyasām
avadhūtena veṣeṇa
gūḍhāv iha samāgatau

śrī-rājā uvāca—King Citraketu said; *kau*—who; *yuvām*—you two; *jñāna-sampannau*—fully developed in knowledge; *mahiṣṭhau*—the greatest; *ca*

—also; *mahīyasām*—among other great personalities; *avadhūtena*—of the liberated wandering mendicants; *veṣeṇa*—by the dress; *gūḍhau*—disguised; *iha*—in this place; *samāgatau*—arrived.

TRANSLATION

King Citraketu said: You have both come here dressed like avadhūtas, liberated persons, just to cover your identities, but I see that of all men, you are the most elevated in awareness. You know everything as it is. Therefore you are the greatest of all great personalities.

TEXT 11

चरन्ति ह्यवनौ कामं ब्राह्मणा भगवत्प्रियाः ।
मादृशां ग्राम्यबुद्धीनां बोधायोन्मत्तलिङ्गिनः ॥ ११ ॥

caranti hy avanau kāmaṁ
brāhmaṇā bhagavat-priyāḥ
mādṛśāṁ grāmya-buddhīnāṁ
bodhāyonmatta-liṅginaḥ

caranti—wander; *hi*—indeed; *avanau*—on the surface of the world; *kāmam*—according to desire; *brāhmaṇāḥ*—the *brāhmaṇas; bhagavat-priyāḥ* —who are also Vaiṣṇavas, very dear to the Personality of Godhead; *mā-dṛśām* —of those like me; *grāmya-buddhīnām*—who are obsessed with temporary material consciousness; *bodhāya*—for the awakening; *unmatta-liṅginaḥ*—who dress as if madmen.

TRANSLATION

Brāhmaṇas who are exalted to the position of Vaiṣṇavas, the most dear servants of Kṛṣṇa, sometimes dress like madmen. Just to benefit materialists like us, who are always attached to sense gratification, and just to dissipate our ignorance, these Vaiṣṇavas wander on the surface of the globe according to their desire.

TEXTS 12–15

कुमारो नारद ऋभुरङ्गिरा देवलोऽसितः ।
अपान्तरतमा व्यासो मार्कण्डेयोऽथ गौतमः ॥ १२ ॥
वसिष्ठो भगवान् रामः कपिलो बादरायणिः ।
दुर्वासा याज्ञवल्क्यश्च जातुकर्णस्तथारुणिः ॥ १३ ॥

रोमशश्च्यवनो दत्त आसुरिः सपतञ्जलिः ।
ऋषिर्वेदशिरा धौम्यो मुनिः पञ्चशिखस्तथा ॥ १४ ॥
हिरण्यनाभः कौशल्यः श्रुतदेव ऋतध्वजः ।
एते परे च सिद्धेशाश्चरन्ति ज्ञानहेतवः ॥ १५ ॥

kumāro nārada ṛbhur
aṅgirā devalo'sitaḥ
apāntaratamā vyāso
mārkaṇḍeyo'tha gautamaḥ

vasiṣṭho bhagavān rāmaḥ
kapilo bādarāyaṇiḥ
durvāsā yājñavalkyaś ca
jātukarṇas tathāruṇiḥ

romaśaś cyavano datta
āsuriḥ sapatañjaliḥ
ṛṣir veda-śirā dhaumyo
muniḥ pañcaśikhas tathā

hiraṇyanābhaḥ kauśalyaḥ
śrutadeva ṛtadhvajaḥ
ete pare ca siddheśāś
caranti jñāna-hetavaḥ

kumāraḥ—Sanat-kumāra; *nāradaḥ*—Nārada Muni; *ṛbhuḥ*—Ṛbhu; *aṅgirāḥ*—Aṅgirā; *devalaḥ*—Devala; *asitaḥ*—Asita; *apāntaratamāḥ*—Vyāsa's previous name, Apāntaratamā; *vyāsaḥ*—Vyāsa; *mārkaṇḍeyaḥ*—Mārkaṇḍeya; *atha*—and; *gautamaḥ*—Gautama; *vasiṣṭhaḥ*—Vasiṣṭha; *bhagavān rāmaḥ*—Lord Paraśurāma; *kapilaḥ*—Kapila; *bādarāyaṇiḥ*—Śukadeva Gosvāmī; *durvāsāḥ*—Durvāsā; *yājñavalkyaḥ*—Yājñavalkya; *ca*—also; *jātukarṇaḥ*—Jātukarṇa; *tathā*—as well as; *aruṇiḥ*—Aruṇi; *romaśaḥ*—Romaśa; *cyavanaḥ*—Cyavana; *dattaḥ*—Dattātreya; *āsuriḥ*—Āsuri; *sa-patañjaliḥ*—with Patañjali Ṛṣi; *ṛṣiḥ*—the sage; *veda-śirāḥ*—the head of the *Vedas; dhaumyaḥ*—Dhaumya; *muniḥ*—the sage; *pañcaśikhaḥ*—Pañcaśikha; *tathā*—so also; *hiraṇyanābhaḥ*—Hiraṇyanābha; *kauśalyaḥ*—Kauśalya; *śrutadevaḥ*—Śrutadeva; *ṛtadhvajaḥ*—Ṛtadhvaja; *ete*—all of these; *pare*—others; *ca*—and; *siddha-īśāḥ*—the masters of mystic power; *caranti*—wander; *jñāna-hetavaḥ*—very learned persons who preach all over the world.

TRANSLATION

O great souls, I have heard that among the great and perfect persons wandering the surface of the earth to instruct knowledge to people covered by ignorance are Sanat-kumāra, Nārada, Ṛbhu, Aṅgirā, Devala, Asita, Apāntaratamā [Vyāsadeva], Mārkaṇḍeya, Gautama, Vasiṣṭha, Bhagavān Paraśurāma, Kapila, Śukadeva, Durvāsā, Yājñavalkya, Jātukarṇa and Aruṇi. Others are Romaśa, Cyavana, Dattātreya, Āsuri, Patañjali, the great sage Dhaumya who is like the head of the Vedas, the sage Pañcaśikha, Hiraṇyanābha, Kauśalya, Śrutadeva and Ṛtadhvaja. You must certainly be among them.

PURPORT

The word *jñāna-hetavaḥ* is very significant because great personalities like those listed in these verses wander on the surface of the globe not to mislead the populace, but to distribute real knowledge. Without this knowledge, human life is wasted. The human form of life is meant for realization of one's relationship with Kṛṣṇa, or God. One who lacks this knowledge is categorized among the animals. The Lord Himself says in *Bhagavad-gītā* (7.15):

na māṁ duṣkṛtino mūḍhāḥ
prapadyante narādhamāḥ
māyayāpahṛta-jñānā
āsuraṁ bhāvam āśritāḥ

"Those miscreants who are grossly foolish, lowest among mankind, whose knowledge is stolen by illusion, and who partake of the atheistic nature of demons, do not surrender unto Me."

Ignorance is the bodily conception of life (*yasyātma-buddhiḥ kuṇape tri-dhātuke ... sa eva go-kharaḥ*). Practically everyone throughout the universe, especially on this planet, Bhūrloka, thinks that there is no separate existence of the body and soul and therefore no need of self-realization. But that is not a fact. Therefore all the *brāhmaṇas* listed here, being devotees, travel all over the world to awaken Kṛṣṇa consciousness in the hearts of such foolish materialists.

The *ācāryas* mentioned in these verses are described in the *Mahābhārata*. The word *pañcaśikha* is also important. One who is liberated from the conceptions of *annamaya, prāṇamaya, manomaya, vijñānamaya* and *ānandamaya* and who is perfectly aware of the subtle coverings of the soul is called *pañcaśikha.* According to the statements of the *Mahābhārata* (*Śānti-parva,* Chapters 218–219), an *ācārya* named Pañcaśikha took birth in the family of Mahārāja Janaka, the ruler of Mithila. The Sāṅkhya philosophers accept Pañcaśikhācārya as one of them. Real knowledge pertains to the living entity dwelling within the body. Unfortunately, because of ignorance, the living entity identifies himself with the body and therefore feels pleasure and pain.

TEXT 16

तस्माद्युवां ग्राम्यपशोर्मम मूढधियः प्रभू ।
अन्धे तमसि मग्नस्य ज्ञानदीप उदीर्यताम् ॥ १६ ॥

tasmād yuvāṁ grāmya-paśor
mama mūḍha-dhiyaḥ prabhū
andhe tamasi magnasya
jñāna-dīpa udīryatām

tasmāt—therefore; *yuvām*—both of you; *grāmya-paśoḥ*—of an animal like a hog, pig or dog; *mama*—me; *mūḍha-dhiyaḥ*—who am very foolish (due to having no spiritual knowledge); *prabhū*—O my two lords; *andhe*—in blind; *tamasi*—darkness; *magnasya*—of one who is absorbed; *jñāna-dīpaḥ*—the torchlight of knowledge; *udīryatām*—let it be ignited.

TRANSLATION

Because you are great personalities, you can give me real knowledge. I am as foolish as a village animal like a pig or dog because I am merged in the darkness of ignorance. Therefore, please ignite the torch of knowledge to save me.

PURPORT

This is the way to receive knowledge. One must submit oneself at the lotus feet of great personalities who can actually deliver transcendental knowledge. It is therefore said, *tasmād guruṁ prapadyeta jijñāsuḥ śreya uttamam:* "One who is inquisitive to understand the highest goal and benefit of life must approach a bona fide spiritual master and surrender unto him." Only one who is actually eager to receive knowledge to eradicate the darkness of ignorance is eligible to approach a *guru,* or spiritual master. The *guru* should not be approached for material benefits. One should not approach a *guru* just to cure some disease or receive some miraculous benefit. This is not the way to approach the *guru. Tad-vijñānārtham:* one should approach the *guru* to understand the transcendental science of spiritual life. Unfortunately, in this age of Kali there are many bogus *gurus* who display magic to their disciples, and many foolish disciples want to see such magic for material benefits. These disciples are not interested in pursuing spiritual life to save themselves from the darkness of ignorance. It is said:

oṁ ajñāna-timirāndhasya
jñānāñjana-śalākayā
cakṣur unmīlitaṁ yena
tasmai śrī-gurave namaḥ

"I was born in the darkest ignorance, and my spiritual master opened my eyes with the torch of knowledge. I offer my respectful obeisances unto him." This gives the definition of the *guru.* Everyone is in the darkness of ignorance. Therefore everyone needs to be enlightened with transcendental knowledge. One who enlightens his disciple and saves him from rotting in the darkness of ignorance in this material world is a true *guru.*

TEXT 17

श्रीअङ्गिरा उवाच
अहं ते पुत्रकामस्य पुत्रदोऽस्म्यङ्गिरा नृप ।
एष ब्रह्मसुतः साक्षान्नारदो भगवानृषिः ॥ १७ ॥

śrī-aṅgirā uvāca
ahaṁ te putra-kāmasya
putrado'smy aṅgirā nṛpa
eṣa brahma-sutaḥ sākṣān
nārado bhagavān ṛṣiḥ

śrī-aṅgirāḥ uvāca—the great sage Aṅgirā said; *aham*—I; *te*—of you; *putra-kāmasya*—desiring to have a son; *putra-daḥ*—the giver of the son; *asmi*—am; *aṅgirāḥ*—Aṅgirā Ṛṣi; *nṛpa*—O King; *eṣaḥ*—this; *brahma-sutaḥ*—the son of Lord Brahmā; *sākṣāt*—directly; *nāradaḥ*—Nārada Muni; *bhagavān*—the most powerful; *ṛṣiḥ*—sage.

TRANSLATION

Aṅgirā said: My dear King, when you desired to have a son, I approached you. Indeed, I am the same Aṅgirā Ṛṣi who gave you this son. As for this ṛṣi, he is the great sage Nārada, the direct son of Lord Brahmā.

TEXTS 18–19

इत्थं त्वां पुत्रशोकेन मग्नं तमसि दुस्तरे ।
अतदर्हमनुस्मृत्य महापुरुषगोचरम् ॥ १८ ॥
अनुग्रहाय भवतः प्राप्तावावामिह प्रभो ।
ब्रह्मण्यो भगवद्भक्तो नावासादितुमर्हसि ॥ १९ ॥

itthaṁ tvāṁ putra-śokena
magnaṁ tamasi dustare
atad-arham anusmṛtya
mahāpuruṣa-gocaram

anugrahāya bhavataḥ
prāptāv āvām iha prabho
brahmaṇyo bhagavad-bhakto
nāvāsāditum arhasi

ittham—in this way; *tvām*—you; *putra-śokena*—because of grief at the death of your son; *magnam*—merged; *tamasi*—in darkness; *dustare*—insurmountable; *a-tat-arham*—unsuitable for a person like you; *anusmṛtya*—remembering; *mahā-puruṣa*—the Supreme Personality of Godhead; *gocaram*—who are advanced in understanding; *anugrahāya*—just to show favor; *bhavataḥ*—toward you; *prāptau*—arrived; *āvām*—we two; *iha*—in this place; *prabho*—O King; *brahmaṇyaḥ*—one who is situated in the Supreme Absolute Truth; *bhagavat-bhaktaḥ*—an advanced devotee of the Supreme Personality of Godhead; *na*—not; *avāsāditum*—to lament; *arhasi*—you deserve.

TRANSLATION

My dear King, you are an advanced devotee of the Supreme Personality of Godhead. To be absorbed in lamentation for the loss of something material is unsuitable for a person like you. Therefore we have both come to relieve you from this false lamentation, which is due to your being merged in the darkness of ignorance. For those who are advanced in spiritual knowledge to be affected by material loss and gain is not at all desirable.

PURPORT

Several words in this verse are very important. The word *mahā-puruṣa* refers to advanced devotees and also to the Supreme Personality of Godhead.

Mahā means "the supreme," and *puruṣa* means "person." One who always engages in the service of the Supreme Lord is called *mahā-pauruṣika.* Śukadeva Gosvāmī and Mahārāja Parīkṣit are sometimes addressed as *mahā-pauruṣika.* A devotee should always aspire to engage in the service of advanced devotees. As Śrīla Narottama dāsa Ṭhākura has sung:

tāṅdera caraṇa sevi bhakta-sane vāsa
janame janame haya, ei abhilāṣa

A devotee should always aspire to live in the association of advanced devotees and engage in the service of the Lord through the *paramparā* system. One should serve the mission of Śrī Caitanya Mahāprabhu through the instructions of the great Gosvāmīs of Vṛndāvana. This is called *tāṅdera caraṇa sevi.* While serving the lotus feet of the Gosvāmīs, one should live in the association of devotees (*bhakta-sane vāsa*). This is the business of a devotee. A devotee should not aspire for material profit or lament for material loss. When Aṅgirā Ṛṣi and Nārada saw that Mahārāja Citraketu, an advanced devotee, had fallen in the darkness of ignorance and was lamenting for the material body of his son, by their causeless mercy they came to advise him so that he could be saved from this ignorance.

Another significant word is *brahmaṇya.* The Supreme Personality of Godhead is sometimes addressed by the prayer *namo brahmaṇya-devāya,* which offers obeisances unto the Lord because He is served by the devotees. Therefore this verse states, *brahmaṇyo bhagavad-bhakto nāvāsāditum arhasi.* This is the symptom of an advanced devotee. *Brahma-bhūtaḥ prasannātmā.* For a devotee—an advanced, self-realized soul—there is no cause for material jubilation or lamentation. He is always transcendental to conditional life.

TEXT 20

तदैव ते परं ज्ञानं ददामि गृहमागतः ।
ज्ञात्वान्याभिनिवेशं ते पुत्रमेव ददाम्यहम् ॥ २० ॥

tadaiva te paraṁ jñānaṁ
dadāmi gṛham āgataḥ
jñātvānyābhiniveśaṁ te
putram eva dadāmy aham

tadā—then; *eva*—indeed; *te*—unto you; *param*—transcendental; *jñānam*—knowledge; *dadāmi*—I would have delivered; *gṛham*—to your home; *āgataḥ*—came; *jñātvā*—knowing; *anya-abhiniveśam*—absorption in something else (in material things); *te*—your; *putram*—a son; *eva*—only; *dadāmi*—gave; *aham*—I.

TRANSLATION

When I first came to your home, I could have given you the supreme transcendental knowledge, but when I saw that your mind was absorbed in material things, I gave you only a son, who caused you jubilation and lamentation.

TEXTS 21–23

अधुना पुत्रिणां तापो भवतैवानुभूयते ।
एवं दारा गृहा रायो विविधैश्वर्यसम्पदः ॥ २१ ॥
शब्दादयश्च विषयाश्चला राज्यविभूतयः ।
मही राज्यं बलं कोषो भृत्यामात्यसुहृज्जनाः ॥ २२ ॥
सर्वेऽपि शूरसेनेमे शोकमोहभयार्तिदाः ।
गन्धर्वनगरप्रख्याः स्वप्नमायामनोरथाः ॥ २३ ॥

adhunā putriṇāṁ tāpo
bhavataivānubhūyate
evaṁ dārā gṛhā rāyo
vividhaiśvarya-sampadaḥ

śabdādayaś ca viṣayāś
calā rājya-vibhūtayaḥ
mahī rājyaṁ balaṁ koṣo
bhṛtyāmātya-suhṛj-janāḥ

sarve'pi śūraseneme
śoka-moha-bhayārtidāḥ
gandharva-nagara-prakhyāḥ
svapna-māyā-manorathāḥ

adhunā—at the present moment; *putriṇām*—of persons who have children; *tāpaḥ*—the tribulation; *bhavatā*—by you; *eva*—indeed; *anubhūyate*—is experienced; *evam*—in this way; *dārāḥ*—good wife; *gṛhāḥ*—residence; *rāyaḥ*—riches; *vividha*—various; *aiśvarya*—opulences; *sampadaḥ*—prosperities; *śabda-ādayaḥ*—sound and so on; *ca*—and; *viṣayāḥ*—the objects of sense gratification; *calāḥ*—temporary; *rājya*—of the kingdom; *vibhūtayaḥ*—opulences; *mahī*—land; *rājyam*—kingdom; *balam*—strength; *koṣaḥ*—treasury; *bhṛtya*—servants; *amātya*—ministers; *suhṛt-janāḥ*—allies; *sarve*—all; *api*—indeed; *śūrasena*—O King of Śūrasena; *ime*—these; *śoka*—of lamentation; *moha*—of illusion; *bhaya*—of fear; *arti*—and distress; *dāḥ*—givers; *gandharva-nagara-prakhyāḥ*—headed by the illusory sight of a *gandharva-nagara,* a big palace within the forest; *svapna*—dreams; *māyā*—illusions; *manorathāḥ*—and concoctions of the mind.

TRANSLATION

My dear King, now you are actually experiencing the misery of a person who has sons and daughters. O King, owner of the state of Śūrasena, one's wife, his house, the opulence of his kingdom, and his various other opulences and objects of sense perception are all the same in that they are temporary. One's kingdom, military power, treasury, servants, ministers, friends and relatives are all causes of fear, illusion, lamentation and distress. They are like a gandharva-nagara, a nonexistent palace that one imagines to exist in the forest. Because they are impermanent, they are no better than illusions, dreams and mental concoctions.

PURPORT

This verse describes the entanglement of material existence. In material existence, the living entity possesses many things—the material body, children, wife and so on (*dehāpatya-kalatrādiṣu*). One may think that these will give him protection, but that is impossible. In spite of all these possessions, the spirit soul has to give up his present situation and accept another. The next situation may be unfavorable, but even if it is favorable, one must give it up and again accept another body. In this way, one's tribulation in material existence continues. A sane man should be perfectly aware that these things will never be able to give him happiness. One must be situated in his spiritual identity and eternally serve the Supreme Personality of Godhead as a devotee. Aṅgirā Ṛṣi and Nārada Muni gave this instruction to Mahārāja Citraketu.

TEXT 24

दृश्यमाना विनार्थेन न दृश्यन्ते मनोभवाः ।
कर्मभिर्ध्यायतो नानाकर्माणि मनसोऽभवन् ॥ २४ ॥

dṛśyamānā vinārthena
na dṛśyante manobhavāḥ

karmabhir dhyāyato nānā-
karmāṇi manaso'bhavan

dṛśyamānāḥ—being perceived; *vinā*—without; *arthena*—substance or reality; *na*—not; *dṛśyante*—are seen; *manobhavāḥ*—creations of mental concoction; *karmabhiḥ*—by fruitive activities; *dhyāyataḥ*—meditating upon; *nānā*—various; *karmāṇi*—fruitive activities; *manasaḥ*—from the mind; *abhavan*—appear.

TRANSLATION

These visible objects like wife, children and property are like dreams and mental concoctions. Actually what we see has no permanent existence. It is sometimes seen and sometimes not. Only because of our past actions do we create such mental concoctions, and because of these concoctions, we perform further activities.

PURPORT

Everything material is a mental concoction because it is sometimes visible and sometimes not. At night when we dream of tigers and snakes, they are not actually present, but we are afraid because we are affected by what we envision in our dreams. Everything material is like a dream because it actually has no permanent existence.

Śrīla Viśvanātha Cakravartī Ṭhākura writes as follows in his commentary: *arthena vyāghra-sarpādinā vinaiva dṛśyamānāḥ svapnādi-bhaṅge sati na dṛśyante tad evaṁ dārādayo'vāstava-vastu-bhūtāḥ svapnādayo'vastu-bhūtāś ca sarve manobhavāḥ mano-vāsanā janyatvān manobhavāḥ.* At night one dreams of tigers and snakes, and while dreaming he actually sees them, but as soon as the dream is broken they no longer exist. Similarly, the material world is a creation of our mental concoctions. We have come to this material world to enjoy material resources, and by mental concoction we discover many, many objects of enjoyment because our minds are absorbed in material things. This is why we receive various bodies. According to our mental concoctions we work in various ways, desiring various achievements, and by nature and the order of the Supreme Personality of Godhead (*karmaṇā-daiva-netreṇa*) we get the advantages we desire. Thus we become more and more involved with material concoctions. This is the reason for our suffering in the material world. By one kind of activity we create another, and they are all products of our mental concoctions.

TEXT 25

अयं हि देहिनो देहो द्रव्यज्ञानक्रियात्मकः ।
देहिनो विविधक्लेशसन्तापकृदुदाहृतः ॥ २५ ॥

ayaṁ hi dehino deho
dravya-jñāna-kriyātmakaḥ
dehino vividha-kleśa-
santāpa-kṛd udāhṛtaḥ

ayam—this; *hi*—certainly; *dehinaḥ*—of the living entity; *dehaḥ*—body; *dravya-jñāna-kriyā-ātmakaḥ*—consisting of the material elements, the senses for acquiring knowledge, and the acting senses; *dehinaḥ*—of the living entity; *vividha*—various; *kleśa*—sufferings; *santāpa*—and of pains; *kṛt*—the cause; *udāhṛtaḥ*—is declared.

TRANSLATION

The living entity in the bodily conception of life is absorbed in the body, which is a combination of the physical elements, the five senses for gathering knowledge, and the five senses of action, along with the mind. Through the mind the living entity suffers three kinds of tribulations—adhibhautika, adhidaivika and adhyātmika. Therefore this body is a source of all miseries.

PURPORT

In the Fifth Canto (5.5.4), while instructing his sons, Ṛṣabhadeva said, *asann api kleśada āsa dehaḥ:* the body, although temporary, is the cause of all the miseries of material existence. As already discussed in the previous verse, the entire material creation is based on mental concoction. The mind sometimes induces us to think that if we purchase an automobile we can enjoy the physical elements, such as earth, water, air and fire, combined in forms of iron, plastic, petrol and so on. Working with the five material elements (*pañca-bhūtas*), as well as with our five knowledge-gathering senses like the eyes, ears and tongue and our five active senses like the hands and legs, we become involved in the material condition. Thus we are subjected to the tribulations known as *adhyātmika, adhidaivika* and *adhibhautika.* The mind is the center because the mind creates all these things. As soon as the material object is struck, however, the mind is affected, and we suffer. For example, with the material elements, the working senses and the knowledge-gathering senses we create a very nice car, and when the car is accidentally smashed in a collision, the mind suffers, and through the mind the living entity suffers.

The fact is that the living entity, while concocting with the mind, creates the material condition. Because matter is destructible, through the material condition the living entity suffers. Otherwise, the living entity is detached from all material conditions. When one comes to the Brahman platform, the platform of spiritual life, fully understanding that he is a spiritual soul (*ahaṁ brahmāsmi*), he is no longer affected by lamentation or hankering. As the Lord says in *Bhagavad-gītā* (18.54):

brahma-bhūtaḥ prasannātmā
na śocati na kāṅkṣati

"One who is thus transcendentally situated at once realizes the Supreme Brahman and becomes fully joyful. He never laments nor desires to have anything." Elsewhere in *Bhagavad-gītā* (15.7) the Lord says:

mamaivāṁśo jīva-loke
jīva-bhūtaḥ sanātanaḥ
manaḥ-ṣaṣṭhānīndriyāṇi
prakṛti-sthāni karṣati

"The living entities in this conditioned world are My eternal fragmental parts. Due to conditioned life, they are struggling very hard with the six senses, which include the mind." The living entity is actually part and parcel of the Supreme Personality of Godhead and is unaffected by material conditions, but because the mind (*manaḥ*) is affected, the senses are affected, and the living entity struggles for existence within this material world.

TEXT 26

तस्मात् स्वस्थेन मनसा विमृश्य गतिमात्मनः ।
द्वैते ध्रुवार्थविश्रम्भं त्यजोपशममाविश ॥ २६ ॥

tasmāt svasthena manasā
vimṛśya gatim ātmanaḥ
dvaite dhruvārtha-viśrambhaṁ
tyajopaśamam āviśa

tasmāt—therefore; *svasthena*—with a careful; *manasā*—mind; *vimṛśya*—considering; *gatim*—real position; *ātmanaḥ*—of yourself; *dvaite*—in the duality; *dhruva*—as permanent; *artha*—object; *viśrambham*—belief; *tyaja* —give up; *upaśamam*—a peaceful condition; *āviśa*—take to.

TRANSLATION

Therefore, O King Citraketu, carefully consider the position of the ātmā. In other words, try to understand who you are—whether body, mind or soul. Consider where you have come from, where you are going after giving up this body, and why you are under the control of material lamentation. Try to understand your real position in this way, and then you will be able to give up your unnecessary attachment. You will also be able to give up the belief that this material world, or anything not directly in touch with service to Kṛṣṇa, is eternal. Thus you will obtain peace.

PURPORT

The Kṛṣṇa consciousness movement is factually endeavoring to bring human society to a sober condition. Because of a misdirected civilization, people are jumping in materialistic life like cats and dogs, performing all sorts of abominable, sinful actions and becoming increasingly entangled. The Kṛṣṇa consciousness movement includes self-realization because one is first directed by Lord Kṛṣṇa to understand that one is not the body but the owner of the body. When one understands this simple fact, he can direct himself toward the goal of life. Because people are not educated in terms of the goal of life, they are working like madmen and becoming more and more attached to the material atmosphere. The misguided man accepts the material condition as everlasting. One must give up his faith in material things and give up attachment for them. Then one will be sober and peaceful.

TEXT 27

श्रीनारद उवाच
एतां मन्त्रोपनिषदं प्रतीच्छ प्रयतो मम ।
यां धारयन् सप्तरात्राद् द्रष्टा सङ्कर्षणं विभुम् ॥ २७ ॥

śrī-nārada uvāca
etāṁ mantropaniṣadaṁ
pratīccha prayato mama
yāṁ dhārayan sapta-rātrād
draṣṭā saṅkarṣaṇaṁ vibhum

śrī-nāradaḥ uvāca—Śrī Nārada Muni said; *etām*—this; *mantra-upaniṣadam*—*Upaniṣad* in the form of a *mantra* by which one can achieve the highest goal of life; *pratīccha*—accept; *prayataḥ*—with great attention (after finishing the funeral ceremony of your dead son); *mama*—from me; *yām*—which; *dhārayan*—accepting; *sapta-rātrāt*—after seven nights; *draṣṭā*—you will see; *saṅkarṣaṇam*—the Supreme Personality of Godhead, Saṅkarṣaṇa; *vibhum*—the Lord.

TRANSLATION

The great sage Nārada continued: My dear King, attentively receive from me a mantra, which is most auspicious. After accepting it from me, in seven nights you will be able to see the Lord face to face.

TEXT 28

यत्पादमूलमुपसृत्य नरेन्द्र पूर्वे
शर्वादयो भ्रममिमं द्वितयं विसृज्य ।
सद्यस्तदीयमतुलानधिकं महित्वं
प्राप्पुर्भवानपि परं न चिरादुपैति ॥ २८ ॥

yat-pāda-mūlam upasṛtya narendra pūrve
śarvādayo bhramam imaṁ dvitayaṁ visṛjya
sadyas tadīyam atulānadhikaṁ mahitvaṁ
prāpur bhavān api paraṁ na cirād upaiti

yat-pāda-mūlam—the lotus feet of whom (Lord Saṅkarṣaṇa); *upasṛtya*—obtaining shelter at; *nara-indra*—O King; *pūrve*—formerly; *śarva-ādayaḥ*—great demigods like Lord Mahādeva; *bhramam*—illusion; *imam*—this; *dvitayam*—consisting of duality; *visṛjya*—giving up; *sadyaḥ*—immediately; *tadīyam*—His; *atula*—unequaled; *anadhikam*—unsurpassed; *mahitvam*—glories; *prāpuḥ*—achieved; *bhavān*—yourself; *api*—also; *param*—the supreme abode; *na*—not; *cirāt*—after a long time; *upaiti*—will obtain.

TRANSLATION

My dear King, in former days Lord Śiva and other demigods took shelter of the lotus feet of Saṅkarṣaṇa. Thus they immediately got free from the illusion of duality and achieved unequaled and unsurpassed glories in spiritual life. You will very soon attain that very same position.

Thus end the Bhaktivedanta purports of the Sixth Canto, Fifteenth Chapter, of the Śrīmad-Bhāgavatam, *entitled "The Saints Nārada and Aṅgirā Instruct King Citraketu."*

CHAPTER SIXTEEN

King Citraketu Meets the Supreme Lord

As related in this chapter, Citraketu was able to talk with his dead son and hear from him the truth of life. When Citraketu was appeased, the great sage Nārada gave him a *mantra,* and by chanting this *mantra* Citraketu found shelter at the lotus feet of Saṅkarṣaṇa.

The living entity is eternal. Thus he has neither birth nor death (*na hanyate hanyamāne śarīre*). According to the reactions of one's fruitive activities, one takes birth in various species of life among the birds, beasts, trees, human beings, demigods and so on, thus rotating through various bodies. For a certain period of time, one receives a particular type of body as a son or father in a false relationship. All our relationships in this material world with friends, relatives or enemies consist of duality, in which one feels happy and distressed on the basis of illusion. The living entity is actually a spiritual soul who is part and parcel of God and has nothing to do with relationships in the world of duality. Therefore Nārada Muni advised Citraketu not to lament for his so-called dead son.

After hearing instructions from their dead child, Citraketu and his wife could understand that all relationships in this material world are causes of misery. The queens who had administered poison to the son of Kṛtadyuti were very much ashamed. They atoned for the sinful act of killing a child and gave up their aspiration to have sons. Thereafter, Nārada Muni chanted prayers to Nārāyaṇa, who exists as *catur-vyūha,* and instructed Citraketu about the Supreme Lord, who creates, maintains and annihilates everything and who is the master of the material nature. After instructing King Citraketu in this way, he returned to Brahmaloka. These instructions about the Absolute Truth are called the *mahā-vidyā.* After being initiated by Nārada Muni, King Citraketu chanted the *mahā-vidyā,* and after one week he attained the presence of Lord Saṅkarṣaṇa, who was surrounded by the four Kumāras. The Lord was nicely dressed in bluish garments, with a helmet and ornaments of gold. His face appeared very happy. In the presence of Lord Saṅkarṣaṇa, Citraketu offered his obeisances and began to offer prayers.

In his prayers, Citraketu said that millions of universes rest in the pores of Saṅkarṣaṇa, who is limitless, having no beginning and end. The Lord is well known to the devotees for His eternity. The difference between worshiping the Lord and worshiping the demigods is that the worshiper of the Lord also becomes eternal, whereas whatever benedictions one can get from the demigods are impermanent. Unless one becomes a devotee, one cannot understand the Supreme Personality of Godhead.

After Citraketu finished his prayers, the unlimited Supreme Lord explained knowledge of Himself to Citraketu.

TEXT 1

श्रीबादरायणिरुवाच

अथ देवऋषी राजन् सम्परेतं नृपात्मजम् ।
दर्शयित्वेति होवाच ज्ञातीनामनुशोचताम् ॥ १ ॥

śrī-bādarāyaṇir uvāca
atha deva-ṛṣī rājan
samparetaṁ nṛpātmajam
darśayitveti hovāca
jñātīnām anuśocatām

śrī-bādarāyaṇiḥ uvāca—Śrī Śukadeva Gosvāmī said; *atha*—thus; *deva-ṛṣiḥ*—the great sage Nārada; *rājan*—O King; *samparetam*—dead; *nṛpa-ātmajam*—the son of the King; *darśayitvā*—making visible; *iti*—thus; *ha*—indeed; *uvāca*—explained; *jñātīnām*—to all the relatives; *anuśocatām*—who were lamenting.

TRANSLATION

Śrī Śukadeva Gosvāmī said: My dear King Parīkṣit, by his mystic power the great sage Nārada brought the dead son into the vision of all the lamenting relatives and then spoke as follows.

TEXT 2

श्रीनारद उवाच

जीवात्मन् पश्य भद्रं ते मातरं पितरं च ते ।
सुहृदो बान्धवास्तप्ताः शुचा त्वत्कृतया भृशम् ॥ २ ॥

śrī-nārada uvāca
jīvātman paśya bhadraṁ te
mātaraṁ pitaraṁ ca te

suhṛdo bāndhavās taptāḥ
śucā tvat-kṛtayā bhṛśam

śrī-nāradaḥ uvāca—Śrī Nārada Muni said; *jīva-ātman*—O living entity; *paśya*—just see; *bhadram*—good fortune; *te*—unto you; *mātaram*—the mother; *pitaram*—the father; *ca*—and; *te*—of you; *suhṛdaḥ*—friends; *bāndhavāḥ*—relatives; *taptāḥ*—aggrieved; *śucā*—by lamentation; *tvat-kṛtayā*—because of you; *bhṛśam*—very greatly.

TRANSLATION

Śrī Nārada Muni said: O living entity, all good fortune unto you. Just see your father and mother. All your friends and relatives are overwhelmed with grief because of your passing away.

TEXT 3

कलेवरं स्वमाविश्य शेषमायुः सुहृद्वृतः ।
भुङ्क्ष्व भोगान् पितृप्रत्तानधितिष्ठ नृपासनम् ॥ ३ ॥

kalevaraṁ svam āviśya
śeṣam āyuḥ suhṛd-vṛtaḥ
bhuṅkṣva bhogān pitṛ-prattān
adhitiṣṭha nṛpāsanam

kalevaram—body; *svam*—your own; *āviśya*—entering; *śeṣam*—the balance; *āyuḥ*—duration of life; *suhṛt-vṛtaḥ*—surrounded by your friends and relatives; *bhuṅkṣva*—just enjoy; *bhogān*—all enjoyable opulences; *pitṛ*—by your father; *prattān*—awarded; *adhitiṣṭha*—accept; *nṛpa-āsanam*—the throne of the king.

TRANSLATION

Because you died untimely, the balance of your lifetime still remains. Therefore you may reenter your body and enjoy the remainder of your life, surrounded by your friends and relatives. Accept the royal throne and all the opulences given by your father.

TEXT 4

जीव उवाच
कस्मिञ्जन्मन्यमी मह्यं पितरो मातरोऽभवन् ।
कर्मभिर्भ्राम्यमाणस्य देवतिर्यङ्नृयोनिषु ॥ ४ ॥

jīva uvāca
kasmiñ janmany amī mahyaṁ
pitaro mātaro'bhavan
karmabhir bhrāmyamāṇasya
deva-tiryaṅ-nṛ-yoniṣu

jīvaḥ uvāca—the living entity said; *kasmin*—in which; *janmani*—birth; *amī*—all those; *mahyam*—to me; *pitaraḥ*—fathers; *mātaraḥ*—mothers; *abhavan*—were; *karmabhiḥ*—by the results of fruitive action; *bhrāmyamāṇasya*—who am wandering; *deva-tiryak*—of the demigods and the lower animals; *nṛ*—and of the human species; *yoniṣu*—in the wombs.

TRANSLATION

By the mystic power of Nārada Muni, the living entity reentered his dead body for a short time and spoke in reply to Nārada Muni's request. He said: According to the results of my fruitive activities, I, the living being, transmigrate from one body to another, sometimes going to the species of the demigods, sometimes to the species of lower animals, sometimes among the vegetables, and sometimes to the human species. Therefore, in which birth were these my mother and father? No one is actually my mother and father. How can I accept these two people as my parents?

PURPORT

Here it is made clear that the living being enters a material body that is like a machine created by the five gross elements of material nature (earth, water, fire, air and sky) and the three subtle elements (mind, intelligence and ego). As confirmed in *Bhagavad-gītā,* there are two separate identities, called the inferior and superior natures, which both belong to the Supreme Personality of Godhead. According to the results of a living entity's fruitive actions, he is forced to enter the material elements in different types of bodies.

This time the living entity was supposed to have been the son of Mahārāja Citraketu and Queen Kṛtadyuti because according to the laws of nature he had entered a body made by the King and Queen. Actually, however, he was not their son. The living entity is the son of the Supreme Personality of Godhead, and because he wants to enjoy this material world, the Supreme Lord gives him a chance to enter various bodies. The living entity has no true relationship with the material body he gets from his material father and mother. He is part and parcel of the Supreme Lord, but he is allowed to go through different bodies. The body created by the so-called father and mother actually has nothing to do with its so-called creators. Therefore the living entity flatly denied that Mahārāja Citraketu and his wife were his father and mother.

TEXT 5

बन्धुज्ञात्यरिमध्यस्थमित्रोदासीनविद्विषः ।
सर्व एव हि सर्वेषां भवन्ति क्रमशो मिथः ॥ ५ ॥

bandhu-jñāty-ari-madhyastha-
mitrodāsīna-vidviṣaḥ
sarva eva hi sarveṣāṁ
bhavanti kramaśo mithaḥ

bandhu—friends; *jñāti*—family members; *ari*—enemies; *madhyastha*—neutrals; *mitra*—well-wishers; *udāsīna*—indifferent; *vidviṣaḥ*—or envious persons; *sarve*—all; *eva*—indeed; *hi*—certainly; *sarveṣām*—of all; *bhavanti*—become; *kramaśaḥ*—gradually; *mithaḥ*—of one another.

TRANSLATION

In this material world, which advances like a river that carries away the living entity, all people become friends, relatives and enemies in due course of time. They also act neutrally, they mediate, they despise one another, and they act in many other relationships. Nonetheless, despite these various transactions, no one is permanently related.

PURPORT

It is our practical experience in this material world that the same person who is one's friend today becomes one's enemy tomorrow. Our relationships as friends or enemies, family men or outsiders, are actually the results of our different dealings. Citraketu Mahārāja was lamenting for his son, who was now dead, but he could have considered the situation otherwise. "This living entity," he could have thought, "was my enemy in my last life, and now, having appeared as my son, he is prematurely leaving just to give me pain and agony." Why should he not consider his dead son his former enemy and instead of lamenting be jubilant because of an enemy's death? As stated in *Bhagavad-gītā* (3.27), *prakṛteḥ kriyamāṇāni guṇaiḥ karmāṇi sarvaśaḥ:* factually everything is happening because of our association with the modes of material nature. Therefore one who is my friend today in association with the mode of goodness may be my enemy tomorrow in association with the modes of passion and ignorance. As the modes of material nature work, in illusion we accept others as friends, enemies, sons or fathers in terms of the reactions of different dealings under different conditions.

TEXT 6

यथा वस्तूनि पण्यानि हेमादीनि ततस्ततः ।
पर्यटन्ति नरेष्वेवं जीवो योनिषु कर्तृषु ॥ ६ ॥

yathā vastūni paṇyāni
hemādīni tatas tataḥ
paryaṭanti nareṣv evaṁ
jīvo yoniṣu kartṛṣu

yathā—just as; *vastūni*—commodities; *paṇyāni*—meant for trading; *hema-ādīni*—such as gold; *tataḥ tataḥ*—from here to there; *paryaṭanti*—move about; *nareṣu*—among men; *evam*—in this way; *jīvaḥ*—the living entity; *yoniṣu*—in different species of life; *kartṛṣu*—in different material fathers.

TRANSLATION

Just as gold and other commodities are continually transferred from one place to another in due course of purchase and sale, so the living entity, as a result of his fruitive activities, wanders throughout the entire universe, being injected into various bodies in different species of life by one kind of father after another.

PURPORT

It has already been explained that Citraketu's son was his enemy in a past life and had now appeared as his son just to give him more severe pain. Indeed, the untimely death of the son caused severe lamentation for the father. One may put forward the argument, "If the King's son was his enemy, how could the King have so much affection for him?" In answer, the example is given that when someone's wealth falls into the hands of his enemy, the money becomes the enemy's friend. Then the enemy can use it for his own purposes. Indeed, he can even use it to harm its previous owner. Therefore the money belongs neither to the one party nor to the other. The money is always money, but in different situations it can be used as an enemy or a friend.

As explained in *Bhagavad-gītā,* it is not by any father or mother that the living entity is given his birth. The living entity is a completely separate identity from the so-called father and mother. By the laws of nature, the living entity is forced to enter the semen of a father and be injected into the womb of the mother. He is not in control of selecting what kind of father he will accept. *Prakṛteḥ kriyamāṇāni:* the laws of nature force him to go to different fathers and mothers, just like a consumer commodity that is purchased and sold. Therefore the so-called relationship of father and son is an arrangement of *prakṛti,* or nature. It has no meaning, and therefore it is called illusion.

The same living entity sometimes takes shelter of an animal father and mother and sometimes a human father and mother. Sometimes he accepts a father and mother among the birds, and sometimes he accepts a demigod father and mother. Śrī Caitanya Mahāprabhu therefore says:

brahmāṇḍa bhramite kona bhāgyavān jīva
guru-kṛṣṇa-prasāde pāya bhakti-latā-bīja

Harassed life after life by the laws of nature, the living entity wanders throughout the entire universe in different planets and different species of life. Somehow or other, if he is fortunate enough, he comes in touch with a devotee who reforms his entire life. Then the living entity goes back home, back to Godhead. Therefore it is said:

janame janame sabe pitā mātā pāya
kṛṣṇa guru nahi mile baja hari ei

In the transmigration of the soul through different bodies, everyone, in every form of life—be it human, animal, tree or demigod—gets a father and mother. This is not very difficult. The difficulty is to obtain a bona fide spiritual master and Kṛṣṇa. Therefore the duty of a human being is to capture the opportunity to come in touch with Kṛṣṇa's representative, the bona fide spiritual master. Under the guidance of the spiritual master, the spiritual father, one can return home, back to Godhead.

TEXT 7

नित्यस्यार्थस्य सम्बन्धो ह्यनित्यो दृश्यते नृषु ।
यावद्यस्य हि सम्बन्धो ममत्वं तावदेव हि ॥ ७ ॥

nityasyārthasya sambandho
hy anityo dṛśyate nṛṣu

yāvad yasya hi sambandho
mamatvaṁ tāvad eva hi

nityasya—of the eternal; *arthasya*—thing; *sambandhaḥ*—relationship; *hi*—indeed; *anityaḥ*—temporary; *dṛśyate*—is seen; *nṛṣu*—in human society; *yāvat*—as long as; *yasya*—of whom; *hi*—indeed; *sambandhaḥ*—relationship; *mamatvam*—ownership; *tāvat*—that long; *eva*—indeed; *hi*—certainly.

TRANSLATION

A few living entities are born in the human species, and others are born as animals. Although both are living entities, their relationships are impermanent. An animal may remain in the custody of a human being for some time, and then the same animal may be transferred to the possession of other human beings. As soon as the animal goes away, the former proprietor no longer has a sense of ownership. As long as the animal is in his possession he certainly has an affinity for it, but as soon as the animal is sold, the affinity is lost.

PURPORT

Aside from the fact that the soul transmigrates from one body to another, even in this life the relationships between living entities are impermanent, as exemplified in this verse. The son of Citraketu was named Harṣaśoka, or "jubilation and lamentation." The living entity is certainly eternal, but because he is covered by a temporary dress, the body, his eternity is not observed. *Dehino'smin yathā dehe kaumāraṁ yauvanaṁ jarā:* "The embodied soul continually passes, in this body, from boyhood to youth to old age." Thus the bodily dress is impermanent. The living entity, however, is permanent. As an animal is transferred from one owner to another, the living entity who was the son of Citraketu lived as his son for some time, but as soon as he was transferred to another body, the affectionate relationship was broken. As stated in the example given in the previous verse, when one has a commodity in his hands he considers it his, but as soon as it is transferred it becomes someone else's commodity. Then one no longer has a relationship with it; he has no affection for it, nor does he lament for it.

TEXT 8

एवं योनिगतो जीवः स नित्यो निरहङ्कृतः ।
यावद्यत्रोपलभ्येत तावत्स्वत्वं हि तस्य तत् ॥ ८ ॥

evaṁ yoni-gato jīvaḥ
sa nityo nirahaṅkṛtaḥ
yāvad yatropalabhyeta
tāvat svatvaṁ hi tasya tat

evam—thus; *yoni-gataḥ*—being within a specific species of life; *jīvaḥ*—the living entity; *saḥ*—he; *nityaḥ*—eternal; *nirahaṅkṛtaḥ*—without identification with the body; *yāvat*—as long as; *yatra*—where; *upalabhyeta*—he may be found; *tāvat*—that long; *svatvam*—the concept of self; *hi*—indeed; *tasya*—of him; *tat*—that.

TRANSLATION

Even though one living entity becomes connected with another because of a relationship based on bodies that are perishable, the living entity is eternal. Actually it is the body that is born or lost, not the living entity. One should not accept that the living entity takes birth or dies. The living being actually has no relationship with so-called fathers and mothers. As long as he appears as the son of a certain father and mother as a result of his past fruitive activities, he has a connection with the body given by that father and mother. Thus he falsely accepts himself as their son and acts affectionately. After he dies, however, the relationship is finished.Under these circumstances, one should not be falsely involved with jubilation and lamentation.

PURPORT

When the living entity lives within the material body, he falsely thinks that he is the body, although actually he is not. His relationship with his body and his so-called father and mother are false, illusory conceptions. These illusions continue as long as one is not enlightened about the situation of the living entity.

TEXT 9

एष नित्योऽव्ययः सूक्ष्म एष सर्वाश्रयः स्वदृक् ।
आत्ममायागुणैर्विश्वमात्मानं सृजते प्रभुः ॥ ९ ॥

eṣa nityo'vyayaḥ sūkṣma
eṣa sarvāśrayaḥ svadṛk
ātmamāyā-guṇair viśvam
ātmānaṁ sṛjate prabhuḥ

eṣaḥ—this living entity; *nityaḥ*—eternal; *avyayaḥ*—imperishable; *sūkṣmaḥ*—very, very fine (not seen by the material eyes); *eṣaḥ*—this living entity; *sarva-āśrayaḥ*—the cause of different types of bodies; *sva-dṛk*—self-effulgent; *ātma-māyā-guṇaiḥ*—by the Supreme Personality of Godhead's modes of material nature; *viśvam*—this material world; *ātmānam*—himself; *sṛjate*—appears; *prabhuḥ*—the master.

TRANSLATION

The living entity is eternal and imperishable because he actually has no beginning and no end. He never takes birth or dies. He is the basic principle of all types of bodies, yet he does not belong to the bodily category. The living being is so sublime that he is equal in quality to the Supreme Lord. Nonetheless, because he is extremely small, he is prone to be illusioned by the external energy, and thus he creates various bodies for himself according to his different desires.

PURPORT

In this verse the philosophy of *acintya-bhedābheda*—simultaneous oneness and difference—is described. The living entity is eternal (*nitya*) like the Supreme Personality of Godhead, but the difference is that the Supreme Lord is the greatest, no one being equal to or greater than Him, whereas the living entity is *sūkṣma,* or extremely small. The *śāstra* describes that the magnitude of the living entity is one ten-thousandth the size of the tip of a hair. The Supreme Lord is all-pervading (*aṇḍāntara-stha-paramāṇu-cayāntara-stham*). Relatively, if the living entity is accepted as the smallest, there should naturally be inquiry about the greatest. The greatest is the Supreme Personality of Godhead, and the smallest is the living entity.

Another peculiar characteristic of the *jīva* is that he becomes covered by *māyā. Ātmamāyā-guṇaiḥ:* he is prone to being covered by the Supreme Lord's illusory energy. The living entity is responsible for his conditional life in the material world, and therefore he is described as *prabhu* ("the master"). If he likes he can come to this material world, and if he likes he can return home, back to Godhead. Because he wanted to enjoy this material world, the Supreme Personality of Godhead gave him a material body through the agency of the material energy. As the Lord Himself says in *Bhagavad-gītā* (18.61):

īśvaraḥ sarva-bhūtānāṁ
hṛd-deśe'rjuna tiṣṭhati

bhrāmayan sarva-bhūtāni
yantrārūḍhāni māyayā

"The Supreme Lord is situated in everyone's heart, O Arjuna, and is directing the wanderings of all living entities, who are seated as on a machine, made of the material energy." The Supreme Lord gives the living entity a chance to enjoy in this material world as he desires, but He openly expresses His own desire that the living entity give up all material aspirations, fully surrender unto Him and return home, back to Godhead.

The living entity is the smallest (*sūkṣma*). Jīva Gosvāmī says in this connection that the living entity within the body is extremely difficult for materialistic scientists to find, although we understand from authorities that the living entity is within the body. The body is different from the living entity.

TEXT 10

न ह्यस्यास्तिप्रियः कश्चिन्नाप्रियः स्वः परोऽपि वा ।
एकः सर्वधियां द्रष्टा कर्तॄणां गुणदोषयोः ॥ १० ॥

na hy asyāsti priyaḥ kaścin
nāpriyaḥ svaḥ paro'pi vā
ekaḥ sarva-dhiyāṁ draṣṭā
kartṝṇāṁ guṇa-doṣayoḥ

na—not; *hi*—indeed; *asya*—to the living entity; *asti*—there is; *priyaḥ*—dear; *kaścit*—someone; *na*—not; *apriyaḥ*—not dear; *svaḥ*—own; *paraḥ*—other; *api*—also; *vā*—or; *ekaḥ*—the one; *sarva-dhiyām*—of the varieties of intelligence; *draṣṭā*—the seer; *kartṝṇām*—of the performers; *guṇa-doṣayoḥ*—of right and wrong activities.

TRANSLATION

For this living entity, no one is dear, nor is anyone unfavorable. He makes no distinction between that which is his own and that which belongs to anyone else. He is one without a second; in other words, he is not affected by friends and enemies, well-wishers or mischief-mongers. He is only an observer, a witness, of the different qualities of men.

PURPORT

As explained in the previous verse, the living entity has the same qualities as the Supreme Personality of Godhead, but he has them in minute quantities because he is a small particle (*sūkṣma*) whereas the Supreme Lord is all-pervading and great. For the Supreme Lord there are no friends, enemies or relatives, for He is completely free from all the disqualifications of ignorance that characterize the conditioned souls. On the other hand, He is extremely kind and favorable to His devotees, and He is not at all satisfied with persons who are envious of His devotees. As the Lord Himself confirms in *Bhagavad-gītā* (9.29):

samo 'haṁ sarva-bhūteṣu
na me dveṣyo 'sti na priyaḥ
ye bhajanti tu māṁ bhaktyā
mayi te teṣu cāpy aham

"I envy no one, nor am I partial to anyone. I am equal to all. But whoever renders service unto Me in devotion is a friend, is in Me, and I am also a friend to him." The Supreme Lord has no enemy or friend, but He is inclined toward a devotee who always engages in His devotional service. Similarly, elsewhere in the *Gītā* (16.19) the Lord says:

tān ahaṁ dviṣataḥ krūrān
saṁsāreṣu narādhamān
kṣipāmy ajasram aśubhān
āsurīṣv eva yoniṣu

"Those who are envious and mischievous, who are the lowest among men, are cast by Me into the ocean of material existence, into various demoniac species of life." The Lord is extremely antagonistic toward those who are envious of His devotees. To protect His devotees, the Lord sometimes has to kill their enemies. For example, to protect Prahlāda Mahārāja, the Lord had to kill his enemy Hiraṇyakaśipu, although Hiraṇyakaśipu attained salvation because of being killed by the Lord. Since the Lord is the witness of everyone's activities, He witnesses the actions of the enemies of His devotees, and He is inclined to punish them. In other cases, however, He simply witnesses what the living entities do and gives the results of one's sinful or pious actions.

TEXT 11

नादत्त आत्मा हि गुणं न दोषं न क्रियाफलम् ।
उदासीनवदासीनः परावरदृगीश्वरः ॥ ११ ॥

nādatta ātmā hi guṇaṁ
na doṣaṁ na kriyā-phalam

udāsīnavad āsīnaḥ
parāvara-dṛg īśvaraḥ

na—not; *ādatte*—accepts; *ātmā*—the Supreme Lord; *hi*—indeed; *guṇam* —happiness; *na*—not; *doṣam*—unhappiness; *na*—nor; *kriyā-phalam*—the result of any fruitive activity; *udāsīna-vat*—exactly like a neutral man; *āsīnaḥ* —sitting (in the core of the heart); *para-avara-dṛk*—seeing the cause and effect; *īśvaraḥ*—the Supreme Lord.

TRANSLATION

The Supreme Lord [ātmā], the creator of cause and effect, does not accept the happiness and distress that result from fruitive actions. He is completely independent of having to accept a material body, and because He has no material body, He is always neutral. The living entities, being part and parcel of the Lord, possess His qualities in a minute quantity. Therefore one should not be affected by lamentation.

PURPORT

The conditioned soul has friends and enemies. He is affected by the good qualities and the faults of his position. The Supreme Lord, however, is always transcendental. Because He is the *īśvara,* the supreme controller, He is not affected by duality. It may therefore be said that He sits in the core of everyone's heart as the neutral witness of the causes and effects of one's activities, good and bad. We should also understand that *udāsīna,* neutral, does not mean that He takes no action. Rather, it means that He is not personally affected. For example, a court judge is neutral when two opposing parties appear before him, but he still takes action as the case warrants. To become completely neutral, indifferent, to material activities, we should simply seek shelter at the lotus feet of the supreme neutral person.

Mahārāja Citraketu was advised that remaining neutral in such trying circumstances as the death of one's son is impossible. Nevertheless, since the Lord knows how to adjust everything, the best course is to depend upon Him and do one's duty in devotional service to the Lord. In all circumstances, one should be undisturbed by duality. As stated in *Bhagavad-gītā* (2.47):

karmaṇy evādhikāras te
mā phaleṣu kadācana
mā karma-phala-hetur bhūr
mā te saṅgo'stv akarmaṇi

"You have a right to perform your prescribed duty, but you are not entitled to the fruits of action. Never consider yourself to be the cause of the results of your activities, and never be attached to not doing your duty." One should execute one's devotional duty, and for the results of one's actions one should depend upon the Supreme Personality of Godhead.

TEXT 12

श्रीबादरायणिरुवाच
इत्युदीर्य गतो जीवो ज्ञातयस्तस्य ते तदा ।
विस्मिता मुमुचुः शोकं छित्त्वात्मस्नेहशृङ्खलाम् ॥ १२ ॥

śrī-bādarāyaṇir uvāca
ity udīrya gato jīvo
jñātayas tasya te tadā
vismitā mumucuḥ śokaṁ
chittvātma-sneha-śṛṅkhalām

śrī-bādarāyaṇiḥ uvāca—Śrī Śukadeva Gosvāmī said; *iti*—in this way; *udīrya*—speaking; *gataḥ*—went; *jīvaḥ*—the living entity (who had appeared as the son of Mahārāja Citraketu); *jñātayaḥ*—the relatives and family members; *tasya*—of him; *te*—they; *tadā*—at that time; *vismitāḥ*—being astonished; *mumucuḥ*—gave up; *śokam*—lamentation; *chittvā*—cutting off; *ātma-sneha*—of affection due to a relationship; *śṛṅkhalām*—the iron shackles.

TRANSLATION

Śrī Śukadeva Gosvāmī continued: When the conditioned soul [jīva] in the form of Mahārāja Citraketu's son had spoken in this way and then left, Citraketu and the other relatives of the dead son were all astonished. Thus they cut off the shackles of their affection, which was due to their relationship with him, and gave up their lamentation.

TEXT 13

निर्हृत्य ज्ञातयो ज्ञातेर्देहं कृत्वोचिताः क्रियाः ।
तत्यजुर्दुस्त्यजं स्नेहं शोकमोहभयार्तिदम् ॥ १३ ॥

nirhṛtya jñātayo jñāter
dehaṁ kṛtvocitāḥ kriyāḥ

tatyajur dustyajaṁ snehaṁ
śoka-moha-bhayārtidam

nirhṛtya—removing; *jñātayaḥ*—King Citraketu and all the other relatives; *jñāteḥ*—of the son; *deham*—the body; *kṛtvā*—performing; *ucitāḥ*—suitable; *kriyāḥ*—activities; *tatyajuḥ*—gave up; *dustyajam*—very difficult to give up; *sneham*—affection; *śoka*—lamentation; *moha*—illusion; *bhaya*—fear; *arti*—and distress; *dam*—giving.

TRANSLATION

After the relatives had discharged their duties by performing the proper funeral ceremonies and burning the dead child's body, they gave up the affection that leads to illusion, lamentation, fear and pain. Such affection is undoubtedly difficult to give up, but they gave it up very easily.

TEXT 14

बालघ्न्यो व्रीडितास्तत्र बालहत्याहतप्रभाः ।
बालहत्याव्रतं चेरुर्ब्राह्मणैर्यन्निरूपितम् ।
यमुनायां महाराज स्मरन्त्यो द्विजभाषितम् ॥ १४ ॥

bāla-ghnyo vrīḍitās tatra
bāla-hatyā-hata-prabhāḥ
bāla-hatyā-vrataṁ cerur
brāhmaṇair yan nirūpitam
yamunāyāṁ mahārāja
smarantyo dvija-bhāṣitam

bāla-ghnyaḥ—the killers of the child; *vrīḍitāḥ*—being very much ashamed; *tatra*—there; *bāla-hatyā*—because of killing the child; *hata*—having lost; *prabhāḥ*—all bodily luster; *bāla-hatyā-vratam*—the atonement for killing the child; *ceruḥ*—executed; *brāhmaṇaiḥ*—by the priests; *yat*—which; *nirūpitam*—described; *yamunāyām*—at the River Yamunā; *mahā-rāja*—O King Parīkṣit; *smarantyaḥ*—remembering; *dvija-bhāṣitam*—the statement given by the *brāhmaṇa.*

TRANSLATION

Queen Kṛtyadyuti's co-wives, who had poisoned the child, were very much ashamed, and they lost all their bodily luster. While lamenting, O

King, they remembered the instructions of Aṅgirā and gave up their ambition to bear children. Following the directions of the brāhmaṇas, they went to the bank of the Yamunā, where they bathed and atoned for their sinful activities.

PURPORT

In this verse the word *bāla-hatyā-hata-prabhāḥ* is to be particularly noted. The practice of killing children has existed in human society for a long time—since time immemorial—but in the days of yore it was very rarely performed. At the present moment, however, in this age of Kali, abortion—killing of the child within the womb—has become very common, and sometimes a child is even killed after birth. If a woman performs such an abominable act, she gradually loses all her bodily luster (*bāla-hatyā-hata-prabhāḥ*). It is also to be noted that the ladies who had committed the sinful act of administering poison to the child were very much ashamed, and according to the directions of the *brāhmaṇas,* they had to undergo atonement for killing the child. Any woman who has ever performed such an infamously sinful act must atone for it, but no one now is doing that. Under the circumstances, the women responsible must suffer in this life and the next. Those who are sincere souls, after hearing this incident, should refrain from such child-killing and should atone for their sinful activities by taking to Kṛṣṇa consciousness very seriously. If one chants the Hare Kṛṣṇa *mahā-mantra* without offenses, all of one's sinful actions are surely atoned for immediately, but one should not commit such deeds again, for that is an offense.

TEXT 15

स इत्थं प्रतिबुद्धात्मा चित्रकेतुर्द्विजोक्तिभिः ।
गृहान्धकूपान्निष्क्रान्तः सरःपङ्कादिव द्विपः ॥ १५ ॥

sa itthaṁ pratibuddhātmā
citraketur dvijoktibhiḥ
gṛhāndha-kūpān niṣkrāntaḥ
saraḥ-paṅkād iva dvipaḥ

saḥ—he; *ittham*—in this way; *pratibuddha-ātmā*—being fully aware of spiritual knowledge; *citraketuḥ*—King Citraketu; *dvija-uktibhiḥ*—by the instructions of the perfect *brāhmaṇas* (Aṅgirā and Nārada Muni); *gṛha-andha-kūpāt*—from the dark well of family life; *niṣkrāntaḥ*—came out; *saraḥ*—of a lake or reservoir of water; *paṅkāt*—from the mud; *iva*—like; *dvipaḥ*—an elephant.

TRANSLATION

Thus enlightened by the instructions of the brāhmaṇas Aṅgirā and Nārada, King Citraketu became fully aware of spiritual knowledge. As an elephant becomes free from a muddy reservoir of water, King Citraketu came out of the dark well of family life.

TEXT 16

कालिन्द्यां विधिवत् स्नात्वा कृतपुण्यजलक्रियः ।
मौनेन संयतप्राणो ब्रह्मपुत्राववन्दत ॥ १६ ॥

kālindyāṁ vidhivat snātvā
kṛta-puṇya-jala-kriyaḥ
maunena saṁyata-prāṇo
brahma-putrāv avandata

kālindyām—in the River Yamunā; *vidhi-vat*—according to prescribed regulations; *snātvā*—bathing; *kṛta*—performing; *puṇya*—pious; *jala-kriyaḥ*—oblations by offering water; *maunena*—with gravity; *saṁyata-prāṇaḥ*—controlling the mind and senses; *brahma-putrau*—unto the two sons of Lord Brahmā (Aṅgirā and Nārada); *avandata*—offered his prayers and obeisances.

TRANSLATION

The King bathed in the water of the Yamunā, and according to prescribed duties, he offered oblations of water to the forefathers and demigods. Very gravely controlling his senses and mind, he then offered his respects and obeisances to the sons of Lord Brahmā [Aṅgirā and Nārada].

TEXT 17

अथ तस्मै प्रपन्नाय भक्ताय प्रयतात्मने ।
भगवान्नारदः प्रीतो विद्यामेतामुवाच ह ॥ १७ ॥

atha tasmai prapannāya
bhaktāya prayatātmane
bhagavān nāradaḥ prīto
vidyām etām uvāca ha

atha—thereafter; *tasmai*—unto him; *prapannāya*—who was surrendered; *bhaktāya*—being a devotee; *prayata-ātmane*—who was self-controlled; *bhagavān*—the most powerful; *nāradaḥ*—Nārada; *prītaḥ*—being very pleased; *vidyām*—transcendental knowledge; *etām*—this; *uvāca*—spoke; *ha*—indeed.

TRANSLATION

Thereafter, being very much pleased with Citraketu, who was a self-controlled devotee and surrendered soul, Nārada, the most powerful sage, spoke to him the following transcendental instructions.

TEXTS 18–19

ॐ नमस्तुभ्यं भगवते वासुदेवाय धीमहि ।
प्रद्युम्नायानिरुद्धाय नमः सङ्कर्षणाय च ॥ १८ ॥
नमो विज्ञानमात्राय परमानन्दमूर्तये ।
आत्मारामाय शान्ताय निवृत्तद्वैतदृष्टये ॥ १९ ॥

oṁ namas tubhyaṁ bhagavate
vāsudevāya dhīmahi
pradyumnāyāniruddhāya
namaḥ saṅkarṣaṇāya ca

namo vijñāna-mātrāya
paramānanda-mūrtaye
ātmārāmāya śāntāya
nivṛtta-dvaita-dṛṣṭaye

oṁ—O my Lord; *namaḥ*—obeisances; *tubhyam*—unto You; *bhagavate*—the Supreme Personality of Godhead; *vāsudevāya*—Kṛṣṇa, the son of Vasudeva; *dhīmahi*—let me meditate upon; *pradyumnāya*—unto Pradyumna; *aniruddhāya*—unto Aniruddha; *namaḥ*—respectful obeisances; *saṅkarṣaṇāya*—unto Lord Saṅkarṣaṇa; *ca*—also; *namaḥ*—all obeisances; *vijñāna-mātrāya*—unto the form full of knowledge; *parama-ānanda-mūrtaye*—full of transcendental bliss; *ātma-ārāmāya*—unto the Lord, who is self-sufficient; *śāntāya*—and free from disturbances; *nivṛtta-dvaita-dṛṣṭaye*—whose vision turns away from duality, or who is one without a second.

TRANSLATION

[Nārada gave Citraketu the following mantra.] O Lord, O Supreme Personality of Godhead, who are addressed by the oṁkāra [praṇava], I offer my respectful obeisances unto You. O Lord Vāsudeva, I meditate upon You. O Lord Pradyumna, Lord Aniruddha and Lord Saṅkarṣaṇa, I offer You my respectful obeisances. O reservoir of spiritual potency, O supreme bliss, I offer my respectful obeisances unto You, who are self-sufficient and most peaceful. O ultimate truth, one without a second, You are realized as Brahman, Paramātmā and Bhagavān and are therefore the reservoir of all knowledge. I offer my respectful obeisances unto You.

PURPORT

In *Bhagavad-gītā* Kṛṣṇa says that He is *praṇavaḥ sarva-vedeṣu,* the syllable *oṁ* in the Vedic *mantras.* In transcendental knowledge, the Lord is addressed as *praṇava, oṁkāra,* which is a symbolic representation of the Lord in sound. *Oṁ namo bhagavate vāsudevāya.* Vāsudeva, who is an expansion of Nārāyaṇa, expands Himself as Pradyumna, Aniruddha and Saṅkarṣaṇa. From Saṅkarṣaṇa comes a second Nārāyaṇa expansion, and from this Nārāyaṇa come further expansions of Vāsudeva, Pradyumna, Saṅkarṣaṇa and Aniruddha. The Saṅkarṣaṇa in this group is the original cause of the three *puruṣas,* namely Kāraṇodakaśāyī Viṣṇu, Garbhodakaśāyī Viṣṇu and Kṣīrodakaśāyī Viṣṇu. Kṣīrodakaśāyī Viṣṇu is situated in every universe in a special planet called Śvetadvīpa. This is confirmed in the *Brahma-saṁhitā: aṇḍāntara-stha.* The word *aṇḍa* means this universe. Within this universe is a planet called Śvetadvīpa, where Kṣīrodakaśāyī Viṣṇu is situated. From Him come all the incarnations within this universe.

As confirmed in the *Brahma-saṁhitā,* all these forms of the Supreme Personality of Godhead are *advaita,* nondifferent, and they are also *acyuta,* infallible; they do not fall down like the conditioned souls. The ordinary living entity is prone to falling into the clutches of *māyā,* but the Supreme Lord in His different incarnations and forms is *acyuta,* infallible. Therefore His body is different from the material body possessed by the conditioned soul.

The word *mātrā* is explained in the Medinī dictionary as follows: *mātrā karṇa-vibhūṣāyāṁ vitte māne paricchade.* The word *mātrā,* in its different imports, is used to indicate the decoration of the ear, possession, respect, and the possession of a covering. As stated in *Bhagavad-gītā* (2.14):

mātrā-sparśās tu kaunteya
śītoṣṇa-sukha-duḥkha-dāḥ
āgamāpāyino'nityās
tāṁs titikṣasva bhārata

"O son of Kuntī, the nonpermanent appearance of happiness and distress, and their disappearance in due course, are like the appearance and disappearance of winter and summer seasons. They arise from sense perception, O scion of Bharata, and one must learn to tolerate them without being disturbed." In the conditioned state of life, the body is used as our dress, and as one needs different dresses during the summer and winter, we conditioned souls are changing bodies according to our desires. However, because the body of the Supreme Lord is full of knowledge, it needs no covering. The idea that Kṛṣṇa's body is like ours—in other words, that His body and soul are different—is a misunderstanding. There are no such differences for Kṛṣṇa, because His body is full of knowledge. Here we receive material bodies because of a lack of knowledge, but because Kṛṣṇa, Vāsudeva, is full of knowledge, there is no difference between His body and His soul. Kṛṣṇa remembers what He said forty million years ago to the sun-god, but an ordinary being cannot remember what he said the day before yesterday. This is the difference between Kṛṣṇa's body and our body. Therefore the Lord is addressed as *vijñāna-mātrāya paramānanda-mūrtaye.*

Because the Lord's body is full of knowledge, He always enjoys transcendental bliss. Indeed, His very form is *paramānanda.* This is confirmed in the *Vedānta-sūtra: ānandamayo 'bhyāsāt.* By nature the Lord is *ānandamaya.* Whenever we see Kṛṣṇa, He is always full of *ānanda* in all circumstances. No one can make Him morose. *Ātmārāmāya:* He does not need to search for external enjoyment, because He is self-sufficient. *Śāntāya:* He has no anxiety. One who has to seek pleasure from other sources is always full of anxiety. *Karmīs, jñānīs* and *yogīs* are full of anxiety because they want something, but a devotee does not want anything; he is simply satisfied in the service of the Lord, who is fully blissful.

Nivṛtta-dvaita-dṛṣṭaye: in our conditioned life our bodies have different parts, but although Kṛṣṇa apparently has different bodily parts, no part of His body is different from any other part. Kṛṣṇa can see with His eyes, and Kṛṣṇa can see without His eyes. Therefore in the *Śvetāśvatara Upaniṣad* it is said, *paśyaty acakṣuḥ.* He can see with His hands and legs. He does not need a particular bodily part to perform a particular action. *Aṅgāni yasya sakalendriya-vṛttimanti:* He can do anything He desires with any part of His body, and therefore He is called almighty.

TEXT 20

आत्मानन्दानुभूत्यैव न्यस्तशक्त्यूर्मये नमः ।
हृषीकेशाय महते नमस्तेऽनन्तमूर्तये ॥ २० ॥

ātmānandānubhūtyaiva
nyasta-śakty-ūrmaye namaḥ
hṛṣīkeśāya mahate
namas te'nanta-mūrtaye

ātma-ānanda—of Your personal bliss; *anubhūtyā*—by perception; *eva*—certainly; *nyasta*—given up; *śakti-ūrmaye*—the waves of material nature; *namaḥ*—respectful obeisances; *hṛṣīkeśāya*—unto the supreme controller of the senses; *mahate*—unto the Supreme; *namaḥ*—respectful obeisances; *te*—unto You; *ananta*—unlimited; *mūrtaye*—whose expansions.

TRANSLATION

Perceiving Your personal bliss, You are always transcendental to the waves of material nature. Therefore, my Lord, I offer my respectful obeisances unto You. You are the supreme controller of the senses, and Your expansions of form are unlimited. You are the greatest, and therefore I offer my respectful obeisances unto You.

PURPORT

This verse analytically differentiates the living entity from the Supreme Lord. The form of the Lord and the form of the conditioned soul are different because the Lord is always blissful whereas the conditioned soul is always under the threefold miseries of the material world. The Supreme Lord is *sac-cid-ānanda-vigraha.* He derives *ānanda,* bliss, from His own self. The Lord's body is transcendental, spiritual, but because the conditioned soul has a material body, he has many bodily and mental troubles. The conditioned soul is always perturbed by attachment and detachment, whereas the Supreme Lord is always free from such dualities. The Lord is the supreme master of all the senses, whereas the conditioned soul is controlled by the senses. The Lord is the greatest, whereas the living entity is the smallest. The living entity is conditioned by the waves of material nature, but the Supreme Lord is transcendental to all actions and reactions. The expansions of the Supreme Lord's body are innumerable (*advaitam acyutam anādim ananta-rūpam*), but the conditioned soul is limited to only one form. From history we learn that a conditioned soul, by mystic power, can sometimes expand into eight forms, but the Lord's bodily expansions are unlimited. This means that the bodies of the Supreme Personality of Godhead have no beginning and no end, unlike the bodies of the living entities.

TEXT 21

वचस्युपरतेऽप्राप्य य एको मनसा सह ।
अनामरूपश्चिन्मात्रः सोऽव्यान्नः सदसत्परः ॥ २१ ॥

vacasy uparate'prāpya
ya eko manasā saha
anāma-rūpaś cin-mātraḥ
so'vyān naḥ sad-asat-paraḥ

vacasi—when the words; *uparate*—cease; *aprāpya*—not achieving the goal; *yaḥ*—He who; *ekaḥ*—one without a second; *manasā*—the mind; *saha*—with; *anāma*—with no material name; *rūpaḥ*—or material form; *cit-mātraḥ*—totally spiritual; *saḥ*—He; *avyāt*—may kindly protect; *naḥ*—us; *sat-asat-paraḥ*—who is the cause of all causes (the supreme cause).

TRANSLATION

The words and mind of the conditioned soul cannot approach the Supreme Personality of Godhead, for material names and forms are not applicable to the Lord, who is entirely spiritual, beyond the conception of gross and subtle forms. The impersonal Brahman is another of His forms. May He, by His pleasure, protect us.

PURPORT

The impersonal Brahman, which is the effulgence of the Lord, is described in this verse.

TEXT 22

यस्मिन्निदं यतश्चेदं तिष्ठत्यप्येति जायते ।
मृण्मयेष्विव मृज्जातिस्तस्मै ते ब्रह्मणे नमः ॥ २२ ॥

yasminn idaṁ yataś cedaṁ
tiṣṭhaty apyeti jāyate
mṛṇmayeṣv iva mṛj-jātis
tasmai te brahmaṇe namaḥ

yasmin—in whom; *idam*—this (cosmic manifestation); *yataḥ*—from whom; *ca*—also; *idam*—this (cosmic manifestation); *tiṣṭhati*—stands; *apyeti*—dissolves; *jāyate*—is born; *mṛt-mayeṣu*—in things made of earth; *iva*—like; *mṛt-jātiḥ*—birth from earth; *tasmai*—unto Him; *te*—You; *brahmaṇe*—the supreme cause; *namaḥ*—respectful obeisances.

TRANSLATION

As pots made completely of earth are situated on earth after being created and are transformed into earth again when broken, this cosmic manifestation is caused by the Supreme Brahman, situated in the Supreme Brahman, and annihilated in the same Supreme Brahman. Therefore, since the Supreme Lord is the cause of Brahman, let us offer Him our respectful obeisances.

PURPORT

The Supreme Lord is the cause of the cosmic manifestation, He maintains it after creation, and after annihilation the Lord is the reservoir of everything.

TEXT 23

यन्न स्पृशन्ति न विदुर्मनोबुद्धीन्द्रियासवः ।
अन्तर्बहिश्च विततं व्योमवत्तन्नतोऽस्म्यहम् ॥ २३ ॥

yan na spṛśanti na vidur
mano-buddhīndriyāsavaḥ
antar bahiś ca vitataṁ
vyomavat tan nato 'smy aham

yat—whom; *na*—not; *spṛśanti*—can touch; *na*—nor; *viduḥ*—can know; *manaḥ*—the mind; *buddhi*—the intelligence; *indriya*—the senses; *asavaḥ*—the life airs; *antaḥ*—within; *bahiḥ*—outside; *ca*—also; *vitatam*—expanded; *vyoma-vat*—like the sky; *tat*—unto Him; *nataḥ*—bowed; *asmi*—am; *aham*—I.

TRANSLATION

The Supreme Brahman emanates from the Supreme Personality of Godhead and expands like the sky. Although untouched by anything material, it exists within and without. Nonetheless, the mind, intelligence, senses and living force can neither touch Him nor know Him. I offer unto Him my respectful obeisances.

TEXT 24

देहेन्द्रियप्राणमनोधियोऽमी
यदंशविद्धाः प्रचरन्ति कर्मसु ।
नैवान्यदा लौहमिवाप्रतप्तं
स्थानेषु तद् द्रष्ट्रपदेशमेति ॥ २४ ॥

dehendriya-prāṇa-mano-dhiyo'mī
yad-aṁśa-viddhāḥ pracaranti karmasu
naivānyadā lauham ivāprataptaṁ
sthāneṣu tad draṣṭrapadeśam eti

deha—the body; *indriya*—senses; *prāṇa*—life airs; *manaḥ*—mind; *dhiyaḥ*—and intelligence; *amī*—all those; *yat-aṁśa-viddhāḥ*—being influenced by rays of Brahman, or the Supreme Lord; *pracaranti*—they move; *karmasu*—in various activities; *na*—not; *eva*—indeed; *anyadā*—at other times; *lauham*—iron; *iva*—like; *aprataptam*—not heated (by fire); *sthāneṣu*—in those circumstances; *tat*—that; *draṣṭṛ-apadeśam*—the name of a subject matter; *eti*—achieves.

TRANSLATION

As iron has the power to burn when made red-hot in the association of fire, so the body, senses, living force, mind and intelligence, although merely lumps of matter, can function in their activities when infused with a particle of consciousness by the Supreme Personality of Godhead. As iron cannot burn unless heated by fire, the bodily senses cannot act unless favored by the Supreme Brahman.

PURPORT

Red-hot iron can burn, but it cannot burn the original fire. Therefore the consciousness of the small particle of Brahman is fully dependent on the power of the Supreme Brahman. In *Bhagavad-gītā* the Lord says, *mattaḥ smṛtir jñānam apohanaṁ ca:* "From Me the conditioned soul receives memory, knowledge and forgetfulness." The power for activities comes from the Supreme Lord, and when the Lord withdraws this power, the conditioned soul no longer has energy with which to act through his various senses. The body includes five knowledge-acquiring senses, five active senses and the mind, but actually these are merely lumps of matter. For example, the brain is nothing but matter, but when electrified by the energy of the Supreme Personality of Godhead, the brain can act, just as iron can burn when made red-hot by the influence of fire. The brain can act while we are awake or even while we are dreaming, but when we are fast asleep or unconscious the brain is inactive. Since the brain is a lump of matter, it does not have independent power with which to act. It can act only when favored by the influence of the Supreme Personality of Godhead, who is Brahman or Parabrahman. This is the way to understand how the Supreme Brahman, Kṛṣṇa, is present everywhere, just as the sunshine is present because of the sun god in the sun globe. The Supreme Lord is called Hṛṣīkeśa; He is the only conductor of the senses. Unless empowered by His energy, our senses cannot act. In other words, He is the only seer, the only worker, the only listener, and the only active principle or supreme controller.

TEXT 25

ॐ नमो भगवते महापुरुषाय महानुभावाय महाविभूतिपतये सकल-
सात्वतपरिवृढनिकरकरकमलकुड्मलोपलालितचरणारविन्दयुगल परमपरमेष्ठि-
न्नमस्ते ॥ २५ ॥

oṁ namo bhagavate mahā-puruṣāya mahānubhāvāya mahā-vibhūti-
pataye sakala-sātvata-parivṛḍha-nikara-kara-kamala-kuḍmalopalālita-
caraṇāravinda-yugala parama-parameṣṭhin namas te.

oṁ—O Supreme Personality of Godhead; *namaḥ*—respectful obeisances; *bhagavate*—unto You, the Lord, who are full in six opulences; *mahā-puruṣāya*—the supreme enjoyer; *mahā-anubhāvāya*—the most perfect realized soul, or the Supersoul; *mahā-vibhūti-pataye*—the master of all mystic power; *sakala-sātvata-parivṛḍha*—of all the best devotees; *nikara*—of the multitude; *kara-kamala*—of the lotus hands; *kuḍmala*—by the buds; *upalālita*—served; *caraṇa-aravinda-yugala*—whose two lotus feet; *parama*—topmost; *parame-*

ṣṭhin—who are situated in the spiritual planet; *namaḥ te*—respectful obeisances unto You.

TRANSLATION

O transcendental Lord, who are situated in the topmost planet of the spiritual world, Your two lotus feet are always massaged by a multitude of the best devotees with their lotus-bud hands. You are the Supreme Personality of Godhead, complete in six opulences. You are the supreme person mentioned in the Puruṣa-sūkta prayers. You are the most perfect, self-realized master of all mystic power. Let me offer my respectful obeisances unto You.

PURPORT

It is said that the Absolute Truth is one, but is manifested in different features as Brahman, Paramātmā and Bhagavān. The previous verses described the Brahman and Paramātmā features of the Absolute Truth. Now this prayer is offered in *bhakti-yoga* to the Absolute Supreme Person. The words used in this regard are *sakala-sātvata-parivṛḍha.* The word *sātvata* means "devotees," and *sakala* means "all together." The devotees, who also have lotus feet, serve the lotus feet of the Lord with their lotus hands. The devotees may sometimes not be competent to serve the lotus feet of the Lord, and therefore the Lord is addressed as *parama-parameṣṭhin.* He is the Supreme Person, yet He is very kind to the devotees. No one is competent to serve the Lord, but even if a devotee is not competent, the merciful Lord accepts the humble attempt of the devotee.

TEXT 26

श्रीशुक उवाच

भक्तायैतां प्रपन्नाय विद्यामादिश्य नारदः ।
ययावङ्गिरसा साकं धाम स्वायम्भुवं प्रभो ॥ २६ ॥

śrī-śuka uvāca
bhaktāyaitāṁ prapannāya
vidyām ādiśya nāradaḥ
yayāv aṅgirasā sākaṁ
dhāma svāyambhuvaṁ prabho

śrī-śukaḥ uvāca—Śrī Śukadeva Gosvāmī said; *bhaktāya*—unto the devotee; *etām*—this; *prapannāya*—unto one who fully surrendered; *vidyām*—transcendental knowledge; *ādiśya*—instructing; *nāradaḥ*—the great sage Nārada; *yayau*—left; *aṅgirasā*—the great saint Aṅgirā; *sākam*—with; *dhāma*—for the topmost planet; *svāyambhuvam*—belonging to Lord Brahmā; *prabho*—O King.

TRANSLATION

Śrī Śukadeva Gosvāmī continued: Nārada, having become the spiritual master of Citraketu, instructed him fully in this prayer because Citraketu was fully surrendered. O King Parīkṣit, Nārada then left with the great sage Aṅgirā for the topmost planet, known as Brahmaloka.

PURPORT

When Aṅgirā had first come to visit King Citraketu, he did not bring Nārada with him. However, after the death of Citraketu's son, Aṅgirā brought Nārada to instruct King Citraketu about *bhakti-yoga.* The difference was that in the beginning Citraketu was not in a temperament of renunciation, but after the death of his son, when he was overwhelmed by his great plight, he was awakened to the platform of renunciation by instructions regarding the falsity of this material world and material possessions. It is only at this stage that *bhakti-yoga* can be instructed. As long as one is attached to material enjoyment, *bhakti-yoga* cannot be understood. This is confirmed in *Bhagavad-gītā* (2.44):

bhogaiśvarya-prasaktānāṁ
tayāpahṛta-cetasām
vyavasāyātmikā buddhiḥ
samādhau na vidhīyate

"In the minds of those who are too attached to sense enjoyment and material opulence, and who are bewildered by such things, the resolute determination of devotional service to the Supreme Lord does not take place." As long as one is very much attached to material enjoyment, one cannot concentrate his mind on the subject matter of devotional service.

The Kṛṣṇa consciousness movement is progressing successfully in the Western countries at the present moment because the youth in the West have reached the stage of *vairāgya,* or renunciation. They are practically disgusted with material pleasure from material sources, and this has resulted in a population of hippies throughout the Western countries. Now if these young people are instructed about *bhakti-yoga,* Kṛṣṇa consciousness, the instructions will certainly be effective.

As soon as Citraketu understood the philosophy of *vairāgya-vidyā,* the knowledge of renunciation, he could understand the process of *bhakti-yoga.* In this regard Śrīla Sārvabhauma Bhaṭṭācārya has said, *vairāgya-vidyā-nija-bhakti-yoga. Vairāgya-vidyā* and *bhakti-yoga* are parallel lines. One is essential for understanding the other. It is also said, *bhaktiḥ pareśānubhavo viraktir anyatra ca* (*Bhāg.* 11.2.42). Advancement in devotional service, or Kṛṣṇa consciousness, is characterized by increasing renunciation of material enjoyment. Nārada Muni is the father of devotional service, and therefore, just to bestow causeless mercy upon King Citraketu, Aṅgirā brought Nārada Muni to instruct the King. These instructions were extremely effective. Anyone who follows in the footsteps of Nārada Muni is certainly a pure devotee.

TEXT 27

चित्रकेतुस्तु तां विद्यां यथा नारदभाषिताम् ।
धारयामास सप्ताहमब्भक्षः सुसमाहितः ॥ २७ ॥

citraketus tu tāṁ vidyāṁ
yathā nārada-bhāṣitām
dhārayām āsa saptāham
ab-bhakṣaḥ susamāhitaḥ

citraketuḥ—King Citraketu; *tu*—indeed; *tām*—that; *vidyām*—transcendental knowledge; *yathā*—just as; *nārada-bhāṣitām*—instructed by the great sage Nārada; *dhārayām āsa*—chanted; *sapta-aham*—continuously for one week; *ap-bhakṣaḥ*—only drinking water; *su-samāhitaḥ*—with great attention and care.

TRANSLATION

Fasting and drinking only water, Citraketu for one week continuously chanted with great care and attention the mantra given by Nārada Muni.

TEXT 28

ततः स सप्तरात्रान्ते विद्यया धार्यमाणया ।
विद्याधराधिपत्यं च लेभेऽप्रतिहतं नृप ॥ २८ ॥

tataḥ sa sapta-rātrānte
vidyayā dhāryamāṇayā
vidyādharādhipatyaṁ ca
lebhe'pratihataṁ nṛpa

tataḥ—from this; *saḥ*—he; *sapta-rātra-ante*—at the end of seven nights; *vidyayā*—by the prayers; *dhāryamāṇayā*—being carefully practiced; *vidyādhara-adhipatyam*—mastership of the Vidyādharas (as an intermediate result); *ca*—also; *lebhe*—achieved; *apratihatam*—undeviated from the instructions of the spiritual master; *nṛpa*—O King Parīkṣit.

TRANSLATION

O King Parīkṣit, after only one week of repeatedly practicing the mantra received from the spiritual master, Citraketu achieved the rule of the planet of the Vidyādharas as an intermediate product of his spiritual advancement in knowledge.

PURPORT

If a devotee, after being initiated, adheres rigidly to the instructions of the spiritual master, he is naturally endowed with the material opulences of *vidyādhara-adhipatyam* and similar posts as by-products. A devotee need not practice *yoga, karma* or *jñāna* to achieve a successful result. Devotional service alone is competent to award a devotee all material power. A pure devotee, however, is never attached to material power, although he gets it very easily without personal endeavor. Citraketu received this side benefit of his devotional service, which he rigidly performed in accordance with the instructions of Nārada.

TEXT 29

ततः कतिपयाहोभिर्विद्ययेद्धमनोगतिः ।
जगाम देवदेवस्य शेषस्य चरणान्तिकम् ॥ २९ ॥

tataḥ katipayāhobhir
vidyayeddha-mano-gatiḥ
jagāma deva-devasya
śeṣasya caraṇāntikam

tataḥ—thereafter; *katipaya-ahobhiḥ*—within a few days; *vidyayā*—by the spiritual *mantra; iddha-manaḥ-gatiḥ*—the course of his mind being enlightened; *jagāma*—went; *deva-devasya*—of the master of all other lords or demigods; *śeṣasya*—Lord Śeṣa; *caraṇa-antikam*—to the shelter of the lotus feet.

TRANSLATION

Thereafter, within a very few days, by the influence of the mantra that Citraketu had practiced, his mind became increasingly enlightened in spiritual progress, and he attained shelter at the lotus feet of Anantadeva.

PURPORT

A devotee's ultimate achievement is to take shelter of the lotus feet of the Lord in any one of the planets in the spiritual sky. As a result of rigid execution of devotional service, a devotee receives all material opulences if these are required; otherwise, the devotee is not interested in material opulences, nor does the Supreme Lord award them. When a devotee is actually engaged in the devotional service of the Lord, his apparently material opulences are not material; they are all spiritual. For example, if a devotee spends money to construct a beautiful and costly temple, the construction is not material but spiritual (*nirbandhaḥ kṛṣṇa-sambandhe yuktaṁ vairāgyam ucyate*). A devotee's mind is never diverted to the material side of the temple. The bricks, stone and wood used in the construction of the temple are spiritual, just as the Deity, although made of stone, is not stone but the Supreme Personality of Godhead Himself. The more one advances in spiritual consciousness, the more he can understand the elements of devotional service. Nothing in devotional service is material; everything is spiritual. Consequently a devotee is awarded so-called material opulence for spiritual advancement. This opulence is an aid to help the devotee advance toward the spiritual kingdom. Thus Mahārāja Citraketu remained in material opulence as a *vidyādhara-pati,* master of the Vidyādharas, and by executing devotional service he became perfect within a very few days and returned home, back to Godhead, taking shelter of the lotus feet of Lord Śeṣa, Ananta.

A *karmī's* material opulence and a devotee's material opulence are not on the same level. Śrīla Madhvācārya comments in this way:

anyāntaryāmiṇaṁ viṣṇum
upāsyānya-samīpagaḥ
bhaved yogyatayā tasya
padaṁ vā prāpnuyān naraḥ

By worshiping Lord Viṣṇu one can get whatever he desires, but a pure devotee never asks Lord Viṣṇu for any material profit. Instead he serves Lord Viṣṇu without material desires and is therefore ultimately transferred to the spiritual kingdom. In this regard, Śrīla Vīrarāghava Ācārya comments, *yatheṣṭa-gatir ity arthaḥ:* by worshiping Viṣṇu, a devotee can get whatever he likes. Mahārāja Citraketu wanted only to return home, back to Godhead, and therefore he achieved success in that way.

TEXT 30

मृणालगौरं शितिवाससं स्फुरत्-
किरीटकेयूरकटित्रकङ्कणम् ।
प्रसन्नवक्त्रारुणलोचनं वृतं
ददर्श सिद्धेश्वरमण्डलैः प्रभुम् ॥ ३० ॥

mṛṇāla-gauraṁ śiti-vāsasaṁ sphurat-
kirīṭa-keyūra-kaṭitra-kaṅkaṇam
prasanna-vaktrāruṇa-locanaṁ vṛtaṁ
dadarśa siddheśvara-maṇḍalaiḥ prabhum

mṛṇāla-gauram—white like the fibers of a lotus; *śiti-vāsasam*—wearing garments of blue silk; *sphurat*—glittering; *kirīṭa*—helmet; *keyūra*—armlets; *kaṭitra*—belt; *kaṅkaṇam*—whose bangles; *prasanna-vaktra*—smiling face; *aruṇa-locanam*—having reddish eyes; *vṛtam*—surrounded; *dadarśa*—he saw; *siddha-īśvara-maṇḍalaiḥ*—by the most perfect devotees; *prabhum*—the Supreme Personality of Godhead.

TRANSLATION

Upon reaching the shelter of Lord Śeṣa, the Supreme Personality of Godhead, Citraketu saw that He was as white as the white fibers of a lotus flower. He was dressed in bluish garments and adorned with a brilliantly glittering helmet, armlets, belt and bangles. His face was smiling, and His eyes were reddish. He was surrounded by such exalted liberated persons as Sanat-kumāra.

TEXT 31

तद्दर्शनध्वस्तसमस्तकिल्बिषः
स्वस्थामलान्तःकरणोऽभ्ययान्मुनिः ।

प्रवृद्धभक्त्या प्रणयाश्रुलोचनः
प्रहृष्टरोमानमदादिपुरुषम् ॥ ३१ ॥

tad-darśana-dhvasta-samasta-kilbiṣaḥ
svasthāmalāntaḥkaraṇo'bhyayān muniḥ
pravṛddha-bhaktyā praṇayāśru-locanaḥ
prahṛṣṭa-romānamad ādi-puruṣam

tat-darśana—by the sight of the Supreme Personality of Godhead; *dhvasta*—destroyed; *samasta-kilbiṣaḥ*—having all sins; *svastha*—healthy; *amala*—and pure; *antaḥkaraṇaḥ*—the core of whose heart; *abhyayāt*—approached face to face; *muniḥ*—the King, who was silent due to full mental satisfaction; *pravṛddha-bhaktyā*—with an attitude of increased devotional service; *praṇaya-aśru-locanaḥ*—with tears in his eyes because of love; *prahṛṣṭa-roma*—his hairs standing on end due to jubilation; *anamat*—offered respectful obeisances; *ādi-puruṣam*—unto the expansion of the original personality.

TRANSLATION

As soon as Mahārāja Citraketu saw the Supreme Lord, he was cleansed of all material contamination and situated in his original Kṛṣṇa consciousness, being completely purified. He became silent and grave, and because of love for the Lord, tears fell from his eyes, and his hairs stood on end. With great devotion and love, he offered his respectful obeisances unto the original Personality of Godhead.

PURPORT

The word *tad-darśana-dhvasta-samasta-kilbiṣaḥ* is very important in this verse. If one regularly sees the Supreme Personality of Godhead in the temple, one will gradually be disinfected of all material desires simply by visiting the temple and seeing the Deity. When one is freed from all the results of sinful activities, one will be purified, and with a healthy mind, completely cleansed, he will increasingly make progress in Kṛṣṇa consciousness.

TEXT 32

स उत्तमश्लोकपदाब्जविष्टरं
प्रेमाश्रुलेशैरुपमेहयन्मुहुः ।
प्रेमोपरुद्धाखिलवर्णनिर्गमो
नैवाशकत्तं प्रसमीडितुं चिरम् ॥ ३२ ॥

sa uttamaśloka-padābja-viṣṭaraṁ
premāśru-leśair upamehayan muhuḥ
premoparuddhākhila-varṇa-nirgamo
naivāśakat taṁ prasamīḍituṁ ciram

saḥ—he; *uttamaśloka*—of the Supreme Personality of Godhead; *pada-abja*—of the lotus feet; *viṣṭaram*—the resting place; *prema-aśru*—of tears of pure love; *leśaiḥ*—by drops; *upamehayan*—moistening; *muhuḥ*—again and again; *prema-uparuddha*—choked with love; *akhila*—all; *varṇa*—of the letters; *nirgamaḥ*—the coming out; *na*—not; *eva*—indeed; *aśakat*—was able; *tam*—unto Him; *prasamīḍitum*—to offer prayers; *ciram*—for a long time.

TRANSLATION

With tears of love and affection, Citraketu repeatedly moistened the resting place of the Supreme Lord's lotus feet. Because his voice was choked in ecstasy, for a considerable time he was unable to utter any of the letters of the alphabet to offer the Lord suitable prayers.

PURPORT

All the letters of the alphabet and the words constructed by those letters are meant for offering prayers to the Supreme Personality of Godhead. Mahārāja Citraketu had the opportunity to offer prayers to the Lord by composing nice verses from the letters of the alphabet, but because of his ecstasy, for a considerable time he could not join those letters to offer prayers to the Lord. As stated in *Śrīmad-Bhāgavatam* (1.5.22):

idaṁ hi puṁsas tapasaḥ śrutasya vā
sviṣṭasya sūktasya ca buddhi-dattayoḥ
avicyuto'rthaḥ kavibhir nirūpito
yad uttamaśloka-guṇānuvarṇanam

If one has scientific, philosophical, political, economic or any other abilities and wants perfection in his knowledge, he should offer prayers to the Supreme Personality of Godhead by composing first-class poetry or engaging his talents in the service of the Lord. Citraketu wanted to do this, but he was unable because of loving ecstasy. Therefore he had to wait for a considerable time before be could offer prayers.

TEXT 33

ततः समाधाय मनो मनीषया
बभाष एतत्प्रतिलब्धवागसौ ।
नियम्य सर्वेन्द्रियबाह्यवर्तनं
जगद्गुरुं सात्वतशास्त्रविग्रहम् ॥ ३३ ॥

tataḥ samādhāya mano manīṣayā
babhāṣa etat pratilabdha-vāg asau
niyamya sarvendriya-bāhya-vartanaṁ
jagad-guruṁ sātvata-śāstra-vigraham

tataḥ—thereafter; *samādhāya*—controlling; *manaḥ*—the mind; *manīṣayā*—by his intelligence; *babhāṣa*—spoke; *etat*—this; *pratilabdha*—recovering; *vāk*—speech; *asau*—that one (King Citraketu); *niyamya*—controlling; *sarva-indriya*—of all the senses; *bāhya*—external; *vartanam*—the wandering; *jagat gurum*—who is the spiritual master of everyone; *sātvata*—of devotional service; *śāstra*—of the holy scriptures; *vigraham*—the personified form.

TRANSLATION

Thereafter, by controlling his mind with his intelligence and thus restricting his senses from external engagements, he recovered suitable words with which to express his feelings. Thus he began offering prayers to the Lord, who is the personification of the holy scriptures [the sātvata-saṁhitās like the Brahma-saṁhitā and the Nārada-pañcarātra] and who is the spiritual master of all. He offered his prayers as follows.

PURPORT

One cannot offer prayers to the Lord with mundane words. One must become spiritually advanced by controlling the mind and senses. Then he can find suitable words to offer in prayers to the Lord. Quoting the following verse from the *Padma Purāṇa,* Śrīla Sanātana Gosvāmī forbids us to sing any song not sung by authorized devotees.

avaiṣṇava-mukhodgīrṇaṁ
pūtaṁ hari-kathāmṛtam
śravaṇaṁ naiva kartavyaṁ
sarpocchiṣṭaṁ yathā payaḥ

The words or songs of a person not fixed in Vaiṣṇava behavior, not strictly following the rules and regulations and chanting the Hare Kṛṣṇa *mantra* should not be accepted by pure devotees. The words *sātvata-śāstra-vigraham* indicate that the *sac-cid-ānanda* body of the Lord can never be accepted to be made of *māyā.* Devotees do not offer prayers to the Lord in an imaginary form. The existence of the Lord's form is supported by all Vedic literature.

TEXT 34

चित्रकेतुरुवाच
अजित जितः सममतिभिः
साधुभिर्भवान् जितात्मभिर्भवता ।
विजितास्तेऽपि च भजता-
मकामात्मनां य आत्मदोऽतिकरुणः ॥ ३४ ॥

citraketur uvāca
ajita jitaḥ sama-matibhiḥ
sādhubhir bhavān jitātmabhir bhavatā
vijitās te'pi ca bhajatām
akāmātmanāṁ ya ātmado'ti-karuṇaḥ

citraketuḥ uvāca—King Citraketu said; *ajita*—O my unconquerable Lord; *jitaḥ*—conquered; *sama-matibhiḥ*—by persons who have conquered the mind; *sādhubhiḥ*—the devotees; *bhavān*—Your Lordship; *jita-ātmabhiḥ*—who have completely controlled the senses; *bhavatā*—by You; *vijitāḥ*—conquered; *te*—they; *api*—also; *ca*—and; *bhajatām*—to those who always engage in Your service; *akāma-ātmanām*—with no motives for material profit; *yaḥ*—who; *ātma-daḥ*—giving Yourself; *ati-karuṇaḥ*—extremely merciful.

TRANSLATION

Citraketu said: O unconquerable Lord, although You cannot be conquered by anyone, You are certainly conquered by devotees who have control of the mind and senses. They can keep You under their control because You are causelessly merciful to devotees who desire no material profit from You. Indeed, You give Yourself to them, and because of this You also have full control over Your devotees.

PURPORT

The Lord and the devotees both conquer. The Lord is conquered by the devotees, and the devotees are conquered by the Lord. Because of being conquered by one another, they both derive transcendental bliss from their relationship. The highest perfection of this mutual conquering is exhibited by Kṛṣṇa and the *gopīs.* The *gopīs* conquered Kṛṣṇa, and Kṛṣṇa conquered the *gopīs.* Thus whenever Kṛṣṇa played His flute, He conquered the minds of the *gopīs,* and without seeing the *gopīs* Kṛṣṇa could not be happy. Other transcendentalists, such as *jñānīs* and *yogīs,* cannot conquer the Supreme Personality of Godhead; only pure devotees can conquer Him.

Pure devotees are described as *sama-mati,* which means that they never deviate from devotional service under any circumstances. It is not that devotees worship the Supreme Lord only when happy; they worship Him even when in distress. Happiness and distress do not hamper the process of devotional service. Therefore *Śrīmad-Bhāgavatam* says that devotional service is *ahaituky apratihatā,* unmotivated and uninterrupted. When a devotee offers devotional service to the Lord without any motive (*anyābhilāṣitā-śūnyam*), his service cannot be hampered by any material condition (*apratihatā*). Thus a devotee who offers service in all conditions of life can conquer the Supreme Personality of Godhead.

A special distinction between devotees and the other transcendentalists, namely the *jñānīs* and *yogīs,* is that *jñānīs* and *yogīs* artificially try to become one with the Supreme, whereas devotees never aspire for such an impossible accomplishment. Devotees know that their position is to be eternally servants of the Supreme Lord and never to be one with Him. Therefore they are called *sama-mati* or *jitātmā.* They detest oneness with the Supreme. They have no lusty desires for oneness; instead, their desire is to be freed from all material hankering. Therefore they are called *niṣkāma,* desireless. A living entity cannot exist without desires, but desires that can never be fulfilled are called *kāma,* lusty desires. *Kāmais tais tair hṛta jñānāḥ:* because of lusty desires, nondevotees are deprived of their intelligence. Thus they are unable to conquer the Supreme Lord, whereas devotees, being freed from such unreasonable desires, can conquer the Lord. Such devotees are also conquered by the Supreme Personality of Godhead. Because they are pure, being free from all material desires, they fully surrender to the Supreme Lord, and therefore the Lord conquers them. Such devotees never aspire for liberation. They simply desire to serve the lotus feet of the Lord. Because they serve the

Lord without desires for remuneration, they can conquer the mercy of the Lord. The Lord is by nature very merciful, and when He sees that His servant is working without desires for material profit, naturally He is conquered.

Devotees are always engaged in service.

sa vai manaḥ kṛṣṇa-padāravindayor
vacāṁsi vaikuṇṭha-guṇānuvarṇane

All the activities of their senses are engaged in the service of the Lord. Because of such devotion, the Lord gives Himself to His devotees as if they could use Him for any purpose they might desire. Of course, devotees have no purpose other than to serve. When a devotee fully surrenders and has no aspiration for material profit, the Lord certainly gives him all opportunities for service. This is the position of the Lord when conquered by His devotees.

TEXT 35

तव विभवः खलु भगवन्
जगदुदयस्थितिलयादीनि ।
विश्वसृजस्तेंऽशांशा-
स्तत्र मृषा स्पर्धन्ति पृथगभिमत्या ॥ ३५ ॥

tava vibhavaḥ khalu bhagavan
jagad-udaya-sthiti-layādīni
viśva-sṛjas te'ṁśāṁśās
tatra mṛṣā spardhanti pṛthag abhimatyā

tava—Your; *vibhavaḥ*—opulences; *khalu*—indeed; *bhagavan*—O Supreme Personality of Godhead; *jagat*—of the cosmic manifestation; *udaya*—the creation; *sthiti*—maintenance; *laya-ādīni*—dissolution and so on; *viśva-sṛjaḥ*—the creators of the manifested world; *te*—they; *aṁśa-aṁśāḥ*—parts of Your plenary portion; *tatra*—in that; *mṛṣā*—in vain; *spardhanti*—rival one another; *pṛthak*—of separateness; *abhimatyā*—by a false conception.

TRANSLATION

My dear Lord, this cosmic manifestation and its creation, maintenance and annihilation are all but Your opulences. Since Lord Brahmā and the other creators are nothing but small portions of a portion of You, their partial power to create does not make them God [īśvara]. Their consciousness of themselves as separate Lords is therefore merely false prestige. It is not valid.

PURPORT

A devotee who has fully surrendered to the lotus feet of the Lord knows very well that the creative energy of the living entities, from Lord Brahmā down to the small ant, exists because the living entities are part and parcel of the Lord. In *Bhagavad-gītā* (15.7) the Lord says, *mamaivāṁśo jīva-loke jīva-bhūtaḥ sanātanaḥ:* "The living entities in this conditioned world are My eternal, fragmental parts." The living entities are nothing but very small portions of the supreme spirit, like sparks of a fire. Because they are part of the Supreme, they have a creative quality in a very minute quantity.

The so-called scientists of the modern materialistic world are proud because they have created modern facilities like great airplanes, but the credit for creating the airplanes should go to the Supreme Personality of Godhead, not to the scientists who have invented or created the so-called wonderful products. The first consideration is the intelligence of the scientist; one must be elevated by the dictation of the Supreme Lord, who says in *Bhagavad-gītā* (15.15), *mattaḥ smṛtir jñānam apohanaṁ ca:* "From Me come remembrance, knowledge and forgetfulness." Because the Supreme Lord, as Supersoul, sits within the core of every living entity's heart, the dictation by which one advances in scientific knowledge or creative faculties comes from Him. Furthermore, the ingredients to manufacture wonderful machines like airplanes are also supplied by the Lord, not by the scientists. Before the airplane was created, its ingredients already existed, having been caused by the Supreme Personality of Godhead, but when the manifested creation of the airplane is ruined, the remaining debris is a problem for the so-called creators. Another example is that the West is creating many automobiles. The ingredients for these cars are supplied, of course, by the Supreme Lord, and the intelligence for the so-called creation is also supplied by the Lord. Ultimately, when the cars are demolished, the so-called creators are faced with the problem of what to do with their ingredients. The actual creator, the original creator, is the Personality of Godhead. Only in the interim does someone create something with intelligence supplied by the Lord, and later the creation again becomes a problem. Therefore the so-called creator is not to be credited with the act of creation; the only credit goes to the Supreme Personality of Godhead. It is rightly stated herein that the credit for all the opulences of creation, maintenance and annihilation belongs to the Supreme Lord, not to the living entities.

TEXT 36

परमाणुपरममहतो-
स्त्वमाद्यन्तान्तरवर्ती त्रयविधुरः ।
आदावन्तेऽपि च सत्त्वानां
यद् ध्रुवं तदेवान्तरालेऽपि ॥ ३६ ॥

paramāṇu-parama-mahatos
tvam ādy-antāntara-vartī traya-vidhuraḥ
ādāv ante'pi ca sattvānāṁ
yad dhruvaṁ tad evāntarāle'pi

parama-aṇu—of the atomic particle; *parama-mahatoḥ*—and of the biggest (the result of the combination of atoms); *tvam*—You; *ādi-anta*—in both the beginning and the end; *antara*—and in the middle; *vartī*—existing; *traya-vidhuraḥ*—although without beginning, end or middle; *ādau*—in the beginning; *ante*—at the end; *api*—also; *ca*—and; *sattvānām*—of all existences; *yat*—which; *dhruvam*—permanent; *tat*—that; *eva*—certainly; *antarāle*—in the middle; *api*—also.

TRANSLATION

You exist in the beginning, middle and end of everything, from the most minute particle of the cosmic manifestation—the atom—to the gigantic universes and total material energy. Nonetheless, You are eternal, having no beginning, end or middle. You are perceived to exist in these three phases, and thus You are permanent. When the cosmic manifestation does not exist, You exist as the original potency.

PURPORT

The *Brahma-saṁhitā* (5.33) says:

advaitam acyutam anādim ananta-rūpam
ādyaṁ purāṇa-puruṣaṁ nava-yauvanaṁ ca
vedeṣu durlabham adurlabham ātma-bhaktau
govindam ādi-puruṣaṁ tam ahaṁ bhajāmi

"I worship the Supreme Personality of Godhead, Govinda [Kṛṣṇa], who is the original person—absolute, infallible, without beginning, although expanded into unlimited forms, still the same original, the oldest, and the person always appearing as a fresh youth. Such eternal, blissful, all-knowing forms of the Lord cannot be understood even by the best Vedic scholars, but they are always manifest to pure, unalloyed devotees." The Supreme Personality of Godhead has no cause, for He is the cause of everything. The Lord is beyond the workings of cause and effect. He is eternally existing. In another verse the *Brahma-saṁhitā* says, *aṇḍāntara-stha-paramāṇu-cayāntara-stham:* the Lord exists within the gigantic universe and within the atom. The descent of the Lord into the atom and the universe indicates that without His presence, nothing could factually exist. Scientists say that water is a combination of hydrogen and oxygen, but when they see a vast ocean they are puzzled about where such a quantity of hydrogen and oxygen could have come from. They think that everything evolved from chemicals, but where did the chemicals come from? That they do not know. Since the Supreme Personality of Godhead is the cause of all causes, He can produce immense quantities of chemicals to create a situation for chemical evolution. We actually see that chemicals are produced from living entities. For example, a lemon tree produces many tons of citric acid. The citric acid is not the cause of the tree; rather, the tree is the cause of the acid. Similarly, the Supreme Personality of Godhead is the cause of everything. He is the cause of the tree that produces the citric acid (*bījaṁ māṁ sarva-bhūtānām*). Devotees can see that the original potencies causing the cosmic manifestation are not in chemicals but in the Supreme Personality of Godhead, for He is the cause of the chemicals.

Everything is caused or manifested by the energy of the Supreme Lord, and when everything is annihilated or dissolved, the original potency enters the body of the Supreme Lord. Therefore this verse says, *ādāv ante'pi ca sattvānāṁ yad dhruvaṁ tad evāntarāle'pi.* The word *dhruvam* means "permanent." The permanent reality is Kṛṣṇa, not this cosmic manifestation. As stated in *Bhagavad-gītā, aham ādir hi devānām* and *mattaḥ sarvaṁ pravartate:* Kṛṣṇa is the original cause of everything. Arjuna recognized Lord Śrī Kṛṣṇa as the original person (*puruṣaṁ śāśvataṁ divyam ādi-devam ajaṁ vibhum*), and the *Brahma-saṁhitā* describes Him as the original person (*govindam ādi-puruṣam*). He is the cause of all causes, whether at the beginning, at the end or in the middle.

TEXT 37

क्षित्यादिभिरेष किलावृतः
सप्तभिर्दशगुणोत्तरैरण्डकोशः ।

यत्र पतत्यणुकल्पः
सहाण्डकोटिकोटिभिस्तदनन्तः ॥ ३७ ॥

kṣity-ādibhir eṣa kilāvṛtaḥ
saptabhir daśa-guṇottarair aṇḍa-kośaḥ
yatra pataty aṇu-kalpaḥ
sahāṇḍa-koṭi-koṭibhis tad anantaḥ

kṣiti-ādibhiḥ—by the ingredients of the material world, headed by earth; *eṣaḥ*—this; *kila*—indeed; *āvṛtaḥ*—covered; *saptabhiḥ*—seven; *daśa-guṇa-uttaraiḥ*—each ten times more than the previous one; *aṇḍa-kośaḥ*—egg-shaped universe; *yatra*—in whom; *patati*—falls; *aṇu-kalpaḥ*—like a minute atom; *saha*—with; *aṇḍa-koṭi-koṭibhiḥ*—millions of such universes; *tat*—therefore; *anantaḥ*—(You are called) unlimited.

TRANSLATION

Every universe is covered by seven layers—earth, water, fire, air, sky, the total energy and false ego—each ten times greater than the previous one. There are innumerable universes besides this one, and although they are unlimitedly large, they move about like atoms in You. Therefore You are called unlimited [ananta].

PURPORT

The *Brahma-saṁhitā* (5.48) says:

yasyaika-niśvasita-kālam athāvalambya
jīvanti loma-vilajā jagad-aṇḍa-nāthāḥ
viṣṇur mahān sa iha yasya kalā-viśeṣo
govindam ādi-puruṣaṁ tam ahaṁ bhajāmi

The origin of the material creation is Mahā-Viṣṇu, who lies in the Causal Ocean. While He sleeps in that ocean, millions of universes are generated as He exhales, and they are all annihilated when He inhales. This Mahā-Viṣṇu is a plenary portion of a portion of Viṣṇu, Govinda (*yasya kalā-viśeṣaḥ*). The word *kalā* refers to a plenary portion of a plenary portion. From Kṛṣṇa, or Govinda, comes Balarāma; from Balarāma comes Saṅkarṣaṇa; from Saṅkarṣaṇa, Nārāyaṇa; from Nārāyaṇa, the second Saṅkarṣaṇa; from the second Saṅkarṣaṇa, Mahā-Viṣṇu; from Mahā-Viṣṇu, Garbhodakaśāyī Viṣṇu; and from Garbhodakaśāyī Viṣṇu, Kṣīrodakaśāyī Viṣṇu. Kṣīrodakaśāyī Viṣṇu controls every universe. This gives an idea of the meaning of *ananta,* unlimited. What is to be said of the unlimited potency and existence of the Lord? This verse describes the coverings of the universe (*saptabhir daśa-guṇottarair aṇḍa-kośaḥ*). The first covering is earth, the second is water, the third is fire, the fourth is air, the fifth is sky, the sixth is the total material energy, and the seventh is the false ego. Beginning with the covering of earth, each covering is ten times greater than the previous one. Thus we can only imagine how great each universe is, and there are many millions of universes. As confirmed by the Lord Himself in *Bhagavad-gītā* (10.42):

athavā bahunaitena
kiṁ jñātena tavārjuna
viṣṭabhyāham idaṁ kṛtsnam
ekāṁśena sthito jagat

"But what need is there, Arjuna, for all this detailed knowledge? With a single fragment of Myself I pervade and support this entire universe." The entire material world manifests only one fourth of the Supreme Lord's energy. Therefore He is called *ananta.*

TEXT 38

विषयतृषो नरपशवो
य उपासते विभूतीर्न परं त्वाम् ।
तेषामाशिष ईश
तदनु विनश्यन्ति यथा राजकुलम्॥ ३८ ॥

viṣaya-tṛṣo nara-paśavo
ya upāsate vibhūtīr na paraṁ tvām
teṣām āśiṣa īśa
tad anu vinaśyanti yathā rāja-kulam

viṣaya-tṛṣaḥ—eager to enjoy sense gratification; *nara-paśavaḥ*—manlike animals; *ye*—who; *upāsate*—worship very gorgeously; *vibhūtīḥ*—small particles of the Supreme Lord (the demigods); *na*—not; *param*—the Supreme; *tvām*—You; *teṣām*—of them; *āśiṣaḥ*—the benedictions; *īśa*—O supreme controller; *tat*—them (the demigods); *anu*—after; *vinaśyanti*—will be vanquished; *yathā*—just as; *rāja-kulam*—those who are supported by the government (when the government is finished).

TRANSLATION

O Lord, O Supreme, unintelligent persons who thirst for sense enjoyment and who worship various demigods are no better than animals in the human form of life. Because of their animalistic propensities, they fail to worship Your Lordship, and instead they worship the insignificant demigods, who are but small sparks of Your glory. With the destruction of the entire universe, including the demigods, the benedictions received from the demigods also vanish, just like the nobility when a king is no longer in power.

PURPORT

Bhagavad-gītā (7.20) says, *kāmais tais tair hṛta jñānāḥ prapadyante 'nya-devatāḥ:* "Those whose minds are distorted by material desires surrender unto the demigods." Similarly, this verse condemns worship of the demigods. We may show our respect to the demigods, but the demigods are not worshipable. The intelligence of those who worship the demigods is lost (*hṛta jñānāḥ*) because these worshipers do not know that when the entire material cosmic manifestation is annihilated, the demigods, who are the departmental heads of that manifestation, will be vanquished. When the demigods are vanquished, the benedictions given by the demigods to unintelligent men will also be vanquished. Therefore a devotee should not hanker to obtain material opulence by worshiping the demigods, but should engage in the service of the Lord, who will satisfy all his desires.

akāmaḥ sarva-kāmo vā
mokṣa-kāma udāra-dhīḥ
tīvreṇa bhakti-yogena
yajeta puruṣaṁ param

"Whether full of all material desires, free from material desires or desiring liberation, a person who has broader intelligence must by all means worship the supreme whole, the Personality of Godhead." (*Bhāg.* 2.3.10) This is the duty of a perfect human being. One who has the shape of a human being but whose actions are nothing but those of an animal is called *nara-paśu* or *dvipada-paśu,* a two-legged animal. A human being who is not interested in Kṛṣṇa consciousness is condemned herewith as a *nara-paśu.*

TEXT 39

कामधियस्त्वयि रचिता
 न परम रोहन्ति यथा करम्भबीजानि।
ज्ञानात्मन्यगुणमये
 गुणगणतोऽस्य द्वन्द्वजालानि ॥ ३९ ॥

kāma-dhiyas tvayi racitā
na parama rohanti yathā karambha-bījāni
jñānātmany aguṇamaye
guṇa-gaṇato'sya dvandva-jālāni

kāma-dhiyaḥ—desires for sense gratification; *tvayi*—in You; *racitāḥ*—performed; *na*—not; *parama*—O Supreme Personality of Godhead; *rohanti*—do grow (produce other bodies); *yathā*—just as; *karambha-bījāni*—sterilized or fried seeds; *jñāna-ātmani*—in You, whose existence is in full knowledge; *aguṇa-maye*—who is not affected by the material qualities; *guṇa-gaṇataḥ*—from the material qualities; *asya*—of a person; *dvandva-jālāni*—the networks of duality.

TRANSLATION

O Supreme Lord, if persons obsessed with material desires for sense gratification through material opulence worship You, who are the source of all knowledge and are transcendental to material qualities, they are not subject to material rebirth, just as sterilized or fried seeds do not produce plants. Living entities are subjected to the repetition of birth and death because they are conditioned by material nature, but since You are transcendental, one who is inclined to associate with You in transcendence escapes the conditions of material nature.

PURPORT

This is confirmed in *Bhagavad-gītā* (4.9), wherein the Lord says:

janma karma ca me divyam
evaṁ yo vetti tattvataḥ
tyaktvā dehaṁ punar janma
naiti mām eti so'rjuna

"One who knows the transcendental nature of My appearance and activities does not, upon leaving the body, take his birth again in this material world, but attains My eternal abode, O Arjuna." If one simply engages in Kṛṣṇa consciousness to understand Kṛṣṇa, he surely becomes immune to the process of repeated birth and death. As clearly stated in *Bhagavad-gītā, tyaktvā dehaṁ punar janma naiti:* such a person, simply by engaging in Kṛṣṇa consciousness or understanding the Supreme Personality of Godhead, Kṛṣṇa, becomes quite fit to return home, back to Godhead. Even those who are obsessed with material desires may also come to worship the Supreme Personality of Godhead so steadily that they go back to Godhead. The fact is that if one comes to Kṛṣṇa consciousness, although he may have many material desires, he becomes increasingly attracted to the lotus feet of Kṛṣṇa through associating with the Supreme Lord by chanting His holy name. The Supreme Lord and His holy name are identical. Thus he becomes uninterested in attachment to material enjoyment. The perfection of life is to be uninterested in material enjoyment and interested in Kṛṣṇa. If one comes to Kṛṣṇa consciousness somehow or other, even for material gain, the result is that he will be liberated. *Kāmād dveṣād bhayāt snehāt.* Whether for the satisfaction of material desires, because of the influence of envy, because of fear, because of affection or because of any other reason, if one comes to Kṛṣṇa, his life is successful.

TEXT 40

जितमजित तदा भवता
    यदाह भागवतं धर्ममनवद्यम्   ।
निष्किञ्चना ये मुनय
    आत्मारामा यमुपासतेऽपवर्गाय ॥ ४० ॥

jitam ajita tadā bhavatā
    yadāha bhāgavataṁ dharmam anavadyam
niṣkiñcanā ye munaya
    ātmārāmā yam upāsate'pavargāya

jitam—conquered; *ajita*—O unconquerable one; *tadā*—then; *bhavatā*—by Your Lordship; *yadā*—when; *āha*—spoke; *bhāgavatam*—which helps the devotee approach the Supreme Personality of Godhead; *dharmam*—the religious process; *anavadyam*—faultless (free from contamination); *niṣkiñcanāḥ*—who have no desire to be happy with material opulences; *ye*—

those who; *munayaḥ*—great philosophers and exalted sages; *ātma-ārāmāḥ* —who are self-satisfied (being completely aware of their constitutional position as eternal servants of the Lord); *yam*—whom; *upāsate*—worship; *apavargāya*—for achieving liberation from material bondage.

TRANSLATION

O unconquerable one, when You spoke about bhāgavata-dharma, which is the uncontaminated religious system for achieving the shelter of Your lotus feet, that was Your victory. Persons who have no material desires, like the Kumāras, who are self-satisfied sages, worship You to be liberated from material contamination. In other words, they accept the process of bhāgavata-dharma to achieve shelter at Your lotus feet.

PURPORT

As stated by Śrīla Rūpa Gosvāmī in *Bhakti-rasāmṛta-sindhu:*

anyābhilāṣitā-śūnyaṁ
jñāna-karmādy-anāvṛtam
ānukūlyena kṛṣṇānu-
śīlanaṁ bhaktir uttamā

"One should render transcendental loving service to the Supreme Lord Kṛṣṇa favorably and without desires for material profit or gain through fruitive activities or philosophical speculation. That is called pure devotional service."

The *Nārada-pañcarātra* also says:

sarvopādhi-vinirmuktaṁ
tat-paratvena nirmalam
hṛṣīkeṇa hṛṣīkeśa-
sevanaṁ bhaktir ucyate

"One should be free from all material designations and cleansed of all material contamination. He should be restored to his pure identity, in which he engages his senses in the service of the proprietor of the senses. That is called devotional service." This is also called *bhāgavata-dharma.* Without material aspirations, one should simply serve Kṛṣṇa, as advised in *Bhagavad-gītā, Nārada-pañcarātra* and *Śrīmad-Bhāgavatam. Bhāgavata-dharma* is the process of religion enunciated by pure devotees, direct representatives of the Supreme Personality of Godhead like Nārada, Śukadeva Gosvāmī and their humble servants in the disciplic succession. By understanding *bhāgavata-*

dharma, one immediately becomes free from material contamination. Living entities, who are part and parcel of the Supreme Personality of Godhead, are loitering in this material world suffering. When they are instructed by the Lord Himself about *bhāgavata-dharma* and they adopt it, that is victory for the Lord, for He then reclaims these fallen souls. A devotee following the principles of *bhāgavata-dharma* feels very much obligated to the Supreme Personality of Godhead. He can understand the difference between life without *bhāgavata-dharma* and life with *bhāgavata-dharma* and thus he ever remains obliged to the Lord. Taking to Kṛṣṇa consciousness and bringing fallen souls to Kṛṣṇa consciousness is victory for Lord Kṛṣṇa.

sa vai puṁsāṁ paro dharmo
yato bhaktir adhokṣaje
ahaituky apratihatā
yayātmā suprasīdati

"The supreme occupation [*dharma*] for all humanity is that by which men can attain to loving devotional service unto the transcendent Lord. Such devotional service must be unmotivated and uninterrupted in order to completely satisfy the self." (*Bhāg.* 1.2.6) Therefore *Śrīmad-Bhāgavatam* is the pure transcendental process of religion.

TEXT 41

विषममतिर्न यत्र नृणां
त्वमहमिति मम तवेति च यदन्यत्र ।
विषमधिया रचितो यः
स ह्यविशुद्धः क्षयिष्णुरधर्मबहुलः ॥ ४१ ॥

viṣama-matir na yatra nṛṇāṁ
tvam aham iti mama taveti ca yad anyatra
viṣama-dhiyā racito yaḥ
sa hy aviśuddhaḥ kṣayiṣṇur adharma-bahulaḥ

viṣama—unequal (your religion, my religion; your belief, my belief); *matiḥ*—consciousness; *na*—not; *yatra*—in which; *nṛṇām*—of human society; *tvam*—you; *aham*—I; *iti*—thus; *mama*—my; *tava*—your; *iti*—thus; *ca*—also; *yat*—which; *anyatra*—elsewhere (in religious systems other than *bhāgavata-dharma*); *viṣama-dhiyā*—by this unequal intelligence; *racitaḥ*—made; *yaḥ*

—that which; *saḥ*—that system of religion; *hi*—indeed; *aviśuddhaḥ*—not pure; *kṣayiṣṇuḥ*—temporary; *adharma-bahulaḥ*—full of irreligion.

TRANSLATION

Being full of contradictions, all forms of religion but bhāgavata-dharma work under conceptions of fruitive results and distinctions of "you and I" and "yours and mine." The followers of Śrīmad-Bhāgavatam have no such consciousness. They are all Kṛṣṇa conscious, thinking that they are Kṛṣṇa's and Kṛṣṇa is theirs. There are other, low-class religious systems, which are contemplated for the killing of enemies or the gain of mystic power, but such religious systems, being full of passion and envy, are impure and temporary. Because they are full of envy, they are full of irreligion.

PURPORT

Bhāgavata-dharma has no contradictions. Conceptions of "your religion" and "my religion" are completely absent from *bhāgavata-dharma. Bhāgavata-dharma* means following the orders given by the Supreme Lord, Bhagavān, as stated in *Bhagavad-gītā: sarva-dharmān parityajya mām ekaṁ śaraṇaṁ vraja.* God is one, and God is for everyone. Therefore everyone must surrender to God. That is the pure conception of religion. Whatever God orders constitutes religion (*dharmaṁ tu sākṣād bhagavat-praṇītam*). In *bhāgavata-dharma* there is no question of "what you believe" and "what I believe." Everyone must believe in the Supreme Lord and carry out His orders. *Ānukūlyena kṛṣṇānuśīlanam:* whatever Kṛṣṇa says—whatever God says—should be directly carried out. That is *dharma,* religion.

If one is actually Kṛṣṇa conscious, he cannot have any enemies. Since his only engagement is to induce others to surrender to Kṛṣṇa, or God, how can he have enemies? If one advocates the Hindu religion, the Muslim religion, the Christian religion, this religion or that religion, there will be conflicts. History shows that the followers of religious systems without a clear conception of God have fought with one another. There are many instances of this in human history, but systems of religion that do not concentrate upon service to the Supreme are temporary and cannot last for long because they are full of envy. There are many activities directed against such religious systems, and therefore one must give up the idea of "my belief" and "your belief." Everyone should believe in God and surrender unto Him. That is *bhāgavata-dharma.*

Bhāgavata-dharma is not a concocted sectarian belief, for it entails research to find how everything is connected with Kṛṣṇa (*īśāvāsyam idaṁ sarvam*). According to the Vedic injunctions, *sarvaṁ khalv idaṁ brahma:* Brahman, the Supreme, is present in everything. *Bhāgavata-dharma* captures this presence of the Supreme. *Bhāgavata-dharma* does not consider everything in the world to be false. Because everything emanates from the Supreme, nothing can be false; everything has some use in the service of the Supreme. For example, we are now dictating into a microphone and recording on a dictating machine, and thus we are finding how the machine can be connected to the Supreme Brahman. Since we are using this machine in the service of the Lord, it is Brahman. This is the meaning of *sarvaṁ khalv idaṁ brahma.* Everything is Brahman because everything can be used for the service of the Supreme Lord. Nothing is *mithyā,* false; everything is factual.

Bhāgavata-dharma is called *sarvotkṛṣṭa,* the best of all religious systems, because those who follow *bhāgavata-dharma* are not envious of anyone. Pure *bhāgavatas,* pure devotees, invite everyone, without envy, to join the Kṛṣṇa consciousness movement. A devotee is therefore exactly like the Supreme Personality of Godhead. *Suhṛdaṁ sarva-bhūtānām:* he is the friend of all living entities. Therefore this is the best of all religious systems. Whereas so-called religions are meant for a particular type of person who believes in a particular way, such discrimination has no place in Kṛṣṇa consciousness, or *bhāgavata-dharma.* If we scrutinize the religious systems meant for worship of demigods or anyone else but the Supreme Personality of Godhead, we will find that they are full of envy and therefore impure.

TEXT 42

कः क्षेमो निजपरयोः
कियान् वार्थः स्वपरद्रुहा धर्मेण ।
स्वद्रोहात्तव कोपः
परसम्पीडया च तथाधर्मः ॥ ४२ ॥

kaḥ kṣemo nija-parayoḥ
kiyān vārthaḥ sva-para-druhā dharmeṇa
sva-drohāt tava kopaḥ
para-sampīḍayā ca tathādharmaḥ

kaḥ—what; *kṣemaḥ*—benefit; *nija*—to oneself; *parayoḥ*—and to others; *kiyān*—how much; *vā*—or; *arthaḥ*—purpose; *sva-para-druhā*—which is envious of the performer and of others; *dharmeṇa*—with the religious system;

sva-drohāt—from being envious of one's own self; *tava*—of You; *kopaḥ*—anger; *para-sampīḍayā*—by giving pain to others; *ca*—also; *tathā*—as well as; *adharmaḥ*—irreligion.

TRANSLATION

How can a religious system that produces envy of one's self and of others be beneficial for oneself and for them? What is auspicious about following such a system? What is actually to be gained? By causing pain to one's own self due to self-envy and by causing pain to others, one arouses Your anger and practices irreligion.

PURPORT

Any religious system but the process of *bhāgavata-dharma*—service as an eternal servant of the Supreme Personality of Godhead—is a system of envy of one's own self and of others. For example, there are many systems of religion in which animal sacrifices are recommended. Such animal sacrifices are inauspicious both for the performer and for the animal. Although one is sometimes permitted to sacrifice an animal before the goddess Kālī and eat it instead of purchasing meat from a slaughterhouse, permission to eat meat after a sacrifice in the presence of the goddess Kālī is not the order of the Supreme Personality of Godhead. It is simply a concession for the miserable person who will not give up eating meat. It is meant to restrict his desire for unrestricted meat-eating. Such a religious system is condemned. Therefore Kṛṣṇa says, *sarva-dharmān parityajya mām ekaṁ śaraṇaṁ vraja:* "Give up all other duties and surrender unto Me." That is the last word in religion.

One may argue that the sacrifice of animals is recommended in the *Vedas.* This recommendation, however, is a restriction. Without Vedic restrictions on the purchase of meat, people will purchase meat from the market, which will be overflooded with meat shops, and slaughterhouses will increase. To restrict this, sometimes the *Vedas* say that one may eat meat after sacrificing an insignificant animal like a goat before the goddess Kālī. In any case, a system of religion in which animal sacrifices are recommended is inauspicious for those who perform the sacrifices and for the animals. Envious persons who perform ostentatious animal sacrifices are condemned in *Bhagavad-gītā* (16.17) as follows:

ātma-sambhāvitāḥ stabdhā
dhana-māna-madānvitāḥ

yajante nāma-yajñais te
dambhenāvidhi-pūrvakam

"Self-complacent and always impudent, deluded by wealth and false prestige, they sometimes perform sacrifices in name only without following any rules or regulations." Sometimes animal sacrifices are performed very gorgeously with grand arrangements for worshiping the goddess Kālī, but such festivals, although performed in the name of *yajña,* are not actually *yajña,* for *yajña* means to satisfy the Supreme Personality of Godhead. Therefore it is recommended that in this age specifically, *yajñaiḥ saṅkīrtana-prāyair yajanti hi sumedhasaḥ:* those who have good intelligence satisfy the *yajña-puruṣa,* Viṣṇu, by chanting the Hare Kṛṣṇa *mantra.* Envious persons, however, are condemned by the Supreme Personality of Godhead as follows:

ahaṅkāraṁ balaṁ darpaṁ
kāmaṁ krodhaṁ ca saṁśritāḥ
mām ātma-para-deheṣu
pradviṣanto 'bhyasūyakāḥ

tān ahaṁ dviṣataḥ krūrān
saṁsāreṣu narādhamān
kṣipāmy ajasram aśubhān
āsurīṣv eva yoniṣu

"Bewildered by false ego, strength, pride, lust and anger, the demon becomes envious of the Supreme Personality of Godhead, who is situated in his own body and in the bodies of others, and blasphemes against the real religion. Those who are envious and mischievous, who are the lowest among men, are cast by Me into the ocean of material existence, into various demoniac species of life." (Bg. 16.18–19) These persons are condemned by the Supreme Personality of Godhead, as indicated by the words *tava kopaḥ.* A person who commits murder is envious of himself and also the person he has killed, for the result of committing murder is that he will be arrested and hanged. If one transgresses the laws of a man-made government, he may escape being killed by the state, but one cannot escape the laws of God. A killer of any animal must be killed in his next life by the same animal. This is the law of nature. One must follow the instructions of the Supreme Lord: *sarva-dharmān parityajya mām ekaṁ śaraṇaṁ vraja.* If one follows any other system of religion, he is subject to punishment by the Supreme Personality of Godhead in many different ways.

Therefore if one follows a concocted system of religion, he is envious not only of others but also of himself. Consequently his system of religion is useless.

Śrīmad-Bhāgavatam (1.2.8) says:

dharmaḥ svanuṣṭhitaḥ puṁsāṁ
viṣvaksena-kathāsu yaḥ
notpādayed yadi ratiṁ
śrama eva hi kevalam

"Duties (*dharma*) executed by men, regardless of occupation, are only so much useless labor if they do not provoke attraction for the message of the Supreme Lord." Following a system of religion that does not awaken one's Kṛṣṇa consciousness, or God consciousness, is merely a waste of time and labor.

TEXT 43

न व्यभिचरति तवेक्षा
यया ह्यभिहितो भागवतो धर्मः ।
स्थिरचरसत्त्वकदम्बे-
ष्वपृथग्धियो यमुपासते त्वार्याः ॥ ४३ ॥

na vyabhicarati tavekṣā
yayā hy abhihito bhāgavato dharmaḥ
sthira-cara-sattva-kadambeṣv
apṛthag-dhiyo yam upāsate tv āryāḥ

na—not; *vyabhicarati*—fails; *tava*—Your; *īkṣā*—outlook; *yayā*—by which; *hi*—indeed; *abhihitaḥ*—declared; *bhāgavataḥ*—in relationship with Your instructions and activities; *dharmaḥ*—religious principle; *sthira*—nonmoving; *cara*—moving; *sattva-kadambeṣu*—among the living entities; *apṛthak-dhiyaḥ*—who do not consider distinctions; *yam*—which; *upāsate*—follow; *tu*—certainly; *āryāḥ*—those who are advanced in civilization.

TRANSLATION

My dear Lord, one's occupational duty is instructed in Śrīmad-Bhāgavatam and Bhagavad-gītā according to Your point of view, which never deviates from the highest goal of life. Those who follow their occupational duties under Your supervision, being equal to all living entities, moving and nonmoving, and not considering high and low, are

called Āryans. Such Āryans worship You, the Supreme Personality of Godhead.

PURPORT

Bhāgavata-dharma and *kṛṣṇa-kathā* are identical. Śrī Caitanya Mahāprabhu wanted everyone to become a *guru* and preach the instructions of Kṛṣṇa everywhere from *Bhagavad-gītā, Śrīmad-Bhāgavatam,* the *Purāṇas, Vedānta-sūtra* and similar Vedic literatures. Āryans, who are advanced in civilization, follow *bhāgavata-dharma.* Prahlāda Mahārāja, although merely a child of five years, recommended:

kaumāra ācaret prājño
dharmān bhāgavatān iha
durlabhaṁ mānuṣaṁ janma
tad apy adhruvam arthadam
(Bhāg. 7.6.1)

Prahlāda Mahārāja preached *bhāgavata-dharma* among his classmates as soon as an opportunity was afforded by the absence of his teachers from the classroom. He said that from the very beginning of life, from the age of five, children should be instructed about *bhāgavata-dharma* because the human form of life, which is very rarely obtained, is meant for understanding this subject.

Bhāgavata-dharma means living according to the instructions of the Supreme Personality of Godhead. In *Bhagavad-gītā* we find that the Supreme Lord has arranged human society in four social divisions, namely *brāhmaṇa, kṣatriya, vaiśya* and *śūdra.* Again, the *Purāṇas* and other Vedic literatures set forth four *āśramas,* which are the divisions of spiritual life. Therefore *bhāgavata-dharma* means the *varṇāśrama-dharma* of the four social and four spiritual divisions.

The members of human society who strictly follow the principles of *bhāgavata-dharma* and live according to the instructions of the Supreme Personality of Godhead are called Āryans or *ārya.* A civilization of Āryans who strictly follow the instructions of the Lord and never deviate from those instructions is perfect. Such civilized men do not discriminate between trees, animals, human beings and other living entities. *Paṇḍitāḥ sama-darśinaḥ:* because they are completely educated in Kṛṣṇa consciousness, they see all living beings equally. Āryans do not kill even a small plant unnecessarily, not to speak of cutting trees for sense gratification. At the present moment, throughout the world, killing is prominent. Men are killing trees, they are killing animals, and they are killing other human beings also, all for sense gratification. This is not an Āryan civilization. As stated here, *sthira-cara-sattva-kadambeṣv apṛthag-dhiyaḥ.* The word *apṛthag-dhiyaḥ* indicates that Āryans do not distinguish between lower and higher grades of life. All life should be protected. All living beings have a right to live, even the trees and plants. This is the basic principle of an Āryan civilization. Apart from the lower living entities, those who have come to the platform of human civilization should be divided into a society of *brāhmaṇas, kṣatriyas, vaiśyas* and *śūdras.* The *brāhmaṇas* should follow the instructions of the Supreme Personality of Godhead as stated in *Bhagavad-gītā* and other Vedic literatures. The criterion must be *guṇa* and *karma.* In other words, one should acquire the qualities of a *brāhmaṇa, kṣatriya, vaiśya* or *śūdra* and act accordingly. This is the civilization accepted by the Āryans. Why do they accept it? They accept it because they are very much eager to satisfy Kṛṣṇa. This is perfect civilization.

Āryans do not deviate from the instructions of Kṛṣṇa, nor do they have doubts about Kṛṣṇa, but non-Āryans and other demoniac people fail to follow the instructions of *Bhagavad-gītā* and *Śrīmad-Bhāgavatam.* This is because they have been trained in sense gratification at the cost of all other living entities. *Nūnaṁ pramattaḥ kurute vikarma:* their only business is to indulge in all kinds of forbidden activities for sense gratification. *Yad indriya-prītaya āpṛṇoti:* they deviate in this way because they want to gratify their senses. They have no other occupation or ambition. Their method of civilization is condemned in the previous verse. *Kaḥ kṣemo nija-parayoḥ kiyān vārthaḥ sva-para-druhā dharmeṇa:* "What is the meaning of a civilization that kills oneself and others?"

This verse, therefore, advises that everyone become a member of the Āryan civilization and accept the instructions of the Supreme Personality of Godhead. One should conduct his social, political and religious affairs according to His instructions. We are spreading the Kṛṣṇa consciousness movement to try to establish a society the way that Kṛṣṇa wants it. This is the meaning of Kṛṣṇa consciousness. We are therefore presenting *Bhagavad-gītā* as it is and kicking out all kinds of mental concoction. Fools and rascals interpret *Bhagavad-gītā* in their own way. When Kṛṣṇa says, *man-manā bhava mad-bhakto mad-yājī māṁ namaskuru*—"Always think of Me, become My devotee, worship Me and offer your homage unto Me"—they comment that it is not Kṛṣṇa to whom we must surrender. Thus they derive imaginary meanings from *Bhagavad-gītā.* The Kṛṣṇa consciousness movement, however, strictly follows *bhāgavata-dharma,* the instructions of *Bhagavad-gītā* and *Śrīmad-Bhāgavatam* for the complete welfare of human society. One who misinterprets *Bhagavad-gītā,* twisting out some meaning for his sense gratification, is a non-Āryan. Therefore commentaries on *Bhagavad-gītā* by such persons should be immediately rejected. One should try to follow *Bhagavad-gītā* as it is. In *Bhagavad-gītā* (12.6–7) Lord Śrī Kṛṣṇa says:

ye tu sarvāṇi karmāṇi
mayi sannyasya mat-parāḥ
ananyenaiva yogena
māṁ dhyāyanta upāsate

teṣām ahaṁ samuddhartā
mṛtyu-saṁsāra-sāgarāt
bhavāmi na cirāt pārtha
mayy āveśita-cetasām

"For one who worships Me, giving up all his activities unto Me and being devoted to Me without deviation, engaged in devotional service and always meditating upon Me, who has fixed his mind upon Me, O son of Pṛthā, for him I am the swift deliverer from the ocean of birth and death."

TEXT 44

न हि भगवन्नघटितमिदं
त्वद्दर्शनान्नृणामखिलपापक्षयः ।
यन्नामसकृच्छ्रवणात्
पुक्कशोऽपि विमुच्यते संसारात् ॥ ४४ ॥

na hi bhagavann aghaṭitam idaṁ
tvad-darśanān nṛṇām akhila-pāpa-kṣayaḥ
yan-nāma sakṛc chravaṇāt
pukkaśo'pi vimucyate saṁsārāt

na—not; *hi*—indeed; *bhagavan*—O my Lord; *aghaṭitam*—not occurred; *idam*—this; *tvat*—of You; *darśanāt*—by seeing; *nṛṇām*—of all human beings; *akhila*—all; *pāpa*—of sins; *kṣayaḥ*—annihilation; *yat-nāma*—whose name; *sakṛt*—only once; *śravaṇāt*—by hearing; *pukkaśaḥ*—the lowest class, the *caṇḍāla; api*—also; *vimucyate*—is delivered; *saṁsārāt*—from the entanglement of material existence.

TRANSLATION

My Lord, it is not impossible for one to be immediately freed from all material contamination by seeing You. Not to speak of seeing You personally, merely by hearing the holy name of Your Lordship only once, even caṇḍālas, men of the lowest class, are freed from all material contamination. Under the circumstances, who will not be freed from material contamination simply by seeing You?

PURPORT

As stated in the *Śrīmad-Bhāgavatam* (9.5.16), *yan-nāma-śruti-mātreṇa pumān bhavati nirmalaḥ:* simply by hearing the holy name of the Lord, one is immediately purified. Therefore, in this age of Kali, when all people are very contaminated, the chanting of the holy name of the Lord is recommended as the only means of improvement.

harer nāma harer nāma
harer nāmaiva kevalam
kalau nāsty eva nāsty eva
nāsty eva gatir anyathā

"In this age of quarrel and hypocrisy the only means of deliverance is the chanting of the holy name of the Lord. There is no other way. There is no other way. There is no other way." (*Bṛhan-nāradīya Purāṇa*) Śrī Caitanya Mahāprabhu introduced this chanting of the holy name five hundred years ago, and now through the Kṛṣṇa consciousness movement, the Hare Kṛṣṇa movement, we are actually seeing that men who are considered to belong to the lowest class are being delivered from all sinful activities simply by hearing the holy name of the Lord. *Saṁsāra,* material existence, is a result of sinful actions. Everyone in this material world is condemned, yet as there are different grades of prisoners, there are different grades of men. All of them, in all statuses of life, are suffering. To stop the suffering of material existence, one must take to the Hare Kṛṣṇa movement of *saṅkīrtana* or Kṛṣṇa conscious life.

Herein it is said, *yan-nāma sakṛc chravaṇāt:* the holy name of the Supreme Personality of Godhead is so powerful that if once heard without offenses, it can purify the lowest of men (*kirāta-hūṇāndhra-pulinda-pulkaśāḥ*). Such men, who are called *caṇḍālas,* are less than *śūdras,* but they also can be purified simply by hearing the holy name of the Lord, not to speak of personally seeing the Lord. From our present position, the Supreme Personality of Godhead can be personally seen as the Deity in the temple. The Deity of the Lord is not different from the Supreme Lord. Because we cannot see the Supreme Lord with our present blunt eyes, the Lord has kindly consented to come before us in a form we can see. Therefore the Deity in the temple should not be considered material. By offering food to the Deity and by decorating and serving the Deity, one gets the same result that one derives from serving the Lord personally in Vaikuṇṭha.

TEXT 45

अथ भगवन् वयमधुना
त्वदवलोकपरिमृष्टाशयमलाः ।
सुरऋषिणा यत् कथितं
तावकेन कथमन्यथा भवति ॥ ४५ ॥

atha bhagavan vayam adhunā
tvad-avaloka-parimṛṣṭāśaya-malāḥ
sura-ṛṣiṇā yat kathitaṁ
tāvakena katham anyathā bhavati

atha—therefore; *bhagavan*—O Supreme Personality of Godhead; *vayam*—we; *adhunā*—at the present moment; *tvat-avaloka*—by seeing You; *parimṛṣṭa*—wiped away; *āśaya-malāḥ*—contaminated desires in the heart; *sura-ṛṣiṇā*—by the great sage of the demigods (Nārada); *yat*—which; *kathitam*—spoken; *tāvakena*—who is Your devotee; *katham*—how; *anyathā*—otherwise; *bhavati*—can it be.

TRANSLATION

Therefore, my dear Lord, simply seeing You has now wiped away all the contamination of sinful activities and their results of material attachment and lusty desires, which always filled my mind and the core of my heart. Whatever is predicted by the great sage Nārada Muni cannot be otherwise. In other words, I have obtained Your audience as a result of being trained by Nārada Muni.

PURPORT

This is the process of the perfect way. One must take lessons from authorities like Nārada, Vyāsa and Asita, and follow their principles. Then one will be able to see the Supreme Personality of Godhead even with one's own eyes. One only needs training. *Ataḥ śrī-kṛṣṇa-nāmādi na bhaved grāhyam indriyaiḥ.* With our blunt eyes and other senses we cannot perceive the Supreme Personality of Godhead, but if we engage our senses in the service of the Lord according to the instructions of the authorities, it will be possible to see Him. As soon as one sees the Supreme Personality of Godhead, all the sinful reactions in the core of one's heart are certainly vanquished.

TEXT 46

विदितमनन्त समस्तं
तव जगदात्मनो जनैरिहाचरितम्।
विज्ञाप्यं परमगुरोः
कियदिव सवितुरिव खद्योतैः ॥ ४६ ॥

viditam ananta samastaṁ
tava jagad-ātmano janair ihācaritam
vijñāpyaṁ parama-guroḥ
kiyad iva savitur iva khadyotaiḥ

viditam—well known; *ananta*—O unlimited; *samastam*—everything; *tava*—to You; *jagat-ātmanaḥ*—who are the Supersoul of all living entities; *janaiḥ*—by the mass of people, or all living entities; *iha*—within this material world; *ācaritam*—performed; *vijñāpyam*—to be informed; *parama-guroḥ*—to the Supreme Personality of Godhead, the supreme master; *kiyat*—how much; *iva*—certainly; *savituḥ*—to the sun; *iva*—like; *khadyotaiḥ*—by the fireflies.

TRANSLATION

O unlimited Supreme Personality of Godhead, whatever a living entity does in this material world is well known to You because You are the Supersoul. In the presence of the sun there is nothing to be revealed by the light of a glowworm. Similarly, because You know everything, in Your presence there is nothing for me to make known.

TEXT 47

नमस्तुभ्यं भगवते
सकलजगत्स्थितिलयोदयेशाय।
दुरवसितात्मगतये
कुयोगिनां भिदा परमहंसाय ॥ ४७ ॥

namas tubhyaṁ bhagavate
sakala-jagat-sthiti-layodayeśāya
duravasitātma-gataye
kuyogināṁ bhidā paramahaṁsāya

namaḥ—all obeisances; *tubhyam*—unto You; *bhagavate*—Your Lordship; *sakala*—all; *jagat*—of the cosmic manifestation; *sthiti*—of the maintenance; *laya*—dissolution; *udaya*—and creation; *īśāya*—unto the Supreme Lord; *duravasita*—impossible to understand; *ātma-gataye*—whose own position; *ku-yoginām*—of those who are attached to the objects of the senses; *bhidā*—by the false understanding of separateness; *parama-haṁsāya*—unto the supreme pure.

TRANSLATION

My dear Lord, You are the creator, maintainer and annihilator of this cosmic manifestation, but persons who are too materialistic and who always see separateness do not have eyes with which to see You. They cannot understand Your real position, and therefore they conclude that the cosmic manifestation is independent of Your opulence. My Lord, You are the supreme pure, and You are full in all six opulences. Therefore I offer my respectful obeisances unto You.

PURPORT

Atheistic men think that the cosmic manifestation has come about by chance, by a combination of matter, without reference to God. Materialistic so-called chemists and atheistic philosophers always try to avoid even the name of God in relation to the cosmic manifestation. For them God's creation is impossible to understand because they are too materialistic. The Supreme Personality of Godhead is *paramahaṁsa,* or the supreme pure, whereas those who are sinful, being very much attached to material sense enjoyment and therefore engaging in material activities like asses, are the lowest of men. All their so-called scientific knowledge is null and void because of their atheistic temperament. Thus they cannot understand the Supreme Personality of Godhead.

TEXT 48

यं वै श्वसन्तमनु विश्वसृजः श्वसन्ति
यं चेकितानमनु चित्तय उच्चकन्ति ।

भूमण्डलं सर्षपायति यस्य मूर्ध्नि
तस्मै नमो भगवतेऽस्तु सहस्रमूर्ध्ने ॥ ४८ ॥

yaṁ vai śvasantam anu viśva-sṛjaḥ śvasanti
yaṁ cekitānam anu cittaya uccakanti
bhū-maṇḍalaṁ sarṣapāyati yasya mūrdhni
tasmai namo bhagavate'stu sahasra-mūrdhne

yam—whom; *vai*—indeed; *śvasantam*—endeavoring; *anu*—after; *viśva-sṛjaḥ*—the directors of the cosmic creation; *śvasanti*—also endeavor; *yam*—whom; *cekitānam*—perceiving; *anu*—after; *cittayaḥ*—all the knowledge-gathering senses; *uccakanti*—perceive; *bhū-maṇḍalam*—the huge universe; *sarṣapāyati*—become like seeds of mustard; *yasya*—of whom; *mūrdhni*—on the head; *tasmai*—unto Him; *namaḥ*—obeisances; *bhagavate*—the Supreme Personality of Godhead, full with six opulences; *astu*—may there be; *sahasra-mūrdhne*—who has thousands of hoods.

TRANSLATION

My dear Lord, it is after You endeavor that Lord Brahmā, Indra and the other directors of the cosmic manifestation become occupied with their activities. It is after You perceive the material energy, My Lord, that the senses begin to perceive. The Supreme Personality of Godhead holds all the universes on His heads like seeds of mustard. I offer my respectful obeisances unto You, that Supreme Personality, who has thousands of hoods.

TEXT 49

श्रीशुक उवाच
संस्तुतो भगवानेवमनन्तस्तमभाषत ।
विद्याधरपतिं प्रीतश्चित्रकेतुं कुरूद्वह ॥ ४९ ॥

śrī-śuka uvāca
saṁstuto bhagavān evam
anantas tam abhāṣata
vidyādhara-patiṁ prītaś
citraketuṁ kurūdvaha

śrī-śukaḥ uvāca—Śrī Śukadeva Gosvāmī said; *saṁstutaḥ*—being worshiped; *bhagavān*—the Supreme Personality of Godhead; *evam*—in this way; *anantaḥ*—Lord Ananta; *tam*—unto him; *abhāṣata*—replied;

vidyādhara-patim—the King of the Vidyādharas; *prītaḥ*—being very pleased; *citraketum*—King Citraketu; *kuru-udvaha*—O best of the Kuru dynasty, Mahārāja Parīkṣit.

TRANSLATION

Śukadeva Gosvāmī continued: The Lord, the Supreme Personality of Godhead, Anantadeva, being very much pleased with the prayers offered by Citraketu, the King of the Vidyādharas, replied to him as follows, O best of the Kuru dynasty, Mahārāja Parīkṣit.

TEXT 50

श्रीभगवानुवाच
यन्नारदाङ्गिरोभ्यां ते व्याहृतं मेऽनुशासनम् ।
संसिद्धोऽसि तया राजन् विद्यया दर्शनाच्च मे ॥ ५० ॥

śrī-bhagavān uvāca
yan nāradāṅgirobhyāṁ te
vyāhṛtaṁ me'nuśāsanam
saṁsiddho'si tayā rājan
vidyayā darśanāc ca me

śrī-bhagavān uvāca—the Supreme Personality of Godhead, Saṅkarṣaṇa, replied; *yat*—which; *nārada-aṅgirobhyām*—by the great sages Nārada and Aṅgirā; *te*—unto you; *vyāhṛtam*—spoken; *me*—of Me; *anuśāsanam*—the worship; *saṁsiddhaḥ*—completely perfected; *asi*—you are; *tayā*—by that; *rājan*—O King; *vidyayā—mantra; darśanāt*—from the direct sight; *ca*—as well as; *me*—of Me.

TRANSLATION

The Supreme Personality of Godhead, Anantadeva, replied as follows: O King, as a result of your having accepted the instructions spoken about Me by the great sages Nārada and Aṅgirā, you have become completely aware of transcendental knowledge. Because you are now educated in the spiritual science, you have seen Me face to face. Therefore you are now completely perfect.

PURPORT

The perfection of life is to be spiritually educated and to understand the existence of the Lord and how He creates, maintains and annihilates the cosmic manifestation. When one is perfect in knowledge, he can develop his love of Godhead through the association of such perfect persons as Nārada and Aṅgirā and the members of their disciplic succession. Then one is able to see the unlimited Supreme Personality of Godhead face to face. Although the Lord is unlimited, by His causeless mercy He becomes visible to the devotee, who is then able to see Him. In our present position of conditioned life we cannot see or understand the Supreme Personality of Godhead.

ataḥ śrī-kṛṣṇa-nāmādi
na bhaved grāhyam indriyaiḥ
sevonmukhe hi jihvādau
svayam eva sphuraty adaḥ

"No one can understand the transcendental nature of the name, form, quality and pastimes of Śrī Kṛṣṇa through his materially contaminated senses. Only when one becomes spiritually saturated by transcendental service to the Lord are the transcendental name, form, quality and pastimes of the Lord revealed to him." (*Bhakti-rasāmṛta-sindhu* 1.2.234) If one takes to spiritual life under the direction of Nārada Muni or his representative and thus engages himself in the service of the Lord, he qualifies himself to see the Lord face to face. The *Brahma-saṁhitā* (5.38) states:

premāñjana-cchurita-bhakti-vilocanena
santaḥ sadaiva hṛdayeṣu vilokayanti
yaṁ śyāmasundaram acintya-guṇa-svarūpaṁ
govindam ādi-puruṣaṁ tam ahaṁ bhajāmi

"I worship the primeval Lord, Govinda, who is always seen by the devotee whose eyes are anointed with the pulp of love. He is seen in His eternal form of Śyāmasundara situated within the heart of the devotee." One must follow the instructions of the spiritual master. Thus one becomes qualified and later sees the Supreme Personality of Godhead, as evinced by Mahārāja Citraketu.

TEXT 51

अहं वै सर्वभूतानि भूतात्मा भूतभावनः ।
शब्दब्रह्म परं ब्रह्म ममोभे शाश्वती तनू ॥ ५१ ॥

ahaṁ vai sarva-bhūtāni
bhūtātmā bhūta-bhāvanaḥ

śabda-brahma paraṁ brahma
mamobhe śāśvatī tanū

aham—I; *vai*—indeed; *sarva-bhūtāni*—expanded in different forms of living entities; *bhūta-ātmā*—the Supersoul of all living entities (the supreme director and enjoyer of them); *bhūta-bhāvanaḥ*—the cause for the manifestation of all living entities; *śabda-brahma*—the transcendental sound vibration (the Hare Kṛṣṇa *mantra*); *param brahma*—the Supreme Absolute Truth; *mama*—My; *ubhe*—both (namely, the form of sound and the form of spiritual identity); *śāśvatī*—eternal; *tanū*—two bodies.

TRANSLATION

All living entities, moving and nonmoving, are My expansions and are separate from Me. I am the Supersoul of all living beings, who exist because I manifest them. I am the form of the transcendental vibrations like oṁkāra and Hare Kṛṣṇa Hare Rāma, and I am the Supreme Absolute Truth. These two forms of Mine—namely, the transcendental sound and the eternally blissful spiritual form of the Deity, are My eternal forms; they are not material.

PURPORT

The science of devotional service has been instructed by Nārada and Aṅgirā to Citraketu. Now, because of Citraketu's devotional service, he has seen the Supreme Personality of Godhead. By performing devotional service, one advances step by step, and when one is on the platform of love of Godhead (*premā pumartho mahān*) he sees the Supreme Lord at every moment. As stated in *Bhagavad-gītā,* when one engages in devotional service twenty-four hours a day (*teṣāṁ satata-yuktānāṁ bhajatāṁ prīti-pūrvakam*) in accordance with the instructions of the spiritual master, his devotional service becomes more and more pleasing. Then the Supreme Personality of Godhead, who is within the core of everyone's heart, speaks to the devotee (*dadāmi buddhi-yogaṁ taṁ yena māṁ upayānti te*). Citraketu Mahārāja was first instructed by his *gurus,* Aṅgirā and Nārada, and now, having followed their instructions, he has come to the stage of seeing the Supreme Lord face to face. Therefore the Lord is now instructing him in the essence of knowledge.

The essence of knowledge is that there are two kinds of *vastu,* or substances. One is real, and the other, being illusory or temporary, is sometimes called nonfactual. One must consider these two kinds of existence.

The real *tattva,* or truth, consists of Brahman, Paramātmā, and Bhagavān. As stated in *Śrīmad-Bhāgavatam* (1.2.11):

vadanti tat tattva-vidas
tattvaṁ yaj jñānam advayam
brahmeti paramātmeti
bhagavān iti śabdyate

"Learned transcendentalists who know the Absolute Truth call this nondual substance Brahman, Paramātmā or Bhagavān." The Absolute Truth exists eternally in three features. Therefore, Brahman, Paramātmā and Bhagavān combined are the substance.

The categories of emanations from the nonsubstance are two—activities and forbidden activities (*karma* and *vikarma*). *Karma* refers to the pious life or material activities performed during the day and the mental activities of dreams at night. These are more or less desired activities. *Vikarma,* however, refers to illusory activities, which are something like the will-o'-the-wisp. These are activities that have no meaning. For example, modern scientists imagine that life can be produced from chemical combinations, and they are very busy trying to prove this in laboratories throughout the world, although no one in history has been able to produce the substance of life from material combinations. Such activities are called *vikarma.*

All material activities are actually illusory, and progress in illusion is simply a waste of time. These illusory activities are called *akārya,* and one must learn of them from the instructions of the Supreme Personality of Godhead. As stated in *Bhagavad-gītā* (4.17):

karmaṇo hy api boddhavyaṁ
boddhavyaṁ ca vikarmaṇaḥ
akarmaṇaś ca boddhavyaṁ
gahanā karmaṇo gatiḥ

"The intricacies of action are very hard to understand. Therefore one should know properly what action is, what forbidden action is, and what inaction is." One must learn of these directly from the Supreme Personality of Godhead, who, as Anantadeva, is instructing King Citraketu because of the advanced stage of devotional service he achieved by following the instructions of Nārada and Aṅgirā.

Herein it is said, *ahaṁ vai sarva-bhūtāni:* the Lord is everything (*sarva-bhūtāni*), including the living entities and the material or physical elements. As the Lord says in *Bhagavad-gītā* (7.4–5):

bhūmir āpo'nalo vāyuḥ
khaṁ mano buddhir eva ca
ahaṅkāra itīyaṁ me
bhinnā prakṛtir aṣṭadhā

apareyam itas tv anyāṁ
prakṛtiṁ viddhi me parām
jīva-bhūtāṁ mahā-bāho
yayedaṁ dhāryate jagat

"Earth, water, fire, air, ether, mind, intelligence and false ego—all together these eight comprise My separated material energies. Besides this inferior nature, O mighty-armed Arjuna, there is a superior energy of Mine, which consists of the living entities, who are struggling with material nature and are sustaining the universe." The living entity tries to lord it over the material or physical elements, but both the physical elements and the spiritual spark are energies emanating from the Supreme Personality of Godhead. Therefore the Lord says, *ahaṁ vai sarva-bhūtāni:* "I am everything." Just as heat and light emanate from fire, these two energies—the physical elements and the living entities—emanate from the Supreme Lord. Therefore the Lord says, *ahaṁ vai sarva-bhūtāni:* "I expand the physical and spiritual categories."

Again, the Lord, as the Supersoul, guides the living entities who are conditioned by the physical atmosphere. Therefore he is called *bhūtātmā bhūta-bhāvanaḥ.* He gives the living entity the intelligence with which to improve his position so that he may return home, back to Godhead, or if he does not want to go back to Godhead, the Lord gives him the intelligence with which to improve his material position. This is confirmed by the Lord Himself in *Bhagavad-gītā* (15.15). *Sarvasya cāhaṁ hṛdi sanniviṣṭo mattaḥ smṛtir jñānam apohanaṁ ca:* "I am seated in everyone's heart, and from Me come remembrance, knowledge and forgetfulness." From within, the Lord gives the living being the intelligence with which to work. Therefore the previous verse said that after the Supreme Personality of Godhead endeavors, our endeavors begin. We cannot independently endeavor or act upon anything. Therefore the Lord is *bhūta-bhāvanaḥ.*

Another specific feature of the knowledge given in this verse is that *śabda-brahma* is also a form of the Supreme Lord. In His eternal, blissful form, Lord Kṛṣṇa is accepted by Arjuna as *paraṁ brahma.* A living entity in the conditioned stage accepts something illusory as substantial. This is called *māyā* or *avidyā*—ignorance. Therefore according to the Vedic knowledge, one must become a devotee, and one must then distinguish between *avidyā* and *vidyā,* which are elaborately explained in the *Īśopaniṣad.* When one is actually on the platform of *vidyā,* he can personally understand the Personality of Godhead in His forms like those of Lord Rāma, Lord Kṛṣṇa and Saṅkarṣaṇa. The Vedic knowledge is described as the breathing of the Supreme Lord, and activities begin on the basis of Vedic knowledge. Therefore the Lord says that when He endeavors or breathes, the material universes come into existence, and various activities gradually develop. The Lord says in *Bhagavad-gītā, praṇavaḥ sarva-vedeṣu:* "I am the syllable *oṁ* in all the Vedic *mantras."* Vedic knowledge begins with the vibration of the transcendental sound *praṇava, oṁkāra.* The same transcendental sound is Hare Kṛṣṇa, Hare Kṛṣṇa, Kṛṣṇa Kṛṣṇa, Hare Hare/ Hare Rāma, Hare Rāma, Rāma Rāma, Hare Hare. *Abhinnatvān nāma-nāminoḥ:* there is no difference between the holy name of the Lord and the Lord Himself.

TEXT 52

लोके विततमात्मानं लोकं चात्मनि सन्ततम् ।
उभयं च मया व्याप्तं मयि चैवोभयं कृतम् ॥ ५२ ॥

loke vitatam ātmānaṁ
lokaṁ cātmani santatam
ubhayaṁ ca mayā vyāptaṁ
mayi caivobhayaṁ kṛtam

loke—in this material world; *vitatam*—expanded (in the spirit of material enjoyment); *ātmānam*—the living entity; *lokam*—the material world; *ca*—also; *ātmani*—in the living entity; *santatam*—spread; *ubhayam*—both (the material world of material elements and the living entity); *ca*—and; *mayā*—by Me; *vyāptam*—pervaded; *mayi*—in Me; *ca*—also; *eva*—indeed; *ubhayam*—both of them; *kṛtam*—created.

TRANSLATION

In this world of matter, which the conditioned soul accepts as consisting of enjoyable resources, the conditioned soul expands, thinking that he is

the enjoyer of the material world. Similarly, the material world expands in the living entity as a source of enjoyment. In this way they both expand, but because they are My energies, they are both pervaded by Me. As the Supreme Lord, I am the cause of these effects, and one should know that both of them rest in Me.

PURPORT

The Māyāvāda philosophy sees everything as being equal in quality with the Supreme Personality of Godhead, or the Supreme Brahman, and therefore sees everything as worshipable. This dangerous theory of the Māyāvāda school has turned people in general toward atheism. On the strength of this theory, one thinks that he is God, but this is not a fact. As stated in *Bhagavad-gītā* (*mayā tatam idaṁ sarvaṁ jagad avyakta-mūrtinā*), the fact is that the entire cosmic manifestation is an expansion of the Supreme Lord's energies, which are manifested in the physical elements and the living entities. The living entities wrongly consider the physical elements to be resources meant for their enjoyment, and they think themselves to be the enjoyers. However, neither of them is independent; they are both energies of the Lord. The original cause for the material energy and spiritual energy is the Supreme Personality of Godhead. However, although the expansion of the Lord's energies is the original cause, one should not think that the Lord Himself has expanded in different ways. To condemn the theories of the Māyāvādīs, the Lord clearly says in *Bhagavad-gītā, mat-sthāni sarva-bhūtāni na cāhaṁ teṣv avasthitaḥ:* "All beings are in Me, but I am not in them." Everything rests upon Him, and everything is but an expansion of His energies, but this does not mean that everything is as worshipable as the Lord Himself. The material expansion is temporary, but the Lord is not temporary. The living entities are parts of the Lord, but they are not the Lord Himself. The living entities in this material world are not inconceivable, but the Lord is. The theory that the Lord's energies, being expansions of the Lord, are as good as the Lord is mistaken.

TEXTS 53–54

यथा सुषुप्तः पुरुषो विश्वं पश्यति चात्मनि ।
आत्मानमेकदेशस्थं मन्यते स्वप्न उत्थितः ॥ ५३ ॥
एवं जागरणादीनि जीवस्थानानि चात्मनः ।
मायामात्राणि विज्ञाय तद्द्रष्टारं परं स्मरेत् ॥ ५४ ॥

yathā suṣuptaḥ puruṣo
viśvaṁ paśyati cātmani
ātmānam eka-deśa-sthaṁ
manyate svapna utthitaḥ

evaṁ jāgaraṇādīni
jīva-sthānāni cātmanaḥ
māyā-mātrāṇi vijñāya
tad-draṣṭāraṁ paraṁ smaret

yathā—just as; *suṣuptaḥ*—sleeping; *puruṣaḥ*—a person; *viśvam*—the whole universe; *paśyati*—perceives; *ca*—also; *ātmani*—in himself; *ātmānam*—himself; *eka-deśa-stham*—lying down in one place; *manyate*—he considers; *svapne*—in the dreaming condition; *utthitaḥ*—waking up; *evam*—in this way; *jāgaraṇa-ādīni*—the states of wakefulness and so on; *jīva-sthānāni*—the living entity's different conditions of existence; *ca*—also; *ātmanaḥ*—of the Supreme Personality of Godhead; *māyā-mātrāṇi*—the exhibitions of the illusory potency; *vijñāya*—knowing; *tat*—of them; *draṣṭāram*—the creator or seer of all such conditions; *param*—the Supreme; *smaret*—one should always remember.

TRANSLATION

When a person is in deep sleep, he dreams and sees in himself many other objects, such as great mountains and rivers or perhaps even the entire universe, although they are far away. Sometimes when one awakens from a dream he sees that he is in a human form, lying in his bed in one place. Then he sees himself, in terms of various conditions, as belonging to a particular nationality, family and so on. All the conditions of deep sleep, dreaming and wakefulness are but energies of the Supreme Personality of Godhead. One should always remember the original creator of these conditions, the Supreme Lord, who is unaffected by them.

PURPORT

None of these conditions of the living entities—namely, deep sleep, dreaming and wakefulness—is substantial. They are simply displays of various phases of conditional life. There may be many mountains, rivers, trees, bees, tigers and snakes that are situated far away, but in a dream one may imagine them to be nearby. Similarly, as one has subtle dreams at night, when the living entity is awake he lives in gross dreams of nation, community, society, possessions, skyscrapers, bank balance, position and honor. Under the circumstances, one should know that his position is due to his contact with the material world. One is situated in different positions in various forms of life that are all but creations of the illusory energy, which works under the direction of the Supreme Personality of Godhead. Therefore the Supreme Lord is the ultimate actor, and the conditioned living entity should simply remember this original actor, Śrī Kṛṣṇa. As living entities, we are being carried away by the waves of *prakṛti,* or nature, which works under the Lord's direction (*mayādhyakṣeṇa prakṛtiḥ sūyate sa-carācaram*). Bhaktivinoda Ṭhākura sings, *(miche) māyāra vaśe, yāccha bhese', khāccha hābuḍubu, bhāi:* "Why are you being carried away by the waves of the illusory energy in various phases of dreaming and wakefulness? These are all creations of *māyā.*" Our only duty is to remember the supreme director of this illusory energy—Kṛṣṇa. For us to do this, the *śāstra* advises us, *harer nāma harer nāma harer nāmaiva kevalam:* one should constantly chant the holy name of the Lord—Hare Kṛṣṇa, Hare Kṛṣṇa, Kṛṣṇa Kṛṣṇa, Hare Hare/ Hare Rāma, Hare Rāma, Rāma Rāma, Hare Hare. The Supreme Lord is realized in three different phases, as Brahman, Paramātmā and Bhagavān, but Bhagavān is the ultimate realization. One who realizes Bhagavān—the Supreme Personality of Godhead, Kṛṣṇa—is the most perfect *mahātmā* (*vāsudevaḥ sarvam iti sa mahātmā sudurlabhaḥ*). In the human form of life, one should understand the Supreme Personality of Godhead, for then one will understand everything else. *kasmin bhagavo vijñāte sarvam idaṁ vijñātaṁ bhavati*. According to this Vedic injunction, simply by understanding Kṛṣṇa one understands Brahman, Paramātmā, *prakṛti,* the illusory energy, the spiritual energy and everything else. Everything will be revealed. *Prakṛti,* the material nature, is working under the direction of the Supreme Lord, and we living entities are being carried away by various phases of *prakṛti.* For self-realization, one should always remember Kṛṣṇa. As stated in *Padma Purāṇa, smartavyaḥ satataṁ viṣṇuḥ:* we should always remember Lord Viṣṇu. *Vismartavyo na jātucit:* we should never forget the Lord. This is the perfection of life.

TEXT 55

येन प्रसुप्तः पुरुषः स्वापं वेदात्मनस्तदा ।
सुखं च निर्गुणं ब्रह्म तमात्मानमवेहि माम् ॥ ५५ ॥

yena prasuptaḥ puruṣaḥ
svāpaṁ vedātmanas tadā
sukhaṁ ca nirguṇaṁ brahma
tam ātmānam avehi mām

yena—by whom (the Supreme Brahman); *prasuptaḥ*—sleeping; *puruṣaḥ*—a man; *svāpam*—the subject of a dream; *veda*—knows; *ātmanaḥ*—of himself; *tadā*—at that time; *sukham*—happiness; *ca*—also; *nirguṇam*—without contact with the material environment; *brahma*—the supreme spirit; *tam*—Him; *ātmānam*—the pervader; *avehi*—just know; *mām*—Me.

TRANSLATION

Know Me to be the Supreme Brahman, the all-pervading Supersoul through whom the sleeping living entity can understand his dreaming condition and his happiness beyond the activities of the material senses. That is to say, I am the cause of the activities of the sleeping living being.

PURPORT

When the living entity becomes free from false ego, he understands his superior position as a spirit soul, part and parcel of the pleasure potency of the Lord. Thus, due to Brahman, even while sleeping the living entity can enjoy. The Lord says, "That Brahman, that Paramātmā and that Bhagavān are I Myself." This is noted by Śrīla Jīva Gosvāmī in his *Krama-sandarbha.*

TEXT 56

उभयं स्मरतः पुंसः प्रस्वापप्रतिबोधयोः ।
अन्वेति व्यतिरिच्येत तज्ज्ञानं ब्रह्म तत् परम् ॥ ५६ ॥

ubhayaṁ smarataḥ puṁsaḥ
prasvāpa-pratibodhayoḥ
anveti vyatiricyeta
taj jñānaṁ brahma tat param

ubhayam—both types of consciousness (sleep and wakefulness); *smarataḥ*—remembering; *puṁsaḥ*—of the person; *prasvāpa*—of consciousness during sleep; *pratibodhayoḥ*—and of consciousness while awake; *anveti*—extends through; *vyatiricyeta*—may reach beyond; *tat*—that; *jñānam*—knowledge; *brahma*—the Supreme Brahman; *tat*—that; *param*—transcendental.

TRANSLATION

If one's dreams during sleep are merely subject matters witnessed by the Supersoul, how can the living entity, who is different from the Supersoul, remember the activities of dreams? The experiences of one person cannot be understood by another. Therefore the knower of the facts, the living entity who inquires into the incidents manifested in dreams and wakefulness, is different from the circumstantial activities. That knowing factor is Brahman. In other words, the quality of knowing belongs to the living entities and to the Supreme Soul. Thus the living entity can also experience the activities of dreams and wakefulness. In both stages the knower is unchanged, but is qualitatively one with the Supreme Brahman.

PURPORT

In knowledge the living entity is qualitatively one with the Supreme Brahman, but the quantity of the Supreme Brahman is not the same as that of the living entity, who is part of Brahman. Because the living entity is Brahman in quality, he can remember the past activities of dreams and also know the present activities of wakefulness.

TEXT 57

यदेतद्विस्मृतं पुंसो मद्भावं भिन्नमात्मनः ।
ततः संसार एतस्य देहाद्देहो मृतेर्मृतिः ॥ ५७ ॥

yad etad vismṛtaṁ puṁso
mad-bhāvaṁ bhinnam ātmanaḥ
tataḥ saṁsāra etasya
dehād deho mṛter mṛtiḥ

yat—which; *etat*—this; *vismṛtam*—forgotten; *puṁsaḥ*—of the living entity; *mat-bhāvam*—My spiritual position; *bhinnam*—separation; *ātmanaḥ*—from the Supreme Soul; *tataḥ*—from that; *saṁsāraḥ*—material, conditional life; *etasya*—of the living entity; *dehāt*—from one body; *dehaḥ*—another body; *mṛteḥ*—from one death; *mṛtiḥ*—another death.

TRANSLATION

When a living entity, thinking himself different from Me, forgets his spiritual identity of qualitative oneness with Me in eternity, knowledge

and bliss, his material, conditional life begins. In other words, instead of identifying his interest with Mine, he becomes interested in his bodily expansions like his wife, children and material possessions. In this way, by the influence of his actions, one body comes from another, and after one death, another death takes place.

PURPORT

Generally the Māyāvādī philosophers or persons influenced by Māyāvādī philosophers think themselves as good as the Supreme Personality of Godhead. This is the cause of their conditional life. As stated by the Vaiṣṇava poet Jagadānanda Paṇḍita in his *Prema-vivarta:*

kṛṣṇa-bahirmukha hañā bhoga vāñchā kare
nikaṭa-stha māyā tāre jāpaṭiyā dhare

As soon as a living entity forgets his constitutional position and endeavors to become one with the Supreme, his conditional life begins. The conception that the Supreme Brahman and the living entity are equal not only in quality but also in quantity is the cause of conditional life. If one forgets the difference between the Supreme Lord and the living entity, his conditional life begins. Conditional life means giving up one body to accept another and undergoing death to accept death again. The Māyāvādī philosopher teaches the philosophy of *tat tvam asi,* saying, "You are the same as God." He forgets that *tat tvam asi* applies in terms of the marginal position of the living entity, who is like sunshine. There is heat and light in the sun, and there is heat and light in the sunshine, and thus they are qualitatively one. But one should not forget that the sunshine rests on the sun. As the Lord says in *Bhagavad-gītā, brahmaṇo hi pratiṣṭhāham:* "I am the original source of Brahman." The sunshine is important because of the presence of the sun globe. It is not that the sun globe is important because of the all-pervasiveness of the sunshine. Forgetfulness and misunderstanding of this fact is called *māyā.* Because of forgetfulness of one's constitutional position and that of the Supreme Lord, one comes into *māyā,* or *saṁsāra*—conditional life. In this regard, Madhvācārya says:

sarva-bhinnaṁ parātmānaṁ
vismaran saṁsared iha
abhinnaṁ saṁsmaran yāti
tamo nāsty atra saṁśayaḥ

When one thinks that the living entity is nondifferent in all respects from the Supreme Lord, there is no doubt that he is in ignorance (*tamaḥ*).

TEXT 58

लब्ध्वेह मानुषीं योनिं ज्ञानविज्ञानसम्भवाम् ।
आत्मानं यो न बुद्ध्येत न क्वचित् क्षेममाप्नुयात् ॥ ५८ ॥

labdhveha mānuṣīṁ yoniṁ
jñāna-vijñāna-sambhavām
ātmānaṁ yo na buddhyeta
na kvacit kṣemam āpnuyāt

labdhvā—achieving; *iha*—in this material world (especially in this pious land of Bhārata-varṣa, India); *mānuṣīm*—the human; *yonim*—species; *jñāna*—of knowledge through Vedic scriptures; *vijñāna*—and practical application of that knowledge in life; *sambhavām*—wherein there is a possibility; *ātmānam*—one's real identity; *yaḥ*—anyone who; *na*—not; *buddhyeta*—understands; *na*—never; *kvacit*—at any time; *kṣemam*—success in life; *āpnuyāt*—can obtain.

TRANSLATION

A human being can attain perfection in life by self-realization through the Vedic literature and its practical application. This is possible especially for a human being born in India, the land of piety. A man who obtains birth in such a convenient position but does not understand his self is unable to achieve the highest perfection, even if he is exalted to life in the higher planetary systems.

PURPORT

This statement is confirmed in *Caitanya-caritāmṛta* (*Ādi* 9.41). Lord Caitanya said:

bhārata-bhūmite haila manuṣya-janma yāra
janma sārthaka kari' kara para-upakāra

Everyone born in India, especially as a human being, can achieve the supreme success through the Vedic literature and its practical application in life. When one is perfect, he can render a service for the self-realization of the entire human society. This is the best way to perform humanitarian work.

TEXT 59

स्मृत्वेहायां परिक्लेशं ततः फलविपर्ययम् ।
अभयं चाप्यनीहायां सङ्कल्पाद्विरमेत्कविः ॥ ५९ ॥

smṛtvehāyāṁ parikleśaṁ
tataḥ phala-viparyayam
abhayaṁ cāpy anīhāyāṁ
saṅkalpād viramet kaviḥ

smṛtvā—remembering; *īhāyām*—in the field of activities with fruitive results; *parikleśam*—the waste of energy and the miserable conditions; *tataḥ*—from that; *phala-viparyayam*—the opposite of the desired result; *abhayam*—fearlessness; *ca*—also; *api*—indeed; *anīhāyām*—when there is no desire for fruitive results; *saṅkalpāt*—from material desire; *viramet*—should cease; *kaviḥ*—one who is advanced in knowledge.

TRANSLATION

Remembering the great trouble found in the field of activities performed for fruitive results, and remembering how one receives the reverse of the results one desires—whether from material actions or from the fruitive activities recommended in the Vedic literatures—an intelligent man should cease from the desire for fruitive actions, for by such endeavors one cannot achieve the ultimate goal of life. On the other hand, if one acts without desires for fruitive results—in other words, if one engages in devotional activities—he can achieve the highest goal of life with freedom from miserable conditions. Considering this, one should cease from material desires.

TEXT 60

सुखाय दुःखमोक्षाय कुर्वाते दम्पती क्रियाः ।
ततोऽनिवृत्तिरप्राप्तिर्दुःखस्य च सुखस्य च ॥ ६० ॥

sukhāya duḥkha-mokṣāya
kurvāte dampatī kriyāḥ
tato'nivṛttir aprāptir
duḥkhasya ca sukhasya ca

sukhāya—for happiness; *duḥkha-mokṣāya*—for release from the unhappy state; *kurvāte*—perform; *dam-patī*—the wife and husband; *kriyāḥ*—activities; *tataḥ*—from that; *anivṛttiḥ*—no cessation; *aprāptiḥ*—no achievement; *duḥkhasya*—of distress; *ca*—also; *sukhasya*—of happiness; *ca*—also.

TRANSLATION

As husband and wife, a man and woman plan together to attain happiness and decrease unhappiness, working jointly in many ways, but because their activities are full of desires, these activities are never a source of happiness, and they never diminish distress. On the contrary, they are a cause of great unhappiness.

TEXTS 61–62

एवं विपर्ययं बुद्ध्वा नृणां विज्ञाभिमानिनाम् ।
आत्मनश्च गतिं सूक्ष्मां स्थानत्रयविलक्षणाम् ॥ ६१ ॥
दृष्टश्रुताभिर्मात्राभिर्निर्मुक्तः स्वेन तेजसा ।
ज्ञानविज्ञानसन्तृप्तो मद्भक्तः पुरुषो भवेत् ॥ ६२ ॥

evaṁ viparyayaṁ buddhvā
nṛṇāṁ vijñābhimāninām
ātmanaś ca gatiṁ sūkṣmāṁ
sthāna-traya-vilakṣaṇām

dṛṣṭa-śrutābhir mātrābhir
nirmuktaḥ svena tejasā
jñāna-vijñāna-santṛpto
mad-bhaktaḥ puruṣo bhavet

evam—in this way; *viparyayam*—reversal; *buddhvā*—realizing; *nṛṇām*—of men; *vijña-abhimāninām*—who think of themselves as full of scientific knowledge; *ātmanaḥ*—of the self; *ca*—also; *gatim*—the progress; *sūkṣmām*—extremely difficult to understand; *sthāna-traya*—the three conditions of life (deep sleep, dreaming and wakefulness); *vilakṣaṇām*—apart from; *dṛṣṭa*—directly perceived; *śrutābhiḥ*—or understood by information from authorities; *mātrābhiḥ*—from objects; *nirmuktaḥ*—being freed; *svena*—by one's own; *tejasā*—strength of consideration; *jñāna-vijñāna*—with knowledge and practical application of the knowledge; *santṛptaḥ*—being fully satisfied; *mat-bhaktaḥ*—My devotee; *puruṣaḥ*—a person; *bhavet*—should become.

TRANSLATION

One should understand that the activities of persons who are proud of their material experience bring only results contradictory to those such persons conceive while awake, sleeping and deeply sleeping. One should further understand that the spirit soul, although very difficult for the materialist to perceive, is above all these conditions, and by the strength of one's discrimination, one should give up the desire for fruitive results in the present life and in the next. Thus becoming experienced in transcendental knowledge, one should become My devotee.

TEXT 63

एतावानेव मनुजैर्योगनैपुण्यबुद्धिभिः ।
स्वार्थः सर्वात्मना ज्ञेयो यत्परात्मैकदर्शनम् ॥ ६३ ॥

etāvān eva manujair
yoga-naipuṇya-buddhibhiḥ
svārthaḥ sarvātmanā jñeyo
yat parātmaika-darśanam

etāvān—this much; *eva*—indeed; *manujaiḥ*—by human beings; *yoga*—by the process of linking with the Supreme by *bhakti-yoga; naipuṇya*—endowed with expertise; *buddhibhiḥ*—who have intelligence; *sva-arthaḥ*—the ultimate goal of life; *sarva-ātmanā*—by all means; *jñeyaḥ*—to be known; *yat*—which; *para*—of the transcendental Lord; *ātma*—and of the soul; *eka*—of the oneness; *darśanam*—understanding.

TRANSLATION

Persons who try to reach the ultimate goal of life must expertly observe the Supreme Absolute Person and the living entity, who are one in quality in their relationship as part and whole. This is the ultimate understanding of life. There is no better truth than this.

TEXT 64

त्वमेतच्छ्रद्धया राजन्नप्रमत्तो वचो मम ।
ज्ञानविज्ञानसम्पन्नो धारयन्नाशु सिध्यसि ॥ ६४ ॥

tvam etac chraddhayā rājann
apramatto vaco mama
jñāna-vijñāna-sampanno
dhārayann āśu sidhyasi

tvam—you; *etat*—this; *śraddhayā*—with great faith and allegiance; *rājan*—O King; *apramattaḥ*—without being mad or deviated to any other conclusion; *vacaḥ*—instruction; *mama*—of Me; *jñāna-vijñāna-sampannaḥ*—being fully aware of knowledge and its practical application in life; *dhārayan*—accepting; *āśu*—very soon; *sidhyasi*—you will become the most perfect.

TRANSLATION

O King, if you accept this conclusion of Mine, being unattached to material enjoyment, adhering to Me with great faith and thus becoming proficient and fully aware of knowledge and its practical application in life, you will achieve the highest perfection by attaining Me.

TEXT 65

श्रीशुक उवाच
आश्वास्य भगवानित्थं चित्रकेतुं जगद्गुरुः ।
पश्यतस्तस्य विश्वात्मा ततश्चान्तर्दधे हरिः ॥ ६५ ॥

śrī-śuka uvāca
āśvāsya bhagavān itthaṁ
citraketuṁ jagad-guruḥ
paśyatas tasya viśvātmā
tataś cāntardadhe hariḥ

śrī-śukaḥ uvāca—Śrī Śukadeva Gosvāmī said; *āśvāsya*—assuring; *bhagavān*—the Supreme Personality of Godhead; *ittham*—thus; *citraketum*—King Citraketu; *jagat-guruḥ*—the supreme spiritual master; *paśyataḥ*—while looking on; *tasya*—he; *viśva-ātmā*—the Supersoul of the whole universe; *tataḥ*—from there; *ca*—also; *antardadhe*—disappeared; *hariḥ*—Lord Hari.

TRANSLATION

Śrī Śukadeva Gosvāmī continued: After thus instructing Citraketu and assuring him of perfection in this way, the Supreme Personality of

Godhead, who is the supreme spiritual master, the supreme soul, Saṅkarṣaṇa, disappeared from that place as Citraketu looked on.

Thus end the Bhaktivedanta purports of the Sixth Canto, Sixteenth Chapter, of the Śrīmad-Bhāgavatam, *entitled "King Citraketu Meets the Supreme Lord."*

CHAPTER SEVENTEEN

Mother Pārvatī Curses Citraketu

The Seventeenth Chapter is summarized as follows. This chapter describes Citraketu's receiving the body of an *asura,* or demon, because of joking with Lord Śiva.

After personally talking with the Supreme Personality of Godhead, King Citraketu enjoyed life in his airplane with the women of the Vidyādhara planet. Engaging in the congregational chanting of the glories of the Lord, he began flying his plane and traveling in outer space. One day while traveling like this, he wandered into the bowers of Sumeru Mountain, where he came upon Lord Śiva embracing Pārvatī, surrounded by an assembly of Siddhas, Cāraṇas and great sages. Seeing Lord Śiva in that situation, Citraketu laughed very loudly, but Pārvatī became very angry at him and cursed him. Because of this curse, Citraketu later appeared as the demon Vṛtrāsura.

Citraketu, however, was not at all afraid of Pārvatī's curse, and thus he spoke as follows: "Everyone in human society enjoys happiness and distress according to his past deeds and in this way travels in the material world. Therefore no one is responsible for his happiness and distress. One is controlled by the influence of material nature in the material world, yet one thinks himself the doer of everything. In this material world, which is made of the external energy of the Supreme Lord, one is sometimes cursed and sometimes favored, and thus he sometimes enjoys in the upper planetary systems and sometimes suffers in the lower planets, but all these situations are the same because they are within this material world. None of these positions has any factual existence, for all of them are temporary. The Supreme Personality of Godhead is the ultimate controller because the material world is created, maintained and annihilated under His control while He nonetheless remains neutral to these different transformations of the material world in time and space. The material, external energy of the Supreme Personality of Godhead is in charge of this material world. The Lord helps the world by creating situations for the living entities within it."

When Citraketu spoke in this way, all the members in the great assembly in which Lord Śiva and Pārvatī were present were astonished. Then Lord Śiva began speaking about the devotees of the Lord. A devotee is neutral in all conditions of life, whether in the heavenly planets or hellish planets, whether liberated from the material world or conditioned by it, and whether blessed with happiness or subjected to distress. These are all merely dualities created by the external energy. Being influenced by the external energy, the living entity accepts a gross and subtle material body, and in this illusory position he apparently suffers miseries, although everyone is part and parcel of the Supreme Lord. The so-called demigods consider themselves independent lords, and in this way they are misled from understanding that all living entities are part of the Supreme. This chapter concludes by glorifying the devotee and the Supreme Personality of Godhead.

TEXT 1

श्रीशुक उवाच
यतश्चान्तर्हितोऽनन्तस्तस्यै कृत्वा दिशे नमः ।
विद्याधरश्चित्रकेतुश्चचार गगनेचरः ॥ १ ॥

śrī-śuka uvāca
yataś cāntarhito'nantas
tasyai kṛtvā diśe namaḥ
vidyādharaś citraketuś
cacāra gagane caraḥ

śrī-śukaḥ uvāca—Śrī Śukadeva Gosvāmī said; *yataḥ*—in which (direction); *ca*—and; *antarhitaḥ*—disappeared; *anantaḥ*—the unlimited Supreme Personality of Godhead; *tasyai*—unto that; *kṛtvā*—after offering; *diśe*—direction; *namaḥ*—obeisances; *vidyādharaḥ*—the King of the Vidyādhara planet; *citraketuḥ*—Citraketu; *cacāra*—traveled; *gagane*—in outer space; *caraḥ*—moving.

TRANSLATION

Śrīla Śukadeva Gosvāmī said: After offering obeisances to the direction from which Ananta, the Supreme Personality of Godhead, had disappeared, Citraketu began traveling in outer space as the head of the Vidyādharas.

TEXTS 2–3

स लक्षं वर्षलक्षाणामव्याहतबलेन्द्रियः ।
स्तूयमानो महायोगी मुनिभिः सिद्धचारणैः ॥ २ ॥

कुलाचलेन्द्रद्रोणीषु नानासङ्कल्पसिद्धिषु ।
रेमे विद्याधरस्त्रीभिर्गापयन् हरिमीश्वरम् ॥ ३ ॥

sa lakṣaṁ varṣa-lakṣāṇām
avyāhata-balendriyaḥ
stūyamāno mahā-yogī
munibhiḥ siddha-cāraṇaiḥ

kulācalendra-droṇīṣu
nānā-saṅkalpa-siddhiṣu
reme vidyādhara-strībhir
gāpayan harim īśvaram

saḥ—he (Citraketu); *lakṣam*—one hundred thousand; *varṣa*—of years; *lakṣāṇām*—one hundred thousand; *avyāhata*—without hindrance; *bala-indriyaḥ*—whose strength and power of the senses; *stūyamānaḥ*—being praised; *mahā-yogī*—the great mystic *yogī; munibhiḥ*—by saintly persons; *siddha-cāraṇaiḥ*—by the Siddhas and Cāraṇas; *kulācalendra-droṇīṣu*—within the valleys of the great mountain known as Kulācalendra, or Sumeru; *nānā-saṅkalpa-siddhiṣu*—where one becomes perfect in all kinds of mystic power; *reme*—enjoyed; *vidyādhara-strībhiḥ*—with the women of the Vidyādhara planet; *gāpayan*—causing to praise; *harim*—the Supreme Personality of Godhead, Hari; *īśvaram*—the controller.

TRANSLATION

Being praised by great sages and saints and by the inhabitants of Siddhaloka and Cāraṇaloka, Citraketu, the most powerful mystic yogī, wandered about enjoying life for millions of years. With bodily strength and senses free from deterioration, he traveled within the valleys of Sumeru Mountain, which is the place of perfection for various kinds of mystic power. In those valleys he enjoyed life with the women of Vidyādhara-loka by chanting the glories of the Supreme Lord, Hari.

PURPORT

It is to be understood that Mahārāja Citraketu, although surrounded by beautiful women from Vidyādhara-loka, did not forget to glorify the Lord by chanting the holy name of the Lord. It has been proved in many places that one who is not contaminated by any material condition, who is a pure devotee engaged in chanting the glories of the Lord, should be understood to be perfect.

TEXTS 4–5

एकदा स विमानेन विष्णुदत्तेन भास्वता ।
गिरिशं ददृशे गच्छन् परीतं सिद्धचारणैः ॥ ४ ॥
आलिङ्ग्याङ्कीकृतां देवीं बाहुना मुनिसंसदि ।
उवाच देव्याः शृण्वन्त्या जहासोच्चैस्तदन्तिके ॥ ५ ॥

ekadā sa vimānena
viṣṇu-dattena bhāsvatā
giriśaṁ dadṛśe gacchan
parītaṁ siddha-cāraṇaiḥ

āliṅgyāṅkīkṛtāṁ devīṁ
bāhunā muni-saṁsadi
uvāca devyāḥ śṛṇvantyā
jahāsoccais tad-antike

ekadā—one time; *saḥ*—he (King Citraketu); *vimānena*—with his airplane; *viṣṇu-dattena*—given to him by Lord Viṣṇu; *bhāsvatā*—shining brilliantly; *giriśam*—Lord Śiva; *dadṛśe*—he saw; *gacchan*—going; *parītam*—surrounded; *siddha*—by the inhabitants of Siddhaloka; *cāraṇaiḥ*—and the inhabitants of Cāraṇaloka; *āliṅgya*—embracing; *aṅkīkṛtām*—sitting on his lap; *devīm*—his wife, Pārvatī; *bāhunā*—with his arm; *muni-saṁsadi*—in the presence of great saintly persons; *uvāca*—he said; *devyāḥ*—while the goddess Pārvatī; *śṛṇvantyāḥ*—was hearing; *jahāsa*—he laughed; *uccaiḥ*—very loudly; *tad-antike*—in the vicinity.

TRANSLATION

One time while King Citraketu was traveling in outer space on a brilliantly effulgent airplane given to him by Lord Viṣṇu, he saw Lord Śiva, surrounded by Siddhas and Cāraṇas. Lord Śiva was sitting in an assembly of great saintly persons and embracing Pārvatī on his lap with his arm. Citraketu laughed loudly and spoke, within the hearing of Pārvatī.

PURPORT

Śrīla Viśvanātha Cakravartī Ṭhākura says in this connection,

bhaktiṁ bhūtiṁ harir dattvā
sva-vicchedānubhūtaye
devyāḥ śāpena vṛtratvaṁ
nītvā taṁ svāntike'nayat

The purport is that the Supreme Personality of Godhead wanted to bring Citraketu to Vaikuṇṭhaloka as soon as possible. The Lord's plan was that Citraketu be cursed by Pārvatī to become Vṛtrāsura so that in his next life he could quickly return home, back to Godhead. There have been many instances in which a devotee acting as a demon has been brought to the kingdom of God by the mercy of the Lord. For Pārvatī to be embraced by Lord Śiva was natural in a relationship between husband and wife; this was nothing extraordinary for Citraketu to see. Nonetheless, Citraketu laughed loudly to see Lord Śiva in that situation, even though he should not have done so. Thus he was eventually cursed, and this curse was the cause of his returning home, back to Godhead.

TEXT 6

चित्रकेतुरुवाच
एष लोकगुरुः साक्षाद्धर्मं वक्ता शरीरिणाम् ।
आस्ते मुख्यः सभायां वै मिथुनीभूय भार्यया ॥ ६ ॥

citraketur uvāca
eṣa loka-guruḥ sākṣād
dharmaṁ vaktā śarīriṇām
āste mukhyaḥ sabhāyāṁ vai
mithunī-bhūya bhāryayā

citraketuḥ uvāca—King Citraketu said; *eṣaḥ*—this; *loka-guruḥ*—the spiritual master of the people who follow Vedic instructions; *sākṣāt*—directly; *dharmam*—of religion; *vaktā*—the speaker; *śarīriṇām*—for all living entities who have accepted material bodies; *āste*—sits; *mukhyaḥ*—the chief; *sabhāyām*—in an assembly; *vai*—indeed; *mithunī-bhūya*—embracing; *bhāryayā*—with his wife.

TRANSLATION

Citraketu said: Lord Śiva, the spiritual master of the general populace, is the best of all living entities who have accepted material bodies. He enunciates the system of religion. Yet how wonderful it is that he is embracing his wife, Pārvatī, in the midst of an assembly of great saintly persons.

TEXT 7

जटाधरस्तीव्रतपा ब्रह्मवादिसभापतिः ।
अङ्कीकृत्य स्त्रियं चास्ते गतह्रीः प्राकृतो यथा ॥ ७ ॥

jaṭā-dharas tīvra-tapā
brahmavādi-sabhā-patiḥ
aṅkīkṛtya striyaṁ cāste
gata-hrīḥ prākṛto yathā

jaṭā-dharaḥ—keeping matted locks of hair; *tīvra-tapāḥ*—highly elevated due to undergoing fierce austerities and penances; *brahma-vādi*—of strict followers of the Vedic principles; *sabhā-patiḥ*—the president of an assembly; *aṅkīkṛtya*—embracing; *striyam*—a woman; *ca*—and; *āste*—sits; *gata-hrīḥ*—without shame; *prākṛtaḥ*—a person conditioned by material nature; *yathā*—just as.

TRANSLATION

Lord Śiva, whose hair is matted on his head, has certainly undergone great austerities and penances. Indeed, he is the president in the assembly of strict followers of Vedic principles. Nonetheless, he is seated with his wife on his lap in the midst of saintly persons and is embracing her as if he were a shameless, ordinary human being.

PURPORT

Citraketu appreciated the exalted position of Lord Śiva, and therefore he remarked at how wonderful it was that Lord Śiva was acting like an ordinary human being. He appreciated Lord Śiva's position, but when he saw Lord Śiva sitting in the midst of saintly persons and acting like a shameless, ordinary man, he was astonished. Śrīla Viśvanātha Cakravartī Ṭhākura remarks that although Citraketu criticized Lord Śiva, he did not offend Lord Śiva like Dakṣa. Dakṣa considered Lord Śiva insignificant, but Citraketu expressed his wonder at Lord Śiva's being situated in that way.

TEXT 8

प्रायशः प्राकृताश्चापि स्त्रियं रहसि बिभ्रति ।
अयं महाव्रतधरो बिभर्ति सदसि स्त्रियम् ॥ ८ ॥

prāyaśaḥ prākṛtāś cāpi
striyaṁ rahasi bibhrati

ayaṁ mahā-vrata-dharo
bibharti sadasi striyam

prāyaśaḥ—generally; *prākṛtāḥ*—conditioned souls; *ca*—also; *api*—although; *striyam*—a woman; *rahasi*—in a solitary place; *bibhrati*—embrace; *ayam*—this (Lord Śiva); *mahā-vrata-dharaḥ*—the master of great vows and austerities; *bibharti*—enjoys; *sadasi*—in an assembly of great saintly persons; *striyam*—his wife.

TRANSLATION

Ordinary conditioned persons generally embrace their wives and enjoy their company in solitary places. How wonderful it is that Lord Mahādeva, although a great master of austerity, is embracing his wife openly in the midst of an assembly of great saints.

PURPORT

The word *mahā-vrata-dharaḥ* indicates a *brahmacārī* who has never fallen down. Lord Śiva is counted among the best of *yogīs,* yet he embraced his wife in the midst of great saintly persons. Citraketu appreciated how great Lord Śiva was to be unaffected even in that situation. Therefore Citraketu was not an offender; he merely expressed his wonder.

TEXT 9

श्रीशुक उवाच
भगवानपि तच्छ्रुत्वा प्रहस्यागाधधीर्नृप ।
तूष्णीं बभूव सदसि सभ्याश्च तदनुव्रताः ॥ ९ ॥

śrī-śuka uvāca
bhagavān api tac chrutvā
prahasyāgādha-dhīr nṛpa
tūṣṇīṁ babhūva sadasi
sabhyāś ca tad-anuvratāḥ

śrī-śukaḥ uvāca—Śrī Śukadeva Gosvāmī said; *bhagavān*—Lord Śiva; *api*—also; *tat*—that; *śrutvā*—hearing; *prahasya*—smiling; *agādha-dhīḥ*—whose intelligence is unfathomed; *nṛpa*—O King; *tūṣṇīm*—silent; *babhūva*—remained; *sadasi*—in the assembly; *sabhyāḥ*—everyone assembled there; *ca*—and; *tat-anuvratāḥ*—followed Lord Śiva (remained silent).

TRANSLATION

Śrīla Śukadeva Gosvāmī continued: My dear King, after hearing Citraketu's statement, Lord Śiva, the most powerful personality, whose knowledge is fathomless, simply smiled and remained silent, and all the members of the assembly followed the lord by not saying anything.

PURPORT

Citraketu's purpose in criticizing Lord Śiva is somewhat mysterious and cannot be understood by a common man. Śrīla Viśvanātha Cakravartī Ṭhākura, however, has made the following observations. Lord Śiva, being the most exalted Vaiṣṇava and one of the most powerful demigods, is able to do anything he desires. Although he was externally exhibiting the behavior of a common man and not following etiquette, such actions cannot diminish his exalted position. The difficulty is that a common man, seeing Lord Śiva's behavior, might follow his example. As stated in *Bhagavad-gītā* (3.21):

yad yad ācarati śreṣṭhas
tat tad evetaro janaḥ
sa yat pramāṇaṁ kurute
lokas tad anuvartate

"Whatever action a great man performs, common men follow. And whatever standards he sets by exemplary acts, all the world pursues." A common man might also criticize Lord Śiva, like Dakṣa, who suffered the consequences for his criticism. King Citraketu desired that Lord Śiva cease this external behavior so that others might be saved from criticizing him and thus becoming offenders. If one thinks that Viṣṇu, the Supreme Personality of Godhead, is the only perfect personality whereas the demigods, even such demigods as Lord Śiva, are inclined to improper social affairs, he is an offender. Considering all this, King Citraketu was somewhat harsh in his behavior with Lord Śiva.

Lord Śiva, who is always deep in knowledge, could understand Citraketu's purpose, and therefore he was not at all angry; rather, he simply smiled and remained silent. The members of the assembly surrounding Lord Śiva could also understand Citraketu's purpose. Consequently, following the behavior of Lord Śiva, they did not protest; instead, following their master, they remained silent. If the members of the assembly thought that Citraketu had blasphemed Lord Śiva, they would certainly have left at once, blocking their ears with their hands.

TEXT 10

इत्यतद्वीर्यविदुषि ब्रुवाणे बह्वशोभनम् ।
रुषाह देवी धृष्टाय निर्जितात्माभिमानिने ॥ १० ॥

ity atad-vīrya-viduṣi
bruvāṇe bahv-aśobhanam
ruṣāha devī dhṛṣṭāya
nirjitātmābhimānine

iti—thus; *a-tat-vīrya-viduṣi*—when Citraketu, who did not know the prowess of Lord Śiva; *bruvāṇe*—spoke; *bahu-aśobhanam*—that which is not up to the standard of etiquette (the criticism of the exalted Lord Śiva); *ruṣā*—with anger; *āha*—said; *devī*—the goddess Pārvatī; *dhṛṣṭāya*—unto Citraketu, who was quite shameless; *nirjita-ātma*—as one who has controlled his senses; *abhimānine*—thinking of himself.

TRANSLATION

Not knowing the prowess of Lord Śiva and Pārvatī, Citraketu strongly criticized them. His statements were not at all pleasing, and therefore the goddess Pārvatī, being very angry, spoke as follows to Citraketu, who thought himself better than Lord Śiva in controlling the senses.

PURPORT

Although Citraketu never meant to insult Lord Śiva, he should not have criticized the lord, even though the lord was transgressing social customs. It is said, *tejīyasāṁ na doṣāya:* one who is very powerful should be understood to be faultless. For example, one should not find faults with the sun, although it evaporates urine from the street. The most powerful cannot be criticized by an ordinary man, or even by a great personality. Citraketu should have known that Lord Śiva, although sitting in that way, was not to be criticized. The difficulty was that Citraketu, having become a great devotee of Lord Viṣṇu, Saṅkarṣaṇa, was somewhat proud at having achieved Lord Saṅkarṣaṇa's favor and therefore thought that he could now criticize anyone, even Lord Śiva. This kind of pride in a devotee is never tolerated. A Vaiṣṇava should always remain very humble and meek and offer respect to others.

tṛṇād api sunīcena
taror api sahiṣṇunā

amāninā mānadena
kīrtanīyaḥ sadā hariḥ

"One should chant the holy name of the Lord in a humble state of mind, thinking oneself lower than the straw in the street; one should be more tolerant than a tree, devoid of all sense of false prestige and ready to offer all respect to others. In such a state of mind one can chant the holy name of the Lord constantly." A Vaiṣṇava should not try to minimize anyone else's position. It is better to remain humble and meek and chant the Hare Kṛṣṇa *mantra.* The word *nirjitātmābhimānine* indicates that Citraketu thought himself a better controller of the senses than Lord Śiva, although actually he was not. Because of all these considerations, mother Pārvatī was somewhat angry at Citraketu.

TEXT 11

श्रीपार्वत्युवाच
अयं किमधुना लोके शास्ता दण्डधरः प्रभुः ।
अस्मद्विधानां दुष्टानां निर्लज्जानां च विप्रकृत् ॥ ११ ॥

śrī-pārvaty uvāca
ayaṁ kim adhunā loke
śāstā daṇḍa-dharaḥ prabhuḥ
asmad-vidhānāṁ duṣṭānāṁ
nirlajjānāṁ ca viprakṛt

śrī-pārvatī uvāca—the goddess Pārvatī said; *ayam*—this; *kim*—whether; *adhunā*—now; *loke*—in the world; *śāstā*—the supreme controller; *daṇḍa-dharaḥ*—the carrier of the rod of punishment; *prabhuḥ*—the master; *asmat-vidhānām*—of persons like us; *duṣṭānām*—criminals; *nirlajjānām*—who have no shame; *ca*—and; *viprakṛt*—the restrainer.

TRANSLATION

The goddess Pārvatī said: Alas, has this upstart now received a post from which to punish shameless persons like us? Has he been appointed ruler, carrier of the rod of punishment? Is he now the only master of everything?

TEXT 12

न वेद धर्मं किल पद्मयोनि-
र्न ब्रह्मपुत्रा भृगुनारदाद्याः ।

न वै कुमारः कपिलो मनुश्च
ये नो निषेधन्त्यतिवर्तिनं हरम् ॥ १२ ॥

na veda dharmaṁ kila padmayonir
na brahma-putrā bhṛgu-nāradādyāḥ
na vai kumāraḥ kapilo manuś ca
ye no niṣedhanty ati-vartinaṁ haram

na—not; *veda*—knows; *dharmam*—the religious principles; *kila*—indeed; *padma-yoniḥ*—Lord Brahmā; *na*—nor; *brahma-putrāḥ*—the sons of Lord Brahmā; *bhṛgu*—Bhṛgu; *nārada*—Nārada; *ādyāḥ*—and so on; *na*—nor; *vai*—indeed; *kumāraḥ*—the four Kumāras (Sanaka, Sanat-kumāra, Sananda and Sanātana); *kapilaḥ*—Lord Kapila; *manuḥ*—Manu himself; *ca*—and; *ye*—who; *no*—not; *niṣedhanti*—order to stop; *ati-vartinam*—who is beyond laws and orders; *haram*—Lord Śiva.

TRANSLATION

Alas, Lord Brahmā, who has taken his birth from the lotus flower, does not know the principles of religion, nor do the great saints like Bhṛgu and Nārada, nor the four Kumāras, headed by Sanat-kumāra. Manu and Kapila have also forgotten the religious principles. I suppose it to be because of this that they have not tried to stop Lord Śiva from behaving improperly.

TEXT 13

एषामनुध्येयपदाब्जयुग्मं
जगद्गुरुं मङ्गलमङ्गलं स्वयम् ।
यः क्षत्रबन्धुः परिभूय सूरीन्
प्रशास्ति धृष्टस्तदयं हि दण्ड्यः ॥ १३ ॥

eṣām anudhyeya-padābja-yugmaṁ
jagad-guruṁ maṅgala-maṅgalaṁ svayam
yaḥ kṣatra-bandhuḥ paribhūya sūrīn
praśāsti dhṛṣṭas tad ayaṁ hi daṇḍyaḥ

eṣām—of all these (exalted personalities); *anudhyeya*—to be constantly meditated upon; *pada-abja-yugmam*—whose two lotus feet; *jagat-gurum*—the spiritual master of the whole world; *maṅgala-maṅgalam*—personification of the topmost religious principle; *svayam*—himself; *yaḥ*—he who; *kṣatra-bandhuḥ*—the lowest of the *kṣatriyas; paribhūya*—overriding; *sūrīn*—the demigods (like Brahmā and the others); *praśāsti*—chastises; *dhṛṣṭaḥ*—impudent; *tat*—therefore; *ayam*—this person; *hi*—indeed; *daṇḍyaḥ*—to be punished.

TRANSLATION

This Citraketu is the lowest of kṣatriyas, for he has impudently overridden Brahmā and the other demigods by insulting Lord Śiva, upon whose lotus feet they always meditate. Lord Śiva is personified religion and the spiritual master of the entire world, and therefore Citraketu must be punished.

PURPORT

All the members of the assembly were exalted *brāhmaṇas* and self-realized souls, but they did not say anything about the conduct of Lord Śiva, who was embracing the goddess Pārvatī on his lap. Citraketu nonetheless criticized Lord Śiva, and therefore the opinion of Pārvatī was that he should be punished.

TEXT 14

नायमर्हति वैकुण्ठपादमूलोपसर्पणम् ।
सम्भावितमतिः स्तब्धः साधुभिः पर्युपासितम् ॥ १४ ॥

nāyam arhati vaikuṇṭha-
pāda-mūlopasarpaṇam
sambhāvita-matiḥ stabdhaḥ
sādhubhiḥ paryupāsitam

na—not; *ayam*—this person; *arhati*—deserves; *vaikuṇṭha-pāda-mūla-upasarpaṇam*—the approaching of the shelter of Lord Viṣṇu's lotus feet; *sambhāvita-matiḥ*—considering himself highly esteemed; *stabdhaḥ*—impudent; *sādhubhiḥ*—by great saintly persons; *paryupāsitam*—worshiped.

TRANSLATION

This person is puffed up because of his achievements, thinking, "I am the best." He does not deserve to approach the shelter of Lord Viṣṇu's lotus feet, which are worshiped by all saintly persons, for he is impudent, thinking himself greatly important.

PURPORT

If a devotee thinks that he is very much advanced in devotional service, he is considered puffed up and unfit to sit beneath the shelter of the Lord's lotus feet. Again, this instruction by Lord Caitanya is applicable:

tṛṇād api sunīcena
taror api sahiṣṇunā
amāninā mānadena
kīrtanīyaḥ sadā hariḥ

"One should chant the holy name of the Lord in a humble state of mind, thinking oneself lower than the straw in the street; one should be more tolerant than a tree, devoid of all sense of false prestige and ready to offer all respect to others. In such a state of mind one can chant the holy name of the Lord constantly." Unless one is humble and meek, one cannot qualify to sit at the lotus feet of the Lord.

TEXT 15

अतः पापीयसीं योनिमासुरीं याहि दुर्मते ।
यथेह भूयो महतां न कर्ता पुत्र किल्बिषम् ॥ १५ ॥

ataḥ pāpīyasīṁ yonim
āsurīṁ yāhi durmate
yatheha bhūyo mahatāṁ
na kartā putra kilbiṣam

ataḥ—therefore; *pāpīyasīm*—most sinful; *yonim*—to the species of life; *āsurīm*—demoniac; *yāhi*—go; *durmate*—O impudent one; *yathā*—so that; *iha*—in this world; *bhūyaḥ*—again; *mahatām*—to great personalities; *na*—not; *kartā*—will commit; *putra*—my dear son; *kilbiṣam*—any offense.

TRANSLATION

O impudent one, my dear son, now take birth in a low, sinful family of demons so that you will not commit such an offense again toward exalted, saintly persons in this world.

PURPORT

One should be very careful not to commit offenses at the lotus feet of Vaiṣṇavas, of whom Lord Śiva is the best. While instructing Śrīla Rūpa Gosvāmī,

Śrī Caitanya Mahāprabhu described an offense at the lotus feet of a Vaiṣṇava as *hātī mātā,* a mad elephant. When a mad elephant enters a nice garden, it spoils the entire garden. Similarly, if one becomes like a mad elephant and commits offenses at the lotus feet of a Vaiṣṇava, his entire spiritual career is halted. One should therefore be very careful not to commit offenses at the lotus feet of a Vaiṣṇava.

Mother Pārvatī was justified in punishing Citraketu, for Citraketu impudently criticized the supreme father, Mahādeva, who is the father of the living entities conditioned within this material world. The goddess Durgā is called mother, and Lord Śiva is called father. A pure Vaiṣṇava should be very careful to engage in his specific duty without criticizing others. This is the safest position. Otherwise, if one tends to criticize others, he may commit the great offense of criticizing a Vaiṣṇava.

Because Citraketu was undoubtedly a Vaiṣṇava, he might have been surprised that Pārvatī had cursed him. Therefore the goddess Pārvatī addressed him as *putra,* or son. Everyone is the son of mother Durgā, but she is not an ordinary mother. As soon as there is a small discrepancy in a demon's behavior, mother Durgā immediately punishes the demon so that he may come to his senses. This is explained by Lord Kṛṣṇa in *Bhagavad-gītā* (7.14):

daivī hy eṣā guṇa-mayī
mama māyā duratyayā
mām eva ye prapadyante
māyām etāṁ taranti te

"This divine energy of Mine, consisting of the three modes of material nature, is difficult to overcome. But those who have surrendered unto Me can easily cross beyond it." To surrender to Kṛṣṇa means to surrender to His devotees also, for no one can be a proper servant of Kṛṣṇa unless he is a proper servant of a devotee. *Chāḍiyā vaiṣṇava-sevā nistāra pāyeche kebā:* without serving a servant of Kṛṣṇa, one cannot be elevated to being a servant of Kṛṣṇa Himself. Therefore mother Pārvatī spoke to Citraketu exactly like a mother who says to her naughty child, "My dear child, I am punishing you so that you won't do anything like this again." This tendency of a mother to punish her child is found even in mother Yaśodā, who became the mother of the Supreme Personality of Godhead. Mother Yaśodā punished Kṛṣṇa by binding Him and showing Him a stick. Thus it is the duty of a mother to chastise her beloved son, even in the case of the Supreme Lord. It is to be understood that mother Durgā was justified in punishing Citraketu. This punishment was a boon to Citraketu because after taking birth as the demon Vṛtrāsura, he was promoted directly to Vaikuṇṭha.

TEXT 16

श्रीशुक उवाच
एवं शप्तश्चित्रकेतुर्विमानादवरुह्य सः ।
प्रसादयामास सतीं मूर्ध्ना नम्रेण भारत ॥ १६ ॥

śrī-śuka uvāca
evaṁ śaptaś citraketur
vimānād avaruhya saḥ
prasādayām āsa satīṁ
mūrdhnā namreṇa bhārata

śrī-śukaḥ uvāca—Śrī Śukadeva Gosvāmī said; *evam*—thus; *śaptaḥ*—cursed; *citraketuḥ*—King Citraketu; *vimānāt*—from his airplane; *avaruhya*—coming down; *saḥ*—he; *prasādayām āsa*—completely pleased; *satīm*—Pārvatī; *mūrdhnā*—by his head; *namreṇa*—bent low; *bhārata*—O King Parīkṣit.

TRANSLATION

Śrī Śukadeva Gosvāmī continued: My dear King Parīkṣit, when Citraketu was cursed by Pārvatī, he descended from his airplane, bowed before her with great humility and pleased her completely.

TEXT 17

चित्रकेतुरुवाच
प्रतिगृह्णामि ते शापमात्मनोऽञ्जलिनाम्बिके ।
देवैर्मर्त्याय यत्प्रोक्तं पूर्वदिष्टं हि तस्य तत् ॥ १७ ॥

citraketur uvāca
pratigṛhṇāmi te śāpam
ātmano 'ñjalināmbike
devair martyāya yat proktaṁ
pūrva-diṣṭaṁ hi tasya tat

citraketuḥ uvāca—King Citraketu said; *pratigṛhṇāmi*—I accept; *te*—your; *śāpam*—curse; *ātmanaḥ*—my own; *añjalinā*—with folded bands; *ambike*—

O mother; *devaiḥ*—by the demigods; *martyāya*—unto a mortal; *yat*—which; *proktam*—prescribed; *pūrva-diṣṭam*—fixed previously according to one's past deeds; *hi*—indeed; *tasya*—of him; *tat*—that.

TRANSLATION

Citraketu said: My dear mother, with my own hands folded together I accept the curse upon me. I do not mind the curse, for happiness and distress are given by the demigods as a result of one's past deeds.

PURPORT

Since Citraketu was a devotee of the Lord, he was not at all disturbed by the curse of mother Pārvatī. He knew very well that one suffers or enjoys the results of one's past deeds as ordained by *daiva-netra*—superior authority, or the agents of the Supreme Personality of Godhead. He knew that he had not committed any offense at the lotus feet of Lord Śiva or the goddess Pārvatī, yet he had been punished, and this means that the punishment had been ordained. Thus the King did not mind it. A devotee is naturally so humble and meek that he accepts any condition of life as a blessing from the Lord. *Tat te'nukampāṁ susamīkṣamāṇaḥ* (*Bhāg.* 10.14.8). A devotee always accepts punishment from anyone as the mercy of the Lord. If one lives in this conception of life, he sees whatever reverses occur to be due to his past misdeeds, and therefore he never accuses anyone. On the contrary, he becomes increasingly attached to the Supreme Personality of Godhead because of his being purified by his suffering. Suffering, therefore, is also a process of purification.

Śrīla Viśvanātha Cakravartī Ṭhākura says in this connection that one who has developed Kṛṣṇa consciousness and who exists in love with Kṛṣṇa is no longer subject to suffering and happiness under the laws of *karma.* Indeed, he is beyond *karma.* The *Brahma-saṁhitā* says, *karmāṇi nirdahati kintu ca bhakti-bhājām:* a devotee is free from the reactions of his *karma* because he has taken to devotional service. This same principle is confirmed in *Bhagavad-gītā* (14.26). *Sa guṇān samatītyaitān brahma-bhūyāya kalpate:* one who is engaged in devotional service has already been freed from the reactions of his material *karma,* and thus he immediately becomes *brahma-bhūta,* or transcendental. This is also expressed in *Śrīmad-Bhāgavatam* (1.2.21). *Kṣīyante cāsya karmāṇi:* before attaining the stage of love, one becomes free from all the results of *karma.*

The Lord is very kind and affectionate toward His devotees, and therefore a devotee, in any condition, is not subjected to the results of *karma.* A devotee never aspires for the heavenly planets. The heavenly planets, liberation and hell are nondifferent for a devotee, for he does not discriminate between different positions in the material world. A devotee is always eager to return home, back to Godhead, and remain there as the Lord's associate. This ambition becomes increasingly fervent in his heart, and therefore he does not care about material changes in his life. Śrīla Viśvanātha Cakravartī Ṭhākura comments that Mahārāja Citraketu's being cursed by Pārvatī should be considered the mercy of the Lord. The Lord wanted Citraketu to return to Godhead as soon as possible, and therefore he terminated all the reactions of his past deeds. Acting through the heart of Pārvatī, the Lord, who is situated in everyone's heart, cursed Citraketu in order to end all his material reactions. Thus Citraketu became Vṛtrāsura in his next life and returned home, back to Godhead.

TEXT 18

संसारचक्र एतस्मिञ्जन्तुरज्ञानमोहितः ।
भ्राम्यन् सुखं च दुःखं च भुङ्क्ते सर्वत्र सर्वदा ॥ १८ ॥

saṁsāra-cakra etasmiñ
jantur ajñāna-mohitaḥ
bhrāmyan sukhaṁ ca duḥkhaṁ ca
bhuṅkte sarvatra sarvadā

saṁsāra-cakre—in the wheel of material existence; *etasmin*—this; *jantuḥ*—the living entity; *ajñāna-mohitaḥ*—being bewildered by ignorance; *bhrāmyan*—wandering; *sukham*—happiness; *ca*—and; *duḥkham*—distress; *ca*—also; *bhuṅkte*—he undergoes; *sarvatra*—everywhere; *sarvadā*—always.

TRANSLATION

Deluded by ignorance, the living entity wanders in the forest of this material world, enjoying the happiness and distress resulting from his past deeds, everywhere and at all times. [Therefore, my dear mother, neither you nor I am to be blamed for this incident.]

PURPORT

As confirmed in *Bhagavad-gītā* (3.27):

prakṛteḥ kriyamāṇāni
guṇaiḥ karmāṇi sarvaśaḥ
ahaṅkāra-vimūḍhātmā
kartāham iti manyate

"The bewildered soul, under the influence of the three modes of material nature, thinks himself the doer of activities that are in actuality carried out by nature." Actually a conditioned soul is completely under the control of material nature. Wandering here and there—always and everywhere—he is subjected to the results of his past deeds. This is carried out by the laws of nature, but one foolishly thinks himself the doer, which in fact he is not. To get free from the *karma-cakra,* the wheel of the results of one's *karma,* one should take to *bhakti-mārga*—devotional service, or Kṛṣṇa consciousness. That is the only remedy. *Sarva-dharmān parityajya mām ekaṁ śaraṇaṁ vraja.*

TEXT 19

नैवात्मा न परश्चापि कर्ता स्यात् सुखदुःखयोः ।
कर्तारं मन्यतेऽत्राज्ञ आत्मानं परमेव च ॥ १९ ॥

naivātmā na paraś cāpi
kartā syāt sukha-duḥkhayoḥ
kartāraṁ manyate'trājña
ātmānaṁ param eva ca

na—not; *eva*—indeed; *ātmā*—the spirit soul; *na*—nor; *paraḥ*—another (friend or enemy); *ca*—also; *api*—indeed; *kartā*—the doer; *syāt*—can be; *sukha-duḥkhayoḥ*—of happiness and distress; *kartāram*—the doer; *manyate*—considers; *atra*—in this connection; *ajñaḥ*—a person not aware of the real fact; *ātmānam*—himself; *param*—another; *eva*—indeed; *ca*—also.

TRANSLATION

In this material world, neither the living entity himself nor others [friends and enemies] are the cause of material happiness and distress. But because of gross ignorance, the living entity thinks that he and others are the cause.

PURPORT

In this verse the word *ajña* is very significant. In the material world, all living entities are *ajña,* ignorant, in different degrees. This ignorance continues very strongly in the mode of ignorance presented by material nature. One must therefore promote himself to the stage of goodness through his character and behavior and then gradually come to the transcendental platform, or *adhokṣaja* platform, in which he realizes both his position and the position of others. Everything is done under the superintendence of the Supreme Personality of Godhead. The process by which the results of action are ordained is called *niyatam,* always working.

TEXT 20

गुणप्रवाह एतस्मिन् कः शापः को न्वनुग्रहः ।
कः स्वर्गो नरकः को वा किं सुखं दुःखमेव वा ॥ २० ॥

guṇa-pravāha etasmin
kaḥ śāpaḥ ko nv anugrahaḥ
kaḥ svargo narakaḥ ko vā
kiṁ sukhaṁ duḥkham eva vā

guṇa-pravāhe—in the current of the modes of material nature; *etasmin*—this; *kaḥ*—what; *śāpaḥ*—a curse; *kaḥ*—what; *nu*—indeed; *anugrahaḥ*—a favor; *kaḥ*—what; *svargaḥ*—elevation to heavenly planets; *narakaḥ*—hell; *kaḥ*—what; *vā*—or; *kim*—what; *sukham*—happiness; *duḥkham*—distress; *eva*—indeed; *vā*—or.

TRANSLATION

This material world resembles the waves of a constantly flowing river. Therefore, what is a curse and what is a favor? What are the heavenly planets, and what are the hellish planets? What is actually happiness, and what is actually distress? Because the waves flow constantly, none of them has an eternal effect.

PURPORT

Śrīla Bhaktivinoda Ṭhākura sings, *(miche) māyāra vaśe, yāccha bhese', khāccha hābuḍubu, bhāi:* "My dear living entities within this material world, why are you being carried away by the waves of the modes of material nature?" *(Jīva) kṛṣṇa-dāsa, ei viśvāsa, karle ta' āra duḥkha nāi:* "If the living entity tries to understand that he is an eternal servant of Kṛṣṇa, there will no longer be misery for him." Kṛṣṇa wants us to give up all other engagements and surrender unto Him. If we do so, where will the cause and effect of this material world be? There is nothing like cause and effect for the surrendered soul. Śrīla Viśvanātha Cakravartī Ṭhākura says in this regard that being put into this material world is like being thrown into a mine of salt. If one falls into a mine of salt, he tastes only salt wherever he goes. Similarly, this material world is full of miseries. The so-called temporary happiness of the world is also misery, but in ignorance we cannot understand this. That is the actual position. When one comes to his senses—when he becomes Kṛṣṇa conscious—he is no longer concerned with the various conditions of this material world. He is not concerned with happiness or distress, curses or favors, or heavenly or hellish planets. He sees no distinction between them.

TEXT 21

एकः सृजति भूतानि भगवानात्ममायया ।
एषां बन्धं च मोक्षं च सुखं दुःखं च निष्कलः ॥ २१ ॥

ekaḥ sṛjati bhūtāni
bhagavān ātma-māyayā
eṣāṁ bandhaṁ ca mokṣaṁ ca
sukhaṁ duḥkhaṁ ca niṣkalaḥ

ekaḥ—one; *sṛjati*—creates; *bhūtāni*—different varieties of living entities; *bhagavān*—the Supreme Personality of Godhead; *ātma-māyayā*—by His personal potencies; *eṣām*—of all the conditioned souls; *bandham*—the conditional life; *ca*—and; *mokṣam*—the liberated life; *ca*—also; *sukham*—happiness; *duḥkham*—distresses; *ca*—and; *niṣkalaḥ*—not affected by the material qualities.

TRANSLATION

The Supreme Personality of Godhead is one. Unaffected by the conditions of the material world, He creates all the conditioned souls by His own personal potency. Because of being contaminated by the material energy, the living entity is put into ignorance and thus into different conditions of bondage. Sometimes, by knowledge, the living entity is given liberation. In sattva-guṇa and rajo-guṇa, he is subjected to happiness and distress.

PURPORT

The question may be raised why the living entities are situated in different conditions and who has arranged this. The answer is that it has been done by the Supreme Personality of Godhead, without anyone's help. The Lord has His own energies (*parāsya śaktir vividhaiva śrūyate*), and one of them, namely the external energy, creates the material world and the varieties of happiness and distress for the conditioned souls under the supervision of the Lord. The material world consists of three modes of material nature—*sattva-guṇa, rajo-guṇa* and *tamo-guṇa. By sattva-guṇa* the Lord maintains the material world, by *rajo-guṇa* He creates it, and by *tamo-guṇa* He annihilates it. After the varieties of living entities are created, they are subject to happiness and distress according to their association. When they are in *sattva-guṇa,* the mode of goodness, they feel happiness, when in *rajo-guṇa* they are distressed, and when in *tamo-guṇa* they have no sense of what to do or what is right and wrong.

TEXT 22

न तस्य कश्चिद्दयितः प्रतीपो
न ज्ञातिबन्धुर्न परो न च स्वः ।
समस्य सर्वत्र निरञ्जनस्य
सुखे न रागः कुत एव रोषः ॥ २२ ॥

na tasya kaścid dayitaḥ pratīpo
na jñāti-bandhur na paro na ca svaḥ
samasya sarvatra nirañjanasya
sukhe na rāgaḥ kuta eva roṣaḥ

na—not; *tasya*—of Him (the Supreme Lord); *kaścit*—anyone; *dayitaḥ*—dear; *pratīpaḥ*—not dear; *na*—nor; *jñāti*—kinsman; *bandhuḥ*—friend; *na*—nor; *paraḥ*—other; *na*—nor; *ca*—also; *svaḥ*—own; *samasya*—who is equal; *sarvatra*—everywhere; *nirañjanasya*—without being affected by material nature; *sukhe*—in happiness; *na*—not; *rāgaḥ*—attachment; *kutaḥ*—from where; *eva*—indeed; *roṣaḥ*—anger.

TRANSLATION

The Supreme Personality of Godhead is equally disposed toward all living entities. Therefore no one is very dear to Him, and no one is a great enemy for Him; no one is His friend, and no one is His relative. Being unattached to the material world, He has no affection for so-called happiness or hatred for so-called distress. The two terms happiness and distress are relative. Since the Lord is always happy, for Him there is no question of distress.

TEXT 23

तथापि तच्छक्तिविसर्ग एषां
सुखाय दुःखाय हिताहिताय ।
बन्धाय मोक्षाय च मृत्युजन्मनोः
शरीरिणां संसृतयेऽवकल्पते ॥ २३ ॥

tathāpi tac-chakti-visarga eṣāṁ
sukhāya duḥkhāya hitāhitāya
bandhāya mokṣāya ca mṛtyu-janmanoḥ
śarīriṇāṁ saṁsṛtaye'vakalpate

tathāpi—still; *tat-śakti*—of the Lord's energy; *visargaḥ*—the creation; *eṣām*—of these (conditioned souls); *sukhāya*—for the happiness; *duḥkhāya*—for the distress; *hita-ahitāya*—for the profit and loss; *bandhāya*—for the bondage; *mokṣāya*—for the liberation; *ca*—also; *mṛtyu*—of death; *janmanoḥ*—and birth; *śarīriṇām*—of all those who accept material bodies; *saṁsṛtaye*—for the repetition; *avakalpate*—acts.

TRANSLATION

Although the Supreme Lord is unattached to our happiness and distress according to karma, and although no one is His enemy or favorite, He creates pious and impious activities through the agency of His material potency. Thus for the continuation of the materialistic way of life He creates happiness and distress, good fortune and bad, bondage and liberation, birth and death.

PURPORT

Although the Supreme Personality of Godhead is the ultimate doer of everything, in His original transcendental existence He is not responsible for the happiness and distress, or bondage and liberation, of the conditioned souls. These are due to the results of the fruitive activities of the living entities within this material world. By the order of a judge, one person is released from jail, and another is imprisoned, but the judge is not responsible, for the distress and happiness of these different people is due to their own activities. Although the government is ultimately the supreme authority, the justice is administered by the departments of the government, and the government is not responsible for the individual judgments. Therefore the government is equal to all the citizens. Similarly, the Supreme Lord is neutral to everyone, but for the maintenance of law and order His supreme government has various departments, which control the activities of the living entities. Another example given in this regard is that lilies open or close because of the sunshine, and thus the bumblebees enjoy or suffer, but the sunshine and the sun globe are not responsible for the happiness and distress of the bumblebees.

TEXT 24

अथ प्रसादये न त्वां शापमोक्षाय भामिनि।
यन्मन्यसे ह्यसाधूक्तं मम तत्क्षम्यतां सति ॥ २४॥

atha prasādaye na tvāṁ
śāpa-mokṣāya bhāmini
yan manyase hy asādhūktaṁ
mama tat kṣamyatāṁ sati

atha—therefore; *prasādaye*—I am trying to please; *na*—not; *tvām*—you; *śāpa-mokṣāya*—for being released from your curse; *bhāmini*—O most angry one; *yat*—which; *manyase*—you consider; *hi*—indeed; *asādhu-uktam*—improper speech; *mama*—my; *tat*—that; *kṣamyatām*—let it be excused; *sati*—O most chaste one.

TRANSLATION

O mother, you are now unnecessarily angry, but since all my happiness and distress are destined by my past activities, I do not plead to be excused or relieved from your curse. Although what I have said is not wrong, please let whatever you think is wrong be pardoned.

PURPORT

Being fully aware of how the results of one's *karma* accrue by the laws of nature, Citraketu did not want to be released from Pārvatī's curse. Nonetheless, he wanted to satisfy her because although his verdict was natural, she was displeased with him. As a matter of course, Mahārāja Citraketu begged pardon from Pārvatī.

TEXT 25

श्रीशुक उवाच

इति प्रसाद्य गिरिशौ चित्रकेतुररिन्दम ।
जगाम स्वविमानेन पश्यतोः स्मयतोस्तयोः ॥ २५॥

śrī-śuka uvāca
iti prasādya giriśau
citraketur arindama
jagāma sva-vimānena
paśyatoḥ smayatos tayoḥ

śrī-śukaḥ uvāca—Śrī Śukadeva Gosvāmī said; *iti*—thus; *prasādya*—after satisfying; *giriśau*—Lord Śiva and his wife, Pārvatī; *citraketuḥ*—King Citraketu; *arim-dama*—O King Parīkṣit, who are always able to subdue the enemy; *jagāma*—went away; *sva-vimānena*—by his own airplane; *paśyatoḥ*—were watching; *smayatoḥ*—were smiling; *tayoḥ*—while Lord Śiva and Pārvatī.

TRANSLATION

Śrī Śukadeva Gosvāmī continued: O King Parīkṣit, subduer of the enemy, after Citraketu satisfied Lord Śiva and his wife, Pārvatī, he boarded his airplane and left as they looked on. When Lord Śiva and Pārvatī saw that Citraketu, although informed of the curse, was unafraid, they smiled, being fully astonished by his behavior.

TEXT 26

ततस्तु भगवान् रुद्रो रुद्राणीमिदमब्रवीत् ।
देवर्षिदैत्यसिद्धानां पार्षदानां च शृण्वताम् ॥ २६ ॥

tatas tu bhagavān rudro
rudrāṇīm idam abravīt
devarṣi-daitya-siddhānāṁ
pārṣadānāṁ ca śṛṇvatām

tataḥ—thereafter; *tu*—then; *bhagavān*—the most powerful; *rudraḥ*—Lord Śiva; *rudrāṇīm*—unto his wife, Pārvatī; *idam*—this; *abravīt*—said; *devarṣi*—while the great sage Nārada; *daitya*—the demons; *siddhānām*—and the inhabitants of Siddhaloka, who are expert in yogic power; *pārṣadānām*—his personal associates; *ca*—also; *śṛṇvatām*—were listening.

TRANSLATION

Thereafter, in the presence of the great sage Nārada, the demons, the inhabitants of Siddhaloka, and his personal associates, Lord Śiva, who is most powerful, spoke to his wife, Pārvatī, while they all listened.

TEXT 27

श्रीरुद्र उवाच
दृष्टवत्यसि सुश्रोणि हरेरद्भुतकर्मणः ।
माहात्म्यं भृत्यभृत्यानां निःस्पृहाणां महात्मनाम् ॥ २७ ॥

śrī-rudra uvāca
dṛṣṭavaty asi suśroṇi
harer adbhuta-karmaṇaḥ
māhātmyaṁ bhṛtya-bhṛtyānāṁ
niḥspṛhāṇāṁ mahātmanām

śrī-rudraḥ uvāca—Lord Śiva said; *dṛṣṭavatī asi*—have you seen; *su-śroṇi*—O beautiful Pārvatī; *hareḥ*—of the Supreme Personality of Godhead; *adbhuta-karmaṇaḥ*—whose acts are wonderful; *māhātmyam*—the greatness; *bhṛtya-bhṛtyānām*—of the servants of the servants; *niḥspṛhāṇām*—who are without ambitions for sense gratification; *mahātmanām*—great souls.

TRANSLATION

Lord Śiva said: My dear beautiful Pārvatī, have you seen the greatness of the Vaiṣṇavas? Being servants of the servants of the Supreme Personality of Godhead, Hari, they are great souls and are not interested in any kind of material happiness.

PURPORT

Lord Śiva, the husband of Pārvatī, told his wife, "My dear Pārvatī, you are very beautiful in your bodily features. Certainly you are glorious. But I do not think that you can compete with the beauty and glory of devotees who have become servants of the servants of the Supreme Personality of Godhead." Of course, Lord Śiva smiled when he joked with his wife in that way, for others cannot speak like that. "The Supreme Lord," Śiva continued, "is always exalted in His activities, and here is another example of His wonderful influence upon King Citraketu, His devotee. Just see, although you cursed the King, he was not at all afraid or sorry. Rather, he offered respect to you, called you mother and accepted your curse, thinking himself faulty. He did not say anything in retaliation. This is the excellence of a devotee. By mildly tolerating your curse, he has certainly excelled the glory of your beauty and your power to curse him.

I can impartially judge that this devotee, Citraketu, has defeated you and your excellence simply by becoming a pure devotee of the Lord." As stated by Śrī Caitanya Mahāprabhu, *taror api sahiṣṇunā.* Just like a tree, a devotee can tolerate all kinds of curses and reversals in life. This is the excellence of a devotee. Indirectly, Lord Śiva forbade Pārvatī to commit the mistake of cursing a devotee like Citraketu. He indicated that although she was powerful, the King, without showing any power, had excelled her power by his tolerance.

TEXT 28

नारायणपराः सर्वे न कुतश्चन बिभ्यति ।
स्वर्गापवर्गनरकेष्वपि तुल्यार्थदर्शिनः ॥ २८ ॥

nārāyaṇa-parāḥ sarve
na kutaścana bibhyati
svargāpavarga-narakeṣv
api tulyārtha-darśinaḥ

nārāyaṇa-parāḥ—pure devotees, who are interested only in the service of Nārāyaṇa, the Supreme Personality of Godhead; *sarve*—all; *na*—not; *kutaścana*—anywhere; *bibhyati*—are afraid; *svarga*—in the higher planetary systems; *apavarga*—in liberation; *narakeṣu*—and in hell; *api*—even; *tulya*—equal; *artha*—value; *darśinaḥ*—who see.

TRANSLATION

Devotees solely engaged in the devotional service of the Supreme Personality of Godhead, Nārāyaṇa, never fear any condition of life. For them the heavenly planets, liberation and the hellish planets are all the same, for such devotees are interested only in the service of the Lord.

PURPORT

Pārvatī might naturally have inquired how devotees become so exalted. Therefore this verse explains that they are *nārāyaṇa-para,* simply dependent on Nārāyaṇa. They do not mind reverses in life because in the service of Nārāyaṇa they have learned to tolerate whatever hardships there may be. They do not care whether they are in heaven or in hell: they simply engage in the service of the Lord. This is their excellence. *Ānukūlyena kṛṣṇānuśīlanam:* they are liberally engaged in the service of the Lord, and therefore they are excellent. By using the word *bhṛtya-bhṛtyānām,* Lord Śiva pointed out that although Citraketu provided one example of tolerance and excellence, all the devotees who have taken shelter of the Lord as eternal servants are glorious. They have no eagerness to be happy by being placed in the heavenly planets, becoming liberated or becoming one with Brahman, the supreme effulgence. These benefits do not appeal to their minds. They are simply interested in giving direct service to the Lord.

TEXT 29

देहिनां देहसंयोगाद् द्वन्द्वानीश्वरलीलया ।
सुखं दुःखं मृतिर्जन्म शापोऽनुग्रह एव च ॥ २९ ॥

dehināṁ deha-saṁyogād
dvandvānīśvara-līlayā
sukhaṁ duḥkhaṁ mṛtir janma
śāpo'nugraha eva ca

dehinām—of all those who have accepted material bodies; *deha-saṁyogāt*—because of contact with the material body; *dvandvāni*—dualities; *īśvara-līlayā*—by the supreme will of the Lord; *sukham*—happiness; *duḥkham*—distress; *mṛtiḥ*—death; *janma*—birth; *śāpaḥ*—curse; *anugrahaḥ*—favor; *eva*—certainly; *ca*—and.

TRANSLATION

Because of the actions of the Supreme Lord's external energy, the living entities are conditioned in contact with material bodies. The dualities of happiness and distress, birth and death, curses and favors, are natural by-products of this contact in the material world.

PURPORT

In *Bhagavad-gītā* we find, *mayādhyakṣeṇa prakṛtiḥ sūyate sa-carācaram:* the material world works under the direction of the goddess Durgā, the material energy of the Lord, but she acts under the direction of the Supreme Personality of Godhead. This is also confirmed in the *Brahma-saṁhitā* (5.44):

sṛṣṭi-sthiti-pralaya-sādhana-śaktir ekā
chāyeva yasya bhuvanāni bibharti durgā

Durgā—the goddess Pārvatī, the wife of Lord Śiva—is extremely powerful. She can create, maintain and annihilate any number of universes by her sweet will, but she acts under the direction of the Supreme Personality of Godhead, Kṛṣṇa, not independently. Kṛṣṇa is impartial, but because this is the material world of duality, such relative terms as happiness and distress, curses and favors, are created by the will of the Supreme. Those who are not *nārāyaṇa-para,* pure devotees, must be disturbed by this duality of the material world, whereas devotees who are simply attached to the service of the Lord are not at all disturbed by it. For example, Haridāsa Ṭhākura was beaten with cane in twenty-two bazaars, but he was never disturbed; instead, he smilingly tolerated the beating. Despite the disturbing dualities of the material world, devotees are not disturbed at all. Because they fix their minds on the lotus feet of the Lord and concentrate on the holy name of the Lord, they do not feel the so-called pains and pleasures caused by the dualities of this material world.

TEXT 30

अविवेककृतः पुंसो ह्यर्थभेद इवात्मनि ।
गुणदोषविकल्पश्च भिदेव स्रजिवत्कृतः ॥ ३० ॥

aviveka-kṛtaḥ puṁso
hy artha-bheda ivātmani
guṇa-doṣa-vikalpaś ca
bhid eva srajivat kṛtaḥ

aviveka-kṛtaḥ—done in ignorance, without mature consideration; *puṁsaḥ*—of the living entity; *hi*—indeed; *artha-bhedaḥ*—differentiation of value; *iva*—like; *ātmani*—in himself; *guṇa-doṣa*—of quality and fault; *vikalpaḥ*—imagination; *ca*—and; *bhit*—difference; *eva*—certainly; *sraji*—in a garland; *vat*—like; *kṛtaḥ*—made.

TRANSLATION

As one mistakenly considers a flower garland to be a snake or experiences happiness and distress in a dream, so, in the material world, by a lack of careful consideration, we differentiate between happiness and distress, considering one good and the other bad.

PURPORT

The happiness and distress of the material world of duality are both mistaken ideas. In the *Caitanya-caritāmṛta* (*Antya* 4.176) it is said:

"dvaite" bhadrābhadra-jñāna, saba—"manodharma"
"ei bhāla, ei manda",—ei saba "bhrama"

The distinctions between happiness and distress in the material world of duality are simply mental concoctions, for the so-called happiness and distress are actually one and the same. They are like the happiness and distress in dreams. A sleeping man creates his happiness and distress by dreaming, although actually they have no existence.

The other example given in this verse is that a flower garland is originally very nice, but by mistake, for want of mature knowledge, one may consider it a snake. In this connection there is a statement by Prabodhānanda Sarasvatī: *viśvaṁ pūrṇa-sukhāyate.* Everyone in this material world is distressed by miserable conditions, but Śrīla Prabodhānanda Sarasvatī says that this world is full of happiness. How is this possible? He answers, *yat-kāruṇya-kaṭākṣa-vaibhavavatāṁ taṁ gauram eva stumaḥ.* A devotee accepts the distress of this material world as happiness only due to the causeless mercy of Śrī Caitanya Mahāprabhu. By His personal behavior, Śrī Caitanya Mahāprabhu showed that He was never distressed but always happy in chanting the Hare Kṛṣṇa *mahā-mantra.* One should follow in the footsteps of Śrī Caitanya Mahāprabhu and engage constantly in chanting the *mahā-mantra*—Hare Kṛṣṇa, Hare Kṛṣṇa, Kṛṣṇa Kṛṣṇa, Hare Hare/ Hare Rāma, Hare Rāma, Rāma Rāma, Hare Hare. Then he will never feel the distresses of the world of duality. In any condition of life one will be happy if he chants the holy name of the Lord.

In dreams we sometimes enjoy eating sweet rice and sometimes suffer as if one of our beloved family members had died. Because the same mind and body exist in the same material world of duality when we are awake, the so-called happiness and distress of this world are no better than the false, superficial happiness of dreams. The mind is the via medium in both dreams and wakefulness, and everything created by the mind in terms of *saṅkalpa* and *vikalpa,* acceptance and rejection, is called *manodharma,* or mental concoction.

TEXT 31

वासुदेवे भगवति भक्तिमुद्वहतां नृणाम् ।
ज्ञानवैराग्यवीर्याणां न हि कश्चिद् व्यपाश्रयः ॥ ३१ ॥

vāsudeve bhagavati
bhaktim udvahatāṁ nṛṇām

jñāna-vairāgya-vīryāṇāṁ
na hi kaścid vyapāśrayaḥ

vāsudeve—to Lord Vāsudeva, Kṛṣṇa; *bhagavati*—the Supreme Personality of Godhead; *bhaktim*—love and faith in devotional service; *udvahatām*—for those who are carrying; *nṛṇām*—men; *jñāna-vairāgya*—of real knowledge and detachment; *vīryāṇām*—possessing the powerful strength; *na*—not; *hi*—indeed; *kaścit*—anything; *vyapāśrayaḥ*—as interest or shelter.

TRANSLATION

Persons engaged in devotional service to Lord Vāsudeva, Kṛṣṇa, have naturally perfect knowledge and detachment from this material world. Therefore such devotees are not interested in the so-called happiness or so-called distress of this world.

PURPORT

Here is the distinction between a devotee and a philosopher who speculates on the subject matter of transcendence. A devotee does not need to cultivate knowledge to understand the falsity or temporary existence of this material world. Because of his unalloyed devotion to Vāsudeva, this knowledge and detachment are automatically manifested in his person. As confirmed elsewhere in *Śrīmad-Bhāgavatam* (1.2.7):

vāsudeve bhagavati
bhakti-yogaḥ prayojitaḥ
janayaty āśu vairāgyaṁ
jñānaṁ ca yad ahaitukam

One who engages in unalloyed devotional service to Vāsudeva, Kṛṣṇa, automatically becomes aware of this material world, and therefore he is naturally detached. This detachment is possible because of his high standard of knowledge. The speculative philosopher tries to understand that this material world is false by cultivating knowledge, but this understanding is automatically manifested in the person of a devotee, without separate endeavor. The Māyāvādī philosophers may be very proud of their so-called knowledge, but because they do not understand Vāsudeva (*vāsudevaḥ sarvam iti*), they do not understand the world of duality, which is a manifestation of Vāsudeva's external energy. Therefore, unless the so-called *jñānīs* take shelter of Vāsudeva, their speculative knowledge is imperfect. *Ye'nye'ravindākṣa vimukta-māninaḥ.* They simply think of becoming free from the contamination of the material world, but because they do not take shelter at the lotus feet of Vāsudeva, their knowledge is impure. When they actually become pure, they surrender to the lotus feet of Vāsudeva. Therefore, the Absolute Truth is easier to understand for a devotee than for *jñānīs* who simply speculate to understand Vāsudeva. Lord Śiva confirms this statement in the following verse.

TEXT 32

नाहं विरिञ्चो न कुमारनारदौ
न ब्रह्मपुत्रा मुनयः सुरेशाः ।
विदाम यस्येहितमंशकांशका
न तत्स्वरूपं पृथगीशमानिनः ॥ ३२ ॥

nāhaṁ viriñco na kumāra-nāradau
na brahma-putrā munayaḥ sureśāḥ
vidāma yasyehitam aṁśakāṁśakā
na tat-svarūpaṁ pṛthag-īśa-māninaḥ

na—not; *aham*—I (Lord Śiva); *viriñcaḥ*—Lord Brahmā; *na*—nor; *kumāra*—the Aśvinī-kumāras; *nāradau*—the great saint Nārada; *na*—nor; *brahma-putrāḥ*—the sons of Lord Brahmā; *munayaḥ*—great saintly persons; *sura-īśāḥ*—all the great demigods; *vidāma*—know; *yasya*—of whom; *īhitam*—activity; *aṁśaka-aṁśakāḥ*—those who are parts of the parts; *na*—not; *tat*—His; *sva-rūpam*—real personality; *pṛthak*—separate; *īśa*—rulers; *māninaḥ*—who consider ourselves to be.

TRANSLATION

Neither I [Lord Śiva], nor Brahmā, nor the Aśvinī-kumāras, nor Nārada or the other great sages who are Brahmā's sons, nor even the demigods can understand the pastimes and personality of the Supreme Lord. Although we are part of the Supreme Lord, we consider ourselves independent, separate controllers, and thus we cannot understand His identity.

PURPORT

Brahma-saṁhitā (5.33) states:

advaitam acyutam anādim ananta-rūpam
ādyaṁ purāṇa-puruṣaṁ nava-yauvanaṁ ca

vedeṣu durlabham adurlabham ātma-bhaktau
govindam ādi-puruṣaṁ tam ahaṁ bhajāmi

"I worship the Supreme Personality of Godhead, Govinda, who is the original person. He is absolute, infallible and beginningless, and although expanded into unlimited forms, He is still the same original person, the oldest person, who always appears as a fresh youth. The eternal, blissful, all-knowing forms of the Lord cannot be understood even by the best Vedic scholars, but they are always manifest to pure, unalloyed devotees." Lord Śiva places himself as one of the nondevotees, who cannot understand the identity of the Supreme Lord. The Lord, being *ananta,* has an unlimited number of forms. Therefore, how is it possible for an ordinary, common man to understand Him? Lord Śiva, of course, is above the ordinary human beings, yet he is unable to understand the Supreme Personality of Godhead. Lord Śiva is not among the ordinary living entities, nor is he in the category of Lord Viṣṇu. He is between Lord Viṣṇu and the common living entity.

TEXT 33

न ह्यस्यास्ति प्रियः कश्चिन्नाप्रियः स्वः परोऽपि वा।
आत्मत्वात्सर्वभूतानां सर्वभूतप्रियो हरिः ॥ ३३ ॥

na hy asyāsti priyaḥ kaścin
nāpriyaḥ svaḥ paro'pi vā
ātmatvāt sarva-bhūtānāṁ
sarva-bhūta-priyo hariḥ

na—not; *hi*—indeed; *asya*—of the Lord; *asti*—there is; *priyaḥ*—very dear; *kaścit*—anyone; *na*—nor; *apriyaḥ*—not dear; *svaḥ*—own; *paraḥ*—other; *api*—even; *vā*—or; *ātmatvāt*—due to being the soul of the soul; *sarva-bhūtānām*—of all living entities; *sarva-bhūta*—to all living entities; *priyaḥ*—very, very dear; *hariḥ*—Lord Hari.

TRANSLATION

He holds no one as very dear and no one as inimical. He has no one for His own relative, and no one is alien to Him. He is actually the soul of the soul of all living entities. Thus He is the auspicious friend of all living beings and is very near and dear to all of them.

PURPORT

The Supreme Personality of Godhead, in His second feature, is the Supersoul of all living entities. As one's self is extremely dear, the Superself of the self is still more dear. No one can be the enemy of the friendly Superself, who is equal to everyone. Relationships of dearness or enmity between the Supreme Lord and the living beings are due to the intervention of the illusory energy. Because the three modes of material nature intervene between the Lord and the living beings, these different relationships appear. Actually, the living entity in his pure condition is always very near and dear to the Lord, and the Lord is dear to him. There is no question of partiality or enmity.

TEXTS 34–35

तस्य चायं महाभागश्चित्रकेतुः प्रियोऽनुगः ।
सर्वत्र समदृक् शान्तो ह्यहं चैवाच्युतप्रियः ॥ ३४ ॥
तस्मान्न विस्मयः कार्यः पुरुषेषु महात्मसु ।
महापुरुषभक्तेषु शान्तेषु समदर्शिषु ॥ ३५ ॥

tasya cāyaṁ mahā-bhāgaś
citraketuḥ priyo'nugaḥ
sarvatra sama-dṛk śānto
hy ahaṁ caivācyuta-priyaḥ

tasmān na vismayaḥ kāryaḥ
puruṣeṣu mahātmasu
mahāpuruṣa-bhakteṣu
śānteṣu sama-darśiṣu

tasya—of Him (the Lord); *ca*—and; *ayam*—this; *mahā-bhāgaḥ*—the most fortunate; *citraketuḥ*—King Citraketu; *priyaḥ*—beloved; *anugaḥ*—most obedient servant; *sarvatra*—everywhere; *sama-dṛk*—sees equally; *śāntaḥ*—very peaceful; *hi*—indeed; *aham*—I; *ca*—also; *eva*—certainly; *acyuta-priyaḥ*—very dear to Lord Kṛṣṇa, who never fails; *tasmāt*—therefore; *na*—no; *vismayaḥ*—wonder; *kāryaḥ*—to be done; *puruṣeṣu*—among persons; *mahā-ātmasu*—who are exalted souls; *mahā-puruṣa-bhakteṣu*—devotees of Lord Viṣṇu; *śānteṣu*—peaceful; *sama-darśiṣu*—equal to everyone.

TRANSLATION

This magnanimous Citraketu is a dear devotee of the Lord. He is equal to all living entities and is free from attachment and hatred. Similarly, I am also very dear to Lord Nārāyaṇa. Therefore, no one should be astonished to see the activities of the most exalted devotees of Nārāyaṇa, for they are free from attachment and envy. They are always peaceful, and they are equal to everyone.

PURPORT

It is said, *vaiṣṇavera kriyā, mudrā vijñeha nā bujhaya:* one should not be astonished to see the activities of exalted, liberated Vaiṣṇavas. As one should not be misled by the activities of the Supreme Personality of Godhead, one should also not be misled by the activities of His devotees. Both the Lord and His devotees are liberated. They are on the same platform, the only difference being that the Lord is the master and the devotees are servants. Qualitatively, they are one and the same. In *Bhagavad-gītā* (9.29) the Lord says:

samo 'haṁ sarva-bhūteṣu
na me dveṣyo 'sti na priyaḥ
ye bhajanti tu māṁ bhaktyā
mayi te teṣu cāpy aham

"I envy no one, nor am I partial to anyone. I am equal to all. But whoever renders service unto Me in devotion is a friend, is in Me, and I am also a friend to him." From this statement by the Supreme Personality of Godhead, it is clear that the devotees of the Lord are always extremely dear to Him. In effect, Lord Śiva told Pārvatī, "Both Citraketu and I are always very dear to the Supreme Lord. In other words, both he and I are on the same level as servants of the Lord. We are always friends, and sometimes we enjoy joking words between us. When Citraketu loudly laughed at my behavior, he did so on friendly terms, and therefore there was no reason to curse him." Thus Lord Śiva tried to convince his wife, Pārvatī, that her cursing of Citraketu was not very sensible.

Here is a difference between male and female that exists even in the higher statuses of life—in fact, even between Lord Śiva and his wife. Lord Śiva could understand Citraketu very nicely, but Pārvatī could not. Thus even in the higher statuses of life there is a difference between the understanding of a male and that of a female. It may be clearly said that the understanding of a woman is always inferior to the understanding of a man. In the Western countries there is now agitation to the effect that man and woman should be considered equal, but from this verse it appears that woman is always less intelligent than man.

It is clear that Citraketu wanted to criticize the behavior of his friend Lord Śiva because Lord Śiva was sitting with his wife on his lap. Then, too, Lord Śiva wanted to criticize Citraketu for externally posing as a great devotee but being interested in enjoying with the Vidyādharī women. These were all friendly jokes; there was nothing serious for which Citraketu should have been cursed by Pārvatī. Upon hearing the instructions of Lord Śiva, Pārvatī must have been very much ashamed for cursing Citraketu to become a demon. Mother Pārvatī could not appreciate Citraketu's position, and therefore she cursed him, but when she understood the instructions of Lord Śiva she was ashamed.

TEXT 36

श्रीशुक उवाच
इति श्रुत्वा भगवतः शिवस्योमाभिभाषितम्।
बभूव शान्तधी राजन् देवी विगतविस्मया ॥ ३६ ॥

śrī-śuka uvāca
iti śrutvā bhagavataḥ
śivasyomābhibhāṣitam
babhūva śānta-dhī rājan
devī vigata-vismayā

śrī-śukaḥ uvāca—Śrī Śukadeva Gosvāmī said; *iti*—thus; *śrutvā*—hearing; *bhagavataḥ*—of the most powerful demigod; *śivasya*—of Lord Śiva; *umā*—Pārvatī; *abhibhāṣitam*—instruction; *babhūva*—became; *śānta-dhīḥ*—very peaceful; *rājan*—O King Parīkṣit; *devī*—the goddess; *vigata-vismayā*—released from astonishment.

TRANSLATION

Śrī Śukadeva Gosvāmī said: O King, after hearing this speech by her husband, the demigoddess [Umā, the wife of Lord Śiva] gave up her astonishment at the behavior of King Citraketu and became steady in intelligence.

PURPORT

Śrīla Viśvanātha Cakravartī Ṭhākura remarks that the word *śānta-dhīḥ* means *svīya-pūrva-svabhāva-smṛtyā.* When Pārvatī remembered her former behavior in cursing Citraketu, she became very much ashamed and covered her face with the skirt of her sari, admitting that she was wrong in cursing Citraketu.

TEXT 37

इति भागवतो देव्याः प्रतिशप्तुमलन्तमः ।
मूर्ध्ना स जगृहे शापमेतावत्साधुलक्षणम् ॥ ३७ ॥

iti bhāgavato devyāḥ
pratiśaptum alantamaḥ
mūrdhnā sa jagṛhe śāpam
etāvat sādhu-lakṣaṇam

iti—thus; *bhāgavataḥ*—the most exalted devotee; *devyāḥ*—of Pārvatī; *pratiśaptum*—to make a counter-curse; *alantamaḥ*—able in all respects; *mūrdhnā*—with his head; *saḥ*—he (Citraketu); *jagṛhe*—accepted; *śāpam*—the curse; *etāvat*—this much; *sādhu-lakṣaṇam*—the symptom of a devotee.

TRANSLATION

The great devotee Citraketu was so powerful that he was quite competent to curse mother Pārvatī in retaliation, but instead of doing so he very humbly accepted the curse and bowed his head before Lord Śiva and his wife. This is very much to be appreciated as the standard behavior of a Vaiṣṇava.

PURPORT

Upon being informed by Lord Śiva, mother Pārvatī could understand that she was wrong in cursing Citraketu. King Citraketu was so exalted in his character that in spite of being wrongly cursed by Pārvatī, he immediately descended from his airplane and bowed his head before the mother, accepting her curse. This has already been explained: *nārāyaṇa-parāḥ sarve na kutaścana bibhyati.* Citraketu very sportingly felt that since the mother wanted to curse him, he could accept this curse just to please her. This is called *sādhu-lakṣaṇam,* the characteristic of a *sādhu,* or a devotee. As explained by Śrī Caitanya Mahāprabhu, *tṛṇād api sunīcena taror api sahiṣṇunā.* A devotee should always be very humble and meek and should offer all respect to others, especially to superiors. Being protected by the Supreme Personality of Godhead, a devotee is always powerful, but a devotee does not wish to show his power unnecessarily. However, when a less intelligent person has some power, he wants to use it for sense gratification. This is not the behavior of a devotee.

TEXT 38

जज्ञे त्वष्टुर्दक्षिणाग्नौ दानवीं योनिमाश्रितः ।
वृत्र इत्यभिविख्यातो ज्ञानविज्ञानसंयुतः ॥ ३८ ॥

jajñe tvaṣṭur dakṣiṇāgnau
dānavīṁ yonim āśritaḥ
vṛtra ity abhivikhyāto
jñāna-vijñāna-saṁyutaḥ

jajñe—was born; *tvaṣṭuḥ*—of the *brāhmaṇa* known as Tvaṣṭā; *dakṣiṇa-agnau*—in the fire sacrifice known as *dakṣiṇāgni; dānavīm*—demoniac; *yonim*—species of life; *āśritaḥ*—taking shelter of; *vṛtraḥ*—Vṛtra; *iti*—thus; *abhivikhyātaḥ*—celebrated; *jñāna-vijñāna-saṁyutaḥ*—fully equipped with transcendental knowledge and practical application of that knowledge in life.

TRANSLATION

Being cursed by mother Durgā [Bhavānī, the wife of Lord Śiva], that same Citraketu accepted birth in a demoniac species of life. Although still fully equipped with transcendental knowledge and practical application of that knowledge in life, he appeared as a demon at the fire sacrifice performed by Tvaṣṭā, and thus he became famous as Vṛtrāsura.

PURPORT

The word *yoni* is generally understood to mean *jāti*—family, group or species. Although Vṛtrāsura appeared in a family of demons, it is clearly said that his knowledge of spiritual life still existed. *Jñāna-vijñāna-saṁyutaḥ:* his spiritual knowledge and the practical application of that knowledge in life were not lost. Therefore it is said that even if a devotee falls down for some reason, he is still not lost.

yatra kva vābhadram abhūd amuṣya kiṁ
ko vārtha āpto'bhajatāṁ sva-dharmataḥ
(Bhāg. 1.5.17)

Once one is advanced in devotional service, his spiritual assets are never lost under any circumstances. Whatever spiritual advancement he has achieved continues. This is confirmed in *Bhagavad-gītā.* Even if a *bhakti-yogī* falls, he takes birth in a rich family or family of *brāhmaṇas,* in which he again starts devotional activities from the point where he left off. Although Vṛtrāsura was known as an *asura,* or demon, he did not lose his consciousness of Kṛṣṇa or devotional service.

TEXT 39

एतत्ते सर्वमाख्यातं यन्मां त्वं परिपृच्छसि ।
वृत्रस्यासुरजातेश्च कारणं भगवन्मतेः ॥ ३९ ॥

etat te sarvam ākhyātaṁ
yan māṁ tvaṁ paripṛcchasi
vṛtrasyāsura-jāteś ca
kāraṇaṁ bhagavan-mateḥ

etat—this; *te*—unto you; *sarvam*—all; *ākhyātam*—explained; *yat*—which; *mām*—me; *tvam*—you; *paripṛcchasi*—asked; *vṛtrasya*—of Vṛtrāsura; *asura-jāteḥ*—whose birth was in a species of *asuras; ca*—and; *kāraṇam*—the cause; *bhagavat-mateḥ*—of exalted intelligence in Kṛṣṇa consciousness.

TRANSLATION

My dear King Parīkṣit, you inquired from me how Vṛtrāsura, a great devotee, took birth in a demoniac family. Thus I have tried to explain to you everything about this.

TEXT 40

इतिहासमिमं पुण्यं चित्रकेतोर्महात्मनः ।
माहात्म्यं विष्णुभक्तानां श्रुत्वा बन्धाद्विमुच्यते ॥ ४० ॥

itihāsam imaṁ puṇyaṁ
citraketor mahātmanaḥ
māhātmyaṁ viṣṇu-bhaktānāṁ
śrutvā bandhād vimucyate

itihāsam—history; *imam*—this; *puṇyam*—very pious; *citraketoḥ*—of Citraketu; *mahā-ātmanaḥ*—the exalted devotee; *māhātmyam*—containing glory; *viṣṇu-bhaktānām*—from the devotees of Viṣṇu; *śrutvā*—hearing; *bandhāt*—from bondage or conditional, material life; *vimucyate*—is freed.

TRANSLATION

Citraketu was a great devotee [mahātmā]. If one hears this history of Citraketu from a pure devotee, the listener also is freed from the conditional life of material existence.

PURPORT

The historical incidents in the *Purāṇas,* such as the history of Citraketu explained in the *Bhāgavata Purāṇa,* are sometimes misunderstood by outsiders, or nondevotees. Therefore Śukadeva Gosvāmī advised that the history of Citraketu be heard from a devotee. Anything about devotional service or the characteristics of the Lord and His devotees must be heard from a devotee, not from a professional reciter. This is advised herein. Śrī Caitanya Mahāprabhu's secretary also advised that one learn the history of *Śrīmad-Bhāgavatam* from a devotee: *yāha, bhāgavata pada vaiṣṇavera sthāne.* One should not hear the statements of *Śrīmad-Bhāgavatam* from professional reciters, or else they will not be effective. Quoting from *Padma Purāṇa,* Śrī Sanātana Gosvāmī has strictly forbidden us to hear about the activities of the Lord and His devotees from the mouths of nondevotees:

avaiṣṇava-mukhodgīrṇaṁ
pūtaṁ hari-kathāmṛtam
śravaṇaṁ naiva kartavyaṁ
sarpocchiṣṭaṁ yathā payaḥ

"One should not hear anything about Kṛṣṇa from a non-Vaiṣṇava. Milk touched by the lips of a serpent has poisonous effects; similarly, talks about Kṛṣṇa given by a non-Vaiṣṇava are also poisonous." One must be a bona fide devotee, and then he can preach and impress devotional service upon his listeners.

TEXT 41

य एतत्प्रातरुत्थाय श्रद्धया वाग्यतः पठेत् ।
इतिहासं हरिं स्मृत्वा स याति परमां गतिम् ॥ ४१ ॥

ya etat prātar utthāya
śraddhayā vāg-yataḥ paṭhet
itihāsaṁ hariṁ smṛtvā
sa yāti paramāṁ gatim

yaḥ—any person who; *etat*—this; *prātaḥ*—early in the morning; *utthāya*—rising; *śraddhayā*—with faith; *vāk-yataḥ*—controlling the mind and words; *paṭhet*—may read; *itihāsam*—history; *harim*—the Supreme Lord; *smṛtvā*—remembering; *saḥ*—that person; *yāti*—goes; *paramām gatim*—back home, back to Godhead.

TRANSLATION

One who rises from bed early in the morning and recites this history of Citraketu, controlling his words and mind and remembering the Supreme Personality of Godhead, will return home, back to Godhead, without difficulty.

Thus end the Bhaktivedanta purports of the Sixth Canto, Seventeenth Chapter, of the Śrīmad-Bhāgavatam *entitled, "Mother Pārvatī Curses Citraketu."*

CHAPTER EIGHTEEN

Diti Vows to Kill King Indra

This chapter gives the history of Diti, the wife of Kaśyapa, and how she followed a vow to have a son who would kill Indra. It also describes how Indra attempted to foil her plan by cutting to pieces the son within her womb.

In relation to Tvaṣṭā and his descendants, there is a description of the dynasty of the Ādityas (sons of Aditi) and other demigods. Pṛśni, the wife of Aditi's fifth son named Savitā, had three daughters—Sāvitrī, Vyāhṛti and Trayī—and very exalted sons named Agnihotra, Paśu, Soma, Cātur-māsya and the five Mahāyajñas. Siddhi, the wife of Bhaga, had three sons, named Mahimā, Vibhu and Prabhu, and she also had one daughter, whose name was Āśī. Dhātā had four wives—Kuhū, Sinīvālī, Rākā and Anumati—who had four sons, named Sāyam, Darśa, Prātaḥ and Pūrṇa-māsa respectively. Kriyā, the wife of Vidhātā, gave birth to the five Purīṣyas, who are representatives of five kinds of fire gods. Bhṛgu, the mind-born son of Brahmā, took his birth again from Carṣaṇī, the wife of Varuṇa, and the great sage Vālmīki appeared from Varuṇa's semen. Agastya and Vasiṣṭha were two sons of Varuṇa and Mitra. Upon seeing the beauty of Urvaśī, Mitra and Varuṇa discharged semen, which they kept in an earthen pot. From that pot, Agastya and Vasiṣṭha appeared. Mitra had a wife named Revatī, who gave birth to three sons—Utsarga, Ariṣṭa and Pippala. Aditi had twelve sons, of whom Indra was the eleventh. Indra's wife was named Paulomī (Śacīdevī). She gave birth to three sons—Jayanta, Ṛṣabha and Mīḍhuṣa. By His own powers, the Supreme Personality of Godhead appeared as Vāmana-deva. From His wife, whose name was Kīrti, appeared a son named Bṛhatśloka. Bṛhatśloka's first son was known as Saubhaga. This is a description of the sons of Aditi. A description of Āditya Urukrama, who is an incarnation of the Supreme Personality of Godhead, will be offered in the Eighth Canto.

The demons born of Diti are also described in this chapter. In the dynasty of Diti appeared the great saintly devotee Prahlāda and also Bali, Prahlāda's grandson. Hiraṇyakaśipu and Hiraṇyākṣa were the first sons of Diti. Hiraṇyakaśipu and his wife, whose name was Kayādhu, had four sons—Saṁhlāda, Anuhlāda, Hlāda and Prahlāda. They also had one daughter, whose name was Siṁhikā. In association with the demon Vipracit, Siṁhikā bore a son named Rāhu, whose head was severed by the Supreme

Personality of Godhead. Kṛti, the wife of Saṁhlāda, bore a son named Pañcajana. Hlāda's wife, whose name was Dhamani, gave birth to two sons—Vātāpi and Ilvala. Ilvala put Vātāpi into the form of a ram and gave him to Agastya to eat. Anuhlāda, in the womb of his wife, Sūryā, begot two sons, named Bāṣkala and Mahiṣa. Prahlāda's son was known as Virocana, and his grandson was known as Bali Mahārāja. Bali Mahārāja had one hundred sons, of whom Bāṇa was the eldest.

After describing the dynasty of the Ādityas and the other demigods, Śukadeva Gosvāmī describes Diti's sons known as the Maruts and how they were elevated to the position of demigods. Just to help Indra, Lord Viṣṇu had killed Hiraṇyākṣa and Hiraṇyakaśipu. Because of this, Diti was very envious, and she was eager to have a son who could kill Indra. By her service, she enchanted Kaśyapa Muni in order to beg from him a greater son to do this. In corroboration of the Vedic injunction *vidvāṁsam api karṣati,* Kaśyapa Muni was attracted to his beautiful wife and promised to grant her any request. When, however, she requested a son who would kill Indra, he condemned himself, and he advised his wife Diti to follow the Vaiṣṇava ritualistic ceremonies to purify herself. When Diti, following the instructions of Kaśyapa, engaged in devotional service, Indra could understand her purpose, and he began observing all her activities. One day, Indra had the opportunity to see her deviating from devotional service. Thus he entered her womb and cut her son into forty-nine parts. In this way the forty-nine kinds of air known as the Maruts appeared, but because Diti had performed the Vaiṣṇava ritualistic ceremonies, all the sons became Vaiṣṇavas.

TEXT 1

श्रीशुक उवाच
पृश्निस्तु पत्नी सवितुः सावित्रीं व्याहृतिं त्रयीम् ।
अग्निहोत्रं पशुं सोमं चातुर्मास्यं महामखान् ॥ १ ॥

śrī-śuka uvāca
pṛśnis tu patnī savituḥ
sāvitrīṁ vyāhṛtiṁ trayīm
agnihotraṁ paśuṁ somaṁ
cātur-māsyaṁ mahā-makhān

śrī-śukaḥ uvāca—Śrī Śukadeva Gosvāmī said; *pṛśniḥ*—Pṛśni; *tu*—then; *patnī*—wife; *savituḥ*—of Savitā; *sāvitrīm*—Sāvitrī; *vyāhṛtim*—Vyāhṛti; *trayīm*

—Trayī; *agnihotram*—Agnihotra; *paśum*—Paśu; *somam*—Soma; *cātur-māsyam*—Cātur-māsya; *mahā-makhān*—the five Mahāyajñas.

TRANSLATION

Śrī Śukadeva Gosvāmī said: Pṛśni, who was the wife of Savitā, the fifth of the twelve sons of Aditi, gave birth to three daughters—Sāvitrī, Vyāhṛti and Trayī—and the sons named Agnihotra, Paśu, Soma, Cātur-māsya and the five Mahāyajñas.

TEXT 2

सिद्धिर्भगस्य भार्याङ्ग महिमानं विभुं प्रभुम्।
आशिषं च वरारोहां कन्यां प्रासूत सुव्रताम्॥ २॥

siddhir bhagasya bhāryāṅga
mahimānaṁ vibhuṁ prabhum
āśiṣaṁ ca varārohāṁ
kanyāṁ prāsūta suvratām

siddhiḥ—Siddhi; *bhagasya*—of Bhaga; *bhāryā*—the wife; *aṅga*—my dear King; *mahimānam*—Mahimā; *vibhum*—Vibhu; *prabhum*—Prabhu; *āśiṣam*—Āśī; *ca*—and; *varārohām*—very beautiful; *kanyām*—daughter; *prāsūta*—bore; *su-vratām*—virtuous.

TRANSLATION

O King, Siddhi, who was the wife of Bhaga, the sixth son of Aditi, bore three sons, named Mahimā, Vibhu and Prabhu, and one extremely beautiful daughter, whose name was Āśī.

TEXTS 3–4

धातुः कुहूः सिनीवाली राका चानुमतिस्तथा ।
सायं दर्शमथ प्रातः पूर्णमासमनुक्रमात् ॥ ३॥
अग्नीन् पुरीष्यानाधत्त क्रियायां समनन्तरः ।
चर्षणी वरुणस्यासीद्यस्यां जातो भृगुः पुनः ॥ ४॥

dhātuḥ kuhūḥ sinīvālī
rākā cānumatis tathā
sāyaṁ darśam atha prātaḥ
pūrṇa-māsam anukramāt

agnīn purīṣyān ādhatta
kriyāyāṁ samanantaraḥ
carṣaṇī varuṇasyāsīd
yasyāṁ jāto bhṛguḥ punaḥ

dhātuḥ—of Dhātā; *kuhūḥ*—Kuhū; *sinīvālī*—Sinīvālī; *rākā*—Rākā; *ca*—and; *anumatiḥ*—Anumati; *tathā*—also; *sāyam*—Sāyam; *darśam*—Darśa; *atha*—also; *prātaḥ*—Prātaḥ; *pūrṇa-māsam*—Pūrṇa-māsa; *anukramāt*—respectively; *agnīn*—fire gods; *purīṣyān*—called the Purīṣyas; *ādhatta*—begot; *kriyāyām*—in Kriyā; *samanantaraḥ*—the next son, Vidhātā; *carṣaṇī*—Carṣaṇī; *varuṇasya*—of Varuṇa; *āsīt*—was; *yasyām*—in whom; *jātaḥ*—took birth; *bhṛguḥ*—Bhṛgu; *punaḥ*—again.

TRANSLATION

Dhātā, the seventh son of Aditi, had four wives, named Kuhū, Sinīvālī, Rākā and Anumati. These wives begot four sons, named Sāyam, Darśa, Prātaḥ and Pūrṇa-māsa respectively. The wife of Vidhātā, the eighth son of Aditi, was named Kriyā. In her Vidhātā begot the five fire gods named the Purīṣyas. The wife of Varuṇa, the ninth son of Aditi, was named Carṣaṇī. Bhṛgu, the son of Brahmā, took birth again in her womb.

TEXT 5

वाल्मीकिश्च महायोगी वल्मीकादभवत्किल ।
अगस्त्यश्च वसिष्ठश्च मित्रावरुणयोर्ऋषी ॥ ५ ॥

vālmīkiś ca mahā-yogī
valmīkād abhavat kila
agastyaś ca vasiṣṭhaś ca
mitrā-varuṇayor ṛṣī

vālmīkiḥ—Vālmīki; *ca*—and; *mahā-yogī*—the great mystic; *valmīkāt*—from an anthill; *abhavat*—took birth; *kila*—indeed; *agastyaḥ*—Agastya; *ca*—and; *vasiṣṭhaḥ*—Vasiṣṭha; *ca*—also; *mitrā-varuṇayoḥ*—of Mitra and Varuṇa; *ṛṣī*—the two sages.

TRANSLATION

By the semen of Varuṇa, the great mystic Vālmīki took birth from an anthill. Bhṛgu and Vālmīki were specific sons of Varuṇa, whereas Agastya

and Vasiṣṭha Ṛṣis were the common sons of Varuṇa and Mitra, the tenth son of Aditi.

TEXT 6

रेतः सिषिचतुःकुम्भे उर्वश्याः सन्निधौ द्रुतम् ।
रेवत्यां मित्र उत्सर्गमरिष्टं पिप्पलं व्यधात् ॥ ६ ॥

retaḥ siṣicatuḥ kumbhe
urvaśyāḥ sannidhau drutam
revatyāṁ mitra utsargam
ariṣṭaṁ pippalaṁ vyadhāt

retaḥ—semen; *siṣicatuḥ*—discharged; *kumbhe*—in an earthen pot; *urvaśyāḥ*—of Urvaśī; *sannidhau*—in the presence; *drutam*—flown; *revatyām*—in Revatī; *mitraḥ*—Mitra; *utsargam*—Utsarga; *ariṣṭam*—Ariṣṭa; *pippalam*—Pippala; *vyadhāt*—begot.

TRANSLATION

Upon seeing Urvaśī, the celestial society girl, both Mitra and Varuṇa discharged semen, which they preserved in an earthen pot. The two sons Agastya and Vasiṣṭha later appeared from that pot, and they are therefore the common sons of Mitra and Varuṇa. Mitra begot three sons in the womb of his wife, whose name was Revatī. Their names were Utsarga, Ariṣṭa and Pippala.

PURPORT

Modern science is trying to generate living entities in test tubes by processing semen, but even long, long ago it was possible for semen kept in a pot to develop into a child.

TEXT 7

पौलोम्यामिन्द्र आधत्त त्रीन् पुत्रानिति नः श्रुतम् ।
जयन्तमृषभं तात तृतीयं मीढुषं प्रभुः ॥ ७ ॥

paulomyām indra ādhatta
trīn putrān iti naḥ śrutam
jayantam ṛṣabhaṁ tāta
tṛtīyaṁ mīḍhuṣaṁ prabhuḥ

paulomyām—in Paulomī (Śacīdevī); *indraḥ*—Indra; *ādhatta*—begot; *trīn*—three; *putrān*—sons; *iti*—thus; *naḥ*—by us; *śrutam*—heard; *jayantam*—Jayanta; *ṛṣabham*—Ṛṣabha; *tāta*—my dear King; *tṛtīyam*—third; *mīḍhuṣam*—Mīḍhuṣa; *prabhuḥ*—the lord.

TRANSLATION

O King Parīkṣit, Indra, the King of the heavenly planets and eleventh son of Aditi, begot three sons, named Jayanta, Ṛṣabha and Mīḍhuṣa, in the womb of his wife, Paulomī. Thus we have heard.

TEXT 8

उरुक्रमस्य देवस्य मायावामनरूपिणः ।
कीर्तौ पत्न्यां बृहच्छ्लोकस्तस्यासन् सौभगादयः ॥ ८ ॥

urukramasya devasya
māyā-vāmana-rūpiṇaḥ
kīrtau patnyāṁ bṛhacchlokas
tasyāsan saubhagādayaḥ

urukramasya—of Urukrama; *devasya*—the Lord; *māyā*—by His internal potency; *vāmana-rūpiṇaḥ*—having the form of a dwarf; *kīrtau*—in Kīrti; *patnyām*—His wife; *bṛhacchlokaḥ*—Bṛhatśloka; *tasya*—of him; *āsan*—were; *saubhaga-ādayaḥ*—sons beginning with Saubhaga.

TRANSLATION

By His own potency, the Supreme Personality of Godhead, who has multifarious potencies, appeared in the form of a dwarf as Urukrama, the twelfth son of Aditi. In the womb of His wife, whose name was Kīrti, He begot one son, named Bṛhatśloka, who had many sons, headed by Saubhaga.

PURPORT

As the Lord says in *Bhagavad-gītā* (4.6):

ajo'pi sann avyayātmā
bhūtānām īśvaro'pi san
prakṛtiṁ svām adhiṣṭhāya
sambhavāmy ātma-māyayā

"Although I am unborn and My transcendental body never deteriorates, and although I am the Lord of all sentient beings, I still appear in every millennium in My original transcendental form." When the Supreme Personality of Godhead incarnates, He does not need any help from the external energy, for He appears as He is by His own potency. The spiritual potency is also called *māyā.* It is said, *ato māyāmayaṁ viṣṇuṁ pravadanti manīṣiṇaḥ:* the body accepted by the Supreme Personality of Godhead is called *māyāmaya.* This does not mean that He is formed of the external energy; this *māyā* refers to His internal potency.

TEXT 9

तत्कर्मगुणवीर्याणि काश्यपस्य महात्मनः ।
पश्चाद्वक्ष्यामहेऽदित्यां यथैवावततार ह ॥ ९ ॥

tat-karma-guṇa-vīryāṇi
kāśyapasya mahātmanaḥ
paścād vakṣyāmahe 'dityāṁ
yathaivāvatatāra ha

tat—His; *karma*—activities; *guṇa*—qualities; *vīryāṇi*—and power; *kāśyapasya*—of the son of Kaśyapa; *mahā-ātmanaḥ*—the great soul; *paścāt*—later; *vakṣyāmahe*—I shall describe; *adityām*—in Aditi; *yathā*—how; *eva*—certainly; *avatatāra*—descended; *ha*—indeed.

TRANSLATION

Later [in the Eighth Canto of Śrīmad-Bhāgavatam] I shall describe how Urukrama, Lord Vāmana-deva, appeared as the son of the great sage Kaśyapa and how He covered the three worlds with three steps. I shall describe the uncommon activities He performed, His qualities, His power and how He took birth from the womb of Aditi.

TEXT 10

अथ कश्यपदायादान् दैतेयान् कीर्तयामि ते ।
यत्र भागवतः श्रीमान् प्रह्लादो बलिरेव च ॥ १० ॥

atha kaśyapa-dāyādān
daiteyān kīrtayāmi te
yatra bhāgavataḥ śrīmān
prahrādo balir eva ca

atha—now; *kaśyapa-dāyādān*—the sons of Kaśyapa; *daiteyān*—born of Diti; *kīrtayāmi*—I shall describe; *te*—to you; *yatra*—where; *bhāgavataḥ*—the great devotee; *śrī-mān*—glorious; *prahrādaḥ*—Prahlāda; *baliḥ*—Bali; *eva*—certainly; *ca*—also.

TRANSLATION

Now let me describe the sons of Diti, who were begotten by Kaśyapa but who became demons. In this demoniac family the great devotee Prahlāda Mahārāja appeared, and Bali Mahārāja also appeared in that family. The demons are technically known as Daityas because they proceeded from the womb of Diti.

TEXT 11

दितेर्द्वावेव दायादौ दैत्यदानववन्दितौ ।
हिरण्यकशिपुर्नाम हिरण्याक्षश्च कीर्तितौ ॥ ११ ॥

diter dvāv eva dāyādau
daitya-dānava-vanditau
hiraṇyakaśipur nāma
hiraṇyākṣaś ca kīrtitau

diteḥ—of Diti; *dvau*—two; *eva*—certainly; *dāyādau*—sons; *daitya-dānava*—by the Daityas and Dānavas; *vanditau*—worshiped; *hiraṇyakaśipuḥ*—Hiraṇyakaśipu; *nāma*—named; *hiraṇyākṣaḥ*—Hiraṇyākṣa; *ca*—also; *kīrtitau*—known.

TRANSLATION

First the two sons named Hiraṇyakaśipu and Hiraṇyākṣa took birth from Diti's womb. Both of them were very powerful and were worshiped by the Daityas and Dānavas.

TEXTS 12–13

हिरण्यकशिपोर्भार्या कयाधुर्नाम दानवी ।
जम्भस्य तनया सा तु सुषुवे चतुरः सुतान् ॥ १२ ॥
संह्लादं प्रागनुह्लादं ह्लादं प्रह्लादमेव च ।
तत्स्वसा सिंहिका नाम राहुं विप्रचितोऽग्रहीत् ॥ १३ ॥

hiraṇyakaśipor bhāryā
kayādhur nāma dānavī
jambhasya tanayā sā tu
suṣuve caturaḥ sutān

saṁhrādaṁ prāg anuhrādaṁ
hrādaṁ prahrādam eva ca
tat-svasā siṁhikā nāma
rāhuṁ vipracito'grahīt

hiraṇyakaśipoḥ—of Hiraṇyakaśipu; *bhāryā*—the wife; *kayādhuḥ*—Kayādhu; *nāma*—named; *dānavī*—descendant of Danu; *jambhasya*—of Jambha; *tanayā*—daughter; *sā*—she; *tu*—indeed; *suṣuve*—gave birth to; *caturaḥ*—four; *sutān*—sons; *saṁhrādam*—Saṁhlāda; *prāk*—first; *anuhrādam*—Anuhlāda; *hrādam*—Hlāda; *prahrādam*—Prahlāda; *eva*—also; *ca*—and; *tat-svasā*—his sister; *siṁhikā*—Siṁhikā; *nāma*—named; *rāhum*—Rāhu; *vipracitaḥ*—from Vipracit; *agrahīt*—received.

TRANSLATION

The wife of Hiraṇyakaśipu was known as Kayādhu. She was the daughter of Jambha and a descendant of Danu. She gave birth to four consecutive sons, known as Saṁhlāda, Anuhlāda, Hlāda and Prahlāda. The sister of these four sons was known as Siṁhikā. She married the demon named Vipracit and gave birth to another demon, named Rāhu.

TEXT 14

शिरोऽहरद्यस्य हरिश्चक्रेण पिबतोऽमृतम् ।
संह्लादस्य कृतिर्भार्यासूत पञ्चजनं ततः ॥ १४ ॥

śiro'harad yasya hariś
cakreṇa pibato'mṛtam
saṁhrādasya kṛtir bhāryā-
sūta pañcajanaṁ tataḥ

śiraḥ—the head; *aharat*—cut off; *yasya*—of whom; *hariḥ*—Hari; *cakreṇa*—with the disc; *pibataḥ*—drinking; *amṛtam*—nectar; *saṁhrādasya*—of Saṁhlāda; *kṛtiḥ*—Kṛti; *bhāryā*—the wife; *asūta*—gave birth to; *pañcajanam*—Pañcajana; *tataḥ*—from him.

TRANSLATION

While Rāhu, in disguise, was drinking nectar among the demigods, the Supreme Personality of Godhead severed his head. The wife of Saṁhlāda was named Kṛti. By union with Saṁhlāda, Kṛti gave birth to a son named Pañcajana.

TEXT 15

ह्रादस्य धमनिर्भार्यासूत वातापिमिल्वलम् ।
योऽगस्त्याय त्वतिथये पेचे वातापिमिल्वलः ॥ १५ ॥

hrādasya dhamanir bhāryā-
sūta vātāpim ilvalam
yo'gastyāya tv atithaye
pece vātāpim ilvalaḥ

hrādasya—of Hlāda; *dhamaniḥ*—Dhamani; *bhāryā*—the wife; *asūta*—gave birth to; *vātāpim*—Vātāpi; *ilvalam*—Ilvala; *yaḥ*—he who; *agastyāya*—to Agastya; *tu*—but; *atithaye*—his guest; *pece*—cooked; *vātāpim*—Vātāpi; *ilvalaḥ*—Ilvala.

TRANSLATION

The wife of Hlāda was named Dhamani. She gave birth to two sons, named Vātāpi and Ilvala. When Agastya Muni became Ilvala's guest, Ilvala served him a feast by cooking Vātāpi, who was in the shape of a ram.

TEXT 16

अनुह्रादस्य सूर्यायां बाष्कलो महिषस्तथा ।
विरोचनस्तु प्राह्रादिर्देव्यां तस्याभवद्बलिः ॥ १६ ॥

anuhrādasya sūryāyāṁ
bāṣkalo mahiṣas tathā
virocanas tu prāhrādir
devyāṁ tasyābhavad baliḥ

anuhrādasya—of Anuhlāda; *sūryāyām*—through Sūryā; *bāṣkalaḥ*—Bāṣkala; *mahiṣaḥ*—Mahiṣa; *tathā*—also; *virocanaḥ*—Virocana; *tu*—indeed; *prāhrādiḥ*—the son of Prahlāda; *devyām*—through his wife; *tasya*—of him; *abhavat*—was; *baliḥ*—Bali.

TRANSLATION

The wife of Anuhlāda was named Sūryā. She gave birth to two sons, named Bāṣkala and Mahiṣa. Prahlāda had one son, Virocana, whose wife gave birth to Bali Mahārāja.

TEXT 17

बाणज्येष्ठं पुत्रशतमशनायां ततोऽभवत् ।
तस्यानुभावं सुश्लोक्यं पश्चादेवाभिधास्यते ॥ १७ ॥

bāṇa-jyeṣṭhaṁ putra-śatam
aśanāyāṁ tato'bhavat
tasyānubhāvaṁ suślokyaṁ
paścād evābhidhāsyate

bāṇa-jyeṣṭham—having Bāṇa as the eldest; *putra-śatam*—one hundred sons; *aśanāyām*—through Aśanā; *tataḥ*—from him; *abhavat*—there were; *tasya*—his; *anubhāvam*—character; *su-ślokyam*—laudable; *paścāt*—later; *eva*—certainly; *abhidhāsyate*—will be described.

TRANSLATION

Thereafter, Bali Mahārāja begot one hundred sons in the womb of Aśanā. Of these one hundred sons, King Bāṇa was the eldest. The activities of Bali Mahārāja, which are very laudable, will be described later [in the Eighth Canto].

TEXT 18

बाण आराध्य गिरिशं लेभे तद्गणमुख्यताम् ।
यत्पार्श्वे भगवानास्ते ह्यद्यापि पुरपालकः ॥ १८ ॥

bāṇa ārādhya giriśaṁ
lebhe tad-gaṇa-mukhyatām
yat-pārśve bhagavān āste
hy adyāpi pura-pālakaḥ

bāṇaḥ—Bāṇa; *ārādhya*—having worshiped; *giriśam*—Lord Śiva; *lebhe*—obtained; *tat*—of him (Lord Śiva); *gaṇa-mukhyatām*—the platform of being one of the chief associates; *yat-pārśve*—beside whom; *bhagavān*—Lord Śiva; *āste*—remains; *hi*—because of which; *adya*—now; *api*—even; *pura-pālakaḥ*—the protector of the capital.

TRANSLATION

Since King Bāṇa was a great worshiper of Lord Śiva, he became one of Lord Śiva's most celebrated associates. Even now, Lord Śiva protects King Bāṇa's capital and always stands beside him.

TEXT 19

मरुतश्च दितेः पुत्राश्चत्वारिंशन्नवाधिकाः ।
त आसन्नप्रजाः सर्वे नीता इन्द्रेण सात्मताम् ॥ १९ ॥

marutaś ca diteḥ putrāś
catvāriṁśan navādhikāḥ
ta āsann aprajāḥ sarve
nītā indreṇa sātmatām

marutaḥ—the Maruts; *ca*—and; *diteḥ*—of Diti; *putrāḥ*—sons; *catvāriṁśat*—forty; *nava-adhikāḥ*—plus nine; *te*—they; *āsan*—were; *aprajāḥ*—without sons; *sarve*—all; *nītāḥ*—were brought; *indreṇa*—by Indra; *sa-ātmatām*—to the position of demigods.

TRANSLATION

The forty-nine Marut demigods were also born from the womb of Diti. None of them had sons. Although they were born of Diti, King Indra gave them a position as demigods.

PURPORT

Apparently even demons can be elevated to positions as demigods when their atheistic character is reformed. There are two kinds of men throughout the universe. Those who are devotees of Lord Viṣṇu are called demigods, and those who are just the opposite are called demons. Even the demons can be transformed into demigods, as the statement of this verse proves.

TEXT 20

श्रीराजोवाच

कथं त आसुरं भावमपोह्यौत्पत्तिकं गुरो ।
इन्द्रेण प्रापिताः सात्म्यं किं तत्साधु कृतं हि तैः ॥ २० ॥

śrī-rājovāca
kathaṁ ta āsuraṁ bhāvam
apohyautpattikaṁ guro

indreṇa prāpitāḥ sātmyaṁ
kiṁ tat sādhu kṛtaṁ hi taiḥ

śrī-rājā uvāca—King Parīkṣit said; *katham*—why; *te*—they; *āsuram*—demoniac; *bhāvam*—mentality; *apohya*—giving up; *autpattikam*—due to birth; *guro*—my dear lord; *indreṇa*—by Indra; *prāpitāḥ*—were converted; *sa-ātmyam*—to demigods; *kim*—whether; *tat*—therefore; *sādhu*—pious activities; *kṛtam*—performed; *hi*—indeed; *taiḥ*—by them.

TRANSLATION

King Parīkṣit inquired: My dear lord, due to their birth, the forty-nine Maruts must have been obsessed with a demoniac mentality. Why did Indra, the King of heaven, convert them into demigods? Did they perform any rituals or pious activities?

TEXT 21

इमे श्रद्दधते ब्रह्मन्नृषयो हि मया सह ।
परिज्ञानाय भगवंस्तन्नो व्याख्यातुमर्हसि ॥ २१ ॥

ime śraddadhate brahmann
ṛṣayo hi mayā saha
parijñānāya bhagavaṁs
tan no vyākhyātum arhasi

ime—these; *śraddadhate*—are eager; *brahman*—O *brāhmaṇa; ṛṣayaḥ*—sages; *hi*—indeed; *mayā saha*—with me; *parijñānāya*—to know; *bhagavan*—O great soul; *tat*—therefore; *naḥ*—to us; *vyākhyātum arhasi*—please explain.

TRANSLATION

My dear brāhmaṇa, I and all the sages present with me are eager to know about this. Therefore, O great soul, kindly explain to us the reason.

TEXT 22

श्रीसूत उवाच
तद्विष्णुरातस्य स बादरायणि-
र्वचो निशम्याहृतमल्पमर्थवत् ।

सभाजयन् संनिभृतेन चेतसा
जगाद सत्रायण सर्वदर्शनः ॥ २२ ॥

śrī-sūta uvāca
tad viṣṇurātasya sa bādarāyaṇir
vaco niśamyādṛtam alpam arthavat
sabhājayan san nibhṛtena cetasā
jagāda satrāyaṇa sarva-darśanaḥ

śrī-sūtaḥ uvāca—Śrī Sūta Gosvāmī said; *tat*—those; *viṣṇurātasya*—of Mahārāja Parīkṣit; *saḥ*—he; *bādarāyaṇiḥ*—Śukadeva Gosvāmī; *vacaḥ*—words; *niśamya*—hearing; *ādṛtam*—respectful; *alpam*—brief; *artha-vat*—meaningful; *sabhājayan san*—praising; *nibhṛtena cetasā*—with great pleasure; *jagāda*—replied; *satrāyaṇa*—O Śaunaka; *sarva-darśanaḥ*—who is aware of everything.

TRANSLATION

Śrī Sūta Gosvāmī said: O great sage Śaunaka, after hearing Mahārāja Parīkṣit speak respectfully and briefly on topics essential to hear, Śukadeva Gosvāmī, who was well aware of everything, praised his endeavor with great pleasure and replied.

PURPORT

Mahārāja Parīkṣit's question was very much appreciated by Śukadeva Gosvāmī because although it was composed of a small number of words, it contained meaningful inquiries about how the sons of Diti, although born as demons, became demigods. Śrīla Viśvanātha Cakravartī Ṭhākura stresses that even though Diti was very envious, her heart was purified because of a devotional attitude. Another significant topic is that although Kaśyapa Muni was a learned scholar and was advanced in spiritual consciousness, he nonetheless fell a victim to the inducement of his beautiful wife. All these questions were posed in a small number of words, and therefore Śukadeva Gosvāmī very much appreciated Mahārāja Parīkṣit's inquiry.

TEXT 23

श्रीशुक उवाच
हतपुत्रा दितिः शक्रपार्ष्णिग्राहेण विष्णुना ।
मन्युना शोकदीप्तेन ज्वलन्ती पर्यचिन्तयत् ॥ २३ ॥

śrī-śuka uvāca
hata-putrā ditiḥ śakra-
pārṣṇi-grāheṇa viṣṇunā
manyunā śoka-dīptena
jvalantī paryacintayat

śrī-śukaḥ uvāca—Śrī Śukadeva Gosvāmī said; *hata-putrā*—whose sons were killed; *ditiḥ*—Diti; *śakra-pārṣṇi-grāheṇa*—who was helping Lord Indra; *viṣṇunā*—by Lord Viṣṇu; *manyunā*—with anger; *śoka-dīptena*—kindled by lamentation; *jvalantī*—burning; *paryacintayat*—thought.

TRANSLATION

Śrī Śukadeva Gosvāmī said: Just to help Indra, Lord Viṣṇu killed the two brothers Hiraṇyākṣa and Hiraṇyakaśipu. Because of their being killed, their mother, Diti, overwhelmed with lamentation and anger, contemplated as follows.

TEXT 24

कदा नु भ्रातृहन्तारमिन्द्रियाराममुल्बणम् ।
अक्लिन्नहृदयं पापं घातयित्वा शये सुखम् ॥ २४ ॥

kadā nu bhrātṛ-hantāram
indriyārāmam ulbaṇam
aklinna-hṛdayaṁ pāpaṁ
ghātayitvā śaye sukham

kadā—when; *nu*—indeed; *bhrātṛ-hantāram*—the killer of the brothers; *indriya-ārāmam*—very fond of sense gratification; *ulbaṇam*—cruel; *aklinna-hṛdayam*—hard hearted; *pāpam*—sinful; *ghātayitvā*—having caused to be killed; *śaye*—shall I rest; *sukham*—happily.

TRANSLATION

Lord Indra, who is very much fond of sense gratification, has killed the two brothers Hiraṇyākṣa and Hiraṇyakaśipu by means of Lord Viṣṇu. Therefore Indra is cruel, hardhearted and sinful. When will I, having killed him, rest with a pacified mind?

TEXT 25

कृमिविड्भस्मसंज्ञासीद्यस्येशाभिहितस्य च ।
भूतध्रुक् तत्कृते स्वार्थं किं वेद निरयो यतः ॥ २५ ॥

kṛmi-viḍ-bhasma-saṁjñāsīd
yasyeśābhihitasya ca
bhūta-dhruk tat-kṛte svārthaṁ
kiṁ veda nirayo yataḥ

kṛmi—worms; *viṭ*—stool; *bhasma*—ashes; *saṁjñā*—name; *āsīt*—becomes; *yasya*—of which (body); *īśa-abhihitasya*—although designated as king; *ca*—also; *bhūta-dhruk*—he who harms others; *tat-kṛte*—for the sake of that; *sva-artham*—his self-interest; *kim veda*—does he know; *nirayaḥ*—punishment in hell; *yataḥ*—from which.

TRANSLATION

When dead, the bodies of all the rulers known as kings and great leaders will be transformed into worms, stool or ashes. If one enviously kills others for the protection of such a body, does he actually know the true interest of life? Certainly he does not, for if one is envious of other entities, he surely goes to hell.

PURPORT

The material body, even if possessed by a great king, is ultimately transformed into stool, worms or ashes. When one is too attached to the bodily conception of life, he is certainly not very intelligent.

TEXT 26

आशासानस्य तस्येदं ध्रुवमुन्नद्धचेतसः ।
मदशोषक इन्द्रस्य भूयाद्येन सुतो हि मे ॥ २६ ॥

āśāsānasya tasyedaṁ
dhruvam unnaddha-cetasaḥ
mada-śoṣaka indrasya
bhūyād yena suto hi me

āśāsānasya—thinking; *tasya*—of him; *idam*—this (body); *dhruvam*—eternal; *unnaddha-cetasaḥ*—whose mind is unrestrained; *mada-śoṣakaḥ*

—who can remove the madness; *indrasya*—of Indra; *bhūyāt*—may there be; *yena*—by which; *sutaḥ*—a son; *hi*—certainly; *me*—of me.

TRANSLATION

Diti thought: Indra considers his body eternal, and thus he has become unrestrained. I therefore wish to have a son who can remove Indra's madness. Let me adopt some means to help me in this.

PURPORT

One who is in the bodily conception of life is compared in the *śāstras* to animals like cows and asses. Diti wanted to punish Indra, who had become like a lower animal.

TEXTS 27–28

इति भावेन सा भर्तुराचचारासकृत्प्रियम् ।
शुश्रूषयानुरागेण प्रश्रयेण दमेन च ॥ २७ ॥
भक्त्या परमया राजन् मनोज्ञैर्वल्गुभाषितैः ।
मनो जग्राह भावज्ञा सस्मितापाङ्गवीक्षणैः ॥ २८ ॥

iti bhāvena sā bhartur
ācacārāsakṛt priyam
śuśrūṣayānurāgeṇa
praśrayeṇa damena ca

bhaktyā paramayā rājan
manojñair valgu-bhāṣitaiḥ
mano jagrāha bhāva-jñā
sasmitāpāṅga-vīkṣaṇaiḥ

iti—thus; *bhāvena*—with the intention; *sā*—she; *bhartuḥ*—of the husband; *ācacāra*—performed; *asakṛt*—constantly; *priyam*—pleasing activities; *śuśrūṣayā*—with service; *anurāgeṇa*—with love; *praśrayeṇa*—with humility; *damena*—with self-control; *ca*—also; *bhaktyā*—with devotion; *paramayā*—great; *rājan*—O King; *manojñaiḥ*—charming; *valgu-bhāṣitaiḥ*—with sweet words; *manaḥ*—his mind; *jagrāha*—brought under her control; *bhāva-jñā*—knowing his nature; *sa-smita*—with smiling; *apāṅga-vīkṣaṇaiḥ*—by glancing.

TRANSLATION

Thinking in this way [with a desire for a son to kill Indra], Diti began constantly acting to satisfy Kaśyapa by her pleasing behavior. O King, Diti always carried out Kaśyapa's orders very faithfully, as he desired. With service, love, humility and control, with words spoken very sweetly to satisfy her husband, and with smiles and glances at him, Diti attracted his mind and brought it under her control.

PURPORT

When a woman wants to endear herself to her husband and make him very faithful, she must try to please him in all respects. When the husband is pleased with his wife, the wife can receive all necessities, ornaments and full satisfaction for her senses. Herein this is indicated by the behavior of Diti.

TEXT 29

एवं स्त्रिया जडीभूतो विद्वानपि मनोज्ञया ।
बाढमित्याह विवशो न तच्चित्रं हि योषिति ॥ २९ ॥

evaṁ striyā jaḍībhūto
vidvān api manojñayā
bāḍham ity āha vivaśo
na tac citraṁ hi yoṣiti

evam—thus; *striyā*—by the woman; *jaḍībhūtaḥ*—enchanted; *vidvān*—very learned; *api*—although; *manojñayā*—very expert; *bāḍham*—yes; *iti*—thus; *āha*—said; *vivaśaḥ*—under her control; *na*—not; *tat*—that; *citram*—astonishing; *hi*—indeed; *yoṣiti*—in the matter of women.

TRANSLATION

Although Kaśyapa Muni was a learned scholar, he was captivated by Diti's artificial behavior, which brought him under her control. Therefore he assured his wife that he would fulfill her desires. Such a promise by a husband is not at all astonishing.

TEXT 30

विलोक्यैकान्तभूतानि भूतान्यादौ प्रजापतिः ।
स्त्रियं चक्रे स्वदेहार्धं यया पुंसां मतिर्हृता ॥ ३० ॥

vilokyaikānta-bhūtāni
bhūtāny ādau prajāpatiḥ
striyaṁ cakre sva-dehārdhaṁ
yayā puṁsāṁ matir hṛtā

vilokya—seeing; *ekānta-bhūtāni*—detached; *bhūtāni*—the living entities; *ādau*—in the beginning; *prajāpatiḥ*—Lord Brahmā; *striyam*—the woman; *cakre*—created; *sva-deha*—of his body; *ardham*—half; *yayā*—by whom; *puṁsām*—of men; *matiḥ*—the mind; *hṛtā*—carried away.

TRANSLATION

In the beginning of creation, Lord Brahmā, the father of the living entities of the universe, saw that all the living entities were unattached. To increase population, he then created woman from the better half of man's body, for woman's behavior carries away a man's mind.

PURPORT

This entire universe is going on under the spell of sexual attachment, which was created by Lord Brahmā to increase the population of the entire universe, not only in human society but also in other species. As stated by Ṛṣabha-deva in the Fifth Canto, *puṁsaḥ striyā mithunī-bhāvam etam:* the entire world is going on under the spell of sexual attraction and desire between man and woman. When man and woman unite, the hard knot of this attraction becomes increasingly tight, and thus a man is implicated in the materialistic way of life. This is the illusion of the material world. This illusion acted upon Kaśyapa Muni, although he was very learned and advanced in spiritual knowledge. As stated in the *Manu-saṁhitā* (2.215) and *Śrīmad-Bhāgavatam* (9.19.17):

mātrā svasrā duhitrā vā
nāviviktāsano bhavet
balavān indriya-grāmo
vidvāṁsam api karṣati

"A man should not associate with a woman in a solitary place, not even with his mother, sister or daughter, for the senses are so strong that they lead astray even a person advanced in knowledge." When a man remains in a solitary place with a woman, his sexual desires undoubtedly increase. Therefore the words *ekānta-bhūtāni,* which are used here, indicate that to avoid sexual desires one should avoid the company of women as far as possible. Sexual desire is so powerful that one is saturated with it if he stays in a solitary place with any woman, even his mother, sister or daughter.

TEXT 31

एवं शुश्रूषितस्तात भगवान् कश्यपः स्त्रिया ।
प्रहस्य परमप्रीतो दितिमाहाभिनन्द्य च ॥ ३१ ॥

evaṁ śuśrūṣitas tāta
bhagavān kaśyapaḥ striyā
prahasya parama-prīto
ditim āhābhinandya ca

evam—thus; *śuśrūṣitaḥ*—being served; *tāta*—O dear one; *bhagavān*—the powerful; *kaśyapaḥ*—Kaśyapa; *striyā*—by the woman; *prahasya*—smiling; *parama-prītaḥ*—being very pleased; *ditim*—to Diti; *āha*—said; *abhinandya*—approving; *ca*—also.

TRANSLATION

O my dear one, the most powerful sage Kaśyapa, being extremely pleased by the mild behavior of his wife Diti, smiled and spoke to her as follows.

TEXT 32

श्रीकश्यप उवाच
वरं वरय वामोरु प्रीतस्तेऽहमनिन्दिते ।
स्त्रिया भर्तरि सुप्रीते कः काम इह चागमः ॥ ३२ ॥

śrī-kaśyapa uvāca
varaṁ varaya vāmoru
prītas te'ham anindite
striyā bhartari suprīte
kaḥ kāma iha cāgamaḥ

śrī-kaśyapaḥ uvāca—Kaśyapa Muni said; *varam*—benediction; *varaya*—ask; *vāmoru*—O beautiful woman; *prītaḥ*—pleased; *te*—with you; *aham*—I; *anindite*—O irreproachable lady; *striyāḥ*—for the woman; *bhartari*—when the husband; *su-prīte*—pleased; *kaḥ*—what; *kāmaḥ*—desire; *iha*—here; *ca*—and; *agamaḥ*—difficult to obtain.

TRANSLATION

Kaśyapa Muni said: O beautiful woman, O irreproachable lady, since I am very much pleased by your behavior, you may ask me for any benediction you want. If a husband is pleased, what desires are difficult for his wife to obtain, either in this world or in the next?

TEXTS 33–34

पतिरेव हि नारीणां दैवतं परमं स्मृतम् ।
मानसः सर्वभूतानां वासुदेवः श्रियः पतिः ॥ ३३ ॥
स एव देवतालिङ्गैर्नामरूपविकल्पितैः ।
इज्यते भगवान् पुम्भिः स्त्रीभिश्च पतिरूपधृक् ॥ ३४ ॥

patir eva hi nārīṇāṁ
daivataṁ paramaṁ smṛtam
mānasaḥ sarva-bhūtānāṁ
vāsudevaḥ śriyaḥ patiḥ

sa eva devatā-liṅgair
nāma-rūpa-vikalpitaiḥ
ijyate bhagavān pumbhiḥ
strībhiś ca pati-rūpa-dhṛk

patiḥ—the husband; *eva*—indeed; *hi*—certainly; *nārīṇām*—of women; *daivatam*—demigod; *paramam*—supreme; *smṛtam*—is considered; *mānasaḥ*—situated in the heart; *sarva-bhūtānām*—of all living entities; *vāsudevaḥ*—Vāsudeva; *śriyaḥ*—of the goddess of fortune; *patiḥ*—the husband; *saḥ*—He; *eva*—certainly; *devatā-liṅgaiḥ*—by the forms of the demigods; *nāma*—names; *rūpa*—forms; *vikalpitaiḥ*—conceived; *ijyate*—is worshiped; *bhagavān*—the Supreme Personality of Godhead; *pumbhiḥ*—by men; *strībhiḥ*—by women; *ca*—also; *pati-rūpa-dhṛk*—in the form of the husband.

TRANSLATION

A husband is the supreme demigod for a woman. The Supreme Personality of Godhead, Lord Vāsudeva, the husband of the goddess of fortune, is situated in everyone's heart and is worshiped through the various names and forms of the demigods by fruitive workers. Similarly, a husband represents the Lord as the object of worship for a woman.

PURPORT

The Lord says in *Bhagavad-gītā* (9.23):

ye'py anya-devatā-bhaktā
yajante śraddhayānvitāḥ
te'pi mām eva kaunteya
yajanty avidhi-pūrvakam

"Whatever a man may sacrifice to other gods, O son of Kuntī, is really meant for Me alone, but it is offered without true understanding." The demigods are various assistants who act like the hands and legs of the Supreme Personality of Godhead. One who is not in direct touch with the Supreme Lord and cannot conceive of the exalted position of the Lord is sometimes advised to worship the demigods as various parts of the Lord. If women, who are usually very much attached to their husbands, worship their husbands as representatives of Vāsudeva, the women benefit, just as Ajāmila benefited by calling for Nārāyaṇa, his son. Ajāmila was concerned with his son, but because of his attachment to the name of Nārāyaṇa, he attained salvation simply by chanting that name. In India a husband is still called *pati-guru,* the husband spiritual master. If husband and wife are attached to one another for advancement in Kṛṣṇa consciousness, their relationship of cooperation is very effective for such advancement. Although the names of Indra and Agni are sometimes uttered in the Vedic *mantras* (*indrāya svāhā, agnaye svāhā*), the Vedic sacrifices are actually performed for the satisfaction of Lord Viṣṇu. As long as one is very much attached to material sense gratification, the worship of the demigods or the worship of one's husband is recommended.

TEXT 35

तस्मात्पतिव्रता नार्यः श्रेयस्कामाः सुमध्यमे।
यजन्तेऽनन्यभावेन पतिमात्मानमीश्वरम् ॥ ३५ ॥

tasmāt pati-vratā nāryaḥ
śreyas-kāmāḥ sumadhyame
yajante'nanya-bhāvena
patim ātmānam īśvaram

tasmāt—therefore; *pati-vratāḥ*—devoted to the husband; *nāryaḥ*—women; *śreyaḥ-kāmāḥ*—conscientious; *su-madhyame*—O thin-waisted woman; *yajante*—worship; *ananya-bhāvena*—with devotion; *patim*—the husband; *ātmānam*—the Supersoul; *īśvaram*—representative of the Supreme Personality of Godhead.

TRANSLATION

My dear wife, whose body is so beautiful, your waist being thin, a conscientious wife should be chaste and should abide by the orders of her husband. She should very devoutly worship her husband as a representative of Vāsudeva.

TEXT 36

सोऽहं त्वयार्चितो भद्रे ईदृग्भावेन भक्तितः ।
तं ते सम्पादये काममसतीनां सुदुर्लभम् ॥ ३६ ॥

so'haṁ tvayārcito bhadre
īdṛg-bhāvena bhaktitaḥ
taṁ te sampādaye kāmam
asatīnāṁ sudurlabham

saḥ—such a person; *aham*—I; *tvayā*—by you; *arcitaḥ*—worshiped; *bhadre*—O gentle woman; *īdṛk-bhāvena*—in such a way; *bhaktitaḥ*—with devotion; *tam*—that; *te*—your; *sampādaye*—shall fulfill; *kāmam*—desire; *asatīnām*—for unchaste women; *su-durlabham*—not obtainable.

TRANSLATION

My dear gentle wife, because you have worshiped me with great devotion, considering me a representative of the Supreme Personality of Godhead, I shall reward you by fulfilling your desires, which are unobtainable for an unchaste wife.

TEXT 37

दितिरुवाच
वरदो यदि मे ब्रह्मन् पुत्रमिन्द्रहणं वृणे ।
अमृत्युं मृतपुत्राहं येन मे घातितौ सुतौ ॥ ३७ ॥

ditir uvāca
varado yadi me brahman
putram indra-haṇaṁ vṛṇe

amṛtyuṁ mṛta-putrāhaṁ
yena me ghātitau sutau

ditiḥ uvāca—Diti said; *vara-daḥ*—the giver of benedictions; *yadi*—if; *me*—to me; *brahman*—O great soul; *putram*—a son; *indra-haṇam*—who can kill Indra; *vṛṇe*—I am asking for; *amṛtyum*—immortal; *mṛta-putrā*—whose sons are dead; *aham*—I; *yena*—by whom; *me*—my; *ghātitau*—were caused to be killed; *sutau*—two sons.

TRANSLATION

Diti replied: O my husband, O great soul, I have now lost my sons. If you want to give me a benediction, I ask you for an immortal son who can kill Indra. I pray for this because Indra, with the help of Viṣṇu, has killed my two sons Hiraṇyākṣa and Hiraṇyakaśipu.

PURPORT

The word *indra-haṇam* means "one who can kill Indra," but it also means "one who follows Indra." The word *amṛtyum* refers to the demigods, who do not die like ordinary human beings because they have extremely long durations of life. For example, the duration of Lord Brahmā's life is stated in *Bhagavad-gītā: sahasra-yuga-paryantam ahar yad brahmaṇo viduḥ.* Even the duration of one day, or twelve hours, of Brahmā is 4,300,000 years multiplied by one thousand. Thus the duration of his life is inconceivable for an ordinary human being. The demigods are therefore sometimes called *amara,* which means "one who has no death." In this material world, however, everyone has to die. Therefore the word *amṛtyum* indicates that Diti wanted a son who would be equal in status to the demigods.

TEXT 38

निशम्य तद्वचो विप्रो विमनाः पर्यतप्यत ।
अहो अधर्मः सुमहानद्य मे समुपस्थितः ॥ ३८ ॥

niśamya tad-vaco vipro
vimanāḥ paryatapyata
aho adharmaḥ sumahān
adya me samupasthitaḥ

niśamya—hearing; *tat-vacaḥ*—her words; *vipraḥ*—the *brāhmaṇa; vimanāḥ*—aggrieved; *paryatapyata*—lamented; *aho*—alas; *adharmaḥ*—

impiety; *su-mahān*—very great; *adya*—today; *me*—upon me; *samupasthitaḥ*—has come.

TRANSLATION

Upon hearing Diti's request, Kaśyapa Muni was very much aggrieved. "Alas," he lamented, "now I face the danger of the impious act of killing Indra."

PURPORT

Although Kaśyapa Muni was eager to fulfill the desire of his wife Diti, when he heard that she wanted a son to kill Indra his jubilation was immediately reduced to nothing because he was averse to the idea.

TEXT 39

अहो अर्थेन्द्रियारामो योषिन्मय्येह मायया ।
गृहीतचेताः कृपणः पतिष्ये नरके ध्रुवम् ॥ ३९ ॥

aho arthendriyārāmo
yoṣin-mayyeha māyayā
gṛhīta-cetāḥ kṛpaṇaḥ
patiṣye narake dhruvam

aho—alas; *artha-indriya-ārāmaḥ*—too attached to material enjoyment; *yoṣit-mayyā*—in the form of a woman; *iha*—here; *māyayā*—by the illusory energy; *gṛhīta-cetāḥ*—my mind being captivated; *kṛpaṇaḥ*—wretched; *patiṣye*—I shall fall; *narake*—to hell; *dhruvam*—surely.

TRANSLATION

Kaśyapa Muni thought: Alas, I have now become too attached to material enjoyment. Taking advantage of this, my mind has been attracted by the illusory energy of the Supreme Personality of Godhead in the form of a woman [my wife]. Therefore I am surely a wretched person who will glide down toward hell.

TEXT 40

कोऽतिक्रमोऽनुवर्तन्त्याः स्वभावमिह योषितः ।
धिङ् मां बताबुधं स्वार्थे यदहं त्वजितेन्द्रियः ॥ ४० ॥

ko'tikramo'nuvartantyāḥ
svabhāvam iha yoṣitaḥ
dhiṅ māṁ batābudhaṁ svārthe
yad ahaṁ tv ajitendriyaḥ

kaḥ—what; *atikramaḥ*—offense; *anuvartantyāḥ*—following; *sva-bhāvam*—her nature; *iha*—here; *yoṣitaḥ*—of the woman; *dhik*—condemnation; *mām*—unto me; *bata*—alas; *abudham*—not conversant; *sva-arthe*—in what is good for me; *yat*—because; *aham*—I; *tu*—indeed; *ajita-indriyaḥ*—unable to control my senses.

TRANSLATION

This woman, my wife, has adopted a means that follows her nature, and therefore she is not to be blamed. But I am a man. Therefore, all condemnation upon me! I am not at all conversant with what is good for me, since I could not control my senses.

PURPORT

The natural instinct of a woman is to enjoy the material world. She induces her husband to enjoy this world by satisfying his tongue, belly and genitals, which are called *jihvā, udara* and *upastha.* A woman is expert in cooking palatable dishes so that she can easily satisfy her husband in eating. When one eats nicely, his belly is satisfied, and as soon as the belly is satisfied the genitals become strong. Especially when a man is accustomed to eating meat and drinking wine and similar passionate things, he certainly becomes sexually inclined. It should be understood that sexual inclinations are meant not for spiritual progress but for gliding down to hell. Thus Kaśyapa Muni considered his situation and lamented. In other words, to be a householder is very risky unless one is trained and the wife is a follower of her husband. A husband should be trained at the very beginning of his life. *Kaumāra ācaret prājño dharmān bhāgavatān iha* (*Bhāg.* 7.6.1). During the time of *brahmacarya,* or student life, a *brahmacārī* should be taught to be expert in *bhāgavata-dharma,* devotional service. Then when he marries, if his wife is faithful to her husband and follows him in such life, the relationship between husband and wife is very desirable. However, a relationship between husband and wife without spiritual consciousness but strictly for sense gratification is not at all good. It is said in *Śrīmad-Bhāgavatam* (12.2.3) that especially in this age, Kali-yuga, *dām-patye'bhirucir hetuḥ:* the relationship between husband and wife will be based on sexual power. Therefore householder life in this Kali-yuga is extremely dangerous unless both the wife and husband take to Kṛṣṇa consciousness.

TEXT 41

शरत्पद्मोत्सवं वक्त्रं वचश्च श्रवणामृतम् ।
हृदयं क्षुरधाराभं स्त्रीणां को वेद चेष्टितम् ॥ ४१ ॥

śarat-padmotsavaṁ vaktraṁ
vacaś ca śravaṇāmṛtam
hṛdayaṁ kṣura-dhārābhaṁ
strīṇāṁ ko veda ceṣṭitam

śarat—in the autumn; *padma*—a lotus flower; *utsavam*—blossoming; *vaktram*—face; *vacaḥ*—words; *ca*—and; *śravaṇa*—to the ear; *amṛtam*—giving pleasure; *hṛdayam*—heart; *kṣura-dhārā*—the blade of a razor; *ābham*—like; *strīṇām*—of women; *kaḥ*—who; *veda*—knows; *ceṣṭitam*—the dealings.

TRANSLATION

A woman's face is as attractive and beautiful as a blossoming lotus flower during autumn. Her words are very sweet, and they give pleasure to the ear, but if we study a woman's heart, we can understand it to be extremely sharp, like the blade of a razor. In these circumstances, who could understand the dealings of a woman?

PURPORT

Woman is now depicted very well from the materialistic point of view by Kaśyapa Muni. Women are generally known as the fair sex, and especially in youth, at the age of sixteen or seventeen, women are very attractive to men. Therefore a woman's face is compared to a blooming lotus flower in autumn. Just as a lotus is extremely beautiful in autumn, a woman at the threshold of youthful beauty is extremely attractive. In Sanskrit a woman's voice is called *nārī-svara* because women generally sing and their singing is very attractive. At the present moment, cinema artists, especially female singers, are especially welcome. Some of them earn fabulous amounts of money simply by singing. Therefore, as taught by Śrī Caitanya Mahāprabhu, a woman's singing is dangerous because it can make a *sannyāsī* fall a victim to the woman. *Sannyāsa* means giving up the company of women, but if a *sannyāsī* hears the voice of a woman and sees her beautiful face, he certainly becomes attracted and is sure to fall down. There have been many examples. Even the great sage Viśvāmitra fell a victim to Menakā. Therefore a person desiring to advance in spiritual consciousness must be especially careful not to see a woman's face or hear a woman's voice. To see a woman's face and appreciate its beauty or to hear a woman's voice and appreciate her singing as very nice is a subtle falldown for a *brahmacārī* or *sannyāsī.* Thus the description of a woman's features by Kaśyapa Muni is very instructive.

When a woman's bodily features are attractive, when her face is beautiful and when her voice is sweet, she is naturally a trap for a man. The *śāstras* advise that when such a woman comes to serve a man, she should be considered to be like a dark well covered by grass. In the fields there are many such wells, and a man who does not know about them drops through the grass and falls down. Thus there are many such instructions. Since the attraction of the material world is based on attraction for women, Kaśyapa Muni thought, "Under the circumstances, who can understand the heart of a woman?" Cāṇakya Paṇḍita has also advised, *viśvāso naiva kartavyaḥ strīṣu rāja-kuleṣu ca:* "There are two persons one should not trust—a politician and a woman." These, of course, are authoritative śāstric injunctions, and we should therefore be very careful in our dealings with women.

Sometimes our Kṛṣṇa consciousness movement is criticized for mingling men and women, but Kṛṣṇa consciousness is meant for anyone. Whether one is a man or woman does not matter. Lord Kṛṣṇa personally says, *striyo vaiśyās tathā śūdrās te'pi yānti parāṁ gatim:* whether one is a woman, *śūdra* or *vaiśya,* not to speak of being a *brāhmaṇa* or *kṣatriya,* everyone is fit to return home, back to Godhead, if he strictly follows the instructions of the spiritual master and *śāstra.* We therefore request all the members of the Kṛṣṇa consciousness movement—both men and women—not to be attracted by bodily features but only to be attracted by Kṛṣṇa. Then everything will be all right. Otherwise there will be danger.

TEXT 42

न हि कश्चित्प्रियः स्त्रीणामञ्जसा स्वाशिषात्मनाम् ।
पतिं पुत्रं भ्रातरं वा घ्नन्त्यर्थे घातयन्ति च ॥ ४२ ॥

na hi kaścit priyaḥ strīṇām
añjasā svāśiṣātmanām

patiṁ putraṁ bhrātaraṁ vā
ghnanty arthe ghātayanti ca

na—not; *hi*—certainly; *kaścit*—anyone; *priyaḥ*—dear; *strīṇām*—to women; *añjasā*—actually; *sva-āśiṣā*—for their own interests; *ātmanām*—most dear; *patim*—husband; *putram*—son; *bhrātaram*—brother; *vā*—or; *ghnanti*—they kill; *arthe*—for their own interests; *ghātayanti*—cause to be killed; *ca*—also.

TRANSLATION

To satisfy their own interests, women deal with men as if the men were most dear to them, but no one is actually dear to them. Women are supposed to be very saintly, but for their own interests they can kill even their husbands, sons or brothers, or cause them to be killed by others.

PURPORT

A woman's nature has been particularly well studied by Kaśyapa Muni. Women are self-interested by nature, and therefore they should be protected by all means so that their natural inclination to be too self-interested will not be manifested. Women need to be protected by men. A woman should be cared for by her father in her childhood, by her husband in her youth and by her grown sons in her old age. This is the injunction of Manu, who says that a woman should not be given independence at any stage. Women must be cared for so that they will not be free to manifest their natural tendency for gross selfishness. There have been many cases, even in the present day, in which women have killed their husbands to take advantage of their insurance policies. This is not a criticism of women but a practical study of their nature. Such natural instincts of a woman or a man are manifested only in the bodily conception of life. When either a man or a woman is advanced in spiritual consciousness, the bodily conception of life practically vanishes. We should see all women as spiritual units (*ahaṁ brahmāsmi*), whose only duty is to satisfy Kṛṣṇa. Then the influences of the different modes of material nature, which result from one's possessing a material body, will not act.

The Kṛṣṇa consciousness movement is so beneficial that it can very easily counteract the contamination of material nature, which results from one's possessing a material body. *Bhagavad-gītā* therefore teaches, in the very beginning, that whether one is a man or a woman, one must know that he or she is not the body but a spiritual soul. Everyone should be interested in the activities of the spirit soul, not the body. As long as one is activated by the bodily conception of life, there is always the danger of being misled, whether one is a man or a woman. The soul is sometimes described as *puruṣa* because whether one is dressed as a man or a woman, one is inclined to enjoy this material world. One who has this spirit of enjoyment is described as *puruṣa.* Whether one is a man or a woman, he is not interested in serving others; everyone is interested in satisfying his or her own senses. Kṛṣṇa consciousness, however, provides first-class training for a man or a woman. A man should be trained to be a first-class devotee of Lord Kṛṣṇa, and a woman should be trained to be a very chaste follower of her husband. That will make the lives of both of them happy.

TEXT 43

प्रतिश्रुतं ददामीति वचस्तन्न मृषा भवेत् ।
वधं नार्हति चेन्द्रोऽपि तत्रेदमुपकल्पते ॥ ४३ ॥

pratiśrutaṁ dadāmīti
vacas tan na mṛṣā bhavet
vadhaṁ nārhati cendro'pi
tatredam upakalpate

pratiśrutam—promised; *dadāmi*—I shall give; *iti*—thus; *vacaḥ*—statement; *tat*—that; *na*—not; *mṛṣā*—false; *bhavet*—can be; *vadham*—killing; *na*—not; *arhati*—is suitable; *ca*—and; *indraḥ*—Indra; *api*—also; *tatra*—in that connection; *idam*—this; *upakalpate*—is suitable.

TRANSLATION

I promised to give her a benediction, and this promise cannot be violated, but Indra does not deserve to be killed. In these circumstances, the solution I have is quite suitable.

PURPORT

Kaśyapa Muni concluded, "Diti is eager to have a son who can kill Indra, since she is a woman, after all, and is not very intelligent. I shall train her in such a way that instead of always thinking of how to kill Indra, she will become a Vaiṣṇava, a devotee of Kṛṣṇa. If she agrees to follow the rules and regulations of the Vaiṣṇava principles, the unclean core of her heart will certainly be cleansed." *Ceto-darpaṇa-mārjanam.* This is the process of devotional service.

Anyone can be purified by following the principles of devotional service in Kṛṣṇa consciousness, for Kṛṣṇa consciousness is so powerful that it can purify even the dirtiest class of men and transform them into the topmost Vaiṣṇavas. Śrī Caitanya Mahāprabhu's movement aims at this purpose. Narottama dāsa Ṭhākura says:

vrajendra-nandana yei, śacī-suta haila sei,
balarāma ha-ila nitāi
dīna-hīna yata chila, hari-nāme uddhārila,
ta'ra sākṣī jagāi-mādhāi

The appearance of Śrī Caitanya Mahāprabhu in this Kali-yuga is especially meant to deliver the fallen souls, who are always planning something for material enjoyment. He gave the people of this age the advantage of being able to chant the Hare Kṛṣṇa *mantra* and thus become fully pure, free from all material contamination. Once one becomes a pure Vaiṣṇava, he transcends all material conceptions of life. Thus Kaśyapa Muni tried to transform his wife into a Vaiṣṇavī so that she might give up the idea of killing Indra. He wanted both her and her sons to be purified so that they would be fit to become pure Vaiṣṇavas. Of course, sometimes a practitioner deviates from the Vaiṣṇava principles, and there is a chance that he may fall down, but Kaśyapa Muni thought that even if one falls while practicing the Vaiṣṇava principles, he is still not a loser. Even a fallen Vaiṣṇava is eligible for better results, as confirmed in *Bhagavad-gītā. Svalpam apy asya dharmasya trāyate mahato bhayāt:* even practicing the Vaiṣṇava principles to a small extent can save one from the greatest danger of material existence. Thus Kaśyapa Muni planned to instruct his wife Diti to become a Vaiṣṇava because he wanted to save the life of Indra.

TEXT 44

इति संचिन्त्य भगवान्मारीचः कुरुनन्दन ।
उवाच किञ्चित् कुपित आत्मानं च विगर्हयन् ॥ ४४ ॥

iti sañcintya bhagavān
mārīcaḥ kurunandana
uvāca kiñcit kupita
ātmānaṁ ca vigarhayan

iti—thus; *sañcintya*—thinking; *bhagavān*—the powerful; *mārīcaḥ*—Kaśyapa Muni; *kuru-nandana*—O descendant of Kuru; *uvāca*—spoke; *kiñcit*—somewhat; *kupitaḥ*—angry; *ātmānam*—himself; *ca*—and; *vigarhayan*—condemning.

TRANSLATION

Śrī Śukadeva Gosvāmī said: Kaśyapa Muni, thinking in this way, became somewhat angry. Condemning himself, O Mahārāja Parīkṣit, descendant of Kuru, he spoke to Diti as follows.

TEXT 45

श्रीकश्यप उवाच
पुत्रस्ते भविता भद्रे इन्द्रहादेवबान्धवः ।
संवत्सरं व्रतमिदं यद्यञ्जो धारयिष्यसि ॥ ४५ ॥

śrī-kaśyapa uvāca
putras te bhavitā bhadre
indra-hādeva-bāndhavaḥ
saṁvatsaraṁ vratam idaṁ
yady añjo dhārayiṣyasi

śrī-kaśyapaḥ uvāca—Kaśyapa Muni said; *putraḥ*—son; *te*—your; *bhavitā*—will be; *bhadre*—O gentle woman; *indra-hā*—killer of Indra, or follower of Indra; *adeva-bāndhavaḥ*—friend of the demons (or *deva-bāndhavaḥ*—friend of the demigods); *saṁvatsaram*—for a year; *vratam*—vow; *idam*—this; *yadi*—if; *añjaḥ*—properly; *dhārayiṣyasi*—you will execute.

TRANSLATION

Kaśyapa Muni said: My dear gentle wife, if you follow my instructions regarding this vow for at least one year, you will surely get a son who will be able to kill Indra. However, if you deviate from this vow of following the Vaiṣṇava principles, you will get a son who will be favorable to Indra.

PURPORT

The word *indra-hā* refers to an *asura* who is always eager to kill Indra. An enemy of Indra is naturally a friend to the *asuras,* but the word *indra-hā* also refers to one who follows Indra or who is obedient to him. When one becomes a devotee of Indra, he is certainly a friend to the demigods. Thus the words *indra-hādeva-bāndhavaḥ* are equivocal, for they say, "Your son will kill Indra, but he will be very friendly to the demigods." If a person actually became a friend of the demigods, he certainly would not be able to kill Indra.

TEXT 46

दितिरुवाच
धारयिष्ये व्रतं ब्रह्मन्ब्रूहि कार्याणि यानि मे ।
यानि चेह निषिद्धानि न व्रतं घ्नन्ति यान्युत ॥ ४६ ॥

ditir uvāca
dhārayiṣye vrataṁ brahman
brūhi kāryāṇi yāni me
yāni ceha niṣiddhāni
na vrataṁ ghnanti yāny uta

ditiḥ uvāca—Diti said; *dhārayiṣye*—I shall accept; *vratam*—vow; *brahman*—my dear *brāhmaṇa; brūhi*—please state; *kāryāṇi*—must be done; *yāni*—what; *me*—to me; *yāni*—what; *ca*—and; *iha*—here; *niṣiddhāni*—is forbidden; *na*—not; *vratam*—the vow; *ghnanti*—break; *yāni*—what; *uta*—also.

TRANSLATION

Diti replied: My dear brāhmaṇa, I must accept your advice and follow the vow. Now let me understand what I have to do, what is forbidden and what will not break the vow. Please clearly state all this to me.

PURPORT

As stated above, a woman is generally inclined to serve her own purposes. Kaśyapa Muni proposed to train Diti to fulfill her desires within one year, and since she was eager to kill Indra, she immediately agreed, saying, "Please let me know what the vow is and how I have to follow it. I promise that I shall do the needful and not break the vow." This is another side of a woman's psychology. Even though a woman is very fond of fulfilling her own plans, when someone instructs her, especially her husband, she innocently follows, and thus she can be trained for better purposes. By nature a woman wants to be a follower of a man; therefore if the man is good the woman can be trained for a good purpose.

TEXT 47

श्रीकश्यप उवाच
न हिंस्याद्भूतजातानि न शपेन्नानृतं वदेत् ।
नछिन्द्यान्नखरोमाणि न स्पृशेद्यदमङ्गलम् ॥ ४७ ॥

śrī-kaśyapa uvāca
na hiṁsyād bhūta-jātāni
na śapen nānṛtaṁ vadet
na chindyān nakha-romāṇi
na spṛśed yad amaṅgalam

śrī-kaśyapaḥ uvāca—Kaśyapa Muni said; *na hiṁsyāt*—must not harm; *bhūta-jātāni*—the living entities; *na śapet*—must not curse; *na*—not; *anṛtam*—a lie; *vadet*—must speak; *na chindyāt*—must not cut; *nakha-romāṇi*—the nails and hair; *na spṛśet*—must not touch; *yat*—that which; *amaṅgalam*—impure.

TRANSLATION

Kaśyapa Muni said: My dear wife, to follow this vow, do not be violent or cause harm to anyone. Do not curse anyone, and do not speak lies. Do not cut your nails and hair, and do not touch impure things like skulls and bones.

PURPORT

Kaśyapa Muni's first instruction to his wife was not to be envious. The general tendency of anyone within this material world is to be envious, and therefore, to become a Kṛṣṇa conscious person, one must curb this tendency, as stated in *Śrīmad-Bhāgavatam* (*paramo nirmatsarāṇām*). A Kṛṣṇa conscious person is always nonenvious, whereas others are always envious. Thus Kaśyapa Muni's instruction that his wife not be envious indicates that this is the first stage of advancement in Kṛṣṇa consciousness. Kaśyapa Muni desired to train his wife to be a Kṛṣṇa conscious person, for this would suffice to protect both her and Indra.

TEXT 48

नाप्सु स्नायान्न कुप्येत न सम्भाषेत दुर्जनैः ।
न वसीताधौतवासः स्त्रजं च विधृतां क्वचित् ॥ ४८ ॥

nāpsu snāyān na kupyeta
na sambhāṣeta durjanaiḥ
na vasītādhauta-vāsaḥ
srajaṁ ca vidhṛtāṁ kvacit

na—not; *apsu*—in water; *snāyāt*—must bathe; *na kupyeta*—must not become angry; *na sambhāṣeta*—must not speak; *durjanaiḥ*—with wicked persons; *na vasīta*—must not wear; *adhauta-vāsaḥ*—unwashed clothes; *srajam*—flower garland; *ca*—and; *vidhṛtām*—which was already worn; *kvacit*—ever.

TRANSLATION

Kaśyapa Muni continued: My dear gentle wife, never enter the water while bathing, never be angry, and do not even speak or associate with wicked people. Never wear clothes that have not been properly washed, and do not put on a garland that has already been worn.

TEXT 49

नोच्छिष्टं चण्डिकान्नं च सामिषं वृषलाहृतम् ।
भुञ्जीतोदक्यया दृष्टं पिबेन्नाञ्जलिना त्वपः ॥ ४९ ॥

nocchiṣṭaṁ caṇḍikānnaṁ ca
sāmiṣaṁ vṛṣalāhṛtam
bhuñjītodakyayā dṛṣṭaṁ
piben nāñjalinā tv apaḥ

na—not; *ucchiṣṭam*—leftover food; *caṇḍikā-annam*—food offered to the goddess Kālī; *ca*—and; *sa-āmiṣam*—mixed with flesh; *vṛṣala-āhṛtam*—brought by a *śūdra; bhuñjīta*—must eat; *udakyayā*—by a woman in her menstrual period; *dṛṣṭam*—seen; *pibet na*—must not drink; *añjalinā*—by joining and cupping the two palms; *tu*—also; *apaḥ*—water.

TRANSLATION

Never eat leftover food, never eat prasāda offered to the goddess Kālī [Durgā], and do not eat anything contaminated by flesh or fish. Do not eat anything brought or touched by a śūdra nor anything seen by a woman in her menstrual period. Do not drink water by joining your palms.

PURPORT

Generally the goddess Kālī is offered food containing meat and fish, and therefore Kaśyapa Muni strictly forbade his wife to take the remnants of such food. Actually a Vaiṣṇava is not allowed to take any food offered to the demigods. A Vaiṣṇava is always fixed in accepting *prasāda* offered to Lord Viṣṇu. Through all these instructions, Kaśyapa Muni, in a negative way, instructed his wife Diti how to become a Vaiṣṇavī.

TEXT 50

नोच्छिष्टास्पृष्टसलिला सन्ध्यायां मुक्तमूर्धजा ।
अनर्चितासंयतवाक् नासंवीता बहिश्चरेत् ॥ ५० ॥

nocchiṣṭāspṛṣṭa-salilā
sandhyāyāṁ mukta-mūrdhajā
anarcitāsaṁyata-vāk
nāsaṁvītā bahiś caret

na—not; *ucchiṣṭā*—after eating; *aspṛṣṭa-salilā*—without washing; *sandhyāyām*—in the evening; *mukta-mūrdhajā*—with the hair loose; *anarcitā*—without ornaments; *asaṁyata-vāk*—without being grave; *na*—not; *asaṁvītā*—without being covered; *bahiḥ*—outside; *caret*—should go.

TRANSLATION

After eating, you should not go out to the street without having washed your mouth, hands and feet. You should not go out in the evening or with your hair loose, nor should you go out unless you are properly decorated with ornaments. You should not leave the house unless you are very grave and are sufficiently covered.

PURPORT

Kaśyapa Muni advised his wife not to go out onto the street unless she was well decorated and well dressed. He did not encourage the miniskirts that have now become fashionable. In Oriental civilization, when a woman goes out onto the street, she must be fully covered so that no man will recognize who she is. All these methods are to be accepted for purification. If one takes to Kṛṣṇa consciousness, one is fully purified, and thus one remains always transcendental to the contamination of the material world.

TEXT 51

नाधौतपादाप्रयता नार्द्रपादा उदक्शिराः ।
शयीत नापराङ्नान्यैर्न नग्ना न च सन्ध्ययोः ॥ ५१ ॥

nādhauta-pādāprayatā
nārdra-pādā udak-śirāḥ
śayīta nāparāṅ nānyair
na nagnā na ca sandhyayoḥ

na—not; *adhauta-pādā*—without washing the feet; *aprayatā*—without being purified; *na*—not; *ardra-pādā*—with wet feet; *udak-śirāḥ*—with the head toward the north; *śayīta*—should lie down; *na*—not; *aparāk*—with the head pointed west; *na*—not; *anyaiḥ*—with other women; *na*—not; *nagnā*—naked; *na*—not; *ca*—and; *sandhyayoḥ*—at sunrise and sunset.

TRANSLATION

You should not lie down without having washed both of your feet or without being purified, nor with wet feet or with your head pointed west or north. You should not lie naked, or with other women, or during the sunrise or sunset.

TEXT 52

धौतवासा शुचिर्नित्यं सर्वमङ्गलसंयुता ।
पूजयेत्प्रातराशात्प्राग्गोविप्राञ् श्रियमच्युतम् ॥ ५२ ॥

dhauta-vāsā śucir nityaṁ
sarva-maṅgala-saṁyutā
pūjayet prātarāśāt prāg
go-viprāñ śriyam acyutam

dhauta-vāsā—wearing washed cloth; *śuciḥ*—being purified; *nityam*—always; *sarva-maṅgala*—with all auspicious items; *saṁyutā*—adorned; *pūjayet*—one should worship; *prātaḥ-āśāt prāk*—before breakfast; *go-viprān*—the cows and *brāhmaṇas; śriyam*—the goddess of fortune; *acyutam*—the Supreme Personality of Godhead.

TRANSLATION

Putting on washed clothing, being always pure and being adorned with turmeric, sandalwood pulp and other auspicious items, before breakfast one should worship the cows, the brāhmaṇas, the goddess of fortune and the Supreme Personality of Godhead.

PURPORT

If one is trained to honor and worship the cows and *brāhmaṇas,* he is actually civilized. The worship of the Supreme Lord is recommended, and the Lord is very fond of the cows and *brāhmaṇas* (*namo brahmaṇya-devāya go-brāhmaṇa-hitāya ca*). In other words, a civilization in which there is no respect for the cows and *brāhmaṇas* is condemned. One cannot become spiritually advanced without acquiring the brahminical qualifications and giving protection to cows. Cow protection insures sufficient food prepared with milk, which is needed for an advanced civilization. One should not pollute civilization by eating the flesh of cows. A civilization must do something progressive, and then it is an Āryan civilization. Instead of killing the cow to eat flesh, civilized men must prepare various milk products that will enhance the condition of society. If one follows the brahminical culture, he will become competent in Kṛṣṇa consciousness.

TEXT 53

स्त्रियो वीरवतीश्चार्चेत्स्रग्गन्धबलिमण्डनैः ।
पतिं चार्च्योपतिष्ठेत ध्यायेत्कोष्ठगतं च तम् ॥५३॥

striyo vīravatīś cārcet
srag-gandha-bali-maṇḍanaiḥ
patiṁ cārcyopatiṣṭheta
dhyāyet koṣṭha-gataṁ ca tam

striyaḥ—women; *vīra-vatīḥ*—possessing husbands and sons; *ca*—and; *arcet*—she should worship; *srak*—with garlands; *gandha*—sandalwood; *bali*—presentations; *maṇḍanaiḥ*—and with ornaments; *patim*—the husband; *ca*—and; *ārcya*—worshiping; *upatiṣṭheta*—should offer prayers; *dhyāyet*—should meditate; *koṣṭha-gatam*—situated in the womb; *ca*—also; *tam*—upon him.

TRANSLATION

With flower garlands, sandalwood pulp, ornaments and other paraphernalia, a woman following this vow should worship women who have sons and whose husbands are living. The pregnant wife should worship her husband and offer him prayers. She should meditate upon him, thinking that he is situated in her womb.

PURPORT

The child in the womb is a part of the husband's body. Therefore the husband, through his representative, indirectly remains within the womb of his pregnant wife.

TEXT 54

सांवत्सरं पुंसवनं व्रतमेतदविप्लुतम् ।
धारयिष्यसि चेत्तुभ्यं शक्रहा भविता सुतः ॥ ५४ ॥

sāṁvatsaraṁ puṁsavanaṁ
vratam etad aviplutam
dhārayiṣyasi cet tubhyaṁ
śakra-hā bhavitā sutaḥ

sāṁvatsaram—for one year; *puṁsavanam*—called *puṁsavana; vratam*—vow; *etat*—this; *aviplutam*—without violation; *dhārayiṣyasi*—you will perform; *cet*—if; *tubhyam*—for you; *śakra-hā*—the killer of Indra; *bhavitā*—will be; *sutaḥ*—a son.

TRANSLATION

Kaśyapa Muni continued: If you perform this ceremony called puṁsavana, adhering to the vow with faith for at least one year, you will give birth to a son destined to kill Indra. But if there is any discrepancy in the discharge of this vow, the son will be a friend to Indra.

TEXT 55

बाढमित्यभ्युपेत्याथ दिती राजन् महामनाः ।
कश्यपाद् गर्भमाधत्त व्रतं चाञ्जो दधार सा ॥ ५५ ॥

bāḍham ity abhyupetyātha
ditī rājan mahā-manāḥ

kaśyapād garbham ādhatta
vrataṁ cāñjo dadhāra sā

bāḍham—yes; *iti*—thus; *abhyupetya*—accepting; *atha*—then; *ditiḥ*—Diti; *rājan*—O King; *mahā-manāḥ*—jubilant; *kaśyapāt*—from Kaśyapa; *garbham*—semen; *ādhatta*—obtained; *vratam*—the vow; *ca*—and; *añjaḥ*—properly; *dadhāra*—discharged; *sā*—she.

TRANSLATION

O King Parīkṣit, Diti, the wife of Kaśyapa, agreed to undergo the purificatory process known as puṁsavana. "Yes," she said, "I shall do everything according to your instructions." With great jubilation she became pregnant, having taken semen from Kaśyapa, and faithfully began discharging the vow.

TEXT 56

मातृष्वसुरभिप्रायमिन्द्र आज्ञाय मानद ।
शुश्रूषणेनाश्रमस्थां दितिं पर्यचरत्कविः ॥ ५६ ॥

mātṛ-ṣvasur abhiprāyam
indra ājñāya mānada
śuśrūṣaṇenāśrama-sthāṁ
ditiṁ paryacarat kaviḥ

mātṛ-svasuḥ—of his mother's sister; *abhiprāyam*—the intention; *indraḥ*—Indra; *ājñāya*—understanding; *māna-da*—O King Parīkṣit, who give respect to everyone; *śuśrūṣaṇena*—with service; *āśrama-sthām*—residing in an *āśrama; ditim*—Diti; *paryacarat*—attended upon; *kaviḥ*—seeing his own interest.

TRANSLATION

O King, who are respectful to everyone, Indra understood Diti's purpose, and thus he contrived to fulfill his own interests. Following the logic that self-preservation is the first law of nature, he wanted to break Diti's promise. Thus he engaged himself in the service of Diti, his aunt, who was residing in an āśrama.

TEXT 57

नित्यं वनात्सुमनसः फलमूलसमित्कुशान् ।
पत्राङ्कुरमृदोऽपश्च काले काल उपाहरत् ॥ ५७ ॥

nityaṁ vanāt sumanasaḥ
phala-mūla-samit-kuśān
patrāṅkura-mṛdo'paś ca
kāle kāla upāharat

nityam—daily; *vanāt*—from the forest; *sumanasaḥ*—flowers; *phala*—fruits; *mūla*—roots; *samit*—wood for the sacrificial fire; *kuśān*—and *kuśa* grass; *patra*—leaves; *aṅkura*—sprouts; *mṛdaḥ*—and earth; *apaḥ*—water; *ca*—also; *kāle kāle*—at the proper time; *upāharat*—brought.

TRANSLATION

Indra served his aunt daily by bringing flowers, fruits, roots and wood for yajñas from the forest. He also brought kuśa grass, leaves, sprouts, earth and water exactly at the proper time.

TEXT 58

एवं तस्या व्रतस्थाया व्रतच्छिद्रं हरिर्नृप ।
प्रेप्सुः पर्यचरज्जिह्मो मृगहेव मृगाकृतिः ॥ ५८ ॥

evaṁ tasyā vrata-sthāyā
vrata-cchidraṁ harir nṛpa
prepsuḥ paryacaraj jihmo
mṛga-heva mṛgākṛtiḥ

evam—thus; *tasyāḥ*—of her; *vrata-sthāyāḥ*—who was faithfully discharging her vow; *vrata-chidram*—a fault in the execution of the vow; *hariḥ*—Indra; *nṛpa*—O King; *prepsuḥ*—desiring to find; *paryacarat*—served; *jihmaḥ*—deceitful; *mṛga-hā*—a hunter; *iva*—like; *mṛga-ākṛtiḥ*—in the form of a deer.

TRANSLATION

O King Parīkṣit, as the hunter of a deer becomes like a deer by covering his body with deerskin and serving the deer, so Indra, although at heart the enemy of the sons of Diti, became outwardly friendly and served Diti in a faithful way. Indra's purpose was to cheat Diti as soon as he could find some fault in the way she discharged the vows of the ritualistic ceremony. However, he wanted to be undetected, and therefore he served her very carefully.

TEXT 59

नाध्यगच्छद्व्रतच्छिद्रं तत्परोऽथ महीपते ।
चिन्तां तीव्रां गतः शक्रः केन मे स्याच्छिवं त्विह ॥ ५९ ॥

nādhyagacchad vrata-cchidraṁ
tat-paro'tha mahī-pate
cintāṁ tīvrāṁ gataḥ śakraḥ
kena me syāc chivaṁ tv iha

na—not; *adhyagacchat*—could find; *vrata-chidram*—a fault in the execution of the vow; *tat-paraḥ*—intent upon that; *atha*—thereupon; *mahī-pate*—O master of the world; *cintām*—anxiety; *tīvrām*—intense; *gataḥ*—obtained; *śakraḥ*—Indra; *kena*—how; *me*—my; *syāt*—can there be; *śivam*—well-being; *tu*—then; *iha*—here.

TRANSLATION

O master of the entire world, when Indra could find no faults, he thought, "How will there be good fortune for me?" Thus he was full of deep anxiety.

TEXT 60

एकदा सा तु सन्ध्यायामुच्छिष्टा व्रतकर्शिता ।
अस्पृष्टवार्यधौताङ्घ्रिः सुष्वाप विधिमोहिता ॥ ६० ॥

ekadā sā tu sandhyāyām
ucchiṣṭā vrata-karśitā
aspṛṣṭa-vāry-adhautāṅghriḥ
suṣvāpa vidhi-mohitā

ekadā—once; *sā*—she; *tu*—but; *sandhyāyām*—during the evening twilight; *ucchiṣṭā*—just after eating; *vrata*—from the vow; *karśitā*—weak and thin; *aspṛṣṭa*—not touched; *vāri*—water; *adhauta*—not washed; *aṅghriḥ*—her feet; *suṣvāpa*—went to sleep; *vidhi*—by fate; *mohitā*—bewildered.

TRANSLATION

Having grown weak and thin because of strictly following the principles of the vow, Diti once unfortunately neglected to wash her mouth, hands and feet after eating and went to sleep during the evening twilight.

TEXT 61

लब्ध्वा तदन्तरं शक्रो निद्रापहृतचेतसः ।
दितेः प्रविष्ट उदरं योगेशो योगमायया ॥ ६१ ॥

labdhvā tad-antaraṁ śakro
nidrāpahṛta-cetasaḥ
diteḥ praviṣṭa udaraṁ
yogeśo yoga-māyayā

labdhvā—finding; *tat-antaram*—after that; *śakraḥ*—Indra; *nidrā*—by sleep; *apahṛta-cetasaḥ*—unconscious; *diteḥ*—of Diti; *praviṣṭaḥ*—entered; *udaram*—the womb; *yoga-īśaḥ*—the master of *yoga; yoga*—of yogic perfections; *māyayā*—by the power.

TRANSLATION

Finding this fault, Indra, who has all the mystic powers [the yoga-siddhis such as aṇimā and laghimā], entered Diti's womb while she was unconscious, being fast asleep.

PURPORT

A perfectly successful *yogī* is expert in eight kinds of perfection. By one of them, called *aṇimā-siddhi,* he can become smaller than an atom, and in that state he can enter anywhere. With this yogic power, Indra entered the womb of Diti while she was pregnant.

TEXT 62

चकर्त सप्तधा गर्भं वज्रेण कनकप्रभम् ।
रुदन्तं सप्तधैकैकं मा रोदीरिति तान् पुनः ॥ ६२ ॥

cakarta saptadhā garbhaṁ
vajreṇa kanaka-prabham
rudantaṁ saptadhaikaikaṁ
mā rodīr iti tān punaḥ

cakarta—he cut; *sapta-dhā*—into seven pieces; *garbham*—the embryo; *vajreṇa*—by his thunderbolt; *kanaka*—of gold; *prabham*—which had the appearance; *rudantam*—crying; *sapta-dhā*—into seven pieces; *eka-ekam*—each one; *mā rodīḥ*—do not cry; *iti*—thus; *tān*—them; *punaḥ*—again.

TRANSLATION

After entering Diti's womb, Indra, with the help of his thunderbolt, cut into seven pieces her embryo, which appeared like glowing gold. In seven places, seven different living beings began crying. Indra told them, "Do not cry," and then he cut each of them into seven pieces again.

PURPORT

Śrīla Viśvanātha Cakravartī Ṭhākura remarks that Indra, by his yogic power, first expanded the body of the one Marut into seven, and then when he cut each of the seven parts of the original body into pieces, there were forty-nine. When each body was cut into seven, other living entities entered the new bodies, and thus they were like plants, which become separate entities when cut into various parts and planted on a hill. The first body was one, and when it was cut into many pieces, many other living entities entered the new bodies.

TEXT 63

तमूचुः पाट्यमानास्ते सर्वे प्राञ्जलयो नृप ।
किं न इन्द्र जिघांससि भ्रातरो मरुतस्तव ॥ ६३ ॥

tam ūcuḥ pāṭyamānās te
sarve prāñjalayo nṛpa
kiṁ na indra jighāṁsasi
bhrātaro marutas tava

tam—to him; *ūcuḥ*—said; *pāṭyamānāḥ*—being aggrieved; *te*—they; *sarve*—all; *prāñjalayaḥ*—with folded hands; *nṛpa*—O King; *kim*—why; *naḥ*—us; *indra*—O Indra; *jighāṁsasi*—do you want to kill; *bhrātaraḥ*—brothers; *marutaḥ*—Maruts; *tava*—your.

TRANSLATION

O King, being very much aggrieved, they pleaded to Indra with folded hands, saying, "Dear Indra, we are the Maruts, your brothers. Why are you trying to kill us?"

TEXT 64

मा भैष्ट भ्रातरो मह्यं यूयमित्याह कौशिकः ।
अनन्यभावान् पार्षदानात्मनो मरुतां गणान् ॥ ६४ ॥

mā bhaiṣṭa bhrātaro mahyaṁ
yūyam ity āha kauśikaḥ
ananya-bhāvān pārṣadān
ātmano marutāṁ gaṇān

mā bhaiṣṭa—do not fear; *bhrātaraḥ*—brothers; *mahyam*—my; *yūyam*—you; *iti*—thus; *āha*—said; *kauśikaḥ*—Indra; *ananya-bhāvān*—devoted; *pārṣadān*—followers; *ātmanaḥ*—his; *marutām gaṇān*—the Maruts.

TRANSLATION

When Indra saw that actually they were his devoted followers, he said to them: If you are all my brothers, you have nothing more to fear from me.

TEXT 65

न ममार दितेर्गर्भः श्रीनिवासानुकम्पया ।
बहुधा कुलिशक्षुण्णो द्रौण्यस्त्रेण यथा भवान् ॥ ६५ ॥

na mamāra diter garbhaḥ
śrīnivāsānukampayā
bahudhā kuliśa-kṣuṇṇo
drauṇy-astreṇa yathā bhavān

na—not; *mamāra*—died; *diteḥ*—of Diti; *garbhaḥ*—the embryo; *śrīnivāsa*—of Lord Viṣṇu, the resting place of the goddess of fortune; *anukampayā*—by the mercy; *bahu-dhā*—into many pieces; *kuliśa*—by the thunderbolt; *kṣuṇṇaḥ*—cut; *drauṇi*—of Aśvatthāmā; *astreṇa*—by the weapon; *yathā*—just as; *bhavān*—you.

TRANSLATION

Śukadeva Gosvāmī said: My dear King Parīkṣit, you were burned by the brahmāstra of Aśvatthāmā, but when Lord Kṛṣṇa entered the womb of your mother, you were saved. Similarly, although the one embryo was cut into forty-nine pieces by the thunderbolt of Indra, they were all saved by the mercy of the Supreme Personality of Godhead.

TEXTS 66–67

सकृदिष्ट्वादिपुरुषं पुरुषो याति साम्यताम् ।
संवत्सरं किञ्चिदूनं दित्या यद्धरिरर्चितः ॥ ६६ ॥

सजूरिन्द्रेण पञ्चाशद्देवास्ते मरुतोऽभवन् ।
व्यपोह्य मातृदोषं ते हरिणा सोमपाः कृताः ॥ ६७ ॥

sakṛd iṣṭvādi-puruṣaṁ
puruṣo yāti sāmyatām
saṁvatsaraṁ kiñcid ūnaṁ
dityā yad dharir arcitaḥ

sajūr indreṇa pañcāśad
devās te maruto'bhavan
vyapohya mātṛ-doṣaṁ te
hariṇā soma-pāḥ kṛtāḥ

sakṛt—once; *iṣṭvā*—worshiping; *ādi-puruṣam*—the original person; *puruṣaḥ*—a person; *yāti*—goes to; *sāmyatām*—possessing the same bodily feature as the Lord; *saṁvatsaram*—a year; *kiñcit ūnam*—a little less than; *dityā*—by Diti; *yat*—because; *hariḥ*—Lord Hari; *arcitaḥ*—was worshiped; *sajūḥ*—with; *indreṇa*—Indra; *pañcāśat*—fifty; *devāḥ*—demigods; *te*—they; *marutaḥ*—the Maruts; *abhavan*—became; *vyapohya*—removing; *mātṛ-doṣam*—the fault of their mother; *te*—they; *hariṇā*—by Lord Hari; *soma-pāḥ*—drinkers of *soma-rasa; kṛtāḥ*—were made.

TRANSLATION

If one worships the Supreme Personality of Godhead, the original person, even once, he receives the benefit of being promoted to the spiritual world and possessing the same bodily features as Viṣṇu. Diti worshiped Lord Viṣṇu for almost one year, adhering to a great vow. Because of such strength in spiritual life, the forty-nine Maruts were born. How, then, is it wonderful that the Maruts, although born from the womb of Diti, became equal to the demigods by the mercy of the Supreme Lord?

TEXT 68

दितिरुत्थाय ददृशे कुमाराननलप्रभान् ।
इन्द्रेण सहितान् देवी पर्यतुष्यदनिन्दिता ॥ ६८ ॥

ditir utthāya dadṛśe
kumārān anala-prabhān
indreṇa sahitān devī
paryatuṣyad aninditā

ditiḥ—Diti; *utthāya*—getting up; *dadṛśe*—saw; *kumārān*—children; *anala-prabhān*—as brilliant as fire; *indreṇa sahitān*—with Indra; *devī*—the goddess; *paryatuṣyat*—was pleased; *aninditā*—being purified.

TRANSLATION

Because of worshiping the Supreme Personality of Godhead, Diti was completely purified. When she got up from bed, she saw her forty-nine sons along with Indra. These forty-nine sons were all as brilliant as fire and were in friendship with Indra, and therefore she was very pleased.

TEXT 69

अथेन्द्रमाह ताताहमादित्यानां भयावहम् ।
अपत्यमिच्छन्त्यचरं व्रतमेतत्सुदुष्करम् ॥ ६९ ॥

athendram āha tātāham
ādityānāṁ bhayāvaham
apatyam icchanty acaraṁ
vratam etat suduṣkaram

atha—thereafter; *indram*—to Indra; *āha*—spoke; *tāta*—dear one; *aham*—I; *ādityānām*—to the Ādityas; *bhaya-āvaham*—fearful; *apatyam*—a son; *icchantī*—desiring; *acaram*—executed; *vratam*—vow; *etat*—this; *su-duṣkaram*—very difficult to perform.

TRANSLATION

Thereafter, Diti said to Indra: My dear son, I adhered to this difficult vow just to get a son to kill you twelve Ādityas.

TEXT 70

एकः सङ्कल्पितः पुत्रः सप्त सप्ताभवन् कथम् ।
यदि ते विदितं पुत्र सत्यं कथय मा मृषा ॥ ७० ॥

ekaḥ saṅkalpitaḥ putraḥ
sapta saptābhavan katham
yadi te viditaṁ putra
satyaṁ kathaya mā mṛṣā

ekaḥ—one; *saṅkalpitaḥ*—was prayed for; *putraḥ*—son; *sapta sapta*—forty-nine; *abhavan*—came to be; *katham*—how; *yadi*—if; *te*—by you;

viditam—known; *putra*—my dear son; *satyam*—the truth; *kathaya*—speak; *mā*—do not (speak); *mṛṣā*—lies.

TRANSLATION

I prayed for only one son, but now I see that there are forty-nine. How has this happened? My dear son Indra, if you know, please tell me the truth. Do not try to speak lies.

TEXT 71

इन्द्र उवाच
अम्ब तेऽहं व्यवसितमुपधार्यागतोऽन्तिकम् ।
लब्धान्तरोऽच्छिदं गर्भमर्थबुद्धिर्न धर्मदृक् ॥ ७१ ॥

indra uvāca
amba te'haṁ vyavasitam
upadhāryāgato'ntikam
labdhāntaro'cchidaṁ garbham
artha-buddhir na dharma-dṛk

indraḥ uvāca—Indra said; *amba*—O mother; *te*—your; *aham*—I; *vyavasitam*—vow; *upadhārya*—understanding; *āgataḥ*—came; *antikam*—nearby; *labdha*—having found; *antaraḥ*—a fault; *acchidam*—I cut; *garbham*—the embryo; *artha-buddhiḥ*—being self-interested; *na*—not; *dharma-dṛk*—possessing vision of religion.

TRANSLATION

Indra replied: My dear mother, because I was grossly blinded by selfish interests, I lost sight of religion. When I understood that you were observing a great vow in spiritual life, I wanted to find some fault in you. When I found such a fault, I entered your womb and cut the embryo to pieces.

PURPORT

When Diti, Indra's aunt, explained to Indra without reservations what she had wanted to do, Indra explained his intentions to her. Thus both of them, instead of being enemies, freely spoke the truth. This is the qualification that results from contact with Viṣṇu. As stated in *Śrīmad-Bhāgavatam* (5.18.12):

yasyāsti bhaktir bhagavaty akiñcanā
sarvair guṇais tatra samāsate surāḥ

If one develops a devotional attitude and becomes purified by worshiping the Supreme Lord, all the good qualities are certainly manifested in his body. Because of being touched by worship of Viṣṇu, both Diti and Indra were purified.

TEXT 72

कृत्तो मे सप्तधा गर्भ आसन् सप्त कुमारकाः ।
तेऽपि चैकैकशो वृक्णाः सप्तधा नापि मम्रिरे ॥ ७२ ॥

kṛtto me saptadhā garbha
āsan sapta kumārakāḥ
te'pi caikaikaśo vṛkṇāḥ
saptadhā nāpi mamrire

kṛttaḥ—cut; *me*—by me; *sapta-dhā*—into seven; *garbhaḥ*—the embryo; *āsan*—there came to be; *sapta*—seven; *kumārakāḥ*—babies; *te*—they; *api*—although; *ca*—also; *eka-ekaśaḥ*—each one; *vṛkṇāḥ*—cut; *sapta-dhā*—into seven; *na*—not; *api*—still; *mamrire*—died.

TRANSLATION

First I cut the child in the womb into seven pieces, which became seven children. Then I cut each of the children into seven pieces again. By the grace of the Supreme Lord, however, none of them died.

TEXT 73

ततस्तत्परमाश्चर्यं वीक्ष्य व्यवसितं मया ।
महापुरुषपूजायाः सिद्धिः काप्यानुषङ्गिणी ॥ ७३ ॥

tatas tat paramāścaryaṁ
vīkṣya vyavasitaṁ mayā
mahāpuruṣa-pūjāyāḥ
siddhiḥ kāpy ānuṣaṅgiṇī

tataḥ—then; *tat*—that; *parama-āścaryam*—great wonder; *vīkṣya*—seeing; *vyavasitam*—it was decided; *mayā*—by me; *mahā-puruṣa*—of Lord Viṣṇu; *pūjāyāḥ*—of worship; *siddhiḥ*—result; *kāpi*—some; *ānuṣaṅgiṇī*—secondary.

TRANSLATION

My dear mother, when I saw that all forty-nine sons were alive, I was certainly struck with wonder. I decided that this was a secondary result of your having regularly executed devotional service in worship of Lord Viṣṇu.

PURPORT

For one who engages in worshiping Lord Viṣṇu, nothing is very wonderful. This is a fact. In *Bhagavad-gītā* (18.78) it is said:

yatra yogeśvaraḥ kṛṣṇo
yatra pārtho dhanur-dharaḥ
tatra śrīr vijayo bhūtir
dhruvā nītir matir mama

"Wherever there is Kṛṣṇa, the master of all mystics, and wherever there is Arjuna, the supreme archer, there will also certainly be opulence, victory, extraordinary power, and morality. That is my opinion." Yogeśvara is the Supreme Personality of Godhead, the master of all mystic *yoga,* who can do anything and everything He likes. This is the omnipotence of the Supreme Lord. For one who pleases the Supreme Lord, no achievement is wonderful. Everything is possible for him.

TEXT 74

आराधनं भगवत ईहमाना निराशिषः ।
ये तु नेच्छन्त्यपि परं ते स्वार्थकुशलाः स्मृताः ॥ ७४ ॥

ārādhanaṁ bhagavata
īhamānā nirāśiṣaḥ
ye tu necchanty api paraṁ
te svārtha-kuśalāḥ smṛtāḥ

ārādhanam—the worship; *bhagavataḥ*—of the Supreme Personality of Godhead; *īhamānāḥ*—being interested in; *nirāśiṣaḥ*—without material desires; *ye*—those who; *tu*—indeed; *na icchanti*—do not desire; *api*—even; *param*—liberation; *te*—they; *sva-artha*—in their own interest; *kuśalāḥ*—expert; *smṛtāḥ*—are considered.

TRANSLATION

Although those who are interested only in worshiping the Supreme Personality of Godhead do not desire anything material from the Lord and do not even want liberation, Lord Kṛṣṇa fulfills all their desires.

PURPORT

When Dhruva Mahārāja saw Lord Viṣṇu, he declined to take any benedictions from Him, for he was fully satisfied by seeing the Lord. Nonetheless, the Lord is so kind that because Dhruva Mahārāja, in the beginning, had desired a kingdom greater than his father's, he was promoted to Dhruvaloka, the best planet in the universe. Therefore in the *śāstra* it is said:

akāmaḥ sarva-kāmo vā
mokṣa-kāma udāra-dhīḥ
tīvreṇa bhakti-yogena
yajeta puruṣaṁ param

"A person who has broader intelligence, whether he is full of material desires, free from material desires, or desiring liberation, must by all means worship the supreme whole, the Personality of Godhead." (*Bhāg.* 2.3.10) One should engage in full devotional service. Then, even though he has no desires, whatever desires he previously had can all be fulfilled simply by his worship of the Lord. The actual devotee does not desire even liberation (*anyābhilāṣitā-śūnyam*). The Lord, however, fulfills the desire of the devotee by awarding him opulence that will never be destroyed. A *karmī's* opulence is destroyed, but the opulence of a devotee is never destroyed. A devotee becomes more and more opulent as he increases his devotional service to the Lord.

TEXT 75

आराध्यात्मप्रदं देवं स्वात्मानं जगदीश्वरम् ।
को वृणीत गुणस्पर्शं बुधः स्यान्नरकेऽपि यत् ॥ ७५ ॥

ārādhyātma-pradaṁ devaṁ
svātmānaṁ jagad-īśvaram
ko vṛṇīta guṇa-sparśaṁ
budhaḥ syān narake'pi yat

ārādhya—after worshiping; *ātma-pradam*—who gives Himself; *devam*—the Lord; *sva-ātmānam*—the most dear; *jagat-īśvaram*—the Lord of the universe; *kaḥ*—what; *vṛṇīta*—would choose; *guṇa-sparśam*—material happiness; *budhaḥ*—intelligent person; *syāt*—is; *narake*—in hell; *api*—even; *yat*—which.

TRANSLATION

The ultimate goal of all ambitions is to become a servant of the Supreme Personality of Godhead. If an intelligent man serves the most dear Lord, who gives Himself to His devotees, how can he desire material happiness, which is available even in hell?

PURPORT

An intelligent man will never aspire to become a devotee to achieve material happiness. That is the test of a devotee. As Śrī Caitanya Mahāprabhu teaches:

na dhanaṁ na janaṁ na sundarīṁ
kavitāṁ vā jagad-īśa kāmaye
mama janmani janmanīśvare
bhavatād bhaktir ahaitukī tvayi

"O almighty Lord, I have no desire to accumulate wealth, nor do I desire beautiful women, nor do I want any number of followers. I only want Your causeless devotional service birth after birth." A pure devotee never begs the Lord for material happiness in the shape of riches, followers, a good wife or even *mukti.* The Lord promises, however, *yoga-kṣemaṁ vahāmy aham:* "I voluntarily bring everything necessary for My service."

TEXT 76

तदिदं मम दौर्जन्यं बालिशस्य महीयसि ।
क्षन्तुमर्हसि मातस्त्वं दिष्ट्या गर्भो मृतोत्थितः ॥ ७६ ॥

tad idaṁ mama daurjanyaṁ
bāliśasya mahīyasi
kṣantum arhasi mātas tvaṁ
diṣṭyā garbho mṛtotthitaḥ

tat—that; *idam*—this; *mama*—of me; *daurjanyam*—evil deed; *bāliśasya*—a fool; *mahīyasi*—O best of women; *kṣantum arhasi*—please excuse;

mātaḥ—O mother; *tvam*—you; *diṣṭyā*—by fortune; *garbhaḥ*—the child within the womb; *mṛta*—killed; *utthitaḥ*—became alive.

TRANSLATION

O my mother, O best of all women, I am a fool. Kindly excuse me for whatever offenses I have committed. Your forty-nine sons have been born unhurt because of your devotional service. As an enemy, I cut them to pieces, but because of your great devotional service they did not die.

TEXT 77

श्रीशुक उवाच
इन्द्रस्तयाभ्यनुज्ञातः शुद्धभावेन तुष्टया ।
मरुद्भिः सह तां नत्वा जगाम त्रिदिवं प्रभुः ॥ ७७ ॥

śrī-śuka uvāca
indras tayābhyanujñātaḥ
śuddha-bhāvena tuṣṭayā
marudbhiḥ saha tāṁ natvā
jagāma tri-divaṁ prabhuḥ

śrī-śukaḥ uvāca—Śrī Śukadeva Gosvāmī said; *indraḥ*—Indra; *tayā*—by her; *abhyanujñātaḥ*—being permitted; *śuddha-bhāvena*—by the good behavior; *tuṣṭayā*—satisfied; *marudbhiḥ saha*—with the Maruts; *tām*—to her; *natvā*—having offered obeisances; *jagāma*—he went; *tri-divam*—to the heavenly planets; *prabhuḥ*—the Lord.

TRANSLATION

Śrī Śukadeva Gosvāmī continued: Diti was extremely satisfied by Indra's good behavior. Then Indra offered his respects to his aunt with profuse obeisances, and with her permission he went away to the heavenly planets with his brothers the Maruts.

TEXT 78

एवं ते सर्वमाख्यातं यन्मां त्वं परिपृच्छसि ।
मङ्गलं मरुतां जन्म किं भूयः कथयामि ते ॥ ७८ ॥

evaṁ te sarvam ākhyātaṁ
yan māṁ tvaṁ paripṛcchasi

maṅgalaṁ marutāṁ janma
kiṁ bhūyaḥ kathayāmi te

evam—thus; *te*—to you; *sarvam*—all; *ākhyātam*—narrated; *yat*—which; *mām*—me; *tvam*—you; *paripṛcchasi*—asked; *maṅgalam*—auspicious; *marutām*—of the Maruts; *janma*—the birth; *kim*—what; *bhūyaḥ*—further; *kathayāmi*—shall I speak; *te*—to you.

TRANSLATION

My dear King Parīkṣit, I have replied as far as possible to the questions you have asked me, especially in regard to this pure, auspicious narration about the Maruts. Now you may inquire further, and I shall explain more.

Thus end the Bhaktivedanta purports to the Sixth Canto, Eighteenth Chapter, of the Śrīmad-Bhāgavatam, *entitled "Diti Vows to Kill King Indra."*

CHAPTER NINETEEN

Performing the Puṁsavana Ritualistic Ceremony

This chapter explains how Diti, Kaśyapa Muni's wife, executed Kaśyapa Muni's instructions on devotional service. During the first day of the bright fortnight of the moon in the month of Agrahāyaṇa (November–December), every woman, following in the footsteps of Diti and following the instructions of her own husband, should begin this *puṁsavana-vrata.* In the morning, after washing her teeth, bathing and thus becoming purified, she should hear about the birth mystery of the Maruts. Then, covering her body with a white dress and being properly ornamented, before breakfast she should worship Lord Viṣṇu and mother Lakṣmī, the goddess of fortune, Lord Viṣṇu's wife, by glorifying Lord Viṣṇu for His mercy, patience, prowess, ability, greatness and other glories and for how He can bestow all mystic benedictions. While offering the Lord all paraphernalia for worship, such as ornaments, a sacred thread, scents, nice flowers, incense and water for bathing and washing His feet, hands and mouth, one should invite the Lord with this *mantra: oṁ namo bhagavate mahā-puruṣāya mahānubhāvāya mahāvibhūtipataye saha mahā-vibhūtibhir balim upaharāmi.* Then one should offer twelve oblations in the fire while chanting this *mantra: oṁ namo bhagavate mahā-puruṣāya mahāvibhūti-pataye svāhā.* One should offer obeisances while chanting this *mantra* ten times. Then one should chant the Lakṣmī-Nārāyaṇa *mantra.*

If either a pregnant woman or her husband regularly discharges this devotional service, both of them will receive the result. After continuing this process for one full year, the chaste wife should fast on the *pūrṇimā,* the full-moon day, of Kārttika. On the following day, the husband should worship the Lord as before and then observe a festival by cooking nice food and distributing *prasāda* to the *brāhmaṇas.* Then, with the permission of the *brāhmaṇas,* the husband and wife should take *prasāda.* This chapter ends by glorifying the results of the *puṁsavana* function.

TEXT 1

श्रीराजोवाच

व्रतं पुंसवनं ब्रह्मन् भवता यदुदीरितम् ।
तस्य वेदितुमिच्छामि येन विष्णुः प्रसीदति ॥ १ ॥

śrī-rājovāca
vrataṁ puṁsavanaṁ brahman
bhavatā yad udīritam
tasya veditum icchāmi
yena viṣṇuḥ prasīdati

śrī-rājā uvāca—Mahārāja Parīkṣit said; *vratam*—the vow; *puṁsavanam*—called *puṁsavana; brahman*—O *brāhmaṇa; bhavatā*—by you; *yat*—which; *udīritam*—was spoken of; *tasya*—of that; *veditum*—to know; *icchāmi*—I want; *yena*—by which; *viṣṇuḥ*—Lord Viṣṇu; *prasīdati*—is pleased.

TRANSLATION

Mahārāja Parīkṣit said: My dear lord, you have already spoken about the puṁsavana vow. Now I want to hear about it in detail, for I understand that by observing this vow one can please the Supreme Lord, Viṣṇu.

TEXTS 2–3

श्रीशुक उवाच
शुक्ले मार्गशिरे पक्षे योषिद्भर्तुरनुज्ञया ।
आरभेत व्रतमिदं सार्वकामिकमादितः ॥ २ ॥
निशम्य मरुतां जन्म ब्राह्मणाननुमन्त्र्य च ।
स्नात्वा शुक्लदती शुक्ले वसीतालङ्कृताम्बरे ।
पूजयेत्प्रातराशात्प्राग्भगवन्तं श्रिया सह ॥ ३ ॥

śrī-śuka uvāca
śukle mārgaśire pakṣe
yoṣid bhartur anujñayā
ārabheta vratam idaṁ
sārva-kāmikam āditaḥ

niśamya marutāṁ janma
brāhmaṇān anumantrya ca
snātvā śukla-datī śukle
vasītālaṅkṛtāmbare
pūjayet prātarāśāt prāg
bhagavantaṁ śriyā saha

śrī-śukaḥ uvāca—Śrī Śukadeva Gosvāmī said; *śukle*—bright; *mārgaśire*—during the month of November–December; *pakṣe*—during the fortnight; *yoṣit*

—a woman; *bhartuḥ*—of the husband; *anujñayā*—with the permission; *ārabheta*—should begin; *vratam*—vow; *idam*—this; *sārva-kāmikam*—which fulfills all desires; *āditaḥ*—from the first day; *niśamya*—hearing; *marutām*—of the Maruts; *janma*—the birth; *brāhmaṇān*—the *brāhmaṇas; anumantrya*—taking instruction from; *ca*—and; *snātvā*—bathing; *śukla-datī*—having cleaned the teeth; *śukle*—white; *vasīta*—should put on; *alaṅkṛtā*—wearing ornaments; *ambare*—garments; *pūjayet*—should worship; *prātaḥ-āśāt prāk*—before breakfast; *bhagavantam*—the Supreme Personality of Godhead; *śriyā saha*—with the goddess of fortune.

TRANSLATION

Śukadeva Gosvāmī said: On the first day of the bright fortnight of the month of Agrahāyaṇa [November–December], following the instructions of her husband, a woman should begin this regulative devotional service with a vow of penance, for it can fulfill all one's desires. Before beginning the worship of Lord Viṣṇu, the woman should hear the story of how the Maruts were born. Under the instructions of qualified brāhmaṇas, in the morning she should wash her teeth, bathe, and dress herself with white cloth and ornaments, and before taking breakfast she should worship Lord Viṣṇu and Lakṣmī.

TEXT 4

अलं ते निरपेक्षाय पूर्णकाम नमोऽस्तु ते ।
महाविभूतिपतये नमः सकलसिद्धये ॥ ४ ॥

alaṁ te nirapekṣāya
pūrṇa-kāma namo'stu te
mahāvibhūti-pataye
namaḥ sakala-siddhaye

alam—enough; *te*—to You; *nirapekṣāya*—indifferent; *pūrṇa-kāma*—O Lord, whose desire is always fulfilled; *namaḥ*—obeisances; *astu*—may there be; *te*—unto You; *mahā-vibhūti*—of Lakṣmī; *pataye*—unto the husband; *namaḥ*—obeisances; *sakala-siddhaye*—unto the master of all mystic perfections.

TRANSLATION

[She should then pray to the Lord as follows.] My dear Lord, You are full in all opulences, but I do not beg You for opulence. I simply offer my

respectful obeisances unto You. You are the husband and master of Lakṣmīdevī, the goddess of fortune, who has all opulences. Therefore You are the master of all mystic yoga. I simply offer my obeisances unto You.

PURPORT

A devotee knows how to appreciate the Supreme Personality of Godhead.

oṁ pūrṇam adaḥ pūrṇam idaṁ
pūrṇāt pūrṇam udacyate
pūrṇasya pūrṇam ādāya
pūrṇam evāvaśiṣyate

"The Personality of Godhead is perfect and complete, and because He is completely perfect, all emanations from Him, such as this phenomenal world, are perfectly equipped as complete wholes. Whatever is produced of the complete whole is also complete in itself. Because He is the complete whole, even though so many complete units emanate from Him, He remains the complete balance." Therefore, to take shelter of the Supreme Lord is required. Whatever a devotee needs will be supplied by the complete Supreme Personality of Godhead (*teṣāṁ nityābhiyuktānāṁ yoga-kṣemaṁ vahāmy aham*). Therefore a pure devotee will not ask anything from the Lord. He simply offers the Lord his respectful obeisances, and the Lord is prepared to accept whatever the devotee can secure to worship Him, even *patraṁ puṣpaṁ phalaṁ toyam* -a leaf, flower, fruit or water. There is no need to artificially exert oneself. It is better to be plain and simple and with respectful obeisances offer to the Lord whatever one can secure. The Lord is completely able to bless the devotee with all opulences.

TEXT 5

यथा त्वं कृपया भूत्या तेजसा महिमौजसा ।
जुष्ट ईश गुणैः सर्वैस्ततोऽसि भगवान् प्रभुः ॥ ५॥

yathā tvaṁ kṛpayā bhūtyā
tejasā mahimaujasā
juṣṭa īśa guṇaiḥ sarvais
tato'si bhagavān prabhuḥ

yathā—as; *tvam*—You; *kṛpayā*—with mercy; *bhūtyā*—with opulences; *tejasā*—with prowess; *mahima-ojasā*—with glory and strength; *juṣṭaḥ*—

endowed; *īśa*—O my Lord; *guṇaiḥ*—with transcendental qualities; *sarvaiḥ*—all; *tataḥ*—therefore; *asi*—You are; *bhagavān*—the Supreme Personality of Godhead; *prabhuḥ*—the master.

TRANSLATION

O my Lord, because You are endowed with causeless mercy, all opulences, all prowess and all glories, strength and transcendental qualities, You are the Supreme Personality of Godhead, the master of everyone.

PURPORT

In this verse the words *tato'si bhagavān prabhuḥ* mean "Therefore You are the Supreme Personality of Godhead, the master of everyone." The Supreme Personality of Godhead is endowed with all six opulences in full, and moreover He is extremely kind to His devotee. Although He is full in Himself, He nonetheless wants all the living entities to surrender unto Him so that they may engage in His service. Thus He becomes satisfied. Although He is full in Himself, He nonetheless becomes pleased when His devotee offers Him *patraṁ puṣpaṁ phalaṁ toyam*—a leaf, flower, fruit or water—in devotion. Sometimes the Lord, as the child of mother Yaśodā, requests His devotee for some food, as if He were very hungry. Sometimes He tells His devotee in a dream that His temple and His garden are now very old and that He cannot enjoy them very nicely. Thus He requests the devotee to repair them. Sometimes He is buried in the earth, and as if unable to come out Himself, He requests His devotee to rescue Him. Sometimes He requests His devotee to preach His glories all over the world, although He alone is quite competent to perform this task. Even though the Supreme Personality of Godhead is endowed with all possessions and is self-sufficient, He depends on His devotees. Therefore the relationship of the Lord with His devotees is extremely confidential. Only the devotee can perceive how the Lord, although full in Himself, depends on His devotee for some particular work. This is explained in *Bhagavad-gītā* (11.33), where the Lord tells Arjuna, *nimitta-mātraṁ bhava savyasācin:* "O Arjuna, merely be an instrument in the fight." Lord Kṛṣṇa had the competence to win the Battle of Kurukṣetra, but nonetheless He induced His devotee Arjuna to fight and become the cause of victory. Śrī Caitanya Mahāprabhu was quite competent enough to spread His name and mission all over the world, but still He depended upon His devotee to do this work. Considering all these points, the most important aspect of the Supreme Lord's self-sufficiency is that He depends on His devotees. This is called His causeless mercy. The devotee who has perceived this causeless mercy of the Supreme Personality of Godhead by realization can understand the master and the servant.

TEXT 6

विष्णुपत्नि महामाये महापुरुषलक्षणे ।
प्रीयेथा मे महाभागे लोकमातर्नमोऽस्तु ते ॥ ६ ॥

viṣṇu-patni mahā-māye
mahāpuruṣa-lakṣaṇe
prīyethā me mahā-bhāge
loka-mātar namo'stu te

viṣṇu-patni—O wife of Lord Viṣṇu; *mahā-māye*—O energy of Lord Viṣṇu; *mahā-puruṣa-lakṣaṇe*—possessing the qualities and opulences of Lord Viṣṇu; *prīyethāḥ*—kindly be pleased; *me*—upon me; *mahā-bhāge*—O goddess of fortune; *loka-mātaḥ*—O mother of the world; *namaḥ*—obeisances; *astu*—may there be; *te*—unto you.

TRANSLATION

[After profusely offering obeisances unto Lord Viṣṇu, the devotee should offer respectful obeisances unto mother Lakṣmī, the goddess of fortune, and pray as follows.] O wife of Lord Viṣṇu, O internal energy of Lord Viṣṇu, you are as good as Lord Viṣṇu Himself, for you have all of His qualities and opulences. O goddess of fortune, please be kind to me. O mother of the entire world, I offer my respectful obeisances unto you.

PURPORT

The Lord has multifarious potencies (*parāsya śaktir vividhaiva śrūyate*). Since mother Lakṣmī, the goddess of fortune, is the Lord's very precious potency, she is addressed here as *mahā-māye.* The word *māyā* means *śakti.* Lord Viṣṇu, the Supreme, cannot exhibit His power everywhere without His principal energy. It is said, *śakti śaktimān abheda:* the power and the powerful are identical. Therefore mother Lakṣmī, the goddess of fortune, is the constant companion of Lord Viṣṇu; they remain together constantly. One cannot keep Lakṣmī in one's home without Lord Viṣṇu. To think that one can do so is very dangerous. To keep Lakṣmī, or the riches of the Lord, without the service of the Lord is always dangerous, for then Lakṣmī becomes the illusory energy. With Lord Viṣṇu, however, Lakṣmī is the spiritual energy.

TEXT 7

ॐ नमो भगवते महापुरुषाय महानुभावाय महाविभूतिपतये सह महाविभूतिभिर्बलिमुपहरामीति। अनेनाहरहर्मन्त्रेण विष्णोरावाहनार्घ्य-पाद्योपस्पर्शनस्नानवासउपवीतविभूषणगन्धपुष्पधूपदीपोपहाराद्युपचारान् सुसमाहितोपाहरेत् ॥ ७॥

oṁ namo bhagavate mahā-puruṣāya mahānubhāvāya mahāvibhūti-pataye saha mahā-vibhūtibhir balim upaharāmīti; anenāhar-ahar mantreṇa viṣṇor āvāhanārghya-pādyopasparśana-snāna-vāsa-upavīta-vibhūṣaṇa-gandha-puṣpa-dhūpa-dīpopahārādy-upacārān susamā-hitopāharet.

oṁ—O my Lord; *namaḥ*—obeisances; *bhagavate*—unto the Supreme Personality of Godhead, full with six opulences; *mahā-puruṣāya*—the best of enjoyers; *mahā-anubhāvāya*—the most powerful; *mahā-vibhūti*—of the goddess of fortune; *pataye*—the husband; *saha*—with; *mahā-vibhūtibhiḥ*—associates; *balim*—presentations; *upaharāmi*—I am offering; *iti*—thus; *anena*—by this; *ahaḥ-ahaḥ*—every day; *mantreṇa*—*mantra; viṣṇoḥ*—of Lord Viṣṇu; *āvāhana*—invocations; *arghya-pādya-upasparśana*—water for washing the hands, feet and mouth; *snāna*—water for bathing; *vāsa*—garments; *upavīta*—a sacred thread; *vibhūṣaṇa*—ornaments; *gandha*—scents; *puṣpa*—flowers; *dhūpa*—incense; *dīpa*—lamps; *upahāra*—gifts; *ādi*—and so on; *upacārān*—presentations; *su-samāhitā*—with great attention; *upāharet*—she must offer.

TRANSLATION

"My Lord Viṣṇu, full in six opulences, You are the best of all enjoyers and the most powerful. O husband of mother Lakṣmī, I offer my respectful obeisances unto You, who are accompanied by many associates, such as Viśvaksena. I offer all the paraphernalia for worshiping You." One should chant this mantra every day with great attention while worshiping Lord Viṣṇu with all paraphernalia, such as water for washing His feet, hands and mouth and water for His bath. One must offer Him various presentations for His worship, such as garments, a sacred thread, ornaments, scents, flowers, incense and lamps.

PURPORT

This *mantra* is very important. Anyone engaged in Deity worship should chant this *mantra,* as quoted above, beginning with *oṁ namo bhagavate mahā-puruṣāya.*

TEXT 8

हविःशेषं च जुहुयादनले द्वादशाहुती : ।
ॐ नमो भगवते महापुरुषाय महाविभूतिपतये स्वाहेति ॥ ८ ॥

haviḥ-śeṣaṁ ca juhuyād anale dvādaśāhutīḥ
oṁ namo bhagavate mahā-puruṣāya mahāvibhūti-pataye svāheti

haviḥ-śeṣam—remnants of the offering; *ca*—and; *juhuyāt*—one should offer; *anale*—in the fire; *dvādaśa*—twelve; *āhutīḥ*—oblations; *oṁ*—O my Lord; *namaḥ*—obeisances; *bhagavate*—unto the Supreme Personality of Godhead; *mahā-puruṣāya*—the supreme enjoyer; *mahā-vibhūti*—of the goddess of fortune; *pataye*—the husband; *svāhā*—hail; *iti*—thus.

TRANSLATION

Śukadeva Gosvāmī continued: After worshiping the Lord with all the paraphernalia mentioned above, one should chant the following mantra while offering twelve oblations of ghee on the sacred fire: oṁ namo bhagavate mahā-puruṣāya mahāvibhūti-pataye svāhā.

TEXT 9

श्रियं विष्णुं च वरदावाशिषां प्रभवावुभौ ।
भक्त्या सम्पूजयेन्नित्यं यदीच्छेत्सर्वसम्पदः ॥ ९ ॥

śriyaṁ viṣṇuṁ ca varadāv
āśiṣāṁ prabhavāv ubhau
bhaktyā sampūjayen nityaṁ
yadīcchet sarva-sampadaḥ

śriyam—the goddess of fortune; *viṣṇum*—Lord Viṣṇu; *ca*—and; *vara-dau*—the bestowers of benedictions; *āśiṣām*—of blessings; *prabhavau*—the sources; *ubhau*—both; *bhaktyā*—with devotion; *sampūjayet*—should worship; *nityam*—daily; *yadi*—if; *icchet*—desires; *sarva*—all; *sampadaḥ*—opulences.

TRANSLATION

If one desires all opulences, his duty is to daily worship Lord Viṣṇu with His wife, Lakṣmī. With great devotion one should worship Him according to the above-mentioned process. Lord Viṣṇu and the goddess of fortune are an immensely powerful combination. They are the bestowers of all benedictions and the sources of all good fortune. Therefore the duty of everyone is to worship Lakṣmī-Nārāyaṇa.

PURPORT

Lakṣmī-Nārāyaṇa—Lord Viṣṇu and mother Lakṣmī—are always situated in everyone's heart (*īśvaraḥ sarva-bhūtānāṁ hṛd-deśe'rjuna tiṣṭhati*). However, because nondevotees do not realize that Lord Viṣṇu stays with His eternal consort, Lakṣmī, within the hearts of all living entities, they are not endowed with the opulence of Lord Viṣṇu. Unscrupulous men sometimes address a poor man as *daridra-nārāyaṇa,* or "poor Nārāyaṇa." This is most unscientific. Lord Viṣṇu and Lakṣmī are always situated in everyone's heart, but this does not mean that everyone is Nārāyaṇa, especially not those in poverty. This is a most abominable term to use in connection with Nārāyaṇa. Nārāyaṇa never becomes poor, and therefore He can never be called *daridra-nārāyaṇa.* Nārāyaṇa is certainly situated in everyone's heart, but He is neither poor nor rich. Only unscrupulous persons who do not know the opulence of Nārāyaṇa try to afflict Him with poverty.

TEXT 10

प्रणमेद्दण्डवद्भूमौ भक्तिप्रह्वेण चेतसा ।
दशवारं जपेन्मन्त्रं ततः स्तोत्रमुदीरयेत् ॥ १० ॥

praṇamed daṇḍavad bhūmau
bhakti-prahveṇa cetasā
daśa-vāraṁ japen mantraṁ
tataḥ stotram udīrayet

praṇamet—should offer obeisances; *daṇḍa-vat*—like a stick; *bhūmau*—on the ground; *bhakti*—through devotion; *prahveṇa*—humble; *cetasā*—with a mind; *daśa-vāram*—ten times; *japet*—should utter; *mantram*—the *mantra;* *tataḥ*—then; *stotram*—prayer; *udīrayet*—should chant.

TRANSLATION

One should offer obeisances unto the Lord with a mind humbled through devotion. While offering daṇḍavats by falling on the ground like a rod, one should chant the above mantra ten times. Then one should chant the following prayer.

TEXT 11

युवां तु विश्वस्य विभू जगतः कारणं परम् ।
इयं हि प्रकृतिः सूक्ष्मा मायाशक्तिर्दुरत्यया ॥ ११ ॥

yuvāṁ tu viśvasya vibhū
jagataḥ kāraṇaṁ param
iyaṁ hi prakṛtiḥ sūkṣmā
māyā-śaktir duratyayā

yuvām—both of you; *tu*—indeed; *viśvasya*—of the universe; *vibhū*—the proprietors; *jagataḥ*—of the universe; *kāraṇam*—the cause; *param*—supreme; *iyam*—this; *hi*—certainly; *prakṛtiḥ*—energy; *sūkṣmā*—difficult to understand; *māyā-śaktiḥ*—the internal energy; *duratyayā*—difficult to overcome.

TRANSLATION

My Lord Viṣṇu and mother Lakṣmī, goddess of fortune, you are the proprietors of the entire creation. Indeed, you are the cause of the creation. Mother Lakṣmī is extremely difficult to understand because she is so powerful that the jurisdiction of her power is difficult to overcome. Mother Lakṣmī is represented in the material world as the external energy, but actually she is always the internal energy of the Lord.

TEXT 12

तस्या अधीश्वरः साक्षात्त्वमेव पुरुषः परः ।
त्वं सर्वयज्ञ इज्येयं क्रियेयं फलभुग्भवान् ॥ १२ ॥

tasyā adhīśvaraḥ sākṣāt
tvam eva puruṣaḥ paraḥ
tvaṁ sarva-yajña ijyeyaṁ
kriyeyaṁ phala-bhug bhavān

tasyāḥ—of her; *adhīśvaraḥ*—the master; *sākṣāt*—directly; *tvam*—You; *eva*—certainly; *puruṣaḥ*—the person; *paraḥ*—supreme; *tvam*—You; *sarva-yajñaḥ*—personified sacrifice; *ijyā*—worship; *iyam*—this (Lakṣmī); *kriyā*—activities; *iyam*—this; *phala-bhuk*—the enjoyer of the fruits; *bhavān*—You.

TRANSLATION

My Lord, You are the master of energy, and therefore You are the Supreme Person. You are sacrifice [yajña] personified. Lakṣmī, the embodiment of spiritual activities, is the original form of worship offered unto You, whereas You are the enjoyer of all sacrifices.

TEXT 13

गुणव्यक्तिरियं देवी व्यञ्जको गुणभुग्भवान् ।
त्वं हि सर्वशरीर्यात्मा श्रीः शरीरेन्द्रियाशयाः ।
नामरूपे भगवती प्रत्ययस्त्वमपाश्रयः ॥ १३ ॥

guṇa-vyaktir iyaṁ devī
vyañjako guṇa-bhug bhavān
tvaṁ hi sarva-śarīry ātmā
śrīḥ śarīrendriyāśayāḥ
nāma-rūpe bhagavatī
pratyayas tvam apāśrayaḥ

guṇa-vyaktiḥ—the reservoir of qualities; *iyam*—this; *devī*—goddess; *vyañjakaḥ*—manifester; *guṇa-bhuk*—the enjoyer of the qualities; *bhavān*—You; *tvam*—You; *hi*—indeed; *sarva-śarīrī ātmā*—the Supersoul of all living entities; *śrīḥ*—the goddess of fortune; *śarīra*—the body; *indriya*—senses; *āśayāḥ*—and the mind; *nāma*—name; *rūpe*—and form; *bhagavatī*—Lakṣmī; *pratyayaḥ*—the cause of manifestation; *tvam*—You; *apāśrayaḥ*—the support.

TRANSLATION

Mother Lakṣmī, who is here, is the reservoir of all spiritual qualities, whereas You manifest and enjoy all these qualities. Indeed, You are actually the enjoyer of everything. You live as the Supersoul of all living entities, and the goddess of fortune is the form of their bodies, senses and minds. She also has a holy name and form, whereas You are the support of all such names and forms and the cause for their manifestation.

PURPORT

Madhvācārya, the *ācārya* of the Tattvavādīs, has described this verse in the following way: "Viṣṇu is described as *yajña* personified, and mother Lakṣmī is described as spiritual activities and the original form of worship. In fact, they represent spiritual activities and the Supersoul of all *yajña.* Lord Viṣṇu is the Supersoul even of Lakṣmīdevī, but no one can be the Supersoul of Lord Viṣṇu, for Lord Viṣṇu Himself is the spiritual Supersoul of everyone."

According to Madhvācārya, there are two *tattvas,* or factors. One is independent, and the other is dependent. The first *tattva* is the Supreme Lord, Viṣṇu, and the second is the *jīva-tattva.* Lakṣmīdevī, being dependent on Lord Viṣṇu, is sometimes counted among the *jīvas.* The Gauḍīya Vaiṣṇavas, however, describe Lakṣmīdevī in accordance with the following two verses from the *Prameya-ratnāvalī* of Baladeva Vidyābhūṣaṇa. The first verse is a quotation from the *Viṣṇu Purāṇa.*

nityaiva sā jagan-mātā
viṣṇoḥ śrīr anapāyinī
yathā sarva-gato viṣṇus
tathaiveyaṁ dvijottama

viṣṇoḥ syuḥ śaktayas tisras
tāsu yā kīrtitā parā
saiva śrīs tad-abhinneti
prāha śiṣyān prabhur mahān

"O best of the *brāhmaṇas,* Lakṣmījī is the constant companion of the Supreme Personality of Godhead, Viṣṇu, and therefore she is called *anapāyinī.* She is the mother of all creation. As Lord Viṣṇu is all-pervading, His spiritual potency, mother Lakṣmī, is also all-pervading. Lord Viṣṇu has three principal potencies—internal, external and marginal. Śrī Caitanya Mahāprabhu has accepted *parā-śakti,* the spiritual energy of the Lord, as being identical with the Lord. Thus she is also included in the independent *viṣṇu-tattva.*"

In the *Kānti-mālā* commentary on the *Prameya-ratnāvalī* there is this statement: *nanu kvacit nitya-mukta-jīvatvaṁ lakṣmyāḥ svīkṛtaṁ, tatrāha-prāheti; nityaiveti padye sarva-vyāpti-kathanena kalākāṣṭhety ādi-padya-dvaye, śuddho'pīty uktā ca mahāprabhunā svaśiṣyān prati lakṣmyā bhagavad-advaitam upadiṣṭam; kvacid yat tasyās tu dvaitam uktaṁ, tat tu tad-āviṣṭa-nitya-mukta jīvam ādāya saṅgatamas tu.* "Although some authoritative Vaiṣṇava disciplic successions count the goddess of fortune among the ever-liberated living entities (*jīvas*) in Vaikuṇṭha, Śrī Caitanya Mahāprabhu, in accordance with the statement in the *Viṣṇu Purāṇa,* has described Lakṣmī as being identical with the *viṣṇu-tattva.* The correct conclusion is that the descriptions of Lakṣmī as being different from Viṣṇu are stated when an eternally liberated living entity is imbued with the quality of Lakṣmī; they do not pertain to mother Lakṣmī, the eternal consort of Lord Viṣṇu."

TEXT 14

यथा युवां त्रिलोकस्य वरदौ परमेष्ठिनौ ।
तथा म उत्तमश्लोक सन्तु सत्या महाशिषः ॥ १४ ॥

yathā yuvāṁ tri-lokasya
varadau parameṣṭhinau
tathā ma uttamaśloka
santu satyā mahāśiṣaḥ

yathā—since; *yuvām*—both of you; *tri-lokasya*—of the three worlds; *vara-dau*—givers of benedictions; *parame-ṣṭhinau*—the supreme rulers; *tathā*—therefore; *me*—my; *uttama-śloka*—O Lord, who are praised with excellent verses; *santu*—may become; *satyāḥ*—fulfilled; *mahā-āśiṣaḥ*—great ambitions.

TRANSLATION

You are both the supreme rulers and benedictors of the three worlds. Therefore, my Lord, Uttamaśloka, may my ambitions be fulfilled by Your grace.

TEXT 15

इत्यभिष्टूय वरदं श्रीनिवासं श्रिया सह ।
तन्निःसार्योपहरणं दत्त्वाचमनमर्चयेत् ॥ १५ ॥

ity abhiṣṭūya varadaṁ
śrīnivāsaṁ śriyā saha
tan niḥsāryopaharaṇaṁ
dattvācamanam arcayet

iti—thus; *abhiṣṭūya*—offering prayers; *vara-dam*—who bestows benedictions; *śrī-nivāsam*—unto Lord Viṣṇu, the abode of the goddess of fortune; *śriyā saha*—with Lakṣmī; *tat*—then; *niḥsārya*—removing; *upaharaṇam*—the paraphernalia for worship; *dattvā*—after offering; *ācamanam*—water for washing the hands and mouth; *arcayet*—one should worship.

TRANSLATION

Śrī Śukadeva Gosvāmī continued: Thus one should worship Lord Viṣṇu, who is known as Śrīnivāsa, along with mother Lakṣmī, the goddess of fortune, by offering prayers according to the process mentioned above. After removing all the paraphernalia of worship, one should offer them water to wash their hands and mouths, and then one should worship them again.

TEXT 16

ततः स्तुवीत स्तोत्रेण भक्तिप्रह्वेण चेतसा ।
यज्ञोच्छिष्टमवघ्राय पुनरभ्यर्चयेद्धरिम् ॥ १६ ॥

tataḥ stuvīta stotreṇa
bhakti-prahveṇa cetasā
yajñocchiṣṭam avaghrāya
punar abhyarcayed dharim

tataḥ—then; *stuvīta*—one should praise; *stotreṇa*—with prayers; *bhakti*—with devotion; *prahveṇa*—humble; *cetasā*—with a mind; *yajña-ucchiṣṭam*—the remnants of sacrifice; *avaghrāya*—smelling; *punaḥ*—again; *abhyarcayet*—one should worship; *harim*—Lord Viṣṇu.

TRANSLATION

Thereafter, with devotion and humility, one should offer prayers to the Lord and mother Lakṣmī. Then one should smell the remnants of the food offered and then again worship the Lord and Lakṣmījī.

TEXT 17

पतिं च परया भक्त्या महापुरुषचेतसा ।
प्रियैस्तैस्तैरुपनमेत् प्रेमशीलः स्वयं पतिः ।
बिभृयात् सर्वकर्माणि पत्न्या उच्चावचानि च ॥ १७ ॥

patiṁ ca parayā bhaktyā
mahāpuruṣa-cetasā

priyais tais tair upanamet
prema-śīlaḥ svayaṁ patiḥ
bibhṛyāt sarva-karmāṇi
patnyā uccāvacāni ca

patim—the husband; *ca*—and; *parayā*—supreme; *bhaktyā*—with devotion; *mahā-puruṣa-cetasā*—accepting as the Supreme Person; *priyaiḥ*—dear; *taiḥ taiḥ*—by those (offerings); *upanamet*—should worship; *prema-śīlaḥ*—being affectionate; *svayam*—himself; *patiḥ*—the husband; *bibhṛyāt*—should execute; *sarva-karmāṇi*—all activities; *patnyāḥ*—of the wife; *ucca-avacāni*—high and low; *ca*—also.

TRANSLATION

Accepting her husband as the representative of the Supreme Person, a wife should worship him with unalloyed devotion by offering him prasāda. The husband, being very pleased with his wife, should engage himself in the affairs of his family.

PURPORT

The family relationship of husband and wife should be established spiritually according to the process mentioned above.

TEXT 18

कृतमेकतरेणापि दम्पत्योरुभयोरपि ।
पत्न्यां कुर्यादनर्हायां पतिरेतत् समाहितः ॥ १८ ॥

kṛtam ekatareṇāpi
dam-patyor ubhayor api
patnyāṁ kuryād anarhāyāṁ
patir etat samāhitaḥ

kṛtam—executed; *ekatareṇa*—by one; *api*—even; *dam-patyoḥ*—of the wife and husband; *ubhayoḥ*—of both; *api*—still; *patnyām*—when the wife; *kuryāt*—he should execute; *anarhāyām*—is unable; *patiḥ*—the husband; *etat*—this; *samāhitaḥ*—with attention.

TRANSLATION

Between the husband and wife, one person is sufficient to execute this devotional service. Because of their good relationship, both of them

will enjoy the result. Therefore if the wife is unable to execute this process, the husband should carefully do so, and the faithful wife will share the result.

PURPORT

The relationship between husband and wife is firmly established when the wife is faithful and the husband sincere. Then even if the wife, being weaker, is unable to execute devotional service with her husband, if she is chaste and sincere she shares half of her husband's activities.

TEXTS 19–20

विष्णोर्व्रतमिदं बिभ्रन्न विहन्यात् कथञ्चन ।
विप्रान् स्त्रियो वीरवतीः स्रग्गन्धबलिमण्डनैः ।
अर्चेदहरहर्भक्त्या देवं नियममास्थिता ॥ १९ ॥
उद्वास्य देवं स्वे धाम्नि तन्निवेदितमग्रतः ।
अद्यादात्मविशुद्ध्यर्थं सर्वकामसमृद्धये ॥ २० ॥

viṣṇor vratam idaṁ bibhran
na vihanyāt kathañcana
viprān striyo vīravatīḥ
srag-gandha-bali-maṇḍanaiḥ
arced ahar-ahar bhaktyā
devaṁ niyamam āsthitā

udvāsya devaṁ sve dhāmni
tan-niveditam agrataḥ
adyād ātma-viśuddhy-arthaṁ
sarva-kāma-samṛddhaye

viṣṇoḥ—of Lord Viṣṇu; *vratam*—vow; *idam*—this; *bibhrat*—executing; *na*—not; *vihanyāt*—should break; *kathañcana*—for any reason; *viprān*—the *brāhmaṇas; striyaḥ*—women; *vīra-vatīḥ*—who have their husband and sons; *srak*—with garlands; *gandha*—sandalwood; *bali*—offerings of food; *maṇḍanaiḥ*—and with ornaments; *arcet*—one should worship; *ahaḥ-ahaḥ*—daily; *bhaktyā*—with devotion; *devam*—Lord Viṣṇu; *niyamam*—the regulative principles; *āsthitā*—following; *udvāsya*—placing; *devam*—the Lord; *sve*—in His own; *dhāmni*—resting place; *tat*—to Him; *niveditam*—

what was offered; *agrataḥ*—after dividing first among the others; *adyāt*—one should eat; *ātma-viśuddhi-artham*—for self-purification; *sarva-kāma*—all desires; *samṛddhaye*—for fulfilling.

TRANSLATION

One should accept this viṣṇu-vrata, which is a vow in devotional service, and should not deviate from its execution to engage in anything else. By offering the remnants of prasāda, flower garlands, sandalwood pulp and ornaments, one should daily worship the brāhmaṇas and worship women who peacefully live with their husbands and children. Every day the wife must continue following the regulative principles to worship Lord Viṣṇu with great devotion. Thereafter, Lord Viṣṇu should be laid in His bed, and then one should take prasāda. In this way, husband and wife will be purified and will have all their desires fulfilled.

TEXT 21

एतेन पूजाविधिना मासान् द्वादश हायनम् ।
नीत्वाथोपरमेत्साध्वी कार्तिके चरमेऽहनि ॥ २१ ॥

etena pūjā-vidhinā
māsān dvādaśa hāyanam
nītvāthoparamet sādhvī
kārtike carame'hani

etena—with this; *pūjā-vidhinā*—regulated worship; *māsān dvādaśa*—twelve months; *hāyanam*—a year; *nītvā*—after passing; *atha*—then; *uparamet*—should fast; *sādhvī*—the chaste wife; *kārtike*—in Kārttika; *carame ahani*—on the final day.

TRANSLATION

The chaste wife must perform such devotional service continuously for one year. After one year passes, she should fast on the full-moon day in the month of Kārttika [October–November].

TEXT 22

श्वोभूतेऽप उपस्पृश्य कृष्णमभ्यर्च्य पूर्ववत् ।
पयःशृतेन जुहुयाच्चरुणा सह सर्पिषा ।
पाकयज्ञविधानेन द्वादशैवाहुतीः पतिः ॥ २२ ॥

śvo-bhūte'pa upaspṛśya
kṛṣṇam abhyarcya pūrvavat
payaḥ-śṛtena juhuyāc
caruṇā saha sarpiṣā
pāka-yajña-vidhānena
dvādaśaivāhutīḥ patiḥ

śvaḥ-bhūte—on the following morning; *apaḥ*—water; *upaspṛśya*—contacting; *kṛṣṇam*—Lord Kṛṣṇa; *abhyarcya*—worshiping; *pūrva-vat*—as previously; *payaḥ-śṛtena*—with boiled milk; *juhuyāt*—one should offer; *caruṇā*—with an offering of sweetrice; *saha*—with; *sarpiṣā*—ghee; *pāka-yajña-vidhānena*—according to the injunctions of the *Gṛhya-sūtras; dvādaśa*—twelve; *eva*—indeed; *āhutīḥ*—oblations; *patiḥ*—the husband.

TRANSLATION

On the morning of the next day, one should wash oneself, and after worshiping Lord Kṛṣṇa as before, one should cook as one cooks for festivals as stated in the Gṛhya-sūtras. Sweet rice should be cooked with ghee, and with this preparation the husband should offer oblations to the fire twelve times.

TEXT 23

आशिषः शिरसादाय द्विजैः प्रीतैः समीरिताः ।
प्रणम्य शिरसा भक्त्या भुञ्जीत तदनुज्ञया ॥ २३ ॥

āśiṣaḥ śirasādāya
dvijaiḥ prītaiḥ samīritāḥ
praṇamya śirasā bhaktyā
bhuñjīta tad-anujñayā

āśiṣaḥ—blessings; *śirasā*—with the head; *ādāya*—accepting; *dvijaiḥ*—by the *brāhmaṇas; prītaiḥ*—who are pleased; *samīritāḥ*—spoken; *praṇamya*—after offering obeisances; *śirasā*—with the head; *bhaktyā*—with devotion; *bhuñjīta*—he should eat; *tat-anujñayā*—with their permission.

TRANSLATION

Thereafter, he should satisfy the brāhmaṇas. When the satisfied brāhmaṇas bestow their blessings, he should devotedly offer them

respectful obeisances with his head, and with their permission he should take prasāda.

TEXT 24

आचार्यमग्रतः कृत्वा वाग्यतः सह बन्धुभिः ।
दद्यात्पत्न्यै चरोः शेषं सुप्रजास्त्वं सुसौभगम् ॥ २४ ॥

ācāryam agrataḥ kṛtvā
vāg-yataḥ saha bandhubhiḥ
dadyāt patnyai caroḥ śeṣaṁ
suprajāstvaṁ susaubhagam

ācāryam—the *ācārya; agrataḥ*—first of all; *kṛtvā*—receiving properly; *vāk-yataḥ*—controlling speech; *saha*—with; *bandhubhiḥ*—friends and relatives; *dadyāt*—he should give; *patnyai*—to the wife; *caroḥ*—of the oblation of sweet rice; *śeṣam*—the remnant; *su-prajāstvam*—which insures good progeny; *su-saubhagam*—which insures good fortune.

TRANSLATION

Before taking his meal, the husband must first seat the ācārya comfortably, and, along with his relatives and friends, should control his speech and offer prasāda to the guru. Then the wife should eat the remnants of the oblation of sweet rice cooked with ghee. Eating the remnants insures a learned, devoted son and all good fortune.

TEXT 25

एतच्चरित्वा विधिवद्व्रतं विभो
रभीप्सितार्थं लभते पुमानिह ।
स्त्री चैतदास्थाय लभेत सौभगं
श्रियं प्रजां जीवपतिं यशो गृहम् ॥ २५ ॥

etac caritvā vidhivad vrataṁ vibhor
abhīpsitārthaṁ labhate pumān iha
strī caitad āsthāya labheta saubhagaṁ
śriyaṁ prajāṁ jīva-patiṁ yaśo gṛham

etat—this; *caritvā*—performing; *vidhi-vat*—according to the injunctions of *śāstra; vratam*—vow; *vibhoḥ*—from the Lord; *abhīpsita*—desired; *artham*

—object; *labhate*—gets; *pumān*—a man; *iha*—in this life; *strī*—a woman; *ca*—and; *etat*—this; *āsthāya*—performing; *labheta*—can get; *saubhagam*—good fortune; *śriyam*—opulence; *prajām*—progeny; *jīva-patim*—a husband with a long duration of life; *yaśaḥ*—good reputation; *gṛham*—home.

TRANSLATION

If this vow or ritualistic ceremony is observed according to the description of śāstra, even in this life a man will be able to achieve all the benedictions he desires from the Lord. A wife who performs this ritualistic ceremony will surely receive good fortune, opulence, sons, a long-living husband, a good reputation and a good home.

PURPORT

In Bengal even today if a woman lives for a long time with her husband, she is considered very fortunate. A woman generally desires a good husband, good children, a good home, prosperity, opulence and so on. As recommended in this verse, a woman will receive all these desirable benedictions, and a man will also be able to receive all benedictions, from the Supreme Personality of Godhead. Thus by performing this particular type of *vrata,* a man and a woman in Kṛṣṇa consciousness will be happy in this material world, and because of being Kṛṣṇa conscious they will be promoted to the spiritual world.

TEXTS 26–28

कन्या च विन्देत समग्रलक्षणं
पतिं त्ववीरा हतकिल्बिषां गतिम् ।
मृतप्रजा जीवसुता धनेश्वरी
सुदुर्भगा सुभगा रूपमग्र्यम् ॥ २६ ॥
विन्देद् विरूपा विरुजा विमुच्यते
य आमयावीन्द्रियकल्यदेहम् ।
एतत्पठन्नभ्युदये च कर्म-
ण्यनन्ततृप्तिः पितृदेवतानाम् ॥ २७ ॥
तुष्टाः प्रयच्छन्ति समस्तकामान्
होमावसाने हुतभुक् श्रीहरिश्च ।
राजन् महन्मरुतां जन्म पुण्यं
दितेर्व्रतं चाभिहितं महत्ते ॥ २८ ॥

kanyā ca vindeta samagra-lakṣaṇaṁ
patiṁ tv avīrā hata-kilbiṣāṁ gatim
mṛta-prajā jīva-sutā dhaneśvarī
sudurbhagā subhagā rūpam agryam

vinded virūpā virujā vimucyate
ya āmayāvīndriya-kalya-deham
etat paṭhann abhyudaye ca karmaṇy
ananta-tṛptiḥ pitṛ-devatānām

tuṣṭāḥ prayacchanti samasta-kāmān
homāvasāne huta-bhuk śrī-hariś ca
rājan mahan marutāṁ janma puṇyaṁ
diter vrataṁ cābhihitaṁ mahat te

kanyā—an unmarried girl; *ca*—and; *vindeta*—can get; *samagralakṣaṇam*—possessing all good qualities; *patim*—a husband; *tu*—and; *avīrā*—a woman without a husband or son; *hata-kilbiṣām*—free from fault; *gatim*—the destination; *mṛta-prajā*—a woman whose children are dead; *jīva-sutā*—a woman whose child has a long duration of life; *dhana-īśvarī*—possessing wealth; *su-durbhagā*—unfortunate; *su-bhagā*—fortunate; *rūpam*—beauty; *agryam*—excellent; *vindet*—can get; *virūpā*—an ugly woman; *virujā*—from the disease; *vimucyate*—is freed; *yaḥ*—he who; *āmayā-vī*—a diseased man; *indriya-kalya-deham*—an able body; *etat*—this; *paṭhan*—reciting; *abhyudaye ca karmaṇi*—and in a sacrificial ceremony in which oblations are offered to the forefathers and demigods; *ananta*—unlimited; *tṛptiḥ*—satisfaction; *pitṛ-devatānām*—of the forefathers and demigods; *tuṣṭāḥ*—being pleased; *prayacchanti*—they bestow; *samasta*—all; *kāmān*—desires; *homa-avasāne*—on the completion of the ceremony; *huta-bhuk*—the enjoyer of the sacrifice; *śrī-hariḥ*—Lord Viṣṇu; *ca*—also; *rājan*—O King; *mahat*—great; *marutām*—of the Maruts; *janma*—birth; *puṇyam*—pious; *diteḥ*—of Diti; *vratam*—the vow; *ca*—also; *abhihitam*—explained; *mahat*—great; *te*—to you.

TRANSLATION

If an unmarried girl observes this vrata, she will be able to get a very good husband. If a woman who is avīrā—who has no husband or son—executes this ritualistic ceremony, she can be promoted to the spiritual world. A woman whose children have died after birth can get a child with

a long duration of life and also become very fortunate in possessing wealth. If a woman is unfortunate she will become fortunate, and if ugly she will become beautiful. By observing this vrata, a diseased man can gain relief from his disease and have an able body with which to work. If one recites this narration while offering oblations to the pitās and demigods, especially during the śrāddha ceremony, the demigods and inhabitants of Pitṛloka will be extremely pleased with him and bestow upon him the fulfillment of all desires. After one performs this ritualistic ceremony, Lord Viṣṇu and His wife, mother Lakṣmī, the goddess of fortune, are very pleased with him. O King Parīkṣit, now I have completely described how Diti performed this ceremony and had good children—the Maruts—and a happy life. I have tried to explain this to you as elaborately as possible.

Thus end the Bhaktivedanta purports of the Sixth Canto, Nineteenth Chapter, of the Śrīmad-Bhāgavatam, *entitled "Performing the Puṁsavana Ritualistic Ceremony."*

END OF THE SIXTH CANTO

Appendixes

About the Author

His Divine Grace A.C. Bhaktivedanta Swami Prabhupāda appeared in this world in 1896 in Calcutta, India. He first met his spiritual master, Śrīla Bhaktisiddhānta Sarasvatī Gosvāmi, in Calcutta in 1922. Śrīla Bhaktisiddhānta Sarasvatī, a prominent religious scholar and the founder of sixty-four Gauḍīya Maṭhas (Vedic institutes) in India, liked this educated young man and convinced him to dedicate his life to teaching Vedic knowledge. Śrīla Prabhupāda became his student and, in 1933, his formally initiated disciple.

At their first meeting, Śrīla Bhaktisiddhānta Sarasvatī requested Śrīla Prabhupāda to broadcast Vedic knowledge in English. In the years that followed, Śrīla Prabhupāda wrote a commentary on the *Bhagavad-gītā,* assisted the Gauḍīya Maṭha in its work, and, in 1944, started *Back to Godhead,* an English fortnightly magazine. Single-handedly, Śrīla Prabhupāda edited it, typed the manuscripts, checked the galley proofs, and even distributed the individual copies. The magazine is now being continued by his disciples all over the world.

In 1950 Śrīla Prabhupāda retired from married life, adopting the *vānaprastha* (retired) order to devote more time to his studies and writing. He traveled to the holy city of Vṛndāvana, where he lived in humble circumstances in the historic temple of Rādhā-Dāmodara. There he engaged for several years in deep study and writing. He accepted the renounced order of life (*sannyāsa*) in 1959. At Rādhā-Dāmodara, Śrīla Prabhupāda began work on his life's masterpiece: a multivolume commentated translation of the eighteen-thousand-verse *Śrīmad-Bhāgavatam* (*Bhāgavata Purāṇa*). He also wrote *Easy Journey to Other Planets.*

After publishing three volumes of the *Bhāgavatam,* Śrīla Prabhupāda came to the United States, in September 1965, to fulfill the mission of his spiritual master. Subsequently, His Divine Grace wrote more than sixty volumes of authoritative commentated translations and summary studies of the philosophical and religious classics of India.

When he first arrived by freighter in New York City, Śrīla Prabhupāda was practically penniless. It was after almost a year of great difficulty that he established the International Society for Krishna Consciousness in July of 1966. Before he passed away on November 14, 1977, he had guided the Society and seen it grow to a worldwide confederation of more than one hundred *ashrams,* schools, temples, institutes, and farm communities.

In 1972 His Divine Grace introduced the Vedic system of primary and secondary education in the West by founding the *gurukula* school in Dallas, Texas. Since then his disciples have established similar schools throughout the United States and the rest of the world.

Śrīla Prabhupāda also inspired the construction of several large international cultural centers in India. The center at Śrīdhāma Māyāpur is the site for a planned spiritual city, an ambitious project for which construction will extend over many years to come. In Vṛndāvana are the magnificent Kṛṣṇa-Balarāma Temple and International Guesthouse, *gurukula* school, and Śrīla Prabhupāda Memorial and Museum. There is also a major cultural and educational center in Mumbai. There are beautiful temples in Delhi, Bangalore, Ahmedabad and Vadodara besides many other centers throughout India.

Śrīla Prabhupāda's most significant contribution, however, is his books. Highly respected by scholars for their authority, depth, and clarity, they are used as textbooks in numerous college courses. His writings have been translated into over fifty languages. The Bhaktivedanta Book Trust, established in 1972 exclusively to publish the works of His Divine Grace, has thus become the world's largest publisher of books in the field of Indian religion and philosophy.

In just twelve years, despite his advanced age, Śrīla Prabhupāda circled the globe fourteen times on lecture tours that took him to six continents. In spite of such a vigorous schedule, Śrīla Prabhupāda continued to write prolifically. His writings constitute a veritable library of Vedic philosophy, religion, literature, and culture.

References

The purports of *Śrīmad-Bhāgavatam* are all confirmed by standard Vedic authorities. The following authentic scriptures are cited in this volume. For specific page references, consult the general index.

Amara-kośa dictionary

Bhagavad-gītā

Bhakti-rasāmṛta-sindhu

Brahmāṇḍa Purāṇa

Brahma-saṁhitā

Brahma-yāmala

Bṛhad-viṣṇu Purāṇa

Bṛhan-nāradīya Purāṇa

Caitanya-caritāmṛta

Cāṇakya-śloka

Daśāvatāra-stotra. See: Gīta-govinda

Garuḍa Purāṇa

Gīta-govinda

Īśopaniṣad

Mahābhārata

Manu-saṁhitā

Matsya Purāṇa

Nārada-pañcarātra

Nāradīya Purāṇa

Padma Purāṇa

Prameya-ratnāvalī

Prema-vivarta

Śikṣāṣṭaka

Skanda Purāṇa

Śrīmad-Bhāgavatam

Śvetāśvatara Upaniṣad

Tantra Bhāgavata

Tantra-nirṇaya

Vedānta-sūtra

Viṣṇu Purāṇa

GENEALOGICAL TABLE-CHART ONE

The Plenary Expansions of Godhead and Descendants of Brahmā up to the Sons and Daughters of Dakṣa

Kṛṣṇa is the source of all forms of Godhead as well as all living entities. His first expansion is Balarama. The first part of this simplified chart portrays the different expansions of Lord Kṛṣṇa through the Puruṣa avatāras, or expansions for material creation, such as Mahā-Viṣṇu. From the second Puruṣa avatāra, Garbhodakaśāyī Viṣṇu, is born Lord Brahmā, the first created personality within the material world. Brahmā is empowered creator of the manifested universe and everything within it. The second part of this chart depicts Brahmā's descendants as far as the sons and daughters of Dakṣa.

The daughters of Dakṣa and their descendants are shown in the second chart (pp 794-795 following). As described in this volume, Prajāpati Dakṣa begot sixty daughters in the womb of his wife Asiknī. One should know that it is because of the union of these sixty daughters with various exalted personalities that the entire universe was filled with various kinds of living entities, such as human beings, demigods, demons, beasts, birds and serpents.

Lord brahmā and subsequent personalities in these charts are jīvas, or ordinary living entities, except as noted. All expansions from Kṛṣṇa to Garbhodakaśāyī Viṣṇu are infinite forms of the Supreme Personality of Godhead, Śrī Kṛṣṇa.

References. *See also index to this volume*
From Kṛṣṇa to Garbhodakaśāyī Viṣṇu : *Śrī Caitanya – caritāmṛta, Ādi-līlā*
From Brahmā to Dakṣa and Asiknī : *Śrimad-Bhāgavatam*, Canto Four

KṚṢṆA
- Balarāma
  - Saṅkarṣaṇa
    - Mahā- Saṅkarṣaṇa
      - Mahā-Viṣṇu
        - Garbhodakaśāyī Viṣṇu
          - Brahmā
            - Svāyambhuva Manu + Śatarūpā
              - Uttānapāda + Suruci & Sunītu
                - Uttama (of Suruci)
                - Dhruva (of Sunītu) + Bhrami (daughter of Prajāpati Śiśumāra) & Ilā (daughter of Vāyu)
                  - Vatsara + Svarvīthi
                    - Iṣa
                    - Urja
                    - Vasu
                    - Jaya
                    - Tigmaketu
                    - Puṣpārna + Doṣā & Prabhā
                      - Pradoṣa
                      - Niśitha
                      - Vyuṣṭa + Puṣkariṇī
                      - Prātaḥ
                      - Madhyandinam
                      - Sāyam
                  - Kalpa
                  - Utkala

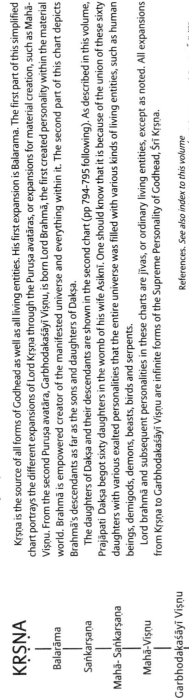

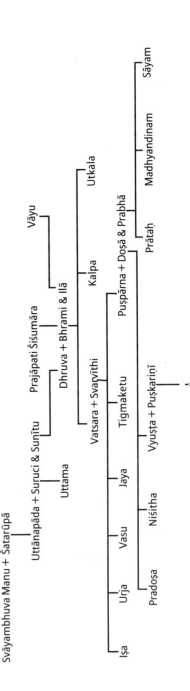

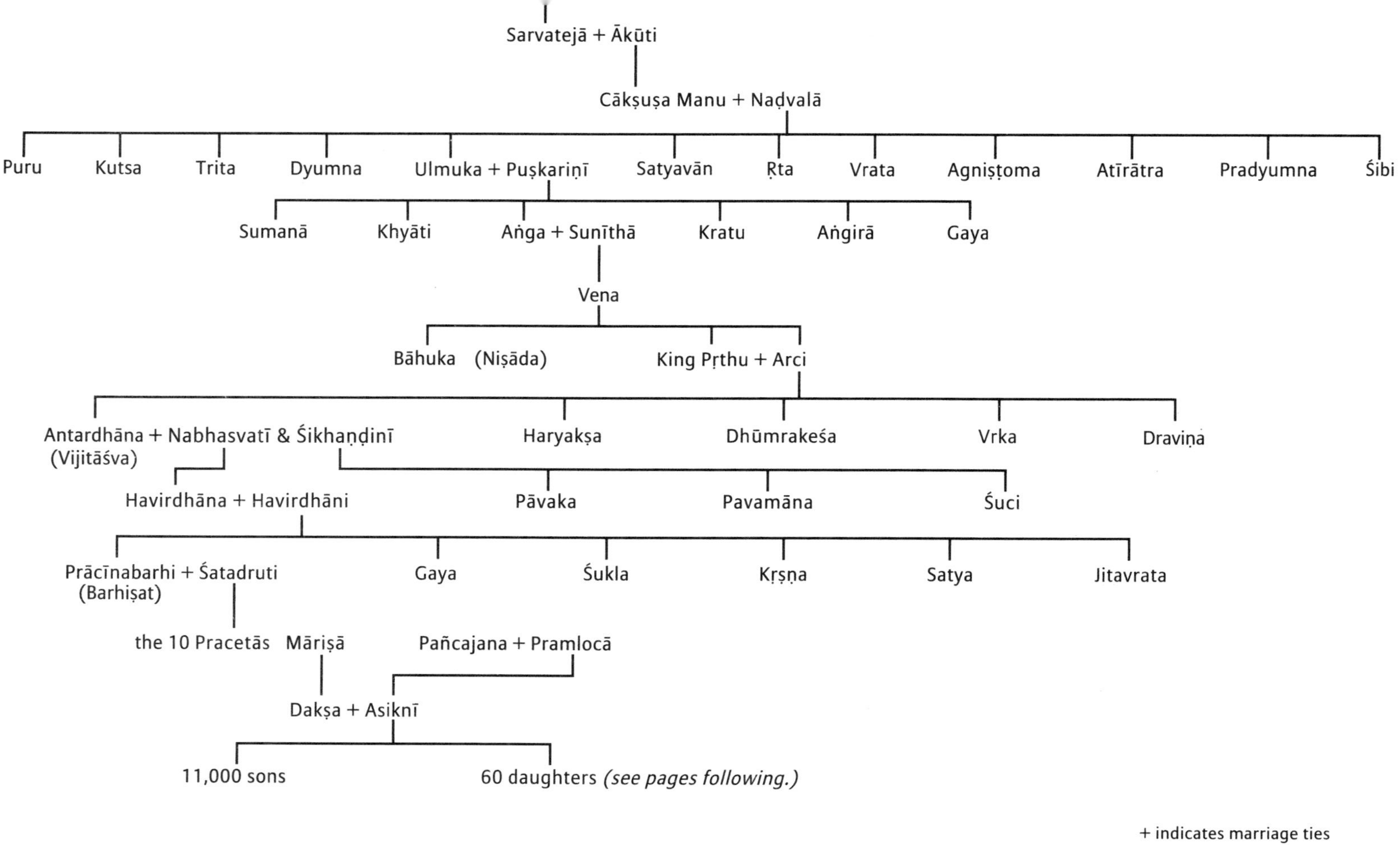
Sarvatejā + Ākūti
Cākṣuṣa Manu + Naḍvalā
Puru
Kutsa
Trita
Dyumna
Ulmuka + Puṣkariṇī
Satyavān
Ṛta
Vrata
Agniṣṭoma
Atīrātra
Pradyumna
Śibi
Sumanā
Khyāti
Aṅga + Sunīthā
Kratu
Aṅgirā
Gaya
Vena
Bāhuka
(Niṣāda)
King Pṛthu + Arci
Antardhāna + Nabhasvatī & Śikhaṇḍinī
(Vijitāśva)
Haryakṣa
Dhūmrakeśa
Vrka
Draviṇa
Havirdhāna + Havirdhāni
Pāvaka
Pavamāna
Śuci
Prācīnabarhi + Śatadruti
(Barhiṣat)
Gaya
Śukla
Kṛṣṇa
Satya
Jitavrata
the 10 Pracetās
Māriṣā
Pañcajana + Pramlocā
Dakṣa + Asiknī
11,000 sons
60 daughters *(see pages following.)*
+ indicates marriage ties

GENEALOGICAL TABLE-CHART TWO

The Progeny of the Daughters of Dakṣa

Kaśyapa (received 17 wives)

Wife		Progeny
Timi	→	aquatics
Vinatā	→	Garuḍa, Anūru (Aruṇa)
Kadrū	→	serpents
Pataṅgī	→	birds
Yāminī	→	locusts
Diti	→	Hiraṇyākṣa, Hiraṇyakaśipu, etc.
Kāṣṭhā	→	single-hooved animals
Ariṣṭā	→	Gandharvas
Surasā	→	Rākṣasas
Ilā	→	creepers & trees
Muni	→	angels
Krodhavaśā	→	mosquitoes, serpents (dandaśūka & others)
Tāmrā	→	large birds of prey
Surabhi	→	cow, buffalo, etc.
Saramā	→	ferocious animals

Danu → Aruṇa, Anutāpana, Dvimūrdhā, Śambara, Vibhāvasu, Ayomukha Śaṅkuśirā, Kapila, Durjaya, Dhūmrakeśa, Ekacakra, Virūpākṣa,

- Svarbhānu + NS → Suprabā + Namuci
- Vṛṣaparvā + NS → Śarmiṣṭhā + Yayāti
- Vipracitti + Siṁhikā → Rāhu & the one hundred Ketus

Hayagrīva (demon), Pulomā, Ariṣṭa,

- Vaiśvānara + NS → Upadānavī + Hiraṇyākṣa; Hayaśirā + Karatu; Pulomā, Kālakā + Kaśyapa → the Paulomas & the Kālakeyas, *headed by* Nivātakavaca

Aṅgirā (received 2 wives) + { **Svadhā** → the Pitās; **Satī** → Atharvāṅgirasa Veda }

Bhūta (received 2 wives) + { **NS** → ghosts & goblins; **Sarūpā** → the ten milion Rudras, *of whom eleven are prominent*: Raivata, Aja, Bhava, Bhīma, Vāma, Ugra, Ajaikapāt, Ahirbradhna Vṛṣākapi, Mahān, Baharūpa }

Kṛśāśva (received 2 wives) + { **Arcis** → Dhūmaketu; **Dhiṣanā** → Vedaśirā, Devala, Vayuna, Manu }

Moon-God (received 27 wives) + { the **Kṛttikā** constellations }

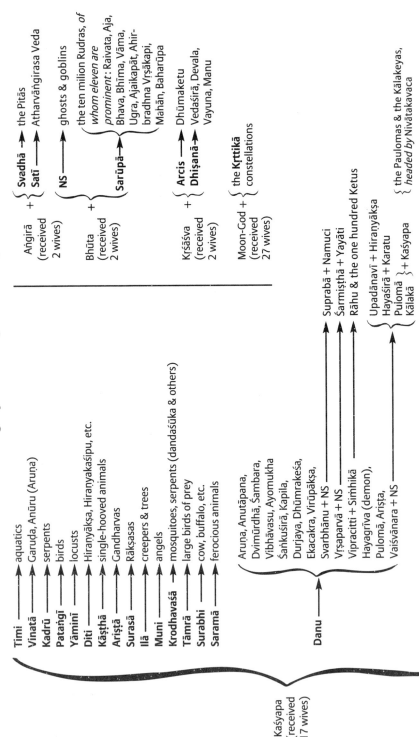

* foster son. Actual father is Śiva.
→ indicates offspring.
NS not specified.
Dakṣa's daughters are indicated by boldface type.

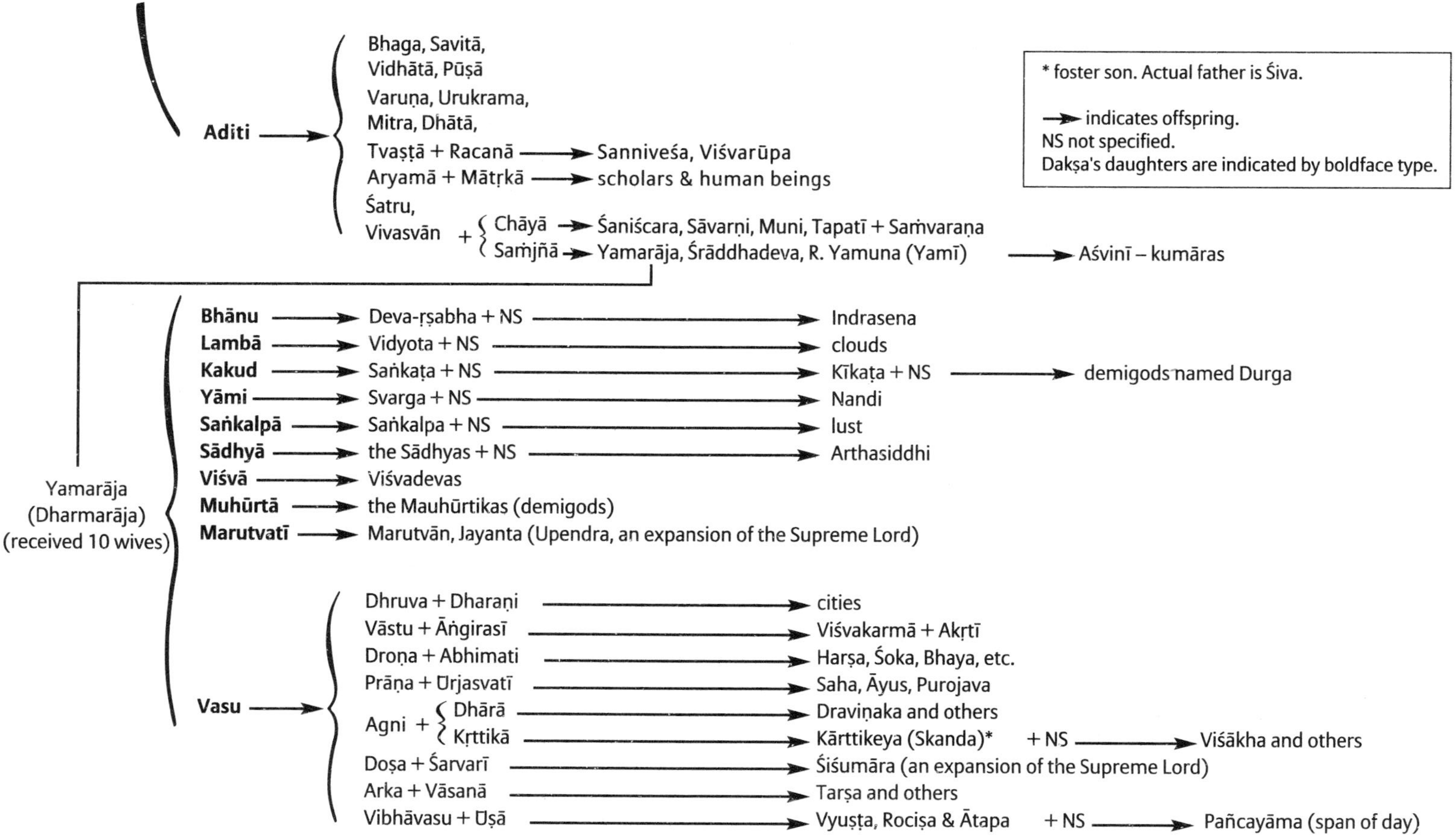

Aditi →

Bhaga, Savitā, Vidhātā, Pūṣā
Varuṇa, Urukrama, Mitra, Dhātā,
Tvaṣṭā + Racanā → Sanniveśa, Viśvarūpa
Aryamā + Mātṛkā → scholars & human beings
Śatru,
Vivasvān + ⎰ Chāyā → Śaniścara, Sāvarṇi, Muni, Tapatī + Saṁvaraṇa
                     ⎱ Saṁjñā → Yamarāja, Śrāddhadeva, R. Yamuna (Yamī)
                       → Aśvinī – kumāras

Bhānu → Deva-ṛṣabha + NS → Indrasena
Lambā → Vidyota + NS → clouds
Kakud → Saṅkaṭa + NS → Kīkaṭa + NS → demigods named Durga
Yāmi → Svarga + NS → Nandi
Saṅkalpā → Saṅkalpa + NS → lust
Sādhyā → the Sādhyas + NS → Arthasiddhi
Viśvā → Viśvadevas
Muhūrtā → the Mauhūrtikas (demigods)
Marutvatī → Marutvān, Jayanta (Upendra, an expansion of the Supreme Lord)

Yamarāja (Dharmarāja) (received 10 wives)

Vasu →

Dhruva + Dharaṇi → cities
Vāstu + Āṅgirasī → Viśvakarmā + Ākṛtī
Droṇa + Abhimati → Harṣa, Śoka, Bhaya, etc.
Prāṇa + Ūrjasvatī → Saha, Āyus, Purojava
Agni + ⎰ Dhārā → Draviṇaka and others
       ⎱ Kṛttikā → Kārttikeya (Skanda)* → Viśākha and others + NS
Doṣa + Śarvarī → Śiśumāra (an expansion of the Supreme Lord)
Arka + Vāsanā → Tarṣa and others
Vibhāvasu + Ūṣā → Vyuṣṭa, Rociṣa & Ātapa + NS → Pañcayāma (span of day)

GENEALOGICAL TABLE CHART THREE
The Descendants of Kaśyapa Muni

This chart shows the descendants of Kaśyapa Muni, whose father, Marīci, was born from the mind of Lord Brahmā, the first created being in the universe. Kaśyapa's wives helped to populate the universe with different species of life. Two of his wives, Diti and Aditi, are especially important : Diti was the mother of many great demons, and Aditi, many great demigods. An incarnation of the Supreme Personality of Godhead, Urukrama, also appeared from Aditi's womb.

Kaśyapa +

- Timi → aquatics
- Vinatā → Garuḍa, Anūru (Aruṇa)
- Kadrū → serpents
- Pataṅgī → birds
- Yāminī → locusts
- Kāṣṭhā → single-hooved animals
- Ariṣṭā → Gandharvas
- Surasā → Rākṣasas
- Ilā → creepers & trees
- Muni → angels
- Surabhi → cow, buffalo, etc.
- Tāmrā → large birds of prey
- Krodhavaśā → mosquitoes, serpents (dandaśūka & others)
- Saramā → ferocious animals
- Diti →
  - Hiraṇyākṣa + Upadānavī
  - Hiraṇyakaśipu + Kayadhu →
    - Saṁhlāda + Kṛti → Pañcajana
    - Anuhlāda + Sūryā → Bāṣkala, Mahiṣa
    - Hlāda + Dhamani → Vātāpi, Ilvala
    - Prahlāda + NS → Virocana + NS → Bali + Aśanā → Bāṇa & 99 others
    - Siṁhikā
  - Maruts
- Danu →
  - Ariṣṭa, Anutāpana,
  - Dvimūrdhā, Śambara, Vipracitti + Siṁhikā → Rāhu & the one hundred Ketus
  - Dhūmrakeśa, Aruṇa,
  - Vibhāvasu, Ayomukha
  - Svarbhānu + NS → Suprabā + Namuci
  - Vṛṣaparvā + NS → Śarmiṣṭhā + Yayāti
  - Śaṅkuśirā, Kapila,
  - Durjaya, Pulomā,
  - Vaiśvānara + NS →
    - Upadānavī
    - Hayaśirā + Karatu
    - Pulomā, Kālakā } Kaśyapa → the Paulomas & the Kālakeyas, *headed by* Nivātakavaca
  - Hayagrīva (demon),
  - Ekacakra, Virūpākṣa,

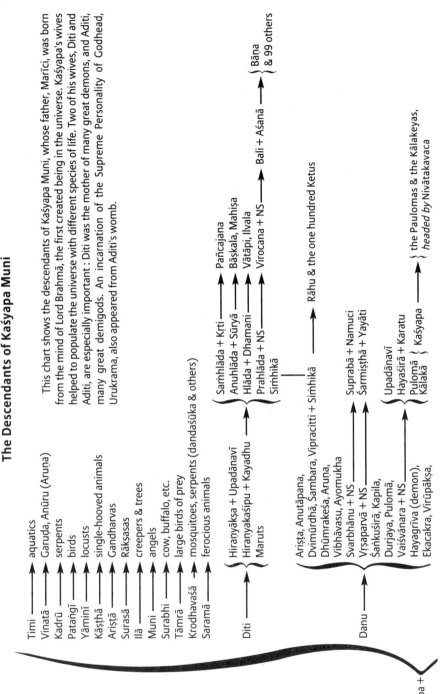

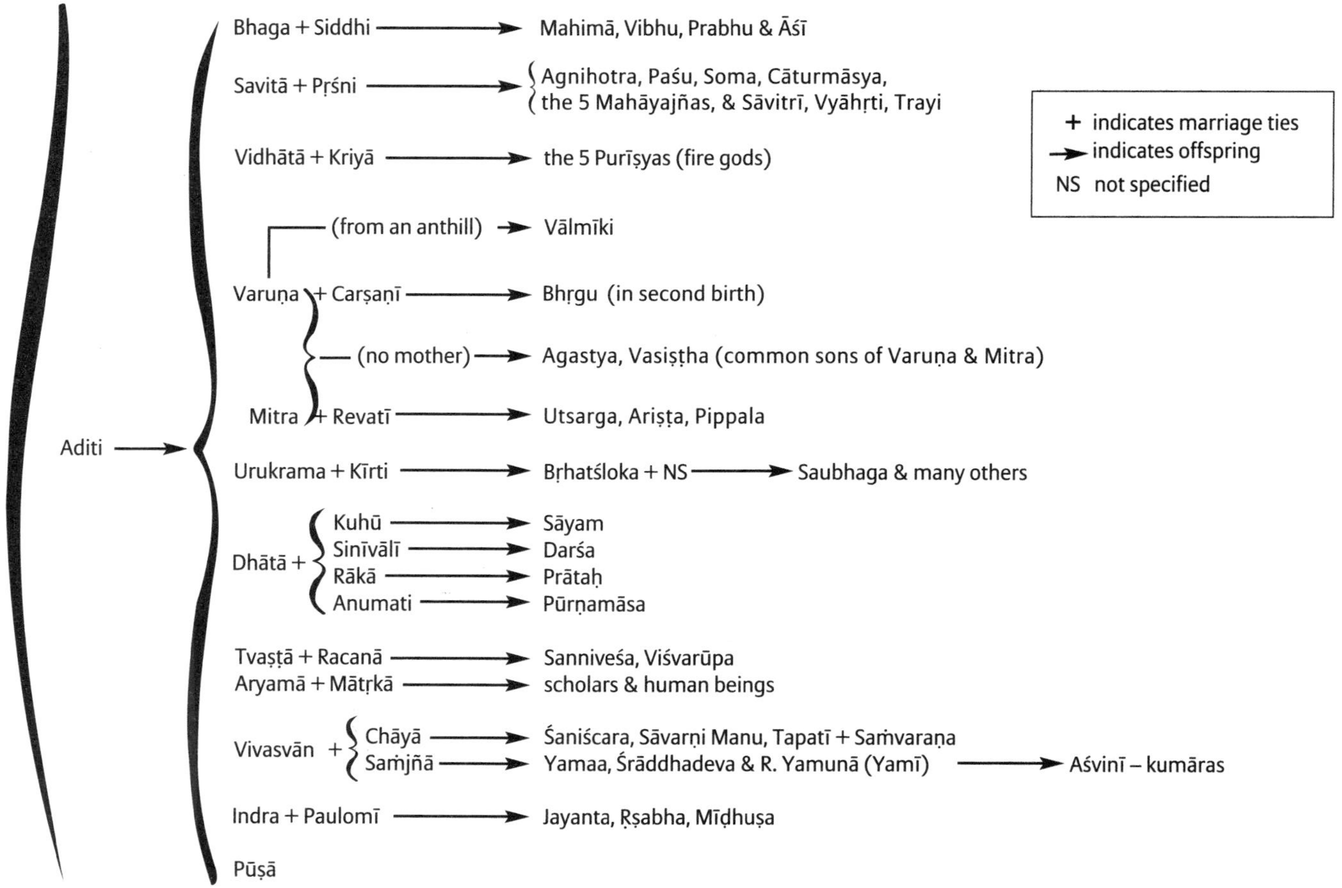
Aditi
Bhaga + Siddhi
Mahimā, Vibhu, Prabhu & Āśī
Savitā + Pṛśni
Agnihotra, Paśu, Soma, Cāturmāsya,
the 5 Mahāyajñas, & Sāvitrī, Vyāhṛti, Trayi
Vidhātā + Kriyā
the 5 Purīṣyas (fire gods)
(from an anthill)
Vālmīki
Varuṇa + Carṣaṇī
Bhṛgu (in second birth)
(no mother)
Agastya, Vasiṣṭha (common sons of Varuṇa & Mitra)
Mitra + Revatī
Utsarga, Ariṣṭa, Pippala
Urukrama + Kīrti
Bṛhatśloka + NS
Saubhaga & many others
Dhātā +
Kuhū
Sāyam
Sinīvālī
Darśa
Rākā
Prātaḥ
Anumati
Pūrṇamāsa
Tvaṣṭā + Racanā
Sanniveśa, Viśvarūpa
Aryamā + Mātṛkā
scholars & human beings
Vivasvān +
Chāyā
Śaniścara, Sāvarṇi Manu, Tapatī + Saṁvaraṇa
Saṁjñā
Yamaa, Śrāddhadeva & R. Yamunā (Yamī)
Aśvinī – kumāras
Indra + Paulomī
Jayanta, Ṛṣabha, Mīḍhuṣa
Pūṣā
+ indicates marriage ties
indicates offspring
NS not specified

Glossary

A

Ācamana—a ritual of purification in which one sips water and simultaneously chants names of the Supreme Lord.

Ācārya—a spiritual master who teaches by his own example, and who sets the proper religious example for all human beings.

Adharma—irreligion.

Adhibhautika—(misery) caused by other living beings.

Adhidaivika—(misery) caused by nature.

Adhyātmika—(misery) caused by one's own body and mind.

Ādityas—the demigods who are descendants of Kaśyapa Muni's wife, Aditi.

Advaita-vādīs—atheistic philosophers who propound the philosophy of *advaita-vāda* or *māyāvāda*. See: *Māyāvāda*

Ajñāta-sukṛti—pious or devotional activity performed accidentally, without knowledge of its effect.

Ānandamaya—full of bliss in spiritual realization; Kṛṣṇa consciousness.

Aṇimā-siddhi—mystic power by which one can become as small as an atom.

Annamaya—(consciousness) absorbed only in food.

Apsarā—a heavenly courtesan. The most beautiful women in the heavenly planets, who are expert at dancing.

Ārati— a ceremony in which one greets and worships the Lord in His form of a Deity by offerings such as incense, a flame, water, a fine cloth, a fragrant flower, a peacock-feather, and yak-tail whisk, accompanied by ringing of a bell and chanting of *mantras*.

Arcana—the procedures followed for worshiping the *arcā-vigraha*, the Deity in the temple; engaging all the senses in the service of the Lord.

Āśrama—a spiritual order of life. The four *āśramas* are *brahmacārī* or student life, *gṛhastha* or married life, *vānaprastha* or retired life, and *sannyāsa* or the renounced order of life; the home of the spiritual master, a place where spiritual practices are executed.

Asura—demon, one who does not follow the principles of scripture, an atheist, a gross materialist. One who is envious of God, and is averse to the supremacy and service of the Supreme Lord, Viṣṇu.

Avatāra—literally "one who descends." A partially or fully empowered incarnation of Lord Kṛṣṇa who descends from the spiritual sky to the material universe with a particular mission described in scriptures. Lord Śrī Kṛṣṇa is the original Personality of Godhead from whom all *avatāras* originate. There are two broad categories of *avatāras*. Some, like Śrī Kṛṣṇa, Śrī Rāma and Śrī Nṛsiṁha, are Viṣṇu-tattva, i.e. direct forms of God Himself, the source of all power. Others are ordinary souls (*jīva-tattva*) who are called *śaktyāveśa avatāras*, and are empowered by the Lord to execute a certain purpose.

B

Balarāma (Baladeva)—the first plenary expansion of the Supreme Personality of Godhead, Lord Kṛṣṇa. He appeared as the son of Rohiṇī and elder brother of Lord Kṛṣṇa. Also known as Balabhadra or Baladeva, He is worshipped in Pūri along with His younger brother Kṛṣṇa and sister Subhadra.

Bhagavad-gītā—a seven-hundred verse record of a conversation between Lord Kṛṣṇa and His disciple, Arjuna, from the *Bhīṣma Parva* of the *Mahābhārata* of Vedavyāsa. The conversation took place between two armies minutes before the start of an immense fratricidal battle. Kṛṣṇa teaches the science of the Absolute Truth and the importance of devotional service to the despondent Arjuna, and it contains the essence of all Vedic wisdom. Śrīla Prabhupāda's annotated English translation is called *Bhagavad-gītā As It Is*; This most essential text of spiritual knowledge, The Song of the Lord, contains Kṛṣṇa's instructions to Arjuna at Kurukṣetra. It is found in the *Mahābhārata*. The *Mahābhārata* is classified as *smṛti-śāstra*, a supplement of the *śruti-śāstra*. *Śruti*, the core Vedic literature, includes the four *Vedas* (*Ṛg, Sāma, Yajur* and *Atharva*) and the *Upaniṣads*. *Śruti* advances the understanding of the absolute. B*hagavad-gītā* is also known as *Gītopaniṣad*, or a *śruti* text spoken by the Supreme Personality of Godhead Himself. Therefore, Śrīla Prabhupāda wrote in a letter, the *Gītā* should be taken as *śruti*. But they take it as smṛti because it is part of the *smṛti* (*Mahābhārata*). In one sense it is both *śruti* and *smṛti*. In only 700 verses, the *Bhagavad-gītā* summarizes all Vedic knowledge about the soul, God, *sanātana-dharma*, sacrifice, *yoga*, *karma*, reincarnation, the modes of material nature, *Vedānta* and pure devotion.

Bhagavān—the Supreme Personality of Godhead, an epithet of the Supreme

Person; the Personality of Godhead, the possessor (*vān*) of six opulences (*bhaga*) in unlimited fullness: wealth (*aiśvarya*), strength (*vīrya*), fame (*yaśaḥ*), beauty (*śriyaḥ*), knowledge (*jñāna*), and renunciation (*vairāgya*).

Bhāgavata-dharma—the science of devotional service to the Supreme Lord; the religious principles enunciated by the Lord; the eternal function of the living being.

Bhakta—a devotee of the Lord; one who performs devotional service (*bhakti*).

Bhakti-yoga—the system of cultivation of pure devotional service to the Supreme Personality of Godhead, Lord Kṛṣṇa, which is not tinged by sense gratification or philosophical speculation. It consists of nine *aṅgas* or parts: (1) *śravaṇaṁ*–hearing about the transcendental holy name, form, and other qualities of the Lord (2) *kīrtanaṁ*– chanting about these qualities, (3) *viṣṇoḥ smaraṇaṁ*–remembering them, (4) *pāda-sevanam*–serving the lotus feet of the Lord, (5) *arcanaṁ*–worshipping the Deity of the Lord, (6) *vandanaṁ*–offering prayers to the Lord, (7) *dāsyaṁ*–serving His mission, (8) *sakhyam*–making friends with the Lord, and (9) *ātma-nivedanam*–surrendering everything unto Him.

Bhoga—material sense enjoyment; food before it has been offered to the Deity.

Brahmacarya—celibate student life, the first order of Vedic spiritual life; the vow of strict abstinence from sex indulgence.

Brahmaloka— the highest planet of the universe, the abode of Lord Brahmā.

Brahman—(1) the infinitesimal spiritual individual soul, (2) the impersonal, all-pervasive aspect of the Supreme, (3) the Supreme Personality of Godhead and (4) the *mahat-tattva*, or total material substance; this Sanskrit term comes from the root *bṛh*, which means to grow or to evolve. The *Cāndogya Upaniṣad* describes Brahman as *tajjalān*, as that (*tat*) from which the world arises (*ja*), into which it returns (*la*), and by which is supported and lives (*an*). Impersonalists equate Brahman with the *brahmajyoti*. But in its fullest sense, Brahman is the *vastu*, the actual substance of the world: (1) Viṣṇu as the Supreme Soul (*paraṁ brahmạn*), (2) the individual self as the subordinate soul (*jīva-brahman*), and (3) matter as creative nature (*mahad-brahman*). Viṣṇu is accepted by all schools of Vaiṣṇava *Vedānta* as the transcendental, unlimited *Puruṣottama* (Supreme Person), while the individual souls and matter are His conscious and unconscious energies (*cid-acid-śakti*).

Brāhmaṇa—a member of the intellectual, priestly class; a person wise in Vedic knowledge, fixed in goodness and knowledge of Brahman, the Absolute Truth; one of the four orders of Vedic society. Their occupation consists of learning and teaching Vedic literature, learning and teaching Deity worship, and receiving and giving charity.

Buddha—incarnation of Kṛṣṇa, the founder of Buddhism who lived during the 5th century B.C. He appeared in this world to bewilder atheists and dissuade them from performing unnecessary animal sacrifices., He took birth in Kapilavastu (in present-day Nepal) as Siddhārtha Gautama, the son of King Śuddhodana. At age twenty-nine he renounced the world and embarked upon a mission to preach *ahiṁsā* (nonviolence) and *śūnyatā* (extinction of the self). He especially opposed the prevailing *karma-mīmāṁsā* philosophy of his time, which distorted Vedic knowledge and promoted unnecessary animal sacrifice.

C

Caitanya-caritāmṛta—translated as "the character of the living force in immortality," it is the authorized biography of Lord Caitanya Mahāprabhu written in the late sixteenth century by Śrīla Kṛṣṇadāsa Kavirāja Gosvāmī, presenting the Lord's pastimes and teachings. It is written in Bengali, with many Sanskrit verses, and is considered the postgraduate study of spiritual knowledge. Ideally, one begins with *Bhagavad-gītā* and advances through *Śrīmad-Bhāgavatam* to the *Śrī Caitanya-caritāmṛta.*

Cakra—one of six centers of vital energy located in the body.

Cāraṇaloka—the heavenly planet of the Cāraṇa demigods.

D

Daivī māyā—the Lord's divine deluding potency, the material energy.

Dāna—charity, one of the six duties of a *brāhmaṇa*

Daṇḍavats—respectful prostrated obeisances offered to an elevated personality, such as one's spiritual master or the Supreme Personality of Godhead. The word literally means falling flat like a rod.

Daridra-nārāyaṇa—"poor Nārāyaṇa," an offensive term used by Māyāvādīs to equate poor men with the Supreme Lord.

Dāsya-rasa—the servitor relationship with the Lord.

Dhanvantari—the incarnation of the Supreme Lord who is the father of Āyurveda, the Vedic medical science.

Dharma—religious principles; one's natural occupation; the quality of rendering service, which is the essential, eternal quality of the soul, regarded as inseparable from it. The Sanskrit term *dharma* is variously translated as duty, virtue, morality, righteousness, or religion, but no single English word conveys the actual import of *dharma*. Dharma ultimately means to surrender to the Supreme Lord, as Lord Kṛṣṇa commands Arjuna in the *Gīta*.

Dharma-śāstras—religious scriptures that prescribe regulations of social organization and religion.

Dharmī—one who abides by Vedic law, or religious principles.

Dhīra—one who is undisturbed by the material energy in all circumstances; ecstasy of sober love for Kṛṣṇa.

Dhruvaloka—the polestar, which is a spiritual planet within the material universe, and is presided over by Dhruva Mahārāja.

E

Ekādaśī—Directly presided over by Lord Hari, Ekādaśī is a holy day for Vaiṣṇavas. It falls on the eleventh day after both the full and new moon days. Abstinence from grains and beans is prescribed. One should utilize this day for fasting and increasing one's devotion to Lord Kṛṣṇa by intensifying the chanting of the Hare Kṛṣṇa *mantra* and other devotional activities.

G

Gandharvas—the celestial demigod dancers, singers, and musicians of the heavenly planets.

Garbhodakaśāyī Viṣṇu—the second Viṣṇu expansion, who enters each universe and from whose navel grows a lotus upon which Lord Brahmā appears. Brahmā then creates the diverse material manifestations.

Gauḍīya Madhva sampradāya—the authorized Vaiṣṇava disciplic succession of bona fide spiritual masters from Bengal coming through Śrīla Madhvācārya and Lord Śrī Caitanya Mahāprabhu; the followers in that tradition.

Goloka Vṛndāvana (Kṛṣṇaloka)—the highest spiritual planet in the kingdom of God, Lord Kṛṣṇa's personal abode.

Gopīs—the cowherd girls of Vraja, who are generally the counterparts of Śrī

Kṛṣṇa's *hlādini-sākti*, Śrīmatī Rādhārāṇī, and His most surrendered and confidential devotees. They assist Her as maidservants in her conjugal pastimes with the Supreme Personality of Godhead.

Gosvāmī—a person who has his senses under full control: the title of a *sannyāsi*, a person in the renounced order of life.

Govinda—a name of the Supreme Lord Kṛṣṇa meaning "one who gives pleasure to the land, the cows and the senses."

Gṛhamedhi—materialistic householder who lives only for sense gratification.

Gṛhastha—regulated householder life. One who leads a God conscious married life and raises a family in Kṛṣṇa consciousness according to the Vedic social system; the second order of Vedic spiritual life.

Guṇas— there are three *guṇas*, or modes of material nature: goodness (*sattva-guṇa*), passion (*rajo-guṇa*) and ignorance (*tamo-guṇa*). The modes are three measures of interaction between conscious spirit and unconscious matter. The modes may be compared to the three primary colors, yellow, red and blue, and consciousness may be compared to clear light. The color yellow symbolizes *sattva-guṇa*, the mode of goodness. This mode is pure, illuminating, and sinless. The color red symbolizes *rajo-guṇa*, the mode of passion, full of longings and desires. The color blue symbolizes *tamo-guṇa*, the mode of ignorance, which binds the soul to madness, indolence and sleep. The three modes combine to produce the vast spectrum of states of conditioned consciousness that encompasses all living entities within the universe.

Guru—spiritual master; one of the three spiritual authorities for a Vaiṣṇava. Literally, this term means heavy. The spiritual master is heavy with knowledge.

H

Hare Kṛṣṇa mantra—a sixteen-word prayer composed of the names Hare, Kṛṣṇa, and Rāma: Hare Kṛṣṇa, Hare Kṛṣṇa, Kṛṣṇa Kṛṣṇa, Hare Hare, Hare Rāma, Hare Rāma, Rāma Rāma, Hare Hare. Hare is an address to Harā, another name for His eternal consort, Śrīmatī Rādhārāṇī. Kṛṣṇa, "the all-attractive one," and Rāma, "the all-pleasing one," are names of God. The chanting of this *mantra* is the most recommended means for spiritual progress in this age of Kali, as it cleanses the mind of all impurities, and helps to understand one's true identity as an eternal spiritual being. Lord Caitanya personally designated it as the *mahā-mantra* and practically demonstrated the effects of the chanting.

Hari—the Supreme Lord, who removes all obstacles to spiritual progress; Lord Viṣṇu.

Hayagriva (Hayaśīrṣā) Lord—the horse-headed incarnation of Lord Kṛṣṇa who returned the stolen *Vedas* to Brahmā and spoke the *Vedas* to him.

J

Jīva-tattva—the living entities, atomic parts of the Supreme Lord.

Jñāna—knowledge. Material *jñāna* does not go beyond the material body and its expansions. Transcendental *jñāna* discriminates between matter and spirit. Perfect *jñāna* is knowledge of the body, the soul and the Supreme Lord.

Jñāna-yoga—the process of approaching the Supreme by the cultivation of knowledge; the predominantly empirical process of linking with the Supreme, which is executed when one is still attached to mental speculation.

Jñānī—one who is engaged in the cultivation of knowledge (especially by philosophical speculation). Upon attaining perfection, a *jñānī* surrenders to Kṛṣṇa.

K

Kali-yuga—the present age, the Age of Kalī, the Age of Quarrel and Hypocrisy. The fourth and last age in the cycle of a *mahā-yuga*. It began 5,000 years ago, and lasts for a total of 432,000 years. It is characterized by irreligious practice and stringent material miseries.

Kalki—He is the tenth incarnation of Lord Viṣṇu. He arrives on a white horse at the end of *Kali-yuga* to annihilate all the demons and atheists.

Kapila—an incarnation of Kṛṣṇa who appeared in Satya-yuga as the son of Devahūti and Kardama Muni and expounded the devotional Sāṅkhya philosophy, the analysis of matter and spirit, as a means of cultivating devotional service to the Lord. (There is also an atheist philosopher named Kapila, but he is not an incarnation of the Lord.)

Kāraṇodakaśāyī Viṣṇu—Mahā-Viṣṇu, the expansion of the Supreme Lord from whom all material universes emanate. He lies within the Causal Ocean and breathes out innumerable universes.

Karatālas—hand cymbals used in *kīrtana*.

Karma—1. material action performed according to scriptural regulations; 2. action pertaining to the development of the material body; 3. any material action which will incur a subsequent reaction and 4. the material reaction one incurs due to fruitive activities. The soul receives due reaction to work by taking his next birth in a lower species, or the human species, or a higher species. Or the soul may be liberated from birth and death altogether. All this depends upon whether the *karma* performed within this lifetime is ignorant, passionate, good or transcendental.

Karma-kāṇḍa—the division of the *Vedas* which deals with fruitive activities performed for the purpose of gradual purification of the grossly entangled materialist; the path of fruitive work.

Karma-yoga—action in devotional service; the path of God realization through dedicating the fruits of one's work to God.

Karmī—a fruitive laborer, one who is attached to the fruits of work, a materialist who works hard to enjoy material life.

Kīrtana—glorification of the Supreme Lord; narrating or singing the glories of the Supreme Personality of Godhead and His Holy Names; the devotional process of chanting the names and glories of the Supreme Lord.

Kṣatriya—second of the four social orders of the *varṇāśrama* system; a warrior who is inclined to fight and lead others; the administrative or protective occupation.

Kṣīrodakaśāyī Viṣṇu—*See:* Supersoul.

Kūrma—the Supreme Lord's incarnation as a tortoise.

Kuśa—an auspicious grass used in Vedic rituals and sacrifices.

L

Laghima-siddhi—mystic ability to make one's body very light

Liṅga—the subtle body: mind, intelligence and false ego.

M

Mādhurya-rasa—the spiritual relationship in conjugal love which the Supreme Lord and His devotee reciprocate as lovers.

Mahā-mantra—*See:* Hare Kṛṣṇa mantra

Mahā-puruṣa—the Supreme Lord, who is the supreme enjoyer.

Maha-Viṣṇu—the expansion of the Supreme Lord Viṣṇu reclining on Ādi-Sesa, from whom all material universes emanate.

Mahābhārata—an important and famous *itihāsa* (historical) scripture belonging to the *smṛti* section of the Vedic scriptures; an ancient, epic history of Bhārata or India composed in 100,000 verses by Kṛṣṇa Dvaipāyana Vyāsadeva, the literary incarnation of Godhead. The essence of all Vedic philosophy, the *Bhagavad-gītā*, is a part of this great work. *Mahābhārata* is a history of the earth from its creation to the great Kurukṣetra war fought between the Kuru and Pāṇḍava factions of the Kaurava dynasty, which took place about five thousand years ago.

Mahājana—one of the twelve great self-realized souls, an authority in the science of Kṛṣṇa Consciousness, who preaches the path of devotional service to the people in general; one who understands the Absolute Truth.

Mahat-tattva—the original, undifferentiated form of the total material energy, from which the material world is manifested when the three modes of material nature are activated by the glance of Mahā-Viṣṇu.

Mahātmā—a "great soul," an exalted devotee of Lord Kṛṣṇa, free from material contamination. He factually understands that Kṛṣṇa is everything, and therefore surrenders unto Him.

Manomaya—(consciousness) absorbed in mental activity.

Mantra—a transcendental sound or Vedic hymn, a prayer or chant; a pure sound vibration when repeated over and over delivers the mind from its material inclinations and illusion. The Vedic scriptures are composed of many thousands of *mantras*.

Manu-saṁhitā—the scriptural law-book for mankind, written by Manu, the administrative demigod, and father of mankind.

Manvantara—duration of each Manu' s reign, comprising 306,720,000 years.

Marudloka—the planet of the Maruts, associates of King Indra.

Maruts—the demigod associates of King Indra, the gods of the air. They number forty-nine and are sons of Diti.

Mathurā—Lord Kṛṣṇa's abode, and birth place, surrounding Vṛndāvana. Lord Krsṇa displayed many of His pastimes here after leaving Vṛndāvana. At the end of Lord Kṛṣṇa's manifest *līlā*, Vajranābha, His grandson, was put in charge of this sacred city.

Māyā—Māyāvāda philosophy. Māyāvāda in Sanskrit means doctrine of illusion. In India, the philosophies of the Buddha and of Śaṅkarācārya are called Māyāvāda. The second grew out of the first. The fundamental principles accepted by both are the following: (1) name, form, individuality, thoughts, desires and words arise from *māyā* or illusion, not God; (2) *māyā* cannot be rationally explained, since the very idea that anything needs explaining is itself *māyā*; (3) the individual self or soul is not eternal, because upon liberation it ceases to exist; (4) like *māyā*, the state of liberation is beyond all explanation. The main difference between the two is that Śaṅkarācārya's Māyāvāda asserts that beyond *māyā* is an eternal impersonal monistic reality, Brahman, the nature of which is the self. Buddhism, however, aims at extinction (*nirodha*) as the final goal. Of the two, Śaṅkarācārya's Māyāvāda is more dangerous, as it apparently derives its authority from the *Vedas*. Much word-jugglery is employed to defend the Vedic origins of Śaṅkarācārya's Māyāvāda. But ultimately Māyāvādīs dispense with Vedic authority by concluding that the Supreme cannot be known through *śabda*, that the name of Kṛṣṇa is a material vibration, that the form of Kṛṣṇa is illusion, and so on. The Śaṅkarites agree with the Buddhists that *nāma-rūpa* (name and form) must always be *māyā*. Therefore Vaiṣṇavas reject both kinds of Māyāvāda as atheism. Buddhists generally do not deny that they are atheists, whereas the Śaṅkarite Māyāvādīs claim to be theists. But actually they are monists and pantheists. Their claim to theism is refuted by their belief that the Supreme Self is overcome by *māyā* and becomes the bound soul. Śaṅkarācārya's Māyāvāda is similar in significant ways to the Western doctrine of solipsism. Like solipsism, it arrives at a philosophical dead end. The questions that remain unanswered are: If my consciousness is the only reality, why can't I change the universe at will, simply by thought? And if my own self is the only reality, why am I dependent for my life, learning and happiness upon a world full of living entities that refuse to acknowledge this reality?

Māyā—illusion; an energy of Kṛṣṇa's which deludes the living entity into forgetfulness of the Supreme Lord. That which is not, unreality, deception, forgetfulness, material illusion. Under illusion a man thinks he can be happy in this temporary material world. The nature of the material world is that the more a man tries to exploit the material situation, the more he is bound by *māyā's* complexities; This is a Sanskrit term of many meanings. It may mean energy; *yoga-māyā* is the spiritual energy sustaining the transcendental manifestation of the spiritual Vaikuṇṭha world, while the reflection, *mahā-māyā*, is the energy of the material world. The Lord's twofold *māyā* bewilders the jīva, hence *māyā* also means bewilderment or illusion. Transcendental bewilderment is in love, by which the devotee sees God as his master, friend, dependent or amorous beloved. The material bewilderment of the living entity begins with his attraction to the glare of the brahmajyoti. That attraction leads to his entanglement in the modes of material nature. According to Bhaktisiddhānta Sarasvatī Ṭhākura, *māyā* also means that which can be measured. This is the feature of Lord Kṛṣṇa's *prakṛti* that captures the minds of scientific materialists. The Vaiṣṇava and Māyāvāda explanations of *māyā* are not the same.

Māyā-ṣukha—material happiness, which is illusory and temporary.

Māyāvāda—the impersonal philosophy propounded by Śaṅkarācārya, which proposes the unqualified oneness of God and the living entities (who are both conceived of as being ultimately formless) and the non-reality of manifest nature; the philosophy that everything is one and that the Absolute Truth is not a person.

Mayāvādī—one who propounds the impersonal philosophy of Māyāvāda.

Mīmāṁsakas—atheistic philosophers who say that even if God exists He is obliged to give us the fruits of our work, and there is no need to worship Him separately.

Mleccha—uncivilized humans, outside the Vedic system of society, who are generally meat-eaters, and whose consciousness is lower than a *śūdra.*

Mṛdaṅga—a two-headed clay drum used for *kīrtana* performances and congregational chanting.

Mukti—liberation of a conditioned soul from material consciousness and bondage.

N

Nāma-aparādha—an offense against the holy name of the Lord.

Nārada Muni—a pure devotee of the Lord, one of the sons of Lord Brahmā, who travels throughout the universes in his eternal body, glorifying devotional service while delivering the science of *bhakti.* He is the spiritual master of Vyāsadeva and of many other great devotees. A great sage among the demigods and one of the foremost authorities on *viṣṇu-bhakti.* Among Nārada's other prominent disciples are Prahlāda, Dhruva, Citraketu (Vṛtrāsura), and the Haryaśvas.

Nārāyaṇa—the majestic four-armed expansion of the Supreme Personality of Godhead who is the resting place of all living entities, and presides over the Vaikuṇṭha planets.

Nitya-muktas (Nitya-siddhas)—eternally liberated soul, associates of the Lord who never come in contact with the external energy, and who never forget Kṛṣṇa at any time.

Nivṛtti-mārga—the path of renunciation, which leads to liberation; directions for giving up the material world for higher spiritual understanding.

Nṛsiṁha Purāṇa—one of the eighteen *Purāṇas.* It describes the pastimes of the Supreme Lord in His half-lion, half-man incarnation as Lord Nṛsiṁha.

Nyāya—logic; one of the six systems of Vedic philosophy, taught by sage Gautama Muni, which explains that the combination of atoms is the cause of everything.

O

Oṁkāra—oṁ, the root of Vedic knowledge; known as the *mahā-vākya,* the supreme sound; the transcendental syllable which represents Kṛṣṇa, and which is vibrated by transcendentalists for attainment of the Supreme while undertaking sacrifices, charities and penances; it denotes the Personality of Godhead as the root of the creation, maintenance and destruction of the cosmic manifestation.

P

Pañcopāsanā—worship by impersonalist Māyāvādīs of five deities (Viṣṇu, Durgā, Brahmā, Gaṇeśa and Vivasvān) that is motivated by the desire to ultimately abandon all conceptions of a personal Absolute.

Param Brahman—the Supreme Brahman, the Personality of Godhead, Lord Śrī Kṛṣṇa.

Paramātmā—*See:* Supersoul.

Paramparā—the disciplic succession, beginning with Kṛṣṇa, through which spiritual knowledge is transmitted by bonafide spiritual masters; literally, one after the other.

Paraśurāma—the incarnation of Lord Kṛṣṇa, who appeared in ancient times to overthrow the warrior class when they had become degraded, who destroyed twenty-one consecutive generations of lawless members of the ruling class. He taught the science of weapons to Droṇa and Karṇa.

Pāṣaṇḍī—an offender or atheist; a non-believer who thinks God and the demigods are on the same level, or who considers devotional activities to be material.

Paṭhana—a *brāhmaṇa's* duty to be conversant with the Vedic scriptures; study of the scriptures.

Prajāpatis—the progenitors of living entities, chief of whom is Lord Brahmā; the demigods in charge of populating the universe.

Prajā—citizens of a state, which in Vedic times included all species of life such as animals and birds.

Prakṛti—material nature, the energy of the Supreme (literally that which is predominated); the female principle enjoyed by the male *puruṣa*. There are two *prakṛtis*—*apara-prakṛti* or the material nature, and *para-prakṛti* or the spiritual nature (living entities)—which are both predominated over by the Supreme Personality of Godhead; one of the five *tattvas* or Vedic ontological truths.

Prāṇa-maya—(consciousness) absorbed in maintaining one's bodily existence.

Prasāda, or prasādam—"the mercy of Lord Kṛṣṇa." Food spiritualized by being prepared for the pleasure of Kṛṣṇa, and by offering with love and devotion. Ordinary food subjects one to karmic reactions, one of the reasons being the many living entities that gave up their lives during the preparation. But food offered to Kṛṣṇa is freed of sin and invokes an attraction to Him.

Pratigraha—accepting charity; the duty of a *brāhmaṇa* to accept contributions from his followers for pursuing his transcendental duties.

Pravṛtti-mārga—the path of sense enjoyment in accordance with Vedic regulations.

Prāyaścitta—atonement for sinful acts.

Purāṇas— Literally, very old; the eighteen major and eighteen minor ancient Vedic literatures compiled about five thousand years ago in India by Śrīla Vyāsadeva that are histories of this and other planets; literatures supplementary to the *Vedas*, discussing such topics as the creation of the universe, incarnations of the Supreme Lord and demigods, and the history of dynasties of saintly kings. The eighteen principal *Purāṇas* discuss ten primary subject matters: (1) the primary creation, (2) the secondary creation, (3) the planetary systems, (4) protection and maintenance by the *avatāras*, (5) the Manus. (6) dynasties of great kings, (7) noble character and activities of great kings, (8) dissolution of the universe and liberation of the living entity, (9) the *jīva* (the spirit soul), (10) the Supreme Lord.

Puruṣa—the enjoyer, or male; the living entity or the Supreme Lord; Viṣṇu, the incarnation of the Lord for material creation; the male or controlling principle. This term may be applied to both, the individual living being and the Supreme Personality of Godhead.

Puruṣa-avatāras—the primary expansions of Lord Viṣṇu who effect the creation, maintenance and destruction of the material universes.

R

Rajoguṇa—the mode of passion of material nature.

Rākṣasa—a class of *asura* or ungodly people. The *rākṣasas* are always opposed to God's will. Generally, they are man-eaters and have grotesque forms.

Rasa—relationship between the Lord and the living entities; mellow, or the sweet taste of a relationship, especially between the Lord and the living entities. There are five principal varieties of *rasa*—neutral relationship (*śānta-rasa*), relationship as servant (*dāsya-rasa*), as friend (*sākhya-rasa*), as parent (*vātsalya-rasa*) and conjugal lover (*mādhurya-rasa*). Just as our present material body permits us to engage in karma (physical activities), the spiritual *rasa*-body permits us to engage in *līlā*, Kṛṣṇa's endlessly expanding spiritual activities.

Ṛṣabhadeva—an incarnation of the Supreme Lord as a devotee king who, after instructing his sons in spiritual life, renounced His kingdom for a life of austerity.

Ṛṣi—a sage who performs austerities.

Rūdra—the expansions of Lord Śiva who rule over the material mode of ignorance. *See:* Śiva

S

Sac-cid-ānanda-vigraha—the Lord's transcendental form, which is eternal and full of knowledge and bliss; the eternal transcendental form of the living entity.

Sādhu—a saint or Krishna conscious devotee, or Vaiṣṇava. A wandering holy man; a saintly person, one of the three authorities for a Vaiṣṇava. *See:* Guru, Śāstra.

Sakhya-rasa—a relationship with the Supreme Lord in devotional friendship.

Sālokya—the liberation of residing on the same planet as the Supreme Lord.

Samādhi—total absorption, and trance of the mind and senses in consciousness of the Supreme Godhead and service to Him. Also also refers to the tomb where a great soul's body is laid after his departure from this world.

Sāmīpya-mukti—liberation of living as a personal associate of the Lord.

Sampradāya—a disciplic succession of spiritual masters, along with the followers in that tradition, through which spiritual knowledge is transmitted; school of thought.

Saṁsṛti—the cycle of repeated birth and death.

Sanātana-dhāma—the eternal abode, the Vaikuṇṭha planets in the spiritual sky.

Sāṅkhya—analytical discrimination between spirit and matter and the path of devotional service as described by Lord Kapila, the son of Devahūti.

Saṅkīrtana—congregational or public glorification of the Supreme Lord Kṛṣṇa through chanting of His holy names, and glorification of His fame and pastimes.

Sannyāsa—the renounced order, the fourth stage of Vedic spiritual life in the Vedic system of *varṇāsrama-dharma*, which is free from family relationships, and in which all activities are completely dedicated to Kṛṣṇa. It is the order of ascetics who travel and constantly preach the message of Godhead for the benefit of all. It is usually accepted at age fifty, after a man has fulfilled his household responsibilities.

Śānta-rasa—the marginal stage of devotional service, passive love of God; the relationship with the Supreme Lord in neutrality.

Sārṣṭi—the liberation of achieving equal opulence with the Lord.

Sārūpya—the liberation of attaining a spiritual form like that of the Supreme Lord.

Śāstra—the revealed scriptures, obeyed by all those who follow the Vedic teachings. Śās means "to regulate and direct" and tra means "an instrument"; Vedic literature; The Vedic scriptures; one of the three authorities for a Vaiṣṇava. In his purport to *Cc., Ādi-līlā* 17.157, Śrīla Prabhupāda writes: The word *śāstra* is derived from the dhātu, or verbal root, śas. *Sas-dhātu* pertains to controlling or ruling. A government's ruling through force or weapons is called *śastra*. Thus whenever there is ruling, either by weapons or by injunctions, the *śas-dhātu* is the basic principle. Between *śastra* (ruling through weapons) and *śāstra* (ruling through the injunctions of the scriptures), the better is *śāstra*. Our Vedic scriptures are not ordinary law books of human common sense; they are the statements of factually liberated persons unaffected by the imperfectness of the senses. *Śāstra* must be correct always, not sometimes correct and sometimes incorrect. In the Vedic scriptures, the cow is described as a mother. Therefore she is a mother for all time; it is not, as some rascals say, that in the Vedic age she was a mother but she is not in this age. If *śāstra* is an authority, the cow is a mother always; she was a mother in the Vedic age, and she is a mother in this age also. If one acts according to the injunctions of *śāstra*, he is freed from the reactions of sinful activity. For example, the propensities for eating flesh, drinking wine and enjoying sex life are all natural to the conditioned soul. The path of such enjoyment is called *pravṛtti-mārga*. The *śāstra* says, *pravṛttir eṣāṁ bhūtānāṁ nivṛttis tu mahā-phalā:* one should not be carried away by the propensities of defective conditioned life; one should be guided by the principles of the *śāstras*. A child's propensity is to play all day long, but it is the injunction of the *śāstras* that the parents should take care to educate him. The *śāstras* are there just to guide the activities of human society. But because people do not refer to the instructions of *śāstras*, which are free from defects and imperfections, they are therefore misguided by so-called educated teachers and leaders who are full of the deficiencies of conditioned life.

Sattva-guṇa—the mode of material goodness, predominated by Lord Viṣṇu.

Sāyujya-mukti—the liberation of merging into the Brahman effulgence of the Lord.

Śeṣa Nāga—an expansion of Lord Balarāma or Saṅkarṣaṇa who takes the form of a many-hooded serpent and serves as Lord Viṣṇu's couch and other paraphernalia. He also holds the unlimited number of universes on His hoods.

Siddha—a perfected person or mystic; a demigod from Siddhaloka; one who has realized the Brahman effulgence; a perfect devotee.

Siddhaloka—the heavenly planet whose inhabitants possess all mystic powers; the planets of materially perfect beings.

Śiva—also known as Hara, Mahādeva, Maheśvara, Āśutoṣa (one who is easily pleased), Giriśa (lord of the mountains) and Gopīśvara, he is the *guṇa-avatāra* who is the superintendent of the mode of ignorance (*tamoguṇa*) and who takes charge of destroying the universe at the time of annihilation. He is also considered the greatest Vaiṣṇava, or devotee, of Lord Kṛṣṇa. He is confused by some with the Supreme Lord.

Smārta-brāhmaṇa—a *brāhmaṇa* interested more in the external performance of the rules and rituals of the Vedas than in attaining Lord Kṛṣṇa who is the goal of the *Vedas*; one who strictly follows the Vedic principles on the mundane platform.

Smṛti—remembrance, a *vyabhicāri-bhāva*; revealed scriptures supplementary to the *śruti*, or original Vedic scriptures, which are the *Vedas* and *Upaniṣads*; scriptures compiled by living entities under transcendental direction; the corollaries of the *Vedas*; one of the five functions of *buddhi.*

Soma-rasa—a life-extending heavenly beverage available on the moon to demigods on the higher planets.

Sravaṇam kīrtanaṁ viṣṇoḥ—the devotional process of hearing and chanting about Lord Viṣṇu, or Kṛṣṇa.

Śrīvatsa—the sign on the chest of Lord Viṣṇu and Nārāyaṇa, indicating the goddess of fortune, Lakṣmī.

Śuddha-sattva—the spiritual platform of pure goodness; the transcendental mode of purified goodness. *See:* Guṇas.

Śūdra—a member of the fourth social order, laborer class, in the traditional Vedic social system. They render service to the three higher classes, namely the *brāhmaṇas*, the *kṣatriyas*, and the *vaiśyas*.

Supersoul—Paramātmā, the localized aspect of Viṣṇu; expansion of the Supreme Lord known as Kṣīrodakaśāyī Viṣṇu, who expands into the heart of every living entity and every atom within the universe, pervading the entire material nature. His spiritual form is four-armed and the size of a thumb. From Him come the living entity's knowledge, remembrance and forgetfulness. The Supersoul is the witness and the one who sanctions all *karma*.

Suṣupti—deep sleep, one of the levels of material consciousness.

Svāmī—*See:* Gosvāmī.

Svāṁśa—Kṛṣṇa's plenary portion.

Svargaloka—the heavenly planets or abodes of the demigods in the material world.

T

Tamo-guṇa—the mode of ignorance, or darkness of material nature. It is controlled by Lord Śiva.

Tapasya— the voluntary acceptance of hardships for spiritual realization, such as rising early in the morning and taking a bath, fasting on certain days of the month etc.

Tilaka—sacred clay markings placed on the forehead and other parts of the body to designate one as a follower of Viṣṇu, Rāma, Śiva etc.

Trayī—the three *Vedas*. (*Ṛg*, *Sāma* and *Yajur*), which explain fruitive activities for material benefits.

U

Upaniṣads—Considered the most significant philosophical sections and crest jewels of the Vedas, the *Upaniṣads*, 108 in number, are found in the *Āraṇyaka* and *Brāhmaṇa* portions of the *Vedas*. The term *upaniṣad* literally means that which is learned by sitting close to the teacher. The *Upaniṣads* teach the philosophy of the Absolute Truth (Brahman) to those seeking liberation from birth and death, and the study of the *Upaniṣads* is known as *Vedānta*, the conclusion of the *Veda*. Because the *Upaniṣads* contain many apparently contradictory statements, the great sage Vyāsa systematized the Upaniṣadic teachings in the *Vedānta-sūtra*. His natural commentary on the *Vedānta-sūtra* is the *Śrīmad-Bhāgavatam*.

V

Vaikuṇṭha—the eternal planets of the spiritual world, the abode of Lord Nārāyaṇa, which lies beyond the coverings of the material universe. Literally, "the place with no anxiety."

Vairāgya—renunciation; detachment from matter and engagement of the mind in spirit.

Vaiṣṇava—a devotee of the Supreme Lord, Viṣṇu, or Kṛṣṇa.

Vaiśya—member of the mercantile or agricultural class, according to the system of four social orders and four spiritual orders.

Vāmanadeva—the Supreme Lord's incarnation as a dwarf *brāhmaṇa* to reclaim the heavenly kingdom, which the king of the demons Bali Mahārāja had conquered. Bali Mahārāja surrendered all his possessions to Lord Vāmanadeva, and became celebrated as one of the *mahājanas*, or great spiritual authorities.

Vānaprastha—A retired householder, a member of the third Vedic spiritual order or *āśrama*, who quits home to cultivate renunciation and travels to holy places, in preparation for the renounced order of life.

Varṇa—the four socio-occupational divisions of Vedic society. Contrary to popular misconception, *varṇas* are nor fixed by birth, but are determined by a person's inclination toward different types of work and his psychological qualities. The four *varṇas* are *brāhmaṇas*, *kṣatriyas*, *vaiśyas* and *śūdras*.

Varṇāśrama-dharma—the system of four social and four spiritual orders of

Vedic society, based on the individual's psycho-physical qualities and tendencies toward particular types of work.

Varuṇa—the demigod in charge of the oceans.

Vāsudeva-parāyaṇa—one whose desire is fixed on the Supreme Lord.

Vātsalya-rasa—the relationship with Kṛṣṇa as His parent.

Vedānta—literally, the end of all knowledge; one the six systems of Vedic philosophy, traditionally reserved for the *sannyāsīs* (renunciates). It is based on the philosophy of the *Vedānta-sūtra*, is the conclusion of Vedic philosophy, and shows Kṛṣṇa as the goal of all philosophy.

Vedānta-sūtra—also known as *Brahma-sūtra*, it is Śrīla Vyāsadeva's conclusive summary of Vedic philosophical knowledge, written in brief codes. All apparent contradictory statements of the vast literature of the *Vedas* are resolved in this work. There are four divisions: (1) reconciliation of all scriptures (2) the consistent reconciliation of apparently conflicting hymns (3) the means or process of attaining the goal (spiritual realization) and (4) the object (or desired fruit) achieved by the spiritual process. The codes of the *Vedānta-sūtra* are very terse, and without a fuller explanation or commentary, their meaning is difficult to grasp. In India all the five main schools of *Vedānta* have explained the *sūtras* through their respective *bhāṣyas* (commentaries). The natural commentary on the *Vedānta-sūtra* is the *Śrīmad-Bhāgavatam*.

Vedas—the original *Veda* was divided into four by Śrīla Vyāsadeva. The four original Vedic scriptures, *Saṁhitās* (*Ṛg, Sāma, Atharva* and *Yajur*) and the 108 *Upaniṣads, Mahābhārata, Vedānta-sūtra*, etc. The system of eternal wisdom compiled by Śrīla Vyāsadeva, the literary incarnation of the Supreme Lord, for the gradual upliftment of all mankind from the state of bondage to the state of liberation. The word *veda* literally means "knowledge", and thus in a wider sense it refers to the whole body of Indian Sanskrit religious literature that is in harmony with the philosophical conclusions found in the original four Vedic *Saṁhitās* and *Upaniṣads*. The message of the transcendental realm that has come down to this phenomenal world through the medium of sound is known as the *Veda*. Being the very words of Godhead Himself, the *Vedas* have existed from eternity. Lord Kṛṣṇa originally revealed the *Vedas* to Brahmā, the first soul to appear in the realm of physical nature, and by him they were subsequently made available to other souls through the channel of spiritual disciplic succession; *Veda, Vedas,* Vedic knowledge. The Sanskrit root of the word *Veda* is *vid*, knowledge. This root is widespread even in modern

Western language: e.g. *video* (from the Latin word to see) and idea (Gr. *ida*). The term Vedic refers to the teachings of the Vedic literatures. From these literatures we learn that this universe, along with countless others, was produced from the breath of Mahā-Viṣṇu some 155,250,000,000,000 years ago. The Lord's divine breath simultaneously transmitted all the knowledge mankind requires to meet his material needs and revive his dormant God consciousness. This knowledge is called *Veda*. Caturmukha (four-faced) Brahmā, the first created being within this universe, received *Veda* from Viṣṇu. Brahmā, acting as an obedient servant of the Supreme Lord, populated the planetary systems with all species of life. He spoke four *Vedas*, one from each of his mouths, to guide human beings in their spiritual and material progress. The *Vedas* are thus traced to the very beginning of the cosmos. Some of the most basic Vedic teachings are: (1) every living creature is an eternal soul covered by a material body; (2) as long as the souls are bewildered by *māyā* (the illusion of identifying the self with the body) they must reincarnate from body to body, life after life; (3) to accept a material body means to suffer the four-fold pangs of birth, old age, disease and death; (4) depending upon the quality of work (*karma*) in the human form, a soul may take its next birth in a subhuman species, or the human species, or a superhuman species, or it may be freed from birth and death altogether; (5) *karma* dedicated in sacrifice to Viṣṇu as directed by Vedic injunctions elevates and liberates the soul.

Vibhinnāṁśa—the separated expansions of the Supreme Lord, the minute living entities, who are part and parcel of Kṛṣṇa.

Vibhūti—a secondary incarnation indirectly empowered by the Supreme Lord; opulence by which Kṛṣṇa controls the entire material manifestation.

Vidyādharas—a race of celestial beings who are attendants of Lord Śiva, and who possess mystic knowledge.

Vijñānamaya—with full knowledge; conscious of the self as different from matter.

Vipra—a *brahmaṇa*, a member of the intellectual, priestly class, wise in Vedic knowledge, and fixed in goodness and knowledgeable of Brahman, the Absolute Truth.

Virāṭ-rupa—the universal form of the Supreme Lord containing the totality of the entire material manifestation.

Viṣṇu— literally, the all-pervading God; the Supreme Personality of Godhead in His four-armed expansion in Vaikuṇṭha. A plenary expansion of the original Supreme Personality of Godhead, Śrī Kṛṣṇa, He supervises the maintenance of the created universe, and enters into the material universe before creation. He is worshiped by all the demigods and sages, and described throughout the *Vedas* as the summum bonum of all knowledge.

Viṣṇudūtas—the messengers of Lord Viṣṇu who come to take perfected devotees back to the spiritual world at the time of death, the personal servants of Lord Viṣṇu, they closely resemble Him in appearance.

Viśuddha-sattva—the spiritual platform of pure goodness.

Vṛndāvana—Kṛṣṇa's eternal abode, where He fully manifests His quality of sweetness; the village on this earth in which He enacted His childhood pastimes five thousand years ago; the topmost transcendental abode of the Supreme Lord. It is His personal spiritual abode descended to the earthly plane. It is situated on the western bank of the river Yamunā.

Vyāsadeva—the literary incarnation of God, and the greatest philosopher of ancient times. The son of Parāśara Muni and Satyavatīdevī, he rendered the *Vedas* into written texts some 5000 years ago. He divided the *Veda* into four parts, the Ṛg, *Yajur*, *Sāma* and *Atharva Veda*, and also compiled the supplementary Vedic literature such as the eighteen *Purāṇas*, *Vedānta-sūtra*, and the *Mahābhārata*. He played a very important part in guiding the Pāṇḍavas during crucial times. He gave the vision of the battle of Kurukṣetra to Sañjaya so that he could relate it to Dhṛtarāṣṭra. He is still living in this world; is also known as Vedavyāsa, Bādarāyaṇa and Dvaipāyana Vyāsa.

Y

Yajamāna—one for whom a priest executes sacrifices.

Yajña—a Vedic sacrifice; also a name for the Supreme Lord meaning "the personification of sacrifice"; the goal and enjoyer of all sacrifices.

Yamadūtas—the messengers of Yamarāja, the lord of death.

Yavana—class of people who do not follow the Vedic principles of life; a low-class person, generally a meat-eater.

Yogī—a transcendentalist who practices one of the many authorized forms of *yoga* or processes of spiritual purification; one who practices the eightfold mystic *yoga* process to gain mystic *siddhis* or Paramātmā realization.

Yuga—one of the four ages of the universe; they differ in length and rotate like calendar months.

Z

Zamindār—a wealthy landowner.

Sanskrit Pronunciation Guide

Throughout the centuries, the Sanskrit language has been written in a variety of alphabets. The mode of writing most widely used throughout India, however, is called *devanāgarī*, which means, literally, the writing used in "the cities of the demigods." The *devanāgarī* alphabet consists of forty-eight characters: thirteen vowels and thirty-five consonants. Ancient Sanskrit grammarians arranged this alphabet according to practical linguistic principles, and this order has been accepted by all Western scholars. The system of transliteration used in this book conforms to a system that scholars have accepted to indicate the pronunciation of each Sanskrit sound.

Vowels

अ a आ ā इ i ई ī उ u ऊ ū ऋ ṛ ॠ ṝ ऌ ḷ

ए e ऐ ai ओ o औ au

Consonants

Guttarals:	क ka	ख kha	ग ga	घ gha	ङ ṅa
Palatals:	च ca	छ cha	ज ja	झ jha	ञ ña
Cerebrals:	ट ṭa	ठ ṭha	ड ḍa	ढ ḍha	ण ṇa
Dentals:	त ta	थ tha	द da	ध dha	न na
Labials:	प pa	फ pha	ब ba	भ bha	म ma
Semivowels:	य ya	र ra	ल la	व va	
Sibilants:	श śa	ष ṣa	स sa		
Aspirate :	ह ha	Anusvāra : ं ṁ	Visarga : ः ḥ		

Numerals

०–0 १–1 २–2 ३–3 ४–4 ५–5 ६–6 ७–7 ८–8 ९–9

The vowels are written as follows after a consonant:

ा ā ि i ी ī ु u ू ū ृ ṛ ॄ ṝ े e ै ai ो o ौ au

For example : क ka का kā कि ki की kī कु ku कू kū
कृ kṛ कॄ kṝ के ke कै kai को ko कौ kau

Generally two or more consonants in conjunction are written together in a special form, as for example: **क्ष kṣa त्र tra**

The vowel "a" is implied after a consonant with no vowel symbol.

The symbol virāma (्) indicates that there is no final vowel: क्

The vowels are pronounced as follows:.

a	—	as in b**u**t
ā	—	as in f**a**r but held twice as long as **a**
ai	—	as in **ai**sle
au	—	as in h**ow**
e	—	as in th**ey**
i	—	as in p**i**n
ī	—	as in pique but held twice as long as **i**
ḷ	—	as in **lree**
o	—	as in **go**
ṛ	—	as in **ri**m
ṝ	—	as in **ree**d but held twice as long as **ṛ**
u	—	as in p**u**sh
ū	—	as in r**u**le but held twice as long as **u**

The consonants are pronounced as follows:

Gutterals
(pronounced from the throat)

k	—	as in **k**ite
kh	—	as in Ec**kh**art
g	—	as in **g**ive
gh	—	as in di**g-h**ard
ṅ	—	as in si**ng**

Labials
(pronounced with the lips)

p	—	as in **p**ine
ph	—	as in u**p-h**ill
b	—	as in **b**ird
bh	—	as in ru**b-h**ard
m	—	as in **m**other

Cerebrals
(pronounced with the tip of the tongue against the roof of the mouth)

ṭ	—	as in **t**ub
ṭh	—	as in ligh**t-h**eart
ḍ	—	as in **d**ove
ḍh	—	as in re**d-h**ot
ṇ	—	as in si**ng**

Palatals
(pronounced with the middle of the tongue against the palate)

c	—	as in **ch**air
ch	—	as in staun**ch-h**eart
j	—	as in **j**oy
jh	—	as in he**dgeh**og
ñ	—	as in ca**ny**on

Dentals
(pronounced like the cerebrals but with the tongue against the teeth)

t	—	as in **t**ub
th	—	as in ligh**t-h**eart
d	—	as in **d**ove
dh	—	as in re**d-h**ot
n	—	as in **n**ut

Semivowels

y	—	as in **y**es
r	—	as in **r**un
l	—	as in **l**ight
v	—	as in **v**ine, except when preceded in the same syllable by a consonant, then like in s**w**an

Aspirate

h	—	as in **h**ome

Sibilants

ś	—	as in the German word *sprechen*
ṣ	—	as in **sh**ine
s	—	as in **s**un

Anusvāra

ṁ	—	a resonant nasal sound as in the French word *bon*

Visarga

ḥ	—	a final **h**-sound: **aḥ** is pronounced like **aha**; **iḥ** like **ihi**.

There is no strong accentuation of syllables in Sanskrit, or pausing between words in a line, only a flowing of short and long syllables (the long twice as long as the short). A long syllable is one whose vowel is long (**ā, ai, au, e , ī, o, ṝ, ū**) or whose short vowel is followed by more than one consonant (including **ḥ** and **ṁ**). Aspirated consonants (consonants followed by an **h**) count as single consonants.

Index of Sanskrit Verses

This index constitutes a complete listing of the first and third lines of each of the Sanskrit poetry verses of this volume of *Śrīmad-Bhāgavatam*, arranged in English alphabetical order. The first column gives the Sanskrit transliteration; the second, the chapter-verse reference. Apostrophes are alphabetized as a's.

B

C

D

E

G

H

I

J

K

L

M

N

O

P

Index of Verses Quoted

This index lists the verses quoted in the purports of this volume of *Śrīmad-Bhāgavatam*. Numerals in boldface type refer to the first or third lines of verses quoted in full; numerals in roman type refer to partially quoted verses.

General Index

The references to the translations and purports of the verses of *Śrīmad-Bhāgavatam* are presented in the following format: "xx.yy (para n)", where 'xx' is the chapter number, 'yy' is the verse number (text number) and 'n' is the paragraph number in the purport. Numerals in the boldface type indicate the translations and those in regular type indicate the purports. Numerals in the mixed type indicate both translation and purports. While counting the paragraphs in the purports, please remember that, the new paragraph begins (in the purport) only where the first word is indented.

A

Abhaya, Kṛṣṇa as, 9.21
Abhimati, sons of, **6.10–12**
Abortion
  atonement for, 16.14
  at contraceptive's failure, 15.4 (para 2)
Absolute Truth
  aspects of, 5.17 (para 1)
  atonement by understanding, **1.11**
  devotee's approach to, compared with *jñānī's,* 17.31
  features of, three defined, 9.42, 16.25, 16.51 (para 2)
  as seen by personalists & impersonalists, **4.32**–33
  Supreme Lord as, 4.47 (para 3)
  See also: Kṛṣṇa; Supreme Lord
Ācārya(s). See: Spiritual master(s); *specific spiritual masters*
Activities of Kṛṣṇa. *See:* Kṛṣṇa, pastime(s) of
Activity (activities)
  caused by Lord, 16.51 (para 6)
  illusion of soul concerning, 15.6
  material, as mental concoction, **15.21**–25
  Nārāyaṇa cause of, 1.41 (para 2)
  pious & forbidden, 16.51 (para 3)
  understanding, via Lord, 16.51 (para 4)
  witnesses of, **1.42**
  Yamarāja observes, **1.48**
  See also: Fruitive activity (activities); *Karma*
Acyuta, Kṛṣṇa's forms as, 16.18–19 (para 2)
Aditi, **6.26**
  descendants of, 18 Intro–**18.9**
  sons of, **6.38–39**
Ādityas, **10.17–18**
Advaita, Kṛṣṇa's forms as, 16.18–19 (para 2)
Agastya, 3.35
Agastya Muni, **18.5**, **18.6**
  Vātāpi &, **18.15**
Agents of Lord, father & king as, **15.6**
Age of Kali. *See:* Kali-yuga
Agni, **6.10–12**
  personified by invited guest, **7.29–30**
  wife, sons, & grandsons of, **6.13**
Agnihotra, **18.1**
Agriculture, 4.4 (para 2)
Ahaituky apratihatā defined, 16.34 (para 2)
Ahaṅgrahopāsanā defined, 8.12
Ahirbradhna, **6.17–18**
Air
  compared to Lord's appearance, **4.34**
  element, **9.21**, 10.11
  See also: Elements, material
Airāvata, **10.13–14**, **11.10–11**
Airplane as example of false creation, 16.35 (para 2)
Airplane, spiritual, **2.44**
Aja, **6.17–18**
Ajaikapāt, **6.17–18**
Ajāmila
  attached to his son, **1.25–30**
  attachment of, compared with woman's attachment to husband, 18.33–34
  brahminical life abandoned by, 1.63–**64**
  chanting of "Nārāyaṇa" by, 1.25–**30**, **2.7**, 2.49 (para 6)
  contemplates deliverance, **2.30–32**
  degraded life of, **1.21–24**
  as determined in devotional service, **2.35–38**
  former goodness of, **1.56–57**, 2.32–**33**
  inspired to name his son, 2.32

Brahman (impersonal absolute) (*continued*)
oneness in quality with, **16.56**
as one phase of Absolute, 5.17 (para 1)
origin of, 9.42
perspectives on, **4.32**
realization of, 9.33
source of, 16.57
suffering absent in understanding, 15.25 (para 2)
See also: Monism
Brāhmaṇa of Kṛṣṇanagara, 7.36
Brahmāṇḍa Purāṇa quoted
on Kṛṣṇa always being in Vṛndāvana, 9.34
on Kṛṣṇa as supreme controller & cause, 9.26–27 (para 2), 9.26–28 (para 2)
on Kṛṣṇa's expansions, 9.45 (para 1)
Brahman effulgence. *See:* Brahman (impersonal absolute)
Brahman, Supreme
connecting everything with, 16.41 (para 3)
Kṛṣṇa as, **4.30**, 4.31 (para 3), 16.24
living entity different from, 16.57
soul's dependency on, **16.24**
universe in, **16.22**
See also: Kṛṣṇa; Supreme Lord
Brahma-saṁhitā, Lord personifies, **16.33**
Brahma-saṁhitā quoted
on devotional service without *karma,* 14.55
on Durgā, 5.16 (para 2), 17.29
on forms of Godhead, 16.18–19 (para 1)
on Kṛṣṇa
in atoms & universes, 16.9 (para 1), 16.36 (para 1)
body of, 16.18–19 (para 5)
expansions of, 16.20, 16.36 (para 1)
greatness of, known to devotees, 16.36 (para 1), 17.32
as Maha-Viṣṇu's source, 16.37
as original person, 16.36 (para 2)
seen by love, 16.50
as supreme controller, 1.41 (para 3), 4.30 (para 2)
as supreme controller , 10.11, 12.10
on materialist's not knowing God, 4.23
on Viṣṇu in Śvetadvīpa, 16.18–19 (para 1)
Brahma *sampradāya,* 8.42
Brahma satyaṁ jagan mithyā, 15.5
Brahma-sūtra, 8.19 (para 1)
Brahma-vidyā. See: Knowledge, spiritual
Brahma-yāmala quoted on unauthorized devotional service, 1.20
Brahmin(s). *See: Brāhmaṇa(s)*
Brain as material, 16.24
Bṛghu, **18.3–4**, **18.5**
Bṛhad-viṣṇu Purāṇa quoted on chanting, 2.7 (para 1), 13.8–9 (para 1)
Bṛhan-nāradīya Purāṇa quoted on chanting, 16.44 (para 1), 16.53–54
Bṛhaspati
Brahmā praises, **7.21**
Indra abandoned by, **6.45**, **7.16**–17
neglected by Indra, **7.2–8**
Bṛhatśloka, **18.8**
Brother(s)
Indra personified by, **7.29–30**
religious principles for, **5.30**, **5.31**
Bubbles & foam as sinful reaction, **9.10**
Buddha, Lord
mission of, 7.39 (para 3), 8.19 (para 2)
nonviolence of, 10.9 (para 1)
protection by, **8.19**

C

Caitanya-caritāmṛta quoted
on association with devotees, 2.32
on conditioned soul's plight, 4.44 (para 2)
on duty of Indians, 10.10 (para 1)
on happiness & distress, 17.30 (para 1)
on India's duty, 16.58
on Kṛṣṇa as sole master, 12.10
on Lord's not giving material prosperity, 9.49
on *sādhus* of all *āśramas,* 5.36 (para 1)
on spiritual master, 7.33
on wandering of living entities, 1.2
Caitanya Mahāprabhu
chanting introduced by, 16.44 (para 1)
compassion in renunciation of, 10.8 (para 1)
delivers fallen souls, 18.43
depends on devotees, 19.5
devotees should serve, 15.18–19 (para 1)
duty to, 12.7 (para 3)
example of, in serving Kṛṣṇa's servants, 11.24
Lakṣmī as *viṣṇu-tattva* accepted by, 19.13 (para 2)
prayer to Kṛṣṇa by, 1.50 (para 1)
preaching desired by, 16.43 (para 1)
Caitanya Mahāprabhu quoted
on chanting, 1.21, 3.24 (para 9)
on Hare Kṛṣṇa *mantra,* 5.26
on humility while chanting, 17.10, 17.14, 17.27, 17.37
on India's special aptitude, 16.58
on living entity as Kṛṣṇa's servant, 10.11
on living entity finding mercy, 16.6 (para 3)
on Māyāvādīs as offenders, 14.5 (para 2)

D

F

Face as index of mind, 14.22
Faith
  government's betrayal of, **2.5–6**
  in Lord & spiritual master, 1.49 (para 2)
Family life
  entangling nature of, 5.6–8
  son needed in, 14.12
  See also: Gṛhastha(s)
Fashion, mundane & transcendental, 5.14 (para 2)
Fasting, 1.13–14 (para 2)
Father(s)
  Brahmā personified by, **7.29–30**
  duty of, 5.25
  as false creator, 12.12
  Haryaśvas' understanding of their, **5.20**
  scriptures compared to, **5.9**, **5.20**
  son's debt to, 5.37
  value of, 5.20 (para 4)
  See also: Parents; *specific fathers*
Fear
  in animals, **1.51**
  bhakti free from, **1.17**, 1.19 (para 3), 1.19 (para 4)
  causes of, **15.21–23**, 15.25 (para 2)
  of death, freedom from, 9.21
  in demigods, of Vṛtrāsura, **11.6**–8
  in demons, of demigods, **11.1**
  inspired by Lord, **9.37**
  killing enemy who is in, **11.4**
  in nondevotees, 9.37
Ferocious animals as offspring of Kaśyapa, **6.24–27**
Fighting, proper conduct in, **11.4**
Fire
  element, **9.21**, 10.11
  Kṛṣṇa compared to, 8.32–33
  Lord's name compared to, **2.18**
  sparks of, compared to demigods, **9.42**
  Supersoul compared to, **4.27–28**
  as witness, **1.42**
Fire god, Indra visited by, **13.15**
Fish as offspring of Kaśyapa, **6.24–27**
Fish incarnation. *See:* Matsya
Flood at beginning of creation, **9.23**
Flower garland mistaken for snake, compared to material illusion, **17.30**
Flying mountains, **12.26**
Food
  for living entities, **4.9**
  offered to Lord. *See: Prasāda*
Food (*continued*)
  unclean, eaten by Ajāmila, **1.67**
Form of Supreme Lord. *See:* Supreme Lord, form(s) of
Freedom. *See:* Liberation
Fruitive activity (activities)
  as atonement, 1.7 (para 2), 1.10, 1.11
  birth determined via, **16.4**
  blindly performed, **5.11**
  bodies caused via, 1.31 (para 2), **1.54**
  ceasing of, **16.59**, **16.61–62**
  contradictory results of, **16.59**–62
  devotee finds distasteful, 1.15 (para 1)
  devotional service superior to, 1.13–14 (para 2)
  liberation from, **2.12**
  punishment for performers of, **1.43**
  trap living entity, **1.52**
  See also: Karma; Vikarma
Fruitive worker(s). *See: Karma; Karmī(s)*

G

Gambling match, compared to battle of Vṛtrāsura & Indra, 12.17
Gandharva-nagara defined, **15.21–23**
Gandharvas, **6.29–31**
  celebrate Indra's victory, **12.34**
  king of, **8.39**
Ganges River, 5.27–28, 10.16 (para 1)
Garbhodakaśāyī Viṣṇu
  as expansion of Mahā-Viṣṇu, 16.37
  as expansion of Saṅkarṣaṇa, 16.18–19 (para 1)
  Kṛṣṇa directs, **12.11**
Garuḍa, **4.35–39**, **6.21–22**, **8.12**
  protection by, **8.29**, **8.30**
Garuḍa Purāṇa quoted on chanting, 2.7 (para 1)
Gautama, **15.12–15**
Ghosts & goblins, as offspring of Bhūta, **6.17–18**
Glorification of Supreme Lord
  for protection, **8.27–28**
  See also: Chanting holy name(s) of Lord
Glowworm in sun, Citraketu compares himself to, **16.46**
Goal of life
  humanitarians must know, 10.10 (para 2)
  See also: Perfection
God consciousness. *See:* Kṛṣṇa consciousness
Goddess of fortune. *See:* Lakṣmī
Godhead, return to
  via devotee's grace, 11.18

H

I

J

K

L

M

Material nature (*continued*)
- strength of, 5.41
- understanding of, necessary, 5.15 (para 2)
- *See also:* Creation; Material world

Material world
- annihilation of. *See:* Annihilation of universe(s)
- cause of, **9.26–27**
- compared to river, **16.5**
- controlled by Kṛṣṇa, 3.12 (para 1)
- as creation of Lord, **1.4–5**
- devotees indifferent in, 17.17 (para 3), 17.20
- as dream, 15.5, **15.21–23**
- duality in, **17.19**–21, **17.29**–31
- as expansion of Lord's energy, **8.32–33**
- false happiness in, 4.27–28 (para 5)
- freedom from, **2.46**
- illusion in, 15.5, **15.21**–26, **16.53–54**
- living entities in, 1.2, 1.39
- living entity's struggle in, 4.44 (para 1)
- Lord creates but transcends, **4.29**
- Lord's disinterest in, **15.6**
- as Lord's energy, **16.52**
- Lord understood via, 4.46 (para 2)
- as mental concoction, **15.21**–26
- modern attachment for, 15.26
- modes of nature in, 17.21
- as nondifferent from Lord, **8.31**
- purpose of, 4.44 (para 1)
- relativity in, **17.19**–21, **17.29**–31
- relief from, **9.43**
- renunciation of, advised by scriptures, 5.20 (para 1)
- suffering in. *See:* Suffering
- transcendental cause of, **4.29–30**
- Viṣṇu forms for, 9.33

Mathurā, 8.20

Mātṛkā, **6.42**
- offspring of, **6.42**

Matsya, Lord
- as aquatic incarnation, **9.26–27**, **9.40**
- demigods pray to, **9.23**
- protection by, **8.13**

Mauhūrtikas, **6.9**

Māyā
- baffles true understanding, 5.11 (para 2)
- beginning of, **16.57**
- bodies created via, 1.31 (para 3)
- compared to ocean, 1.53
- compared to river, **5.16**
- devotee understands, 16.51 (para 7)
- illusions of, **16.53–54**

Māyā (*continued*)
- liberation from, via association of *mahātmās,* 1.16 (para 1)
- material life arranged via, 15.4 (para 2)
- as spiritual potency, 18.8
- understanding baffled via, 5.11 (para 2)
- understanding of, as necessary, **5.16**
- *See also:* Illusion; Material world; Nature, material

Maya (demon) & Vṛtrāsura, **10.31**

Māyāpur, Kṛṣṇa consciousness center in, 2.39

Māyāvādī(s). *See:* Impersonalist(s)

Meat-eating
- civilized men avoid, 18.52
- Kaśyapa's instructions against, **18.49**
- restricted by sacrifice, 16.42 (para 1)
- *See also:* Animal slaughter

Meditation
- at death, 11.21
- highest form of, 2.41
- on oneness in quality with Lord, **8.11**, 8.12
- useless for knowing Lord, 4.47 (para 1)
- useless without *bhakti,* **2.46**
- *See also:* Chanting holy name(s) of Lord

Mellows, types of, five listed, 9.45 (para 3)

Men, demigods & demons classes of, 18.19
- *See also:* Demigod(s); Demon(s); Human being(s)

Menstruation as sinful reaction, **9.9**

Mental speculation. *See:* Speculative knowledge

Mercy
- of devotee, 1.1 (para 3), 1.2, 2.32, 2.35
- of Lord. *See:* Supreme Lord, mercy of
- personified by sister, **7.29–30**
- of spiritual master, 7.23

Merging of body, 10.11

Merging of soul, 10.11

Merging with God. *See:* Liberation; Māyavādī(s); Monism

Mīḍhuṣa, **18.7**

Military science, proper dealings in, **11.4**

Milk
- need of, 18.52
- touched by serpent's lips, compared to hearing from nondevotees, 17.40

Millennium, defined, 10.16 (para 2)

Millionaire compared to devotee, 13.3 (para 3)

Mind
- at death, duty concerning, 11.21
- in devotional service, 11.24
- discipline of, for happiness, **14.19–20**
- discipline of, via austerity, **1.13–14**
- as element, sixteenth, **1.50**

O

Praṇava in Nārāyaṇa-kavaca *mantra,* **8.4**–10
Prasāda
as offered by devotees, **18.49**
in *puṁsavana-vrata,* **19.16**, **19.17–18**, **19.19–21**, **19.23–24**
Prātaḥ, **18.3–4**
Prāyaścitta. See: Atonement
Prayer(s)
by Dakṣa, **4.23**–34
by demigods, Lord pleased by, **9.46**
by demigods, quoted, **9.21**–27 , **9.31**–45
ignorance of goal in, 9.32
impersonalists offer, indirectly, 9.47
to Lakṣmī in *puṁsavana-vrata,* **19.6**, **19.9**, **19.10–11**, **19.13**, **19.14–15**
to Lord
Anantadeva by Citraketu, **16.34**–48
Citraketu receives, from Nārada, **16.18**–25
by demigods, **9.21**–27 , **9.31**–45 , **9.46**
mundaners incapable of, 16.33
as perfection of words, etc., 16.32
in *puṁsavana-vrata,* **19.4**, **19.7**, **19.10–11**, **19.14**–16
personal, devotees offer, 9.47
protective. *See:* Nārāyaṇa-kavaca
by Vṛtrāsura, **11.24**–27
Preacher(s), Kṛṣṇa conscious
attitude of, 2.34, 2.36–37, 4.5, 5.44 (para 1)
Caitanya's formula for, 4.5, 5.44 (para 1)
curse on author may be accepted by, 5.43
devotee's duty to be, 3.18
knowledge required for, 1.38 (para 2)
Kṛṣṇa satisfied by, 5.39 (para 1)
opposition to, 2.2 (para 2)
protected by Kṛṣṇa, 2.36–37
recognized by Lord, 4.44 (para 3)
tolerance recommended for, 5.44 (para 1)
as tolerant & fearless, 5.39 (para 1)
See also: Devotee(s); *specific preachers*
Preaching of Kṛṣṇa consciousness
Caitanya depends on devotees for, 19.5
material possessions used in, 11.22
sacrifice for, 10.6, **10.8**
from Vedic literatures, 16.43 (para 1)
See also: Preacher(s)
Pregnant woman, example of, 5.41
Prema-vivarta quoted
on beginning of conditioned life, 16.57
on chanting, 13.8–9 (para 1)
Pretas, **8.25**
Pride
in Citraketu, 17.10
disqualifies devotee, 17.10
Priesthood
brāhmaṇas reject, 7.35–36
duty of, 7.38
offered by demigods to Viśvarūpa, **7.32**
selfless, 7.36
Viśvarūpa accepts, **7.35**, **7.37**
Principles of holy life. *See:* Regulative principles
Prostitute, intelligence compared to, **5.6–8**, **5.14–15**
Protection
in all directions, **8.14**
at all times, 8.12
from animals, **8.27–28**
from aquatics, **8.13**
from bad eatables, **8.18**
from bad planets, **8.27–28**
by boar incarnation, **8.15**
of cows, 4.9
at day, **8.20**
from defamation, **8.18**
by Dhanvantari incarnation, **8.18**
by dwarf incarnation, **8.13**
from envious persons, 8.18, **8.27–28**
at evening, **8.21**
from falldown in *bhakti-yoga,* **8.19**
from falling from duty, **8.16**
from false religion, **8.16**
from fear in heat or cold, **8.18**
by fish incarnation, **8.13**
in foreign countries, **8.15**
in forest & battlefront, **8.15**
by Garuḍa, **8.29**
from ghosts, **8.27–28**
by glorifying Supreme Lord, **8.27–28**
from heat & cold, fear in, **8.18**
from hellish planets, **8.17**
from ignorance, **8.19**
from illness, **8.18**
of intelligence, **8.30**
at junction of day & night, **8.22**
from Kali-yuga, **8.19**
by Lakṣmaṇa, **8.15**
in land areas, **8.13**
from laziness & forgetting *Vedas,* **8.19**
of life airs, **8.30**
of life by governments, 4.7, 4.11
from lightning, **8.27–28**
by Lord
Balarāma (as Śeṣa), **8.18**
Buddhadeva, **8.19**
Dāmodara, **8.22**
Dattātraya, **8.16**
Govinda, **8.20**
Hayagrīva, **8.17**

S

T

W

Y